Exploring
English
Lyrics

Exploring English Lyrics

SELECTION AND PRONUNCIATION OF ENGLISH ART SONG REPERTOIRE

Cheri Montgomery *and* Allen Henderson

ROWMAN & LITTLEFIELD
Lanham • Boulder • New York • London

Published by Rowman & Littlefield
An imprint of The Rowman & Littlefield Publishing Group, Inc.
4501 Forbes Boulevard, Suite 200, Lanham, Maryland 20706
www.rowman.com

86-90 Paul Street, London EC2A 4NE

British Library Cataloguing in Publication Information Available

Library of Congress Cataloging-in-Publication Data

Names: Montgomery, Cheri, author. | Henderson, Allen, 1963- author.
Title: Exploring English lyrics : selection and pronunciation of English art song repertoire / Cheri Montgomery and Allen Henderson.
Description: Lanham : Rowman & Littlefield Publishers, 2024. | Includes bibliographical references and index.
Identifiers: LCCN 2024003361 (print) | LCCN 2024003362 (ebook) | ISBN 9781538192689 (cloth) | ISBN 9781538192696 (paperback) |
    ISBN 9781538192702 (ebook)
Subjects: LCSH: Songs, English--Texts. | Singing--Diction. | English language--Pronunciation. | LCGFT: Song texts.
Classification: LCC ML54.6 .E98 2024 (print) | LCC ML54.6 (ebook) | DDC 782.42168/143--dc23/eng/20240123
LC record available at https://lccn.loc.gov/2024003361
LC ebook record available at https://lccn.loc.gov/2024003362

All things bright and beautiful,

[ɔl θɪŋz bɹɑːɪt ænd ˈbjutɪfʊl]

All creatures great and small,

[ɔl ˈkɹiʧʊz gɹɛːɪt ænd smɔl]

All things wise and wonderful,

[ɔl θɪŋz wɑːɪz ænd ˈwʌndʌfʊl]

The Lord God made them all.

[ðʌ lɔd gɑd mɛːɪd ðɛm ɔl]

~Cecil Francis Alexander

Contents

Introduction

Dr. Allen Henderson and Cheri Montgomery

Exploring English Lyrics provides pronunciation for 790 English art song texts. Selections include masterworks that span nearly five hundred years of art song history. Diverse segments of British, American, African American, Canadian, Scottish, Irish, and Australian cultures are represented.

The scope of the lyrics selected includes works appropriate for beginners as well as those being performed by the world's most prominent professional singers. Texts of frequently performed songs from the Royal Conservatory of Music Development Program adjudications, new composers' collected works, as well as lyrics from major anthologies such as Joan Boytim's First Book series are included.

The geographic range and time periods spanned within this resource are vast. Lengthy discussions addressing the many dialects of the English language and how pronunciation has changed over time would be necessary were this text intended for speech. Diction for singers maintains a different purpose. The phonetic indications within represent a pronunciation that is ideal for singing. We maintain the opinion that fine singing is dialect-free. Our basic premise in creating this resource is to preserve a pronunciation of the English language that is ideal for singing. Specific instances in which dialect or character voice pronunciation must be indicated are addressed on a case-by-case basis. A discussion of the differences between spoken and sung pronunciation is published in the January/February 2020 issue of the *Journal of Singing*: "Diction (Still) Belongs in the Music Department."

The pronunciation of the schwa is indicated throughout the text. The schwa is useful for speech but not ideal for singing. It exists due to the vowel reduction that occurs in unstressed syllables. The schwa serves as a place holder for those sounds that are difficult to define. Vowel obscurity is not acceptable for singing. Singers must sustain vowel sounds in unstressed syllables. Indicating pronunciation of the schwa is particularly helpful for non-native speakers learning to sing in English. Additional information regarding the schwa is published in the September/October 2022 issue of the *Journal of Singing*: "Defining the Schwa for English, German, French, and Russian Lyric Diction."

This text uses a refined set of symbols. Symbols that are unfavorable for singing are not included. A limited lexicon is best for both the student and international audience. It provides a non-native approach to the discovery of proper pronunciation. We hope students will begin to think of English transcription for lyric diction as a specific entity that is uniquely suited for the purpose of singing. This approach standardizes pronunciation and helps native English-speaking singers disassociate problematic speech patterns that hinder technique and limit clear communication of the text. Using transcriptions specifically designed for lyric diction, whether in lessons or while learning songs in the singer's native language, assists to quickly minimize dialectical differences that may become stumbling blocks to learning. Having a proficient knowledge of the International Phonetic Alphabet (IPA) strengthens the delivery of the text, helps students discover more ease in singing, elevates elegance, and enhances details in the final performance.

The following features ensure accuracy of the IPA, specify the pronunciation of vowels in unstressed syllables, and provide options for the pronunciation of *r*:

- The phonetics are computer-generated from a database of 87,000-plus words transcribed according to rules established by Madeleine Marshall, author of *The Singer's Manual of English Diction*. The transcriptions were further edited to reflect certain dialects and to accommodate fine details within the phrase.

- Vowels in unstressed syllables (transcribed with a schwa in the dictionary) are given a specific vowel sound. Reduced vowels are indicated with a vowel in parentheses. The vowel in parentheses replaces (or mixes with) the preceding vowel.

- Vowel *r* is indicated for the words *or*, *for*, and *nor* when intervocalic within the phrase. Vowel *r* is also indicated for intervocalic *r* in American texts. The vowel [ʁ] symbol (established by Dr. William Odom from *Siebs* 1969 edition) is used to represent an *r* formed with the tongue tip touching the lower front teeth and the sides of the tongue touching the upper molars. This helps the singer avoid a retroflex tongue formation in spellings where it would negatively affect a preceding vowel. A flipped *r* option is given in superscript.

The "Transcription Rules" on page xi provide a list of English spellings with IPA as recommended for lyric diction. The "English Pronunciation Guide" on page xv contains sample words with links to sound examples. The indices enable readers to search by composer, song cycle, first line, or song title. References to settings of texts by multiple composers are indicated throughout this book.

The artistic communication of art song lyrics can be challenging for both native and non-native speakers of any language. *Exploring English Lyrics* assists the singer and teacher with repertoire selections while providing an easily accessible and reliable transcription source.

This is the most unified collection of English lyrics with transcriptions available and an invaluable resource for English-speaking singers and teachers who may have previously assumed that just speaking the text in one's own native language is enough. The pronunciations were designed to enhance the sung delivery of the text while honoring the intentions of the poet and composer.

Dr. Allen Henderson and Cheri Montgomery

Note concerning the IPA for titles: The spoken pronunciation (provided beneath each title) may differ from the sung pronunciation of the same words. The sustained nature of singing and its effect on the pronunciation of *r* and vowels in unstressed syllables necessitates adjustments to the IPA.

Transcription Rules

(FROM *A PICTURE WORKBOOK OF ENGLISH SPELLINGS AND PHONETICS* BY CHERI MONTGOMERY)

A   *a* + one consonant + vowel = [ɛːɪ]: *lake*

a + two consonants or one final consonant = [æ]: *add*, *map*

a exception words: a [ʌ], *ache* [ɛːɪ], *father* [ɑ], *gauge* [ɛːɪ], *have* [æ], *yacht* [ɑ]

ai = [ɛːɪ]: *faith*

air = [ɛːʌ]: *pair*

alk = [ɔk]: *talk*

all = [ɔl]: *call*

alm = [ɑm]: *palm*

als = [ɔls]: *false*

alt = [ɔlt]: *salt*

ange = [ɛːɪndʒ]: *change*

ar + consonant = [ɑ]: *smart*

ar + silent *e* = [ɛːʌ]: *care* (except: *are* [ɑ])

ar/arr + vowel = [æɾ]: *marry* (American: [æʁ(ɾ)])

aste = [ɛːɪst]: *taste*

athe = [ɛːɪð]: *bathe*

au = [ɔ]: *August*

aw = [ɔ]: *fawn*

ay = [ɛːɪ]: *may* (except: *says* [ɛ])

B   *b, bb* = [b]: *babble*

C   *c* + consonant = [k]: *clap*

ca = [k]: *candle*

ce = [s]: *peace*

ch = [tʃ]: *chair* (except: *choir, choral, chorus, chord, echo, loch, school* = [k])

ci = [s]: *cinch*

co = [k]: *coach*

cr initial = [kɾ] in dramatic words: *cringe*

cu = [k]: *cute*

D   *d, dd* = [d]: *daddy*

d preceded by a voiceless consonant = [t]: *missed*

dg + silent *e* = [dʒ]: *judge*

du, dew = [dju]: *duty, dew*

E   *e* + consonant + silent *e* in single syllable words = [i]: *eve*

e final: the *e* is silent in the sequence: consonant + vowel + consonant + *e*: *love*

e final of two or three letter words = [i]: *me* (except: *the* = [ʌ/ʊ]; *the* + initial vowel = [i])

e in single syllable words = [ɛ]: *egg, net*

ea = [i] in single syllable words: *team* (check dictionary for *ea* words with multiple syllables)

ea exceptions: *break* [ɛːɪ], *breast* [ɛ], *great* [ɛːɪ], *cleanse* [ɛ], *deaf* [ɛ], *dealt* [ɛ], *death* [ɛ], *dreamt* [ɛ], *heart* [ɑ], *hearth* [ɑ], *leapt* [ɛ], *meant* [ɛ], *realm* [ɛ], *steak* [ɛːɪ], *sweat* [ɛ], *threat* [ɛ]

ead, ealth = [ɛ]: *bread, health* (exceptions: *bead, read, plead, knead, lead* = [i])

ear = [ɪːʌ] or [ɜ]: *fear, earn* (exceptions: *bear, pear, swear, tear, wear* = [ɛːʌ])

ed: the *e* is silent in the following sequence: consonant + vowel + consonant + *ed*: *loved* (except when preceded by a stop: *faded*)

ee = [i]: *see*

eer = [ɪːʌ]: *cheer*

ei = [i]: *receive* (exceptions: *beige, deign, eight, feign, feint, freight, reign, sleigh, veil, vein, weigh* = [ɛːɪ], *height* [hɑːɪt])

eir words: *heir, their* = [ɛːʌ]

er = [ɜ] in single syllable word or in stressed syllable: *her* (*er* + initial vowel word = [ɜɾ])

er = [ʌ] in an unstressed syllable: *letter*

er + silent *e* = [ɪːʌ]: *here* (except: *there, where* = [ɛːʌ])

eri, ery = [ɛɾɪ]: *very* (American is [ɛʁ(ɾ)ɪ])

ero = [ɪɾoːʊ]: *hero* (American is [hɪʁ(ɾ)oːʊ])

err + vowel = [ɛɾ]: *error* (American is [ɛʁ(ɾ)])

es: the *e* is silent in the following sequence:
  consonant + vowel + consonant + *es*: *lives*
  (except when preceded by [s]: *laces*)

eu words: *deuce, feud* = [u]

ew = [ju]: *view* (except: *sew* [oːʊ])

ew exception: consonant + *l* + *ew* = [u]: *flew*

ey final = [i] for single syllable words: *key*
  (except: *grey, hey, prey, they* = [ɛːɪ])

F   *f, ff* = [f]: *feather* (except: *of* [ʌv])

G   *g* + consonant, *a, i, o, u* = [g]: *green*
  (exception word: *giant* [ˈdʒɑːɪæ(ɪ)nt])

g + *e, y* = [dʒ]: *sage, gym* (except: *geese, get*
  = [g])

gh = silent: *caught* (except: *cough, laugh,*
  tough, rough = [f])

gn = [n]: *sign* (initial *gn* = [n]: *gnome*)

gr initial = [gɾ] in dramatic words: *grieve*

H   *h* initial = [h]: *hand*

h initial is silent: *heir, herb, honest* (except:
herb: *h* is pronounced in British English)

I   *i* + one consonant + vowel = [ɑːɪ]: *pine*

i + two consonants or one final cons. = [ɪ]: *bit*
  (except: *isle, tithe, writhe, wind* = [ɑːɪ])

i final in single syllable words = [ɑːɪ]: *I*
  (exception word: *ski* [ski])

ie = [i]: *piece* (exception word: *friend* = [ɛ])

ie, ies, ied final in single syllable words with
  no other vowels = [ɑːɪ]: *pie, cries, lied*

ie, ies, ied final in polysyllabic words = [ɪ]:
  prairie, ladies, fancied

ier = [ɪːʌ]: *fierce*

ieu exception word: *lieu* [ju]

igh = [ɑːɪ]: *light*

ign = [ɑːɪn]: *sign*

ild = [ɑːɪld]: *mild*

imb = [ɑːɪm]: *climb* (except: *limb* [ɪ])

ind = [ɑːɪnd]: *kind*

int = [ɑːɪnt]: *pint* (except: *mint, tint* = [ɪ])

ir + consonant = [ɜ]: *bird*

ir + silent *e* = [ɑːɪʌ]: *fire*

is exception word: *isle* [ɑːɪl]

J   *j* = [dʒ]: *jet*

K   *k* = [k]: *kite*

kn = [n]: *knee*

L   *l, ll* = [l]: *little*

lu, lew = [lju]: *lute*

M   *m* = [m]: *mammoth*

mb final = [m]: *climb*

N   *nc, nk, nqu, nx* = [ŋk]: *ink, lynx*

ng = [ŋ]: *song*

ng exceptions: *finger* [ˈfɪŋʌ], *linger*

ng + *er* for adjectives = [ŋg]: *stronger*

ng + *est* for adjectives = [ŋg]: *strongest*

nu, new = [nju]: *numerous, knew*

O   *o* + one consonant + vowel = [oːʊ]: *rope*
  (exceptions: *come* [ʌ], *done* [ʌ], *dove* [ʌ],
  glove [ʌ], *lose* [u], *love* [ʌ], *move* [u],
  one [ʌ], *prove* [u], *shove* [ʌ], *some* [ʌ])

o + two consonants or one final consonant =
  [ɑ]: *odd, top* (exceptions: *both* [oːʊ],
  comb [oːʊ], *does* [ʌ], *folk* [oːʊ], *from* [ʌ],
  front [ʌ], *ghost* [oːʊ], *gross* [oːʊ],
  host [oːʊ], *loth* [oːʊ], *monk* [ʌ], *month* [ʌ],
  moss [ɔ], *most* [oːʊ], *of* [ʌ], *once* [ʌ],
  post [oːʊ], *son* [ʌ], *tomb* [u], *ton* [ʌ],
  wolf [ʊ], *womb* [u], *won* [ʌ], *yolk* [oːʊ])

o first or middle unstressed syllable = [o]: *obey*

o initial or final = [oːʊ]: *open, so* (exceptions:
  do [u], *to* [u], *too* [u], *two* [u], *who* [u])

o as [w] exceptions: *one, once*

oa = [oːʊ]: *oath* (except: *board, broad, coarse*
  = [ɔ])

oar = [ɔːʌ]: *soar*

oi = [ɔːɪ]: *join*

ol = [oːʊl]: *cold*

oo = [u]: *boot* (except: *blood, flood* = [ʌ])

ood = [ʊ] exceptions: *good, hood, stood, wood*

ook = [ʊ] exceptions: *book, brook, cook,*
  crook, hook, look, nook, rook, shook, took

ool = [ʊ] exception: *wool*

oor = [ɔːʌ]: *door* (except: *poor, moor* = [ʊːʌ])

oot = [ʊ] exceptions: *foot, soot*

or + consonant = [ɔ]: *born*

or + silent *e* = [ɔːʌ]: *core*

or, for, nor = [ɔ] (intervocalic is [ɔʁ⁽ᶜ⁾])

orr = [ɑɾ]: *tomorrow* (American: [ɑʁ⁽ᶜ⁾])

ou = [ɑːʊ]: *out*

ough = [ɔ]: *cough*

ought = [ɔt]: *thought*

ould = [ʊd]: *could*

oup = [up]: *group*

ou exception words: *dough* [oːʊ], *rough* [ʌ],
  soul [oːʊ], *though* [oːʊ], *through* [u],
  touch [ʌ], *tough* [ʌ], *wound* [u], *you* [u],
  young [ʌ], *youth* [u]

our final = [ɑːʊʌ]: *sour* (exceptions: *four* [ɔːʌ],
  pour [ʊːʌ], *tour* [ʊːʌ], *your* [ɔːʌ])

our + consonant = [ɔ]: *course*

ow initial = [oːʊ]: *own* (exception: *owl* [ɑːʊ])

ow medial = [ɑːʊ]: *town* (except: *bowl* [oːʊ])

ow final = [oːʊ]: *shadow*

ow exceptions: *bow* = [ɑːʊ]/[oːʊ], *brow, chow,*
  cow, how, now, plow, vow, wow = [ɑːʊ])

oy = [ɔːɪ]: *boy*

P   *p, pp* = [p]: *paper*

ph = [f]: *sphere*

ps initial = [s]: *psalm*

Q *qu* = [kw]: *question*

R *r* + vowel = [ɹ]: *ring*

r: consonant + *r* = silent *r*: *heart*

r or *rr* when intervocalic = [ɾ]: *glory, sorry* (American: [ʁ⁽ʳ⁾])

r + [u] = [ɾu]: *truth* (American: [ɹ⁽ʳ⁾u])

r + [u] initial = [ɾru]: *rue* (American: [ɹ⁽ʳ⁾u])

S *s, ss* = [s]: *sister*

s preceded by a voiced consonant = [z]: *birds*

s final = [z]: *eyes* (exceptions: *gas, this, thus, us, yes* = [s])

s as [z]: vowel + *s* + vowel = [z]: *rose, use* (except: *cease, close, geese, loose, use* = [s])

sh = [ʃ]: *shine*

sion final = [ʒ]: *vision*

ssion final = [ʃ]: *passion*

sure unstressed and final in a polysyllable = [ʒʌ]: *pleasure*

su = [sju]: *suit*

T *t, tt* = [t]: *tattle* (intervocalic *t* is often [d] for American English: *little*)

th = [θ]: *thought* (except: *baths, births, cloths, moths, paths, smooth, than, that, the, thee, them, then, thence, these, this, thus, tithe, truths, with, wreaths, youths* = [ð])

th: vowel + *th* + vowel = [ð]: *breathe*

thu, thew = [θju]: *enthuse*

tion = [ʃʌn]: *motion*

tu, tew = [tju]: *tune*

ture final and unstressed = [ʧʌ]: *picture*

U *u* + consonant + vowel = [ju]: *music*

u + two consonants or one final consonant = [ʌ]: *must, from* (exceptions: *bull, bush, full, pull, push, put* = [ʊ])

u in unstressed syllables = [u]: *fortunate*

u: consonant + *l* + *u* = [u]: *flew* (not [ju])

ui = [ɪ]: *build* (except: *bruise, cruise, fruit, juice, suit* = [u]/[ju])

ur = [ɜ]: *turn*

ur + silent *e* in one syllable word = [ʊːʌ]: *sure*

ure in unstressed syllable = [ʌ]: *pasture*

uy exception word: *buy* [bɑːɪ]

V *v* = [v]: *vase*

W *w* = [w]: *win* (exception word: *two* [tu])

wa = [wɑ]: *wash* (exception word: *water* [ɔ])

war = [wɔ]: *swarm*

wh = [ʍ] *what* (except: *who, whole, whom, whose* = [h])

wha = [ʍɑ]: *what*

wor + consonant = [wɜ] in stressed syllable or single syllable word: *world* (exceptions: *sword* = [ɔ], *sworn, worn* = [wɔ])

wr = [ɹ]: *wrong*

X *x* + consonant = [ks]: *next*

x + vowel = [gz]: *exile*

Y *y* initial = [j]: *yes*

y + one consonant + vowel = [ɑːɪ]: *type*

y + final silent *e* = [ɑːɪ]: *bye*

y + one final consonant = [ɪ]: *gym*

y final in single syllable words = [ɑːɪ]: *my*

y final in polysyllabic words = [ɪ]: *baby*

Z *z, zz* = [z]: *prize, buzz*

GENERAL RULES FOR POLYSYLLABIC WORDS

POLYSYLLABIC WORDS WITH A SINGLE CONSONANTS				
a			[ɛ]/[ɛːɪ]	any [ˈɛnɪ]/nature [ˈnɛːɪʧʊ(ʌ)]
e			[ɛ]/[i]	ever [ˈɛvʌ]/even [ˈivɛ(ɪ)n]
i, y	+ one consonant + vowel =		[ɪ]/[ɑːɪ]	river [ˈɹɪvʌ]/silent [ˈsɑːɪlɛnt]
o			[oːʊ]	over [ˈoːʊvʌ]
u			[ju]/[u]	music [ˈmjuzɪk]/ruby [ˈɾrubɪ]

POLYSYLLABIC WORDS WITH CONSONANT CLUSTERS				
a			[æ]/[ɛːɪ]	happy [ˈhæpɪ]/angel [ˈɛːɪndʒʊl]
e			[ɛ]	gentle [ˈdʒɛntʊl]
i, y	+ two consonants + vowel =		[ɪ]	silver [ˈsɪlvʌ]
o			[oːʊ]/[ʌ]	only [ˈoːʊnlɪ]/mother [ˈmʌðʌ]
u			[ʌ]	summer [ˈsʌmʌ]

POLYSYLLABIC WORDS WITH INTERVOCALIC R			
a		[ær]	tarry [ˈtæɾɪ]
e	+ *r/rr* + vowel =	[ɛɾ]/[ɪɾ]	berry [ˈbɛɾɪ]/hero [ˈhɪːʌɾoːʊ]
o		[ɔɾ]/[ɑɾ]	glory [ˈglɔɾɪ]/sorrow [ˈsɑɾoːʊ]
u		[ʊɾ]	hurry [ˈhʊɾɪ]

A vowel *r* option is provided for intervocalic *r* in American English: [ʁ⁽ʳ⁾]

WHEN TO SING [ɑ]

Specified spellings that have an [æ] sound in American English are pronounced with dark [ɑ] for British English.

I.   Spellings: *a* + [f]: *after* [ˈɑftʌ], *a* + [s]: *fast* [fɑst], *a* + [ntʃ]: *branch* [ˈbɹɑntʃ], *a* + [ns]: *dance* [dɑns], *a* + th: *bath* [bɑθ]

II.   Spellings *-and*, *-ant*, and *-ample* are [ɑ] in these words only:
     -and: *command, demand, reprimand*
     -ant: *can't, shan't, aunt, advantage, chant, enchant, grant, plant, slant*
     -ample: *sample, example*

III.   Exceptions to section I include: *alas, ant, asp, aspect, aspen, aspiration, ass, baffle, blaspheme, cancel, cascade, chastise, circumstance, classic, classify, contrast, daffodil, enhance, expanse, fancy, fantastic, fathom, gather, graphic, hast, hath, lass, mass, math, passage, passenger, passive, pasture, ranch, riffraff, romance, sarcastic, scaffold, stance, trans-* (as a prefix), *traffic*

DEFINING THE SCHWA

Rules for defining the schwa are discussed in the September/October 2022 issue of the *Journal of Singing*: "Defining the Schwa for English, German, French, and Russian Lyric Diction" by Cheri Montgomery.

English Pronunciation Guide

(FROM *SINGER'S DICTION* BY CHERI MONTGOMERY)

Terms

IPA. The International Phonetic Alphabet was designed by linguists for speech. Singers adopted the IPA for lyric diction. Precise pronunciation must be defined within the respective language then further defined for lyric diction.

Phoneme. Each IPA symbol represents one phoneme. A phoneme is the smallest element of sound within a language. For example, [t] is the first phoneme in the word *time* [tɑːɪm]. IPA symbols are enclosed in brackets in this text.

Monosyllable: a word with one syllable

Polysyllable: a word with two or more syllables

Monophthong: a vowel sound that maintains one articulatory position throughout the course of the syllable

Falling Diphthong: two vowel sounds in the same syllable with a lengthening of the first vowel

Rising Diphthong: two vowel sounds in the same syllable with a lengthening of the second vowel

Triphthong: three vowel sounds within the same syllable

Hiatus: adjacent vowel sounds that occupy consecutive syllables

Intervocalic: a consonant that stands between vowels

Initial: the first letter or sound of a word

Medial: a letter or sound in the middle of a word

Final: the last letter or sound of a word

Dialect

Dialect is the source of much confusion in the lyric diction classroom. Students often state: "But I don't say it that way." This observation implies that the singer expects lyric diction to feel "natural." Singing formations may not feel "natural" especially when spoken practice provides the standard for what is considered "normal." English lyric diction rules offer a prescribed pronunciation that is ideal for singing. Dialect is imperceptible in fine singing. Lyric diction should not reflect speech formation or regional dialects (exceptions for the character voice are indicated within the text). These points are addressed through the informed critique of performances by classically trained singers.

Note concerning the IPA for titles: the spoken pronunciation (provided beneath each title) may differ from the sung pronunciation of the same words. The sustained nature of singing and its effect on the pronunciation of *r* and vowels in unstressed syllables necessitates adjustments to the IPA.

Choice of Symbols

There are fourteen vowel sounds in English: [i ɪ e ɛ u ʊ o ɔ ɒ ɑ a æ ʌ ɜ]. This text uses symbols that are most favorable for singing. Uniformity, clarity, and ease of production are enhanced by replacing the bright [a] and back [ɒ] vowels with dark [ɑ]. The words *night* [nɑːɪt], *song* [sɒŋ], and *father* [ˈfɑðʌ] are transcribed with a dark [ɑ] for lyric diction. Vowel clarity and distinction are enhanced by applying an open vowel transcription to the diphthongs. For example, words like *fate* [fɛːɪt] and *lane* [lɛːɪn] could be mistaken for *feet* [fit] and *lean* [lin] if closed [eːi] were applied.

Sound Links

Sounds for symbols of multiple languages are available in one location at https://www.stmpublishers.com/listening.

Symbol	Audio Example	Symbol	Audio Example	Symbol	Audio Example
[ʌ]	bit.ly/2Wtvv93	[j]	bit.ly/2yzX2O7	[s]	bit.ly/2YD76QR
[ɑ]	bit.ly/2WuU5q2	[k]	bit.ly/35B6FrO	[ʃ]	bit.ly/3dmEXSs
[æ]	bit.ly/3fpGZmA	[l]	bit.ly/35BOHWe	[t]	bit.ly/2SI9MZX
[b]	bit.ly/3c9R5WG	[m]	bit.ly/3beJdlD	[θ] [ð]	bit.ly/2L5gDsg
[d]	bit.ly/35APdUe	[n]	bit.ly/2YHrrVh	[ʧ]	bit.ly/35ChxG8
[e]	bit.ly/2WupTex	[ŋ]	bit.ly/2SE2gPN	[ʤ]	bit.ly/3djkUnS
[ɛ]	bit.ly/3b1FWWA	[o]	bit.ly/3bb6q7Y	[u]	bit.ly/2SHwcdF
[f]	bit.ly/2L30LX3	[ɔ]	bit.ly/3diCQ1U	[ʊ]	bit.ly/2SJ3V6G
[g]	bit.ly/2SHAcuJ	[p]	bit.ly/3dlWDh4	[v]	bit.ly/2L62Sti
[h]	bit.ly/3cbRckG	[ɹ]	bit.ly/2SGfw6n	[w]	bit.ly/2YHtbhh
[ʔ]	bit.ly/35LBKtb	[ʁ]	bit.ly/2SFsQrP	[ʍ]	bit.ly/35zvbJW
[i]	bit.ly/2YCmFs8	[ɾ]	bit.ly/2xDxsHz	[z]	bit.ly/2SFvgqg
[ɪ]	bit.ly/3b8PiQ8	[ɜ]	bit.ly/2YBkLrE	[ʒ]	bit.ly/3b8OOd9

Characteristics of the English language with a comparison between speech and singing

1. The qualities of spoken English include: a weighted accentuation of the stressed syllable, a rise in pitch of the stressed syllable, and variable vowel lengths. The composer's setting dictates the pitch, vowel length, and weight of English pronunciation for singing.

2. Spoken English is medial in placement with a lax formation of the vowel. English for singing maintains a released jaw position, intentional lip rounding for back vowels, and forward tongue arch for front vowels.

3. Vowels are typically weak in formation for speech. They must be precise, pure, and highly resonated for singing. Vowel clarity and distinction are required.

4. The consonants *p*, *t*, and *k* are aspirate in both the spoken and sung forms of English.

5. The upward curled tongue position of the English lateral *l* and retroflex *r* have an undesirable effect on preceding vowel sounds. Dental *l* and vowel [ʁ] replacements (for postvocalic *l* and *r*) are recommended.

6. As a general rule, diction for singing is dialect-free. Dialect affects specified words, and the *a*, *r*, and *wh* spellings in American English. An [ʁ] pronunciation is indicated for intervocalic *r*, an [æ] pronunciation is indicated for specified *a* spellings, and a [w] pronunciation may be preferable for the *wh* spelling.

7. This text indicates precise pronunciation of the schwa. Specified spellings have an alternate pronunciation. The correct choice is dependent on duration of the note. The sustained pronunciation is provided first. The rapidly enunciated pronunciation is indicated in parenthesis. The two vowels may also mix.

Audio

ENGLISH PRONUNCIATION CHART

FRONT VOWELS Front tongue arch		BACK VOWELS Lip rounding		SEMI CONSONANTS Front tongue arch		DIACRITICAL MARKS	
[i]	eat, greet [it] [gɹit]	[u]	food, blue [fud] [blu]	[j]	yet, year [jɛt] [jɪːʌ]	[:] Length	day, shadow [dɛːɪ] [ˈʃædoːʊ]
[ɪ]	bit, quick [bɪt] [kwɪk]	[ʊ]	look, put [lʊk] [pʊt]	Lip rounding		[ˈ] 1st Stress	return, again [ɹɪˈtɜn] [ʌˈgɛn]
[e]	chaos, décor [ˈkeɑs] [deˈkɔːʌ]	[o]	obey, protect [oˈbɛːɪ] [pɹoˈtɛkt]	[w]	web, winter [wɛb] [ˈwɪntʌ]	[ˌ] 2nd Stress	melancholy [ˈmɛlɪnˌkɑlɪ]
				Voiceless lip consonant			
[ɛ]	met, friend [mɛt] [fɹɛnd]	[ɔ]	talk, ought [tɔk] [ɔt]	[ʍ]	wheat, whistle [ʍit] [ˈʍɪsʊl]	Parentheses: Reduced vowel	heaven [ˈhɛvɛ(ɪ)n]

CENTRAL VOWELS

[æ]	hat, lamb [hæt] [læm]	[ɑ]	father, top [ˈfɑðʌ] [tɑp]	[ʌ]	up, love [ʌp] [lʌv]	[ɜ] Vowel *r*	bird, worth [bɜd] [wɜθ]

The following symbols are not included in the English transcriptions: [a] (voilà), [ɒ] (hot), and [e:i] (fate). The [a] vowel has a sound that is between the [ɑ] and [æ] vowels; [ɒ] is between [ɔ] and [ɑ]; and [e] is between [ɛ] and [i].

ENGLISH R		FRICATIVES		AFFRICATES		DENTAL	
[r]	thread, throne [θrɛd] [θroːʊn]	[ʃ]	short, passion [ʃɔt] [ˈpæʃʌn]	[ʧ]	chair, latch [ʧɛːʌ] [læʧ]	[θ]	think, youth [θɪŋk] [juθ]
[ɹ]	ring, dream [ɹɪŋ] [dɹim]	[ʒ]	asure, vision [ˈæʒʊ(ʌ)] [ˈvɪʒʌn]	[ʤ]	judge, gentle [ʤʌʤ] [ˈʤɛntʊl]	[ð]	they, breathe, with [ðɛːɪ] [bɹɪð] [wɪð]
*[ʁ]	around [ʌˈʁ⁽ʳ⁾ɑːʊnd]	GLOTTAL A glottal stop [ʔ] is a grunt sound (not indicated in this text)				VELAR	
Silent *r*	star, morning [stɑ] [ˈmɔnɪŋ]	[h]	home, heart [hoːʊm] [hɑt]	[ʔ]	age, ever [ʔɛːɪʤ] [ˈʔɛvʌ]	[ŋ]	finger, thank [ˈfɪŋgʌ] [θæŋk]

* Intervocalic *r* is transcribed with a vowel [ʁ] for the unstressed words *or, for,* and *nor,* and for intervocalic *r* in American English. The [ʁ] symbol is selected for lyric diction to describe a vowel formation not identified on the official IPA chart. The lips are rounded, the tongue tip touches the lower front teeth, and the sides touch the upper molars. This will alleviate the adverse effect that a retroflex tongue formation would have on a preceding vowel.

A

Adam, Adolphe (Fr. 1803-1856)

Song Selection

"O Holy Night"
[oːʊ ˈhoːʊlɪ naːɪt]
Translation of "Minuit, chrétiens" by Placide Cappeau
(Fr. 1808-1877)

O holy night! The stars are brightly shining,
[oːʊ ˈhoːʊlɪ naːɪt ðʊ staz a ˈbɹaːɪtlɪ ˈʃaːɪnɪŋ]
It is the night of the dear Saviour's birth.
[ɪt ɪz ðʊ naːɪt ʌv ðʊ diːʌ ˈseːɪvjɔ(ʌ)z bɜθ]
Long lay the world in sin and error pining,
[laŋ leːɪ ðʊ wɜld ɪn sɪn ænd ˈɛɹɔ(ʌ) ˈpaːɪnɪŋ]
Till He appeared and the soul felt its worth.
[tɪl hi ʌˈpɪːʌd ænd ðʊ soːʊl fɛlt ɪts wɜθ]
A thrill of hope the weary world rejoices,
[ʌ θɹɪl ʌv hoːʊp ðʊ ˈwɪːʌɹɪ wɜld ɹɪˈdʒɔːɪsɛ(ɪ)z]
For yonder breaks a new and glorious morn;
[fɔ ˈjandʌ bɹeːɪks ʌ nju ænd ˈglɔɹɪʌs mɔn]
Fall on your knees, O hear the angel voices!
[fɔl an jɔːʌ niz oːʊ hɪːʌ ði ˈeːɪndʒɛ(ʊ)l ˈvɔːɪsɛ(ɪ)z]
O night divine, O night when Christ was born!
[oːʊ naːɪt dɪˈvaːɪn oːʊ naːɪt ʍɛn kɹaːɪst waz bɔn]
O night divine, O night, O night divine!
[oːʊ naːɪt dɪˈvaːɪn oːʊ naːɪt oːʊ naːɪt dɪˈvaːɪn]
Led by the light of Faith serenely beaming,
[lɛd baːɪ ðʊ laːɪt ʌv feːɪθ sɪˈɹinlɪ ˈbimɪŋ]
With glowing hearts by His cradle we stand.
[wɪð ˈgloːʊɪŋ hats baːɪ hɪz ˈkɹeːɪdʊl wi stænd]
So, led by light of a star sweetly gleaming,
[soːʊ lɛd baːɪ laːɪt ʌv ʌ sta ˈswitlɪ ˈglimɪŋ]
Here came the wise men from the Orient land.
[hɪːʌ keːɪm ðʊ waːɪz mɛn fɹʌm ði ˈɔɹɪɛnt lænd]
The King of kings lay thus in lowly manger,
[ðʊ kɪŋ ʌv kɪŋz leːɪ ðʌs ɪn ˈloːʊlɪ ˈmeːɪndʒʌ]
In all our trials born to be our friend;
[ɪn ɔl aːʊʌ ˈtɹaːɪʌlz bɔn tu bi aːʊʌ fɹɛnd]
He knows our need, to our weakness no stranger
[hi noːʊz aːʊʌ nid tu aːʊʌ ˈwiknɛ(ɪ)s noːʊ ˈstɹeːɪndʒʌ]
Behold your King! Before Him lowly bend!
[bɪˈhoːʊld jɔːʌ kɪŋ bɪˈfɔːʌ hɪm ˈloːʊlɪ bɛnd]
Truly He taught us to love one another,
[ˈtɹulɪ hi tɔt ʌs tu lʌv wʌn ʌˈnʌðʌ]
His law is love, and His gospel is peace;
[hɪz lɔ ɪz lʌv ænd hɪz ˈgaspʊl ɪz pis]
Chains shall He break, for the slave is our brother,
[tʃeːɪnz ʃæl hi bɹeːɪk fɔ ðʊ sleːɪv ɪz aːʊʌ ˈbɹʌðʌ]
And in His name all oppression shall cease.
[ænd ɪn hɪz neːɪm ɔl oˈpɹɛʃʌn ʃæl sis]
Sweet hymns of joy in grateful chorus raise we,
[swit hɪmz ʌv dʒɔːɪ ɪn ˈgɹeːɪtfʊl ˈkɔɹʌs ɹɛːɪz wi]

Let all within us praise His holy name;
[lɛt ɔl wɪðˈɪn ʌs pɹɛːɪz hɪz ˈhoːʊlɪ neːɪm]
Christ is the Lord, Sing praise to Him forever,
[kɹaːɪst ɪz ðʊ lɔd sɪŋ pɹɛːɪz tu hɪm fɔʁ⁽ʳ⁾ˈɛvʌ]
His pow'r and glory evermore proclaim!
[hɪz paːʊʌɾ ænd ˈglɔɹɪ ɛvʌˈmɔːʌ pɹʊˈklɛːɪm]

 ## Adams, H. Leslie (Am. b. 1932)

Five Millay Songs (Song Cycle)
[faːɪv mɪˈlɛːɪ saŋz]
Millay, Edna St. Vincent (Am. 1892-1950)

1. Wild Swans
[waːɪld swanz]

I looked in my heart while the swans went over.
[aːɪ lʊkt ɪn maːɪ hat ʍaːɪl ðʌ swanz wɛnt ˈoːʊvʌ]
And what did I see I had not seen before?
[ænd ʍat dɪd aːɪ si aːɪ hæd nat sin bɪˈfɔːʌ]
Only a question less or a question more:
[ˈoːʊnlɪ ʌ ˈkwɛstʃʌn lɛs ɔʁ⁽ʳ⁾ ʌ ˈkwɛstʃʌn mɔːʌ]
Nothing to match the flight of wild birds flying.
[ˈnʌθɪŋ tu mætʃ ðʌ flaːɪt ʌv waːɪld bɜdz ˈflaːɪɪŋ]
Tiresome heart, forever living and dying,
[ˈtaːɪʌsʌm hat fɔʁ⁽ʳ⁾ˈɛvʌ ˈlɪvɪŋ ænd ˈdaːɪɪŋ]
House without air, I lock your door.
[haːʊs wɪðˈaːʊt ɛːʌ aːɪ lak jɔːʌ dɔːʌ]
Wild swans, come over the town, come over
[waːɪld swanz kʌm ˈoːʊvʌ ðʌ taːʊn kʌm ˈoːʊvʌ]
The town again, trailing your legs and crying!
[ðʌ taːʊn ʌˈgɛn ˈtɹɛːɪlɪŋ jɔːʌ lɛgz ænd ˈkɹaːɪɪŋ]

2. Branch by Branch
[bɹæntʃ baːɪ bɹæntʃ]

Branch by branch this tree has died.
[bɹæntʃ baːɪ bɹæntʃ ðɪs tɹi hæz daːɪd]
Green only is one last bough,
[gɹin ˈoːʊnlɪ ɪz wʌn læst baːʊ]
Moving its leaves in the sun.
[ˈmuvɪŋ ɪts livz ɪn ðʌ sʌn]
What evil ate its root, what blight,
[ʍat ˈivɪ(ʊ)l ɛːɪt ɪts ɹ⁽ʳʳ⁾ut ʍat blaːɪt]
What ugly thing,
[ʍat ˈʌglɪ θɪŋ]
Let the mole say, the bird sing;
[lɛt ðʌ moːʊl sɛːɪ ðʌ bɜd sɪŋ]
Or the white worm behind the shedding bark
[ɔ ðʌ ʍaːɪt wɜm bɪˈhaːɪnd ðʌ ˈʃɛdɪŋ bak]
Tick in the dark.
[tɪk ɪn ðʌ dak]
You and I have only one thing to do:
[ju ænd aːɪ hæv ˈoːʊnlɪ wʌn θɪŋ tu du]
Saw, saw, saw the trunk through.
[sɔ sɔ sɔ ðʌ tɹʌŋk θɹu]

3. For You There Is No Song

[fɔʁ ju ðɛːʁ ɪz noːʊ saŋ]

For you there is no song,
[fɔ ju ðɛːʌʁ⁽ʳ⁾ ɪz noːʊ saŋ]
Only the shaking of the voice that meant to sing;
[ˈoːʊnlɪ ðʌ ˈʃɛːɪkɪŋ ʌv ðʌ vɔːɪs ðæt mɛnt tu sɪŋ]
The sound of the strong voice breaking.
[ðʌ saːʊnd ʌv ðʌ stɹaŋ vɔːɪs ˈbɹɛːɪkɪŋ]
Strange in my hand appears the pen,
[stɹɛːɪndʒ ɪn maːɪ hænd ʌˈpɪːʌz ðʌ pɛn]
And yours broken
[ænd jɔːʌz ˈbɹoːʊkɛ(ɪ)n]
There are ink and tears on the page;
[ðɛːʌʁ⁽ʳ⁾ aʁ⁽ʳ⁾ ɪŋk ænd tɪːʌz an ðʌ pɛːɪdʒ]
Only the tears have spoken.
[ˈoːʊnlɪ ðʌ tɪːʌz hæv ˈspoːʊkɛ(ɪ)n]

4. The Return from Town

[ðʌ ɹɪˈtɜn fɹʌm taːʊn]

As I sat down by Saddle Stream
[æz aːɪ sæt daːʊn baːɪ ˈsædʊl stɹim]
To bathe my dusty feet there,
[tu bɛːɪð maːɪ ˈdʌstɪ fit ðɛːʌ]
A girl was standing on the bridge
[ʌ ɡɜl waz ˈstændɪŋ an ðʌ bɹɪdʒ]
Any boy would meet there.
[ˈɛnɪ bɔːɪ wʊd mit ðɛːʌ]
As I went over Woody Knob
[æz aːɪ wɛnt ˈoːʊvʌ ˈwʊdɪ nab]
And dipped into the Hollow,
[ænd dɪpt ˈɪntu ðʌ ˈhaloːʊ]
A youth was coming up the hill
[ʌ juθ waz ˈkʌmɪŋ ʌp ðʌ hɪl]
Any lad would follow.
[ˈɛnɪ læd wʊd ˈfaloːʊ]
Then in I turned at my own gate,–
[ðɛn ɪn aːɪ tɜnd æt maːɪ oːʊn ɡɛːɪt]
And nothing to be sad for–
[ænd ˈnʌθɪŋ tu bi sæd fɔːʌ]
To such a wife as any man
[tu sʌtʃ ʌ waːɪf æz ˈɛnɪ mæn]
Would pass a pretty lass for.
[wʊd pæs ʌ ˈpɹɪtɪ læs fɔːʌ]

5. Gone Again Is Summer the Lovely

[ɡan ʌˈɡɛn ɪz ˈsʌmʁ ðʌ ˈlʌvli]

Gone, gone again is Summer the lovely,
[ɡan ɡan ʌˈɡɛn ɪz ˈsʌmʌ ðʌ ˈlʌvli]
She that knew not where to hide,
[ʃi ðæt nju nat ʍɛːʌ tu haːɪd]
Is gone again like a jeweled fish from the hand,
[ɪz ɡan ʌˈɡɛn laːɪk ʌ ˈdʒuːɛ(ʊ)ld fɪʃ fɹʌm ðʌ hænd]

Is lost on every side.
[ɪz last an ˈɛvɹɪ saːɪd]
Mute, mute, I make my way to the garden,
[mjut mjut aːɪ mɛːɪk maːɪ wɛːɪ tu ðʌ ˈɡadɛ(ɪ)n]
Thither where she last was seen;
[ˈθɪðʌ ʍɛːʌ ʃi læst waz sin]
The heavy foot of the frost is on the flags there,
[ðʌ ˈhɛvɪ fʊt ʌv ðʌ fɹast ɪz an ðʌ flægz ðɛːʌ]
Where her light step has been.
[ʍɛːʌ hɜ laːɪt stɛp hæz bɪn]
Gone, gone again is Summer the lovely,
[ɡan ɡan ʌˈɡɛn ɪz ˈsʌmʌ ðʌ ˈlʌvli]
Gone again on every side,
[ɡan ʌˈɡɛn an ˈɛvɹɪ saːɪd]
Lost again like a shining fish from the hand
[last ʌˈɡɛn laːɪk ʌ ˈʃaːɪnɪŋ fɪʃ fɹʌm ðʌ hænd]
Into the shadowy tide.
[ˈɪntu ðʌ ˈʃædoːʊɪ taːɪd]

Song Selections

"Love Response"

[lʌv ɹɪˈspans]
Dunbar, Paul Lawrence (Am. 1872-1906)

When Phyllis sighs
[ʍɛn ˈfɪlɪs saːɪz]
And from her eyes the light dies out:
[ænd fɹʌm hɜ aːɪz ðʌ laːɪt daːɪz aːʊt]
My soul replies
[maːɪ soːʊl ɹɪˈplaːɪz]
with misery of deep-drawn breath,
[wɪð ˈmɪzʌʁ⁽ʳ⁾ɪ ʌv dip dɹɔn bɹɛθ]
Even as it were at war with death.
[ˈivɛ(ɪ)n æz ɪt wɜ⁽ʳ⁾ æt wɔ wɪð dɛθ]
When Phyllis smiles,
[ʍɛn ˈfɪlɪs smaːɪlz]
Her glance beguiles my heart
[hɜ glæns bɪˈɡaːɪlz maːɪ hat]
thru love-lit woodland aisles,
[θru lʌv lɪt ˈwʊdlæ(ʌ)nd aːɪlz]
And thru the silence high and clear,
[ænd θru ðʌ ˈsaːɪlɛ(ɪ)ns haːɪ ænd klɪːʌ]
A wooing warbler's song, I hear.
[ʌ ˈwuɪŋ ˈwɔblʌz saŋ aːɪ hɪːʌ]
But if she frown, despair comes down
[bʌt ɪf ʃi fɹaːʊn dɪˈspɛːʌ kʌmz daːʊn]
I put me on my sack-cloth gown.
[aːɪ pʊt mi an maːɪ sæk klaθ ɡaːʊn]
So frown not, Phyllis, lest I die,
[soːʊ fɹaːʊn nat ˈfɪlɪs lɛst aːɪ daːɪ]
But look on me with smile or sigh.
[bʌt lʊk an mi wɪð smaːɪl ɔ saːɪ]

"Night Song" (Nightsongs)
[naːɪt sɑŋ]
Delany, Clarissa M. Scott (Am. 1901-1927)

The night was made for rest and sleep,
[ðʌ naːɪt wɑz mɛːɪd fɔ ɹɛst ænd slip]
For winds that softly sigh;
[fɔ wɪndz ðæt ˈsɑftlɪ saːɪ]
It was not made for grief and tears;
[ɪt wɑz nɑt mɛːɪd fɔ ɡɹⁱⁿif ænd tɪːʌz]
So then why do I cry?
[soːʊ ðɛn ʍaːɪ du ɑːɪ kɹⁱⁿaːɪ]
The wind that blows through leafy trees
[ðʌ wɪnd ðæt bloːʊz θɾu ˈlifɪ tɹiz]
Is soft and warm and sweet;
[ɪz sɑft ænd wɔm ænd swit]
For me the night is a gracious cloak
[fɔ mi ðʌ naːɪt ɪz ʌ ˈɡɹɛːɪʃʌs kloːʊk]
To hide my soul's defeat.
[tu haːɪd maːɪ soːʊlz dɪˈfit]
Just one dark hour of shaken depths,
[dʒʌst wʌn dɑk ɑːʊʌʁⁱⁿ ʌv ˈʃɛːɪkɛⁱⁿn dɛpθs]
Of bitter black despair–
[ʌv ˈbɪtʌ blæk dɪˈspɛːʌ]
Another day will find me brave,
[ʌˈnʌðʌ dɛːɪ wɪl faːɪnd mi bɹɛːɪv]
And not afraid to dare.
[ænd nɑt ʌˈfɹɛːɪd tu dɛːʌ]

"Sence You Went Away" (Nightsongs)
[sɛns ju wɛnt ʌˈwɛːɪ]
Johnson, James Weldon (Am. 1871-1938)

Seems lak to me de stars don't shine so bright,
[sim(z) laːɪk tʊ mi dʌ stɑz doːʊn(t) ʃaːɪn soːʊ bɹaːɪt]
Seems lak to me de sun done loss his light,
[sim(z) laːɪk tʊ mi dʌ sʌn dʌn lɑs hɪz laːɪt]
Seems lak to me der's nothin' goin' right,
[sim(z) laːɪk tʊ mi dɛːʌz ˈnʌθɪn ˈɡoːʊɪn ɹaːɪt]
Sence you went away.
[sɛns ju wɛnt ʌˈwɛːɪ]
Seems lak to me de sky ain't half so blue,
[sim(z) laːɪk tʊ mi dʌ skaːɪ ɛːɪnt hæf soːʊ blu]
Seems lak to me dat ev'thing wants you,
[sim(z) laːɪk tʊ mi dæt ˈɛvɹɪθɪŋ wɑnts ju]
Seems lak to me I don't know what to do,
[sim(z) laːɪk tʊ mi a doːʊnt noːʊ wɑt tʊ du]
Sence you went away.
[sɛns ju wɛnt ʌˈwɛːɪ]
Oh, ev'ything is wrong, De day's jes twice as long,
[oːʊ ˈɛvɹɪθɪŋ ɪz ɹɑŋ dʌ dɛːɪz dʒɛs twaːɪs æz lɑŋ]
De bird's forgot his song, Sence you went away.
[dʌ bɜdz fɔˈɡɑt hɪz sɑŋ sɛns ju wɛnt ʌˈwɛːɪ]
Seems lak to me I jes can't he'p but sigh,
[sim(z) laːɪk tʊ mi a dʒɛs kɛːɪnt hɛp bʌt saːɪ]

Seems lak to me ma th'oat keeps gittin' dry,
[sim(z) laːɪk tʊ mi ma θoːʊt kips ˈɡɛ(d)ɪn dɹaːɪ]
Seems lak to me a tear stays in my eye,
[sim(z) laːɪk tʊ mi ʌ tɪːʌ stɛːɪz ɪn ma ɑ]
Sence you went away.
[sɛns ju wɛnt ʌˈwɛːɪ]

"The Heart of a Woman" (Nightsongs)
[ðʌ hɑʁt ʌv ʌ ˈwʊmʌn]
Johnson, Georgia Douglas (Am. 1880-1966)

The heart of a woman goes forth with the dawn
[ðʌ hɑt ʌv ʌ ˈwʊmæ(ʌ)n ɡoːʊz fɔθ wɪð ðʌ dɔn]
As a lone bird, soft winging so restlessly on.
[æz ʌ loːʊn bɜd sɑft ˈwɪŋɪŋ soːʊ ˈɹɛstlɛ(ɪ)slɪ ɑn]
Afar o'er life's turrets and vales does it roam
[ʌˈfaʁⁱⁿ ɔːʌ laːɪfs ˈtʊʁⁱⁿɛ(ɪ)ts ænd vɛːɪlz dʌz ɪt ɹoːʊm]
In the wake of those echoes the heart calls home.
[ɪn ðʌ wɛːɪk ʌv ðoːʊz ˈɛkoːʊz ðʌ hɑt kɔlz hoːʊm]
The heart of a woman falls back with the night
[ðʌ hɑt ʌv ʌ ˈwʊmæ(ʌ)n fɔlz bæk wɪð ðʌ naːɪt]
And enters some alien cage in its plight,
[ænd ˈɛntʌz sʌm ˈɛːɪlɪɛ(ɪ)n kɛːɪdʒ ɪn ɪts plaːɪt]
And tries to forget it has dreamed of the stars
[ænd tɹaːɪz tu fɔˈɡɛt ɪt hæz dɹimd ʌv ðʌ stɑz]
While it breaks, breaks on the sheltering bars.
[ʍaːɪl ɪt bɹɛːɪks bɹɛːɪks ɑn ðʌ ˈʃɛltʌʁⁱⁿɪŋ bɑz]

Adler, Samuel (Am. b. 1928)

Four Poems of James Stephens (Song Cycle)
[fɔːʁ ˈpoɛmz ʌv dʒɛːɪmz ˈstivɪnz]
Stephens, James (Ir. 1882-1950)

1. The Wind
[ðʌ wɪnd]

The wind stood up and gave a shout,
[ðʌ wɪnd stʊd ʌp ænd ɡɛːɪv ʌ ʃaːʊt]
He whistled on his fingers
[hi ˈʍɪsʊld ɑn hɪz ˈfɪŋɡʌz]
And kicked the withered leaves about.
[ænd kɪkt ðʌ ˈwɪðʌd livz ʌˈbaːʊt]
And thumped the branches with his hand,
[ænd θʌmpt ðʌ ˈbɹænʧɛ(ɪ)z wɪð hɪz hænd]
And said he'll kill and kill; And so he will.
[ænd sɛd hil kɪl ænd kɪl ænd soːʊ hi wɪl]

2. Chill of the Eve
[ʧil ʌv ði iv]

A long, green swell
[ʌ lɑŋ ɡɹin swɛl]

Slopes soft to the sea;
[sloːʊps saft tu ðʌ si]
And a far-off bell
[ænd ʌ faʁ⁽ʳ⁾ af bɛl]
Swings sweet to me.
[swɪŋz swit tu mi]
As the grey chill day
[æz ðʌ ɡɹɛːɪ ʧil dɛːɪ]
Slips away from the lea.
[slɪps ʌˈwɛːɪ fɹʌm ðʌ li]
Spread cold and far,
[spɹɛd koːʊld ænd fɑ]
Without one glow
[wɪðˈaːʊt wʌn gloːʊ]
From a mild pale star,
[fɹʌm ʌ maːɪld pɛːɪl stɑ]
Is the sky's steel brow;
[ɪz ðʌ skaːɪz stil bɹɑːʊ]
And the grey chill day,
[ænd ðʌ ɡɹɛːɪ ʧil dɛːɪ]
Slips away below.
[slɪps ʌˈwɛːɪ bɪˈloːʊ]
Yon green tree grieves,
[jɑn ɡɹin tɹi ɡɹ⁽ʳ⁾ivz]
To the air around;
[tu ði ɛːʌʁ⁽ʳ⁾ ʌˈʁaːʊnd]
And the whispering leaves
[ænd ðʌ ˈʍɪspʌʁ⁽ʳ⁾ɪŋ livz]
Have a lonely sound
[hæv ʌ ˈloːʊnlɪ saːʊnd]
As the grey chill day,
[æz ðʌ ɡɹɛːɪ ʧil dɛːɪ]
Slips away from the ground.
[slɪps ʌˈwɛːɪ fɹʌm ðʌ ɡɹɑːʊnd]
And dark, more dark,
[ænd dak mɔːʌ dak]
The shades settle down;
[ðʌ ʃɛːɪdz ˈsɛtʊl daːʊn]
Far off is a spark
[faʁ⁽ʳ⁾ af ɪz ʌ spak]
From the lamp-lit town,
[fɹʌm ðʌ læmp lɪt taːʊn]
As the grey chill day,
[æz ðʌ ɡɹɛːɪ ʧil dɛːɪ]
Slips away with a frown.
[slɪps ʌˈwɛːɪ wɪð ʌ fɹaːʊn]

3. The Piper
[ðʌ ˈpaːɪpʁ]

Shepherd! While the lambs do feed,
[ˈʃɛpʌd ʍaːɪl ðʌ læmz du fid]
Do not sulk beneath a tree,
[du nɑt sʌlk bɪˈniθ ʌ tɹi]
But upon your oaten reed,
[bʌt ʌˈpɑn jɔːʁ⁽ʳ⁾ ˈoːʊtɛ⁽ɪ⁾n ɹid]

Pipe us merrily.
[paːɪp ʌs ˈmɛʁ⁽ʳ⁾ɪli]
Though it rain do not forbear!
[ðoːʊ ɪt ɹɛːɪn du nɑt fɔˈbɛːʌ]
Sun and rain are from the sky
[sʌn ænd ɹɛːɪn ɑ fɹʌm ðʌ skaːɪ]
Pipe a silly merry air,
[paːɪp ʌ ˈsɪlɪ ˈmɛʁ⁽ʳ⁾ɪ ɛːʌ]
Till the shower passes by.
[tɪl ðʌ ʃaːʊʌ ˈpæsɛ⁽ɪ⁾z baːɪ]
The sun will come again in gold!
[ðʌ sʌn wɪl kʌm ʌˈgɛn ɪn goːʊld]
Pipe us merrily, Pipe us merrily
[paːɪp ʌs ˈmɛʁ⁽ʳ⁾ɪli paːɪp ʌs ˈmɛʁ⁽ʳ⁾ɪli]
Until evening brings the lambs to fold.
[ʌnˈtɪl ˈivnɪŋ bɹɪŋz ðʌ læmz tu foːʊld]
You may weep then, if you will.
[ju mɛːɪ wip ðɛn ɪf ju wɪl]

4. And It Was Stormy Weather
[ænd ɪt waz ˈstɔʁmi ˈwɛðʁ]

Now the winds are riding by,
[naːʊ ðʌ wɪndz ʌ ˈɹaːɪdɪŋ baːɪ]
Clouds are galloping the sky,
[klaːʊdz ʌ ˈgælʌpɪŋ ðʌ skaːɪ]
Bush and tree are lashing bare,
[bʊʃ ænd tɹi ʌ ˈlæʃɪŋ bɛːʌ]
Savage boughs on savage air!
[ˈsævæ⁽ɪ⁾ʤ baːʊz an ˈsævæ⁽ɪ⁾ʤ ɛːʌ]
Crying as they lash and sway;
[ˈkɹ⁽ʳ⁾aːɪŋ æz ðɛːɪ læʃ ænd swɛːɪ]
Pull the roots out of the clay!
[pʊl ðʌ ɹ⁽ʳʳ⁾uts aːʊt ʌv ðʌ klɛːɪ]
Lift away, away, away!
[lɪft ʌˈwɛːɪ ʌˈwɛːɪ ʌˈwɛːɪ]
Leave security and speed
[liv sɪˈkjʊːʁ⁽ʳ⁾ɪtɪ ænd spid]
From the roots, the mud, the mead!
[fɹʌm ðʌ ɹ⁽ʳʳ⁾uts ðʌ mʌd ðʌ mid]
Into the sea and air we go!
[ˈɪntu ðʌ si ænd ɛːʌ wi goːʊ]
To chase the gull! the moon, and know,
[tu ʧɛːɪs ðʌ gʌl ðʌ mun ænd noːʊ]
Flying high, flying high!
[ˈflaːɪŋ haːɪ ˈflaːɪŋ haːɪ]
All the freedom of the sky.
[ɔl ðʌ ˈfɹidʌm ʌv ðʌ skaːɪ]

Unholy Sonnets (Song Cycle)
[ˌʌnˈhoːʊli ˈsɑnɪts]
Donne, John (Eng. 1572-1631)

1. The Good Morrow
[ðʊ gʊd ˈmaʁoːʊ]

I wonder, by my troth, what thou, and I
[ɑːɪ ˈwʌndʌ baːɪ maːɪ tɹoːʊθ ʍɑt ðɑːʊ ænd ɑːɪ]
Did, till we lov'd? Were we not wean'd till then?
[dɪd tɪl wi lʌvd wɜ wi nɑt wind tɪl ðɛn]
But suck'd on country pleasures, childishly?
[bʌt sʌkt ɑn ˈkʌntɹɪ ˈplɛʒʊ(ʌ)z ˈʧɑːɪldɪʃlɪ]
Or snorted we in the seven sleepers' den?
[ɔ ˈsnɔtɛ(ɪ)d wi ɪn ðʊ ˈsɛvɛ(ɪ)n ˈslipʌz dɛn]
'Twas so; but this, all pleasures fancies be.
[twɑz soːʊ bʌt ðɪs ɔl ˈplɛʒʊ(ʌ)z ˈfænsɪz bi]
If ever any beauty I did see,
[ɪf ˈɛvʌɾ ˈɛnɪ ˈbjutɪ ɑːɪ dɪd si]
Which I desir'd and got, 'twas but a dream of thee.
[ʍɪʧ ɑːɪ dɪˈzɑːɪɑd ænd gɑt twɑz bʌt ʌ dɹim ʌv ði]
And now good morrow to our waking souls,
[ænd naːʊ gʊd ˈmaɾoːʊ tu ɑːʊʌ ˈwɛːɪkɪŋ soːʊlz]
Which watch not one another out of fear;
[ʍɪʧ wɑʧ nɑt wʌn ʌˈnʌðʌɾ ɑːʊt ʌv fiːʌ]
For love, all love of other sights controls,
[fɔ lʌv ɔl lʌv ʌv ˈʌðʌ sɑːɪts kʌnˈtɹoːʊlz]
And makes one little room, an everywhere.
[ænd mɛːɪks wʌn ˈlɪtʊl ɾɾum æn ˈɛvɹɪʍɛːʌ]
Let sea-discoverers to new worlds have gone,
[lɛt si dɪsˈkʌvʌɾʌz tu nju wɜldz hæv gɑn]
Let maps to other, worlds on worlds have shown,
[lɛt mæps tu ˈʌðʌ wɜldz ɑn wɜldz hæv ʃoːʊn]
Let us possess a world, each hath one, and is one.
[lɛt ʌs poˈzɛs ʌ wɜld iʧ hæθ wʌn ænd ɪz wʌn]
My face in thine eye, thine in mine appears,
[maːɪ fɛːɪs ɪn ðɑːɪn ɑːɪ ðɑːɪn ɪn maːɪn ʌˈpɪːʌz]
And true plain hearts do in the faces rest
[ænd tru plɛːɪn hɑts du ɪn ðʊ ˈfɛːɪsɛ(ɪ)z ɹɛst]
Where can we find two better hemispheres
[ʍɛːʌ kæn wi fɑːɪnd tu ˈbɛtʌ ˈhɛmɪsfiːʌz]
Without sharp North, without declining West?
[wɪðˈɑːʊt ʃɑp nɔθ wɪðˈɑːʊt dɪˈklɑːɪnɪŋ wɛst]
Whatever dies was not mixed equally;
[ʍɑtˈɛvʌ dɑːɪz wɑz nɑt mɪkst ˈikwʊlɪ]
If our two loves be one, or thou and I
[ɪf ɑːʊʌ tu lʌvz bi wʌn ɔ ðɑːʊ ænd ɑːɪ]
Love so alike, that none do slacken, none can die.
[lʌv soːʊ ʌˈlɑːɪk ðæt nʌn du ˈslækɛ(ɪ)n nʌn kæn dɑːɪ]

2. The Broken Heart
[ðʊ ˈbɹoːʊkɪn hɑʁt]

He is stark mad, who ever says,
[hi ɪz stɑk mæd hu ˈɛvʌ sɛz]

That he hath been in love an hour,
[ðæt hi hæθ bin ɪn lʌv æn ɑːʊ]
Yet not that love so soon decays,
[jɛt nɑt ðæt lʌv soːʊ sun dɪˈkɛːɪz]
But that it can ten in less space devour;
[bʌt ðæt ɪt kæn tɛn ɪn lɛs spɛːɪs dɪˈvaːʊʌ]
Who will believe me, if I swear
[hu wɪl bɪˈliv mi ɪf ɑːɪ swɛːʌ]
That I have had the plague a year?
[ðæt ɑːɪ hæv hæd ðʊ plɛːɪg ʌ jiːʌ]
Who would not laugh at me, if I should say,
[hu wʊd nɑt laf æt mi ɪf ɑːɪ ʃʊd sɛːɪ]
I saw a flask of powder burn a day?
[ɑːɪ sɔ ʌ flask ʌv ˈpaːʊdʌ bɜn ʌ dɛːɪ]
Ah, what a trifle is a heart,
[a ʍɑt ʌ ˈtɹɑːɪfʊl ɪz ʌ hat]
If once into love's hands it come!
[ɪf wʌns ˈɪntu lʌvz hændz ɪt kʌm]
All other griefs allow a part
[ɔl ˈʌðʌ gɹifs ʌˈlaːʊ ʌ pat]
To other griefs, and ask themselves but some;
[tu ˈʌðʌ gɹifs ænd ask ðɛmˈsɛlvz bʌt sʌm]
They come to us, but us Love draws,
[ðɛːɪ kʌm tu ʌs bʌt ʌs lʌv dɹɔz]
He swallows us, and never chaws:
[hi ˈswɑloːʊz ʌs ænd ˈnɛvʌ ʧɔz]
By him, as by chain'd shot, whole ranks to die,
[baːɪ hɪm æz baːɪ ʧɛːɪnd ʃɑt hoːʊl ɹæŋks tu dɑːɪ]
He is the tyrant pike, our hearts the fry.
[hi ɪz ðʊ ˈtɑːɪɾæ(ɪ)nt pɑːɪk ɑːʊʌ hats ðʊ fɹɑːɪ]
If 'twere not so, what did become
[ɪf twɜ nɑt soːʊ ʍɑt dɪd bɪˈkʌm]
Of my heart, when I first saw thee?
[ʌv maːɪ hat ʍɛn ɑːɪ fɜst sɔ ði]
I brought a heart into the room,
[ɑːɪ bɹɔt ʌ hat ˈɪntu ðʊ ɹɾum]
But from the room, I carried none with me:
[bʌt fɹʌm ðʊ ɹɾum ɑːɪ ˈkæɾɪd nʌn wɪð mi]
If it had gone to thee, I know
[ɪf ɪt hæd gɑn tu ði ɑːɪ noːʊ]
Mine would have taught thine heart to show
[maːɪn wʊd hæv tɔt ðɑːɪn hat tu ʃoːʊ]
More pity unto me: but Love, alas,
[mɔːʌ ˈpɪtɪ ˈʌntu mi bʌt lʌv ʌˈlæs]
At one first blow did shiver it as glass
[æt wʌn fɜst bloːʊ dɪd ˈʃɪvʌ ɪt æz glas]
Yet nothing can to nothing fall,
[jɛt ˈnʌθɪŋ kæn tu ˈnʌθɪŋ fɔl]
Nor any place be empty quite,
[nɔʁ⁽ʳ⁾ ˈɛnɪ plɛːɪs bi ˈɛmptɪ kwaːɪt]
Therefore I think my breast hath all
[ˈðɛːʌfɔːʌ ɑːɪ θɪŋk maːɪ bɹɛst hæθ ɔl]
Those pieces still, though they be not unite;
[ðoːʊz ˈpisɛ(ɪ)z stɪl ðoːʊ ðɛːɪ bi nɑt juˈnɑːɪt]
And now as broken glasses show
[ænd naːʊ æz ˈbɹoːʊkɛ(ɪ)n ˈglasɛ(ɪ)z ʃoːʊ]

A hundred lesser faces, so
[ʌ ˈhʌndɹɛ(ɪ)d ˈlɛsʌ ˈfɛːɪsɛ(ɪ)z soːʊ]
My rags of heart can like, wish, and adore
[maːɪ ɹægz ʌv hat kæn laːɪk wɪʃ ænd ʌˈdɔːʌ]
But after one such love, can love no more.
[bʌt ˈaftʌ wʌn sʌtʃ lʌv kæn lʌv noːʊ mɔːʌ]

3. Woman's Constancy
[ˈwʊmʌnz ˈkanstɪnsi]

Now thou hast loved me one whole day,
[naːʊ ðaːʊ hæst lʌvd mi wʌn hoːʊl dɛːɪ]
Tomorrow when thou leav'st, what wilt thou say?
[tuˈmaɾoːʊ ʍɛn ðaːʊ livst ʍat wɪlt ðaːʊ sɛːɪ]
Wilt thou then antedate some new made vow?
[wɪlt ðaːʊ ðɛn ˌæntiˈdeːɪt sʌm nju meːɪd vaːʊ]
Or say that now
[ɔ sɛːɪ ðæt naːʊ]
We are not just those persons, which we were?
[wi a nat dʒʌst ðoːʊz ˈpɜsʌnz ʍɪtʃ wi wɜ]
Or, that oaths made in reverential fear
[ɔ ðæt oːʊðz meːɪd ɪn ˌɹɛvʌˈɹɛnʃʊl fiːʌ]
Of Love, and his wrath, any may forswear?
[ʌv lʌv ænd hɪz ɹæθ ˈɛni meːɪ fɔˈswɛːʌ]
Or, as true deaths, true marriages untie,
[ɔʁ⁽ʳ⁾ æz tru dɛθs tru ˈmæræ(ɪ)dʒɛ(ɪ)z ʌnˈtaːɪ]
So lovers' contracts, images of those,
[soːʊ ˈlʌvʌz ˈkantɹækts ˈɪmæ(ɪ)dʒɛ(ɪ)z ʌv ðoːʊz]
Bind but till sleep, death's image, them unloose?
[baːɪnd bʌt tɪl slip dɛθs ˈɪmæ(ɪ)dʒ ðɛm ʌnˈlus]
Or, your own end to justify,
[ɔ jɔːʌɾ oːʊn ɛnd tu ˈdʒʌstɪfaːɪ]
For having purposed change, and falsehood, you
[fɔ ˈhævɪŋ ˈpɜpʌst tʃɛːɪndʒ ænd ˈfɔlsˌhʊd ju]
Can have no way but falsehood to be true?
[kæn hæv noːʊ wɛːɪ bʌt ˈfɔlsˌhʊd tu bi tru]
Vain lunatic, against these 'scapes I could
[vɛːɪn ˈlunʌtɪk ʌˈgɛnst ðiz skɛːɪps aːɪ kʊd]
Dispute, and conquer, if I would,
[dɪˈspjut ænd ˈkaŋkʌɾ if aːɪ wʊd]
Which I abstain to do,
[ʍɪtʃ aːɪ æbˈstɛːɪn tu du]
For by tomorrow, I may think so too.
[fɔ baːɪ tuˈmaɾoːʊ aːɪ mɛːɪ θɪŋk soːʊ tu]

4. The Indifferent
[ði ɪnˈdɪfɹɛnt]

I can love both fair and brown,
[aːɪ kæn lʌv boːʊθ fɛːʌɾ ænd bɹaːʊn]
Her whom abundance melts,
[hɜ hum ʌˈbʌndæ(ɪ)ns mɛlts]
and her whom want betrays,
[ænd hɜ hum want bɪˈtɹɛːɪz]
Her who loves loneness best,
[hɜ hu lʌvz ˈloːʊnɛ(ɪ)s bɛst]

and her who masks and plays,
[ænd hɜ hu masks ænd plɛːɪz]
Her whom the country formed, and whom the town,
[hɜ hum ðʊ ˈkʌntɹi fɔmd ænd hum ðʊ taːʊn]
Her who believes, and her who tries,
[hɜ hu bɪˈlivz ænd hɜ hu tɹaːɪz]
Her who still weeps with spongy eyes,
[hɜ hu stɪl wips wɪð ˈspʌndʒi aːɪz]
And her who is dry cork, and never cries;
[ænd hɜ hu ɪz dɹaːɪ kɔk ænd ˈnɛvʌ kɹaːɪz]
I can love her, and her, and you, and you,
[aːɪ kæn lʌv hɜ ænd hɜ ænd ju ænd ju]
I can love any, so she be not true.
[aːɪ kæn lʌv ˈɛni soːʊ ʃi bi nat tru]
Will no other vice content you?
[wɪl noːʊ ˈʌðʌ vaːɪs kʌnˈtɛnt ju]
Will it not serve your turn to do as did your mothers?
[wɪl ɪt nat sɜv jɔːʌ tɜn tu du æz dɪd jɔːʌ ˈmʌðʌz]
Or have you old vices spent,
[ɔ hæv ju oːʊld ˈvaːɪsɛ(ɪ)z spɛnt]
and now would find out others?
[ænd naːʊ wʊd faːɪnd aːʊt ˈʌðʌz]
Or doth a fear, that men are true, torment you?
[ɔ dʌθ ʌ fiːʌ ðæt mɛn a tru tɔˈmɛnt ju]
Oh we are not, be not you so;
[oːʊ wi a nat bi nat ju soːʊ]
Let me, and do you, twenty know.
[lɛt mi ænd du ju ˈtwɛnti noːʊ]
Rob me, but bind me not, and let me go.
[ɹab mi bʌt baːɪnd mi nat ænd lɛt mi goːʊ]
Must I, who came to travel through you,
[mʌst aːɪ hu kɛːɪm tu ˈtɹævol θɹu ju]
Grow your fixed subject, because you are true?
[gɹoːʊ jɔːʌ fikst ˈsʌbdʒɛkt bɪˈkɔz ju a tru]
Venus heard me sigh this song,
[ˈvinʊs hɜd mi saːɪ ðɪs saŋ]
And by Love's sweetest part, Variety, she swore
[ænd baːɪ lʌvz ˈswitɛ(ɪ)st pat vʌˈɹaːɪɪti ʃi swɔːʌ]
She heard not this till now;
[ʃi hɜd nat ðɪs tɪl naːʊ]
and that it should be so no more.
[ænd ðæt ɪt ʃʊd bi soːʊ noːʊ mɔːʌ]
She went, examined, and returned ere long,
[ʃi wɛnt ɪgˈzæmɪnd ænd ɹɪˈtɜnd ɛːʌ laŋ]
And said, "Alas, some two or three
[ænd sɛd ʌˈlæs sʌm tu ɔ θɹi]
Poor heretics in love there be,
[pʊːʌ ˈhɛɾɛ(ɪ)tɪks ɪn lʌv ðɛːʌ bi]
Which think to 'stablish dangerous constancy.
[ʍɪtʃ θɪŋk tu ˈstæblɪʃ ˈdɛːɪndʒʌɾʌs ˈkanstæ(ɪ)nsi]
But I have told them, Since you will be true,
[bʌt aːɪ hæv toːʊld ðɛm sɪns ju wɪl bi tru]
You shall be true to them who're false to you.
[ju ʃæl bi tru tu ðɛm huːʌ fɔls tu ju]

5. The Triple Foole [ðʊ ˈtɹɪpʊl ful]

I am two fools, I know–
[ɑːɪ æm tu fulz ɑːɪ noːʊ]
For loving, and for saying so in whining poetry;
[fɔ ˈlʌvɪŋ ænd fɔ ˈseːɪŋ soːʊ ɪn ˈʍɑːɪnɪŋ ˈpoːʊɛ(ɪ)tɹɪ]
But where's that wiseman that would not be I,
[bʌt ʍɛːʌz ðæt ˈwɑːɪzmæn ðæt wʊd nat bi ɑːɪ]
If she would not deny?
[ɪf ʃi wʊd nat dɪˈnɑːɪ]
Then, as th' earths inward narrow crooked lanes
[ðɛn æz ðɜːs ˈɪnwʊd ˈnæroːʊ ˈkɹʊkɛ(ɪ)d lɛːɪnz]
Do purge sea water's fretful salt away,
[du pɜɹdʒ si ˈwɔtʌz ˈfɹɛtfʊl sɔlt ʌˈwɛːɪ]
I thought, if I could draw my pains
[ɑːɪ θɔt ɪf ɑːɪ kʊd dɹɔ mɑːɪ pɛːɪnz]
Through rhymes vexation, I should them allay.
[θru ɹɑːɪmz vɛkˈseːɪʃʌn ɑːɪ ʃʊd ðɛm ʌˈlɛːɪ]
Grief brought to numbers cannot be so fierce,
[ɡrif bɹɔt tu ˈnʌmbʌz kæˈnat bi soːʊ fɪːʌs]
For he tames it that fetters it in verse.
[fɔ hi tɛːɪmz ɪt ðæt ˈfɛtʌz ɪt ɪn vɜs]
But when I have done so,
[bʌt ʍɛn ɑːɪ hæv dʌn soːʊ]
Some man, his art and voice to show,
[sʌm mæn hɪz at ænd vɔːɪs tu ʃoːʊ]
Doth set and sing my pain,
[dʌθ sɛt ænd sɪŋ mɑːɪ pɛːɪn]
And, by delighting many, frees again
[ænd bɑːɪ dɪˈlɑːɪtɪŋ ˈmɛnɪ fɹiz ʌˈɡɛːɪn]
Grief, which verse did restrain.
[ɡrif ʍɪtʃ vɜs dɪd ɹɪˈstɹɛːɪn]
To Love and Grief tribute of verse belongs,
[tu lʌv ænd ɡrif ˈtɹɪbjut ʌv vɜs bɪˈlaŋz]
But not of such as pleases when 'tis read;
[bʌt nat ʌv sʌtʃ æz ˈplizɛ(ɪ)z ʍɛn tɪz ɹɛd]
Both are increased by such songs,
[boːʊθ ɑr ɪnˈkɹist bɑːɪ sʌtʃ saŋz]
For both their triumphs so are published;
[fɔ boːʊθ ðɛːʌ ˈtɹɑːɪʌmfs soːʊ ɑ ˈpʌblɪʃt]
And I, which was two fools, do so grow three;
[ænd ɑːɪ ʍɪtʃ waz tu fulz du soːʊ ɡɹoːʊ θri]
Who are a little wise, the best fools be.
[hu ɑr ʌ ˈlɪtʊl wɑːɪz ðʊ bɛst fulz bi]

 Althouse, Jay, arr. (Am. b. 1951)

Song Selection for Youth

"The Stars Are with the Voyager"
[ðʌ stɑɹz ɑʁ wɪθ ðʌ ˈvɔːɹɪdʒʁ]
Hood, Thomas (Eng. 1789-1845)

* *The stars are with the voyager*
  [ðʌ staz ɑ wɪð ðʌ ˈvɔːɹæ(ɪ)dʒʌ]

Wherever he may sail;
[ʍɛːʌˈɛvʌ hi mɛːɪ sɛːɪl]
And wherever he may sail;
[ænd ʍɛːʌˈɛvʌ hi mɛːɪ sɛːɪl]
So love is with the lover's heart,
[soːʊ lʌv ɪz wɪð ðʌ ˈlʌvʌz hat]
Wherever he may be.
[ʍɛːʌˈɛvʌ hi mɛːɪ bi]
And wherever he may be.
[ænd ʍɛːʌˈɛvʌ hi mɛːɪ bi]
The moon is constant to her time;
[ðʌ mun ɪz ˈkanstæ(ɪ)nt tu hɜ tɑːɪm]
The sun will never fail;
[ðʌ sʌn wɪl ˈnɛvʌ fɛːɪl]
But follow, follow round the world,
[bʌt ˈfaloːʊ ˈfaloːʊ ɹɑːʊnd ðʌ wɜld]
The great green earth and the sea,
[ðʌ ɡɹɛːɪt ɡɹin ɜθ ænd ðʌ si]
The stars are with the voyager
[ðʌ staz ɑ wɪð ðʌ ˈvɔːɹæ(ɪ)dʒʌ]
Wherever he may sail;
[ʍɛːʌˈɛvʌ hi mɛːɪ sɛːɪl]
And wherever he may sail;
[ænd ʍɛːʌˈɛvʌ hi mɛːɪ sɛːɪl]
And so the night is never dark
[ænd soːʊ ðʌ nɑːɪt ɪz ˈnɛvʌ dak]
And day is brighter day
[ænd dɛːɪ ɪz ˈbɹɑːɪtʌ dɛːɪ]
The sun may set the love will shine
[ðʌ sʌn mɛːɪ sɛt bʌt lʌv wɪl ʃɑːɪn]
And day is brighter day
[ænd dɛːɪ ɪz ˈbɹɑːɪtʌ dɛːɪ]

Anonymous

Song Selections

"False Phillis"
[fɔls ˈfɪlɪs]
Anonymous

Exact to appointment I went to the grove,
[ɪɡˈzækt tu ʌˈpɔːɪntmɛnt ɑːɪ wɛnt tu ðʊ ɡɹoːʊv]
To meet my fair Phillis, and tell tales of love,
[tu mit mɑːɪ fɛːʌ ˈfɪlɪs ænd tɛl tɛːɪlz ʌv lʌv]
But judge of my anguish, my rage and despair,
[bʌt dʒʌdʒ ʌv mɑːɪ ˈæŋɡwɪʃ mɑːɪ ɹɛːɪdʒ ænd dɪˈspɛːʌ]
When I found on arrival no Phillis was there.
[ʍɛn ɑːɪ fɑːʊnd an ʌˈɹɑːɪvʊl noːʊ ˈfɪlɪs waz ðɛːʌ]
I waited a while, which increased but my rage,
[ɑːɪ ˈwɛːɪtɛ(ɪ)d ʌ ʍɑːɪl ʍɪtʃ ɪnˈkɹist bʌt mɑːɪ ɹɛːɪdʒ]
With lovers you know ev'ry moment's an age,
[wɪð ˈlʌvʌz ju noːʊ ˈɛvɹɪ ˈmoːʊmɛnts æn ɛːɪdʒ]
I sighed and I cried, and I looked far and near,
[ɑːɪ sɑːɪd ænd ɑːɪ kɹɑːɪd ænd ɑːɪ lʊkt far ænd nɪːʌ]

But in vain was my looking, no Phillis was there!
[bʌt ɪn veːɪn waz maːɪ 'lʊkɪŋ noːʊ 'fɪlɪs waz ðɛːʌ]
To wait any longer I thought was in vain,
[tu weːɪt 'ɛnɪ 'laŋgʌɾ aːɪ θɔt waz ɪn veːɪn]
So I trudged o'er the fields to my cottage again;
[soːʊ aːɪ tɹʌdʒd ɔːʌ ðʊ fildz tu maːɪ 'katæ(ɪ)dʒ ʌ'gɛːɪn]
When Oh! to my grief, in a grove that was near,
[ʍɛn oːʊ tu maːɪ grif ɪn ʌ gɹoːʊv ðæt waz nɪːʌ]
I beheld the false Phillis with Damon was there.
[aːɪ bɪ'hɛld ðʊ fɔls 'fɪlɪs wɪð 'dɛːɪmʌn waz ðɛːʌ]
I glowed with resentment, and proudly passed by,
[aːɪ gloːʊd wɪð ɹɪ'zɛntmɛnt ænd 'pɹaːʊdlɪ past baːɪ]
When sweet as the morning, young Kate caught my eye;
[ʍɛn swit æz ðʊ 'mɔnɪŋ jʌŋ kɛːɪt kɔt maːɪ aːɪ]
I told her my story, she banished my care;
[aːɪ toːʊld hɜ maːɪ 'stɔrɪ ʃi 'bænɪʃt maːɪ kɛːʌ]
Bade me go to the grove, she would surely be there.
[bæd mi goːʊ tu ðʊ gɹoːʊv ʃi wʊd 'ʃʊːʌlɪ bi ðɛːʌ]

"Have You Seen but a White Lily Grow"
[hæv ju sin bʌt ʌ ʍaːɪt 'lɪli gɹoːʊ]
Jonson, Ben (Eng. 1572-1637)

Have you seen but a white Lilie grow,
[hæv ju sin bʌt ʌ ʍaːɪt 'lɪli gɹoːʊ]
Before rude hands have touch'd it?
[bɪ'fɔːʌ rrud hændz hæv tʌʧt ɪt]
Have you mark'd but the fall of the snow,
[hæv ju makt bʌt ðʊ fɔl ʌv ðʊ snoːʊ]
Before the earth hath smucht it?
[bɪ'fɔːʌ ði ɜθ hæθ smʌʧt ɪt]
Have you felt the wool of Beaver?
[hæv ju fɛlt ðʊ wʊl ʌv 'bivʌ]
Or swan's down ever?
[ɔ swanz daːʊn 'ɛvʌ]
Or have smelt of the bud of the bryer?
[ɔ hæv smɛlt ʌv ðʊ bʌd ʌv ðʊ 'bɹaːɪʌ]
Or the nard in the fire?
[ɔ ðʊ nad ɪn ðʊ faːɪʌ]
Or have tasted the bag of the bee?
[ɔ hæv 'tɛːɪstɛ(ɪ)d ðʊ bæg ʌv ðʊ bi]
O so white, O so soft, O so sweet, is she.
[oːʊ soːʊ ʍaːɪt oːʊ soːʊ saft oːʊ soːʊ swit ɪz ʃi]

Argento, Dominick (Am. 1927-2019)

Six Elizabethan Songs (Song Cycle)
[sɪks ˌɛlɪzʌ'biθɪn saŋz]

1. Spring
[spɹɪŋ]
Nashe, Thomas (Eng. 1567-1601)

Spring, the sweet Spring, is the year's pleasant king:
[spɹɪŋ ðʌ swit spɹɪŋ ɪz ðʌ jɪːʌz 'plɛzæ(ɪ)nt kɪŋ]

Then blooms each thing, then maids dance in a ring,
[ðɛn blumz iʧ θɪŋ ðɛn mɛːɪdz dæns ɪn ʌ ɹɪŋ]
Cold doth not sting, the pretty birds do sing,
[koːʊld dʌθ nat stɪŋ ðʌ 'pɹɪtɪ bɜdz du sɪŋ]
Cuckoo, jug-jug, pu-we, to-witta-woo!
['kuku dʒʌg dʒʌg pu wi tu 'wɪttʌ wu]
The palm and may make country houses gay,
[ðʌ pam ænd mɛːɪ mɛːɪk 'kʌntɹɪ 'haːʊzɛ(ɪ)z gɛːɪ]
Lambs frisk and play, the shepherd pipes all day,
[læmz fɹɪsk ænd plɛːɪ ðʌ 'ʃɛpʌd paːɪps ɔl dɛːɪ]
And we hear aye birds tune this merry lay,
[ænd wi hɪːʌʁ(ɾ) aːɪ bɜdz tjun ðɪs 'mɛʁ(ɾ)ɪ lɛːɪ]
Cuckoo, jug-jug, pu-we, to-witta-woo!
['kuku dʒʌg dʒʌg pu wi tu 'wɪttʌ wu]
The fields breathe sweet, the daisies kiss our feet,
[ðʌ fildz bɹɪð swit ðʌ 'dɛːɪzɪz kɪs aːʊʌ fit]
Young lovers meet, old wives a-sunning sit,
[jʌŋ 'lʌvʌz mit oːʊld waːɪvz ʌ 'sʌnɪŋ sɪt]
In every street, these tunes our ears do greet,
[ɪn 'ɛvɹɪ stɹit ðiz tjunz aːʊʌʁ(ɾ) ɪːʌz du gɹit]
Cuckoo, jug-jug, pu-we, to-witta-woo!
['kuku dʒʌg dʒʌg pu wi tu 'wɪttʌ wu]
Spring! The sweet Spring!
[spɹɪŋ ðʌ swit spɹɪŋ]

2. Sleep [slip]
Daniel, Samuel (Eng. 1562-1619)

Care-charmer Sleep, son of the sable Night,
[kɛːʌ 'ʧamʌ slip sʌn ʌv ðʌ 'sɛːɪbʊl naːɪt]
Brother to Death, in silent darkness born,
['bɹʌðʌ tu dɛθ ɪn 'saːɪlɛnt 'dakne(ɪ)s bɔn]
Relieve my anguish and restore thy light;
[ɹɪ'liv maːɪ 'æŋgwɪʃ ænd ɹɪ'stɔːʌ ðaːɪ laːɪt]
With dark forgetting of my care return.
[wɪð dak fɔ'gɛtɪŋ ʌv maːɪ kɛːʌ ɹɪ'tɜn]
And let the day be time enough to mourn
[ænd lɛt ðʌ dɛːɪ bi taːɪm ɪ'nʌf tu mɔn]
The shipwreck of my ill-adventured youth:
[ðʌ 'ʃɪpɹɛk ʌv maːɪ ɪl æd'vɛnʧʊ(ʌ)d juθ]
Let waking eyes suffice to wail their scorn
[lɛt 'wɛːɪkɪŋ aːɪz sʌ'faːɪs tu wɛːɪl ðɛːʌ skɔn]
Without the torment of the night's untruth.
[wɪð 'aːʊt ðʌ 'tɔmɛnt ʌv ðʌ naːɪts ʌn'tɹɪ(ɾ)uθ]
Cease, dreams, the images of day-desires
[sis dɹimz ði 'ɪmæ(ɪ)dʒɛ(ɪ)z ʌv dɛːɪ dɪ'zaːɪʌz]
To model forth the passions of the morrow;
[tu 'madʊl fɔθ ðʌ 'pæʃʌnz ʌv ðʌ 'maʁ(ɾ)oːʊ]
Never let rising sun approve you liars
['nɛvʌ lɛt 'ɹaːɪzɪŋ sʌn ʌ'pɹɪ(ɾ)uv ju 'laːɪʌz]
To add more grief to aggravate my sorrow:
[tu æd mɔːʌ gɹɪ(ɾ)if tu 'ægɹʌvɛːɪt maːɪ 'saʁ(ɾ)oːʊ]
Still let me sleep, embracing clouds in vain,
[stɪl lɛt mi slip ɪm'bɹɛːɪsɪŋ klaːʊdz ɪn vɛːɪn]
And never wake to feel the day's disdain.
[ænd 'nɛvʌ wɛːɪk tu fil ðʌ dɛːɪz dɪs'dɛːɪn]

3. Winter
[ˈwɪntʁ]
Shakespeare, William (Eng. 1564-1616)

When icicles hang by the wall
[ʍɛn ˈɑːɪsɪkʊlz hæŋ bɑːɪ ðʌ wɔl]
And Dick the shepherd blows his nail,
[ænd dɪk ðʌ ˈʃɛpʌd bloːʊz hɪz nɛːɪl]
And Tom bears logs into the hall,
[ænd tɑm bɛːʌz lɑgz ˈɪntu ðʌ hɔl]
And milk comes frozen home in pail;
[ænd mɪlk kʌmz ˈfɹoːʊzɛ(ɪ)n hoːʊm ɪn pɛːɪl]
When blood is nipt and ways be foul,
[ʍɛn blʌd ɪz nɪpt ænd wɛːɪz bi fɑːʊl]
Then nightly sings the staring owl Tu-whoo!
[ðɛn ˈnɑːɪtlɪ sɪŋz ðʌ ˈstɛːʌʁ(ʳ)ɪŋ ɑːʊl tu ʍu]
Tu-whit! Tu-whoo! A merry note!
[tu ʍɪt tu ʍu ʌ ˈmɛʁ(ʳ)ɪ noːʊt]
While greasy Joan doth keel the pot
[ʍɑːɪl ˈgɹɪsɪ ʤoːʊn dʌθ kil ðʌ pɑt]
When all aloud the wind doth blow,
[ʍɛn ɔl ʌˈlɑːʊd ðʌ wɪnd dʌθ bloːʊ]
And coughing drowns the parson's saw,
[ænd ˈkɔfɪŋ dɹɑːʊnz ðʌ ˈpɑsʌnz sɔ]
And birds sit brooding in the snow,
[ænd bɜdz sɪt ˈbɹ(ʳ)udɪŋ ɪn ðʌ snoːʊ]
And Marian's nose looks red and raw;
[ænd ˈmæʁ(ʳ)ɪæ(ɪ)nz noːʊz lʊks ɹɛd ænd ɹɔ]
When roasted crabs hiss in the bowl
[ʍɛn ˈɹoːʊstɛ(ɪ)d kɹæbz hɪs ɪn ðʌ boːʊl]
Then nightly sings the staring owl Tu-whoo!
[ðɛn ˈnɑːɪtlɪ sɪŋz ðʌ ˈstɛːʌʁ(ʳ)ɪŋ ɑːʊl tu ʍu]
Tu-whit! Tu-whoo! A merry note!
[tu ʍɪt tu ʍu ʌ ˈmɛʁ(ʳ)ɪ noːʊt]
While greasy Joan doth keel the pot.
[ʍɑːɪl ˈgɹɪsɪ ʤoːʊn dʌθ kil ðʌ pɑt]

4. Dirge [dɜʤ]
Shakespeare, William (Eng. 1564-1616)

Come away, Come away, Death,
[kʌm ʌˈwɛːɪ kʌm ʌˈwɛːɪ dɛθ]
And in sad cypress let me be laid;
[ænd ɪn sæd ˈsɑːɪpɹɛ(ɪ)s lɛt mi bi lɛːɪd]
Fly away, Fly away, breath;
[flɑːɪ ʌˈwɛːɪ flɑːɪ ʌˈwɛːɪ bɹɛθ]
I am slain by a fair cruel maid.
[ɑːɪ æm slɛːɪn bɑːɪ ʌ fɛːʌ ˈkɹ(ʳ)uːɛ(ʊ)l mɛːɪd]
My shroud of white stuck all with yew,
[mɑːɪ ʃɹɑːʊd ʌv ʍɑːɪt stʌk ɔl wɪð ju]
O prepare it!
[oːʊ pɹɪˈpɛːʌʁ(ʳ) ɪt]
My part of death, no one so true
[mɑːɪ pɑt ʌv dɛθ noːʊ wʌn soːʊ tɹ(ʳ)u]
Did share it.
[dɪd ʃɛːʌʁ(ʳ) ɪt]

Not a flower, not a flower sweet
[nat ʌ flɑːʊʌ nat ʌ flɑːʊʌ swit]
On my black coffin let there be strown;
[ɑn mɑːɪ blæk ˈkɑfɪn lɛt ðɛːʌ bi stɹoːʊn]
Not a friend, not a friend greet
[nat ʌ fɹɛnd nat ʌ fɹɛnd gɹit]
My poor corpse, where my bones shall be thrown:
[mɑːɪ pʊːʌ kɔps ʍɛːʌ mɑːɪ boːʊnz ʃæl bi θɹoːʊn]
A thousand thousand sighs to save,
[ʌ ˈθɑːʊzæ(ʌ)nd ˈθɑːʊzæ(ʌ)nd sɑːɪz tu sɛːɪv]
Lay me, O where
[lɛːɪ mi oːʊ ʍɛːʌ]
Sad true lover never find my grave,
[sæd tɹ(ʳ)u ˈlʌvʌ ˈnɛvʌ fɑːɪnd mɑːɪ gɹ(ʳ)ɛːɪv]
To weep there.
[tu wip ðɛːʌ]

5. Diaphenia
[ˌdɑːɪʌˈfɪnɪʌ]
Anonymous

Diaphenia, like the daffadowndilly,
[ˌdɑːɪʌˈfɪnɪʌ lɑːɪk ðʌ ˌdæfʌdɑːʊnˈdɪlɪ]
White as the sun, fair as the lily,
[ʍɑːɪt æz ðʌ sʌn fɛːʌʁ(ʳ) æz ðʌ ˈlɪlɪ]
Heigh ho, how I do love thee!
[hɛːɪ hoːʊ hɑːʊ ɑːɪ du lʌv ði]
I do love thee as my lambs
[ɑːɪ du lʌv ði æz mɑːɪ læmz]
Are beloved of their dams;
[ɑ bɪˈlʌvɛ(ɪ)d ʌv ðɛːʌ dæmz]
How blest were I if thou would'st prove me.
[hɑːʊ blɛst wɜ ɑːɪ ɪf ðɑːʊ wʊdst pɹ(ʳ)uv mi]
Diaphenia, like the spreading roses,
[ˌdɑːɪʌˈfɪnɪʌ lɑːɪk ðʌ ˈspɹɛdɪŋ ˈɹoːʊzɛ(ɪ)z]
That in thy sweets all sweets incloses,
[ðæt ɪn ðɑːɪ swits ɔl swits ɪnˈkloːʊzɛ(ɪ)z]
Fair sweet, how I do love thee!
[fɛːʌ swit hɑːʊ ɑːɪ du lʌv ði]
I do love thee as each flower
[ɑːɪ du lʌv ði æz iʧ flɑːʊʌ]
loves the sun's life-giving power;
[lʌvz ðʌ sʌnz lɑːɪf ˈgɪvɪŋ pɑːʊʌ]
For dead, thy breath to life might move me.
[fɔ dɛd ðɑːɪ bɹɛθ tu lɑːɪf mɑːɪt muv mi]
Diaphenia like to all things blessed
[ˌdɑːɪʌˈfɪnɪʌ lɑːɪk tu ɔl θɪŋz ˈblɛsɛ(ɪ)d]
When all thy praises are expressed
[ʍɛn ɔl ðɑːɪ ˈpɹɛːɪzɛ(ɪ)z ɑʁ(ʳ) ɪkˈspɹɛsɛ(ɪ)d]
Dear joy, how I do love thee!
[dɪːʌ ʤɔːɪ hɑːʊ ɑːɪ du lʌv ði]
As the birds do love the spring,
[æz ðʌ bɜdz du lʌv ðʌ spɹɪŋ]
Or the bees their careful king:
[ɔ ðʌ biz ðɛːʌ ˈkɛːʌfʊl kɪŋ]

Then in requite, sweet virgin, love me!
[ðɛn ɪn ɹɪˈkwɑːɪt swit ˈvɜdʒɪn lʌv mi]

6. Hymn
[hɪm]
Jonson, Ben (Eng. 1572-1637)

Queen and Huntress, chaste and fair,
[kwin ænd ˈhʌntɹɛ(ɪ)s tʃɛːɪst ænd fɛːʌ]
Now the sun is laid to sleep,
[nɑːʊ ðʌ sʌn ɪz lɛːɪd tu slip]
Seated in thy silver chair
[ˈsitɛ(ɪ)d ɪn ðɑːɪ ˈsɪlvʌ tʃɛːɪ]
State in wonted manner keep:
[stɛːɪt ɪn ˈwɑntɛ(ɪ)d ˈmænʌ kip]
Hesperus entreats thy light,
[ˈhɛspʌʁ⁽ʳ⁾ʊs ɪnˈtɹits ðɑːɪ lɑːɪt]
Goddess excellently bright.
[ˈɡɑdɛ(ɪ)s ˈɛksɛ(ɪ)lɛntlɪ bɹɑːɪt]
Earth, let not thy envious shade'
[ɜθ lɛt nɑt ðɑːɪ ˈɛnvɪʌs ʃɛːɪd]
Dare itself to interpose;
[dɛːʌʁ⁽ʳ⁾ ɪtˈsɛlf tu ɪntʌˈpoːʊz]
Cynthia's shining orb was made
[ˈsɪnθɪʌz ˈʃɑːɪnɪŋ ɔb wɑz mɛːɪd]
Heaven to clear when day did close:
[ˈhɛvɪn tu klɪːʌ ʍɛn dɛːɪ dɪd kloːʊz]
Bless us then with wished sight
[blɛs ʌs ðɛn wɪð ˈwɪʃɛ(ɪ)d sɑːɪt]
Goddess, excellently bright.
[ˈɡɑdɛ(ɪ)s ˈɛksɛ(ɪ)lɛntlɪ bɹɑːɪt]
Lay thy bow of pearl apart
[lɛːɪ ðɑːɪ boːʊ ʌv pɜl ʌˈpat]
And thy crystal shining quiver;
[ænd ðɑːɪ ˈkɹɪstʊl ˈʃɑːɪnɪŋ ˈkwɪvʌ]
Give unto the flying hart
[ɡɪv ˈʌntu ðʌ ˈflɑːɪŋ hat]
Space to breathe, how short so ever:
[spɛːɪs tu bɹɪð hɑːʊ ʃɔt soːʊ ˈɛvʌ]
Thou that mak'st a day of night,
[ðɑːʊ ðæt mɛːɪkst ʌ dɛːɪ ʌv nɑːɪt]
Goddess, excellently bright!
[ˈɡɑdɛ(ɪ)s ˈɛksɛ(ɪ)lɛntlɪ bɹɑːɪt]

Song Selection

"The Devon Maid" (see Bridge)

Arne, Thomas (Eng. 1710-1778)

Song Selections

"Barbara Allen" (see Quilter)

"Under the Greenwood Tree" (see Quilter)

"When Daisies Pied"
[ʍɛn ˈdɛːɪziz pɑːɪd]
Shakespeare, William (Eng. 1564-1616)

1. When daisies pied, and violets blue,
[ʍɛn ˈdɛːɪziz pɑːɪd ænd ˈvɑːɪo(ʌ)lɛ(ɪ)ts blu]
And lady smocks all silver white,
[ænd ˈlɛːɪdɪ smɑks ɔl ˈsɪlvʌ ʍɑːɪt]
And cuckoo buds of yellow hue,
[ænd ˈkuku bʌdz ʌv ˈjɛloːʊ hju]
Do paint the meadow with delight:
[du pɛːɪnt ðʊ ˈmɛdoːʊ wɪð dɪˈlɑːɪt]
REFRAIN:
The cuckoo then, on ev'ry tree,
[ðʊ ˈkuku ðɛn ɑn ˈɛvɹɪ tɹi]
Mocks married men; for thus sings he:
[mɑks ˈmærɪd mɛn fɔ ðʌs sɪŋz hi]
Cuckoo, cuckoo, cuckoo!
[ˈkuku ˈkuku ˈkuku]
O word of fear,
[oːʊ wɜd ʌv fɪːʌ]
Unpleasing to a married ear.
[ʌnˈplizɪŋ tu ʌ ˈmærɪd ɪːʌ]
2. When shepherds pipe on oaten straws,
[ʍɛn ˈʃɛpʌdz pɑːɪp ɑn ˈoːʊtɛ(ɪ)n stɹɔz]
And merry larks are ploughmen's clocks,
[ænd ˈmɛɹɪ lɑks ɑ ˈplɑːʊmɛ(ɪ)nz klɑks]
And turtles tread, and rooks, and daws,
[ænd ˈtɜtʊlz tɹɛd ænd ɹʊks ænd dɔz]
And maidens bleach their summer smocks:
[ænd ˈmɛːɪdɛ(ɪ)nz blitʃ ðɛːʌ ˈsʌmʌ smɑks]
REFRAIN:
The cuckoo then, on ev'ry tree,
[ðʊ ˈkuku ðɛn ɑn ˈɛvɹɪ tɹi]
Mocks married men; for thus sings he:
[mɑks ˈmærɪd mɛn fɔ ðʌs sɪŋz hi]
Cuckoo, cuckoo, cuckoo!
[ˈkuku ˈkuku ˈkuku]
O word of fear,
[oːʊ wɜd ʌv fɪːʌ]
Unpleasing to a married ear.
[ʌnˈplizɪŋ tu ʌ ˈmærɪd ɪːʌ]

"Where the Bee Sucks"
[ʍɛːʌ ðʊ bi sʌks]
Shakespeare, William (Eng. 1564-1616)

Where the bee sucks there lurk I;
[ʍɛːʌ ðʊ bi sʌks ðɛːʌ lɜk ɑːɪ]
In a cow-slip's bell I lie:
[ɪn ʌ kɑːʊ slɪps bɛl ɑːɪ lɑːɪ]
There I couch when owls do cry,
[ðɛːʌɾ ɑːɪ kɑːʊtʃ ʍɛn ɑːʊlz du kɹɑːɪ]
On the bat's back do I fly
[ɑn ðʊ bæts bæk du ɑːɪ flɑːɪ]

After summer merrily,
[ˈaftʌ ˈsʌmʌ ˈmɛɹɪlɪ]
Merrily, merrily, shall I live now,
[ˈmɛɹɪlɪ ˈmɛɹɪlɪ ʃæl ɑːɪ lɪv naːʊ]
Under the blossom that hangs on the bough.
[ˈʌndʌ ðʊ ˈblasʌm ðæt hæŋz ɑn ðʊ baːʊ]

"Why So Pale and Wan" (see Quilter)

Aylward, Florence (Eng. 1862-1950)

Song Selection

"The Window"
[ðʊ ˈwɪndoːʊ]
Grogan, Walter E. (flourished 1909-1923)

Sweet maid, fair maid,
[swit mɛːɪd fɛːʌ mɛːɪd]
open the window
[ˈoːʊpɛ(ɪ)n ðʊ ˈwɪndoːʊ]
See, here we wait, the morn and I
[si hɪːʌ wi wɛːɪt ðʊ mɔn ænd ɑːɪ]
Eager to greet
[ˈigʌ tu gɹit]
maiden so sweet
[ˈmɛːɪdɛ(ɪ)n soːʊ swit]
So shyly sweet,
[soːʊ ˈʃaːɪlɪ swit]
so sweetly shy
[soːʊ ˈswitlɪ ʃaːɪ]
Sweet maid, rare maid,
[swit mɛːɪd ɹɛːʌ mɛːɪd]
open the window,
[ˈoːʊpɛ(ɪ)n ðʊ ˈwɪndoːʊ]
See, here are roses for thy prize
[si hɪːʌɾ ɑ ˈɾoːʊzɛ(ɪ)z fɔ ðaːɪ pɹɑːɪz]
Blooming and fair
[ˈblumɪŋ ænd fɛːʌ]
with fragrance rare
[wɪð ˈfɹɛːɪgɹæ(ɪ)ns ɹɛːʌ]
All waiting for thy sunny eyes.
[ɔl ˈwɛːɪtɪŋ fɔ ðaːɪ ˈsʌnɪ ɑːɪz]
Sweet maid, dear maid,
[swit mɛːɪd dɪːʌ mɛːɪd]
open the window,
[ˈoːʊpɛ(ɪ)n ðʊ ˈwɪndoːʊ]
Here they arose newborn from sleep,
[hɪːʌ ðɛːɪ ʌˈɾoːʊz ˈnjubɔn fɹʌm slip]
Look down and see
[lʊk daːʊn ænd si]
our gifts to thee
[aːʊʌ gɪfts tu ði]
A rose to wear, a heart to keep.
[ʌ ɾoːʊz tu wɛːʌɾ ʌ hɑt tu kip]

B

Bach, Johann S. (Gr. 1685-1750)

Song Selections

"Jesu, Joy of Man's Desiring"
[ˈjezu dʒɔːɪ ʌv mænz dɪˈzaːɪʁɪŋ]
Bridges, Robert Seymour (Eng. 1844-1930)

Jesu, joy of man's desiring
[ˈjezu dʒɔːɪ ʌv mænz dɪˈzaːɪɾɪŋ]
Holy wisdom, love most bright
[ˈhoːʊlɪ ˈwɪzdʌm lʌv moːʊst bɹaːɪt]
Drawn by Thee, our souls aspiring
[dɹɔn baːɪ ði aːʊʌ soːʊlz ʌˈspaːɪʌɾɪŋ]
Soar to uncreated light
[sɔːʌ tu ˌʌnkɹɪˈɛːɪtɛ(ɪ)d laːɪt]
Word of God, our flesh that fashioned
[wɜd ʌv gad aːʊʌ flɛʃ ðæt ˈfæʃʌnd]
With the fire of life impassioned
[wɪð ðʊ faːɪʌɾ ʌv laːɪf ɪmˈpæʃʌnd]
Striving still to truth unknown
[ˈstɹaːɪvɪŋ stɪl tu tɹuθ ʌnˈnoːʊn]
Soaring, dying round Thy throne
[ˈsɔːʌɾɪŋ ˈdaːɪŋ ɹaːʊnd ðaːɪ θɾoːʊn]

"Sheep May Safely Graze"
[ʃip mɛːɪ ˈsɛːɪflɪ gɹɛːɪz]
(Arr. Christopher Ruck)

Sheep may safely graze unceasing
[ʃip mɛːɪ ˈsɛːɪflɪ gɹɛːɪz ʌnˈsisɪŋ]
In a steadfast shepherd's sight.
[ɪn ʌ ˈstɛdfast ˈʃɛpʌdz saːɪt]
He who rules with vision guiding
[hi hu ɾrulz wɪð ˈvɪʒʌn ˈgaːɪdɪŋ]
Brings us rest and peace abiding
[bɹɪŋz ʌs ɹɛst ænd pis ʌˈbaːɪdɪŋ]
Saves our souls from endless night.
[sɛːɪvz aːʊʌ soːʊlz fɹʌm ˈɛndlɛ(ɪ)s naːɪt]

 ## Bacon, Ernst (Am. 1898-1990)

Five Poems by Emily Dickinson (Song Cycle)
[faːɪv ˈpoːʊɪmz baːɪ ˈɛmɪlɪ ˈdɪkɪnsʌn]
Dickinson, Emily (Am. 1830-1886)

1. It's All I Have to Bring
[ɪts ɔl ɑːɪ hæv tu bɹɪŋ]

It's all I have to bring today,
[ɪts ɔl ɑːɪ hæv tu bɹɪŋ tuˈdɛːɪ]

This, and my heart beside,
[ðɪs ænd mɑːɪ hɑt bɪˈsɑːɪd]
This, and my heart, and all the fields,
[ðɪs ænd mɑːɪ hɑt ænd ɔl ðʌ fildz]
And all the meadows wide.
[ænd ɔl ðʌ ˈmɛdoːʊz wɑːɪd]
Be sure you count, should I forget,
[bi ʃʊːʌ ju kɑːʊnt ʃʊd ɑːɪ fɔˈgɛt]
Someone the sum could tell,–
[ˈsʌmwʌn ðʌ sʌm kʊd tɛl]
This, and my heart, and all the bees
[ðɪs ænd mɑːɪ hɑt ænd ɔl ðʌ biz]
Which in the clover dwell.
[ʌɪʧ ɪn ðʌ ˈkloːʊvʌ dwɛl]

2. So Bashful
[soːʊ ˈbæʃfʊl]

So bashful when I spied her,
[soːʊ ˈbæʃfʊl ʌɛn ɑːɪ spɑːɪd hɜ]
So pretty, so ashamed!
[soːʊ ˈpɹɪti soːʊ ʌˈʃɛːɪmd]
So hidden in her leaflets,
[soːʊ ˈhɪdɛ(ɪ)n ɪn hɜ ˈliflɛ(ɪ)ts]
Lest anybody find;
[lɛst ˈɛnɪbadɪ fɑːɪnd]
So breathless till I passed her,
[soːʊ ˈbɹɛθlɛ(ɪ)s tɪl ɑːɪ pæst hɜ]
So helpless when I turned
[soːʊ ˈhɛlplɛ(ɪ)s ʌɛn ɑːɪ tɜnd]
And bore her, struggling, blushing,
[ænd bɔːʌ hɜ ˈstɹʌglɪŋ ˈblʌʃɪŋ]
Her simple haunts beyond!
[hɜ ˈsɪmpʊl hɔnts bɪˈjand]
For whom I robbed the dingle,
[fɔ hum ɑːɪ ɹabd ðʌ ˈdɪŋgʊl]
For whom betrayed the dell,
[fɔ hum bɪˈtɹɛːɪd ðʌ dɛl]
Many will doubtless ask me,
[ˈmɛnɪ wɪl ˈdɑːʊtlɛ(ɪ)s æsk mi]
But I shall never tell!
[bʌt ɑːɪ ʃæl ˈnɛvʌ tɛl]

3. Poor Little Heart! (see Gordon)

4. To Make a Prairie
[tu mɛːɪk ʌ ˈpɹɛʁi]

To make a prairie it takes
[tu mɛːɪk ʌ ˈpɹɛʁ(ɾ)ɪ ɪt tɛːɪks]
a clover and one bee,
[ʌ ˈkloːʊvʌ ænd wʌn bi]
One clover, and a bee,
[wʌn ˈkloːʊvʌ ænd ʌ bi]
And revery.
[ænd ˈɹɛvʌʁ(ɾ)ɪ]

The revery alone will do, If bees are few.
[ðʌ ˈɹɛvʌʁ(ɾ)ɪ ʌˈloːʊn wɪl du ɪf biz ɑ fju]

5. And This of All My Hopes
[ænd ðɪs ʌv ɔl mɑːɪ hoːʊps]

And this of all my hopes,
[ænd ðɪs ʌv ɔl mɑːɪ hoːʊps]
This is the silent end.
[ðɪs ɪz ðʌ ˈsɑːɪlɛnt ɛnd]
Bountiful colored my morning rose,
[ˈbɑːʊntɪfʊl ˈkʌlɔ(ʌ)d mɑːɪ ˈmɔnɪŋ ɹoːʊz]
Early and sere its end.
[ˈɜlɪ ænd sɪːʌʁ(ɾ) ɪts ɛnd]
Never bud from a stem
[ˈnɛvʌ bʌd fɹʌm ʌ stɛm]
Stepped with so gay a foot,
[stɛpt wɪð soːʊ gɛːɪ ʌ fʊt]
Never a worm so confident
[ˈnɛvʌʁ(ɾ) ʌ wɜm soːʊ ˈkanfɪdɛnt]
Bored at so brave a root.
[bɔd æt soːʊ bɹɛːɪv ʌ ɹ(ɾɾ)ut]

Barab, Seymour (Am. 1921-2014)

The Rivals (Song Cycle)
[ðʌ ˈɹɑːɪvʊlz]
Stephens, James (Ir. 1880-1950)

1. The Daisies [ðʌ ˈdɛːɪziz]

In the scented bud of the morning O,
[ɪn ðʌ ˈsɛntɛ(ɪ)d bʌd ʌv ðʌ ˈmɔnɪŋ oːʊ]
When the windy grass went rippling far!
[ʌɛn ðʌ ˈwɪndɪ gɹæs wɛnt ˈɹɪplɪŋ fa]
I saw my dear one walking slow
[ɑːɪ sɔ mɑːɪ dɪːʌ wʌn ˈwɔkɪŋ sloːʊ]
In the field where the daisies are.
[ɪn ðʌ fild ʌɛːʌ ðʌ ˈdɛːɪziz a]
We did not laugh, and we did not speak,
[wi dɪd nat læf ænd wi dɪd nat spik]
As we wandered happily, to and fro,
[æz wi ˈwandʌd ˈhæpɪlɪ tu ænd fɹoːʊ]
I kissed my dear on either cheek,
[ɑːɪ kɪst mɑːɪ dɪːʌʁ(ɾ) an ˈɑːɪðʌ ʧik]
In the bud of the morning O!
[ɪn ðʌ bʌd ʌv ðʌ ˈmɔnɪŋ oːʊ]
A lark sang up, from the breezy land;
[ʌ lak sæŋ ʌp fɹʌm ðʌ ˈbɹizɪ lænd]
A lark sang down, from a cloud afar;
[ʌ lak sæŋ dɑːʊn fɹʌm ʌ klɑːʊd ʌˈfa]
As she and I went, hand in hand,
[æz ʃi ænd ɑːɪ wɛnt hænd ɪn hænd]
In the field where the daisies are.
[ɪn ðʌ fild ʌɛːʌ ðʌ ˈdɛːɪziz a]

2. The Rose in the Wind
[ðʌ ɹoːʊz ɪn ðʌ wɪnd]

Dip and swing!
[dɪp ænd swɪŋ]
Lift and sway!
[lɪft ænd swɛːɪ]
Dream a life
[dɹim ʌ lɑːɪf]
In a dream, away!
[ɪn ʌ dɹim ʌˈwɛːɪ]
Like a dream
[lɑːɪk ʌ dɹim]
In a sleep
[ɪn ʌ slip]
Is the rose
[ɪz ðʌ ɹoːʊz]
In the wind!
[ɪn ðʌ wɪnd]
And a fish
[ænd ʌ fɪʃ]
In the deep;
[ɪn ðʌ dip]
And a man
[ænd ʌ mæn]
In the mind!
[ɪn ðʌ mɑːɪnd]
Dreaming to lack
[ˈdɹimɪŋ tu læk]
All that is his!
[ɔl ðæt ɪz hɪz]
Dreaming to gain
[ˈdɹimɪŋ tu gɛːɪn]
All that he is!
[ɔl ðæt hi ɪz]
Dreaming a life,
[ˈdɹimɪŋ ʌ lɑːɪf]
In a dream, away!
[ɪn ʌ dɹim ʌˈwɛːɪ]
Dip and swing,
[dɪp ænd swɪŋ]
Lift and sway!
[lɪft ænd swɛːɪ]

3. The Hawk
[ðʌ hɔk]

A bird is singing now;
[ʌ bɜd ɪz ˈsɪŋɪŋ nɑːʊ]
Merrily sings he.
[ˈmɛʁ⁽ʳ⁾ɪlɪ sɪŋz hi]
Of his mate on the bough,
[ʌv hɪz mɛːɪt an ðʌ bɑːʊ]
And her eggs in the tree:
[ænd hɜ ɛgz ɪn ðʌ tɹi]

But yonder a hawk
[bʌt ˈjandʌ ʌ hɔk]
Swings down from the blue,
[swɪŋz dɑːʊn fɹʌm ðʌ blu]
And the bird's song is finished
[ænd ðʌ bɜdz saŋ ɪz ˈfɪnɪʃt]
- is this story true?
[ɪz ðɪs ˈstɔʁ⁽ʳ⁾ɪ tɹ⁽ʳ⁾u]
God now have mercy
[gad nɑːʊ hæv ˈmɜsɪ]
On me, and on you!
[an mi ænd an ju]

4. The Rivals
[ðʌ ˈɹɑːɪvʊlz]

I heard a bird at dawn
[ɑːɪ hɜd ʌ bɜd æt dɔn]
Singing sweetly on a tree,
[ˈsɪŋɪŋ ˈswitlɪ an ʌ tɹi]
That the dew was on the lawn,
[ðæt ðʌ dju waz an ðʌ lɔn]
And the wind was on the lea;
[ænd ðʌ wɪnd waz an ðʌ li]
But I did not listen to him,
[bʌt ɑːɪ dɪd nat ˈlɪsɛ(ɪ)n tu hɪm]
For he did not sing to me.
[fɔ hi dɪd nat sɪŋ tu mi]
I did not listen to him,
[ɑːɪ dɪd nat ˈlɪsɛ(ɪ)n tu hɪm]
For he did not sing to me
[fɔ hi dɪd nat sɪŋ tu mi]
That the dew was on the lawn
[ðæt ðʌ dju waz an ðʌ lɔn]
And the wind was on the lea;
[ænd ðʌ wɪnd waz an ðʌ li]
I was singing at the time
[ɑːɪ waz ˈsɪŋɪŋ æt ðʌ tɑːɪm]
Just as prettily as he.
[dʒʌst æz ˈpɹɪtɪlɪ æz hi]
I was singing all the time,
[ɑːɪ waz ˈsɪŋɪŋ ɔl ðʌ tɑːɪm]
Just as prettily as he,
[dʒʌst æz ˈpɹɪtɪlɪ æz hi]
About the dew upon the lawn
[ʌˈbɑːʊt ðʌ dju ʌˈpan ðʌ lɔn]
And the wind upon the lea;
[ænd ðʌ wɪnd ʌˈpan ðʌ li]
So I did not listen to him
[soːʊ ɑːɪ dɪd nat ˈlɪsɛ(ɪ)n tu hɪm]
As he sang upon a tree.
[æz hi sæŋ ʌˈpan ʌ tɹi]

Song Selection for Youth

"At the Seaside" (A Child's Garden of Verses)
[æt ðʌ ˈsiˌsɑːɪd]
Stevenson, Robert Louis (Sc. 1850-1894)

When I was down beside the sea
[ʍɛn ɑːɪ waz dɑːʊn bɪˈsɑːɪd ðʌ si]
A wooden spade they gave to me
[ʌ ˈwʊdɛ(ɪ)n spɛːɪd ðɛːʊ gɛːɪv tu mi]
To dig the sandy shore.
[tu dɪg ðʌ ˈsændɪ ʃɔːʌ]
My holes were empty like a cup.
[mɑːɪ hoːʊlz wɜ ˈɛmptɪ lɑːɪk ʌ kʌp]
In every hole the sea came up.
[ɪn ˈɛvɹɪ hoːʊl ðʌ si kɛːɪm ʌp]
Till it could come no more.
[tɪl ɪt kʊd kʌm noːʊ mɔːʌ]

Barber, Samuel (Am. 1910-1981)

Song Selections

"A Nun Takes the Veil"
[ʌ nʌn tɛːɪks ðʌ vɛːɪl]
Hopkins, Gerard Manley (Eng. 1844-1889)

I have desired to go
[ɑːɪ hæv dɪˈzɑːɪʌd tu goːʊ]
Where springs not fail,
[ʍɛːʌ spɹɪŋz nat fɛːɪl]
To fields where flies no sharp and sided hail
[tu fildz ʍɛːʌ flɑːɪz noːʊ ʃap ænd ˈsɑːɪdɛ(ɪ)d hɛːɪl]
And a few lilies blow.
[ænd ʌ fju ˈlɪlɪz bloːʊ]
And I have asked to be
[ænd ɑːɪ hæv æskt tu bi]
Where no storms come,
[ʍɛːʌ noːʊ stɔmz kʌm]
Where the green swell is in the havens dumb,
[ʍɛːʌ ðʌ gɹin swɛl ɪz ɪn ðʌ ˈhɛːɪvɛ(ɪ)nz dʌm]
And out of the swing of the sea.
[ænd ɑːʊt ʌv ðʌ swɪŋ ʌv ðʌ si]

"A Slumber Song of the Madonna"
[ʌ ˈslʌmbʁ saŋ ʌv ðʌ mʌˈdanʌ]
Keel, J. Frederick (Eng. 1871-1954)

Sleep, little baby, I love thee;
[slip ˈlɪdʊl ˈbɛːɪbɪ ɑːɪ lʌv ði]
Sleep, little king, I am bending above thee;
[slip ˈlɪdʊl kɪŋ ɑːɪ æm ˈbɛndɪŋ ʌˈbʌv ði]
How should I know what to sing?
[hɑːʊ ʃʊd ɑːɪ noːʊ ʍat tu sɪŋ]

Here in my arms as I sing thee to sleep!
[hiːʌʁ⁽ʳ⁾ ɪn mɑːɪ amz æz ɑːɪ sɪŋ ði tu slip]
Hushaby low, Rockaby so.
[ˈhʌʃʌbɑːɪ loːʊ ˈɹakʌbɑːɪ soːʊ]
Kings may have wonderful jewels to bring!
[kɪŋz mɛːɪ hæv ˈwʌndʌfʊl ˈdʒuːɛ(ʊ)lz tu bɹɪŋ]
Mother has only a kiss for her king.
[ˈmʌðʌ hæz ˈoːʊnlɪ ʌ kɪs fɔ hɜ kɪŋ]
Why should my singing so make me to weep?
[ʍɑːɪ ʃʊd mɑːɪ ˈsɪŋɪŋ soːʊ mɛːɪk mi tu wip]
Only I know that I love thee, I love thee!
[ˈoːʊnlɪ ɑːɪ noːʊ ðæt ɑːɪ lʌv ði ɑːɪ lʌv ði]
Love thee, my little one, Sleep!
[lʌv ði mɑːɪ ˈlɪtʊl wʌn slip]

"Bessie Bobtail"
[ˈbɛsi ˈbabtɛːɪl]
Stephens, James (Ir. 1882-1950)

As down the road she wambled slow,
[æz dɑːʊn ðʌ ɹoːʊd ʃi ˈwambʊld sloːʊ]
She had not got a place to go:
[ʃi hæd nat gat ʌ plɛːɪs tu goːʊ]
She had not got a place to fall
[ʃi hæd nat gat ʌ plɛːɪs tu fɔl]
And rest herself- no place at all.
[ænd ɹɛst hɜˈsɛlf noːʊ plɛːɪs æt ɔl]
She stumped along, and wagged her pate;
[ʃi stʌmpt ʌˈlaŋ ænd wægd hɜ pɛːɪt]
And said a thing was desperate.
[ænd sɛd ʌ θɪŋ waz ˈdɛspʌʁ⁽ʳ⁾æ(ɪ)t]
Her face was screwed and wrinkled tight
[hɜ fɛːɪs waz skɹɪ⁽ʳ⁾ud ænd ˈɹɪŋkʊld tɑːɪt]
Just like a nut- and, left and right,
[dʒʌst lɑːɪk ʌ nʌt ænd lɛft ænd ɹɑːɪt]
On either side she wagged her head,
[an ˈɑːɪðʌ sɑːɪd ʃi wægd hɜ hɛd]
And said a thing; and what she said
[ænd sɛd ʌ θɪŋ ænd ʍat ʃi sɛd]
Was desperate as any word
[waz ˈdɛspʌʁ⁽ʳ⁾æ(ɪ)t æz ˈɛnɪ wɜd]
That ever yet a person heard.
[ðæt ˈɛvʌ jɛt ʌ ˈpɜsʌn hɜd]
I walked behind her for a while
[ɑːɪ wɔkt bɪˈhaːɪnd hɜ fɔʁ⁽ʳ⁾ ʌ ʍɑːɪl]
And watched the people nudge and smile.
[ænd waʧt ðʌ ˈpipʊl nʌdʒ ænd smɑːɪl]
But ever, as she went she said,
[bʌt ˈɛvʌʁ⁽ʳ⁾ æz ʃi wɛnt ʃi sɛd]
As left and right she swung her head,
[æz lɛft ænd ɹɑːɪt ʃi swʌŋ hɜ hɛd]
"Oh, God He knows," and "God He knows:"
[oːʊ gad hi noːʊz ænd gad hi noːʊz]
And, surely God Almighty knows.
[ænd ˈʃʊːʌlɪ gad ɔlˈmɑːɪtɪ noːʊz]

"Dover Beach"
[ˈdoːʊvʁ biʧ]
Arnold, Matthew (Eng. 1822-1888)

The sea is calm tonight,
[ðʌ si ɪz kɑm tuˈnɑːɪt]
The tide is full, the moon lies fair
[ðʌ tɑːɪd ɪz fʊl ðʌ mun lɑːɪz fɛːʌ]
Upon the straights;– on the French coast the light
[ʌˈpɑn ðʌ stɹɛːɪts an ðʌ fɹɛnʧ koːʊst ðʌ lɑːɪt]
Gleams and is gone; the cliffs of England stand,
[glimz ænd ɪz gan ðʌ klɪfs ʌv ˈɪŋglæ(ʌ)nd stænd]
Glimm'ring and vast, out in the tranquil bay.
[ˈglɪmɹɪŋ ænd væst ɑːʊt ɪn ðʌ ˈtɹæŋkwɪ(ʊ)l bɛːɪ]
Come to the window, sweet is the night-air!
[kʌm tu ðʌ ˈwɪndoːʊ swit ɪz ðʌ nɑːɪt ɛːʌ]
Only, from the long line of spray
[ˈoːʊnlɪ fɹʌm ðʌ laŋ lɑːɪn ʌv spɹɛːɪ]
Where the sea meets the moon-blanch'd land,
[ʍɛːʌ ðʌ si mits ðʌ mun blænʧt lænd]
Listen! you hear the grating roar
[ˈlɪsɛ(ɪ)n ju hɪːʌ ðʌ ˈgɹɛːɪtɪŋ ɹoːʌ]
Of pebbles which the waves draw back, and fling,
[ʌv ˈpɛbʊlz ʍɪʧ ðʌ wɛːɪvz dɹɔ bæk ænd flɪŋ]
At their return, up the high strand,
[æt ðɛːʌ ɹɪˈtɜn ʌp ðʌ hɑːɪ stɹænd]
Begin, and cease, and then again begin,
[bɪˈgɪn ænd sis ænd ðɛn ʌˈgɛn bɪˈgɪn]
With tremulous cadence slow, and bring
[wɪð ˈtɹɛmjulʌs ˈkɛːɪdɛ(ɪ)ns sloːʊ ænd bɹɪŋ]
The eternal note of sadness in.
[ði ɪˈtɜnʊl noːʊt ʌv ˈsædnɛ(ɪ)s ɪn]
Sophocles long ago
[ˈsafo(ʌ)ˌkliz laŋ ʌˈgoːʊ]
Heard it on the Ægean, and it brought
[hɜd ɪt an ði ʌˈʤiæ(ɪ)n ænd ɪt bɹɔt]
Into his mind the turbid ebb and flow
[ˈɪntu hɪz mɑːɪnd ðʌ ˈtɜbɪd ɛb ænd floːʊ]
Of human misery; we
[ʌv ˈhjumæ(ʌ)n ˈmɪzʌʁ(ʳ)ɪ wi]
Find also in the sound a thought,
[fɑːɪnd ˈɔlsoːʊ ɪn ðʌ sɑːʊnd ʌ θɔt]
Hearing it by this distant northern sea.
[ˈhɪːʌʁ(ʳ)ɪŋ ɪt bɑːɪ ðɪs ˈdɪstæ(ɪ)nt ˈnɔðʌn si]
The Sea of Faith
[ðʌ si ʌv fɛːɪθ]
Was once, too, at the full, and round earth's shore
[waz wʌns tu æt ðʌ fʊl ænd ɹɑːʊnd ɜθs ʃɔːʌ]
Lay like the folds of a bright girdle furled.
[lɛːɪ lɑːɪk ðʌ foːʊldz ʌv ʌ bɹɑːɪt ˈgɜdʊl fɜld]
But now I only hear
[bʌt nɑːʊ ɑːɪ ˈoːʊnlɪ hɪːʌ]
Its melancholy, long, withdrawing roar,
[ɪts ˈmɛlæ(ɪ)nˌkalɪ laŋ wɪðˈdɹɔɪŋ ɹoːʌ]
Retreating, to the breath
[ɹɪˈtɹitɪŋ tu ðʌ bɹɛθ]

Of the night-wind, down the vast edges drear
[ʌv ðʌ nɑːɪt wɪnd dɑːʊn ðʌ væst ˈɛʤɛ(ɪ)z dɹɪːʌ]
And naked shingles of the world.
[ænd ˈnɛːɪkɛ(ɪ)d ˈʃɪŋgʊlz ʌv ðʌ wɜld]
Ah, love, let us be true
[ɑ lʌv lɛt ʌs bi tɹ(ʳ)u]
To one another! for the world, which seems
[tu wʌn ʌˈnʌðʌ fɔ ðʌ wɜld ʍɪʧ simz]
To lie before us like a land of dreams,
[tu lɑːɪ bɪˈfɔːʁ(ʳ) ʌs lɑːɪk ʌ lænd ʌv dɹimz]
So various, so beautiful, so new,
[soːʊ ˈvæʁ(ʳ)ɪʌs soːʊ ˈbjutɪfʊl soːʊ nju]
Hath really neither joy, nor love, nor light,
[hæθ ˈɹɪːʌlɪ ˈnɑːɪðʌ ʤɔːɪ nɔ lʌv nɔ lɑːɪt]
Nor certitude, nor peace, nor help for pain;
[nɔ ˈsɜtɪtjud nɔ pis nɔ hɛlp fɔ pɛːɪn]
And we are here as on a darkling plain
[ænd wi ɑ hɪːʁ(ʳ) æz an ʌ ˈdaklɪŋ plɛːɪn]
Swept with confused alarms of struggle and flight,
[swɛpt wɪð kʌnˈfjuzd ʌˈlamz ʌv ˈstɹʌgʊl ænd flɑːɪt]
Where ignorant armies clash by night.
[ʍɛːʁ(ʳ) ˈɪgnɔʁ(ʳ)æ(ɪ)nt ˈɑmɪz klæʃ bɑːɪ nɑːɪt]

"I Hear an Army"
[ɑːɪ hɪːʁ æn ˈɑʁmi]
Joyce, James (Ir. 1882-1941)

I hear an army charging upon the land,
[ɑːɪ hɪːʌʁ(ʳ) æn ˈɑmɪ ˈʧɑʤɪŋ ʌˈpan ðʌ lænd]
And the thunder of horses plunging,
[ænd ðʌ ˈθʌndʌʁ(ʳ) ʌv ˈhɔsɛ(ɪ)z ˈplʌnʤɪŋ]
foam about their knees:
[foːʊm ʌˈbɑːʊt ðɛːʌ niz]
Arrogant, in black armour, behind them stand,
[ˈæʁ(ʳ)ogæ(ɪ)nt ɪn blæk ˈɑmʌ bɪˈhɑːɪnd ðɛm stænd]
Disdaining the reins, with fluttering whips,
[dɪsˈdɛːɪnɪŋ ðʌ ɹɛːɪnz wɪð ˈflʌtʌʁ(ʳ)ɪŋ ʍɪps]
the charioteers.
[ðʌ ʧæʁ(ʳ)ɪʌˈtɪːʌz]
They cry unto the night their battlename:
[ðɛːɪ kɹ(ʳ)ɑːɪ ˈʌntu ðʌ nɑːɪt ðɛːʌ ˈbætʊlnɛːɪm]
I moan in sleep when I hear afar
[ɑːɪ moːʊn ɪn slip ʍɛn ɑːɪ hɪːʌʁ(ʳ) ʌˈfɑ]
their whirling laughter.
[ðɛːʌ ˈʍɜlɪŋ ˈlæftʌ]
They cleave the gloom of dreams, a blinding flame,
[ðɛːɪ kliv ðʌ glum ʌv dɹimz ʌ ˈblɑːɪndɪŋ flɛːɪm]
Clanging, clanging upon the heart as upon an anvil.
[ˈklæŋɪŋ ˈklæŋɪŋ ʌˈpan ðʌ hat æz ʌˈpan æn ˈænvɪ(ʊ)l]
They come shaking in triumph their long, green hair:
[ðɛːɪ kʌm ˈʃɛːɪkɪŋ ɪn ˈtɹɑːɪʌmf ðɛːʌ laŋ gɹin hɛːʌ]
They come out of the sea and run shouting by the shore.
[ðɛːɪ kʌm ɑːʊt ʌv ðʌ si ænd ɹʌn ˈʃɑːʊtɪŋ bɑːɪ ðʌ ʃɔːʌ]
My heart, have you no wisdom thus to despair?
[mɑːɪ hat hæv ju noːʊ ˈwɪzdʌm ðʌs tu dɪˈspɛːʌ]

My love, my love, why have you left me alone?
[mɑːɪ lʌv mɑːɪ lʌv ʍɑːɪ hæv ju lɛft mi ʌˈloːʊn]

"Mother, I Cannot Mind My Wheel"
[ˈmʌðɐ ɑːɪ kæˈnɑt mɑːɪnd mɑːɪ ʍil]
Landor, Walter Savage (Eng. 1775-1864)

Mother, I cannot mind my wheel;
[ˈmʌðʌ ɑːɪ kæˈnɑt mɑːɪnd mɑːɪ ʍil]
My fingers ache, my lips are dry:
[mɑːɪ ˈfɪŋgʌz ɛːɪk mɑːɪ lɪps ɑ dɹɑːɪ]
O, if you felt the pain I feel!
[oːʊ ɪf ju fɛlt ðʌ pɛːɪn ɑːɪ fil]
But O, who ever felt as I?
[bʌt oːʊ hu ˈɛvʌ fɛlt æz ɑːɪ]
No longer could I doubt him true–
[noːʊ ˈlɑŋgʌ kʊd ɑːɪ dɑːʊt hɪm tɹⁱⁱu]
All other men may use deceit;
[ɔl ˈʌðʌ mɛn mɛːɪ juz dɪˈsit]
He always said my eyes were blue,
[hi ˈɔlwɛːɪz sɛd mɑːɪ ɑːɪz wɜ blu]
And often swore my lips were sweet.
[ænd ˈɑfɛ(ɪ)n swɔːʌ mɑːɪ lɪps wɜ swit]

"Now Have I Fed and Eaten up the Rose"
[nɑːʊ hæv ɑːɪ fɛd ænd ˈitɪn ʌp ðʌ ɹoːʊz]
Joyce, James (Ir. 1882-1941)

Now have I fed and eaten up the rose
[nɑːʊ hæv ɑːɪ fɛd ænd ˈitɛ(ɪ)n ʌp ðʌ ɹoːʊz]
Which then she laid within my stiff-cold hand.
[ʍɪtʃ ðɛn ʃi lɛːɪd wɪðˈɪn mɑːɪ stɪf koːʊld hænd]
That I should ever feed upon a rose
[ðæt ɑːɪ ʃʊd ˈɛvʌ fid ʌˈpɑn ʌ ɹoːʊz]
I never had believed in liveman's land.
[ɑːɪ ˈnɛvʌ hæd bɪˈlivd ɪn ˈlɑːɪvmænz lænd]
Only I wonder was it white or red
[ˈoːʊnlɪ ɑːɪ ˈwʌndʌ wɑz ɪt ʍɑːɪt ɔ ɹɛd]
The flow'r that in the darkness my food has been.
[ðʌ flɑːʊʌ ðæt ɪn ðʌ ˈdɑknɛ(ɪ)s mɑːɪ fud hæz bɪn]
Give us, and if Thou give, thy daily bread,
[gɪv ʌs ænd ɪf ðɑːʊ gɪv ðɑːɪ ˈdɛːɪlɪ bɹɛd]
Deliver us from evil, Lord, Amen.
[dɪˈlɪvʌʁⁱ ʌs fɹʌm ˈivɪ(ʊ)l lɔd ɑˈmɛn]

"Sleep Now"
[slip nɑːʊ]
Joyce, James (Ir. 1882-1941)

Sleep now, O sleep now,
[slip nɑːʊ oːʊ slip nɑːʊ]
O you unquiet heart!
[oːʊ ju ʌnˈkwɑːɪɛ(ɪ)t hɑt]
A voice crying "Sleep now"
[ʌ vɔːɪs ˈkɹⁱɑːɪɪŋ slip nɑːʊ]

Is heard in my heart.
[ɪz hɜd ɪn mɑːɪ hɑt]
The voice of the winter
[ðʌ vɔːɪs ʌv ðʌ ˈwɪntʌ]
Is heard at the door.
[ɪz hɜd æt ðʌ dɔːʌ]
O sleep, for the winter
[oːʊ slip fɔ ðʌ ˈwɪntʌʁⁱ]
Is crying "Sleep no more."
[ɪz ˈkɹⁱɑːɪɪŋ slip noːʊ mɔːʌ]
My kiss will give peace now
[mɑːɪ kɪs wɪl gɪv pis nɑːʊ]
And quiet to your heart-
[ænd ˈkwɑːɪɛ(ɪ)t tu jɔːʌ hɑt]
Sleep on in peace now,
[slip ɑn ɪn pis nɑːʊ]
O you unquiet heart!
[oːʊ ju ʌnˈkwɑːɪɛ(ɪ)t hɑt]

"The Daisies" (see Barab)

"The Secrets of the Old"
[ðʌ ˈsikɹɪts ʌv ði oːʊld]
Yeats, William Butler (Ir. 1865-1939)

I have old women's secrets now
[ɑːɪ hæv oːʊld ˈwɪmɛ(ɪ)nz ˈsikɹɛ(ɪ)ts nɑːʊ]
That had those of the young;
[ðæt hæd ðoːʊz ʌv ðʌ jʌŋ]
Madge tells me what I dared not think
[mædʒ tɛlz mi ʍɑt ɑːɪ dɛːʌd nɑt θɪŋk]
When my blood was strong,
[ʍɛn mɑːɪ blʌd wɑz stɹɑŋ]
And what had drowned a lover once
[ænd ʍɑt hæd dɹɑːʊnd ʌ ˈlʌvʌ wʌns]
Sounds like an old song.
[sɑːʊndz lɑːɪk æn oːʊld sɑŋ]
Though Marg'ry is stricken dumb
[ðoːʊ ˈmɑdʒɹɪ ɪz ˈstɹɪkɛ(ɪ)n dʌm]
If thrown in Madge's way,
[ɪf θɹoːʊn ɪn ˈmædʒɛ(ɪ)z wɛːɪ]
We three make up a solitude;
[wi θɾi mɛːɪk ʌp ʌ ˈsɑlɪtjud]
For none alive today
[fɔ nʌn ʌˈlɑːɪv tuˈdɛːɪ]
Can know the stories that we know
[kæn noːʊ ðʌ ˈstɔʁⁱɪz ðæt wi noːʊ]
Or say the things we say:
[ɔ sɛːɪ ðʌ θɪŋz wi sɛːɪ]
How such a man pleased women most
[hɑːʊ sʌtʃ ʌ mæn plizd ˈwɪmɛ(ɪ)n moːʊst]
Of all that are gone,
[ʌv ɔl ðæt ɑ gɑn]
How such a pair loved many years
[hɑːʊ sʌtʃ ʌ pɛːʌ lʌvd ˈmɛnɪ jɪːʌz]

And such a pair but one,
[ænd sʌʧ ʌ pɛːʌ bʌt wʌn]
Stories of the bed of straw
[ˈstɔʁ⁽ʳ⁾ɪz ʌv ðʌ bɛd ʌv stɹɔ]
Or the bed of down.
[ɔ ðʌ bɛd ʌv daːʊn]

 # Bax, Arnold (Eng. 1883-1953)

The Bard of the Dimbovitza (Song Cycle)
[ðʊ bad ʌv ðʊ ˈdimbovitsa]
Translation of Romanian folksongs by Alma Strettell
(Eng. 1856-1939)

1. Gipsy Song
[ˈʤɪpsi saŋ]

There where the path to the plain goes by
[ðɛːʌ ʍɛːʌ ðʊ paθ tu ðʊ plɛːɪn goːʊz baːɪ]
Where deep in the thicket my hut doth lie
[ʍɛːʌ dip ɪn ðʊ ˈθɪkɛ⁽ɪ⁾t maːɪ hʌt dʌθ laːɪ]
Where corn stands green in the garden plot,
[ʍɛːʌ kɔn stændz ɡɹin ɪn ðʊ ˈɡadɛ⁽ɪ⁾n plat]
The brook ripples by so clear there,
[ðʊ bɹʊk ˈɹɪpʊlz baːɪ soːʊ klɪːʌ ðɛːʌ]
The way is open so white and fair,
[ðʊ wɛːɪ ɪz ˈoːʊpɛ⁽ɪ⁾n soːʊ ʍaːɪt ænd fɛːʌ]
My heart's best beloved he takes it not.
[maːɪ hats bɛst bɪˈlʌvɛ⁽ɪ⁾d hi tɛːɪks ɪt nat]
There where I sit by my door and spin
[ðɛːʌ ʍɛːʌɾ aːɪ sɪt baːɪ maːɪ dɔːʌɾ ænd spɪn]
While morning winds that blow out and in
[ʍaːɪl ˈmɔnɪŋ wɪndz ðæt bloːʊ aːʊt ænd ɪn]
With scent of roses enfold the spot.
[wɪð sɛnt ʌv ˈɹoːʊzɛ⁽ɪ⁾z ɪnˈfoːʊld ðʊ spat]
When at evening I softly sing my lay
[ʍɛn æt ˈivnɪŋ aːɪ ˈsaftlɪ sɪŋ maːɪ lɛːɪ]
That the wanderer hears as he goes his way
[ðæt ðʊ ˈwandʌɾʌ hɪːʌz æz hi goːʊz hɪz wɛːɪ]
My heart's best beloved he hears me not.
[maːɪ hats bɛst bɪˈlʌvɛ⁽ɪ⁾d hi hɪːʌz mi nat]
There where on Sundays I go alone
[ðɛːʌ ʍɛːʌɾ an ˈsʌndeːɪz aːɪ goːʊ ʌˈloːʊn]
To the old, old well with the milk-white stone
[tu ði oːʊld oːʊld wɛl wɪð ðʊ mɪlk ʍaːɪt stoːʊn]
Where by the fence in a nook forgot
[ʍɛːʌ baːɪ ðʊ fɛns ɪn ʌ nʊk fʌˈɡat]
Rises a spring in the daisied grass
[ˈɹaːɪzɛ⁽ɪ⁾z ʌ spɹɪŋ ɪn ðʊ ˈdɛːɪzid ɡɹas]
That makes who so drinks of it love alas!
[ðæt mɛːɪks hu soːʊ dɹɪŋks ʌv ɪt lʌv ʌˈlæs]
My heart's best beloved he drinks it not.
[maːɪ hats bɛst bɪˈlʌvɛ⁽ɪ⁾d hi dɹɪŋks ɪt nat]
There by my window where day by day
[ðɛːʌ baːɪ maːɪ ˈwɪndoːʊ ʍɛːʌ dɛːɪ baːɪ dɛːɪ]

When the sunbeams first brighten the morning's grey
[ʍɛn ðʊ ˈsʌnbimz fɜst ˈbɹaːɪtɛ⁽ɪ⁾n ðʊ ˈmɔnɪŋz ɡɹɛːɪ]
I lean and dream of my weary lot
[aːɪ lin ænd dɹim ʌv maːɪ ˈwɪːʌɾi lat]
And wait his coming and softly cry
[ænd wɛːɪt hɪz ˈkʌmɪŋ ænd ˈsaftlɪ kɹaːɪ]
Because of love's longing that makes one die,
[bɪˈkɔz ʌv lʌvz ˈlaŋɪŋ ðæt mɛːɪks wʌn daːɪ]
My heart's best beloved he dieth not.
[maːɪ hats bɛst bɪˈlʌvɛ⁽ɪ⁾d hi ˈdaːɪɛ⁽ɪ⁾θ nat]

2. The Well of Tears
[ðʊ wɛl ʌv tɪːʌz]

The night is coming, let thy spindle be.
[ðʊ naːɪt ɪz ˈkʌmɪŋ lɛt ðaːɪ ˈspɪndʊl bi]
Those who went by this way
[ðoːʊz hu wɛnt baːɪ ðɪs wɛːɪ]
Spoke of their huts together, and the huts
[spoːʊk ʌv ðɛːʌ hʌts tuˈɡɛðʌ ænd ðʊ hʌts]
Seemed far, so far away.
[simd fa soːʊ far ʌˈwɛːɪ]
What saw'st thou at the bottom of the well?
[ʍat ˈsɔɪst ðaːʊ æt ðʊ ˈbatʌm ʌv ðʊ wɛl]
I saw my face, my bodice, and my chain.
[aːɪ sɔ maːɪ fɛːɪs maːɪ ˈbadɪs ænd maːɪ ʧɛːɪn]
Child, didst thou see aught else?
[ʧaːɪld dɪdst ðaːʊ si ɔt ɛls]
I saw there at the bottom of the well
[aːɪ sɔ ðɛːʌ æt ðʊ ˈbatʌm ʌv ðʊ wɛl]
A man who wept.
[ʌ mæn hu wɛpt]
My face, down there, was sore afraid of him;
[maːɪ fɛːɪs daːʊn ðɛːʌ waz sɔːʌɾ ʌˈfɹɛːɪd ʌv hɪm]
And all the water in the well was naught
[ænd ɔl ðʊ ˈwɔtʌɾ ɪn ðʊ wɛl waz nɔt]
But this man's tears.
[bʌt ðɪs mænz tɪːʌz]
I was afraid, and would not draw those tears.
[aːɪ waz ʌˈfɹɛːɪd ænd wʊd nat dɹɔ ðoːʊz tɪːʌz]
Then came a woman, and I went aside,
[ðɛn kɛːɪm ʌ ˈwʊmɛ⁽ʌ⁾n ænd aːɪ wɛnt ʌˈsaːɪd]
But yet I saw, how she drew up those tears.
[bʌt jɛt aːɪ sɔ haːʊ ʃi dɹu ʌp ðoːʊz tɪːʌz]
And how she drank them, looking all the while
[ænd haːʊ ʃi dɹæŋk ðɛm ˈlʊkɪŋ ɔl ðʊ ʍaːɪl]
Up at the sky.
[ʌp æt ðʊ skaːɪ]
Then with her apron she did wipe her lips,
[ðɛn wɪð hɜ ˈɛːɪpɹʌn ʃi dɪd waːɪp hɜ lɪps]
And went from thence– and I, too, went my way.
[ænd wɛnt fɹʌm ðɛns ænd aːɪ tu wɛnt maːɪ wɛːɪ]
The night cometh, let thy spindle be.
[ðʊ naːɪt ˈkʌmɛ⁽ɪ⁾θ lɛt ðaːɪ ˈspɪndʊl bi]
Those who went by this way
[ðoːʊz hu wɛnt baːɪ ðɪs wɛːɪ]

Spoke of their huts together, and the huts
[spoːʊk ʌv ðɛːʌ hʌts tuˈgɛðʌ ænd ðʊ hʌts]
Seemed far, too far away.
[simd faʌ tu faʌ ʌˈwɛːɪ]

3. Misconception
[mɪskʌnˈsɛpʃʌn]

What hath he done the luckless fellow
[ʍat hæθ hi dʌn ðʊ ˈlʌklɛ(ɪ)s ˈfɛloːʊ]
That thou wilt speak to him no more?
[ðæt ðaːʊ wɪlt spik tu hɪm noːʊ mɔːʌ]
Are ye not of the self-same village?
[ɑ ji nat ʌv ðʊ sɛlf sɛːɪm ˈvɪlæ(ɪ)dʒ]
Why wilt thou sister, not sit down by me
[ʍaːɪ wɪlt ðaːʊ ˈsɪstʌ nat sɪt daːʊn baːɪ mi]
And what awaitest thou to stand so long?
[ænd ʍat ʌˈwɛːɪtɛ(ɪ)st ðaːʊ tu stænd soːʊ laŋ]
Look down the way no longer,
[lʊk daːʊn ðʊ wɛːɪ noːʊ ˈlaŋgʌ]
Watch the old well no longer,
[watʃ ði oːʊld wɛl noːʊ ˈlaŋgʌ]
But rather hearken to me the while I sing.
[bʌt ˈɹaðʌ ˈhakɛ(ɪ)n tu mi ðʊ ʍaːɪl aːɪ sɪŋ]
What hath he done, the luckless fellow
[ʍat hæθ hi dʌn ðʊ ˈlʌklɛ(ɪ)s ˈfɛloːʊ]
That thou wilt speak to him no more?
[ðæt ðaːʊ wɪlt spik tu hɪm noːʊ mɔːʌ]
Are ye not of the self-same village?
[ɑ ji nat ʌv ðʊ sɛlf sɛːɪm ˈvɪlæ(ɪ)dʒ]
Down to the riverside we went together.
[daːʊn tu ðʊ ˈɹɪvʌsaːɪd wi wɛnt tuˈgɛðʌ]
He said: "Now hearken,
[hi sɛd naːʊ ˈhakɛ(ɪ)n]
hearken to the wind that rustles thro' the leaves."
[ˈhakɛ(ɪ)n tu ðʊ wɪnd ðæt ˈɹʌsʊlz θɹu ðʊ livz]
I said "O see, O see the merry sunshine
[aːɪ sɛd oːʊ si oːʊ si ðʊ ˈmɛɹɪ ˈsʌnʃaːɪn]
that shineth thro' the wavelet."
[ðæt ˈʃaːɪnɛ(ɪ)θ θɹu ðʊ ˈwɛːɪvlɛ(ɪ)t]
He said "I love, I swear I love a woman
[hi sɛd aːɪ lʌv aːɪ swɛːʌɹ aːɪ lʌv ʌ ˈwʊmæ(ʌ)n]
whom thou knowest not."
[hum ðaːʊ ˈnoːʊɛ(ɪ)st nat]
I said "I love, I swear, I love a lad
[aːɪ sɛd aːɪ lʌv aːɪ swɛːʌɹ aːɪ lʌv ʌ læd]
of whom thou knowest naught."
[ʌv hum ðaːʊ ˈnoːʊɛ(ɪ)st nɔt]
He said "That woman ceaseless weeps for me."
[hi sɛd ðæt ˈwʊmæ(ʌ)n ˈsislɛ(ɪ)s wips fɔ mi]
And I replied "That lad awaiteth me."
[ænd aːɪ ɹɪˈplaːɪd ðæt læd ʌˈwɛːɪtɛ(ɪ)θ mi]
Then from the river we went hence together.
[ðɛn fɹʌm ðʊ ˈɹɪvʌ wi wɛnt hɛns tuˈgɛðʌ]
And I, I knew full well that he was my lad
[ænd aːɪ aːɪ nju fʊl wɛl ðæt hi waz maːɪ læd]

And he, he surely knew I was that woman.
[ænd hi hi ˈʃʊːʌlɪ nju aːɪ waz ðæt ˈwʊmæ(ʌ)n]
But yet because of all that sunshine in the water
[bʌt jɛt bɪˈkɔz ʌv ɔl ðæt ˈsʌnʃaːɪn ɪn ðʊ ˈwɔtʌ]
And of the wind that rustled thro' the leaves
[ænd ʌv ðʊ wɪnd ðæt ˈɹʌsʊld θɹu ðʊ livz]
We both were silent. We kept silence both.
[wi boːʊθ wɜ ˈsaːɪlɛnt wi kɛpt ˈsaːɪlɛ(ɪ)ns boːʊθ]
What hath he done the luckless fellow
[ʍat hæθ hi dʌn ðʊ ˈlʌklɛ(ɪ)s ˈfɛloːʊ]
That thou wilt speak to him no more?
[ðæt ðaːʊ wɪlt spik tu hɪm noːʊ mɔːʌ]
Are ye not of the self-same village?
[ɑ ji nat ʌv ðʊ sɛlf sɛːɪm ˈvɪlæ(ɪ)dʒ]

4. My Girdle I Hung on a Tree Top Tall
[maːɪ ˈgɜdʊl aːɪ hʌŋ an ʌ tɹi tap tɔl]

My girdle I hung on a tree-top tall,
[maːɪ ˈgɜdʊl aːɪ hʌŋ an ʌ tɹi tap tɔl]
So the songs of the birds, it hears them all.
[soːʊ ðʊ saŋz ʌv ðʊ bɜdz ɪt hiːʌz ðɛm ɔl]
O maiden, who gave thee those lips so red,
[oːʊ ˈmɛːɪdɛ(ɪ)n hu gɛːɪv ði ðoːʊz lɪps soːʊ ɹɛd]
That smile, and those songs?–
[ðæt smaːɪl ænd ðoːʊz saŋz]
– Lad, what is it to thee
[læd ʍat ɪz ɪt tu ði]
Or why wouldst thou know who hath given them me?–
[ɔ ʍaːɪ wʊdst ðaːʊ noːʊ hu hæθ ˈgɪvɛ(ɪ)n ðɛm mi]
– And whither, O maiden, so fast art thou sped?
[ænd ˈʍɪðʌ oːʊ ˈmɛːɪdɛ(ɪ)n soːʊ fast at ðaːʊ spɛd]
To the plum-tree groves in the valley below,
[tu ðʊ plʌm tɹi gɹoːʊvz ɪn ðʊ ˈvælɪ bɪˈloːʊ]
Or there, where the orchards of apple-trees grow
[ɔ ðɛːʌ ʍɛːʌ ði ˈɔtʃʌdz ʌv ˈæpʊl tɹiz gɹoːʊ]
Overhanging the cliff?–
[ˈoːʊvʌˌhæŋɪŋ ðʊ klɪf]
– Lad, what is it to thee,
[læd ʍat ɪz ɪt tu ði]
Since it is not thou that shall go with me?–
[sɪns ɪt ɪz nat ðaːʊ ðæt ʃæl goːʊ wɪð mi]
My girdle I hung on a tree-top tall,
[maːɪ ˈgɜdʊl aːɪ hʌŋ an ʌ tɹi tap tɔl]
So the songs of the birds, it hears them all.
[soːʊ ðʊ saŋz ʌv ðʊ bɜdz ɪt hiːʌz ðɛm ɔl]
O maiden, what in thy heart dost thou bear?
[oːʊ ˈmɛːɪdɛ(ɪ)n ʍat ɪn ðaːɪ hat dʌst ðaːʊ bɛːʌ]
A song, or a love?–
[ʌ saŋ ɔʁ(r) ʌ lʌv]
– Lad, what is it to thee?
[læd ʍat ɪz ɪt tu ði]
If there's one I love, sure, thou art not he.–
[ɪf ðɛːʌz wʌn aːɪ lʌv ʃʊːʌ ðaːʊ at nat hi]
Where wouldst thou I died of my love, then, where?
[ʍɛːʌ wʊdst ðaːʊ aːɪ daːɪd ʌv maːɪ lʌv ðɛn ʍɛːʌ]

By the river, where over me flowers shall weep?
[baːɪ ðʊ ˈɾɪvʌ ʍɛːʌɾ ˈoːʊvʌ mi flaːʊɑz ʃæl wip]
In the hut, where my mother who lulled me to sleep,
[ɪn ðʊ hʌt ʍɛːʌ maːɪ ˈmʌðʌ hu lʌld mi tu slip]
Shall sing me my dirge?–
[ʃæl sɪŋ mi maːɪ dʒɜdʒ]
–Lad, what is it to me,
[læd ʍat ɪz ɪt tu mi]
Since I am not going to weep over thee?–
[sɪns aːɪ æm nat ˈgoːʊɪŋ tu wip ˈoːʊvʌ ði]
My girdle I hung on a tree-top tall,
[maːɪ ˈgɜdʊl aːɪ hʌŋ an ʌ tɹi tap tɔl]
So the songs of the birds, it hears them all.
[soːʊ ðʊ saŋz ʌv ðʊ bɜdz ɪt hiːʌz ðɛm ɔl]

5. Spinning Song
[ˈspɪnɪŋ saŋ]

THE DAUGHTER:
What didst thou mother when thou wert a maiden?
[ʍat dɪdst ðaːʊ ˈmʌðʌ ʍɛn ðaːʊ wɜt ʌ ˈmeːɪdɛ(ɪ)n]
THE MOTHER:
I was young.
[aːɪ waz jʌŋ]
THE DAUGHTER:
Didst thou, like me,
[dɪdst ðaːʊ laːɪk mi]
Hark to the moon's soft footfalls across the sky,
[hak tu ðʊ munz saft ˈfʊtfɔlz ʌˈkɹas ðʊ skaːɪ]
Or didst thou watch the little star's betrothals?
[ɔ dɪdst ðaːʊ watʃ ðʊ ˈlɪtʊl staz bɪˈtɹoːʊðʊlz]
THE MOTHER:
Thy father cometh home,
[ðaːɪ ˈfaðʌ ˈkʌmɛ(ɪ)θ hoːʊm]
Leave the door open.
[liv ðʊ dɔːʌɾ ˈoːʊpɛ(ɪ)n]
THE DAUGHTER:
Down to the fountain, didst thou go
[daːʊn tu ðʊ ˈfaːʊntæ(ɪ)n dɪdst ðaːʊ goːʊ]
and there thy wooden pitcher filled
[ænd ðɛːʌ ðaːɪ ˈwʊdɛ(ɪ)n ˈpɪtʃʌ fɪld]
Didst thou yet linger another hour
[dɪdst ðaːʊ jɛt ˈlɪŋgʌɾ ʌˈnʌðʌ aːʊʌ]
With the full pitcher by thee?
[wɪð ðʊ fʊl ˈpɪtʃʌ baːɪ ði]
THE MOTHER:
I was young.
[aːɪ waz jʌŋ]
THE DAUGHTER:
And did thy tears make glad thy countenance?
[ænd dɪd ðaːɪ tɪːʌz meːɪk glæd ðaːɪ ˈkaːʊntɛ(ɪ)næ(ɪ)ns]
And didst thy sleep bring gladness to the night?
[ænd dɪdst ðaːɪ slip bɹɪŋ ˈglædnɛ(ɪ)s tu ðʊ naːɪt]
And didst thy dreams bring gladness to thy sleep?
[ænd dɪdst ðaːɪ dɹimz bɹɪŋ ˈglædnɛ(ɪ)s tu ðaːɪ slip]

And didst thou smile even by graves
[ænd dɪdst ðaːʊ smaːɪl ˈivɛ(ɪ)n baːɪ gɾeːɪvz]
Despite thy pity, thy pity for the dead?
[dɪˈspaːɪt ðaːɪ ˈpɪtɪ ðaːɪ ˈpɪtɪ fɔ ðʊ dɛd]
THE MOTHER:
Thy father cometh home,
[ðaːɪ ˈfaðʌ ˈkʌmɛ(ɪ)θ hoːʊm]
Leave the door open.
[liv ðʊ dɔːʌɾ ˈoːʊpɛ(ɪ)n]
THE DAUGHTER:
Lovedst thou strawberries and raspberries
[ˈlʌvɛ(ɪ)dst ðaːʊ ˈstɹɔbɛɾɪz ænd ˈɹæzbɛɾɪz]
Because they are as red as maiden's lips?
[bɪˈkɔz ðɛːɪ ɑɾ æz ɹɛd æz ˈmeːɪdɛ(ɪ)nz lɪps]
Didst love the girdle for its many pearls
[dɪdst lʌv ðʊ ˈgɜdʊl fɔʁ⁽ʳ⁾ ɪts ˈmɛnɪ pɜlz]
The river and the wood, because they lie so close
[ðʊ ˈɾɪvʌɾ ænd ðʊ wʊd bɪˈkɔz ðɛːɪ laːɪ soːʊ kloːʊs]
behind the village?
[bɪˈhaːɪnd ðʊ ˈvɪlæ(ɪ)dʒ]
Didst love the beating of the heart
[dɪdst lʌv ðʊ ˈbitɪŋ ʌv ðʊ hat]
There close beneath thy bodice,
[ðɛːʌ kloːʊs bɪˈniθ ðaːɪ ˈbadɪs]
Even although t'were not thy Sunday bodice?
[ˈivɛ(ɪ)n ɔlˈðoːʊ twɜ nat ðaːɪ ˈsʌndɛːɪ ˈbadɪs]
THE MOTHER:
Thy father cometh home
[ðaːɪ ˈfaðʌ ˈkʌmɛ(ɪ)θ hoːʊm]
Leave the door open.
[liv ðʊ dɔːʌɾ ˈoːʊpɛ(ɪ)n]

Song Selections

"A Christmas Carol"
[ʌ ˈkɹɪsmʌs ˈkæʁʊl]
Anonymous 15th Century

There is no rose of such virtue
[ðɛːʌɾ ɪz noːʊ ɾoːʊz ʌv sʌtʃ ˈvɜtju]
As is the rose that bare Jesu:
[æz ɪz ðʊ ɾoːʊz ðæt bɛːʌ ˈjezu]
Res miranda Alleluia.
[ɾɛs mɪˈɾanda alɛˈluja]
For in this rose contained was
[fɔʁ⁽ʳ⁾ ɪn ðɪs ɹoːʊz kʌnˈtɛːɪnɛ(ɪ)d waz]
Heaven and earth in little space:
[ˈhɛvɛ(ɪ)n ænd ɜθ ɪn ˈlɪtʊl spɛːɪs]
Res miranda Alleluia.
[ɾɛs mɪˈɾanda alɛˈluja]
By that rose we may well see
[baːɪ ðæt ɹoːʊz wi meːɪ wɛl si]
There be one God in Persons three:
[ðɛːʌ bi wʌn gad ɪn ˈpɜsʌnz θɹi]
Pares forma, Alleluia.
[ˈpaɾɛs ˈfɔrma alɛˈluja]

The angels sungen the shepherds unto:
[ði ˈɛːɪndʒɛ(ʊ)lz ˈsʌŋɪn ðʊ ˈʃɛpʌdz ˈʌntu]
Gloria in excelsis Deo, Gaudeamus, Alleluia.
[ˈglɔrɪa in ɛgˈʃɛlsɪs ˈdɛɔ gaːʊdɛˈamus alɛˈluja]
Then leave we all this worldly mirth,
[ðɛn liv wi ɔl ðɪs ˈwɜldlɪ mɜθ]
And follow we this joyous birth,
[ænd ˈfaloːʊ wi ðɪs ˈdʒɔːɪʌs bɜθ]
Transeamus Alleluia.
[trɑnsɛˈamus alɛˈluja]

"A Milking Sian"
[ʌ ˈmɪlkɪŋ ʃan]
Sharp, William (Sc. 1855-1905)

Give up thy milk to her who calls
[gɪv ʌp ðaːɪ mɪlk tu hɜ hu kɔlz]
Across the low green hills of Heaven,
[ʌˈkɹas ðʊ loːʊ gɹin hɪlz ʌv ˈhɛvɪn]
And stream-cool meads of Paradise!
[ænd stɹim kul midz ʌv ˈpærʌdaːɪs]
Across the low green hills of Heaven
[ʌˈkɹas ðʊ loːʊ gɹin hɪlz ʌv ˈhɛvɪn]
How sweet to hear the milking call,
[haːʊ swit tu hiːʌ ðʊ ˈmɪlkɪŋ kɔl]
The milking call i' the hills of Heaven:
[ðʊ ˈmɪlkɪŋ kɔl ɪ ðʊ hɪlz ʌv ˈhɛvɪn]
Stream-cool the meads of Paradise,
[stɹim kul ðʊ midz ʌv ˈpærʌdaːɪs]
Across the low green hills of Heaven.
[ʌˈkɹas ðʊ loːʊ gɹin hɪlz ʌv ˈhɛvɪn]
Give up thy milk to her who calls,
[gɪv ʌp ðaːɪ mɪlk tu hɜ hu kɔlz]
Sweet voiced amid the Starry Seven,
[swit vɔːɪst ʌˈmɪd ðʊ ˈstarɪ ˈsɛvɪn]
Give up thy milk to her who calls.
[gɪv ʌp ðaːɪ mɪlk tu hɜ hu kɔlz]

"Far in a Western Brookland"
[faʁ ɪn ʌ ˈwɛstʌn ˈbɹʊklʌnd]
Housman, Alfred Edward (Eng. 1859-1936)

Far in a western brookland
[far ɪn ʌ ˈwɛstʌn ˈbɹʊklæ(ʌ)nd]
That bred me long ago
[ðæt bɹɛd mi laŋ ʌˈgoːʊ]
The poplars stand and tremble
[ðʊ ˈpaplʌz stænd ænd ˈtɹɛmbʊl]
By pools I used to know.
[baːɪ pulz aːɪ just tu noːʊ]
There, in the windless night-time,
[ðɛːʌr ɪn ðʊ ˈwɪndlɛ(ɪ)s naːɪt taːɪm]
The wanderer, marvelling why,
[ðʊ ˈwand(ʌ)rʌ ˈmavlɪŋ ʍaːɪ]
Halts on the bridge to hearken
[hɔlts an ðʊ bɹɪdʒ tu ˈhakɛ(ɪ)n]

How soft the poplars sigh.
[haːʊ saft ðʊ ˈpaplʌz saːɪ]
He hears long since forgotten
[hi hiːʌz laŋ sɪns fɔˈgatɛ(ɪ)n]
In fields where I was known,
[ɪn fildz ʍɛːʌr aːɪ waz noːʊn]
Here I lie down in London
[hiːʌr aːɪ laːɪ daːʊn ɪn ˈlʌndʌn]
And turn to rest alone.
[ænd tɜn tu rɛst ʌˈloːʊn]
There, by the starlit fences,
[ðɛːʌ baːɪ ðʊ ˈstalɪt ˈfɛnsɛ(ɪ)z]
The wanderer halts and hears
[ðʊ ˈwand(ʌ)rʌ hɔlts ænd hiːʌz]
My soul that lingers sighing
[maːɪ soːʊl ðæt ˈlɪŋʌz ˈsaːɪɪŋ]
About the glimmering weirs.
[ʌˈbaːʊt ðʊ ˈglɪmɹɪŋ wiːʌz]

"I Heard a Piper Piping" (Five Irish Songs)
[aːɪ hɜd ʌ ˈpaːɪpʌ ˈpaːɪpɪŋ]
Campbell, Joseph (Ir. 1881-1944)

I heard a piper piping
[aːɪ hɜd ʌ ˈpaːɪpʌ ˈpaːɪpɪŋ]
The blue hills among –
[ðʊ blu hɪlz ʌˈmʌŋ]
And never heard I half
[ænd ˈnɛvʌ hɜd aːɪ haf]
So plaintive a song –
[soːʊ ˈplɛːɪntɪv ʌ saŋ]
It seemed but a part
[ɪt simd bʌt ʌ pat]
Of the hills' melancholy
[ʌv ðʊ hɪlz ˈmɛlæ(ɪ)n̩ˌkalɪ]
No piper piping there
[noːʊ ˈpaːɪpʌ ˈpaːɪpɪŋ ðɛːʌ]
Could ever be jolly.
[kʊd ˈɛvʌ bi ˈdʒalɪ]
And still the piper piped
[ænd stɪl ðʊ ˈpaːɪpʌ paːɪpt]
The blue hills among,
[ðʊ blu hɪlz ʌˈmʌŋ]
And all the birds were quiet –
[ænd ɔl ðʊ bɜdz wɜ ˈkwaːɪɛ(ɪ)t]
To listen to his song.
[tu ˈlɪsɛ(ɪ)n tu hɪz saŋ]

"Sheiling Song"
[ˈʃilɪŋ saŋ]
Sharp, William (Sc. 1855-1905)

I go where the sheep go,
[aːɪ goːʊ ʍɛːʌ ðʊ ʃip goːʊ]
With the sheep are my feet
[wɪð ðʊ ʃip a maːɪ fit]

I go where the kye go,
[ɑːɪ goːʊ ʍɛːʌ ðʊ kɑːɪ goːʊ]
Their breath is so sweet.
[ðɛːʌ bɹɛθ ɪz soːʊ swit]
O lover who loves me,
[oːʊ ˈlʌvʌ hu lʌvz mi]
Art thou half so fleet?
[ɑt ðɑːʊ haf soːʊ flit]
Where the sheep climb, the kye go,
[ʍɛːʌ ðʊ ʃip klɑːɪm ðʊ kɑːɪ goːʊ]
There we shall meet.
[ðɛːʌ wi ʃæl mit]

"Slumber-Song"
[ˈslʌmbʌ saŋ]
Bax, Arnold (Eng. 1883-1953)

Still my baby, hush my darling,
[stɪl mɑːɪ ˈbɛːɪbɪ hʌʃ mɑːɪ ˈdalɪŋ]
Golden stars drift all about your bed;
[ˈgoːʊldɛ(ɪ)n staz dɹɪft ɔl ʌˈbɑːʊt jɔːʌ bɛd]
And while the soft grey veils of sleep
[ænd ʍɑːɪl ðʊ saft gɹɛːɪ vɛːɪlz ʌv slip]
Over your little helpless body creep
[ˈoːʊvʌ jɔːʌ ˈlɪtʊl ˈhɛlplɛ(ɪ)s ˈbɑdɪ kɹip]
Mine arms shall fold you close, and hold you
[mɑːɪn amz ʃæl foːʊld ju kloːʊs ænd hoːʊld ju]
Bathed in the dews of the spirit's fountain head.
[bɛːɪðd ɪn ðʊ djuz ʌv ðʊ ˈspɪɹɪts ˈfɑːʊntæ(ɪ)n hɛd]
From your sleepy world of dreams and stars
[fɹʌm jɔːʌ ˈslipɪ wɜld ʌv dɹimz ænd staz]
Stretch out your tiny hands rememb'ring me.
[stɹɛtʃ ɑːʊt jɔːʌ ˈtɑːɪnɪ hændz ɹɪˈmɛmbɹɪŋ mi]
Through pallid mists and memories
[θɹu ˈpælɪd mɪsts ænd ˈmɛmɔɹɪz]
My sweet dead stars fall in the sighing seas.
[mɑːɪ swit dɛd staz fɔl ɪn ðʊ ˈsɑːɪŋ siz]
You have I only, I that am lonely,
[ju hæv ɑːɪ ˈoːʊnlɪ ɑːɪ ðæt æm ˈloːʊnlɪ]
O give me love as I give love to thee!
[oːʊ gɪv mi lʌv æz ɑːɪ gɪv lʌv tu ði]

"The Song in the Twilight"
[ðʊ saŋ ɪn ðʊ ˈtwɑːɪlɑːɪt]
Bax, Freda (Eng. d. 1928)

I have heard a music,
[ɑːɪ hæv hɜd ʌ ˈmjuzɪk]
Strange and wild and tender,
[stɹɛːɪndʒ ænd wɑːɪld ænd ˈtɛndʌ]
Through the mystic splendour,
[θɹu ðʊ ˈmɪstɪk ˈsplɛndʊ(ʌ)]
of the twilight stealing
[ʌv ðʊ ˈtwɑːɪlɑːɪt ˈstilɪŋ]
Like the spell entrancing of a magic potion
[lɑːɪk ðʊ spɛl ɪnˈtɹansɪŋ ʌv ʌ ˈmædʒɪk ˈpoːʊʃʌn]

Slowly it enwound me,
[ˈsloːʊlɪ ɪt ɪnˈwɑːʊnd mi]
Twirling, twining, dancing,
[ˈtwɜlɪŋ ˈtwɑːɪnɪŋ ˈdansɪŋ]
In a mazy motion,
[ɪn ʌ ˈmɛːɪzɪ ˈmoːʊʃʌn]
Whirling all around me
[ˈʍɜlɪŋ ɔl ʌˈɹɑːʊnd mi]
Thro' the deep'ning twilight
[θɹu ðʊ ˈdipnɪŋ ˈtwɑːɪlɑːɪt]
Aery voices calling
[ˈɛːʌɪ ˈvɔːɪsɛ(ɪ)z ˈkɔlɪŋ]
And dim shadows falling
[ænd dɪm ˈʃædoːʊz ˈfɔlɪŋ]
Clustered all around me
[ˈklʌstʌd ɔl ʌˈɹɑːʊnd mi]
But I heeded only
[bʌt ɑːɪ ˈhidɛ(ɪ)d ˈoːʊnlɪ]
That wild music burning
[ðæt wɑːɪld ˈmjuzɪk ˈbɜnɪŋ]
With an infinite yearning
[wɪð æn ˈɪnfɪnɪt ˈjɜnɪŋ]
all the heart of me
[ɔl ðʊ hat ʌv mi]
And I wandered lonely
[ænd ɑːɪ ˈwandʌd ˈloːʊnlɪ]
Lonely, ah so lonely,
[ˈloːʊnlɪ a soːʊ ˈloːʊnlɪ]
Down the pathway weeping
[dɑːʊn ðʊ ˈpaθwɛːɪ ˈwipɪŋ]
While the world lay sleeping
[ʍɑːɪl ðʊ wɜld lɛːɪ ˈslipɪŋ]
Dreaming at my feet.
[ˈdɹimɪŋ æt mɑːɪ fit]

"The White Peace"
[ðʊ ʍɑːɪt pis]
Sharp, William (Sc. 1855-1905)

It lies not on the sunlit hill
[ɪt lɑːɪz nat an ðʊ ˈsʌnlɪt hɪl]
Nor on the sunlit plain:
[nɔʁ⁽ʳ⁾ an ðʊ ˈsʌnlɪt plɛːɪn]
Nor ever on any running stream
[nɔʁ⁽ʳ⁾ ˈɛvʌɪ an ˈɛnɪ ˈɹʌnɪŋ stɹim]
Nor on the unclouded main
[nɔʁ⁽ʳ⁾ an ði ʌnˈklɑːʊdɛ(ɪ)d mɛːɪn]
But sometimes, through the Soul of Man,
[bʌt ˈsʌmtɑːɪmz θɹu ðʊ soːʊl ʌv mæn]
Slow moving o'er his pain,
[sloːʊ ˈmuvɪŋ ɔːʌ hɪz pɛːɪn]
The moonlight of a perfect peace
[ðʊ ˈmunlɑːɪt ʌv ʌ ˈpɜfɛ(ɪ)kt pis]
Floods heart and brain.
[flʌdz hat ænd bɹɛːɪn]

Beach, Amy Marcy (Am. 1867-1944)

Three Browning Songs (Song Cycle)
[θɾi ˈbɹɑːʊnɪŋ sɑŋz]
Browning, Robert (Eng. 1812-1889)

1. The Year's at the Spring
[ðʌ jiːʁz æt ðʌ spɹɪŋ]

The year's at the spring,
[ðʌ jiːʌz æt ðʌ spɹɪŋ]
And day's at the morn;
[ænd dɛːɪz æt ðʌ mɔn]
Morning's at seven;
[ˈmɔnɪŋz æt ˈsɛvɛ(ɪ)n]
The hillside's dew-pearled;
[ðʌ ˈhɪlsɑːɪdz dju pɜld]
The lark's on the wing;
[ðʌ lɑks ɑn ðʌ wɪŋ]
The snail's on the thorn;
[ðʌ snɛːɪlz ɑn ðʌ θɔn]
God's in His heaven,
[gɑdz ɪn hɪz ˈhɛvɛ(ɪ)n]
All's right with the world!
[ɔlz ɹɑːɪt wɪð ðʌ wɜld]

2. Ah, Love, but a Day!
[ɑ lʌv bʌt ʌ dɛːɪ]

Ah, Love, but a day,
[ɑ lʌv bʌt ʌ dɛːɪ]
And the world has changed!
[ænd ðʌ wɜld hæz ʧɛːɪnʤd]
The sun's away,
[ðʌ sʌnz ʌˈwɛːɪ]
And the bird estranged;
[ænd ðʌ bɜd ɪˈstɹɛːɪnʤd]
The wind has dropped,
[ðʌ wɪnd hæz dɹɑpt]
And the sky's deranged;
[ænd ðʌ skɑːɪz dɪˈʁ(ʳ)ɛːɪnʤd]
Summer has stopped.
[ˈsʌmʌ hæz stɑpt]
Look in my eyes!
[lʊk ɪn mɑːɪ ɑːɪz]
Wilt thou change too?
[wɪlt ðɑːʊ ʧɛːɪnʤ tu]
Should I fear surprise?
[ʃʊd ɑːɪ fiːʌ sɜˈpɹɑːɪz]
Shall I find aught new
[ʃæl ɑːɪ fɑːɪnd ɔt nju]
In the old and dear,
[ɪn ði oːʊld ænd dɪːʌ]
In the good and true,
[ɪn ðʌ gʊd ænd tɹ(ʳ)u]

With the changing year?
[wɪð ðʌ ˈʧɛːɪnʤɪŋ jiːʌ]
Ah, Love, Look in my eyes,
[ɑ lʌv lʊk ɪn mɑːɪ ɑːɪz]
Wilt thou change too?
[wɪlt ðɑːʊ ʧɛːɪnʤ tu]

3. I Send My Heart up to Thee!
[ɑːɪ sɛnd mɑːɪ hɑʁt ʌp tu ði]

I send my heart up to thee, all my heart
[ɑːɪ sɛnd mɑːɪ hɑt ʌp tu ði ɔl mɑːɪ hɑt]
In this my singing.
[ɪn ðɪs mɑːɪ ˈsɪŋɪŋ]
For the stars help me,
[fɔ ðʌ stɑz hɛlp mi]
and the sea bears part;
[ænd ðʌ si bɛːʌz pɑt]
The very night is clinging
[ðʌ ˈvɛʁ(ʳ)ɪ nɑːɪt ɪz ˈklɪŋɪŋ]
Closer to Venice' streets to leave one space
[ˈkloːʊsʌ tu ˈvɛnɪs stɹɪts tu liv wʌn spɛːɪs]
Above me, whence thy face
[ʌˈbʌv mi ʍɛns ðɑːɪ fɛːɪs]
May light my joyous heart to thee,
[mɛːɪ lɑːɪt mɑːɪ ˈʤɔːɪʌs hɑt tu ði]
To thee its dwelling place,
[tu ði ɪts ˈdwɛlɪŋ plɛːɪs]
Thy face may light my joyous heart
[ðɑːɪ fɛːɪs mɛːɪ lɑːɪt mɑːɪ ˈʤɔːɪʌs hɑt]
To thee, my heart, to thee its dwelling place.
[tu ði mɑːɪ hɑt tu ði ɪts ˈdwɛlɪŋ plɛːɪs]

Song Selections

"Dark Is the Night"
[dɑk ɪz ðʌ nɑːɪt]
Henley, William Ernest (Eng. 1849-1903)

The sea is full of wand'ring foam,
[ðʌ si ɪz fʊl ʌv ˈwandɹɪŋ foːʊm]
The sky of driving cloud;
[ðʌ skɑːɪ ʌv ˈdɹɑːɪvɪŋ klɑːʊd]
My restless thoughts among them roam.
[mɑːɪ ˈɹɛstlɛ(ɪ)s θɔts ʌˈmʌŋ ðɛm ɹoːʊm]
The night is dark and loud.
[ðʌ nɑːɪt ɪz dɑk ænd lɑːʊd]
Where are the hours that came to me
[ʍɛːʌʁ(ʳ) ɑ ði ɑːʊʌz ðæt kɛːɪm tu mi]
So beautiful and bright?
[soːʊ ˈbjutɪfʊl ænd bɹɑːɪt]
A wild wind shakes the wilder sea.
[ʌ wɑːɪld wɪnd ʃɛːɪks ðʌ ˈwɑːɪldʌ si]
O dark and loud's the night!
[oːʊ dɑk ænd lɑːʊdz ðʌ nɑːɪt]

"My Sweetheart and I"
[maːɪ ˈswithaʁt ænd aːɪ]
Translation of *Elle et moi* by Félix Bovet (1824-1903)

Like springtime with colors so fair,
[laːɪk ˈspɹɪ̈ŋtaːɪm wɪð ˈkʌlɔ(ʌ)z soːʊ fɛːʌ]
Like rosy flame entrancing,
[laːɪk ˈɹoːʊzɪ fleːɪm ɪnˈtɹænsɪŋ]
With its bright, joyous dancing,
[wɪð ɪts bɹaːɪt ˈdʒɔːʌs ˈdænsɪŋ]
Like the flow'ret pale, whose perfume fills the air,
[laːɪk ðʌ ˈflaːʊʌʁ⁽ʳ⁾ɛ(ɪ)t peːɪl huz pɜˈfjum fɪlz ðɪ ɛːʌ]
So lovely thou art,
[soːʊ ˈlʌvlɪ ðaːʊ at]
Ah! My sweetheart!
[a maːɪ ˈswithat]
Like the swallow that heralds the coming of May
[laːɪk ðʌ ˈswaloːʊ ðæt ˈhɛʁ⁽ʳ⁾ʊldz ðʌ ˈkʌmɪŋ ʌv meːɪ]
Like the fawn that doth follow
[laːɪk ðʌ fɔn ðæt dʌθ ˈfaloːʊ]
the white flower alway, Ah!
[ðʌ ʍaːɪt flaːʊʌʁ⁽ʳ⁾ ˈɔlweːɪ a]
Its beauteous charm his heart alluring;
[ɪts ˈbjutɪʌs tʃam hɪz hat ʌˈljʊːʌʁ⁽ʳ⁾ɪŋ]
Like fearless moth who soon must fly
[laːɪk ˈfɪːʌlɛ(ɪ)s maθ hu sun mʌst flaːɪ]
Through the flame, his wings consuming,
[θɾu ðʌ fleːɪm hɪz wɪŋz kʌnˈsjumɪŋ]
Ah! Am I!
[a æm aːɪ]

"Now Sleeps the Crimson Petal" (see Quilter)

"Take, O Take Those Lips Away"
[tɛːɪk oːʊ tɛːɪk ðoːʊz lɪps ʌˈweːɪ]
Shakespeare, William (Eng. 1564-1616)

Take, O take those lips away,
[tɛːɪk oːʊ tɛːɪk ðoːʊz lɪps ʌˈweːɪ]
That so sweetly were forsworn,
[ðæt soːʊ ˈswitlɪ wɜ fɔˈswɔn]
And those eyes, the break of day,
[ænd ðoːʊz aːɪz ðʌ bɹeːɪk ʌv dɛːɪ]
Lights that do mislead the morn:
[laːɪts ðæt du mɪsˈlid ðʌ mɔn]
But my kisses bring again,
[bʌt maːɪ ˈkɪsɛ(ɪ)z bɹɪŋ ʌˈgɛn]
Seals of love, but seal'd in vain.
[silz ʌv lʌv bʌt sild ɪn vɛːɪn]

Beck, John Ness (Am. 1930-1987)

Song Selection

"Song of Devotion"
[saŋ ʌv dɪˈvoːʊʃʌn]
Philippians 1:3-11

I thank my God on ev'ry remembrance of you,
[aːɪ θæŋk maːɪ gad an ˈɛvɹɪ ɹɪˈmembɹæ(ɪ)ns ʌv ju]
always in ev'ry prayer of mine for you with joy;
[ˈɔlweːɪz ɪn ˈɛvɹɪ pɹæːʁ⁽ʳ⁾ ʌv maːɪn fɔ ju wɪð dʒɔːɪ]
I have you in my heart. And this I pray,
[aːɪ hæv ju ɪn maːɪ hat ænd ðɪs aːɪ pɹeːɪ]
that your love may abound yet more and more
[ðæt jɔːʌ lʌv meːɪ ʌˈbaːʊnd jet mɔːʌʁ⁽ʳ⁾ ænd mɔːʌ]
in knowledge and in all judgment,
[ɪn ˈnalɛ(ɪ)dʒ ænd ɪn ɔl ˈdʒʌdʒmɛnt]
that ye may approve things that are excellent,
[ðæt ji meːɪ ʌˈpɹ⁽ʳ⁾uv θɪŋz ðæt aʁ⁽ʳ⁾ ˈɛksɛ(ɪ)lɛnt]
that ye may be sincere, being filled
[ðæt ji meːɪ bi sɪnˈsɪːʌ ˈbiɪŋ fɪld]
with the fruits of righteousness
[wɪð ðʌ fɹ⁽ʳ⁾uts ʌv ˈɹɑːɪtʃʌsnɛ(ɪ)s]
unto the glory and praise of God.
[ˈʌntu ðʌ ˈglɔʁ⁽ʳ⁾ɪ ænd pɹɛːɪz ʌv gad]
I thank my God on ev'ry remembrance of you...

Bennett, Richard R. (Eng. 1936-2012)

Song Selections

"The Birds' Lament" (The Aviary)
[ðʊ bɜdz lʌˈmɛnt]
Clare, John (Eng. 1793-1864)

Oh, says the linnet, if I sing,
[oːʊ sɛz ðʊ ˈlɪnɛ(ɪ)t ɪf aːɪ sɪŋ]
My love forsook me in the spring,
[maːɪ lʌv fɔˈsʊk mi ɪn ðʊ spɹɪŋ]
And nevermore will I be seen
[ænd ˈnevʌmɔːʌ wɪl aːɪ bi sin]
without my satin gown of green.
[wɪðˈaːʊt maːɪ ˈsætɪn gaːʊn ʌv gɹin]
Oh, says the pretty feathered jay,
[oːʊ sɛz ðʊ ˈpɹɪtɪ ˈfɛðʌd dʒɛːɪ]
Now my love is gone away
[naːʊ maːɪ lʌv ɪz gan ʌˈweːɪ]
And for the memory of my dear
[ænd fɔ ðʊ ˈmemɔɹɪ ʌv maːɪ dɪːʌ]
A feather of each sort I'll wear.
[ʌ ˈfɛðʌɾ ʌv itʃ sɔt aːɪl wɛːʌ]
Oh, says the rook and eke the crow,
[oːʊ sɛz ðʊ ɾʊk ænd ik ðʊ kɹoːʊ]

The reason why in black we go
[ðʊ ˈrizʌn ʍaːɪ ɪn blæk wi goːʊ]
Because our love has us forsook,
[bɪˈkɔz aːʊʌ lʌv hæz ʌs fɔˈsʊk]
So pity us poor crow and rook.
[soːʊ ˈpɪti ʌs pʊːʌ kɹoːʊ ænd ɹʊk]
Oh, says the pretty speckled thrush
[oːʊ sɛz ðʊ ˈpɹɪti ˈspɛkʊld θɹʌʃ]
that changes its note from bush to bush,
[ðæt ˈʧɛːɪndʒɛ(ɪ)z ɪts noːʊt fɹʌm bʊʃ tu bʊʃ]
My love has left me here alone,
[maːɪ lʌv hæz lɛft mi hɪːʌɾ ʌˈloːʊn]
I fear she never will return.
[aːɪ fɪːʌ ʃi ˈnɛvʌ wɪl ɹɪˈtɜn]

"The Lark" (The Aviary)
[ðʊ lɑk]
Coleridge, Samuel Taylor (Eng. 1772-1834)

Do you ask what the birds say? The sparrow, the dove,
[du ju ask ʍɑt ðʊ bɜdz seːɪ ðʊ ˈspæroːʊ ðʊ dʌv]
The linnet and thrush say, "I love and I love."
[ðʊ ˈlɪnɛ(ɪ)t ænd θɹʌʃ seːɪ aːɪ lʌv ænd aːɪ lʌv]
In the winter they're silent, the wind is so strong;
[ɪn ðʊ ˈwɪntʌ ðɛːʌ ˈsaːɪlɛnt ðʊ wɪnd ɪz soːʊ stɹaŋ]
What it says, I don't know, but it sings a loud song.
[ʍɑt ɪt sɛz aːɪ doːʊnt noːʊ bʌt ɪt sɪŋz ʌ laːʊd saŋ]
But green leaves, and blossoms,
[bʌt ɡɹin livz ænd ˈblasʌmz]
and sunny warm weather,
[ænd ˈsʌnɪ wɔm ˈwɛðʌ]
And singing and loving all come back together.
[ænd ˈsɪŋɪŋ ænd ˈlʌvɪŋ ɔl kʌm bæk tuˈɡɛðʌ]
But the lark is so brimful of gladness and love,
[bʌt ðʊ lɑk ɪz soːʊ ˈbɹɪmfʊl ʌv ˈɡlædnɛ(ɪ)s ænd lʌv]
The green fields below him, the blue sky above,
[ðʊ ɡɹin fildz bɪˈloːʊ hɪm ðʊ blu skaːɪ ʌˈbʌv]
That he sings, and he sings, and forever sings he,
[ðæt hi sɪŋz ænd hi sɪŋz ænd fɔʀ⁽ʳ⁾ˈɛvʌ sɪŋz hi]
"I love my Love, and my Love loves me!"
[aːɪ lʌv maːɪ lʌv ænd maːɪ lʌv lʌvz mi]

"The Owl" (The Aviary)
[ðɪ aːʊl]
Tennyson, Lord Alfred (Eng. 1809-1892)

When cats run home and light is come,
[ʍɛn kæts ɹʌn hoːʊm ænd laːɪt ɪz kʌm]
And dew is cold upon the ground,
[ænd dju ɪz koːʊld ʌˈpɑn ðʊ ɡɹaːʊnd]
And the far-off stream is dumb,
[ænd ðʊ fɑr af stɹim ɪz dʌm]
And the whirring sail goes round;
[ænd ðʊ ˈʍʊrɪŋ seːɪl goːʊz ɹaːʊnd]
Alone and warming his five wits,
[ʌˈloːʊn ænd ˈwɔmɪŋ hɪz faːɪv wɪts]

The white owl in the belfry sits.
[ðʊ ʍaːɪt aːʊl ɪn ðʊ ˈbɛlfɹɪ sɪts]
When merry milkmaids click the latch,
[ʍɛn ˈmɛrɪ ˈmɪlkmɛːɪdz klɪk ðʊ læʧ]
And rarely smells the new-mown hay,
[ænd ˈɹɛːʌlɪ smɛlz ðʊ nju moːʊn hɛːɪ]
And the cock hath sung beneath the thatch
[ænd ðʊ kɑk hæθ sʌŋ bɪˈniθ ðʊ θæʧ]
Twice or thrice his round-e-lay;
[twaːɪs ɔ θɹaːɪs hɪz ɹaːʊnd ʌ lɛːɪ]
Alone and warming his five wits,
[ʌˈloːʊn ænd ˈwɔmɪŋ hɪz faːɪv wɪts]
The white owl in the belfry sits.
[ðʊ ʍaːɪt aːʊl ɪn ðʊ ˈbɛlfɹɪ sɪts]

Bernstein, Leonard (Am. 1918-1990)

Two Love Songs (Song Cycle)
[tu lʌv saŋz]

1. Extinguish My Eyes
[ɪkˈstɪŋgwɪʃ maːɪ aːɪz]
Lemont, Jessie (Am. 1872-1947)

Extinguish my eyes I still can see you:
[ɪkˈstɪŋgwɪʃ maːɪ aːɪz aːɪ stɪl kæn si ju]
Close my ears I can hear your footsteps fall:
[kloːʊz maːɪ ɪːʌz aːɪ kæn hɪːʌ jɔːʌ ˈfʊtstɛps fɔl]
And without feet I still can follow you:
[ænd wɪðˈaːʊt fit aːɪ stɪl kæn ˈfaloːʊ ju]
Voiceless I can still return your call.
[ˈvɔːɪslɛ(ɪ)s aːɪ kæn stɪl ɹɪˈtɜn jɔːʌ kɔl]
Break off my arms, and I can embrace you:
[bɹɛːɪk af maːɪ amz ænd aːɪ kæn ɪmˈbɹɛːɪs ju]
Enfold you with my heart as with a hand:
[ɪnˈfoːʊld ju wɪð maːɪ hat æz wɪð ʌ hænd]
Hold my heart, my brain will take fire of you,
[hoːʊld maːɪ hat maːɪ bɹɛːɪn wɪl tɛːɪk faːɪʌʀ⁽ʳ⁾ ʌv ju]
As flax takes fire from a brand!
[æz flæks tɛːɪks faːɪʌ fɹʌm ʌ bɹænd]
And flame will sweep in a flood:
[ænd flɛːɪm wɪl swip ɪn ʌ flʌd]
Through all the singing currents of my blood:
[θɹu ɔl ðʌ ˈsɪŋɪŋ ˈkʊʀ⁽ʳ⁾ɛnts ʌv maːɪ blʌd]
Mmmm...
[m]

2. When My Soul Touches Yours
[ʍɛn maːɪ soːʊl ˈtʌʧɪz jɔːʀz]
Adaptation by Jessie Lemont (Am. 1872-1947)

When my soul touches yours a great chord sings:
[ʍɛn maːɪ soːʊl ˈtʌʧɛ(ɪ)z jɔːʌz ʌ ɡɹɛːɪt kɔd sɪŋz]
How can I tune it then to other things?
[haːʊ kæn aːɪ tjun ɪt ðɛn tu ˈʌðʌ θɪŋz]

Oh, if some spot in darkness could be found
[oːʊ ɪf sʌm spat ɪn ˈdaknɛ(ɹ)s kʊd bi faːʊnd]
That does not vibrate when your depths sound!
[ðæt dʌz nat ˈvaːɪbɹɛːɪt ʍɛn jɔːʌ dɛpθs saːʊnd]
But ev'rything that touches you and me welds us
[bʌt ˈɛvɹɪθɪŋ ðæt ˈtʌʧɛ(ɹ)z ju ænd mi wɛldz ʌs]
as played strings sound one melody.
[æz plɛːɪd stɹɪŋz saːʊnd wʌn ˈmɛlodɪ]
Where, where is the instrument
[ʍɛːʌ ʍɛːʌʁ(ɾ) ɪz ði ˈɪnstɹ(ɾ)u(ʌ)mɛnt]
whence the sounds flow?
[ʍɛns ðʌ saːʊndz floːʊ]
And whose the magic hand that holds the bow?
[ænd huz ðʌ ˈmæʤɪk hænd ðæt hoːʊldz ðʌ boːʊ]
Oh, sweet song! Oh!
[oːʊ swit saŋ oːʊ]

Song Selection

"Music I Heard with You" (see Hageman)

Bishop, Henry (Eng. 1785-1855)

Song Selection

"Love Has Eyes"
[lʌv hæz aːɪz]
Dibdin, Charles (Eng. 1745-1815)

1. Love's blind, they say, Oh! never! nay,
[lʌvz blaːɪnd ðɛːɪ sɛːɪ oːʊ ˈnɛvʌ nɛːɪ]
Can words love's grace impart?
[kæn wɜdz lʌvz ɡɹɛːɪs ɪmˈpat]
The fancy weak, The tongue may speak,
[ðʊ ˈfænsɪ wik ðʊ tʌŋ mɛːɪ spik]
But eyes alone the heart,
[bʌt aːɪz ʌˈloːʊn ðʊ hat]
In one soft look what language lies,
[ɪn wʌn saft lʊk ʍat ˈlæŋɡwæ(ɹ)ʤ laːɪz]
Oh, yes, believe me, Love has eyes.
[oːʊ jɛs bɪˈliv mi lʌv hæz aːɪz]
2. Love's wing'd, they cry, Oh! never! I,
[lʌvz wɪŋgd ðɛːɪ kɹaːɪ oːʊ ˈnɛvʌ aːɪ]
No pinions have to soar; Deceivers rove,
[noːʊ ˈpɪnjʌnz hæv tu sɔːʌ dɪˈsivʌz ɹoːʊv]
But never love, Attach'd, he roves no more:
[bʌt ˈnɛvʌ lʌv ʌˈtæʧt hi ɹoːʊvz noːʊ mɔːʌ]
Can he have wings who never flies?
[kæn hi hæv wɪŋz hu ˈnɛvʌ flaːɪz]
And yet, believe me, Love has eyes.
[ænd jɛt bɪˈliv mi lʌv hæz aːɪz]

Bolcom, William (Am. b. 1938)

Song Selection

"'Tis Not That Dying Hurts Us So"
[tɪz nat ðæt ˈdaːɪɪŋ hɜts ʌs soːʊ]
(Let Evening Come)
Dickinson, Emily (Am. 1830-1886)

'Tis not that Dying hurts us so–
[tɪz nat ðæt ˈdaːɪɪŋ hɜts ʌs soːʊ]
'Tis Living– hurts us more–
[tɪz ˈlɪvɪŋ hɜts ʌs mɔːʌ]
But Dying– is a different way–
[bʌt ˈdaːɪɪŋ ɪz ʌ ˈdɪfɹɛnt wɛːɪ]
A Kind behind the Door–
[ʌ kaːɪnd bɪˈhaːɪnd ðʌ dɔːʌ]
The Southern Custom– of the Bird–
[ðʌ ˈsʌðʌn ˈkʌstʌm ʌv ðʌ bɜd]
That ere the Frosts are due–
[ðæt ɛːʌ ðʌ fɹasts a dju]
Accepts a better Latitude–
[ækˈsɛpts ʌ ˈbɛtʌ ˈlætɪtjud]
We– are the Birds– that stay.
[wi a ðʌ bɜdz ðæt stɛːɪ]
The Shrivers round Farmers' doors–
[ðʌ ˈʃɹɪvʌz ɹaːʊnd ˈfamʌz dɔːʌz]
For whose reluctant Crumb–
[fɔ huz ɹɪˈlʌktæ(ɹ)nt kɹ(ɾ)ʌm]
We stipulate– till pitying Snows
[wi ˈstɪpjulɛːɪt tɪl ˈpɪtɪɪŋ snoːʊz]
Persuade our Feathers Home.
[pɜˈswɛːɪd aːʊʌ ˈfɛðʌz hoːʊm]

Boughton, Rutland (Eng. 1878-1960)

Song Selection

"Faery Song" (The Immortal Hour)
[ˈfɛʁi saŋ]
Sharp, William (Sc. 1855-1905)

How beautiful they are, the lordly ones
[haːʊ ˈbjutɪfʊl ðɛːɪ a ðʊ ˈlɔdlɪ wʌnz]
Who dwell in the hills, in the hollow hills.
[hu dwɛl ɪn ðʊ hɪlz ɪn ðʊ ˈhaloːʊ hɪlz]
They have faces like flowers
[ðɛːɪ hæv ˈfɛːɪsɛ(ɹ)z laːɪk flaːʊʌz]
And their breath is a wind
[ænd ðɛːʌ bɹɛθ ɪz ʌ wɪnd]
That blows over summer meadows
[ðæt bloːʊz ˈoːʊvʌ ˈsʌmʌ ˈmɛdoːʊz]
Filled with dewy clover.
[fɪld wɪð ˈdjuɹ ˈkloːʊvʌ]

Their limbs are more white than shafts of moonshine,
[ðɛːʌ lɪmz a mɔːʌ ʍaːɪt ðæn ʃafts ʌv 'munʃaːɪn]
They are more fleet than the March wind
[ðɛːɪ a mɔːʌ flit ðæn ðʊ maʧ wɪnd]
They laugh and are glad and are terrible
[ðɛːɪ laf ænd a glæd ænd a 'tɛrɪbʊl]
When their lances shake and glitter
[ʍɛn ðɛːʌ 'lansɛ(ɪ)z ʃɛːɪk ænd 'glɪtʌ]
Every green reed quivers.
['ɛvɹɪ gɹin ɹid 'kwɪvʌz]
How beautiful they are, How beautiful,
[haːʊ 'bjutɪfʊl ðɛːɪ a haːʊ 'bjutɪfʊl]
The lordly ones in the hollow hills.
[ðʊ 'lɔdlɪ wʌnz ɪn ðʊ 'haloːʊ hɪlz]

Boyce, William (Eng. 1710-1779)

Song Selection

"Tell Me, Lovely Shepherd"
[tɛl mi 'lʌvli 'ʃɛpʌd]
Moore, Edward (Eng. 1712-1757)

Tell me, lovely shepherd, where, where?
[tɛl mi 'lʌvli 'ʃɛpʌd ʍɛːʌ ʍɛːʌ]
Tell me, where thou feed'st at noon thy fleecy care.
[tɛl mi ʍɛːʌ ðaːʊ fidst æt nun ðaːɪ 'flisɪ kɛːʌ]
Direct me to the sweet retreat,
[daːɪ'rɛkt mi tu ðʊ swit ɹɪ'tɹit]
That guards thee from the mid-day heat.
[ðæt gadz ði fɹʌm ðʊ 'mɪdeːɪ hit]
Left by the flocks I lonely stray
[lɛft baːɪ ðʊ flaks aːɪ 'loːʊnlɪ stɹeːɪ]
Without a guide and lose my way.
[wɪð'aːʊt ʌ gaːɪd ænd luz maːɪ weːɪ]
Where rest at noon thy bleating care?
[ʍɛːʌ ɹɛst æt nun ðaːɪ 'blitɪŋ kɛːʌ]
Gentle shepherd, tell me where?
['ʤɛntʊl 'ʃɛpʌd tɛl mi ʍɛːʌ]

Bray, Kenneth Ira (Ca. 1919-1999)

Song Selection

"White Butterflies"
[ʍaːɪt 'bʌtʁflaːɪz]
Swinburne, Algernon Charles (Eng. 1837-1909)

Fly, white butterflies, out to sea,
[flaːɪ ʍaːɪt 'bʌtʌflaːɪz aːʊt tu si]
Frail pale wings for the winds to try,
[fɹɛːɪl pɛːɪl wɪŋz fɔ ðʌ wɪndz tu tɹaːɪ]

Small white wings that we scarce can see,
[smɔl ʍaːɪt wɪŋz ðæt wi skɛːʌs kæn si]
Fly fly fly.
[flaːɪ flaːɪ flaːɪ]
Some fly light as a laugh of glee,
[sʌm flaːɪ laːɪt æz ʌ læf ʌv gli]
Some fly soft as a long low sigh:
[sʌm flaːɪ saft æz ʌ laŋ loːʊ saːɪ]
All to the haven where each would be,
[ɔl tu ðʌ 'hɛːɪvɛ(ɪ)n ʍɛːʌʁ⁽ʳ⁾ iʧ wʊd bi]
Fly fly fly.
[flaːɪ flaːɪ flaːɪ]

Bridge, Frank (Eng. 1879-1941)

Song Selections

"E'en as a Lovely Flower"
['iin æz ʌ 'lʌvli flaːʊʌ]
Kroeker, Kate Freiligrath (Gr. 1845-1904)

E'en as a lovely flower,
['iin æz ʌ 'lʌvli flaːʊʌ]
So fair, so pure thou art,
[soːʊ fɛːʌ soːʊ pjʊːʌ ðaːʊ at]
I gaze on thee, and sadness
[aːɪ gɛːɪz an ði ænd 'sædnɛ(ɪ)s]
Comes stealing o'er my heart.
[kʌmz 'stilɪŋ ɔːʌ maːɪ hat]
My hands I fain had folded
[maːɪ hændz aːɪ fɛːɪn hæd 'foːʊldɛ(ɪ)d]
Upon thy soft brown hair,
[ʌ'pan ðaːɪ saft bɹaːʊn hɛːʌ]
Praying that God may keep thee
['pɹɛːɪɪŋ ðæt gad mɛːɪ kip ði]
So lovely, pure and fair.
[soːʊ 'lʌvli pjʊːʌ ænd fɛːʌ]

"Love Went A-Riding"
[lʌv wɛnt ʌ'ʁaːɪdɪŋ]
Coleridge, Mary (Eng. 1861-1907)

Love went a-riding over the earth,
[lʌv wɛnt ʌ'ɹaːɪdɪŋ 'oːʊvʌ ði ɜθ]
On Pegasus he rode.
[an 'pɛgʌsʊs hi ɹoːʊd]
The flowers before him sprang to birth,
[ðʊ flaːʊʌz bɪ'fɔːʌ hɪm spɹæŋ tu bɜθ]
And the frozen rivers flowed.
[ænd ðʊ 'fɹoːʊzɛ(ɪ)n 'ɹɪvʌz floːʊd]
Then all the youths and the maidens cried,
[ðɛn ɔl ðʊ juðz ænd ðʊ 'mɛːɪdɛ(ɪ)nz kɹaːɪd]
"Stay here with us, King of Kings."
[stɛːɪ hɪːʌ wɪð ʌs kɪŋ ʌv kɪŋz]

But Love said, "No! for the horse I ride has wings."
[bʌt lʌv sɛd noːʊ fɔ ðʊ hɔs aːɪ ɾaːɪd hæz wɪŋz]

"The Devon Maid"
[ðʊ ˈdɛvʌn mɛːɪd]
Keats, John (Eng. 1795-1821)

Where be you going, you Devon Maid?
[ʍɛːʌ bi ju ˈgoːʊɪŋ ju ˈdɛvʌn mɛːɪd]
And what have ye there in the Basket?
[ænd ʍat hæv ji ðɛːʌɾ ɪn ðʊ ˈbaskɛ(ɪ)t]
Ye tight little fairy, just fresh from the dairy,
[ji taːɪt ˈlɪtʊl ˈfɛːʌɾɪ dʒʌst fɹɛʃ fɹʌm ðʊ ˈdɛːʌɾɪ]
Will you give me some cream if I ask it?
[wɪl ju gɪv mi sʌm kɹim ɪf aːɪ ask ɪt]
I love your hills and I love your dales,
[aːɪ lʌv jɔːʌ hɪlz ænd aːɪ lʌv jɔːʌ dɛːɪlz]
And I love your flocks a-bleating;
[ænd aːɪ lʌv jɔːʌ flaks ʌ ˈblitɪŋ]
But Oh, on the heather to lie together,
[bʌt oːʊ an ðʊ ˈhɛðʌ tu laːɪ tuˈgɛðʌ]
With both our hearts a-beating!
[wɪð boːʊθ aːʊʌ hats ʌ ˈbitɪŋ]
I'll put your basket all safe in a nook;
[aːɪl pʊt jɔːʌ ˈbaskɛ(ɪ)t ɔl sɛːɪf ɪn ʌ nʊk]
Your shawl I'll hang on the willow,
[jɔːʌ ʃɔl aːɪl hæŋ an ðʊ ˈwɪloːʊ]
And we will sigh in the daisy's eye
[ænd wi wɪl saːɪ ɪn ðʊ ˈdɛːɪzɪz aːɪ]
and kiss on the grass green pillow.
[ænd kɪs an ðʊ gɹas gɹin ˈpɪloːʊ]

Britten, Benjamin (Eng. 1913-1976)

A Charm of Lullabies (Song Cycle)
[ʌ tʃam ʌv ˈlʌlʌbaːɪz]

1. A Cradle Song
[ʌ ˈkɹɛːɪdʊl saŋ]
Blake, William (Eng. 1757-1827)

Sleep! Sleep! beauty bright,
[slip slip ˈbjutɪ bɹaːɪt]
Dreaming o'er the joys of night;
[ˈdɹimɪŋ ɔːʌ ðʊ dʒɔːɪz ʌv naːɪt]
Sleep! Sleep! in thy sleep
[slip slip ɪn ðaːɪ slip]
Little sorrows sit and weep.
[ˈlɪtʊl ˈsaɾoːʊz sɪt ænd wip]
Sweet Babe, in thy face
[swit bɛːɪb ɪn ðaːɪ fɛːɪs]
Soft desires I can trace,
[saft dɪˈzaːɪʌz aːɪ kæn tɹɛːɪs]
Secret joys and secret smiles,
[ˈsikɹɛ(ɪ)t dʒɔːɪz ænd ˈsikɹɛ(ɪ)t smaːɪlz]

Little pretty infant wiles.
[ˈlɪtʊl ˈpɹɪtɪ ˈɪnfæ(ɪ)nt waːɪlz]
O, the cunning wiles that creep
[oːʊ ðʊ ˈkʌnɪŋ waːɪlz ðæt kɹip]
In thy little heart asleep.
[ɪn ðaːɪ ˈlɪtʊl hat ʌˈslip]
When thy little heart does wake
[ʍɛn ðaːɪ ˈlɪtʊl hat dʌz wɛːɪk]
Then the dreadful lightnings break,
[ðɛn ðʊ ˈdɹɛdfʊl ˈlaːɪtnɪŋz bɹɛːɪk]
From thy cheek and from thy eye,
[fɹʌm ðaːɪ tʃik ænd fɹʌm ðaːɪ aːɪ]
O'er the youthful harvests nigh.
[ɔːʌ ðʊ ˈjuθfʊl ˈhavɛ(ɪ)sts naːɪ]
Infant wiles and infant smiles
[ˈɪnfæ(ɪ)nt waːɪlz ænd ˈɪnfæ(ɪ)nt smaːɪlz]
Heav'n and Earth of peace beguiles.
[hɛvn ænd ɜθ ʌv pis bɪˈgaːɪlz]

2. The Highland Balou
[ðʊ ˈhaːɪlʌnd baˈlu]
Burns, Robert (Sc. 1759-1796)

Hee Balou, my sweet wee Donald,
[hi baˈlu ma swit wi ˈdanʊld]
Picture o' the great Clanronald!
[ˈpɪktʊr oːʊ ðʊ gɹɛːɪt klanˈɾanʊld]
Brawlie kens our wanton Chief
[ˈbɹɔlɪ kɛnz aːʊr ˈwantʌn tʃif]
What gat my young Highland thief.
[ʍʌt gat maːɪ jʌŋ ˈhilæ(ʌ)nd θif]
(Hee Balou!)
[hi baˈlu]
Leeze me on thy bonnie craigie!
[liz mi an ðaːɪ ˈbanɪ ˈkɹɛːɪgɪ]
And thou live, thou'll steal a naigie,
[ænd ðaːʊ lɪv ðaːʊl stil ʌ ˈnɛːɪgɪ]
Travel the country thro' and thro',
[ˈtɹævʊl ðʊ ˈkʌntrɪ θɾu ænd θɾu]
and bring hame a Carlisle cow!
[ænd bɹɪŋ hɛːɪm ʌ ˈkarlaːɪl ku]
Thro' the Lawlands, o'er the Border,
[θɾu ðʊ ˈlɔlæ(ʌ)ndz ɔːʌ ðʊ ˈbɔrdʊ]
Weel, my babie, may thou furder!
[wil ma ˈbabɪ mɛːɪ ðaːʊ ˈfʊrdʊ]
Herry the louns o' the laigh Countrie,
[ˈhɛrɪ ðʊ lunz oːʊ ðʊ lɛːɪ ˈkʌntrɪ]
Syne to the Highlands hame to me!
[saːɪn tʊ ðʊ ˈhilæ(ʌ)ndz hɛːɪm tʊ mi]

3. Sephestia's Lullaby
[sɪˈfɛstjaz ˈlʌlʌbaːɪ]
Greene, Robert (Eng. 1558-1592)

Weep not, my wanton, smile upon my knee;
[wip nat maːɪ ˈwantʌn smaːɪl ʌˈpan maːɪ ni]

When thou art old there's grief enough for thee.
[ʍɛn ðaːʊ at oːʊld ðɛːʌz grif ɪˈnʌf fɔ ði]
Mother's wag, pretty boy,
[ˈmʌðʌz wæg ˈpɹɪtɪ bɔːɪ]
Father's sorrow, father's joy;
[ˈfaðʌz ˈsaroːʊ ˈfaðʌz dʒɔːɪ]
When thy father first did see
[ʍɛn ðaːɪ ˈfaðʌ fɜst dɪd si]
Such a boy by him and me,
[sʌʧ ʌ bɔːɪ baːɪ hɪm ænd mi]
He was glad, I was woe;
[hi waz glæd aːɪ waz woːʊ]
Fortune changed made him so,
[ˈfɔʧʌn ˈʧɛːɪndʒɛ(ɪ)d meːɪd hɪm soːʊ]
When he left his pretty boy,
[ʍɛn hi lɛft hɪz ˈpɹɪtɪ bɔːɪ]
Last his sorrow, first his joy.
[last hɪz ˈsaroːʊ fɜst hɪz dʒɔːɪ]
Weep not, my wanton, smile upon my knee;
[wip nat maːɪ ˈwantʌn smaːɪl ʌˈpan maːɪ ni]
When thou art old there's grief enough for thee.
[ʍɛn ðaːʊ at oːʊld ðɛːʌz grif ɪˈnʌf fɔ ði]
The wanton smiled, father wept,
[ðʊ ˈwantʌn smaːɪld ˈfaðʌ wɛpt]
Mother cried, baby leapt;
[ˈmʌðʌ kraːɪd ˈbɛːɪbɪ lɛpt]
More he crowed, more we cried,
[mɔːʌ hi ˈkɹoːʊɛ(ɪ)d mɔːʌ wi kraːɪd]
Nature could not sorrow hide:
[ˈnɛːɪʧʊ(ʌ) kʊd nat ˈsaroːʊ haːɪd]
He must go, he must kiss
[hi mʌst goːʊ hi mʌst kɪs]
Child and mother, baby bliss,
[ʧaːɪld ænd ˈmʌðʌ ˈbɛːɪbɪ blɪs]
For he left his pretty boy,
[fɔ hi lɛft hɪz ˈpɹɪtɪ bɔːɪ]
Father's sorrow, father's joy.
[ˈfaðʌz ˈsaroːʊ ˈfaðʌz dʒɔːɪ]
Weep not, my wanton, Smile upon my knee,
[wip nat maːɪ ˈwantʌn smaːɪl ʌˈpan maːɪ ni]
When thou art old There's grief enough for thee.
[ʍɛn ðaːʊ at oːʊld ðɛːʌz grif ɪˈnʌf fɔ ði]

4. A Charm
[ʌ ʧam]
Randolph, Thomas (Eng. 1605-1635)

Quiet! Sleep!
[ˈkwaːɪɛ(ɪ)t slip]
Or I will make
[ɔʁ⁽ʳ⁾ aːɪ wɪl mɛːɪk]
Erinnys whip thee with a snake,
[ɛˈrɪnɪz ʍɪp ði wɪð ʌ snɛːɪk]
And cruel Rhadamanthus take
[ænd ˈkruːɛ(ʊ)l ɹaˈdamanʊs tɛːɪk]

Thy body to the boiling lake,
[ðaːɪ ˈbadɪ tu ðʊ ˈbɔːɪlɪŋ lɛːɪk]
Where fire and brimstones never slake;
[ʍɛːʌ faːɪʌr ænd ˈbɹɪmstoːʊnz ˈnɛvʌ slɛːɪk]
Thy heart shall burn, thy head shall ache,
[ðaːɪ hat ʃæl bɜn ðaːɪ hɛd ʃæl ɛːɪk]
And ev'ry joint about thee quake;
[ænd ˈɛvɹɪ dʒɔːɪnt ʌˈbaːʊt ði kwɛːɪk]
And therefore dare not yet to wake!
[ænd ˈðɛːʌfɔːʌ dɛːʌ nat jɛt tu wɛːɪk]
Quiet, sleep! Quiet, sleep!
[ˈkwaːɪɛ(ɪ)t slip ˈkwaːɪɛ(ɪ)t slip]
Quiet!
[ˈkwaːɪɛ(ɪ)t]
Quiet, sleep! Or thou shalt see
[ˈkwaːɪɛ(ɪ)t slip ɔ ðaːʊ ʃælt si]
The horrid hags of Tartary,
[ðʊ ˈhɔrɪd hægz ʌv ˈtartarɪ]
Whose tresses ugly serpents be,
[huz ˈtɹɛsɛ(ɪ)z ˈʌglɪ ˈsɜpɛnts bi]
And Cerberus shall bark at thee,
[ænd ˈsɛrbɛrʊs ʃæl bak æt ði]
And all the Furies that are three
[ænd ɔl ðʊ ˈfjʊːʌrɪz ðæt a θɹi]
The worst is called Tisiphone,
[ðʊ wɜst ɪz kɔld tɪˈsɪfonɪ]
Shall lash thee to eternity;
[ʃæl læʃ ði tu ɪˈtɜnɪtɪ]
And therefore sleep thou peacefully
[ænd ˈðɛːʌfɔːʌ slip ðaːʊ ˈpisfʊlɪ]
Quiet, sleep! Quiet, sleep!
[ˈkwaːɪɛ(ɪ)t slip ˈkwaːɪɛ(ɪ)t slip]
Quiet!
[ˈkwaːɪɛ(ɪ)t]

5. The Nurse's Song
[ðʊ ˈnɜsɪz saŋ]
Phillip, John (Eng. flourished 1561)

Lullaby baby,
[ˈlʌlʌbaːɪ ˈbɛːɪbɪ]
Thy nurse will tend thee as duly as may be.
[ðaːɪ nɜs wɪl tɛnd ði æz ˈdjulɪ æz mɛːɪ bi]
Lullaby baby!
[ˈlʌlʌbaːɪ ˈbɛːɪbɪ]
Be still, my sweet sweeting, no longer do cry;
[bi stɪl maːɪ swit ˈswitɪŋ noːʊ ˈlaŋgʌ du kraːɪ]
Sing lullaby baby, lullaby baby.
[sɪŋ ˈlʌlʌbaːɪ ˈbɛːɪbɪ ˈlʌlʌbaːɪ ˈbɛːɪbɪ]
Let dolours be fleeting, I fancy thee, I...
[lɛt ˈdɔlʊz bi ˈflitɪŋ aːɪ ˈfænsɪ ði aːɪ]
To rock and to lull thee I will not delay me.
[tu rak ænd tu lʌl ði aːɪ wɪl nat dɪˈlɛːɪ mi]
Lullaby baby,
[ˈlʌlʌbaːɪ ˈbɛːɪbɪ]

Lullabylabylaby baby,
[ˈlʌlʌbaːɪlʌbaːɪlʌbaːɪ ˈbɛːɪbi]
Thy nurse will tend thee as duly as may be
[ðaːɪ nɜs wɪl tɛnd ði æz ˈdjuli æz mɛːɪ bi]
Lullabylabylaby baby
[ˈlʌlʌbaːɪlʌbaːɪlʌbaːɪ ˈbɛːɪbi]
The gods be thy shield and comfort in need!
[ðʊ gadz bi ðaːɪ ʃild ænd ˈkʌmfɔ(ʌ)t ɪn nid]
Sing lullaby baby,
[sɪŋ ˈlʌlʌbaːɪ ˈbɛːɪbi]
Lullabylaby baby
[ˈlʌlʌbaːɪlʌbaːɪ ˈbɛːɪbi]
They give thee good fortune and well for to speed,
[ðɛːɪ gɪv ði gʊd ˈfɔʧʌn ænd wɛl fɔ tu spid]
And this to desire... I will not delay me.
[ænd ðɪs tu dɪˈzaːɪʌ aːɪ wɪl nat dɪˈlɛːɪ mi]
This to desire... I will not delay me.
[ðɪs tu dɪˈzaːɪʌ aːɪ wɪl nat dɪˈlɛːɪ mi]
Lullaby baby,
[ˈlʌlʌbaːɪ ˈbɛːɪbi]
Lullabylaby baby,
[ˈlʌlʌbaːɪlʌbaːɪ ˈbɛːɪbi]
Thy nurse will tend thee as duly as may be.
[ðaːɪ nɜs wɪl tɛnd ði æz ˈdjuli æz mɛːɪ bi]
Lullabylabylaby baby.
[ˈlʌlʌbaːɪlʌbaːɪlʌbaːɪlʌbaːɪ ˈbɛːɪbi]

The Holy Sonnets of John Donne (Song Cycle)
[ðʊ ˈhoːʊli ˈsanɪts ʌv ʤan dʌn]
Donne, John (Eng. 1572-1631)

1. Oh My Blacke Soule!
[oːʊ maːɪ blæk soːʊl]

Oh my blacke Soule! now thou art summoned
[oːʊ maːɪ blæk soːʊl naːʊ ðaːʊ at ˈsʌmʌnɛ(ɪ)d]
By sicknesse, death's herald, and champion;
[baːɪ ˈsɪknɛ(ɪ)s dɛθs ˈhɛrʊld ænd ˈʧæmpɪːʌn]
Thou art like a pilgrim, which abroad hath done
[ðaːʊ at laːɪk ʌ ˈpilgrɪm ʍɪʧ ʌˈbrɔd hæθ dʌn]
Treason, and durst not turne to whence hee is fled,
[ˈtrizʌn ænd dɜst nat tɜn tu ʍɛns hi ɪz flɛd]
Or like a thiefe, which till death's doome be read,
[ɔ laːɪk ʌ θif ʍɪʧ tɪl dɛθs dum bi rɛd]
Wisheth himselfe deliver'd from prison;
[ˈwɪʃɛ(ɪ)θ hɪmˈsɛlf dɪˈlivʌd frʌm ˈprizʌn]
But dam'd and hal'd to execution,
[bʌt dæmd ænd hɛːɪld tu ɛksɪˈkjuʃɪʌn]
Wisheth that still he might be imprisoned.
[ˈwɪʃɛ(ɪ)θ ðæt stɪl hi maːɪt bi ɪmˈprizʌnɛ(ɪ)d]
Yet grace, if thou repent, thou canst not lacke;
[jɛt grɛːɪs ɪf ðaːʊ rɪˈpɛnt ðaːʊ kænst nat læk]
But who shall give thee that grace to beginne?
[bʌt hu ʃæl gɪv ði ðæt grɛːɪs tu bɪˈgɪn]
Oh make thyselfe with holy mourning blaçke,
[oːʊ mɛːɪk ðaːɪˈsɛlf wɪð ˈhoːʊli ˈmɔnɪŋ blæk]

And red with blushing as thou art with sinne;
[ænd rɛd wɪð ˈblʌʃɪŋ æz ðaːʊ at wɪð sɪn]
Or wash thee in Christ's blood, which hath this might
[ɔ waʃ ði ɪn kraːɪsts blʌd ʍɪʧ hæθ ðɪs maːɪt]
That being red, it dyes red soules to white.
[ðæt ˈbiɪŋ rɛd ɪt daːɪz rɛd soːʊlz tu ʍaːɪt]

2. Batter My Heart
[ˈbætʌ maːɪ hat]

Batter my heart, three person'd God; for, you
[ˈbætʌ maːɪ hat θri ˈpɜsʌnd gad fɔ ju]
As yet but knocke, breathe, shine, and seeke to mend;
[æz jɛt bʌt nak brið ʃaːɪn ænd sik tu mɛnd]
That I may rise, and stand,
[ðæt aːɪ mɛːɪ raːɪz ænd stænd]
O'erthrow me, and bend
[ɔːʌˈθroːʊ mi ænd bɛnd]
Your force, to breake, blowe, burn and make me new.
[jɔːʌ fɔs tu brɛːɪk bloːʊ bɜn ænd mɛːɪk mi nju]
I, like an usurpt towne, to another due,
[aːɪ laːɪk æn ˌjuˈsɜpt taːʊn tu ʌˈnʌðʌ dju]
Labour to admit you, but Oh, to no end,
[ˈlɛːɪbʊ(ʌ) tu ædˈmɪt ju bʌt oːʊ tu noːʊ ɛnd]
Reason your viceroy in mee, mee should defend
[ˈrizʌn jɔːʌ ˈvaːɪsrɔːɪ ɪn mi mi ʃʊd dɪˈfɛnd]
But is captiv'd, and proves weake or untrue.
[bʌt ɪz ˈkæptɪvd ænd pruvz wik ɔʁ(r) ʌnˈtru]
Yet dearely I love you and would be loved faine,
[jɛt ˈdɪːʌli aːɪ lʌv ju ænd wʊd bi ˈlʌvɛ(ɪ)d fɛːɪn]
But am betroth'd unto your enemie:
[bʌt æm bɪˈtrɔʊðd ˈʌntu jɔːʌr ˈɛnɪ(ʌ)mi]
Divorce mee, untie, or breake that knot againe,
[dɪˈvɔs mi ʌnˈtaːɪ ɔ brɛːɪk ðæt nat ʌˈgɛːɪn]
Take mee to you, imprison mee, for I
[tɛːɪk mi tu ju ɪmˈprizʌn mi fɔʁ(r) aːɪ]
Except you enthrall mee, never shall be free,
[ɪkˈsɛpt ju ɪnˈθrɔl mi ˈnɛvʌ ʃæl bi fri]
Nor ever chaste, except you ravish mee.
[nɔʁ(r) ˈɛvʌ ʧɛːɪst ɪkˈsɛpt ju ˈrævɪʃ mi]

3. O Might Those Sighes and Teares
[oːʊ maːɪt ðoːʊz saːɪz ænd tɪːʌz]

O might those sighes and teares return againe
[oːʊ maːɪt ðoːʊz saːɪz ænd tɪːʌz rɪˈtɜn ʌˈgɛːɪn]
Into my breast and eyes, which I have spent,
[ˈɪntu maːɪ brɛst ænd aːɪz ʍɪʧ aːɪ hæv spɛnt]
That I might in this holy discontent
[ðæt aːɪ maːɪt ɪn ðɪs ˈhoːʊli dɪskʌnˈtɛnt]
Mourne with some fruit, as I have mourn'd in vaine;
[mɔn wɪð sʌm frut æz aːɪ hæv mɔnd ɪn vɛːɪn]
In mine Idolatry what show'rs of rain
[ɪn maːɪn aːɪˈdalʌtrɪ ʍat ʃaːʊʌz ʌv rɛːɪn]
Mine eyes did waste? What griefs my heart did rent?
[maːɪn aːɪz dɪd wɛːɪst ʍat grifs maːɪ hat dɪd rɛnt]

That sufferance was my sinne; now I repent
[ðæt ˈsʌfʌɾæ(ɪ)ns waz maːɪ sɪn naːʊ aːɪ ɾɪˈpɛnt]
'Cause I did suffer, I must suffer paine.
[kɔz aːɪ dɪd ˈsʌfʌ aːɪ mʌst ˈsʌfʌ pɛːɪn]
Th'hydroptique drunkard, and night scouting thiefe,
[ðhaːɪˈdɹaptɪk ˈdɹʌŋkʌd ænd naːɪt ˈskaːʊtɪŋ θif]
The itchy lecher and self tickling proud
[ði ˈɪʧɪ ˈlɛʧʌr ænd sɛlf ˈtɪklɪŋ pɹaːʊd]
Have the remembrance of past joyes, for reliefe
[hæv ðʊ ɾɪˈmɛmbɹæ(ɪ)ns ʌv past dʒɔːɪz fɔ ɾɪˈlif]
Of coming ills. To poore me is allow'd
[ʌv ˈkʌmɪŋ ɪlz tu pʊːʌ miˑɪz ʌˈlaːʊd]
No ease; for, long, yet vehement griefe hath been
[noːʊ iz fɔ laŋ jɛt ˈvɪʌmɛnt grif hæθ bin]
Th'effect and cause, the punishment and sinne.
[ðɪˈfɛkt ænd kɔz ðʊ ˈpʌnɪʃmɛnt ænd sɪn]

4. Oh, to Vex Me
[oːʊ tu vɛks mi]

Oh, to vex me, contraryes meet in one:
[oːʊ tu vɛks mi ˈkantɪɛːʌɾɪz mit ɪn wʌn]
In constancy unnaturally hath begott
[ɪn ˈkanstæ(ɪ)nsɪ ʌnˈnæʧɹʊlɪ hæθ bɪˈgat]
A constant habit; that when I would not
[ʌ ˈkanstæ(ɪ)nt ˈhæbɪt ðæt ʍɛn aːɪ wʊd nat]
I change in vowes, and in devotione.
[aːɪ ʧɛːɪndʒ ɪn vaːʊz ænd ɪn dɪˈvoːʊʃɪʌn]
As humorous is my contritione
[æz ˈhjumɔɾʌs ɪz maːɪ kʌnˈtɹɪʃɪʌn]
As my profane Love and as soone forgott:
[æz maːɪ pɹoˈfɛːɪn lʌv ænd æz sun fɔˈgat]
As ridlingly distemper'd, cold and hott,
[æz ˈɹɪdlɪŋlɪ dɪˈstɛmpʌd koːʊld ænd hat]
As praying, as mute; as infinite, as none.
[æz ˈpɹɛːɪŋ æz mjut æz ˈɪnfɪnɪt æz nʌn]
I durst not view Heav'n yesterday; and today
[aːɪ dɜst nat vju hɛvn ˈjɛstʌdɛːɪ ænd tuˈdɛːɪ]
In prayers, and flatt'ring speeches I court God:
[ɪn pɹɛːaz ænd ˈflætɹɪŋ ˈspiʧɛ(ɪ)z aːɪ kɔt gad]
Tomorrow I quake with true feare of his rod.
[tuˈmaɾoːʊ aːɪ kwɛːɪk wɪð tru fɪːʌr ʌv hɪz ɹad]
So my devout fitts come and go away,
[soːʊ maːɪ dɪˈvaːʊt fits kʌm ænd goːʊ ʌˈwɛːɪ]
Like a fantastique Ague: save that here
[laːɪk ʌ fænˈtæstɪk ˈɛːɪgju sɛːɪv ðæt hɪːʌ]
Those are my best dayes, when I shake with feare.
[ðoːʊz a maːɪ bɛst dɛːɪz ʍɛn aːɪ ʃɛːɪk wɪð fɪːʌ]

5. What If This Present
[ʍat ɪf ðɪs ˈpɹɛzɛnt]

What if this present were the world's last night?
[ʍat ɪf ðɪs ˈpɹɛzɛnt wɜ ðʊ wɜldz last naːɪt]
Marke in my heart, O Soule, where thou dost dwell,
[mak ɪn maːɪ hat oːʊ soːʊl ʍɛːʌ ðaːʊ dʌst dwɛl]

The picture of Christ crucified, and tell
[ðʊ ˈpɪkʧʊ(ʌ)r ʌv kɹaːɪst ˈkɹusɪfaːɪd ænd tɛl]
Whether that countenance can thee affright,
[ˈʍɛðʌ ðæt ˈkaːʊntɛ(ɪ)næ(ɪ)ns kæn ði ʌˈfɹaːɪt]
Teares in his eyes quench the amazing light,
[tiːʌz ɪn hɪz aːɪz kwɛnʧ ði ʌˈmɛːɪzɪŋ laːɪt]
Blood fills his frownes,
[blʌd fɪlz hɪz fɹaːʊnz]
which from his pierc'd head fell.
[ʍɪʧ fɹʌm hɪz pɪːʌst hɛd fɛl]
And can that tongue adjudge thee into hell,
[ænd kæn ðæt tʌŋ ʌˈdʒʌdʒ ði ˈɪntu hɛl]
Which pray'd forgivenesse for his foes fierce spight?
[ʍɪʧ pɹɛːɪd fɔˈgɪvnɛ(ɪ)s fɔ hɪz foːʊz fɪːʌs spaːɪt]
No, no; but as in my idolatrie
[noːʊ noːʊ bʌt æz ɪn maːɪ aːɪˈdalʌtɹɪ]
I said to all my profane mistresses,
[aːɪ sɛd tu ɔl maːɪ pɹoˈfɛːɪn ˈmɪstɹɛ(ɪ)sɛ(ɪ)z]
Beauty, of pity, foulenesse onely is
[ˈbjutɪ ʌv ˈpɪtɪ ˈfaːʊlnɛ(ɪ)s ˈoːʊnlɪ ɪz]
A sign of rigour: so I say to thee,
[ʌ saːɪn ʌv ˈɹɪgʊ(ʌ) soːʊ aːɪ sɛːɪ tu ði]
To wicked spirits are horrid shapes assign'd,
[tu ˈwɪkɛ(ɪ)d ˈspɪɾɪts a ˈhɔɾɪd ʃɛːɪps ʌˈsaːɪnd]
This beauteous forme assures a piteous minde.
[ðɪs ˈbjutɪʌs fɔm ʌˈʃʊːʌz ʌ ˈpɪtɪʌs maːɪnd]

6. Since She Whom I Lov'd
[sɪns ʃi hum aːɪ lʌvd]

Since she whom I lov'd hath pay'd her last debt
[sɪns ʃi hum aːɪ lʌvd hæθ pɛːɪd hɜ last dɛt]
To Nature, and to hers, and my good is dead,
[tu ˈnɛːɪʧʊ(ʌ)r ænd tu hɜz ænd maːɪ gʊd ɪz dɛd]
And her Soule early into Heaven ravished,
[ænd hɜ soːʊl ˈɜlɪ ˈɪntu ˈhɛvɪn ˈɹævɪʃɛ(ɪ)d]
Wholly on heavenly things my mind is sett.
[ˈhoːʊlɪ an ˈhɛvɛ(ɪ)nlɪ θɪŋz maːɪ maːɪnd ɪz sɛt]
Here the admyring her my mind did whett
[hɪːʌ ði ædˈmaːɪʌɾɪŋ hɜ maːɪ maːɪnd dɪd ʍɛt]
To seeke thee God; so streams do shew their head;
[tu sik ði gad soːʊ stɹimz du ʃoːʊ ðɛːʌ hɛd]
But though I have found thee
[bʌt ðoːʊ aːɪ hæv faːʊnd ði]
and thou my thirst hast fed,
[ænd ðaːʊ maːɪ θɜst hæst fɛd]
A holy thirsty dropsy melts mee yett,
[ʌ ˈhoːʊlɪ ˈθɜstɪ ˈdɹapsɪ mɛlts mi jɛt]
But why should I begg more love, when as thou
[bʌt ʍaːɪ ʃʊd aːɪ bɛg mɔːʌ lʌv ʍɛn æz ðaːʊ]
Dost wooe my soul for hers: off'ring all thine:
[dʌst wu maːɪ soːʊl fɔ hɜz ˈafɹɪŋ ɔl ðaːɪn]
And dost not only feare lest I allow
[ænd dʌst nat ˈoːʊnlɪ fɪːʌ lɛst aːɪ ʌˈlaːʊ]
My love to Saints and Angels things divine,
[maːɪ lʌv tu sɛːɪnts ænd ˈɛːɪndʒɛ(ʊ)lz θɪŋz dɪˈvaːɪn]

But in thy tender jealousy dost doubt
[bʌt ɪn ðaːɪ 'tɛndʌ 'ʤɛlʌsɪ dʌst daːʊt]
Lest the world, Fleshe, yea, Devill putt thee out.
[lɛst ðʊ wɜld flɛʃ jɛːɪ 'dɛvɪ(ʊ)l pʊt ði aːʊt]

7. At the Round Earth's Imagined Corners
[æt ðʊ ɹaːʊnd ɜθs ɪ'mæʤɪnd 'kɔnʌz]

At the round earth's imagined corners, blow
[æt ðʊ ɹaʊnd ɜθs ɪ'mæʤɪnd 'kɔnʌz bloːʊ]
Your trumpets, angels, and arise, arise
[jɔːʌ 'tɹʌmpɛ(ɪ)ts 'ɛːɪnʤɛ(ʊ)lz ænd ʌ'raːɪz ʌ'raːɪz]
From death, you numberless infinities
[fɹʌm dɛθ ju 'nʌmbʌlɛ(ɪ)s ɪn'fɪnɪtɪz]
Of souls, and to your scattered bodies goe,
[ʌv soːʊlz ænd tu jɔːʌ 'skætʌd 'bɑdɪz goːʊ]
All whom the flood did, and fire shall o'erthrow,
[ɔl hum ðʊ flʌd dɪd ænd faːɪʌ ʃæl ɔːʌ'θɾoːʊ]
All whom warre, dearth, age, agues, tyrannies,
[ɔl hum wɔ dɜθ ɛːɪʤ 'ɛːɪgjuz 'tɪɾæ(ɪ)nɪz]
Despaire, law, chance hath slaine; and you whose eyes
[dɪ'spɛːʌ lɔ ʧans hæθ slɛːɪn ænd ju huz aːɪz]
Shall behold God and never taste death's woe,
[ʃæl bɪ'hoːʊld gɑd ænd 'nɛvʌ tɛːɪst dɛθs woːʊ]
But let them sleepe, Lord, and mee mourn a space,
[bʌt lɛt ðɛm slip lɔd ænd mi mɔn ʌ spɛːɪs]
For, if above all these, my sins abound,
[fɔʁ(r) ɪf ʌ'bʌv ɔl ðiz maːɪ sɪnz ʌ'baːʊnd]
'Tis late to ask abundance of Thy grace,
[tɪz lɛːɪt tu ask ʌ'bʌndæ(ɪ)ns ʌv ðaːɪ gɹɛːɪs]
When we are there; here on this lowly ground,
[ʌɛn wi a ðɛːʌ hiːʌr an ðɪs 'loːʊlɪ gɹaːʊnd]
Teach me how to repent; for that's as good
[tiʧ mi haːʊ tu ɾɪ'pɛnt fɔ ðæts æz gʊd]
As if Thou hadst seal'd my pardon with Thy blood.
[æz ɪf ðaːʊ hædst sild maːɪ 'padʌn wɪð ðaːɪ blʌd]

8. Thou Hast Made Me
[ðaːʊ hæst mɛːɪd mi]

Thou hast made me, and shall thy work decay?
[ðaːʊ hæst mɛːɪd mi ænd ʃæl ðaːɪ wɜk dɪ'kɛːɪ]
Repaire me now, for now mine end doth haste,
[ɹɪ'pɛːʌ mi naːʊ fɔ naːʊ maːɪn ɛnd dʌθ hɛːɪst]
I runne to death, and death meets me as fast,
[aːɪ ɾʌn tu dɛθ ænd dɛθ mits mi æz fast]
And all my pleasures are like yesterday;
[ænd ɔl maːɪ 'plɛʒʊ(ʌ)z a laːɪk 'jɛstʌdɛːɪ]
I dare not move my dim eyes anyway,
[aːɪ dɛːʌ nat muv maːɪ dɪm aːɪz 'ɛnɪwɛːɪ]
Despaire behind, and death before doth cast
[dɪ'spɛːʌ bɪ'haːɪnd ænd dɛθ bɪ'fɔːʌ dʌθ kast]
Such terror, and my feeble flesh doth waste
[sʌʧ 'tɛɾɔ(ʌ)r ænd maːɪ 'fibʊl flɛʃ dʌθ wɛːɪst]
By sinne in it, which it t'wards Hell doth weigh;
[baːɪ sɪn ɪn ɪt ʌɪʧ ɪt twɔdz hɛl dʌθ wɛːɪ]

Onely thou art above, and when t'wards thee
['oːʊnlɪ ðaːʊ at ʌ'bʌv ænd ʌɛn twɔdz ði]
By thy leave I can looke, I rise againe;
[baːɪ ðaːɪ liv aːɪ kæn lʊk aːɪ raːɪz ʌ'gɛːɪn]
But our old subtle foe so tempteth me,
[bʌt aːʊʌr oːʊld 'sʌtʊl foːʊ soːʊ 'tɛmptɛ(ɪ)θ mi]
That not one houre myselfe can I sustaine;
[ðæt nat wʌn aːʊʌ maːɪ'sɛlf kæn aːɪ sʌ'stɛːɪn]
Thy Grace may wing me to prevent his art,
[ðaːɪ gɹɛːɪs mɛːɪ wɪŋ mi tu pɹɪ'vɛnt hɪz at]
And thou like Adamant draw mine iron heart.
[ænd ðaːʊ laːɪk 'ædʌmæ(ɪ)nt dɹɔ maːɪn 'aːɪʌn hat]

9. Death Be Not Proud
[dɛθ bi nat pɹaːʊd]

Death be not proud, though some have called thee
[dɛθ bi nat pɹaːʊd ðoːʊ sʌm hæv 'kɔlɛ(ɪ)d ði]
Mighty and dreadfull, for, thou art not soe,
['maːɪtɪ ænd 'dɹɛdfʊl fɔ ðaːʊ at nat soːʊ]
For, those, whom thou think'st thou dost over throw,
[fɔ ðoːʊz hum ðaːʊ 'θɪŋkst ðaːʊ dʌst 'oːʊvʌ θɾoːʊ]
Die not, poore death, nor yet canst thou kill mee.
[daːɪ nat pʊːʌ dɛθ nɔ jɛt kænst ðaːʊ kɪl mi]
From rest and sleepe, which but thy pictures be,
[fɹʌm ɹest ænd slip ʌɪʧ bʌt ðaːɪ 'pɪkʧʊ(ʌ)z bi]
Much pleasure; then from thee, much more must flow,
[mʌʧ 'plɛʒʊ(ʌ) ðɛn fɹʌm ði mʌʧ mɔːʌ mʌst floːʊ]
And soonest our best men with thee do goe,
[ænd 'sunɛ(ɪ)st aːʊʌ bɛst mɛn wɪð ði du goːʊ]
Rest of their bones, and souls deliverie.
[ɹest ʌv ðɛːʌ boːʊnz ænd soːʊlz dɪ'lɪvʌɾɪ]
Thou art slave to Fate,
[ðaːʊ at slɛːɪv tu fɛːɪt]
Chance, kings and desperate men,
[ʧans kɪŋz ænd 'dɛspʌɾæ(ɪ)t mɛn]
And dost with poyson, warre, and sickness dwell,
[ænd dʌst wɪð 'pɔːɪzʌn wɔr ænd 'sɪknɛ(ɪ)s dwɛl]
And poppie, or charmes can make us sleepe as well
[ænd 'papɪ ɔ ʧamz kæn mɛːɪk ʌs slip æz wɛl]
And better than thy stroake; why swell'st thou then?
[ænd 'bɛtʌ ðæn ðaːɪ stɹoːʊk ʌaːɪ swɛlst ðaːʊ ðɛn]
One short sleepe past, wee wake eternally,
[wʌn ʃɔt slip past wi wɛːɪk ɪ'tɜnʊlɪ]
And death shall be no more; Death, thou shalt die.
[ænd dɛθ ʃæl bi noːʊ mɔːʌ dɛθ ðaːʊ ʃælt daːɪ]

Winter Words (Song Cycle)
['wɪntʌ wɜdz]
Hardy, Thomas (Eng. 1840-1928)

1. At Day-Close in November
[æt dɛːɪ kloːʊz ɪn no'vɛmbʌ]

The ten hours' light is abating,
[ðʊ tɛn aːʊʌz laːɪt ɪz ʌ'bɛːɪtɪŋ]

And a late bird wings across,
[ænd ʌ leːɪt bɜd wɪŋz ʌ'kɹas]
Where the pines, like waltzers waiting,
[ʍɛːʌ ðʊ paːɪnz laːɪk 'wɔltsʌz 'wɛːɪtɪŋ]
Give their black heads a toss.
[gɪv ðɛːʌ blæk hɛdz ʌ tas]
Beech leaves, that yellow the noon-time,
[biːtʃ livz ðæt 'jɛloːʊ ðʊ nun taːɪm]
Float past like specks in the eye;
[floːʊt past laːɪk spɛks ɪn ði aːɪ]
I set every tree in my June time,
[aːɪ sɛt 'ɛvɹɪ tɹi ɪn maːɪ dʒun taːɪm]
And now they obscure the sky.
[ænd naːʊ ðɛːɪ ʌb'skjʊːʌ ðʊ skaːɪ]
And the children who ramble through here
[ænd ðʊ 'tʃɪldɹɛ(ɪ)n hu 'ɹæmbʊl θɹu hiːʌ]
Conceive that there never has been
[kʌn'siv ðæt ðɛːʌ 'nɛvʌ hæz bin]
A time when no tall trees grew here,
[ʌ taːɪm ʍɛn noːʊ tɔl tɹiz gɹu hiːʌ]
That none will in time be seen.
[ðæt nʌn wɪl ɪn taːɪm bi sin]

2. Midnight on the Great Western
['mɪdnaːɪt an ðʊ gɹeːɪt 'wɛstʌn]

In the third-class seat sat the journeying boy,
[ɪn ðʊ θɜd klas sit sæt ðʊ 'dʒɜnɪɪŋ bɔːɪ]
And the roof-lamp's oily flame
[ænd ðʊ ɹuf læmps 'ɔːɪlɪ fleːɪm]
Played down on his listless form and face,
[pleːɪd daːʊn an hɪz 'lɪstlɛ(ɪ)s fɔm ænd fɛːɪs]
Bewrapt past knowing to what he was going,
[bɪ'ɹæpt past 'noːʊɪŋ tu ʍat hi waz 'goːʊɪŋ]
Or whence he came.
[ɔ ʍɛns hi kɛːɪm]
In the band of his hat the journeying boy,
[ɪn ðʊ bænd ʌv hɪz hæt ðʊ 'dʒɜnɪɪŋ bɔːɪ]
Had a ticket stuck; and a string
[hæd ʌ 'tɪkɛ(ɪ)t stʌk ænd ʌ stɹɪŋ]
Around his neck bore the key of his box,
[ʌ'ɹaːʊnd hɪz nɛk bɔːʌ ðʊ ki ʌv hɪz baks]
That twinkled gleams of the lamp's sad beams
[ðæt 'twɪŋkʊld glimz ʌv ðʊ læmps sæd bimz]
Like a living thing.
[laːɪk ʌ 'lɪvɪŋ θɪŋ]
What past can be yours, O journeying boy
[ʍat past kæn bi jɔːʌz oːʊ 'dʒɜnɪɪŋ bɔːɪ]
Towards a world unknown,
[tu'wɔdz ʌ wɜld ʌn'noːʊn]
Who calmly, as if incurious quite
[hu 'kamlɪ æz ɪf ɪn'kjʊːɹɪʌs kwaːɪt]
On all at stake, can undertake
[an ɔl æt stɛːɪk kæn ʌndʌ'tɛːɪk]
This plunge alone?
[ðɪs plʌndʒ ʌ'loːʊn]

Knows your soul a sphere, O journeying boy,
[noːʊz jɔːʌ soːʊl ʌ sfiːʌ oːʊ 'dʒɜnɪɪŋ bɔːɪ]
Our rude realms far above,
[aːʊʌ ɹʊd ɹɛlmz far ʌ'bʌv]
Whence with spacious vision you mark and mete
[ʍɛns wɪð 'speːɪʃʌs 'vɪʒʌn ju mak ænd mit]
This region of sin that you find you in,
[ðɪs 'ɹidʒʌn ʌv sɪn ðæt ju faːɪnd ju ɪn]
But are not of?
[bʌt a nat ʌv]

3. Wagtail and Baby
['wægtɛːɪl ænd 'bɛːɪbi]

A baby watched a ford, whereto
[ʌ 'bɛːɪbi watʃt ʌ fɔd ʍɛːʌ'tu]
A wagtail came for drinking;
[ʌ 'wægtɛːɪl kɛːɪm fɔ 'dɹɪŋkɪŋ]
A blaring bull went wading through,
[ʌ 'blɛːʌɹɪŋ bʊl wɛnt 'wɛːɪdɪŋ θɹu]
The wagtail showed no shrinking.
[ðʊ 'wægtɛːɪl ʃoːʊd noːʊ 'ʃɹɪŋkɪŋ]
A stallion splashed his way across,
[ʌ 'stæljʌn splæʃt hɪz wɛːɪ ʌ'kɹas]
The birdie nearly sinking;
[ðʊ bɜdɪ 'nɪːʌlɪ 'sɪŋkɪŋ]
He gave his plumes a twitch and toss,
[hi gɛːɪv hɪz plumz ʌ twɪtʃ ænd tas]
And held his own unblinking.
[ænd hɛld hɪz oːʊn ʌn'blɪŋkɪŋ]
Next saw the baby round the spot
[nɛkst sɔ ðʊ 'bɛːɪbɪ ɹaːʊnd ðʊ spat]
A mongrel slowly slinking;
[ʌ 'maŋgɹʊl 'sloːʊlɪ 'slɪŋkɪŋ]
The wagtail gazed, but faltered not
[ðʊ 'wægtɛːɪl gɛːɪzd bʌt 'fɔltʌd nat]
In dip and sip and prinking.
[ɪn dɪp ænd sɪp ænd 'pɹɪŋkɪŋ]
A perfect gentleman then neared;
[ʌ 'pɜfɛ(ɪ)kt 'dʒɛntʊlmæ(ʌ)n ðɛn nɪːʌd]
The wagtail, in a winking,
[ðʊ 'wægtɛːɪl ɪn ʌ 'wɪŋkɪŋ]
With terror rose and disappeared;
[wɪð 'tɛɹɔ(ʌ) ɹoːʊz ænd dɪsʌ'pɪːʌd]
The baby fell a-thinking.
[ðʊ 'bɛːɪbɪ fɛl ʌ 'θɪŋkɪŋ]

4. The Little Old Table
[ðʊ 'lɪtʊl oːʊld 'tɛːɪbʊl]

Creak, little wood thing, creak,
[kɹik 'lɪtʊl wʊd θɪŋ kɹik]
When I touch you with elbow or knee;
[ʍɛn aːɪ tʌtʃ ju wɪð 'ɛlboːʊ ɔ ni]
That is the way you speak
[ðæt ɪz ðʊ wɛːɪ ju spik]

Of one who gave you to me!
[ʌv wʌn hu gɛːɪv ju tu mi]
You, little table, she brought—
[ju ˈlɪtʊl ˈtɛːɪbʊl ʃi bɹɔt]
Brought me with her own hand,
[bɹɔt mi wɪð hɜ⁽ʳ⁾ oːʊn hænd]
As she looked at me with a thought
[æz ʃi lʊkt æt mi wɪð ʌ θɔt]
That I did not understand.
[ðæt ɑːɪ dɪd nɑt ʌndʌˈstænd]
Whoever owns it anon,
[huˈɛvʌɾ oːʊnz ɪt ʌˈnɑn]
And hears it, will never know
[ænd hɪːʌz ɪt wɪl ˈnɛvʌ noːʊ]
What a history hangs upon
[ʍɑt ʌ ˈhɪstɔɾɪ hæŋz ʌˈpɑn]
This creak from long ago.
[ðɪs kɹik fɹʌm lɑŋ ʌˈgoːʊ]

5. The Choirmaster's Burial
[ðʊ ˈkwɑːɪʌmɑstʌz ˈbɛʁɪʊl]

He often would ask us
[hi ˈɑfɛ⁽ɪ⁾n wʊd ask ʌs]
That, when he died,
[ðæt ʍɛn hi dɑːɪd]
After playing so many
[ˈɑftʌ ˈplɛːɪɪŋ soːʊ ˈmɛnɪ]
To their last rest,
[tu ðɛːʌ last ɹɛst]
If out of us any
[ɪf ɑːʊt ʌv ʌs ˈɛnɪ]
Should here abide,
[ʃʊd hɪːʌɾ ʌˈbɑːɪd]
And it would not task us,
[ænd ɪt wʊd nɑt task ʌs]
We would with our lutes
[wi wʊd wɪð ɑːʊʌ ljuts]
Play over him
[plɛːɪ ˈoːʊvʌ hɪm]
By his grave-brim
[bɑːɪ hɪz gɹɛːɪv bɹɪm]
The psalm he liked best —
[ðʊ sɑm hi lɑːɪkt bɛst]
The one whose sense suits
[ðʊ wʌn huz sɛns sjuts]
"Mount Ephraim"
[mɑːʊnt ˈifɹɛɪm]
And perhaps we should seem
[ænd pɜˈhæps wi ʃʊd sim]
To him, in Death's dream,
[tu hɪm ɪn dɛθs dɹɪm]
Like the seraphim.
[lɑːɪk ðʊ ˈsɛɾʌfɪm]
As soon as I knew
[æz sun æz ɑːɪ nju]

That his spirit was gone
[ðæt hɪz ˈspɪɾɪt wɑz gɑn]
I thought this his due,
[ɑːɪ θɔt ðɪs hɪz dju]
And spoke thereupon.
[ænd spoːʊk ˌðɛːʌɾʌˈpɑn]
"I think," said the vicar,
[ɑːɪ θɪŋk sɛd ðʊ ˈvɪkʌ]
"A read service quicker
[ʌ ɾɛd ˈsɜvɪs ˈkwɪkʌ]
Than viols out-of-doors
[ðæn ˈvɑːɪo(ʌ)lz ɑːʊt ʌv dɔːʌz]
In these frosts and hoars.
[ɪn ðiz fɹasts ænd hɔːʌz]
That old-fashioned way
[ðæt oːʊld ˈfæʃʌnd wɛːɪ]
Requires a fine day,
[ɹɪˈkwɑːɪʌz ʌ fɑːɪn dɛːɪ]
And it seems to me
[ænd ɪt simz tu mi]
It had better not be."
[ɪt hæd ˈbɛtʌ nɑt bi]
Hence, that afternoon,
[hɛns ðæt ɑftʌˈnun]
Though never knew he
[ðoːʊ ˈnɛvʌ nju hi]
That his wish could not be,
[ðæt hɪz wɪʃ kʊd nɑt bi]
To get through it faster
[tu gɛt θɹu ɪt ˈfɑstʌ]
They buried the master
[ðɛːɪ ˈbɛɾɪd ðʊ ˈmɑstʌ]
Without any tune.
[wɪðˈɑːʊt ˈɛnɪ tjun]
But 'twas said that, when
[bʌt twɑz sɛd ðæt ʍɛn]
At the dead of next night
[æt ðʊ dɛd ʌv nɛkst nɑːɪt]
The vicar looked out,
[ðʊ ˈvɪkʌ lʊkt ɑːʊt]
There struck on his ken
[ðɛːʌ stɹʌk ɑn hɪz kɛn]
Thronged roundabout,
[θɹɑŋd ˈɹɑːʊndʌbɑːʊt]
Where the frost was graying
[ʍɛːʌ ðʊ fɹɑst wɑz ˈgɹɛːɪŋ]
The headstoned grass,
[ðʊ ˈhɛdstoːʊnd gɹɑs]
A band all in white
[ʌ bænd ɔl ɪn ʍɑːɪt]
Like the saints in church-glass,
[lɑːɪk ðʊ sɛːɪnts ɪn tʃɜtʃ glɑs]
Singing and playing
[ˈsɪŋɪŋ ænd ˈplɛːɪɪŋ]
The ancient stave
[ðɪ ˈɛːɪntʃɛnt stɛːɪv]

By the choirmaster's grave.
[bɑːɪ ðʊ ˈkwɑːɪɑmɑstʌz gɹɛːɪv]
Such the tenor man told
[sʌʧ ðʊ ˈtɛnʌ mæn toːʊld]
When he had grown old.
[ʍɛn hi hæd gɹoːʊn oːʊld]

6. Proud Songstress
[pɹɑːʊd ˈsɑŋstɹɪs]

The thrushes sing as the sun is going,
[ðʊ ˈθɹʌʃɛ(ɪ)z sɪŋ æz ðʊ sʌn ɪz ˈgoːʊɪŋ]
And the finches whistle in ones and pairs,
[ænd ðʊ ˈfɪnʧɛ(ɪ)z ˈʍɪsʊl ɪn wʌnz ænd pɛːʌz]
And as it gets dark loud nightingales
[ænd æz ɪt gɛts dak lɑːʊd ˈnɑːɪtɪngɛːɪlz]
In bushes
[ɪn ˈbʊʃɛ(ɪ)z]
Pipe, as they can when April wears,
[pɑːɪp æz ðɛːɪ kæn ʍɛn ˈɛːɪpɹɪ(ʊ)l wɛːʌz]
As if all Time were theirs.
[æz ɪf ɔl tɑːɪm wɜ ðɛːʌz]
These are brand new birds of twelve-months' growing,
[ðiz ɑ bɹænd nju bɜdz ʌv twɛlv mʌnθs ˈgɹoːʊɪŋ]
Which a year ago, or less than twain,
[ʍɪʧ ʌ jiːʌr ʌˈgoːʊ ɔ lɛs ðæn twɛːɪn]
No finches were, nor nightingales,
[noːʊ ˈfɪnʧɛ(ɪ)z wɜ nɔ ˈnɑːɪtɪngɛːɪlz]
Nor thrushes,
[nɔ ˈθɹʌʃɛ(ɪ)z]
But only particles of grain,
[bʌt ˈoːʊnlɪ ˈpɑtɪkʊlz ʌv gɹɛːɪn]
And earth, and air, and rain.
[ænd ɜθ ænd ɛːʌr ænd ɹɛːɪn]

7. At the Railway Station, Upway
[æt ðʊ ˈɹɛːɪlwɛːɪ ˈstɛːɪʃʌn ˈʌpwɛːɪ]

"There is not much that I can do,
[ðɛːʌr ɪz nɑt mʌʧ ðæt ɑːɪ kæn du]
For I've no money that's quite my own!"
[fɔʁ⁽ᵗ⁾ ɑːɪv noːʊ ˈmʌnɪ ðæts kwɑːɪt mɑːɪ oːʊn]
Spoke up the pitying child–
[spoːʊk ʌp ðʊ ˈpɪtɪɪŋ ʧɑːɪld]
A little boy with a violin
[ʌ ˈlɪtʊl bɔːɪ wɪð ʌ vɑːɪoˈlɪn]
At the station before the train came in,–
[æt ðʊ ˈstɛːɪʃʌn bɪˈfɔːʌ ðʊ tɹɛːɪn kɛːɪm ɪn]
"But I can play my fiddle to you,
[bʌt ɑːɪ kæn plɛːɪ mɑːɪ ˈfɪdʊl tu ju]
And a nice one 'tis, and good in tone!"
[ænd ʌ nɑːɪs wʌn tɪz ænd gʊd ɪn toːʊn]
The man in the handcuffs smiled;
[ðʊ mæn ɪn ðʊ ˈhændkʌfs smɑːɪld]
The constable looked, and he smiled, too,
[ðʊ ˈkɑnstʌbʊl lʊkt ænd hi smɑːɪld tu]

As the fiddle began to twang;
[æz ðʊ ˈfɪdʊl bɪˈgæn tu twæŋ]
And the man in the handcuffs suddenly sang
[ænd ðʊ mæn ɪn ðʊ ˈhændkʌfs ˈsʌdɛ(ɪ)nlɪ sæŋ]
With grimful glee:
[wɪð ˈgɹɪmfʊl gli]
"This life so free
[ðɪs lɑːɪf soːʊ fɹi]
Is the thing for me!"
[ɪz ðʊ θɪŋ fɔ mi]
And the constable smiled, and said no word,
[ænd ðʊ ˈkɑnstʌbʊl smɑːɪld ænd sɛd noːʊ wɜd]
As if unconscious of what he heard;
[æz ɪf ʌnˈkɑnʃʌs ʌv ʍɑt hi hɜd]
And so they went on till the train came in–
[ænd soːʊ ðɛːɪ wɛnt ɑn tɪl ðʊ tɹɛːɪn kɛːɪm ɪn]
The convict, and boy with the violin.
[ðʊ ˈkɑnvɪkt ænd bɔːɪ wɪð ðʊ vɑːɪoˈlɪn]

8. Before Life and After
[bɪˈfɔːʌ lɑːɪf ænd ˈɑftʌ]

A time there was– as one may guess
[ʌ tɑːɪm ðɛːʌ wɑz æz wʌn mɛːɪ gɛs]
And as, indeed, earth's testimonies tell–
[ænd æz ɪnˈdid ɜθs ˈtɛstɪmoːʊnɪz tɛl]
Before the birth of consciousness,
[bɪˈfɔːʌ ðʊ bɜθ ʌv ˈkɑnʃʌsnɛ(ɪ)s]
When all went well.
[ʍɛn ɔl wɛnt wɛl]
None suffered sickness, love, or loss,
[nʌn ˈsʌfʌd ˈsɪknɛ(ɪ)s lʌv ɔ lɑs]
None knew regret, starved hope, or heart-burnings;
[nʌn nju ɹɪˈgɹɛt stɑvd hoːʊp ɔ hat ˈbɜnɪŋz]
None cared whatever crash or cross
[nʌn kɛːʌd ʍɑtˈɛvʌ kɹæʃ ɔ kɹɑs]
Brought wrack to things.
[bɹɔt ɹæk tu θɪŋz]
If something ceased, no tongue bewailed,
[ɪf ˈsʌmθɪŋ sist noːʊ tʌŋ bɪˈwɛːɪld]
If something winced and waned, no heart was wrung;
[ɪf ˈsʌmθɪŋ wɪnst ænd wɛːɪnd noːʊ hat wɑz ɹʌŋ]
If brightness dimmed, and dark prevailed,
[ɪf ˈbɹɑːɪtnɛ(ɪ)s dɪmd ænd dak pɹɪˈvɛːɪld]
No sense was stung.
[noːʊ sɛns wɑz stʌŋ]
But the disease of feeling germed,
[bʌt ðʊ dɪˈziz ʌv ˈfilɪŋ ʤɜmd]
And primal rightness took the tinct of wrong;
[ænd ˈpɹɑːɪmʊl ˈɹɑːɪtnɛ(ɪ)s tʊk ðʊ tɪŋkt ʌv ɹɑŋ]
Ere nescience shall be reaffirmed
[ɛːʌ ˈnɛsɪɛns ʃæl bi ˌɹɪʌˈfɜmd]
How long, how long?
[hɑːʊ lɑŋ hɑːʊ lɑŋ]

Song Selections

"Early One Morning"
[ˈɜli wʌn ˈmɔnɪŋ]
Folksong

Early one morning, just as the sun was rising,
[ˈɜlɪ wʌn ˈmɔnɪŋ dʒʌst æz ðʊ sʌn waz ˈɹɑːɪzɪŋ]
I heard a maid sing in the valley below.
[ɑːɪ hɜd ʌ mɛːɪd sɪŋ ɪn ðʊ ˈvælɪ bɪˈloːʊ]
"Oh, don't deceive me, Oh, never leave me!
[oːʊ doːʊnt dɪˈsiv mi oːʊ ˈnɛvʌ liv mi]
How could you use a poor maiden so?"
[haːʊ kʊd ju juz ʌ pʊːʌ ˈmɛːɪdɛ(ɪ)n soːʊ]
"O gay is the garland, fresh are the roses
[oːʊ gɛːɪ ɪz ðʊ ˈgalæ(ʌ)nd fɹɛʃ a ðʊ ˈroːʊzɛ(ɪ)z]
I've culled from the garden to bind on thy brow.
[ɑːɪv kʌld fɹʌm ðʊ ˈgadɛ(ɪ)n tu baːɪnd an ðɑːɪ bɹɑːʊ]
O don't deceive me, O do not leave me!
[oːʊ doːʊnt dɪˈsiv mi oːʊ du nat liv mi]
How could you use a poor maiden so?
[haːʊ kʊd ju juz ʌ pʊːʌ ˈmɛːɪdɛ(ɪ)n soːʊ]
Remember the vows that you made to your Mary,
[ɹɪˈmɛmbʌ ðʊ vaːʊz ðæt ju mɛːɪd tu jɔːʌ ˈmæɹɪ]
Remember the bow'r where you vowed to be true.
[ɹɪˈmɛmbʌ ðʊ ˈbaːʊʌ ʍɛːʌ ju vaːʊd tu bi tɹu]
O don't deceive me, O never leave me!
[oːʊ doːʊnt dɪˈsiv mi oːʊ ˈnɛvʌ liv mi]
How could you use a poor maiden so!
[haːʊ kʊd ju juz ʌ pʊːʌ ˈmɛːɪdɛ(ɪ)n soːʊ]
Thus sung the poor maiden, her sorrow bewailing,
[ðʌs sʌŋ ðʊ pʊːʌ ˈmɛːɪdɛ(ɪ)n hɜ ˈsaɹoːʊ bɪˈwɛːɪlɪŋ]
Thus sung the poor maid in the valley below;
[ðʌs sʌŋ ðʊ pʊːʌ mɛːɪd ɪn ðʊ ˈvælɪ bɪˈloːʊ]
"O don't deceive me! O do not leave me!
[oːʊ doːʊnt dɪˈsiv mi oːʊ du nat liv mi]
How could you use a poor maiden so?"
[haːʊ kʊd ju juz ʌ pʊːʌ ˈmɛːɪdɛ(ɪ)n soːʊ]

"O Waly, Waly"
[oːʊ ˈwɛːli ˈwɛːli]
Somerset Folksong

The water is wide I cannot get o'er,
[ðʊ ˈwɔtʌɹ ɪz waːɪd ɑːɪ kæˈnat gɛt ɔːʌ]
and neither have I wings to fly.
[ænd ˈnaːɪðʌ hæv ɑːɪ wɪŋz tu flaːɪ]
Give me a boat that will carry two,
[gɪv mi ʌ boːʊt ðæt wɪl ˈkæɹɪ tu]
and both shall row, my love and I.
[ænd boːʊθ ʃæl ɹoːʊ maːɪ lʌv ænd ɑːɪ]
O, down in the meadows the other day,
[oːʊ daːʊn ɪn ðʊ ˈmɛdoːʊz ðɪ ˈʌðʌ dɛːɪ]
A-gath'ring flowers both fine and gay,
[ʌ ˈgæðɹɪŋ flaːʊʌz boːʊθ faːɪn ænd gɛːɪ]

A-gathering flowers both red and blue,
[ʌ ˈgæðʌɹɪŋ flaːʊʌz boːʊθ ɹɛd ænd blu]
I little thought what love can do.
[ɑːɪ ˈlɪtʊl θɔt ʍat lʌv kæn du]
I leaned my back up against some oak
[ɑːɪ lind maːɪ bæk ʌp ʌˈgɛnst sʌm oːʊk]
thinking that he was a trusty tree;
[ˈθɪŋkɪn ðæt hi waz ʌ ˈtɹʌstɪ tɹi]
But first he bended, and then he broke;
[bʌt fɜst hi ˈbɛndɛ(ɪ)d ænd ðɛn hi bɹoːʊk]
and so did my false love to me.
[ænd soːʊ dɪd maːɪ fɔls lʌv tu mi]
A ship there is, and she sails the sea,
[ʌ ʃɪp ðɛːʌɹ ɪz ænd ʃi sɛːɪlz ðʊ si]
She's loaded deep as deep can be,
[ʃiz ˈloːʊdɛ(ɪ)d dip æz dip kæn bi]
But not so deep as the love I'm in:
[bʌt nat soːʊ dip æz ðʊ lʌv ɑːɪm ɪn]
I know not if I sink or swim.
[ɑːɪ noːʊ nat ɪf ɑːɪ sɪŋk ɔ swɪm]
O, love is handsome and love is fine,
[oːʊ lʌv ɪz ˈhænsʌm ænd lʌv ɪz faːɪn]
and love's a jewel while it is new,
[ænd lʌvz ʌ ˈdʒuːɛ(ʊ)l ʍaːɪl ɪt ɪz nju]
But when it is old, it groweth cold,
[bʌt ʍɛn ɪt ɪz oːʊld ɪt ˈgɹoːʊɛ(ɪ)θ koːʊld]
and fades away like morning dew.
[ænd fɛːɪdz ʌˈwɛːɪ laːɪk ˈmɔnɪŋ dju]

"Oliver Cromwell"
[ˈalɪvʌ ˈkɹamwɛl]
Folksong

Oliver Cromwell lay buried and dead,
[ˈalɪvʌ ˈkɹamwɛl lɛːɪ ˈbɛɹɪd ænd dɛd]
Hee-haw– buried and dead,
[hi hɔ ˈbɛɹɪd ænd dɛd]
There grew an old apple-tree over his head,
[ðɛːʌ gɹu æn oːʊld ˈæpʊl tɹi ˈoːʊvʌ hɪz hɛd]
Hee-haw– over his head.
[hi hɔ ˈoːʊvʌ hɪz hɛd]
The apples were ripe and ready to fall;
[ðɪ ˈæpʊlz wɜ ɹaːɪp ænd ˈɹɛdɪ tu fɔl]
Hee-haw– ready to fall;
[hi hɔ ˈɹɛdɪ tu fɔl]
There came an old woman to gather them all,
[ðɛːʌ kɛːɪm æn oːʊld ˈwʊmæ(ʌ)n tu ˈgæðʌ ðɛm ɔl]
Hee-haw– gather them all.
[hi hɔ ˈgæðʌ ðɛm ɔl]
Oliver rose and gave her a drop,
[ˈalɪvʌ ɹoːʊz ænd gɛːɪv hɜ(ʳ) ʌ dɹap]
Hee-haw– gave her a drop,
[hi hɔ gɛːɪv hɜ(ʳ) ʌ dɹap]
Which made the old woman go hippety hop,
[ʍɪtʃ mɛːɪd ðɪ oːʊld ˈwʊmæ(ʌ)n goːʊ ˈhɪpɪtɪ hap]

Hee-haw– hippety hop.
[hi hɔ ˈhɪpɪtɪ hap]
The saddle and bridle, they lie on the shelf,
[ðʊ ˈsædʊl ænd ˈbɹɑːɪdʊl ðɛːɪ lɑːɪ an ðʊ ʃɛlf]
Hee-haw– lie on the shelf,
[hi hɔ lɑːɪ an ðʊ ʃɛlf]
If you want any more you can sing it yourself,
[ɪf ju want ˈɛnɪ mɔːʌ ju kæn sɪŋ ɪt jɔːʌˈsɛlf]
Hee-haw– sing it yourself.
[hi hɔ sɪŋ ɪt jɔːʌˈsɛlf]

"She's Like the Swallow"
[ʃiz lɑːɪk ðʊ ˈswaloːʊ]
Folksongs

She's like the swallow that flies so high,
[ʃiz lɑːɪk ðʊ ˈswaloːʊ ðæt flɑːɪz soːʊ hɑːɪ]
She's like the river that never runs dry,
[ʃiz lɑːɪk ðʊ ˈɾɪvʌ ðæt ˈnɛvʌ ɾʌnz dɹɑːɪ]
She's like the sunshine on the lee shore,
[ʃiz lɑːɪk ðʊ ˈsʌnʃɑːɪn an ðʊ li ʃɔːʌ]
I love my love and love is no more.
[ɑːɪ lʌv mɑːɪ lʌv ænd lʌv ɪz noːʊ mɔːʌ]
'Twas out in the garden this fair maid did go,
[twɑz ɑːʊt ɪn ðʊ ˈgadɛ(ɪ)n ðɪs fɛːʌ mɛːɪd dɪd goːʊ]
A-picking the beautiful primerose;
[ʌ ˈpɪkɪŋ ðʊ ˈbjutɪfʊl ˈpɹɪmʌɾoːʊz]
The more she pluck'd the more she pulled
[ðʊ mɔːʌ ʃi plʌkt ðʊ mɔːʌ ʃi pʊld]
Until she got her aperon full.
[ʌnˈtɪl ʃi gat hɜ ˈɛːɪpʌɾʌn fʊl]
It's out of those roses she made a bed,
[ɪts ɑːʊt ʌv ðoːʊz ˈɹoːʊzɛ(ɪ)z ʃi mɛːɪd ʌ bɛd]
A stony pillow for her head.
[ʌ ˈstoːʊnɪ ˈpɪloːʊ fɔ hɜ hɛd]
She laid her down, no word did say,
[ʃi lɛːɪd hɜ dɑːʊn noːʊ wɜd dɪd sɛːɪ]
Until this fair maid's heart did break.
[ʌnˈtɪl ðɪs fɛːʌ mɛːɪdz hat dɪd bɹɛːɪk]
She's like the swallow that flies so high...

"Sweet Polly Oliver"
[swit ˈpalɪ ˈalɪvʌ]
Folksong

As sweet Polly Oliver lay musing in bed,
[æz swit ˈpalɪ ˈalɪvʌ lɛːɪ ˈmjuzɪŋ ɪn bɛd]
A sudden strange fancy came into her head.
[ʌ ˈsʌdɛ(ɪ)n stɹɛːɪndʒ ˈfænsɪ kɛːɪm ˈɪntu hɜ hɛd]
"Nor father nor mother shall make me false prove,
[nɔ ˈfaðʌ nɔ ˈmʌðʌ ʃæl mɛːɪk mi fɔls pɹʊv]
I'll 'list as a soldier, and follow my love."
[ɑːɪl lɪst æz ʌ ˈsoːʊldjʌɾ ænd ˈfaloːʊ mɑːɪ lʌv]
So early next morning she softly arose
[soːʊ ˈɜlɪ nɛkst ˈmɔnɪŋ ʃi ˈsaftlɪ ʌˈɾoːʊz]

And dressed herself up in her dead brother's clothes.
[ænd dɹɛst hɜˈsɛlf ʌp ɪn hɜ dɛd ˈbɹʌðʌz kloːʊðz]
She cut her hair close and she stained her face brown,
[ʃi kʌt hɜ hɛːʌ kloːʊs ænd ʃi stɛːɪnd hɜ fɛːɪs bɹɑːʊn]
And went for a soldier to fair London Town.
[ænd wɛnt fɔʁ⁽ʳ⁾ ʌ ˈsoːʊldjʌ tu fɛːʌ ˈlʌndʌn tɑːʊn]
Then up spoke the sergeant one day at his drill.
[ðɛn ʌp spoːʊk ðʊ ˈsadʒæ(ɪ)nt wʌn dɛːɪ æt hɪz dɹɪl]
"Now who's good for nursing? A captain, he's ill."
[nɑːʊ huz gʊd fɔ ˈnɜsɪŋ ʌ ˈkæptæ(ɪ)n hiz ɪl]
"I'm ready," said Polly. To nurse him she's gone,
[ɑːɪm ˈɹɛdɪ sɛd ˈpalɪ tu nɜs hɪm ʃiz gan]
And finds it's her true love all wasted and wan.
[ænd fɑːɪndz ɪts hɜ tru lʌv ɔl ˈwɛːɪstɛ(ɪ)d ænd wan]
The first week the doctor kept shaking his head,
[ðʊ fɜst wik ðʊ ˈdaktʌ kɛpt ˈʃɛːɪkɪŋ hɪz hɛd]
"No nursing, young fellow, can save him," he said.
[noːʊ ˈnɜsɪŋ jʌŋ ˈfɛloːʊ kæn sɛːɪv hɪm hi sɛd]
But when Polly Oliver had nursed him back to life,
[bʌt ʍɛn ˈpalɪ ˈalɪvʌ hæd nɜst hɪm bæk tu lɑːɪf]
He cried,
[hi kɾɑːɪd]
"You have cherished him as if you were his wife."
[ju hæv ˈtʃɛɾɪʃt hɪm æz ɪf ju wɜ hɪz wɑːɪf]
Oh, then Polly Oliver, she burst into tears
[oːʊ ðɛn ˈpalɪ ˈalɪvʌ ʃi bɜst ˈɪntu tɪːʌz]
And told the good doctor her hopes and her fears,
[ænd toːʊld ðʊ gʊd ˈdaktʌ hɜ hoːʊps ænd hɜ fɪːʌz]
And very shortly after, for better or for worse,
[ænd ˈvɛɾɪ ˈʃɔtlɪ ˈaftʌ fɔ ˈbɛtʌɾ ɔ fɔ wɜs]
The captain took joyfully his pretty soldier nurse.
[ðʊ ˈkæptæ(ɪ)n tʊk ˈdʒɔːɪfʊlɪ hɪz ˈpɹɪtɪ ˈsoːʊldjʌ nɜs]

"The Ash Grove"
[ði æʃ gɹoːʊv]
Folksong

Down yonder green valley where streamlets meander,
[dɑːʊn ˈjandʌ gɹin ˈvælɪ ʍɛːʌ ˈstɹimlɛ(ɪ)ts mɪˈændʌ]
When twilight is fading, I pensively rove,
[ʍɛn ˈtwɑːɪlɑːɪt ɪz ˈfɛːɪdɪŋ ɑːɪ ˈpɛnsɪvlɪ ɾoːʊv]
Or at the bright noontide in solitude wander
[ɔʁ⁽ʳ⁾ æt ðʊ bɹɑːɪt ˈnuntɑːɪd ɪn ˈsalɪtjud ˈwandʌ]
Amid the dark shades of the lonely Ash grove.
[ʌˈmɪd ðʊ dak ʃɛːɪdz ʌv ðʊ ˈloːʊnlɪ æʃ gɹoːʊv]
'Twas there while the blackbird was joyfully singing,
[twɑz ðɛːʌ ʍɑːɪl ðʊ ˈblækbɜd waz ˈdʒɔːɪfʊlɪ ˈsɪŋɪŋ]
I first met my dear one, the joy of my heart;
[ɑːɪ fɜst mɛt mɑːɪ dɪːʌ wʌn ðʊ dʒɔːɪ ʌv mɑːɪ hat]
Around us for gladness the bluebells were ringing.
[ʌˈɾɑːʊnd ʌs fɔ ˈglædnɛ(ɪ)s ðʊ ˈblubɛlz wɜ ˈɾɪŋɪŋ]
Ah! then little thought I how soon we should part.
[a ðɛn ˈlɪtʊl θɔt ɑːɪ hɑːʊ sun wi ʃʊd pat]
Still glows the bright sunshine
[stɪl gloːʊz ðʊ bɹɑːɪt ˈsʌnʃɑːɪn]

o'er valley and mountain,
[ɔːʌ ˈvælɪ ænd ˈmɑːʊntæ(ɪ)n]
Still warbles the blackbird his note from the tree;
[stɪl ˈwɔbʊlz ðʊ ˈblækbɜd hɪz noːʊt fɪʌm ðʊ tɹi]
Still trembles the moonbeam
[stɪl ˈtɹɛmbʊlz ðʊ ˈmunbim]
on streamlet and fountain,
[ɑn ˈstɹimlɛ(ɪ)t ænd ˈfɑːʊntæ(ɪ)n]
But what are the beauties of nature to me?
[bʌt ʍat ɑ ðʊ ˈbjutɪz ʌv ˈnɛːɪʧʊ(ʌ) tu mi]
With sorrow, deep sorrow, my bosom is laden,
[wɪð ˈsɑɹoːʊ dip ˈsɑɹoːʊ maːɪ ˈbʊzʌm ɪz ˈlɛːɪdɛ(ɪ)n]
All day I go mourning in search of my love.
[ɔl dɛːɪ aːɪ goːʊ ˈmɔnɪŋ ɪn sɜʧ ʌv maːɪ lʌv]
Ye echoes, O tell me, where is the sweet maiden?
[ji ˈɛkoːʊz oːʊ tɛl mi ʍɛːʌɾ ɪz ðʊ swit ˈmɛːɪdɛ(ɪ)n]
She sleeps 'neath the green turf down by the Ash grove.
[ʃi slips niθ ðʊ gɹin tɜf daːʊn baːɪ ði æʃ gɹoːʊv]

"The Brisk Young Widow"
[ðʊ bɹɪsk jʌŋ ˈwɪdoːʊ]
Folksong

In Chester town there liv'd
[ɪn ˈʧɛstʌ taːʊn ðɛːʌ lɪvd]
A brisk young widow.
[ʌ bɹɪsk jʌŋ ˈwɪdoːʊ]
For beauty and fine clothes
[fɔ ˈbjutɪ ænd faːɪn kloːʊðz]
None could excel her.
[nʌn kʊd ɪkˈsɛl hɜ]
She was proper stout and tall,
[ʃi waz ˈpɹɑpʌ staːʊt ænd tɔl]
Her fingers long and small,
[hɜ ˈfɪŋgʌz lɑŋ ænd smɔl]
She's a comely dame withall,
[ʃiz ʌ ˈkʌmlɪ dɛːɪm wɪðˈɔl]
She's a brisk young widow.
[ʃiz ʌ bɹɪsk jʌŋ ˈwɪdoːʊ]
A lover soon there came,
[ʌ ˈlʌvʌ sun ðɛːʌ kɛːɪm]
A brisk young farmer,
[ʌ bɹɪsk jʌŋ ˈfɑmʌ]
With his hat turn'd up all round,
[wɪð hɪz hæt tɜnd ʌp ɔl ɹaːʊnd]
Seeking to gain her.
[ˈsikɪŋ tu gɛːɪn hɜ]
"My dear, for love of you
[maːɪ dɪːʌ fɔ lʌv ʌv ju]
This wide world I'd go through
[ðɪs waːɪd wɜld aːɪd goːʊ θɹu]
If you will but prove true
[ɪf ju wɪl bʌt pɹuv tɹu]
You shall wed a farmer."
[ju ʃæl wɛd ʌ ˈfɑmʌ]

Says she: "I'm not for you
[sɛz ʃi aːɪm nɑt fɔ ju]
Nor no such fellow.
[nɔ noːʊ sʌʧ ˈfɛloːʊ]
I'm for a lively lad
[aːɪm fɔʁ⁽ʳ⁾ ʌ ˈlaːɪvlɪ læd]
With lands and riches,
[wɪð lændz ænd ˈɹɪʧɛ(ɪ)z]
'Tis not your hogs and yowes
[tɪz nɑt jɔːʌ hɑgz ænd jɑːʊz]
Can maintain furbelows,
[kæn mɛːɪnˈtɛːɪn ˈfɜbɪloːʊz]
My silk and satin clothes
[maːɪ sɪlk ænd ˈsætɪn kloːʊðz]
Are all my glory."
[ɑr ɔl maːɪ ˈglɔɹɪ]
"O madam, don't be coy
[oːʊ ˈmædæ(ʌ)m doːʊnt bi kɔːɪ]
For all your glory,
[fɔʁ⁽ʳ⁾ ɔl jɔːʌ ˈglɔɹɪ]
For fear of another day
[fɔ fɪːʌɾ ʌv ʌˈnʌðʌ dɛːɪ]
And another story.
[ænd ʌˈnʌðʌ ˈstɔɹɪ]
If the world on you should frown
[ɪf ðʊ wɜld ɑn ju ʃʊd fɹaːʊn]
Your top-knot must come down
[jɔːʌ tɑp nɑt mʌst kʌm daːʊn]
To a Lindsey-woolsey gown.
[tu ʌ ˈlɪndzɪ ˈwʊlzɪ gɑːʊn]
Where is then your glory?"
[ʍɛːʌɾ ɪz ðɛn jɔːʌ ˈglɔɹɪ]
At last there came that way
[æt last ðɛːʌ kɛːɪm ðæt wɛːɪ]
A sooty collier,
[ʌ ˈsʊtɪ ˈkɑljʌ]
With his hat bent down all round,
[wɪð hɪz hæt bɛnt daːʊn ɔl ɹaːʊnd]
And soon he did gain her:
[ænd sun hi dɪd gɛːɪn hɜ]
Whereat the farmer swore;
[ʍɛːʌɾˈæt ðʊ ˈfɑmʌ swɔːʌ]
"The widow's mazed, I'm sure.
[ðʊ ˈwɪdoːʊz mɛːɪzd aːɪm ʃʊːʌ]
I'll never court no more
[aːɪl ˈnɛvʌ kɔt noːʊ mɔːʌ]
A brisk young widow!"
[ʌ bɹɪsk jʌŋ ˈwɪdoːʊ]

"The Foggy, Foggy Dew"
[ðʊ ˈfɑgi ˈfɑgi dju]
Folksong

When I was a bachelor I lived all alone,
[ʍɛn aːɪ waz ʌ ˈbæʧʊlɔ(ʌ)r aːɪ lɪvd ɔl ʌˈloːʊn]

and worked at the weaver's trade
[ænd wɜkt æt ðʊ 'wivʌz tɹɛːɪd]
And the only, only thing that I ever did wrong,
[ænd ði 'oːʊnlɪ 'oːʊnlɪ θɪŋ ðæt aːɪ 'ɛvʌ dɪd ɹaŋ]
was to woo a fair young maid.
[waz tu wu ʌ fɛːʌ jʌŋ mɛːɪd]
I wooed her in the winter time, and in the summer too.
[aːɪ wud hɜ⁽ʳ⁾ ɪn ðʊ 'wɪntʌ taːɪm ænd ɪn ðʊ 'sʌmʌ tu]
And the only, only thing I did that was wrong,
[ænd ði 'oːʊnlɪ 'oːʊnlɪ θɪŋ aːɪ dɪd ðæt waz ɹaŋ]
was to keep her from the foggy, foggy dew.
[waz tu kip hɜ fɹʌm ðʊ 'fagɪ 'fagɪ dju]
One night she came to my bedside
[wʌn naːɪt ʃi kɛːɪm tu maːɪ 'bɛdsaːɪd]
when I lay fast asleep,
[ʌɛn aːɪ lɛːɪ fast ʌ'slip]
She laid her head upon my bed and she began to weep.
[ʃi lɛːɪd hɜ hɛd ʌ'pan maːɪ bɛd ænd ʃi bɪ'gæn tu wip]
She sighed, she cried, she damn' near died,
[ʃi saːɪd ʃi kɹaːɪd ʃi dæm nɪːʌ daːɪd]
she said: "What shall I do?"
[ʃi sɛd ʌat ʃæl aːɪ du]
So I hauled her into bed and I covered up her head,
[soːʊ aːɪ hɔld hɜ⁽ʳ⁾ 'ɪntu bɛd ænd aːɪ 'kʌvʌd ʌp hɜ hɛd]
just to keep her from the foggy, foggy dew.
[dʒʌst tu kip hɜ fɹʌm ðʊ 'fagɪ 'fagɪ dju]
Oh I am a bachelor and I live with my son,
[oːʊ aːɪ æm ʌ 'bætʃʊlɔ⁽ʌ⁾r ænd aːɪ lɪv wɪð maːɪ sʌn]
and we work at the weaver's trade.
[ænd wi wɜk æt ðʊ 'wivʌz tɹɛːɪd]
And ev'ry single time that I look into his eyes,
[ænd 'ɛvɹɪ 'sɪŋgʊl taːɪm ðæt aːɪ lʊk 'ɪntu hɪz aːɪz]
he reminds me of the fair young maid.
[hi rɪ'maːɪndz mi ʌv ðʊ fɛːʌ jʌŋ mɛːɪd]
He reminds me of the winter time,
[hi rɪ'maːɪndz mi ʌv ðʊ 'wɪntʌ taːɪm]
and of the summer too,
[ænd ʌv ðʊ 'sʌmʌ tu]
And of the many, many times
[ænd ʌv ðʊ 'mɛnɪ 'mɛnɪ taːɪmz]
that I held her in my arms,
[ðæt aːɪ hɛld hɜ⁽ʳ⁾ ɪn maːɪ amz]
just to keep her from the foggy, foggy dew.
[dʒʌst tu kip hɜ fɹʌm ðʊ 'fagɪ 'fagɪ dju]

"The Salley Gardens"
[ðʊ 'sælɪ 'gadɪnz]
Yeats, William Butler (Ir. 1865-1939)

Down by the Salley gardens
[daːʊn baːɪ ðʊ 'sælɪ 'gadɛ(ɪ)nz]
my love and I did meet,
[maːɪ lʌv ænd aːɪ dɪd mit]
She passed the Salley gardens
[ʃi past ðʊ 'sælɪ 'gadɛ(ɪ)nz]

with little snow-white feet.
[wɪð 'lɪtʊl snoːʊ ʌaːɪt fit]
She bid me take love easy,
[ʃi bɪd mi tɛːɪk lʌv 'izɪ]
as the leaves grow on the tree,
[æz ðʊ livz gɹoːʊ an ðʊ tɹi]
But I being young and foolish,
[bʌt aːɪ 'biɪŋ jʌŋ ænd 'fulɪʃ]
with her did not agree.
[wɪð hɜ dɪd nat ʌ'gɹi]
In a field by the river
[ɪn ʌ fild baːɪ ðʊ 'rɪvʌ]
my love and I did stand,
[maːɪ lʌv ænd aːɪ dɪd stænd]
And on my leaning shoulder
[ænd an maːɪ 'linɪŋ 'ʃoːʊldʌ]
she laid her snow-white hand.
[ʃi lɛːɪd hɜ snoːʊ ʌaːɪt hænd]
She bid me take life easy
[ʃi bɪd mi tɛːɪk laːɪf 'izɪ]
as the grass grows on the weirs,
[æz ðʊ gɹas gɹoːʊz an ðʊ wɪːʌz]
But I was young and foolish,
[bʌt aːɪ waz jʌŋ ænd 'fulɪʃ]
and now am full of tears.
[ænd naːʊ æm fʊl ʌv tɪːʌz]

"The Trees They Grow So High"
[ðʊ tɹiz ðɛːɪ gɹoːʊ soːʊ haːɪ]
British Folksong

The trees they grow so high
[ðʊ tɹiz ðɛːɪ gɹoːʊ soːʊ haːɪ]
and the leaves they do grow green,
[ænd ðʊ livz ðɛːɪ du gɹoːʊ gɹin]
And many a cold winter's night
[ænd 'mɛnɪ ʌ koːʊld 'wɪntʌz naːɪt]
my love and I have seen.
[maːɪ lʌv ænd aːɪ hæv sin]
Of a cold winter's night,
[ʌv ʌ koːʊld 'wɪntʌz naːɪt]
my love, you and I alone have been,
[maːɪ lʌv ju ænd aːɪ ʌ'loːʊn hæv bin]
Whilst my bonny boy is young,
[ʌaːɪlst maːɪ 'banɪ bɔːɪ ɪz jʌŋ]
He's a-growing.
[hiz ʌ 'gɹoːʊɪŋ]
Growing, growing,
['gɹoːʊɪŋ 'gɹoːʊɪŋ]
Whilst my bonny boy is young
[ʌaːɪlst maːɪ 'banɪ bɔːɪ ɪz jʌŋ]
he's a-growing.
[hiz ʌ 'gɹoːʊɪŋ]
O father, dearest father,
[oːʊ 'faðʌ 'dɪːʌɹɛ(ɪ)st 'faðʌ]

You've done to me great wrong,
[juv dʌn tu mi gɹɛːɪt ɹaŋ]
You've tied me to a boy
[juv taːɪd mi tu ʌ bɔːɪ]
when you know he is too young.
[ʍɛn ju noːʊ hi ɪz tu jʌŋ]
O daughter, dearest daughter,
[oːʊ 'dɔtʌ 'dɪːʌɾɛ(ɪ)st 'dɔtʌɾ]
If you wait a little while,
[ɪf ju wɛːɪt ʌ 'lɪtʊl ʍaːɪl]
A lady you shall be
[ʌ 'lɛːɪdɪ ju ʃæl bi]
while he's growing.
[ʍaːɪl hiz 'gɹoːʊɪŋ]
Growing, growing,
['gɹoːʊɪŋ 'gɹoːʊɪŋ]
a lady you shall be
[ʌ 'lɛːɪdɪ ju ʃæl bi]
while he's growing.
[ʍaːɪl hiz 'gɹoːʊɪŋ]
I'll send your love to college
[aːɪl sɛnd jɔːʌ lʌv tu 'kalɛ(ɪ)dʒ]
all for a year or two,
[ɔl fɔʁ⁽ʳ⁾ ʌ jiːʌɾ ɔ tu]
And then in the mean-time
[ænd ðɛn ɪn ðʊ min taːɪm]
he will do for you;
[hi wɪl du fɔ ju]
I'll buy him white ribbons,
[aːɪl baːɪ hɪm ʍaːɪt 'ɹɪb(ʌ)nz]
Tie them round his bonny waist
[taːɪ ðɛm ɹaːʊnd hɪz 'banɪ wɛːɪst]
To let the ladies know
[tu lɛt ðʊ 'lɛːɪdɪz noːʊ]
that he's married.
[ðæt hiz 'mæɹɪd]
Married, married,
['mæɹɪd 'mæɹɪd]
to let the ladies know
[tu lɛt ðʊ 'lɛːɪdɪz noːʊ]
that he's married.
[ðæt hiz 'mæɹɪd]
I went up to the college
[aːɪ wɛnt ʌp tu ðʊ 'kalɛ(ɪ)dʒ]
and I looked over the wall,
[ænd aːɪ lʊkt 'oːʊvʌ ðʊ wɔl]
Saw four and twenty gentlemen
[sɔ fɔːʌɾ ænd 'twɛntɪ 'dʒɛntʊlmɛ(ɪ)n]
playing at bat and ball.
['plɛːɪɪŋ æt bæt ænd bɔl]
I called for my true love,
[aːɪ kɔld fɔ maːɪ tru lʌv]
but they would not let him come,
[bʌt ðɛːɪ wʊd nat lɛt hɪm kʌm]
All because he was a young boy
[ɔl bɪ'kɔz hi waz ʌ jʌŋ bɔːɪ]

and growing.
[ænd 'gɹoːʊɪŋ]
Growing, growing,
['gɹoːʊɪŋ 'gɹoːʊɪŋ]
All because he was a young boy
[ɔl bɪ'kɔz hi waz ʌ jʌŋ bɔːɪ]
and growing.
[ænd 'gɹoːʊɪŋ]
At the age of sixteen,
[æt ði ɛːɪdʒ ʌv 'sɪks'tin]
he was a married man
[hi waz ʌ 'mæɹɪd mæn]
And at the age of seventeen
[ænd æt ði ɛːɪdʒ ʌv 'sɛvɛ(ɪ)n'tin]
he was a father to a son.
[hi waz ʌ 'faðʌ tu ʌ sʌn]
And at the age of eighteen
[ænd æt ði ɛːɪdʒ ʌv 'ɛːɪ'tin]
The grass grew over him,
[ðʊ gɹas gɹu 'oːʊvʌ hɪm]
Cruel death soon put an end
['kɹuːɛ(ʊ)l dɛθ sun pʊt æn ɛnd]
to his growing,
[tu hɪz 'gɹoːʊɪŋ]
Growing, growing,
['gɹoːʊɪŋ 'gɹoːʊɪŋ]
cruel death soon put an end
['kɹuːɛ(ʊ)l dɛθ sun pʊt æn ɛnd]
to his growing.
[tu hɪz 'gɹoːʊɪŋ]
And now my love is dead
[ænd naːʊ maːɪ lʌv ɪz dɛd]
and in his grave doth lie.
[ænd ɪn hɪz gɹɛːɪv dʌθ laːɪ]
The green grass grows o'er him
[ðʊ gɹin gɹas gɹoːʊz ɔːʌ hɪm]
So very, very high.
[soːʊ 'vɛɹɪ 'vɛɹɪ haːɪ]
I'll sit and I'll mourn
[aːɪl sɪt ænd aːɪl mɔn]
his fate until the day I die,
[hɪz fɛːɪt ʌn'tɪl ðʊ dɛːɪ aːɪ daːɪ]
and I'll watch all o'er his child
[ænd aːɪl watʃ ɔl ɔːʌ hɪz tʃaːɪld]
while he's growing,
[ʍaːɪl hiz 'gɹoːʊɪŋ]
Growing, growing,
['gɹoːʊɪŋ 'gɹoːʊɪŋ]
and I'll watch all o'er his child
[ænd aːɪl watʃ ɔl ɔːʌ hɪz tʃaːɪld]
while he's growing.
[ʍaːɪl hiz 'gɹoːʊɪŋ]

"Tis the Last Rose of Summer"
[tɪz ðʊ last ɹoːʊz ʌv ˈsʌmʌ]
Moore, Thomas (Ir. 1779-1852)

'Tis the last rose of summer,
[tɪz ðʊ last ɹoːʊz ʌv ˈsʌmʌ]
Left blooming alone;
[lɛft ˈblumɪŋ ʌˈloːʊn]
All her lovely companions
[ɔl hɜ ˈlʌvlɪ kʌmˈpænjʌnz]
Are faded and gone;
[ɑ ˈfɛːɪdɛ(ɪ)d ænd gɑn]
No flow'r of her kindred,
[noːʊ flɑːʊɾ ʌv hɜ ˈkɪndɹɛ(ɪ)d]
No rosebud is nigh
[noːʊ ˈɾoːʊzbʌd ɪz nɑːɪ]
To reflect back her blushes,
[tu ɹɪˈflɛkt bæk hɜ ˈblʌʃɛ(ɪ)z]
Or give sigh for sigh.
[ɔ gɪv sɑːɪ fɔ sɑːɪ]
I'll not leave thee, thou lone one,
[ɑːɪl nɑt liv ði ðɑːʊ loːʊn wʌn]
To pine on the stem;
[tu pɑːɪn ɑn ðʊ stɛm]
Since the lovely are sleeping,
[sɪns ðʊ ˈlʌvlɪ ɑ ˈslipɪŋ]
Go, sleep thou with them;
[goːʊ slip ðɑːʊ wɪð ðɛm]
Thus kindly I scatter
[ðʌs ˈkɑːɪndlɪ ɑːɪ ˈskætʌ]
Thy leaves o'er the bed
[ðɑːɪ livz ɔːʌ ðʊ bɛd]
Where thy mates of the garden
[ʍɛːʌ ðɑːɪ mɛːɪts ʌv ðʊ ˈgɑdɛ(ɪ)n]
Lie senseless and dead.
[lɑːɪ ˈsɛnslɛ(ɪ)s ænd dɛd]
So soon may I follow,
[soːʊ sun mɛːɪ ɑːɪ ˈfaloːʊ]
When friendships decay,
[ʍɛn ˈfɹɛndʃɪps dɪˈkɛːɪ]
And from Love's shining circle
[ænd fɹʌm lʌvz ˈʃɑːɪnɪŋ ˈsɜkʊl]
The gems drop away!
[ðʊ dʒɛmz dɹɑp ʌˈwɛːɪ]
When true hearts lie wither'd.
[ʍɛn tɾu hɑts lɑːɪ ˈwɪðʌd]
And fond ones are flown,
[ænd fɑnd wʌnz ɑ floːʊn]
Oh! who would inhabit
[oːʊ hu wʊd ɪnˈhæbɪt]
This bleak world alone?
[ðɪs blik wɜld ʌˈloːʊn]

Burleigh, Henry (Harry T.)
(Am. 1866-1949)

Song Selections

"Balm in Gilead"
[bɑm ɪn ˈgɪliˌæd]
Spiritual

CHORUS:
There is a balm in Gilead,
[ðɛːʁ ɪz ʌ bɑm ɪn ˈgɪliˌæd]
To make the wounded whole
[tu mɛːɪk ðʌ ˈwundɛ(ɪ)d hoːʊl]
There is a balm in Gilead,
[ðɛːʁ ɪz ʌ bɑm ɪn ˈgɪliˌæd]
To heal the sin sick soul.
[tu hil ðʌ sɪn sɪk soːʊl]
1. Sometimes I feel discouraged,
[ˈsʌmtɑːɪmz ɑːɪ fil dɪsˈkʊʁæ(ɪ)dʒd]
And think my work's in vain,
[ænd θɪŋk mɑːɪ wɜks ɪn vɛːɪn]
But then the Holy Spirit,
[bʌt ðɛn ðʌ ˈhoːʊlɪ ˈspɪʁɪt]
Revives my soul again.
[ɹɪˈvɑːɪvz mɑːɪ soːʊl ʌˈgɛn]
CHORUS
2. If you can preach like Peter,
[ɪf ju kæn pɹitʃ lɑːɪk ˈpidʌ]
If you can pray like Paul,
[ɪf ju kæn pɹɛːɪ lɑːɪk pɔl]
Go home and tell your neighbor,
[goːʊ hoːʊm ænd tɛl jɔːʌ ˈnɛːɪbɔ]
"He died to save us all."
[hi dɑːɪd tu sɛːɪv ʌs ɔl]
CHORUS

"Deep River"
[dip ˈɹɪvʁ]
Spiritual

Deep river, my home is over Jordan,
[dip ˈɹɪvʌ mɑ hoːʊm ɪz ˈoːʊvʌ ˈdʒɔdʌ(ɪ)n]
Deep river, Lord, I want to
[dip ˈɹɪvʌ lɔd ɑ wɑn tu]
cross over into campground.
[kɹɑs ˈoːʊvʌʁ ˈɪntu ˈkæmpgɹɑːʊnd]
Oh, don't you want to go to that gospel feast,
[oːʊ doːʊnt ju wɑnt tu goːʊ tu ðæt ˈgɑspʊl fist]
That promised land where all is peace?
[ðæt ˈpɹɑmɪst lænd wɛːʌʁ ɔl ɪz pis]
Deep river, my home is over Jordan...

"Go Down, Moses"
[goːʊ daːʊn ˈmoːʊzɪs]
Spiritual

When Israel was in Egypt's lan'
[wɛn ˈɪzɹɑɛl waz ɪn ˈɪdʒɪpts læn(d)]
Let my people go,
[lɛt maːɪ ˈpipʊl goːʊ]
Oppress'd so hard they could not stand,
[oˈpɹɛst soːʊ had ðɛːɪ kʊd nat stænd]
Let my people go.
[lɛt maːɪ ˈpipʊl goːʊ]
Go down, Moses,
[goːʊ daːʊn ˈmoːʊzɛ(ɪ)s]
'Way down in Egypt's lan',
[wɛːɪ daːʊn ɪn ˈɪdʒɪpts læn(d)]
Tell ole Pharaoh,
[tɛl oːʊl ˈfɛʁoːʊ]
To let my people go.
[tu lɛt maːɪ ˈpipʊl goːʊ]
Thus saith the Lord, bold Moses said,
[ðʌs ˈsɛːɪɛ(ɪ)θ ðʌ lɔd boːʊld ˈmoːʊzɛ(ɪ)s sɛd]
Let my people go,
[lɛt maːɪ ˈpipʊl goːʊ]
If not I'll smite your first born dead,
[ɪf nat aːɪl smaːɪt jɔːʌ fɜst bɔn dɛd]
Let my people go.
[lɛt maːɪ ˈpipʊl goːʊ]
Go down, Moses,
[goːʊ daːʊn ˈmoːʊzɛ(ɪ)s]
'Way down in Egypt's lan'
[wɛːɪ daːʊn ɪn ˈɪdʒɪpts læn(d)]
Tell ole Pharaoh
[tɛl oːʊl ˈfɛʁoːʊ]
To let my people go!
[tu lɛt maːɪ ˈpipʊl goːʊ]

"Go, Tell It on de Mountains"
[goːʊ tɛl ɪt an dʌ ˈmaːʊntɪnz]
Spiritual

1. When I was a learner,
[wɛn aːɪ waz ʌ ˈlɜnʌ]
I sought both night and day,
[aːɪ sɔt boːʊθ naːɪt ænd dɛːɪ]
I asked the Lord to help me,
[aːɪ æskt ðʌ lɔd tu hɛlp mi]
An' He showed me the way.
[æn hi ʃoːʊd mi ðʌ wɛːɪ]
CHORUS
Go tell it on de mountains;
[goːʊ tɛl ɪt an dʌ ˈmaːʊntæ(ɪ)nz]
Over the hills an' ev'rywhere:
[ˈoːʊvʌ ðʌ hɪlz æn ˈɛvɹɪwɛːʌ]
Go tell it on de mountains,
[goːʊ tɛl ɪt an dʌ ˈmaːʊntæ(ɪ)nz]

Our Jesus Christ is born.
[aːʊʌ ˈdʒizʌs kɹaːɪst ɪz bɔn]
2. While shepherds kept their watching;
[waːɪl ˈʃɛpʌdz kɛpt ðɛːʌ ˈwatʃɪŋ]
O'er wand'ring flock by night;
[ɔːʌ ˈwandɹɪŋ flak baːɪ naːɪt]
Behold! From out the heavens,
[bɪˈhoːʊld fɹʌm aːʊt ðʌ ˈhɛvɛ(ɪ)nz]
There shone a holy light.
[ðɛːʌ ʃoːʊn ʌ ˈhoːʊlɪ laːɪt]

"Little David, Play on Your Harp"
[ˈlɪdʊl ˈdɛːɪvɪd plɛːɪ an jɔːʁ haʁp]
Spiritual

Little David, play on your harp, Hallelu.
[ˈlɪdʊl ˈdɛːɪvɪd plɛːɪ an jɔːʌ hap halɛˈlu]
God told Moses, O Lord!
[gad toːʊld ˈmoːʊzɛ(ɪ)s oːʊ lɔd]
Go down into Egypt, O Lord!
[goːʊ daːʊn ˈɪntu ˈɪdʒɪpt oːʊ lɔd]
Tell ole Pharo', O Lord!
[tɛl oːʊl ˈfɛʁoːʊ oːʊ lɔd]
Loose my people,
[lus maːɪ ˈpipʊl]
O Little David; play on your harp, Hallelu.
[oːʊ ˈlɪdʊl ˈdɛːɪvɪd plɛːɪ an jɔːʌ hap halɛˈlu]
Down in de valley, O Lord!
[daːʊn ɪn dʌ ˈvælɪ oːʊ lɔd]
I didn't go to stay; O Lord!
[ɑ ˈdɪ(d)ɪn(t) goːʊ tu stɛːɪ oːʊ lɔd]
My soul got happy, O Lord!
[ma soːʊl gat ˈhæpɪ oːʊ lɔd]
An' I stay'd all day,
[æn a stɛːɪd ɔl dɛːɪ]
O Little David, play on your harp, Hallelu.
[oːʊ ˈlɪdʊl ˈdɛːɪvɪd plɛːɪ an jɔːʌ hap halɛˈlu]

"My Lord, What a Mornin" (see Johnson)

"Ride on, King Jesus"
[ɹaːɪd an kɪŋ ˈdʒizʌs]
Spiritual

Ride on, King Jesus!
[ɹaːɪd an kɪŋ ˈdʒizʌs]
No man cana hinder me.
[noːʊ mæn ˈkænʌ ˈhɪndʌ mi]
Ride on, King Jesus, Ride on,
[ɹaːɪd an kɪŋ ˈdʒizʌs ɹaːɪd an]
No man cana hinder me.
[noːʊ mæn ˈkænʌ ˈhɪndʌ mi]
De ribber of Jordan He did cross,
[dʌ ˈɹɪbʌʁ ʌv ˈdʒɔdʌ(ɪ)n hi dɪd kɹas]
No man cana hinder me.
[noːʊ mæn ˈkænʌ ˈhɪndʌ mi]

Ride on, King Jesus,
[ɹɑːɪd an kɪŋ ˈʤizʌs]
No man cana hinder me.
[noːʊ mæn ˈkænʌ ˈhɪndʌ mi]

"Sometimes I Feel Like a Motherless Child"
[ˈsʌmtɑːɪmz ɑːɪ fil lɑːɪk ʌ ˈmʌðʁlɪs ʧɑːɪld]
Spiritual

Sometimes I feel like a motherless chile,
[ˈsʌmtɑːɪmz a fil lak ʌ ˈmʌðʌlɛ(ɪ)s ʧɑːɪl]
A long ways from home a long ways from home.
[ʌ laŋ wɛːɪz fɹʌm hoːʊm ʌ laŋ wɛːɪz fɹʌm hoːʊm]
Sometimes I feel like I'm almos' gone
[ˈsʌmtɑːɪmz a fil lak am ˈɔlmoːʊs(t) gan]
A long ways from home, a long ways from home.
[ʌ laŋ wɛːɪz fɹʌm hoːʊm ʌ laŋ wɛːɪz fɹʌm hoːʊm]

"Steal Away"
[stil ʌˈwɛːɪ]
Spiritual

Steal away, steal away, steal away to Jesus!
[stil ʌˈwɛːɪ stil ʌˈwɛːɪ stil ʌˈwɛːɪ tu ˈʤizʌs]
Steal away, steal away home,
[stil ʌˈwɛːɪ stil ʌˈwɛːɪ hoːʊm]
I ain't got long to stay here!
[ɑːɪ ɛːɪn(t) gat laŋ tu stɛːɪ hɪːʌ]
1. My Lord calls me,
[mɑːɪ lɔd kɔlz mi]
He calls me by the thunder;
[hi kɔlz mi bɑːɪ ðʌ ˈθʌndʌ]
The trumpet sounds within-a my soul;
[ðʌ ˈtɹʌmpɛ(ɪ)t sɑːʊndz wɪðˈɪn ʌ mɑːɪ soːʊl]
I ain't got long to stay here.
[ɑːɪ ɛːɪn(t) gat laŋ tu stɛːɪ hɪːʌ]
Steal away, steal away, steal away to Jesus!
[stil ʌˈwɛːɪ stil ʌˈwɛːɪ stil ʌˈwɛːɪ tu ˈʤizʌs]
Steal away, steal away home,
[stil ʌˈwɛːɪ stil ʌˈwɛːɪ hoːʊm]
I ain't got long to stay here!
[ɑːɪ ɛːɪn(t) gat laŋ tu stɛːɪ hɪːʌ]
2. Green trees are bending,
[gɹin tɹiz a ˈbɛndɪŋ]
Poor sinner stands a-trembling;
[pɔ ˈsɪnʌ stændz ʌ ˈtɹɛmblɪŋ]
The trumpet sounds within-a my soul
[ðʌ ˈtɹʌmpɛ(ɪ)t sɑːʊndz wɪðˈɪn ʌ mɑːɪ soːʊl]
I ain't got long to stay here.
[ɑːɪ ɛːɪn(t) gat laŋ tu stɛːɪ hɪːʌ]
Steal away, steal away, steal away to Jesus!
[stil ʌˈwɛːɪ stil ʌˈwɛːɪ stil ʌˈwɛːɪ tu ˈʤizʌs]
Steal away, steal away home,
[stil ʌˈwɛːɪ stil ʌˈwɛːɪ hoːʊm]
I ain't got long to stay here.
[ɑːɪ ɛːɪn(t) gat laŋ tu stɛːɪ hɪːʌ]

"Swing Low, Sweet Chariot"
[swɪŋ loːʊ swit ˈʧæʁɪʌt]
Spiritual

Swing low, sweet chariot,
[swɪŋ loːʊ swit ˈʧæʁɪʌt]
Coming for to carry me home.
[ˈkʌmɪŋ fɔ tʊ ˈkæʁɪ mi hoːʊm]
Swing low, sweet chariot,
[swɪŋ loːʊ swit ˈʧæʁɪʌt]
Coming for to carry me home.
[ˈkʌmɪŋ fɔ tʊ ˈkæʁɪ mi hoːʊm]
I look'd over Jordan, what did I see,
[ɑːɪ lʊkt ˈoːʊvʌ ˈʤɔdʌ(ɪ)n wat dɪd ɑːɪ si]
Coming for to carry me home?
[ˈkʌmɪŋ fɔ tʊ ˈkæʁɪ mi hoːʊm]
A band of angels coming after me,
[ʌ bænd ʌv ˈɛːɪnʤɛ(ʊ)lz ˈkʌmɪŋ ˈæftʌ mi]
Coming for to carry me home.
[ˈkʌmɪŋ fɔ tʊ ˈkæʁɪ mi hoːʊm]
Swing low, sweet chariot,
[swɪŋ loːʊ swit ˈʧæʁɪʌt]
Coming for to carry me home.
[ˈkʌmɪŋ fɔ tʊ ˈkæʁɪ mi hoːʊm]
Swing low, sweet chariot,
[swɪŋ loːʊ swit ˈʧæʁɪʌt]
Coming for to carry me home.
[ˈkʌmɪŋ fɔ tʊ ˈkæʁɪ mi hoːʊm]

Butterworth, George
(Eng. 1885-1916)

Six Songs from a Shropshire Lad (Song Cycle)
[sɪks saŋz fɹʌm ʌ ˈʃɹapʃɑːɪʌ læd]
Housman, Alfred Edward (Eng. 1859-1936)

1. Loveliest of Trees
[ˈlʌvliɪst ʌv tɹiz]

Loveliest of trees, the cherry now
[ˈlʌvlɪɛ(ɪ)st ʌv tɹiz ðʊ ˈʧɛɹɪ nɑːʊ]
Is hung with bloom along the bough,
[ɪz hʌŋ wɪð blum ʌˈlaŋ ðʊ bɑːʊ]
And stands about the woodland ride
[ænd stændz ʌˈbɑːʊt ðʊ ˈwʊdlæ(ʌ)nd ɹɑːɪd]
Wearing white for Eastertide.
[ˈwɛːʌɹɪŋ ʍɑːɪt fɔ ˈistʌtɑːɪd]
Now, of my threescore years and ten,
[nɑːʊ ʌv mɑːɪ ˈθriskɔːʌ jɪːʌz ænd tɛn]
Twenty will not come again,
[ˈtwɛntɪ wɪl nat kʌm ʌˈgɛn]
And take from seventy springs a score,
[ænd tɛːɪk fɹʌm ˈsɛvɛ(ɪ)ntɪ spɹɪŋz ʌ skɔːʌ]

It only leaves me fifty more.
[ɪt 'oːʊnlɪ livz mi 'fɪftɪ mɔːʌ]
And since to look at things in bloom
[ænd sins tu lʊk æt θɪŋz ɪn blum]
Fifty springs are little room,
['fɪftɪ spɹɪŋz ɑ 'lɪtʊl ɹrum]
About the woodlands I will go
[ʌ'baːʊt ðʊ 'wʊdlæ(ʌ)ndz ɑːɪ wɪl goːʊ]
To see the cherry hung with snow.
[tu si ðʊ 'tʃɛɹɪ hʌŋ wɪð snoːʊ]

2. When I Was One-and-Twenty
[ʍɛn ɑːɪ waz wʌn ænd 'twɛnti]

When I was one-and-twenty
[ʍɛn ɑːɪ waz wʌn ænd 'twɛntɪ]
I heard a wise man say,
[ɑːɪ hɜd ʌ waːɪz mæn sɛːɪ]
"Give crowns and pounds and guineas
[gɪv kɹaːʊnz ænd paːʊndz ænd 'gɪnɪz]
But not your heart away;
[bʌt nat jɔːʌ hat ʌ'wɛːɪ]
Give pearls away and rubies
[gɪv pɜlz ʌ'wɛːɪ ænd 'ɹrubɪz]
But keep your fancy free."
[bʌt kip jɔːʌ 'fænsɪ fɹɪ]
But I was one-and-twenty,
[bʌt ɑːɪ waz wʌn ænd 'twɛntɪ]
No use to talk to me.
[noːʊ jus tu tɔk tu mi]
When I was one-and-twenty
[ʍɛn ɑːɪ waz wʌn ænd 'twɛntɪ]
I heard him say again,
[ɑːɪ hɜd hɪm sɛːɪ ʌ'gɛːɪn]
"The heart out of the bosom
[ðʊ hat aːʊt ʌv ðʊ 'bʊzʌm]
Was never given in vain;
[waz 'nɛvʌ 'gɪvɛ(ɪ)n ɪn vɛːɪn]
'Tis paid with sighs a plenty,
[tɪz pɛːɪd wɪð saːɪz ʌ 'plɛntɪ]
And sold for endless rue."
[ænd soːʊld fɔʁ(ʳ) 'ɛndlɛ(ɪ)s ɹru]
And I am two-and-twenty,
[ænd ɑːɪ æm tu ænd 'twɛntɪ]
And oh, 'tis true, 'tis true.
[ænd oːʊ tɪz tru tɪz tru]

3. Look Not in My Eyes
[lʊk nat ɪn maːɪ ɑːɪz]

Look not in my eyes, for fear
[lʊk nat ɪn maːɪ ɑːɪz fɔ fɪːʌ]
They mirror true the sight I see
[ðɛːɪ 'mɪɹɔ(ʌ) tru ðʊ saːɪt ɑːɪ si]
And there you find your face too clear
[ænd ðɛːʌ ju faːɪnd jɔːʌ fɛːɪs tu klɪːʌ]

And love it and be lost like me.
[ænd lʌv ɪt ænd bi last laːɪk mi]
One the long nights through must lie
[wʌn ðʊ laŋ naːɪts θru mʌst laːɪ]
Spent in star-defeated sighs,
[spɛnt ɪn sta dɪ'fitɛ(ɪ)d saːɪz]
But why should you as well as I
[bʌt ʍaːɪ ʃʊd ju æz wɛl æz ɑːɪ]
Perish? Gaze not in my eyes.
['pɛɹɪʃ gɛːɪz nat ɪn maːɪ ɑːɪz]
A Grecian lad, as I hear tell,
[ʌ 'gɹɪʃæ(ɪ)n læd æz ɑːɪ hɪːʌ tɛl]
One that many loved in vain,
[wʌn ðæt 'mɛnɪ lʌvd ɪn vɛːɪn]
Looked into a forest well
[lʊkt 'ɪntu ʌ 'fɔɹɛ(ɪ)st wɛl]
And never looked away again.
[ænd 'nɛvʌ lʊkt ʌ'wɛːɪ ʌ'gɛːɪn]
There, when the turf in spring-time flowers,
[ðɛːʌ ʍɛn ðʊ tɜf ɪn spɹɪŋ taːɪm flaːʊʌz]
With downward eye and gazes sad,
[wɪð 'daːʊnwʊd aːɪ ænd 'gɛːɪzɛ(ɪ)z sæd]
Stands amid the glancing showers
[stændz ʌ'mɪd ðʊ 'glansɪŋ ʃaːʊʌz]
A jonquil, not a Grecian lad.
[ʌ 'dʒaŋkwɪ(ʊ)l nat ʌ 'gɹɪʃæ(ɪ)n læd]

4. Think No More, Lad
[θɪŋk noːʊ mɔːʌ læd]

Think no more, lad; laugh, be jolly:
[θɪŋk noːʊ mɔːʌ læd laf bi 'dʒalɪ]
Why should men make haste to die?
[ʍaːɪ ʃʊd mɛn mɛːɪk hɛːɪst tu daːɪ]
Empty heads and tongues a-talking
['ɛmptɪ hɛdz ænd tʌŋz ʌ 'tɔkɪŋ]
Make the rough road easy walking,
[mɛːɪk ðʊ ɹʌf ɹoːʊd 'izɪ 'wɔkɪŋ]
And the feather pate of folly
[ænd ðʊ 'fɛðʌ pɛːɪt ʌv 'falɪ]
Bears the falling sky.
[bɛːʌz ðʊ 'fɔlɪŋ skaːɪ]
Oh, 'tis jesting, dancing, drinking
[oːʊ tɪz 'dʒestɪŋ 'dansɪŋ 'dɹɪŋkɪŋ]
Spins the heavy world around.
[spɪnz ðʊ 'hɛvɪ wɜld ʌ'raːʊnd]
If young hearts were not so clever,
[ɪf jʌŋ hats wɜ nat soːʊ 'klɛvʌ]
Oh, they would be young for ever:
[oːʊ ðɛːɪ wʊd bi jʌŋ fɔʁ(ʳ) 'ɛvʌ]
Think no more; 'tis only thinking
[θɪŋk noːʊ mɔːʌ tɪz 'oːʊnlɪ 'θɪŋkɪŋ]
Lays lads underground.
[lɛːɪz lædz ʌndʌ'gɹaːʊnd]

5. The Lads in Their Hundreds
[ðʊ lædz ɪn ðɛːʌ ˈhʌndɹɪdz]

The lads in their hundreds to Ludlow
[ðʊ lædz ɪn ðɛːʌ ˈhʌndɹɛ(ɪ)dz tu ˈlʌdloːʊ]
come in for the fair,
[kʌm ɪn fɔ ðʊ fɛːʌ]
There's men from the barn and the forge
[ðɛːʌz mɛn fɹʌm ðʊ ban ænd ðʊ fɔdʒ]
and the mill and the fold,
[ænd ðʊ mɪl ænd ðʊ foːʊld]
The lads for the girls and the lads
[ðʊ lædz fɔ ðʊ gɜlz ænd ðʊ lædz]
for the liquor are there,
[fɔ ðʊ ˈlɪkɔr a ðɛːʌ]
And there with the rest are the lads
[ænd ðɛːʌ wɪð ðʊ ɹɛst a ðʊ lædz]
that will never be old.
[ðæt wɪl ˈnɛvʌ bi oːʊld]
There's chaps from the town and the field
[ðɛːʌz ʧæps fɹʌm ðʊ taːʊn ænd ðʊ fild]
and the till and the cart,
[ænd ðʊ tɪl ænd ðʊ kat]
And many to count are the stalwart,
[ænd ˈmɛnɪ tu kaːʊnt a ðʊ ˈstɔlwat]
and many the brave,
[ænd ˈmɛnɪ ðʊ bɹɛːɪv]
And many the handsome of face
[ænd ˈmɛnɪ ðʊ ˈhænsʌm ʌv fɛːɪs]
and the handsome of heart,
[ænd ðʊ ˈhænsʌm ʌv hat]
And few that will carry their looks
[ænd fju ðæt wɪl ˈkæɹɪ ðɛːʌ lʊks]
or their truth to the grave.
[ɔ ðɛːʌ truθ tu ðʊ gɹɛːɪv]
I wish one could know them,
[aːɪ wɪʃ wʌn kʊd noːʊ ðɛm]
I wish there were tokens to tell
[aːɪ wɪʃ ðɛːʌ wɜ ˈtoːʊkɛ(ɪ)nz tu tɛl]
The fortunate fellows that now
[ðʊ ˈfɔʧu(ʌ)næ(ɪ)t ˈfɛloːʊz ðæt naːʊ]
you can never discern;
[ju kæn ˈnɛvʌ dɪˈsɜn]
And then one could talk with them friendly
[ænd ðɛn wʌn kʊd tɔk wɪð ðɛm ˈfɹɛndlɪ]
and wish them farewell,
[ænd wɪʃ ðɛm fɛːʌˈwɛl]
And watch them depart on the way
[ænd waʧ ðɛm dɪˈpat an ðʊ wɛːɪ]
that they will not return.
[ðæt ðɛːɪ wɪl nat ɹɪˈtɜn]
But now you may stare as you like
[bʌt naːʊ ju mɛːɪ stɛːʌr æz ju laːɪk]
and there's nothing to scan
[ænd ðɛːʌz ˈnʌθɪŋ tu skæn]

And brushing your elbow unguessed at
[ænd ˈbɹʌʃɪŋ jɔːʌ ˈɛlboːʊ ʌnˈgɛst æt]
and not to be told
[ænd nat tu bi toːʊld]
They carry back bright to the coiner
[ðɛːɪ ˈkæɹɪ bæk bɹaːɪt tu ðʊ ˈkɔːɪnʌ]
the mintage of man,
[ðʊ ˈmɪntæ(ɪ)dʒ ʌv mæn]
The lads that will die in their glory
[ðʊ lædz ðæt wɪl daːɪ ɪn ðɛːʌ ˈglɔɹɪ]
and never be old.
[ænd ˈnɛvʌ bi oːʊld]

6. Is My Team Ploughing?
[ɪz maːɪ tim ˈplaːʊɪŋ]

"Is my team ploughing,
[ɪz maːɪ tim ˈplaːʊɪŋ]
That I was used to drive
[ðæt aːɪ waz just tu dɹaːɪv]
And hear the harness jingle
[ænd hiːʌ ðʊ ˈhanɛ(ɪ)s ˈdʒɪŋgʊl]
When I was man alive?"
[ʍɛn aːɪ waz mæn ʌˈlaːɪv]
Ay, the horses trample,
[aːɪ ðʊ ˈhɔsɛ(ɪ)z ˈtɹæmpʊl]
The harness jingles now;
[ðʊ ˈhanɛ(ɪ)s ˈdʒɪŋgʊlz naːʊ]
No change though you lie under
[noːʊ ʧɛːɪndʒ ðoːʊ ju laːɪ ˈʌndʌ]
The land you used to plough.
[ðʊ lænd ju just tu plaːʊ]
"Is football playing
[ɪz ˈfʊtbɔl ˈplɛːɪɪŋ]
Along the river-shore,
[ʌˈlaŋ ðʊ ˈɹɪvʌ ʃɔːʌ]
With lads to chase the leather,
[wɪð lædz tu ʧɛːɪs ðʊ ˈlɛðʌ]
Now I stand up no more?"
[naːʊ aːɪ stænd ʌp noːʊ mɔːʌ]
Ay, the ball is flying,
[aːɪ ðʊ bɔl ɪz ˈflaːɪɪŋ]
The lads play heart and soul;
[ðʊ lædz plɛːɪ hat ænd soːʊl]
The goal stands up, the keeper
[ðʊ goːʊl stændz ʌp ðʊ ˈkipʌ]
Stands up to keep the goal.
[stændz ʌp tu kip ðʊ goːʊl]
"Is my girl happy,
[ɪz maːɪ gɜl ˈhæpɪ]
That I thought hard to leave,
[ðæt aːɪ θɔt had tu liv]
And has she tired of weeping
[ænd hæz ʃi taːɪʌd ʌv ˈwipɪŋ]
As she lies down at eve?"
[æz ʃi laːɪz daːʊn æt iv]

Ay, she lies down lightly,
[ɑːɪ ʃi lɑːɪz dɑːʊn ˈlɑːɪtlɪ]
She lies not down to weep;
[ʃi lɑːɪz nat dɑːʊn tu wip]
Your girl is well contented.
[jɔːʌ ɡɜl ɪz wɛl kʌnˈtɛntɛ(ɪ)d]
Be still, my lad, and sleep.
[bi stɪl mɑːɪ læd ænd slip]
"Is my friend hearty,
[ɪz mɑːɪ fɹɛnd ˈhɑtɪ]
Now I am thin and pine,
[nɑːʊ ɑːɪ æm θɪn ænd pɑːɪn]
And has he found to sleep in
[ænd hæz hi fɑːʊnd tu slip ɪn]
A better bed than mine?"
[ʌ ˈbɛtʌ bɛd ðæn mɑːɪn]
Yes, lad, I lie easy,
[jɛs læd ɑːɪ lɑːɪ ˈizɪ]
I lie as lads would choose;
[ɑːɪ lɑːɪ æz lædz wʊd ʧuz]
I cheer a dead man's sweetheart,
[ɑːɪ ʧɪːʌɾ ʌ dɛd mænz ˈswithɑt]
Never ask me whose.
[ˈnɛvʌɾ ask mi huz]

Song Selections

"A Brisk Young Sailor Courted Me"
[ʌ bɹɪsk jʌŋ ˈsɛːɪlʌ ˈkɔtɪd mi]
Folksong

A brisk young sailor courted me,
[ʌ bɹɪsk jʌŋ ˈsɛːɪlɔ(ʌ) ˈkɔtɛ(ɪ)d mi]
He stole away my liberty,
[hi stoːʊl ʌˈwɛːɪ mɑːɪ ˈlɪbʌtɪ]
He won my heart with a free good-will,
[hi wʌn mɑːɪ hat wɪð ʌ fɹi ɡʊd wɪl]
He's false, I know, but I love him still.
[hiz fɔls ɑːɪ noːʊ bʌt ɑːɪ lʌv hɪm stɪl]
There is an alehouse in yonder town,
[ðɛːʌɾ ɪz æn ˈɛːɪlhɑːʊs ɪn ˈjandʌ tɑːʊn]
Where my love goes and sits him down,
[ʍɛːʌ mɑːɪ lʌv ɡoːʊz ænd sɪts hɪm dɑːʊn]
He takes another girl on his knee,
[hi tɛːɪks ʌˈnʌðʌ ɡɜl an hɪz ni]
And don't you think that's a grief to me?
[ænd doːʊnt ju θɪŋk ðæts ʌ ɡrif tu mi]
A grief to me! I'll tell you why,
[ʌ ɡrif tu mi ɑːɪl tɛl ju ʍɑːɪ]
Because she's got more gold than I,
[bɪˈkɔz ʃiz ɡat mɔːʌ ɡoːʊld ðæn ɑːɪ]
Her gold will waste and her beauty blast,
[hɜ ɡoːʊld wɪl wɛːɪst ænd hɜ ˈbjutɪ blast]
And she'll become like me at last.
[ænd ʃil bɪˈkʌm lɑːɪk mi æt last]

O what a foolish girl was I
[oːʊ ʍat ʌ ˈfulɪʃ ɡɜl waz ɑːɪ]
To give my heart to a sailor boy,
[tu ɡɪv mɑːɪ hat tu ʌ ˈsɛːɪlɔ(ʌ) bɔːɪ]
A sailor boy although he be,
[ʌ ˈsɛːɪlɔ(ʌ) bɔːɪ ɔlˈðoːʊ hi bi]
I love him better than he loves me.
[ɑːɪ lʌv hɪm ˈbɛtʌ ðæn hi lʌvz mi]

"With Rue My Heart Is Laden" (Bredon Hill)
[wɪθ ɹu mɑːɪ hat ɪz ˈlɛːɪdɪn]
Housman, Alfred Edward (Eng. 1859-1936)

With rue my heart is laden
[wɪð ɹɹu mɑːɪ hat ɪz ˈlɛːɪdɛ(ɪ)n]
For golden friends I had,
[fɔ ˈɡoːʊldɛ(ɪ)n fɹɛndz ɑːɪ hæd]
For many a rose-lipt maiden
[fɔ ˈmɛnɪ ʌ ɹoːʊz lɪpt ˈmɛːɪdɛ(ɪ)n]
And many a lightfoot lad.
[ænd ˈmɛnɪ ʌ ˈlɑːɪtfʊt læd]
By brooks too broad for leaping
[bɑːɪ bɹʊks tu bɹɔd fɔ ˈlipɪŋ]
The lightfoot boys are laid;
[ðʊ ˈlɑːɪtfʊt bɔːɪz a lɛːɪd]
The rose-lipt girls are sleeping
[ðʊ ɹoːʊz lɪpt ɡɜlz a ˈslipɪŋ]
In fields where roses fade.
[ɪn fildz ʍɛːʌ ˈɹoːʊzɛ(ɪ)z fɛːɪd]

Byrd, William (Eng. 1539?-1623)

Song Selection

"My Mind to Me a Kingdom Is"
[mɑːɪ mɑːɪnd tu mi ʌ ˈkɪŋdʌm ɪz]
Anonymous

My mind to me a kingdom is:
[mɑːɪ mɑːɪnd tu mi ʌ ˈkɪŋdʌm ɪz]
Such perfect joy therein I find
[sʌʧ ˈpɜfɛ(ɪ)kt ʤɔːɪ ðɛːʌɾ ɪn ɑːɪ fɑːɪnd]
That it excels all other bliss
[ðæt ɪt ɪkˈsɛlz ɔl ˈʌðʌ blɪs]
Which God or nature hath assigned.
[ʍɪʧ ɡad ɔ ˈnɛːɪʧʊ(ʌ) hæθ ʌˈsɑːɪnd]
Though much I want, that most would have,
[ðoːʊ mʌʧ ɑːɪ want ðæt moːʊst wʊd hæv]
Yet still my mind forbids to crave.
[jɛt stɪl mɑːɪ mɑːɪnd fɔˈbɪdz tu kɹɛːɪv]
No princely port, nor wealthy store,
[noːʊ ˈpɹɪnslɪ pɔt nɔ ˈwɛlθɪ stɔːʌ]
No force to win a victory,
[noːʊ fɔs tu wɪn ʌ ˈvɪktɔɪ]

No wily wit to salve a sore,
[noːʊ ˈwaːɪlɪ wɪt tu sælv ʌ sɔːʌ]
No shape to win a loving eye;
[noːʊ ʃɛːɪp tu wɪn ʌ ˈlʌvɪŋ aːɪ]
To none of these I yield as thrall!
[tu nʌn ʌv ðiz aːɪ jild æz θrɔl]
For why my mind despise them all.
[fɔ ʍaːɪ maːɪ maːɪnd dɪˈspaːɪz ðɛm ɔl]
I see that plenty surfeits oft,
[aːɪ si ðæt ˈplɛntɪ ˈsɜfɪts aft]
And hasty climbers soonest fall;
[ænd ˈhɛːɪstɪ ˈklaːɪmʌz ˈsunɛ(ɪ)st fɔl]
I see that such as are aloft,
[aːɪ si ðæt sʌtʃ æz aɾ ʌˈlaft]
Mishap doth threaten most of all.
[ˈmɪʃæp dʌθ ˈθrɛtɛ(ɪ)n moːʊst ʌv ɔl]
These get with toil, and keep with fear:
[ðiz gɛt wɪð tɔːɪl ænd kip wɪð fɪːʌ]
Such cares my mind can never bear.
[sʌtʃ kɛːʌz maːɪ maːɪnd kæn ˈnɛvʌ bɛːʌ]
I press to bear no haughty sway,
[aːɪ pɹɛs tu bɛːʌ noːʊ ˈhɔtɪ swɛːɪ]
I wish no more than may suffice,
[aːɪ wɪʃ noːʊ mɔːʌ ðæn mɛːɪ sʌˈfaːɪs]
I do no more, than well I may;
[aːɪ du noːʊ mɔːʌ ðæn wɛl aːɪ mɛːɪ]
Look, what I want, my mind supplies.
[lʊk ʍat aːɪ want maːɪ maːɪnd sʌˈplaːɪz]
Lo, thus I triumph as a king,
[loːʊ ðʌs aːɪ ˈtɹaːɪʌmf æz ʌ kɪŋ]
My mind content with any thing.
[maːɪ maːɪnd kʌntɛnt wɪð ˈɛnɪ θɪŋ]
I laugh not at another's loss,
[aːɪ laf nat æt ʌˈnʌðʌz las]
Nor grudge not at another's gain.
[nɔ grʌdʒ nat æt ʌˈnʌðʌz gɛːɪn]
No worldly waves my mind can toss,
[noːʊ ˈwɜldlɪ wɛːɪvz maːɪ maːɪnd kæn tas]
I brook that is another's bane;
[aːɪ bɹʊk ðæt ɪz ʌˈnʌðʌz bɛːɪn]
I fear no foe, nor fawn on friend,
[aːɪ fɪːʌ noːʊ foːʊ nɔ fɔn an fɹɛnd]
I loathe not life nor dread mine end.
[aːɪ loːʊð nat laːɪf nɔ dɹɛd maːɪn ɛnd]
My wealth is health and perfect ease;
[maːɪ wɛlθ ɪz hɛlθ ænd ˈpɜfɛ(ɪ)kt iz]
And conscience clear my chief defense;
[ænd ˈkanʃɛ(ɪ)ns klɪːʌ maːɪ tʃif dɪˈfɛns]
I never seek by bribes to please,
[aːɪ ˈnɛvʌ sik baːɪ bɹaːɪbz tu pliz]
Nor by deserts to give offence,
[nɔ baːɪ dɪˈzɜts tu gɪv oˈfɛns]
Thus do I live, thus will I die:
[ðʌs du aːɪ lɪv ðʌs wɪl aːɪ daːɪ]
Would all did so as well as I!
[wʊd ɔl dɪd soːʊ æz wɛl æz aːɪ]

C

Cadman, Charles Wakefield
(Am. 1881-1946)

Song Selection

"From the Land of the Sky-Blue Water"
[fɪʌm ðʌ lænd ʌv ðʌ skaːɪ blu ˈwɒtʁ]
(Four American Indian Songs)
Eberhart, Nelle Richmond (Am. 1871-1944)

From the Land of the Sky-blue Water,
[fɪʌm ðʌ lænd ʌv ðʌ skaːɪ blu ˈwɒtʌ]
They brought a captive maid;
[ðɛːɪ bɹɔt ʌ ˈkæptɪv mɛːɪd]
And her eyes they are lit with lightnings,
[ænd hɜ aːɪz ðɛːɪ a lɪt wɪð ˈlaːɪtnɪŋz]
Her heart is not afraid!
[hɜ hat ɪz nat ʌˈfɪɛːɪd]
But I steal to her lodge at dawning,
[bʌt aːɪ stil tu hɜ ladʒ æt ˈdɔnɪŋ]
I woo her with my flute;
[aːɪ wu hɜ wɪð maːɪ flut]
She is sick for the Sky-blue Water,
[ʃi ɪz sɪk fɔ ðʌ skaːɪ blu ˈwɒtʌ]
The captive maid is mute.
[ðʌ ˈkæptɪv mɛːɪd ɪz mjut]

"O Mistress Mine" (see Quilter)

 ## Cage, John (Am. 1912-1992)

Song Selection

"The Wonderful Widow of Eighteen Springs"
[ðʌ ˈwʌndʁfʊl ˈwɪdoːʊ ʌv ˈɛːɪtin spɹɪŋz]
Joyce, James (Ir. 1882-1941)

Night by silent sailing night, Isobel,
[naːɪt baːɪ ˈsaːɪlɛnt ˈsɛːɪlɪŋ naːɪt izoˈbɛl]
wildwoods eyes and primarose hair,
[ˈwaːɪldwʊdz aːɪz ænd ˈpɹɪmʌʁ⁽ʳ⁾oːʊz hɛːʌ]
quietly, all the woods so wild
[ˈkwaːɪɛ(ɪ)tlɪ ɔl ðʌ wʊdz soːʊ waːɪld]
in mauves of moss and Daphne dews
[ɪn mɔvz ʌv mɔs ænd ˈdæfnɪ djuz]
how all so still she lay
[haːʊ ɔl soːʊ stɪl ʃi lɛːɪ]
'neath of the white thorn,
[niθ ʌv ðʌ ʍaːɪt θɔn]

child of tree
[ʧɑːɪld ʌv tɹi]
like some lost happy leaf
[lɑːɪk sʌm lɑst 'hæpɪ lif]
like blowing flower stilled
[lɑːɪk 'bloːʊŋ flɑːʊʌ stɪld]
as fain would she anon
[æz fɛːɪn wʊd ʃi ʌ'nɑn]
for soon again 'twill be,
[fɔ sun ʌ'gɛn twɪl bi]
win me, woo me, wed me,
[wɪn mi wu mi wɛd mi]
ah! weary me deeply,
[ɑ 'wɪːʌʁ⁽ʳ⁾ɪ mi 'dipli]
now even calm lay sleeping
[nɑːʊ 'ivɛ(ɪ)n kɑm lɛːɪ 'slipŋ]
night, Isobel,
[nɑːɪt izɔ'bɛl]
Sister Isobel, Saintette Isobel,
['sɪstʌ izɔ'bɛl sẽ'tɛt izɔ'bɛl]
Madame Isa Veuve La Belle.
[ma'dam i'za 'vœvə la bɛl]

Campion, Thomas (Eng. 1567-1620)

Song Selections

"If Thou Long'st So Much to Learn"
[ɪf ðɑːʊ lɑŋst soːʊ mʌʧ tu lɜn]
(The Third Booke of Ayres)
Campion, Thomas (Eng. 1567-1620)

If thou long'st so much to learn,
[ɪf ðɑːʊ lɑŋst soːʊ mʌʧ tu lɜn]
sweet boy, what 'tis to love,
[swit bɔːɪ ʍat tɪz tu lʌv]
Do but fix thy thought on me,
[du bʌt fɪks ðɑːɪ θɔt ɑn mi]
and thou shalt quickly prove.
[ænd ðɑːʊ ʃælt 'kwɪklɪ pɹuv]
Little suit at first shall win
['lɪtʊl sjut æt fɜst ʃæl wɪn]
Way to thy abashed desire;
[wɛːɪ tu ðɑːɪ ʌ'bæʃt dɪ'zɑːɪʌ]
But then will I hedge thee in
[bʌt ðɛn wɪl ɑːɪ hɛʤ ði ɪn]
Salamander-like, with fire.
[ˌsælʌ'mændʌ lɑːɪk wɪð fɑːɪʌ]
With thee dance I will and sing,
[wɪð ði dɑns ɑːɪ wɪl ænd sɪŋ]
and thy fond dalliance bear;
[ænd ðɑːɪ fɑnd 'dæljæ(ɪ)ns bɛːʌ]
We the grovy hills will climb
[wi ðʊ 'gɹoːʊvɪ hɪlz wɪl klɑːɪm]

and play the wantons there.
[ænd plɛːɪ ðʊ 'wantʌnz ðɛːʌ]
Otherwhiles we'll gather flowers,
['ʌðʌʍɑːɪlz wil 'gæðʌ flɑːʊʌz]
Lying dallying on the grass,
['lɑːɪŋ 'dælɪŋ ɑn ðʊ gɹɑs]
And thus our delightful hours
[ænd ðʌs ɑːʊʌ dɪ'lɑːɪtfʊl ɑːʊʌz]
Full of waking dreams shall pass.
[fʊl ʌv 'wɛːɪkɪŋ dɹimz ʃæl pɑs]
When thy joys were thus at height
[ʍɛn ðɑːɪ ʤɔːɪz wɜ ðʌs æt hɑːɪt]
my love should turn from thee;
[mɑːɪ lʌv ʃʊd tɜn fɹʌm ði]
Old acquaintance then should grow
[oːʊld ʌ'kwɛːɪntæ(ɪ)ns ðɛn ʃʊd gɹoːʊ]
as strange as strange might be;
[æz stɹɛːɪnʤ æz stɹɛːɪnʤ mɑːɪt bi]
Twenty rivals thou should'st find
['twɛntɪ 'ɹɑːɪvʊlz ðɑːʊ ʃʊdst fɑːɪnd]
Breaking all their hearts for me;
['bɹɛːɪkɪŋ ɔl ðɛːʌ hɑts fɔ mi]
When to all I'll prove more kind
[ʍɛn tu ɔl ɑːɪl pɹuv mɔːʌ kɑːɪnd]
And more forward than to thee.
[ænd mɔːʌ 'fɔwʊd ðæn tu ði]
Thus thy silly youth enraged would soon my love defy.
[ðʌs ðɑːɪ 'sɪlɪ juθ ɪn'ɹɛːɪʤd wʊd sun mɑːɪ lʌv dɪ'fɑːɪ]
But alas, poor soul, too late;
[bʌt ʌ'læs pʊːʌ soːʊl tu lɛːɪt]
clipped wings can never fly.
[klɪpt wɪŋz kæn 'nɛvʌ flɑːɪ]
Those sweet hours which we had passed,
[ðoːʊz swit ɑːʊʌz ʍɪʧ wi hæd pɑst]
Called to mind thy heart would burn;
[kɔld tu mɑːɪnd ðɑːɪ hɑt wʊd bɜn]
And could'st thou fly ne'er so fast,
[ænd kʊdst ðɑːʊ flɑːɪ nɛːʌ soːʊ fast]
They would make thee straight return.
[ðɛːɪ wʊd mɛːɪk ði stɹɛːɪt ɹɪ'tɜn]

"Oft Have I Sighed" (The Third Booke of Ayres)
[ɑft hæv ɑːɪ sɑːɪd]
Campion, Thomas (Eng. 1567-1620)

Oft have I sighed for him that hears me not:
[ɑft hæv ɑːɪ sɑːɪd fɔ hɪm ðæt hɪːʌz mi nɑt]
Who, absent, hath both love and me forgot.
[hu 'æbsɛnt hæθ boːʊθ lʌv ænd mi fɔ'gat]
O yet I languish still through his delay.
[oːʊ jɛt ɑːɪ 'læŋgwɪʃ stɪl θɹu hɪz dɪ'lɛːɪ]
Days seem as years
[dɛːɪz sim æz jɪːʌz]
when wished friends break their day.
[ʍɛn wɪʃt fɹɛndz bɹɛːɪk ðɛːʌ dɛːɪ]

Had he but loved as common lovers use,
[hæd hi bʌt lʌvd æz ˈkamʌn ˈlʌvʌz juz]
His faithless stay some kindness would excuse.
[hɪz ˈfeːɪθlɛ(ɪ)s steːɪ sʌm ˈkaːɪndnɛ(ɪ)s wʊd ɪkˈskjuz]
O yet I languish still, still constant mourn
[oːʊ jɛt aːɪ ˈlæŋgwɪʃ stɪl stɪl ˈkanstæ(ɪ)nt mɔn]
For him that can break vows, but not return.
[fɔ hɪm ðæt kæn bɹeːɪk vaːʊz bʌt nat ɹɪˈtɜn]

"When to Her Lute Corinna Sings"
[ʍɛn tu hɜ ljut kɔˈʁinʌ sɪŋz]
Campion, Thomas (Eng. 1567-1620)

When to her lute Corrina sings,
[ʍɛn tu hɜ ljut kɔˈrinʌ sɪŋz]
Her voice revives the leaden strings,
[hɜ vɔːɪs ɹɪˈvaːɪvz ðʊ ˈlɛdɛ(ɪ)n stɹɪŋz]
And doth in highest notes appear,
[ænd dʌθ ɪn ˈhaːɪɛ(ɪ)st noːʊts ʌˈpɪʌ]
As any challeng'd echo clear;
[æz ˈɛnɪ ˈʧælɛ(ɪ)nʤd ˈɛkoːʊ klɪːʌ]
But when she doth of mourning speak,
[bʌt ʍɛn ʃi dʌθ ʌv ˈmɔnɪŋ spik]
Even with her sighs the strings do break.
[ˈivɛ(ɪ)n wɪð hɜ saːɪz ðʊ stɹɪŋz du bɹeːɪk]
And, as her lute doth live or die,
[ænd æz hɜ ljut dʌθ lɪv ɔ daːɪ]
Led by her passion, so must I:
[lɛd baːɪ hɜ ˈpæʃʌn soːʊ mʌst aːɪ]
For when of pleasure she doth sing,
[fɔ ʍɛn ʌv ˈplɛʒʊ(ʌ) ʃi dʌθ sɪŋ]
My thoughts enjoy a sudden spring;
[maːɪ θɔts ɪnˈʤɔːɪ ʌ ˈsʌdɛ(ɪ)n spɹɪŋ]
But if she doth of sorrow speak,
[bʌt ɪf ʃi dʌθ ʌv ˈsaroːʊ spik]
Even from my heart the strings do break.
[ˈivɛ(ɪ)n fɹʌm maːɪ hat ðʊ stɹɪŋz du bɹeːɪk]

Carpenter, John Alden
(Am. 1876-1951)

Gitanjali (Song Cycle)
[giˈtanʤali]
Tagore, Rabindrath (Bengali 1861-1941)

1. When I Bring to You Colour'd Toys
[ʍɛn aːɪ bɹɪŋ tu ju ˈkʌlʁd tɔːɪz]

When I bring to you colour'd toys, my child,
[ʍɛn aːɪ bɹɪŋ tu ju ˈkʌlʊ(ʌ)d tɔːɪz maːɪ ʧaːɪld]
I understand why there is such a play
[aːɪ ʌndʌˈstænd ʍaːɪ ðɛːʌʁ⁽ʳ⁾ ɪz sʌʧ ʌ pleːɪ]
of colours on clouds, on water,
[ʌv ˈkʌlʊ(ʌ)z an klaːʊdz an ˈwɔtʌ]

and why flow'rs are painted in tints:
[ænd ʍaːɪ flaːʊʌz ʌ ˈpeːɪntɛ(ɪ)d ɪn tɪnts]
when I give colour'd toys to you, my child.
[ʍɛn aːɪ gɪv ˈkʌlʊ(ʌ)d tɔːɪz tu ju maːɪ ʧaːɪld]
When I sing to make you dance,
[ʍɛn aːɪ sɪŋ tu meːɪk ju dæns]
I truly know why there is music in leaves,
[aːɪ ˈtɹ⁽ʳ⁾ulɪ noːʊ ʍaːɪ ðɛːʌʁ⁽ʳ⁾ ɪz ˈmjuzɪk ɪn livz]
and why waves send their chorus of voices
[ænd ʍaːɪ wɛːɪvz sɛnd ðɛːʌ ˈkɔʁ⁽ʳ⁾ʌs ʌv ˈvɔːɪsɛ(ɪ)z]
to the heart of the listening earth:
[tu ðʌ hat ʌv ðʌ ˈlɪsɛ(ɪ)nɪŋ ɜθ]
when I sing to make you dance.
[ʍɛn aːɪ sɪŋ tu meːɪk ju dæns]
When I bring sweet things to your greedy hands,
[ʍɛn aːɪ bɹɪŋ swit θɪŋz tu jɔːʌ ˈgɹidɪ hændz]
I know why there is honey in the cup of the flower
[aːɪ noːʊ ʍaːɪ ðɛːʌʁ⁽ʳ⁾ ɪz ˈhʌnɪ ɪn ðʌ kʌp ʌv ðʌ flaːʊʌ]
and why fruits are secretly filled with sweet juice:
[ænd ʍaːɪ fɹ⁽ʳ⁾uts ʌ ˈsikɹɛ(ɪ)tlɪ fɪld wɪð swit ʤus]
when I bring sweet things to your greedy hands.
[ʍɛn aːɪ bɹɪŋ swit θɪŋz tu jɔːʌ ˈgɹidɪ hændz]

2. On the Day When Death Will Knock at Your Door
[an ðʌ dɛːɪ ʍɛn dɛθ wɪl nak æt jɔːʁ dɔːʁ]

On the day when death will knock at thy door,
[an ðʌ dɛːɪ ʍɛn dɛθ wɪl nak æt ðaːɪ dɔːʌ]
what wilt thou offer to him?
[ʍat wɪlt ðaːʊ ˈafʌ tu hɪm]
Oh, I will set before my guest
[oːʊ aːɪ wɪl sɛt bɪˈfɔːʌ maːɪ gɛst]
the full vessel of my life;
[ðʌ fʊl ˈvɛsʊl ʌv maːɪ laːɪf]
I will never let him go with empty hands.
[aːɪ wɪl ˈnɛvʌ lɛt hɪm goːʊ wɪð ˈɛmptɪ hændz]
All the sweet vintage of all my autumn days
[ɔl ðʌ swit ˈvɪntæ(ɪ)ʤ ʌv ɔl maːɪ ˈɔtʌm dɛːɪz]
and summer nights,
[ænd ˈsʌmʌ naːɪts]
all the earnings and gleanings of my busy life,
[ɔl ði ˈɜnɪŋz ænd ˈglinɪŋz ʌv maːɪ ˈbɪzɪ laːɪf]
will I place before him at the close of my days
[wɪl aːɪ pleːɪs bɪˈfɔːʌ hɪm æt ðʌ kloːʊz ʌv maːɪ dɛːɪz]
when death will knock at my door.
[ʍɛn dɛθ wɪl nak æt maːɪ dɔːʌ]

3. The Sleep That Flits on Baby's Eyes
[ðʌ slip ðæt flɪts an ˈbeːɪbiz aːɪz]

The sleep that flits on baby's eyes,
[ðʌ slip ðæt flɪts an ˈbeːɪbɪz aːɪz]
does anybody know from where it comes?
[dʌz ˈɛnɪbadɪ noːʊ fɹʌm ʍɛːʌʁ⁽ʳ⁾ ɪt kʌmz]
Yes, there is a rumour
[jɛs ðɛːʌʁ⁽ʳ⁾ ɪz ʌ ˈɹumʊ(ʌ)]

that it has its dwelling where,
[ðæt ɪt hæz ɪts ˈdwɛlɪŋ ʍɛːʌʁ⁽ʳ⁾]
in the fairy village among the shadows
[ɪn ðʌ ˈfɛʁ⁽ʳ⁾ɪ ˈvɪlæ⁽ɪ⁾dʒ ʌˈmʌŋ ðʌ ˈʃædoːʊz]
of the forest dimly lit with glow-worms,
[ʌv ðʌ ˈfɔʁ⁽ʳ⁾ɛ⁽ɪ⁾st ˈdɪmlɪ lɪt wɪð gloːʊ wɜmz]
there hang two timid buds of enchantment.
[ðɛːʌ hæŋ tu ˈtɪmɪd bʌdz ʌv ɪnˈtʃæntmɛnt]
From there it comes to kiss baby's eyes.
[fɹʌm ðɛːʌʁ⁽ʳ⁾ ɪt kʌmz tu kɪs ˈbɛːɪbɪz ɑːɪz]

4. I Am Like a Remnant on a Cloud of Autumn
[ɑːɪ æm lɑːɪk ʌ ˈɹɛmnɪnt an ʌ klɑːʊd ʌv ˈɔtʌm]

I am like a remnant of a cloud of autumn
[ɑːɪ æm lɑːɪk ʌ ˈɹɛmnæ⁽ɪ⁾nt ʌv ʌ klɑːʊd ʌv ˈɔtʌm]
uselessly roaming in the sky,
[ˈjuslɛ⁽ɪ⁾slɪ ˈɹoːʊmɪŋ ɪn ðʌ skɑːɪ]
O my sun ever-glorious!
[oːʊ mɑːɪ sʌn ˈɛvʌ ˈglɔʁ⁽ʳ⁾ɪʌs]
Thy touch has not yet melted my vapour,
[ðɑːɪ tʌtʃ hæz nat jɛt mɛltɛ⁽ɪ⁾d mɑːɪ ˈvɛːɪpʊ⁽ʌ⁾]
making me one with thy light,
[ˈmɛːɪkɪŋ mi wʌn wɪð ðɑːɪ lɑːɪt]
and thus I count months and years
[ænd ðʌs ɑːɪ kɑːʊnt mʌnθs ænd jɪːʌz]
separated from thee.
[ˈsɛpʌʁ⁽ʳ⁾ɛːɪtɛ⁽ɪ⁾d fɹʌm ði]
If this be thy wish and if this be thy play,
[ɪf ðɪs bi ðɑːɪ wɪʃ ænd ɪf ðɪs bi ðɑːɪ plɛːɪ]
then take this fleeting emptiness of mine,
[ðɛn tɛːɪk ðɪs ˈflitɪŋ ˈɛmptɪnɛ⁽ɪ⁾s ʌv mɑːɪn]
paint it with colours, gild it with gold,
[pɛːɪnt ɪt wɪð ˈkʌlʊ⁽ʌ⁾z gɪld ɪt wɪð goːʊld]
float it on the wanton wind
[floːʊt ɪt an ðʌ ˈwantʌn wɪnd]
and spread it in varied wonders.
[ænd spɹɛd ɪt ɪn ˈvæʁ⁽ʳ⁾ɪd ˈwʌndʌz]
And again, when it shall be thy wish
[ænd ʌˈgɛn ʍɛn ɪt ʃæl bi ðɑːɪ wɪʃ]
to end this play at night,
[tu ɛnd ðɪs plɛːɪ æt nɑːɪt]
I shall melt and vanish away in the dark,
[ɑːɪ ʃæl mɛlt ænd ˈvænɪʃ ʌˈwɛːɪ ɪn ðʌ dak]
or it may be in a smile of the white morning,
[ɔʁ⁽ʳ⁾ ɪt mɛːɪ bi ɪn ʌ smɑːɪl ʌv ðʌ ʍɑːɪt ˈmɔnɪŋ]
in a coolness of purity transparent.
[ɪn ʌ ˈkulnɛ⁽ɪ⁾s ʌv ˈpjʊːʌʁ⁽ʳ⁾ɪtɪ tɹæn ˈspæʁ⁽ʳ⁾ɛnt]

5. On the Seashore of Endless Worlds
[an ðʌ ˈsiʃɔːʁ ʌv ˈɛndlɪs wɜldz]

On the seashore of endless worlds children meet.
[an ðʌ ˈsiʃɔːʁ⁽ʳ⁾ ʌv ˈɛndlɛ⁽ɪ⁾s wɜldz ˈtʃɪldɹɛ⁽ɪ⁾n mit]
The infinite sky is motionless overhead
[ði ˈɪnfɪnɪt skɑːɪ ɪz ˈmoːʊʃʌnlɛ⁽ɪ⁾s ˈoːʊvʌhɛd]

and the restless water is boisterous.
[ænd ðʌ ˈɹɛstlɛ⁽ɪ⁾s ˈwɔtʌʁ⁽ʳ⁾ ɪz ˈbɔːɪstʌʁ⁽ʳ⁾ʌs]
On the seashore of endless worlds
[an ðʌ ˈsiʃɔːʁ⁽ʳ⁾ ʌv ˈɛndlɛ⁽ɪ⁾s wɜldz]
the children meet with shouts and dances.
[ðʌ ˈtʃɪldɹɛ⁽ɪ⁾n mit wɪð ʃɑːʊts ænd ˈdænsɛ⁽ɪ⁾z]
They build their houses with sand
[ðɛːɪ bɪld ðɛːʌ ˈhɑːʊzɛ⁽ɪ⁾z wɪð sænd]
and they play with empty shells.
[ænd ðɛːɪ plɛːɪ wɪð ˈɛmptɪ ʃɛlz]
With withered leaves they weave their boats
[wɪð ˈwɪðʌd livz ðɛːɪ wiv ðɛːʌ boːʊts]
and smilingly float them on the vast deep.
[ænd ˈsmɑːɪlɪŋlɪ floːʊt ðɛm an ðʌ væst dip]
Children have their play on the seashore of worlds.
[ˈtʃɪldɹɛ⁽ɪ⁾n hæv ðɛːʌ plɛːɪ an ðʌ ˈsiʃɔːʁ⁽ʳ⁾ ʌv wɜldz]
They know not how to swim,
[ðɛːɪ noːʊ nat hɑːʊ tu swɪm]
they know not how to cast nets.
[ðɛːɪ noːʊ nat hɑːʊ tu kæst nɛts]
Pearl fishers dive for pearls,
[pɜl ˈfɪʃʌz dɑːɪv fɔ pɜlz]
merchants sail in their ships,
[ˈmɜtʃæ⁽ɪ⁾nts sɛːɪl ɪn ðɛːʌ ʃɪps]
while children gather pebbles
[ʍɑːɪl ˈtʃɪldɹɛ⁽ɪ⁾n ˈgæðʌ ˈpɛbʊlz]
and scatter them again.
[ænd ˈskætʌ ðɛm ʌˈgɛn]
They seek not for hidden treasures,
[ðɛːɪ sik nat fɔ ˈhɪdɛ⁽ɪ⁾n ˈtɹɛʒʊ⁽ʌ⁾z]
they know not how to cast nets.
[ðɛːɪ noːʊ nat hɑːʊ tu kæst nɛts]
The sea surges up with laughter,
[ðʌ si ˈsɜdʒɛ⁽ɪ⁾z ʌp wɪð ˈlæftʌ]
and pale gleams the smile of the sea-beach.
[ænd pɛːɪl glimz ðʌ smɑːɪl ʌv ðʌ si bitʃ]
Death-dealing waves sing meaningless ballads
[dɛθ ˈdilɪŋ wɛːɪvz sɪŋ ˈminɪŋlɛ⁽ɪ⁾s ˈbælæ⁽ɪ⁾dz]
to the children, even like a mother
[tu ðʌ ˈtʃɪldɹɛ⁽ɪ⁾n ˈivɛ⁽ɪ⁾n lɑːɪk ʌ ˈmʌðʌ]
while rocking her baby's cradle.
[ʍɑːɪl ˈɹakɪŋ hɜ ˈbɛːɪbɪz ˈkɹɛːɪdʊl]
The sea plays with children,
[ðʌ si plɛːɪz wɪð ˈtʃɪldɹɛ⁽ɪ⁾n]
and pale gleams the smile of the sea-beach.
[ænd pɛːɪl glimz ðʌ smɑːɪl ʌv ðʌ si bitʃ]
On the seashore of endless worlds children meet.
[an ðʌ ˈsiʃɔːʁ⁽ʳ⁾ ʌv ˈɛndlɛ⁽ɪ⁾s wɜldz ˈtʃɪldɹɛ⁽ɪ⁾n mit]
Tempest roams in the pathless sky,
[ˈtɛmpɛ⁽ɪ⁾st ɹoːʊmz ɪn ðʌ ˈpæθlɛ⁽ɪ⁾s skɑːɪ]
ships get wrecked in the trackless water,
[ʃɪps gɛt ɹɛkt ɪn ðʌ ˈtɹæklɛ⁽ɪ⁾s ˈwɔtʌ]
death is abroad and children play.
[dɛθ ɪz ʌˈbɹɔd ænd ˈtʃɪldɹɛ⁽ɪ⁾n plɛːɪ]
On the seashore of endless worlds
[an ðʌ ˈsiʃɔːʁ⁽ʳ⁾ ʌv ˈɛndlɛ⁽ɪ⁾s wɜldz]

is the great meeting of children.
[ɪz ðʌ gɹɛːɪt ˈmitɪŋ ʌv ˈtʃɪldɹɛ(ɪ)n]

6. Light, My Light
[lɑːɪt mɑːɪ lɑːɪt]

Light, my light, the world-filling light,
[lɑːɪt mɑːɪ lɑːɪt ðʌ wɜld ˈfɪlɪŋ lɑːɪt]
the eye-kissing light, heart-sweetening light!
[ði ɑːɪ ˈkɪsɪŋ lɑːɪt hɑt ˈswitɛ(ɪ)nɪŋ lɑːɪt]
Ah, the light dances, my darling,
[ɑ ðʌ lɑːɪt ˈdænsɛ(ɪ)z mɑːɪ ˈdɑlɪŋ]
at the centre of my life;
[æt ðʌ ˈsɛntʌʁ⁽ʳ⁾ ʌv mɑːɪ lɑːɪf]
the light strikes, my darling, the chords of my love;
[ðʌ lɑːɪt stɹɑːɪks mɑːɪ ˈdɑlɪŋ ðʌ kɔdz ʌv mɑːɪ lʌv]
the sky opens, the wind runs wild,
[ðʌ skɑːɪ ˈoːʊpɛ(ɪ)nz ðʌ wɪnd ɹʌnz wɑːɪld]
laughter passes over the earth.
[ˈlæftʌ ˈpæsɛ(ɪ)z ˈoːʊvʌ ði ɜθ]
The butterflies spread their sails on the sea of light.
[ðʌ ˈbʌtʌflɑːɪz spɹɛd ðɛːʌ sɛːɪlz an ðʌ si ʌv lɑːɪt]
Lilies and jasmines surge up on the crest
[ˈlɪlɪz ænd ˈdʒæzmɪnz sɜdʒ ʌp an ðʌ kɹɛst]
of the waves of light.
[ʌv ðʌ wɛːɪvz ʌv lɑːɪt]
The light is shattered into gold on every cloud,
[ðʌ lɑːɪt ɪz ˈʃætʌd ˈɪntu goːʊld an ˈɛvɹɪ klɑːʊd]
my darling,
[mɑːɪ ˈdɑlɪŋ]
and it scatters gems in profusion.
[ænd ɪt ˈskætʌz dʒɛmz ɪn pɹoˈfjuʒʌn]
Mirth spreads from leaf to leaf, my darling,
[mɜθ spɹɛdz fɹʌm lif tu lif mɑːɪ ˈdɑlɪŋ]
and gladness without measure.
[ænd ˈglædnɛ(ɪ)s wɪðˈɑːʊt ˈmɛʒʊ(ʌ)]
The heaven's river has drowned its banks
[ðʌ ˈhɛvɛ(ɪ)nz ˈɹɪvʌ hæz dɹɑːʊnd ɪts bæŋks]
and the flood of joy is abroad.
[ænd ðʌ flʌd ʌv dʒɔːɪ ɪz ʌˈbɹɔd]

Song Selections

"Go, Lovely Rose" (see "Song" by Rorem)

"Little Fly"
[ˈlɪtʊl flɑːɪ]
Blake, William (Eng. 1757-1827)

Little fly,
[ˈlɪtʊl flɑːɪ]
Thy summer's play
[ðɑːɪ ˈsʌmʌz plɛːɪ]
My thoughtless hand
[mɑːɪ ˈθɔtlɛ(ɪ)s hænd]

Has brush'd away.
[hæz bɹʌʃt ʌˈwɛːɪ]
Am not I
[æm nat ɑːɪ]
A fly like thee?
[ʌ flɑːɪ lɑːɪk ði]
Or art not thou
[ɔʁ⁽ʳ⁾ ɑt nat ðɑːʊ]
A man like me?
[ʌ mæn lɑːɪk mi]
For I dance,
[fɔʁ⁽ʳ⁾ ɑːɪ dæns]
And drink and sing,
[ænd dɹɪŋk ænd sɪŋ]
Till some blind hand
[tɪl sʌm blɑːɪnd hænd]
Shall brush my wing.
[ʃæl bɹʌʃ mɑːɪ wɪŋ]
If thought is life
[ɪf θɔt ɪz lɑːɪf]
And strength and breath,
[ænd stɹɛŋθ ænd bɹɛθ]
And the want
[ænd ðʌ want]
Of thought is Death;
[ʌv θɔt ɪz dɛθ]
Then am I
[ðɛn æm ɑːɪ]
A happy fly,
[ʌ ˈhæpɪ flɑːɪ]
If I live,
[ɪf ɑːɪ lɪv]
Or if I die.
[ɔʁ⁽ʳ⁾ ɪf ɑːɪ dɑːɪ]

"Looking-Glass River"
[ˈlʊkɪŋ glæs ˈɹɪvʁ]
Stevenson, Robert Louis (Sc. 1850-1894)

Smooth it slides upon its travel,
[smuð ɪt slɑːɪdz ʌˈpan ɪts ˈtɹævʊl]
Here a wimple, there a gleam–
[hɪːʌʁ⁽ʳ⁾ ʌ ˈwɪmpʊl ðɛːʌʁ⁽ʳ⁾ ʌ glim]
O the clean gravel!
[oːʊ ðʌ klin ˈgɹævʊl]
O the smooth stream!
[oːʊ ðʌ smuð stɹim]
Sailing blossoms, silver fishes,
[ˈsɛːɪlɪŋ ˈblasʌmz ˈsɪlvʌ ˈfɪʃɛ(ɪ)z]
Paven pools as clear as air–
[ˈpɛːɪvɛ(ɪ)n pulz æz klɪːʌʁ⁽ʳ⁾ æz ɛːʌ]
How a child wishes
[hɑːʊ ʌ tʃɑːɪld ˈwɪʃɛ(ɪ)z]
To live down there.
[tu lɪv dɑːʊn ðɛːʌ]

"The Green River"
[ðʌ gɹin ˈɹɪvʁ]
Douglas, Lord Alfred (Eng. 1870-1945)

I know a green grass path that leaves the field
[ɑːɪ noːʊ ʌ gɹin gɹæs pæθ ðæt livz ðʌ fild]
And, like a running river, winds along
[ænd lɑːɪk ʌ ˈɹʌnɪŋ ˈɹɪvʌ wɑːɪndz ʌˈlɑŋ]
Into a leafy wood, where is no throng
[ˈɪntu ʌ ˈlifɪ wʊd ʍɛːʌʁ⁽ʳ⁾ ɪz noːʊ θɹɑŋ]
Of birds at noon-day; and no soft throats yield
[ʌv bɜdz æt nun dɛːɪ ænd noːʊ sɑft θɹoːʊts jild]
Their music to the moon. The place is sealed,
[ðɛːʌ ˈmjuzɪk tu ðʌ mun ðʌ plɛːɪs ɪz sild]
An unclaimed sovereignty of voiceless song,
[æn ʌnˈklɛːɪmd ˈsɑvɹɛ(ɪ)ntɪ ʌv ˈvɔːɪslɛ(ɪ)s sɑŋ]
And all th' unravished silences belong
[ænd ɔl ðʌnˈɹævɪʃt ˈsɑːɪlɛ(ɪ)nsɛ(ɪ)z bɪˈlɑŋ]
To some sweet singer lost, or unrevealed.
[tu sʌm swit ˈsɪŋʌ lɑst ɔʁ⁽ʳ⁾ ʌnɹɪˈvild]
So is my soul become a silent place.
[soːʊ ɪz mɑːɪ soːʊl bɪˈkʌm ʌ ˈsɑːɪlɛnt plɛːɪs]
Oh, may I awake from this uneasy night
[oːʊ mɛːɪ ɑːɪ ʌˈwɛːɪk fɹʌm ðɪs ʌnˈizɪ nɑːɪt]
To find some voice of music manifold.
[tu fɑːɪnd sʌm vɔːɪs ʌv ˈmjuzɪk ˈmænɪfoːʊld]
Let it be shape of sorrow with wan face,
[lɛt ɪt bi ʃɛːɪp ʌv ˈsɑʁ⁽ʳ⁾oːʊ wɪð wɑn fɛːɪs]
Or love, that swoons on sleep, or else delight
[ɔ lʌv ðæt swunz ɑn slip ɔʁ⁽ʳ⁾ ɛls dɪˈlɑːɪt]
That is as wide-eyed as a marigold.
[ðæt ɪz æz wɑːɪd ɑːɪd æz ʌ ˈmæʁ⁽ʳ⁾ɪgoːʊld]

Chanler, Theodore (Am. 1902-1961)

Eight Epitaphs (Song Cycle)
[ɛːɪt ˈɛpɪtæfs]
Mare, Walter de la (Eng. 1873-1956)

1. Alice Rodd
[ˈælɪs ɹɑd]

Here lyeth our infant, Alice Rodd;
[hɪːʌ ˈlɑːɪɛ(ɪ)θ ɑːʊʁ⁽ʳ⁾ ˈɪnfæ(ɪ)nt ˈælɪs ɹɑd]
She was so small, Scarce aught at all,
[ʃi wɑz soːʊ smɔl skɛːʌs ɔt æt ɔl]
But a mere breath of sweetness sent from God.
[bʌt ʌ mɪːʌ bɹɛθ ʌv ˈswitnɛ(ɪ)s sɛnt fɹʌm gɑd]
Sore we did weep; our hearts on sorrow set.
[sɔːʌ wi dɪd wip ɑːʊʌ hɑts ɑn ˈsɑʁ⁽ʳ⁾oːʊ sɛt]
Till on our knees, God sent us ease:
[tɪl ɑn ɑːʊʌ niz gɑd sɛnt ʌs iz]
And now we weep no more than we forget.
[ænd nɑːʊ wi wip noːʊ mɔːʌ ðæn wi fɔˈgɛt]

2. Susannah Fry
[suˈzænʌ fɹɑːɪ]

Here sleep I, Susannah Fry,
[hɪːʌ slip ɑːɪ suˈzænʌ fɹɑːɪ]
No one near me, No one nigh:
[noːʊ wʌn nɪːʌ mi noːʊ wʌn nɑːɪ]
Alone, alone Under my stone,
[ʌˈloːʊn ʌˈloːʊn ˈʌndʌ mɑːɪ stoːʊn]
Dreaming on, Still dreaming on,
[ˈdɹimɪŋ ɑn stɪl ˈdɹimɪŋ ɑn]
Grass for my valance And coverlid,
[gɹæs fɔ mɑːɪ ˈvælæ(ɪ)ns ænd ˈkʌvʌlɪd]
Dreaming on As I always did.
[ˈdɹimɪŋ ɑn æz ɑːɪ ˈɔlwɛːɪz dɪd]
'Weak in the head' Maybe. Who knows?
[wik ɪn ðʌ hɛd ˈmɛːɪˈbi hu noːʊz]
Susannah Fry Under the rose.
[suˈzænʌ fɹɑːɪ ˈʌndʌ ðʌ ɹoːʊz]

3. Three Sisters
[θɹi ˈsɪstʁz]

Three sisters rest beneath
[θɹi ˈsɪstʌz ɹɛst bɪˈniθ]
This cypress shade,
[ðɪs ˈsɑːɪpɹɛ(ɪ)s ʃɛːɪd]
Sprightly Rebecca, Anne,
[ˈspɹɑːɪtlɪ ɹʌˈbɛkʌ æn]
And Adelaide.
[ænd ædʌˈlɛːɪd]
Gentle their hearts to all
[ˈdʒɛntʊl ðɛːʌ hɑts tu ɔl]
On earth, save Man;
[ɑn ɜθ sɛːɪv mæn]
In Him, they said, all Grief,
[ɪn hɪm ðɛːɪ sɛd ɔl gɹ⁽ʳ⁾if]
All Woe began.
[ɔl woːʊ bɪˈgæn]
Spinsters they lived, and spinsters
[ˈspɪnstʌz ðɛːɪ lɪvd ænd ˈspɪnstʌz]
Here are laid;
[hɪːʌʁ⁽ʳ⁾ ɑ lɛːɪd]
Sprightly Rebecca, Anne,
[ˈspɹɑːɪtlɪ ɹʌˈbɛkʌ æn]
And Adelaide.
[ænd ædʌˈlɛːɪd]

4. Thomas Logge
[ˈtɑmʌs lɑg]

Here lies Thomas Logge–A rascally dogge;
[hɪːʌ lɑːɪz ˈtɑmʌs lɑg ʌ ˈɹæskʊlɪ dɑg]
A poor useless creature–by choice as by nature;
[ʌ pʊːʌ ˈjuslɛ(ɪ)s ˈkɹitʃʊ(ʌ) bɑːɪ tʃɔːɪs æz bɑːɪ ˈnɛːɪtʃʊ(ʌ)]

Who never served God– for kindness or Rod;
[hu ˈnɛvʌ sɜvd gɑd fɔ ˈkɑːɪndnɛ(ɪ)s ɔ ɹɑd]
Who, for pleasure or penny,– never did any
[hu fɔ ˈplɛʒʊ(ʌ)ʁ(r) ɔ ˈpɛnɪ ˈnɛvʌ dɪd ˈɛnɪ]
Work in his life– but to marry a Wife,
[wɜk ɪn hɪz lɑːɪf bʌt tu ˈmæʁ(r)ɪ ʌ wɑːɪf]
And live aye in strife:
[ænd lɪv ɑːɪ ɪn stɹɑːɪf]
And all this he says– at the end of his days
[ænd ɔl ðɪs hi sɛz æt ði ɛnd ʌv hɪz dɛːɪz]
Lest some fine canting pen Should be at him again.
[lɛst sʌm fɑːɪn ˈkæntɪŋ pɛn ʃʊd bi æt hɪm ʌˈgɛn]

5. A Midget
[ʌ ˈmɪdʒɪt]

Just a span and half a span
[dʒʌst ʌ spæn ænd hæf ʌ spæn]
From head to heel was this little man.
[fɹʌm hɛd tu hil wɑz ðɪs ˈlɪtʊl mæn]
Scarcely a capful of small bones
[ˈskɛːʌslɪ ʌ ˈkæpfʊl ʌv smɔl boːʊnz]
Raised up erect this midget once.
[ɹɛːɪzd ʌp ɪˈʁ(r)ɛkt ðɪs ˈmɪdʒɛ(ɪ)t wʌns]
Yet not a knuckle was askew;
[jɛt nɑt ʌ ˈnʌkʊl wɑz ʌˈskju]
Inches for feet God made him true;
[ˈɪntʃɛ(ɪ)z fɔ fit gɑd mɛːɪd hɪm tɹ(r)u]
And something handsome put between
[ænd ˈsʌmθɪŋ ˈhænsʌm pʊt bɪˈtwin]
His coal-black hair and beardless chin.
[hɪz koːʊl blæk hɛːʌʁ(r) ænd ˈbɪːʌdlɛ(ɪ)s tʃɪn]
But now, forsooth, with mole and mouse,
[bʌt nɑːʊ fɔˈsuθ wɪð moːʊl ænd mɑːʊs]
He keeps his own small darkened home
[hi kips hɪz oːʊn smɔl ˈdɑkɛ(ɪ)nd hoːʊm]

6. No Voice to Scold
[noːʊ vɔːɪs tu skoːʊld]

No Voice to scold;
[noːʊ vɔːɪs tu skoːʊld]
No face to frown;
[noːʊ fɛːɪs tu fɹɑːʊn]
No hand to smite
[noːʊ hænd tu smɑːɪt]
The helpless down:
[ðʌ ˈhɛlplɛ(ɪ)s dɑːʊn]
Ay, Stranger, here
[ɑːɪ ˈstɹɛːɪndʒʌ hɪːʌʁ(r)]
An Infant lies,
[æn ˈɪnfæ(ɪ)nt lɑːɪz]
With worms for
[wɪð wɜmz fɔ]
Welcome Paradise.
[ˈwɛlkʌm ˈpæʁ(r)ʌdɑːɪs]

7. Ann Poverty
[æn ˈpɑvʁtɪ]

Stranger, here lies Ann Poverty;
[ˈstɹɛːɪndʒʌ hɪːʌ lɑːɪz æn ˈpɑvʌtɪ]
Such was her name, And such was she.
[sʌtʃ wɑz hɜ nɛːɪm ænd sʌtʃ wɑz ʃi]
May Jesu pity Poverty.
[mɛːɪ ˈjezu ˈpɪtɪ ˈpɑvʌtɪ]

8. Be Very Quiet Now
[bi ˈvɛʁi ˈkwɑːɪt nɑːʊ]

Be very quiet now:
[bi ˈvɛʁ(r)ɪ ˈkwɑːɪɛ(ɪ)t nɑːʊ]
A child's asleep
[ʌ tʃɑːɪldz ʌˈslip]
In this small cradle,
[ɪn ðɪs smɔl ˈkɹɛːɪdʊl]
In this shadow deep!
[ɪn ðɪs ˈʃædoːʊ dip]

Song Selections

"O Mistress Mine" (see Quilter)

"The Lamb" (see Hoiby)

"Tillie"
[ˈtɪli]
Mare, Walter de la (Eng. 1873-1956)

Old Tillie Turveycombe sat to sew,
[oːʊld ˈtɪlɪ ˈtɜvɪkoːʊm sæt tu soːʊ]
Just where a patch of fern did grow;
[dʒʌst ʍɛːʌʁ(r) ʌ pætʃ ʌv fɜn dɪd gɹoːʊ]
There, as she yawned, and yawn wide did she,
[ðɛːʌʁ(r) æz ʃi jɔnd ænd jɔn wɑːɪd dɪd ʃi]
Floated some seed down her gull-e-t;
[ˈfloːʊtɛ(ɪ)d sʌm sid dɑːʊn hɜ gʌl i ti]
And look you once,
[ænd lʊk ju wʌns]
And look you twice,
[ænd lʊk ju twɑːɪs]
Poor old Tillie was gone in a trice.
[pʊːʌʁ(r) oːʊld ˈtɪlɪ wɑz gɑn ɪn ʌ tɹɑːɪs]
But oh, when the wind do a-moaning come,
[bʌt oːʊ ʍɛn ðʌ wɪnd du ʌ ˈmoːʊnɪŋ kʌm]
'Tis poor old Tillie sick for home;
[tɪz pʊːʌʁ(r) oːʊld ˈtɪlɪ sɪk fɔ hoːʊm]
And oh, when a voice in the mist do sigh,
[ænd oːʊ ʍɛn ʌ vɔːɪs ɪn ðʌ mɪst du sɑːɪ]
Old Tillie Turveycombe's floating by.
[oːʊld ˈtɪlɪ ˈtɜvɪkoːʊmz ˈfloːʊtɪŋ bɑːɪ]

"Wind"
[wɪnd]
Feeney, Leonard (Am. 1897-1978)

Wind is to show
[wɪnd ɪz tu ʃoːʊ]
How a thing can blow,
[haːʊ ʌ θɪŋ kæn bloːʊ]
And especially through trees;
[ænd ɪ'spɛʃʊlɪ θru tɹiz]
When it is fast
[ʍɛn ɪt ɪz fæst]
It is called a blast,
[ɪt ɪz kɔld ʌ blæst]
And it's otherwise known as a breeze.
[ænd ɪts 'ʌðʌwaːɪz noːʊn æz ʌ bɹiz]
It begins somewhere in the sky,
[ɪt bɪ'ɡɪnz 'sʌmʍɛːʌʁ⁽ʳ⁾ ɪn ðʌ skaːɪ]
Like a sigh,
[laːɪk ʌ saːɪ]
Then it turns to a roar,
[ðɛn ɪt tɜnz tu ʌ ɹɔːʌ]
And returns to a sigh once more.
[ænd ɹɪ'tɜnz tu ʌ saːɪ wʌns mɔːʌ]
Wind is the air
[wɪnd ɪz ði ɛːʌʁ⁽ʳ⁾]
In your hair,
[ɪn jɔːʌ hɛːʌ]
When you stand
[ʍɛn ju stænd]
On the sand
[ɑn ðʌ sænd]
By the shore.
[baːɪ ðʌ ʃɔːʌ]
Wind will shake the lattices late at night,
[wɪnd wɪl ʃɛːɪk ðʌ 'lætɪsɛ(ɪ)z lɛːɪt æt naːɪt]
It will make the clouds go by;
[ɪt wɪl mɛːɪk ðʌ klaːʊdz goːʊ baːɪ]
Anything easy that's hard to do,
['ɛnɪθɪŋ 'izɪ ðæts hɑd tu du]
It is pretty sure to try:
[ɪt ɪz 'pɹɪtɪ ʃʊːʌ tu tɹaːɪ]
Blow down a pine,
[bloːʊ daːʊn ʌ paːɪn]
Clothes from a line,
[kloːʊðz fɹʌm ʌ laːɪn]
Tumble a chimney top.
['tʌmbʊl ʌ 'ʧɪmnɪ tɑp]
Wind is the general sound
[wɪnd ɪz ðʌ 'dʒɛnʌʁ⁽ʳ⁾ʊl saːʊnd]
You hear around,
[ju hɪːʌʁ⁽ʳ⁾ ʌ'ʁ⁽ʳ⁾aːʊnd]
That suddenly likes to stop.
[ðæt 'sʌdɛ(ɪ)nlɪ laːɪks tu stɑp]

Charles, Ernest (Am. 1895-1984)

Song Selections

"And So, Goodbye"
[ænd soːʊ ɡʊd'baːɪ]
Charles, Ernest (Am. 1895-1984)

And so, goodbye!
[ænd soːʊ ɡʊd'baːɪ]
Go now; no, do not say a word.
[ɡoːʊ naːʊ noːʊ du nɑt sɛːɪ ʌ wɜd]
I do not care to know the reason why:
[aːɪ du nɑt kɛːʌ tu noːʊ ðʌ 'ɹizʌn ʍaːɪ]
Too deep the grief that now my heart must bear;
[tu dip ðʌ ɡɹ⁽ʳ⁾if ðæt naːʊ maːɪ hɑt mʌst bɛːʌ]
Enough to know my dreams are all awry,
[ɪ'nʌf tu noːʊ maːɪ dɹimz aʁ⁽ʳ⁾ ɔl ʌ'ʁ⁽ʳ⁾aːɪ]
And so, goodbye.
[ænd soːʊ ɡʊd'baːɪ]
Go now; no, do not touch my hand.
[ɡoːʊ naːʊ noːʊ du nɑt tʌʧ maːɪ hænd]
I could not stand that added bit of pain:
[aːɪ kʊd nɑt stænd ðæt 'ædɛ(ɪ)d bɪt ʌv pɛːɪn]
Enough to remember one hour of joy,
[ɪ'nʌf tu ɹɪ'mɛmbʌ wʌn aːʊʁ⁽ʳ⁾ ʌv dʒɔːɪ]
One hour of ecstasy
[wʌn aːʊʁ⁽ʳ⁾ ʌv 'ɛkstʌsɪ]
And so, goodbye, goodbye.
[ænd soːʊ ɡʊd'baːɪ ɡʊd'baːɪ]

"Clouds"
[klaːʊdz]
Anonymous

Clouds adrift in the summer sky
[klaːʊdz ʌ'dɹɪft ɪn ðʌ 'sʌmʌ skaːɪ]
Resemble Life, as they wander by.
[ɹɪ'zɛmbʊl laːɪf æz ðɛːɪ 'wandʌ baːɪ]
Whence they come and whither they go
[ʍɛns ðɛːɪ kʌm ænd 'ʍɪðʌ ðɛːɪ ɡoːʊ]
We often wonder but never know;
[wi 'ɑfɛ(ɪ)n 'wʌndʌ bʌt 'nɛvʌ noːʊ]
One little hour we know their grace–
[wʌn 'lɪtʊl aːʊʌ wi noːʊ ðɛːʌ ɡɹɛːɪs]
They pass like shadows, nor hold their place,
[ðɛːɪ pæs laːɪk 'ʃædoːʊz nɔ hoːʊld ðɛːʌ plɛːɪs]
Ever recurring, like the dawn,
['ɛvʌ ɹɪ'kʊʁ⁽ʳ⁾ɪŋ laːɪk ðʌ dɔn]
Never enduring, but always gone,
['nɛvʌʁ⁽ʳ⁾ ɪn'djuːʌʁ⁽ʳ⁾ɪŋ bʌt 'ɔlwɛːɪz ɡan]
Part of the infinite, shall we say,
[pɑt ʌv ði 'ɪnfɪnɪt ʃæl wi sɛːɪ]
Part of the moment we call today.
[pɑt ʌv ðʌ 'moːʊmɛnt wi kɔl tu'dɛːɪ]

"Let My Song Fill Your Heart"
[lɛt maːɪ saŋ fil jɔːʁ haʁt]
Anonymous

Let my song fill your heart
[lɛt maːɪ saŋ fil jɔːʌ hat]
With its melody oh so divine,
[wɪð ɪts ˈmɛlodɪ oːʊ soːʊ dɪˈvaːɪn]
That thrills me like a dream
[ðæt θrɪlz mi laːɪk ʌ dɹim]
Of happiness supreme.
[ʌv ˈhæpɪnɛ(ɪ)s suˈpɹim]
It's enchanting, it's sublime!
[ɪts ɪnˈʧæntɪŋ ɪts sʌˈblaːɪm]
Let my song say the words
[lɛt maːɪ saŋ sɛːɪ ðʌ wɜdz]
That my lips are afraid to say-
[ðæt maːɪ lɪps aʁ(ʳ) ʌˈfɹɛːɪd tu sɛːɪ]
Of the yearning
[ʌv ðʌ ˈjɜnɪŋ]
And of desires burning
[ænd ʌv dɪˈzaːɪʌz ˈbɜnɪŋ]
To hold you and to fold you
[tu hoːʊld ju ænd tu foːʊld ju]
So close, close to my heart!
[soːʊ kloːʊs kloːʊs tu maːɪ hat]
The evening falls,
[ði ˈivnɪŋ fɔlz]
So come to me-
[soːʊ kʌm tu mi]
Come like the sighing wind from the sea,
[kʌm laːɪk ðʌ ˈsaːɪŋ wɪnd fɹʌm ðʌ si]
And brightly, so lightly,
[ænd ˈbɹaːɪtlɪ soːʊ ˈlaːɪtlɪ]
We'll dance on the shining sand.
[wil dæns an ðʌ ˈʃaːɪnɪŋ sænd]
All thro' the night
[ɔl θru ðʌ naːɪt]
That's filled with sheer delight,
[ðæts fild wɪð ʃiːʌ dɪˈlaːɪt]
Our lamp of love will ever be bright,
[aːʊʌ læmp ʌv lʌv wɪl ˈɛvʌ bi bɹaːɪt]
And so all thro' life we will walk hand in hand.
[ænd soːʊ ɔl θru laːɪf wi wɪl wɔk hænd ɪn hænd]

"My Lady Walks in Loveliness"
[maːɪ ˈlɛːɪdi wɔks ɪn ˈlʌvlinɪs]
Charles, Ernest (Am. 1895-1984)

My Lady walks in loveliness
[maːɪ ˈlɛːɪdi wɔks ɪn ˈlʌvlinɛ(ɪ)s]
And shames the moon's cold grace.
[ænd ʃɛːɪmz ðʌ munz koːʊld ɡɹɛːɪs]
A thousand songs dwell in her voice,
[ʌ ˈθaːʊzæ(ʌ)nd saŋz dwɛl ɪn hɜ vɔːɪs]

Enchantment in her face,
[ɪnˈʧæntmɛnt ɪn hɜ fɛːɪs]
And Love himself lays down his lute
[ænd lʌv hɪmˈsɛlf lɛːɪz daːʊn hɪz ljut]
To mark her passing there,
[tu mɑk hɜ ˈpæsɪŋ ðɛːʌ]
A lovely lyric lady
[ʌ ˈlʌvlɪ ˈlɪʁ(ʳ)ɪk ˈlɛːɪdi]
With sun beams in her hair.
[wɪð sʌn bimz ɪn hɜ hɛːʌ]

 # Cipullo, Tom (Am. b. 1956)

A Visit with Emily (Song Cycle)
[ʌ ˈvɪzɪt wɪθ ˈɛmɪli]
Dickinson, Emily (Am. 1830-1886) and
letters from T.W. Higginson

1. Cavatina (letter from T.W. Higginson to his wife,
[kavaˈtina ˈlɛtʁ fɹʌm ti ˈdʌbʊlju ˈhɪɡɪnsʌn tu hɪz waːɪf]
quoting Emily Dickinson)
[ˈkwoːʊtɪŋ ˈɛmɪli ˈdɪkɪnsʌn]

If I read a book and it makes
[ɪf aːɪ ɹid ʌ bʊk ænd ɪt mɛːɪks]
my whole body so cold
[maːɪ hoːʊl ˈbɑdɪ soːʊ koːʊld]
no fire ever can warm me,
[noːʊ faːɪʌʁ(ʳ) ˈɛvʌ kæn wɔm mi]
I know that is poetry.
[aːɪ noːʊ ðæt ɪz ˈpoːʊɛ(ɪ)tɹɪ]
If I feel physically as if the top of my head
[ɪf aːɪ fil ˈfɪzɪklɪ æz ɪf ðʌ tɑp ʌv maːɪ hɛd]
were taken off, I know that is poetry.
[wɜ ˈtɛːɪke(ɪ)n ɑf aːɪ noːʊ ðæt ɪz ˈpoːʊɛ(ɪ)tɹɪ]
These are the only ways I know it.
[ðiz a ði ˈoːʊnlɪ wɛːɪz aːɪ noːʊ ɪt]
Is there any other way?
[ɪz ðɛːʌʁ(ʳ) ˈɛni ˈʌðʌ wɛːɪ]

2. Arietta parlante (letter from Dickinson to T.W.
[aˈrjetta parˈlante ˈlɛtʁ fɹʌm ˈdɪkɪnsʌn tu ti ˈdʌbʊlju]
Higginson, 7 June 1862)
[ˈhɪɡɪnsʌn ˈsɛvɪn dʒun ˈɛːɪtin ˈsɪksti tu]

Dear friend, – Your letter gave no drunkenness,
[dɪʌ fɹɛnd jɔːʌ ˈlɛtʌ ɡɛːɪv noːʊ ˈdɹʌŋke(ɪ)nɛ(ɪ)s]
because I tasted rum before.
[bɪˈkɔz aːɪ ˈtɛːɪstɛ(ɪ)d ɹʌm bɪˈfɔːʌ]
Domingo comes but once;
[doˈmiŋɡoːʊ kʌmz bʌt wʌns]
yet I have had few pleasures
[jɛt aːɪ hæv hæd fju ˈplɛʒʊ(ʌ)z]
so deep as your opinion,
[soːʊ dip æz jɔːʌʁ(ʳ) oˈpɪnjʌn]

and if I tried to thank you,
[ænd ɪf ɑːɪ tɹɑːɪd tu θæŋk ju]
my tears would block my tongue.
[mɑːɪ tiːʌz wʊd blɑk mɑːɪ tʌŋ]
If fame belonged to me, I could not escape her;
[ɪf fɛːɪm bɪˈlɑŋd tu mi ɑːɪ kʊd nɑt ɪˈskɛːɪp hɜ]
if she did not,
[ɪf ʃi dɪd nɑt]
the longest day would pass me on the chase,
[ðʌ ˈlɑŋgɛ(ɪ)st dɛːɪ wʊd pæs mi ɑn ðʌ ʧɛːɪs]
and the approbation of my dog
[ænd ði ˌæpɹoˈbɛːɪʃʌn ʌv mɑːɪ dɑg]
would forsake me then.
[wʊd fɔˈsɛːɪk mi ðɛn]
My barefoot rank is better.
[mɑːɪ ˈbɛːʌfʊt ɹæŋk ɪz ˈbɛtʌ]

3. Aria (Fame Is a Fickle Food)
[ˈɑɾia fɛːɪm ɪz ʌ ˈfɪkʊl fud]

Fame is a fickle food
[fɛːɪm ɪz ʌ ˈfɪkʊl fud]
Upon a shifting plate
[ʌˈpɑn ʌ ˈʃɪftɪŋ plɛːɪt]
Whose table once a
[huz ˈtɛːɪbʊl wʌns ʌ]
Guest but not
[gɛst bʌt nɑt]
The second time is set
[ðʌ ˈsɛkʌnd tɑːɪm ɪz sɛt]
Whose crumbs the crows inspect
[huz kɹʌmz ðʌ kɹoːʊz ɪnˈspɛkt]
And with ironic caw
[ænd wɪð ɑːɪˈʁ(ʳ)ɑnɪk kɔ]
Flap past it to the
[flæp pæst ɪt tu ðʌ]
Farmer's corn
[ˈfɑmʌz kɔn]
Men eat of it and die
[mɛn it ʌv ɪt ænd dɑːɪ]

4. Moto perpetuo
[ˈmɔto perˈpɛtuo]
(Fame Is the One That Does Not Stay)
[fɛːɪm ɪz ðʌ wʌn ðæt dʌz nɑt stɛːɪ]

Fame is the one that does not stay –
[fɛːɪm ɪz ðʌ wʌn ðæt dʌz nɑt stɛːɪ]
It's occupant must die
[ɪts ˈɑkjupæ(ɪ)nt mʌst dɑːɪ]
Or out of sight of estimate
[ɔʁ(ʳ) ɑːʊt ʌv sɑːɪt ʌv ˈɛstɪmɪt]
Ascend incessantly –
[ʌˈsɛnd ɪnˈsɛsæ(ɪ)ntlɪ]
Or be that most insolvent thing
[ɔ bi ðæt moːʊst ɪnˈsɑlvɛnt θɪŋ]

A Lightning in the Germ –
[ʌ ˈlɑːɪtnɪŋ ɪn ðʌ dʒɜm]
Electrical the embryo
[ɪˈlɛktɹɪkʊl ði ˈɛmbɹɪoːʊ]
But we demand the Flame
[bʌt wi dɪˈmænd ðʌ flɛːɪm]

5. Arietta (Fame Is a Bee)
[aˈɾjetta fɛːɪm ɪz ʌ bi]

Fame is a bee.
[fɛːɪm ɪz ʌ bi]
It has a song–
[ɪt hæz ʌ sɑŋ]
It has a sting–
[ɪt hæz ʌ stɪŋ]
Ah, too, it has a wing.
[ɑ tu ɪt hæz ʌ wɪŋ]

6. Quodlibet I–
[ˈkwɑdlɪˌbɛt wʌn]

7. Arioso (letter to T.W. Higginson,
[aˈɾjoso ˈlɛtʁ tu ti ˈdʌbʊlju ˈhɪgɪnsʌn]
July 1862)
[dʒuˈlɑːɪ ˈɛːɪtin ˈsɪksti tu]

Could you believe me-without?
[kʊd ju bɪˈliv mi wɪðˈɑːʊt]
I had no portrait, now, but am small, like the Wren,
[ɑːɪ hæd noːʊ ˈpɔtɹæ(ɪ)t nɑːʊ bʌt æm smɔl lɑːɪk ðʌ ɹɛn]
and my Hair is bold, like the Chestnut Bur-
[ænd mɑːɪ hɛːʌʁ(ʳ) ɪz boːʊld lɑːɪk ðʌ ˈʧɛsnʌt bɜ]
and my eyes, like the Sherry in the Glass,
[ænd mɑːɪ ɑːɪz lɑːɪk ðʌ ˈʃɛʁ(ʳ)ɪ ɪn ðʌ glæs]
that the Guest leaves- Would this do just as well?
[ðæt ðʌ gɛst livz wʊd ðɪs du dʒʌst æz wɛl]

8. Aria di campane (letter to T.W. Higginson,
[ˈɑɾia di kamˈpane ˈlɛtʁ tu ti ˈdʌbʊlju ˈhɪgɪnsʌn]
16 August 1870)
[sɪksˈtin ˈɔgʌst ˈɛːɪtin ˈsɛvɪndi]

Dear friend, I will be at Home and glad.
[dɪːʌ fɹɛnd ɑːɪ wɪl bi æt hoːʊm ænd glæd]
I think you said the 15th.
[ɑːɪ θɪŋk ju sɛd ðʌ fɪfˈtinθ]
The incredible never surprises us
[ði ɪnˈkɹɛdɪbʊl ˈnɛvʌ sɜˈpɹɑːɪzɛ(ɪ)z ʌs]
because it is the incredible.
[bɪˈkɔz ɪt ɪz ði ɪnˈkɹɛdɪbʊl]

56 Cipullo

9. Recitative (letter from Higginson to his wife,
[ˌɹɛsɪtaˈtiv ˈlɛtɐ fɹʌm ˈhɪɡɪnsʌn tu hɪz wɑːɪf]
describing his first visit to Emily Dickinson)
[dɪˈskɹɑːɪbɪŋ hɪz fɜst ˈvɪzɪt tu ˈɛmɪli ˈdɪkɪnsʌn]

A large county lawyer's house, brown brick,
[ʌ lɑdʒ ˈkaːʊntɪ ˈlɔjʌz haːʊs bɹaːɒn bɹɪk]
with great trees & a garden– I sent up my card.
[wɪð ɡɹeːɪt tɹiz ænd ʌ ˈɡadɛ(ɪ)n aːɪ sɛnt ʌp maːɪ kɑd]
A parlor dark & cool & stiffish,
[ʌ ˈpalɔ(ʌ) dak ænd kul ænd ˈstɪfɪʃ]
a few books & engravings
[ʌ fju bʊks ænd ɪnˈɡɹeːɪvɪŋz]
& an open piano–
[ænd æn ˈoːʊpɛ(ɪ)n ˈpjænoːʊ]
Malbone & Out Door Papers among other books.
[ˈmælboːʊn ænd aːʊt dɔːʌ ˈpɛːɪpʌz ʌˈmʌŋ ˈʌðʌ bʊks]
A step like a pattering child's in entry
[ʌ stɛp laːɪk ʌ ˈpætʌɐ⁽ʳ⁾ɪŋ ʧaːɪldz ɪn ˈɛntɹɪ]
& in glided a
[ænd ɪn ˈɡlaːɪdɛ(ɪ)d ʌ]
little plain woman with two smooth bands
[ˈlɪtʊl plɛːɪn ˈwʊmæ(ʌ)n wɪð tu smuð bændz]
of reddish hair & a face a little like Belle Dove's;
[ʌv ˈɹɛdɪʃ hɛːʌ ænd ʌ fɛːɪs ʌ ˈlɪtʊl laːɪk bɛl dʌvz]
not plainer– with no good feature–
[nat ˈplɛːɪnʌ wɪð noːʊ ɡʊd ˈfiʧʊ(ʌ)]
in a very plain & exquisitely clean white pique
[ɪn ʌ ˈvɛɐ⁽ʳ⁾ɪ plɛːɪn ænd ɪkˈskwɪzɪtlɪ klin ʍaːɪt pik]
& a blue net worsted shawl.
[ænd ʌ blu nɛt ˈwʊstɛ(ɪ)d ʃɔl]
She came to me with two day lilies
[ʃi kɛːɪm tu mi wɪð tu dɛːɪ ˈlɪlɪz]
which she put in a sort of childlike way
[ʍɪʧ ʃi pʊt ɪn ʌ sɔt ʌv ˈʧaːɪldlaːɪk wɛːɪ]
into my hand & said "These are my introduction"
[ˈɪntu maːɪ hænd ænd sɛd ðiz ɑ maːɪ ɪntɹoˈdʌkʃʌn]
in a soft breathless childlike voice–
[ɪn ʌ saft ˈbɹɛθlɛ(ɪ)s ˈʧaːɪldlaːɪk vɔːɪs]
& added under her breath
[ænd ˈædɛ(ɪ)d ˈʌndʌ hɜ bɹɛθ]
Forgive me if I am frightened;
[fɔˈɡɪv mi ɪf aːɪ æm ˈfɹaːɪtɛ(ɪ)nd]
I never see strangers
[aːɪ ˈnɛvʌ si ˈstɹɛːɪndʒʌz]
& I hardly know what I say–
[ænd aːɪ ˈhadlɪ noːʊ ʍat aːɪ sɛːɪ]
but she talked soon & thenceforward continuously–
[bʌt ʃi tɔkt sun ænd ˈðɛnsfɔwʊd kʌnˈtɪnjuʌslɪ]
& deferentially– sometimes stopping to ask me
[ænd ˌdɛfʌˈɐ⁽ʳ⁾ɛnʃʊlɪ ˈsʌmtaːɪmz ˈstapɪŋ tu æsk mi]
to talk instead of her– but readily recommencing.
[tu tɔk ɪnˈstɛd ʌv hɜ bʌt ˈɹɛdɪlɪ ˌɹikʌˈmɛnsɪŋ]

10. Catch (Higginson's letter continued,
[kæʧ ˈhɪɡɪnsʌnz ˈlɛtɐ kʌnˈtɪnjud]
quoting Dickinson)
[ˈkwoːʊtɪŋ ˈdɪkɪnsʌn]

Women talk: men are silent:
[ˈwɪmɛ(ɪ)n tɔk mɛn ɑ ˈsaːɪlɛnt]
that is why I dread women;
[ðæt ɪz ʍaːɪ aːɪ dɹɛd ˈwɪmɛ(ɪ)n]

11. Chaconne
[ʃaˈkɔn]
(Your Thoughts Don't Have Words Every Day)
[jɔːɐ θɔts doːʊnt hæv wɜdz ˈɛvɹɪ dɛːɪ]

Your thoughts don't have words every day
[jɔːʌ θɔts doːʊnt hæv wɜdz ˈɛvɹɪ dɛːɪ]
They come a single time
[ðɛːɪ kʌm ʌ ˈsɪŋɡʊl taːɪm]
Like signal esoteric sips
[laːɪk ˈsɪɡnʊl ˌɛsoˈtɛɐ⁽ʳ⁾ɪk sɪps]
Of the communion Wine ˉ
[ʌv ðʌ kʌˈmjunjʌn waːɪn]
Which while you taste so native seems
[ʍɪʧ ʍaːɪl ju tɛːɪst soːʊ ˈnɛːɪtɪv simz]
So easy so to be
[soːʊ ˈizɪ soːʊ tu bi]
You cannot comprehend its price
[ju kæˈnat kampɹɪˈhɛnd ɪts pɹaːɪs]
Nor its infrequency
[nɔɐ⁽ʳ⁾ ɪts ɪnˈfɹikwɪnsɪ]

12. Coranto (Forbidden Fruit a Flavor Has)
[koˈranto fɔɐˈbɪdɪn fɹut ʌ ˈflɛːɪvɐ hæz]

Forbidden fruit a flavor has
[fɔˈbɪdɛ(ɪ)n fɹ⁽ʳ⁾ut ʌ ˈflɛːɪvɔ(ʌ) hæz]
That lawful orchards mocks;
[ðæt ˈlɔfʊl ˈɔʧʌdz maks]
How luscious lies within the pod
[haːʊ ˈlʌʃʌs laːɪz wɪðˈɪn ðʌ pad]
The pea that Duty locks!
[ðʌ pi ðæt ˈdjutɪ laks]

13. Passacaglia (Higginson's letter to his wife)
[passaˈkaʎʎa ˈhɪɡɪnsʌnz ˈlɛtɐ tu hɪz waːɪf]

When I said,
[ʍɛn aːɪ sɛd]
I would come again sometime,
[aːɪ wʊd kʌm ʌˈɡɛn ˈsʌmtaːɪm]
she said, "Say, in a long time; that will be nearer.
[ʃi sɛd sɛːɪ ɪn ʌ laŋ taːɪm ðæt wɪl bi ˈnɪːɐ⁽ʳ⁾ʌ]
Some time is nothing."
[sʌm taːɪm ɪz ˈnʌθɪŋ]

14. Trio (If You Were Coming in the Fall)
['tɹio ɪf ju wɜ 'kʌmɪŋ ɪn ðʌ fɔl]

If you were coming in the Fall,
[ɪf ju wɜ 'kʌmɪŋ ɪn ðʌ fɔl]
I'd brush the Summer by
[ɑːɪd bɹʌʃ ðʌ 'sʌmʌ bɑːɪ]
With half a smile, and half a spurn,
[wɪð hæf ʌ smɑːɪl ænd hæf ʌ spɜn]
As Housewives do, a Fly.
[æz 'hɑːʊswɑːɪvz du ʌ flɑːɪ]
If I could see you in a year,
[ɪf ɑːɪ kʊd si ju ɪn ʌ jɪːʌ]
I'd wind the months in balls–
[ɑːɪd wɑːɪnd ðʌ mʌnθs ɪn bɔlz]
And put them each in separate Drawers,
[ænd pʊt ðɛm iʃ ɪn 'sɛpʌʁ⁽ʳ⁾æ(ɪ)t dɹɔːʌz]
For fear the numbers fuse–
[fɔ fɪːʌ ðʌ 'nʌmbʌz fjuz]
If only Centuries, delayed,
[ɪf 'oːʊnlɪ 'sɛntʃʊʁ⁽ʳ⁾ɪz dɪ'lɛːɪd]
I'd count them on my Hand,
[ɑːɪd kɑːʊnt ðɛm ɑn mɑːɪ hænd]
Subtracting, til my fingers dropped
[sʌb'tɹæktɪŋ tɪl mɑːɪ 'fɪŋgʌz dɹɑpt]
Into Van Dieman's Land,
['ɪntu væn 'dimæ(ʌ)nz lænd]
If certain, when this life was out–
[ɪf 'sɜtæ(ɪ)n ʍɛn ðɪs lɑːɪf wɑz ɑːʊt]
That yours and mine, should be
[ðæt jɔːʌz ænd mɑːɪn ʃʊd bi]
I'd toss it yonder, like a Rind,
[ɑːɪd tɑs ɪt 'jɑndʌ lɑːɪk ʌ ɹɑːɪnd]
And take Eternity–
[ænd tɛːɪk ɪ'tɜnɪtɪ]
But, now, uncertain of the length
[bʌt nɑːʊ ʌn'sɜtæ(ɪ)n ʌv ðʌ lɛŋθ]
Of this, that is between,
[ʌv ðɪs ðæt ɪz bɪ'twin]
It goads me, like the Goblin Bee–
[ɪt goːʊdz mi lɑːɪk ðʌ 'gɑblɪn bi]
That will not state– its sting.
[ðæt wɪl nɑt stɛːɪt ɪts stɪŋ]

15. Cantilena I
[kanti'lɛna wʌn]
(letter to T.W. Higginson, June 1878)
['lɛtʁ tu ti 'dʌbʊlju 'hɪgɪnsʌn dʒun 'ɛːɪtin 'sɛvɪndi ɛːt]

When you wrote you would come in November,
[ʍɛn ju ɹoːʊt ju wʊd kʌm ɪn no'vɛmbʌ]
it would please me it were November then–
[ɪt wʊd pliz mi ɪt wɜ no'vɛmbʌ ðɛn]
but time has moved–
[bʌt tɑːɪm hæz muvd]

You went with the coming of the Birds–
[ju wɛnt wɪð ðʌ 'kʌmɪŋ ʌv ðʌ bɜdz]
they will go with your coming–
[ðɛːɪ wɪl goːʊ wɪð jɔːʌ 'kʌmɪŋ]
but to see you is so much sweeter than Birds,
[bʌt tu si ju ɪz soːʊ mʌtʃ 'swɪtʌ ðæn bɜdz]
I could excuse the spring.
[ɑːɪ kʊd ɪk'skjuz ðʌ spɹɪŋ]

16. Cantilena II (As Imperceptibly as Grief)
[kanti'lɛna tu æz ɪmpɜ'sɛptɪbli æz gɹif]

As imperceptibly as Grief
[æz ɪmpɜ'sɛptɪblɪ æz gɹ⁽ʳ⁾if]
The Summer lapsed away –
[ðʌ 'sʌmʌ læpst ʌ'wɛːɪ]
Too imperceptible, at last
[tu ɪmpɜ'sɛptɪbʊl æt læst]
To seem like Perfidy –
[tu sim lɑːɪk 'pɜfɪdɪ]
A Quietness distilled
[ʌ 'kwɑːɪɛ(ɪ)tnɛ(ɪ)s dɪ'stɪld]
As Twilight long begun
[æz 'twɑːɪlɑːɪt lɑŋ bɪ'gʌn]
Or Nature spending with herself
[ɔ 'nɛːɪtʃʊ(ʌ) 'spɛndɪŋ wɪð hɜ'sɛlf]
Sequestered Afternoon –
[sɪ'kwɛstʌd æftʌ'nun]
The Dusk drew earlier in –
[ðʌ dʌsk dɹ⁽ʳ⁾u 'ɜlɪʌʁ⁽ʳ⁾ ɪn]
The Morning foreign shone –
[ðʌ 'mɔnɪŋ 'fɔʁ⁽ʳ⁾ɛ(ɪ)n ʃoːʊn]
A courteous, yet harrowing Grace
[ʌ 'kɜtɪʌs jɛt 'hæʁ⁽ʳ⁾oːʊɪŋ gɹɛːɪs]
As Guest that would be gone –
[æz gɛst ðæt wʊd bi gɑn]
And thus without a Wing
[ænd ðʌs wɪð'ɑːʊt ʌ wɪŋ]
Or service of a Keel
[ɔ 'sɜvɪs ʌv ʌ kil]
Our Summer made her light escape
[ɑːʊʌ 'sʌmʌ mɛːɪd hɜ lɑːɪt ɪ'skɛːɪp]
Into the Beautiful
['ɪntu ðʌ 'bjutɪfʊl]

17. Aria (Wonder– Is Not Precisely Knowing)
['aria 'wʌndʁ ɪz nat pɹɪ'sɑːɪsli 'noːʊɪŋ]

Wonder – is not precisely Knowing
['wʌndʌʁ⁽ʳ⁾ ɪz nat pɹɪ'sɑːɪslɪ 'noːʊɪŋ]
And not precisely Knowing not –
[ænd nat pɹɪ'sɑːɪslɪ 'noːʊɪŋ nat]
A beautiful but bleak condition
[ʌ 'bjutɪfʊl bʌt blik kʌn'dɪʃʌn]
He has not lived who has not felt –
[hi hæz nat lɪvd hu hæz nat fɛlt]

Suspense – is his maturer Sister –
[sʌˈspɛns ɪz hɪz mʌˈtjʊːʌʁ⁽ʳ⁾ʌ ˈsɪstʌ]
Whether Adult Delight is Pain
[ˈʍɛðʌʁ⁽ʳ⁾ ʌˈdʌlt dɪˈlaːɪt ɪz pɛːɪn]
Or of itself a new misgiving –
[ɔʁ⁽ʳ⁾ ʌv ɪtˈsɛlf ʌ nju mɪsˈɡɪvɪŋ]
This is the Gnat that mangles men –
[ðɪs ɪz ðʌ næt ðæt ˈmæŋɡʊlz mɛn]

18. Aria (Whether They Have Forgotten)
[ˈaria ˈʍɛðʁ ðɛːɪ hæv fʌʁˈɡatɪn]

Whether they have forgotten
[ˈʍɛðʌ ðɛːɪ hæv fɔˈɡate⁽ɪ⁾n]
Or are forgetting now
[ɔʁ⁽ʳ⁾ ɑ fɔˈɡɛtɪŋ naːʊ]
Or never remembered –
[ɔ ˈnɛvʌ ɹɪˈmɛmbʌd]
Safer not to know –
[ˈsɛːɪfʌ nɑt tu noːʊ]
Miseries of conjecture
[ˈmɪzʌʁ⁽ʳ⁾ɪz ʌv kʌnˈdʒɛktʃʊ⁽ʌ⁾]
Are a softer woe
[aʁ⁽ʳ⁾ ʌ ˈsaftʌ woːʊ]
Than a Fact of iron
[ðæn ʌ fækt ʌv ˈaːɪʌn]
Hardened with I know –
[ˈhade⁽ɪ⁾nd wɪð aːɪ noːʊ]

19. Quodlibet II
[ˈkwɑdlɪˌbɛt tu]

20. Hymn (We Never Know How High We Are)
[hɪm wi ˈnɛvʁ noːʊ haːʊ haːɪ wi aʁ]

We never know how high we are
[wi ˈnɛvʌ noːʊ haːʊ haːɪ wi ɑ]
Till we are called to rise;
[tɪl wi ɑ kɔld tu ɹaːɪz]
And then, if we are true to plan,
[ænd ðɛn ɪf wi ɑ tɹ⁽ʳ⁾u tu plæn]
Our statures touch the skies–
[ɑːʊʌ ˈstætʃʊ⁽ʌ⁾z tʌtʃ ðʌ skaːɪz]

21. Epilogue (Nature– the Gentlest Mother Is)
see Copland

Song Selections

"A Clear Midnight" (Insomnia)
[ʌ klɪːʁ ˈmɪdnaːɪt]
Whitman, Walt (Am. 1819-1892)

This is thy hour, O Soul,
[ðɪs ɪz ðaːɪ aːʊʌʁ⁽ʳ⁾ oːʊ soːʊl]

thy free flight into the wordless,
[ðaːɪ fɹi flaːɪt ˈɪntu ðʌ ˈwɜdlɛ⁽ɪ⁾s]
Away from books, away from art, the day erased,
[ʌˈwɛːɪ fɹʌm bʊks ʌˈwɛːɪ fɹʌm ɑt ðʌ dɛːɪ ɪˈʁ⁽ʳ⁾ɛːɪst]
the lesson done,
[ðʌ ˈlɛsʌn dʌn]
Thee fully forth emerging, silent, gazing,
[ði ˈfʊlɪ fɔθ ɪˈmɜdʒɪŋ ˈsaːɪlɛnt ˈɡɛːɪzɪŋ]
pondering the themes thou lovest best,
[ˈpandʌʁ⁽ʳ⁾ɪŋ ðʌ θimz ðaːʊ ˈlʌvɛ⁽ɪ⁾st bɛst]
Night, sleep, death, and the stars.
[naːɪt slip dɛθ ænd ðʌ staz]

"As Summer into Autumn Slips" (Late Summer)
[æz ˈsʌmʁ ˈɪntu ˈɔtʌm slɪps]
Dickinson, Emily (Am. 1830-1886)

As Summer into Autumn slips
[æz ˈsʌmʌʁ⁽ʳ⁾ ˈɪntu ˈɔtʌm slɪps]
And yet we sooner say
[ænd jɛt wi ˈsunʌ sɛːɪ]
"The Summer" than "the Autumn," lest
[ðʌ ˈsʌmʌ ðæn ði ˈɔtʌm lɛst]
We turn the sun away,
[wi tɜn ðʌ sʌn ʌˈwɛːɪ]
And almost count it an Affront
[ænd ˈɔlmoːʊst kaːʊnt ɪt æn ʌˈfɹʌnt]
The presence to concede
[ðʌ ˈpɹɛze⁽ɪ⁾ns tu kʌnˈsid]
Of one however lovely, not
[ʌv wʌn haːʊˈɛvʌ ˈlʌvlɪ nɑt]
The one that we have loved –
[ðʌ wʌn ðæt wi hæv lʌvd]

"For the Bed at Kelmscott" (Insomnia)
[fɔʁ ðʌ bɛd æt ˈkɛlmskɑt]
Morris, William (Eng. 1834-1896)

The wind's on the wold
[ðʌ wɪndz ɑn ðʌ woːʊld]
And the night is a-cold,
[ænd ðʌ naːɪt ɪz ʌ koːʊld]
And Thames runs chill
[ænd tɛmz ɹʌnz tʃɪl]
'Twixt mead and hill.
[twɪkst mid ænd hɪl]
But kind and dear
[bʌt kaːɪnd ænd dɪːʌ]
Is the old house here
[ɪz ði oːʊld haːʊs hɪːʌ]
And my heart is warm
[ænd maːɪ hɑt ɪz wɔm]
'Midst winter's harm.
[mɪdst ˈwɪntʌz ham]
Rest then and rest,
[ɹɛst ðɛn ænd ɹɛst]

And think of the best
[ænd θɪŋk ʌv ðʌ bɛst]
'Twixt summer and spring,
[twɪkst ˈsʌmʌʁ⁽ʳ⁾ ænd spɹɪŋ]
When all birds sing
[ʍɛn ɔl bɜdz sɪŋ]
In the town of the tree,
[ɪn ðʌ taːʊn ʌv ðʌ tɹi]
As ye lie in me
[æz ji laːɪ ɪn mi]
And scarce doth move,
[ænd skɛːʌs dʌθ muv]
Lest earth and its love
[lɛst ɜθ ænd ɪts lʌv]
Should fade away
[ʃʊd fɛːɪd ʌˈwɛːɪ]
Ere the full of the day.
[ɛːʌ ðʌ fʊl ʌv ðʌ dɛːɪ]
I am old and have seen
[aːɪ æm oːʊld ænd hæv sin]
Many things that have been;
[ˈmɛnɪ θɪŋz ðæt hæv bɪn]
Both grief and peace
[boːʊθ gɹɪ⁽ʳ⁾if ænd pis]
And wane and increase
[ænd wɛːɪn ænd ɪnˈkɹis]
No tale I tell, Of ill or well,
[noːʊ tɛːɪl aːɪ tɛl ʌv ɪl ɔ wɛl]
But this I say: Night treadeth on day,
[bʌt ðɪs aːɪ sɛːɪ naːɪt ˈtɹɛdɛ⁽ɪ⁾θ ɑn dɛːɪ]
And for worst or best
[ænd fɔ wɜst ɔ bɛst]
Right good is rest.
[ɹaːɪt gʊd ɪz ɹɛst]

"The White Rose"
[ðʌ ʍaːɪt ɹoːʊz]
O'Reilly, John Boyle (Ir. 1844-1890)

The red rose whispers of passion,
[ðʌ ɹɛd ɹoːʊz ˈʍɪspʌz ʌv ˈpæʃʌn]
And the white rose breathes of love;
[ænd ðʌ ʍaːɪt ɹoːʊz bɹiðz ʌv lʌv]
O, the red rose is a falcon,
[oːʊ ðʌ ɹɛd ɹoːʊz ɪz ʌ ˈfælkʌn]
And the white rose is a dove.
[ænd ðʌ ʍaːɪt ɹoːʊz ɪz ʌ dʌv]
But I send you a cream-white rosebud
[bʌt aːɪ sɛnd ju ʌ kɹim ʍaːɪt ˈɹoːʊzbʌd]
With a flush on its petal tips;
[wɪð ʌ flʌʃ ɑn ɪts ˈpɛtʊl tɪps]
For the love that is purest and sweetest
[fɔ ðʌ lʌv ðæt ɪz ˈpjʊːʌʁ⁽ʳ⁾ɛ⁽ɪ⁾st ænd ˈswitɛ⁽ɪ⁾st]
Has a kiss of desire on the lips
[hæz ʌ kɪs ʌv dɪˈzaːɪʌ ɑn ðʌ lɪps]

 Clarke, Rebecca (Eng. 1886-1979)

Three Irish Country Songs (Song Cycle)
[θɹi ˈaːɪʁɪʃ ˈkʌntɹi sɑŋz]
Irish Folksongs

1. I Know My Love
[aːɪ noːʊ maːɪ lʌv]

1. I know my love by his way of walkin'
[aːɪ noːʊ maːɪ lʌv baːɪ hɪz wɛːɪ ʌv ˈwɔkɪn]
And I know my love by his way of talkin'
[ænd aːɪ noːʊ maːɪ lʌv baːɪ hɪz wɛːɪ ʌv ˈtɔkɪn]
And I know my love dressed in a suit o' blue,
[ænd aːɪ noːʊ maːɪ lʌv dɹɛst ɪn ʌ sjut ʌ blu]
And if my love leaves me what will I do?
[ænd ɪf maːɪ lʌv livz mi ʍat wɪl aːɪ du]
REFRAIN:
And still she cried "I love him the best,
[ænd stɪl ʃi kɹaːɪd aːɪ lʌv hɪm ðʊ bɛst]
And a troubled mind, sure, can know no rest."
[ænd ʌ ˈtɹʌbʊld maːɪnd ʃʊːʌ kæn noːʊ noːʊ ɹɛst]
And still she cried, "Bonny boys are few,
[ænd stɪl ʃi kɹaːɪd ˈbɑnɪ bɔːɪz a fju]
And if my love leaves me, what will I do?"
[ænd ɪf maːɪ lʌv livz mi ʍat wɪl aːɪ du]
2. There is a dance house in Maradyke
[ðɛːʌɾ ɪz ʌ dans haːʊs ɪn mæɾʌˈdaːɪk]
And there my true love goes every night,
[ænd ðɛːʌ maːɪ tru lʌv goːʊz ˈɛvɹɪ naːɪt]
He takes a strange one upon his knee,
[hi tɛːɪks ʌ stɹɛːɪndʒ wʌn ʌˈpɑn hɪz ni]
And don't you think now that vexes me?
[ænd doːʊnt ju θɪŋk naːʊ ðæt ˈvɛksɛ⁽ɪ⁾z mi]
REFRAIN
3. If my love knew I could wash and wring,
[ɪf maːɪ lʌv nju aːɪ kʊd waʃ ænd ɹɪŋ]
If my love knew I could weave and spin,
[ɪf maːɪ lʌv nju aːɪ kʊd wiv ænd spɪn]
I'd make a coat all of the finest kind,
[aːɪd mɛːɪk ʌ koːʊt ɔl ʌv ðʊ ˈfaːɪnɛ⁽ɪ⁾st kaːɪnd]
But the want of money sure leaves me behind.
[bʌt ðʊ want ʌv ˈmʌnɪ ʃʊːʌ livz mi bɪˈhaːɪnd]
REFRAIN

2. I Know Where I'm Goin'
[aːɪ noːʊ ʍɛːʁ aːɪm ˈgoːʊɪn]

"I know where I'm goin'," she said
[aːɪ noːʊ ʍɛːʌɾ aːɪm ˈgoːʊɪn ʃi sɛd]
"And I know who's goin' with me,
[ænd aːɪ noːʊ huz ˈgoːʊɪn wɪð mi]
I know who I love,
[aːɪ noːʊ hu aːɪ lʌv]
But the dear knows who I'll marry.
[bʌt ðʊ dɹːʌ noːʊz hu aːɪl ˈmæɾɪ]

I have stockings of silk,
[ɑːɪ hæv ˈstɑkɪŋz ʌv sɪlk]
Shoes of fine green leather,
[ʃuz ʌv fɑːɪn gɹin ˈlɛðʌ]
Combs to buckle my hair,
[koːʊmz tu ˈbʌkʊl mɑːɪ hɛːʌ]
And a ring for every finger.
[ænd ʌ ɾɪŋ fɔʁ⁽ʳ⁾ ˈɛvɹɪ ˈfɪŋgʌ]
Some say he's black,
[sʌm sɛːɪ hiz blæk]
But I say he's bonny,
[bʌt ɑːɪ sɛːɪ hiz ˈbɑnɪ]
The fairest of them all,
[ðʊ ˈfɛːʌɾɛ⁽ɪ⁾st ʌv ðɛm ɔl]
My handsome, winsome Johnny.
[mɑːɪ ˈhænsʌm ˈwɪnsʌm ˈdʒɑnɪ]
Feather beds are soft,
[ˈfɛðʌ bɛdz ɑ sɑft]
And painted rooms are bonny,
[ænd ˈpɛːɪntɛ⁽ɪ⁾d ɾɾumz ɑ ˈbɑnɪ]
But I would leave them all
[bʌt ɑːɪ wʊd liv ðɛm ɔl]
To go with my love Johnny.
[tu goːʊ wɪð mɑːɪ lʌv ˈdʒɑnɪ]

3. As I Was Goin' to Ballynure
[æz ɑːɪ wɑz ˈgoːʊɪn tu ˈbælɪnʊːʌ]

As I was goin' to Ballynure
[æz ɑːɪ wɑz ˈgoːʊɪn tu ˈbælɪnʊːʌ]
the day I well remember
[ðʊ dɛːɪ ɑːɪ wɛl ɹɪˈmɛmbʌ]
For to view the lads and lasses on
[fɔ tu vju ðʊ lædz ænd ˈlæsɛ⁽ɪ⁾z ɑn]
the fifth day of November
[ðʊ fɪfθ dɛːɪ ʌv noˈvɛmbʌ]
With a ma ring-doo-a-day,
[wɪð ʌ mɑ ɾɪŋ du ʌ dɛːɪ]
With a ma ring-a-doo-a daddy oh.
[wɪð ʌ mɑ ɾɪŋ ʌ du ʌ ˈdædɪ oːʊ]
As I was goin' along the road
[æz ɑːɪ wɑz ˈgoːʊɪn ʌˈlɑŋ ðʊ roːʊd]
as homeward I was walkin'
[æz ˈhoːʊmwʊd ɑːɪ wɑz ˈwɔkɪn]
I heard a wee lad behind a ditch
[ɑːɪ hɜd ʌ wi læd bɪˈhɑːɪnd ʌ dɪtʃ]
a to his wee lass was talkin',
[ʌ tu hɪz wi læs wɑz ˈtɔkɪn]
With a ma ring-doo-a-day,
[wɪð ʌ mɑ ɾɪŋ du ʌ dɛːɪ]
With a ma ring-a-doo-a daddy oh.
[wɪð ʌ mɑ ɾɪŋ ʌ du ʌ ˈdædɪ oːʊ]
Said the wee lad to the wee lass,
[sɛd ðʊ wi læd tu ðʊ wi læs]
"It's will ye let me kiss ye?
[ɪts wɪl ji lɛt mi kɪs ji]

for it's I have got the cordial eye
[fɔʁ⁽ʳ⁾ ɪts ɑːɪ hæv gɑt ðʊ ˈkɔdjʊl ɑːɪ]
that far exceeds the whiskey."
[ðæt fɑr ɪkˈsidz ðʊ ˈʍɪskɪ]
With a ma ring-doo-a-day,
[wɪð ʌ mɑ ɾɪŋ du ʌ dɛːɪ]
With a ma ring-a-doo-a daddy oh.
[wɪð ʌ mɑ ɾɪŋ ʌ du ʌ ˈdædɪ oːʊ]
"This cordial that ye talk about
[ðɪs ˈkɔdjʊl ðæt ji tɔk ʌˈbɑːʊt]
There's very few o' them gets it,
[ðɛːz ˈvɛɾɪ fju ʌ ðɛm gɛts ɪt]
For there's nothin' now but crooked combs
[fɔ ðɛːz ˈnʌθɪn nɑːʊ bʌt ˈkɾʊkɛ⁽ɪ⁾d koːʊmz]
And muslin gowns can catch it."
[ænd ˈmʌzlɪn gɑːʊnz kæn kætʃ ɪt]
With a ma ring-doo-a-day,
[wɪð ʌ mɑ ɾɪŋ du ʌ dɛːɪ]
With a ma ring-a-doo-a daddy oh.
[wɪð ʌ mɑ ɾɪŋ ʌ du ʌ ˈdædɪ oːʊ]
As I was goin' along the road
[æz ɑːɪ wɑz ˈgoːʊɪn ʌˈlɑŋ ðʊ roːʊd]
as homeward I was walkin'
[æz ˈhoːʊmwʊd ɑːɪ wɑz ˈwɔkɪn]
I heard a wee lad behind a ditch–
[ɑːɪ hɜd ʌ wi læd bɪˈhɑːɪnd ʌ dɪtʃ]
a to his wee lass was talkin'
[ʌ tu hɪz wi læs wɑz ˈtɔkɪn]
With a ma ring-doo-a-day,
[wɪð ʌ mɑ ɾɪŋ du ʌ dɛːɪ]
With a ma ring-a-doo-a daddy oh.
[wɪð ʌ mɑ ɾɪŋ ʌ du ʌ ˈdædɪ oːʊ]

Song Selection

"The Cloths of Heaven"
[ðʊ klɑθs ʌv ˈhɛvɪn]
Yeats, William Butler (Ir. 1865-1939)

Had I the heavens' embroidered cloths
[hæd ɑːɪ ðʊ ˈhɛvɛ⁽ɪ⁾nz ɪmˈbɹɔːɪdʌd klɑθs]
Enwrought with golden and silver light
[ɪnˈɹɔt wɪð ˈgoːʊldɛ⁽ɪ⁾n ænd ˈsɪlvʌ lɑːɪt]
The blue and the dim and the dark cloths
[ðʊ blu ænd ðʊ dɪm ænd ðʊ dɑk klɑθs]
Of night and light and the half-light
[ʌv nɑːɪt ænd lɑːɪt ænd ðʊ hɑf lɑːɪt]
I would spread the cloths under your feet
[ɑːɪ wʊd spɹɛd ðʊ klɑθs ˈʌndʌ jɔːʌ fit]
But I, being poor, have only my dreams;
[bʌt ɑːɪ ˈbiɪŋ pʊːʌ hæv ˈoːʊnlɪ mɑːɪ dɹimz]
I have spread my dreams under your feet;
[ɑːɪ hæv spɹɛd mɑːɪ dɹimz ˈʌndʌ jɔːʌ fit]
Tread softly because you tread on my dreams.
[tɹɛd ˈsaftlɪ bɪˈkɔz ju tɹɛd ɑn mɑːɪ dɹimz]

Cloud, Judith (Am. 1954-2023)

I Spill My Soul (Song Cycle)
[ɑːɪ spɪl maːɪ soːʊl]
Cummings, E. E. (Am. 1894-1962)

1. thy fingers make early flowers of all things
(see Walker)

2. this is the garden; colours come and go
[ðɪs ɪz ðʌ ˈgaʁdɪn ˈkʌlʁz kʌm ænd goːʊ]

this is the garden: colours come and go,
[ðɪs ɪz ðʌ ˈgadɛ(ɪ)n ˈkʌlʊ(ʌ)z kʌm ænd goːʊ]
frail azures fluttering from night's outer wing
[fɪɛːɪl ˈæʒʊ(ʌ)z ˈflʌtʌʁ⁽ʳ⁾ɪŋ fɪʌm naːɪts ˈaːʊtʌ wɪŋ]
strong silent greens silently lingering,
[stɪaŋ ˈsaːɪlɛnt gɪinz ˈsaːɪlɛntlɪ ˈlɪŋgʌʁ⁽ʳ⁾ɪŋ]
Absolute lights like baths of golden snow.
[ˈæbso(ʌ)ljut laːɪts laːɪk bæðz ʌv ˈgoːʊldɛ(ɪ)n snoːʊ]
This is the garden: pursed lips do blow
[ðɪs ɪz ðʌ ˈgadɛ(ɪ)n pɜst lɪps du bloːʊ]
upon cool flutes within wide glooms, and sing
[ʌˈpan kul fluts wɪðˈɪn waːɪd glumz ænd sɪŋ]
(of harps celestial to the quivering string)
[ʌv haps sɪˈlɛstʃʊl tu ðʌ ˈkwɪvʌʁ⁽ʳ⁾ɪŋ stɪɪŋ]
invisible faces hauntingly and slow.
[ɪnˈvɪzɪbʊl ˈfɛːɪsɛ(ɪ)z ˈhɔntɪŋlɪ ænd sloːʊ]
This is the garden. Time shall surely reap
[ðɪs ɪz ðʌ ˈgadɛ(ɪ)n taːɪm ʃæl ˈʃʊːʌlɪ ɪip]
and on Death's blade lies many a flower curled,
[ænd an dɛθs blɛːɪd laːɪz ˈmɛnɪ ʌ flaːʊʌ kɜld]
in other lands where other songs be sung;
[ɪn ˈʌðʌ lændz ʍɛːʌʁ⁽ʳ⁾ ˈʌðʌ saŋz bi sʌŋ]
yet stand they here enraptured, as among
[jɛt stænd ðɛːɪ hɪːʌ ɪnˈɪæptʃʊ(ʌ)d æz ʌˈmʌŋ]
the slow deep trees perpetual of sleep
[ðʌ sloːʊ dip tɪiz pɜˈpɛtʃʊʊl ʌv slip]
some silver fingered fountain steals the world.
[sʌm ˈsɪlvʌ ˈfɪŋgʌd ˈfaːʊntæ(ɪ)n stilz ðʌ wɜld]

3. (sitting in a tree-)
[ˈsɪtɪŋ ɪn ʌ tɪi]

(sitting in a tree-)
[ˈsɪtɪŋ ɪn ʌ tɪi]
o small you
[oːʊ smɔl ju]
sitting in a tree-
[ˈsɪtɪŋ ɪn ʌ tɪi]
sitting in a treetop
[ˈsɪtɪŋ ɪn ʌ ˈtɪi ˌtap]
riding on a greenest
[ˈɪaːɪdɪŋ an ʌ ˈgɪinɛ(ɪ)st]
riding on a greener
[ˈɪaːɪdɪŋ an ʌ ˈgɪinʌ]

(o little i)
[oːʊ ˈlɪtʊl ɑːɪ]
riding on a leaf
[ˈɪaːɪdɪŋ an ʌ lif]
o least who
[oːʊ list hu]
sing small thing
[sɪŋ smɔl θɪŋ]
dance little joy
[dæns ˈlɪtʊl dʒɔːɪ]
(shine most prayer)
[ʃaːɪn moːʊst pɪɛːʌ]

4. Thou to whom the musical white spring
[ðaːʊ tu hum ðʌ ˈmjuzɪkʊl ʍaːɪt spɪɪŋ]

O Thou to whom the musical white spring
[oːʊ ðaːʊ tu hum ðʌ ˈmjuzɪkʊl ʍaːɪt spɪɪŋ]
offers her lily inextinguishable,
[ˈafʌz hɜ ˈlɪlɪ ɪnˌɛkˈstɪŋgwɪʃʌbʊl]
taught by thy tremulous grace bravely to fling
[tɔt baːɪ ðaːɪ ˈtɪɛmjulʌs gɪɛːɪs ˈbɪɛːɪvlɪ tu flɪŋ]
implacable death's mysteriously sable
[ɪmˈplækʌbʊl dɛθs mɪˈstɪʁ⁽ʳ⁾ɪʌslɪ ˈsɛːɪbʊl]
robe from her redolent shoulders,
[ɪoːʊb fɪʌm hɜ ˈɪedo(ʌ)lɛnt ˈʃoːʊldʌz]
Thou from whose
[ðaːʊ fɪʌm huz]
feet reincarnate song suddenly leaping
[fit ˌɪiinˈkaˌnɛːɪt saŋ ˈsʌdɛ(ɪ)nlɪ ˈlipɪŋ]
flame flung, mounts, inimitably to lose
[flɛːɪm flʌŋ maːʊnts ɪˈnɪmɪtʌblɪ tu luz]
herself where the wet stars softly are keeping
[hɜˈsɛlf ʍɛːʌ ðʌ wɛt staz ˈsaftlɪ ɑ ˈkipɪŋ]
their exquisite dream – O Love! upon thy dim
[ðɛːʌʁ⁽ʳ⁾ ɪkˈskwɪzɪt dɪiim oːʊ lʌv ʌˈpan ðaːɪ dɪm]
shrine of intangible commemoration,
[ʃɪaːɪn ʌv ɪnˈtænd ɪbʊl kʌmɛmoˈʁ⁽ʳ⁾ɛːɪʃʌn]
(from whose faint close as some grave languorous
[fɪʌm huz fɛːɪnt kloːʊz æz sʌm gɪ⁽ʳ⁾ɛːɪv ˈlæŋgoʁ⁽ʳ⁾ʌs]
hymn pledged to illimitable dissipation
[hɪm plɛdʒd tu ɪˈlɪmɪtʌbʊl ˌdɪsɪˈpɛːɪʃʌn]
unhurried clouds of incense fleetly roll)
[ʌnˈhʊʁ⁽ʳ⁾ɪd klaːʊdz ʌv ˈɪnsɛns ˈflitlɪ ɪoːʊl]
I spill my bright incalculable soul.
[ɑːɪ spɪl maːɪ bɪaːɪt ɪnˈkælkjulʌbʊl soːʊl]

Five Edgar Allen Poe Songs (Song Cycle)
[faːɪv ˈɛdgʁ ˈælɪn poːʊ saŋz]
Poe, Edgar Allan (Am. 1809-1849)

1. Hear the Sledges with the Bells
[ɑːɪ hɪːʁ ðʌ ˈslɛdʒɪz wɪθ ðʌ bɛlz]

Hear the sledges with the bells,
[hɪːʌ ðʌ ˈslɛdʒɛ(ɪ)z wɪð ðʌ bɛlz]

Silver bells!
[ˈsɪlvʌ bɛlz]
What a world of merriment
[ʍat ʌ wɜld ʌv ˈmɛʁ⁽ʳ⁾ɪmɛnt]
Their melody foretells!
[ðɛːʌ ˈmɛlodɪ fɔˈtɛlz]
How they tinkle, tinkle, tinkle,
[haːʊ ðɛːɪ ˈtɪŋkʊl ˈtɪŋkʊl ˈtɪŋkʊl]
In the icy air of night!
[ɪn ði ˈɑːɪsɪ ɛːʌʁ⁽ʳ⁾ ʌv naːɪt]
While the stars that oversprinkle
[ʍaːɪl ðʌ staz ðæt oːʊvʌˈspɹɪŋkʊl]
All the heavens seem to twinkle
[ɔl ðʌ ˈhɛvɛ⁽ɪ⁾nz sim tu ˈtwɪŋkʊl]
With a crystalline delight;
[wɪð ʌ ˈkɹɪstʊlɪn dɪˈlaːɪt]
Keeping time, time, time,
[ˈkipɪŋ taːɪm taːɪm taːɪm]
In a sort of Runic rhyme,
[ɪn ʌ sɔt ʌv ˈɹ⁽ʳʳ⁾unɪk ɹaːɪm]
To the tintinabulation that so musically wells
[tu ðʌ tɪntɪnæbjuˈlɛːɪʃʌn ðæt soːʊ ˈmjuzɪklɪ wɛlz]
From the bells, bells, bells, bells, bells, bells, bells–
[fɹʌm ðʌ bɛlz bɛlz bɛlz bɛlz bɛlz bɛlz bɛlz]
From the jingling and the tinkling of the bells.
[fɹʌm ðʌ ˈdʒɪŋglɪŋ ænd ðʌ ˈtɪŋklɪŋ ʌv ðʌ bɛlz]

2. Evening Star
[ˈivnɪŋ staʁ]

'Twas noontide of summer,
[twaz ˈnuntaːɪd ʌv ˈsʌmʌ]
And mid-time of night;
[ænd mɪd taːɪm ʌv naːɪt]
And stars, in their orbits,
[ænd staz ɪn ðɛːʌʁ⁽ʳ⁾ ˈɔbɪts]
Shone pale, thro' the light
[ʃoːʊn pɛːɪl θru ðʌ laːɪt]
Of the brighter, cold, moon,
[ʌv ðʌ ˈbɹaːɪtʌ koːʊld mun]
'Mid planets her slaves,
[mɪd ˈplænɛ⁽ɪ⁾ts hɜ slɛːɪvz]
Herself in the Heavens,
[hɜˈsɛlf ɪn ðʌ ˈhɛvɛ⁽ɪ⁾nz]
Her beam on the waves.
[hɜ bim an ðʌ wɛːɪvz]
I gazed awhile
[aːɪ gɛːɪzd ʌˈʍaːɪl]
On her cold smile;
[an hɜ koːʊld smaːɪl]
Too cold, too cold for me,
[tu koːʊld tu koːʊld fɔ mi]
There passed, as a shroud,
[ðɛːʌ pæst æz ʌ ʃɹaːʊd]
A fleecy cloud,
[ʌ ˈflisɪ klaːʊd]

And I turned away to thee,
[ænd aːɪ tɜnd ʌˈwɛːɪ tu ði]
Proud Evening Star,
[pɹaːʊd ˈivnɪŋ sta]
In thy glory afar,
[ɪn ðaːɪ ˈglɔʁ⁽ʳ⁾ɪ ʌˈfa]
And dearer thy beam shall be;
[ænd ˈdiːʌʁ⁽ʳ⁾ʌ ðaːɪ bim ʃæl bi]
For joy to my heart
[fɔ dʒɔːɪ tu maːɪ hat]
Is the proud part
[ɪz ðʌ pɹaːʊd pat]
Thou bearest in Heav'n at night,
[ðaːʊ ˈbɛːʌʁ⁽ʳ⁾ɛ⁽ɪ⁾st ɪn hɛvn æt naːɪt]
And more I admire
[ænd mɔːʌʁ⁽ʳ⁾ aːɪ ædˈmaːɪʌ]
Thy distant fire,
[ðaːɪ ˈdɪstæ⁽ɪ⁾nt faːɪʌ]
Than that colder, colder light.
[ðæn ðæt ˈkoːʊldʌ ˈkoːʊldʌ laːɪt]

3. Romance
[ɹoˈmæns]

Romance, who loves to nod and sing,
[ɹoˈmæns hu lʌvz tu nad ænd sɪŋ]
With drowsy head and folded wing,
[wɪð ˈdɹaːʊzɪ hɛd ænd ˈfoːʊldɛ⁽ɪ⁾d wɪŋ]
Among the green leaves as they shake
[ʌˈmʌŋ ðʌ gɹin livz æz ðɛːɪ ʃɛːɪk]
Far down some shadowy lake,
[fa daːʊn sʌm ˈʃædoːʊɪ lɛːɪk]
To me a painted paroquet
[tu mi ʌ ˈpɛːɪntɛ⁽ɪ⁾d ˈpæʁ⁽ʳ⁾okɛt]
Hath been– a most familiar bird–
[hæθ bɪn ʌ moːʊst fʌˈmɪljʌ bɜd]
Taught me my alphabet to say–
[tɔt mi maːɪ ˈælfʌbɛt tu sɛːɪ]
To lisp my very earliest word
[tu lɪsp maːɪ ˈvɛʁ⁽ʳ⁾ɪ ˈɜlɪɛ⁽ɪ⁾st wɜd]
While in the wild wood I did lie,
[ʍaːɪl ɪn ðʌ waːɪld wʊd aːɪ dɪd laːɪ]
A child– with a most knowing eye.
[ʌ tʃaːɪld wɪð ʌ moːʊst ˈnoːʊɪŋ aːɪ]
Of late, eternal Condor years
[ʌv lɛːɪt ɪˈtɜnʊl ˈkandɔ jɪːʌz]
So shake the very Heav'n on high
[soːʊ ʃɛːɪk ðʌ ˈvɛʁ⁽ʳ⁾ɪ hɛvn an haːɪ]
With tumult as they thunder by,
[wɪð ˈtjumʊlt æz ðɛːɪ ˈθʌndʌ baːɪ]
I have no time for idle cares
[aːɪ hæv noːʊ taːɪm fɔʁ⁽ʳ⁾ ˈaːɪdʊl kɛːʌz]
Through gazing on the unquiet sky.
[θru ˈgɛːɪzɪŋ an ði ʌnˈkwaːɪɛ⁽ɪ⁾t skaːɪ]
And when an hour with calmer wings
[ænd ʍɛn æn aːʊʌ wɪð ˈkamʌ wɪŋz]

Its down upon my spirit flings–
[ɪts daːʊn ʌˈpɑn maːɪ ˈspɪʁ⁽ʳ⁾ɪt flɪŋz]
That little time with lyre and rhyme
[ðæt ˈlɪtʊl taːɪm wɪð ˈlaːɪʌʁ⁽ʳ⁾ ænd ʁaːɪm]
To while away – forbidden things!
[tu ʍaːɪl ʌˈwɛːɪ fɔˈbɪdɛ⁽ɪ⁾n θɪŋz]
My heart would feel to be a crime
[maːɪ hɑt wʊd fil tu bi ʌ kʁ⁽ʳ⁾aːɪm]
Unless it trembled with the strings.
[ʌnˈlɛs ɪt ˈtʁɛmbʊld wɪð ðʌ stʁɪŋz]

4. Alone
[ʌˈloːʊn]

From childhood's hour I have not been
[fʁʌm ˈtʃaːɪldhʊdz aːʊʌ aːɪ hæv nɑt bɪn]
As others were; I have not seen
[æz ˈʌðʌz wɝ aːɪ hæv nɑt sin]
As others saw – I could not bring
[æz ˈʌðʌz sɔ aːɪ kʊd nɑt bʁɪŋ]
My passions from a common spring.
[maːɪ ˈpæʃʌnz fʁʌm ʌ ˈkɑmʌn spʁɪŋ]
From the same source I have not taken
[fʁʌm ðʌ sɛːɪm sɔs aːɪ hæv nɑt ˈtɛːɪkɛ⁽ɪ⁾n]
My sorrow – I could not awaken
[maːɪ ˈsaʁ⁽ʳ⁾oːʊ aːɪ kʊd nɑt ʌˈwɛːɪkɛ⁽ɪ⁾n]
My heart to joy at the same tone. –
[maːɪ hɑt tu dʒɔːɪ æt ðʌ sɛːɪm toːʊn]
And all I loved – I lov'd alone –
[ænd ɔl aːɪ lʌvd aːɪ lʌvd ʌˈloːʊn]
Then – in my childhood – in the dawn
[ðɛn ɪn maːɪ ˈtʃaːɪldhʊd ɪn ðʌ dɔn]
Of a most stormy life – was drawn
[ʌv ʌ moːʊst ˈstɔmi laːɪf wɑz dʁɔn]
From ev'ry depth of good and ill
[fʁʌm ˈɛvʁi dɛpθ ʌv gʊd ænd ɪl]
The mystery which binds me still –
[ðʌ ˈmɪstʌʁ⁽ʳ⁾i ʍɪtʃ baːɪndz mi stɪl]
From the torrent of the fountain –
[fʁʌm ðʌ ˈtɔʁ⁽ʳ⁾ɛnt ʌv ðʌ ˈfaːʊntæ⁽ɪ⁾n]
From the red cliff of the mountain, –
[fʁʌm ðʌ ʁɛd klɪf ʌv ðʌ ˈmaːʊntæ⁽ɪ⁾n]
From the sun that 'round me roll'd
[fʁʌm ðʌ sʌn ðæt ʁaːʊnd mi ʁoːʊld]
In its autumn tint of gold –
[ɪn ɪts ˈɔtʌm tɪnt ʌv goːʊld]
From the lightning in the sky
[fʁʌm ðʌ ˈlaːɪtnɪŋ ɪn ðʌ skaːɪ]
As it pass'd me flying by,
[æz ɪt pæst mi ˈflaːɪŋ baːɪ]
From the thunder, and the storm,
[fʁʌm ðʌ ˈθʌndʌʁ⁽ʳ⁾ ænd ðʌ stɔm]
And the cloud that took the form
[ænd ðʌ klaːʊd ðæt tʊk ðʌ fɔm]
(When the rest of heaven was blue)
[ʍɛn ðʌ ʁɛst ʌv ˈhɛvɛ⁽ɪ⁾n wɑz blu]

Of a demon in my view.
[ʌv ʌ ˈdimʌn ɪn maːɪ vju]

5. Dream within a Dream (see "A Dream within a Dream" by Hagen)

Song Selections

"A Short History of Medicine" (Songs for Toby)
[ʌ ʃɔʁt ˈhɪstɔʁi ʌv ˈmɛdɪsɪn]
Anonymous

"I have an earache!"
[aːɪ hæv æn ˈiːʌʁ⁽ʳ⁾ɛːɪk]
2000 B. C.– "Here, eat this root."
[tu ˈθaːʊzæ⁽ʌ⁾nd bi si hiːʌ it ðɪs ʁ⁽ʳʳ⁾ut]
1000 B. C.– "That root is heathen,
[wʌn ˈθaːʊzæ⁽ʌ⁾nd bi si ðæt ʁ⁽ʳʳ⁾ut ɪz ˈhiðɛ⁽ɪ⁾n]
say this prayer."
[sɛːɪ ðɪs pʁɛːʌ]
1850 A. D.– "That prayer is superstition,
[ˈɛːɪtin ˈfɪfti ɛːɪ di ðæt pʁɛːʌʁ⁽ʳ⁾ ɪz ˌsupʌˈstɪʃʌn]
drink this potion."
[dʁɪŋk ðɪs ˈpoːʊʃʌn]
1940 A. D.– "The potion is snake oil,
[ˈnaːɪntin ˈfɔʁdi ɛːɪ di ðʌ ˈpoːʊʃʌn ɪz snɛːɪk ɔːɪl]
swallow this pill."
[ˈswaloːʊ ðɪs pɪl]
1985 A. D.– "That pill is ineffective,
[ˈnaːɪntin ˈɛːɪdi faːɪv ɛːɪ di ðæt pɪl ɪz ɪnɪˈfɛktɪv]
take this antibiotic."
[tɛːɪk ðɪs ˌæntɪbaːɪˈɑtɪk]
2000 A. D.– "That antibiotic is artificial.
[tu ˈθaːʊzæ⁽ʌ⁾nd ɛːɪ di ðæt ˌæntɪbaːɪˈɑtɪk ɪz ɑtɪˈfɪʃʊl]
Here, eat this root."
[hiːʌ it ðɪs ʁ⁽ʳʳ⁾ut]

"Didn't You Hear My Lord When He Called?"
[ˈdɪdɪnt ju hiːʁ maːɪ lɔʁd wɛn hi kɔld]
Traditional

Didn't you hear my Lord when He called?
[ˈdɪ(d)ɪn ju hiːʌ maːɪ lɔd wɛn hi kɔld]
Yes, I heard my Lord call,
[jɛs aːɪ hɝd maːɪ lɔd kɔl]
My Lord callin in my soul.
[maːɪ lɔd ˈkɔlɪn ɪn maːɪ soːʊl]
Can you hear them angels moan?
[kæn ju hiːʌ ðɛm ˈɛːɪndʒɛ⁽ʊ⁾lz moːʊn]
Yes I heard the angels moan.
[jɛs aːɪ hɝd ðɪ ˈɛːɪndʒɛ⁽ʊ⁾lz moːʊn]
Angels moanin in my soul.
[ˈɛːɪndʒɛ⁽ʊ⁾lz ˈmoːʊnɪn ɪn maːɪ soːʊl]
Didn't you hear them turtle doves moan
[ˈdɪ(d)ɪn ju hiːʌ ðɛm ˈtɝtʊl dʌvz moːʊn]
Yes I heard the turtle doves moan
[jɛs aːɪ hɝd ðʌ ˈtɝtʊl dʌvz moːʊn]

Didn't you hear them heaven bell's ring?
[ˈdɪ(d)ɪn ju hiːʌ ðɛm ˈhɛvɛ(ɪ)n bɛlz ɹɪŋ]
Yes I heard the heaven bell's ring.
[jɛs ɑːɪ hɜd ðʌ ˈhɛvɛ(ɪ)n bɛlz ɹɪŋ]
Angels moanin in my soul.
[ˈɛːɪndʒɛ(ʊ)lz ˈmoːʊnɪn ɪn mɑːɪ soːʊl]

"Perplexed Music"
[pɜˈplɛkst ˈmjuzɪk]
Browning, Elizabeth Barrett (Eng. 1806-1861)

Experience, like a pale musician, holds
[ɪkˈspiːʌʁ⁽ʳ⁾ɪˌɛ(ɪ)ns lɑːɪk ʌ pɛːɪl mjuˈzɪʃæ(ɪ)n hoːʊldz]
A dulcimer of patience in his hand,
[ʌ ˈdʌlsɪmʌ ʌv ˈpɛːɪʃɛ(ɪ)ns ɪn hɪz hænd]
Whence harmonies, we cannot understand
[ʍɛns ˈhamo(ʌ)nɪz wi kæˈnat ʌndʌˈstænd]
Of God's will in his worlds, the strain unfolds
[ʌv gadz wɪl ɪn hɪz wɜldz ðʌ stɹɛːɪn ʌnˈfoːʊldz]
In sad-perplexed minors: deathly colds
[ɪn sæd pɜˈplɛksɛ(ɪ)d ˈmɑːɪnɔ(ʌ)z ˈdɛθlɪ koːʊldz]
Fall on us while we hear, and countermand
[fɔl an ʌs ʍɑːɪl wi hiːʌ ænd ˈkɑːʊntʌmænd]
Our sanguine heart back from the fancyland
[ɑːʊʌ ˈsæŋgwɪn hat bæk fɹʌm ðʌ ˈfænsɪlæ(ʌ)nd]
With nightingale in visionary wolds.
[wɪð ˈnɑːɪtɪŋgɛːɪl ɪn ˈvɪʒʌnɛʁ⁽ʳ⁾ɪ woːʊldz]
We murmur 'Where is any certain tune
[wi ˈmɜmʊ(ʌ) ʍɛːʌʁ⁽ʳ⁾ ɪz ˈɛnɪ ˈsɜtæ(ɪ)n tjun]
Or measured music in such notes as these?'
[ɔ ˈmɛʒʊ(ʌ)d ˈmjuzɪk ɪn sʌtʃ noːʊts æz ðiz]
But angels, leaning from their golden seat,
[bʌt ˈɛːɪndʒɛ(ʊ)lz ˈlinɪŋ fɹʌm ðɛːʌ ˈgoːʊldɛ(ɪ)n sit]
Are not so minded; their fine ear hath won
[ɑ nat soːʊ ˈmɑːɪndɛ(ɪ)d ðɛːʌ fɑːɪn iːʌ hæθ wʌn]
The issue of completed cadences,
[ði ˈɪʃu ʌv kʌmˈplitɛ(ɪ)d ˈkɛːɪdɛ(ɪ)nsɛ(ɪ)z]
And, smiling down the stars, they whisper– SWEET
[ænd ˈsmɑːɪlɪŋ dɑːʊn ðʌ staz ðɛːɪ ˈʍɪspʌ swit]

"You are tired (I think)"
[ju aʁ tɑːɪʁd ɑːɪ θɪŋk]
Cummings, E. E. (Am. 1894-1962)

You are tired,
[ju ɑ tɑːɪʌd]
(I think)
[ɑːɪ θɪŋk]
Of the always puzzle of living and doing;
[ʌv ði ˈɔlwɛːɪz ˈpʌzʊl ʌv ˈlɪvɪŋ ænd ˈduɪŋ]
And so am I.
[ænd soːʊ æm ɑːɪ]
Come with me, then,
[kʌm wɪð mi ðɛn]
And we'll leave it far and far away–
[ænd wil liv ɪt faʁ⁽ʳ⁾ ænd faʁ⁽ʳ⁾ ʌˈwɛːɪ]

(Only you and I, understand!)
[ˈoːʊnlɪ ju ænd ɑːɪ ʌndʌˈstænd]
You have played,
[ju hæv plɛːɪd]
(I think)
[ɑːɪ θɪŋk]
And broke the toys you were fondest of,
[ænd bɹoːʊk ðʌ tɔːɪz ju wɜ ˈfandɛ(ɪ)st ʌv]
And are a little tired now;
[ænd aʁ⁽ʳ⁾ ʌ ˈlɪtʊl tɑːɪʌd nɑːʊ]
Tired of things that break, and–
[tɑːɪʌd ʌv θɪŋz ðæt bɹɛːɪk ænd]
Just tired.
[dʒʌst tɑːɪʌd]
So am I.
[soːʊ æm ɑːɪ]
But I come with a dream in my eyes tonight,
[bʌt ɑːɪ kʌm wɪð ʌ dɹim ɪn mɑːɪ ɑːɪz tuˈnɑːɪt]
And I knock with a rose
[ænd ɑːɪ nak wɪð ʌ ɹoːʊz]
at the hopeless gate of your heart–
[æt ðʌ ˈhoːʊplɛ(ɪ)s gɛːɪt ʌv jɔːʌ hat]
Open to me!
[ˈoːʊpɛ(ɪ)n tu mi]
For I will show you the places Nobody knows,
[fɔʁ⁽ʳ⁾ ɑːɪ wɪl ʃoːʊ ju ðʌ ˈplɛːɪsɛ(ɪ)z ˈnoːʊbadɪ noːʊz]
And, if you like,
[ænd ɪf ju lɑːɪk]
The perfect places of Sleep.
[ðʌ ˈpɜfɛ(ɪ)kt ˈplɛːɪsɛ(ɪ)z ʌv slip]
Ah, come with me!
[ɑ kʌm wɪð mi]
I'll blow you that wonderful bubble, the moon,
[ɑːɪl bloːʊ ju ðæt ˈwʌndʌfʊl ˈbʌbʊl ðʌ mun]
That floats forever and a day;
[ðæt floːʊts fɔʁ⁽ʳ⁾ˈɛvʌʁ⁽ʳ⁾ ænd ʌ dɛːɪ]
I'll sing you the jacinth song
[ɑːɪl sɪŋ ju ðʌ ˈdʒɛːɪsɪnθ saŋ]
Of the probable stars;
[ʌv ðʌ ˈpɹabʌbʊl staz]
I will attempt the unstartled steppes of dream,
[ɑːɪ wɪl ʌˈtɛmpt ði ʌnˈstatʊld stɛps ʌv dɹim]
Until I find the only Flower,
[ʌnˈtɪl ɑːɪ fɑːɪnd ði ˈoːʊnlɪ flɑːʊʌ]
Which shall keep (I think) your little heart
[ʍɪtʃ ʃæl kip ɑːɪ θɪŋk jɔːʌ ˈlɪtʊl hat]
While the moon comes out of the sea.
[ʍɑːɪl ðʌ mun kʌmz ɑːʊt ʌv ðʌ si]

Coates, Eric (Eng. 1886-1957)

Song Selections

"Bird Songs at Eventide"
[bɜd saŋz æt ˈivɪntɑːɪd]
Bennett, Harry Rodney (1890-1948)

Over the quiet hills
[ˈoːʊvʌ ðʊ ˈkwɑːɪɛ(ɪ)t hɪlz]
Slowly the shadows fall;
[ˈsloːʊlɪ ðʊ ˈʃædoːʊz fɔl]
Far down the echoing vale
[fɑ dɑːʊn ði ˈɛkoːʊɪŋ veːɪl]
Birds softly call;
[bɜdz ˈsɑftlɪ kɔl]
Slowly the golden sun
[ˈsloːʊlɪ ðʊ ˈgoːʊldɛ(ɪ)n sʌn]
Sinks in the dreaming west;
[sɪŋks ɪn ðʊ ˈdɹimɪŋ wɛst]
Bird songs at eventide
[bɜd saŋz æt ˈivɛ(ɪ)ntɑːɪd]
Call me to rest.
[kɔl mi tu ɾɛst]
Love, through the hours of day
[lʌv ðɾu ði ɑːʊʌz ʌv deːɪ]
Sadness of heart may bring,
[ˈsædnɛ(ɪ)s ʌv hɑt meːɪ bɹɪŋ]
When twilight comes again
[ʍɛn ˈtwɑːɪlɑːɪt kʌmz ʌˈgeːɪn]
Sorrows take wing;
[ˈsaɾoːʊz teːɪk wɪŋ]
For when the dusk of dreams
[fɔ ʍɛn ðʊ dʌsk ʌv dɹimz]
Comes with the falling dew,
[kʌmz wɪð ðʊ ˈfɔlɪŋ dju]
Bird songs at eventide
[bɜd saŋz æt ˈivɛ(ɪ)ntɑːɪd]
Call me to you.
[kɔl mi tu ju]

"Who Is Sylvia?" [hu ɪz ˈsɪlvia]
Shakespeare, William (Eng. 1564-1616)

Who is Silvia? What is she,
[hu ɪz ˈsɪlvɑ ʍat ɪz ʃi]
That all our swains commend her?
[ðæt ɔl ɑːʊʌ sweːɪnz kʌˈmɛnd hɜ]
Holy, fair and wise is she;
[ˈhoːʊlɪ fɛːʌr ænd wɑːɪz ɪz ʃi]
The heavens such grace did lend her,
[ðʊ ˈhɛvɛ(ɪ)nz sʌʧ gɹeːɪs dɪd lɛnd hɜ]
That she might admiréd be.
[ðæt ʃi mɑːɪt ædˈmɑːɪʌɾɛ(ɪ)d bi]
Is she kind as she is fair?
[ɪz ʃi kɑːɪnd æz ʃi ɪz fɛːʌ]

For beauty lives with kindness.
[fɔ ˈbjutɪ lɪvz wɪð ˈkɑːɪndnɛ(ɪ)s]
Love doth to her eyes repair,
[lʌv dʌθ tu hɜ ɑːɪz ɹɪˈpeːʌ]
To help him of his blindness,
[tu hɛlp hɪm ʌv hɪz ˈblɑːɪndnɛ(ɪ)s]
And being helped, inhabits there.
[ænd ˈbiɪŋ hɛlpt ɪnˈhæbɪts ðɛːʌ]
Then to Silvia let us sing,
[ðɛn tu ˈsɪlvɪɑ lɛt ʌs sɪŋ]
That Silvia is excelling;
[ðæt ˈsɪlvɪɑ ɪz ɪkˈsɛlɪŋ]
She excels each mortal thing
[ʃi ɪkˈsɛlz iʧ ˈmɔtʊl θɪŋ]
Upon the dull earth dwelling;
[ʌˈpan ðʊ dʌl ɜθ ˈdwɛlɪŋ]
To her let us garlands bring.
[tu hɜ lɛt ʌs ˈgɑlæ(ʌ)ndz bɹɪŋ]

Coleridge-Taylor, Samuel (Eng. 1875-1912)

Song Selections

"Oh What Comes over the Sea"
[oːʊ ʍat kʌmz ˈoːʊvʌ ðʊ si]
Rossetti, Christina Georgina (Eng. 1830-1894)

Oh what comes over the sea,
[oːʊ ʍat kʌmz ˈoːʊvʌ ðʊ si]
Shoals and quicksands past;
[ʃoːʊlz ænd ˈkwɪksændz pɑst]
And what comes home to me,
[ænd ʍat kʌmz hoːʊm tu mi]
Sailing slow, sailing fast?
[ˈseːɪlɪŋ sloːʊ ˈseːɪlɪŋ fɑst]
A wind comes over the sea
[ʌ wɪnd kʌmz ˈoːʊvʌ ðʊ si]
With a moan in its blast;
[wɪð ʌ moːʊn ɪn ɪts blɑst]
But nothing comes home to me,
[bʌt ˈnʌθɪŋ kʌmz hoːʊm tu mi]
Sailing slow, sailing fast.
[ˈseːɪlɪŋ sloːʊ ˈseːɪlɪŋ fɑst]
Let me be, let me be,
[lɛt mi bi lɛt mi bi]
For my lot is cast:
[fɔ mɑːɪ lat ɪz kɑst]
Land or sea all's one to me,
[lænd ɔ si ɔlz wʌn tu mi]
And sail it slow or fast.
[ænd seːɪl ɪt sloːʊ ɔ fɑst]
Let me be, let me be,
[lɛt mi bi lɛt mi bi]

"The Willow Song"
[ðʊ ˈwɪloːʊ sɑŋ]
Shakespeare, William (Eng. 1564-1616)

The poor soul sat sighing by a sycamore tree,
[ðʊ puːʌ soːʊl sæt ˈsaːɪŋ baːɪ ʌ ˈsɪkʌmɔːʌ tɹi]
Sing all a green willow, willow, willow;
[sɪŋ ɔl ʌ gɹin ˈwɪloːʊ ˈwɪloːʊ ˈwɪloːʊ]
Her hand on her bosom, her head on her knee,
[hɜ hænd ɑn hɜ ˈbʊzʌm hɜ hɛd ɑn hɜ ni]
Sing willow, willow, willow:
[sɪŋ ˈwɪloːʊ ˈwɪloːʊ ˈwɪloːʊ]
The fresh streams ran by her,
[ðʊ fɹɛʃ stɹimz ɹæn baːɪ hɜ]
and murmur'd her moans;
[ænd ˈmɜmʊ(ʌ)d hɜ moːʊnz]
Sing willow, willow, willow:
[sɪŋ ˈwɪloːʊ ˈwɪloːʊ ˈwɪloːʊ]
Her salt tears fell from her, and soften'd the stones;
[hɜ sɔlt tɪːʌz fɛl fɹʌm hɜ ænd ˈsafɛ(ɪ)nd ðʊ stoːʊnz]
Sing willow, willow, willow:
[sɪŋ ˈwɪloːʊ ˈwɪloːʊ ˈwɪloːʊ]
Sing all a green willow must be my garland.
[sɪŋ ɔl ʌ gɹin ˈwɪloːʊ mʌst bi maːɪ ˈgalæ(ʌ)nd]
Let nobody blame him, his scorn I approve,
[lɛt ˈnoːʊbadɪ blɛːɪm hɪm hɪz skɔn aːɪ ʌˈpɹuv]
I call'd my love false love; but what said he then?
[aːɪ kɔld maːɪ lʌv fɔls lʌv bʌt ʍat sɛd hi ðɛn]
Sing willow, willow, willow.
[sɪŋ ˈwɪloːʊ ˈwɪloːʊ ˈwɪloːʊ]

"This Is the Island of Gardens"
[ðɪs ɪz ði ˈaːɪlʌnd ʌv ˈgadɪnz]
Radclyffe-Hall, Marguerite (Eng. 1880-1943)

This is the island of gardens,
[ðɪs ɪz ði ˈaːɪlæ(ʌ)nd ʌv ˈgadɛ(ɪ)nz]
Filled with a marvelous fragrance,
[fɪld wɪð ʌ ˈmavʊlʌs ˈfɹɛːɪgɹæ(ɪ)ns]
O! the pale scent of the jasmine!
[oːʊ ðʊ pɛːɪl sɛnt ʌv ðʊ ˈʤæzmɪn]
O! the delicious mimosa!
[oːʊ ðʊ dɪˈlɪʃʌs mɪˈmoːʊsʌ]
Beating soft pinions together,
[ˈbitɪŋ saft ˈpɪnjʌnz tuˈgɛðʌ]
Cometh a wind from the mountains;
[ˈkʌmɛ(ɪ)θ ʌ wɪnd fɹʌm ðʊ ˈmaːʊntæ(ɪ)nz]
Why wouldst thou leave us, O small wind?
[ʍaːɪ wʊdst ðaːʊ liv ʌs oːʊ smɔl wɪnd]
Rest thee awhile 'mid the laurels.
[ɹɛst ði ʌˈʍaːɪl mɪd ðʊ ˈlɔɹʊlz]
Even as thou, have I wandered
[ˈivɛ(ɪ)n æz ðaːʊ hæv aːɪ ˈwandʌd]
Over the earth and the ocean,
[ˈoːʊvʌ ði ɜθ ænd ði ˈoːʊʃæ(ɪ)n]

Pondering many things deeply,
[ˈpandʌɹɪŋ ˈmɛnɪ θɪŋz ˈdipli]
Now I lie down in the sunshine.
[naːʊ aːɪ laːɪ daːʊn ɪn ðʊ ˈsʌnʃaːɪn]

 # Conte, David (Am. b. 1955)

American Death Ballads (Song Cycle)
[ʌˈmɛɹɪkɪn dɛθ ˈbælɪdz]
Anonymous

I. Wicked Polly
[ˈwɪkɪd ˈpɑli]

Young people who delight in sin,
[jʌŋ ˈpipʊl hu dɪˈlaːɪt ɪn sɪn]
I'll tell you what has lately been:
[aːɪl tɛl ju ʍat hæz ˈlɛːɪtlɪ bɪn]
A woman who was young and fair
[ʌ ˈwʊmæ(ʌ)n hu waz jʌŋ ænd fɛːʌ]
died in sin and deep despair.
[daːɪd ɪn sɪn ænd dip dɪˈspɛːʌ]
She went to frolics, dances and play,
[ʃi wɛnt tu ˈfɹɑlɪks ˈdænsɛ(ɪ)z ænd plɛːɪ]
in spite of all her friends could say.
[ɪn spaːɪt ʌv ɔl hɜ fɹɛndz kʊd sɛːɪ]
"I'll turn to God when I get old,
[aːɪl tɜn tu gad ʍɛn aːɪ gɛt oːʊld]
and He will then receive my soul."
[ænd hi wɪl ðɛn ɹɪˈsiv maːɪ soːʊl]
One Friday morning she took sick,
[wʌn ˈfɹaːɪdɛːɪ ˈmɔnɪŋ ʃi tʊk sɪk]
her stubborn heart began to break.
[hɜ ˈstʌbɔn hat bɪˈgæn tu bɹɛːɪk]
She called her mother to her bed,
[ʃi kɔld hɜ ˈmʌðʌ tu hɜ bɛd]
her eyes were rolling in her head:
[hɜ aːɪz wɜ ˈɹoːʊlɪŋ ɪn hɜ hɛd]
"O mother, mother, fare you well,
[oːʊ ˈmʌðʌ ˈmʌðʌ fɛːʌ ju wɛl]
your wicked Polly's doomed to hell,
[jɔːʌ ˈwɪkɛ(ɪ)d ˈpɑlɪz dumd tu hɛl]
The tears are lost you shed for me;
[ðʌ tɪːʌz a last ju ʃɛd fɔ mi]
my soul is lost, I plainly see."
[maːɪ soːʊl ɪz last aːɪ ˈplɛːɪnlɪ si]
"My earthly father, fare you well;
[maːɪ ˈɜθlɪ ˈfaðʌ fɛːʌ ju wɛl]
your wicked Polly's doomed to hell.
[jɔːʌ ˈwɪkɛ(ɪ)d ˈpɑlɪz dumd tu hɛl]
The flaming wrath begins to roll;
[ðʌ ˈflɛːɪmɪŋ ɹæθ bɪˈgɪnz tu ɹoːʊl]
I'm a lost and ruined soul."
[aːɪm ʌ last ænd ˈɹ⁽ʳʳ⁾uɪnd soːʊl]

"Your counsels I have slipped all,
[jɔːʌ 'kaːʊnsʊlz aːɪ hæv slɪpt ɔl]
my carnal appetite to fill.
[maːɪ 'kanʊl 'æpɪ(ʌ)ˌtaːɪt tu fɪl]
When I am dead, remember well,
[ʍɛn aːɪ æm dɛd ɹɪ'mɛmbʌ wɛl]
your wicked Polly groans in hell."
[jɔːʌ 'wɪkɛ(ɪ)d 'palɪ gɹ⁽ʳ⁾oːʊnz ɪn hɛl]
She wrung her hands and groaned and cried
[ʃi ɹʌŋ hɜ hændz ænd gɹ⁽ʳ⁾oːʊnd ænd kɹ⁽ʳ⁾aːɪd]
and gnawed her tongue before she died;
[ænd nɔd hɜ tʌŋ bɪ'fɔːʌ ʃi daːɪd]
Her nails turned black, her voice did fail,
[hɜ nɛːɪlz tɜnd blæk hɜ vɔːɪs dɪd fɛːɪl]
she died and left this lower vale.
[ʃi daːɪd ænd lɛft ðɪs 'loːʊʌ vɛːɪl]
Young people, let this be your case,
[jʌŋ 'pipʊl lɛt ðɪs bi jɔːʌ kɛːɪs]
Oh, turn to God and trust His grace.
[oːʊ tɜn tu gad ænd tɹʌst hɪz gɹɛːɪs]
Down on your knees for mercy cry,
[daːʊn an jɔːʌ niz fɔ 'mɜsɪ kɹ⁽ʳ⁾aːɪ]
lest you in sin like Polly die.
[lɛst ju ɪn sɪn laːɪk 'palɪ daːɪ]

II. The Unquiet Grave

[ði ʌn'kwaːɪt gɹɛːɪv]

"The wind doth blow today, my love,
[ðʌ wɪnd dʌθ bloːʊ tu'dɛːɪ maːɪ lʌv]
And a few small drops of rain;
[ænd ʌ fju smɔl dɹaps ʌv ɹɛːɪn]
I never had but one true-love,
[aːɪ 'nɛvʌ hæd bʌt wʌn tɹ⁽ʳ⁾u lʌv]
In cold grave she was lain.
[ɪn koːʊld gɹ⁽ʳ⁾ɛːɪv ʃi waz lɛːɪn]
"I'll do as much for my true-love
[aːɪl du æz mʌtʃ fɔ maːɪ tɹ⁽ʳ⁾u lʌv]
As any young man may;
[æz 'ɛnɪ jʌŋ mæn mɛːɪ]
I'll sit and mourn all at her grave
[aːɪl sɪt ænd mɔn ɔl æt hɜ gɹ⁽ʳ⁾ɛːɪv]
For a twelvemonth and a day."
[fɔʁ⁽ʳ⁾ ʌ 'twɛlvmʌnθ ænd ʌ dɛːɪ]
The twelvemonth and a day being up,
[ðʌ 'twɛlvmʌnθ ænd ʌ dɛːɪ 'biɪŋ ʌp]
The dead began to speak:
[ðʌ dɛd bɪ'gæn tu spik]
"Oh who sits weeping on my grave,
[oːʊ hu sɪts 'wipɪŋ an maːɪ gɹ⁽ʳ⁾ɛːɪv]
And will not let me sleep?"
[ænd wɪl nat lɛt mi slip]
"'Tis I, my love, sits on your grave,
[tɪz aːɪ maːɪ lʌv sɪts an jɔːʌ gɹ⁽ʳ⁾ɛːɪv]
And will not let you sleep;
[ænd wɪl nat lɛt ju slip]

For I crave one kiss of your clay-cold lips,
[fɔʁ⁽ʳ⁾ aːɪ kɹɛːɪv wʌn kɪs ʌv jɔːʌ klɛːɪ koːʊld lɪps]
And that is all I seek."
[ænd ðæt ɪz ɔl aːɪ sik]
"You crave one kiss of my clay-cold lips,
[ju kɹɛːɪv wʌn kɪs ʌv maːɪ klɛːɪ koːʊld lɪps]
But my breath smells earthy strong;
[bʌt maːɪ bɹɛθ smɛlz 'ɜθɪ stɹaŋ]
If you have one kiss of my clay-cold lips,
[ɪf ju hæv wʌn kɪs ʌv maːɪ klɛːɪ koːʊld lɪps]
Your time will not be long."
[jɔːʌ taːɪm wɪl nat bi laŋ]
"'Tis down in yonder garden green,
[tɪz daːʊn ɪn 'jandʌ 'gadɛ(ɪ)n gɹin]
Love, where we used to walk,
[lʌv ʍɛːʌ wi just tu wɔk]
The finest flower that e're was seen
[ðʌ 'faːɪnɛ(ɪ)st flaːʊʌ ðæt ɛːʌ waz sin]
Is withered to a stalk."
[ɪz 'wɪðʌd tu ʌ stɔk]
"The stalk is withered dry, my love,
[ðʌ stɔk ɪz 'wɪðʌd dɹaːɪ maːɪ lʌv]
So will our hearts decay;
[soːʊ wɪl aːʊʌ hats dɪ'kɛːɪ]
So make yourself content, my love,
[soːʊ mɛːɪk jɔːʌ'sɛlf kʌn'tɛnt maːɪ lʌv]
Till God calls you away."
[tɪl gad kɔlz ju ʌ'wɛːɪ]

III. The Dying Californian

[ðʌ 'daːɪɪŋ kælɪ'fɔʁnjɪn]

Lay up nearer, brother, nearer,
[lɛːɪ ʌp 'nɪːʌʁ⁽ʳ⁾ʌ 'bɹʌðʌ 'nɪːʌʁ⁽ʳ⁾ʌ]
For my limbs are growing cold;
[fɔ maːɪ lɪmz a 'gɹoːʊɪŋ koːʊld]
And thy presence seemeth dearer
[ænd ðaːɪ 'pɹɛzɛ(ɪ)ns 'simɛ(ɪ)θ 'dɪːʌʁ⁽ʳ⁾ʌ]
When thine arms around me fold.
[ʍɛn ðaːɪn amz ʌ'ʁ⁽ʳ⁾aːʊnd mi foːʊld]
I am dying, brother, dying,
[aːɪ æm 'daːɪɪŋ 'bɹʌðʌ 'daːɪɪŋ]
Soon you'll miss me in your berth,
[sun jul mɪs mi ɪn jɔːʌ bɜθ]
For my form will soon be lying
[fɔ maːɪ fɔm wɪl sun bi 'laːɪŋ]
'Neath the ocean's briny surf.
[niθ ði 'oːʊʃæ(ɪ)nz 'bɹaːɪnɪ sɜf]
Tell my father when you see him
[tɛl maːɪ 'faðʌ ʍɛn ju si hɪm]
That in death I prayed for him,
[ðæt ɪn dɛθ aːɪ pɹɛːɪd fɔ hɪm]
Prayed that I might only meet him
[pɹɛːɪd ðæt aːɪ maːɪt 'oːʊnlɪ mit hɪm]
In a world that's free from sin.
[ɪn ʌ wɜld ðæts fɹi fɹʌm sɪn]

Tell my mother– God assist her,
[tɛl maːɪ ˈmʌðʌ gad ʌˈsɪst hɜ]
Now that she is growing old–
[naːʊ ðæt ʃi ɪz ˈɡɹoːʊɪŋ oːʊld]
That her child would glad have kissed her
[ðæt hɜ ʧaːɪld wʊd glæd hæv kɪst hɜ]
When his lips grew pale and cold.
[ʍɛn hɪz lɪps ɡɹ⁽ʳ⁾u pɛːɪl ænd koːʊld]
Listen, brother, catch each whisper,
[ˈlɪsɛ(ɪ)n ˈbɹʌðʌ kæʧ iʧ ˈʍɪspʌ]
'Tis my wife I speak of now;
[tɪz maːɪ waːɪf aːɪ spik ʌv naːʊ]
Tell, O tell her how I missed her
[tɛl oːʊ tɛl hɜ haːʊ aːɪ mɪst hɜ]
When the fever burned my brow.
[ʍɛn ðʌ ˈfivʌ bɜnd maːɪ bɹaːʊ]
Tell her she must kiss my children
[tɛl hɜ ʃi mʌst kɪs maːɪ ˈʧɪldɹɛ(ɪ)n]
Like the kiss I last impressed,
[laːɪk ðʌ kɪs aːɪ læst ɪmˈpɹɛst]
Hold them as when I last held them,
[hoːʊld ðɛm æz ʍɛn aːɪ læst hɛld ðɛm]
Held them closely to my breast.
[hɛld ðɛm ˈkloːʊslɪ tu maːɪ bɹɛst]
It was for them I crossed the ocean,
[ɪt wɑz fɔ ðɛm aːɪ kɹɑst ði ˈoːʊʃæ(ɪ)n]
What my hopes were I'll not tell;
[ʍat maːɪ hoːʊps wɜ aːɪl nat tɛl]
But they gained an orphan's portion,
[bʌt ðɛːɪ ɡɛːɪnd æn ˈɔfæ(ɪ)nz ˈpɔʃʌn]
Yet He doeth all things well.
[jɛt hi ˈduɛ(ɪ)θ ɔl θɪŋz wɛl]
Tell them I have reached the haven
[tɛl ðɛm aːɪ hæv ɹiʧt ðʌ ˈhɛːɪvɛ(ɪ)n]
Where I sought the precious dust,
[ʍɛːʌʁ⁽ʳ⁾ aːɪ sɔt ðʌ ˈpɹɛʃʌs dʌst]
And I gained a port called Heaven
[ænd aːɪ ɡɛːɪnd ʌ pɔt kɔld ˈhɛvɛ(ɪ)n]
Where the gold will never rust.
[ʍɛːʌ ðʌ goːʊld wɪl ˈnɛvʌ ɹʌst]

IV. Captain Kidd
[ˈkæptɪn kɪd]

"My name was Robert Kidd, as I sailed, as I sailed,
[maːɪ nɛːɪm wɑz ˈɹabʌt kɪd æz aːɪ sɛːɪld æz aːɪ sɛːɪld]
My name was Robert Kidd, as I sailed.
[maːɪ nɛːɪm wɑz ˈɹabʌt kɪd æz aːɪ sɛːɪld]
My name was Robert Kidd, God's laws I did forbid,
[maːɪ nɛːɪm wɑz ˈɹabʌt kɪd gadz lɔz aːɪ dɪd fɔˈbɪd]
And so wickedly I did, as I sailed, as I sailed,
[ænd soːʊ ˈwɪkɛ(ɪ)dlɪ aːɪ dɪd æz aːɪ sɛːɪld æz aːɪ sɛːɪld]
And so wickedly I did as I sailed!"
[ænd soːʊ ˈwɪkɛ(ɪ)dlɪ aːɪ dɪd æz aːɪ sɛːɪld]
"My parents taught me well, as I sailed, as I sailed,
[maːɪ ˈpæʁ⁽ʳ⁾ɛnts tɔt mi wɛl æz aːɪ sɛːɪld æz aːɪ sɛːɪld]

My parents taught me well, as I sailed.
[maːɪ ˈpæʁ⁽ʳ⁾ɛnts tɔt mi wɛl æz aːɪ sɛːɪld]
I cursed my father dear, and her that did me bear,
[aːɪ kɜst maːɪ ˈfaðʌ dɪːʌ ænd hɜ ðæt dɪd mi bɛːʌ]
And so wickedly did swear, as I sailed, as I sailed,
[ænd soːʊ ˈwɪkɛ(ɪ)dlɪ dɪd swɛːʌ æz aːɪ sɛːɪld]
And so wickedly did swear as I sailed.
[ænd soːʊ ˈwɪkɛ(ɪ)dlɪ dɪd swɛːʌ æz aːɪ sɛːɪld]
I'd a Bible in my hand, as I sailed, as I sailed,
[aːɪd ʌ ˈbaːɪbʊl ɪn maːɪ hænd æz aːɪ sɛːɪld æz aːɪ sɛːɪld]
But I sunk it in the sand, as I sailed.
[bʌt aːɪ sʌŋk ɪt ɪn ðʌ sænd æz aːɪ sɛːɪld]
I made a solemn vow, to God I would not bow,
[aːɪ mɛːɪd ʌ ˈsalʌm vaːʊ tu gad aːɪ wʊd nat baːʊ]
Nor myself one prayer allow, when I sailed.
[nɔ maːɪˈsɛlf wʌn pɹɛːʌʁ⁽ʳ⁾ ʌˈlaːʊ ʍɛn aːɪ sɛːɪld]
I murdered William Moore, as I sailed.
[aːɪ ˈmɜdʌd ˈwɪljæ(ɪ)m mɔːʌʁ⁽ʳ⁾ æz aːɪ sɛːɪld]
And being cruel still, my gunner did I kill,
[ænd ˈbiŋ ˈkɹ⁽ʳ⁾uːʊl stɪl maːɪ ˈgʌnʌ dɪd aːɪ kɪl]
And much precious blood did I spill, as I sailed,
[ænd mʌʧ ˈpɹɛʃʌs blʌd dɪd aːɪ spɪl æz aːɪ sɛːɪld]
To Execution Dock, I must go, I must go,
[tu ɛksɪˈkjuʃʌn dak aːɪ mʌst goːʊ aːɪ mʌst goːʊ]
To Execution Dock, I must go,
[tu ɛksɪˈkjuʃʌn dak aːɪ mʌst goːʊ]
To Execution Dock,
[tu ɛksɪˈkjuʃʌn dak]
where many thousands flock,
[ʍɛːʌ ˈmɛni ˈθaːʊzæ(ʌ)ndz flak]
But I must bear my shock, and must die.
[bʌt aːɪ mʌst bɛːʌ maːɪ ʃak ænd mʌst daːɪ]
Come all ye young and old, see me die, see me die,
[kʌm ɔl ji jʌŋ ænd oːʊld si mi daːɪ si mi daːɪ]
Come all ye young and old, see me die.
[kʌm ɔl ji jʌŋ ænd oːʊld si mi daːɪ]
Come all ye young and old,
[kʌm ɔl ji jʌŋ ænd oːʊld]
you're welcome to my gold,
[jɔːʌ ˈwɛlkʌm tu maːɪ goːʊld]
For by it I've lost my soul, and must die,
[fɔ baːɪ ɪt aːɪv last maːɪ soːʊl ænd mʌst daːɪ]
Take warning now by me, for I must die,
[tɛːɪk ˈwɔnɪŋ naːʊ baːɪ mi fɔʁ⁽ʳ⁾ aːɪ mʌst daːɪ]
Take warning now by me,
[tɛːɪk ˈwɔnɪŋ naːʊ baːɪ mi]
and shun bad company,
[ænd ʃʌn bæd ˈkʌmpæ(ɪ)nɪ]
Lest you come to hell with me, for I must die.
[lɛst ju kʌm tu hɛl wɪð mi fɔʁ⁽ʳ⁾ aːɪ mʌst daːɪ]

Song Selection

"Echo" (see Faith)

Copland, Aaron (Am. 1900-1990)

Old American Songs, Set 1 (Song Cycle)
[oːʊld ʌˈmɛʁɪkɪn sɑŋz sɛt wʌn]
Folksongs

1. The Boatman's Dance
[ðʌ ˈboːʊtmʌnz dæns]

High row the boatmen row,
[haːɪ ɹoːʊ ðʌ ˈboːʊtmɛ(ɪ)n ɹoːʊ]
Floatin' down the river the Ohio.
[ˈfloːʊ(t)ɪn daːʊn ðʌ ˈɹɪvʌ ði oːʊˈhaːɪoːʊ]
The boatmen dance, the boatmen sing,
[ðʌ ˈboːʊtmɛ(ɪ)n dæns ðʌ ˈboːʊtmɛ(ɪ)n sɪŋ]
The boatmen up to ev'rything,
[ðʌ ˈboːʊtmɛ(ɪ)n ʌp tʊ ˈɛvɹɪθɪŋ]
And when the boatman gets on shore
[ænd ʍɛn ðʌ ˈboːʊtmæ(ʌ)n gɛts ɑn ʃɔːʌ]
He spends his cash and works for more.
[hi spɛndz hɪz kæʃ ænd wɜks fɔ mɔːʌ]
Then dance the boatmen dance,
[ðɛn dæns ðʌ ˈboːʊtmɛ(ɪ)n dæns]
O dance the boatmen dance.
[oːʊ dæns ðʌ ˈboːʊtmɛ(ɪ)n dæns]
O dance all night 'til broad daylight,
[oːʊ dæns ɔl naːɪt tɪl bɹɑd ˈdeːɪlaːɪt]
And go home with the gals in the mornin'.
[ænd goːʊ hoːʊm wɪð ðʌ gælz ɪn ðʌ ˈmɔnɪn]
High row the boatmen row,
[haːɪ ɹoːʊ ðʌ ˈboːʊtmɛ(ɪ)n ɹoːʊ]
Floatin' down the river the Ohio.
[ˈfloːʊ(t)ɪn daːʊn ðʌ ˈɹɪvʌ ði oːʊˈhaːɪoːʊ]
I went on board the other day
[aːɪ wɛnt ɑn bɔd ði ˈʌðʌ dɛːɪ]
To see what the boatmen had to say.
[tu si ʍɑt ðʌ ˈboːʊtmɛ(ɪ)n hæd tʊ sɛːɪ]
There I let my passion loose,
[ðɛːʌʁ⁽ʳ⁾ aːɪ lɛt maːɪ ˈpæʃʌn lus]
An' they cram me in the callaboose.
[æn ðɛːɪ kɹæm mi ɪn ðʌ ˈkælʌˌbus]
O dance the boatmen dance. . .
[oːʊ dæns ðʌ ˈboːʊtmɛ(ɪ)n dæns]
The boatman is a thrifty man,
[ðʌ ˈboːʊtmæ(ʌ)n ɪz ʌ ˈθɹɪftɪ mæn]
There's none can do as the boatman can.
[ðɛːʌz nʌn kæn du æz ðʌ ˈboːʊtmæ(ʌ)n kæn]
I never see a pretty gal in my life
[aːɪ ˈnɛvʌ si ʌ ˈpɹɪtɪ gæl ɪn maːɪ laːɪf]
But that she was a boatman's wife.
[bʌt ðæt ʃi wɑz ʌ ˈboːʊtmæ(ʌ)nz waːɪf]
O dance the boatmen dance. . .
[oːʊ dæns ðʌ ˈboːʊtmɛ(ɪ)n dæns]

2. The Dodger
[ðʌ ˈdɑdʒʁ]

Yes the candidate's a dodger,
[jɛs ðʌ ˈkændɪdɛːɪts ʌ ˈdɑdʒʌ]
Yes a well known dodger,
[jɛs ʌ wɛl noːʊn ˈdɑdʒʌ]
Yes the candidate's a dodger,
[jɛs ðʌ ˈkændɪdɛːɪts ʌ ˈdɑdʒʌ]
Yes and I'm a dodger too.
[jɛs ænd aːɪm ʌ ˈdɑdʒʌ tu]
He'll meet you and treat you
[hil mit ju ænd tɹit ju]
And ask you for your vote
[ænd æsk ju fɔ jɔːʌ voːʊt]
But look out boys
[bʌt lʊk aːʊt bɔːɪz]
He's a dodgin' for a note.
[hiz ʌ ˈdɑdʒɪn fɔʁ⁽ʳ⁾ ʌ noːʊt]
Yes we're all dodgin'
[jɛs wɪːʌʁ⁽ʳ⁾ ɔl ˈdɑdʒɪn]
A dodgin', dodgin', dodgin'
[ʌ ˈdɑdʒɪn ˈdɑdʒɪn ˈdɑdʒɪn]
Yes we're all dodgin'
[jɛs wɪːʌʁ⁽ʳ⁾ ɔl ˈdɑdʒɪn]
Out away through the world.
[aːʊt ʌˈwɛːɪ θru ðʌ wɜld]
Yes the preacher he's a dodger,
[jɛs ðʌ ˈpɹitʃʌ hiz ʌ ˈdɑdʒʌ]
Yes a well known dodger,
[jɛs ʌ wɛl noːʊn ˈdɑdʒʌ]
Yes the preacher he's a dodger
[jɛs ðʌ ˈpɹitʃʌ hiz ʌ ˈdɑdʒʌ]
Yes and I'm a dodger too.
[jɛs ænd aːɪm ʌ ˈdɑdʒʌ tu]
He'll preach you a gospel,
[hil pɹitʃ ju ʌ ˈgɑspʊl]
And tell you of your crimes.
[ænd tɛl ju ʌv jɔːʌ kɹaːɪmz]
But look out boys
[bʌt lʊk aːʊt bɔːɪz]
He's a dodgin' for your dimes,
[hiz ʌ ˈdɑdʒɪn fɔ jɔːʌ daːɪmz]
Yes we're all dodgin'...
[jɛs wɪːʌʁ⁽ʳ⁾ ɔl ˈdɑdʒɪn]
Yes the lover he's a dodger,
[jɛs ðʌ ˈlʌvʌ hiz ʌ ˈdɑdʒʌ]
Yes a well known dodger
[jɛs ʌ wɛl noːʊn ˈdɑdʒʌ]
Yes the lover he's a dodger
[jɛs ðʌ ˈlʌvʌ hiz ʌ ˈdɑdʒʌ]
Yes and I'm a dodger too.
[jɛs ænd aːɪm ʌ ˈdɑdʒʌ tu]
He'll hug you and kiss you
[hil hʌg ju ænd kɪs ju]

And call you his bride
[ænd kɔl ju hɪz bɹɑːɪd]
But look out girls
[bʌt lʊk ɑːʊt gɜlz]
He's a tellin' you a lie.
[hiz ʌ ˈtɛlɪn ju ʌ lɑːɪ]
Yes we're all dodgin'...
[jɛs wɪːʌʁ⁽ʳ⁾ ɔl ˈdɑdʒɪn]

3. Long Time Ago
[lɑŋ tɑːɪm ʌˈgoːʊ]

On the lake where droop'd the willow
[ɑn ðʌ lɛːɪk ʍɛːʌ dɹ⁽ʳ⁾ʊpt ðʌ ˈwɪloːʊ]
Long time ago
[lɑŋ tɑːɪm ʌˈgoːʊ]
Where the rock threw back the billow
[ʍɛːʌ ðʌ ɹɑk θɹu bæk ðʌ ˈbɪloːʊ]
Brighter than snow.
[ˈbɹɑːɪtʌ ðæn snoːʊ]
Dwelt a maid beloved and cherish'd
[dwɛlt ʌ mɛːɪd bɪˈlʌvd ænd ˈtʃɛʁ⁽ʳ⁾ɪʃt]
By high and low
[bɑːɪ hɑːɪ ænd loːʊ]
But the autumn leaf she perish'd
[bʌt ði ˈɔtʌm lif ʃi ˈpɛʁ⁽ʳ⁾ɪʃt]
Long time ago.
[lɑŋ tɑːɪm ʌˈgoːʊ]
Rock and tree and flowing water
[ɹɑk ænd tɹi ænd ˈfloːʊɪŋ ˈwɔtʌ]
Long time ago
[lɑŋ tɑːɪm ʌˈgoːʊ]
Bird and bee and blossom taught her
[bɜd ænd bi ænd ˈblɑsʌm tɔt hɜ]
Love's spell to know.
[lʌvz spɛl tu noːʊ]
While to my fond words she listen'd
[ʍɑːɪl tu mɑːɪ fɑnd wɜdz ʃi ˈlɪsɛ⁽ʳ⁾nd]
Murmuring low
[ˈmɜmʊʁ⁽ʳ⁾ɪŋ loːʊ]
Tenderly her blue eyes glisten'd
[ˈtɛndʌlɪ hɜ blu ɑːɪz ˈglɪsɛ⁽ʳ⁾nd]
Long time ago.
[lɑŋ tɑːɪm ʌˈgoːʊ]

4. Simple Gifts
[ˈsɪmpʊl gɪfts]

'Tis the gift to be simple 'tis the gift to be free
[tɪz ðʌ gɪft tu bi ˈsɪmpʊl tɪz ðʌ gɪft tu bi fɹi]
'Tis the gift to come down where you ought to be
[tɪz ðʌ gɪft tu kʌm dɑːʊn ʍɛːʌ ju ɔt tu bi]
And when we find ourselves in that place just right
[ænd ʍɛn wi fɑːɪnd ɑːʊʌˈsɛlvz ɪn ðæt plɛːɪs dʒʌst ɹɑːɪt]
'Twill be in the valley of love and delight.
[twɪl bi ɪn ðʌ ˈvælɪ ʌv lʌv ænd dɪˈlɑːɪt]

When true simplicity is gained
[ʍɛn tɹ⁽ʳ⁾u sɪmˈplɪsɪtɪ ɪz gɛːɪnd]
To bow and to bend we shan't be ashamed
[tu bɑːʊ ænd tu bɛnd wi ʃænt bi ʌˈʃɛːɪmd]
To turn, turn will be our delight
[tu tɜn tɜn wɪl bi ɑːʊʌ dɪˈlɑːɪt]
'Till by turning, turning we come round right.
[tɪl bɑːɪ ˈtɜnɪŋ ˈtɜnɪŋ wi kʌm ɹɑːʊnd ɹɑːɪt]

5. I Bought Me a Cat
[ɑ bɔt mi ʌ kæt]

I bought me a cat, my cat pleased me,
[ɑ bɔt mi ʌ kæt mɑ kæt plizd mi]
I fed my cat under yonder tree.
[ɑ fɛd mɑ kæt ˈʌndʌ ˈjɑndʌ tɹi]
My cat says fiddle eye fee.
[mɑ kæt sɛz ˈfɪdʊl ɑːɪ fi]
I bought me a duck, my duck pleased me,
[ɑ bɔt mi ʌ dʌk mɑ dʌk plizd mi]
I fed my duck under yonder tree.
[ɑ fɛd mɑ dʌk ˈʌndʌ ˈjɑndʌ tɹi]
My duck says, "Quaa, quaa,"
[mɑ dʌk sɛz kwæ̃ kwæ̃]
My cat says fiddle eye fee.
[mɑ kæt sɛz ˈfɪdʊl ɑːɪ fi]
I bought me a goose, my goose pleased me,
[ɑ bɔt mi ʌ gus mɑ gus plizd mi]
I fed my goose under yonder tree.
[ɑ fɛd mɑ gus ˈʌndʌ ˈjɑndʌ tɹi]
My goose says, "Quaw, quaw," My duck says. . .
[mɑ gus sɛz kwɔ kwɔ mɑ dʌk sɛz]
I bought me a hen, my hen pleased me.
[ɑ bɔt mi ʌ hɛn mɑ hɛn plizd mi]
I fed my hen under yonder tree.
[ɑ fɛd mɑ hɛn ˈʌndʌ ˈjɑndʌ tɹi]
My hen says, Shimmy shack, shimmy shack,"
[mɑ hɛn sɛz ˈʃɪmɪ ʃæk ˈʃɪmɪ ʃæk]
My goose says. . .
[mɑ gus sɛz]
I bought me a pig, my pig pleased me.
[ɑ bɔt mi ʌ pɪg mɑ pɪg plizd mi]
I fed my pig under yonder tree.
[ɑ fɛd mɑ pɪg ˈʌndʌ ˈjɑndʌ tɹi]
My pig says, "Griffey, griffey." My hen says. . .
[mɑ pɪg sɛz ˈgɹɪfɪ ˈgɹɪfɪ mɑ hɛn sɛz]
I bought me a cow, my cow pleased me.
[ɑ bɔt mi ʌ kɑːʊ mɑ kɑːʊ plizd mi]
I fed my cow under yonder tree.
[ɑ fɛd mɑ kɑːʊ ˈʌndʌ ˈjɑndʌ tɹi]
My cow says "Baw, baw," my pig says . . .
[mɑ kɑːʊ sɛz bɔ bɔ mɑ pɪg sɛz]
I bought me a horse, my horse pleased me.
[ɑ bɔt mi ʌ hɔs mɑ hɔs plizd mi]
I fed my horse under yonder tree.
[ɑ fɛd mɑ hɔs ˈʌndʌ ˈjɑndʌ tɹi]

My horse says, "Neigh, neigh," My cow says. . .
[mɑ hɔs sɛz nɛːɪ nɛːɪ mɑ kɑːʊ sɛz]
I bought me a wife, my wife pleased me.
[ɑ bɔt mi ʌ wɑːɪf mɑ wɑːɪf plizd mi]
I fed my wife under yonder tree.
[ɑ fɛd mɑ wɑːɪf ˈʌndʌ ˈjɑndʌ tɹi]
My wife says, "Honey, honey," My horse says. . .
[mɑ wɑːɪf sɛz ˈhʌnɪ ˈhʌnɪ mɑ hɔs sɛz]

Old American Songs, Set 2 (Song Cycle)
[oːʊld ʌˈmɛʁɪkɪn sɑŋz sɛt tu]
Folksongs

1. The Little Horses
[ðʌ ˈlɪtʊl ˈhɔʁsɪz]

Hush you bye,
[hʌʃ ju bɑːɪ]
Don't you cry,
[doːʊnt ju kɹɑːɪ]
Go to sleepy little baby.
[goːʊ tu ˈslipɪ ˈlɪdʊl ˈbɛːɪbɪ]
When you wake,
[ʍɛn ju wɛːɪk]
You shall have,
[ju ʃæl hæv]
All the pretty little horses.
[ɔl ðʌ ˈpɹɪtɪ ˈlɪdʊl ˈhɔsɛ(ɪ)z]
Blacks and bays,
[blæks ænd bɛːɪz]
Dapples and grays,
[ˈdæpʊlz ænd gɹɛːɪz]
Coach and six-a little horses.
[koːʊtʃ ænd sɪks ʌ ˈlɪdʊl ˈhɔsɛ(ɪ)z]
Blacks and bays,
[blæks ænd bɛːɪz]
Dapples and grays,
[ˈdæpʊlz ænd gɹɛːɪz]
Coach and six-a little horses.
[koːʊtʃ ænd sɪks ʌ ˈlɪdʊl ˈhɔsɛ(ɪ)z]
Hush you bye,
[hʌʃ ju bɑːɪ]
Don't you cry,
[doːʊnt ju kɹɑːɪ]
Go to sleepy little baby.
[goːʊ tu ˈslipɪ ˈlɪdʊl ˈbɛːɪbɪ]
When you wake,
[ʍɛn ju wɛːɪk]
You'll have sweet cake, and
[jul hæv swit kɛːɪk ænd]
All the pretty little horses.
[ɔl ðʌ ˈpɹɪtɪ ˈlɪdʊl ˈhɔsɛ(ɪ)z]
A brown and gray and a black and a bay and a
[ʌ bɹɑːʊn ænd gɹɛːɪ ænd ʌ blæk ænd ʌ bɛːɪ ænd ʌ]
Coach and six-a little horses.
[koːʊtʃ ænd sɪks ʌ ˈlɪdʊl ˈhɔsɛ(ɪ)z]

A black and a bay and a brown and a gray and a
[ʌ blæk ænd ʌ bɛːɪ ænd ʌ bɹɑːʊn ænd ʌ gɹɛːɪ ænd ʌ]
Coach and six-a little horses.
[koːʊtʃ ænd sɪks ʌ ˈlɪdʊl ˈhɔsɛ(ɪ)z]
Hush you bye,
[hʌʃ ju bɑːɪ]
Don't you cry,
[doːʊnt ju kɹɑːɪ]
Oh you pretty little baby.
[oːʊ ju ˈpɹɪtɪ ˈlɪdʊl ˈbɛːɪbɪ]
Go to sleepy little baby.
[goːʊ tu ˈslipɪ ˈlɪdʊl ˈbɛːɪbɪ]
Oh you pretty little baby.
[oːʊ ju ˈpɹɪtɪ ˈlɪdʊl ˈbɛːɪbɪ]

2. Zion's Walls
[ˈzɑːɪʌnz wɔlz]

Come fathers and mothers come,
[kʌm ˈfɑðʌz ænd ˈmʌðʌz]
Sisters and brothers come,
[ˈsɪstʌz ænd ˈbɹʌðʌz kʌm]
Join us in singing the praises of Zion.
[dʒɔːɪn ʌs ɪn ˈsɪŋɪŋ ðʌ ˈpɹɛːɪzɛ(ɪ)z ʌv ˈzɑːɪʌn]
O fathers don't you feel determined
[oːʊ ˈfɑðʌz doːʊnt ju fil dɪ ˈtɜmɪnd]
To meet within the walls of Zion?
[tu mit wɪðˈɪn ðʌ wɔlz ʌv ˈzɑːɪʌn]
We'll shout and go round
[wil ʃɑːʊt ænd goːʊ ɹɑːʊnd]
The walls of Zion.
[ðʌ wɔlz ʌv ˈzɑːɪʌn]

3. The Golden Willow Tree
[ðʌ ˈgoːʊldɪn ˈwɪloːʊ tɹi]

There was a little ship in South Amerikee,
[ðɛːʌ wɑz ʌ ˈlɪtʊl ʃɪp ɪn sɑːʊθ ʌˈmɛʁ(ʳ)ɪˈki]
Crying O the land that lies so low,
[ˈkɹɑːɪɪŋ oːʊ ðʌ lænd ðæt lɑːɪz soːʊ loːʊ]
There was a little ship in South Amerikee,
[ðɛːʌ wɑz ʌ ˈlɪtʊl ʃɪp ɪn sɑːʊθ ʌˈmɛʁ(ʳ)ɪˈki]
She went by the name of the Golden Willow Tree,
[ʃi wɛnt bɑːɪ ðʌ nɛːɪm ʌv ðʌ ˈgoːʊldɛ(ɪ)n ˈwɪloːʊ tɹi]
As she sailed in the lowland lonesome low,
[æz ʃi sɛːɪld ɪn ðʌ ˈloːʊlæ(ʌ)nd ˈloːʊnsʌm loːʊ]
As she sailed in the lowland so low.
[æz ʃi sɛːɪld ɪn ðʌ ˈloːʊlæ(ʌ)nd soːʊ loːʊ]
We hadn't been a sailin' more than two weeks or three,
[wi ˈhæ(d)ɪnt bɪn ʌ ˈsɛːɪlɪn mɔːʌ ðæn tu wiks ɔ θɹi]
Till we came in sight of the British Roverie,
[tɪl wi kɛːɪm ɪn sɑːɪt ʌv ðʌ ˈbɹɪtɪʃ ˈɹoːʊvʌ ʁ(ʳ)i]
As she sailed in the lowland lonesome low,
[æz ʃi sɛːɪld ɪn ðʌ ˈloːʊlæ(ʌ)nd ˈloːʊnsʌm loːʊ]
As she sailed in the lowland so low.
[æz ʃi sɛːɪld ɪn ðʌ ˈloːʊlæ(ʌ)nd soːʊ loːʊ]

Up stepped a little carpenter boy, Says
[ʌp stɛpt ʌ ˈlɪtʊl ˈkɑpɛntʌ bɔːɪ sɛz]
"What will you give me for the ship that I'll destroy?"
[ʍɑt wɪl ju gɪv mi fɔ ðʌ ʃɪp ðæt ɑːɪl dɪˈstɹɔːɪ]
"I'll give you gold or I'll give thee,
[ɑːɪl gɪv ju goːʊld ɔʁ⁽ʳ⁾ ɑːɪl gɪv ði]
The fairest of my daughters as she sails upon the sea,
[ðʌ ˈfɛːʌʁ⁽ʳ⁾ɛ⁽ɪ⁾st ʌv mɑːɪ ˈdɔtʌz æz ʃi seːɪlz ʌˈpɑn ðʌ si]
If you'll sink 'em in the lowland lonesome low,
[ɪf jul sɪŋk ɛm ɪn ðʌ ˈloːʊlæ(ʌ)nd ˈloːʊnsʌm loːʊ]
If you'll sink 'em in the land that lies so low."
[ɪf jul sɪŋk ɛm ɪn ðʌ lænd ðæt lɑːɪz soːʊ loːʊ]
He turned upon his back and away swum he,
[hi tɜnd ʌˈpɑn hɪz bæk ænd ʌˈwɛːɪ swʌm hi]
He swum till he came to the British Roverie,
[hi swʌm tɪl hi kɛːɪm tu ðʌ ˈbɹɪtɪʃ ˈɹoːʊvʌˈʁ⁽ʳ⁾i]
He had a little instrument fitted for his use,
[hi hæd ʌ ˈlɪtʊl ˈɪnstɹ⁽ʳ⁾u(ʌ)mɛnt ˈfɪtɛ(ɪ)d fɔ hɪz jus]
He bored nine holes and he bored them all at once.
[hi bɔd nɑːɪn hoːʊlz ænd hi bɔd ðɛm ɔl æt wʌns]
He turned upon his breast and back swum he,
[hi tɜnd ʌˈpɑn hɪz bɹɛst ænd bæk swʌm hi]
He swum till he came to the Golden Willow Tree.
[hi swʌm tɪl hi kɛːɪm tu ðʌ ˈgoːʊldɛ(ɪ)n ˈwɪloːʊ tɹi]
"Captain, O Captain, come take me on board,
[ˈkæptæ(ɪ)n oːʊ ˈkæptæ(ɪ)n kʌm tɛːɪk mi ɑn bɔd]
And do unto me as good as your word
[ænd du ˈʌntu mi æz gʊd æz jɔːʌ wɜd]
For I sank 'em in the lowland lonesome low,
[fɔʁ⁽ʳ⁾ ɑːɪ sæŋk ɛm ɪn ðʌ ˈloːʊlæ(ʌ)nd ˈloːʊnsʌm loːʊ]
I sank 'em in the lowland so low."
[ɑːɪ sæŋk ɛm ɪn ðʌ ˈloːʊlæ(ʌ)nd soːʊ loːʊ]
"Oh no, I won't take you on board,
[oːʊ noːʊ ɑːɪ woːʊnt tɛːɪk ju ɑn bɔd]
Nor do unto you as good as my word,
[nɔ du ˈʌntu ju æz gʊd æz mɑːɪ wɜd]
Though you sank 'em in the lowland lonesome low,
[ðoːʊ ju sæŋk ɛm ɪn ðʌ ˈloːʊlæ(ʌ)nd ˈloːʊnsʌm loːʊ]
Though you sank 'em in the land that lies so low."
[ðoːʊ ju sæŋk ɛm ɪn ðʌ lænd ðæt lɑːɪz soːʊ loːʊ]
"If it wasn't for the love that I have for your men,
[ɪf ɪt ˈwɑzɛ(ɪ)nt fɔ ðʌ lʌv ðæt ɑːɪ hæv fɔ jɔːʌ mɛn]
I'd do unto you as I done unto them,
[ɑːɪd du ˈʌntu ju æz ɑːɪ dʌn ˈʌntu ðɛm]
I'd sink you in the lowland lonesome low,
[ɑːɪd sɪŋk ju ɪn ðʌ ˈloːʊlæ(ʌ)nd ˈloːʊnsʌm loːʊ]
I'd sink you in the lowland so low."
[ɑːɪd sɪŋk ju ɪn ðʌ ˈloːʊlæ(ʌ)nd soːʊ loːʊ]
He turned upon his head and down swum he,
[hi tɜnd ʌˈpɑn hɪz hɛd ænd dɑːʊn swʌm hi]
He swum till he came to the bottom of the sea.
[hi swʌm tɪl hi kɛːɪm tu ðʌ ˈbatʌm ʌv ðʌ si]
Sank himself in the lowland lonesome low,
[sæŋk hɪmˈsɛlf ɪn ðʌ ˈloːʊlæ(ʌ)nd ˈloːʊnsʌm loːʊ]
Sank himself in the land that lies so low.
[sæŋk hɪmˈsɛlf ɪn ðʌ lænd ðæt lɑːɪz soːʊ loːʊ]

4. At the River
[æt ðʌ ˈɹɪvʁ]
Lowry, Robert (Am. 1826-1899)

Shall we gather by the river,
[ʃæl wi ˈgæðʌ bɑːɪ ðʌ ˈɹɪvʌ]
Where bright angel's feet have trod,
[ʍɛːʌ bɹɑːɪt ˈɛːɪndʒɛ(ʊ)lz fit hæv tɹɑd]
With its crystal tide forever
[wɪð ɪts ˈkɹɪstʊl tɑːɪd fɔʁ⁽ʳ⁾ˈɛvʌ]
Flowing by the throne of God.
[ˈfloːʊɪŋ bɑːɪ ðʌ θroːʊn ʌv gad]
Yes, we'll gather by the river,
[jɛs wil ˈgæðʌ bɑːɪ ðʌ ˈɹɪvʌ]
The beautiful, the beautiful river,
[ðʌ ˈbjutɪfʊl ðʌ ˈbjutɪfʊl ˈɹɪvʌ]
Gather with the saints by the river
[ˈgæðʌ wɪð ðʌ sɛːɪnts bɑːɪ ðʌ ˈɹɪvʌ]
That flows by the throne of God.
[ðæt floːʊz bɑːɪ ðʌ θroːʊn ʌv gad]
Soon we'll reach the shining river,
[sun wil ɹiʧ ðʌ ˈʃɑːɪnɪŋ ˈɹɪvʌ]
Soon our pilgrimage will cease,
[sun ɑːʊʌ ˈpɪlgɹɪmæ(ɪ)dʒ wɪl sis]
Soon our happy hearts will quiver
[sun ɑːʊʌ ˈhæpɪ hɑts wɪl ˈkwɪvʌ]
With the melody of peace.
[wɪð ðʌ ˈmɛlodɪ ʌv pis]

5. Ching-a-Ring Chaw
[ʧɪŋ ʌ ɹɪŋ ʧɔ]

Ching-a-ring-a ring ching ching,
[ʧɪŋ ʌ ɹɪŋ ʌ ɹɪŋ ʧɪŋ ʧɪŋ]
Hoa dinga ding kum larkee,
[ˈhoːʊʌ ˈdɪŋʌ dɪŋ kum ˈlaˈki]
Ching-a-ring-a ring ching ching,
[ʧɪŋ ʌ ɹɪŋ ʌ ɹɪŋ ʧɪŋ ʧɪŋ]
Hoa ding(a) kum larkee.
[ˈhoːʊʌ dɪŋ(ʌ) kum ˈlaˈki]
Brothers gather round,
[ˈbɹʌðʌz ˈgæðʌ ɹɑːʊnd]
Listen to this story,
[ˈlɪsɛ(ɪ)n tu ðɪs ˈstɔʁ⁽ʳ⁾ɪ]
'Bout the promised land,
[bɑːʊt ðʌ ˈpɹɑmɪst lænd]
An' the promised glory.
[æn ðʌ ˈpɹɑmɪst ˈglɔʁ⁽ʳ⁾ɪ]
You don' need to fear,
[jʊ doːʊn nid tʊ fiːʌ]
If you have no money,
[ɪf jʊ hæv noːʊ ˈmʌnɪ]
You don' need none there,
[jʊ doːʊn nid nʌn ðeːʌ]
To buy you milk and honey.
[tʊ bɑːɪ ju mɪlk ænd ˈhʌnɪ]

There you'll ride in style,
[ðeːʌ jul ɹaːɪd ɪn staːɪl]
Coach with four white horses,
[koːʊʧ wɪð fɔːʌ ʍaːɪt ˈhɔsɛ(ɪ)z]
There the evenin' meal,
[ðeːʌ ði ˈivnɪn mil]
Has one two three four courses.
[hæz wʌn tu θri fɔːʌ ˈkɔsɛ(ɪ)z]
Ching-a-ring-a ring ching ching,
[ʧɪŋ ʌ ɹɪŋ ʌ ɹɪŋ ʧɪŋ ʧɪŋ]
Hoa ding(a) kum larkee.
[ˈhoːʊʌ dɪŋ(ʌ) kum ˈlaːki]
Nights we all will dance,
[naːɪts wi ɔl wɪl dæns]
To the harp and fiddle,
[tu ðʌ hap ænd ˈfɪdʊl]
Waltz and jig and prance,
[wɔlts ænd ʤɪg ænd pɹæns]
"Cast off down the middle!"
[kæst af daːʊn ðʌ ˈmɪdʊl]
When the mornin' come,
[ʍɛn ðʌ ˈmɔnɪn kʌm]
All in grand and splendour,
[ɔl ɪn gɹænd ænd ˈsplɛndʊ(ʌ)]
Stand out in the sun,
[stænd aːʊt ɪn ðʌ sʌn]
And hear the holy thunder.
[ænd hɪːʌ ðʌ ˈhoːʊlɪ ˈθʌndʌ]
Brothers hear me out,
[ˈbɹʌðʌz hɪːʌ mi aːʊt]
The promised land's a-comin',
[ðʌ ˈpɹɑmɪst lændz ʌ ˈkʌmɪn]
Dance and sing and shout,
[dæns ænd sɪŋ ænd ʃaːʊt]
I hear them harps a strummin'.
[aːɪ hɪːʌ ðɛm haps ʌ ˈstɹʌmɪn]
Ching-a-ring-a ring ching ching Chaw.
[ʧɪŋ ʌ ɹɪŋ ʌ ɹɪŋ ʧɪŋ ʧɪŋ ʧɔ]

Twelve Poems of Emily Dickinson (Song Cycle)
[twɛlv ˈpoːʊɪmz ʌv ˈɛmɪli ˈdɪkɪnsʌn]
Dickinson, Emily (Am. 1830-1886)

1. Nature, the Gentlest Mother
[ˈneːɪʧʁ ðʌ ˈʤɛntlɪst ˈmʌðʁ]

Nature, the gentlest mother
[ˈneːɪʧʊ(ʌ) ðʌ ˈʤɛntlɛ(ɪ)st ˈmʌðʌ]
Impatient of no child,
[ɪmˈpeːɪʃent ʌv noːʊ ʧaːɪld]
The feeblest or the waywardest,–
[ðʌ ˈfiblɛ(ɪ)st ɔ ðʌ ˈweːɪwʊdɛ(ɪ)st]
Her admonition mild
[hɜ ædmo(ʌ)ˈnɪʃʌn maːɪld]
In forest and the hill
[ɪn ˈfɔʁ(ʳ)ɛ(ɪ)st ænd ðʌ hɪl]

By traveller is heard,
[baːɪ ˈtɹævʊlʌʁ(ʳ) ɪz hɜd]
Restraining rampant squirrel
[ɹɪˈstɹeːɪnɪŋ ˈɹæmpæ(ɪ)nt ˈskwʊʁ(ʳ)ʊl]
Or too impetuous bird.
[ɔ tu ɪmˈpɛʧuʌs bɜd]
How fair her conversation,
[haːʊ feːʌ hɜ kɑnvɜˈseːɪʃʌn]
A summer afternoon.
[ʌ ˈsʌmʌʁ(ʳ) æftʌˈnun]
Her household, her assembly;
[hɜ ˈhaːʊshoːʊld hɜ ʌˈsɛmblɪ]
And when the sun goes down
[ænd ʍɛn ðʌ sʌn goːʊz daːʊn]
Her voice among the aisles
[hɜ vɔːɪs ʌˈmʌŋ ði aːɪlz]
Incites the timid prayer
[ɪnˈsaːɪts ðʌ ˈtɪmɪd pɹɛːʌ]
Of the minutest cricket,
[ʌv ðʌ maːɪˈnjutɛ(ɪ)st ˈkɹɪkɛ(ɪ)t]
The most unworthy flower.
[ðʌ moːʊst ʌnˈwɜðɪ flaːʊʌ]
When all the children sleep,
[ʍɛn ɔl ðʌ ˈʧɪldɹɛ(ɪ)n slip]
She turns as long away,
[ʃi tɜnz æz lɑŋ ʌˈweːɪ]
As will suffice to light her lamps;
[æz wɪl sʌˈfaːɪs tu laːɪt hɜ læmps]
Then, bending from the sky,
[ðɛn ˈbɛndɪŋ fɹʌm ðʌ skaːɪ]
With infinite affection
[wɪð ˈɪnfɪnɪt ʌˈfɛkʃʌn]
And infiniter care,
[ænd ˈɪnfɪnaːɪtʌ kɛːʌ]
Her golden finger on her lip,
[hɜ ˈgoːʊldɛ(ɪ)n ˈfɪŋgʌʁ(ʳ) ɑn hɜ lɪp]
Wills silence everywhere.
[wɪlz ˈsaːɪlɛ(ɪ)ns ˈɛvɹɪʍɛːʌ]

2. There Came a Wind like a Bugle
[ðeːʁ keːɪm ʌ wɪnd laːɪk ʌ ˈbjugʊl]

There came a wind like a bugle,
[ðeːʌ keːɪm ʌ wɪnd laːɪk ʌ ˈbjugʊl]
It quivered through the grass,
[ɪt ˈkwɪvʌd θru ðʌ gɹæs]
And a green chill upon the heat
[ænd ʌ gɹin ʧɪl ʌˈpɑn ðʌ hit]
So ominous did pass.
[soːʊ ˈɑmɪnʌs dɪd pæs]
We barred the windows and the doors
[wi bɑd ðʌ ˈwɪndoːʊz ænd ðʌ dɔːʌz]
As from an emerald ghost
[æz fɹʌm æn ˈɛmɹʊld goːʊst]
The doom's electric moccasin
[ðʌ dumz ɪˈlɛktɹɪk ˈmɑkʌsɪn]

That very instant passed.
[ðæt ˈvɛʁ⁽ʳ⁾ɪ ˈɪnstæ(ɪ)nt pæst]
On a strange mob of panting trees
[ɑn ʌ stɹɛːɪndʒ mɑb ʌv ˈpæntɪŋ tɹiz]
And fences fled away.
[ænd ˈfɛnsɛ(ɪ)z flɛd ʌˈwɛːɪ]
And rivers where the houses ran
[ænd ˈɹɪvʌz ʍɛːʌ ðʌ ˈhɑːʊzɛ(ɪ)z ɹæn]
The living looked that day,
[ðʌ ˈlɪvɪŋ lʊkt ðæt dɛːɪ]
The bell within the steeple wild,
[ðʌ bɛl wɪðˈɪn ðʌ ˈstipʊl wɑːɪld]
The flying tidings whirled.
[ðʌ ˈflɑːɪɪŋ ˈtɑːɪdɪŋz ʍ3ld]
How much can come and much can go,
[hɑːʊ mʌtʃ kæn kʌm ænd mʌtʃ kæn goːʊ]
And yet abide the world.
[ænd jɛt ʌˈbɑːɪd ðʌ w3ld]

3. Why Do They Shut Me out of Heaven
[ʍɑːɪ du ðɛːɪ ʃʌt mi ɑːʊt ʌv ˈhɛvɪn]

Why do they shut me out of Heaven?
[ʍɑːɪ du ðɛːɪ ʃʌt mi ɑːʊt ʌv ˈhɛvɛ(ɪ)n]
Did I sing too loud?
[dɪd ɑːɪ sɪŋ tu lɑːʊd]
But I can sing a little minor,
[bʌt ɑːɪ kæn sɪŋ ʌ ˈlɪtʊl ˈmɑːɪnɔ(ʌ)]
Timid as a bird.
[ˈtɪmɪd æz ʌ b3d]
Wouldn't the angels try me
[ˈwʊdɛ(ɪ)nt ði ˈɛːɪndʒɛ(ʊ)lz tɹɑːɪ mi]
just once more
[dʒʌst wʌns mɔːʌ]
Just see if I troubled them
[dʒʌst si ɪf ɑːɪ ˈtɹʌbʊld ðɛm]
But don't shut the door.
[bʌt doːʊnt ʃʌt ðʌ dɔːʌ]
Oh if I were the gentlemen
[oːʊ ɪf ɑːɪ w3 ðʌ ˈdʒɛntʊlmɛ(ɪ)n]
in the white robes
[ɪn ðʌ ʍɑːɪt ɹoːʊbz]
and they were the little hand that knocked,
[ænd ðɛːɪ w3 ðʌ ˈlɪtʊl hænd ðæt nɑkt]
Could I forbid?
[kʊd ɑːɪ fɔˈbɪd]
Why do they shut me out of Heaven,
[ʍɑːɪ du ðɛːɪ ʃʌt mi ɑːʊt ʌv ˈhɛvɛ(ɪ)n]
Did I sing too loud?
[dɪd ɑːɪ sɪŋ tu lɑːʊd]

4. The World Feels Dusty
[ðʌ w3ld filz ˈdʌsti]

The world feels dusty,
[ðʌ w3ld filz ˈdʌstɪ]

when we stop to die
[ʍɛn wi stɑp tu dɑːɪ]
We want the dew then
[wi want ðʌ dju ðɛn]
Honors taste dry.
[ˈɑnɔ(ʌ)z tɛːɪst dɹɑːɪ]
Flags vex a dying face
[flægz vɛks ʌ ˈdɑːɪɪŋ fɛːɪs]
But the least fan
[bʌt ðʌ list fæn]
stirred by a friend's hand
[st3d bɑːɪ ʌ fɹɛndz hænd]
Cools like the rain
[kulz lɑːɪk ðʌ ɹɛːɪn]
Mine be the ministry
[mɑːɪn bi ðʌ ˈmɪnɪstɹɪ]
when thy thirst comes
[ʍɛn ðɑːɪ θ3st kʌmz]
Dews of thyself to fetch
[djuz ʌv ðɑːɪˈsɛlf tu fɛtʃ]
and holy balms.
[ænd ˈhoːʊlɪ bɑmz]

5. Heart, We Will Forget Him
[hɑʁt wi wɪl fɔʁˈgɛt hɪm]

Heart, we will forget him
[hɑt wi wɪl fɔˈgɛt hɪm]
You and I, tonight.
[ju ænd ɑːɪ tuˈnɑːɪt]
You may forget the warmth he gave,
[ju mɛːɪ fɔˈgɛt ðʌ wɔmθ hi gɛːɪv]
I will forget the light.
[ɑːɪ wɪl fɔˈgɛt ðʌ lɑːɪt]
When you have done, pray tell me,
[ʍɛn ju hæv dʌn pɹɛːɪ tɛl mi]
That I my thoughts may dim;
[ðæt ɑːɪ mɑːɪ θɔts mɛːɪ dɪm]
Haste... lest while you're lagging,
[hɛːɪst lɛst ʍɑːɪl jɔːʌ ˈlægɪŋ]
I may remember him.
[ɑːɪ mɛːɪ ɹɪˈmɛmbʌ hɪm]

6. Dear March, Come In!
[diːʁ mɑʁtʃ kʌm ɪn]

Dear March, come in!
[diːʌ mɑtʃ kʌm ɪn]
How glad I am!
[hɑːʊ glæd ɑːɪ æm]
I looked for you before.
[ɑːɪ lʊkt fɔ ju bɪˈfɔːʌ]
Put down your hat—
[pʊt dɑːʊn jɔːʌ hæt]
You must have walked—
[ju mʌst hæv wɔkt]

How out of breath you are.
[haːʊ aːʊt ʌv bɹɛθ ju ɑ]
Dear March, how are you?
[dɪːʌ maʧ haːʊ a ju]
And the rest?
[ænd ðʌ ɹest]
Did you leave Nature well?
[dɪd ju liv ˈnɛːɪʧʊ(ʌ) wɛl]
Oh, March, come right upstairs with me,
[oːʊ maʧ kʌm ɹaːɪt ʌpˈstɛːʌz wɪð mi]
I have so much to tell.
[aːɪ hæv soːʊ mʌʧ tu tɛl]
I got your letter, and the bird's;
[aːɪ gat jɔːʌ ˈlɛtʌ ænd ðʌ bɜdz]
The maples never knew
[ðʌ ˈmɛːɪpʊlz ˈnɛvʌ nju]
That you were coming,– I declare,
[ðæt ju wɜ ˈkʌmɪŋ aːɪ dɪˈklɛːʌ]
How red their faces grew,
[haːʊ ɹed ðɛːʌ ˈfɛːɪsɛ(ɪ)z gɹ(r)u]
But March, forgive me.
[bʌt maʧ fɔˈgɪv mi]
And all those hills
[ænd ɔl ðoːʊz hɪlz]
You left for me to hue,
[ju lɛft fɔ mi tu hju]
There was no purple suitable,
[ðɛːʌ waz noːʊ ˈpɜpʊl ˈsjutʌbʊl]
You took it all with you.
[ju tʊk ɪt ɔl wɪð ju]
Who knocks? that April?
[hu naks ðæt ˈɛːɪpɹɪ(ʊ)l]
Lock the door,
[lak ðʌ dɔːʌ]
I will not be pursued
[aːɪ wɪl nat bi pɜˈsjud]
He stayed away a year, to call
[hi stɛːɪd ʌˈwɛːɪ ʌ jɪːʌ tu kɔl]
When I am occupied
[ʍɛn aːɪ æm ˈakjupaːɪd]
But trifles look so trivial
[bʌt ˈtɹaːɪfʊlz lʊk soːʊ ˈtɹɪvɪʊl]
As soon as you have come
[æz sun æz ju hæv kʌm]
And blame is just as dear as praise
[ænd blɛːɪm ɪz ʤʌst æz dɪːʌʁ(r) æz pɹɛːɪz]
And praise as mere as blame.
[ænd pɹɛːɪz æz mɪːʌ æz blɛːɪm]

7. Sleep Is Supposed to Be
[slip ɪz sʌˈpoːʊzd tu bi]

Sleep is supposed to be,
[slip ɪz sʌˈpoːʊzd tu bi]
By souls of sanity,
[baːɪ soːʊlz ʌv ˈsænɪtɪ]

The shutting of the eye.
[ðʌ ˈʃʌtɪŋ ʌv ði aːɪ]
Sleep is the station grand
[slip ɪz ðʌ ˈstɛːɪʃʌn gɹænd]
Down which on either hand
[daːʊn ʍɪʧ an ˈaːɪðʌ hænd]
The hosts of witness stand.
[ðʌ hoːʊsts ʌv ˈwɪtnɛ(ɪ)s stænd]
Morn is supposed to be,
[mɔn ɪz sʌˈpoːʊzd tu bi]
By people of degree,
[baːɪ ˈpipʊl ʌv dɪˈgɹi]
The breaking of the day.
[ðʌ ˈbɹɛːɪkɪŋ ʌv ðʌ dɛːɪ]
Morning has not occurred.
[ˈmɔnɪŋ hæz nat ʌˈkɜd]
That shall aurora be
[ðæt ʃæl ɔˈʁ(r)ɔʁ(r)ʌ bi]
East of Eternity;
[ist ʌv ɪˈtɜnɪtɪ]
One with the banner gay,
[wʌn wɪð ðʌ ˈbænʌ gɛːɪ]
One in the red array,
[wʌn ɪn ðʌ ɹed ʌˈʁ(r)ɛːɪ]
That is the break of day.
[ðæt ɪz ðʌ bɹɛːɪk ʌv dɛːɪ]

8. When They Come Back
[ʍɛn ðɛːɪ kʌm bæk]

When they come back– if Blossoms do,
[ʍɛn ðɛːɪ kʌm bæk ɪf ˈblasʌmz du]
I always feel a doubt
[aːɪ ˈɔlwɛːɪz fil ʌ daːʊt]
If Blossoms can be born again
[ɪf ˈblasʌmz kæn bi bɔn ʌˈgɛn]
When once the art is out.
[ʍɛn wʌns ði at ɪz aːʊt]
When they begin, if Robins do,
[ʍɛn ðɛːɪ bɪˈgɪn ɪf ˈɹabɪnz du]
I always had a fear
[aːɪ ˈɔlwɛːɪz hæd ʌ fɪːʌ]
I did not tell, it was their last Experiment
[aːɪ dɪd nat tɛl ɪt waz ðɛːʌ læst ɪkˈspɛʁ(r)ɪmɛnt]
Last year.
[læst jɪːʌ]
When it is May, if May return,
[ʍɛn ɪt ɪz mɛːɪ ɪf mɛːɪ ɹɪˈtɜn]
Has nobody a pang
[hæz ˈnoːʊbadɪ ʌ pæŋ]
That on a face so beautiful
[ðæt an ʌ fɛːɪs soːʊ ˈbjutɪfʊl]
We might not look again?
[wi maːɪt nat lʊk ʌˈgɛn]
If I am there, one does not know
[ɪf aːɪ æm ðɛːʌ wʌn dʌz nat noːʊ]

What party one may be
[ʍɑt ˈpɑtɪ wʌn mɛːɪ bi]
Tomorrow, But if I am there,
[tuˈmaʁ⁽ʳ⁾oːʊ bʌt ɪf ɑːɪ æm ðɛːʌ]
I take back all I say!
[ɑːɪ tɛːʊk bæk ɔl ɑːɪ sɛːɪ]

9. I Felt a Funeral in My Brain
[ɑːɪ fɛlt ʌ ˈfjunɹʊl ɪn mɑːɪ bɹɛːɪn]

I felt a funeral in my brain,
[ɑːɪ fɛlt ʌ ˈfjunʌʁ⁽ʳ⁾ʊl ɪn mɑːɪ bɹɛːɪn]
And mourners to and fro,
[ænd ˈmɔnʌz tu ænd fɹoːʊ]
Kept treading, treading till it seemed
[kɛpt ˈtɹɛdɪŋ ˈtɹɛdɪŋ tɪl ɪt simd]
That sense was breaking through.
[ðæt sɛns wɑz ˈbɹɛːɪkɪŋ θɹu]
And when they all were seated
[ænd ʍɛn ðɛːɪ ɔl wɜ ˈsitɛ(ɪ)d]
A service like a drum
[ʌ ˈsɜvɪs lɑːɪk ʌ dɹʌm]
Kept beating, beating till I thought
[kɛpt ˈbitɪŋ ˈbitɪŋ tɪl ɑːɪ θɔt]
My mind was going numb.
[mɑːɪ mɑːɪnd wɑz ˈgoːʊɪŋ nʌm]
And then I heard them lift a box,
[ænd ðɛn ɑːɪ hɜd ðɛm lɪft ʌ bɑks]
And creak across my soul
[ænd kɹik ʌˈkɹɑs mɑːɪ soːʊl]
With those same boots of lead again,
[wɪð ðoːʊz sɛːɪm buts ʌv lɛd ʌˈgɛn]
Then space began to toll
[ðɛn spɛːɪs bɪˈgæn tu toːʊl]
As all the heavens were a bell,
[æz ɔl ðʌ ˈhɛvɛ(ɪ)nz wɜ⁽ʳ⁾ ʌ bɛl]
And Being but an ear.
[ænd ˈbiɪŋ bʌt æn ɪːʌ]
And I and silence some strange race,
[ænd ɑːɪ ænd ˈsɑːɪlɛ(ɪ)ns sʌm stɹɛːɪndʒ ɹɛːɪs]
Wrecked, solitary here.
[ɹɛkt ˈsɑlɪtɛʁ⁽ʳ⁾ɪ hɪːʌ]

10. I've Heard an Organ Talk Sometimes
[ɑːɪv hɜd æn ˈɔʁgɪn tɔk ˈsʌmtɑːɪmz]

I've heard an organ talk sometimes
[ɑːɪv hɜd æn ˈɔgæ(ɪ)n tɔk ˈsʌmtɑːɪmz]
In a cathedral aisle
[ɪn ʌ kʌˈθidɹʊl ɑːɪl]
And understood no word it said
[ænd ʌndʌˈstʊd noːʊ wɜd ɪt sɛd]
Yet held my breath the while
[jɛt hɛld mɑːɪ bɹɛθ ðʌ ʍɑːɪl]
And risen up and gone away,
[ænd ˈɹɪzɛ(ɪ)n ʌp ænd gɑn ʌˈwɛːɪ]

A more Bernardine girl
[ʌ mɔːʌ bɜˈnaˌdin gɜl]
And know not what was done to me
[ænd noːʊ nɑt ʍɑt wɑz dʌn tu mi]
In that old hallowed aisle.
[ɪn ðæt oːʊld ˈhæloːʊd ɑːɪl]

11. Going to Heaven!
[ˈgoːʊɪŋ tu ˈhɛvɪn]

Going to Heaven!
[ˈgoːʊɪŋ tu ˈhɛvɛ(ɪ)n]
I don't know when,
[ɑːɪ doːʊnt noːʊ ʍɛn]
Pray do not ask me how,
[pɹɛːɪ du nɑt æsk mi hɑːʊ]
Indeed I'm too astonished
[ɪnˈdid ɑːɪm tu ʌˈstɑnɪʃt]
To think of answering you.
[tu θɪŋk ʌv ˈænsʌʁ⁽ʳ⁾ɪŋ ju]
Going to Heaven!
[ˈgoːʊɪŋ tu ˈhɛvɛ(ɪ)n]
How dim it sounds.
[hɑːʊ dɪm ɪt sɑːʊndz]
And yet it will be done
[ænd jɛt ɪt wɪl bi dʌn]
As sure as flocks go home at night
[æz ʃʊːʌʁ⁽ʳ⁾ æz flɑks goːʊ hoːʊm æt nɑːɪt]
Unto the shepherd's arm!
[ˈʌntu ðʌ ˈʃɛpʌdz am]
Perhaps you're going too!
[pɜˈhæps jɔːʌ ˈgoːʊɪŋ tu]
Who knows?
[hu noːʊz]
If you should get there first
[ɪf ju ʃʊd gɛt ðɛːʌ fɜst]
Save just a little place for me,
[sɛːɪv dʒʌst ʌ ˈlɪtʊl plɛːɪs fɔ mi]
Close to the two I lost.
[kloːʊs tu ðʌ tu ɑːɪ last]
The smallest "robe" will fit me,
[ðʌ ˈsmɔlɛ(ɪ)st ɹoːʊb wɪl fit mi]
And just a bit of "crown";
[ænd dʒʌst ʌ bɪt ʌv kɹɑːʊn]
For you know we do not mind our dress
[fɔ ju noːʊ wi du nɑt mɑːɪnd ɑːʊʌ dɹɛs]
When we are going home.
[ʍɛn wi a ˈgoːʊɪŋ hoːʊm]
Going to Heaven!
[ˈgoːʊɪŋ tu ˈhɛvɛ(ɪ)n]
I'm glad I don't believe it
[ɑːɪm glæd ɑːɪ doːʊnt bɪˈliv ɪt]
For it would stop my breath,
[fɔʁ⁽ʳ⁾ ɪt wʊd stɑp mɑːɪ bɹɛθ]
And I'd like to look a little more
[ænd ɑːɪd lɑːɪk tu lʊk ʌ ˈlɪtʊl mɔːʌ]

At such a curious earth.
[æt sʌʧ ʌ 'kjʊːʌʁ⁽ʳ⁾ɪʌs ɜθ]
I am glad they did believe it
[ɑːɪ æm glæd ðɛːɪ dɪd bɪ'liv ɪt]
Whom I have never found
[hum ɑːɪ hæv 'nɛvʌ fɑːʊnd]
Since the mighty autumn afternoon,
[sɪns ðʌ 'mɑːɪtɪ 'ɔtʌm æftʌ'nun]
I left them in the ground.
[ɑːɪ lɛft ðɛm ɪn ðʌ gɹɑːʊnd]

12. The Chariot
[ðʌ 'ʧæʁɪʌt]

Because I would not stop for Death,
[bɪ'kɔz ɑːɪ wʊd nɑt stɑp fɔ dɛθ]
He kindly stopped for me.
[hi 'kɑːɪndlɪ stɑpt fɔ mi]
The carriage held but just ourselves–
[ðʌ 'kæʁ⁽ʳ⁾æ⁽ɪ⁾ʤ hɛld bʌt ʤʌst ɑːʊʌ'sɛlvz]
and Immortality.
[ænd ɪmɔ'tælɪtɪ]
We slowly drove– he knew no haste,
[wi 'sloːʊlɪ dɹoːʊv hi nju noːʊ heːɪst]
And I had put away
[ænd ɑːɪ hæd pʊt ʌ'wɛːɪ]
My labour, and my leisure too
[mɑːɪ 'leːɪbʊ(ʌ)ʁ⁽ʳ⁾ ænd mɑːɪ 'liʒʊ(ʌ) tu]
For his civility.
[fɔ hɪz sɪ'vɪlɪtɪ]
We passed the school where children played,
[wi pæst ðʌ skul ʍɛːʌ 'ʧɪldɹɛ⁽ɪ⁾n pleːɪd]
Their lessons scarcely done
[ðɛːʌ 'lɛsʌnz 'skɛːʌslɪ dʌn]
We passed the fields of gazing grain,
[wi pæst ðʌ fildz ʌv 'geːɪzɪŋ gɹeːɪn]
We passed the setting sun,
[wi pæst ðʌ 'sɛtɪŋ sʌn]
We paused before a house that seemed
[wi pɔzd bɪ'fɔːʁ⁽ʳ⁾ ʌ hɑːʊs ðæt simd]
a swelling of the ground;
[ʌ 'swɛlɪŋ ʌv ðʌ gɹɑːʊnd]
The roof was scarcely visible,
[ðʌ ɹ⁽ʳʳ⁾uf wɑz 'skɛːʌslɪ 'vɪzɪbʊl]
The cornice but a mound,
[ðʌ 'kɔnɪs bʌt ʌ mɑːʊnd]
Since then 'tis centuries; but each
[sɪns ðɛn tɪz 'sɛnʧʊʁ⁽ʳ⁾ɪz bʌt iʧ]
Feels shorter than the day,
[filz 'ʃɔtʌ ðæn ðʌ dɛːɪ]
I first surmised the horses' heads
[ɑːɪ fɜst sɜ'mɑːɪzd ðʌ 'hɔsɛ(ɪ)z hɛdz]
Were toward eternity.
[wɜ twɔd ɪ'tɜnɪtɪ]

Crawley, Clifford (Ca. 1929-2016)

Song Selections for Youth

"Little Leprechaun"
['lɪtʊl 'lɛpɹɪ ̩kɑn]
Crawley, Clifford (Ca. 1929-2016)

Little, little, little, little Leprechaun,
['lɪtʊl 'lɪtʊl 'lɪtʊl 'lɪtʊl 'lɛpɹɪ ̩kɑn]
Don't sit there looking all forlorn,
[doːʊnt sɪt ðɛːʌ 'lʊkɪŋ ɔl fɔ'lɔn]
1. Come and play with me!
[kʌm ænd pleːɪ wɪð mi]
We'll play games, and I'll let you choose
[wil pleːɪ geːɪmz ænd ɑːɪl lɛt ju ʧuz]
So you can win and I will lose;
[soːʊ ju kæn wɪn ænd ɑːɪ wɪl luz]
2. Come and dance with me!
[kʌm ænd dæns wɪð mi]
Please don't worry because you're small,
[pliz doːʊnt 'wʊʁ⁽ʳ⁾ɪ bɪ'kɔz jɔːʌ smɔl]
It's just that I am much too tall;
[ɪts ʤʌst ðæt ɑːɪ æm mʌʧ tu tɔl]
3. Come and sing with me!
[kʌm ænd sɪŋ wɪð mi]
You sing high notes and I'll sing low,
[ju sɪŋ hɑːɪ noːʊts ænd ɑːɪl sɪŋ loːʊ]
And you sing quick and I'll sing slow;
[ænd ju sɪŋ kwɪk ænd ɑːɪl sɪŋ sloːʊ]
Little, little, little, little Leprechaun,
['lɪtʊl 'lɪtʊl 'lɪtʊl 'lɪtʊl 'lɛpɹɪ ̩kɑn]
Now you're not feeling so forlorn,
[nɑːʊ jɔːʌ nɑt 'filɪŋ soːʊ fɔ'lɔn]
Little, little, little, little Leprechaun,
['lɪtʊl 'lɪtʊl 'lɪtʊl 'lɪtʊl 'lɛpɹɪ ̩kɑn]
Have a happy day!
[hæv ʌ 'hæpɪ dɛːɪ]

Reprinted by permission of Leslie Music Publications

"My Dog Spot"
[mɑːɪ dɑg spɑt]
Bennett, Rodney (Eng. 1936-2012)

I have a white dog whose name is Spot,
[ɑːɪ hæv ʌ wɑːɪt dɑg huz neːɪm ɪz spɑt]
And he's sometimes white and he's sometimes not.
[ænd hɪz 'sʌmtɑːɪmz wɑːɪt ænd hɪz 'sʌmtɑːɪmz nɑt]
But whether he's white or whether he's not,
[bʌt 'wɛðʌ hɪz wɑːɪt ɔ 'wɛðʌ hɪz nɑt]
There's a patch on his ear that makes him Spot.
[ðɛːʌz ʌ pæʧ ɑn hɪz ɪːʌ ðæt meːɪks hɪm spɑt]
He has a tongue that is long and pink,
[hi hæz ʌ tʌŋ ðæt ɪz lɑŋ ænd pɪŋk]

And he lolls it out when he wants to think.
[ænd hi lɑlz ɪt ɑːʊt wɛn hi wɑnts tu θɪŋk]
He seems to think most when the weather is hot,
[hi simz tu θɪŋk moːʊst wɛn ðʌ ˈwɛðʌʁ⁽ʳ⁾ ɪz hɑt]
He's a wise sort of dog is my dog, Spot.
[hiz ʌ wɑːɪz sɔt ʌv dɑg ɪz mɑːɪ dɑg spɑt]
He likes a bone and he likes a ball,
[hi lɑːɪks ʌ boːʊn ænd hi lɑːɪks ʌ bɔl]
But he doesn't care for a cat at all.
[bʌt hi ˈdʌzɛ⁽ɪ⁾nt kɛːʌ fɔʁ⁽ʳ⁾ ʌ kæt æt ɔl]
He waggles his tail and he knows what's what,
[hi ˈwægʊlz hɪz teːɪl ænd hi noːʊz wɑts wɑt]
So I'm glad that he's my dog, My dog, Spot.
[soːʊ ɑːɪm glæd ðæt hiz mɑːɪ dɑg mɑːɪ dɑg spɑt]

Reprinted by permission of Leslie Music Publications

Crockart, Eric (Eng. b. 1952)

Song Selection for Youth

"On a Star Bright Winter Night"
[ɑn ʌ stɑ bɹɑːɪt ˈwɪntʌ nɑːɪt]
Folksong

On a star bright winter night, Hush my baby
[ɑn ʌ stɑ bɹɑːɪt ˈwɪntʌ nɑːɪt hʌʃ mɑːɪ ˈbeːɪbi]
To a cold land snowy white, Hush my baby
[tu ʌ koːʊld lænd ˈsnoːʊɪ wɑːɪt hʌʃ mɑːɪ ˈbeːɪbi]
He came down to save us all;
[hi kɛːɪm dɑːʊn tu sɛːɪv ʌs ɔl]
To save us and redeem us.
[tu sɛːɪv ʌs ænd ɹɪˈdim ʌs]
Yet he once was just like you, Hush my baby.
[jɛt hi wʌns wɑz dʒʌst lɑːɪk ju hʌʃ mɑːɪ ˈbeːɪbi]
In a stable in a town, Hush my baby.
[ɪn ʌ ˈstɛːɪbʊl ɪn ʌ tɑːʊn hʌʃ mɑːɪ ˈbeːɪbi]
Gleams the light that won't die down, Hush my baby.
[glimz ðʊ lɑːɪt ðæt woːʊnt dɑːɪ dɑːʊn hʌʃ mɑːɪ ˈbeːɪbi]
See how Joseph bends to kiss
[si hɑːʊ ˈdʒoːʊsɛ⁽ɪ⁾f bɛndz tu kɪs]
The child that Mary rocks now.
[ðʊ tʃɑːɪld ðæt ˈmæɹɪ ɹɑks nɑːʊ]
They were once like me and you, Hush my baby.
[ðɛːɪ wɜ wʌns lɑːɪk mi ænd ju hʌʃ mɑːɪ ˈbeːɪbi]
Little Jesus smiles in sleep, Hush my baby.
[ˈlɪtʊl ˈdʒizʌs smɑːɪlz ɪn slip hʌʃ mɑːɪ ˈbeːɪbi]
hears the angels laugh and weep, Hush my baby.
[hɪːʌz ði ˈɛːɪndʒɛ⁽ʊ⁾lz lɑf ænd wip hʌʃ mɑːɪ ˈbeːɪbi]
he must take a long hard road,
[hi mʌst teːɪk ʌ lɑŋ hɑd ɹoːʊd]
Yet God's love will not falter.
[jɛt gɑdz lʌv wɪl nɑt ˈfɔltʌ]
But tonight he's just like you, Hush my baby.
[bʌt tuˈnɑːɪt hiz dʒʌst lɑːɪk ju hʌʃ mɑːɪ ˈbeːɪbi]

D

Delius, Frederick (Eng. 1862-1934)

Three Songs, the Words by Shelley (Song Cycle)
[θɹi sɑŋz ðʊ wɜdz bɑːɪ ˈʃɛli]
Shelley, Percy Bysshe (Eng. 1792-1822)

1. Indian Love Song
[ˈɪndiʌn lʌv sɑŋ]

I arise from dreams of thee
[ɑːɪ ʌˈɾɑːɪz fɹʌm dɹimz ʌv ði]
In the first sweet sleep of night,
[ɪn ðʊ fɜst swit slip ʌv nɑːɪt]
When the winds are breathing low,
[ʍɛn ðʊ wɪndz ʌ ˈbɹiðɪŋ loːʊ]
And the stars are shining bright:
[ænd ðʊ stɑz ʌ ˈʃɑːɪnɪŋ bɹɑːɪt]
I arise from dreams of thee,
[ɑːɪ ʌˈɾɑːɪz fɹʌm dɹimz ʌv ði]
And a spirit in my feet
[ænd ʌ ˈspɪɾɪt ɪn mɑːɪ fit]
Hath led me, who knows how?
[hæθ lɛd mi hu noːʊz hɑːʊ]
To thy chamber window, Sweet!
[tu ðɑːɪ ˈtʃɛːɪmbʌ ˈwɪndoːʊ swit]
The wand'ring airs they faint
[ðʊ ˈwɑndɪŋ ɛːʌz ðɛːɪ fɛːɪnt]
On the dark, the silent stream
[ɑn ðʊ dɑk ðʊ ˈsɑːɪlɛnt stɹim]
The Champak odours fail
[ðʊ ˈtʃæmpæk ˈoːʊdʊz fɛːɪl]
Like sweet thoughts in a dream;
[lɑːɪk swit θɔts ɪn ʌ dɹim]
The nightingale's complaint,
[ðʊ ˈnɑːɪtɪngɛːɪlz kʌmˈplɛːɪnt]
It dies upon her heart;
[ɪt dɑːɪz ʌˈpɑn hɜ hɑt]
As I must die on thine,
[æz ɑːɪ mʌst dɑːɪ ɑn ðɑːɪn]
Beloved as thou art!
[bɪˈlʌvɛ⁽ɪ⁾d æz ðɑːʊ at]
Oh lift me from the grass!
[oːʊ lɪft mi fɹʌm ðʊ gɹɑs]
I die! I faint! I fail!
[ɑːɪ dɑːɪ ɑːɪ fɛːɪnt ɑːɪ fɛːɪl]
Let thy love in kisses rain
[lɛt ðɑːɪ lʌv ɪn ˈkɪsɛ⁽ɪ⁾z ɹɛːɪn]
On my lips and eyelids pale.
[ɑn mɑːɪ lɪps ænd ˈɑːɪlɪdz pɛːɪl]
My cheek is cold and white, alas!
[mɑːɪ tʃik ɪz koːʊld ænd ʍɑːɪt ʌˈlæs]

My heart beats loud and fast;
[maːɪ hɑt bits laːʊd ænd fast]
Oh! press it close to thine again,
[oːʊ pɹɛs ɪt kloːʊs tu ðaːɪn ʌˈgeːɪn]
Where it will break, at last.
[ʍɛːʌɾ ɪt wɪl bɹeːɪk æt last]

2. Love's Philosophy (see Quilter)

3. To the Queen of My Heart
[tu ðʊ kwin ʌv maːɪ hat]

Shall we roam, my love,
[ʃæl wi roːʊm maːɪ lʌv]
To the twilight grove,
[tu ðʊ ˈtwaːɪlɑːɪt gɹoːʊv]
When the moon is rising bright?
[ʍɛn ðʊ mun ɪz ˈɹɑːɪzɪŋ bɹɑːɪt]
Oh, I'll whisper there,
[oːʊ aːɪl ˈʍɪspʌ ðɛːʌ]
In the cool night air,
[ɪn ðʊ kul nɑːɪt ɛːʌ]
What I dare not in broad daylight!
[ʍat aːɪ dɛːʌ nat ɪn bɹɔd ˈdeːɪlɑːɪt]
I'll tell thee a part
[aːɪl tɛl ði ʌ pat]
Of the thoughts that start
[ʌv ðʊ θɔts ðæt stat]
To being when thou art nigh;
[tu ˈbiɪŋ ʍɛn ðaːʊ at naːɪ]
And thy beauty, more bright
[ænd ðaːɪ ˈbjuti mɔːʌ bɹaːɪt]
Than the stars' soft light,
[ðæn ðʊ staz saft laːɪt]
Shall seem as a weft from the sky.
[ʃæl sim æz ʌ wɛft fɹʌm ðʊ skaːɪ]
When the pale moonbeam
[ʍɛn ðʊ peːɪl ˈmunbim]
On tower and stream
[an taːʊʌɾ ænd stɹim]
Sheds a flood of silver sheen,
[ʃɛdz ʌ flʌd ʌv ˈsɪlvʌ ʃin]
How I love to gaze
[haːʊ aːɪ lʌv tu geːɪz]
As the cold ray strays
[æz ðʊ koːʊld ɹeːɪ stɹeːɪz]
O'er thy face, my heart's throned queen!
[ɔːʌ ðaːɪ feːɪs maːɪ hats θɹoːʊnd kwin]
Wilt thou roam with me
[wɪlt ðaːʊ roːʊm wɪð mi]
To the restless sea,
[tu ðʊ ˈɹɛstlɛ(ɪ)s si]
And linger upon the steep,
[ænd ˈlɪŋgʌɾ ʌˈpan ðʊ stip]
And list to the flow
[ænd lɪst tu ðʊ floːʊ]

Of the waves below
[ʌv ðʊ weːɪvz bɪˈloːʊ]
How they toss and roar and leap?
[haːʊ ðeːɪ tas ænd ɹɔːʌɾ ænd lip]
Those boiling waves,
[ðoːʊz ˈbɔːɪlɪŋ weːɪvz]
And the storm that raves
[ænd ðʊ stɔm ðæt ɹeːɪvz]
At night o'er their foaming crest,
[æt naːɪt ɔːʌ ðɛːʌ ˈfoːʊmɪŋ kɹɛst]
Resemble the strife
[ɹɪˈzɛmbʊl ðʊ stɹɑːɪf]
That, from earliest life,
[ðæt fɹʌm ˈɜlɪɛ(ɪ)st lɑːɪf]
The passions have waged in my breast.
[ðʊ ˈpæʃʌnz hæv weːɪdʒd ɪn maːɪ bɹɛst]
Oh, come then, and rove
[oːʊ kʌm ðɛn ænd ɹoːʊv]
To the sea or the grove,
[tu ðʊ si ɔ ðʊ gɹoːʊv]
When the moon is rising bright,
[ʍɛn ðʊ mun ɪz ˈɹɑːɪzɪŋ bɹɑːɪt]
And I'll whisper there,
[ænd aːɪl ˈʍɪspʌ ðɛːʌ]
In the cool night air,
[ɪn ðʊ kul nɑːɪt ɛːʌ]
What I dare not in broad daylight.
[ʍat aːɪ dɛːʌ nat ɪn bɹɔd ˈdeːɪlɑːɪt]
Oh, come then, and rove
[oːʊ kʌm ðɛn ænd ɹoːʊv]
To the sea and the grove.
[tu ðʊ si ænd ðʊ gɹoːʊv]

Dello Joio, Norman (Am. 1913-2008)

Three Songs of Adieu (Song Cycle)
[θri saŋz ʌv aˈdjø]

1. After Love [ˈæftʁ lʌv]
Symons, Arthur (Eng. 1865-1945)

Born now to part and parting now,
[bɔn naːʊ tu pat ænd ˈpatɪŋ naːʊ]
Never to meet again;
[ˈnɛvʌ tu mit ʌˈgɛn]
To have done for ever; I and thou,
[tu hæv dʌn fɔʁ⁽ʳ⁾ ˈɛvʌ aːɪ ænd ðaːʊ]
With joy, and so in pain.
[wɪð dʒɔːɪ ænd soːʊ ɪn peːɪn]
It is too hard, too hard to meet
[ɪt ɪz tu had tu had tu mit]
As friends and love no more;
[æz fɹɛndz ænd lʌv noːʊ mɔːʌ]
Those other meetings were too sweet
[ðoːʊz ˈʌðʌ ˈmitɪŋz wɜ tu swit]

Too sweet, that went before.
[tu swit ðæt wɛnt bɪˈfɔːʌ]
And I would have, now love is over,
[ænd ɑːɪ wʊd hæv naːʊ lʌv ɪz ˈoːʊvʌ]
An end to all, and end:
[æn ɛnd tu ɔl ænd ɛnd]
I cannot, having been your lover,
[ɑːɪ kæˈnat ˈhævɪŋ bɪn jɔːʌ ˈlʌvʌ]
Stoop to become your friend!
[stup tu bɪˈkʌm jɔːʌ fɹɛnd]

2. Fade, Vision Bright
[fɛːɪd ˈvɪʒʌn bɹɑːɪt]
Anonymous

Fade, vision bright!
[fɛːɪd ˈvɪʒʌn bɹɑːɪt]
No clinging hands can stay thee.
[noːʊ ˈklɪŋɪŋ hændz kæn stɛːɪ ði]
Die, dream of light!
[dɑːɪ dɹim ʌv lɑːɪt]
No clasping hands can pray thee;
[noːʊ ˈklæspɪŋ hændz kæn pɹɛːɪ ði]
Farewell, delight!
[fɛːʌˈwɛl dɪˈlɑːɪt]
I have no more to say to thee.
[ɑːɪ hæv noːʊ mɔːʌ tu sɛːɪ tu ði]
The gold was gold the little while it lasted,
[ðʌ goːʊld waz goːʊld ðʌ ˈlɪtʊl ʍɑːɪl ɪt ˈlæstɛ(ɪ)d]
The dream was true, although its joy be blasted.
[ðʌ dɹim waz tɹˈ(ʳ)u ɔlˈðoːʊ ɪts dʒɔːɪ bi ˈblæstɛ(ɪ)d]
That hour was mine so swift a time it lasted.
[ðæt ɑːʊʌ waz mɑːɪn soːʊ swɪft ʌ tɑːɪm ɪt ˈlæstɛ(ɪ)d]
Fade, vision bright!
[fɛːɪd ˈvɪʒʌn bɹɑːɪt]
Die, dream of light! Farewell, Farewell.
[dɑːɪ dɹim ʌv lɑːɪt fɛːʌˈwɛl fɛːʌˈwɛl]

3. Farewell
[fɛːʁˈwɛl]
Symonds, John Addington (Eng. 1840-1893)

Farewell; to what distant place
[fɛːʌˈwɛl tu ʍat ˈdɪstæ(ɪ)nt plɛːɪs]
Wilt thou thy sunlight carry?
[wɪlt ðɑːʊ ðɑːɪ ˈsʌnlɑːɪt ˈkæʁ(ʳ)ɪ]
I stay with cold and clouded face:
[ɑːɪ stɛːɪ wɪð koːʊld ænd ˈklɑːʊdɛ(ɪ)d fɛːɪs]
How long am I to tarry?
[hɑːʊ laŋ æm ɑːɪ tu ˈtæʁ(ʳ)ɪ]
Where thou goest, morn will be;
[ʍɛːʌ ðɑːʊ ˈgoːʊɛ(ɪ)st mɔn wɪl bi]
Thou leavest night and gloom to me.
[ðɑːʊ ˈlivɛ(ɪ)st nɑːɪt ænd glum tu mi]
The night and gloom I can't take;
[ðʌ nɑːɪt ænd glum ɑːɪ kænt tɛːɪk]

I do not grudge thy splendor:
[ɑːɪ du nat gɹˈ(ʳ)ʌdʒ ðɑːɪ ˈsplɛndɔ(ʌ)]
Bid souls of eager men awake;
[bɪd soːʊlz ʌv ˈigʌ mɛn ʌˈwɛːɪk]
Be kind and bright and tender.
[bi kɑːɪnd ænd bɹɑːɪt ænd ˈtɛndʌ]
Give day to other worlds; for me
[gɪv dɛːɪ tu ˈʌðʌ wɜldz fɔ mi]
It must suffice to dream of thee.
[ɪt mʌst sʌˈfɑːɪs tu dɹim ʌv ði]

Song Selection

"There Is a Lady Sweet and Kind"
[ðɛːʁ ɪz ʌ ˈlɛːɪdi swit ænd kɑːɪnd]
Ford, Thomas (Eng. 1580-1648)

There is a Lady sweet and kind,
[ðɛːʌʁ(ʳ) ɪz ʌ ˈlɛːɪdi swit ænd kɑːɪnd]
Was never face so pleased my mind;
[waz ˈnɛvʌ fɛːɪs soːʊ plizd mɑːɪ mɑːɪnd]
I did but see her passing by,
[ɑːɪ dɪd bʌt si hɜ ˈpæsɪŋ bɑːɪ]
And yet I love her till I die.
[ænd jɛt ɑːɪ lʌv hɜ tɪl ɑːɪ dɑːɪ]
Her gesture, her motion and her smile,
[hɜ ˈdʒɛstʃʊ(ʌ) hɜ ˈmoːʊʃʌn ænd hɜ smɑːɪl]
Her wit, her voice, my heart beguile;
[hɜ wɪt hɜ vɔːɪs mɑːɪ hat bɪˈgɑːɪl]
Beguile my heart, I know not why,
[bɪˈgɑːɪl mɑːɪ hat ɑːɪ noːʊ nat ʍɑːɪ]
And yet I love her till I die.
[ænd jɛt ɑːɪ lʌv hɜ tɪl ɑːɪ dɑːɪ]
There is a Lady sweet and kind,
[ðɛːʌʁ(ʳ) ɪz ʌ ˈlɛːɪdi swit ænd kɑːɪnd]
Was never face so pleased my mind;
[waz ˈnɛvʌ fɛːɪs soːʊ plizd mɑːɪ mɑːɪnd]
If she should change the earth,
[ɪf ʃi ʃʊd tʃɛːɪndʒ ði ɜθ]
Should change the earth or sky,
[ʃʊd tʃɛːɪndʒ ði ɜθ ɔ skɑːɪ]
Yet will I love her till I die.
[jɛt wɪl ɑːɪ lʌv hɜ tɪl ɑːɪ dɑːɪ]

 # Dougherty, Celius (Am. 1902-1986)

Song Selections

"Across the Western Ocean"
[ʌˈkɹas ðʌ ˈwɛstʁn ˈoːʊʃɪn]
Folksong

Oh, the times are hard and the wages low,
[oːʊ ðʌ tɑːɪmz ɑ had ænd ðʌ ˈwɛːɪdʒɛ(ɪ)z loːʊ]

Oh, sailor, where you bound to?
[oːʊ ˈsɛːɪlɔ(ʌ) ʍɛːʌ ju bɑːʊnd tu]
The Rocky Mountains are my home,
[ðʌ ˈɹɑkɪ ˈmɑːʊntæ(ɪ)nz ɑ mɑːɪ hoːʊm]
Across the western ocean.
[ʌˈkɹɑs ðʌ ˈwɛstʌn ˈoːʊʃæ(ɪ)n]
We are going away from friends and home,
[wi ɑ ˈgoːʊɪŋ ʌˈwɛːɪ fɹʌm fɹɛndz ænd hoːʊm]
Oh, sailor, where you bound to?
[oːʊ ˈsɛːɪlɔ(ʌ) ʍɛːʌ ju bɑːʊnd tu]
We're going away to search for gold,
[wɪːʌ ˈgoːʊɪŋ ʌˈwɛːɪ tu sɝʧ fɔ goːʊld]
Across the western ocean.
[ʌˈkɹɑs ðʌ ˈwɛstʌn ˈoːʊʃæ(ɪ)n]
Fathers, mothers, say goodbye,
[ˈfɑðʌz ˈmʌðʌz sɛːɪ gʊdˈbɑːɪ]
Oh, sailor, where you bound to?
[oːʊ ˈsɛːɪlɔ(ʌ) ʍɛːʌ ju bɑːʊnd tu]
Sisters, brothers, don't you cry,
[ˈsɪstʌz ˈbɹʌðʌz doːʊnt ju kɹɑːɪ]
O'er the western ocean.
[ɔːʌ ðʌ ˈwɛstʌn ˈoːʊʃæ(ɪ)n]

"Love in the Dictionary"
[lʌv ɪn ðʌ ˈdɪkʃʌnɛʁi]
Anonymous

Love: A strong, complex emotion
[lʌv ʌ stɹɑŋ ˈkɑmˈplɛks ɪˈmoːʊʃʌn]
or feeling of personal attachment,
[ɔ ˈfilɪŋ ʌv ˈpɝsʌnʊl ʌˈtæʧmɛnt]
causing one to appreciate, delight in,
[ˈkɔzɪŋ wʌn tu ʌˈpɹɪʃiːɪt dɪˈlɑːɪt ɪn]
or crave the presence
[ɔ kɹɛːɪv ðʌ ˈpɹɛzɛ(ɪ)ns]
or possession of the object,
[ɔ poˈzɛʃʌn ʌv ði ˈɑbʤɛkt]
and to please and promote the welfare
[ænd tu pliz ænd pɹoˈmoːʊt ðʌ ˈwɛlfɛːʌ]
of that object;
[ʌv ðæt ˈɑbʤɛkt]
devoted affection or attachment;
[dɪˈvoːʊtɛ(ɪ)d ʌˈfɛkʃʌn ɔʁ(ʳ) ʌˈtæʧmɛnt]
specifically, the feeling between husband and wife;
[spɪˈsɪfɪklɪ ðʌ ˈfilɪŋ bɪˈtwin ˈhʌzbæ(ɪ)nd ænd wɑːɪf]
brother and sister;
[ˈbɹʌðʌ ænd ˈsɪstʌ]
or lover and sweetheart;
[ɔ ˈlʌvʌʁ(ʳ) ænd ˈswithɑt]
One who is beloved;
[wʌn hu ɪz bɪˈlʌvd]
a sweetheart;
[ʌ ˈswithɑt]
animal passion;
[ˈænɪmʊl ˈpæʃʌn̩]

the personification of the love-passion;
[ðʌ pɝsɑnɪfɪˈkɛːɪʃʌn ʌv ðʌ lʌv ˈpæʃʌn]
Cupid;
[ˈkjupɪd]
in some games, as tennis, nothing.
[ɪn sʌm gɛːɪmz æz ˈtɛnɪs ˈnʌθɪŋ]

"Shady Grove"
[ˈʃɛːɪdi gɹoːʊv]
Folksong

CHORUS:
Shady grove, my true love
[ˈʃɛːɪdɪ gɹoːʊv mɑːɪ tɹ(ʳ)u lʌv]
Shady grove I know
[ˈʃɛːɪdɪ gɹoːʊv ɑːɪ noːʊ]
Shady grove, my true love
[ˈʃɛːɪdɪ gɹoːʊv mɑːɪ tɹ(ʳ)u lʌv]
I'm bound for the shady grove
[ɑːɪm bɑːʊnd fɔ ðʌ ˈʃɛːɪdɪ gɹoːʊv]
1. Some come here to fiddle and dance
[sʌm kʌm hɪːʌ tu ˈfɪdʊl ænd dæns]
Some come here to tarry
[sʌm kʌm hɪːʌ tu ˈtæʁ(ʳ)ɪ]
Some come here to fiddle and dance
[sʌm kʌm hɪːʌ tu ˈfɪdʊl ænd dæns]
I come here to marry
[ɑːɪ kʌm hɪːʌ tu ˈmæʁ(ʳ)ɪ]
CHORUS
2. Wish I had a fiddle and string
[wɪʃ ɑːɪ hæd ʌ ˈfɪdʊl ænd stɹɪŋ]
Made of golden twine
[mɛːɪd ʌv ˈgoːʊldɛ(ɪ)n twɑːɪn]
Every tune I pick on it
[ˈɛvɹɪ tjun ɑːɪ pɪk ɑn ɪt]
Is I wish that girl were mine.
[ɪz ɑːɪ wɪʃ ðæt gɝl wɝ mɑːɪn]
CHORUS
3. Teachers in the summer time
[ˈtiʧʌz ɪn ðʌ ˈsʌmʌ tɑːɪm]
Apples in the fall
[ˈæpʊlz ɪn ðʌ fɔl]
If I can't have the girl I love
[ɪf ɑːɪ kænt hæv ðʌ gɝl ɑːɪ lʌv]
I won't have none at all.
[ɑːɪ woːʊnt hæv nʌn æt ɔl]
CHORUS

"Shenandoah"
[ʃɛnænˈdoːʊʌ]
Anonymous

O Shenandoah, I hear you calling,
[oːʊ ʃɛnænˈdoːʊʌ ɑːɪ hɪːʌ ju ˈkɔlɪŋ]
Hio! you rolling river,
[ˈhɑːɪoːʊ ju ˈɹoːʊlɪŋ ˈɹɪvʌ]

O Shenandoah, I long to hear you,
[oːʊ ʃɛnænˈdoːʊʌ ɑːɪ laŋ tu hɪːʌ ju]
Hio! I'm bound away,
[ˈhaːɪoːʊ ɑːɪm baːʊnd ʌˈwɛːɪ]
'Cross the wide Missouri.
[kɹɑs ðʌ waːɪd mɪˈzʊʁ⁽ʳ⁾ɪ]
Missouri she's a mighty river,
[mɪˈzʊʁ⁽ʳ⁾ɪ ʃiz ʌ ˈmaːɪtɪ ˈɹɪvʌ]
Hio! you rolling river,
[ˈhaːɪoːʊ ju ˈɹoːʊlɪŋ ˈɹɪvʌ]
When she rolls down her topsails shiver,
[ʍɛn ʃi ɹoːʊlz daːʊn hɜ ˈtɑpsɛːɪlz ˈʃɪvʌ]
Hio! I'm bound away,
[ˈhaːɪoːʊ ɑːɪm baːʊnd ʌˈwɛːɪ]
'Cross the wide Missouri.
[kɹɑs ðʌ waːɪd mɪˈzʊʁ⁽ʳ⁾ɪ]
Farewell, my dearest, I'm bound to leave you;
[fɛːʌˈwɛl maːɪ ˈdɪːʁ⁽ʳ⁾ɛ⁽ɪ⁾st ɑːɪm baːʊnd tu liv ju]
Hio! you rolling river,
[ˈhaːɪoːʊ ju ˈɹoːʊlɪŋ ˈɹɪvʌ]
O Shenandoah, I'll not deceive you,
[oːʊ ʃɛnænˈdoːʊʌ ɑːɪl nɑt dɪˈsiv ju]
Hio! I'm bound away,
[ˈhaːɪoːʊ ɑːɪm baːʊnd ʌˈwɛːɪ]
'Cross the wide Missouri.
[kɹɑs ðʌ waːɪd mɪˈzʊʁ⁽ʳ⁾ɪ]

"The K'e"
[ðʌ kɛːɪ]
Anonymous

The K'e still ripples to its banks,
[ðʌ kɛːɪ stɪl ˈɹɪpʊlz tu ɪts bæŋks]
The moorfowl cry.
[ðʌ ˈmʊːʌfaːʊl kɹɑːɪ]
My hair was gathered in a knot,
[maːɪ hɛːʌ wɑz ˈgæðʌd ɪn ʌ nɑt]
And you came by.
[ænd ju kɛːɪm baːɪ]
Selling of silks you were,
[ˈsɛlɪŋ ʌv sɪlks ju wɜ]
A lad not of our kin;
[ʌ læd nɑt ʌv aːʊʌ kɪn]
You passed at sunset on the road
[ju pæst æt ˈsʌnsɛt ɑn ðʌ ɹoːʊd]
From far off Ts'in.
[fɪʌm fɑʁ⁽ʳ⁾ ɑf tsɪn]
The frogs were croaking in the dusk;
[ðʌ fɹɑgz wɜ ˈkɹoːʊkɪŋ ɪn ðʌ dʌsk]
The grass was wet.
[ðʌ gɹæs wɑz wɛt]
We talked together, and I laughed;
[wi tɔkt tuˈgɛðʌ ænd ɑːɪ læft]
I hear it yet.
[ɑːɪ hɪːʌʁ⁽ʳ⁾ ɪt jɛt]

I thought that I would be your wife;
[ɑːɪ θɔt ðæt ɑːɪ wʊd bi jɔːʌ waːɪf]
I had your word.
[ɑːɪ hæd jɔːʌ wɜd]
And so I took the road with you,
[ænd soːʊ ɑːɪ tʊk ðʌ ɹoːʊd wɪð ju]
And cross the ford.
[ænd kɹɑs ðʌ fɔd]
I do not know when first it was
[ɑːɪ du nɑt noːʊ ʍɛn fɜst ɪt wɑz]
your eyes looked cold.
[jɔːʌʁ⁽ʳ⁾ ɑːɪz lʊkt koːʊld]
But all this was three years ago,
[bʌt ɔl ðɪs wɑz θri jɪːʌz ʌˈgoːʊ]
And I am old.
[ænd ɑːɪ æm oːʊld]

Dowland, John (Eng. 1563-1626)

Song Selections

"Come Again, Sweet Love"
[kʌm ʌˈgɛn swit lʌv]
Anonymous

1. Come again,
[kʌm ʌˈgɛːɪn]
Sweet love doth now invite
[swit lʌv dʌθ naːʊ ɪnˈvaːɪt]
Thy graces that refrain
[ðaːɪ ˈgɹɛːɪsɛ⁽ɪ⁾z ðæt ɹɪˈfɹɛːɪn]
To do me due delight,
[tu du mi dju dɪˈlaːɪt]
To see, to hear, to touch, to kiss, to die
[tu si tu hɪːʌ tu tʌʧ tu kɪs tu daːɪ]
With thee again in sweetest sympathy.
[wɪð ði ʌˈgɛːɪn ɪn ˈswitɛ⁽ɪ⁾st ˈsɪmpæ⁽ʌ⁾θɪ]
2. Come again,
[kʌm ʌˈgɛːɪn]
That I may cease to mourn
[ðæt ɑːɪ mɛːɪ sis tu mɔn]
Thro' thy unkind disdain;
[θɹu ðaːɪ ʌnˈkaːɪnd dɪsˈdɛːɪn]
For now, left and forlorn,
[fɔ naːʊ lɛft ænd fɔˈlɔn]
I sit, I sigh, I weep, I faint, I die
[ɑːɪ sɪt ɑːɪ saːɪ ɑːɪ wip ɑːɪ fɛːɪnt ɑːɪ daːɪ]
In deadly pain and endless misery.
[ɪn ˈdɛdlɪ pɛːɪn ænd ˈɛndlɛ⁽ɪ⁾s ˈmɪzʌɹɪ]
3. Gentle Love,
[ˈʤɛntʊl lʌv]
Draw forth thy wounding dart,
[dɹɔ fɔθ ðaːɪ ˈwundɪŋ dat]
Thou canst not pierce her heart,
[ðaːʊ kænst nɑt pɪːʌs hɜ hat]

For I that do approve,
[fɔʁ⁽ʳ⁾ ɑːɪ ðæt du ʌˈpɹuv]
By sighs and tears more hot than are thy shafts,
[bɑːɪ sɑːɪz ænd tɪːʌz mɔːʌ hat ðæn ɑ ðɑːɪ ʃafts]
Did tempt, while she for triumph laughs.
[dɪd tɛmpt ʍɑːɪl ʃi fɔ ˈtɪɑːɪʌmf lafs]

"Fine Knacks for Ladies"
[fɑːɪn næks fɔ ˈlɛːɪdiz]
Anonymous

Fine knacks for ladies, cheap, choice, brave and new,
[fɑːɪn næks fɔ ˈlɛːɪdiz ʧip ʧɔːɪs bɹɛːɪv ænd nju]
Good pennyworths but money cannot move,
[gʊd ˈpɛnɪwɜθs bʌt ˈmʌnɪ kæˈnat muv]
I keep a fair but for the fair to view,
[ɑːɪ kip ʌ fɛːʌ bʌt fɔ ðʊ fɛːʌ tu vju]
A beggar may be liberal of love.
[ʌ ˈbɛgʌ mɛːɪ bi ˈlɪbʌɾʊl ʌv lʌv]
Though all my wares be trash, the heart is true.
[ðoːʊ ɔl mɑːɪ ʍɛːʌz bi tɹæʃ ðʊ hat ɪz tru]
Great gifts are guiles and look for gifts again,
[gɹɛːɪt gɪfts ɑ gɑːɪlz ænd lʊk fɔ gɪfts ʌˈgɛːɪn]
My trifles come, as treasures from my mind,
[mɑːɪ ˈtɹɑːɪfʊlz kʌm æz ˈtɹɛʒʊ(ʌ)z fɹʌm mɑːɪ mɑːɪnd]
It is a precious jewel to be plain,
[ɪt ɪz ʌ ˈpɹɛʃʌs ˈʤuːɛ(ʊ)l tu bi plɛːɪn]
Sometimes in shell the orient's pearls we find.
[ˈsʌmtɑːɪmz ɪn ʃɛl ði ˈɔɹɪɛnts pɜlz wi fɑːɪnd]
Of others take a sheaf, of me a grain.
[ʌv ˈʌðʌz tɛːɪk ʌ ʃif ʌv mi ʌ gɹɛːɪn]
Within this pack pins, points, laces and gloves,
[wɪðˈɪn ðɪs pæk pɪnz pɔːɪnts ˈlɛːɪsɛ(ɪ)z ænd glʌvz]
And divers toys fitting a country fair,
[ænd ˈdɑːɪvʌz tɔːɪz ˈfɪtɪŋ ʌ ˈkʌntɹɪ fɛːʌ]
But in my heart where duty serves and loves,
[bʌt ɪn mɑːɪ hat ʍɛːʌ ˈdjutɪ sɜvz ænd lʌvz]
Turtles and twins, court's brood, a heav'nly pair.
[ˈtɜtʊlz ænd twɪnz kɔts brud ʌ ˈhɛvnlɪ pɛːʌ]
Happy the heart that thinks of no removes.
[ˈhæpɪ ðʊ hat ðæt θɪŋks ʌv noːʊ ɹɪˈmuvz]

"Flow, My Tears"
[floːʊ mɑːɪ tɪːʌz]
Anonymous

Flow, my tears, fall from your springs!
[floːʊ mɑːɪ tɪːʌz fɔl fɹʌm jɔːʌ spɹɪŋz]
Exiled for ever, let me mourn;
[ˈɛgzɑːɪld fɔʁ⁽ʳ⁾ ˈɛvʌ lɛt mi mɔn]
Where night's black bird her sad infamy sings,
[ʍɛːʌ nɑːɪts blæk bɜd hɜ sæd ˈɪnfæ(ʌ)mɪ sɪŋz]
There let me live forlorn.
[ðɛːʌ lɛt mi lɪv fɔˈlɔn]
Down vain lights, shine you no more!
[dɑːʊn vɛːɪn lɑːɪts ʃɑːɪn ju noːʊ mɔːʌ]

No nights are dark enough for those
[noːʊ nɑːɪts ɑ dak ɪˈnʌf fɔ ðoːʊz]
That in despair their lost fortunes deplore.
[ðæt ɪn dɪˈspɛːʌ ðɛːʌ last ˈfɔʧʌnz dɪˈplɔːʌ]
Light doth but shame disclose.
[lɑːɪt dʌθ bʌt ʃɛːɪm dɪsˈkloːʊz]
Never may my woes be relieved,
[ˈnɛvʌ mɛːɪ mɑːɪ woːʊz bi ɹɪˈlivɛ(ɪ)d]
Since pity is fled;
[sɪns ˈpɪtɪ ɪz flɛd]
And tears and sighs and groans my weary days
[ænd tɪːʌz ænd sɑːɪz ænd groːʊnz mɑːɪ ˈwɪːʌɾɪ dɛːɪz]
Of all joys have deprived.
[ʌv ɔl ʤɔːɪz hæv dɪˈpɹɑːɪvɛ(ɪ)d]
From the highest spire of contentment,
[fɹʌm ðʊ ˈhɑːɪɛ(ɪ)st spɑːɪʌɾ ʌv kʌnˈtɛntmɛnt]
My fortune is thrown;
[mɑːɪ ˈfɔʧʌn ɪz θroːʊn]
And fear and grief and pain for my deserts
[ænd fɪːʌ ænd grif ænd pɛːɪn fɔ mɑːɪ dɪˈzɜts]
Are my hopes, since hope is gone.
[ɑ mɑːɪ hoːʊps sɪns hoːʊp ɪz gan]
Hark you shadows that in darkness dwell,
[hak ju ˈʃædoːʊz ðæt ɪn ˈdaknɛ(ɪ)s dwɛl]
Learn to contemn light,
[lɜn tu kʌnˈtɛm lɑːɪt]
Happy, happy they that in hell
[ˈhæpɪ ˈhæpɪ ðɛːɪ ðæt ɪn hɛl]
Feel not the world's despite.
[fil nat ðʊ wɜldz dɪˈspɑːɪt]

"I Saw My Lady Weep"
[ɑːɪ sɔ mɑːɪ ˈlɛːɪdi wip]
Anonymous

I saw my lady weep,
[ɑːɪ sɔ mɑːɪ ˈlɛːɪdi wip]
And Sorrow proud to be advanced so,
[ænd ˈsaroːʊ pɹɑːʊd tu bi ædˈvansɛ(ɪ)d soːʊ]
In those fair eyes where all perfections keep,
[ɪn ðoːʊz fɛːʌ ɑːɪz ʍɛːʌɾ ɔl pɜˈfɛkʃʌnz kip]
Her face was full of woe;
[hɜ fɛːɪs waz fʊl ʌv woːʊ]
But such a woe (believe me) as wins more hearts,
[bʌt sʌʧ ʌ woːʊ bɪˈliv mi æz wɪnz mɔːʌ hats]
Than Mirth can do with her enticing parts.
[ðæn mɜθ kæn du wɪð hɜ⁽ʳ⁾ ɪnˈtɑːɪsɪŋ pats]
Sorrow was there made fair,
[ˈsaroːʊ waz ðɛːʌ mɛːɪd fɛːʌ]
And Passion wise, tears a delightful thing,
[ænd ˈpæʃʌn wɑːɪz tɪːʌz ʌ dɪˈlɑːɪtfʊl θɪŋ]
Silence beyond all speech a wisdom rare,
[ˈsɑːɪlɛ(ɪ)ns bɪˈjand ɔl spiʧ ʌ ˈwɪzdʌm ɹɛːʌ]
She made her sighs to sing,
[ʃi mɛːɪd hɜ sɑːɪz tu sɪŋ]

And all things with so sweet a sadness move,
[ænd ɔl θɪŋz wɪð soːʊ swit ʌ ˈsædnɛ(ɪ)s muv]
As made my heart at once both grieve and love.
[æz mɛːɪd maːɪ hat æt wʌns boːʊθ gɹiv ænd lʌv]
O fairer than aught else,
[oːʊ ˈfɛːʌɾʌ ðæn ɔt ɛls]
The world can show, leave off in time to grieve,
[ðʊ wɜld kæn ʃoːʊ liv af ɪn taːɪm tu gɹiv]
Enough, enough, your joyful looks excel,
[ɪˈnʌf ɪˈnʌf jɔːʌ ˈdʒɔːɪfʊl lʊks ɪkˈsɛl]
Tears kill the heart believe, kill the heart.
[tɪːʌz kɪl ðʊ hat bɪˈliv kɪl ðʊ hat]
O strive not to be excellent in woe,
[oːʊ stɹaːɪv nat tu bi ˈɛksɛ(ɪ)lɛnt ɪn woːʊ]
Which only breeds your beauty's overthrow.
[ʌɪʧ ˈoːʊnlɪ bɹɪdz jɔːʌ ˈbjutɪz ˌoːʊvʌˈθɾoːʊ]

"In Darkness Let Me Dwell"
[ɪn ˈdaknɪs lɛt·mi dwɛl]
Anonymous

In darkness let me dwell, the ground shall sorrow be,
[ɪn ˈdaknɛ(ɪ)s lɛt mi dwɛl ðʊ gɹaːʊnd ʃæl ˈsaɾoːʊ bi]
The roof despair to bar all cheerful light from me,
[ðʊ ɹɹuf dɪˈspɛːʌ tu baɾ ɔl ˈʧɪːʌfʊl laːɪt fɹʌm mi]
The walls of marble black
[ðʊ wɔlz ʌv ˈmabʊl blæk]
that moistened still shall weep,
[ðæt ˈmɔːɪsɛ(ɪ)nd stɪl ʃæl wip]
My music hellish jarring sounds
[maːɪ ˈmjuzɪk ˈhɛlɪʃ ˈdʒaɹɪŋ saːʊndz]
to banish friendly sleep.
[tu ˈbænɪʃ ˈfɹɛndlɪ slip]
Thus wedded to my woes,
[ðʌs ˈwɛdɛ(ɪ)d tu maːɪ woːʊz]
and bedded to my tomb,
[ænd ˈbɛdɛ(ɪ)d tu maːɪ tum]
O, let me, living, die, till death do come.
[oːʊ lɛt mi ˈlɪvɪŋ daːɪ tɪl dɛθ du kʌm]

"Sigh No More Ladies"
[saːɪ noːʊ mɔːʌ ˈlɛːɪdiz]
Shakespeare, William (Eng. 1564-1616)

Sigh no more, ladies, sigh no more,
[saːɪ noːʊ mɔːʌ ˈlɛːɪdɪz saːɪ noːʊ mɔːʌ]
Men were deceivers ever;
[mɛn wɜ dɪˈsivʌz ˈɛvʌ]
One foot in sea and one on shore;
[wʌn fʊt ɪn si ænd wʌn an ʃɔːʌ]
To one thing constant never.
[tu wʌn θɪŋ ˈkanstæ(ɪ)nt ˈnɛvʌ]
Then sigh not so,
[ðɛn saːɪ nat soːʊ]
But let them go,
[bʌt lɛt ðɛm goːʊ]

And be you blithe and bonny;
[ænd bi ju blaːɪð ænd ˈbanɪ]
Converting all your sounds of woe
[kʌnˈvɜtɪŋ ɔl jɔːʌ saːʊndz ʌv woːʊ]
Into Hey nonny, nonny.
[ˈɪntu hɛːɪ ˈnoːʊnɪ ˈnoːʊnɪ]
Sing no more ditties, sing no more,
[sɪŋ noːʊ mɔːʌ ˈdɪtɪz sɪŋ noːʊ mɔːʌ]
Of dumps so dull and heavy;
[ʌv dʌmps soːʊ dʌl ænd ˈhɛvɪ]
The fraud of men was ever so
[ðʊ fɹɔd ʌv mɛn waz ˈɛvʌ soːʊ]
Since summer first was leafy.
[sɪns ˈsʌmʌ fɜst waz ˈlifɪ]
Then sigh not so,
[ðɛn saːɪ nat soːʊ]
But let them go,
[bʌt lɛt ðɛm goːʊ]
And be you blithe and bonny;
[ænd bi ju blaːɪð ænd ˈbanɪ]
Converting all your sounds of woe
[kʌnˈvɜtɪŋ ɔl jɔːʌ saːʊndz ʌv woːʊ]
Into Hey nonny, nonny.
[ˈɪntu hɛːɪ ˈnoːʊnɪ ˈnoːʊnɪ]

"Weep You No More, Sad Fountains" (see Quilter)

"Who Ever Thinks Or Hopes for Love"
[hu ˈɛvʌ θɪŋks ɔ hoːʊps fɔ lʌv]
Brooke, Baron Fulke Grenville (Eng. 1554-1628)

Who ever thinks or hopes of love for love,
[hu ˈɛvʌ θɪŋks ɔ hoːʊps ʌv lʌv fɔ lʌv]
Or who belov'd, in Cupid's laws doth glory,
[ɔ hu bɪˈlʌvd ɪn ˈkjupɪdz lɔz dʌθ ˈglɔɹɪ]
Who joys in vows or vows not to remove,
[hu dʒɔːɪz ɪn vaːʊz ɔ vaːʊz nat tu ɹɪˈmuv]
Who by this light God hath not been made sorry:
[hu baːɪ ðɪs laːɪt gad hæθ nat bin mɛːɪd ˈsaɹɪ]
Let him see me eclipsed from my sun
[lɛt hɪm si mi ɪˈklɪpsɛ(ɪ)d fɹʌm maːɪ sʌn]
With dark clouds of an earth quite overrun.
[wɪð dak klaːʊdz ʌv æn ɜθ kwaːɪt ˌoːʊvʌˈɹʌn]
Who thinks that sorrows felt, desires hidd'n,
[hu θɪŋks ðæt ˈsaɾoːʊz fɛlt dɪˈzaːɪʌz ˈhɪdɛ(ɪ)n]
Or humble faith in constant honour arm'd
[ɔ ˈhʌmbʊl fɛːɪθ ɪn ˈkanstæ(ɪ)nt ˈanʊ(ʌ) amd]
Can keep love from the fruit that is forbidd'n,
[kæn kip lʌv fɹʌm ðʊ fɹut ðæt ɪz fɔˈbɪdɛ(ɪ)n]
Who thinks that change is by entreaty charm'd,
[hu θɪŋks ðæt ʧɛːɪndʒ ɪz baːɪ ɪnˈtɹitɪ ʧamd]
Looking on me let him know love's delights
[ˈlʊkɪŋ an mi lɛt hɪm noːʊ lʌvz dɪˈlaːɪts]
Are treasures hid in caves but kept by sprites.
[a ˈtɹɛʒʊ(ʌ)z hɪd ɪn kɛːɪvz bʌt kɛpt baːɪ spɹaːɪts]

Dring, Madeleine (Eng. 1923-1977)

Song Selection

"Crabbed Age and Youth"
[ˈkɹæbɪd ɛːɪʤ ænd juθ]
Shakespeare, William (Eng. 1564-1616)

Crabbed age and youth cannot live together:
[ˈkɹæbɛ(ɪ)d ɛːɪʤ ænd juθ kæˈnat lɪv tuˈgɛðʌ]
Youth is full of pleasance, age is full of care;
[juθ ɪz fʊl ʌv ˈplɛzæ(ɪ)ns ɛːɪʤ ɪz fʊl ʌv kɛːʌ]
Youth like summer morn, age like winter weather;
[juθ laːɪk ˈsʌmʌ mɔn ɛːɪʤ laːɪk ˈwɪntʌ ˈwɛðʌ]
Youth like summer brave, age like winter bare.
[juθ laːɪk ˈsʌmʌ bɹɛːɪv ɛːɪʤ laːɪk ˈwɪntʌ bɛːʌ]
Youth is full of sport, age's breath is short;
[juθ ɪz fʊl ʌv spɔt ˈɛːɪʤɛ(ɪ)z bɹɛθ ɪz ʃɔt]
Youth is nimble, age is lame;
[juθ ɪz ˈnɪmbʊl ɛːɪʤ ɪz lɛːɪm]
Youth is hot and bold, age is weak and cold;
[juθ ɪz hat ænd boːʊld ɛːɪʤ ɪz wik ænd koːʊld]
Youth is wild, and age is tame.
[juθ ɪz waːɪld ænd ɛːɪʤ ɪz tɛːɪm]
Age, I do abhor thee; youth, I do adore thee;
[ɛːɪʤ aːɪ du æbˈhɔːʌ ði juθ aːɪ du ʌˈdɔːʌ ði]
O, my love, my love is young!
[oːʊ maːɪ lʌv maːɪ lʌv ɪz jʌŋ]
Age, I do defy thee: O, sweet shepherd, hie thee,
[ɛːɪʤ aːɪ du dɪˈfaːɪ ði oːʊ swit ˈʃɛpʌd haːɪ ði]
For methinks thou stay'st too long.
[fɔ ˈmiˈθɪŋks ðaːʊ stɛːɪst tu laŋ]

"I Feed a Flame Within"
[aːɪ fid ʌ flɛːɪm wɪðˈɪn]
Dryden, John (Eng. 1631-1700)

I feed a flame within which so torments me
[aːɪ fid ʌ flɛːɪm wɪðˈɪn ʍɪʧ soːʊ tɔˈmɛnts mi]
That it both pains my heart, and yet contents me:
[ðæt ɪt boːʊθ pɛːɪnz maːɪ hat ænd jɛt kʌnˈtɛnts mi]
'Tis such a pleasing smart, and I so love it,
[tɪz sʌʧ ʌ ˈplizɪŋ smat ænd aːɪ soːʊ lʌv ɪt]
That I had rather die than once remove it.
[ðæt aːɪ hæd ˈɹaðʌ daːɪ ðæn wʌns ɹɪˈmuv ɪt]
Yet he for whom I grieve shall never know it
[jɛt hi fɔ hum aːɪ gɹiv ʃæl ˈnɛvʌ noːʊ ɪt]
My tongue does not betray nor my eyes show it
[maːɪ tʌŋ dʌz nat bɪˈtɹɛːɪ nɔ maːɪ aːɪz ʃoːʊ ɪt]
Not a sigh, nor a tear my pain discloses
[nat ʌ saːɪ nɔʁ(r) ʌ tiːʌ maːɪ pɛːɪn dɪsˈkloːʊzɛ(ɪ)z]
But they fall silently like dew on roses
[bʌt ðɛːɪ fɔl ˈsaːɪlɛntlɪ laːɪk dju an ˈɹoːʊzɛ(ɪ)z]
Thus, to prevent my love from being cruel
[ðʌs tu pɹɪˈvɛnt maːɪ lʌv fɹʌm ˈbiɪŋ ˈkruːɛ(ʊ)l]

My heart's the sacrifice as it's the fuel.
[maːɪ hats ðʌ ˈsækɹɪfaːɪs æz ɪts ðʌ ˈfjuːʊl]
And while I suffer thus to give him quiet
[ænd ʍaːɪl aːɪ ˈsʌfʌ ðʌs tu gɪv hɪm ˈkwaːɪɛ(ɪ)t]
My faith rewards my love though he deny it
[maːɪ fɛːɪθ ɹɪˈwɔdz maːɪ lʌv ðoːʊ hi dɪˈnaːɪ ɪt]
On his eyes will I gaze, and there delight me
[an hɪz aːɪz wɪl aːɪ gɛːɪz ænd ðɛːʌ dɪˈlaːɪt mi]
While I conceal my love no frown can fright me.
[ʍaːɪl aːɪ kʌnˈsil maːɪ lʌv noːʊ fɹaːʊn kæn fɹaːɪt mi]
To be more happy I dare not aspire
[tu bi mɔːʌ ˈhæpɪ aːɪ dɛːʌ nat ʌˈspaːɪʌ]
Nor can I fall more low mounting no higher.
[nɔ kæn aːɪ fɔl mɔːʌ loːʊ ˈmaːʊntɪŋ noːʊ ˈhaːɪʌ]

"The Cuckoo" (see "When Daisies Pied" by Arne)

"To Daffodils"
[tu ˈdæfʌdɪlz]
(Dedications: 5 Poems by Robert Herrick)
Herrick, Robert (Eng. 1591-1674)

Fair daffodils, we weep to see
[fɛːʌ ˈdæfo(ʌ)dɪlz wi wip tu si]
You haste away so soon;
[ju hɛːɪst ʌˈwɛːɪ soːʊ sun]
As yet the early-rising sun
[æz jɛt ði ˈɜlɪ ˈɹaːɪzɪŋ sʌn]
Has not attain'd his noon. Stay, stay
[hæz nat ʌˈtɛːɪnd hɪz nun stɛːɪ stɛːɪ]
Until the hasting day has run
[ʌnˈtɪl ðʌ ˈhɛːɪstɪŋ dɛːɪ hæz ɹʌn]
But to the evensong,
[bʌt tu ði ˈivɛ(ɪ)nsaŋ]
And, having pray'd together, we
[ænd ˈhævɪŋ pɹɛːɪd tuˈgɛðʌ wi]
Will go with you along.
[wɪl goːʊ wɪð ju ʌˈlaŋ]
We have short time to stay, as you,
[wi hæv ʃɔt taːɪm tu stɛːɪ æz ju]
We have as short a spring;
[wi hæv æz ʃɔt ʌ spɹɪŋ]
As quick a growth to meet decay,
[æz kwɪk ʌ gɹoːʊθ tu mit dɪˈkɛːɪ]
As you, or anything. We die,
[æz ju ɔʁ(r) ˈɛnɪθɪŋ wi daːɪ]
As your hours do, and dry, Away,
[æz jɔːʌ aːʊʌz du ænd dɹaːɪ ʌˈwɛːɪ]
Like to the summer's rain,
[laːɪk tu ðʌ ˈsʌmʌz ɹɛːɪn]
Or as the pearls of morning's dew,
[ɔʁ(r) æz ðʌ pɜlz ʌv ˈmɔnɪŋz dju]
Ne'er to be found again.
[nɛːʌ tu bi faːʊnd ʌˈgɛːɪn]

"To the Willow Tree" (see Rorem)

Duke, John (Am. 1899-1984)

Four Poems by Edward Arlington Robinson
[fɔːʁ ˈpoːʊɪmz baːɪ ˈɛdwʁd ˈɑʁlɪŋtʌn ˈʁɑbɪnsʌn]
(Song Cycle)
Robinson, Edward Arlington (Am. 1869-1935)

1. Richard Cory
[ˈʁɪʧʁd ˈkɔʁi]

Whenever Richard Cory went down town,
[ʍɛnˈɛvʌ ˈʁɪʧʌd ˈkɔʁ⁽ʳ⁾i wɛnt daːʊn taːʊn]
We people on the pavement looked at him:
[wi ˈpipʊl an ðʌ ˈpɛːɪvmɛnt lʊkt æt hɪm]
He was a gentleman from sole to crown,
[hi waz ʌ ˈʤɛntʊlmæ⁽ʌ⁾n fʁʌm soːʊl tu kʁaːʊn]
Clean favored and imperially slim.
[klin ˈfɛːɪvɔ⁽ʌ⁾d ænd ɪmˈpɪːʁⁱⁱʊlɪ slɪm]
And he was always quietly arrayed,
[ænd hi waz ˈɔlwɛːɪz ˈkwaːɪɛ⁽ɪ⁾tlɪ ʌˈʁ⁽ʳ⁾ɛːɪd]
And he was always human when he talked;
[ænd hi waz ˈɔlwɛːɪz ˈhjumæ⁽ʌ⁾n ʍɛn hi tɔkt]
But still he fluttered pulses when he said,
[bʌt stɪl hi ˈflʌtʌd ˈpʌlsɛ⁽ɪ⁾z ʍɛn hi sɛd]
"Good morning," And he glittered when he walked.
[gʊd ˈmɔnɪŋ ænd hi ˈglɪtʌd ʍɛn hi wɔkt]
And he was rich, yes richer than a king,
[ænd hi waz ʁɪʧ jɛs ˈʁɪʧʌ ðæn ʌ kɪŋ]
And admirably schooled in every grace:
[ænd ˈædmɪʁ⁽ʳ⁾ʌblɪ skʊld ɪn ˈɛvʁɪ gʁɛːɪs]
In fine, we thought that he was everything
[ɪn faːɪn wi θɔt ðæt hi waz ˈɛvʁɪθɪŋ]
To make us wish that we were in his place.
[tu mɛːɪk ʌs wɪʃ ðæt wi wɜ⁽ʳ⁾ ɪn hɪz plɛːɪs]
So on we worked, and waited for the light,
[soːʊ an wi wɜkt ænd ˈwɛːɪtɛ⁽ɪ⁾d fɔ ðʌ laːɪt]
And went without the meat and cursed the bread;
[ænd wɛnt wɪðˈaːʊt ðʌ mit ænd kɜst ðʌ bʁɛd]
And Richard Cory one calm summer night,
[ænd ˈʁɪʧʌd ˈkɔʁ⁽ʳ⁾i wʌn kam ˈsʌmʌ naːɪt]
Went home and put a bullet through his head.
[wɛnt hoːʊm ænd pʊt ʌ ˈbʊlɛ⁽ɪ⁾t θʁu hɪz hɛd]

2. Miniver Cheevy
[ˈmɪnɪvʁ ˈʧivi]

Miniver Cheevy, child of scorn,
[ˈmɪnɪvʌ ˈʧivi ʧaːɪld ʌv skɔn]
Grew lean while he assailed the seasons;
[gʁ⁽ʳ⁾u lin ʍaːɪl hi ʌˈsɛːɪld ðʌ ˈsizʌnz]
He wept that he was ever born,
[hi wɛpt ðæt hi waz ˈɛvʌ bɔn]
And he had reasons.
[ænd hi hæd ˈʁizʌnz]
Miniver loved the days of old
[ˈmɪnɪvʌ lʌvd ðʌ dɛːɪz ʌv oːʊld]

When swords were bright and steeds were prancing;
[ʍɛn sɔdz wɜ bʁaːɪt ænd stidz wɜ ˈpʁænsɪŋ]
The vision of a warrior bold
[ðʌ ˈvɪʒʌn ʌv ʌ ˈwɔjɔ⁽ʌ⁾ boːʊld]
Would set him dancing.
[wʊd sɛt hɪm ˈdænsɪŋ]
Miniver sighed for what was not,
[ˈmɪnɪvʌ saːɪd fɔ ʍat waz nat]
And dreamed, and rested from his labors;
[ænd dʁimd ænd ˈʁɛstɛ⁽ɪ⁾d fʁʌm hɪz ˈlɛːɪbɔ⁽ʌ⁾z]
He dreamed of Thebes and Camelot,
[hi dʁimd ʌv θibz ænd ˈkæmʌlat]
And Priam's neighbors.
[ænd ˈpʁaːɪæ⁽ɪ⁾mz ˈnɛːɪbɔ⁽ʌ⁾z]
Miniver mourned the ripe renown
[ˈmɪnɪvʌ mɔnd ðʌ ʁaːɪp ʁɪˈnaːʊn]
That made so many a name so fragrant;
[ðæt mɛːɪd soːʊ ˈmɛnɪ ʌ nɛːɪm soːʊ ˈfʁɛːɪgʁæ⁽ɪ⁾nt]
He mourned Romance, now on the town,
[hi mɔnd ʁoˈmæns naːʊ an ðʌ taːʊn]
And Art, a vagrant.
[ænd at ʌ ˈvɛːɪgʁæ⁽ɪ⁾nt]
Miniver loved the Medici,
[ˈmɪnɪvʌ lʌvd ðʌ ˈmɛdɪʧi]
Albeit he had never seen one;
[ɔlˈbiɪt hi hæd ˈnɛvʌ sin wʌn]
He would have sinned incessantly
[hi wʊd hæv sɪnd ɪnˈsɛsæ⁽ɪ⁾ntlɪ]
Could he have been one.
[kʊd hi hæv bɪn wʌn]
Miniver cursed the commonplace
[ˈmɪnɪvʌ kɜst ðʌ ˈkamʌnplɛːɪs]
And eyed a khaki suit with loathing;
[ænd aːɪd ʌ ˈkækɪ sjut wɪð ˈloːʊðɪŋ]
He missed the mediaeval grace
[hi mɪst ðʌ ˌmɛdɪˈivʊl gʁɛːɪs]
Of iron clothing.
[ʌv ˈaːɪʌn ˈkloːʊðɪŋ]
Miniver scorned the gold he sought,
[ˈmɪnɪvʌ skɔnd ðʌ goːʊld hi sɔt]
But sore annoyed was he without it;
[bʌt sɔːʁ⁽ʳ⁾ ʌˈnɔːɪd waz hi wɪðˈaːʊt ɪt]
Miniver thought, and thought, and thought,
[ˈmɪnɪvʌ θɔt ænd θɔt ænd θɔt]
And thought about it.
[ænd θɔt ʌˈbaːʊt ɪt]
Miniver Cheevy, born too late,
[ˈmɪnɪvʌ ˈʧivi bɔn tu lɛːɪt]
Scratched his head and kept on thinking:
[skʁæʧt hɪz hɛd ænd kɛpt an ˈθɪŋkɪŋ]
Miniver coughed, and called it fate,
[ˈmɪnɪvʌ kɔft ænd kɔld ɪt fɛːɪt]
And kept on drinking.
[ænd kɛpt an ˈdʁɪŋkɪŋ]

3. Luke Havergal

[luk ˈhævʁˌɡɔl]

Go to the western gate, Luke Havergal,
[ɡoːʊ tu ðʌ ˈwɛstʌn ɡɛːɪt luk ˈhævʌˌɡɔl]
There where the vines cling crimson on the wall,
[ðɛːʌ ʍɛːʌ ðʌ vɑːɪnz klɪŋ ˈkɹɪmzʌn ɑn ðʌ wɔl]
And in the twilight wait for what will come.
[ænd ɪn ðʌ ˈtwɑːɪlɑːɪt wɛːɪt fɔ ʍat wɪl kʌm]
The leaves will whisper there of her, and some,
[ðʌ livz wɪl ˈʍɪspʌ ðɛːʌʁ⁽ʳ⁾ ʌv hɜ ænd sʌm]
Like flying words, will strike you as they fall;
[lɑːɪk ˈflɑːɪɪŋ wɜdz wɪl stɹɑːɪk ju æz ðɛːɪ fɔl]
But go, and if you listen she will call.
[bʌt ɡoːʊ ænd ɪf ju ˈlɪsɛ⁽ɪ⁾n ʃi wɪl kɔl]
Out of a grave I come to tell you this,
[ɑːʊt ʌv ʌ ɡɹ⁽ʳ⁾ɛːɪv ɑːɪ kʌm tu tɛl ju ðɪs]
Out of a grave I come to quench the kiss
[ɑːʊt ʌv ʌ ɡɹ⁽ʳ⁾ɛːɪv ɑːɪ kʌm tu kwɛnʧ ðʌ kɪs]
That flames upon your forehead with a glow
[ðæt flɛːɪmz ʌˈpɑn jɔːʌ ˈfɔːʌhɛd wɪð ʌ ɡloːʊ]
That blinds you to the way that you must go.
[ðæt blɑːɪndz ju tu ðʌ wɛːɪ ðæt ju mʌst ɡoːʊ]
Yes, there is yet one way to where she is,
[jɛs ðɛːʌʁ⁽ʳ⁾ ɪz jɛt wʌn wɛːɪ tu ʍɛːʌ ʃi ɪz]
Bitter, but one that faith may never miss.
[ˈbɪtʌ bʌt wʌn ðæt fɛːɪθ mɛːɪ ˈnɛvʌ mɪs]
Out of a grave I come to tell you this,
[ɑːʊt ʌv ʌ ɡɹ⁽ʳ⁾ɛːɪv ɑːɪ kʌm tu tɛl ju ðɪs]
There is the western gate, Luke Havergal,
[ðɛːʌʁ⁽ʳ⁾ ɪz ðʌ ˈwɛstʌn ɡɛːɪt luk ˈhævʌˌɡɔl]
There are the crimson leaves upon the wall.
[ðɛːʌʁ⁽ʳ⁾ ɑ ðʌ ˈkɹɪmzʌn livz ʌˈpɑn ðʌ wɔl]
Go, for the winds are tearing them away,–
[ɡoːʊ fɔ ðʌ wɪndz ɑ ˈtɛːʌʁ⁽ʳ⁾ɪŋ ðɛm ʌˈwɛːɪ]
Nor think to riddle the dead words they say,
[nɔ θɪŋk tu ˈɹɪdʊl ðʌ dɛd wɜdz ðɛːɪ sɛːɪ]
But go, and if you trust her she will call.
[bʌt ɡoːʊ ænd ɪf ju tɹʌst hɜ ʃi wɪl kɔl]
There is the western gate, Luke Havergal–
[ðɛːʌʁ⁽ʳ⁾ ɪz ðʌ ˈwɛstʌn ɡɛːɪt luk ˈhævʌˌɡɔl]

Six Poems of Emily Dickinson (Song Cycle)

[sɪks ˈpoːʊɪmz ʌv ˈɛmɪli ˈdɪkɪnsʌn]
Dickinson, Emily (Am. 1830-1886)

1. Good Morning, Midnight

[ɡʊd ˈmɔʁnɪŋ ˈmɪdnɑːɪt]

Good morning, midnight,
[ɡʊd ˈmɔnɪŋ ˈmɪdnɑːɪt]
I'm coming home.
[ɑːɪm ˈkʌmɪŋ hoːʊm]
Day got tired of me
[dɛːɪ ɡat tɑːɪʌd ʌv mi]

How could I of him?
[hɑːʊ kʊd ɑːɪ ʌv hɪm]
Sunshine was a sweet place–
[ˈsʌnʃɑːɪn wɑz ʌ swit plɛːɪs]
I liked to stay.
[ɑːɪ lɑːɪkt tu stɛːɪ]
But morn didn't want me now,
[bʌt mɔn ˈdɪdɛ⁽ɪ⁾nt want mi nɑːʊ]
So goodnight day!
[soːʊ ˌɡʊdˈnɑːɪt dɛːɪ]
I can look –can't I –
[ɑːɪ kæn lʊk kænt ɑːɪ]
When the East is red?
[ʍɛn ði ist ɪz ɹɛd]
The hills– have a way then
[ðʌ hɪlz hæv ʌ wɛːɪ ðɛn]
That puts the heart– abroad,
[ðæt pʊts ðʌ hat ʌˈbɹɔd]
You– are not so fair, midnight,
[ju ɑ nat soːʊ fɛːʌ ˈmɪdnɑːɪt]
I chose Day.
[ɑːɪ ʧoːʊz dɛːɪ]
But please take a little girl–
[bʌt pliz tɛːɪk ʌ ˈlɪtʊl ɡɜl]
He turned away!
[hi tɜnd ʌˈwɛːɪ]

2. Heart! We Will Forget Him (see Copland)

3. Let Down the Bars, Oh Death

[lɛt dɑːʊn ðʌ baʁz oːʊ dɛθ]

Let down the bars, Oh Death!
[lɛt dɑːʊn ðʌ baz oːʊ dɛθ]
The tired flocks come in
[ðʌ tɑːɪʌd flaks kʌm ɪn]
Whose bleating ceases to repeat,
[huz ˈblitɪŋ ˈsisɛ⁽ɪ⁾z tu ɹɪˈpit]
Whose wandering is done.
[huz ˈwandʌʁ⁽ʳ⁾ɪŋ ɪz dʌn]
Thine is the stillest night,
[ðɑːɪn ɪz ðʌ ˈstɪlɛ⁽ɪ⁾st nɑːɪt]
Thine the securest fold;
[ðɑːɪn ðʌ sɪˈkjʊːʌʁ⁽ʳ⁾ɛ⁽ɪ⁾st foːʊld]
Too near thou art for seeking thee,
[tu niːʌ ðɑːʊ at fɔ ˈsikɪŋ ði]
Too tender to be told.
[tu ˈtɛndʌ tu bi toːʊld]

4. An Awful Tempest Mashed the Air

[æn ˈɔfʊl ˈtɛmpɪst mæʃt ði ɛːʁ]

An awful tempest mashed the air–
[æn ˈɔfʊl ˈtɛmpɛ⁽ɪ⁾st mæʃt ði ɛːʌ]
The clouds were gaunt, and few. –
[ðʌ klɑːʊdz wɜ ɡɔnt ænd fju]

A black– as of a spectre's cloak–
[ʌ blæk æz ʌv ʌ 'spɛktʌz kloːʊk]
Hid heav'n and earth from view.
[hɪd hɛvn ænd ɝθ fɹʌm vju]
The creatures chuckled on the roofs–
[ðʌ 'kɹitʃʊ(ʌ)z 'tʃʌkʊld an ðʌ ɹ⁽ʳʳ⁾ufs]
And whistled in the air–
[ænd 'ʍɪsʊld ɪn ði ɛːʌ]
And shook their fists–
[ænd ʃʊk ðɛːʌ fɪsts]
And gnashed their teeth–
[ænd næʃt ðɛːʌ tiθ]
And swung their frenzied hair.
[ænd swʌŋ ðɛːʌ 'fɹɛnzɪd hɛːʌ]
The morning lit, the birds arose,
[ðʌ 'mɔnɪŋ lɪt ðʌ bɝdz ʌˈʁ⁽ʳ⁾oːʊz]
The monster's faded eyes
[ðʌ 'manstʌz 'fɛːɪdɛ(ɪ)d aːɪz]
Turned slowly to his native coast–
[tɝnd 'sloːʊlɪ tu hɪz 'nɛːɪtɪv koːʊst]
And peace– was Paradise!
[ænd pis wʌz 'pæʁ⁽ʳ⁾ʌdaːɪs]

5. Nobody Knows This Little Rose
['noːʊbadɪ noːʊz ðɪs 'lɪtʊl ɹoːʊz]

Nobody knows this little rose,
['noːʊbadɪ noːʊz ðɪs 'lɪtʊl ɹoːʊz]
It might a pilgrim be.
[ɪt maːɪt ʌ 'pɪlgɹɪm bi]
Did I not take it from the ways
[dɪd aːɪ nat tɛːɪk ɪt fɹʌm ðʌ wɛːz]
And lift it up to thee.
[ænd lɪft ɪt ʌp tu ði]
Only a bee will miss it,
['oːʊnlɪ ʌ bi wɪl mɪs ɪt]
Only a butterfly,
['oːʊnlɪ ʌ 'bʌtʌflaːɪ]
Hastening from far journey
['hɛːɪsɛ(ɪ)nɪŋ fɹʌm fa 'dʒɝnɪ]
On its breast to lie.
[an ɪts bɹɛst tu laːɪ]
Only a bird will wonder,
['oːʊnlɪ ʌ bɝd wɪl 'wʌndʌ]
Only a breeze will sigh.
['oːʊnlɪ ʌ bɹiz wɪl saːɪ]
Ah, little rose, how easy
[a 'lɪtʊl ɹoːʊz haːʊ 'izɪ]
For such as thee to die!
[fɔ sʌtʃ æz ði tu daːɪ]

6. Bee! I'm Expecting You (see Gordon)

Song Selections

"Bells in the Rain"
[bɛlz ɪn ðʌ ɹɛːɪn]
Wylie, Elinor (Am. 1885-1928)

Sleep falls, with limpid drops of rain,
[slip fɔlz wɪð 'lɪmpɪd dɹaps ʌv ɹɛːɪn]
Upon the steep cliffs of the town.
[ʌ'pan ðʌ stip klɪfs ʌv ðʌ taːʊn]
Sleep falls; men are at peace again
[slip fɔlz mɛn aʁ⁽ʳ⁾ æt pis ʌ'gɛn]
While the small drops fall softly down.
[ʍaːɪl ðʌ smɔl dɹaps fɔl 'saftlɪ daːʊn]
The bright drops ring like bells of glass
[ðʌ bɹaːɪt dɹaps ɹɪŋ laːɪk bɛlz ʌv glæs]
Thinned by the wind, and lightly blown;
[θɪnd baːɪ ðʌ wɪnd ænd 'laːɪtlɪ bloːʊn]
Sleep cannot fall on peaceful grass
[slip kæ'nat fɔl an 'pisfʊl gɹæs]
So softly as it falls on stone.
[soːʊ 'saftlɪ æz ɪt fɔlz an stoːʊn]
Peace falls unheeded on the dead
[pis fɔlz ʌn'hidɛ(ɪ)d an ðʌ dɛd]
Asleep; they have had peace to drink;
[ʌ'slip ðɛːɪ hæv hæd pis tu dɹɪŋk]
Upon a live man's bloody head
[ʌ'pan ʌ laːɪv mænz 'blʌdɪ hɛd]
It falls most tenderly, I think.
[ɪt fɔlz moːʊst 'tɛndʌlɪ aːɪ θɪŋk]

"Loveliest of Trees" (see Somervell)

"The Bird"
[ðʌ bɝd]
Wylie, Elinor (Am. 1885-1928)

O clear and musical,
[oːʊ klɪːʌʁ⁽ʳ⁾ ænd 'mjuzɪkʊl]
Sing again! Sing again!
[sɪŋ ʌ'gɛn sɪŋ ʌ'gɛn]
Hear the rain fall
[hɪːʌ ðʌ ɹɛːɪn fɔl]
Through the long night,
[θɹu ðʌ laŋ naːɪt]
Bring me your song again,
[bɹɪŋ mi jɔːʌ saŋ ʌ'gɛn]
O dear delight!
[oːʊ dɪːʌ dɪ'laːɪt]
O dear and comforting,
[oːʊ dɪːʌʁ⁽ʳ⁾ ænd 'kʌmfɔ(ʌ)tɪŋ]
Mine again! Mine again!
[maːɪn ʌ'gɛn maːɪn ʌ'gɛn]
Hear the rain sing
[hɪːʌ ðʌ ɹɛːɪn sɪŋ]

And the dark rejoice!
[ænd ðʌ dak ɹɪˈdʒɔːɪs]
Shine like a spark again,
[ʃaːɪn laːɪk ʌ spak ʌˈgɛn]
O clearest voice!
[oːʊ ˈklɪːʌʁ⁽ʳ⁾ɛ(ɪ)st vɔːɪs]
O clearest voice!
[oːʊ ˈklɪːʌʁ⁽ʳ⁾ɛ(ɪ)st vɔːɪs]

E

Elgar, Edward (Eng. 1857-1934)

Sea Pictures (Song Cycle)
[si ˈpɪktʃʌz]

1. Sea Slumber Song
[si ˈslʌmbʌ saŋ]
Noel, Roden Berkeley Wriothesley (Eng. 1834-1894)

Sea-birds are asleep,
[si bɜdz ɑɾ ʌˈslip]
The world forgets to weep,
[ðʊ wɜld fɔˈgɛts tu wip]
Sea murmurs her soft slumber-song
[si ˈmɜmʊ(ʌ)z hɜ saft ˈslʌmbʌ saŋ]
On the shadowy sand
[an ðʊ ˈʃædoːʊɪ sænd]
Of this elfin land;
[ʌv ðɪs ˈɛlfɪn lænd]
"I, the Mother mild,
[aːɪ ðʊ ˈmʌðʌ maːɪld]
Hush thee, O my child,
[hʌʃ ði oːʊ maːɪ tʃaːɪld]
Forget the voices wild!
[fɔˈgɛt ðʊ ˈvɔːɪsɛ(ɪ)z waːɪld]
Isles in elfin light
[aːɪlz ɪn ˈɛlfɪn laːɪt]
Dream, the rocks and caves,
[dɹim ðʊ ɾaks ænd kɛːɪvz]
Lulled by whispering waves,
[lʌld baːɪ ˈʍɪsp(ʌ)ɾɪŋ wɛːɪvz]
Veil their marbles bright,
[vɛːɪl ðɛːʌ ˈmabʊlz bɹaːɪt]
Foam glimmers faintly white
[foːʊm ˈglɪmʌz ˈfɛːɪntlɪ ʍaːɪt]
Upon the shelly sand
[ʌˈpan ðʊ ˈʃɛlɪ sænd]
Of this elfin land;
[ʌv ðɪs ˈɛlfɪn lænd]
Sea-sound, like violins,
[si saːʊnd laːɪk vaːɪoˈlɪnz]

To slumber woos and wins,
[tu ˈslʌmbʌ wuz ænd wɪnz]
I murmur my soft slumber-song,
[aːɪ ˈmɜmʊ(ʌ) maːɪ saft ˈslʌmbʌ saŋ]
Leave woes, and wails, and sins,
[liv woːʊz ænd wɛːɪlz ænd sɪnz]
Ocean's shadowy might
[oːʊʃæ(ɪ)nz ˈʃædoːʊɪ maːɪt]
Breathes good-night,
[bɹiðz gʊd naːɪt]
Good night!"
[gʊd naːɪt]

2. In Haven (Capri)
[ɪn ˈhɛːɪvɪn kʌˈpɹi]
Elgar, Caroline Alice (Eng. 1848-1920)

Closely let me hold thy hand,
[ˈkloːʊslɪ lɛt mi hoːʊld ðaːɪ hænd]
Storms are sweeping sea and land;
[stɔmz ɑ ˈswipɪŋ si ænd lænd]
Love alone will stand.
[lʌv ʌˈloːʊn wɪl stænd]
Closely cling, for waves beat fast,
[ˈkloːʊslɪ klɪŋ fɔ wɛːɪvz bit fast]
Foam-flakes cloud the hurrying blast;
[foːʊm flɛːɪks klaːʊd ðʊ ˈhʊɾɪŋ blast]
Love alone will last.
[lʌv ʌˈloːʊn wɪl last]
Kiss my lips, and softly say:
[kɪs maːɪ lɪps ænd ˈsaftlɪ sɛːɪ]
"Joy, sea-swept, may fade to-day;
[dʒɔːɪ si swɛpt mɛːɪ fɛːɪd tu dɛːɪ]
Love alone will stay."
[lʌv ʌˈloːʊn wɪl stɛːɪ]

3. Sabbath Morning at Sea
[ˈsæbʌθ ˈmɔnɪŋ æt si]
Browning, Elizabeth Barrett (Eng. 1806-1861)

The ship went on with solemn face:
[ðʊ ʃɪp wɛnt an wɪð ˈsalʌm fɛːɪs]
To meet the darkness on the deep,
[tu mit ðʊ ˈdaknɛ(ɪ)s an ðʊ dip]
The solemn ship went onward.
[ðʊ ˈsalʌm ʃɪp wɛnt ˈanwʊd]
I bowed down weary in the place;
[aːɪ baːʊd daːʊn ˈwɪːʌɾɪ ɪn ðʊ plɛːɪs]
For parting tears and present sleep
[fɔ ˈpatɪŋ tɪːʌz ænd ˈpɹɛzɛnt slip]
Had weighed mine eyelids downward.
[hæd wɛːɪd maːɪn ˈaːɪlɪdz ˈdaːʊnwʊd]
The new sight, the new wondrous sight!
[ðʊ nju saːɪt ðʊ nju ˈwʌndɹʌs saːɪt]
The waters around me, turbulent,
[ðʊ ˈwɔtʌz ʌˈɾaːʊnd mi ˈtɜbjulɛnt]

The skies, impassive o'er me,
[ðʊ skɑːɪz ɪmˈpæsɪv ɔːʌ mi]
Calm in a moonless, sunless light,
[kɑm ɪn ʌ ˈmunlɛ(ɪ)s ˈsʌnlɛ(ɪ)s lɑːɪt]
As glorified by even the intent
[æz ˈglɔɪfɑːɪd bɑːɪ ˈivɛ(ɪ)n ðɪ ɪnˈtɛnt]
Of holding the day glory!
[ʌv ˈhoːʊldɪŋ ðʊ dɛːɪ ˈglɔɪ]
Love me, sweet friends, this sabbath day.
[lʌv mi swit fɪɛndz ðɪs ˈsæbæ(ʌ)θ dɛːɪ]
The sea sings round me while ye roll
[ðʊ si sɪŋz ɪɑːʊnd mi ʍɑːɪl ji roːʊl]
Afar the hymn, unaltered,
[ʌˈfɑ ðʊ hɪm ʌnˈɔltʌd]
And kneel, where once I knelt to pray,
[ænd nil ʍɛːʌ ʍʌns ɑːɪ nɛlt tu pɪɛːɪ]
And bless me deeper in your soul
[ænd blɛs mi ˈdipʌɪ ɪn jɔːʌ soːʊl]
Because your voice has faltered.
[bɪˈkɔz jɔːʌ vɔːɪs hæz ˈfɔltʌd]
And though this sabbath comes to me
[ænd ðoːʊ ðɪs ˈsæbæ(ʌ)θ kʌmz tu mi]
Without the stolèd minister,
[wɪðˈɑːʊt ðʊ ˈstoːʊlɛ(ɪ)d ˈmɪnɪstʌ]
And chanting congregation,
[ænd ˈʧɑntɪŋ kɑŋgɪɪˈgeːɪʃʌn]
God's Spirit shall give comfort. HE
[gɑdz ˈspɪɪɪt ʃæl gɪv ˈkʌmfɔ(ʌ)t hi]
Who brooded soft on waters drear,
[hu ˈbɪudɛ(ɪ)d sɑft ɑn ˈwɔtʌz dɪɪːʌ]
Creator on creation.
[kɪɪˈɛːɪtɔ(ʌ)r ɑn kɪɪˈɛːɪʃʌn]
He shall assist me to look higher,
[hi ʃæl ʌˈsɪst mi tu lʊk ˈhɑːɪʌ]
Where keep the saints, with harp and song,
[ʍɛːʌ kip ðʊ sɛːɪnts wɪð hɑp ænd sɑŋ]
An endless sabbath morning,
[æn ˈɛndlɛ(ɪ)s ˈsæbæ(ʌ)θ ˈmɔnɪŋ]
An endless sabbath morning,
[æn ˈɛndlɛ(ɪ)s ˈsæbæ(ʌ)θ ˈmɔnɪŋ]
And, on that sea commixed with fire,
[ænd ɑn ðæt si kʌˈmɪkst wɪð fɑːɪʌ]
And that sea commixed with fire,
[ænd ðæt si kʌˈmɪkst wɪð fɑːɪʌ]
Oft drop their eyelids raised too long
[ɑft dɪɑp ðɛːʌ ˈɑːɪlɪdz ɪɛːɪzd tu lɑŋ]
To the full Godhead's burning.
[tu ðʊ fʊl ˈgɑdhɛdz ˈbɜnɪŋ]

4. Where Corals Lie
[ʍɛːʌ ˈkɔʁʊlz lɑːɪ]
Garnett, Richard (1835-1906)

The deeps have music soft and low
[ðʊ dips hæv ˈmjuzɪk sɑft ænd loːʊ]

When winds awake the airy spry,
[ʍɛn wɪndz ʌˈweːɪk ðɪ ˈɛːʌɪ spɪɑːɪ]
It lures me, lures me on to go
[ɪt ljʊːʌz mi ljʊːʌz mi ɑn tu goːʊ]
And see the land where corals lie.
[ænd si ðʊ lænd ʍɛːʌ ˈkɔʁʊlz lɑːɪ]
By mount and mead, by lawn and rill,
[bɑːɪ mɑːʊnt ænd mid bɑːɪ lɔn ænd ɪɪl]
When night is deep and moon is high,
[ʍɛn nɑːɪt ɪz dip ænd mun ɪz hɑːɪ]
That music seeks and finds me still,
[ðæt ˈmjuzɪk siks ænd fɑːɪndz mi stɪl]
And tells me where the corals lie.
[ænd tɛlz mi ʍɛːʌ ðʊ ˈkɔʁʊlz lɑːɪ]
Yes, press my eyelids close, 'tis well;
[jɛs pɪɛs mɑːɪ ˈɑːɪlɪdz kloːʊz tɪz wɛl]
But far the rapid fancies fly
[bʌt fɑ ðʊ ˈɪæpɪd ˈfænsɪz flɑːɪ]
To rolling worlds of wave and shell,
[tu ˈɪoːʊlɪŋ wɜldz ʌv weːɪv ænd ʃɛl]
And all the land where corals lie.
[ænd ɔl ðʊ lænd ʍɛːʌ ˈkɔʁʊlz lɑːɪ]
Thy lips are like a sunset glow,
[ðɑːɪ lɪps ɑ lɑːɪk ʌ ˈsʌnsɛt gloːʊ]
Thy smile is like a morning sky,
[ðɑːɪ smɑːɪl ɪz lɑːɪk ʌ ˈmɔnɪŋ skɑːɪ]
Yet leave me, leave me, let me go
[jɛt liv mi liv mi lɛt mi goːʊ]
And see the land where corals lie.
[ænd si ðʊ lænd ʍɛːʌ ˈkɔʁʊlz lɑːɪ]

5. The Swimmer
[ðʊ ˈswɪmʌ]
Gordon, Adam Lindsay (Eng. 1833-1870)

With short, sharp, violent lights made vivid,
[wɪð ʃɔt ʃɑp ˈvɑːɪo(ʌ)lɛnt lɑːɪts meːɪd ˈvɪvɪd]
To southward far as the sight can roam,
[tu ˈsɑːʊθwʊd fɑr æz ðʊ sɑːɪt kæn ɪoːʊm]
Only the swirl of the surges livid,
[ˈoːʊnlɪ ðʊ swɜl ʌv ðʊ ˈsɜdʒɛ(ɪ)z ˈlɪvɪd]
The seas that climb and the surfs that comb.
[ðʊ siz ðæt klɑːɪm ænd ðʊ sɜfs ðæt koːʊm]
Only the crag and the cliff to nor'ward,
[ˈoːʊnlɪ ðʊ kʁæg ænd ðʊ klɪf tu ˈnɔwʊd]
The rocks receding, and reefs flung forward,
[ðʊ ɪɑks ɪɪˈsidɪŋ ænd ɪɪfs flʌŋ ˈfɔwʊd]
waifs wreck'd seaward and wasted shoreward,
[wɛːɪfs ɪɛkt ˈsiwʊd ænd ˈwɛːɪstɛ(ɪ)d ˈʃɔːʌwʊd]
On shallows sheeted with flaming foam.
[ɑn ˈʃæloːʊz ˈʃitɛ(ɪ)d wɪð ˈflɛːɪmɪŋ foːʊm]
A grim, gray coast and a seaboard ghastly,
[ʌ grɪm grɛːɪ koːʊst ænd ʌ ˈsibɔd ˈgɑstlɪ]
And shores trod seldom by feet of men–
[ænd ʃɔːʌz tɪɑd ˈsɛldʌm bɑːɪ fit ʌv mɛn]

Where the batter'd hull and the broken mast lie,
[ʍɛːʌ ðʊ ˈbætʌd hʌl ænd ðʊ ˈbɹoːʊkɛ(ɪ)n mɑst lɑːɪ]
They have lain embedded these long years ten.
[ðɛːɪ hæv lɛːɪn ɪmˈbɛdɛ(ɪ)d ðiz lɑŋ jɪːʌz tɛn]
Love! when we wandered here together,
[lʌv ʍɛn wi ˈwɑndʌd hɪːʌ tuˈgɛðʌ]
Hand in hand through the sparkling weather,
[hænd ɪn hænd θɾu ðʊ ˈspɑklɪŋ ˈwɛðʌ]
From the heights and hollows of fern and heather,
[fɪʌm ðʊ hɑːɪts ænd ˈhɑloːʊz ʌv fɜn ænd ˈhɛðʌ]
God surely loved us a little then.
[gɑd ˈʃʊːʌlɪ lʌvd ʌs ʌ ˈlɪtʊl ðɛn]
The skies were fairer and shores were firmer–
[ðʊ skɑːɪz wɜ ˈfɛːʌɾʌ ænd ʃɔːʌz wɜ ˈfɜmʌ]
The blue sea over the bright sand roll'd;
[ðʊ blu si ˈoːʊvʌ ðʊ bɹɑːɪt sænd ɹoːʊld]
Babble and prattle, and ripple and murmur,
[ˈbæbʊl ænd ˈpɹætʊl ænd ˈɹɪpʊl ænd ˈmɜmʊ(ʌ)]
Sheen of silver and glamour of gold.
[ʃin ʌv ˈsɪlvʌ ænd ˈglæmʊ(ʌ)r ʌv goːʊld]
So, girt with tempest and wing'd with thunder
[soːʊ gɜt wɪð ˈtɛmpɛ(ɪ)st ænd wɪŋgd wɪð ˈθʌndʌ]
And clad with lightning and shod with sleet,
[ænd klæd wɪð ˈlɑːɪtnɪŋ ænd ʃɑd wɪð slit]
And strong winds treading the swift waves under
[ænd stɹɑŋ wɪndz ˈtɹɛdɪŋ ðʊ swɪft wɛːɪvz ˈʌndʌ]
The flying rollers with frothy feet.
[ðʊ ˈflɑːɪŋ ˈɹoːʊlʌz wɪð ˈfɹɑθɪ fit]
One gleam like a bloodshot sword-blade swims on
[wʌn glim lɑːɪk ʌ ˈblʌdʃɑt sɔd blɛːɪd swɪmz ɑn]
The sky line, staining the green gulf crimson,
[ðʊ skɑːɪ lɑːɪn ˈstɛːɪnɪŋ ðʊ gɹin gʌlf ˈkɹɪmzʌn]
A death-stroke fiercely dealt by a dim sun
[ʌ dɛθ stɹoːʊk ˈfɪːʌʃlɪ dɛlt bɑːɪ ʌ dɪm sʌn]
That strikes through his stormy winding sheet.
[ðæt stɹɑːɪks θɾu hɪz ˈstɔmɪ ˈwɑːɪndɪŋ ʃit]
O, brave white horses! you gather and gallop,
[oːʊ bɹɛːɪv ʍɑːɪt ˈhɔsɛ(ɪ)z ju ˈgæðʌ⁽ʳ⁾ ænd ˈgælʌp]
The storm sprite loosens the gusty reins;
[ðʊ stɔm spɹɑːɪt ˈlusɛ(ɪ)nz ðʊ ˈgʌstɪ ɾɛːɪnz]
Now the stoutest ship were the frailest shallop
[nɑːʊ ðʊ ˈstɑːʊtɛ(ɪ)st ʃɪp wɜ ðʊ ˈfɹɛːɪlɛ(ɪ)st ˈʃælʌp]
In your hollow backs, on your high-arched manes.
[ɪn jɔːʌ ˈhɑloːʊ bæks ɑn jɔːʌ hɑːɪ ɑʧt mɛːɪnz]
I would ride as never man has ridden
[ɑːɪ wʊd ɹɑːɪd æz ˈnɛvʌ mæn hæz ˈɹɪdɛ(ɪ)n]
In your sleepy, swirling surges hidden;
[ɪn jɔːʌ ˈslipɪ ˈswɜlɪŋ ˈsɜʤɛ(ɪ)z ˈhɪdɛ(ɪ)n]
I would ride as never man has ridden
[ɑːɪ wʊd ɹɑːɪd æz ˈnɛvʌ mæn hæz ˈɹɪdɛ(ɪ)n]
To gulfs foreshadow'd thro' strifes forbidden,
[tu gʌlfs fɔˈʃædoːʊd θɾu stɹɑːɪfs fɔˈbɪdɛ(ɪ)n]
Where no light wearies and no love wanes.
[ʍɛːʌ noːʊ lɑːɪt ˈwɪːʌɾɪz ænd noːʊ lʌv wɛːɪnz]

Song Selection

"Speak, Music!" Op. 41, No. 2
[spik ˈmjuzɪk]
Benson, Arthur Christopher (Eng. 1862-1925)

Speak, speak, music, and bring to me
[spik spik ˈmjuzɪk ænd bɹɪŋ tu mi]
Fancies too fleet for me,
[ˈfænsɪz tu flit fɔ mi]
Sweetness too sweet for me,
[ˈswitnɛ(ɪ)s tu swit fɔ mi]
Wake, wake, voices, and sing to me,
[wɛːɪk wɛːɪk ˈvɔːɪsɛ(ɪ)z ænd sɪŋ tu mi]
Sing to me tenderly; bid me rest.
[sɪŋ tu mi ˈtɛndʌlɪ bɪd mi ɾɛst]
Rest, Rest! ah, I am fain of it!
[ɹɛst ɹɛst ɑ ɑːɪ æm fɛːɪn ʌv ɪt]
Die, Hope! small was my gain of it!
[dɑːɪ hoːʊp smɔl wɑz mɑːɪ gɛːɪn ʌv ɪt]
Song, take thy parable,
[sɑŋ tɛːɪk ðɑːɪ ˈpæɾʌbʊl]
Whisper, whisper that all is well,
[ˈʍɪspʌ ˈʍɪspʌ ðæt ɔl ɪz wɛl]
Say, say that there tarrieth
[sɛːɪ sɛːɪ ðæt ðɛːʌ ˈtæɾɪɛ(ɪ)θ]
Something, something more true than death,
[ˈsʌmθɪŋ ˈsʌmθɪŋ mɔːʌ tru ðæn dɛθ]
Waiting to smile for me; bright and blest.
[ˈwɛːɪtɪŋ tu smɑːɪl fɔ mi bɹɑːɪt ænd blɛst]
Thrill, thrill, string: echo and play for me
[θɾɪl θɾɪl stɹɪŋ ˈɛkoːʊ ænd plɛːɪ fɔ mi]
All, all that the poet, the priest cannot say for me;
[ɔl ɔl ðæt ðʊ ˈpoːʊɛ(ɪ)t ðʊ pɹist kæˈnɑt sɛːɪ fɔ mi]
Soar, voice, soar, heavenwards, and pray for me,
[sɔːʌ vɔːɪs sɔːʌ ˈhɛvɪnwʊdz ænd pɹɛːɪ fɔ mi]
Wondering, wandering; bid me rest.
[ˈwʌndʌɾɪŋ ˈwɑndʌɾɪŋ bɪd mi ɾɛst]

F

Faith, Richard (Am. 1926-2021)

Song Selections

"Echo"
[ˈɛkoːʊ]
Rossetti, Christina Georgina (Eng. 1830-1894)

Come to me in the silence of the night;
[kʌm tu mi ɪn ðʌ ˈsɑːɪlɛ(ɪ)ns ʌv ðʌ nɑːɪt]
Come in the speaking silence of a dream;
[kʌm ɪn ðʌ ˈspikɪŋ ˈsɑːɪlɛ(ɪ)ns ʌv ʌ dɹim]

Come with soft rounded cheeks and eyes as bright
[kʌm wɪð saft ˈɹɑːʊndɛ(ɪ)d ʧiks ænd ɑːɪz æz bɹɑːɪt]
As sunlight on a stream; Come back in tears,
[æz ˈsʌnlɑːɪt ɑn ʌ stɹim kʌm bæk ɪn tɪːʌz]
O memory, hope, love of finished years.
[oːʊ ˈmɛmɔʁ(ʳ)ɪ hoːʊp lʌv ʌv ˈfɪnɪʃt jɪːʌz]
O dream how sweet, too sweet, too bitter sweet,
[oːʊ dɹim hɑːʊ swit tu swit tu ˈbɪtʌ swit]
Whose wakening should have been in Paradise,
[huz ˈwɛːɪkɛ(ɪ)nɪŋ ʃʊd hæv bɪn ɪn ˈpæʁ(ʳ)ʌdɑːɪs]
Where souls brim full of love abide and meet;
[ʍɛːʌ soːʊlz bɹɪm fʊl ʌv lʌv ʌˈbɑːɪd ænd mit]
Where thirsting longing eyes
[ʍɛːʌ ˈθɜstɪŋ ˈlɑŋɪŋ ɑːɪz]
Watch the slow door
[wɑʧ ðʌ sloːʊ dɔːʌ]
That opening, letting in, lets out no more.
[ðæt ˈoːʊpɛ(ɪ)nɪŋ ˈlɛtɪŋ ɪn lɛts ɑːʊt noːʊ mɔːʌ]
Yet come to me in dreams, that I may live
[jɛt kʌm tu mi ɪn dɹimz ðæt ɑːɪ mɛːɪ lɪv]
My very life again though cold in death:
[mɑːɪ ˈvɛʁ(ʳ)ɪ lɑːɪf ʌˈgɛn ðoːʊ koːʊld ɪn dɛθ]
Come back to me in dreams, that I may give
[kʌm bæk tu mi ɪn dɹimz ðæt ɑːɪ mɛːɪ gɪv]
Pulse for pulse, breath for breath:
[pʌls fɔ pʌls bɹɛθ fɔ bɹɛθ]
Speak low, lean low,
[spik loːʊ lin loːʊ]
As long ago, my love, how long ago.
[æz lɑŋ ʌˈgoːʊ mɑːɪ lʌv hɑːʊ lɑŋ ʌˈgoːʊ]

"It Was a Lover and His Lass" (see Morley)

"Music I Heard with You" (see Hageman)

"Remember Me"
[ɹɪˈmɛmbʁ mi]
Rossetti, Christina Georgina (Eng. 1830-1894)

Remember me when I am gone away,
[ɹɪˈmɛmbʌ mi ʍɛn ɑːɪ æm gɑn ʌˈwɛːɪ]
Gone far away into the silent land;
[gɑn fɑʁ(ʳ) ʌˈwɛːɪ ˈɪntu ðʌ ˈsɑːɪlɛnt lænd]
When you can no more hold me by the hand,
[ʍɛn ju kæn noːʊ mɔːʌ hoːʊld mi bɑːɪ ðʌ hænd]
Nor I half turn to go yet turning stay.
[nɔʁ(ʳ) ɑːɪ hæf tɜn tu goːʊ jɛt ˈtɜnɪŋ stɛːɪ]
Remember me when no more day by day
[ɹɪˈmɛmbʌ mi ʍɛn noːʊ mɔːʌ dɛːɪ bɑːɪ dɛːɪ]
You tell me of our future that you planned:
[ju tɛl mi ʌv ɑːʊʌ ˈfjuʧʊ(ʌ) ðæt ju plænd]
Only remember me.
[ˈoːʊnlɪ ɹɪˈmɛmbʌ mi]
Remember me when I am gone away.
[ɹɪˈmɛmbʌ mi ʍɛn ɑːɪ æm gɑn ʌˈwɛːɪ]

"Spring, the Sweet Spring" (see "Spring" by Argento)

"The Blackbird"
[ðʌ ˈblækbɜd]
Henley, William Ernest (Eng. 1849-1903)

The Nightingale has a lyre of gold,
[ðʌ ˈnɑːɪtɪŋɛːɪl hæz ʌ ˈlɑːɪʁ(ʳ) ʌv goːʊld]
The lark's is a clarion call,
[ðʌ lɑks ɪz ʌ ˈklæʁ(ʳ)ɪʌn kɔl]
And the blackbird plays but a boxwood flute,
[ænd ðʌ ˈblækbɜd plɛːɪz bʌt ʌ ˈbɑksˌwʊd flut]
But I love him best of all.
[bʌt ɑːɪ lʌv hɪm bɛst ʌv ɔl]
For his song is all of the joy of life.
[fɔ hɪz sɑŋ ɪz ɔl ʌv ðʌ ʤɔːɪ ʌv lɑːɪf]
And we in the mad spring weather,
[ænd wi ɪn ðʌ mæd spɹɪŋ ˈwɛðʌ]
We two have listened till he sang
[wi tu hæv ˈlɪsɛ(ɪ)nd tɪl hi sæŋ]
Our heart and lips together.
[ɑːʊʌ hɑt ænd lɪps tuˈgɛðʌ]

"The Lake Isle of Innisfree"
[ðʌ lɛːɪk ɑːɪl ʌv ˈɪnɪʃˌfɹi]
Yeats, William Butler (Ir. 1865-1939)

I will arise and go now, and go to Innisfree,
[ɑːɪ wɪl ʌˈʁ(ʳ)ɑːɪz ænd goːʊ nɑːʊ ænd goːʊ tu ˈɪnɪʃˌfɹi]
And a small cabin build there,
[ænd ʌ smɔl ˈkæbɪn bɪld ðɛːʌʁ(ʳ)]
of clay and wattles made;
[ʌv klɛːɪ ænd ˈwɑtʊlz mɛːɪd]
Nine bean rows will I have there,
[nɑːɪn bin ɹoːʊz wɪl ɑːɪ hæv ðɛːʌ]
a hive for the honey bee,
[ʌ hɑːɪv fɔ ðʌ ˈhʌni bi]
And live alone in the bee-loud glade.
[ænd lɪv ʌˈloːʊn ɪn ðʌ bi lɑːʊd glɛːɪd]
And I shall have some peace there,
[ænd ɑːɪ ʃæl hæv sʌm pis ðɛːʌ]
for peace comes dropping slow,
[fɔ pis kʌmz ˈdɹɑpɪŋ sloːʊ]
Dropping from the veils of morning
[ˈdɹɑpɪŋ fɹʌm ðʌ vɛːɪlz ʌv ˈmɔnɪŋ]
to where the cricket sings;
[tu ʍɛːʌ ðʌ ˈkɹɪkɛ(ɪ)t sɪŋz]
There midnight's all a glimmer,
[ðɛːʌ ˈmɪdnɑːɪts ɔl ʌ ˈglɪmʌ]
and noon a purple glow,
[ænd nun ʌ ˈpɜpʊl gloːʊ]
And evening full of linnet's wing.
[ænd ˈivnɪŋ fʊl ʌv ˈlɪnɛ(ɪ)ts wɪŋ]
I will arise and go now,
[ɑːɪ wɪl ʌˈʁ(ʳ)ɑːɪz ænd goːʊ nɑːʊ]

for always night and day
[fɔʁ⁽ʳ⁾ 'ɔlwɛːɪz naːɪt ænd dɛːɪ]
I hear lake water lapping
[aːɪ hiːʌ lɛːɪk 'wɔtʌ 'læpɪŋ]
with low sounds by the shore;
[wɪð loːʊ saːʊndz baːɪ ðʌ ʃɔːʌ]
While I stand on the roadway,
[ʍaːɪl aːɪ stænd an ðʌ 'ɹoːʊdwɛːɪ]
or on the pavements gray,
[ɔʁ⁽ʳ⁾ an ðʌ 'pɛːɪvmɛnts gɹɛːɪ]
I hear it in the deep heart's core.
[aːɪ hiːʌʁ⁽ʳ⁾ ɪt ɪn ðʌ dip hats kɔːʌ]

 # Fine, Irving (Am. 1914-1962)

Childhood Fables for Grownups (Song Cycle)
['tʃaːɪldhʊd 'fɛːɪbʊlz fɔʁ 'gɹoːʊnʌps]
Norman, Gertrude (Am. 1847-1946)

1. Polaroli
['poːʊlʌʁoːʊli]

Polaroli the polar bear,
['poːʊlʌʁ⁽ʳ⁾oːʊli ðʌ 'poːʊlʌ bɛːʌ]
He finds the cold so nice
[hi faːɪndz ðʌ koːʊld soːʊ naːɪs]
He loves to roll in the deepest snow
[hi lʌvz tu roːʊl ɪn ðʌ 'dipɛ(ɪ)st snoːʊ]
And sleep on a heap of ice.
[ænd slip an ʌ hip ʌv aːɪs]
In ice-water he loves to swim
[ɪn aːɪs 'wɔtʌ hi lʌvz tu swɪm]
and splish and splash and splush,
[ænd splɪʃ ænd splæʃ ænd splʌʃ]
And mush the cold snow under him
[ænd mʌʃ ðʌ koːʊld snoːʊ 'ʌndʌ hɪm]
And snuggle in the slush.
[ænd 'snʌgʊl ɪn ðʌ slʌʃ]
His favorite dish is frozen fish
[hɪz 'fɛːɪvɔʁ⁽ʳ⁾ɪt dɪʃ ɪz 'fɹoːʊzɛ(ɪ)n fɪʃ]
With icicles and spicicles
[wɪð 'aːɪsɪkʊlz ænd 'spaːɪsɪkʊlz]
and other little nicicles
[ænd 'ʌðʌ 'lɪtʊl 'naːɪsɪkʊlz]
And that's his favorite dish.
[ænd ðæts hɪz 'fɛːɪvɔʁ⁽ʳ⁾ɪt dɪʃ]
And if he had his wish
[ænd ɪf hi hæd hɪz wɪʃ]
Just one thing he would wish:
[dʒʌst wʌn θɪŋ hi wʊd wɪʃ]
That all the world were made of snow
[ðæt ɔl ðʌ wɜld wɜ mɛːɪd ʌv snoːʊ]
And ice and frozen fish.
[ænd aːɪs ænd 'fɹoːʊzɛ(ɪ)n fɪʃ]

2. Tigeroo
['taːɪgʌˌʁu]

There once was a tiger named Tigeroo
[ðɛːʌ wʌns waz ʌ 'taːɪgʌ nɛːɪmd 'taːɪgʌˌʁ⁽ʳ⁾u]
The hungriest tiger in the zoo,
[ðʌ 'hʌŋgɹɪɛ(ɪ)st 'taːɪgʌʁ⁽ʳ⁾ ɪn ðʌ zu]
All day long he liked to eat
[ɔl dɛːɪ laŋ hi laːɪkt tu it]
Not cake, not cookies, but only meat.
[nat kɛːɪk nat 'kʊkɪz bʌt 'oːʊnlɪ mit]
The keeper said, "Now Tigeroo
[ðʌ 'kipʌ sɛd naːʊ 'taːɪgʌˌʁ⁽ʳ⁾u]
You eat too much, You know you do,
[ju it tu mʌtʃ ju noːʊ ju du]
If you eat anymore and you get sick,
[ɪf ju it ˌɛnɪ'mɔːʁ⁽ʳ⁾ ænd ju gɛt sɪk]
I'll call the tiger-doctor quick."
[aːɪl kɔl ðʌ 'taːɪgʌ 'daktɔ(ʌ) kwɪk]
"I'll eat all I like" said Tigeroo
[aːɪl it ɔl aːɪ laːɪk sɛd 'taːɪgʌˌʁ⁽ʳ⁾u]
"I'm the hungriest tiger in the zoo,
[aːɪm ðʌ 'hʌŋgɹɪɛ(ɪ)st 'taːɪgʌʁ⁽ʳ⁾ ɪn ðʌ zu]
You tell that doctor I said Pooh!
[ju tɛl ðæt 'daktɔ(ʌ) aːɪ sɛd pu]
If he comes in my cage I'll eat him, too"
[ɪf hi kʌmz ɪn maːɪ kɛːɪdʒ aːɪl it hɪm tu]

3. Lenny the Leopard
['lɛni ðʌ 'lɛpʁd]

Lenny the Leopard hated his spots
['lɛni ðʌ 'lɛpʌd 'hɛːɪtɛ(ɪ)d hɪz spats]
He covered them over with purple blots
[hi 'kʌvʌd ðɛm 'oːʊvʌ wɪð 'pɜpʊl blats]
And tied his tail in a hundred knots.
[ænd taːɪd hɪz tɛːɪl ɪn ʌ 'hʌndɹɛ(ɪ)d nats]
He painted his ears, one red, one blue,
[hi 'pɛːɪntɛ(ɪ)d hɪz iːʌz wʌn ɹɛd wʌn blu]
And dipped his nose in a pot of glue,
[ænd dɪpt hɪz noːʊz ɪn ʌ pat ʌv glu]
And ev'rything else bad leopards do.
[ænd 'ɛvɹɪθɪŋ ɛls bæd 'lɛpʌdz du]
But his mother said, Lenny I still love you,
[bʌt hɪz 'mʌðʌ sɛd 'lɛni aːɪ stɪl lʌv ju]
You're my baby and I love you.
[jɔːʌ maːɪ 'bɛːɪbɪ ænd aːɪ lʌv ju]

4. The Frog and the Snake
[ðʌ fɹag ænd ðʌ snɛːɪk]

There was a little frog, He jumped upon a log
[ðɛːʌ waz ʌ 'lɪtʊl fɹag hi dʒʌmpt ʌ'pan ʌ lag]
Tried to splash and splatter and quack, quack, quack.
[tɹaːɪd tu splæʃ ænd 'splætʌʁ⁽ʳ⁾ ænd kwæk kwæk kwæk]

And sat there smiling in the soft summer sun.
[ænd sæt ðɛːʌ ˈsmaːɪlɪŋ ɪn ðʌ saft ˈsʌmʌ sʌn]
Along came a snake, The frog began to shake,
[ʌˈlaŋ kɛːɪm ʌ sneːɪk ðʌ fɹag bɪˈgæn tu ʃɛːɪk]
He didn't know which way first to run.
[hi ˈdɪdɪnt noːʊ ʍɪtʃwɛːɪ fɜst tu ɹʌn]
"Look here," said the frog, "You may think I'm a frog,
[lʊk hɪːʌ sɛd ðʌ fɹag ju mɛːɪ θɪŋk aːɪm ʌ fɹag]
But I'm really not, I'm a golliwogg,
[bʌt aːɪm ˈɹɪlɪ nat aːɪm ʌ ˈgalɪwag]
And if a golliwogg gets eaten by a snake
[ænd ɪf ʌ ˈgalɪwag gɛts ˈite(ɪ)n baːɪ ʌ sneːɪk]
That snake will die of a tummy ache."
[ðæt sneːɪk wɪl daːɪ ʌv ʌ ˈtʌmɪ ɛːɪk]
"Oh goodness," said the snake
[oːʊ ˈgʊdnɛ(ɪ)s sɛd ðʌ sneːɪk]
"What a terrible mistake,"
[ʍat ʌ ˈtɛʁ⁽ʳ⁾ɪbʊl mɪˈsteːɪk]
And he quivered and shivered
[ænd hi ˈkwɪvʌd ænd ˈʃɪvʌd]
and quivered and shivered and away did run
[ænd ˈkwɪvʌd ænd ˈʃɪvʌd ænd ʌˈwɛːɪ dɪd ɹʌn]
While the frog sat there smiling
[ʍaːɪl ðʌ fɹag sæt ðɛːʌ ˈsmaːɪlɪŋ]
and laughing and beaming,
[ænd ˈlæfɪŋ ænd ˈbimɪŋ]
Smiling and beaming, laughing and beaming,
[ˈsmaːɪlɪŋ ænd ˈbimɪŋ ˈlæfɪŋ ænd ˈbimɪŋ]
Smiling and beaming in the soft summer sun.
[ˈsmaːɪlɪŋ ænd ˈbimɪŋ ɪn ðʌ saft ˈsʌmʌ sʌn]

5. Two Worms
[tu wɜmz]

A lonely little worm
[ʌ ˈloːʊnlɪ ˈlɪtʊl wɜm]
Didn't wiggle or squirm,
[ˈdɪdɪnt ˈwɪgʊl ɔ skwɜm]
Lay in the grass
[lɛːɪ ɪn ðʌ gɹæs]
And cried, alas!
[ænd kɹaːɪd ʌˈlæs]
Nobody loves me.
[ˈnoːʊbadɪ lʌvz mi]
Not one dog or cat,
[nat wʌn dag ɔ kæt]
Not one mouse or rat,
[nat wʌn maːʊs ɔ ɹæt]
Not one dandelion.
[nat wʌn ˈdændɪlaːɪʌn]
That is that.
[ðæt ɪz ðæt]
Nobody wants me,
[ˈnoːʊbadɪ wants mi]
Nobody needs me,
[ˈnoːʊbadɪ nidz mi]

Nobody loves me,
[ˈnoːʊbadɪ lʌvz mi]
Needs me,
[nidz mi]
Nobody wants me now.
[ˈnoːʊbadɪ wants mi naːʊ]
He saw another worm,
[hi sɔ ʌˈnʌðʌ wɜm]
Looked too sad to squirm,
[lʊkt tu sæd tu skwɜm]
"Worm!" he cried,
[wɜm hi kɹaːɪd]
"Oh be my friend,
[oːʊ bi maːɪ fɹɛnd]
Loneliness will end,
[ˈloːʊnlɪnɛ(ɪ)s wɪl ɛnd]
loneliness, loneliness will end."
[ˈloːʊnlɪnɛ(ɪ)s ˈloːʊnlɪnɛ(ɪ)s wɪl ɛnd]
And so each little worm
[ænd soːʊ itʃ ˈlɪtʊl wɜm]
Began to sing and squirm,
[bɪˈgæn tu sɪŋ ænd skwɜm]
To sing and squirm,
[tu sɪŋ ænd skwɜm]
A husband and devoted wife
[ʌ ˈhʌzbæ(ɪ)nd ænd dɪˈvoːʊtɛ(ɪ)d waːɪf]
They wiggled their way through life.
[ðɛːɪ ˈwɪgʊld ðɛːʌ wɛːɪ θru laːɪf]
They wiggled,
[ðɛːɪ ˈwɪgʊld]
They squiggled,
[ðɛːɪ ˈskwɪgʊld]
They wiggled, miggled, squiggled, wriggled,
[ðɛːɪ ˈwɪgʊld ˈmɪgʊld ˈskwɪgʊld ˈɹɪgʊld]
Wiggled their way through life.
[ˈwɪgʊld ðɛːʌ wɛːɪ θru laːɪf]

6. The Duck and the Yak
[ðʌ dʌk ænd ðʌ jæk]

Once there was a baby duck,
[wʌns ðɛːʌ waz ʌ ˈbɛːɪbɪ dʌk]
Used to wish he was a yak,
[just tu wɪʃ hi waz ʌ jæk]
Cried for horns and a great big back.
[kɹaːɪd fɔ hɔnz ænd ʌ gɹɛːɪt bɪg bæk]
But the little baby duck
[bʌt ðʌ ˈlɪtʊl ˈbɛːɪbɪ dʌk]
Was completely out of luck;
[waz kʌmˈplitlɪ aːʊt ʌv lʌk]
A duckling can only become a duck.
[ʌ ˈdʌklɪŋ kæn ˈoːʊnlɪ bɪˈkʌm ʌ dʌk]
Once there was a baby yak,
[wʌns ðɛːʌ waz ʌ ˈbɛːɪbɪ jæk]
Used to wish he was a duck,
[just tu wɪʃ hi waz ʌ dʌk]

But the little baby yak,
[bʌt ðʌ ˈlɪtʊl ˈbɛːɪbɪ jæk]
Was completely off the track;
[wɑz kʌmˈplitlɪ ɑf ðʌ tɹæk]
A yakling can only become a yak.
[ʌ ˈjæklɪŋ kæn ˈoːʊnlɪ bɪˈkʌm ʌ jæk]
When sometimes you get tired of you
[ʍɛn ˈsʌmtaːɪmz ju gɛt taːɪʌd ʌv ju]
And wish for things that can't come true,
[ænd wɪʃ fɔ θɪŋz ðæt kænt kʌm tɹ⁽ʳ⁾u]
Don't you cry alas, alack!
[doːʊnt ju kɹaːɪ ʌˈlæs ʌˈlæk]
Remember the story of the duck and the yak.
[ɹɪˈmɛmbʌ ðʌ ˈstɔʁ⁽ʳ⁾ɪ ʌv ðʌ dʌk ænd ðʌ jæk]
Snails will never learn to fly.
[snɛːɪlz wɪl ˈnɛvʌ lɜn tu flaːɪ]
Wouldn't do for birds to try to crawl.
[ˈwʊdɪnt du fɔ bɜdz tu tɹaːɪ tu kɹɔl]
Not at all, not at all, not at all.
[nɑt æt ɔl nɑt æt ɔl nɑt æt ɔl]
A monkey will never become an auk,
[ʌ ˈmʌŋkɪ wɪl ˈnɛvʌ bɪˈkʌm æn ɔk]
And a donkey will never become a hawk,
[ænd ʌ ˈdɑŋkɪ wɪl ˈnɛvʌ bɪˈkʌm ʌ hɔk]
And a duckling can never become a yak.
[ænd ʌ ˈdʌklɪŋ kæn ˈnɛvʌ bɪˈkʌm ʌ jæk]
Remember the story that I tell
[ɹɪˈmɛmbʌ ðʌ ˈstɔʁ⁽ʳ⁾ɪ ðæt aːɪ tɛl]
Of the duck and the yak.
[ʌv ðʌ dʌk ænd ðʌ jæk]
Remember this lesson, learn it well.
[ɹɪˈmɛmbʌ ðɪs ˈlɛsʌn lɜn ɪt wɛl]
Hail the duck, alas, alack and the yak.
[hɛːɪl ðʌ dʌk ʌˈlæs ʌˈlæk ænd ðʌ jæk]

 # Finzi, Gerald (Eng. 1901-1956)

I Said to Love (Song Cycle)
[aːɪ sɛd tu lʌv]
Hardy, Thomas (Eng. 1840-1928)

1. I Need Not Go
[aːɪ nid nɑt goːʊ]

I need not go
[aːɪ nid nɑt goːʊ]
Through sleet and snow
[θɹu slit ænd snoːʊ]
To where I know
[tu ʍɛːʌr aːɪ noːʊ]
She waits for me;
[ʃi wɛːɪts fɔ mi]
She will tarry me there
[ʃi wɪl ˈtærɪ mi ðɛːʌ]

Till I find it fair,
[tɪl aːɪ faːɪnd ɪt fɛːʌ]
And have time to spare
[ænd hæv taːɪm tu spɛːʌ]
From company.
[fɹʌm ˈkʌmpæ⁽ɪ⁾nɪ]
When I've overgot
[ʍɛn aːɪv ˈoːʊvʌgat]
The world somewhat,
[ðʊ wɜld ˈsʌmʍat]
When things cost not
[ʍɛn θɪŋz kast nɑt]
Such stress and strain,
[sʌʧ stɹɛs ænd stɹɛːɪn]
Is soon enough
[ɪz sun ɪˈnʌf]
By cypress sough
[baːɪ ˈsaːɪpɹɛ⁽ɪ⁾s sʌf]
To tell my Love
[tu tɛl maːɪ lʌv]
I am come again.
[aːɪ æm kʌm ʌˈgɛːɪn]
And if someday,
[ænd ɪf ˈsʌmdeːɪ]
When none cries nay,
[ʍɛn nʌn kɹaːɪz nɛːɪ]
I still delay
[aːɪ stɪl dɪˈlɛːɪ]
To seek her side,
[tu sik hɜ saːɪd]
(Though ample measure
[ðoːʊ ˈæmpʊl ˈmɛʒʊ⁽ʌ⁾]
Of fitting leisure
[ʌv ˈfɪtɪŋ ˈlɛʒʊ⁽ʌ⁾]
Await my pleasure)
[ʌˈwɛːɪt maːɪ ˈplɛʒʊ⁽ʌ⁾]
She will not chide.
[ʃi wɪl nɑt ʧaːɪd]
What not upbraid me
[ʍat nɑt ʌpˈbɹɛːɪd mi]
That I delayed me,
[ðæt aːɪ dɪˈlɛːɪd mi]
Nor ask what stayed me
[nɔʁ⁽ʳ⁾ ask ʍat stɛːɪd mi]
So long? Ah, no!
[soːʊ laŋ ɑ noːʊ]
New cares may claim me,
[nju kɛːʌz mɛːɪ klɛːɪm mi]
New loves inflame me,
[nju lʌvz ɪnˈflɛːɪm mi]
She will not blame me,
[ʃi wɪl nɑt blɛːɪm mi]
But suffer it so.
[bʌt ˈsʌfʌr ɪt soːʊ]

2. At Middlegate-Field in February
[æt ˈmɪdʊlgɛːɪt fild ɪn ˈfɛbɹuɛʁi aːɪ sɛd tu lʌv]

The bars are thick with drops that show
[ðʊ baz ɑ θɪk wɪð dɹaps ðæt ʃoːʊ]
As they gather themselves from the fog
[æz ðɛːɪ ˈgæðʌ ðɛmˈsɛlvz fɹʌm ðʊ fag]
Like silver buttons ranged in a row,
[laːɪk ˈsɪlvʌ ˈbʌtʌnz ɹɛːɪndʒd ɪn ʌ roːʊ]
And as evenly spaced as if measured, although
[ænd æz ˈiːvɛ(ɪ)nlɪ spɛːɪst æz ɪf ˈmɛʒʊ(ʌ)d ɔlˈðoːʊ]
They fall at the feeblest jog.
[ðɛːɪ fɔl æt ðʊ ˈfiblɛ(ɪ)st dʒag]
They load the leafless hedge hard by,
[ðɛːɪ loːʊd ðʊ ˈliflɛ(ɪ)s hɛdʒ had baːɪ]
And the blades of last year's grass,
[ænd ðʊ blɛːɪdz ʌv last jiːʌz gɹas]
While the fallow ploughland turned up nigh
[ʍaːɪl ðʊ ˈfæloːʊ ˈplaːʊlæ(ʌ)nd tɜnd ʌp naːɪ]
In raw rolls, clammy and clogging lie–
[ɪn ɹɔ roːʊlz ˈklæmɪ ænd ˈklagɪŋ laːɪ]
Too clogging for feet to pass.
[tu ˈklagɪŋ fɔ fit tu pas]
How dry it was on a farback day
[haːʊ dɹaːɪ ɪt waz an ʌ ˈfabæk dɛːɪ]
When straws hung the hedge and around,
[ʍɛn stɹɔz hʌŋ ðʊ hɛdʒ ænd ʌˈraːʊnd]
When amid the sheaves in amorous play
[ʍɛn ʌˈmɪd ðʊ ʃivz ɪn ˈæmɔɹʌs plɛːɪ]
In curtained bonnets and light array
[ɪn ˈkɜtæ(ɪ)nd ˈbanɛ(ɪ)ts ænd laːɪt ʌˈrɛːɪ]
Bloomed a bevy now underground!
[blumd ʌ ˈbɛvɪ naːʊ ʌndʌˈgɹaːʊnd]

3. Two Lips
[tu lɪps]

I kissed them in fancy as I came
[aːɪ kɪst ðɛm ɪn ˈfænsɪ æz aːɪ kɛːɪm]
Away in the morning glow:
[ʌˈwɛːɪ ɪn ðʊ ˈmɔnɪŋ gloːʊ]
I kissed them through the glass of her picture-frame:
[aːɪ kɪst ðɛm θɾu ðʊ glas ʌv hɜ ˈpɪktʃʊ(ʌ) fɹɛːɪm]
She did not know.
[ʃi dɪd nat noːʊ]
I kissed them in love, in troth, in laughter,
[aːɪ kɪst ðɛm ɪn lʌv ɪn tɹoːʊθ ɪn ˈlaftʌ]
When she knew all; long so!
[ʍɛn ʃi nju ɔl laŋ soːʊ]
That I should kiss them in a shroud thereafter
[ðæt aːɪ ʃʊd kɪs ðɛm ɪn ʌ ʃɹaːʊd ðɛːʌɾˈaftʌ]
She did not know.
[ʃi dɪd nat noːʊ]

4. In Five-Score Summers
[ɪn faːɪv skɔːʌ ˈsʌmʌz]

In five-score summers! All new eyes,
[ɪn faːɪv skɔːʌ ˈsʌmʌz ɔl nju aːɪz]
New minds, new modes, new fools, new wise;
[nju maːɪndz nju moːʊdz nju fulz nju waːɪz]
New woes to weep, new joys to prize;
[nju woːʊz tu wip nju dʒɔːɪz tu pɹaːɪz]
With nothing left of me and you
[wɪð ˈnʌθɪŋ lɛft ʌv mi ænd ju]
In that live century's vivid view
[ɪn ðæt laːɪv ˈsɛntʃʊɹɪz ˈvɪvɪd vju]
Beyond a pinch of dust or two;
[bɪˈjand ʌ pɪntʃ ʌv dʌst ɔ tu]
A century which, if not sublime,
[ʌ ˈsɛntʃʊɹɪ ʍɪtʃ ɪf nat sʌˈblaːɪm]
Will show, I doubt not, at its prime,
[wɪl ʃoːʊ aːɪ daːʊt nat æt ɪts pɹaːɪm]
A scope above this blinkered time.
[ʌ skoːʊp ʌˈbʌv ðɪs ˈblɪŋkʌd taːɪm]
–Yet what to me how far above?
[jɛt ʍat tu mi haːʊ faɾ ʌˈbʌv]
For I would only ask thereof
[fɔʁ⁽ʳ⁾ aːɪ wʊd ˈoːʊnlɪ ask ðɛːʌɾˈʌv]
That thy worm should be my worm, Love!
[ðæt ðaːɪ wɜm ʃʊd bi maːɪ wɜm lʌv]

5. For Life I Had Never Cared Greatly
[fɔ laːɪf aːɪ hæd ˈnɛvʌ kɛːʌd ˈgɹɛːɪtlɪ]

For Life I had never cared greatly,
[fɔ laːɪf aːɪ hæd ˈnɛvʌ kɛːʌd ˈgɹɛːɪtlɪ]
As worth a man's while;
[æz wɜθ ʌ mænz ʍaːɪl]
Peradventures unsought,
[pɛɾædˈvɛntʃʊ(ʌ)z ʌnˈsɔt]
Peradventures that finished in nought,
[pɛɾædˈvɛntʃʊ(ʌ)z ðæt ˈfɪnɪʃt ɪn nɔt]
Had kept me from youth
[hæd kɛpt mi fɹʌm juθ]
and through manhood till lately
[ænd θɾu ˈmænhʊd tɪl ˈlɛːɪtlɪ]
Unwon by its style.
[ʌnˈwʌn baːɪ ɪts staːɪl]
In earliest years– why I know not–
[ɪn ˈɜlɪɛ(ɪ)st jiːʌz ʍaːɪ aːɪ noːʊ nat]
I viewed it askance;
[aːɪ vjud ɪt ʌˈskans]
Conditions of doubt,
[kʌnˈdɪʃʌnz ʌv daːʊt]
Conditions that leaked slowly out,
[kʌnˈdɪʃʌnz ðæt likt ˈsloːʊlɪ aːʊt]
May haply have bent me to stand and to show not
[mɛːɪ ˈhæplɪ hæv bɛnt mi tu stænd ænd tu ʃoːʊ nat]

Much zest for its dance.
[mʌtʃ zɛst fɔʁ⁽ⁱ⁾ ɪts dɑns]
With symphonies soft and sweet colour
[wɪð ˈsɪmfo(ʌ)nɪz sɑft ænd swit ˈkʌlʊ(ʌ)]
It courted me then,
[ɪt ˈkɔtɛ(ɪ)d mi ðɛn]
Till evasions seemed wrong,
[tɪl ɪˈvɛːɪʒʌnz simd ɹɑŋ]
Till evasions gave in to its song,
[tɪl ɪˈvɛːɪʒʌnz gɛːɪv ɪn tu ɪts sɑŋ]
And I warmed, until living aloofly loomed duller
[ænd ɑːɪ wɔmd ʌnˈtɪl ˈlɪvɪŋ ʌˈluflɪ lumd ˈdʌlʌ]
Than life among men.
[ðæn lɑːɪf ʌˈmʌŋ mɛn]
Anew I found nought to set eyes on,
[ʌˈnju ɑːɪ fɑːʊnd nɔt tu sɛt ɑːɪz ɑn]
When, lifting its hand,
[ʍɛn ˈlɪftɪŋ ɪts hænd]
It uncloaked a star,
[ɪt ʌnˈkloːʊkt ʌ stɑ]
Uncloaked it from fog-damps afar,
[ʌnˈkloːʊkt ɪt fɹʌm fɑg dæmps ʌˈfɑ]
And showed its beams burning from pole to horizon
[ænd ʃoːʊd ɪts bimz ˈbɜnɪŋ fɹʌm poːʊl tu hɔˈɹɑːɪzʌn]
As bright as a brand.
[æz bɹɑːɪt æz ʌ bɹænd]
And so, the rough highway forgetting,
[ænd soːʊ ðʊ ɹʌf ˈhɑːɪwɛːɪ fɔˈgɛtɪŋ]
I pace hill and dale
[ɑːɪ pɛːɪs hɪl ænd dɛːɪl]
Regarding the sky,
[ɹɪˈgɑdɪŋ ðʊ skɑːɪ]
Regarding the vision on high,
[ɹɪˈgɑdɪŋ ðʊ ˈvɪʒʌn ɑn hɑːɪ]
And thus re-illumed have no humour for letting
[ænd ðʌs ˌɹiːˈljumd hæv noːʊ ˈhjumʊ(ʌ) fɔ ˈlɛtɪŋ]
My pilgrimage fail.
[mɑːɪ ˈpɪlgɹɪmæ(ɪ)dʒ fɛːɪl]

6. I Said to Love
[ɑːɪ sɛd tu lʌv]

I said to Love,
[ɑːɪ sɛd tu lʌv]
"It is not now as in old days
[ɪt ɪz nɑt nɑːʊ æz ɪn oːʊld dɛːɪz]
When men adored thee and thy ways
[ʍɛn mɛn ʌˈdɔːɑd ði ænd ðɑːɪ wɛːɪz]
All else above;
[ɔl ɛls ʌˈbʌv]
Named thee the Boy, the Bright, the One
[nɛːɪmd ði ðʊ bɔːɪ ðʊ bɹɑːɪt ðʊ wʌn]
Who spread a heaven beneath the sun,"
[hu spɹɛd ʌ ˈhɛvɛ(ɪ)n bɪˈniθ ðʊ sʌn]
I said to Love.
[ɑːɪ sɛd tu lʌv]

I said to him,
[ɑːɪ sɛd tu hɪm]
"We now know more of thee than then;
[wi nɑːʊ noːʊ mɔːʌɾ ʌv ði ðæn ðɛn]
We were but weak in judgment when,
[wi wɜ bʌt wik ɪn ˈdʒʌdʒmɛnt ʍɛn]
With hearts abrim,
[wɪð hɑts ʌˈbɹɪm]
We clamoured thee that thou would'st please
[wi ˈklæmʊ(ʌ)d ði ðæt ðɑːʊ wʊdst pliz]
Inflict on us thine agonies,"
[ɪnˈflɪkt ɑn ʌs ðɑːɪn ˈægo(ʌ)nɪz]
I said to him.
[ɑːɪ sɛd tu hɪm]
I said to Love,
[ɑːɪ sɛd tu lʌv]
"Thou art not young, thou art not fair,
[ðɑːʊ ɑt nɑt jʌŋ ðɑːʊ ɑt nɑt fɛːʌ]
No elfin darts, no cherub air,
[noːʊ ˈɛlfɪn dɑts noːʊ ˈtʃɛɾʌb ɛːʌ]
Nor swan, nor dove
[nɔ swɑn nɔ dʌv]
Are thine; but features pitiless,
[ɑ ðɑːɪn bʌt ˈfitʃʊ(ʌ)z ˈpɪtɪlɛ(ɪ)s]
And iron daggers of distress,"
[ænd ˈɑːɪʌn ˈdægʌz ʌv dɪˈstɹɛs]
I said to Love.
[ɑːɪ sɛd tu lʌv]
"Depart then, Love!
[dɪˈpɑt ðɛn lʌv]
—Man's race shall perish, threatenest thou,
[mænz ɹɛːɪs ʃæl ˈpɛɹɪʃ ˈθɹɛtɛ(ɪ)nɛ(ɪ)st ðɑːʊ]
Without thy kindling coupling-vow?
[wɪðˈɑːʊt ðɑːɪ ˈkɪndlɪŋ ˈkʌplɪŋ vɑːʊ]
The age to come the man of now
[ði ɛːɪdʒ tu kʌm ðʊ mæn ʌv nɑːʊ]
Know nothing of? –
[noːʊ ˈnʌθɪŋ ʌv]
We fear not such a threat from thee;
[wi fiːʌ nɑt sʌtʃ ʌ θɹɛt fɹʌm ði]
We are too old in apathy!
[wi ɑ tu oːʊld ɪn ˈæpʌθɪ]
Mankind shall cease. –
[mænˈkɑːɪnd ʃæl sis]
So let it be,"
[soːʊ lɛt ɪt bi]
I said to Love.
[ɑːɪ sɛd tu lʌv]

Till Earth Outwears (Song Cycle)
[tɪl ɜθ ɑːʊtˈweːʌz]
Hardy, Thomas (Eng. 1840-1928)

1. Let Me Enjoy the Earth
[lɛt mi ɪnˈʤɔːɪ ði ɜθ]

Let me enjoy the earth no less
[lɛt mi ɪnˈʤɔːɪ ði ɜθ noːʊ lɛs]
Because the all-enacting Might
[bɪˈkɔz ði ɔl ɪˈnæktɪŋ maːɪt]
That fashioned forth its loveliness
[ðæt ˈfæʃʌnd fɔθ ɪts ˈlʌvlɪnɛ(ɪ)s]
Had other aims than my delight.
[hæd ˈʌðʌɾ ɛːɪmz ðæn maːɪ dɪˈlaːɪt]
About my path there flits a Fair,
[ʌˈbaːʊt maːɪ paθ ðɛːʌ flɪts ʌ fɛːʌ]
Who throws me not a word or sign;
[hu θroːʊz mi nɑt ʌ wɜd ɔ saːɪn]
I'll charm me with her ignoring air,
[aːɪl ʧɑm mi wɪð hɜ(ʳ) ɪgˈnɔːʌɾɪŋ ɛːʌ]
And laud the lips not meant for mine.
[ænd lɔd ðʊ lɪps nɑt mɛnt fɔ maːɪn]
From manuscripts of moving song
[fɹʌm ˈmænjuˌskɹɪpts ʌv ˈmuvɪŋ sɑŋ]
Inspired by scenes and dreams unknown
[ɪnˈspaːɪʌd baːɪ sinz ænd dɹimz ʌnˈnoːʊn]
I'll pour out raptures that belong
[aːɪl pɔːʌɾ aːʊt ˈɹæpʧʊ(ʌ)z ðæt bɪˈlɑŋ]
To others, as they were my own.
[tu ˈʌðʌz æz ðɛːɪ wɜ maːɪ oːʊn]
And some day hence, towards Paradise
[ænd sʌm dɛːɪ hɛns twɔdz ˈpæɾʌdaːɪs]
And all its blest– if such should be–
[ænd ɔl ɪts blɛst ɪf sʌʧ ʃʊd bi]
I will lift glad, a far-off eyes,
[aːɪ wɪl lɪft glæd ʌ far ɑf aːɪz]
Though it contain no place for me.
[ðoːʊ ɪt kʌnˈteːɪn noːʊ plɛːɪs fɔ mi]

2. In Years Defaced
[ɪn jɪːʌz dɪˈfeːɪst]

In years defaced and lost,
[ɪn jɪːʌz dɪˈfeːɪst ænd lɑst]
Two sat here, transport-tossed,
[tu sæt hiːʌ ˈtɹænspɔt tɑst]
Lit by a living love
[lɪt baːɪ ʌ ˈlɪvɪŋ lʌv]
The wilted world knew nothing of:
[ðʊ ˈwɪltɛ(ɪ)d wɜld nju ˈnʌθɪŋ ʌv]
Scared momently
[skɛːʌd ˈmoːʊmɛntlɪ]
By gain-givings,
[baːɪ gɛːɪn ˈgɪvɪŋz]

Then hoping things
[ðɛn ˈhoːʊpɪŋ θɪŋz]
That could not be.
[ðæt kʊd nɑt bi]
Of love and us no trace
[ʌv lʌv ænd ʌs noːʊ tɹɛːɪs]
Abides upon the place;
[ʌˈbaːɪdz ʌˈpɑn ðʊ plɛːɪs]
The sun and shadows wheel,
[ðʊ sʌn ænd ˈʃædoːʊz ʍil]
Season and season sereward steal:
[ˈsizʌn ænd ˈsizʌn ˈsɪːʌwʊd stil]
Foul days and fair
[faːʊl dɛːɪz ænd fɛːʌ]
Here, too, prevail,
[hɪːʌ tu pɹɪˈveːɪl]
And gust and gale
[ænd gʌst ænd gɛːɪl]
As everywhere.
[æz ˈɛvɹɪʍɛːʌ]
But lonely shepherd souls
[bʌt ˈloːʊnlɪ ˈʃɛpʌd soːʊlz]
Who bask amid these knolls
[hu bask ʌˈmɪd ðiz noːʊlz]
May catch a faery sound
[mɛːɪ kæʧ ʌ ˈfɛːʌɾɪ saːʊnd]
On sleepy noon-tides from the ground:
[ɑn ˈslipɪ nun taːɪdz fɹʌm ðʊ gɹaːʊnd]
"O not again
[oːʊ nɑt ʌˈgɛn]
Till Earth outwears
[tɪl ɜθ ɑːʊtˈweːʌz]
Shall love like theirs
[ʃæl lʌv laːɪk ðɛːʌz]
Suffuse this glen!"
[sʌˈfjuz ðɪs glɛn]

3. The Market-Girl
[ðʊ ˈmɑkɪt gɜl]

Nobody took any notice of her
[ˈnoːʊbɑdɪ tʊk ˈɛnɪ ˈnoːʊtɪs ʌv hɜ]
as she stood on the causey kerb,
[æz ʃi stʊd ɑn ðʊ ˈkɔzɪ kɜb]
All eager to sell her honey and apples
[ɔl ˈigʌ tu sɛl hɜ ˈhʌnɪ ænd ˈæpʊlz]
and bunches of garden herb;
[ænd ˈbʌnʧɛ(ɪ)z ʌv ˈgɑdɛ(ɪ)n ɜb]
And if she had offered to give her wares
[ænd ɪf ʃi hæd ˈɑfʌd tu gɪv hɜ wɛːʌz]
and herself with them too that day,
[ænd hɜˈsɛlf wɪð ðɛm tu ðæt dɛːɪ]
I doubt if a soul would have cared
[aːɪ daːʊt ɪf ʌ soːʊl wʊd hæv kɛːʌd]
to take a bargain so choice away.
[tu tɛːɪk ʌ ˈbagæ(ɪ)n soːʊ ʧɔːɪs ʌˈweːɪ]

But chancing to trace her sunburnt grace
[bʌt ˈtʃansɪŋ tu tɹeːɪs hɜ ˈsʌnbɜnt gɹeːɪs]
that morning as I passed nigh,
[ðæt ˈmɔnɪŋ æz ɑːɪ past naːɪ]
I went and I said, "Poor maidy dear!–
[ɑːɪ wɛnt ænd ɑːɪ sɛd puːʌ ˈmeːɪdɪ dɪːʌɾ]
and will none of the people buy?"
[ænd wɪl nʌn ʌv ðʊ ˈpipʊl baːɪ]
And so it began;
[ænd soːʊ ɪt bɪˈgæn]
and soon we knew what the end of it all must be,
[ænd sun wi nju ʍɑt ði ɛnd ʌv ɪt ɔl mʌst bi]
And I found that though no others had bid,
[ænd ɑːɪ faːʊnd ðæt ðoːʊ noːʊ ˈʌðʌz hæd bɪd]
a prize had been won by me.
[ʌ pɹɑːɪz hæd bin wʌn baːɪ mi]

4. I Look into My Glass
[ɑːɪ lʊk ˈɪntu maːɪ glas]

I look into my glass,
[ɑːɪ lʊk ˈɪntu maːɪ glas]
And view my wasting skin,
[ænd vju maːɪ ˈweːɪstɪŋ skɪn]
And say, "Would God it came to pass
[ænd seːɪ wʊd gad ɪt keːɪm tu pas]
My heart had shrunk as thin!"
[maːɪ hat hæd ʃɹʌŋk æz θɪn]
For then, I, undistrest
[fɔ ðɛn ɑːɪ ʌndɪˈstɹɛst]
By hearts grown cold to me,
[baːɪ hats gɹoːʊn koːʊld tu mi]
Could lonely wait my endless rest
[kʊd ˈloːʊnlɪ weːɪt maːɪ ˈɛndlɛ(ɪ)s ɹɛst]
With equanimity.
[wɪð ˌɛkwʌˈnɪmɪtɪ]
But Time, to make me grieve,
[bʌt taːɪm tu meːɪk mi gɹiv]
Part steals, lets part abide;
[pat stilz lɛts pat ʌˈbaːɪd]
And shakes this fragile frame at eve
[ænd ʃeːɪks ðɪs ˈfɹædʒaːɪl fɹeːɪm æt iv]
With throbbings of noontide.
[wɪð ˈθɹabɪŋz ʌv ˈnuntaːɪd]

5. It Never Looks like Summer
[ɪt ˈnɛvʌ lʊks laːɪk ˈsʌmʌ]

"It never looks like summer here
[ɪt ˈnɛvʌ lʊks laːɪk ˈsʌmʌ hɪːʌɾ]
On Beeny by the sea."
[an ˈbinɪ baːɪ ðʊ si]
But though she saw its look as drear,
[bʌt ðoːʊ ʃi sɔ ɪts lʊk æz dɹɪːʌ]
Summer it seemed to me.
[ˈsʌmʌɾ ɪt simd tu mi]

It never looks like summer now
[ɪt ˈnɛvʌ lʊks laːɪk ˈsʌmʌ naːʊ]
Whatever weather's there;
[ʍat'ɛvʌ ˈwɛðʌz ðɛːʌ]
But ah, it cannot anyhow,
[bʌt ɑ ɪt kæˈnat ˈɛnihaːʊ]
On Beeny or elsewhere!
[an ˈbinɪ ɔʁ⁽ʳ⁾ ˈɛlsʍɛːʌ]

6. At a Lunar Eclipse
[æt ʌ ˈlunʁ ɪˈklɪps]

Thy shadow, Earth, from Pole to Central Sea,
[ðaːɪ ˈʃædoːʊ ɜθ fɹʌm poːʊl tu ˈsɛntɹol si]
Now steals along upon the Moon's meek shine
[naːʊ stilz ʌˈlaŋ ʌˈpan ðʊ munz mik ʃaːɪn]
In even monochrome and curving line
[ɪn ˈivɛ(ɪ)n ˈmano(ʌ)ˌkɹoːʊm ænd ˈkɜvɪŋ laːɪn]
Of imperturbable serenity.
[ʌv ɪmpɜˈtɜbʌbʊl sɜˈɹɛnɪtɪ]
How shall I link such suncast symmetry
[haːʊ ʃæl ɑːɪ lɪŋk sʌtʃ ˈsʌnkast ˈsɪmɛ(ɪ)tɹɪ]
With the torn troubled form I know as thine,
[wɪð ðʊ tɔn ˈtɹʌbʊld fɔm ɑːɪ noːʊ æz ðaːɪn]
That profile, placid as a brow divine,
[ðæt ˈpɹoːʊfaːɪl ˈplæsɪd æz ʌ bɹaːʊ dɪˈvaːɪn]
With continents of moil and misery?
[wɪð ˈkantɪnɛnts ʌv mɔːɪl ænd ˈmɪzʌɾɪ]
And can immense Mortality but throw
[ænd kæn ɪˈmɛns mɔˈtælɪtɪ bʌt θɹoːʊ]
So small a shade,
[soːʊ smɔl ʌ ʃɛːɪd]
and Heaven's high human scheme
[ænd ˈhɛvɛ(ɪ)nz haːɪ ˈhjumæ(ʌ)n skim]
Be hemmed within the coasts yon arc implies?
[bi hɛmd wɪðˈɪn ðʊ koːʊsts jan ak ɪmˈplaːɪz]
Is such the stellar gauge of earthly show,
[ɪz sʌtʃ ðʊ ˈstɛlʌ gɛːɪdʒ ʌv ˈɜθlɪ ʃoːʊ]
Nation at war with nation, brains that teem,
[ˈnɛːɪʃʌn æt wɔ wɪð ˈnɛːɪʃʌn bɹɛːɪnz ðæt tim]
Heroes, and women fairer than the skies?
[ˈhɪːʌɾoːʊz ænd ˈwɪmɛ(ɪ)n ˈfɛːʌɾʌ ðæn ðʊ skaːɪz]

7. Life Laughs Onward
[laːɪf lafs ˈɑnwʊd]

Rambling I looked for an old abode
[ˈɹæmblɪŋ ɑːɪ lʊkt fɔʁ⁽ʳ⁾ æn oːʊld ʌˈboːʊd]
Where, years back, one had lived I knew;
[ʍɛːʌ jɪːʌz bæk wʌn hæd lɪvd ɑːɪ nju]
Its site a dwelling duly showed,
[ɪts saːɪt ʌ ˈdwɛlɪŋ ˈdjulɪ ʃoːʊd]
But it was new.
[bʌt ɪt waz nju]
I went where, not so long ago,
[ɑːɪ wɛnt ʍɛːʌ nat soːʊ laŋ ʌˈgoːʊ]

The sod had riven two breasts asunder;
[ðʊ sad hæd ˈɹɪvɛ(ɪ)n tu bɹɛsts ʌˈsʌndʌ]
Daisies throve gaily there, as though
[ˈdɛːɪzɪz θɹoːʊv ˈgɛːɪlɪ ðɛːʌ æz ðoːʊ]
No grave were under.
[noːʊ gɹɛːɪv wɜ ˈʌndʌ]
I walked along a terrace where
[ɑːɪ wɔkt ʌˈlɑŋ ʌ ˈtɛɹæ(ɪ)s ʍɛːʌ]
Loud children gambolled in the sun:
[lɑːʊd ˈʧɪldɹɛ(ɪ)n ˈgæmbʊld ɪn ðʊ sʌn]
The figure that had once sat there
[ðʊ ˈfɪgʊ(ʌ) ðæt hæd wʌns sæt ðɛːʌ]
Was missed by none.
[wɑz mɪst bɑːɪ nʌn]
Life laughed and moved on unsubdued,
[lɑːɪf laft ænd muvd ɑn ˌʌnsʌbˈdjud]
I saw that Old succumbed to Young:
[ɑːɪ sɔ ðæt oːʊld sʌˈkʌmd tu jʌŋ]
'Twas well my too regretful mood
[twɑz wɛl mɑːɪ tu ɹɪˈgɹɛtfʊl mud]
Died on my tongue.
[dɑːɪd ɑn mɑːɪ tʌŋ]

Oh Fair to See (Song Cycle)
[oːʊ fɛːʌ tu si]

1. I Say I'll Seek Her
[ɑːɪ sɛːɪ ɑːɪl sik hɜ]
Hardy, Thomas (Eng. 1840-1928)

I say "I'll seek her side
[ɑːɪ sɛːɪ ɑːɪl sik hɜ sɑːɪd]
Ere hindrance interposes;"
[ɛːʌ ˈhɪndɹæ(ɪ)ns ɪntʌˈpoːʊzɛ(ɪ)z]
But eve in midnight closes,
[bʌt iv ɪn ˈmɪdnɑːɪt ˈkloːʊzɛ(ɪ)z]
And here I still abide.
[ænd hɪːʌ ɑːɪ stɪl ʌˈbɑːɪd]
When darkness wears I see
[ʍɛn ˈdaknɛ(ɪ)s wɛːʌz ɑːɪ si]
Her sad eyes in a vision;
[hɜ sæd ɑːɪz ɪn ʌ ˈvɪʒʌn]
They ask, "What indecision
[ðɛːɪ ask ʍat ɪndɪˈsɪʒʌn]
Detains you, Love, from me?–
[dɪˈtɛːɪnz ju lʌv fɹʌm mi]
The creaking hinge is oiled,
[ðʊ ˈkɹikɪŋ hɪndʒ ɪz ɔːɪld]
I have unbarred the backway,
[ɑːɪ hæv ʌnˈbad ðʊ ˈbækwɛːɪ]
But you tread not the trackway;
[bʌt ju tɹɛd nat ðʊ ˈtɹækwɛːɪ]
And shall the thing be spoiled?
[ænd ʃæl ðʊ θɪŋ bi spɔːɪld]
Far cockcrows echo shrill,
[fa ˈkakkɹoːʊz ˈɛkoːʊ ʃɹɪl]

The shadows are abating,
[ðʊ ˈʃædoːʊz ɑɹ ʌˈbɛːɪtɪŋ]
And I am waiting, waiting;
[ænd ɑːɪ æm ˈwɛːɪtɪŋ ˈwɛːɪtɪŋ]
But O, you tarry still."
[bʌt oːʊ ju ˈtæɹɪ stɪl]

2. Oh Fair to See
[oːʊ fɛːʌ tu si]
Rossetti, Christina Georgina (Eng. 1830-1894)

Oh fair to see
[oːʊ fɛːʌ tu si]
Bloom-laden cherry tree,
[blum ˈlɛːɪdɛ(ɪ)n ˈʧɛɹɪ tɹi]
Arrayed in sunny white,
[ʌˈɹɛːɪd ɪn ˈsʌnɪ ʍɑːɪt]
An April day's delight;
[æn ˈɛːɪpɹɪ(ʊ)l dɛːɪz dɪˈlɑːɪt]
Oh fair to see!
[oːʊ fɛːʌ tu si]
Fruit-laden cherry tree,
[fɹut ˈlɛːɪdɛ(ɪ)n ˈʧɛɹɪ tɹi]
With balls of shining red
[wɪð bɔlz ʌv ˈʃɑːɪnɪŋ ɹɛd]
Decking a leafy head;
[ˈdɛkɪŋ ʌ ˈlifɪ hɛd]
Oh fair to see!
[oːʊ fɛːʌ tu si]

3. As I Lay in the Early Sun
[æz ɑːɪ lɛːɪ ɪn ði ˈɜli sʌn]
Shanks, Edward (Eng. 1892-1953)

As I lay in the early sun,
[æz ɑːɪ lɛːɪ ɪn ði ˈɜli sʌn]
Stretched in the grass, I thought upon
[stɹɛʧt ɪn ðʊ gɹas ɑːɪ θɔt ʌˈpan]
My true love, my dear love,
[mɑːɪ tru lʌv mɑːɪ dɪːʌ lʌv]
Who has my heart forever
[hu hæz mɑːɪ hat fɔʁ⁽ʳ⁾ˈɛvʌ]
Who is my happiness when we meet,
[hu ɪz mɑːɪ ˈhæpɪnɛ(ɪ)s ʍɛn wi mit]
My sorrow when we sever.
[mɑːɪ ˈsaɹoːʊ ʍɛn wi ˈsɛvʌ]
She is all fire when I do burn,
[ʃi ɪz ɔl fɑːɪʌ ʍɛn ɑːɪ du bɜn]
Gentle when I moody turn,
[ˈdʒɛntʊl ʍɛn ɑːɪ ˈmudɪ tɜn]
Brave when I am sad and heavy
[bɹɛːɪv ʍɛn ɑːɪ æm sæd ænd ˈhɛvɪ]
And all laughter when I am merry.
[ænd ɔl ˈlaftʌ ʍɛn ɑːɪ æm ˈmɛɹɪ]
And so I lay and dreamed and dreamed,
[ænd soːʊ ɑːɪ lɛːɪ ænd dɹimd ænd dɹimd]

And so the day wheeled on,
[ænd soːʊ ðʊ dɛːɪ ʍild ɑn]
While all the birds with thoughts like mine
[ʍɑːɪl ɔl ðʊ bɜdz wɪð θɔts lɑːɪk mɑːɪn]
Were singing to the sun.
[wɜ ˈsɪŋɪŋ tu ðʊ sʌn]

4. Only the Wanderer
[ˈoːʊnli ðʊ ˈwandʌʁʌ]
Gurney, Ivor (Bertie) (Eng. 1890-1937)

Only the wanderer
[ˈoːʊnlɪ ðʊ ˈwandʌʁʌ]
Knows England's graces,
[noːʊz ˈɪŋglæ(ʌ)ndz ˈgʁɛːɪsɛ(ɪ)z]
Or can anew see clear
[ɔ kæn ʌˈnju si klɪːʌ]
Familiar faces.
[fʌˈmɪljʌ ˈfɛːɪsɛ(ɪ)z]
And who loves joy as he
[ænd hu lʌvz dʒɔːɪ æz hi]
That dwells in shadows?
[ðæt dwɛlz ɪn ˈʃædoːʊz]
Do not forget me quite,
[du nɑt fɔˈgɛt mi kwɑːɪt]
O Severn meadows.
[oːʊ ˈsɛvʌn ˈmɛdoːʊz]

5. To Joy (copyright)

6. Harvest (copyright)

7. Since We Loved
[sɪns wi lʌvd]
Bridges, Robert Seymour (Eng. 1844-1930)

Since we loved,– (the earth that shook
[sɪns wi lʌvd ði ɜθ ðæt ʃʊk]
As we kissed, fresh beauty took)–
[æz wi kɪst fʁɛʃ ˈbjutɪ tʊk]
Love hath been as poets paint,
[lʌv hæθ bin æz ˈpoːʊɛ(ɪ)ts pɛːɪnt]
Life as heaven is to a saint;
[lɑːɪf æz ˈhɛvɛ(ɪ)n ɪz tu ʌ sɛːɪnt]
All my joys my hope excel,
[ɔl mɑːɪ dʒɔːɪz mɑːɪ hoːʊp ɪkˈsɛl]
All my work hath prosper'd well,
[ɔl mɑːɪ wɜk hæθ ˈpʁaspʌd wɛl]
All my songs have happy been,
[ɔl mɑːɪ sɑŋz hæv ˈhæpɪ bin]
O my love, my life, my queen.
[oːʊ mɑːɪ lʌv mɑːɪ lɑːɪf mɑːɪ kwin]

Song Selection

"Who Is Sylvia?" (see Coates)

 # Fletcher, Linda, arr. (Ca. b. 1954)

Song Selection

"Olde Irish Blessing"
[oːʊld ˈɑːɪʁɪʃ ˈblɛsɪŋ]
Traditional

May the road rise to meet you;
[mɛːɪ ðʌ ʁoːʊd ʁɑːɪz tu mit ju]
May the wind be always at your back;
[mɛːɪ ðʌ wind bi ˈɔlwɛːɪz æt jɔːʌ bæk]
May the sun shine warm upon your face;
[mɛːɪ ðʌ sʌn ʃɑːɪn wɔm ʌˈpan jɔːʌ fɛːɪs]
May the rain fall soft upon your fields;
[mɛːɪ ðʌ ʁɛːɪn fɔl saft ʌˈpan jɔːʌ fildz]
And until we meet again;
[ænd ʌnˈtɪl wi mit ʌˈgɛn]
May God hold you in the palm of his hand.
[mɛːɪ gad hoːʊld ju ɪn ðʌ pam ʌv hɪz hænd]

Foster, Stephen (Am. 1826-1864)

Song Selections

"Ah! May the Red Rose Live Alway"
[ɑ mɛːɪ ðʌ ʁɛd ʁoːʊz lɪv ˈɔlwɛːɪ]
Foster, Stephen (Am. 1826-1864)

Ah! may the red rose live alway,
[ɑ mɛːɪ ðʌ ʁɛd ʁoːʊz lɪv ˈɔlwɛːɪ]
To smile upon earth and sky!
[tu smɑːɪl ʌˈpan ɜθ ænd skɑːɪ]
Why should the beautiful ever weep?
[ʍɑːɪ ʃʊd ðʌ ˈbjutɪfʊl ˈɛvʌ wip]
Why should the beautiful die?
[ʍɑːɪ ʃʊd ðʌ ˈbjutɪfʊl dɑːɪ]
Lending a charm to ev'ry ray
[ˈlɛndɪŋ ʌ tʃam tu ˈɛvʁɪ ʁɛːɪ]
That falls on her cheeks of light,
[ðæt fɔlz an hɜ tʃiks ʌv lɑːɪt]
Giving the zephyr kiss for kiss,
[ˈgɪvɪŋ ðʌ ˈzɛfʌ kɪs fɔ kɪs]
And nursing the dew-drop bright–
[ænd ˈnɜsɪŋ ðʌ dju dʁap bʁɑːɪt]
Ah! may the red rose live alway,
[ɑ mɛːɪ ðʌ ʁɛd ʁoːʊz lɪv ˈɔlwɛːɪ]
To smile upon earth and sky!
[tu smɑːɪl ʌˈpan ɜθ ænd skɑːɪ]

Why should the beautiful ever weep?
[ʍaːɪ ʃʊd ðʌ 'bjutɪfʊl 'ɛvʌ wip]
Why should the beautiful die?
[ʍaːɪ ʃʊd ðʌ 'bjutɪfʊl daːɪ]
Long may the daisies dance the field,
[laŋ mɛːɪ ðʌ 'dɛːɪzɪz dæns ðʌ fild]
Frolicking far and near!
['fɹɑlɪkɪŋ faʁ⁽ʳ⁾ ænd nɪːʌ]
Why should the innocent hide their heads?
[ʍaːɪ ʃʊd ði 'ɪno(ʌ)sɛnt haːɪd ðɛːʌ hɛdz]
Why should the innocent fear?
[ʍaːɪ ʃʊd ði 'ɪno(ʌ)sɛnt fɪːʌ]
Spreading their petals in mute delight
['spɹɛdɪŋ ðɛːʌ 'pɛtʊlz ɪn mjut dɪ'laːɪt]
When morn in its radiance breaks,
[ʍɛn mɔn ɪn ɪts 'ɹɛːɪdɪæ(ɪ)ns bɹɛːɪks]
Keeping a floral festival
['kipɪŋ ʌ 'flɔʁ⁽ʳ⁾ʊl 'fɛstɪvʊl]
Till the night-loving primrose wakes–
[tɪl ðʌ naːɪt 'lʌvɪŋ 'pɹɪmɹoːʊz wɛːɪks]
Long may the daisies dance the field,
[laŋ mɛːɪ ðʌ 'dɛːɪzɪz dæns ðʌ fild]
Frolicking far and near!
['fɹɑlɪkɪŋ faʁ⁽ʳ⁾ ænd nɪːʌ]
Why should the innocent hide their heads?
[ʍaːɪ ʃʊd ði 'ɪno(ʌ)sɛnt haːɪd ðɛːʌ hɛdz]
Why should the innocent fear?
[ʍaːɪ ʃʊd ði 'ɪno(ʌ)sɛnt fɪːʌ]
Lulled be the dirge in the cypress bough,
[lʌld bi ðʌ dɜdʒ ɪn ðʌ 'saːɪpɹɛ(ɪ)s baːʊ]
That tells of departed flowers!
[ðæt tɛlz ʌv dɪ'pɑtɛ(ɪ)d flaːʊʌz]
Ah! that the butterfly's gilded wing
[ɑ ðæt ðʌ 'bʌtʌflaːɪz 'gɪldɛ(ɪ)d wɪŋ]
Fluttered in evergreen bowers!
['flʌtʌd ɪn 'ɛvʌgɹin 'baːʊʌz]
Sad is my heart for the blighted plants–
[sæd ɪz maːɪ hɑt fɔ ðʌ 'blaːɪtɛ(ɪ)d plænts]
Its pleasures are aye as brief–
[ɪts 'plɛʒʊ(ʌ)z aʁ⁽ʳ⁾ ɛːɪ æz bɹif]
They bloom at the young year's joyful call,
[ðɛːɪ blum æt ðʌ jʌŋ jɪːʌz 'dʒɔːɪfʊl kɔl]
And fade with the autumn leaf:
[ænd fɛːɪd wɪð ði 'ɔtʌm lif]
Ah! may the red rose live alway,
[ɑ mɛːɪ ðʌ ɹɛd ɹoːʊz lɪv 'ɔlwɛːɪ]
To smile upon earth and sky!
[tu smaːɪl ʌ'pan ɜθ ænd skaːɪ]
Why should the beautiful ever weep?
[ʍaːɪ ʃʊd ðʌ 'bjutɪfʊl 'ɛvʌ wip]
Why should the beautiful die?
[ʍaːɪ ʃʊd ðʌ 'bjutɪfʊl daːɪ]

"Beautiful Dreamer"
['bjutɪfʊl 'dɹimʁ]
Foster, Stephen (Am. 1826-1864)

Beautiful Dreamer, wake unto me,
['bjutɪfʊl 'dɹimʌ wɛːk 'ʌntu mi]
Starlight and dewdrops are waiting for thee;
['stalaːɪt ænd 'djudɹaps ɑ 'wɛːɪtɪŋ fɔ ði]
Sounds of the rude world heard in the day,
[saːʊndz ʌv ðʌ ɹ⁽ʳʳ⁾ud wɜld hɜd ɪn ðʌ dɛːɪ]
Lull'd by the moonlight have all pass'd away!
[lʌld baːɪ ðʌ 'munlaːɪt hæv ɔl pæst ʌ'wɛːɪ]
Beautiful dreamer, queen of my song,
['bjutɪfʊl 'dɹimʌ kwin ʌv maːɪ saŋ]
List while I woo thee with soft melody;
[lɪst ʍaːɪl aːɪ wu ði wɪð saft 'mɛlodɪ]
Gone are the cares of life's busy throng,
[gan ɑ ðʌ kɛːʌz ʌv laːɪfs 'bɪzɪ θɹaŋ]
Beautiful dreamer, awake unto me!
['bjutɪfʊl 'dɹimʌʁ⁽ʳ⁾ ʌ'wɛːk 'ʌntu mi]
Beautiful dreamer, out on the sea,
['bjutɪfʊl 'dɹimʌʁ⁽ʳ⁾ aːʊt an ðʌ si]
Mermaids are chanting the wild lorelie;
['mɜmɛːɪdz ɑ 'tʃæntɪŋ ðʌ waːɪld lɔʁ⁽ʳ⁾ʌ'li]
Over the streamlet vapors are borne,
['oːʊvʌ ðʌ 'stɹimlɛ(ɪ)t 'vɛːɪpɔ(ʌ)z ɑ bɔn]
Waiting to fade at the bright coming morn.
['wɛːɪtɪŋ tu fɛːɪd æt ðʌ bɹaːɪt 'kʌmɪŋ mɔn]
Beautiful dreamer, beam on my heart,
['bjutɪfʊl 'dɹimʌ bim an maːɪ hat]
E'en as the morn on the streamlet and sea;
[in æz ðʌ mɔn an ðʌ 'stɹimlɛ(ɪ)t ænd si]
Then will all clouds of sorrow depart,
[ðɛn wɪl ɔl klaːʊdz ʌv 'saʁ⁽ʳ⁾oːʊ dɪ'pat]
Beautiful dreamer, awake unto me!
['bjutɪfʊl 'dɹimʌʁ⁽ʳ⁾ ʌ'wɛːk 'ʌntu mi]

"Gentle Annie"
['dʒɛntʊl 'æni]
Foster, Stephen (Am. 1826-1864)

Thou wilt come no more, gentle Annie,
[ðaːʊ wɪlt kʌm noːʊ mɔːʌ 'dʒɛntʊl 'æni]
Like a flower thy spirit did depart;
[laːɪk ʌ flaːʊʌ ðaːɪ 'spɪʁ⁽ʳ⁾ɪt dɪd dɪ'pat]
Thou are gone, alas! like the many
[ðaːʊ ɑ gan ʌ'læs laːɪk ðʌ 'mɛni]
That have bloomed in the summer of my heart.
[ðæt hæv blumd ɪn ðʌ 'sʌmʌʁ⁽ʳ⁾ ʌv maːɪ hat]
Shall we never more behold thee;
[ʃæl wi 'nɛvʌ mɔːʌ bɪ'hoːʊld ði]
Never hear thy winning voice again–
['nɛvʌ hɪːʌ ðaːɪ 'wɪnɪŋ vɔːɪs ʌ'gɛn]
When the Spring time comes, gentle Annie,
[ʍɛn ðʌ spɹɪŋ taːɪm kʌmz 'dʒɛntʊl 'æni]

When the wild flowers are scattered o'er the plain?
[ʍɛn ðʌ wɑːɪld flaˈʊʌz a ˈskætʌd ɔːʌ ðʌ plɛːɪn]
We have roamed and loved mid the bowers
[wi hæv ɹoːʊmd ænd lʌvd mɪd ðʌ ˈbaːʊʌz]
When thy downy cheeks were in their bloom;
[ʍɛn ðaːɪ ˈdaːʊnɪ tʃiks wɜ⁽ʳ⁾ ɪn ðɛːʌ blum]
Now I stand alone mid the flowers
[naːʊ aːɪ stænd ʌˈloːʊn mɪd ðʌ flaːʊʌz]
While they mingle their perfumes o'er thy tomb.
[ʍaːɪl ðɛːɪ ˈmɪŋgʊl ðɛːʌ pɜˈfjumz ɔːʌ ðaːɪ tum]
Shall we never more behold thee…
[ʃæl wi ˈnɛvʌ mɔːʌ bɪˈhoːʊld ði]
Ah! the hours grow sad while I ponder
[a ði aːʊʌz gɹoːʊ sæd ʍaːɪl aːɪ ˈpandʌ]
Near the silent spot where thou are laid,
[nɪːʌ ðʌ ˈsaːɪlɛnt spat ʍɛːʌ ðaːʊ a lɛːɪd]
And my heart bows down when I wander
[ænd maːɪ hat baːʊz daːʊn ʍɛn aːɪ ˈwandʌ]
By the streams and the meadows where we strayed.
[baːɪ ðʌ stɹimz ænd ðʌ ˈmɛdoːʊz ʍɛːʌ wi stɹɛːɪd]
Shall we never more behold thee…
[ʃæl wi ˈnɛvʌ mɔːʌ bɪˈhoːʊld ði]

"Hard Times Come Again No More"
[haʁd taːɪmz kʌm ʌˈgɛn noːʊ mɔːʁ]
Foster, Stephen (Am. 1826-1864)

1. Let us pause in life's pleasures
[lɛt ʌs pɔz ɪn laːɪfs ˈplɛʒʊ⁽ʌ⁾z]
and count its many tears
[ænd kaːʊnt ɪts ˈmɛnɪ tɪːʌz]
While we all sup sorrow with the poor:
[ʍaːɪl wi ɔl sʌp ˈsaʁ⁽ʳ⁾oːʊ wɪð ðʌ pʊːʌ]
There's a song that will linger forever in our ears;
[ðɛːʌz ʌ saŋ ðæt wɪl ˈlɪŋgʌ fɔʁ⁽ʳ⁾ˈɛvʌʁ⁽ʳ⁾ ɪn aːʊʌʁ⁽ʳ⁾ ɪːʌz]
Oh! Hard Times, come again no more.
[oːʊ had taːɪmz kʌm ʌˈgɛn noːʊ mɔːʌ]
CHORUS:
'Tis the song, the sigh of the weary;
[tɪz ðʌ saŋ ðʌ saːɪ ʌv ðʌ ˈwiːʌʁ⁽ʳ⁾ɪ]
Hard Times, Hard Times, come again no more:
[had taːɪmz had taːɪmz kʌm ʌˈgɛn noːʊ mɔːʌ]
Many days you have lingered
[ˈmɛnɪ dɛːɪz ju hæv ˈlɪŋgʌd]
around my cabin door;
[ʌˈʁ⁽ʳ⁾aːʊnd maːɪ ˈkæbɪn dɔːʌ]
Oh! Hard Times, come again no more.
[oːʊ had taːɪmz kʌm ʌˈgɛn noːʊ mɔːʌ]
2. While we seek mirth and beauty
[ʍaːɪl wi sik mɜθ ænd ˈbjutɪ]
and music light and gay
[ænd ˈmjuzɪk laːɪt ænd gɛːɪ]
There are frail forms fainting at the door:
[ðɛːʌʁ⁽ʳ⁾ a fɹɛːɪl fɔmz ˈfɛːɪntɪŋ æt ðʌ dɔːʌ]
Though their voices are silent,
[ðoːʊ ðɛːʌ ˈvɔːɪsɛ(ɪ)z a ˈsaːɪlɛnt]

their pleading looks will say–
[ðɛːʌ ˈplidɪŋ lʊks wɪl sɛːɪ]
Oh! Hard times, come again no more.
[oːʊ had taːɪmz kʌm ʌˈgɛn noːʊ mɔːʌ]
CHORUS
3. 'Tis a sigh that is wafted across the troubled wave,
[tɪz ʌ saːɪ ðæt ɪz ˈwaftɛ(ɪ)d ʌˈkɹas ðʌ ˈtɹʌbʊld wɛːɪv]
'Tis a wail that is heard upon the shore,
[tɪz ʌ wɛːɪl ðæt ɪz hɜd ʌˈpan ðʌ ʃɔːʌ]
'Tis a dirge that is murmured
[tɪz ʌ dɜdʒ ðæt ɪz ˈmɜmʊ(ʌ)d]
around the lowly grave,–
[ʌˈʁ⁽ʳ⁾aːʊnd ðʌ ˈloːʊlɪ gɹɛːɪv]
Oh! Hard Times, come again no more.
[oːʊ had taːɪmz kʌm ʌˈgɛn noːʊ mɔːʌ]
CHORUS

"If You've Only Got a Moustache"
[ɪf juv ˈoːʊnli gat ʌ mʌˈstæʃ]
Cooper, George (Am. 1840-1927)

Oh! all of you poor single men,
[oːʊ ɔl ʌv ju pʊːʌ ˈsɪŋgʊl mɛn]
Don't ever give up in despair,
[doːʊnt ˈɛvʌ gɪv ʌp ɪn dɪˈspɛːʌ]
For there's always a chance while there's life
[fɔ ðɛːʌz ˈɔlwɛːɪz ʌ tʃæns ʍaːɪl ðɛːʌz laːɪf]
To capture the hearts of the fair,
[tu ˈkæptʃʊ(ʌ) ðʌ hats ʌv ðʌ fɛːʌ]
No matter what may be your age,
[noːʊ ˈmætʌ ʍat mɛːɪ bi jɔːʌʁ⁽ʳ⁾ ɛːɪdʒ]
You always may cut a fine dash,
[ju ˈɔlwɛːɪz mɛːɪ kʌt ʌ faːɪn dæʃ]
You will suit all the girls to a hair
[ju wɪl sjut ɔl ðʌ gɜlz tu ʌ hɛːʌ]
If you've only got a moustache,
[ɪf juv ˈoːʊnlɪ gat ʌ mʌˈstæʃ]
A moustache, a moustache,
[ʌ mʌˈstæʃ ʌ mʌˈstæʃ]
If you've only got a moustache.
[ɪf juv ˈoːʊnlɪ gat ʌ mʌˈstæʃ]
No matter for manners or style,
[noːʊ ˈmætʌ fɔ ˈmænʌz ɔ staːɪl]
No matter for birth or for fame,
[noːʊ ˈmætʌ fɔ bɜθ ɔ fɔ fɛːɪm]
All these used to have something to do
[ɔl ðiz just tu hæv ˈsʌmθɪŋ tu du]
With young ladies changing their name.
[wɪð jʌŋ ˈlɛːɪdɪz ˈtʃɛːɪndʒɪŋ ðɛːʌ nɛːɪm]
There's no reason now to despond,
[ðɛːʌz noːʊ ˈɹizʌn naːʊ tu dɪˈspand]
Or go and do anything rash,
[ɔ goːʊ ænd du ˈɛnɪθɪŋ ɹæʃ]
For you'll do though you can't raise a cent,
[fɔ jul du ðoːʊ ju kænt ɹɛːɪz ʌ sɛnt]

If you'll only raise a moustache!
[ɪf jul ˈoːʊnlɪ ɹɛːɪz ʌ mʌˈstæʃ]
A moustache, a moustache,
[ʌ mʌˈstæʃ ʌ mʌˈstæʃ]
If you'll only raise a moustache.
[ɪf jul ˈoːʊnlɪ ɹɛːɪz ʌ mʌˈstæʃ]
Your head may be thick as a block,
[jɔːʌ hɛd mɛːɪ bi θɪk æz ʌ blak]
And empty as any foot-ball,
[ænd ˈɛmptɪ æz ˈɛnɪ fʊt bɔl]
Oh! your eyes may be green as the grass
[oːʊ jɔːʌʁ⁽ʳ⁾ aːɪz mɛːɪ bi ɡɹin æz ðʌ ɡɹæs]
Your heart just as hard as a wall.
[jɔːʌ hɑt dʒʌst æz had æz ʌ wɔl]
Yet take the advice that I give,
[jɛt tɛːɪk ði ædˈvaːɪs ðæt aːɪ ɡɪv]
You'll soon gain affection and cash,
[jul sun ɡɛːɪn ʌˈfɛkʃʌn ænd kæʃ]
And will be all the rage with the girls,
[ænd wɪl bi ɔl ðʌ ɹɛːɪdʒ wɪð ðʌ ɡɜlz]
If you'll only get a moustache,
[ɪf jul ˈoːʊnlɪ ɡɛt ʌ mʌˈstæʃ]
A moustache, a moustache,
[ʌ mʌˈstæʃ ʌ mʌˈstæʃ]
If you'll only get a moustache.
[ɪf jul ˈoːʊnlɪ ɡɛt ʌ mʌˈstæʃ]
I once was in sorrow and tears
[aːɪ wʌns waz ɪn ˈsaʁ⁽ʳ⁾oːʊ ænd tɪːʌz]
Because I was jilted you know,
[bɪˈkɔz aːɪ waz ˈdʒɪltɛ(ɪ)d ju noːʊ]
So right down to the river I ran
[soːʊ ɹaːɪt daːʊn tu ðʌ ˈɹɪvʌʁ⁽ʳ⁾ aːɪ ɹæn]
To quickly dispose of my woe.
[tu ˈkwɪklɪ dɪˈspoːʊz ʌv maːɪ woːʊ]
A good friend he gave me advice
[ʌ ɡʊd fɹɛnd hi ɡɛːɪv mi ædˈvaːɪs]
And timely prevented the splash,
[ænd ˈtaːɪmlɪ pɹɪˈvɛntɛ(ɪ)d ðʌ splæʃ]
Now at home I've a wife and ten heirs,
[naːʊ æt hoːʊm aːɪv ʌ waːɪf ænd tɛn ɛːʌz]
And all through a handsome moustache,
[ænd ɔl θɹu ʌ ˈhænsʌm mʌˈstæʃ]
A moustache, a moustache,
[ʌ mʌˈstæʃ ʌ mʌˈstæʃ]
And all through a handsome moustache.
[ænd ɔl θɹu ʌ ˈhænsʌm mʌˈstæʃ]

"Jeanie with the Light Brown Hair"
[ˈdʒini wɪθ ðʌ laːɪt bɹaːʊn hɛːʁ]
Foster, Stephen (Am. 1826-1864)

I dream of Jeanie with the light brown hair,
[aːɪ dɹim ʌv ˈdʒini wɪð ðʌ laːɪt bɹaːʊn hɛːʌ]
Borne, like a vapor, on the summer air;
[bɔn laːɪk ʌ ˈvɛːɪpɔ(ʌ)ʁ⁽ʳ⁾ an ðʌ ˈsʌmʌʁ⁽ʳ⁾ ɛːʌ]

I see her tripping where the bright streams play,
[aːɪ si hɜ ˈtɹɪpɪŋ ʍɛːʌ ðʌ bɹaːɪt stɹimz plɛːɪ]
Happy as the daisies that dance on her way.
[ˈhæpɪ æz ðʌ ˈdɛːɪzɪz ðæt dæns an hɜ wɛːɪ]
Many were the wild notes her merry voice would pour,
[ˈmɛnɪ wɜ ðʌ waːɪld noːʊts hɜ ˈmɛʁ⁽ʳ⁾ɪ vɔːɪs wʊd pɔːʌ]
Many were the blithe birds that warbled them o'er:
[ˈmɛnɪ wɜ ðʌ blaːɪð bɜdz ðæt ˈwɔbʊld ðɛm ɔːʌ]
Oh! I dream of Jeanie with the light brown hair,
[oːʊ aːɪ dɹim ʌv ˈdʒini wɪð ðʌ laːɪt bɹaːʊn hɛːʌ]
Floating, like a vapor, on the soft summer air.
[ˈfloːʊtɪŋ laːɪk ʌ ˈvɛːɪpɔ(ʌ)ʁ⁽ʳ⁾ an ðʌ saft ˈsʌmʌʁ⁽ʳ⁾ ɛːʌ]
I sigh for Jeanie, but her light form strayed
[aːɪ saːɪ fɔ ˈdʒini bʌt hɜ laːɪt fɔm stɹɛːɪd]
Far from the fond hearts round her native glade;
[fa fɹʌm ðʌ fand hats ɹaːʊnd hɜ ˈnɛːɪtɪv glɛːɪd]
Her smiles have vanished and her sweet songs flown
[hɜ smaːɪlz hæv ˈvænɪʃt ænd hɜ swit saŋz floːʊn]
Flitting like the dreams that have cheered us and gone
[ˈflɪtɪŋ laːɪk ðʌ dɹimz ðæt hæv ʧiːʌd ʌs ænd gan]
Now the nodding wild flowers
[naːʊ ðʌ ˈnadɪŋ waːɪld flaːʊʌz]
may wither on the shore
[mɛːɪ ˈwɪðʌʁ⁽ʳ⁾ an ðʌ ʃɔːʌ]
While her gentle fingers will cull them no more:
[ʍaːɪl hɜ ˈdʒɛntʊl ˈfɪŋgʌz wɪl kʌl ðɛm noːʊ mɔːʌ]
Oh! I sigh for Jeanie with the light brown hair
[oːʊ aːɪ saːɪ fɔ ˈdʒini wɪð ðʌ laːɪt bɹaːʊn hɛːʌ]
Floating, like a vapor, on the soft summer air.
[ˈfloːʊtɪŋ laːɪk ʌ ˈvɛːɪpɔ(ʌ)ʁ⁽ʳ⁾ an ðʌ saft ˈsʌmʌʁ⁽ʳ⁾ ɛːʌ]

"My Wife Is a Most Knowing Woman"
[maːɪ waːɪf ɪz ʌ moːʊst ˈnoːʊɪŋ ˈwʊmʌn]
Foster, Stephen (Am. 1826-1864)

Note: the silent "r" may be pronounced for the character voice

My wife is a most knowing woman,
[maːɪ waːɪf ɪz ʌ moːʊst ˈnoːʊɪŋ ˈwʊmæ(ʌ)n]
She always is finding me out,
[ʃi ˈɔlwɛːɪz ɪz ˈfaːɪndɪŋ mi aːʊt]
She never will hear explanations
[ʃi ˈnɛvʁ wɪl hɪːʁ ɛksplʌˈnɛːɪʃʌnz]
But instantly puts me to rout,
[bʌt ˈɪnstæ(ɪ)ntlɪ pʊts mi tu ɹaːʊt]
There's no use to try and deceive her,
[ðɛːʁz noːʊ jus tu tɹaːɪ ænd dɪˈsiv hɜ]
If out with my friends, night or day,
[ɪf aːʊt wɪð maːɪ fɹɛndz naːɪt ɜ dɛːɪ]
In the most inconceivable manner
[ɪn ðʌ moːʊst ɪnkʌnˈsivʌbʊl ˈmænʁ]
She knows where I've been right away,
[ʃi noːʊz ʍɛːʁ aːɪv bɪn ɹaːɪt ʌˈwɛːɪ]
She says that I'm "mean" and "inhuman"
[ʃi sɛz ðæt aːɪm min ænd ɪnˈhjumæ(ʌ)n]

Oh! my wife is a most knowing woman.
[oːʊ maːɪ waːɪf ɪz ʌ moːʊst ˈnoːʊɪŋ ˈwʊmæ(ʌ)n]
She would have been hung up for witchcraft
[ʃi wʊd hæv bɪn hʌŋ ʌp fɔ ˈwɪʧkɹæft]
If she had lived sooner, I know,
[ɪf ʃi hæd lɪvd ˈsunʁ aːɪ noːʊ]
There's no hiding anything from her,
[ðɛːʁz noːʊ ˈhaːɪdɪŋ ˈɛnɪθɪŋ fɹʌm hɜ]
She knows what I do–where I go;
[ʃi noːʊz ʍat aːɪ du ʍɛːʁ aːɪ goːʊ]
And if I come in after midnight
[ænd ɪf aːɪ kʌm ɪn ˈæftʁ ˈmɪdnaːɪt]
And say "I have been to the lodge,"
[ænd sɛːɪ aːɪ hæv bɪn tu ðʌ laʤ]
Oh, she says while she flies in a fury,
[oːʊ ʃi sɛz ʍaːɪl ʃi flaːɪz ɪn ʌ ˈfjuːʁɪ]
"Now don't think to play such a dodge!
[naːʊ doːʊnt θɪŋk tu plɛːɪ sʌʧ ʌ daʤ]
It's all very fine, but wont do, man."
[ɪts ɔl ˈvɛʁɪ faːɪn bʌt woːʊnt du mæn]
Oh, my wife is a most knowing woman.
[oːʊ maːɪ waːɪf ɪz ʌ moːʊst ˈnoːʊɪŋ ˈwʊmæ(ʌ)n]
Not often I go out to dinner
[nat ˈafɛ(ɪ)n aːɪ goːʊ aːʊt tu ˈdɪnʁ]
And come home a little "so so,"
[ænd kʌm hoːʊm ʌ ˈlɪtʊl soːʊ soːʊ]
I try to creep up through the hall-way,
[aːɪ tɹaːɪ tu kɹip ʌp θɾu ðʌ hɔl wɛːɪ]
As still as a mouse, on tip-toe,
[æz stɪl æz ʌ maːʊs an tɪp toːʊ]
She's sure to be waiting up for me
[ʃiz ʃʊːʁ tu bi ˈwɛːɪtɪŋ ʌp fɔ mi]
And then comes a nice little scene,
[ænd ðɛn kʌmz ʌ naːɪs ˈlɪtʊl sin]
"What, you tell me you're sober, you wretch you,
[ʍat ju tɛl mi jɔːʁ ˈsoːʊbʁ ju ɹɛʧ ju]
Now don't think that I am so green!
[naːʊ doːʊnt θɪŋk ðæt aːɪ æm soːʊ gɹin]
My life is quite worn out with you, man,"
[maːɪ laːɪf ɪz kwaːɪt wɔn aːʊt wɪð ju mæn]
Oh, my wife is a most knowing woman!
[oːʊ maːɪ waːɪf ɪz ʌ moːʊst ˈnoːʊɪŋ ˈwʊmæ(ʌ)n]
She knows me much better than I do,
[ʃi noːʊz mi mʌʧ ˈbɛtʁ ðæn aːɪ du]
Her eyes are like those of a lynx,
[hɜ aːɪz a laːɪk ðoːʊz ʌv ʌ lɪŋks]
Though how she discovers my secrets
[ðoːʊ haːʊ ʃi dɪsˈkʌvʁz maːɪ ˈsikɹɛ(ɪ)ts]
Is a riddle would puzzle a sphynx,
[ɪz ʌ ˈɹɪdʊl wʊd ˈpʌzʊl ʌ sfɪŋks]
On fair days, when we go out walking,
[an fɛːʁ dɛːɪz ʍɛn wi goːʊ aːʊt ˈwɔkɪŋ]
If ladies look at me askance,
[ɪf ˈlɛːɪdɪz lʊk æt mi ʌˈskæns]
In the most harmless way, I assure you,
[ɪn ðʌ moːʊst ˈhamlɛ(ɪ)s wɛːɪ aːɪ ʌˈʃʊːʁ ju]

My wife gives me, oh! such a glance,
[maːɪ waːɪf gɪvz mi oːʊ sʌʧ ʌ glæns]
And says "all these insults you'll rue, man."
[ænd sɛz ɔl ðiz ˈɪnsʌlts jʊl ɹu mæn]
Oh, my wife is a most knowing woman.
[oːʊ maːɪ waːɪf ɪz ʌ moːʊst ˈnoːʊɪŋ ˈwʊmæ(ʌ)n]
Yes, I must give all my friends up
[jɛs aːɪ mʌst gɪv ɔl maːɪ fɹɛndz ʌp]
If I would live happy and quiet;
[ɪf aːɪ wʊd lɪv ˈhæpɪ ænd ˈkwaːɪɛ(ɪ)t]
One might as well be 'neath a tombstone
[wʌn maːɪt æz wɛl bi niθ ʌ ˈtumstoːʊn]
As live in confusion and riot.
[æz lɪv ɪn kʌnˈfjuʒʌn ænd ˈɹaːɪʌt]
This life we all know is a short one,
[ðɪs laːɪf wi ɔl noːʊ ɪz ʌ ʃɔt wʌn]
While some tongues are long, heaven knows,
[ʍaːɪl sʌm tʌŋz a laŋ ˈhɛvɛ(ɪ)n noːʊz]
And a miserable life is a husbands,
[ænd ʌ ˈmɪzɹʌbʊl laːɪf ɪz ʌ ˈhʌzbæ(ɪ)ndz]
Who numbers his wife with his foes,
[hu ˈnʌmbʁz hɪz waːɪf wɪð hɪz foːʊz]
I'll stay at home now like a true man,
[aːɪl stɛːɪ æt hoːʊm naːʊ laːɪk ʌ tɹu mæn]
For my wife is a most knowing woman.
[fɔ maːɪ waːɪf ɪz ʌ moːʊst ˈnoːʊɪŋ ˈwʊmæ(ʌ)n]

"Some Folks Do"
[sʌm foːʊks du]
Foster, Stephen (Am. 1826-1864)

1. Some folks like to sigh,
[sʌm foːʊks laːɪk tu saːɪ]
Some folks do, some folks do;
[sʌm foːʊks du sʌm foːʊks du]
Some folks long to die,
[sʌm foːʊks laŋ tu daːɪ]
But that's not me nor you.
[bʌt ðæts nat mi nɔ ju]
CHORUS:
Long live the merry merry heart
[laŋ lɪv ðʌ ˈmɛʁ(ʳ)ɪ ˈmɛʁ(ʳ)ɪ hat]
That laughs by night and day,
[ðæt læfs baːɪ naːɪt ænd dɛːɪ]
Like the Queen of Mirth,
[laːɪk ðʌ kwin ʌv mɜθ]
No matter what some folks say.
[noːʊ ˈmætʌ ʍat sʌm foːʊks sɛːɪ]
2. Some folks fear to smile,
[sʌm foːʊks fiːʌ tu smaːɪl]
Some folks do, some folks do,
[sʌm foːʊks du sʌm foːʊks du]
Others laugh through guile,
[ˈʌðʌz læf θɾu gaːɪl]
But that's not me nor you.
[bʌt ðæts nat mi nɔ ju]

CHORUS
3. Some folks get grey hairs,
[sʌm foːʊks get gɹɛːɪ hɛːʌz]
Some folks do, some folks do;
[sʌm foːʊks du sʌm foːʊks du]
Brooding o'er their cares,
[ˈbɹ⁽ᶦ⁾udɪŋ ɔːʌ ðɛːʌ kɛːʌz]
But that's not me nor you.
[bʌt ðæts nɑt mi nɔ ju]
CHORUS
4. Some folks toil and save,
[sʌm foːʊks tɔːɪl ænd sɛːɪv]
Some folks do, some folks do;
[sʌm foːʊks du sʌm foːʊks du]
To buy themselves a grave,
[tu bɑːɪ ðɛmˈsɛlvz ʌ gɹɛːɪv]
But that's not me nor you.
[bʌt ðæts nɑt mi nɔ ju]
CHORUS

G

Gibbons, Orlando (Eng. 1583-1625)

Song Selection

"The Silver Swan"
[ðʊ ˈsɪlvʌ swɑn]
Anonymous

The silver swan who, living, had no note,
[ðʊ ˈsɪlvʌ swɑn hu ˈlɪvɪŋ hæd noːʊ noːʊt]
when death approached unlocked her silent throat.
[ʍɛn dɛθ ʌˈpɹoːʊʧt ʌnˈlɑkt hɜ ˈsɑːɪlɛnt θɹoːʊt]
Leaning her breast against the reedy shore,
[ˈlinɪŋ hɜ bɹɛst ʌˈgɛnst ðʊ ˈɹidɪ ʃɔːʌ]
thus sung her first and last, and sung no more.
[ðʌs sʌŋ hɜ fɜst ænd lɑst ænd sʌŋ noːʊ mɔːʌ]
Farewell all joys, O death come close mine eyes.
[fɛːʌˈwɛl ɔl ʤɔːɪz oːʊ dɛθ kʌm kloːʊz mɑːɪn ɑːɪz]
More geese than swans now live,
[mɔːʌ gis ðæn swɑnz nɑːʊ lɪv]
more fools than wise.
[mɔːʌ fulz ðæn wɑːɪz]

Gibbs, C. Armstrong (Eng. 1889-1960)

Song Selection

"Five Eyes"
[fɑːɪv ɑːɪz]
Mare, Walter de la (Eng. 1873-1956)

In Hans' old mill his three black cats
[ɪn ˈhɑnzɛ⁽ɪ⁾z oːʊld mɪl hɪz θri blæk kæts]
Watch the bins for the thieving rats.
[wɑʧ ðʊ bɪnz fɔ ðʊ ˈθivɪŋ ɹæts]
Whisker and claw they crouch in the night,
[ˈʍɪskʌr ænd klɔ ðɛːɪ kɹɑːʊʧ ɪn ðʊ nɑːɪt]
Their five eyes smould'ring green and bright;
[ðɛːʌ fɑːɪv ɑːɪz ˈsmoːʊldɹɪŋ gɹin ænd bɹɑːɪt]
Squeaks from the floursack, squeaks from where
[skwiks fɹʌm ðʊ ˈflɑːʊʌsæk skwiks fɹʌm ʍɛːʌ]
The cold wind stirs on the empty stair,
[ðʌ koːʊld wɪnd stɜz ɑn ðɪ ˈɛmptɪ stɛːʌ]
Squeaking and scamp'ring, ev'rywhere.
[ˈskwikɪŋ ænd ˈskæmpɹɪŋ ˈɛvɹɪʍɛːʌ]
Then down they pounce, now in, now out
[ðɛn dɑːʊn ðɛːɪ pɑːʊns nɑːʊ ɪn nɑːʊ ɑːʊt]
At whisking tail, and sniffing snout;
[æt ˈʍɪskɪŋ tɛːɪl ænd ˈsnɪfɪŋ snɑːʊt]
While lean old Hans he snores away
[ʍɑːɪl lin oːʊld hɑnz hi snɔːʌz ʌˈwɛːɪ]
Til peep of light at break of day;
[tɪl pip ʌv lɑːɪt æt bɹɛːɪk ʌv dɛːɪ]
Then up he climbs to his creaking mill,
[ðɛn ʌp hi klɑːɪmz tu hɪz ˈkɹikɪŋ mɪl]
Out come his cats all grey with meal;
[ɑːʊt kʌm hɪz kæts ɔl gɹɛːɪ wɪð mil]
Jekkel, and Jessup, and one eyed Jill.
[ˈʤɛkʊl ænd ˈʤɛsʌp ænd wʌn ɑːɪd ʤɪl]

Gordon, Ricky Ian (Am. b. 1956)

Too Few the Mornings Be (Song Cycle)
[tu fju ðʌ ˈmɔʁnɪŋz bi]
(Eleven Songs for Soprano and Piano)
Dickinson, Emily (Am. 1830-1886)

1. Too Few the Mornings Be
[tu fju ðʌ ˈmɔʁnɪŋz bi]

Too few the mornings be,
[tu fju ðʌ ˈmɔnɪŋz bi]
Too scant the nights.
[tu skænt ðʌ nɑːɪts]
No lodging can be had
[noːʊ ˈlɑʤɪŋ kæn bi hæd]

For the delights
[fɔ ðʌ dɪˈlɑːɪts]
That come to earth to stay,
[ðæt kʌm tu ɜθ tu steːɪ]
But no apartment find
[bʌt noːʊ ʌˈpɑtmɛnt fɑːɪnd]
And ride away.
[ænd ɹɑːɪd ʌˈweːɪ]

2. If All the Griefs I Am to Have
[ɪf ɔl ðʌ gɹifs ɑːɪ æm tu hæv]

If all the griefs I am to have
[ɪf ɔl ðʌ gɹ(ɾ)ifs ɑːɪ æm tu hæv]
Would only come today,
[wʊd ˈoːʊnlɪ kʌm tuˈdeːɪ]
I am so happy I believe
[ɑːɪ æm soːʊ ˈhæpɪ ɑːɪ bɪˈliv]
They'd laugh and run away.
[ðeːɪd læf ænd ɹʌn ʌˈweːɪ]
If all the joys I am to have
[ɪf ɔl ðʌ ʤɔːɪz ɑːɪ æm tu hæv]
Would only come today,
[wʊd ˈoːʊnlɪ kʌm tuˈdeːɪ]
They could not be so big as this
[ðeːɪ kʊd nɑt bi soːʊ bɪg æz ðɪs]
That happens to me now.
[ðæt ˈhæpɛ(ɪ)nz tu mi nɑːʊ]

3. The Bustle in a House
[ðʌ ˈbʌsʊl ɪn ʌ hɑːʊs]

The bustle in a house
[ðʌ ˈbʌsʊl ɪn ʌ hɑːʊs]
The morning after death
[ðʌ ˈmɔnɪŋ ˈæftʌ dɛθ]
Is solemnest of industries
[ɪz ˈsɑlʌmɛ(ɪ)st ʌv ˈɪndʌstɹɪz]
Enacted upon earth,–
[ɪˈnæktɛ(ɪ)d ʌˈpɑn ɜθ]
The sweeping up the heart,
[ðʌ ˈswipɪŋ ʌp ðʌ hɑt]
And putting love away
[ænd ˈpʊtɪŋ lʌv ʌˈweːɪ]
We shall not want to use again
[wi ʃæl nɑt wɑnt tu juz ʌˈgɛn]
Until eternity.
[ʌnˈtɪl ɪˈtɜnɪtɪ]

4. This Is My Letter to the World
[ðɪs ɪz mɑːɪ ˈlɛtʁ tu ðʌ wɜld]

This is my letter to the world,
[ðɪs ɪz mɑːɪ ˈlɛtʌ tu ðʌ wɜld]
That never wrote to me,
[ðæt ˈnɛvʌ ɹoːʊt tu mi]

The simple news that nature told,
[ðʌ ˈsɪmpʊl njuz ðæt ˈneːɪʧʊ(ʌ) toːʊld]
With tender majesty.
[wɪð ˈtɛndʌ ˈmæʤɛ(ɪ)stɪ]
Her message is committed
[hɜ ˈmɛsæ(ɪ)ʤ ɪz kʌˈmɪtɛ(ɪ)d]
To hands I cannot see;
[tu hændz ɑːɪ kæˈnɑt si]
For love of her, sweet countrymen,
[fɔ lʌv ʌv hɜ swit ˈkʌntɹɪmɛ(ɪ)n]
Judge tenderly of me.
[ʤʌʤ ˈtɛndʌlɪ ʌv mi]

5. You Cannot Put a Fire Out
[ju kæˈnɑt pʊt ʌ fɑːɪʁ ɑːʊt]

You cannot put a fire out;
[ju kæˈnɑt pʊt ʌ fɑːɪʌʁ(ɾ) ɑːʊt]
A Thing that can ignite
[ʌ θɪŋ ðæt kæn ɪgˈnɑːɪt]
Can go, itself, without a fan–
[kæn goːʊ ɪtˈsɛlf wɪðˈɑːʊt ʌ fæn]
Upon the slowest night–
[ʌˈpɑn ðʌ ˈsloːʊɛ(ɪ)st nɑːɪt]
You cannot fold a flood–
[ju kæˈnɑt foːʊld ʌ flʌd]
And put it in a drawer–
[ænd pʊt ɪt ɪn ʌ dɹɔːʌ]
Because the winds would find it out,
[bɪˈkɔz ðʌ wɪndz wʊd fɑːɪnd ɪt ɑːʊt]
And tell your cedar floor–
[ænd tɛl jɔːʌ ˈsidʌ flɔːʌ]

6. Bee! I'm Expecting You!
[bi ɑːɪm ɪkˈspɛktɪŋ ju]

Bee! I'm expecting you!
[bi ɑːɪm ɪkˈspɛktɪŋ ju]
Was saying yesterday
[wɑz ˈseːɪɪŋ ˈjɛstʌdeːɪ]
To somebody you know
[tu ˈsʌmbɑdɪ ju noːʊ]
That you were due.
[ðæt ju wɜ dju]
The frogs got home last week–
[ðʌ fɹɑgz gɑt hoːʊm læst wik]
Are settled, and at work,
[ɑ ˈsɛtʊld ænd æt wɜk]
Birds, mostly back–
[bɜdz ˈmoːʊstlɪ bæk]
The clover warm and thick–
[ðʌ ˈkloːʊvʌ wɔm ænd θɪk]
You'll get my letter by
[jul gɛt mɑːɪ ˈlɛtʌ bɑːɪ]
The seventeenth; Reply
[ðʌ ˈsɛvɛ(ɪ)nˈtinθ ɹɪˈplɑːɪ]

Or better, Be with me–
[ɔ ˈbɛtʌ bi wɪð mi]
Yours, Fly.
[jɔːʌz flɑːɪ]

7. Poor Little Heart!
[pʊːʁ ˈlɪtʊl haʁt]

Poor little heart!
[pʊːʌ ˈlɪtʊl hat]
Did they forget thee?
[dɪd ðɛːɪ fɔˈgɛt ði]
Then dinna care! Then dinna care!
[ðɛn ˈdɪnʌ kɛːʌ ðɛn ˈdɪnʌ kɛːʌ]
Proud little heart!
[pɹɑːʊd ˈlɪtʊl hat]
Did they forsake thee?
[dɪd ðɛːɪ fɔˈsɛːɪk ði]
Be debonair! Be debonair!
[bi dɛbo(ʌ)ˈnɛːʌ bi dɛbo(ʌ)ˈnɛːʌ]
Frail little heart!
[fɹɛːɪl ˈlɪtʊl hat]
I would not break thee:
[ɑːɪ wʊd nɑt bɹɛːɪk ði]
Could'st credit me? Could'st credit me?
[ˈkʊdɛ(ɪ)st ˈkɹɛdɪt mi ˈkʊdɛ(ɪ)st ˈkɹɛdɪt mi]
Gay little heart!
[gɛːɪ ˈlɪtʊl hat]
Like morning glory
[lɑːɪk ˈmɔnɪŋ ˈglɔʁ(ɾ)ɪ]
Thou'll wilted be; thou'll wilted be!
[ðɑːʊl ˈwɪltɛ(ɪ)d bi ðɑːʊl ˈwɪltɛ(ɪ)d bi]

8. I'm Nobody! Who are you?
[ɑːɪm ˈnoːʊbadi hu ɑ ju]

I'm nobody! Who are you?
[ɑːɪm ˈnoːʊbadɪ hu ɑ ju]
Are you nobody, too?
[ɑ ju ˈnoːʊbadɪ tu]
Then there's a pair of us!– Don't tell!
[ðɛn ðɛːʌz ʌ pɛːʌʁ(ɾ) ʌv ʌs doːʊnt tɛl]
They'd advertise, you know!
[ðɛːɪd ˈædvʌtaːɪz ju noːʊ]
How dreary to be somebody!
[hɑːʊ ˈdɹɪːʌʁ(ɾ)ɪ tu bi ˈsʌmbadɪ]
How public, like a frog
[hɑːʊ ˈpʌblɪk lɑːɪk ʌ fɹag]
To tell your name the livelong June
[tu tɛl jɔːʌ nɛːɪm ðʌ ˈlɪvlʌŋ dʒun]
To an admiring bog!
[tu æn ædˈmɑːɪʁ(ɾ)ɪŋ bag]

9. How Happy Is the Little Stone
[hɑːʊ ˈhæpi ɪz ðʌ ˈlɪtʊl stoːʊn]

How happy is the little stone
[hɑːʊ ˈhæpɪ ɪz ðʌ ˈlɪtʊl stoːʊn]
That rambles in the road alone,
[ðæt ˈɹæmbʊlz ɪn ðʌ ɹoːʊd ʌˈloːʊn]
And doesn't care about careers,
[ænd ˈdʌzɛ(ɪ)nt kɛːʌʁ(ɾ) ʌˈbɑːʊt kʌ ˈʁ(ɾ)ɪːʌz]
And exigencies never fears;
[ænd ˈɛksɪdʒɪnsɪz ˈnɛvʌ fɪːʌz]
Whose coat of elemental brown
[huz koːʊt ʌv ɛlɪ(ʌ)ˈmɛntʊl bɹɑːʊn]
A passing universe put on;
[ʌ ˈpæsɪŋ ˈjunɪˌvɜs pʊt ɑn]
And independent as the sun,
[ænd ɪndɪˈpɛndɛnt æz ðʌ sʌn]
Associates and glows alone,
[ʌˈsoːʊʃɪɛːɪts ænd gloːʊz ʌˈloːʊn]
Fulfilling absolute decree
[fʊlˈfɪlɪŋ ˈæbso(ʌ)ljut dɪˈkɹɪ]
In casual simplicity.
[ɪn ˈkæʒuʊl sɪmˈplɪsɪtɪ]

10. Estranged from Beauty
[ɪˈstɹɛːɪndʒd fɹʌm ˈbjuti]

Estranged from beauty,– none can be,–
[ɪˈstɹɛːɪndʒd fɹʌm ˈbjuti nʌn kæn bi]
For beauty is infinity;–
[fɔ ˈbjutɪ ɪz ɪnˈfɪnɪtɪ]
And power to be finite ceased–
[ænd pɑːʊʌ tu bi ˈfɑːɪnɑːɪt sist]
Before identity was leased–
[bɪˈfɔːʌʁ(ɾ) ɑːɪ ˈdɛntɪtɪ waz list]

11. Will There Really Be a Morning?
[wɪl ðɛːʁ ˈɹɪli bi ʌ ˈmɔʁnɪŋ]

Will there really be a morning?
[wɪl ðɛːʌ ˈɹɪli bi ʌ ˈmɔnɪŋ]
Is there such a thing as day?
[ɪz ðɛːʌ sʌtʃ ʌ θɪŋ æz dɛːɪ]
Could I see it from the mountains,
[kʊd ɑːɪ si ɪt fɹʌm ðʌ ˈmɑːʊntæ(ɪ)nz]
If I were as tall as they?
[ɪf ɑːɪ wɜ(ɾ) æz tɔl æz ðɛːɪ]
Has it feet like water-lilies?
[hæz ɪt fit lɑːɪk ˈwɔtʌ ˈlɪlɪz]
Has it feathers like a bird?
[hæz ɪt ˈfɛðʌz lɑːɪk ʌ bɜd]
Does it come from famous places
[dʌz ɪt kʌm fɹʌm ˈfɛːɪmʌs ˈplɛːɪsɛ(ɪ)z]
Of which I have never heard?
[ʌv ʍɪtʃ ɑːɪ hæv ˈnɛvʌ hɜd]

Oh, some scholar! Oh, some sailor!
[o:ʊ sʌm ˈskalʌ o:ʊ sʌm ˈsɛːɪlɔ(ʌ)]
Oh, some wise man from the skies!
[o:ʊ sʌm waːɪz mæn fɹʌm ðʌ skaːɪz]
Please to tell this little pilgrim
[pliz tu tɛl ðɪs ˈlɪtol ˈpɪlgɹɪm]
Where the place called morning lies!
[ʍɛːʌ ðʌ plɛːɪs kɔld ˈmɔnɪŋ laːɪz]

Gounod, Charles (Fr. 1818-1893)

Song Selections

"O Divine Redeemer"
[o:ʊ dɪˈvaːɪn ɹɪˈdimʌ]
Translation by Alfred W. Phillips (Eng. 1844-1836)

Ah! turn me not away, receive me tho' unworthy,
[a tɜn mi nat ʌˈwɛːɪ ɹɪˈsiv mi ðo:ʊ ʌnˈwɜðɪ]
Ah! turn me not away, receive me tho' unworthy!
[a tɜn mi nat ʌˈwɛːɪ ɹɪˈsiv mi ðo:ʊ ʌnˈwɜðɪ]
Hear Thou my cry, hear Thou my cry,
[hiːʌ ðaːʊ maːɪ kɹaːɪ hiːʌ ðaːʊ maːɪ kɹaːɪ]
Behold, Lord, my distress!
[bɪˈho:ʊld lɔd maːɪ dɪˈstɹɛs]
Answer me from Thy throne,
[ˈansʌ mi fɹʌm ðaːɪ θro:ʊn]
Haste Thee, Lord, to mine aid,
[hɛːɪst ði lɔd tu maːɪn ɛːɪd]
Thy pity show in my deep anguish!
[ðaːɪ ˈpɪtɪ ʃo:ʊ ɪn maːɪ dip ˈæŋgwɪʃ]
Let not the sword of vengeance smite me,
[lɛt nat ðʌ sɔd ʌv ˈvɛndʒæ(ɪ)ns smaːɪt mi]
Tho' righteous Thine anger, O Lord!
[ðo:ʊ ˈɹaːɪtʃʌs ðaːɪn ˈæŋgʌ o:ʊ lɔd]
Shield me in danger, O regard me!
[ʃild mi ɪn ˈdɛːɪndʒʌ o:ʊ ɹɪˈgad mi]
On Thee, Lord, alone will I call.
[an ði lɔd ʌˈlo:ʊn wɪl aːɪ kɔl]
O divine Redeemer! O divine Redeemer!
[o:ʊ dɪˈvaːɪn ɹɪˈdimʌ o:ʊ dɪˈvaːɪn ɹɪˈdimʌ]
I pray Thee, grant me pardon, and remember not,
[aːɪ pɹɛːɪ ði gɹant mi ˈpadʌn ænd ɹɪˈmɛmbʌ nat]
Remember not my sins!
[ɹɪˈmɛmbʌ nat maːɪ sɪnz]
Forgive me,
[fɔˈgɪv mi]
O, divine Redeemer! I pray Thee, grant me pardon,
[o:ʊ dɪˈvaːɪn ɹɪˈdimʌ aːɪ pɹɛːɪ ði gɹant mi ˈpadʌn]
And remember not, remember not, O Lord, my sins!
[ænd ɹɪˈmɛmbʌ nat ɹɪˈmɛmbʌ nat o:ʊ lɔd maːɪ sɪnz]
Night gathers round my soul;
[naːɪt ˈgæðʌz ɹaːʊnd maːɪ so:ʊl]
Fearful, I cry to Thee;
[ˈfiːʌfʊl aːɪ kɹaːɪ tu ði]

Come to mine aid, O Lord!
[kʌm tu maːɪn ɛːɪd o:ʊ lɔd]
Haste Thee, Lord, haste to help me!
[hɛːɪst ði lɔd hɛːɪst tu hɛlp mi]
Hear my cry, hear my cry!
[hiːʌ maːɪ kɹaːɪ hiːʌ maːɪ kɹaːɪ]
Save me, Lord, in Thy mercy;
[sɛːɪv mi lɔd ɪn ðaːɪ ˈmɜsɪ]
Hear my cry, hear my cry!
[hiːʌ maːɪ kɹaːɪ hiːʌ maːɪ kɹaːɪ]
Come and save me, O Lord!
[kʌm ænd sɛːɪv mi o:ʊ lɔd]
O, divine Redeemer! O, divine Redeemer!
[o:ʊ dɪˈvaːɪn ɹɪˈdimʌ o:ʊ dɪˈvaːɪn ɹɪˈdimʌ]
I pray Thee, grant me pardon and remember not,
[aːɪ pɹɛːɪ ði gɹant mi ˈpadʌn ænd ɹɪˈmɛmbʌ nat]
Remember not, O Lord, my sins!
[ɹɪˈmɛmbʌ nat o:ʊ lɔd maːɪ sɪnz]
Save, in the day of retribution,
[sɛːɪv ɪn ðʌ dɛːɪ ʌv ɹɛtɹɪˈbjuʃʌn]
From Death shield Thou me, O my God!
[fɹʌm dɛθ ʃild ðaːʊ mi o:ʊ maːɪ gad]
O, divine Redeemer, have mercy!
[o:ʊ dɪˈvaːɪn ɹɪˈdimʌ hæv ˈmɜsɪ]
Help me, my Savior!
[hɛlp mi maːɪ ˈsɛːɪvjɔ(ʌ)]

"The King of Love My Shepherd Is"
[ðʊ kɪŋ ʌv lʌv maːɪ ˈʃɛpʌd ɪz]
Baker, Henry (Eng. 1821-1877)

The King of Love my Shepherd is,
[ðʊ kɪŋ ʌv lʌv maːɪ ˈʃɛpʌd ɪz]
Whose goodness faileth never;
[huz ˈgʊdnɛ(ɪ)s ˈfɛːɪlɛ(ɪ)θ ˈnɛvʌ]
I nothing lack if I am His,
[aːɪ ˈnʌθɪŋ læk ɪf aːɪ æm hɪz]
And He is mine forever.
[ænd hi ɪz maːɪn fɔʁ(ɾ)ˈɛvʌ]
Where streams of living waters flow,
[ʍɛːʌ stɹimz ʌv ˈlɪvɪŋ ˈwɔtʌz flo:ʊ]
My ransomed soul He leadeth,
[maːɪ ˈɹænsʌmd so:ʊl hi ˈlidɛ(ɪ)θ]
And where the verdant pastures grow,
[ænd ʍɛːʌ ðʊ ˈvɜdæ(ɪ)nt ˈpastʃʊ(ʌ)z gɹo:ʊ]
With food celestial feedeth.
[wɪð fud sɪˈlɛstʃʊl ˈfidɛ(ɪ)θ]
The King of Love my Shepherd is,
[ðʊ kɪŋ ʌv lʌv maːɪ ˈʃɛpʌd ɪz]
Perverse and foolish oft I strayed,
[pɜˈvɜs ænd ˈfulɪʃ aft aːɪ stɹɛːɪd]
But yet in love He sought me,
[bʌt jɛt ɪn lʌv hi sɔt mi]
And on His shoulder gently laid,
[ænd an hɪz ˈʃo:ʊldʌ ˈdʒɛntlɪ lɛːɪd]

And home rejoicing brought me.
[ænd hoːʊm ɹɪˈdʒɔːɪsɪŋ bɹɔt mi]
In death's dark vale I fear no ill
[ɪn dɛθs dɑk veːɪl ɑːɪ fiːʌ noːʊ ɪl]
With Thee, dear Lord, beside me;
[wɪð ðiː dɪːʌ lɔd bɪˈsaːɪd mi]
Thy rod and staff my comfort still,
[ðaːɪ ɾɑd ænd stɑf maːɪ ˈkʌmfɔt stɪl]
Thy cross before to guide me.
[ðaːɪ kɹɑs bɪˈfɔːʌ tu gɑːɪd mi]
And so through all the length of days,
[ænd soːʊ θɾu ɔl ðʊ lɛŋθ ʌv deːɪz]
Thy goodness faileth never;
[ðaːɪ ˈgʊdnɛ(ɪ)s ˈfeːɪlɛ(ɪ)θ ˈnɛvʌ]
Good Shepherd, May I sing Thy praise,
[gʊd ˈʃɛpʌd meːɪ ɑːɪ sɪŋ ðaːɪ pɹɛːɪz]
Forever, and forever!
[fɔʁ⁽ʳ⁾ˈɛvʌɾ ænd fɔʁ⁽ʳ⁾ˈɛvʌ]

Grieg, Edvard (Nor. 1843-1907)

Song Selection

"My Johann"
[maːɪ ˈjoːʊhan]
Epstein, Adele (Nor.)

Tra, la, la, la, la, la, la, la, la,
[tɹɑ lɑ lɑ lɑ lɑ lɑ lɑ lɑ lɑ lɑ]
When I go out to dance,
[ʍɛn ɑːɪ goːʊ aːʊt tu dans]
my Johann meets me.
[maːɪ ˈjoːʊhan mits mi]
Oh! See what he's brought!
[oːʊ si ʍat hiz bɹɔt]
Johann's brought me flowers,
[ˈjoːʊhanz bɹɔt mi flaːʊʌz]
Tra, la, la, la, la, la, la, la, la, la,
[tɹɑ lɑ lɑ lɑ lɑ lɑ lɑ lɑ lɑ lɑ]
And with a kiss the naughty boy would greet me.
[ænd wɪð ʌ kɪs ðʊ ˈnɔtɪ bɔːɪ wʊd gɹit mi]
Oh! Should we be caught,
[oːʊ ʃʊd wi bi kɔt]
We would both catch ours,
[wi wʊd boːʊθ kæʧ aːʊʌz]
Tra, la, la, la, la, la, la, la, la, la,
[tɹɑ lɑ lɑ lɑ lɑ lɑ lɑ lɑ lɑ lɑ]
Heigh! Ho! Thus! So!
[hɛːɪ hoːʊ ðʌs soːʊ]
To and fro, 'round we go!
[tu ænd fɹoːʊ ɾaːʊnd wi goːʊ]
Tra, la, la, la, la, la, la, la, la,
[tɹɑ lɑ lɑ lɑ lɑ lɑ lɑ lɑ lɑ lɑ]

Griffes, Charles Tomlinson (Am. 1884-1920)

Three Poems of Fiona Macleod (Song Cycle)
[θɾi ˈpoːʊɪmz ʌv fiˈoːʊnʌ mʌˈklɔːɪd]
Sharp, William (Sc. 1855-1905)
pseudonym: Fiona Macleod

1. Lament of Ian the Proud
[lʌˈmɛnt ʌv ˈiʌn ðʌ pɹɑːʊd]

What is this crying that I hear in the wind?
[ʍat ɪz ðɪs ˈkɹ⁽ʳ⁾aːɪɪŋ ðæt ɑːɪ hiːʌʁ⁽ʳ⁾ ɪn ðʌ wɪnd]
Is it the old sorrow and the old grief?
[ɪz ɪt ði oːʊld ˈsaʁ⁽ʳ⁾oːʊ ænd ði oːʊld gɹ⁽ʳ⁾if]
Or is it a new thing coming, a whirling leaf
[ɔʁ⁽ʳ⁾ ɪz ɪt ʌ nju θɪŋ ˈkʌmɪŋ ʌ ˈʍɜlɪŋ lif]
About the gray hair of me
[ʌˈbaːʊt ðʌ gɹ⁽ʳ⁾ɛːɪ hɛːʌʁ⁽ʳ⁾ ʌv mi]
who am weary and blind?
[hu æm ˈwiːʌʁ⁽ʳ⁾ɪ ænd blaːɪnd]
I know not what it is, but on the moor above the shore
[ɑːɪ noːʊ nat ʍat ɪt ɪz bʌt an ðʌ mʊːʌʁ⁽ʳ⁾ ʌˈbʌv ðʌ ʃɔːʌ]
There is a stone which the purple nets of heather bind,
[ðɛːʌʁ⁽ʳ⁾ ɪz ʌ stoːʊn ʍɪʧ ðʌ ˈpɜpʊl nɛts ʌv ˈhɛðʌ baːɪnd]
And thereon is writ: She will return no more.
[ænd ðɛːʌʁ⁽ʳ⁾ˈan ɪz ɹɪt ʃi wɪl ɹɪˈtɜn noːʊ mɔːʌ]
O blown, whirling leaf, and the old grief,
[oːʊ bloːʊn ˈʍɜlɪŋ lif ænd ði oːʊld gɹ⁽ʳ⁾if]
And wind crying to me who am old and blind!
[ænd wɪnd ˈkɹ⁽ʳ⁾aːɪɪŋ tu mi hu æm oːʊld ænd blaːɪnd]

2. Thy Dark Eyes to Mine
[ðaːɪ daʁk aːɪz tu maːɪn]

Thy dark eyes to mine, Eilidh,
[ðaːɪ dak aːɪz tu maːɪn ˈɛːɪlɪ]
Lamps of desire!
[læmps ʌv dɪˈzaːɪʌ]
O how my soul leaps,
[oːʊ haːʊ maːɪ soːʊl lips]
Leaps to their fire!
[lips tu ðɛːʌ faːɪʌ]
Sure, now, if I in heaven,
[ʃʊːʌ naːʊ ɪf ɑːɪ ɪn ˈhɛvɛ(ɪ)n]
Dreaming in bliss,
[ˈdɹimɪŋ ɪn blɪs]
Heard but a whisper,
[hɜd bʌt ʌ ˈʍɪspʌ]
But a lost echo even
[bʌt ʌ last ˈɛkoːʊ ˈivɛ(ɪ)n]
Of one such kiss,
[ʌv wʌn sʌʧ kɪs]
All of the soul of me
[ɔl ʌv ðʌ soːʊl ʌv mi]

Would leap afar,
[wʊd lip ʌˈfɑ]
If that called me to thee,
[ɪf ðæt kɔld mi tu ði]
Aye, I would leap afar,
[ɑːɪ ɑːɪ wʊd lip ʌˈfɑ]
A falling star.
[ʌ ˈfɔlɪŋ sta]

3. The Rose of the Night
[ðʌ ɹoːʊz ʌv ðʌ naːɪt]

The dark rose of thy mouth
[ðʌ dak ɹoːʊz ʌv ðɑːɪ maːʊθ]
Draw nigher, draw nigher!
[dɹɔ ˈnaːɪʌ dɹɔ ˈnaːɪʌ]
Thy breath is the wind of the south,
[ðaːɪ bɹɛθ ɪz ðʌ wɪnd ʌv ðʌ saːʊθ]
A wind of fire!
[ʌ wɪnd ʌv faːɪʌ]
The wind and the rose and darkness,
[ðʌ wɪnd ænd ðʌ ɹoːʊz ænd ˈdaknɛ(ɪ)s]
O Rose of my Desire!
[oːʊ ɹoːʊz ʌv maːɪ dɪˈzaːɪʌ]
Deep silence of the night,
[dip ˈsaːɪlɛ(ɪ)ns ʌv ðʌ naːɪt]
Husht like a breathless lyre,
[hʌʃt laːɪk ʌ ˈbɹɛθlɛ(ɪ)s ˈlaːɪʌ]
Save the sea's thunderous might,
[sɛːɪv ðʌ siz ˈθʌndaʁ(r)ʌs maːɪt]
Dim, menacing, dire;
[dim ˈmɛnæ(ɪ)sɪŋ daːɪʌ]
Silence and wind and sea, They are thee,
[ˈsaːɪlɛ(ɪ)ns ænd wɪnd ænd si ðɛːɪ ɑ ði]
O Rose of my Desire!
[oːʊ ɹoːʊz ʌv maːɪ dɪˈzaːɪʌ]
As a wind-eddying flame
[æz ʌ wɪnd ˈɛdɪɪŋ flɛːɪm]
Leaping higher and higher,
[ˈlipɪŋ ˈhaːɪʌʁ(r) ænd ˈhaːɪʌ]
Thy soul, thy secret name,
[ðaːɪ soːʊl ðaːɪ ˈsikɹɛ(ɪ)t nɛːɪm]
Leaps thro' Death's blazing pyre!
[lips θru dɛθs ˈblɛːɪzɪŋ ˈpaːɪʌ]
Kiss me, imperishable Fire, Dark Rose,
[kɪs mi ɪmˈpɛʁ(r)ɪʃʌbʊl faːɪʌ dak ɹoːʊz]
O Rose of my Desire!
[oːʊ ɹoːʊz ʌv maːɪ dɪˈzaːɪʌ]

Gurney, Ivor (Eng. 1890-1937)

Song Selections

"In Flanders"
[ɪn ˈflændʌz]
Harvey, Frederick William (Eng. 1888-1957)

I'm homesick for my hills again–
[aːɪm ˈhoːʊmsɪk fɔ maːɪ hɪlz ʌˈgɛːɪn]
To see above the Severn plain
[tu si ʌˈbʌv ðʊ ˈsɛvʌn plɛːɪn]
Unscabbarded against the sky
[ʌnˈskæbʌdɛ(ɪ)d ʌˈgɛːɪnst ðʊ skaːɪ]
The blue high blade of Cotswold lie;
[ðʊ blu haːɪ blɛːɪd ʌv ˈkatswɔld laːɪ]
The giant clouds go royally
[ðʊ ˈdʒaːɪæ(ɪ)nt klaːʊdz goːʊ ˈɹɔːɪʊli]
By jagged Malvern with a train
[baːɪ ˈdʒægɛ(ɪ)d ˈmɔlvʌn wɪð ʌ tɹɛːɪn]
Of shadows.
[ʌv ˈʃædoːʊz]
Where the land is low
[ʍɛːʌ ðʊ lænd ɪz loːʊ]
Like a huge imprisoning O
[laːɪk ʌ hjudʒ ɪmˈpɹɪzʌnɪŋ oːʊ]
I hear a heart that's sound and high,
[aːɪ hiːʌʁ ʌ hat ðæts saːʊnd ænd haːɪ]
I hear the heart within me cry:
[aːɪ hiːʌ ðʊ hat wɪðˈɪn mi kraːɪ]
"I'm homesick for my hills again–
[aːɪm ˈhoːʊmsɪk fɔ maːɪ hɪlz ʌˈgɛːɪn]
Cotswold or Malvern, sun or rain!
[ˈkatswɔld ɔ ˈmɔlvʌn sʌn ɔ ʁɛːɪn]
My hills again!"
[maːɪ hɪlz ʌˈgɛːɪn]

"Sleep" (Five Elizabethan Songs)
[slip]
Fletcher, John (Eng. 1579-1625)

Come, Sleep, and with thy sweet deceiving
[kʌm slip ænd wɪð ðaːɪ swit dɪˈsivɪŋ]
Lock me in delight awhile;
[lak mi ɪn dɪˈlaːɪt ʌˈʍaːɪl]
Let some pleasing dream beguile
[lɛt sʌm ˈplizɪŋ dɹim bɪˈgaːɪl]
All my fancies; that from thence
[ɔl maːɪ ˈfænsɪz ðæt fɹʌm ðɛns]
I may feel an influence
[aːɪ mɛːɪ fil æn ˈɪnfluɛ(ɪ)ns]
All my powers of care bereaving!
[ɔl maːɪ paːʊʌz ʌv kɛːʌ bɪˈrivɪŋ]
Though but a shadow, but a sliding,
[ðoːʊ bʌt ʌ ˈʃædoːʊ bʌt ʌ ˈslaːɪdɪŋ]

Let me know some little joy!
[lɛt mi noːʊ sʌm ˈlɪtʊl dʒɔːɪ]
We that suffer long annoy
[wi ðæt ˈsʌfʌ laŋ ʌˈnɔːɪ]
Are contented with a thought
[ɑ kʌnˈtɛntɛ(ɪ)d wɪð ʌ θɔt]
Through an idle fancy wrought:
[θɾu æn ˈɑːɪdʊl ˈfænsɪ ɾɔt]
O let my joys have some abiding!
[oːʊ lɛt mɑːɪ dʒɔːɪz hæv sʌm ʌˈbɑːɪdɪŋ]

"Spring" (see Argento)

"The Fields Are Full"
[ðʊ fildz ɑ fʊl]
Shanks, Edward (Eng. 1892-1953)

The fields are full of summer still
[ðʊ fildz ɑ fʊl ʌv ˈsʌmʌ stil]
And breathe again upon the air
[ænd bɹið ʌˈgɛːɪn ʌˈpɑn ði ɛːʌ]
From brown dry side of hedge and hill
[fɹʌm bɹɑːʊn dɹɑːɪ sɑːɪd ʌv hɛdʒ ænd hil]
More sweetness than the sense can bear.
[mɔːʌ ˈswitnɛ(ɪ)s ðæn ðʊ sɛns kæn bɛːʌ]
So some old couple, who in youth
[soːʊ sʌm oːʊld ˈkʌpʊl hu ɪn juθ]
With love were filled and over-full,
[wɪð lʌv wɜ fild ænd ˈoːʊvʌ fʊl]
And loved with strength and loved with truth,
[ænd lʌvd wɪð stɹɛŋθ ænd lʌvd wɪð truθ]
In heavy age are beautiful.
[ɪn ˈhɛvɪ ɛːɪdʒ ɑ ˈbjutɪfʊl]

H

Hageman, Richard (Am. 1882-1966)

Song Selections

"Christ Went up into the Hills"
[kɹɑːɪst wɛnt ʌp ˈɪntu ðʌ hɪlz]
Adams, Katharine (Am.)

Christ went up into the hills alone
[kɹɑːɪst wɛnt ʌp ˈɪntu ðʌ hɪlz ʌˈloːʊn]
Walking slowly the winding way,
[ˈwɔkɪŋ ˈsloːʊlɪ ðʌ ˈwɑːɪndɪŋ wɛːɪ]
Far from the city's dust and stone,
[fɑ fɹʌm ðʌ ˈsɪtɪz dʌst ænd stoːʊn]
To the lonely hills to pray.
[tu ðʌ ˈloːʊnlɪ hɪlz tu pɹɛːɪ]

There was no one to go with Him
[ðɛːʌ waz noːʊ wʌn tu goːʊ wɪð hɪm]
On His lonely walk in the silent night.
[ɑn hɪz ˈloːʊnlɪ wɔk ɪn ðʌ ˈsɑːɪlɛnt nɑːɪt]
Only the hush of the starshine dim,
[ˈoːʊnlɪ ðʌ hʌʃ ʌv ðʌ ˈstɑʃɑːɪn dɪm]
Only the shadowed hill-road white,
[ˈoːʊnlɪ ðʌ ˈʃædoːʊd hɪl ɹoːʊd ʍɑːɪt]
Only the lambs calling each to each,
[ˈoːʊnlɪ ðʌ læmz ˈkɔlɪŋ iʧ tu iʧ]
And the tender goodnight of dreaming birds.
[ænd ðʌ ˈtɛndʌ ˌgʊdˈnɑːɪt ʌv ˈdɹimɪŋ bɜdz]
Only a love too pure for speech,
[ˈoːʊnlɪ ʌ lʌv tu pjʊːʌ fɔ spiʧ]
And a grief too deep for words.
[ænd ʌ gɹ(ʳ)if tu dip fɔ wɜdz]

"Do Not Go, My Love"
[du nat goːʊ mɑːɪ lʌv]
Tagore, Rabindrath (Bengali 1861-1941)

Do not go, my love, without asking my leave.
[du nat goːʊ mɑːɪ lʌv wɪðˈɑːʊt ˈæskɪŋ mɑːɪ liv]
I have watched all night,
[ɑːɪ hæv waʧt ɔl nɑːɪt]
and now my eyes are heavy with sleep;
[ænd nɑːʊ mɑːɪ ɑːɪz ɑ ˈhɛvɪ wɪð slip]
I fear lest I lose you when I am sleeping.
[ɑːɪ fɪːʌ lɛst ɑːɪ luz ju ʍɛn ɑːɪ æm ˈslipɪŋ]
Do not go, my love, without asking my leave.
[du nat goːʊ mɑːɪ lʌv wɪðˈɑːʊt ˈæskɪŋ mɑːɪ liv]
I start up and stretch my hands to touch you.
[ɑːɪ stat ʌp ænd stɹɛʧ mɑːɪ hændz tu tʌʧ ju]
I ask myself, "Is it a dream?"
[ɑːɪ æsk mɑːɪˈsɛlf ɪz ɪt ʌ dɹim]
Could I but entangle your feet with my heart,
[kʊd ɑːɪ bʌt ɪnˈtæŋgʊl jɔːʌ fit wɪð mɑːɪ hat]
And hold them fast to my breast!
[ænd hoːʊld ðɛm fæst tu mɑːɪ bɹɛst]
Do not go, my love, without asking my leave.
[du nat goːʊ mɑːɪ lʌv wɪðˈɑːʊt ˈæskɪŋ mɑːɪ liv]

"Music I Heard with You"
[ˈmjuzɪk ɑːɪ hɜd wɪθ ju]
Aiken, Conrad (Am. 1889-1973)

Music I heard with you was more than music,
[ˈmjuzɪk ɑːɪ hɜd wɪð ju waz mɔːʌ ðæn ˈmjuzɪk]
And bread I broke with you was more than bread;
[ænd bɹɛd ɑːɪ bɹoːʊk wɪð ju waz mɔːʌ ðæn bɹɛd]
Now that I am without you, all is desolate;
[nɑːʊ ðæt ɑːɪ æm wɪðˈɑːʊt ju ɔl ɪz ˈdɛsolæ(ɪ)t]
All that was once so beautiful is dead.
[ɔl ðæt waz wʌns soːʊ ˈbjutɪfʊl ɪz dɛd]
Your hands once touched this table and this silver,
[jɔːʌ hændz wʌns tʌʧt ðɪs ˈtɛːɪbʊl ænd ðɪs ˈsɪlvʌ]

And I have seen your fingers hold this glass.
[ænd ɑːɪ hæv sin jɔːʌ ˈfɪŋɡʌz hoːʊld ðɪs glæs]
These things do not remember you, beloved,
[ðiz θɪŋz du nat ɹɪˈmɛmbʌ ju bɪˈlʌvɛ(ɪ)d]
And yet your touch upon them will not pass.
[ænd jɛt jɔːʌ tʌʧ ʌˈpɑn ðɛm wɪl nat pæs]
For it was in my heart you moved among them,
[fɔʁ(r) ɪt waz ɪn mɑːɪ hat ju muvd ʌˈmʌŋ ðɛm]
And blessed them with your hands and with your eyes;
[ænd blɛst ðɛm wɪð jɔːʌ hændz ænd wɪð jɔːʌʁ(r) ɑːɪz]
And in my heart they will remember always,–
[ænd ɪn mɑːɪ hat ðɛːɪ wɪl ɹɪˈmɛmbʌʁ(r) ˈɔlwɛːɪz]
They knew you once, O beautiful and wise.
[ðɛːɪ nju ju wʌns oːʊ ˈbjutɪfʊl ænd wɑːɪz]

Hagen, Daron (Am. b. 1961)

Song Selections

"A Dream Within a Dream" (Echo's Songs)
[ʌ dɹim wɪðˈɪn ʌ dɹim]
Poe, Edgar Allan (Am. 1809-1849)

Take this kiss upon thy brow!
[tɛːɪk ðɪs kɪs ʌˈpɑn ðɑːɪ bɹɑːʊ]
And in parting from you now,
[ænd ɪn ˈpatɪŋ fɹʌm ju nɑːʊ]
Thus much let me avow–
[ðʌs mʌʧ lɛt mi ʌˈvɑːʊ]
You are not wrong who deem,
[ju ɑ nat ɹʌŋ hu dim]
That my days have been a dream;
[ðæt mɑːɪ dɛːɪz hæv bɪn ʌ dɹim]
Yet if hope has flown away,
[jɛt ɪf hoːʊp hæz floːʊn ʌˈwɛːɪ]
In a night, or in a day,
[ɪn ʌ nɑːɪt ɔʁ(r) ɪn ʌ dɛːɪ]
In a vision, or in a day,
[ɪn ʌ ˈvɪʒʌn ɔʁ(r) ɪn ʌ dɛːɪ]
In a vision, or in none,
[ɪn ʌ ˈvɪʒʌn ɔʁ(r) ɪn nʌn]
Is it therefore the less gone?
[ɪz ɪt ˈðɛːʌfɔːʌ ðʌ lɛs gɑn]
All that we see or seem
[ɔl ðæt wi si ɔ sim]
Is but a dream within a dream.
[ɪz bʌt ʌ dɹim wɪðˈɪn ʌ dɹim]
I stand amid the roar
[ɑːɪ stænd ʌˈmɪd ðʌ ɹɔːʌ]
Of a surf-tormented shore,
[ʌv ʌ sɜf tɔˈmɛntɛ(ɪ)d ʃɔːʌ]
And I hold within my hand
[ænd ɑːɪ hoːʊld wɪðˈɪn mɑːɪ hænd]
Grains of the golden sand–
[ɡɹɛːɪnz ʌv ðʌ ˈɡoːʊldɛ(ɪ)n sænd]

How few! yet how they creep
[hɑːʊ fju jɛt hɑːʊ ðɛːɪ kɹip]
Through my fingers to the deep,
[θɹu mɑːɪ ˈfɪŋɡʌz tu ðʌ dip]
While I weep– while I weep!
[ʍɑːɪl ɑːɪ wip ʍɑːɪl ɑːɪ wip]
O God! can I not grasp
[oːʊ gad kæn ɑːɪ nat ɡɹæsp]
Them with a tighter clasp?
[ðɛm wɪð ʌ ˈtɑːɪtʌ klæsp]
O God! can I not save
[oːʊ gad kæn ɑːɪ nat sɛːɪv]
One from the pitiless wave?
[wʌn fɹʌm ðʌ ˈpɪtɪlɛ(ɪ)s wɛːɪv]
Is all that we see or seem
[ɪz ɔl ðæt wi si ɔ sim]
But a dream within a dream?
[bʌt ʌ dɹim wɪðˈɪn ʌ dɹim]

"Specimen Case" (see "A Specimen Case" by Rorem)

Hailstork, Adolphus Cunningham (Am. b. 1941)

"Longing"
[ˈlaŋɪŋ]
Dunbar, Paul Lawrence (Am. 1872-1906)

If you could sit with me beside the sea to-day,
[ɪf ju kʊd sɪt wɪð mi bɪˈsɑːɪd ðʌ si tu dɛːɪ]
And whisper with me sweetest dreamings o'er and o'er;
[ænd ˈʍɪspʌ wɪð mi ˈswitɛ(ɪ)st ˈdɹimɪŋz ɔːʌʁ(r) ænd ɔːʌ]
I think I should not find the clouds
[ɑːɪ θɪŋk ɑːɪ ʃʊd nat fɑːɪnd ðʌ klɑːʊdz]
so dim and gray,
[soːʊ dɪm ænd ɡɹɛːɪ]
And not so loud the waves complaining
[ænd nat soːʊ lɑːʊd ðʌ wɛːɪvz kʌmˈplɛːɪnɪŋ]
at the shore.
[æt ðʌ ʃɔːʌ]
If you could sit with me upon the shore to-day,
[ɪf ju kʊd sɪt wɪð mi ʌˈpɑn ðʌ ʃɔːʌ tu dɛːɪ]
And hold my hand in yours as in the days of old,
[ænd hoːʊld mɑːɪ hænd ɪn jɔːʌz æz ɪn ðʌ dɛːɪz ʌv oːʊld]
I think I should not mind the chill baptismal spray,
[ɑːɪ θɪŋk ɑːɪ ʃʊd nat mɑːɪnd ðʌ ʧɪl bæpˈtɪzmʊl spɹɛːɪ]
Nor find my hand and heart
[nɔ fɑːɪnd mɑːɪ hænd ænd hat]
and all the world so cold.
[ænd ɔl ðʌ wɜld soːʊ koːʊld]
If you could walk with me beside the strand to-day,
[ɪf ju kʊd wɔk wɪð mi bɪˈsɑːɪd ðʌ stɹænd tu dɛːɪ]
And tell me that my longing love had won your own,
[ænd tɛl mi ðæt mɑːɪ ˈlaŋɪŋ lʌv hæd wʌn jɔːʌʁ(r) oːʊn]

I think all my sad thoughts would then be put away,
[ɑːɪ θɪŋk ɔl mɑːɪ sæd θɔts wʊd ðɛn bi pʊt ʌˈwɛːɪ]
And I could give back laughter for the ocean's moan!
[ænd ɑːɪ kʊd gɪv bæk ˈlæftʌ fɔ ði ˈoːʊʃæ(ɪ)nz moːʊn]

"Love" (Songs of Love and Justice)
[lʌv]
Martin Luther King, Jr. (Am. 1929-1968)

Love is the only force
[lʌv ɪz ði ˈoːʊnlɪ fɔs]
capable of transforming
[ˈkɛːɪpʌbʊl ʌv tɹænsˈfɔmɪŋ]
an enemy into a friend.
[æn ˈɛnɪ(ʌ)mɪ ˈɪntu ʌ fɹɛnd]

"My Heart to Thy Heart"
[mɑːɪ hɑʁt tu ðɑːɪ hɑʁt]
Dunbar, Paul Lawrence (Am. 1872-1906)

My heart to thy heart,
[mɑːɪ hɑt tu ðɑːɪ hɑt]
My hand to thine;
[mɑːɪ hænd tu ðɑːɪn]
My lips to thy lips,
[mɑːɪ lɪps tu ðɑːɪ lɪps]
Kisses are wine
[ˈkɪsɛ(ɪ)z ʌ wɑːɪn]
Brewed for the lover in sunshine and shade;
[bɹ(ʳ)ud fɔ ðʌ ˈlʌvʌ ɪn ˈsʌnʃɑːɪn ænd ʃɛːɪd]
Let me drink deep, then, my African maid.
[lɛt mi dɹɪŋk dip ðɛn mɑːɪ ˈæfɹɪkæ(ɪ)n mɛːɪd]
Lily to lily,
[ˈlɪlɪ tu ˈlɪlɪ]
Rose unto rose;
[ɹoːʊz ˈʌntu ɹoːʊz]
My love to thy love
[mɑːɪ lʌv tu ðɑːɪ lʌv]
Tenderly grows.
[ˈtɛndʌlɪ gɹoːʊz]
Rend not the oak and the ivy in twain,
[ɹɛnd nat ði oːʊk ænd ði ˈɑːɪvɪ ɪn twɛːɪn]
Nor the swart maid from her swarthier swain.
[nɔ ðʌ swɔt mɛːɪd fɹʌm hɜ ˈswɔðɪʌ swɛːɪn]

"The Awakening" (Five Dunbar Lyrics)
[ði ʌˈwɛːɪkɪnɪŋ]
Dunbar, Paul Lawrence (Am. 1872-1906)

I did not know that life could be so sweet,
[ɑːɪ dɪd nat noːʊ ðæt lɑːɪf kʊd bi soːʊ swit]
I did not know the hours could be so fleet,
[ɑːɪ dɪd nat noːʊ ði ɑːʊʌz kʊd bi soːʊ flit]
Till I knew you, and life was sweet again.
[tɪl ɑːɪ nju ju ænd lɑːɪf waz swit ʌˈgɛn]

The days grew brief with love and lack of pain–
[ðʌ dɛːɪz gɹ(ʳ)u bɹɪf wɪð lʌv ænd læk ʌv pɛːɪn]
I was a slave a few short days ago,–
[ɑːɪ waz ʌ slɛːɪv ʌ fju ʃɔt dɛːɪz ʌˈgoːʊ]
The powers of Kings and princes now I know;
[ðʌ pɑːʊʌz ʌv kɪŋz ænd ˈpɹɪnsɛ(ɪ)z nɑːʊ ɑːɪ noːʊ]
I would not be again in bondage
[ɑːɪ wʊd nat bi ʌˈgɛn ɪn ˈbandæ(ɪ)ʤ]
Save I had your smile, the liberty I crave.
[sɛːɪv ɑːɪ hæd jɔʌ smɑːɪl ðʌ ˈlɪbʌtɪ ɑːɪ kɹɛːɪv]

 # Hall, Juliana (Am. b. 1958)

Night Dances (Song Cycle)
[nɑːɪt ˈdænsɪz]
(6 songs for Soprano and Piano)

1. The Cricket Sang
[ðʌ ˈkɹɪkɪt sæŋ]
Dickinson, Emily (Am. 1830-1886)

The cricket sang,
[ðʌ ˈkɹɪkɛ(ɪ)t sæŋ]
And set the sun,
[ænd sɛt ðʌ sʌn]
And workmen finished, one by one,
[ænd ˈwɜkmɛ(ɪ)n ˈfɪnɪʃt wʌn bɑːɪ wʌn]
Their seam the day upon.
[ðɛːʌ sim ðʌ dɛːɪ ʌˈpan]
The low grass loaded with the dew,
[ðʌ loːʊ gɹæs ˈloːʊdɛ(ɪ)d wɪð ðʌ dju]
The twilight stood as strangers do
[ðʌ ˈtwɑːɪlɑːɪt stʊd æz ˈstɹɛːɪnʤʌz du]
With hat in hand, polite and new,
[wɪð hæt ɪn hænd poˈlɑːɪt ænd nju]
To stay as if, or go.
[tu stɛːɪ æz ɪf ɔ goːʊ]
A vastness, as a neighbor, came,
[ʌ ˈvæstnɛ(ɪ)s æz ʌ ˈnɛːɪbɔ(ʌ) kɛːɪm]
A wisdom without face or name,
[ʌ ˈwɪzdʌm wɪðˈɑːʊt fɛːɪs ɔ nɛːɪm]
A peace, as hemispheres at home,
[ʌ pis æz ˈhɛmɪsfɪːʌz æt hoːʊm]
And so the night became.
[ænd soːʊ ðʌ nɑːɪt bɪˈkɛːɪm]

2. Some Things are Dark
[sʌm θɪŋz ɑʁ dɑʁk]
Millay, Edna St. Vincent (Am. 1892-1950)

Some things are dark– or think they are.
[sʌm θɪŋz ɑ dɑk ɔ θɪŋk ðɛːɪ ɑ]
But, in comparison to me,
[bʌt ɪn kʌmˈpæʁ(ʳ)ɪsʌn tu mi]

All things are light enough to see
[ɔl θɪŋz ɑ laːɪt ɪˈnʌf tu si]
In any place, at any hour.
[ɪn ˈɛni plɛːɪs æt ˈɛni aːʊʌ]
For I am Nightmare: where I fly,
[fɔʁ⁽ʳ⁾ aːɪ æm ˈnɑːɪtmɛːʌ ᴍɛːʌʁ⁽ʳ⁾ aːɪ flaːɪ]
Terror and rain stand in the sky
[ˈtɛʁ⁽ʳ⁾ɔʁ⁽ʳ⁾ ænd ɹɛːɪn stænd ɪn ðʌ skaːɪ]
So thick, you could not tell them from
[soːʊ θɪk ju kʊd nɑt tɛl ðɛm fɹʌm]
That blackness out of which you come.
[ðæt ˈblæknɛ(ɪ)s aːʊt ʌv ᴍɪʧ ju kʌm]
So much for "where I fly": but when
[soːʊ mʌʧ fɔ ᴍɛːʌʁ⁽ʳ⁾ aːɪ flaːɪ bʌt ᴍɛn]
I strike, and clutch in claw the brain–
[aːɪ stɹaːɪk ænd klʌʧ ɪn klɔ ðʌ bɹɛːɪn]
Erebus, to such brain, will seem
[ˈɛʁ⁽ʳ⁾ɪbʊs tu sʌʧ bɹɛːɪn wɪl sim]
The thin blue dusk of pleasant dream.
[ðʌ θɪn blu dʌsk ʌv ˈplɛzæ(ɪ)nt dɹim]

3. Song

[sɑŋ]
Brontë, Emily (Eng. 1818-1848)

This shall be thy lullaby
[ðɪs ʃæl bi ðaːɪ ˈlʌlʌbaːɪ]
Rocking on the stormy sea,
[ˈɹakɪŋ an ðʌ ˈstɔmi si]
Though it roar in thunder wild,
[ðoːʊ ɪt ɹɔːʌʁ⁽ʳ⁾ ɪn ˈθʌndʌ waːɪld]
Sleep, stilly sleep, my dark-haired child.
[slip ˈstɪli slip maːɪ dak hɛːʌd ʧaːɪld]
When our shuddering boat was crossing
[ᴍɛn aːʊʌ ˈʃʌdʌʁ⁽ʳ⁾ɪŋ boːʊt waz ˈkɹasɪŋ]
Eldern's lake so rudely tossing,
[ˈɛldʌnz lɛːɪk soːʊ ˈɹ⁽ʳʳ⁾udli ˈtasɪŋ]
Then 'twas first my nursling smiled;
[ðɛn twaz fɜst maːɪ ˈnɜslɪŋ smaːɪld]
Sleep, softly sleep, my fair-browed child.
[slip ˈsaftli slip maːɪ fɛːʌ bɹaːʊd ʧaːɪld]
Waves above thy cradle break,
[wɛːɪvz ʌˈbʌv ðaːɪ ˈkɹɛːɪdʊl bɹɛːɪk]
Foamy tears are on thy cheek,
[ˈfoːʊmi tiːʌz aʁ⁽ʳ⁾ an ðaːɪ ʧik]
Yet the Ocean's self grows mild
[jɛt ði ˈoːʊʃæ(ɪ)nz sɛlf gɹoːʊz maːɪld]
When it bears my slumbering child.
[ᴍɛn ɪt bɛːʌz maːɪ ˈslʌmbʌʁ⁽ʳ⁾ɪŋ ʧaːɪld]

4. Sleep, Mourner, Sleep!

[slip ˈmɔʁnʁ slip]
Brontë, Patrick Branwell (Eng. 1817-1848)

Sleep, mourner, sleep!– I cannot sleep,
[slip ˈmɔnʌ slip aːɪ kæˈnat slip]

My weary mind still wanders on;
[maːɪ ˈwiːʌʁ⁽ʳ⁾i maːɪnd stɪl ˈwandʌz an]
Then silent weep – I cannot weep,
[ðɛn ˈsaːɪlɛnt wip aːɪ kæˈnat wip]
For eyes and tears are turned to stone.
[fɔʁ⁽ʳ⁾ aːɪz ænd tɪːʌz a tɜnd tu stoːʊn]

5. A Spider Sewed at Night

[ʌ ˈspaːɪdʁ soːʊd æt naːɪt]
Dickinson, Emily (Am. 1830-1886)

A spider sewed at night
[ʌ ˈspaːɪdʌ soːʊd æt naːɪt]
Without a light
[wɪðˈaːʊt ʌ laːɪt]
Upon an arc of white.
[ʌˈpan æn ak ʌv ᴍaːɪt]
If ruff it was of dame
[ɪf ɹʌf ɪt waz ʌv dɛːɪm]
Or shroud of gnome,
[ɔ ʃɹaːʊd ʌv noːʊm]
Himself, himself inform.
[hɪmˈsɛlf hɪmˈsɛlf ɪnˈfɔm]
Of immortality
[ʌv ɪmɔˈtælɪti]
His strategy
[hɪz ˈstɹætɛ(ɪ)ʤɪ]
Was physiognomy.
[waz fɪziˈano(ʌ)mɪ]

6. Sonnet (copyright)

Setting Sail (Song Cycle)
[ˈsɛtɪŋ sɛːɪl]
Dickinson, Emily (Am. 1830-1886)

1. Setting Sail

[ˈsɛtɪŋ sɛːɪl]

Exultation is the going
[ɛgzu(ʊ)lˈtɛːɪʃʌn ɪz ðʌ ˈgoːʊɪŋ]
Of an inland soul to sea,–
[ʌv æn ˈɪnlæ(ʌ)nd soːʊl tu si]
Past the houses, past the headlands,
[pæst ðʌ ˈhaːʊzɛ(ɪ)z pæst ðʌ ˈhɛdlæ(ʌ)ndz]
Into deep eternity!
[ˈɪntu dip ɪˈtɜnɪti]
Bred as we, among the mountains,
[bɹɛd æz wi ʌˈmʌŋ ðʌ ˈmaːʊntæ(ɪ)nz]
Can the sailor understand
[kæn ðʌ ˈsɛːɪlɔ(ʌ)ʁ⁽ʳ⁾ ʌndʌˈstænd]
The divine intoxication
[ðʌ dɪˈvaːɪn ɪntaksɪˈkɛːɪʃʌn]
Of the first league out from land?
[ʌv ðʌ fɜst lig aːʊt fɹʌm lænd]

2. A Little Madness in the Spring
[ʌ ˈlɪtʊl ˈmædnɪs ɪn ðʌ spɹɪŋ]

A little madness in the Spring
[ʌ ˈlɪtʊl ˈmædnɛ(ɪ)s ɪn ðʌ spɹɪŋ]
Is wholesome even for the King,
[ɪz ˈhoːʊlsʌm ˈivɛ(ɪ)n fɔ ðʌ kɪŋ]
But God be with the Clown,
[bʌt ɡad bi wɪð ðʌ klaːʊn]
Who ponders this tremendous scene–
[hu ˈpandʌz ðɪs tɹɪˈmɛndʌs sin]
This whole experiment of green,
[ðɪs hoːʊl ɪkˈspɛʁ(ɾ)ɪment ʌv ɡɹin]
As if it were his own!
[æz ɪf ɪt wɜ hɪz oːʊn]

3. If I Can Stop One Heart from Breaking
[ɪf aːɪ kæn stap wʌn haʁt fɹʌm ˈbɹeːɪkɪŋ]

If I can stop one heart from breaking,
[ɪf aːɪ kæn stap wʌn hat fɹʌm ˈbɹeːɪkɪŋ]
I shall not live in vain;
[aːɪ ʃæl nat lɪv ɪn veːɪn]
If I can ease one life the aching,
[ɪf aːɪ kæn iz wʌn laːɪf ði ˈeːɪkɪŋ]
Or cool one pain,
[ɔ kul wʌn peːɪn]
Or help one fainting robin
[ɔ hɛlp wʌn ˈfeːɪntɪŋ ˈɹabɪn]
Unto his nest again,
[ˈʌntu hɪz nɛst ʌˈɡɛn]
I shall not live in vain.
[aːɪ ʃæl nat lɪv ɪn veːɪn]

4. A Book
[ʌ bʊk]

He ate and drank the precious words,
[hi ɛːɪt ænd dɹæŋk ðʌ ˈpɹɛʃʌs w3dz]
His spirit grew robust;
[hɪz ˈspɪʁ(ɾ)ɪt ɡɹ(ɾ)u ɹoˈbʌst]
He knew no more that he was poor,
[hi nju noːʊ mɔːʌ ðæt hi waz pʊːʌ]
Nor that his frame was dust.
[nɔ ðæt hɪz fɹɛːɪm waz dʌst]
He danced along the dingy days,
[hi dænst ʌˈlaŋ ðʌ ˈdɪndʒɪ dɛːɪz]
And this bequest of wings
[ænd ðɪs bɪˈkwɛst ʌv wɪŋz]
Was but a book. What liberty
[waz bʌt ʌ bʊk ʍat ˈlɪbʌtɪ]
A loosened spirit brings!
[ʌ ˈlusɛ(ɪ)nd ˈspɪʁ(ɾ)ɪt bɹɪŋz]

5. Suspense
[sʌˈspɛns]

Elysium is as far as to
[ɪˈlizɪʌm ɪz æz faʁ(ɾ) æz tu]
The very nearest room,
[ðʌ ˈvɛʁ(ɾ)ɪ ˈniːʌʁ(ɾ)ɛ(ɪ)st ɹ(ɾɾ)um]
If in that room a friend await
[ɪf ɪn ðæt ɹ(ɾɾ)um ʌ fɹɛnd ʌˈweːɪt]
Felicity or doom.
[fɪˈlɪsɪtɪ ɔ dum]
What fortitude the soul contains,
[ʍat ˈfɔtɪtjud ðʌ soːʊl kʌnˈteːɪnz]
That it can so endure
[ðæt ɪt kæn soːʊ ɪnˈdjʊːʌ]
The accent of a coming foot,
[ði ˈæksɛnt ʌv ʌ ˈkʌmɪŋ fʊt]
The opening of a door!
[ði ˈoːʊpɛ(ɪ)nɪŋ ʌv ʌ dɔːʌ]

6. I Died for Beauty
[aːɪ daːɪd fɔʁ ˈbjuti]

I died for beauty, but was scarce
[aːɪ daːɪd fɔ ˈbjutɪ bʌt waz skɛːʌs]
Adjusted in the tomb,
[ʌˈdʒʌstɛ(ɪ)d ɪn ðʌ tum]
When one who died
[ʍɛn wʌn hu daːɪd]
for truth was lain
[fɔ tɹ(ɾ)uθ waz lɛːɪn]
In an adjoining room.
[ɪn æn ʌˈdʒɔːɪnɪŋ ɹ(ɾɾ)um]
He questioned softly why I failed?
[hi ˈkwɛstʃʌnd ˈsaftlɪ ʍaːɪ aːɪ fɛːɪld]
"For Beauty," I replied.
[fɔ ˈbjutɪ aːɪ ɹɪˈplaːɪd]
"And I for truth, –the two are one;
[ænd aːɪ fɔ tɹ(ɾ)uθ ðʌ tu a wʌn]
We brethren are," he said.
[wi ˈbɹɛðɹɛ(ɪ)n a hi sɛd]
And so, as kinsmen met a night,
[ænd soːʊ æz ˈkɪnzmɛ(ɪ)n mɛt ʌ naːɪt]
We talked between the rooms,
[wi tɔkt bɪˈtwin ðʌ ɹ(ɾɾ)umz]
Until the moss had reached our lips,
[ʌnˈtɪl ðʌ mɔs hæd ɹiʧt aːʊʌ lɪps]
And covered up our names.
[ænd ˈkʌvʌd ʌp aːʊʌ nɛːɪmz]

7. Down Time's Quaint Stream
[daːʊn taːɪmz kwɛːɪnt stɹim]

Down Time's quaint stream
[daːʊn taːɪmz kwɛːɪnt stɹim]

Without an oar,
[wɪð'ɑːʊt æn ɔːʌ]
We are enforced to sail,
[wi ɑʁ⁽ʳ⁾ ɪn'fɔst tu sɛːɪl]
Our Port—a secret—
[ɑːʊʌ pɔt ʌ 'sikɹɛ(ɪ)t]
Our Perchance—a gale.
[ɑːʊʌ pɜ'ʧæns ʌ gɛːɪl]
What Skipper would
[ʍat 'skɪpʌ wʊd]
Incur the risk,
[ɪn'kɜ ðʌ ɹɪsk]
What Buccaneer would ride,
[ʍat ˌbʌkæ(ʌ)'nɪːʌ wʊd ɹɑːɪd]
Without a surety from the wind
[wɪð'ɑːʊt ʌ 'ʃʊːʌʁ⁽ʳ⁾ɛ(ɪ)tɪ fɹʌm ðʌ wɪnd]
Or schedule of the tide?
[ɔ 'skɛʤʊl ʌv ðʌ tɑːɪd]

8. The Blunder Is to Estimate
[ðʌ 'blʌndʁ ɪz tu 'ɛstɪmɛːɪt]

The Blunder is to estimate,—
[ðʌ 'blʌndʌʁ⁽ʳ⁾ ɪz tu 'ɛstɪmɛːɪt]
"Eternity is Then,"
[ɪ't3nɪtɪ ɪz ðɛn]
We say, as of a station.
[wi sɛːɪ æz ʌv ʌ 'stɛːɪʃʌn]
Meanwhile he is so near,
['minʍɑːɪl hi ɪz soːʊ nɪːʌ]
He joins me in my ramble,
[hi ʤɔːɪnz mi ɪn mɑːɪ 'ɹæmbʊl]
Divides abode with me,
[dɪ'vɑːɪdz ʌ'boːʊd wɪð mi]
No friend have I that so persists
[noːʊ fɹɛnd hæv ɑːɪ ðæt soːʊ pɜ'sɪsts]
As this Eternity.
[æz ðɪs ɪ't3nɪtɪ]

9. Faith Is a Fine Invention
[fɛːɪθ ɪz ʌ fɑːɪn ɪn'vɛnʃʌn]

Faith is a fine invention
[fɛːɪθ ɪz ʌ fɑːɪn ɪn'vɛnʃʌn]
For gentlemen who see;
[fɔ 'ʤɛntʊlmɛ(ɪ)n hu si]
But microscopes are prudent
[bʌt 'mɑːɪkɹʌskoːʊps ʌ 'pɹ⁽ʳ⁾udɛnt]
In an emergency!
[ɪn æn ɪ'm3ʤɛ(ɪ)nsɪ]

10. I Reason, Earth Is Short
[ɑːɪ 'ɹizʌn 3θ ɪz ʃɔʁt]

I reason, earth is short,
[ɑːɪ 'ɹizʌn 3θ ɪz ʃɔt]

And anguish absolute,
[ænd 'æŋgwɪʃ 'æbso(ʌ)ljut]
And many hurt;
[ænd 'mɛnɪ hɜt]
But what of that?
[bʌt ʍat ʌv ðæt]
I reason, we could die:
[ɑːɪ 'ɹizʌn wi kʊd dɑːɪ]
The best vitality
[ðʌ bɛst vɑːɪ'tælɪtɪ]
Cannot excel decay;
[kæ'nɑt ɪk'sɛl dɪ'kɛːɪ]
But what of that?
[bʌt ʍat ʌv ðæt]
I reason, that in heaven
[ɑːɪ 'ɹizʌn ðæt ɪn 'hɛvɛ(ɪ)n]
Somehow, it will be even,
['sʌmhɑːʊ ɪt wɪl bi 'ivɛ(ɪ)n]
Some new equation given;
[sʌm nju ɪ'kwɛːɪʒʌn 'gɪvɛ(ɪ)n]
But what of that?
[bʌt ʍat ʌv ðæt]

11. Look Back on Time with Kindly Eyes
[lʊk bæk ɑn tɑːɪm wɪθ 'kɑːɪndli ɑːɪz]

Look back on time with kindly eyes,
[lʊk bæk ɑn tɑːɪm wɪð 'kɑːɪndlɪ ɑːɪz]
He doubtless did his best;
[hi 'dɑːʊtlɛ(ɪ)s dɪd hɪz bɛst]
How softly sinks his trembling sun
[hɑːʊ 'sɑftlɪ sɪŋks hɪz 'tɹɛmblɪŋ sʌn]
In human nature's west!
[ɪn 'hjumæ(ʌ)n 'nɛːɪʧʊ(ʌ)z wɛst]

12. Playmates
['plɛːɪmɛːɪts]

God permits industrious angels
[gɑd pɜ'mɪts ɪn'dʌstɹɪʌs 'ɛːɪnʤɛ(ʊ)lz]
Afternoons to play.
[æftʌ'nunz tu plɛːɪ]
I met one,—forgot my school-mates,
[ɑːɪ mɛt wʌn fɔ'gɑt mɑːɪ skul mɛːɪts]
All, for him, straightway.
[ɔl fɔ hɪm 'stɹɛːɪtwɛːɪ]
God calls home the angels promptly
[gɑd kɔlz hoːʊm ði 'ɛːɪnʤɛ(ʊ)lz 'pɹɑmptlɪ]
At the setting sun;
[æt ðʌ 'sɛtɪŋ sʌn]
I missed mine. How dreary marbles,
[ɑːɪ mɪst mɑːɪn hɑːʊ 'dɹɪːʌʁ⁽ʳ⁾ɪ 'mɑbʊlz]
After playing Crown!
['æftʌ 'plɛːɪɪŋ kɹɑːʊn]

Song Selections

"A Song" (Winter Windows)
[ʌ sɑŋ]
Shelley, Percy Bysshe (Eng. 1792-1822)

A widow bird sat mourning for her love
[ʌ ˈwɪdoːʊ bɜd sæt ˈmɔnɪŋ fɔ hɜ lʌv]
Upon a wintry bough,
[ʌˈpɑn ʌ ˈwɪntɹɪ bɑːʊ]
The frozen wind crept on above;
[ðʌ ˈfɹoːʊzɛ(ɪ)n wɪnd kɹɪ⁽ᵗ⁾ɛpt ɑn ʌˈbʌv]
The freezing stream below.
[ðʌ ˈfɹizɪŋ stɹim bɪˈloːʊ]
There was no leaf upon the forest bare,
[ðɛːʌ wɑz noːʊ lif ʌˈpɑn ðʌ ˈfɔʁ⁽ᵗ⁾ɛ(ɪ)st bɛːʌ]
No flower upon the ground
[noːʊ flɑːʊʌʁ⁽ᵗ⁾ ʌˈpɑn ðʌ ɡɹɑːʊnd]
And little motion in the air,
[ænd ˈlɪtʊl ˈmoːʊʃʌn ɪn ði ɛːʌ]
Except the mill-wheel's sound.
[ɪkˈsɛpt ðʌ mɪl ʍilz sɑːʊnd]

"I Can No Other Answer Make"
[ɑːɪ kæn noːʊ ˈʌðʁ ˈænsʁ mɛːɪk]
Shakespeare, William (Eng. 1564-1616)

I would not by my will have troubled you,
[ɑːɪ wʊd nɑt bɑːɪ mɑːɪ wɪl hæv ˈtɹʌbʊld ju]
But, since you make your pleasure of your pains,
[bʌt sɪns ju mɛːɪk jɔːʌ ˈplɛʒʊ(ʌ)ʁ⁽ᵗ⁾ ʌv jɔːʌ pɛːɪnz]
I can no other answer make but thanks,
[ɑːɪ kæn noːʊ ˈʌðʌʁ⁽ᵗ⁾ ˈænsʌ mɛːɪk bʌt θæŋks]
And thanks, and ever thanks.
[ænd θæŋks ænd ˈɛvʌ θæŋks]

"I Sing to Use the Waiting" (Paradise)
[ɑːɪ sɪŋ tu juz ðʌ ˈwɛːɪtɪŋ]
Dickinson, Emily (Am. 1830-1886)

I sing to use the waiting,
[ɑːɪ sɪŋ tu juz ðʌ ˈwɛːɪtɪŋ]
My bonnet but to tie,
[mɑːɪ ˈbɑnɛ(ɪ)t bʌt tu tɑːɪ]
And shut the door unto my house;
[ænd ʃʌt ðʌ dɔːʌʁ⁽ᵗ⁾ ˈʌntu mɑːɪ hɑːʊs]
No more to do have I,
[noːʊ mɔːʌ tu du hæv ɑːɪ]
Till, his best step approaching,
[tɪl hɪz bɛst stɛp ʌˈpɹoːʊʧɪŋ]
We journey to the day,
[wi ˈʤɜnɪ tu ðʌ dɛːɪ]
And tell each other how we sang
[ænd tɛl iʧ ˈʌðʌ hɑːʊ wi sæŋ]
To keep the dark away.
[tu kip ðʌ dɑk ʌˈwɛːɪ]

"Theme in Yellow" (Theme in Yellow)
[θim ɪn ˈjɛloːʊ]
Sandburg, Carl (Am. 1878-1967)

I spot the hills
[ɑːɪ spɑt ðʌ hɪlz]
With yellow balls in autumn.
[wɪð ˈjɛloːʊ bɔlz ɪn ˈɔtʌm]
I light the prairie cornfields
[ɑːɪ lɑːɪt ðʌ ˈpɹɛʁ⁽ᵗ⁾ɪ ˈkɔnfildz]
Orange and tawny gold clusters
[ˈɔʁ⁽ᵗ⁾ɪnʤ ænd ˈtɔnɪ ɡoːʊld ˈklʌstʌz]
And I am called pumpkins.
[ænd ɑːɪ æm kɔld ˈpʌmpkɪnz]
On the last of October
[ɑn ðʌ læst ʌv ɑkˈtoːʊbʌ]
When dusk is fallen
[ʍɛn dʌsk ɪz ˈfɔlɛ(ɪ)n]
Children join hands
[ˈʧɪldɹɛ(ɪ)n ʤɔːɪn hændz]
And circle round me
[ænd ˈsɜkʊl ɹɑːʊnd mi]
Singing ghost songs
[ˈsɪŋɪŋ ɡoːʊst sɑŋz]
And love to the harvest moon;
[ænd lʌv tu ðʌ ˈhɑvɛ(ɪ)st mun]
I am a jack-o'-lantern
[ɑːɪ æm ʌ ʤæk oːʊ ˈlæntʌn]
With terrible teeth
[wɪð ˈtɛʁ⁽ᵗ⁾ɪbʊl tiθ]
And the children know
[ænd ðʌ ˈʧɪldɹɛ(ɪ)n noːʊ]
I am fooling.
[ɑːɪ æm ˈfulɪŋ]

"To Susan Gilbert (Dickinson) I"
[tu ˈsuzʌn ˈɡɪlbʁt ˈdɪkɪnsʌn wʌn]
(Syllables of Velvet, Sentences of Plush)
Dickinson, Emily (Am. 1830-1886)

I wept a tear here, Susie, on purpose for you
[ɑːɪ wɛpt ʌ tɪːʌ hɪːʌ ˈsuzi ɑn ˈpɜpʌs fɔ ju]
– because this "sweet silver moon"
[bɪˈkɔz ðɪs swit ˈsɪlvʌ mun]
smiles in on me and Vinnie,
[smɑːɪlz ɪn ɑn mi ænd ˈvɪni]
and then it goes so far before it gets to you
[ænd ðɛn ɪt ɡoːʊz soːʊ fɑ bɪˈfɔːʌʁ⁽ᵗ⁾ ɪt ɡɛts tu ju]
– and then you never told me if there was
[ænd ðɛn ju ˈnɛvʌ toːʊld mi ɪf ðɛːʌ wɑz]
any moon in Baltimore – and how do I know, Susie,
[ˈɛnɪ mun ɪn ˈbɔltɪmɔːʌ ænd hɑːʊ du ɑːɪ noːʊ ˈsuzɪ]
– that you see her sweet face at all?
[ðæt ju si hɜ swit fɛːɪs æt ɔl]
She looks like a fairy tonight,
[ʃi lʊks lɑːɪk ʌ ˈfɛʁ⁽ᵗ⁾ɪ tuˈnɑːɪt]

sailing around the sky in a little silver gondola
[ˈsɛːɪlɪŋ ʌˈʁ⁽ʳ⁾ɑːʊnd ðʌ skaːɪ ɪn ʌ ˈlɪtʊl ˈsɪlvʌ ˈɡandʌlʌ]
with stars for gondoliers.
[wɪð staz fɔ ɡando(ʌ)ˈliːʌz]
I asked her to let me ride a little while ago
[ɑːɪ æskt hɜ tu lɛt mi ɹɑːɪd ʌ ˈlɪtʊl ʍaːɪl ʌˈɡoːʊ]
– and told her I would get out when she got
[ænd toːʊld hɜ ɑːɪ wʊd ɡɛt ɑːʊt ʍɛn ʃi ɡat]
as far as Baltimore,
[æz faʁ⁽ʳ⁾ æz ˈbɔltɪmɔːʌ]
but she only smiled to herself and went sailing on.
[bʌt ʃi ˈoːʊnlɪ smaːɪld tu hɜˈsɛlf ænd wɛnt ˈsɛːɪlɪŋ an]

"Winter Night" (Winter Windows)
[ˈwɪntʁ naːɪt]
Millay, Edna St. Vincent (Am. 1892-1950)

Pile high the hickory and the light
[paːɪl haːɪ ðʌ ˈhɪkɔʁ⁽ʳ⁾ɪ ænd ðʌ laːɪt]
Log of chestnut struck by the blight.
[lag ʌv ˈtʃɛsnʌt stɹʌk baːɪ ðʌ blaːɪt]
Welcome-in the winter night.
[ˈwɛlkʌm ɪn ðʌ ˈwɪntʌ naːɪt]
The day has gone in hewing and felling,
[ðʌ dɛːɪ hæz ɡan ɪn ˈhjuɪŋ ænd ˈfɛlɪŋ]
Sawing and drawing wood to the dwelling
[ˈsɔɪŋ ænd ˈdɹɔɪŋ wʊd tu ðʌ ˈdwɛlɪŋ]
For the night of talk and story-telling.
[fɔ ðʌ naːɪt ʌv tɔk ænd ˈstɔʁ⁽ʳ⁾ɪ ˈtɛlɪŋ]
These are the hours that give the edge
[ðiz a ði aːʊʌz ðæt ɡɪv ði ɛdʒ]
To the blunted axe and the bent wedge,
[tu ðʌ ˈblʌntɛ(ɪ)d æks ænd ðʌ bɛnt wɛdʒ]
Straighten the saw and lighten the sledge.
[ˈstɹɛːɪtɛ(ɪ)n ðʌ sɔ ænd ˈlaːɪtɛ(ɪ)n ðʌ slɛdʒ]
Here are question and reply,
[hiːʌʁ⁽ʳ⁾ a ˈkwɛstʃʌn ænd ɹɪˈplaːɪ]
And the fire reflected in the thinking eye.
[ænd ðʌ faːɪʌ ɹɪˈflɛktɛ(ɪ)d ɪn ðʌ ˈθɪŋkɪŋ aːɪ]
So peace, and let the bob-cat cry.
[soːʊ pis ænd lɛt ðʌ bab kæt kɹ⁽ʳ⁾aːɪ]

Handel, George Frederic
(Gr./Eng. 1685-1759)

Selections

"Art Thou Troubled" (Rodelinda)
[at ðaːʊ ˈtɹʌbʊld]
Anonymous

Art thou troubled? Music will calm thee,
[at ðaːʊ ˈtɹʌbʊld ˈmjuzɪk wɪl kam ði]

Art thou weary? Rest shall be thine.
[at ðaːʊ ˈwɪːʌɹɪ ɹest ʃæl bi ðaːɪn]
Music, source of all gladness, heals thy sadness
[ˈmjuzɪk sɔs ʌv ɔl ˈɡlædnɛ(ɪ)s hilz ðaːɪ ˈsædnɛ(ɪ)s]
At her shrine. Music, music, ever divine.
[æt hɜ ʃɹaːɪn ˈmjuzɪk ˈmjuzɪk ˈɛvʌ dɪˈvaːɪn]
Music, music calleth with voice divine.
[ˈmjuzɪk ˈmjuzɪk ˈkɔlɛ(ɪ)θ wɪð vɔːɪs dɪˈvaːɪn]
When the welcome spring is smiling,
[ʍɛn ðʊ ˈwɛlkʌm spɹɪŋ ɪz ˈsmaːɪlɪŋ]
All the earth with flow'rs beguiling,
[ɔl ði ɜθ wɪð flaːʊʌz bɪˈɡaːɪlɪŋ]
After winter's dreary reign,
[ˈaftʌ ˈwɪntʌz ˈdɹɪːʌɹɪ ɹɛːɪn]
Sweetest music doth attend her,
[ˈswitɛ(ɪ)st ˈmjuzɪk dʌθ ʌˈtɛnd hɜ]
Heav'nly harmonies doth lend her,
[ˈhɛvnlɪ ˈhamo(ʌ)nɪz dʌθ lɛnd hɜ]
Chanting praises in her train.
[ˈtʃantɪŋ ˈpɹɛːɪzɛ(ɪ)z ɪn hɜ tɹɛːɪn]

"Come and Trip It"
[kʌm ænd tɹɪp ɪt]
Jennens, Charles (Eng. 1700-1773)

Come, and trip it as you go,
[kʌm ænd tɹɪp ɪt æz ju ɡoːʊ]
On the light fantastic toe.
[an ðʊ laːɪt fænˈtæstɪk toːʊ]

"Here Amid the Shady Woods"
[hiːʁ ʌˈmɪd ðʊ ˈʃɛːɪdɪ wʊdz]
Morell, Thomas (Eng. 1703-1784)

Here amid the shady woods,
[hiːʌɾ ʌˈmɪd ðʊ ˈʃɛːɪdɪ wʊdz]
Fragrant flow'rs and crystal floods,
[ˈfɹɛːɪɡɹæ(ɪ)nt flaːʊʌz ænd ˈkɹɪstʊl flʌdz]
Taste, my soul, this charming seat,
[tɛːɪst maːɪ soːʊl ðɪs ˈtʃamɪŋ sit]
Love and glory's calm retreat.
[lʌv ænd ˈɡlɔɹɪz kam ɹɪˈtɹit]

"Leave Me, Loathsome Light!" (Semele)
[liv mi ˈloːʊðsʌm laːɪt]
Congreve, William (Eng. 1670-1729)

Leave me loathsome light!
[liv mi ˈloːʊðsʌm laːɪt]
Receive me, silent night.
[ɹɪˈsiv mi ˈsaːɪlɛnt naːɪt]
Lethe, why does thy ling'ring current cease?
[ˈliθɪ ʍaːɪ dʌz ðaːɪ ˈlɪŋɡɹɪŋ ˈkʊɾɛnt sis]
Oh, murmur me again to peace!
[oːʊ ˈmɜmʊ(ʌ) mi ʌˈɡɛːɪn tu pis]

"O Sleep, Why Dost Thou Leave Me?" (Semele)
[oːʊ slip ʍaːɪ dʌst ðaːʊ liv mi]
Congreve, William (Eng. 1670-1729)

Oh sleep, why dost thou leave me?
[oːʊ slip ʍaːɪ dʌst ðaːʊ liv mi]
Why dost thou leave me?
[ʍaːɪ dʌst ðaːʊ liv mi]
Why thy visionary joys remove?
[ʍaːɪ ðaːɪ 'vɪʒʌnɛɾɪ dʒɔːɪz ɹɪ'muv]
Oh sleep, again deceive me,
[oːʊ slip ʌ'gɛːɪn dɪ'siv mi]
To my arms Restore my wand'ring love!
[tu maːɪ amz ɹɪ'stɔːʌ maːɪ 'wandɹɪŋ lʌv]

"Silent Worship" (Tolomeo - Ptolemy)
['saːɪlɛnt 'wɜʃɪp]
Adapted by Somervell, Arthur (Eng. 1863-1937)

Did you not hear my lady
[dɪd ju nat hɪːʌ maːɪ 'lɛːɪdɪ]
Go down the garden singing?
[goːʊ daːʊn ðʊ 'gadɛ(ɪ)n 'sɪŋɪŋ]
Blackbird and thrush were silent
['blækbɜd ænd θɹʌʃ wɜ 'saːɪlɛnt]
To hear the alleys ringing.
[tu hɪːʌ ði 'æliz 'ɹɪŋɪŋ]
O saw you not my lady
[oːʊ sɔ ju nat maːɪ 'lɛːɪdɪ]
Out in the garden there?
[aːʊt ɪn ðʊ 'gadɛ(ɪ)n ðɛːʌ]
Shaming the rose and lily
['ʃɛːɪmɪŋ ðʊ roːʊz ænd 'lɪlɪ]
For she is twice as fair.
[fɔ ʃi ɪz twaːɪs æz fɛːʌ]
Though I am nothing to her,
[ðoːʊ aːɪ æm 'nʌθɪŋ tu hɜ]
Though she must rarely look at me,
[ðoːʊ ʃi mʌst 'ɹɛːʌlɪ lʊk æt mi]
And though I could never woo her,
[ænd ðoːʊ aːɪ kʊd 'nɛvʌ wu hɜ]
I love her till I die.
[aːɪ lʌv hɜ tɪl aːɪ daːɪ]
Surely you heard my lady
['ʃʊːʌlɪ ju hɜd maːɪ 'lɛːɪdɪ]
Go down the garden singing,
[goːʊ daːʊn ðʊ 'gadɛ(ɪ)n 'sɪŋɪŋ]
Silencing all the songbirds:
['saːɪlɛ(ɪ)nsɪŋ ɔl ðʊ 'sɑŋbɜdz]
And setting the alleys ringing,
[ænd 'sɛtɪŋ ði 'æliz 'ɹɪŋɪŋ]
But surely you see my lady
[bʌt 'ʃʊːʌlɪ ju si maːɪ 'lɛːɪdɪ]
Out in the garden there.
[aːʊt ɪn ðʊ 'gadɛ(ɪ)n ðɛːʌ]

Riv'ling the glitt'ring sunshine,
['ɹaːɪvlɪŋ ðʊ 'glɪtɹɪŋ 'sʌnʃaːɪn]
With a glory of golden hair.
[wɪð ʌ 'glɔɾɪ ʌv 'goːʊldɛ(ɪ)n hɛːʌ]

"The Birds No More Shall Sing" (Acis and Galatea)
[ðʊ bɜdz noːʊ mɔːʌ ʃæl sɪŋ]
Gay, John (Eng. 1685-1732)

The birds no more shall sing,
[ðʊ bɜdz noːʊ mɔːʌ ʃæl sɪŋ]
Nor breezes cool the grove,
[nɔ 'bɹizɛ(ɪ)z kul ðʊ gɹoːʊv]
Nor blossoms deck the spring,
[nɔ 'blasʌmz dɛk ðʊ spɹɪŋ]
If I forsake my love.
[ɪf aːɪ fɔ'sɛːɪk maːɪ lʌv]
The sun shall rise at night,
[ðʊ sʌn ʃæl ɹaːɪz æt naːɪt]
The moon her orbit leave,
[ðʊ mun hɜ 'ɔbɪt liv]
And day be turned to night,
[ænd dɛːɪ bi tɜnd tu naːɪt]
When I my love deceive.
[ʍɛn aːɪ maːɪ lʌv dɪ'siv]
Come, then, let's haste away,
[kʌm ðɛn lets hɛːɪst ʌ'wɛːɪ]
And view the charming spring
[ænd vju ðʊ 'ʧamɪŋ spɹɪŋ]
the flow'rs in bright display,
[ðʊ flaːʊʌz ɪn bɹaːɪt dɪ'splɛːɪ]
The birds begin to sing.
[ðʊ bɜdz bɪ'gɪn tu sɪŋ]
'Tis music, all we hear;
[tɪz 'mjuzɪk ɔl wi hɪːʌ]
'Tis beauty, all we see;
[tɪz 'bjutɪ ɔl wi si]
The lovely flow'rs appear:
[ðʊ 'lʌvlɪ flaːʊʌz ʌ'pɪːʌ]
Thy lover waits for thee.
[ðaːɪ 'lʌvʌ wɛːɪts fɔ ði]

"Total Eclipse" (Samson)
['toːʊtʊl ɪ'klɪps]
Handel, George Frederic (Gr./Eng. 1685-1759)

Oh, loss of sight! Of thee I most complain!
[oːʊ las ʌv saːɪt ʌv ði aːɪ moːʊst kʌm'plɛːɪn]
Oh, worse than beggary, old age, or chains!
[oːʊ wɜs ðæn 'bɛgʌɾɪ oːʊld ɛːɪdʒ ɔ ʧɛːɪnz]
My very soul in real darkness dwells.
[maːɪ 'vɛɾɪ soːʊl ɪn ɹɪːʌl 'daknɛ(ɪ)s dwɛlz]
Total eclipse! No sun, no moon,
['toːʊtʊl ɪ'klɪps noːʊ sʌn noːʊ mun]
All dark amidst the blaze of noon!
[ɔl dak ʌ'mɪdst ðʊ blɛːɪz ʌv nun]

O, glorious light! No cheering ray
[oːʊ ˈɡlɔɾɪʌs lɑːɪt noːʊ ˈʧiːʌɾɪŋ ɹɛːɪ]
To glad my eyes with welcome day!
[tu ɡlæd mɑːɪ ɑːɪz wɪð ˈwɛlkʌm dɛːɪ]
Why thus depriv'd Thy prime decree?
[ʍɑːɪ ðʌs dɪˈpɹɑːɪvd ðɑːɪ pɹɑːɪm dɪˈkɹi]
Sun, moon and stars are dark to me!
[sʌn mun ænd stɑz ɑ dɑk tu mi]

"Where'er You Walk" (Semele)
[ʍɛːʁ ɛːʌ ju wɔk]
Congreve, William (Eng. 1670-1729)

Where'er you walk,
[ʍɛːʌ ɛːʌ ju wɔk]
Cool gales shall fan the glade;
[kul ɡɛːɪlz ʃæl fæn ðʊ ɡlɛːɪd]
Trees, where you sit,
[tɹiz ʍɛːʌ ju sɪt]
shall crowd into a shade:
[ʃæl kɹɑːʊd ˈɪntu ʌ ʃɛːɪd]
Where'er you tread,
[ʍɛːʌ ɛːʌ ju tɹɛd]
the blushing flowers shall rise,
[ðʊ ˈblʌʃɪŋ flɑːʊʌz ʃæl ɹɑːɪz]
and all things flourish,
[ænd ɔl θɪŋz ˈflʊɾɪʃ]
Where'er you turn your eyes.
[ʍɛːʌ ɛːʌ ju tɜn jɔːʌ ɑːɪz]

Haydn, Joseph (Aut. 1732-1809)

Song Selections

"A Pastoral Song"
[ʌ ˈpastɔʁʊl saŋ]
Hunter, Anne (Eng. 1742-1821)

My mother bids me bind my hair
[mɑːɪ ˈmʌðʌ bɪdz mi bɑːɪnd mɑːɪ hɛːʌ]
With bands of rosy hue,
[wɪð bændz ʌv ˈɹoːʊzɪ hju]
Tie up my sleeves with ribbons rare,
[tɑːɪ ʌp mɑːɪ slivz wɪð ˈɹɪbʌnz ɹɛːʌ]
And lace my bodice blue.
[ænd lɛːɪs mɑːɪ ˈbɑdɪs blu]
For why, she cries, sit still and weep,
[fɔ ʍɑːɪ ʃi kɹɑːɪz sɪt stɪl ænd wip]
While others dance and play?
[ʍɑːɪl ˈʌðʌz dɑns ænd plɛːɪ]
Alas! I scarce can go or creep,
[ʌˈlæs ɑːɪ skɛːʌs kæn ɡoːʊ ɔ kɹip]
While Lubin is away.
[ʍɑːɪl ˈlubɪn ɪz ʌˈwɛːɪ]

'Tis sad to think the days are gone,
[tɪz sæd tu θɪŋk ðʊ dɛːɪz ɑ ɡɑn]
When those we love were near;
[ʍɛn ðoːʊz wi lʌv wɜ niːʌ]
I sit upon this mossy stone,
[ɑːɪ sɪt ʌˈpɑn ðɪs ˈmɔsɪ stoːʊn]
And sigh when none can hear.
[ænd sɑːɪ ʍɛn nʌn kæn hiːʌ]
And while I spin my flaxen thread,
[ænd ʍɑːɪl ɑːɪ spɪn mɑːɪ ˈflæksɛ(ɪ)n θɾɛd]
And sing my simple lay,
[ænd sɪŋ mɑːɪ ˈsɪmpʊl lɛːɪ]
The village seems asleep, or dead,
[ðʊ ˈvɪlæ(ɪ)ʤ simz ʌˈslip ɔ dɛd]
Now Lubin is away.
[nɑːʊ ˈlubɪn ɪz ʌˈwɛːɪ]

"Despair" [dɪˈspɛːʌ]
Hunter, Anne (Eng. 1742-1821)

The anguish of my bursting heart,
[ði ˈæŋgwɪʃ ʌv mɑːɪ ˈbɜstɪŋ hat]
Till now my tongue hath ne'er betray'd.
[tɪl nɑːʊ mɑːɪ tʌŋ hæθ nɛːʌ bɪˈtɹɛːɪd]
Despair at length reveals the smart
[dɪˈspɛːʌɾ æt lɛŋθ ɹɪˈvilz ðʊ smat]
No time can cure, no hope can aid.
[noːʊ tɑːɪm kæn kjʊːʌ noːʊ hoːʊp kæn ɛːɪd]
My sorrows verging to the grave,
[mɑːɪ ˈsɑɾoːʊz ˈvɜʤɪŋ tu ðʊ ɡɹɛːɪv]
No more shall pain thy gentle breast.
[noːʊ mɔːʌ ʃæl pɛːɪn ðɑːɪ ˈʤɛntʊl bɹɛst]
Think death gives freedom to the slave.
[θɪŋk dɛθ ɡɪvz ˈfɹidʌm tu ðʊ slɛːɪv]
Nor mourn for me when I'm at rest.
[nɔ mɔn fɔ mi ʍɛn ɑːɪm æt ɹɛst]

"Fidelity" [fɪˈdɛlɪti]
Hunter, Anne (Eng. 1742-1821)

While hollow burst the rushing winds,
[ʍɑːɪl ˈhaloːʊ bɜst ðʊ ˈɾʌʃɪŋ wɑːɪndz (wɪndz)]
And heavy beats the show'r,
[ænd ˈhɛvi bits ðʊ ʃɑːʊʌ]
This anxious, aching bosom finds
[ðɪs ˈæŋkʃʌs ˈɛːɪkɪŋ ˈbʊzʌm fɑːɪndz]
No comfort in its pow'r.
[noːʊ ˈkʌmfɔ(ʌ)t ɪn ɪts pɑːʊʌ]
For ah, my love, it little knows
[fɔʁ⁽ʳ⁾ ɑ mɑːɪ lʌv ɪt ˈlɪtʊl noːʊz]
What thy hard fate may be,
[ʍʌt ðɑːɪ had fɛːɪt mɛːɪ bi]
What bitter storm of fortune blows,
[ʍʌt ˈbɪtʌ stɔm ʌv ˈfɔʧʌn bloːʊz]
What tempests trouble thee.
[ʍʌt ˈtɛmpɛ(ɪ)sts ˈtɹʌbʊl ði]

A wayward fate hath spun the thread
[ʌ ˈwɛːɪwʊd fɛːɪt hæθ spʌn ðʊ θrɛd]
On which our days depend,
[ɑn ʍɪʧ ɑːʊʌ dɛːɪz dɪˈpɛnd]
And darkling in the checker'd shade,
[ænd ˈdɑklɪŋ ɪn ðʊ ˈʧɛkʌd ʃɛːɪd]
She draws it to an end.
[ʃi dɹɔz ɪt tu æn ɛnd]
But whatsoe'er may be our doom,
[bʌt ʍatsoˈɛːʌ mɛːɪ bi ɑːʊʌ dum]
The lot is cast for me,
[ðʊ lat ɪz kast fɔ mi]
For in the world or in the tomb,
[fɔʁ⁽ʳ⁾ ɪn ðʊ wɜld ɔʁ⁽ʳ⁾ ɪn ðʊ tum]
My heart is fix'd on thee.
[mɑːɪ hat ɪz fɪkst ɑn ði]

"Love Will Find Out the Way"
[lʌv wɪl fɑːɪnd ɑːʊt ðʊ wɛːɪ]
Folksong

Quite over the mountains,
[kwɑːɪt ˈoːʊvʌ ðʊ ˈmɑːʊntæ⁽ɪ⁾nz]
And over the waves,
[ænd ˈoːʊvʌ ðʊ wɛːɪvz]
Quite over the fountains,
[kwɑːɪt ˈoːʊvʌ ðʊ ˈfɑːʊntæ⁽ɪ⁾nz]
And under the graves;
[ænd ˈʌndʌ ðʊ gɹɛːɪvz]
O'er floods that are deepest,
[ɔːʌ flʌdz ðæt a ˈdipɛ⁽ɪ⁾st]
Which Neptune obey,
[ʍɪʧ ˈnɛptjun oˈbɛːɪ]
O'er rocks that are steepest,
[ɔːʌ ɾaks ðæt a ˈstipɛ⁽ɪ⁾st]
Love will find out the way.
[lʌv wɪl fɑːɪnd ɑːʊt ðʊ wɛːɪ]
Oh, some think to lose him,
[oːʊ sʌm θɪŋk tu luz hɪm]
Which is too unkind;
[ʍɪʧ ɪz tu ʌnˈkɑːɪnd]
And some do suppose him,
[ænd sʌm du sʌˈpoːʊz hɪm]
Poor thing to be blind;
[pʊːʌ θɪŋ tu bi blɑːɪnd]
But if ne'er so close ye wall him,
[bʌt ɪf nɛːʌ soːʊ kloːʊs ji wɔl hɪm]
Do the best that ye may,
[du ðʊ bɛst ðæt ji mɛːɪ]
Blind Love, if so ye call him,
[blɑːɪnd lʌv ɪf soːʊ ji kɔl hɪm]
He will find out the way.
[hi wɪl fɑːɪnd ɑːʊt ðʊ wɛːɪ]

"Night is Falling"
[nɑːɪt ɪz ˈfɔlɪŋ]
Wager, Willis

Night is falling over meadow,
[nɑːɪt ɪz ˈfɔlɪŋ ˈoːʊvʌ ˈmɛdoːʊ]
And no star, the flow'r of shadow,
[ænd noːʊ sta ðʊ flaːʊɾ ʌv ˈʃædoːʊ]
Shines in heaven far above.
[ʃɑːɪnz ɪn ˈhɛvɛ⁽ɪ⁾n far ʌˈbʌv]
But what matter stars in heaven
[bʌt ʍat ˈmætʌ staz ɪn ˈhɛvɛ⁽ɪ⁾n]
When the glimpse to me is given
[ʍɛn ðʊ glɪmps tu mi ɪz ˈgɪvɛ⁽ɪ⁾n]
Of the sparkling eyes of love?
[ʌv ðʊ ˈspaklɪŋ ɑːɪz ʌv lʌv]
Ah, behold, 'tis the hour
[ɑ bɪˈhoːʊld tɪz ði ɑːʊʌ]
Of magic power;
[ʌv ˈmædʒɪk pɑːʊʌ]
All in flower
[ɔl ɪn flɑːʊʌ]
Bids thee come and join our playing,
[bɪdz ði kʌm ænd dʒɔːɪn ɑːʊʌ ˈplɛːɪɪŋ]
Cease delaying.
[sis dɪˈlɛːɪɪŋ]
The lagoon is now forsaken
[ðʊ lʌˈgun ɪz nɑːʊ fɔˈsɛːɪkɛ⁽ɪ⁾n]
As I glide along to thee;
[æz ɑːɪ glaːɪd ʌˈlaŋ tu ði]
Come, my love, softly waken
[kʌm mɑːɪ lʌv ˈsaftlɪ ˈwɛːɪkɛ⁽ɪ⁾n]
While the breezes follow free.
[ʍɑːɪl ðʊ ˈbɹizɛ⁽ɪ⁾z ˈfaloːʊ fɹi]
I do call thee, I implore thee;
[ɑːɪ du kɔl ði ɑːɪ ɪmˈplɔːʌ ði]
When thou knowest I adore thee,
[ʍɛn ðaːʊ ˈnoːʊɛ⁽ɪ⁾st ɑːɪ ʌˈdɔːʌ ði]
What alarm can bring thee fear?
[ʍat ʌˈlam kæn bɹɪŋ ði fiːʌ]
Come, my love, and hasten lightly,
[kʌm mɑːɪ lʌv ænd ˈhɛːɪsɛ⁽ɪ⁾n ˈlaːɪtlɪ]
Never moment smiled more brightly
[ˈnɛvʌ ˈmoːʊment smaːɪld mɔːʌ ˈbɹɑːɪtlɪ]
On our love with blissful cheer.
[ɑn ɑːʊʌ lʌv wɪð ˈblɪsfʊl ʧiːʌ]
All too soon will come the morrow,
[ɔl tu sun wɪl kʌm ðʊ ˈmaɾoːʊ]
All too soon from thee I must fly;
[ɔl tu sun fɹʌm ði ɑːɪ mʌst flaːɪ]
Shall I then implore in sorrow,
[ʃæl ɑːɪ ðɛn ɪmˈplɔːɾ ɪn ˈsaɾoːʊ]
Ah, beloved, and grieving thus die?
[ɑ bɪˈlʌvɛ⁽ɪ⁾d ænd ˈgrivɪŋ ðʌs daːɪ]

"O Tuneful Voice"
[oːʊ ˈtjunfʊl vɔːɪs]
Hunter, Anne (Eng. 1742-1821)

O tuneful voice! I still deplore,
[oːʊ ˈtjunfʊl vɔːɪs aːɪ stɪl dɪˈplɔːʌ]
Thy accents, which though heard no more,
[ðaːɪ ˈæksɛnts ʍɪʧ ðoːʊ hɜd noːʊ mɔːʌ]
Still vibrate on my heart.
[stɪl ˈvaːɪbɹɛːɪt ɑn maːɪ hɑt]
In Echo's cave I long to dwell,
[ɪn ˈɛkoːʊz kɛːɪv aːɪ lɑŋ tu dwɛl]
And still to hear that sad farewell,
[ænd stɪl tu hɪːʌ ðæt sæd fɛːʌˈwɛl]
When we were forc'd to part.
[ʍɛn wi wɜ fɔst tu pɑt]
Bright eyes! O that the task were mine
[bɹaːɪt aːɪz oːʊ ðæt ðʊ tɑsk wɜ maːɪn]
To guard the liquid fires that shine,
[tu gɑd ðʊ ˈlɪkwɪd faːɪʌz ðæt ʃaːɪn]
And round your orbits play!
[ænd ɹaːʊnd jɔːʌ ˈɔbɪts plɛːɪ]
To watch them with a vestal's care,
[tu wɑʧ ðɛm wɪð ʌ ˈvɛstʊlz kɛːʌ]
To feed with smiles a light so fair,
[tu fid wɪð smaːɪlz ʌ laːɪt soːʊ fɛːʌ]
That it may ne'er decay.
[ðæt ɪt mɛːɪ nɛːʌ dɪˈkɛːɪ]

"Piercing Eyes"
[ˈpiːʌsɪŋ ɑːɪz]
Anonymous

Why asks my fair one if I love?
[ʍaːɪ ɑsks maːɪ fɛːʌ wʌn ɪf aːɪ lʌv]
Those eyes so piercing bright!
[ðoːʊz ɑːɪz soːʊ ˈpiːʌsɪŋ bɹaːɪt]
Can ev'ry doubt of that remove
[kæn ˈɛvɹɪ daːʊt ʌv ðæt ɹɪˈmuv]
And need no other light.
[ænd nid noːʊ ˈʌðʌ laːɪt]
Those eyes full well do know my heart
[ðoːʊz ɑːɪz fʊl wɛl du noːʊ maːɪ hɑt]
And all its workings see.
[ænd ɔl ɪts ˈwɜkɪŋz si]
E'er since they play'd the conq'ror's part,
[ɛːʌ sɪns ðɛːɪ plɛːɪd ðʊ ˈkɑŋkɹɔ(ʌ)z pɑt]
And I no more was free.
[ænd aːɪ noːʊ mɔːʌ waz fɹi]

"Pleasing Pain"
[ˈplizɪŋ pɛːɪn]
Hunter, Anne (Eng. 1742-1821)

Far from this throbbing bosom haste,
[fɑ fɹʌm ðɪs ˈθɹɑbɪŋ ˈbʊzʌm hɛːɪst]

Ye doubts, ye fears, that lay it waste;
[ji daːʊts ji fɪːʌz ðæt lɛːɪ ɪt wɛːɪst]
Dear anxious days of pleasing pain,
[dɪːʌɾ ˈæŋkʃʌs dɛːɪz ʌv ˈplizɪŋ pɛːɪn]
Fly never to return again.
[flaːɪ ˈnɛvʌ tu ɾɪˈtɜn ʌˈgɛːɪn]
But ah, return ye smiling hours,
[bʌt ɑ ɾɪˈtɜn ji ˈsmaːɪlɪŋ aːʊʌz]
By careless fancy cron'd with flow'rs;
[baːɪ ˈkɛːʌlɛ(ɪ)s ˈfænsɪ kɹaːʊnd wɪð flaːʊʌz]
Come, fairy joys and wishes gay,
[kʌm ˈfɛːʌɾɪ ʤɔːɪz ænd ˈwɪʃɛ(ɪ)z gɛːɪ]
And dance in sportive rounds away.
[ænd dans ɪn ˈspɔtɪv ɹaːʊndz ʌˈwɛːɪ]
So shall the moments gaily glide
[soːʊ ʃæl ðʊ ˈmoːʊments ˈgɛːɪlɪ glaːɪd]
O'er various life's tumultuous tide,
[ɔːʌ ˈvæɾɪʌs laːɪfs tjuˈmʌlʧuʌs taːɪd]
Nor sad regrets disturb their course
[nɔ sæd ɹɪˈgɹɛts dɪˈstɜb ðɛːʌ kɔs]
To calm oblivion's peaceful source.
[tu kɑm o(ʌ)ˈblɪvɪʌnz ˈpisfʊl sɔs]

"Sailor's Song"
[ˈsɛːɪlʌz sɑŋ]
Hunter, Anne (Eng. 1742-1821)

High on the giddy bending mast
[haːɪ ɑn ðʊ ˈgɪdɪ ˈbɛndɪŋ mɑst]
The seaman furls the rending sail,
[ðʊ ˈsimæ(ʌ)n fɜlz ðʊ ˈɹɛndɪŋ sɛːɪl]
And, fearless of the rushing blast,
[ænd ˈfiːʌlɛ(ɪ)s ʌv ðʊ ˈɾʌʃɪŋ blɑst]
He careless whistles to the gale.
[hi ˈkɛːʌlɛ(ɪ)s ˈʍɪsʊlz tu ðʊ gɛːɪl]
Rattling ropes and rolling seas,
[ˈɹætlɪŋ ɹoːʊps ænd ˈɹoːʊlɪŋ siz]
Hurlyburly, hurlyburly,
[ˈhɜlɪˈbɜlɪ ˈhɜlɪˈbɜlɪ]
War nor death can him displease.
[wɔ nɔ dɛθ kæn hɪm dɪˈspliz]
The hostile foe his vessel seeks,
[ðʊ ˈhɑstaːɪl foːʊ hɪz ˈvɛsʊl siks]
High bounding o'er the raging main,
[haːɪ ˈbaːʊndɪŋ ɔːʌ ðʊ ˈɾɛːɪʤɪŋ mɛːɪn]
The roaring cannon loudly speaks,
[ðʊ ˈɾɔːʌɾɪŋ ˈkænʌn ˈlaːʊdlɪ spiks]
'Tis Britain's glory we maintain.
[tɪz ˈbɹɪtæ(ɪ)nz ˈglɔɹɪ wi mɛːɪnˈtɛːɪn]
Rattling ropes and rolling seas,
[ˈɹætlɪŋ ɹoːʊps ænd ˈɹoːʊlɪŋ siz]
Hurlyburly, hurlyburly,
[ˈhɜlɪˈbɜlɪ ˈhɜlɪˈbɜlɪ]
War nor death can him displease.
[wɔ nɔ dɛθ kæn hɪm dɪˈspliz]

"She Never Told Her Love"
[ʃi 'nɛvʌ toːʊld hɜ lʌv]
Shakespeare, William (Eng. 1564-1616)

She never told her love,
[ʃi 'nɛvʌ toːʊld hɜ lʌv]
But let concealment, like a worm in the bud,
[bʌt lɛt kʌn'silmɛnt laːɪk ʌ wɜm ɪn ðʊ bʌd]
Feed on her damask cheek;
[fid ɑn hɜ 'dæmæ(ɪ)sk ʧik]
She sat like Patience on a monument,
[ʃi sæt laːɪk 'pɛːɪʃɛ(ɪ)ns ɑn ʌ 'mɑnjumɛnt]
Smiling at grief.
['smaːɪlɪŋ æt gɹif]

"Sympathy"
['sɪmpʌθi]
Hoole, John (Eng. 1727-1803)

In thee I bear so dear a part,
[ɪn ði aːɪ bɛːʌ soːʊ dɪːʌɾ ʌ pɑt]
By love so firm, so firm am thine,
[baːɪ lʌv soːʊ fɜm soːʊ fɜm æm ðaːɪn]
That each affection of thy heart,
[ðæt iʧ ʌ'fɛkʃʌn ʌv ðaːɪ hɑt]
By sympathy is mine.
[baːɪ 'sɪmpæ(ʌ)θɪ ɪz maːɪn]
When thou art griev'd, I grieve no less,
[ʍɛn ðaːʊ ɑt gɹivd aːɪ gɹiv noːʊ lɛs]
My joys by thine are known,
[maːɪ ʤɔːɪz baːɪ ðaːɪn ɑ noːʊn]
And ev'ry good thou would'st possess,
[ænd 'ɛvɹɪ gʊd ðaːʊ wʊdst po'zɛs]
Becomes in wish my own.
[bɪ'kʌmz ɪn wɪʃ maːɪ oːʊn]

"The Mermaid's Song"
[ðʊ 'mɜmɛːɪdz sɑŋ]
Hunter, Anne (Eng. 1742-1821)

1. Now the dancing sunbeams play
[naːʊ ðʊ 'dɑnsɪŋ 'sʌnbimz plɛːɪ]
On the green and glassy sea.
[ɑn ðʊ gɹin ænd 'glɑsɪ si]
Come, and I will lead the way,
[kʌm ænd aːɪ wɪl lid ðʊ wɛːɪ]
Where the pearly treasures be.
[ʍɛːʌ ðʊ 'pɜlɪ 'tɹɛʒʊ(ʌ)z bi]
CHORUS:
Come with me, and we will go
[kʌm wɪð mi ænd wi wɪl goːʊ]
Where the rocks of coral grow.
[ʍɛːʌ ðʊ ɾaks ʌv 'kɔɾʊl gɹoːʊ]
Follow, follow, follow me.
['faloːʊ 'faloːʊ 'faloːʊ mi]

2. Come, behold what treasures lie
[kʌm bɪ'hoːʊld ʍat 'tɹɛʒʊ(ʌ)z laːɪ]
Far below the rolling waves;
[fɑ bɪ'loːʊ ðʊ 'roːʊlɪŋ wɛːɪvz]
Riches hid from human eye,
['ɹɪʧɛ(ɪ)z hɪd fɹʌm 'hjumæ(ʌ)n aːɪ]
Dimly shine in ocean's caves.
['dɪmlɪ ʃaːɪn ɪn 'oːʊʃæ(ɪ)nz kɛːɪvz]
Ebbing tides bear no delay,
['ɛbɪŋ taːɪdz bɛːʌ noːʊ dɪ'lɛːɪ]
Stormy winds are far away.
['stɔmɪ wɪndz ɑ fɑɾ ʌ'wɛːɪ]
CHORUS

"The Spirit's Song"
[ðʊ 'spɪʀɪts sɑŋ]
Hunter, Anne (Eng. 1742-1821)

Hark! Hark, what I tell to thee,
[hak hak ʍat aːɪ tɛl tu ði]
Nor sorrow o'er the tomb;
[nɔ 'saɾoːʊ ɔːʌ ðʊ tum]
My spirit wanders free,
[maːɪ 'spɪɾɪt 'wandʌz fɹi]
And waits till thine shall come.
[ænd wɛːɪts tɪl ðaːɪn ʃæl kʌm]
All pensive and alone,
[ɔl 'pɛnsɪv ænd ʌ'loːʊn]
I see thee sit and weep,
[aːɪ si ði sɪt ænd wip]
Thy head upon the stone
[ðaːɪ hɛd ʌ'pɑn ðʊ stoːʊn]
Where my cold ashes sleep.
[ʍɛːʌ maːɪ koːʊld 'æʃɛ(ɪ)z slip]
I watch thy speaking eyes,
[aːɪ waʧ ðaːɪ 'spikɪŋ aːɪz]
And mark each falling tear;
[ænd mak iʧ 'fɔlɪŋ tɪːʌ]
I catch thy passing sighs,
[aːɪ kæʧ ðaːɪ 'pasɪŋ saːɪz]
Ere they are lost in air.
[ɛːʌ ðɛːɪ ɑ last ɪn ɛːʌ]
Hark! Hark, what I tell to thee...
[hak hak ʍat aːɪ tɛl tu ði]

"The Wanderer"
[ðʊ 'wandʌʀʌ]
Hunter, Anne (Eng. 1742-1821)

To wander alone when the moon, faintly beaming
[tu 'wandʌɾ ʌ'loːʊn ʍɛn ðʊ mun 'fɛːɪntlɪ 'bimɪŋ]
With glimmering lustre, darts thro' the dark shade,
[wɪð 'glɪmʌɾɪŋ 'lʌstʌ dats θɾu ðʊ dak ʃɛːɪd]
Where owls seek for covert, and nightbirds complaining
[ʍɛːʌɾ aːʊlz sik fɔ 'kʌvʌt ænd 'naːɪtbɜdz kʌm'plɛːɪnɪŋ]

Add sound to the horror that darkens the glade.
[æd saːʊnd tu ðʊ ˈhɔɾɔ(ʌ) ðæt ˈdakɛ(ɪ)nz ðʊ glɛːɪd]
'Tis not for the happy; come, daughter of sorrow,
[tɪz nat fɔ ðʊ ˈhæpɪ kʌm ˈdɔtʌɾ ʌv ˈsaɾoːʊ]
'Tis here thy sad thoughts are embalm'd in thy tears,
[tɪz hɪːʌ ðaːɪ sæd θɔts aɾ ɪmˈbamd ɪn ðaːɪ tɪːʌz]
Where, lost in the past, disregarding tomorrow,
[ʍɛːʌ last ɪn ðʊ past dɪsɹɪˈgadɪŋ tuˈmaɾoːʊ]
There's nothing for hopes and nothing for fears.
[ðɛːʌz ˈnʌθɪŋ fɔ hoːʊps ænd ˈnʌθɪŋ fɔ fɪːʌz]

Head, Michael (Eng. 1900-1976)

Over the Rim of the Moon (Song Cycle)
[ˈoːʊvʌ ðʊ ɹɪm ʌv ðʊ mun]
Ledwidge, Francis (Ir. 1891-1917)

1. The Ships of Arcady
[ðʊ ʃɪps ʌv ˈakʌˌdi]

Thro' the faintest filigree
[θɾu ðʊ ˈfɛːɪntɛ(ɪ)st ˈfɪlɪˌgɹi]
Over the dim waters go
[ˈoːʊvʌ ðʊ dɪm ˈwɔtʌz goːʊ]
Little ships of Arcady
[ˈlɪtʊl ʃɪps ʌv ˈakʌˌdi]
When the morning moon is low.
[ʍɛn ðʊ ˈmɔnɪŋ mun ɪz loːʊ]
I can hear the sailors' song
[aːɪ kæn hɪːʌ ðʊ ˈsɛːɪlɔ(ʌ)z saŋ]
From the blue edge of the sea,
[fɹʌm ðʊ blu ɛdʒ ʌv ðʊ si]
Passing like the lights a-long
[ˈpasɪŋ laːɪk ðʊ laːɪts ʌ laŋ]
Thro' the dusky filigree.
[θɾu ðʊ ˈdʌskɪ ˈfɪlɪˌgɹi]
Then where moon and waters meet
[ðɛn ʍɛːʌ mun ænd ˈwɔtʌz mit]
Sail by sail they pass away,
[sɛːɪl baːɪ sɛːɪl ðɛːɪ pas ʌˈwɛːɪ]
With little friendly winds replete
[wɪð ˈlɪtʊl ˈfɹɛndlɪ wɪndz ɹɪˈplit]
Blowing from the breaking day.
[ˈbloːʊɪŋ fɹʌm ðʊ ˈbɹɛːɪkɪŋ dɛːɪ]
And when the little ships have flown,
[ænd ʍɛn ðʊ ˈlɪtʊl ʃɪps hæv floːʊn]
Dreaming still of Arcady
[ˈdɹimɪŋ stɪl ʌv ˈakʌˌdi]
I look across the waves, alone
[aːɪ lʊk ʌˈkɹas ðʊ wɛːɪvz ʌˈloːʊn]
In the misty filigree.
[ɪn ðʊ ˈmɪstɪ ˈfɪlɪˌgɹi]
Thro' the faintest filigree,
[θɾu ðʊ ˈfɛːɪntɛ(ɪ)st ˈfɪlɪˌgɹi]

Over the dim waters go
[ˈoːʊvʌ ðʊ dɪm ˈwɔtʌz goːʊ]
Little ships of Arcady
[ˈlɪtʊl ʃɪps ʌv ˈakʌˌdi]
When the morning moon is low.
[ʍɛn ðʊ ˈmɔnɪŋ mun ɪz loːʊ]

2. A Blackbird Singing
[ʌ ˈblækbɜd ˈsɪŋɪŋ]

A blackbird singing
[ʌ ˈblækbɜd ˈsɪŋɪŋ]
On a moss upholstered stone,
[an ʌ mɔs ʌpˈhoːʊlstʌd stoːʊn]
Bluebells swinging,
[ˈblubɛlz ˈswɪŋɪŋ]
Shadows wildly blown,
[ˈʃædoːʊz ˈwaːɪldlɪ bloːʊn]
A song in the wood,
[ʌ saŋ ɪn ðʊ wʊd]
A ship on the sea.
[ʌ ʃɪp an ðʊ si]
The song was for you
[ðʊ saŋ waz fɔ ju]
and the ship was for me.
[ænd ðʊ ʃɪp waz fɔ mi]
A blackbird singing,
[ʌ ˈblækbɜd ˈsɪŋɪŋ]
I hear in my troubled mind,
[aːɪ hɪːʌɾ ɪn maːɪ ˈtɹʌbʊld maːɪnd]
Bluebells swinging
[ˈblubɛlz ˈswɪŋɪŋ]
I see in a distant wind.
[aːɪ si ɪn ʌ ˈdɪstæ(ɪ)nt wɪnd]
But sorrow and silence
[bʌt ˈsaɾoːʊ ænd ˈsaːɪlɛ(ɪ)ns]
Are the wood's threnody,
[a ðʊ wʊdz ˈθɾɛnʌdɪ]
The silence for you
[ðʊ ˈsaːɪlɛ(ɪ)ns fɔ ju]
And the sorrow for me.
[ænd ðʊ ˈsaɾoːʊ fɔ mi]
A blackbird singing
[ʌ ˈblækbɜd ˈsɪŋɪŋ]

3. Beloved
[bɪˈlʌvɪd]

Nothing but sweet music wakes
[ˈnʌθɪŋ bʌt swit ˈmjuzɪk wɛːɪks]
My Beloved, my Beloved.
[maːɪ bɪˈlʌvɛ(ɪ)d maːɪ bɪˈlʌvɛ(ɪ)d]
Sleeping by the blue lakes,
[ˈslipɪŋ baːɪ ðʊ blu lɛːɪks]
My own Beloved!
[maːɪ oːʊn bɪˈlʌvɛ(ɪ)d]

Song of lark and song of thrush,
[saŋ ʌv lak ænd saŋ ʌv θrʌʃ]
My Beloved! my Beloved!
[mɑːɪ bɪˈlʌvɛ(ɪ)d mɑːɪ bɪˈlʌvɛ(ɪ)d]
Sing in morning's rosy blush,
[sɪŋ ɪn ˈmɔnɪŋz ˈɹoːʊzi blʌʃ]
My own Beloved!
[mɑːɪ oːʊn bɪˈlʌvɛ(ɪ)d]
When your eyes dawn blue and clear,
[ʌɛn jɔːʌr ɑːɪz dɔn blu ænd klɪːʌ]
My Beloved! my Beloved!
[mɑːɪ bɪˈlʌvɛ(ɪ)d mɑːɪ bɪˈlʌvɛ(ɪ)d]
You will find me waiting here,
[ju wɪl fɑːɪnd mi ˈwɛːɪtɪŋ hɪːʌ]
My own Beloved!
[mɑːɪ oːʊn bɪˈlʌvɛ(ɪ)d]

4. Nocturne
[ˈnɑktʊn]

The rim of the moon
[ðʊ ɾɪm ʌv ðʊ mun]
Is over the corn.
[ɪz ˈoːʊvʌ ðʊ kɔn]
The beetle's drone
[ðʊ ˈbitʊlz dɹoːʊn]
Is above the thorn.
[ɪz ʌˈbʌv ðʊ θɔn]
Grey days come soon
[ɡɹɛːɪ dɛːɪz kʌm sun]
And I am alone;
[ænd ɑːɪ æm ʌˈloːʊn]
Can you hear my moan
[kæn ju hɪːʌ mɑːɪ moːʊn]
Where you rest, Aroon?
[ʌɛːʌ ju ɾɛst ʌˈrun]
When the wild tree bore
[ʌɛn ðʊ wɑːɪld tɹi bɔːʌ]
The deep blue cherry,
[ðʊ dip blu ˈtʃɛɾɪ]
In night's deep pall
[ɪn nɑːɪts dip pɔl]
Our love kissed merry.
[ɑːʊʌ lʌv kɪst ˈmɛɾɪ]
But you come no more
[bʌt ju kʌm noːʊ mɔːʌ]
Where its woodlands call,
[ʌɛːʌr ɪts ˈwʊdlæ(ʌ)ndz kɔl]
And the grey days fall
[ænd ðʊ ɡɹɛːɪ dɛːɪz fɔl]
On my grief, Asthore!
[ɑn mɑːɪ ɡɾif ˈæstɔːʌ]
The rim of the moon
[ðʊ ɾɪm ʌv ðʊ mun]
is over the corn.
[ɪz ˈoːʊvʌ ðʊ kɔn]

The beetle's drone
[ðʊ ˈbitʊlz dɹoːʊn]
is above the thorn.
[ɪz ʌˈbʌv ðʊ θɔn]
Grey days come soon
[ɡɹɛːɪ dɛːɪz kʌm sun]
and I am alone;
[ænd ɑːɪ æm ʌˈloːʊn]
Can you hear my moan
[kæn ju hɪːʌ mɑːɪ moːʊn]
where you rest, Aroon?
[ʌɛːʌ ju ɾɛst ʌˈrun]

Three Psalms (Song Cycle)
[θɾi sɑmz]

1. I Will Lift up Mine Eyes: Psalm 121
[ɑːɪ wɪl lɪft ʌp mɑːɪn ɑːɪz sɑm wʌn ˈtwɛnti wʌn]

I will lift up mine eyes unto the hills,
[ɑːɪ wɪl lɪft ʌp mɑːɪn ɑːɪz ˈʌntu ðʊ hɪlz]
From whence cometh my help.
[fɹʌm ʌɛns ˈkʌmɛ(ɪ)θ mɑːɪ hɛlp]
My help cometh from the Lord,
[mɑːɪ hɛlp ˈkʌmɛ(ɪ)θ fɹʌm ðʊ lɔd]
Which made heaven and earth,
[ʌɪtʃ mɛːɪd ˈhɛvɪn ænd ɜθ]
He will not suffer thy foot to be moved:
[hi wɪl nɑt ˈsʌfʌ ðɑːɪ fʊt tu bi muvd]
He that keepeth thee will not slumber.
[hi ðæt ˈkipɛ(ɪ)θ ði wɪl nɑt ˈslʌmbʌ]
Behold, he that keepeth Israel
[bɪˈhoːʊld hi ðæt ˈkipɛ(ɪ)θ ˈɪzɹɑɛl]
Shall neither slumber nor sleep.
[ʃæl ˈnɑːɪðʌ ˈslʌmbʌ nɔ slip]
The Lord is thy keeper:
[ðʊ lɔd ɪz ðɑːɪ ˈkipʌ]
The Lord is thy shade upon thy right hand.
[ðʊ lɔd ɪz ðɑːɪ ʃɛːɪd ʌˈpɑn ðɑːɪ ɾɑːɪt hænd]
The sun shall not smite thee by day,
[ðʊ sʌn ʃæl nɑt smɑːɪt ði bɑːɪ dɛːɪ]
Nor the moon by night,
[nɔ ðʊ mun bɑːɪ nɑːɪt]
The Lord shall preserve thee
[ðʊ lɔd ʃæl pɹɪˈzɜv ði]
shall preserve thee from all evil:
[ʃæl pɹɪˈzɜv ði fɹʌm ɔl ˈivɪ(ʊ)l]
He shall preserve thy soul,
[hi ʃæl pɹɪˈzɜv ðɑːɪ soːʊl]
The Lord shall preserve
[ðʊ lɔd ʃæl pɹɪˈzɜv]
thy going out and thy coming in
[ðɑːɪ ˈɡoːʊɪŋ ɑːʊt ænd ðɑːɪ ˈkʌmɪŋ ɪn]
From this day forth,
[fɹʌm ðɪs dɛːɪ fɔθ]

and even for evermore, for evermore.
[ænd ˈivɛ(ɪ)n fɔʁ⁽ʳ⁾ ɛvʌˈmɔːʌ fɔʁ⁽ʳ⁾ ɛvʌˈmɔːʌ]

2. Be Merciful Unto Me O God: Psalm 57
[bi ˈmɜsɪfʊl ˈʌntu mi oːʊ gad sam ˈfɪfti ˈsɛvɪn]

Be merciful unto me, O God, Be merciful unto me,
[bi ˈmɜsɪfʊl ˈʌntu mi oːʊ gad bi ˈmɜsɪfʊl ˈʌntu mi]
For my soul trusteth in thee, Yea,
[fɔ maːɪ soːʊl ˈtɹʌstɛ(ɪ)θ ɪn ði jɛːɪ]
in the shadow of thy wings will I make my refuge,
[ɪn ðʊ ˈʃædoːʊ ʌv ðaːɪ wɪŋz wɪl aːɪ mɛːɪk maːɪ ˈɹɛfjudʒ]
Until these calamities be overpast.
[ʌnˈtɪl ðiz kʌˈlæmɪtɪz bi ˌoːʊvʌˈpast]
I will cry unto God most high,
[aːɪ wɪl kɹaːɪ ˈʌntu gad moːʊst haːɪ]
Unto God that performeth all things for me.
[ˈʌntu gad ðæt pɜˈfɔmɛ(ɪ)θ ɔl θɪŋz fɔ mi]
He shall send from heaven and save me from the
[hi ʃæl sɛnd fɹʌm ˈhɛvɛ(ɪ)n ænd sɛːɪv mi fɹʌm ðʊ]
reproach of him that would swallow me up.
[ɹɪˈpɹoːʊʧ ʌv hɪm ðæt wʊd ˈswaloːʊ mi ʌp]
God shall send forth his mercy and his truth.
[gad ʃæl sɛnd fɔθ hɪz ˈmɜsɪ ænd hɪz tɹuθ]
My soul is among lions,
[maːɪ soːʊl ɪz ʌˈmʌŋ ˈlaːɪʌnz]
and I lie even among them
[ænd aːɪ laːɪ ˈivɛ(ɪ)n ʌˈmʌŋ ðɛm]
that are set on fire, even the sons of men,
[ðæt a sɛt an faːɪʌ ˈivɛ(ɪ)n ðʊ sʌnz ʌv mɛn]
whose teeth are spears and arrows,
[huz tiθ a spɪːʌz ænd ˈæɾoːʊz]
and their tongue a sharp sword.
[ænd ðɛːʌ tʌŋ ʌ ʃap sɔd]
Be thou exalted, O God, above the heavens;
[bi ðaːʊ ɪgˈzɔltɛ(ɪ)d oːʊ gad ʌˈbʌv ðʊ ˈhɛvɛ(ɪ)nz]
Let thy glory be above all the earth.
[lɛt ðaːɪ ˈglɔɾɪ bi ʌˈbʌv ɔl ði ɜθ]
They have prepared a net for my steps;
[ðɛːɪ hæv pɹɪˈpɛːʌd ʌ nɛt fɔ maːɪ stɛps]
my soul is bowed down:
[maːɪ soːʊl ɪz baːʊd daːʊn]
they have digged a pit before me,
[ðɛːɪ hæv dɪgd ʌ pɪt bɪˈfɔːʌ mi]
Into the midst whereof they are fallen themselves.
[ˈɪntu ðʊ mɪdst ʍɛːʌˈɾʌv ðɛːɪ a ˈfɔlɛ(ɪ)n ðɛmˈsɛlvz]
My heart is fixed, O God, my heart is fixed:
[maːɪ hat ɪz fɪkst oːʊ gad maːɪ hat ɪz fɪkst]
I will sing and give praise.
[aːɪ wɪl sɪŋ ænd gɪv pɹɛːɪz]
Awake up, my glory. Awake, psaltery and harp.
[ʌˈwɛːɪk ʌp maːɪ ˈglɔɾɪ ʌˈwɛːɪk ˈsɔltʌɾɪ ænd hap]
I myself will awake early.
[aːɪ maːɪˈsɛlf wɪl ʌˈwɛːɪk ˈɜlɪ]
I will praise thee, O Lord, among the people:
[aːɪ wɪl pɹɛːɪz ði oːʊ lɔd ʌˈmʌŋ ðʊ ˈpipʊl]

I will sing unto thee among the nations.
[aːɪ wɪl sɪŋ ˈʌntu ði ʌˈmʌŋ ðʊ ˈnɛːɪʃʌnz]
For thy mercy is great unto the heavens,
[fɔ ðaːɪ ˈmɜsɪ ɪz gɹɛːɪt ˈʌntu ðʊ ˈhɛvɛ(ɪ)nz]
And thy truth unto the clouds.
[ænd ðaːɪ truθ ˈʌntu ðʊ klaːʊdz]
Be thou exalted, O God, above the heavens:
[bi ðaːʊ ɪgˈzɔltɛ(ɪ)d oːʊ gad ʌˈbʌv ðʊ ˈhɛvɛ(ɪ)nz]
Let thy glory be above all the earth.
[lɛt ðaːɪ ˈglɔɾɪ bi ʌˈbʌv ɔl ði ɜθ]

3. Make a Joyful Noise Unto the Lord: Psalm 100
[mɛːɪk ʌ ˈdʒɔːɪfʊl nɔːɪz ˈʌntu ðʊ lɔd sam wʌn ˈhʌndɹɪd]

Make a joyful noise unto the Lord, all ye lands.
[mɛːɪk ʌ ˈdʒɔːɪfʊl nɔːɪz ˈʌntu ðʊ lɔd ɔl ji lændz]
Serve the Lord with gladness.
[sɜv ðʊ lɔd wɪð ˈglædnɛ(ɪ)s]
Come before his presence with singing.
[kʌm bɪˈfɔːʌ hɪz ˈpɹɛzɛ(ɪ)ns wɪð ˈsɪŋɪŋ]
Know ye that the Lord he is God.
[noːʊ ji ðæt ðʊ lɔd hi ɪz gad]
It is he that hath made us, and not we ourselves.
[ɪt ɪz hi ðæt hæθ mɛːɪd ʌs ænd nat wi aːʊʌˈsɛlvz]
We are his people, and the sheep of his pasture.
[wi a hɪz ˈpipʊl ænd ðʊ ʃip ʌv hɪz ˈpasʧʊ(ʌ)]
Enter into his gates with thanksgiving,
[ˈɛntʌɾ ˈɪntu hɪz gɛːɪts wɪð θæŋksˈgɪvɪŋ]
And into his courts with praise.
[ænd ˈɪntu hɪz kɔts wɪð pɹɛːɪz]
Be thankful unto him and bless his name.
[bi ˈθæŋkfʊl ˈʌntu hɪm ænd blɛs hɪz nɛːɪm]
For the Lord is good. His mercy is everlasting;
[fɔ ðʊ lɔd ɪz gʊd hɪz ˈmɜsɪ ɪz ɛvʌˈlastɪŋ]
And his truth endureth to all generations.
[ænd hɪz truθ ɪnˈdjuːʌɾɛ(ɪ)θ tu ɔl dʒɛnʌˈɾɛːɪʃʌnz]

Song Selections

"A Piper"
[ʌ ˈpaːɪpʌ]
O'Sullivan, Seumas (Ir. 1879-1958)

A piper in the streets today
[ʌ ˈpaːɪpʌɾ ɪn ðʊ stɹits tuˈdɛːɪ]
Set up, and tuned, and started to play,
[sɛt ʌp ænd tjund ænd ˈstatɛ(ɪ)d tu plɛːɪ]
And away, away, away on the tide
[ænd ʌˈwɛːɪ ʌˈwɛːɪ ʌˈwɛːɪ an ðʊ taːɪd]
Of his music we started; on ev'ry side
[ʌv hɪz ˈmjuzɪk wi ˈstatɛ(ɪ)d an ˈɛvɹɪ saːɪd]
Doors and windows were opened wide,
[dɔːʌz ænd ˈwɪndoːʊz wɜ ˈoːʊpɛ(ɪ)nd waːɪd]
And men left down their work and came,
[ænd mɛn lɛft daːʊn ðɛːʌ wɜk ænd kɛːɪm]

And women with petticoats coloured like flame.
[ænd ˈwɪmɛ(ɪ)n wɪð ˈpɛtɪkoːʊts ˈkʌlʊ(ʌ)d laːɪk flɛːɪm]
And little bare feet that were blue with cold,
[ænd ˈlɪtʊl bɛːʌ fit ðæt wɜ blu wɪð koːʊld]
Went dancing back to the age of gold,
[wɛnt ˈdɑnsɪŋ bæk tu ði ɛːɪdʒ ʌv goːʊld]
And all the world went gay, went gay,
[ænd ɔl ðʊ wɜld wɛnt gɛːɪ wɛnt gɛːɪ]
For half an hour in the street today.
[fɔ haf æn ɑːʊʌɾ ɪn ðʊ stɹit tuˈdɛːɪ]

"Acquaint Now Thyself with Him"
[ʌˈkwɛːɪnt naːʊ ðaːɪˈsɛlf wɪθ hɪm]
(I Chronicles 16:29; Job 22:21; Psalms 96:8-9;
Micah 6:6,8)

Acquaint now thyself with Him and be at peace;
[ʌˈkwɛːɪnt naːʊ ðaːɪˈsɛlf wɪð hɪm ænd bi æt pis]
Thereby good shall come unto thee.
[ðɛːʌˈbaːɪ gʊd ʃæl kʌm ˈʌntu ði]
Acquaint now thyself with Him and be at peace.
[ʌˈkwɛːɪnt naːʊ ðaːɪˈsɛlf wɪð hɪm ænd bi æt pis]
Exalt the Lord our God and worship at His holy hill.
[ɪgˈzɔlt ðʊ lɔd ɑːʊʌ gad ænd ˈwɜʃɪp æt hɪz ˈhoːʊlɪ hɪl]
For the Lord our God is holy.
[fɔ ðʊ lɔd ɑːʊʌ gad ɪz ˈhoːʊlɪ]
O worship the Lord in the beauty of holiness.
[oːʊ ˈwɜʃɪp ðʊ lɔd ɪn ðʊ ˈbjutɪ ʌv ˈhoːʊlɪnɛ(ɪ)s]
Fear before Him all the earth.
[fiːʌ bɪˈfɔːʌ hɪm ɔl ði ɜθ]
Give unto the Lord the glory due unto His name.
[gɪv ˈʌntu ðʊ lɔd ðʊ ˈglɔɾɪ dju ˈʌntu hɪz nɛːɪm]
Bring an offering, and come unto His courts.
[bɹɪŋ æn ˈɒfʌɾɪŋ ænd kʌm ˈʌntu hɪz kɔts]
Wherewith shall I come before the Lord,
[ʍɛːʌˈwɪð ʃæl aːɪ kʌm bɪˈfɔːʌ ðʊ lɔd]
And bow myself before the most high God?
[ænd baːʊ maːɪˈsɛlf bɪˈfɔːʌ ðʊ moːʊst haːɪ gad]
Shall I come before Him with burnt offerings?
[ʃæl aːɪ kʌm bɪˈfɔːʌ hɪm wɪð bɜnt ˈɒfʌɾɪŋz]
He hath showed thee O man what is good
[hi hæθ ʃoːʊd ði oːʊ mæn ʍat ɪz gʊd]
And what doth the Lord require of thee,
[ænd ʍat dʌθ ðʊ lɔd ɹɪˈkwaːɪʌɾ ʌv ði]
But to do justly, and to love mercy
[bʌt tu du ˈdʒʌstlɪ ænd tu lʌv ˈmɜsɪ]
And to walk humbly with thy God.
[ænd tu wɔk ˈhʌmblɪ wɪð ðaːɪ gad]
Acquaint now thyself with him and be at peace;
[ʌˈkwɛːɪnt naːʊ ðaːɪˈsɛlf wɪð hɪm ænd bi æt pis]
Thereby good shall come unto thee.
[ðɛːʌˈbaːɪ gʊd ʃæl kʌm ˈʌntu ði]
Acquaint now thyself with Him and be at peace.
[ʌˈkwɛːɪnt naːʊ ðaːɪˈsɛlf wɪð hɪm ænd bi æt pis]

"Money, O!"
[ˈmʌnɪ oːʊ]
Davies, William Henry (Wel. 1871-1940)

When I had money, money, O!
[ʍɛn aːɪ hæd ˈmʌnɪ ˈmʌnɪ oːʊ]
I knew no joy till I went poor;
[aːɪ nju noːʊ dʒɔːɪ tɪl aːɪ wɛnt pʊːʌ]
For many a false man as a friend
[fɔ ˈmɛnɪ ʌ fɔls mæn æz ʌ fɹɛnd]
Came knocking all day at my door.
[kɛːɪm ˈnɑkɪŋ ɔl dɛːɪ æt maːɪ dɔːʌ]
Then felt I like a child that holds
[ðɛn fɛlt aːɪ laːɪk ʌ tʃaːɪld ðæt hoːʊldz]
A trumpet that he must not blow
[ʌ ˈtɹʌmpɛ(ɪ)t ðæt hi mʌst nat bloːʊ]
Because a man is dead; I dared
[bɪˈkɔz ʌ mæn ɪz dɛd aːɪ dɛːʌd]
Not speak to let this false world know.
[nat spik tu lɛt ðɪs fɔls wɜld noːʊ]
Much have I thought of life, and seen
[mʌtʃ hæv aːɪ θɔt ʌv laːɪf ænd sin]
How poor men's hearts are ever light;
[haːʊ pʊːʌ mɛnz hats ɑɾ ˈɛvʌ laːɪt]
And how their wives do hum like bees
[ænd haːʊ ðɛːʌ waːɪvz du hʌm laːɪk biz]
About their work from morn till night.
[ʌˈbaːʊt ðɛːʌ wɜk fɹʌm mɔn tɪl naːɪt]
So, when I hear these poor ones laugh,
[soːʊ ʍɛn aːɪ hiːʌ ðiz pʊːʌ wʌnz laf]
And see the rich ones coldly frown
[ænd si ðʊ ɹɪtʃ wʌnz ˈkoːʊldlɪ fɹaːʊn]
Poor men, think I, need not go up
[pʊːʌ mɛn θɪŋk aːɪ nid nat goːʊ ʌp]
So much as rich men should come down.
[soːʊ mʌtʃ æz ɹɪtʃ mɛn ʃʊd kʌm daːʊn]
When I had money, money, O!
[ʍɛn aːɪ hæd ˈmʌnɪ ˈmʌnɪ oːʊ]
I knew no joy till I went poor;
[aːɪ nju noːʊ dʒɔːɪ tɪl aːɪ wɛnt pʊːʌ]
For many a false man as a friend
[fɔ ˈmɛnɪ ʌ fɔls mæn æz ʌ fɹɛnd]
Came knocking all day at my door.
[kɛːɪm ˈnɑkɪŋ ɔl dɛːɪ æt maːɪ dɔːʌ]

"Sweet Chance" (Songs of the Countryside)
[swit tʃɑns]
Davies, William Henry (Wel. 1871-1940)

Sweet Chance, that led my steps abroad,
[swit tʃɑns ðæt lɛd maːɪ stɛps ʌˈbɹɔd]
Beyond the town, where wild flow'rs grow—
[bɪˈjand ðʊ taːʊn ʍɛːʌ waːɪld flɑːʊʌz gɹoːʊ]
A rainbow and a cuckoo, Lord,
[ʌ ˈɾɛːɪboːʊ ænd ʌ ˈkuku lɔd]

How rich and great the times are now!
[haːʊ rɪtʃ ænd gɹeːɪt ðʊ taːɪmz a naːʊ]
Know, all ye sheep
[noːʊ ɔl ji ʃip]
And cows, that keep
[ænd kaːʊz ðæt kip]
On staring that I stand so long
[an steːʌrɪŋ ðæt aːɪ stænd soːʊ laŋ]
In grass that's wet from heavy rain–
[ɪn gɹas ðæts wɛt fɹʌm 'hɛvɪ ɾeːɪn]
A rainbow, and a cuckoo's song
[ʌ 'ɾeːɪnboːʊ ænd ʌ 'kukuz saŋ]
May never come together again.
[meːɪ 'nɛvʌ kʌm tu'geðʌr ʌ'geːɪn]
May never come
[meːɪ 'nɛvʌ kʌm]
This side the tomb.
[ðɪs saːɪd ðʊ tum]
A rainbow, and a cuckoo's song
[ʌ 'ɾeːɪnboːʊ ænd ʌ 'kukuz saŋ]
May never come together again...
[meːɪ 'nɛvʌ kʌm tu'geðʌr ʌ'geːɪn]

"The Singer"
[ðʊ 'sɪŋʌ]
Taylor, Bronnie (Aus. 1921-1991)

I met a singer on the hill,
[aːɪ mɛt ʌ 'sɪŋʌr an ðʊ hɪl]
He wore a tattered cloak;
[hi wɔːʌr ʌ 'tætʌd kloːʊk]
His cap was torn,
[hɪz kæp waz tɔn]
His shoes were worn,
[hɪz ʃuz wɜ wɔn]
And dreamily he spoke.
[ænd 'dɹimɪlɪ hi spoːʊk]
Fa la la la la la...
[fa la la la la la]
A wrinkled face, a cheery smile,
[ʌ 'rɪŋkʊld feːɪs ʌ 'tʃiːʌrɪ smaːɪl]
And a nobby stick had he;
[ænd ʌ 'nabɪ stɪk hæd hi]
His eyes were grey and far away
[hɪz aːɪz wɜ gɹeːɪ ænd far ʌ'weːɪ]
And changeful as the sea.
[ænd 'tʃeːɪndʒfʊl æz ðʊ si]
I offered him a piece of gold
[aːɪ 'afʌd hɪm ʌ pis ʌv goːʊld]
And hoped that he would stay.
[ænd hoːʊpt ðæt hi wʊd steːɪ]
No word he spoke, But shook his head
[noːʊ wɜd hi spoːʊk bʌt ʃʊk hɪz hɛd]
And smiled and went his way.
[ænd smaːɪld ænd wɛnt hɪz weːɪ]

Fa la la la la la...
[fa la la la la la]
I watched the singer down the hill.
[aːɪ watʃt ðʊ 'sɪŋʌ daːʊn ðʊ hɪl]
My eyes went following after,
[maːɪ aːɪz wɛnt 'faloːʊɪŋ 'aftʌ]
I thought I heard a fairy flute
[aːɪ θɔt aːɪ hɜd ʌ 'feːʌrɪ flut]
And the sound of fairy laughter,
[ænd ðʊ saːʊnd ʌv 'feːʌrɪ 'laftʌ]
Fa la la la la la...
[fa la la la la la]

"When I Think upon the Maidens"
[ʍɛn aːɪ θɪŋk ʌ'pan ðʊ 'meːɪdɪnz]
Ashbrooke, Philip (?) (Eng. 1875-1941)

When I think upon the maidens
[ʍɛn aːɪ θɪŋk ʌ'pan ðʊ 'meːɪdɛ(ɪ)nz]
Whom I swore to love for aye,
[hum aːɪ swɔːʌ tu lʌv fɔʁ(ʳ) ɛːɪ]
Cynthia, Doris and her cousin,
['sɪnθɪʌ 'dɔrɪs ænd hɜ 'kʌzɪn]
There are still another dozen, Ah!
[ðɛːʌr a stɪl ʌ'nʌðʌ 'dʌzɛ(ɪ)n a]
Debts my heart can never pay.
[dɛts maːɪ hat kæn 'nɛvʌ peːɪ]
Do they scorn me now I wonder,
[du ðeːɪ skɔn mi naːʊ aːɪ 'wʌndʌ]
Did they take it as a game?
[dɪd ðeːɪ teːɪk ɪt æz ʌ geːɪm]
Flora, Olive, and the others,
['flɔrʌ 'alɪv ænd ði 'ʌðʌz]
How I hated all their brothers! Ah!
[haːʊ aːɪ 'heːɪtɛ(ɪ)d ɔl ðeːʌ 'bɹʌðʌz a]
Fickle Cupid you're to blame!
['fɪkʊl 'kjupɪd jɔːʌ tu bleːɪm]
Years have passed and yet I'm single,
[jiːʌz hæv past ænd jɛt aːɪm 'sɪŋgʊl]
Torn and undecided still,
[tɔn ænd ʌndɪ'saːɪdɛ(ɪ)d stɪl]
Clara, Mabel, what a vision!
['klærʌ 'meːɪbʊl ʍat ʌ 'vɪʒʌn]
I can't come to a decision,
[aːɪ kant kʌm tu ʌ dɪ'sɪʒʌn]
And I hope I never will!
[ænd aːɪ hoːʊp aːɪ 'nɛvʌ wɪl]

Heggie, Jake (Am. b. 1961)

How Well I Knew the Light (Song Cycle)
[haːʊ wɛl aːɪ nju ðʌ laːɪt]
Dickinson, Emily (Am. 1830-1886)

1. Ample Make This Bed
[ˈæmpʊl mɛːɪk ðɪs bɛd]

Ample make this Bed–
[ˈæmpʊl mɛːɪk ðɪs bɛd]
Make this Bed with Awe–
[mɛːɪk ðɪs bɛd wɪð ɔ]
In it wait till Judgment break
[ɪn ɪt wɛːɪt tɪl ˈdʒʌdʒmɛnt bɹɛːɪk]
Excellent and Fair.
[ˈɛksɛ(ɪ)lɛnt ænd fɛːʌ]
Be its Mattress straight–
[bi ɪts ˈmætɹɛ(ɪ)s stɹɛːɪt]
Be its Pillow round–
[bi ɪts ˈpɪloːʊ ɹɑːʊnd]
Let no Sunrise' yellow noise–
[lɛt noːʊ ˈsʌnɹɑːɪz ˈjɛloːʊ nɔːɪz]
Interrupt this Ground–
[ɪntʌˈʁ(ʳ)ʌpt ðɪs gɹɑːʊnd]

2. The Sun Kept Setting
[ðʌ sʌn kɛpt ˈsɛtɪŋ]

The Sun kept setting– setting– still
[ðʌ sʌn kɛpt ˈsɛtɪŋ ˈsɛtɪŋ stɪl]
No Hue of Afternoon
[noːʊ hju ʌv æftʌˈnun]
Upon the Village I perceived
[ʌˈpɑn ðʌ ˈvɪlæ(ɪ)dʒ ɑːɪ pɜˈsivd]
From House to House 'twas Noon.
[fɹʌm hɑːʊs tu hɑːʊs twɑz nun]
The Dusk kept dropping– dropping– still
[ðʌ dʌsk kɛpt ˈdɹɑpɪŋ ˈdɹɑpɪŋ stɪl]
No Dew upon the Grass–
[noːʊ dju ʌˈpɑn ðʌ gɹæs]
But only on my Forehead stopped–
[bʌt ˈoːʊnlɪ ɑn mɑːɪ ˈfɔhɛd stɑpt]
And wandered in my Face–
[ænd ˈwɑndʌd ɪn mɑːɪ fɛːɪs]
My Feet kept drowsing– drowsing– still
[mɑːɪ fit kɛpt ˈdɹɑːʊzɪŋ ˈdɹɑːʊzɪŋ stɪl]
My fingers were awake–
[mɑːɪ ˈfɪŋgʌz wɜ(ʳ) ʌˈwɛːɪk]
Yet why so little sound–
[jɛt ʍɑːɪ soːʊ ˈlɪtʊl sɑːʊnd]
Myself unto my Seeming– make?
[mɑːɪˈsɛlf ˈʌntu mɑːɪ ˈsimɪŋ mɛːɪk]
How well I knew the Light before–
[hɑːʊ wɛl ɑːɪ nju ðʌ lɑːɪt bɪˈfɔːʌ]

I could see it now–
[ɑːɪ kʊd si ɪt nɑːʊ]
'Tis Dying– I am doing–
[tɪz ˈdɑːɪɪŋ ɑːɪ æm ˈduɪŋ]
but I'm not afraid to know–
[bʌt ɑːɪm nɑt ʌˈfɹɛːɪd tu noːʊ]

Newer Every Day: Songs for Kiri (Song Cycle)
[ˈnjuʁ ˈɛvɹɪ dɛːɪ sɑŋz fɔʁ ˈkɪʁi]
Dickinson, Emily (Am. 1830-1886)

1. Silence
[ˈsɑːɪlɪns]

Silence is all we dread.
[ˈsɑːɪlɛ(ɪ)ns ɪz ɔl wi dɹɛd]
There's Ransom in a Voice–
[ðɛːʌz ˈɹænsʌm ɪn ʌ vɔːɪs]
But Silence is Infinity.
[bʌt ˈsɑːɪlɛ(ɪ)ns ɪz ɪnˈfɪnɪtɪ]
Himself have not a face.
[hɪmˈsɛlf hæv nɑt ʌ fɛːɪs]

2. I'm Nobody! Who Are You? (see Gordon)

3. Fame (see "Fame Is a Bee" by Cipullo)

4. That I Did Always Love
[ðæt ɑːɪ dɪd ˈɔlwɛːɪz lʌv]

That I did always love
[ðæt ɑːɪ dɪd ˈɔlwɛːɪz lʌv]
I bring thee Proof
[ɑːɪ bɹɪŋ ði pɹ(ʳ)uf]
That till I loved
[ðæt tɪl ɑːɪ lʌvd]
I never lived – Enough –
[ɑːɪ ˈnɛvʌ lɪvd ɪˈnʌf]
That I shall love alway –
[ðæt ɑːɪ ʃæl lʌv ˈɔlwɛːɪ]
I argue thee, That love is life –
[ɑːɪ ˈɑgju ði ðæt lʌv ɪz lɑːɪf]
And life hath Immortality –
[ænd lɑːɪf hæθ ɪmɔˈtælɪtɪ]
This – dost thou doubt – Sweet –
[ðɪs dʌst ðɑːʊ dɑːʊt swit]
Then have I Nothing to show – But Calvary –
[ðɛn hæv ɑːɪ ˈnʌθɪŋ tu ʃoːʊ bʌt ˈkælvɑʁ(ʳ)ɪ]

5. Goodnight
[ˌgʊdˈnɑːɪt]

Some say goodnight at night –
[sʌm sɛːɪ ˌgʊdˈnɑːɪt æt nɑːɪt]
I say goodnight by day –
[ɑːɪ sɛːɪ ˌgʊdˈnɑːɪt bɑːɪ dɛːɪ]

Good-bye – the Going utter me –
[gʊd baːɪ ðʌ ˈgoːʊɪŋ ˈʌtʌ mi]
Goodnight, I still reply –
[ˌgʊdˈnaːɪt aːɪ stɪl ɹɪˈplaːɪ]
For parting, that is night,
[fɔ ˈpatɪŋ ðæt ɪz naːɪt]
And presence, simply dawn –
[ænd ˈpɹɛzɛ(ɪ)ns ˈsɪmplɪ dɔn]
Itself the purple on the height
[ɪtˈsɛlf ðʌ ˈpɜpʊl an ðʌ haːɪt]
Denominated morn.
[dɪˈnamɪˌnɛːɪtɛ(ɪ)d mɔn]
Goodnight, I still reply –
[ˌgʊdˈnaːɪt aːɪ stɪl ɹɪˈplaːɪ]
Good-bye – the Going utter me –
[gʊd baːɪ ðʌ ˈgoːʊɪŋ ˈʌtʌ mi]
Goodnight, I still reply –
[ˌgʊdˈnaːɪt aːɪ stɪl ɹɪˈplaːɪ]
Look back on Time, with kindly eyes–
[lʊk bæk an taːɪm wɪð ˈkaːɪndlɪ aːɪz]
He doubtless did his best–
[hi ˈdaːʊtlɛ(ɪ)s dɪd hɪz bɛst]
How softly sinks that trembling sun
[haːʊ ˈsaftlɪ sɪŋks ðæt ˈtɹɛmblɪŋ sʌn]
In Human Nature's West.
[ɪn ˈhjumæ(ʌ)n ˈnɛːɪtʃʊ(ʌ)z wɛst]

Songs and Sonnets to Ophelia (Song Cycle)
[sɑŋz ænd ˈsanɪts tu oˈfilja]

1. The Spring Is Arisen; Ophelia's Song (copyright)

2. Women Have Loved before as I Love Now
[ˈwɪmɪn hæv lʌvd bɪˈfɔːʁ æz aːɪ lʌv naːʊ]
Millay, Edna St. Vincent (Am. 1892-1950)

Women have loved before as I love now;
[ˈwɪmɛ(ɪ)n hæv lʌvd bɪˈfɔːʁ(ʳ) æz aːɪ lʌv naːʊ]
At least, in lively chronicles of the past–
[æt list ɪn ˈlaːɪvlɪ ˈkɹanɪkʊlz ʌv ðʌ pæst]
Of Irish waters by a Cornish prow
[ʌv ˈaːɪʁ(ʳ)ɪʃ ˈwɔtʌz baːɪ ʌ ˈkɔnɪʃ pɹaːʊ]
Or Trojan waters by a Spartan mast
[ɔ ˈtɹoːʊdʒæ(ɪ)n ˈwɔtʌz baːɪ ʌ ˈspatæ(ɪ)n mæst]
Much to their cost invaded– Here and there,
[mʌtʃ tu ðɛːʌ kast ɪnˈvɛːɪdɛ(ɪ)d hiːʌ ænd ðɛːʌ]
Hunting the amorous line, skimming the rest,
[ˈhʌntɪŋ ðɪ ˈæmɔʁ(ʳ)ʌs laːɪn ˈskɪmɪŋ ðʌ ɹɛst]
I find some woman bearing as I bear
[aːɪ faːɪnd sʌm ˈwɔmæ(ʌ)n ˈbɛːʌʁ(ʳ)ɪŋ æz aːɪ bɛːʌ]
Love like a burning city in the breast.
[lʌv laːɪk ʌ ˈbɜnɪŋ ˈsɪtɪ ɪn ðʌ bɹɛst]
I think however that of all alive
[aːɪ θɪŋk haːʊˈɛvʌ ðæt ʌv ɔl ʌˈlaːɪv]
I only in such utter, ancient way
[aːɪ ˈoːʊnlɪ ɪn sʌtʃ ˈʌtʌ ˈɛːɪntʃɛnt wɛːɪ]

Do suffer love; in me alone survive
[du ˈsʌfʌ lʌv ɪn mi ʌˈloːʊn sɜˈvaːɪv]
The unregenerate passions of a day
[ðɪ ʌnɹɪˈdʒɛnɹæ(ɪ)t ˈpæʃʌnz ʌv ʌ dɛːɪ]
When treacherous queens, with death upon the tread,
[ʍɛn ˈtɹɛtʃʌʁ(ʳ)ʌs kwinz wɪð dɛθ ʌˈpan ðʌ tɹɛd]
Heedless and willful, took their knights to bed.
[ˈhidlɛ(ɪ)s ænd ˈwɪlfʊl tʊk ðɛːʌ naːɪts tu bɛd]

3. Not in a Silver Casket Cool with Pearls
[nat ɪn ʌ ˈsɪlvʁ ˈkæskɪt kul wɪθ pɜlz]
Millay, Edna St. Vincent (Am. 1892-1950)

Not in a silver casket cool with pearls
[nat ɪn ʌ ˈsɪlvʌ ˈkæskɛ(ɪ)t kul wɪð pɜlz]
Or rich with red corundum or with blue,
[ɔ ɹɪtʃ wɪð ɹɛd kɔˈʁ(ʳ)ʌndʌm ɔ wɪð blu]
Locked, and the key withheld, as other girls
[lakt ænd ðʌ ki wɪðˈhɛld æz ˈʌðʌ gɜlz]
Have given their loves, I give my love to you;
[hæv ˈgɪvɛ(ɪ)n ðɛːʌ lʌvz aːɪ gɪv maːɪ lʌv tu ju]
Not in a lovers'-knot, not in a ring
[nat ɪn ʌ ˈlʌvʌz nat nat ɪn ʌ ɹɪŋ]
Worked in such fashion, and the legend plain–
[wɜkt ɪn sʌtʃ ˈfæʃʌn ænd ðʌ ˈlɛdʒɛ(ɪ)nd plɛːɪn]
Semper fidelis, where a secret spring
[ˈsɛmpɛr fiˈdɛlis ʍɛːʌʁ(ʳ) ʌ ˈsikɹɛ(ɪ)t spɹɪŋ]
Kennels a drop of mischief for the brain:
[ˈkɛnʊlz ʌ dɹap ʌv ˈmɪstʃɪf fɔ ðʌ bɹɛːɪn]
Love in the open hand, no thing but that,
[lʌv ɪn ði ˈoːʊpɛ(ɪ)n hænd noːʊ θɪŋ bʌt ðæt]
Ungemmed, unhidden, wishing not to hurt,
[ʌnˈdʒɛmd ʌnˈhɪdɛ(ɪ)n ˈwɪʃɪŋ nat tu hɜt]
As one should bring you cowslips in a hat
[æz wʌn ʃʊd bɹɪŋ ju ˈkaːʊslɪps ɪn ʌ hæt]
Swung from the hand, or apples in her skirt,
[swʌŋ fɹʌm ðʌ hænd ɔʁ(ʳ) ˈæpʊlz ɪn hɜ skɜt]
I bring you, calling out as children do:
[aːɪ bɹɪŋ ju ˈkɔlɪŋ aːʊt æz ˈtʃɪldɹɛ(ɪ)n du]
"Look what I have!– And these are all for you."
[lʊk ʍat aːɪ hæv ænd ðiz aʁ(ʳ) ɔl fɔ ju]

4. Spring
[spɹɪŋ]
Millay, Edna St. Vincent (Am. 1892-1950)

To what purpose, April, do you return again?
[tu ʍat ˈpɜpʌs ˈɛːɪpɹɪl(ʊ)l du ju ɹɪˈtɜn ʌˈgɛn]
Beauty is not enough.
[ˈbjutɪ ɪz nat ɪˈnʌf]
You can no longer quiet me with the redness
[ju kæn noːʊ ˈlaŋgʌ ˈkwaːɪɛ(ɪ)t mi wɪð ðʌ ˈɹɛdnɛ(ɪ)s]
Of little leaves opening stickily.
[ʌv ˈlɪtʊl livz ˈoːʊpnɪŋ ˈstɪkɪlɪ]
I know what I know.
[aːɪ noːʊ ʍat aːɪ noːʊ]

The sun is hot on my neck as I observe
[ðʌ sʌn ɪz hɑt ɑn maːɪ nɛk æz ɑːɪ ʌbˈzɜv]
The spikes of the crocus.
[ðʌ spaːɪks ʌv ðʌ ˈkɹoːʊkʌs]
The smell of the earth is good.
[ðʌ smɛl ʌv ði 3θ ɪz gʊd]
It is apparent that there is no death.
[ɪt ɪz ʌˈpæʁ⁽ʳ⁾ɛnt ðæt ðɛːʌʁ⁽ʳ⁾ ɪz noːʊ dɛθ]
But what does that signify?
[bʌt ʍɑt dʌz ðæt ˈsɪgnɪˌfaːɪ]
Not only under ground are the brains of men
[nɑt ˈoːʊnlɪ ˈʌndʌ gɹɑːʊnd ɑ ðʌ bɹɛːɪnz ʌv mɛn]
Eaten by maggots. Life in itself is nothing,
[ˈiːtɛ⁽ɪ⁾n baːɪ ˈmægʌts laːɪf ɪn ɪtˈsɛlf ɪz ˈnʌθɪŋ]
An empty cup, a flight of uncarpeted stairs.
[æn ˈɛmptɪ kʌp ʌ flaːɪt ʌv ʌnˈkɑpɛ⁽ɪ⁾tɛ⁽ɪ⁾d stɛːʌz]
It is not enough that yearly, down this hill,
[ɪt ɪz nɑt ɪˈnʌf ðæt ˈjɪːʌlɪ daːʊn ðɪs hɪl]
April
[ˈɛːɪpɹɪ⁽ʊ⁾l]
Comes like an idiot, babbling and strewing flowers.
[kʌmz laːɪk æn ˈɪdɪʌt ˈbæbʊlɪŋ ænd ˈstɹ⁽ʳ⁾uɪŋ flaːʊʌz]

Songs to the Moon, Part 1:
[sɑŋz tu ðʌ mun pɑʁt wʌn]
"Fairy-Tales for the Children" (Song Cycle)
[ˈfɛʁɪ tɛːɪlz fɔʁ ðʌ ˈʧɪldɹɪn]
Lindsay, Vachel (Am. 1879-1931)

1. Prologue: Once More– to Gloriana
[ˈpɹoːʊlɑg wʌns mɔːʁ tu glɔʁɪˈænʌ]

Girl with the burning golden eyes,
[gɜl wɪð ðʌ ˈbɜnɪŋ ˈgoːʊldɛ⁽ɪ⁾n aːɪz]
And red-bird song, and snowy throat:
[ænd ɹɛd bɜd sɑŋ ænd ˈsnoːʊɪ θɹoːʊt]
I bring you gold and silver moons –
[aːɪ bɹɪŋ ju goːʊld ænd ˈsɪlvʌ munz]
And diamond stars, and mists that float.
[ænd ˈdaːɪmʌnd stɑz ænd mɪsts ðæt floːʊt]
I bring you moons and snowy clouds,
[aːɪ bɹɪŋ ju munz ænd ˈsnoːʊɪ klaːʊdz]
I bring you prairie skies to-night –
[aːɪ bɹɪŋ ju ˈpɹɛʁ⁽ʳ⁾ɪ skaːɪz tu naːɪt]
To feebly praise your golden eyes
[tu ˈfiblɪ pɹɛːɪz jɔːʌ ˈgoːʊldɛ⁽ɪ⁾n aːɪz]
And red-bird song, and throat so white.
[ænd ɹɛd bɜd sɑŋ ænd θɹoːʊt soːʊ ʍaːɪt]

2. Euclid
[ˈjuklɪd]

Old Euclid drew a circle
[oːʊld ˈjuklɪd dɹ⁽ʳ⁾u ʌ ˈsɜkʊl]
On a sand-beach long ago.
[ɑn ʌ sænd biʧ lɑŋ ʌˈgoːʊ]

He bounded and enclosed it
[hi ˈbɑːʊndɛ⁽ɪ⁾d ænd ɪnˈkloːʊzd ɪt]
With angles thus and so.
[wɪð ˈæŋgʊlz ðʌs ænd soːʊ]
His set of solemn greybeards
[hɪz sɛt ʌv ˈsɑlʌm ˈgɹɛːɪbɪːʌdz]
Nodded and argued much
[ˈnɑdɛ⁽ɪ⁾d ænd ˈɑgjud mʌʧ]
Of arc and of circumference,
[ʌv ɑk ænd ʌv sɜˈkʌmfɹɛ⁽ɪ⁾ns]
Diameter and such.
[daːɪˈæmɪtʌʁ⁽ʳ⁾ ænd sʌʧ]
Ba da ba bee-ba de ba pa (hm)
[ba da ba bi ba dɛːɪ ba pa m]
A silent child stood by them
[ʌ ˈsaːɪlɛnt ʧaːɪld stʊd baːɪ ðɛm]
From morning until noon
[fɹʌm ˈmɔnɪŋ ʌnˈtɪl nun]
Because they drew such charming
[bɪˈkɔz ðɛːɪ dɹ⁽ʳ⁾u sʌʧ ˈʧɑmɪŋ]
Round pictures of the moon.
[ɹaːʊnd ˈpɪkʧʊ⁽ʌ⁾z ʌv ðʌ mun]

3. The Haughty Snail-King
[ðʌ ˈhɔtɪ snɛːɪl kɪŋ]

Twelve snails went walking after night.
[twɛlv snɛːɪlz wɛnt ˈwɔkɪŋ ˈæftʌ naːɪt]
They'd creep an inch or so,
[ðɛːɪd kɹip æn ɪnʧ ɔ soːʊ]
Then stop and bug their eyes, And blow.
[ðɛn stɑp ænd bʌg ðɛːʌʁ aːɪz ænd bloːʊ]
Some folks . . . are . . . deadly . . . slow.
[sʌm foːʊks ɑ ˈdɛdlɪ sloːʊ]
Twelve snails went walking yestereve,
[twɛlv snɛːɪlz wɛnt ˈwɔkɪŋ ˈjɛstʌʁ ˌiv]
Led by their fat old king.
[lɛd baːɪ ðɛːʌ fæt oːʊld kɪŋ]
They were so dull their princeling had
[ðɛːɪ wɜ soːʊ dʌl ðɛːʌ ˈpɹɪnslɪŋ hæd]
No sceptre, robe or ring–
[noːʊ ˈsɛptʌ ɹoːʊb ɔ ɹɪŋ]
Only a paper cap to wear
[ˈoːʊnlɪ ʌ ˈpɛːɪpʌ kæp tu wɛːʌ]
When nightly journeying.
[ʍɛn ˈnaːɪtlɪ ˈʤɜnɪɪŋ]
Shhhh! This king-snail said: "I feel a thought
[ʃ ðɪs kɪŋ snɛːɪl sɛd aːɪ fil ʌ θɔt]
Within. . . . it blossoms soon. . . .
[wɪðˈɪn ɪt ˈblɑsʌmz sun]
O little courtiers of mine, . . .
[oːʊ ˈlɪtʊl ˈkɔtɪʌz ʌv maːɪn]
I crave a pretty boon. . . .
[aːɪ kɹɛːɪv ʌ ˈpɹɪtɪ bun]
Oh, yes . . . (High thoughts with effort come,
[oːʊ jɛs haːɪ θɔts wɪð ˈɛfɔ⁽ʌ⁾t kʌm]

And well-bred snails are almost dumb.)
[æn wɛl bɹɛd sneːɪlz ɑ ˈɔlmoːʊst dʌm]
"I wish I had a yellow crown
[ɑːɪ wɪʃ ɑːɪ hæd ʌ ˈjɛloːʊ kɹɑːʊn]
As glistering as the moon." Shhhh!
[æz ˈɡlɪstɹɪŋ æz ðʌ mun ʃ]

4. What the Rattlesnake Said
[ʍat ðʌ ˈɹætʊl ˌsneːɪk sɛd]

The moon's a little prairie-dog.
[ðʌ munz ʌ ˈlɪtʊl ˈpɹɛʁ⁽ʳ⁾ɪ dɑɡ]
He shivers through the night.
[hi ˈʃɪvʌz θɹu ðʌ naːɪt]
He sits upon his hill and cries
[hi sɪts ʌˈpɑn hɪz hɪl ænd kɹɑːɪz]
For fear that I will bite.
[fɔ fiːʌ ðæt ɑːɪ wɪl baːɪt]
The sun's a broncho. He's afraid
[ðʌ sʌnz ʌ ˈbɹɑŋkoːʊ hiz ʌˈfɹeːɪd]
Like every other thing,
[laːɪk ˈɛvɹɪ ˈʌðʌ θɪŋ]
And trembles, morning, noon and night,
[ænd ˈtɹɛmbʊlz ˈmɔnɪŋ nun ænd naːɪt]
Lest I should spring, and sssssssssssting.
[lɛst ɑːɪ ʃʊd spɹɪŋ ænd stɪŋ]

5. The Moon's the North Wind's Cooky
[ðʌ munz ðʌ nɔʁθ wɪndz ˈkʊki]
(What the Little Girl Said)
[ʍat ðʌ ˈlɪtʊl ɡɜl sɛd]

The Moon's the North Wind's cooky.
[ðʌ munz ðʌ nɔθ wɪndz ˈkʊkɪ]
He bites it, day by day,
[hi baːɪts ɪt deːɪ baːɪ deːɪ]
Until there's but a rim of scraps
[ʌnˈtɪl ðeːʌz bʌt ʌ ɹɪm ʌv skɹæps]
That crumble all away.
[ðæt ˈkɹʌmbʊl ɔl ʌˈweːɪ]
The South Wind is a baker.
[ðʌ saːʊθ wɪnd ɪz ʌ ˈbeːɪkʌ]
He kneads clouds in his den,
[hi nidz klaːʊdz ɪn hɪz dɛn]
And bakes a crisp new moon that... greedy...
[ænd beːɪks ʌ kɹɪsp nju mun ðæt ˈɡɹidɪ]
North Wind... eats... again!
[nɔθ wɪnd its ʌˈɡɛn]

6. What the Scarecrow Said
[ʍat ðʌ ˈskɛːʁkɹoːʊ sɛd]

The dim-winged spirits of the night
[ðʌ dɪm wɪŋgd ˈspɪʁ⁽ʳ⁾ɪts ʌv ðʌ naːɪt]
Do fear and serve me well.
[du fiːʌʁ⁽ʳ⁾ ænd sɜv mi wɛl]

They creep from out the hedges of
[ðeːɪ kɹ⁽ʳ⁾ip fɹʌm aːʊt ðʌ ˈhɛdʒɛ⁽ɪ⁾z ʌv]
The garden where I dwell.
[ðʌ ˈɡadɛ⁽ɪ⁾n ʍɛːʌʁ⁽ʳ⁾ aːɪ dwɛl]
I wave my arms across the walk.
[aːɪ wɛːɪv maːɪ amz ʌˈkɹas ðʌ wɔk]
The troops obey the sign,
[ðʌ tɹ⁽ʳ⁾ups oˈbeːɪ ðʌ saːɪn]
And bring me shimmering shadow-robes
[ænd bɹɪŋ mi ˈʃɪmɹɪŋ ˈʃædoːʊ ɹoːʊbz]
And cups of cowslip-wine.
[ænd kʌps ʌv ˈkaːʊslɪp waːɪn]
Then dig a treasure called the moon,
[ðɛn dɪɡ ʌ ˈtɹɛʒʊ⁽ʌ⁾ kɔld ðʌ mun]
A very precious thing,
[ʌ ˈvɛʁ⁽ʳ⁾ɪ ˈpɹɛʃʌs θɪŋ]
And keep it in the air for me
[ænd kip ɪt ɪn ði ɛːʌ fɔ mi]
Because I am a King.
[bɪˈkɔz aːɪ æm ʌ kɪŋ]

7. What the Gray-Winged Fairy Said
[ʍat ðʌ ɡɹeːɪ wɪŋgd ˈfɛʁi sɛd]

The moon's a gong, hung in the wild,
[ðʌ munz ʌ ɡaŋ hʌŋ ɪn ðʌ waːɪld]
Whose song the fays hold dear.
[huz saŋ ðʌ feːɪz hoːʊld dɪːʌ]
Of course you do not hear it, child.
[ʌv kɔs ju du nat hiːʌʁ⁽ʳ⁾ ɪt tʃaːɪld]
It takes a fairy ear.
[ɪt tɛːɪks ʌ ˈfɛʁ⁽ʳ⁾ɪ iːʌ]
The full moon is a splendid gong
[ðʌ fʊl mun ɪz ʌ ˈsplɛndɪd ɡaŋ]
That beats as night grows still.
[ðæt bits æz naːɪt ɡɹoːʊz stɪl]
It sounds above the evening song
[ɪt saːʊndz ʌˈbʌv ði ˈivnɪŋ saŋ]
Of dove or whippoorwill.
[ʌv dʌv ɔ ˈʍɪpɔwɪl]

8. Yet Gentle Will the Griffin Be
[jɛt ˈdʒɛntʊl wɪl ðʌ ˈɡɹɪfɪn bi]
(What Grandpa Told the Children)
[ʍat ˈɡɹæmpa toːʊld ðʌ ˈtʃɪldɹɪn]

The moon? It is a griffin's egg,
[ðʌ mun ɪt ɪz ʌ ˈɡɹɪfɪnz ɛɡ]
Hatching to-morrow night.
[ˈhætʃɪŋ tuˈmaʁ⁽ʳ⁾oːʊ naːɪt]
And how the little boys will watch
[ænd haːʊ ðʌ ˈlɪtʊl bɔːɪz wɪl watʃ]
With shouting and delight Ah! ha ha ha!
[wɪð ˈʃaːʊtɪŋ ænd dɪˈlaːɪt a ha ha ha]
To see him break the shell and stretch
[tu si hɪm bɹɛːɪk ðʌ ʃɛl ænd stɹɛtʃ]

And creep across the sky.
[ænd kɹip ʌˈkɹɑs ðʌ skaːɪ]
The boys will laugh. The little girls,
[ðʌ bɔːɪz wɪl læf ðʌ ˈlɪtʊl gɜlz]
I fear, may hide and cry. Wah!
[ɑːɪ fiːʌ mɛːɪ haːɪd ænd kɹ(ɾ)aːɪ wɑ]
Yet gentle will the griffin be,
[jɛt ˈdʒɛntʊl wɪl ðʌ ˈgɹɪfɪn bi]
Most decorous and fat,
[moːʊst ˈdɛkoɾ(ɾ)ʌs ænd fæt]
And walk up to the Milky Way
[ænd wɔk ʌp tu ðʌ ˈmɪlkɪ wɛːɪ]
And lap it like a cat.
[ænd læp ɪt laːɪk ʌ kæt]

The Moon Is a Mirror (Song Cycle)
[ðʌ mun ɪz ʌ ˈmɪʀʌʀ]
Lindsay, Vachel (Am. 1879-1931)

1. The Strength of the Lonely
[ðʌ stɹɛŋθ ʌv ðʌ ˈloːʊnli]
(What the Mendicant Said)
[ʍat ðʌ ˈmɛndɪkɪnt sɛd]

The moon's a monk, unmated,
[ðʌ munz ʌ mʌŋk ʌnˈmɛːɪtɛ(ɪ)d]
Who walks his cell, the sky.
[hu wɔks hɪz sɛl ðʌ skaːɪ]
His strength is that of heaven-vowed men
[hɪz stɹɛŋθ ɪz ðæt ʌv ˈhɛvɛ(ɪ)n vaːʊd mɛn]
Who all life's flames defy.
[hu ɔl laːɪfs flɛːɪmz dɪˈfaːɪ]
They turn to stars and shadows,
[ðɛːɪ tɜn tu stɑz ænd ˈʃædoːʊz]
They go like snow or dew–
[ðɛːɪ goːʊ laːɪk snoːʊ ɔ dju]
Oh leaving behind no sorrow–
[oːʊ ˈliviŋ bɪˈhaːɪnd noːʊ ˈsaʀ(ɾ)oːʊ]
Only the arching blue.
[ˈoːʊnlɪ ði ˈɑtʃɪŋ blu]

2. What the Miner in the Desert Said
[ʍat ðʌ ˈmaːɪnʀ ɪn ðʌ ˈdɛzʀt sɛd]

The moon's a brass-hooped water keg,
[ðʌ munz ʌ bɹæs hupt ˈwɔtʌ kɛg]
A wondrous water feast.
[ʌ ˈwʌndɹʌs ˈwɔtʌ fist]
If I could climb the ridge and drink
[ɪf aːɪ kʊd klaːɪm ðʌ ɹɪdʒ ænd dɹɪŋk]
And give drink to my beast;
[ænd gɪv dɹɪŋk tu maːɪ bist]
If I could drain that keg, the flies
[ɪf aːɪ kʊd dɹɛːɪn ðæt kɛg ðʌ flaːɪz]
Would not be biting so,
[wʊd nat bi ˈbaːɪtɪŋ soːʊ]

My burning feet be spry again,
[maːɪ ˈbɜnɪŋ fit bi spɹaːɪ ʌˈgɛn]
My mule no longer slow.
[maːɪ mjul noːʊ ˈlaŋgʌ sloːʊ]
And I could rise and dig for ore,
[ænd aːɪ kʊd ɹaːɪz ænd dɪg foʀ(ɾ) ɔːʌ]
And reach my fatherland,
[ænd ɹitʃ maːɪ ˈfɑðʌˌlænd]
And not be food for ants and hawks
[ænd nat bi fud foʀ(ɾ) ænts ænd hɔks]
And perish in the sand.
[ænd ˈpɛʀ(ɾ)ɪʃ ɪn ðʌ sænd]

3. The Old Horse in the City
[ði oːʊld hɔʀs ɪn ðʌ ˈsɪti]

Note: the silent "r" may be pronounced

The moon's a peck of corn. It lies
[ðʌ munz ʌ pɛk ʌv kɔʀn ɪt laːɪz]
Heaped up for me to eat.
[hipt ʌp foʀ mi tu it]
I wish that I might climb the path
[aːɪ wɪʃ ðæt aːɪ maːɪt klaːɪm ðʌ pæθ]
And taste that supper sweet.
[ænd tɛːɪst ðæt ˈsʌpʀ swit]
Men feed me straw and scanty grain
[mɛn fid mi stɹɔ ænd ˈskæntɪ gɹɛːɪn]
And beat me till I'm sore.
[ænd bit mi tɪl aːɪm sɔːʀ]
Some day I'll break the halter-rope
[sʌm dɛːɪ aːɪl bɹɛːɪk ðʌ ˈhɔltʀ ɹoːʊp]
And smash the stable-door,
[ænd smæʃ ðʌ ˈstɛːɪbʊl dɔːʀ]
Run down the street and mount the hill
[ɹʌn daːʊn ðʌ stɹit ænd maːʊnt ðʌ hɪl]
Just as the corn appears.
[dʒʌst æz ðʌ kɔʀn ʌˈpɪʀz]
I've seen it rise at certain times
[aːɪv sin ɪt ɹaːɪz æt ˈsɜtæ(ɪ)n taːɪmz]
For years and years and years.
[foʀ jɪːʀz ænd jɪːʀz ænd jɪːʀz]

4. What the Forester Said
[ʍat ðʌ ˈfɔʀɪstʀ sɛd]

The moon is but a candle-glow
[ðʌ mun ɪz bʌt ʌ ˈkændʊl gloːʊ]
That flickers through the gloom:
[ðæt ˈflɪkʌz θru ðʌ glum]
The starry space, a castle hall:
[ðʌ ˈstaʀ(ɾ)ɪ spɛːɪs ʌ ˈkæsʊl hɔl]
And Earth, the children's room,
[ænd ɜθ ðʌ ˈtʃɪldɹɛ(ɪ)nz ɹ(ɾɾ)um]
Where all night long the old trees stand
[ʍɛːʌʀ(ɾ) ɔl naːɪt laŋ ði oːʊld tɹiz stænd]

To watch the streams asleep:
[tu wɑʧ ðʌ stɹimz ʌˈslip]
Grandmothers guarding trundle-beds:
[ˈgɹændmʌðʌz ˈgɑdɪŋ ˈtɹʌndʊl bɛdz]
Good shepherds guarding sheep.
[gʊd ˈʃɛpʌdz ˈgɑdɪŋ ʃip]

5. What the Snowman Said
[ʍɑt ðʌ ˈsnoːʊˌmæn sɛd]

The Moon's a snowball. See the drifts
[ðʌ munz ʌ ˈsnoːʊbɔl si ðʌ dɹɪfts]
Of white that cross the sphere.
[ʌv ʍɑːɪt ðæt kɹɑs ðʌ sfɪːʌ]
The Moon's a snowball, melted down
[ðʌ munz ʌ ˈsnoːʊbɔl mɛltɛ(ɪ)d dɑːʊn]
A dozen times a year.
[ʌ ˈdʌzɛ(ɪ)n tɑːɪmz ʌ jɪːʌ]
Yet rolled again in hot July
[jɛt ɹoːʊld ʌˈgɛn ɪn hɑt dʒuˈlɑːɪ]
When all my days are done
[ʍɛn ɔl mɑːɪ dɛːɪz ɑ dʌn]
And cool to greet the weary eye
[ænd kul tu gɹit ðʌ ˈwiːʌʁ(ɾ)ɪ ɑːɪ]
After the scorching sun. La la la...
[ˈæftʌ ðʌ ˈskɔʧɪŋ sʌn lɑ lɑ lɑ]
The moon's a piece of winter fair
[ðʌ munz ʌ pis ʌv ˈwɪntʌ fɛːʌ]
Renewed the year around,
[ɹɪˈnjud ðʌ jɪːʌʁ(ɾ) ʌˈʁ(ɾ)ɑːʊnd]
Behold it, deathless and unstained,
[bɪˈhoːʊld ɪt ˈdɛθlɛ(ɪ)s ænd ʌnˈstɛːɪnd]
Above the grimy ground!
[ʌˈbʌv ðʌ ˈgɹ(ɾ)ɑːɪmɪ gɹɑːʊnd]
It rolls on high so brave and white
[ɪt ɹoːʊlz ɑn hɑːɪ soːʊ bɹɛːɪv ænd ʍɑːɪt]
Where the clear air-rivers flow,
[ʍɛːʌ ðʌ klɪːʌʁ(ɾ) ɛːʌ ˈɹɪvʌz floːʊ]
Proclaiming Christmas all the time
[pɹoˈklɛːɪmɪŋ ˈkɹɪsmʌs ɔl ðʌ tɑːɪm]
And the glory of the snow!
[ænd ðʌ ˈgloʁ(ɾ)ɪ ʌv ðʌ snoːʊ]

Song Selections

"Go Thy Great Way!" (The Starry Night)
[goːʊ ðɑːɪ gɹɛːɪt wɛːɪ]
Dickinson, Emily (Am. 1830-1886)

Go thy great way!
[goːʊ ðɑːɪ gɹɛːɪt wɛːɪ]
The Stars thou meetst
[ðʌ stɑz ðɑːʊ mitst]
Are even as Thyself–
[ɑʁ(ɾ) ˈivɛ(ɪ)n æz ðɑːɪˈsɛlf]

For what are Stars but Asterisks
[fɔ ʍɑt ɑ stɑz bʌt ˈæstɹɪsks]
To point a human Life?
[tu pɔːɪnt ʌ ˈhjumæ(ʌ)n lɑːɪf]

"I Would Not Paint a Picture" (The Starry Night)
[ɑːɪ wʊd nɑt pɛːɪnt ʌ ˈpɪkʧʁ]
Dickinson, Emily (Am. 1830-1886)

I would not paint– a picture–
[ɑːɪ wʊd nɑt pɛːɪnt ʌ ˈpɪkʧʊ(ʌ)]
I'd rather be the one
[ɑːɪd ˈɹæðʌ bi ðʌ wʌn]
Its bright impossibility
[ɪts bɹɑːɪt ɪmpɑsɪˈbɪlɪtɪ]
To dwell– delicious– on–
[tu dwɛl dɪˈlɪʃʌs ɑn]
And wonder how the fingers feel
[ænd ˈwʌndʌ hɑːʊ ðʌ ˈfɪŋgʌz fil]
Whose rare– celestial– stir–
[huz ɹɛːʌ sɪˈlɛsʧʊl stɜ]
Evokes so sweet a Torment–
[ɪˈvoːʊks soːʊ swit ʌ ˈtɔmɛnt]
Such sumptuous– Despair–
[sʌʧ ˈsʌmpʧuʌs dɪˈspɛːʌ]
I would not talk, like Cornets–
[ɑːɪ wʊd nɑt tɔk lɑːɪk kɔˈnɛts]
I'd rather be the one
[ɑːɪd ˈɹæðʌ bi ðʌ wʌn]
Raised softly to the Ceiling–
[ɹɛːɪzd ˈsɑftlɪ tu ðʌ ˈsilɪŋ]
And out, and easy on–
[ænd ɑːʊt ænd ˈizɪ ɑn]
Through Villages of Ether–
[θɹu ˈvɪlæ(ɪ)dʒɛ(ɪ)z ʌv ˈiθʌ]
Myself endued Balloon
[mɑːɪˈsɛlf ɪnˈdjud bʌˈlun]
By but a lip of Metal–
[bɑːɪ bʌt ʌ lɪp ʌv ˈmɛtʊl]
The pier to my Pontoon–
[ðʌ pɪːʌ tu mɑːɪ panˈtun]
Nor would I be a Poet–
[nɔ wʊd ɑːɪ bi ʌ ˈpoːʊɛ(ɪ)t]
'Tis finer– own the Ear–
[tɪz ˈfɑːɪnʌʁ(ɾ) oːʊn ði ɪːʌ]
Enamored– impotent– content–
[ɪˈnæmo(ʌ)d ˈɪmpo(ʌ)tɛnt kʌnˈtɛnt]
The License to revere,
[ðʌ ˈlɑːɪsɛ(ɪ)ns tu ɹɪˈvɪːʌ]
A privilege so awful
[ʌ ˈpɹɪvɪlɛ(ɪ)dʒ soːʊ ˈɔfʊl]
What would the Dower be,
[ʍɑt wʊd ðʌ dɑːʊʌ bi]
Had I the Art to stun myself
[hæd ɑːɪ ði ɑt tu stʌn mɑːɪˈsɛlf]

With Bolts of Melody!
[wɪð boːʊlts ʌv ˈmɛlodɪ]

"In the Midst of Thousands" (These Strangers)
[ɪn ðʌ mɪdst ʌv ˈθaːʊzʌndz]
Douglass, Frederick (Am. 1818-1895)

There I was in the midst of thousands,
[ðɛːʌʁ⁽ʳ⁾ aːɪ waz ɪn ðʌ mɪdst ʌv ˈθaːʊzæ(ʌ)ndz]
and yet a perfect stranger;
[ænd jɛt ʌ ˈpɜfɛ(ɪ)kt ˈstɹɛːɪndʒʌ]
without home and without friends,
[wɪðˈaːʊt hoːʊm ænd wɪðˈaːʊt fɹɛndz]
afraid to speak to anyone,
[ʌˈfɹɛːɪd tu spik tu ˈɛnɪwʌn]
For fear of speaking to the wrong one.
[fɔ fɪːʌʁ⁽ʳ⁾ ʌv ˈspikɪŋ tu ðʌ ɹaŋ wʌn]
I saw in every white man an enemy
[aːɪ sɔ ɪn ˈɛvɹɪ ʍaːɪt mæn æn ˈɛnɪ(ʌ)mɪ]
And in almost every colored man,
[ænd ɪn ˈɔlmoːʊst ˈɛvɹɪ ˈkʌlɔ(ʌ)d mæn]
Cause for distrust.
[kɔz fɔ dɪˈstɹʌst]
In the midst of thousands, a perfect stranger.
[ɪn ðʌ mɪdst ʌv ˈθaːʊzæ(ʌ)ndz ʌ ˈpɜfɛ(ɪ)kt ˈstɹɛːɪndʒʌ]

"It Makes No Difference Abroad" (Faith Disquiet)
[ɪt mɛːɪks noːʊ ˈdɪfɹɪns ʌˈbɹɔd]
Dickinson, Emily (Am. 1830-1886)

It makes no difference abroad–
[ɪt mɛːɪks noːʊ ˈdɪfʌʁ⁽ʳ⁾ɛ(ɪ)ns ʌˈbɹɔd]
The Seasons– fit– the same–
[ðʌ ˈsizʌnz fɪt ðʌ sɛːɪm]
The Mornings blossom into Noons–
[ðʌ ˈmɔnɪŋz ˈblasʌm ˈɪntu nunz]
And split their Pods of Flame–
[ænd splɪt ðɛːʌ padz ʌv flɛːɪm]
Wild flowers– kindle in the Woods–
[waːɪld flaːʊʌz ˈkɪndʊl ɪn ðʌ wʊdz]
The Brooks slam– all the Day–
[ðʌ bɹʊks slæm ɔl ðʌ dɛːɪ]
No Black bird bates his Banjo–
[noːʊ blæk bɜd bɛːɪts hɪz ˈbænˌdʒoːʊ]
For passing Calvary–
[fɔ ˈpæsɪŋ ˈkælvaʁ⁽ʳ⁾ɪ]
Auto da Fe– and Judgment–
[ˈaːʊto da fe ænd ˈdʒʌdʒmɛnt]
Are nothing to the Bee–
[a ˈnʌθɪŋ tu ðʌ bi]
His separation from His Rose–
[hɪz sɛpʌˈʁ⁽ʳ⁾ɛːɪʃʌn fɹʌm hɪz ɹoːʊz]
To Him– sums Misery–
[tu hɪm sʌmz ˈmɪzʌʁ⁽ʳ⁾ɪ]

"It Sounded as If the Streets Were Running"
[ɪt ˈsaːʊndɪd æz ɪf ðʌ stɹits wɜ ˈɹʌnɪŋ]
(Before the Storm)
Dickinson, Emily (Am. 1830-1886)

It sounded as if the Streets were running
[ɪt ˈsaːʊndɛ(ɪ)d æz ɪf ðʌ stɹits wɜ ˈɹʌnɪŋ]
And then the streets stood still
[ænd ðɛn ðʌ stɹits stʊd stɪl]
Eclipse was all we could see at the window
[ɪˈklɪps waz ɔl wi kʊd si æt ðʌ ˈwɪndoːʊ]
And Awe was all we could feel.
[ænd ɔ waz ɔl wi kʊd fil]
By and by the boldest stole out of his covert
[baːɪ ænd baːɪ ðʌ ˈboːʊldɛ(ɪ)st stoːʊl aːʊt ʌv hɪz ˈkʌvʌt]
To see if Time was there
[tu si ɪf taːɪm waz ðɛːʌ]
Nature was in an Opal Apron,
[ˈnɛːɪʧʊ(ʌ) waz ɪn æn ˈoːʊpʊl ˈɛːɪpɹʌn]
Mixing fresher Air.
[ˈmɪksɪŋ ˈfɹɛʃʌʁ⁽ʳ⁾ ɛːʌ]

"The Night Is Freezing Fast"
[ðʌ naːɪt ɪz ˈfɹizɪŋ fæst]
(On the Road to Christmas)
Housman, Alfred Edward (Eng. 1859-1936)

The night is freezing fast,
[ðʌ naːɪt ɪz ˈfɹizɪŋ fæst]
To-morrow comes December;
[tuˈmaʁ⁽ʳ⁾oːʊ kʌmz dɪˈsɛmbʌ]
And winterfalls of old
[ænd ˈwɪntʌfɔlz ʌv oːʊld]
Are with me from the past;
[a wɪð mi fɹʌm ðʌ pæst]
And chiefly I remember
[ænd ˈʧiflɪ aːɪ ɹɪˈmɛmbʌ]
How Dick would hate the cold.
[haːʊ dɪk wʊd hɛːɪt ðʌ koːʊld]
Fall, winter, fall; for he,
[fɔl ˈwɪntʌ fɔl fɔ hi]
Prompt hand and headpiece clever,
[pɹampt hænd ænd ˈhɛdpis ˈklɛvʌ]
Has woven a winter robe,
[hæz ˈwoːʊvɛ(ɪ)n ʌ ˈwɪntʌ ɹoːʊb]
And made of earth and sea
[ænd mɛːɪd ʌv ɜθ ænd si]
His overcoat forever,
[hɪz ˈoːʊvʌkoːʊt fɔʁ⁽ʳ⁾ˈɛvʌ]
And wears the turning globe.
[ænd wɛːʌz ðʌ ˈtɜnɪŋ gloːʊb]

"These Strangers, in a Foreign World"
[ðiz ˈstɹeːɪndʒɐz ɪn ʌ ˈfɔɐɪn wɜld]
(These Strangers)
Dickinson, Emily (Am. 1830-1886)

These Strangers, in a foreign World,
[ðiz ˈstɹeːɪndʒʌz ɪn ʌ ˈfɔɐ⁽ʳ⁾ɛ(ɪ)n wɜld]
Protection asked of me –
[pɹoˈtɛkʃʌn æskt ʌv mi]
Befriend them, lest Yourself in Heaven
[bɪˈfɹɛnd ðɛm lɛst jɔːʌˈsɛlf ɪn ˈhɛvɛ(ɪ)n]
Be found a Refugee –
[bi faːʊnd ʌ ɹɛfjuˈdʒi]

"What Lips My Lips Have Kissed"
[ʍat lɪps maːɪ lɪps hæv kɪst]
(Before the Storm)
Millay, Edna St. Vincent (Am. 1892-1950)

What lips my lips have kissed, and where and why,
[ʍat lɪps maːɪ lɪps hæv kɪst ænd ʍɛːʌɐ⁽ʳ⁾ ænd ʍaːɪ]
I have forgotten, and what arms have lain
[aːɪ hæv fɔˈgatɛ(ɪ)n ænd ʍat amz hæv lɛːɪn]
Under my head till morning; but the rain
[ˈʌndʌ maːɪ hɛd tɪl ˈmɔnɪŋ bʌt ðʌ ɹɛːɪn]
Is full of ghosts tonight, that tap and sigh
[ɪz fʊl ʌv goːʊsts tuˈnaːɪt ðæt tæp ænd saːɪ]
Upon the glass and listen for reply,
[ʌˈpan ðʌ glæs ænd ˈlɪsɛ(ɪ)n fɔ ɹɪˈplaːɪ]
And in my heart there stirs a quiet pain
[ænd ɪn maːɪ hat ðɛːʌ stɜz ʌ ˈkwaːɪɛ(ɪ)t pɛːɪn]
For unremembered lads that not again
[fɔɐ⁽ʳ⁾ ˌʌnɹɪˈmɛmbʌd lædz ðæt nat ʌˈgɛn]
Will turn to me at midnight with a cry.
[wɪl tɜn tu mi æt ˈmɪdnaːɪt wɪð ʌ kɹ⁽ʳ⁾aːɪ]
Thus in the winter stands the lonely tree,
[ðʌs ɪn ðʌ ˈwɪntʌ stændz ðʌ ˈloːʊnlɪ tɹi]
Nor knows what birds have vanished one by one,
[nɔ noːʊz ʍat bɜdz hæv ˈvænɪʃt wʌn baːɪ wʌn]
Yet knows its boughs more silent than before:
[jɛt noːʊz ɪts baːʊz mɔːʌ ˈsaːɪlɛnt ðæn bɪˈfɔːʌ]
I cannot say what loves have come and gone,
[aːɪ kæˈnat sɛːɪ ʍat lʌvz hæv kʌm ænd gan]
I only know that summer sang in me
[aːɪ ˈoːʊnlɪ noːʊ ðæt ˈsʌmʌ sæŋ ɪn mi]
A little while, that in me sings no more.
[ʌ ˈlɪtʊl ʍaːɪl ðæt ɪn mi sɪŋz noːʊ mɔːʌ]

Herbert, Victor (Am. 1859-1924)

Song Selection

"Art is Calling for Me"
[aɐt ɪz ˈkɔlɪŋ fɔɐ mi]
(The Prima Donna Song)
[ðʌ ˈprima ˈdɔnna saŋ]
(The Enchantress)
Herbert, Victor (Am. 1859-1924) and Harry B. Smith

Mama is a queen and Papa is a king;
[ˈmamʌ ɪz ʌ kwin ænd ˈpapʌ ɪz ʌ kɪŋ]
So I am a princess, (and) I know it;
[soːʊ aːɪ æm ʌ ˈpɹɪnsɛ(ɪ)s (ænd) aːɪ noːʊ ɪt]
But court etiquette is a dull dreary thing,
[bʌt kɔt ˈɛtɪkɛ(ɪ)t ɪz ʌ dʌl ˈdɹɪːʌɐ⁽ʳ⁾ɪ θɪŋ]
I just hate it all, and I show it.
[aːɪ dʒʌst hɛːɪt ɪt ɔl ænd aːɪ ʃoːʊ ɪt]
To sing on the stage, that's the one life for me,
[tu sɪŋ an ðʌ stɛːɪdʒ ðæts ðʌ wʌn laːɪf fɔ mi]
My figure's just like Tetrazzini;
[maːɪ ˈfɪgjʊ(ʌ)z dʒʌst laːɪk tetratˈtsini]
I know I'd win fame if I sang in "Bohéme;"
[aːɪ noːʊ aːɪd wɪn fɛːɪm ɪf aːɪ sæŋ ɪn boˈɛm]
That op'ra by Signor Puccini.
[ðæt ˈapɹa baːɪ sɪnˈjɔr putˈtʃini]
I've roulades and the trills
[aːɪv ruˈladz ænd ðʌ trɪlz]
That would send the cold chills
[ðæt wʊd sɛnd ðʌ koːʊld tʃɪlz]
Down the backs of all hearers of my vocal frills.
[daːʊn ðʌ bæks ʌv ɔl ˈhɪːʌɐ⁽ʳ⁾z ʌv maːɪ ˈvoːʊkʊl frɪlz]
Aah-aah-aah-aah-aah-aah-aah-aah-aah-aaaaahhhhh
[a]
I long to be a prima donna, donna, donna
[aːɪ laŋ tu bi ʌ ˈprima ˈdɔnna ˈdɔnna ˈdɔnna]
I long to shine upon the stage,
[aːɪ laŋ tu ʃaːɪn ʌˈpan ðʌ stɛːɪdʒ]
I have the embonpoint
[aːɪ hæv ði ãbõˈpwɛ̃]
To become a queen of song;
[tu bɪˈkʌm ʌ kwin ʌv saŋ]
And my figure would look pretty as a page.
[ænd maːɪ ˈfɪgjʊ(ʌ) wʊd lʊk ˈpɹɪtɪ æz ʌ pɛːɪdʒ]
I want to be a screechy, peachy cantatrice,
[aːɪ want tu bi ʌ ˈskɹiːtʃɪ ˈpitʃɪ kantaˈtritʃe]
Like other plump girls that I see;
[laːɪk ˈʌðʌ plʌmp gɜlz ðæt aːɪ si]
I hate society;
[aːɪ hɛːɪt soˈsaːɪɛ(ɪ)tɪ]
I hate propriety;
[aːɪ hɛːɪt pɹoˈpɹaːɪɛ(ɪ)tɪ]
Art is calling for me.
[at ɪz ˈkɔlɪŋ fɔ mi]

I'm in the elite, and men sigh at my feet;
[ɑːɪm ɪn ði ɪˈlit ænd mɛn saːɪ æt maːɪ fit]
Still I do not fancy my position;
[stɪl ɑːɪ du nɑt ˈfænsɪ maːɪ poˈzɪʃʌn]
I have not much use for the men that I meet,
[ɑːɪ hæv nɑt mʌtʃ jus fɔ ðæt mɛn ðæt ɑːɪ mit]
I quite burn with lyric ambition.
[ɑːɪ kwaːɪt bɜn wɪð ˈlɪʁ⁽ʳ⁾ɪk æmˈbɪʃʌn]
Those tenors so sweet,
[ðoːʊz ˈtɛnɔ⁽ʌ⁾z soːʊ swit]
If they made love to me,
[ɪf ðɛːɪ mɛːɪd lʌv tu mi]
I'd be a success, that I do know;
[ɑːɪd bi ʌ sʌkˈsɛs ðæt ɑːɪ du noːʊ]
And Melba I'd oust if I once sang in "Faust,"
[ænd ˈmɛlbʌ ɑːɪd ɑːʊst ɪf ɑːɪ wʌns sæŋ ɪn faːʊst]
That op'ra so charming by Gounod.
[ðæt ˈɑpɹʌ soːʊ ˈtʃɑmɪŋ baːɪ guˈno]
Girls would be on the brink
[gɜlz wʊd bi ɑn ðʌ bɹɪŋk]
Of hysterics, I think,
[ʌv hɪˈstɛʁ⁽ʳ⁾ɪks ɑːɪ θɪŋk]
Even strong men would have to go out for a drink.
[ˈiːvɛ⁽ɪ⁾n stɹɑŋ mɛn wʊd hæv tu goːʊ ɑːʊt fɔʁ⁽ʳ⁾ ʌ dɹɪŋk]
I long to be a prima donna, donna, donna,
[ɑːɪ lɑŋ tu bi ʌ ˈprima ˈdɔnna ˈdɔnna ˈdɔnna]
I long to shine upon the stage,
[ɑːɪ lɑŋ tu ʃaːɪn ʌˈpɑn ðʌ stɛːɪdʒ]
With my avoirdupois
[wɪð maːɪ avwɑɹdyˈpwa]
And my tra la la la la,
[ænd maːɪ tra la la la la]
I would be the chief sensation of the age.
[ɑːɪ wʊd bi ðʌ tʃif sɛnˈsɛːɪʃʌn ʌv ði ɛːɪdʒ]
I long to hear them shouting: "Viva" to the diva,
[ɑːɪ lɑŋ tu hɪːʌ ðɛm ˈʃaːʊtɪŋ ˈviva tu ðʌ ˈdiva]
Oh, very lovely that must be;
[oːʊ ˈvɛʁ⁽ʳ⁾ɪ ˈlʌvlɪ ðæt mʌst bi]
That's what I'm dying for,
[ðæts ʍɑt ɑːɪm ˈdaːɪŋ fɔ]
That's what I'm sighing for,
[ðæts ʍɑt ɑːɪm ˈsaːɪŋ fɔ]
Art is calling for me.
[ɑt ɪz ˈkɔlɪŋ fɔ mi]

 Higdon, Jennifer (Am. b. 1962)

Love Sweet (Song Cycle)
[lʌv swit]
Lowell, Amy (Am. 1874-1925)

1. Apology [ʌˈpɑlʌdʒi]

Be not angry with me that I bear
[bi nɑt ˈæŋgɹɪ wɪð mi ðæt ɑːɪ bɛːʌ]

Your colours everywhere,
[jɔːʌ ˈkʌlɔ⁽ʌ⁾z ˈɛvɹɪwɛːʌ]
All through each crowded street,
[ɔl θru itʃ ˈkɹɑːʊdɛ⁽ɪ⁾d stɹit]
And meet
[ænd mit]
The wonder-light in every eye,
[ðʌ ˈwʌndʌ laːɪt ɪn ˈɛvɹɪ ɑːɪ]
As I go by.
[æz ɑːɪ goːʊ baːɪ]
Each plodding wayfarer looks up to gaze,
[itʃ ˈplɑdɪŋ ˈwɛːɪˌfɛːʁ⁽ʳ⁾ʌ lʊks ʌp tu gɛːɪz]
Blinded by rainbow haze,
[ˈblɑːɪndɛ⁽ɪ⁾d baːɪ ˈɹɛːɪnboːʊ hɛːɪz]
The stuff of happiness,
[ðʌ stʌf ʌv ˈhæpɪnɛ⁽ɪ⁾s]
No less,
[noːʊ lɛs]
Which wraps me in its glad-hued folds
[ʍɪtʃ ɹæps mi ɪn ɪts glæd hjud foːʊldz]
Of peacock golds.
[ʌv ˈpikɑk goːʊldz]
Before my feet the dusty, rough-paved way
[bɪˈfɔːʌ maːɪ fit ðʌ ˈdʌstɪ ɹʌf pɛːɪvd wɛːɪ]
Flushes beneath its gray.
[ˈflʌʃɛ⁽ɪ⁾z bɪˈniθ ɪts gɹɛːɪ]
My steps fall ringed with light,
[maːɪ stɛps fɔl ɹɪŋd wɪð laːɪt]
So bright,
[soːʊ bɹaːɪt]
It seems a myriad suns are strown
[ɪt simz ʌ ˈmɪʁ⁽ʳ⁾ɪæ⁽ɪ⁾d sʌnz ɑ stɹoːʊn]
About the town.
[ʌˈbaːʊt ðʌ taːʊn]
Before me is the sound of steepled bells,
[bɪˈfɔːʌ mi ɪz ðʌ saːʊnd ʌv ˈstipʊld bɛlz]
And rich perfuméd smells
[ænd ɹɪtʃ pɜˈfjumd smɛlz]
Hang like a wind-forgotten cloud,
[hæŋ laːɪk ʌ wɪnd fɔˈgatɛ⁽ɪ⁾n klaːʊd]
And shroud
[ænd ʃɹaʊd]
Me from close contact with the world.
[mi fɹʌm kloːʊs ˈkɑntækt wɪð ðʌ wɜld]
I dwell impearled.
[ɑːɪ dwɛl ɪmˈpɜld]
You blazon me with jewelled insignia.
[ju ˈblɛːɪzʌn mi wɪð ˈdʒuːɛ⁽ʊ⁾ld ɪnˈsɪgnɪʌ]
A flaming nebula
[ʌ ˈflɛːɪmɪŋ ˈnɛbjulʌ]
Rims in my life. And yet you set
[ɹɪmz ɪn maːɪ laːɪf ænd jɛt ju sɛt]
The word upon me, unconfessed
[ðʌ wɜd ʌˈpɑn mi ʌnkʌnˈfɛst]
To go unguessed.
[tu goːʊ ʌnˈgɛst]

2. The Giver of Stars

[ðʌ ˈɡɪvʀ ʌv staʀz]

Let the quiet of your spirit bathe me
[lɛt ðʌ ˈkwaːɪɛ(ɪ)t ʌv jɔːʌ ˈspɪʀ⁽ʳ⁾ɪt bɛːɪð mi]
With its clear and rippled coolness,
[wɪð ɪts klɪːʌʀ⁽ʳ⁾ ænd ˈʌɪpʊld ˈkʊlnɛ(ɪ)s]
That, loose-limbed and weary, I find rest,
[ðæt lus lɪmd ænd ˈwɪːʌʀ⁽ʳ⁾ɪ aːɪ faːɪnd ʀɛst]
Outstretched upon your peace, as on a bed of ivory.
[aːʊtˈstʀɛʧt ʌˈpɑn jɔːʌ pis æz ɑn ʌ bɛd ʌv ˈaːɪvɔʀ⁽ʳ⁾ɪ]
Let the flickering flame of your soul play about me,
[lɛt ðʌ ˈflɪkʌʀ⁽ʳ⁾ɪŋ flɛːɪm ʌv jɔːʌ soːʊl plɛːɪ ʌˈbaːʊt mi]
That into my limbs may come the keenness of fire,
[ðæt ˈɪntu maːɪ lɪmz mɛːɪ kʌm ðʌ ˈkinɛ(ɪ)s ʌv faːɪʀ]
The life and joy of tongues of flame,
[ðʌ laːɪf ænd dʒɔːɪ ʌv tʌŋz ʌv flɛːɪm]
And, going out from you, tightly strung and in tune,
[ænd ˈɡoːʊɪŋ aːʊt fʀʌm ju ˈtaːɪtlɪ stʌʌŋ ænd ɪn tjun]
I may rouse the blear-eyed world,
[aːɪ mɛːɪ ʀaːʊz ðʌ blɪːʌʀ⁽ʳ⁾ aːɪd wɜld]
And pour into it the beauty which you have begotten.
[ænd pɔːʌʀ⁽ʳ⁾ ˈɪntu ɪt ðʌ ˈbjutɪ ʍɪʧ ju hæv bɪˈɡɑtɛ(ɪ)n]

3. Absence [ˈæbsɪns]

My cup is empty to-night,
[maːɪ kʌp ɪz ˈɛmptɪ tu naːɪt]
Cold and dry are its sides,
[koːʊld ænd dʌaːɪ aʀ⁽ʳ⁾ ɪts saːɪdz]
Chilled by the wind from the open window.
[ʧɪld baːɪ ðʌ wɪnd fʀʌm ði ˈoːʊpɛ(ɪ)n ˈwɪndoːʊ]
Empty and void, it sparkles white in the moonlight.
[ˈɛmptɪ ænd vɔːɪd ɪt ˈspɑkʊlz ʍaːɪt ɪn ðʌ ˈmunlaːɪt]
The room is filled with the strange scent
[ðʌ ʀ⁽ʳʳ⁾um ɪz fɪld wɪð ðʌ stʌɛːɪndʒ sɛnt]
Of wisteria blossoms.
[ʌv wɪˈstɪʀ⁽ʳ⁾ɪʌ ˈblɑsʌmz]
They sway in the moon's radiance
[ðɛːɪ swɛːɪ ɪn ðʌ munz ˈʀɛːɪdɪæ(ɪ)ns]
And tap against the wall.
[ænd tæp ʌˈɡɛnst ðʌ wɔl]
But the cup of my heart is still,
[bʌt ðʌ kʌp ʌv maːɪ hɑt ɪz stɪl]
And old, and empty.
[ænd oːʊld ænd ˈɛmptɪ]
When you come, it brims
[ʍɛn ju kʌm ɪt bʌɪmz]
Red and trembling with blood,
[ʀɛd ænd ˈtʌɛmblɪŋ wɪð blʌd]
Heart's blood for your drinking;
[hɑts blʌd fɔ jɔːʌ ˈdʌɪŋkɪŋ]
To fill your mouth with love
[tu fɪl jɔːʌ maːʊθ wɪð lʌv]
And the bitter-sweet taste of a soul.
[ænd ðʌ ˈbɪtʌ swit tɛːɪst ʌv ʌ soːʊl]

4. A Gift

[ʌ ɡɪft]

See! I give myself to you, Beloved!
[si aːɪ ɡɪv maːɪˈsɛlf tu ju bɪˈlʌvɛ(ɪ)d]
My words are little jars
[maːɪ wɜdz ɑ ˈlɪtʊl dʒɑz]
For you to take and put upon a shelf.
[fɔ ju tu tɛːɪk ænd pʊt ʌˈpɑn ʌ ʃɛlf]
Their shapes are quaint and beautiful,
[ðɛːʌ ʃɛːɪps ɑ kwɛːɪnt ænd ˈbjutɪfʊl]
And they have many pleasant colours and lustres
[ænd ðɛːɪ hæv ˈmɛnɪ ˈplɛzæ(ɪ)nt ˈkʌlɔ(ʌ)z ænd ˈlʌstʌz]
To recommend them.
[tu ʀɛkʌˈmɛnd ðɛm]
Also the scent from them fills the room
[ˈɔlsoːʊ ðʌ sɛnt fʌʌm ðɛm fɪlz ðʌ ʀ⁽ʳʳ⁾um]
With sweetness of flowers and crushed grasses.
[wɪð ˈswitnɛ(ɪ)s ʌv flaːʊʌz ænd kʌ⁽ʳ⁾ʌʃt ˈɡʀæsɛ(ɪ)z]
When I shall have given you the last one
[ʍɛn aːɪ ʃæl hæv ˈɡɪvɛ(ɪ)n ju ðʌ læst wʌn]
You will have the whole of me, But I shall be dead.
[ju wɪl hæv ðʌ hoːʊl ʌv mi bʌt aːɪ ʃæl bi dɛd]

5. A Fixed Idea

[ʌ fɪkst aːɪˈdɪʌ]

What torture lurks within a single thought
[ʍɑt ˈtɔʧʊ(ʌ) lɜks wɪðˈɪn ʌ ˈsɪŋɡʊl θɔt]
When grown too constant, and however kind,
[ʍɛn ɡʌoːʊn tu ˈkɑnstæ(ɪ)nt ænd haːʊˈɛvʌ kaːɪnd]
However welcome and still, the weary mind
[haːʊˈɛvʌ ˈwɛlkʌm ænd stɪl ðʌ ˈwɪːʌʀ⁽ʳ⁾ɪ maːɪnd]
Aches with its presence. Dull remembrance taught
[ɛːɪks wɪð ɪts ˈpʌɛzɛ(ɪ)ns dʌl ʌɪˈmɛmbʌæ(ɪ)ns tɔt]
Remembers on unceasingly; unsought
[ʌɪˈmɛmbʌz ɑn ʌnˈsisɪŋlɪ ʌnˈsɔt]
The old delight is with us but to find
[ði oːʊld dɪˈlaːɪt ɪz wɪð ʌs bʌt tu faːɪnd]
That all recurring joy is pain refined,
[ðæt ɔl ʀɪˈkʊʀ⁽ʳ⁾ɪŋ dʒɔːɪ ɪz pɛːɪn ʀɪˈfaːɪnd]
Become a habit, and we struggle, caught.
[bɪˈkʌm ʌ ˈhæbɪt ænd wi ˈstʌʌɡʊl kɔt]
You lie upon my heart as on a nest,
[ju laːɪ ʌˈpɑn maːɪ hɑt æz ɑn ʌ nɛst]
Folded in peace, for you can never know
[ˈfoːʊldɛ(ɪ)d ɪn pis fɔ ju kæn ˈnɛvʌ noːʊ]
How crushed I am with having you at rest
[haːʊ kʌ⁽ʳ⁾ʌʃt aːɪ æm wɪð ˈhævɪŋ ju æt ʀɛst]
Heavy upon my life. I love you so
[ˈhɛvɪ ʌˈpɑn maːɪ laːɪf aːɪ lʌv ju soːʊ]
You bind my freedom from its rightful quest.
[ju baːɪnd maːɪ ˈfʌidʌm fʌʌm ɪts ˈʀaːɪtfʊl kwɛst]
In mercy lift your drooping wings and go.
[ɪn ˈmɜsɪ lɪft jɔːʌ ˈdʌ⁽ʳ⁾upɪŋ wɪŋz ænd ɡoːʊ]

Hoiby, Lee (Am. 1926-2011)

I Was There (Song Cycle)
[ɑːɪ wɑz ðɛːʁ]
Whitman, Walt (Am. 1819-1892)

1. Beginning My Studies
[bɪˈɡɪnɪŋ mɑːɪ ˈstʌdiz]

Beginning my studies the first step pleas'd me so much.
[bɪˈɡɪnɪŋ mɑːɪ ˈstʌdiz ðʌ fɜst stɛp plizd mi soːʊ mʌʧ]
The mere fact consciousness, these forms,
[ðʌ mɪːʌ fækt ˈkɑnʃʌsnɛ(ɪ)s ðiz fɔmz]
the power of motion,
[ðʌ pɑːʊʁ⁽ʳ⁾ ʌv ˈmoːʊʃʌn]
The least insect or animal, the senses, eyesight, love.
[ðʌ list ˈɪnsɛkt ɔʁ⁽ʳ⁾ ˈænɪmʊl ðʌ ˈsɛnsɛ(ɪ)z ˈɑːɪsɑːɪt lʌv]
The first step I say awed me and pleased me so much,
[ðʌ fɜst stɛp ɑːɪ sɛːɪ ɔd mi ænd plizd mi soːʊ mʌʧ]
I have hardly gone and hardly wish'd to go any farther,
[ɑːɪ hæv ˈhɑdlɪ ɡɑn ænd ˈhɑdlɪ wɪʃt tu ɡoːʊ ˈɛnɪ ˈfɑðʌ]
But stop and loiter all the time
[bʌt stɑp ænd ˈlɔːɪtʌʁ⁽ʳ⁾ ɔl ðʌ tɑːɪm]
to sing it in ecstatic songs.
[tu sɪŋ ɪt ɪn ɪkˈstætɪk sɑŋz]

2. I Was There
[ɑːɪ wɑz ðɛːʁ]

I understand the large hearts of heroes,
[ɑːɪ ʌndʌˈstænd ðʌ lɑdʒ hɑts ʌv ˈhɪʁ⁽ʳ⁾oːʊz]
The courage of present times and all times,
[ðʌ ˈkʊʁ⁽ʳ⁾æ(ɪ)dʒ ʌv ˈpɹɛzɛnt tɑːɪmz ænd ɔl tɑːɪmz]
How the skipper saw the crowded and rudderless wreck
[hɑːʊ ðʌ ˈskɪpʌ sɔ ðʌ ˈkɹɑːʊdɛ(ɪ)d ænd ˈɹʌdʌlɛ(ɪ)s ɹɛk]
of the steam-ship,
[ʌv ðʌ stim ʃɪp]
and Death chasing it up and down the storm,
[ænd dɛθ ˈʧɛːɪsɪŋ ɪt ʌp ænd dɑːʊn ðʌ stɔm]
How he knuckled tight and gave not back an inch,
[hɑːʊ hi ˈnʌkʊld tɑːɪt ænd ɡɛːɪv nɑt bæk æn ɪnʧ]
and was faithful of days and faithful of nights,
[ænd wɑz ˈfɛːɪθfʊl ʌv dɛːɪz ænd ˈfɛːɪθfʊl ʌv nɑːɪts]
And chalked in large letters, on a board,
[ænd ʧɔkt ɪn lɑdʒ ˈlɛtʌz ɑn ʌ bɔd]
Be of good cheer, we will not desert you;
[bi ʌv ɡʊd ʧɪːʌ wi wɪl nɑt dɪˈzɜt ju]
How he followed with them and
[hɑːʊ hi ˈfɑloːʊd wɪð ðɛm ænd]
tacked with them three days and would not give it up,
[tækt wɪð ðɛm θri dɛːɪz ænd wʊd nɑt ɡɪv ɪt ʌp]
How he saved the drifting company at last,
[hɑːʊ hi sɛːɪvd ðʌ ˈdɹɪftɪŋ ˈkʌmpæ(ɪ)nɪ æt læst]
How the lank loose-gown'd women looked when
[hɑːʊ ðʌ læŋk lus ɡɑːʊnd ˈwɪmɛ(ɪ)n lʊkt ʍɛn]

boated from the side
[ˈboːʊtɛ(ɪ)d fɹʌm ðʌ sɑːɪd]
of their prepared graves,
[ʌv ðɛːʌ pɹɪˈpɛːʌʁ⁽ʳ⁾ɛ(ɪ)d ɡɹɛːɪvz]
How the silent old-faced infants,
[hɑːʊ ðʌ ˈsɑːɪlɛnt oːʊld fɛːɪst ˈɪnfæ(ɪ)nts]
and the lifted sick,
[ænd ðʌ ˈlɪftɛ(ɪ)d sɪk]
and the sharp-lipped unshaved men,
[ænd ðʌ ʃɑp lɪpt ʌnˈʃɛːɪvɛ(ɪ)d mɛn]
All this I swallow, it tastes good,
[ɔl ðɪs ɑːɪ ˈswɑloːʊ ɪt tɛːɪsts ɡʊd]
I like it well, it becomes mine,
[ɑːɪ lɑːɪk ɪt wɛl ɪt bɪˈkʌmz mɑːɪn]
I am the man, I suffered, I was there.
[ɑːɪ æm ðʌ mæn ɑːɪ ˈsʌfʌd ɑːɪ wɑz ðɛːʌ]

3. A Clear Midnight (see Cipullo)

4. O Captain! My Captain!
[oːʊ ˈkæptɪn mɑːɪ ˈkæptɪn]

O Captain, my Captain!
[oːʊ ˈkæptæ(ɪ)n mɑːɪ ˈkæptæ(ɪ)n]
Our fearful trip is done.
[ɑːʊʌ ˈfɪːʌfʊl tɹɪp ɪz dʌn]
The ship has weathered every rack,
[ðʌ ʃɪp hæz ˈwɛðʌd ˈɛvɹɪ ɹæk]
the prize we sought is won,
[ðʌ pɹɑːɪz wi sɔt ɪz wʌn]
The port is near, the bells I hear,
[ðʌ pɔt ɪz nɪːʌ ðʌ bɛlz ɑːɪ hɪːʌ]
the people all exulting.
[ðʌ ˈpipʊl ɔl ɪɡˈzʌltɪŋ]
While follow eyes the steady keel,
[ʍɑːɪl ˈfɑloːʊ ɑːɪz ðʌ ˈstɛdɪ kil]
the vessel grim and daring;
[ðʌ ˈvɛsʊl ɡɹ⁽ʳ⁾ɪm ænd ˈdɛːʌʁ⁽ʳ⁾ɪŋ]
But O heart! heart! heart!
[bʌt oːʊ hɑt hɑt hɑt]
O the bleeding drops of red,
[oːʊ ðʌ ˈblidɪŋ dɹɑps ʌv ɹɛd]
Where on the deck my Captain lies,
[ʍɛːʌʁ⁽ʳ⁾ ɑn ðʌ dɛk mɑːɪ ˈkæptæ(ɪ)n lɑːɪz]
Fallen cold and dead.
[ˈfɔlɛ(ɪ)n koːʊld ænd dɛd]
O Captain! my Captain!
[oːʊ ˈkæptæ(ɪ)n mɑːɪ ˈkæptæ(ɪ)n]
Rise up and hear the bells;
[ɹɑːɪz ʌp ænd hɪːʌ ðʌ bɛlz]
Rise up, for you the flag is flung,
[ɹɑːɪz ʌp fɔ ju ðʌ flæɡ ɪz flʌŋ]
for you the bugle trills,
[fɔ ju ðʌ ˈbjuɡʊl tɹɪlz]
For you bouquets and ribboned wreaths,
[fɔ ju buˈkɛːɪz ænd ˈɹɪbʌnd ɹɪðz]

for you the shores a-crowding,
[fɔ ju ðʌ ʃɔːʌz ʌ ˈkɹɑːʊdɪŋ]
For you they call, the swaying mass,
[fɔ ju ðɛːɪ kɔl ðʌ ˈswɛːɪɪŋ mæs]
their eager faces turning;
[ðɛːʌʁ⁽ᵗ⁾ ˈigʌ ˈfɛːɪsɛ(ɪ)z ˈtɜnɪŋ]
Here Captain! dear father!
[hiːʌ ˈkæptæ(ɪ)n diːʌ ˈfɑðʌ]
The arm beneath your head!
[ði ɑm bɪˈniθ jɔːʌ hɛd]
It is some dream that on this deck
[ɪt ɪz sʌm dɹim ðæt ɑn ðɪs dɛk]
You've fallen cold and dead.
[juv ˈfɔlɛ(ɪ)n koːʊld ænd dɛd]
My Captain does not answer,
[mɑːɪ ˈkæptæ(ɪ)n dʌz nɑt ˈænsʌ]
his lips are pale and still,
[hɪz lɪps ɑ pɛːɪl ænd stɪl]
My father does not feel my arm,
[mɑːɪ ˈfɑðʌ dʌz nɑt fil mɑːɪ ɑm]
he has no strength nor will,
[hi hæz noːʊ stɹɛŋθ nɔ wɪl]
The ship is anchored safe and sound,
[ðʌ ʃɪp ɪz ˈæŋkɔ(ʌ)d sɛːɪf ænd sɑːʊnd]
its voyage closed and done,
[ɪts ˈvɔːɪæ(ɪ)ʤ kloːʊzd ænd dʌn]
From fearful trip, the victor ship
[fɹʌm ˈfiːʌfʊl tɹɪp ðʌ ˈvɪktɔ(ʌ) ʃɪp]
comes in with object won:
[kʌmz ɪn wɪð ˈɑbʤɛkt wʌn]
Exult, O shores, and ring, O bells!
[ɪgˈzʌlt oːʊ ʃɔːʌz ænd ɹɪŋ oːʊ bɛlz]
But I, with mournful tread,
[bʌt ɑːɪ wɪð ˈmɔnfʊl tɹɛd]
Walk the deck my Captain lies,
[wɔk ðʌ dɛk mɑːɪ ˈkæptæ(ɪ)n lɑːɪz]
Fallen cold and dead.
[ˈfɔlɛ(ɪ)n koːʊld ænd dɛd]

5. Joy, Shipmate, Joy!
[ʤɔːɪ ˈʃɪpmɛːɪt ʤɔːɪ]

Joy, shipmate, joy!
[ʤɔːɪ ˈʃɪpmɛːɪt ʤɔːɪ]
(Pleas'd to my soul at death I cry,)
[plizd tu mɑːɪ soːʊl æt dɛθ ɑːɪ kɹɑːɪ]
Our life is closed, our life begins,
[ɑːʊʌ lɑːɪf ɪz kloːʊzd ɑːʊʌ lɑːɪf bɪˈgɪnz]
The long, long anchorage we leave,
[ðʌ lɑŋ lɑŋ ˈæŋkɔʁ⁽ᵗ⁾æ(ɪ)ʤ wi liv]
The ship is clear at last, she leaps!
[ðʌ ʃɪp ɪz kliːʌʁ⁽ᵗ⁾ æt læst ʃi lips]
She swiftly courses from the shore,
[ʃi ˈswɪftlɪ ˈkɔsɛ(ɪ)z fɹʌm ðʌ ʃɔːʌ]
Joy, shipmate, joy!
[ʤɔːɪ ˈʃɪpmɛːɪt ʤɔːɪ]

Song Selections

"Jabberwocky"
[ˈʤæbʁwɑki]
Carroll, Lewis (Eng. 1832-1898)

'Twas brillig, and the slithy toves
[twɑz ˈbɹɪlɪg ænd ðʌ ˈslɑːɪði toːʊvz]
Did gyre and gimble in the wabe:
[dɪd ˈgɑːɪʌ ænd ˈgɪmbʊl ɪn ðʌ wɛːɪb]
All mimsy were the borogoves,
[ɔl ˈmɪmzɪ wɜ ðʌ ˈbɑɾoːʊgoːʊvz]
And the momeraths outgrabe.
[ænd ðʌ ˈmoːʊmɹæθs ɑːʊtˈgɹɛːɪb]
"Beware the Jabberwock, my son!
[bɪˈwɛːʌ ðʌ ˈʤæbʌwak mɑːɪ sʌn]
The jaws that bite, the claws that catch!
[ðʌ ʤɔz ðæt bɑːɪt ðʌ klɔz ðæt kæʧ]
Beware the Jubjub bird, and shun
[bɪˈwɛːʌ ðʌ ˈʤʊʤʊb bɜd ænd ʃʌn]
The frumious Bandersnatch!"
[ðʌ ˈfrumjʌs ˈbændʌsnæʧ]
He took his vorpal sword in hand:
[hi tʊk hɪz ˈvɔpʊl sɔd ɪn hænd]
Long time the manxome foe he sought–
[lɑŋ tɑːɪm ðʌ ˈmæŋksʌm foːʊ hi sɔt]
So rested he by the Tumtum tree,
[soːʊ ˈɹɛstɛ(ɪ)d hi bɑːɪ ðʌ ˈtʌmtʌm tɹi]
And stood awhile in thought.
[ænd stʊd ʌˈʍɑːɪl ɪn θɔt]
And, as in uffish thought he stood,
[ænd æz ɪn ˈʌfɪʃ θɔt hi stʊd]
The Jabberwock, with eyes of flame,
[ðʌ ˈʤæbʌwak wɪð ɑːɪz ʌv flɛːɪm]
Came whiffling through the tulgey wood,
[kɛːɪm ˈʍɪflɪŋ θɾu ðʌ ˈtʌlgɪ wʊd]
And burbled as it came!
[ænd ˈbɜbʊld æz ɪt kɛːɪm]
One, two! One, two! And through and through
[wʌn tu wʌn tu ænd θɾu ænd θɾu]
The vorpal blade went snicker-snack!
[ðʌ ˈvɔpʊl blɛːɪd wɛnt ˈsnɪkʌ snæk]
He left it dead, and with its head
[hi lɛft ɪt dɛd ænd wɪð ɪts hɛd]
He went galumphing back.
[hi wɛnt gʌˈlʌmfɪŋ bæk]
"And, hast thou slain the Jabberwock?
[ænd hæst ðɑːʊ slɛːɪn ðʌ ˈʤæbʌwak]
Come to my arms, my beamish boy!
[kʌm tu mɑːɪ amz mɑːɪ ˈbimɪʃ bɔːɪ]
O frabjous day! Callooh! Callay!"
[oːʊ ˈfɹæbʤʌs dɛːɪ kʌˈlu kʌˈlɛːɪ]
He chortled in his joy.
[hi ˈʧɔtʊld ɪn hɪz ʤɔːɪ]
'Twas brillig, and the slithy toves
[twɑz ˈbɹɪlɪg ænd ðʌ ˈslɑːɪði toːʊvz]

Did gyre and gimble in the wabe:
[dɪd ˈgɑːɪɐɾ ænd ˈgɪmbʊl ɪn ðʌ wɛːɪb]
All mimsy were the borogoves,
[ɔl ˈmɪmzɪ wɜ ðʌ ˈbɑɾoːʊgoːʊvz]
And the momeraths outgrabe.
[ænd ðʌ ˈmoːʊmɹæθs ɑːʊtˈgɾɛːɪb]

"The Lamb" (Two Songs of Innocence)
[ðʌ læm]
Blake, William (Eng. 1757-1827)

Little Lamb, who made thee?
[ˈlɪtʊl læm hu mɛːɪd ði]
Dost thou know who made thee?
[dʌst ðɑːʊ noːʊ hu mɛːɪd ði]
Gave thee life and bid thee feed,
[gɛːɪv ði lɑːɪf ænd bɪd ði fid]
By the stream and o'er the mead;
[bɑːɪ ðʌ stɹim ænd ɔːʌ ðʌ mid]
Gave thee clothing of delight,
[gɛːɪv ði ˈkloːʊðɪŋ ʌv dɪˈlɑːɪt]
Softest clothing woolly bright;
[ˈsɑftɛ(ɪ)st ˈkloːʊðɪŋ ˈwʊlɪ bɹɑːɪt]
Gave thee such a tender voice,
[gɛːɪv ði sʌʧ ʌ ˈtɛndʌ vɔːɪs]
Making all the vales rejoice:
[ˈmɛːɪkɪŋ ɔl ðʌ vɛːɪlz ɹɪˈʤɔːɪs]
Little Lamb, who made thee?
[ˈlɪtʊl læm hu mɛːɪd ði]
Dost thou know who made thee?
[dʌst ðɑːʊ noːʊ hu mɛːɪd ði]
Little Lamb, I'll tell thee,
[ˈlɪtʊl læm ɑːɪl tɛl ði]
He is called by thy name,
[hi ɪz ˈkɔlɛ(ɪ)d bɑːɪ ðɑːɪ nɛːɪm]
For He calls Himself a Lamb:
[fɔ hi kɔlz hɪmˈsɛlf ʌ læm]
He is meek and He is mild,
[hi ɪz mik ænd hi ɪz mɑːɪld]
He became a little child:
[hi bɪˈkɛːɪm ʌ ˈlɪtʊl ʧɑːɪld]
I a child and thou a lamb,
[ɑːɪ ʌ ʧɑːɪld ænd ðɑːʊ ʌ læm]
We are called by His name.
[wi ɑ ˈkɔlɛ(ɪ)d bɑːɪ hɪz nɛːɪm]
Little Lamb, God bless thee.
[ˈlɪtʊl læm gɑd blɛs ði]

"The Serpent" (Songs for Leontyne)
[ðʌ ˈsɜpɛnt]
Roethke, Theodore (Am. 1908-1963)

There was a Serpent who had to sing.
[ðɛːʌ wɑz ʌ ˈsɜpɛnt hu hæd tu sɪŋ]
There was. There was.
[ðɛːʌ wɑz ðɛːʌ wɑz]

He simply gave up Serpenting.
[hi ˈsɪmplɪ gɛːɪv ʌp ˈsɜpɛntɪŋ]
Because. Because.
[bɪˈkɔz bɪˈkɔz]
He didn't like his Kind of Life;
[hi ˈdɪdɛ(ɪ)nt lɑːɪk hɪz kɑːɪnd ʌv lɑːɪf]
He couldn't find a proper Wife;
[hi ˈkʊdɛ(ɪ)nt fɑːɪnd ʌ ˈpɹɑpʌ wɑːɪf]
He was a Serpent with a soul;
[hi wɑz ʌ ˈsɜpɛnt wɪð ʌ soːʊl]
He got no Pleasure down his Hole.
[hi gɑt noːʊ ˈplɛʒʊ(ʌ) dɑːʊn hɪz hoːʊl]
And so, of course, he had to Sing,
[ænd soːʊ ʌv kɔs hi hæd tu sɪŋ]
And Sing he did, like Anything!
[ænd sɪŋ hi dɪd lɑːɪk ˈɛnɪθɪŋ]
The Birds, they were, they were astounded;
[ðʌ bɜdz ðɛːɪ wɜ ðɛːɪ wɜ(ɾ) ʌˈstɑːʊndɛ(ɪ)d]
And various Measures Propounded
[ænd ˈvæɹ(ɾ)ɪʌs ˈmɛʒʊ(ʌ)z pɹoˈpɑːʊndɛ(ɪ)d]
To stop the Serpent's Awful Racket:
[tu stɑp ðʌ ˈsɜpɛnts ˈɔfʊl ˈɹækɛ(ɪ)t]
They bought a Drum. He wouldn't Whack it.
[ðɛːɪ bɔt ʌ dɹʌm hi ˈwʊdɛ(ɪ)nt ʍæk ɪt]
They sent, –you always send, –to Cuba
[ðɛːɪ sɛnt ju ˈɔlwɛːɪz sɛnd tu ˈkjubʌ]
And got a Most Commodious Tuba;
[ænd gɑt ʌ moːʊst kʌˈmoːʊdɪʌs ˈtubʌ]
They got a Horn, they got a Flute,
[ðɛːɪ gɑt ʌ hɔn ðɛːɪ gɑt ʌ flut]
But Nothing would suit.
[bʌt ˈnʌθɪŋ wʊd sjut]
He said, "Look, Birds, all this is futile:
[hi sɛd lʊk bɜdz ɔl ðɪs ɪz ˈfjutʊl]
I do not like to Bang or Tootle."
[ɑːɪ du nɑt lɑːɪk tu bæŋ ɔ ˈtutʊl]
And then he cut loose with a Horrible Note
[ænd ðɛn hi kʌt lus wɪð ʌ ˈhɔɹ(ɾ)ɪbʊl noːʊt]
That practically split the Top of his Throat.
[ðæt ˈpɹæktɪklɪ splɪt ðʌ tɑp ʌv hɪz θroːʊt]
"You see," he said, with a Serpent's Leer,
[ju si hi sɛd wɪð ʌ ˈsɜpɛnts lɪːʌ]
"I'm Serious about my Singing Career!"
[ɑːɪm ˈsɪːʌɾɪʌs ʌˈbɑːʊt mɑːɪ ˈsɪŋɪŋ kʌˈɹɪːʌ]
And the Woods Resounded with many a Shriek
[ænd ðʌ wʊdz ɹɪˈzɑːʊndɛ(ɪ)d wɪð ˈmɛnɪ ʌ ʃɹik]
As the Birds flew off to the end of Next Week.
[æz ðʌ bɜdz flu ɑf tu ði ɛnd ʌv nɛkst wik]

"There Came a Wind Like a Bugle" (see Copland)

Holst, Gustav (Eng. 1874-1934)

Four Songs for Voice and Violin (Song Cycle)
[fɔːʌ saŋz fɔ vɔːɪs ænd vɑːɪʌˈlɪn]
Anonymous

1. Jesu Sweet
[ˈʤezju swit]

Jesu Sweet, now will I sing
[ˈʤezju swit nɑːʊ wɪl ɑːɪ sɪŋ]
To Thee a song of love longing;
[tu ði ʌ saŋ ʌv lʌv ˈlaŋɪŋ]
Do in my heart a quick well spring
[du ɪn mɑːɪ hat ʌ kwɪk wɛl spɹɪŋ]
Thee to love above all thing.
[ði tu lʌv ʌˈbʌv ɔl θɪŋ]
Jesu Sweet, my dim heart's gleam
[ˈʤezju swit mɑːɪ dɪm hats glim]
Brighter than the sunnèbeam!
[ˈbɹɑːɪtʌ ðæn ðʊ ˈsʌnʌbim]
As thou wert born in Bethlehem
[æz ðɑːʊ wɜt bɔn ɪn ˈbɛθlɪhɛm]
Make in me thy lovèdream.
[mɛːɪk ɪn mi mi ðɑːɪ ˈlʌvʌdɹim]
Jesu Sweet, my dark heart's light
[ˈʤezju swit mɑːɪ dak hats lɑːɪt]
Thou art day withouten night;
[ðɑːʊ at dɛːɪ wɪðˈɑːʊtʌn nɑːɪt]
Give me strength and eke might
[gɪv mi stɹɛŋθ ænd ˈikʌ mɑːɪt]
For to loven Thee aright.
[fɔ tu ˈlʌvʌn ði ʌˈrɑːɪt]
Jesu Sweet, well may he be
[ˈʤezju swit wɛl mɛːɪ hi bi]
That in Thy bliss Thyself shall see:
[ðæt ɪn ðɑːɪ blɪs ðɑːɪˈsɛlf ʃæl si]
With lovè cords then draw Thou me
[wɪð ˈlʌvʌ kɔdz ðɛn dɹɔ ðɑːʊ mi]
That I may come and dwell with Thee.
[ðæt ɑːɪ mɛːɪ kʌm ænd dwɛl wɪð ði]

2. My Soul Has Nought but Fire and Ice
[mɑːɪ soːʊl hæz nɔt bʌt fɑːɪʁ ænd ɑːɪs]

My soul has nought but fire and ice
[mɑːɪ soːʊl hæz nɔt bʌt fɑːɪʌr ænd ɑːɪs]
And my body earth and wood:
[ænd mɑːɪ ˈbadɪ ɜθ ænd wʊd]
Pray we all the Most High King
[pɹɛːɪ wi ɔl ðʊ moːʊst hɑːɪ kɪŋ]
Who is the Lord of our last doom,
[hu ɪz ðʊ lɔd ʌv ɑːʊʌ last dum]
That He should give us just one thing
[ðæt hi ʃʊd gɪv ʌs ʤʌst wʌn θɪŋ]

That we may do His will.
[ðæt wi mɛːɪ du hɪz wɪl]

3. I Sing of a Maiden
[ɑːɪ sɪŋ ʌv ʌ ˈmɛːɪdɪn]

I sing of a maiden
[ɑːɪ sɪŋ ʌv ʌ ˈmɛːɪdɛ(ɪ)n]
That matchless is.
[ðæt ˈmæʧlɛ(ɪ)s ɪz]
King of all Kings
[kɪŋ ʌv ɔl kɪŋz]
Was her Son iwis.
[waz hɜ sʌn iˈwɪs]
He came all so still
[hi kɛːɪm ɔl soːʊ stɪl]
Where His mother was
[ʍɛːʌ hɪz ˈmʌðʌ waz]
As dew in April
[æz dju ɪn ˈɛːɪpɹɪ(ʊ)l]
That falleth on grass:
[ðæt ˈfɔlɛ(ɪ)θ an gɹas]
He came all so still
[hi kɛːɪm ɔl soːʊ stɪl]
To His mother's bower
[tu hɪz ˈmʌðʌz ˈbɑːʊʌ]
As dew in April
[æz dju ɪn ˈɛːɪpɹɪ(ʊ)l]
That falleth on flower.
[ðæt ˈfɔlɛ(ɪ)θ an flɑːʊʌ]
He came all so still
[hi kɛːɪm ɔl soːʊ stɪl]
Where His mother lay
[ʍɛːʌ hɪz ˈmʌðʌ lɛːɪ]
As dew in April
[æz dju ɪn ˈɛːɪpɹɪ(ʊ)l]
That formeth on spray.
[ðæt ˈfɔmɛ(ɪ)θ an spɹɛːɪ]
Mother and maiden
[ˈmʌðʌr ænd ˈmɛːɪdɛ(ɪ)n]
Was ne'er none but she:
[waz nɛːʌ nʌn bʌt ʃi]
Well may such a lady
[wɛl mɛːɪ sʌʧ ʌ ˈlɛːɪdɪ]
God's mother be.
[gadz ˈmʌðʌ bi]

4. My Leman Is So True
[mɑːɪ ˈlɛːɪmʌn ɪz soːʊ tɹu]

My Leman is so true
[mɑːɪ ˈlɛːɪmæ(ʌ)n ɪz soːʊ tɹu]
Of love and full steadfast
[ʌv lʌv ænd fʊl ˈstɛdfast]
Yet seemeth ever new.
[jɛt ˈsimɛ(ɪ)θ ˈɛvʌ nju]

His love is on us cast.
[hɪz lʌv ɪz ɑn ʌs kast]
I would that all Him knew
[ɑːɪ wʊd ðæt ɔl hɪm nju]
And loved Him firm and fast,
[ænd lʌvd hɪm fɜm ænd fast]
They never would it rue
[ðɛːɪ ˈnɛvʌ wʊd ɪt rru]
But happy be at last.
[bʌt ˈhæpɪ bi æt last]
He lovingly abides
[hi ˈlʌvɪŋlɪ ʌˈbɑːɪdz]
Although I stay full long;
[ɔlˈðoːʊ ɑːɪ stɛːɪ fʊl laŋ]
He will me never chide
[hi wɪl mi ˈnɛvʌ ʧɑːɪd]
Although I choose the wrong.
[ɔlˈðoːʊ ɑːɪ ʧuz ðʊ rɑŋ]
He says "Behold My side
[hi sɛz bɪˈhoːʊld mɑːɪ sɑːɪd]
And why on Rood I hung;
[ænd ʍɑːɪ ɑn rrud ɑːɪ hʌŋ]
For my love leave thy pride
[fɔ mɑːɪ lʌv liv ðɑːɪ prɑːɪd]
And I thee underfong.
[ænd ɑːɪ ði ˈʌndʌfɑŋ]
I'll dwell with Thee believe,"
[ɑːɪl dwɛl wɪð ði bɪˈliv]
Leman, under Thy tree.
[ˈlɛːɪmæ(ʌ)n ˈʌndʌ ðɑːɪ tri]
May no pain e'er me grieve
[mɛːɪ noːʊ pɛːɪn ɛːʌ mi griv]
Nor make me from Thee flee.
[nɔ mɛːɪk mi frʌm ði fli]
I will in at Thy sleeve
[ɑːɪ wɪl ɪn æt ðɑːɪ sliv]
All in Thine heart to be;
[ɔl ɪn ðɑːɪn hat tu bi]
Mine heart shall burst and cleave
[mɑːɪn hat ʃæl bɜst ænd kliv]
Ere untrue Thou me see.
[ɛːʌr ʌnˈtru ðɑːʊ mi si]

Six Songs (Song Cycle)
[sɪks sɑŋz]

1. Calm Is the Morn
[kɑm ɪz ðʊ mɔn]
Tennyson, Lord Alfred (Eng. 1809-1892)

Calm is the morn without a sound,
[kɑm ɪz ðʊ mɔn wɪðˈɑːʊt ʌ sɑːʊnd]
Calm as to suit a calmer grief,
[kɑm æz tu sjut ʌ ˈkɑmʌ grif]
And only thro' the faded leaf
[ænd ˈoːʊnlɪ θru ðʊ ˈfɛːɪdɛ(ɪ)d lif]

The chestnut pattering to the ground:
[ðʊ ˈʧɛsnʌt ˈpætʌrɪŋ tu ðʊ grɑːʊnd]
Calm and deep peace on this high world
[kɑm ænd dip pis ɑn ðɪs hɑːɪ wɜld]
And on these dews that drench the furze
[ænd ɑn ðiz djuz ðæt drɛnʧ ðʊ fɜz]
And all the silvery gossamers
[ænd ɔl ðʊ ˈsɪlvʌrɪ ˈgɑsʌmʌz]
That twinkle into green and gold:
[ðæt ˈtwɪŋkʊl ˈɪntu grin ænd goːʊld]
Calm and still light on yon great plain
[kɑm ænd stɪl lɑːɪt ɑn jɑn grɛːɪt plɛːɪn]
That sweeps with all its autumn bowers,
[ðæt swips wɪð ɔl ɪts ˈɔtʌm ˈbɑːʊʌz]
And crowded farms and lessening towers,
[ænd ˈkrɑːʊdɛ(ɪ)d famz ænd ˈlɛsɛ(ɪ)nɪŋ tɑːʊʌz]
To mingle with the bounding main:
[tu ˈmɪŋgʊl wɪð ðʊ ˈbɑːʊndɪŋ mɛːɪn]
Calm and deep peace in this wide air,
[kɑm ænd dip pis ɪn ðɪs wɑːɪd ɛːʌ]
These leaves that redden to the fall;
[ðiz livz ðæt ˈrɛdɛ(ɪ)n tu ðʊ fɔl]
And in my heart, if calm at all,
[ænd ɪn mɑːɪ hat ɪf kɑm æt ɔl]
If any calm, a calm despair:
[ɪf ˈɛnɪ kɑm ʌ kɑm dɪˈspɛːʌ]
Calm on the seas, and silver sleep,
[kɑm ɑn ðʊ siz ænd ˈsɪlvʌ slip]
And waves that sway themselves in rest,
[ænd wɛːɪvz ðæt swɛːɪ ðɛmˈsɛlvz ɪn rɛst]
And dead calm in that noble breast
[ænd dɛd kɑm ɪn ðæt ˈnoːʊbʊl brɛst]
Which heaves but in the heaving deep.
[ʍɪʧ hivz bʌt ɪn ðʊ ˈhivɪŋ dip]

2. My True Love Hath My Heart (see Ireland)

3. Weep You No More (see Quilter)

4. Lovely Kind and Kindly Loving
[ˈlʌvli kɑːɪnd ænd ˈkɑːɪndli ˈlʌvɪŋ]
Breton, Nicholas (Eng. 1542-1626)

Lovely kind and kindly loving,
[ˈlʌvlɪ kɑːɪnd ænd ˈkɑːɪndlɪ ˈlʌvɪŋ]
Such a mind were worth the moving,
[sʌʧ ʌ mɑːɪnd wɜ wɜθ ðʊ ˈmuvɪŋ]
Truly fair and fairly true
[ˈtrulɪ fɛːʌr ænd ˈfɛːʌlɪ tru]
Where are all these but in you?
[ʍɛːʌr ɑr ɔl ðiz bʌt ɪn ju]
Wisely kind and kindly wise,
[ˈwɑːɪzlɪ kɑːɪnd ænd ˈkɑːɪndlɪ wɑːɪz]
Blessed life where such love lies!
[ˈblɛsɛ(ɪ)d lɑːɪf ʍɛːʌ sʌʧ lʌv lɑːɪz]

Wise and kind and fair and true,
[wɑːɪz ænd kɑːɪnd ænd fɛːʌʳ ænd tʃu]
Lovely live all these in you!
[ˈlʌvlɪ lɪv ɔl ðiz ɪn ju]
Sweetly dear and dearly sweet,
[ˈswitlɪ dɪːʌʳ ænd ˈdɪːʌlɪ swit]
Blessed where these blessings meet
[ˈblɛsɛ(ɪ)d ʍɛːʌ ðiz ˈblɛsɪŋz mit]
Sweet, fair, wise, kind, blessed, true
[swit fɛːʌ wɑːɪz kɑːɪnd ˈblɛsɛ(ɪ)d tʃu]
Blessed be all these in you!
[ˈblɛsɛ(ɪ)d bi ɔl ðiz ɪn ju]

5. Cradle Song
[ˈkʃɛːɪdʊl sɑŋ]
Blake, William (Eng. 1757-1827)

Sweet dreams, form a shade
[swit dʃimz fom ʌ ʃɛːɪd]
O'er my lovely infant's head;
[ɔːʌ mɑːɪ ˈlʌvlɪ ˈɪnfæ(ɪ)nts hɛd]
Sweet dreams of pleasant streams
[swit dʃimz ʌv ˈplɛzæ(ɪ)nt stʃimz]
By happy, silent, moony beams.
[bɑːɪ ˈhæpɪ ˈsɑːɪlɛnt ˈmunɪ bimz]
Sweet sleep, with soft down
[swit slip wɪð saft dɑːʊn]
Weave thy brows an infant crown.
[wiv ðɑːɪ bʃɑːʊz æn ˈɪnfæ(ɪ)nt kʃɑːʊn]
Sweet sleep, Angel mild,
[swit slip ˈɛːɪndʒɛ(ʊ)l mɑːɪld]
Hover o'er my happy child.
[ˈhʌvʌʳ ɔːʌ mɑːɪ ˈhæpɪ ʧɑːɪld]
Sweet smiles, in the night
[swit smɑːɪlz ɪn ðʊ nɑːɪt]
Hover over my delight;
[ˈhʌvʌʳ ˈɔːʊvʌ mɑːɪ dɪˈlɑːɪt]
Sweet smiles, Mother's smile,
[swit smɑːɪlz ˈmʌðʌz smɑːɪl]
All the live long night beguile.
[ɔl ðʊ lɪv lɑŋ nɑːɪt bɪˈgɑːɪl]
Sweet moans, dove-like sighs,
[swit moːʊnz dʌv lɑːɪk sɑːɪz]
Chase not slumber from thine eyes.
[ʧɛːɪs nat ˈslʌmbʌ fʃʌm ðɑːɪn ɑːɪz]
Sweet moan, sweeter smile,
[swit moːʊn ˈswitʌ smɑːɪl]
All the dove-like moans beguile.
[ɔl ðʊ dʌv lɑːɪk moːʊnz bɪˈgɑːɪl]

6. Peace
[pis]
Hyatt, Alfred Henry (Eng. 1870-1911)

The toil of day is done,
[ðʊ tɔːɪl ʌv dɛːɪ ɪz dʌn]

Its stress and stirring cease,
[ɪts stʃɛs ænd ˈstʊrɪŋ sis]
Falls soft a word, the gift of God.
[fɔlz saft ʌ wɜd ðʊ gɪft ʌv gad]
'Peace.'
[pis]
Opal of evening sky,
[ˈoːʊpɔl ʌv ˈivnɪŋ skɑːɪ]
Gold of the fading west,
[goːʊld ʌv ðʊ ˈfɛːɪdɪŋ wɛst]
A single star shining afar. Rest.
[ʌ ˈsɪŋgʊl stɑ ˈʃɑːɪnɪŋ ʌˈfɑ ʃɛst]

Twelve Humbert Wolfe Songs (Song Cycle)
[twɛlv ˈhʌmbʌt wʊlf sɑŋz]
Wolfe, Humbert (Eng. 1885-1940)

1. Persephone
[pɛːʌˈsɛfoni]

Come back Persephone!
[kʌm bæk pɛːʌˈsɛfoni]
As a moonflake thin,
[æz ʌ ˈmunflɛːɪk θɪn]
flutes for the dancers
[fluts fɔ ðʊ ˈdansʌz]
you danced with begin.
[ju danst wɪð bɪˈgɪn]
Leave the deep hellebore
[liv ðʊ dip ˈhɛlɪbɔːʌ]
the dark, the untranquil
[ðʊ dak ði ʌnˈtʃæŋkwɪ(ʊ)l]
for spring's pale primrose
[fɔ spʃɪŋz pɛːɪl ˈpʃɪmʃoːʊz]
and her first jonquil.
[ænd hɜ fɜst ˈdʒaŋkwɪ(ʊ)l]
Again they are singing
[ʌˈgɛːɪn ðɛːɪ ɑ ˈsɪŋɪŋ]
(O will you not heed them?)
[oːʊ wɪl ju nat hid ðɛm]
with none now to answer,
[wɪð nʌn nɑːʊ tu ˈansʌ]
and none to lead them.
[ænd nʌn tu lid ðɛm]
They will grow older,
[ðɛːɪ wɪl gʃoːʊ ˈoːʊldʌ]
till comes a day
[tɪl kʌmz ʌ dɛːɪ]
when the last of your maidens
[ʍɛn ðʊ last ʌv jɔːʌ ˈmɛːɪdɛ(ɪ)nz]
is tired of play:
[ɪz tɑːɪʌd ʌv plɛːɪ]
when the song as it rises
[ʍɛn ðʊ sɑŋ æz ɪt ˈʃɑːɪzɛ(ɪ)z]
faints and droops over,
[fɛːɪnts ænd dʃups ˈoːʊvʌ]

and your playmates go seeking
[ænd jɔːʌ ˈpleːɪmeːɪts goːʊ ˈsikɪŋ]
a gentler lover.
[ʌ ˈdʒentlʌ ˈlʌvʌ]
Listen the dancers!
[ˈlɪseˈ(ɪ)n ðʊ ˈdansʌz]
The flutes oh listen!
[ðʊ fluts oːʊ ˈlɪseˈ(ɪ)n]
Hasten Persephone!
[ˈheːɪseˈ(ɪ)n pɛːʌˈsefonɪ]
Persephone! Hasten!
[pɛːʌˈsefonɪ ˈheːɪseˈ(ɪ)n]

2. Things Lovelier
[θɪŋz ˈlʌvlɪʌ]

You cannot dream
[ju kæˈnɑt dɹim]
things lovelier
[θɪŋz ˈlʌvlɪʌ]
than the first love
[ðæn ðʊ fɜst lʌv]
I had of her.
[ɑːɪ hæd ʌv hɜ]
Nor air is any
[nɔʁ⁽ʳ⁾ ɛːʌɾ ɪz ˈɛnɪ]
as magic shaken
[æz ˈmædʒɪk ˈʃeːɪkeˈ(ɪ)n]
as her breath in
[æz hɜ bɹɛθ ɪn]
the first kiss taken.
[ðʊ fɜst kɪs ˈteːɪkeˈ(ɪ)n]
And who, in dreaming,
[ænd hu ɪn ˈdɹimɪŋ]
understands
[ʌndʌˈstændz]
her hands stretched like
[hɜ hændz stɹetʃt lɑːɪk]
a blind man's hands?
[ʌ blɑːɪnd mænz hændz]
Open, trembling,
[ˈoːʊpeˈ(ɪ)n ˈtɹemblɪŋ]
wise they were—
[wɑːɪz ðɛːɪ wɜ]
You cannot dream
[ju kæˈnɑt dɹim]
things lovelier.
[θɪŋz ˈlʌvlɪʌ]

3. Now in These Fairylands
[nɑːʊ ɪn ðiz ˈfɛʁɪlændz]

Now in these fairylands
[nɑːʊ ɪn ðiz ˈfɛːʌɾɪlændz]
gather your weary hands
[ˈgæðʌ jɔːʌ ˈwiːʌɾɪ hændz]

close to your breast,
[kloːʊs tu jɔːʌ bɹɛst]
and be at rest.
[ænd bi æt ɹest]
Now in these silences
[nɑːʊ ɪn ðiz ˈsaːɪleˈ(ɪ)nseˈ(ɪ)z]
lean to the cadences,
[lin tu ðʊ ˈkɛːɪdeˈ(ɪ)nseˈ(ɪ)z]
moulding their grace
[ˈmoːʊldɪŋ ðɛːʌ gɹeːɪs]
to the line of your face.
[tu ðʊ lɑːɪn ʌv jɔːʌ feːɪs]
Now at the end of all,
[nɑːʊ æt ði ɛnd ʌv ɔl]
loveliest friend of all,
[ˈlʌvlɪeˈ(ɪ)st fɹɛnd ʌv ɔl]
all things are yours
[ɔl θɪŋz a jɔːʌz]
in this peace that endures.
[ɪn ðɪs pis ðæt ɪnˈdjʊːʌz]

4. A Little Music
[ʌ ˈlɪtʊl ˈmjuzɪk]

Since it is evening,
[sɪns ɪt ɪz ˈivnɪŋ]
let us invent
[let ʌs ɪnˈvent]
love's undiscovered
[lʌvz ˌʌndɪˈskʌvʌd]
continent.
[ˈkɑntɪnɛnt]
What shall we steer by,
[ʍat ʃæl wi stɪːʌ bɑːɪ]
having no chart
[ˈhævɪŋ noːʊ tʃat]
but the deliberate
[bʌt ðʊ dɪˈlɪbʌɾæˈ(ɪ)t]
fraud of the heart?
[fɹɔd ʌv ðʊ hɑt]
How shall we find it?
[hɑːʊ ʃæl wi fɑːɪnd ɪt]
Beyond what keys
[bɪˈjɑnd ʍat kiz]
of boyhood's Spanish
[ʌv ˈbɔːɪhʊdz ˈspænɪʃ]
piracies,
[ˈpɑːɪɾæ(ʌ)sɪz]
false Eldorados
[fɔls ɛldɔˈɾados]
dim with the tears
[dɪm wɪð ðʊ tɪːʌz]
of beauty, the last
[ʌv ˈbjutɪ ðʊ last]
of the buccaneers?
[ʌv ðʊ ˌbʌkæ(ʌ)ˈnɪːʌz]

Since it is evening,
[sɪns ɪt ɪz 'ivnɪŋ]
let us design
[lɛt ʌs dɪ'zaːɪn]
what shall be utterly
[ʍat ʃæl bi 'ʌtʌlɪ]
yours and mine.
[jɔːʌz ænd maːɪn]
There will be nothing
[ðɛːʌ wɪl bi 'nʌθɪŋ]
that ever before
[ðæt 'ɛvʌ bɪ'fɔːʌ]
beckoned the sail
['bɛkʌnd ðʊ sɛːɪl]
or from any shore.
[ɔ fɹʌm 'ɛnɪ ʃɔːʌ]
Trees shall be greener
[tɹiz ʃæl bi 'gɹinʌ]
by mountains more pale,
[baːɪ 'maːʊntæ(ɪ)nz mɔːʌ pɛːɪl]
thrushes outsinging
['θɹʌʃɛ(ɪ)z aːʊt'sɪŋɪŋ]
the nightingale,
[ðʊ 'naːɪtɪŋɡɛːɪl]
flowers now butterflies,
[flaːʊʌz naːʊ 'bʌtʌflaːɪz]
now in the grass,
[naːʊ ɪn ðʊ gɹas]
suddenly quiet
['sʌdɛ(ɪ)nlɪ 'kwaːɪɛ(ɪ)t]
as painted glass,
[æz 'pɛːɪntɛ(ɪ)d glas]
and fishes of emerald
[ænd 'fɪʃɛ(ɪ)z ʌv 'ɛmʌʊld]
dive for the moon,
[daːɪv fɔ ðʊ mun]
whose silver is stained
[huz 'sɪlvʌɾ ɪz stɛːɪnd]
by the peacock lagoon.
[baːɪ ðʊ 'pikak lʌ'gun]
Since it is evening,
[sɪns ɪt ɪz 'ivnɪŋ]
and sailing weather,
[ænd 'sɛːɪlɪŋ 'wɛðʌ]
let us set out
[lɛt ʌs sɛt aːʊt]
for the dream together;
[fɔ ðʊ dɹim tu'gɛðʌ]
set for the landfall,
[sɛt fɔ ðʊ 'lændfʌl]
where love and verse
[ʍɛːʌ lʌv ænd vɜs]
enfranchise for ever
[ɪn'fɹæn.tʃaːɪz fɔʁ(ʳ) 'ɛvʌ]
the travellers.
[ðʊ 'tɹævʊlʌz]

5. The Thought
[ðʊ θɔt]

I will not write a poem for you,
[aːɪ wɪl nat ɹaːɪt ʌ 'poːʊɛ(ɪ)m fɔ ju]
because a poem, even the loveliest,
[bɪ'kɔz ʌ 'poːʊɛ(ɪ)m 'ivɛ(ɪ)n ðʊ 'lʌvlɪɛ(ɪ)st]
can only do what words can do–
[kæn 'oːʊnlɪ du ʍat wɜdz kæn du]
stir the air, and dwindle, and be at rest.
[stɜ ði ɛːʌɾ ænd 'dwɪndʊl ænd bi æt ɹɛst]
Nor will I hold you with my hands, because
[nɔ wɪl aːɪ hoːʊld ju wɪð maːɪ hændz bɪ'kɔz]
the bones of my hands on yours would press,
[ðʊ boːʊnz ʌv maːɪ hændz ɑn jɔːʌz wʊd pɹɛs]
and you'd say after "Mortal was,
[ænd jud sɛːɪ 'aftʌ 'mɔtʊl waz]
and crumbling, that lover's tenderness."
[ænd 'kɹʌmblɪŋ ðæt 'lʌvʌz 'tɛndʌnɛ(ɪ)s]
But I will hold you in a thought without moving
[bʌt aːɪ wɪl hoːʊld ju ɪn ʌ θɔt wɪð'aːʊt 'muvɪŋ]
spirit or desire or will–
['spɪɾɪt ɔ dɪ'zaːɪʌɾ ɔ wɪl]
for I know no other way of loving,
[fɔʁ(ʳ) aːɪ noːʊ noːʊ 'ʌðʌ wɛːɪ ʌv 'lʌvɪŋ]
that endures when the heart is still.
[ðæt ɪn'djuːʌz ʍɛn ðʊ hɑt ɪz stɪl]

6. The Floral Bandit
[ðʊ 'flɔʁʊl 'bændɪt]

Beyond the town– oh far! beyond it
[bɪ'jand ðʊ taːʊn oːʊ fa bɪ'jand ɪt]
she walks– that lady– have you seen her?
[ʃi wɔks ðæt 'lɛːɪdɪ hæv ju sin hɜ]
that thief of spring, that floral bandit
[ðæt θif ʌv spɹɪŋ ðæt 'flɔʁʊl 'bændɪt]
who leaves the grass she walks on greener.
[hu livz ðʊ gɹas ʃi wɔks ɑn 'gɹinʌ]
And she can sing– the blackbirds hear her–
[ænd ʃi kæn sɪŋ ðʊ 'blækbɜdz hɪːʌ hɜ]
those little coals with throats of flame–
[ðoːʊz 'lɪtʊl koːʊlz wɪð θɹoːʊts ʌv flɛːɪm]
and they can find, alighting near her,
[ænd ðɛːɪ kæn faːɪnd ʌ'laːɪtɪŋ nɪːʌ hɜ]
no sweeter practice than her name.
[noːʊ 'switʌ 'pɹæktɪs ðæn hɜ nɛːɪm]
What is her name? O ask the linnet,
[ʍat ɪz hɜ nɛːɪm oːʊ ask ðʊ 'lɪnɛ(ɪ)t]
for human tongue would strive in vain
[fɔ 'hjumæ(ʌ)n tʌŋ wʊd stɹaːɪv ɪn vɛːɪn]
to speak the buds uncrumpling in it,
[tu spik ðʊ bʌdz ʌn'kɹʌmplɪŋ ɪn ɪt]
and the small language of the rain.
[ænd ðʊ smɔl 'læŋgwæ(ɪ)dʒ ʌv ðʊ ɾɛːɪn]

Who is this lady? What is she?
[hu ɪz ðɪs ˈlɛːɪdɪ ʍɑt ɪz ʃi]
the Sylvia all our swains adore?
[ðʊ ˈsɪlvɪɑ ɔl ɑːʊʌ swɛːɪnz ʌˈdɔːʌ]
Yes, she is that unchangingly,
[jɛs ʃi ɪz ðæt ʌnˈʧɛːɪndʒɪŋlɪ]
but she is also something more.
[bʌt ʃi ɪz ˈɔlsoːʊ ˈsʌmθɪŋ mɔːʌ]
For buds at best are little green
[fɔ bʌdz æt bɛst ɑ ˈlɪtʊl ɡɹin]
keys on an old thin clavichord,
[kiz ɑn æn oːʊld θɪn ˈklævɪ ̩kɔd]
that only has the one high tune
[ðæt ˈoːʊnlɪ hæz ðʊ wʌn hɑːɪ tjun]
that, since the first, all springs have heard.
[ðæt sɪns ðʊ fɜst ɔl spɹɪŋz hæv hɜd]
And all first love with the same sighing
[ænd ɔl fɜst lʌv wɪð ðʊ sɛːɪm ˈsɑːɪŋ]
tunes, though more sweetly touched, has lingered,
[tjunz ðoːʊ mɔːʌ ˈswitlɪ tʌʧt hæz ˈlɪŋɡʌd]
as though he were for ever trying
[æz ðoːʊ hi wɜ fɔʁ⁽ʳ⁾ ˈɛvʌ ˈtɹɑːɪŋ]
toccatas Purcell might have fingered.
[tʌˈkɑtɑz ˈpɜsɛ(ʊ)l mɑːɪt hæv ˈfɪŋɡʌd]
But no one knows her range nor can
[bʌt noːʊ wʌn noːʊz hɜ ɹɛːɪndʒ nɔ kæn]
guess half the phrases of her fiddle,
[ɡɛs hɑf ðʊ ˈfɹɛːɪzɛ(ɪ)z ʌv hɜ ˈfɪdʊl]
the lady who for ev'ry man
[ðʊ ˈlɛːɪdɪ hu fɔʁ⁽ʳ⁾ ˈɛvɹɪ mæn]
breaks off her music in the middle.
[bɹɛːɪks ɑf hɜ ˈmjuzɪk ɪn ðʊ ˈmɪdʊl]

7. Envoi
[ˈɑnvɔːɪ]

When the spark that glittered
[ʍɛn ðʊ spɑk ðæt ˈɡlɪtʌd]
flakes into ash,
[flɛːɪks ˈɪntu æʃ]
and the spirit unfettered
[ænd ðʊ ˈspɪrɪt ʌnˈfɛtʌd]
is done with flesh,
[ɪz dʌn wɪð flɛʃ]
when all that wonder,
[ʍɛn ɔl ðæt ˈwʌndʌ]
this loveliness
[ðɪs ˈlʌvlɪnɛ(ɪ)s]
of heart lies under
[ʌv hɑt lɑːɪz ˈʌndʌ]
the sleepy grass,
[ðʊ ˈslipɪ ɡɹɑs]
and slow are the swift,
[ænd sloːʊ ɑ ðʊ swɪft]
and dark the fair,
[ænd dɑk ðʊ fɛːʌ]

and sweet voices lift,
[ænd swit ˈvɔːɪsɛ(ɪ)z lɪft]
not on the air,
[nɑt ɑn ði ɛːʌ]
when the long spell
[ʍɛn ðʊ lɑŋ spɛl]
of dust lies on
[ʌv dʌst lɑːɪz ɑn]
all that was well
[ɔl ðæt wɑz wɛl]
bethought upon,
[bɪˈθɔt ʌˈpɑn]
of all that lovely,
[ʌv ɔl ðæt ˈlʌvlɪ]
of all those brief
[ʌv ɔl ðoːʊz bɹif]
hopes that went bravely
[hoːʊps ðæt wɛnt ˈbɹɛːɪvlɪ]
beyond belief,
[bɪˈjɑnd bɪˈlif]
of life's deep blazon
[ʌv lɑːɪfs dip ˈblɛːɪzʌn]
with love's gold stain
[wɪð lʌvz ɡoːʊld stɛːɪn]
passing all reason
[ˈpɑsɪŋ ɔl ˈɹizʌn]
doth aught remain?
[dʌθ ɔt ɹɪˈmɛːɪn]
What need of answer?
[ʍɑt nid ʌv ˈɑnsʌ]
Bird chaunting priest,
[bɜd ˈʧɔntɪŋ pɹist]
dawn swings her censer
[dɔn swɪŋz hɜ ˈsɛnsʌɹ]
of bloom-white mist,
[ʌv blum ʍɑːɪt mɪst]
noon from her shoulder
[nun fɹʌm hɜ ˈʃoːʊldʌ]
lets her sun-shawl
[lɛts hɜ sʌn ʃɔl]
half loose, half hold her,
[hɑf lus hɑf hoːʊld hɜ]
and drifting fall,
[ænd ˈdɹɪftɪŋ fɔl]
and evening slowly
[ænd ˈivnɪŋ ˈsloːʊlɪ]
by hill and wood
[bɑːɪ hɪl ænd wʊd]
perfects her holy
[pɜˈfɛkts hɜ ˈhoːʊlɪ]
solitude,
[ˈsɑlɪtjud]
unasked, undaunted
[ʌnˈɑskt ʌnˈdɔntɛ(ɪ)d]
by love, or what
[bɑːɪ lʌv ɔ ʍɑt]

the heart has wanted,
[ðʊ hɑt hæz ˈwɑntɛ(ɪ)d]
and wanteth not.
[ænd ˈwɑntɛ(ɪ)θ nɑt]
Unasked? Say rather
[ʌnˈɑskt sɛːɪ ˈrɑðʌ]
that these will startle
[ðæt ðiz wɪl ˈstɑtʊl]
tomorrow other
[tuˈmɑɾoːʊ ˈʌðʌ]
hearts with mortal
[hɑts wɪð ˈmɔtʊl]
beauty they had
[ˈbjutɪ ðɛːɪ hæd]
from us, as we
[fɪʌm ʌs æz wi]
inherited
[ɪnˈhɛɾɪtɛ(ɪ)d]
that legacy.
[ðæt ˈlɛgæ(ɪ)sɪ]
Undaunted? Yes,
[ʌnˈdɔntɛ(ɪ)d jɛs]
since death can lend
[sɪns dɛθ kæn lɛnd]
to loveliness
[tu ˈlʌvlɪnɛ(ɪ)s]
only an end
[ˈoːʊnlɪ æn ɛnd]
that with the beginning
[ðæt wɪð ðʊ bɪˈgɪnɪŋ]
is one designed,
[ɪz wʌn dɪˈzɑːɪnd]
one shape, one meaning
[wʌn ʃɛːɪp wʌn ˈminɪŋ]
beyond the mind.
[bɪˈjɑnd ðʊ mɑːɪnd]

8. The Dream-City
[ðʊ dɹim ˈsɪti]

On a dream-hill we'll build our city,
[ɑn ʌ dɹim hɪl wɪl bɪld ɑːʊʌ ˈsɪti]
and we'll build gates that have two keys—
[ænd wɪl bɪld gɛːɪts ðæt hæv tu kiz]
love to let in the vanquished, and pity
[lʌv tu lɛt ɪn ðʊ ˈvæŋkwɪʃt ænd ˈpɪti]
to close the locks that shelter these.
[tu kloːʊz ðʊ lɑks ðæt ˈʃɛltʌ ðiz]
There will be quiet open spaces,
[ðɛːʌ wɪl bi ˈkwɑːɪɛ(ɪ)t ˈoːʊpɛ(ɪ)n ˈspɛːɪsɛ(ɪ)z]
and shady towers sweet with bells,
[ænd ˈʃɛːɪdɪ tɑːʊʌz swit wɪð bɛlz]
and quiet folks with quiet faces,
[ænd ˈkwɑːɪɛ(ɪ)t foːʊks wɪð ˈkwɑːɪɛ(ɪ)t ˈfɛːɪsɛ(ɪ)z]
walking among these miracles.
[ˈwɔkɪŋ ʌˈmʌŋ ðiz ˈmɪɾʌkʊlz]

There'll be a London Square in Maytime
[ˈðɛːʌɾʊl bi ʌ ˈlʌndʌn skwɛːʌɾ ɪn ˈmɛːɪtɑːɪm]
with London lilacs, whose brave light
[wɪð ˈlʌndʌn ˈlɑːɪlæks huz bɹɛːɪv lɑːɪt]
startles with coloured lamps the daytime,
[ˈstɑtʊlz wɪð ˈkʌlɔ(ʌ)d læmps ðʊ ˈdɛːɪtɑːɪm]
with sudden scented wings the night.
[wɪð ˈsʌdɛ(ɪ)n ˈsɛntɛ(ɪ)d wɪŋz ðʊ nɑːɪt]
A silent Square could but a lonely thrush
[ʌ ˈsɑːɪlɛnt skwɛːʌ kʊd bʌt ʌ ˈloːʊnlɪ θɾʌʃ]
on the lilacs bear to cease
[ɑn ðʊ ˈlɑːɪlæks bɛːʌ tu sis]
his song, and no sound else—
[hɪz sɑŋ ænd noːʊ sɑːʊnd ɛls]
save only the traffic of the heart at peace.
[sɛːɪv ˈoːʊnlɪ ðʊ ˈtɹæfɪk ʌv ðʊ hɑt æt pis]
And we will have a river painted
[ænd wi wɪl hæv ʌ ˈɹɪvʌ ˈpɛːɪntɛ(ɪ)d]
with the dawn's wistful stratagems
[wɪð ðʊ dɔnz ˈwɪstfʊl ˈstɹætʌdʒɛ(ɪ)mz]
of dusted gold, and night acquainted
[ʌv ˈdʌstɛ(ɪ)d goːʊld ænd nɑːɪt ʌˈkwɛːɪntɛ(ɪ)d]
with the long purples of the Thames.
[wɪð ðʊ lɑŋ ˈpɜpʊlz ʌv ðʊ tɛmz]
And we will have— oh yes! the gardens
[ænd wi wɪl hæv oːʊ jɛs ðʊ ˈgɑdɛ(ɪ)nz]
Kensington, Richmond Hill and Kew,
[ˈkɛnzɪŋtʌn ˈɹɪtʃmʌnd hɪl ænd kju]
and Hampton, where winter scolds, and pardons
[ænd ˈhæmptʌn ʍɛːʌ ˈwɪntʌ skoːʊldz ænd ˈpɑdʌnz]
the first white crocus breaking through.
[ðʊ fɜst ʍɑːɪt ˈkɹoːʊkʌs ˈbɹɛːɪkɪŋ θɾu]
And where the great their greatness squander,
[ænd ʍɛːʌ ðʊ gɹɛːɪt ðɛːʌ ˈgɹɛːɪtnɛ(ɪ)s ˈskwɑndʌ]
and while the wise their wisdom lose,
[ænd ʍɑːɪl ðʊ wɑːɪz ðɛːʌ ˈwɪzdʌm luz]
squirrels will leap, and deer will wander,
[ˈskwʊɾʊlz wɪl lip ænd dɪːʌ wɪl ˈwɑndʌ]
gracefully, down the avenues.
[ˈgɹɛːɪsfʊlɪ dɑːʊn ði ˈævɪnjuz]

9. Journey's End
[ˈdʒɜniz ɛnd]

What will they give me, when journey's done?
[ʍɑt wɪl ðɛːɪ gɪv mi ʍɛn ˈdʒɜnɪz dʌn]
Your own room to be quiet in, Son!
[jɔːɾ oːʊn ɹum tu bi ˈkwɑːɪɛ(ɪ)t ɪn sʌn]
Who shares it with me? There is none
[hu ʃɛːʌz ɪt wɪð mi ðɛːʌɾ ɪz nʌn]
shares that cool dormitory, Son!
[ʃɛːʌz ðæt kul ˈdɔmɪtɔɾɪ sʌn]
Who turns the sheets? There is but one,
[hu tɜnz ðʊ ʃits ðɛːʌɾ ɪz bʌt wʌn]
and no one needs to turn it, Son!
[ænd noːʊ wʌn nidz tu tɜn ɪt sʌn]

Who lights the candle? Ev'ryone
[hu laːɪts ðʊ 'kændʊl 'ɛvɹɪwʌn]
sleeps without candle all night, Son!
[slips wɪðˈaːʊt 'kændʊl ɔl naːɪt sʌn]
Who calls me after sleeping? Son!
[hu kɔlz mi 'aftʌ 'slipɪŋ sʌn]
You are not called when journey's done.
[ju ɑ nat kɔld ʍɛn 'ʤɜnɪz dʌn]

10. In the Street of Lost Time
[ɪn ðʊ stɹit ʌv last taːɪm]

Rest and have ease;
[ɹɛst ænd hæv iz]
Here are no more voyages;
[hiːʌɾ a noːʊ mɔːʌ 'vɔːɪæ(ɪ)ʤɛ(ɪ)z]
fold, fold your narrow pale hands;
[foːʊld foːʊld jɔːʌ 'næɾoːʊ pɛːɪl hændz]
and under the veil of night lie,
[ænd 'ʌndʌ ðʊ vɛːɪl ʌv naːɪt laːɪ]
as I have seen you
[æz ɑːɪ hæv sin ju]
lie in your deep hair;
[laːɪ ɪn jɔːʌ dip hɛːʌ]
but patiently now that new loves,
[bʌt 'pɛːɪʃɛntlɪ naːʊ ðæt nju lʌvz]
new days, have gone their ways.
[nju dɛːɪz hæv gan ðɛːʌ wɛːɪz]

11. Rhyme
[ɹaːɪm]

Rhyme
[ɹaːɪm]
in your clear chime
[ɪn jɔːʌ klɪːʌ ʧaːɪm]
we hear
[wi hɪːʌ]
ringing, far-off and clear,
['ɹɪŋɪŋ faɾ af ænd klɪːʌ]
in beauty's fairy granges
[ɪn 'bjutɪz 'fɛːʌɪ 'gɹɛːɪnʤɛ(ɪ)z]
at evensong the changes
[æt 'ivɛ(ɪ)nsaŋ ðʊ 'ʧɛːɪnʤɛ(ɪ)z]
and swells
[ænd swɛlz]
of her lost elfin-bells.
[ʌv hɜ last 'ɛlfɪn bɛlz]
You
[ju]
glimmering through,
['glɪmʌɾɪŋ θru]
astir,
[ʌ'stɜ]
wander a lamplighter,
['wandʌ ʌ 'læmplaːɪtʌ]

kindling that lamp and this
['kɪndlɪŋ ðæt læmp ænd ðɪs]
of long-quenched memories
[ʌv laŋ kwɛnʧt 'mɛmɔɹɪz]
with blaze
[wɪð blɛːɪz]
of their auto-da-fés.
[ʌv ðɛːʌɾ 'aːʊto da fe]
Numbers
['nʌmbʌz]
the soul remembers,
[ðʊ soːʊl ɹɪ'mɛmbʌz]
(and moved among them when
[ænd muvd ʌ'mʌŋ ðɛm ʍɛn]
the Sons of Morning sung them)
[ðʊ sʌnz ʌv 'mɔnɪŋ sʌŋ ðɛm]
you echo, while the dim
[ju 'ɛkoːʊ ʍaːɪl ðʊ dɪm]
shadow of Seraphim
['ʃædoːʊ ʌv 'sɛɾʌfɪm]
half floats
[haf floːʊts]
among your muted notes.
[ʌ'mʌŋ jɔːʌ 'mjutɛ(ɪ)d noːʊts]
Tamer
['tɛːɪmʌ]
of love's sweet grammar
[ʌv lʌvz swit 'gɹæmʌ]
you parse,
[ju pas]
and change, his nouns to stars,
[ænd ʧɛːɪnʤ hɪz naːʊnz tu staz]
his verbs you conjugate,
[hɪz vɜbz ju 'kanʤugɛːɪt]
so that they vanish straight
[soːʊ ðæt ðɛːɪ 'vænɪʃ stɹɛːɪt]
from time,
[fɹʌm taːɪm]
and lift a moonlit paradeigm.
[ænd lɪft ʌ 'munlɪt 'pæɾʌdaːɪm]
Rhyme
[ɹaːɪm]
by your clear chime
[baːɪ jɔːʌ klɪːʌ ʧaːɪm]
we climb,
[wi klaːɪm]
clean out of space and time,
[klin aːʊt ʌv spɛːɪs ænd taːɪm]
and the small earth behind us
[ænd ðʊ smɔl ɜθ bɪ'haːɪnd ʌs]
can neither lose nor find us,
[kæn 'naːɪðʌ luz nɔ faːɪnd ʌs]
set free in your eternity.
[sɛt fɹi ɪn jɔːʌɾ ɪ'tɜnɪtɪ]

12. Betelgeuse
[ˈbɛːɪtʊlgɛz]

On Betelgeuse
[ɑn ˈbɛːɪtʊlgɛz]
the gold leaves hang in golden aisles
[ðʊ goːʊld livz hæŋ ɪn ˈgoːʊldɛ(ɪ)n ɑːɪlz]
for twice a hundred million miles,
[fɔ twaːɪs ʌ ˈhʌndɹɛ(ɪ)d ˈmiljʌn mɑːɪlz]
and twice a hundred million years
[ænd twaːɪs ʌ ˈhʌndɹɛ(ɪ)d ˈmiljʌn jɪːʌz]
they golden hang and nothing stirs,
[ðɛːɪ ˈgoːʊldɛ(ɪ)n hæŋ ænd ˈnʌθɪŋ stɜz]
on Betelgeuse.
[ɑn ˈbɛːɪtʊlgɛz]
Space is a wind that does
[spɛːɪs ɪz ʌ wind ðæt dʌz]
not blow on Betelgeuse,
[nat bloːʊ ɑn ˈbɛːɪtʊlgɛz]
and time– oh time– is a bird,
[ænd tɑːɪm oːʊ tɑːɪm ɪz ʌ bɜd]
whose wings have never stirred
[huz wiŋz hæv ˈnɛvʌ stɜd]
the golden avenues of leaves
[ðʊ ˈgoːʊldɛ(ɪ)n ˈævɪnjuz ʌv livz]
on Betelgeuse. On Betelgeuse
[ɑn ˈbɛːɪtʊlgɛz ɑn ˈbɛːɪtʊlgɛz]
there is nothing that joys or grieves
[ðɛːɹ ɪz ˈnʌθɪŋ ðæt dʒɔːɪz ɔ grivz]
the unstirred multitude of leaves,
[ði ʌnˈstɜd ˈmʌltɪtjud ʌv livz]
nor ghost of evil or good haunts
[nɔ goːʊst ʌv ˈivɪ(ʊ)l ɔ gʊd hɔnts]
the gold multitude
[ðʊ goːʊld ˈmʌltɪtjud]
on Betelgeuse.
[ɑn ˈbɛːɪtʊlgɛz]
And birth they do not use
[ænd bɜθ ðɛːɪ du nat juz]
nor death on Betelgeuse,
[nɔ dɛθ ɑn ˈbɛːɪtʊlgɛz]
and the God, of whom we are
[ænd ðʊ gad ʌv hum wi ɑr]
infinite dust, is there
[ˈinfɪnɪt dʌst ɪz ðɛːʌr]
a single leaf of those
[ʌ ˈsiŋgʊl lif ʌv ðoːʊz]
gold leaves on Betelgeuse.
[goːʊld livz ɑn ˈbɛːɪtʊlgɛz]

 # Hundley, Richard (Am. 1931-2018)
Song Selections

"Ballad on Queen Anne's Death"
[ˈbælɪd ɑn kwin ænz dɛθ]
Anonymous

March with his wind hath struck a cedar tall
[mɑtʃ wɪð hɪz wind hæθ stɹʌk ʌ ˈsidʌ tɔl]
And weeping April mourns the cedars fall.
[ænd ˈwipɪŋ ˈɛːɪpɹɪ(ʊ)l mɔnz ðʌ ˈsidʌz fɔl]
And May intends no flow'rs her month shall bring
[ænd mɛːɪ ɪnˈtɛndz noːʊ flaːʊʌz hɜ mʌnθ ʃæl bɹɪŋ]
Since she must lose the flow'r of all the spring.
[sins ʃi mʌst luz ðʌ flaːʊʁ⁽ʳ⁾ ʌv ɔl ðʌ spɹɪŋ]
Thus March's wind hath caused April show'rs,
[ðʌs ˈmɑtʃɛ(ɪ)z wind hæθ kɔzd ˈɛːɪpɹɪ(ʊ)l ʃaːʊʌz]
And yet sad May must lose her flow'r of flow'rs.
[ænd jet sæd mɛːɪ mʌst luz hɜ flaːʊʁ⁽ʳ⁾ ʌv flaːʊʌz]

"Epitaph on a Wife"
[ˈɛpɪtæf ɑn ʌ wɑːɪf]
Anonymous

Here lies my wife
[hɪːʌ lɑːɪz mɑːɪ wɑːɪf]
Semanthia Proctor
[sɪˈmænθiʌ ˈpɹɑktɔ(ʌ)]
She had a cold
[ʃi hæd ʌ koːʊld]
And wouldn't doctor
[ænd ˈwʊdɛ(ɪ)nt ˈdɑktɔ(ʌ)]
She couldn't stay
[ʃi ˈkʊdɛ(ɪ)nt stɛːɪ]
She had to go–
[ʃi hæd tu goːʊ]
Praise God from whom all blessings flow.
[pɹɛːɪz gad fɹʌm hum ɔl ˈblɛsɪŋz floːʊ]

"Isaac Greentree (An Epitaph)"
[ˈɑːɪzɪk ˈgɹintɹi æn ˈɛpɪtæf]
Anonymous

In springtime comes the gentle rain,
[ɪn ˈspɹɪŋtɑːɪm kʌmz ðʌ ˈdʒɛntʊl ɹɛːɪn]
Soothing honey, sweet breeze, and sheltering sun.
[ˈsuðɪŋ ˈhʌni swit bɹiz ænd ˈʃɛltʌʁ⁽ʳ⁾ɪŋ sʌn]
Beneath these trees rising to the skies,
[bɪˈniθ ðiz tɹiz ˈɹɑːɪzɪŋ tu ðʌ skɑːɪz]
The planter of them, Isaac Greentree lies.
[ðʌ ˈplantʌʁ⁽ʳ⁾ ʌv ðɛm ˈɑːɪzɪk ˈgɹintɹi lɑːɪz]
The time shall come when these trees shall fall
[ðʌ tɑːɪm ʃæl kʌm ʍɛn ðiz tɹiz ʃæl fɔl]
And Isaac Greentree rise above them all.
[ænd ˈɑːɪzɪk ˈgɹintɹi ɹɑːɪz ʌ ˈbʌv ðɛm ɔl]

"Orpheus with His Lute"
[ˈɔʁfiʊs wɪθ hɪz ljut]
Shakespeare, William (Eng. 1564-1616)

Orpheus with his lute made trees,
[ˈɔfiʊs wɪð hɪz ljut meːɪd tɹiz]
And the mountain-tops that freeze,
[ænd ðʌ ˈmɑːʊntæ(ɪ)n tɑps ðæt fɹiz]
Bow themselves, when he did sing:
[boːʊ ðɛmˈsɛlvz ʍɛn hi dɪd sɪŋ]
To his music, plants and flowers
[tu hɪz ˈmjuzɪk plænts ænd flaːʊʌz]
Ever sprung; as sun and showers
[ˈɛvʌ spɹʌŋ æz sʌn ænd ʃaːʊʌz]
There had made a lasting spring.
[ðɛːʌ hæd meːɪd ʌ ˈlæstɪŋ spɹɪŋ]
Everything that heard him play,
[ˈɛvɹɪθɪŋ ðæt hɜd hɪm pleːɪ]
Even the billows of the sea,
[ˈivɛ(ɪ)n ðʌ ˈbɪloːʊz ʌv ðʌ si]
Hung their heads, and then lay by.
[hʌŋ ðɛːʌ hɛdz ænd ðɛn lɛːɪ baːɪ]
In sweet music is such art:
[ɪn swit ˈmjuzɪk ɪz sʌtʃ at]
Killing care and grief of heart
[ˈkɪlɪŋ kɛːʌʁ(ʳ) ænd gɹ(ʳ)if ʌv hat]
Fall asleep, or, hearing, die.
[fɔl ʌˈslip ɔ ˈhiːʌʁ(ʳ)ɪŋ daːɪ]

"Strings in the Earth and Air"
[stɹɪŋz ɪn ði ɜθ ænd ɛːʁ]
Joyce, James (Ir. 1882-1941)

Strings in the earth and air
[stɹɪŋz ɪn ði ɜθ ænd ɛːʌ]
Make music sweet;
[mɛːɪk ˈmjuzɪk swit]
Strings by the river where
[stɹɪŋz baːɪ ðʌ ˈɹɪvʌ ʍɛːʌ]
The willows meet.
[ðʌ ˈwɪloːʊz mit]
There's music along the river
[ðɛːʌz ˈmjuzɪk ʌˈlaŋ ðʌ ˈɹɪvʌ]
For love wanders there,
[fɔ lʌv ˈwandʌz ðɛːʌ]
Pale flowers on his mantle,
[pɛːɪl flaːʊʌz an hɪz ˈmæntʊl]
Dark leaves on his hair.
[dak livz an hɪz hɛːʌ]
All softly playing,
[ɔl ˈsaftlɪ ˈpleːɪɪŋ]
With head to the music bent,
[wɪð hɛd tu ðʌ ˈmjuzɪk bɛnt]
And fingers straying, Upon an instrument.
[ænd ˈfɪŋgʌz ˈstɹɛːɪɪŋ ʌˈpan æn ˈɪnstɹ(ʳ)u(ʌ)mɛnt]

"Sweet Suffolk Owl"
[swit ˈsʌfʌk aːʊl]
Vautor, Thomas (Eng. 1590-1625)

Sweet Suffolk owl, so trimly dight,
[swit ˈsʌfʌk aːʊl soːʊ ˈtɹɪmlɪ daːɪt]
With feathers like a lady bright,
[wɪð ˈfɛðʌz laːɪk ʌ ˈlɛːɪdɪ bɹaːɪt]
Thou singest alone, sitting by night,
[ðaːʊ ˈsɪŋɛ(ɪ)st ʌˈloːʊn ˈsɪtɪŋ baːɪ naːɪt]
Te whit, te whoo! Te whit, te whoo!
[tʌ ʍɪt tʌ ʍu tʌ ʍɪt tʌ ʍu]
Thy note that forth so freely rolls
[ðaːɪ noːʊt ðæt fɔθ soːʊ ˈfɹilɪ ɹoːʊlz]
With shrill command the mouse controls
[wɪð ʃɹɪl kʌˈmænd ðʌ maːʊs kʌnˈtɹoːʊlz]
And singest a dirge for dying souls,
[ænd ˈsɪŋɛ(ɪ)st ʌ dɜdʒ fɔ ˈdaːɪɪŋ soːʊlz]
Te whit, te whoo! Te whit, te whoo!
[tʌ ʍɪt tʌ ʍu tʌ ʍɪt tʌ ʍu]

"The Astronomers (An Epitaph)"
[ði ʌˈstɹɑnʌmʁz æn ˈɛpɪtæf]
Anonymous

Susan Campbell eighteen sixty-three nineteen ten
[ˈsuzæ(ʌ)n ˈkæmbʊl ˈɛːɪtin ˈsɪkstɪ θɹi ˈnaːɪntin tɛn]
Brian Campbell eighteen sixty-two nineteen nine
[ˈbɹaːɪæ(ʌ)n ˈkæmbʊl ˈɛːɪtin ˈsɪkstɪ tu ˈnaːɪntin naːɪn]
Astronomers, We have loved the stars too deeply
[ʌˈstɹɑnʌmʌz wi hæv lʌvd ðʌ staz tu ˈdiplɪ]
To be afraid of the night.
[tu bi ʌˈfɹɛːɪd ʌv ðʌ naːɪt]

"Will There Really Be a Morning" (see Gordon)

"When Children Are Playing Alone on the Green"
[ʍɛn ˈtʃɪldɹɪn aʁ ˈpleːɪɪŋ ʌˈloːʊn an ðʌ gɹin]
Stevenson, Robert Louis (Sc. 1850-1894)

When children are playing alone on the green,
[ʍɛn ˈtʃɪldɹɛ(ɪ)n a ˈpleːɪɪŋ ʌˈloːʊn an ðʌ gɹin]
In comes a playmate that never was seen.
[ɪn kʌmz ʌ ˈplɛːɪmɛːɪt ðæt ˈnɛvʌ waz sin]
When children are happy and lonely and good,
[ʍɛn ˈtʃɪldɹɛ(ɪ)n a ˈhæpɪ ænd ˈloːʊnlɪ ænd gʊd]
The friend of the children comes out of the wood.
[ðʌ fɹɛnd ʌv ðʌ ˈtʃɪldɹɛ(ɪ)n kʌmz aːʊt ʌv ðʌ wʊd]
Nobody heard him and nobody saw,
[ˈnoːʊbadɪ hɜd hɪm ænd ˈnoːʊbadɪ sɔ]
His is a picture you never could draw.
[hɪz ɪz ʌ ˈpɪktʃʊ(ʌ) ju ˈnɛvʌ kʊd dɹɔ]
But he's sure to be present, abroad or at home,
[bʌt hiz ʃʊːʌ tu bi ˈpɹɛzɛnt ʌˈbɹɔd ɔʁ(ʳ) æt hoːʊm]
When children are happy and playing alone.
[ʍɛn ˈtʃɪldɹɛ(ɪ)n a ˈhæpɪ ænd ˈpleːɪɪŋ ʌˈloːʊn]

I

 Ireland, John (Eng. 1879-1962)

Song Selections

"I Have Twelve Oxen"
[ɑːɪ hæv twɛlv ˈɑksɪn]
Anonymous (early 16th century)

I have twelve oxen that be fair and brown,
[ɑːɪ hæv twɛlv ˈɑksɪn ðæt bi fɛːʌr ænd bɪɑːʊn]
And they go a-grazing down by the town.
[ænd ðɛːɪ goːʊ ʌ ˈgɪɛːɪzɪŋ dɑːʊn bɑːɪ ðʊ tɑːʊn]
With hey! with ho! with hey! with ho!
[wɪð hɛːɪ wɪð hoːʊ wɪð hɛːɪ wɪð hoːʊ]
Sawest not you mine oxen, you little pretty boy?
[ˈsɔɛ(ɪ)st nɑt ju mɑːɪn ˈɑksɪn ju ˈlɪtʊl ˈpɪɪtɪ bɔːɪ]
I have twelve oxen, they be fair and white,
[ɑːɪ hæv twɛlv ˈɑksɪn ðɛːɪ bi fɛːʌr ænd ʍɑːɪt]
And they go a-grazing down by the dyke.
[ænd ðɛːɪ goːʊ ʌ ˈgɪɛːɪzɪŋ dɑːʊn bɑːɪ ðʊ dɑːɪk]
With hey! with ho! with hey! with ho!
[wɪð hɛːɪ wɪð hoːʊ wɪð hɛːɪ wɪð hoːʊ]
Sawest not you mine oxen, you little pretty boy?
[ˈsɔɛ(ɪ)st nɑt ju mɑːɪn ˈɑksɪn ju ˈlɪtʊl ˈpɪɪtɪ bɔːɪ]
I have twelve oxen, and they be fair and black,
[ɑːɪ hæv twɛlv ˈɑksɪn ænd ðɛːɪ bi fɛːʌr ænd blæk]
And they go a-grazing down by the lake.
[ænd ðɛːɪ goːʊ ʌ ˈgɪɛːɪzɪŋ dɑːʊn bɑːɪ ðʊ lɛːɪk]
With hey! with ho! with hey! with ho!
[wɪð hɛːɪ wɪð hoːʊ wɪð hɛːɪ wɪð hoːʊ]
Sawest not you mine oxen, you little pretty boy?
[ˈsɔɛ(ɪ)st nɑt ju mɑːɪn ˈɑksɪn ju ˈlɪtʊl ˈpɪɪtɪ bɔːɪ]
I have twelve oxen, and they be fair and red,
[ɑːɪ hæv twɛlv ˈɑksɪn ænd ðɛːɪ bi fɛːʌr ænd ɪɛd]
And they go a-grazing down by the mead.
[ænd ðɛːɪ goːʊ ʌ ˈgɪɛːɪzɪŋ dɑːʊn bɑːɪ ðʊ mid]
With hey! with ho! with hey! with ho!
[wɪð hɛːɪ wɪð hoːʊ wɪð hɛːɪ wɪð hoːʊ]
Sawest not you mine oxen, you little pretty boy?
[ˈsɔɛ(ɪ)st nɑt ju mɑːɪn ˈɑksɪn ju ˈlɪtʊl ˈpɪɪtɪ bɔːɪ]

"If There Were Dreams to Sell"
[ɪf ðɛːʌ wɜ dɪɪmz tu sɛl]
Beddoes, Thomas Lovell (Eng. 1803-1849)

If there were dreams to sell,
[ɪf ðɛːʌ wɜ dɪɪmz tu sɛl]
What would you buy?
[ʍɑt wʊd ju bɑːɪ]
Some cost a passing bell;
[sʌm kɑst ʌ ˈpɑsɪŋ bɛl]

Some a light sigh,
[sʌm ʌ lɑːɪt sɑːɪ]
That shakes from Life's fresh crown
[ðæt ʃɛːɪks fɪʌm lɑːɪfs fɪɛʃ kɪɑːʊn]
Only a rose-leaf down.
[ˈoːʊnlɪ ʌ roːʊz lif dɑːʊn]
If there were dreams to sell,
[ɪf ðɛːʌ wɜ dɪɪmz tu sɛl]
Merry and sad to tell,
[ˈmɛɪɪ ænd sæd tu tɛl]
And the crier rang the bell,
[ænd ðʊ ˈkɪɑːɪʌ ræŋ ðʊ bɛl]
What would you buy?
[ʍɑt wʊd ju bɑːɪ]
A cottage lone and still,
[ʌ ˈkɑtæ(ɪ)dʒ loːʊn ænd stɪl]
With bow'rs nigh,
[wɪð ˈbɑːʊʌz nɑːɪ]
Shadowy, my woes to still,
[ˈʃædoːʊɪ mɑːɪ woːʊz tu stɪl]
Until I die.
[ʌnˈtɪl ɑːɪ dɑːɪ]
Such pearl from Life's fresh crown,
[sʌtʃ pɜl fɪʌm lɑːɪfs fɪɛʃ kɪɑːʊn]
Fain would I shake me down.
[fɛːɪn wʊd ɑːɪ ʃɛːɪk mi dɑːʊn]
Were dreams to have at will,
[wɜ dɪɪmz tu hæv æt wɪl]
This best would heal my ill,
[ðɪs bɛst wʊd hil mɑːɪ ɪl]
This would I buy.
[ðɪs wʊd ɑːɪ bɑːɪ]

"My True Love Hath My Heart"
[mɑːɪ tɪu lʌv hæθ mɑːɪ hɑt]
Sidney, Philip Sir (Eng. 1554-1586)

My true love hath my heart, and I have his,
[mɑːɪ tru lʌv hæθ mɑːɪ hɑt ænd ɑːɪ hæv hɪz]
By just exchange one for the other giv'n:
[bɑːɪ dʒʌst ɪksˈtʃɛːɪndʒ wʌn fɔ ðɪ ˈʌðʌ ˈgɪvɛ(ɪ)n]
I hold his dear, and mine he cannot miss,
[ɑːɪ hoːʊld hɪz dɪːʌ ænd mɑːɪn hi kæˈnɑt mɪs]
There never was a better bargain driv'n:
[ðɛːʌ ˈnɛvʌ wɑz ʌ ˈbɛtʌ ˈbɑgæ(ɪ)n ˈdɪɪvɪn]
My true love hath my heart, and I have his.
[mɑːɪ tru lʌv hæθ mɑːɪ hɑt ænd ɑːɪ hæv hɪz]
His heart in me keeps him and me in one,
[hɪz hɑt ɪn mi kips hɪm ænd mi ɪn wʌn]
My heart in him his thoughts and senses guides:
[mɑːɪ hɑt ɪn hɪm hɪz θɔts ænd ˈsɛnsɛ(ɪ)z gɑːɪdz]
He loves my heart, for once it was his own,
[hi lʌvz mɑːɪ hɑt fɔ wʌns ɪt wɑz hɪz oːʊn]
I cherish his because in me it bides:
[ɑːɪ ˈtʃɛɪʃ hɪz bɪˈkɔz ɪn mi ɪt bɑːɪdz]

"Sea Fever"
[si ˈfivʌ]
Masefield, John (Eng. 1878-1967)

I must go down to the seas again,
[ɑːɪ mʌst goːʊ daːʊn tu ðʊ siz ʌˈgɛːɪn]
to the lonely sea and the sky,
[tu ðʊ ˈloːʊnlɪ si ænd ðʊ skaːɪ]
And all I ask is a tall ship and a star to steer her by,
[ænd ɔl ɑːɪ ask ɪz ʌ tɔl ʃɪp ænd ʌ stɑ tu stiːʌ hɜ baːɪ]
And the wheel's kick and the wind's song
[ænd ðʊ ʍilz kɪk ænd ðʊ wɪndz saŋ]
and the white sail's shaking,
[ænd ðʊ ʍaːɪt sɛːɪlz ˈʃɛːɪkɪŋ]
And a grey mist on the sea's face
[ænd ʌ gɹɛːɪ mɪst an ðʊ siz fɛːɪs]
and a grey dawn breaking.
[ænd ʌ gɹɛːɪ dɔn ˈbɹɛːɪkɪŋ]
I must go down to the seas again,
[ɑːɪ mʌst goːʊ daːʊn tu ðʊ siz ʌˈgɛːɪn]
for the call of the running tide
[fɔ ðʊ kɔl ʌv ðʊ ˈɾʌnɪŋ taːɪd]
Is a wild call and a clear call, that may not be denied;
[ɪz ʌ waːɪld kɔl ænd ʌ klɪːʌ kɔl ðæt mɛːɪ nat bi dɪˈnaːɪd]
And all I ask is a windy day
[ænd ɔl ɑːɪ ask ɪz ʌ ˈwɪndɪ dɛːɪ]
with the white clouds flying,
[wɪð ðʊ ʍaːɪt klaːʊdz ˈflaːɪŋ]
And the flung spray and the blown spume,
[ænd ðʊ flʌŋ spɹɛːɪ ænd ðʊ bloːʊn spjum]
and the seagulls crying.
[ænd ðʊ ˈsigʌlz ˈkɾaːɪŋ]
I must go down to the seas again,
[ɑːɪ mʌst goːʊ daːʊn tu ðʊ siz ʌˈgɛːɪn]
to the vagrant gypsy life,
[tu ðʊ ˈvɛːɪgɹæ(ɪ)nt ˈdʒɪpsɪ laːɪf]
To the gull's way and the whale's way,
[tu ðʊ gʌlz wɛːɪ ænd ðʊ ʍɛːɪlz wɛːɪ]
where the wind's like a whetted knife;
[ʍɛːʌ ðʊ wɪndz laːɪk ʌ ˈʍɛtɛ(ɪ)d naːɪf]
And all I ask is a merry yarn
[ænd ɔl ɑːɪ ask ɪz ʌ ˈmɛɾɪ jɑn]
from a laughing fellow-rover,
[fɹʌm ʌ ˈlafɪŋ ˈfɛloːʊ ˈroːʊvʌ]
And quiet sleep and a sweet dream
[ænd ˈkwaːɪɛ(ɪ)t slip ænd ʌ swit dɹim]
when the long trick's over.
[ʍɛn ðʊ laŋ tɹɪks ˈoːʊvʌ]

"Spring Sorrow"
[spɹɪŋ ˈsaʁoːʊ]
Brooke, Rupert (Eng. 1887-1915)

All suddenly the wind comes soft,
[ɔl ˈsʌdɛ(ɪ)nlɪ ðʊ wɪnd kʌmz saft]

And Spring is here again;
[ænd spɹɪŋ ɪz hɪːʌɾ ʌˈgɛːɪn]
And the hawthorn quickens with buds of green,
[ænd ðʊ ˈhɔθɔn ˈkwɪkɛ(ɪ)nz wɪð bʌdz ʌv gɹin]
And my heart with buds of pain.
[ænd maːɪ hɑt wɪð bʌdz ʌv pɛːɪn]
My heart all Winter lay so numb,
[maːɪ hɑt ɔl ˈwɪntʌ lɛːɪ soːʊ nʌm]
The earth so dead and frore,
[ði ɜθ soːʊ dɛd ænd fɹɔːʌ]
That I never thought the Spring would come,
[ðæt ɑːɪ ˈnɛvʌ θɔt ðʊ spɹɪŋ wʊd kʌm]
Or my heart wake any more.
[ɔ maːɪ hɑt wɛːɪk ˈɛnɪ mɔːʌ]
But Winter's broken and earth has woken,
[bʌt ˈwɪntʌz ˈbɹoːʊkɛ(ɪ)n ænd ɜθ hæz ˈwoːʊkɛ(ɪ)n]
And the small birds cry again;
[ænd ðʊ smɔl bɜdz kɹaːɪ ʌˈgɛːɪn]
And the hawthorn hedge puts forth its buds,
[ænd ðʊ ˈhɔθɔn hɛdʒ pʊts fɔθ ɪts bʌdz]
And my heart puts forth its pain.
[ænd maːɪ hɑt pʊts fɔθ ɪts pɛːɪn]

Ives, Charles Edward
(Am. 1874-1954)

Memories (Song Cycle)
[ˈmɛmɔʁiz]
Ives, Charles Edward (Am. 1874-1954)

A. Very Pleasant
[ˈvɛʁɪ ˈplɛzɪnt]

We're sitting in the opera house;
[wɪːʌ ˈsɪtɪŋ ɪn ði ˈapɹa haːʊs]
We're waiting for the curtain to arise
[wɪːʌ ˈwɛːɪtɪŋ fɔ ðʌ ˈkɜtæ(ɪ)n tu ʌˈʁ⁽ʳ⁾aːɪz]
with wonders for our eyes;
[wɪð ˈwʌndʌz fɔʁ⁽ʳ⁾ aːʊʌʁ⁽ʳ⁾ aːɪz]
We're feeling pretty gay,
[wɪːʌ ˈfilɪŋ ˈpɹɪtɪ gɛːɪ]
and well we may,
[ænd wɛl wi mɛːɪ]
"O, Jimmy, look!" I say,
[oːʊ ˈdʒɪmɪ lʊk ɑːɪ sɛːɪ]
"The band is tuning up
[ðʌ bænd ɪz ˈtjunɪŋ ʌp]
and soon will start to play."
[ænd sun wɪl stat tu plɛːɪ]
We whistle and we hum,
[wi ˈʍɪsʊl ænd wi hʌm]
Beat time with the drum.
[bit taːɪm wɪð ðʌ dɹʌm]

We're sitting in the opera house,
[wiːʌ ˈsɪtɪŋ ɪn ði ˈapɹa haːʊs]
awaiting for the curtain to rise
[ʌˈweːɪtɪŋ fɔ ðʌ ˈkɜtæ(ɪ)n tu ɹɑːɪz]
with wonders for our eyes,
[wɪð ˈwʌndʌz fɔʁ⁽ʳ⁾ ɑːʊʌʁ⁽ʳ⁾ ɑːɪz]
a feeling of expectancy,
[ʌ ˈfilɪŋ ʌv ɪkˈspɛktæ(ɪ)nsɪ]
a certain kind of ecstasy,
[ʌ ˈsɜtæ(ɪ)n kɑːɪnd ʌv ˈɛkstʌsɪ]
expectancy and ecstasy– Sh's's's.
[ɪkˈspɛktæ(ɪ)nsɪ ænd ˈɛkstʌsɪ ʃ]
Curtain!
[ˈkɜtæ(ɪ)n]

B. Rather Sad
[ˈɹæðʁ sæd]

From the street a strain on my ear doth fall,
[fɹʌm ðʌ stɹit ʌ stɹeːɪn an maːɪ iːʌ dʌθ fɔl]
A tune as threadbare as that "old red shawl,"
[ʌ tjun æz ˈθɹɛdˌbeːʌʁ⁽ʳ⁾ æz ðæt oːʊld ɹɛd ʃɔl]
It is tattered, it is torn,
[ɪt ɪz ˈtætʌd ɪt ɪz tɔn]
it shows signs of being worn,
[ɪt ʃoːʊz saːɪnz ʌv ˈbiɪŋ wɔn]
It's the tune my uncle hummed from early morn,
[ɪts ðʌ tjun maːɪ ˈʌŋkʊl hʌmd fɹʌm ˈɜlɪ mɔn]
'Twas a common little thing and kind 'a sweet,
[twaz ʌ ˈkamʌn ˈlɪtʊl θɪŋ ænd kɑːɪnd ʌ swit]
But 'twas sad and seemed to slow up both his feet;
[bʌt twaz sæd ænd simd tu sloːʊ ʌp boːʊθ hɪz fit]
I can see him shuffling down
[ɑːɪ kæn si hɪm ˈʃʌflɪŋ daːʊn]
to the barn or to the town, a humming.
[tu ðʌ ban ɔ tu ðʌ taːʊn ʌ ˈhʌmɪŋ]

Song Selections

"At the River" (see Copland)

"Charlie Rutlage" (Cowboy Songs)
[ˈtʃaʁli ˈɹʌtlɪdʒ]
Folk songs collected by John Avery Lomax
(Am. 1867-1948)

Another good cowpuncher has gone to meet his fate,
[ʌˈnʌðʌ gʊd ˈkaːʊpʌntʃʌ hæz gan tu mit hɪz feːɪt]
I hope he'll find a resting place,
[ɑːɪ hoːʊp hil faːɪnd ʌ ˈɹɛstɪŋ pleːɪs]
within the golden gate.
[wɪðˈɪn ðʌ ˈgoːʊldɪn geːɪt]
Another place is vacant
[ʌˈnʌðʌ pleːɪs ɪz ˈveːɪkæ(ɪ)nt]
on the ranch of the XIT,
[an ðʌ ɹæntʃ ʌv ði ɛks ɑːɪ ti]

'Twill be hard to find another that's liked as well as he.
[twɪl bi had tu faːɪnd ʌˈnʌðʌ ðæts laːɪkt æz wɛl æz hi]
The first that died was Kid White,
[ðʌ fɜst ðæt daːɪd waz kɪd ʍaːɪt]
a man both tough and brave,
[ʌ mæn boːʊθ tʌf ænd bɹeːɪv]
While Charlie Rutlage makes the third
[ʍaːɪl ˈtʃaɫɪ ˈɹʌtlæ(ɪ)dʒ meːɪks ðʌ θɜd]
to be sent to his grave,
[tu bi sɛnt tu hɪz gɹeːɪv]
Caused by a cowhorse falling,
[kɔzd baːɪ ʌ ˈkaːʊhɔs ˈfɔlɪŋ]
While running after stock;
[ʍaːɪl ˈɹʌnɪŋ ˈæftʌ stak]
'Twas on the spring round up,
[twaz an ðʌ spɹɪŋ ɹaːʊnd ʌp]
A place where death men mock,
[ʌ pleːɪs ʍɛːʌ dɛθ mɛn mak]
He went forward one morning
[hi wɛnt ˈfɔwʊd ʍʌn ˈmɔnɪŋ]
on a circle through the hills,
[an ʌ ˈsɜkʊl θɹu ðʌ hɪlz]
He was gay and full of glee,
[hi waz geːɪ ænd fʊl ʌv gli]
and free from earthly ills;
[ænd fɹi fɹʌm ˈɜθlɪ ɪlz]
But when it came to finish up the work
[bʌt ʍɛn ɪt keːɪm tu ˈfɪnɪʃ ʌp ðʌ wɜk]
on which he went,
[an ʍɪtʃ hi wɛnt]
Nothing came back from him;
[ˈnʌθɪŋ keːɪm bæk fɹʌm hɪm]
his time on earth was spent.
[hɪz taːɪm an ɜθ waz spɛnt]
'Twas as he rode the round up,
[twaz æz hi ɹoːʊd ðʌ ɹaːʊnd ʌp]
an XIT turned back to the herd;
[æn ɛks ɑːɪ ti tɜnd bæk tu ðʌ hɜd]
Poor Charlie shoved him in again,
[pʊːʌ ˈtʃalɪ ʃʌvd hɪm ɪn ʌˈgɛn]
his cutting horse he spurred;
[hɪz ˈkʌtɪŋ hɔs hi spɜd]
Another turned;
[ʌˈnʌðʌ tɜnd]
at that moment his horse the creature spied
[æt ðæt ˈmoːʊmɛnt hɪz hɔs ðʌ ˈkɹiːtʃʊ(ʌ) spaːɪd]
and turned and fell with him,
[ænd tɜnd ænd fɛl wɪð hɪm]
beneath poor Charlie died.
[bɪˈniθ pʊːʌ ˈtʃalɪ daːɪd]
His relations in Texas his face never more will see,
[hɪz ɹɪˈleːɪʃʌnz ɪn ˈtɛksʌs hɪz feːɪs ˈnɛvʌ mɔːʌ wɪl si]
But I hope he'll meet his loved ones beyond in eternity.
[bʌt ɑːɪ hoːʊp hil mit hɪz lʌvd wʌnz bɪˈjand ɪn ɪˈtɜnɪtɪ]
I hope he'll meet his parents,
[ɑːɪ hoːʊp hil mit hɪz ˈpæʁ⁽ʳ⁾ɛnts]

will meet them face to face,
[wɪl mit ðɛm fɛːɪs tu fɛːɪs]
And that they'll grasp him by the right hand
[ænd ðæt ðɛːɪl gɹæsp hɪm baːɪ ðʌ ɹaːɪt hænd]
at the shining throne of grace.
[æt ðʌ ˈʃaːɪnɪŋ θɹoːʊn ʌv gɹɛːɪs]

"In Flanders Field" (Three Songs of the War)
[ɪn ˈflændɛz fild]
McCrae, John (Ca. 1872-1918)

In Flanders fields the poppies blow,
[ɪn ˈflændʌz fildz ðʌ ˈpɑpɪz bloːʊ]
Between the crosses, row on row
[bɪˈtwin ðʌ ˈkɹɑsɛ(ɪ)z ɹoːʊ ɑn ɹoːʊ]
That mark our place; And in the sky
[ðæt mɑk aːʊʌ plɛːɪs ænd ɪn ðʌ skaːɪ]
the larks still bravely singing fly,
[ðʌ lɑks stɪl ˈbɹɛːɪvlɪ ˈsɪŋɪŋ flaːɪ]
Scarce heard amidst the guns below.
[skɛːʌs hɜd ʌˈmɪdst ðʌ gʌnz bɪˈloːʊ]
We are the Dead. Short days ago
[wi ɑ ðʌ dɛd ʃɔt dɛːɪz ʌˈgoːʊ]
we lived, felt dawn, saw sunset glow,
[wi lɪvd fɛlt dɔn sɔ ˈsʌnsɛt gloːʊ]
Loved and were loved, and now we lie
[lʌvd ænd wɜ lʌvd ænd naːʊ wi laːɪ]
In Flanders fields.
[ɪn ˈflændʌz fildz]
Take up our quarrel with the foe!
[tɛːɪk ʌp aːʊʌ ˈkwɔʁ(ʳ)ʊl wɪð ðʌ foːʊ]
To you from falling hands we throw
[tu ju fɹʌm ˈfɔlɪŋ hændz wi θɹoːʊ]
the torch. Be yours to hold it high.
[ðʌ tɔtʃ bi jɔːʌz tu hoːʊld ɪt haːɪ]
If ye break faith with us who die
[ɪf ji bɹɛːɪk fɛːɪθ wɪð ʌs hu daːɪ]
We shall not sleep though the poppies grow
[wi ʃæl nɑt slip ðoːʊ ðʌ ˈpɑpɪz gɹoːʊ]
In Flanders fields.
[ɪn ˈflændʌz fildz]

"In the Alley" (Five Street Songs)
[ɪn ði ˈæli]
Ives, Charles Edward (Am. 1874-1954)

On my way to work one summer day,
[ɑn maːɪ wɛːɪ tu wɜk wʌn ˈsʌmʌ dɛːɪ]
Just off the main highway,
[dʒʌst ɑf ðʌ mɛːɪn ˈhaːɪwɛːɪ]
Through a window in an alley
[θɹu ʌ ˈwɪndoːʊ ɪn æn ˈæli]
smiled a lass, her name was Sally,
[smaːɪld ʌ læs hɜ nɛːɪm wɑz ˈsæli]
O could it be!
[oːʊ kʊd ɪt bi]

O could it be she smiled on me!
[oːʊ kʊd ɪt bi ʃi smaːɪld ɑn mi]
All that day, before my eyes,
[ɔl ðæt dɛːɪ bɪˈfɔːʌ maːɪ aːɪz]
amidst the busy whirl,
[ʌˈmɪdst ðʌ ˈbɪzi ʍɜl]
came the image of that lovely Irish girl,
[kɛːɪm ði ˈɪmæ(ɪ)dʒ ʌv ðæt ˈlʌvli ˈaːɪʁ(ʳ)ɪʃ gɜl]
And hopes would seem to rise,
[ænd hoːʊps wʊd sim tu ɹaːɪz]
as the clouds rise in the skies,
[æz ðʌ klaːʊdz ɹaːɪz ɪn ðʌ skaːɪz]
When I thought of her and those beaming eyes.
[ʍɛn aːɪ θɔt ʌv hɜ ænd ðoːʊz ˈbimɪŋ aːɪz]
So that evening, dressed up smart and neat,
[soːʊ ðæt ˈivnɪŋ dɹɛst ʌp smat ænd nit]
I wandered down her street,
[aːɪ ˈwandʌd daːʊn hɜ stɹit]
At the corner of the alley
[æt ðʌ ˈkɔnʌʁ(ʳ) ʌv ði ˈæli]
was another man with Sally,
[wɑz ʌˈnʌðʌ mæn wɪð ˈsæli]
and my eyes grew dim,
[ænd maːɪ aːɪz gɹ(ʳ)u dɪm]
She smiles on him, and only on him!
[ʃi smaːɪlz ɑn hɪm ænd ˈoːʊnli ɑn hɪm]

"In the Mornin'"
[ɪn ðʌ ˈmɔʁnɪn]
(Eleven Songs and Two Harmonizations)
Anonymous

In the mornin' when I rise,
[ɪn ðʌ ˈmɔnɪn ʍɛn aːɪ ɹaːɪz]
Give me Jesus!
[gɪv mi ˈdʒizʌs]
You can have all the world, but
[ju kæn hæv ɔl ðʌ wɜld bʌt]
Give me Jesus!
[gɪv mi ˈdʒizʌs]
'Twixt the cradle and the grave,
[twɪkst ðʌ ˈkɹɛːɪdʊl ænd ðʌ gɹ(ʳ)ɛːɪv]
Give me Jesus!
[gɪv mi ˈdʒizʌs]
You can have all the world, but
[ju kæn hæv ɔl ðʌ wɜld bʌt]
Give me Jesus!
[gɪv mi ˈdʒizʌs]

"Serenity"
[sɪˈʁɛnɪti]
Whittier, John Greenleaf (Am. 1807-1892)

O, Sabbath rest of Galilee!
[oːʊ ˈsæbæ(ʌ)θ ɹɛst ʌv ˈgæli̩li]

O, calm of hills above,
[oːʊ kɑm ʌv hɪlz ʌˈbʌv]
Where Jesus knelt to share with Thee,
[ʍɛːʌ ˈdʒizʌs nɛlt tu ʃɛːʌ wɪð ði]
the silence of eternity
[ðʌ ˈsɑːɪlɛ(ɪ)ns ʌv ɪˈtɜnɪti]
Interpreted by love.
[ɪnˈtɜpɹɛ(ɪ)tɛ(ɪ)d bɑːɪ lʌv]
Drop Thy still dews of quietness,
[dɹɑp ðɑːɪ stɪl djuz ʌv ˈkwɑːɪɛ(ɪ)tnɛ(ɪ)s]
till all our strivings cease:
[tɪl ɔl ɑːʊʌ ˈstɹɑːɪvɪŋz sis]
Take from our souls the strain and stress,
[tɛːɪk fɹʌm ɑːʊʌ soːʊlz ðʌ stɹɛːɪn ænd stɹɛs]
and let our ordered lives confess,
[ænd lɛt ɑːʊʌʁ⁽ʳ⁾ ˈɔdʌd lɑːɪvz kʌnˈfɛs]
the beauty of thy peace.
[ðʌ ˈbjuti ʌv ðɑːɪ pis]

"Slow March"
[sloːʊ mɑʁtʃ]
Ives, Charles Edward (Am. 1874-1954)

One evening just at sunset we laid him in the grave;
[wʌn ˈivnɪŋ dʒʌst æt ˈsʌnsɛt wi lɛːɪd hɪm ɪn ðʌ gɹɛːɪv]
Although a humble animal
[ɔlˈðoːʊ ʌ ˈhʌmbʊl ˈænɪmʊl]
his heart was true and brave.
[hɪz hɑt wɑz tɹ⁽ʳ⁾u ænd bɹɛːɪv]
All the family joined us, in solemn march and slow,
[ɔl ðʌ ˈfæmlɪ dʒɔːɪnd ʌs ɪn ˈsɑlʌm mɑtʃ ænd sloːʊ]
from the garden place beneath the trees
[fɹʌm ðʌ ˈgɑdɛ(ɪ)n plɛːɪs bɪˈniθ ðʌ tɹiz]
and where the sunflowers grow.
[ænd ʍɛːʌ ðʌ ˈsʌnflɑːʊʌz gɹoːʊ]

"The Children's Hour"
[ðʌ ˈtʃɪldɹɪnz ɑːʊʁ]
Longfellow, Henry Wadsworth (Am. 1807-1882)

Between the dark and the daylight,
[bɪˈtwin ðʌ dak ænd ðʌ ˈdɛːɪlɑːɪt]
When the night is beginning to lower,
[ʍɛn ðʌ nɑːɪt ɪz bɪˈgɪnɪŋ tu ˈloːʊʌ]
Comes a pause in the days occupations,
[kʌmz ʌ pɔz ɪn ðʌ dɛːɪz ɑkjuˈpɛːɪʃʌnz]
That is known as Children's Hour.
[ðæt ɪz noːʊn æz ˈtʃɪldɹɛ(ɪ)nz ɑːʊʌ]
I hear in the chamber above me
[ɑːɪ hɪːʌʁ⁽ʳ⁾ ɪn ðʌ ˈtʃɛːɪmbʌʁ⁽ʳ⁾ ʌˈbʌv mi]
The patter of little feet
[ðʌ ˈpætʌʁ⁽ʳ⁾ ʌv ˈlɪtʊl fit]
The sound of a door that is opened
[ðʌ sɑːʊnd ʌv ʌ dɔːʌ ðæt ɪz ˈoːʊpɛ(ɪ)nd]
and voices soft and sweet.
[ænd ˈvɔːɪsɛ(ɪ)z saft ænd swit]

From my study I see in the lamplight
[fɹʌm mɑːɪ ˈstʌdɪ ɑːɪ si ɪn ðʌ ˈlæmplɑːɪt]
Descending the broad hall stair,
[dɪˈsɛndɪŋ ðʌ bɹɔd hɔl stɛːʌ]
Grave Alice and laughing Allegra
[gɹɛːɪv ˈælɪs ænd ˈlæfɪŋ ʌˈlɛgɹʌ]
and Edith with golden hair.
[ænd ˈidɛ(ɪ)θ wɪð ˈgoːʊldɛ(ɪ)n hɛːʌ]
Between the dark and daylight,
[bɪˈtwin ðʌ dak ænd ˈdɛːɪlɑːɪt]
Comes a pause,
[kʌmz ʌ pɔz]
That is known as Children's Hour.
[ðæt ɪz noːʊn æz ˈtʃɪldɹɛ(ɪ)nz ɑːʊʌ]

"The Circus Band" (Five Street Songs)
[ðʌ ˈsɜkʌs bænd]
Ives, Charles Edward (Am. 1874-1954)

All summer long, we boys
[ɔl ˈsʌmʌ lɑŋ wi bɔːɪz]
dreamed 'bout big circus joys!
[dɹimd bɑːʊt bɪg ˈsɜkʌs dʒɔːɪz]
Down Main street, comes the band,
[dɑːʊn mɛːɪn stɹit kʌmz ðʌ bænd]
Oh! "Ain't it a grand and glorious noise!"
[oːʊ ɛːɪnt ɪt ʌ gɹænd ænd ˈglɔʁ⁽ʳ⁾ʌs nɔːɪz]
Horses are prancing, Knights advancing;
[ˈhɔsɛ(ɪ)z ɑ ˈpɹænsɪŋ nɑːɪts ædˈvænsɪŋ]
Helmets gleaming, Pennants streaming,
[ˈhɛlmɛ(ɪ)ts ˈglimɪŋ ˈpɛnæ(ɪ)nts ˈstɹimɪŋ]
Cleopatra's on her throne!
[klioˈpætɹʌz ɑn hɜ θɹoːʊn]
That golden hair is all her own.
[ðæt ˈgoːʊldɛ(ɪ)n hɛːʌʁ⁽ʳ⁾ ɪz ɔl hɜ oːʊn]
Where is the lady all in pink?
[ʍɛːʌʁ⁽ʳ⁾ ɪz ðʌ ˈlɛːɪdɪ ɔl ɪn pɪŋk]
Last year she waved to me I think,
[læst jɹʌ ʃi wɛːɪvd tu mi ɑːɪ θɪŋk]
Can she have died? Can! that! rot!
[kæn ʃi hæv dɑːɪd kæn ðæt ɹat]
She is passing but she sees me not.
[ʃi ɪz ˈpæsɪŋ bʌt ʃi siz mi nɑt]

"The Greatest Man"
[ðʌ ˈgɹɛːɪtɪst mæn]
Collins, Anne (Am. b. 1951)

Note: the silent "r" may be pronounced for the character voice

My teacher said us boys should write
[mɑːɪ ˈtitʃʌ sɛd ʌs bɔːɪz ʃʊd ɹɑːɪt]
about some great man, so I thought last night
[ʌˈbɑːʊt sʌm gɹɛːɪt mæn soːʊ ɑːɪ θɔt læst nɑːɪt]
'n thought about heroes and men
[n θɔt ʌˈbɑːʊt ˈhɪʁoːʊz ænd mɛn]

that had done great things,
[ðæt hæd dʌn gɹeːɪt θɪŋz]
'n then I got to thinkin' 'bout my pa;
[n ðɛn aːɪ gat tʊ 'θɪŋkɪn baːʊt maːɪ pɔ]
he ain't a hero 'r anything but pshaw!
[hi ɛːɪnt ʌ 'hɪʁoːʊ ɜ 'ɛnɪθɪŋ bʌt pʃɔ]
Say! He can ride the wildest hoss
[sɛːɪ hi kɪn ɹaːɪd ðʌ 'waːɪldɛ(ɪ)st hɔs]
'n find minners near the moss
[n faːɪnd 'mɪnʁz nɪːʌ ðʌ mɔs]
down by the creek; 'n he can swim
[daːʊn baːɪ ðʌ kɹik n hi kæn swɪm]
'n fish, we ketched five new lights, me 'n him!
[n fɪʃ wi kɛʧt faːɪv nju laːɪts mi n hɪm]
Dad's some hunter too– Oh, my!
[dædz sʌm 'hʌntʌ tu oːʊ maːɪ]
Miss Molly Cottontail sure does fly
[mɪs 'malɪ 'katʌntɛːɪl ʃʊːʌ dʌz flaːɪ]
When he tromps through the fields 'n brush!
[wɛn hi tɹamps θɹu ðʌ fildz n bɹʌʃ]
(Dad won't kill a lark 'r thrush.)
[dæd woːʊnt kɪl ʌ lak ɜ θrʌʃ]
Once when I was sick 'n though his hands were rough
[wʌns wɛn aːɪ waz sɪk n ðoːʊ hɪz hændz wɜ ɹʌf]
he rubbed the pain right out. "That's the stuff!"
[hi ɹʌbd ðʌ pɛːɪn ɹaːɪt aːʊt ðæts ðʌ stʌf]
he said when I winked back the tears. He never cried
[hi sɛd wɛn aːɪ wɪŋkt bæk ðʌ tɪːʌz hi 'nɛvʌ kɹaːɪd]
but once 'n that was when my mother died.
[bʌt wʌns n ðæt waz wɛn maːɪ 'mʌðʌ daːɪd]
There're lots o' great men George Washington 'n Lee,
[ðɛːʌ lats ʌ gɹɛːɪt mɛn dʒɔɹdʒ 'waʃɪŋtʌn n li]
but Dad's got 'em all beat holler, seems to me!
[bʌt dædz gat ɛm ɔl bit 'halʌ simz tu mi]

"The Housatonic at Stockbridge"
[ðʌ husʌ'tanɪk æt 'stakbɹɪdʒ]
Johnson, Robert Underwood (Am. 1858-1937)

Contented river! in thy dreamy realm
[kʌn'tɛntɛ(ɪ)d 'ɹɪvʌ ɪn ðaːɪ 'dɹimɪ ɹɛlm]
The cloudy willow and the plumy elm:
[ðʌ 'klaːʊdɪ 'wɪloːʊ ænd ðʌ 'plumɪ ɛlm]
Thou beautiful! From ev'ry dreamy hill
[ðaːʊ 'bjutɪfʊl fɹʌm 'ɛvɹɪ 'dɹimɪ hɪl]
what eye but wanders with thee at thy will,
[ʍat aːɪ bʌt 'wandʌz wɪð ði æt ðaːɪ wɪl]
Contented river! And yet over-shy
[kʌn'tɛntɛ(ɪ)d 'ɹɪvʌ ænd jɛt 'oːʊvʌ ʃaːɪ]
To mask thy beauty from the eager eye;
[tu mæsk ðaːɪ 'bjutɪ fɹʌm ði 'igʌʁ(ʳ) aːɪ]
Hast thou a thought to hide from field and town?
[hæst ðaːʊ ʌ θɔt tu haːɪd fɹʌm fild ænd taːʊn]
In some deep current of the sunlit brown
[ɪn sʌm dip 'kʊʁ(ʳ)ɛnt ʌv ðʌ 'sʌnlɪt bɹaːʊn]

Ah! there's a restive ripple,
[a ðɛːʌz ʌ 'ɹɛstɪv 'ɹɪpʊl]
and the swift red leaves
[ænd ðʌ swɪft ɹɛd livz]
September's firstlings faster drift;
[sɛp'tɛmbʌz 'fɜstlɪŋz 'fæstʌ dɹɪft]
Wouldst thou away, dear stream?
[wʊdst ðaːʊ ʌ'wɛːɪ dɪːʌ stɹim]
Come, whisper near!
[kʌm 'ʍɪspʌ nɪːʌ]
I also of much resting have a fear:
[aːɪ 'ɔlsoːʊ ʌv mʌʧ 'ɹɛstɪŋ hæv ʌ fɪːʌ]
Let me tomorrow thy companion be,
[lɛt mi tu'maʁ(ʳ)oːʊ ðaːɪ kʌm'pænjʌn bi]
By fall and shallow to the adventurous sea!
[baːɪ fɔl ænd 'ʃæloːʊ tu ði æd'vɛnʧʊʁ(ʳ)ʌs si]

"The Side Show"
[ðʌ saːɪd ʃoːʊ]
Ives, Charles Edward (Am. 1874-1954)

"Is that Mister Riley,
[ɪz ðæt 'mɪstʌ 'ɹaːɪlɪ]
who keeps the hotel?"
[hu kips ðʌ hoˈtɛl]
is the tune that accomp'nies
[ɪz ðʌ tjun ðæt ʌ'kʌmpnɪz]
the trotting-track bell;
[ðʌ 'tɹatɪŋ tɹæk bɛl]
An old horse unsound,
[æn oːʊld hɔs ʌn'saːʊnd]
turns the merry-go-round,
[tɜnz ðʌ 'mɛʁ(ʳ)ɪ goːʊ ɹaːʊnd]
making poor Mister Riley
['mɛːɪkɪŋ pʊːʌ 'mɪstʌ 'ɹaːɪlɪ]
look a bit like a Russian dance,
[lʊk ʌ bɪt laːɪk ʌ 'ɹʌʃæ(ɪ)n dæns]
Some speak of so highly,
[sʌm spik ʌv soːʊ 'haːɪlɪ]
as they do of Riley!
[æz ðɛːɪ du ʌv 'ɹaːɪlɪ]

"The Things Our Fathers Loved"
[ðʌ θɪŋz aːʊʁ 'faðʁz lʌvd]
Ives, Charles Edward (Am. 1874-1954)

I think there must be a place in the soul
[aːɪ θɪŋk ðɛːʌ mʌst bi ʌ plɛːɪs ɪn ðʌ soːʊl]
all made of tunes, of tunes of long ago;
[ɔl mɛːɪd ʌv tjunz ʌv tjunz ʌv laŋ ʌ'goːʊ]
I hear the organ on the Main Street corner,
[aːɪ hɪːʌ ði 'ɔgæ(ɪ)n an ðʌ mɛːɪn stɹit 'kɔnʌ]
Aunt Sarah humming Gospels; Summer evenings,
[ant 'sæʁ(ʳ)ʌ 'hʌmɪŋ 'gaspʊlz 'sʌmʌʁ(ʳ) 'ivnɪŋz]
The village cornet band, playing in the square.
[ðʌ 'vɪlæ(ɪ)dʒ kɔ'nɛt bænd 'plɛːɪŋ ɪn ðʌ skwɛːʌ]

The town's Red, White and Blue,
[ðʌ taːʊnz ɹɛd ʍaːɪt ænd blu]
all Red, White and Blue Now! Hear the songs!
[ɔl ɹɛd ʍaːɪt ænd blu naːʊ hiːʌ ðʌ sɑŋz]
I know not what are the words
[aːɪ noːʊ nɑt ʍat a ðʌ wɝdz]
But they sing in my soul of the things our Fathers loved.
[bʌt ðɛːɪ sɪŋ ɪn maːɪ soːʊl ʌv ðʌ θɪŋz aːʊʌ ˈfɑðʌz lʌvd]

"Tom Sails Away" (Three Songs of the War)
[tɑm sɛːɪlz ʌˈwɛːɪ]
Ives, Charles Edward (Am. 1874-1954)

Scenes from my childhood are with me,
[sinz fɹʌm maːɪ ˈʧɑːɪldhʊd a wɪð mi]
I'm in the lot behind our house upon the hill,
[aːɪm ɪn ðʌ lɑt bɪˈhaːɪnd aːʊʌ haːʊs ʌˈpɑn ðʌ hɪl]
a spring day's sun is setting,
[ʌ spɹɪŋ dɛːɪz sʌn ɪz ˈsɛtɪŋ]
mother with Tom in her arms
[ˈmʌðʌ wɪð tɑm ɪn hɝ ɑmz]
is coming towards the garden;
[ɪz ˈkʌmɪŋ twɔdz ðʌ ˈgɑdɛ(ɪ)n]
the lettuce rows are showing green.
[ðʌ ˈlɛtʌs ɹoːʊz a ˈʃoːʊɪŋ gɹin]
Thinner grows the smoke o'er the town,
[ˈθɪnʌ gɹoːʊz ðʌ smoːʊk ɔːʌ ðʌ taːʊn]
stronger comes the breeze from the ridge,
[ˈstɹɑŋʌ kʌmz ðʌ bɹiz fɹʌm ðʌ ɹɪʤ]
'Tis after six, the whistles have blown,
[tɪz ˈæftʌ sɪks ðʌ ˈʍɪsʊlz hæv bloːʊn]
the milk train's gone down the valley
[ðʌ mɪlk tɹɛːɪnz gɑn daːʊn ðʌ ˈvælɪ]
Daddy is coming up the hill from the mill,
[ˈdædɪ ɪz ˈkʌmɪŋ ʌp ðʌ hɪl fɹʌm ðʌ mɪl]
We run down the lane to meet him
[wi ɹʌn daːʊn ðʌ lɛːɪn tu mit hɪm]
But today! In freedom's cause Tom sailed away
[bʌt tuˈdɛːɪ ɪn ˈfɹidʌmz kɔz tɑm sɛːɪld ʌˈwɛːɪ]
for over there, over there!
[fɔʁ(ⁱ) ˈoːʊvʌ ðɛːʌ ˈoːʊvʌ ðɛːʌ]
Scenes from my childhood
[sinz fɹʌm maːɪ ˈʧɑːɪldhʊd]
are floating before my eyes.
[a ˈfloːʊtɪŋ bɪˈfɔːʌ maːɪ aːɪz]

"Two Little Flowers (and Dedicated to Them)"
[tu ˈlɪtʊl ˈflɑːʊʁz ænd ˈdɛdɪkɛːɪtɪd tu ðɛm]
Ives, Charles Edward (Am. 1874-1954) and
Twitchell, Harmony (Mrs. Ives) (Am. 1876-1979)

On sunny days in our backyard,
[ɑn ˈsʌnɪ dɛːɪz ɪn aːʊʌ ˌbækˈjad]
Two little flowers are seen,
[tu ˈlɪtʊl flɑːʊʌz a sin]

One dressed, at times, in brightest pink
[wʌn dɹɛst æt taːɪmz ɪn ˈbɹɑːɪtɛ(ɪ)st pɪŋk]
and one in green.
[ænd wʌn ɪn gɹin]
The marigold is radiant,
[ðʌ ˈmæʁ(ⁱ)ɪgoːʊld ɪz ˈɹɛːɪdɪæ(ɪ)nt]
the rose passing fair;
[ðʌ ɹoːʊz ˈpæsɪŋ fɛːʌ]
The violet is ever dear,
[ðʌ ˈvaːɪo(ʌ)lɛ(ɪ)t ɪz ˈɛvʌ dɪːʌ]
the orchid, ever rare;
[ði ˈɔkɪd ˈɛvʌ ɹɛːʌ]
There's loveliness in wild flow'rs
[ðɛːʌz ˈlʌvlɪnɛ(ɪ)s ɪn waːɪld flɑːʊʌz]
of field or wide savannah,
[ʌv fild ɔ waːɪd sʌˈvænʌ]
But fairest, rarest of them all
[bʌt ˈfɛːʌʁ(ⁱ)ɛːɪst ˈɹɛːʌʁ(ⁱ)ɛ(ɪ)st ʌv ðɛm ɔl]
are Edith and Susanna.
[a ˈidɛ(ɪ)θ ænd suˈzænʌ]

J

Johnson, Hall (Am. 1888-1970)

Song Selections

"Fix Me"
[fɪks mi]
Spiritual

REFRAIN:
Oh, fix me. Fix me, Jesus, fix me.
[oːʊ fɪks mi fɪks mi ˈʤizʌs fɪks mi]
1. Fix me for my long, white robe;
[fɪks mi fɔ maːɪ lɑŋ waːɪt ɹoːʊb]
Fix me, Jesus, fix me.
[fɪks mi ˈʤizʌs fɪks mi]
Fix me for my starry crown.
[fɪks mi fɔʁ maːɪ ˈstaʁɪ kɹaːʊn]
Fix me, Jesus, fix me.
[fɪks mi ˈʤizʌs fɪks mi]
REFRAIN
2. Fix me for my dyin' bed.
[fɪks mi fɔ maːɪ ˈdaːɪn bɛd]
Fix me, Jesus, fix me.
[fɪks mi ˈʤizʌs fɪks mi]
Fix me for my home on high.
[fɪks mi fɔʁ maːɪ hoːʊm an haːɪ]
Fix me, Jesus, fix me.
[fɪks mi ˈʤizʌs fɪks mi]
REFRAIN

"Give Me Jesus" (see "In the Mornin'" by Ives)

"My God Is So High"
[mɑːɪ gad ɪz soːʊ hɑːɪ]
Spiritual

REFRAIN:
My God is so high,
[mɑːɪ gad ɪz soːʊ hɑːɪ]
You can't get over Him,
[jʊ kɛːɪnt gɛt ˈoːʊvʌ hɪm]
He's so low,
[hiz soːʊ loːʊ]
You can't get under Him,
[jʊ kɛːɪnt gɛt ˈʌndʌ hɪm]
He's so wide–
[hiz soːʊ wɑːɪd]
You can't get around Him,
[jʊ kɛːɪnt gɛt ʌˈʁɑːʊnd hɪm]
You mus' come in by 'n through de Lam'.
[jʊ mʌs kʌm ɪn bɑ n θɾu dʌ læm]
1. One day as I was walkin' along the heb'nly road
[wʌn dɛːɪ æz ɑːɪ waz ˈwɔkɪn ʌˈlaŋ ðʌ ˈhɛbnlɪ ɹoːʊd]
My Savior spoke unto me
[mɑ ˈsɛːɪvjɔ(ʌ) spoːʊk ˈʌntu mi]
An' He filled my heart wid love.
[æn hi fɪld mɑ hat wɪd lʌv]
REFRAIN
2. I'll take my gospel trumpet,
[ɑːɪl tɛːɪk mɑːɪ ˈgaspʊl ˈtɹʌmpɛ(ɪ)t]
an' I'll begin to blow,
[æn ɑːɪl bɪˈgɪn tu bloːʊ]
An' if my Savior help me,
[æn ɪf mɑ ˈsɛːɪvjɔ(ʌ) hɛlp mi]
I'll blow wherever I go.
[ɑːɪl bloːʊ wɛːʌʁˈɛvʌʁ ɑːɪ goːʊ]
REFRAIN

"My Good Lord Done Been Here"
[mɑːɪ gʊd lɔʁd dʌn bɪn hɪːʁ]
Spiritual

REFRAIN:
My good Lord done been here!
[mɑ gʊd lɔ dʌn bɪn hɪːʌ]
Blessed my soul an' gone away.
[blɛs(t) mɑːɪ soːʊl æn gan ʌˈwɛːɪ]
1. When I git up in de Heaven
[wɛn ɑ gɪd ʌp ɪn dʌ ˈhɛvɛ(ɪ)n]
An' my work is done,
[æn mɑ wɜk ɪz dʌn]
Gonna set down 'side Sister Mary,
[ˈgʌnʌ sɛt dɑːʊn sɑːɪd ˈsɪstʌ ˈmæʁɪ]
Gonna chatter wid de darlin' Son. I tell you,
[ˈgʌnʌ ˈtʃætʌ wɪ dʌ ˈdaлɪn sʌn ɑ tɛl ju]
REFRAIN

2. I'm gonna to hol' up de Baptis finger,
[am ˈgʌnʌ hoːʊl ʌp dʌ ˈbæptɪs ˈfɪŋgʌ]
Hol' up de Baptis han',
[hoːʊl ʌp dʌ ˈbæptɪs hæn]
When I git up in de heaven,
[wɛn ɑ gɪd ʌp ɪn dʌ ˈhɛvɛ(ɪ)n]
Gonna jine de Baptis' Ban'. 'Cause
[ˈgʌnʌ dʒɔːɪn dʌ ˈbæptɪs bæn kɔz]
REFRAIN
3. Now you may be a rich man,
[nɑːʊ ju mɛːɪ bi ʌ ɹɪtʃ mæn]
White as the driftin' snow,
[wɑːɪt æz ðʌ ˈdɹɪftɪn snoːʊ]
But ef yo' soul ain't been converted,
[bʌt ɪf jɔːʌ soːʊl ɛːɪnt bɪn kʌnˈvɜtɛ(ɪ)d]
Straight to Hell you' boun' to go.
[stɹɛːɪ tʊ hɛl jʊ bɑːʊn tʊ goːʊ]
REFRAIN

"My Lord, What a Mornin'"
[mɑːɪ lɔʁd wat ʌ ˈmɔʁnɪn]
Spiritual

REFRAIN:
My Lord, what a mornin'!
[mɑːɪ lɔd wat ʌ ˈmɔnɪn]
When de stars begin to fall.
[wɛn dʌ staz bɪˈgɪn tu fɔl]
1. You'll hear de trumpet soun'
[jul hɪːʌ dʌ ˈtɹʌmpɛ(ɪ)t sɑːʊn]
To wake de nations undergroun',
[tu wɛːɪk dʌ ˈnɛːɪʃʌnz ˈʌndʌgɹɑːʊn]
Lookin' to my God's right han',
[ˈlʊkɪn tu mɑːɪ gadz ɹɑːɪt hæn]
When de stars begin to fall.
[wɛn dʌ staz bɪˈgɪn tu fɔl]
2. You'll hear de sinners moan,
[jul hɪːʌ dʌ ˈsɪnʌz moːʊn]
To see de righteous marchin' home,
[tu si dʌ ˈɹɑːɪtʃʌs ˈmatʃɪn hoːʊm]
Lookin' to my God's right han',
[ˈlʊkɪn tu mɑːɪ gadz ɹɑːɪt hæn]
When de stars begin to fall.
[wɛn dʌ staz bɪˈgɪn tu fɔl]

"His Name So Sweet"
[hɪz nɛːɪm soːʊ swit]
Spiritual

REFRAIN:
Oh Lord, I jus' come from de fountain,
[oːʊ lɔd ɑ dʒʌs kʌm fɹʌm dʌ ˈfɑːʊntæ(ɪ)n]
I'm jus' from de fountain, Lord,
[ɑːɪm dʒʌs fɹʌm dʌ ˈfɑːʊntæ(ɪ)n lɔd]
I jus' come from de fountain,
[ɑ dʒʌs kʌm fɹʌm dʌ ˈfɑːʊntæ(ɪ)n]

His Name so sweet.
[hɪz nɛːɪm soːʊ swit]
1. Po' sinner, do you love Jesus?
[poːʊ 'sɪnʌ du ju lʌv 'ʤizʌs]
Yes, yes, I do love m' Jesus.
[jɛs jɛs ɑ du lʌv mɑ 'ʤizʌs]
Sinner, do you love Jesus?
['sɪnʌ du ju lʌv 'ʤizʌs]
His name so sweet.
[hɪz nɛːɪm soːʊ swit]
REFRAIN
2. Class leader, do you love Jesus?
[klæs 'lidʌ du ju lʌv 'ʤizʌs]
Yes, yes, I do love m' Jesus.
[jɛs jɛs ɑ du lʌv mɑ 'ʤizʌs]
Leader, do you love Jesus?
['lidʌ du ju lʌv 'ʤizʌs]
His name so sweet.
[hɪz nɛːɪm soːʊ swit]
REFRAIN
3 'Zid'n Elder, do you love Jesus?
[zɑːɪdn 'ɛldʌ du ju lʌv 'ʤizʌs]
Yes, yes, I do love m' Jesus.
[jɛs jɛs ɑ du lʌv mɑ 'ʤizʌs]
Elder, do you love Jesus?
['ɛldʌ du ju lʌv 'ʤizʌs]
His name so sweet.
[hɪz nɛːɪm soːʊ swit]
REFRAIN

"Oh, Glory!"
[oːʊ 'glɔʁi]
Spiritual

Oh, Glory! There is room enough in Paradise–
[oːʊ 'glɔʁ⁽ʳ⁾ɪ ðɛːʌʁ⁽ʳ⁾ ɪz ɹ⁽ʳʳ⁾um ɪ'nʌf ɪn 'pæʁ⁽ʳ⁾ʌdɑːɪs]
To have a home in Glory.
[tu hæv ʌ hoːʊm ɪn 'glɔʁ⁽ʳ⁾ɪ]
Jesus, my all, to heaven is gone
['ʤizʌs mɑːɪ ɔl tu 'hɛvɛ⁽ɪ⁾n ɪz gɑn]
To have a home in Glory,
[tu hæv ʌ hoːʊm ɪn 'glɔʁ⁽ʳ⁾ɪ]
He whom I fixed my hopes upon,
[hi hum ɑːɪ fɪkst mɑːɪ hoːʊps ʌ'pɑn]
To have a home in Glory.
[tu hæv ʌ hoːʊm ɪn 'glɔʁ⁽ʳ⁾ɪ]
Oh, Glory! There is room enough in Paradise
[oːʊ 'glɔʁ⁽ʳ⁾ɪ ðɛːʌʁ⁽ʳ⁾ ɪz ɹ⁽ʳʳ⁾um ɪ'nʌf ɪn 'pæʁ⁽ʳ⁾ʌdɑːɪs]
To have a home in Glory.
[tu hæv ʌ hoːʊm ɪn 'glɔʁ⁽ʳ⁾ɪ]
His track I see– and I'll pursue,– to have a home,–
[hɪz tʁæk ɑːɪ si ænd ɑːɪl pɜ'sju tu hæv ʌ hoːʊm]
The narrow way– till Him I view.
[ðʌ 'næʁ⁽ʳ⁾oːʊ wɛːɪ tɪl hɪm ɑːɪ vju]
To have a home. Oh, Glory!
[tu hæv ʌ hoːʊm oːʊ 'glɔʁ⁽ʳ⁾ɪ]

There is room enough in Paradise
[ðɛːʌʁ⁽ʳ⁾ ɪz ɹ⁽ʳʳ⁾um ɪ'nʌf ɪn 'pæʁ⁽ʳ⁾ʌdɑːɪs]
To have a home in Glory.
[tu hæv ʌ hoːʊm ɪn 'glɔʁ⁽ʳ⁾ɪ]
Hm... To have a home in Glory.
[m tu hæv ʌ hoːʊm ɪn 'glɔʁ⁽ʳ⁾ɪ]

"Ride On, King Jesus!" (see Burleigh)

"Steal Away" (see Burleigh)

"Witness"
['wɪtnɪs]
Spiritual

Oh, Lord, what manner of man is dis?
[oːʊ lɔd wɑt 'mænʌʁ ʌv mæn ɪz dɪs]
All nations in Him are blest,
[ɔl 'nɛːɪʃʌnz ɪn hɪm ɑ blɛst]
All things are done by His will;
[ɔl θɪŋz ɑ dʌn bɑ hɪz wɪl]
He spoke to de sea an' de sea stood still
[hi spoːʊk tu dʌ si æn dʌ si stʊd stɪl]
Now ain't dat a witness for my Lord?
[nɑːʊ ɛːɪn dæt ʌ 'wɪtnɛ⁽ɪ⁾s fɔ mɑ lɔd]
Ma soul is a witness for my Lord
[mɑ soːʊl ɪz ʌ 'wɪtnɛ⁽ɪ⁾s fɔ mɑ lɔd]
Now dere was a man of de Pharersees
[nɑːʊ dɛːʌ wɑz ʌ mæn ʌv dʌ 'fɛʁʌˌsiz]
His name was Nicodemus an' 'e didn' believe.
[hɪz nɛːɪm wɑz nɪkʌ'dimʌs æn hi 'dɪ(d)ɪn bɪ'liv]
De same came to Chris' by night,
[dʌ sɛːɪm kɛːɪm tu kɪɑːɪs bɑːɪ nɑːɪt]
Wanted to be taught out o' human sight.
['wɑnɪd tu bi tɔt ɑːʊt ʌ 'hjumæ⁽ʌ⁾n sɑːɪt]
Nicodemus was a man desired to know
[nɪkʌ'dimʌs wɑz ʌ mæn dɪ'zɑːɪʌ tʊ noːʊ]
How a man kin be born when he is ol'.
[hɑːʊ ʌ mæn kɪn bi bɔn wɛn hi ɪz oːʊl]
Chris' tol' Nicodemus, as a frien'
[kɪɑːɪs toːʊl nɪkʌ'dimʌs æz ʌ fɪɛn]
"Man, you mus' be born again."
[mæn ju mʌs bi bɔn ʌ'gɛn]
Said, "Marvel not, man, ef you wanna be wise
[sɛd 'mɑvʊl nɑt mæn ɪf ju 'wɑnʌ bi wɑːɪz]
Repent, believe, an' be baptize'."
[ɹɪ'pɛnt bɪ'liv æn bi bæp'tɑːɪz]
Den you'll be a witness for my Lord.
[dɛn jul bi ʌ 'wɪtnɛ⁽ɪ⁾s fɔ mɑ lɔd]
Soul is a witness for my Lord
[soːʊl ɪz ʌ 'wɪtnɛ⁽ɪ⁾s fɔ mɑ lɔd]
You read about Samson, from his birth
[ju ɹid ʌ'bɑːʊt 'sæmsʌn fɪʌm hɪz bɜθ]
The stronges' man dat ever lived on earth.
[ðʌ 'stɪɑŋɛ⁽ɪ⁾s mæn dæt 'ɛvʌ lɪvd ɑn ɜθ]

'Way back yonder in ancien' times
[wɛːɹ bæk ˈjɑndʌʁ ɪn ˈɛːɪnʧɛn tɑːɪmz]
He killed ten thousan' of de Philistines.
[hi kɪld tɛn ˈθɑːʊzæ(ʌ)n ʌv dʌ ˈfɪlɪstɑːɪnz]
Den ol' Samson went wand'rin' about;
[dɛn oːʊl ˈsæmsʌn wɛnt ˈwandɹɪn ʌˈbɑːʊt]
Samson's strength was never found out
[ˈsæmsʌnz stɹɛŋθ wʌz ˈnɛvʌ fɑːʊnd ɑːʊt]
Till 'is wife sat upon 'is knee
[tɪl ɪz wɑːɪf sæt ʌˈpɑn ɪz ni]
She said, "Tell me where yo' strength lies,
[ʃi sɛd tɛl mi wɛːʌ jɔ stɹɛŋθ lɑːɪz]
ef you please."
[ɪf ju pliz]
Now Samson's wife, She talk so fair,
[nɑːʊ ˈsæmsʌnz wɑːɪf ʃi tɔk soːʊ fɛːʌ]
Samson said, "Cut off a my hair.
[ˈsæmsʌn sɛd kʌt af ʌ ma hɛːʌ]
Shave my head jes' as clean as yo' han'
[ʃɛːɪv ma hɛd ʤɛs æz klin æz jɔ hæn]
An' my strength will 'come lak a natchul man.
[æn ma stɹɛŋθ wɪl kʌm lak ʌ ˈnæʧʊl mæn]
Ol' Samson was a witness for my Lord.
[oːʊl ˈsæmsʌn wʌz ʌ ˈwɪtnɛ(ɪ)s fɔ ma lɔd]
Soul is a witness for my Lord.
[soːʊl ɪz ʌ ˈwɪtnɛ(ɪ)s fɔ ma lɔd]
Da's another witness, Now da's another witness,
[dæz ʌˈnʌðʌ ˈwɪtnɛ(ɪ)s nɑːʊ dæz ʌˈnʌðʌ ˈwɪtnɛ(ɪ)s]
Ma soul is a witness for my Lord.
[ma soːʊl ɪz ʌ ˈwɪtnɛ(ɪ)s fɔ ma lɔd]

K

Kingsley, Herbert (Am. 1882-1961)

Song Selection

"The Green Dog"
[ðʌ ɡɹin dɑɡ]
Anonymous

If my dog were green
[ɪf mɑːɪ dɑɡ wɜ ɡɹin]
I never would be seen
[ɑːɪ ˈnɛvʌ wʊd bi sin]
without a sea-green bonnet
[wɪðˈɑːʊt ʌ si ɡɹin ˈbanɛ(ɪ)t]
with an enormous feather upon it.
[wɪð æn ɪˈnɔmʌs ˈfɛðʌʁ(ʳ) ʌˈpɑn ɪt]
Shoes of leaf-green,
[ʃuz ʌv lif ɡɹin]

Hose of tea-green,
[hoːʊz ʌv ti ɡɹin]
Coat of apple-green,
[koːʊt ʌv ˈæpʊl ɡɹin]
Gloves of bottle-green,
[ɡlʌvz ʌv ˈbatʊl ɡɹin]
In fact, I never would be seen except in green–
[ɪn fækt ɑːɪ ˈnɛvʌ wʊd bi sin ɪkˈsɛpt ɪn ɡɹin]
If my dog were green.
[ɪf mɑːɪ dɑɡ wɜ ɡɹin]
But, alas! no matter what you've heard,
[bʌt ʌˈlæs noːʊ ˈmætʌ ʍat juv hɜd]
The facts are consistently absurd,
[ðʌ fækts a kʌnˈsɪstɛ(ɪ)ntlɪ ʌbˈsɜd]
For my dog isn't green,
[fɔ mɑːɪ dɑɡ ˈɪzɛ(ɪ)nt ɡɹin]
And, what sets the matter even more agog–
[ænd ʍat sɛts ðʌ ˈmætʌʁ(ʳ) ˈivɛ(ɪ)n mɔːʌʁ(ʳ) ʌˈɡɑɡ]
I haven't any dog!
[ɑːɪ ˈhævɛ(ɪ)nt ˈɛnɪ dɑɡ]

 # Kohn, Steven Mark (Am. b. 1957)

American Folk Set, Book 1 (Song Cycle)
[ʌˈmɛʁɪkɪn foːʊk sɛt bʊk wʌn]
Folksongs

1. Ten Thousand Miles Away
[tɛn ˈθɑːʊzænd mɑːɪlz ʌˈwɛːɪ]

Sing I for a brave and a gallant barque,
[sɪŋ ɑːɪ fɔʁ(ʳ) ʌ bɹɛːɪv ænd ʌ ˈɡælæ(ɪ)nt bɑk]
for a stiff and a rattling breeze,
[fɔʁ(ʳ) ʌ stɪf ænd ʌ ˈɹætlɪŋ bɹiz]
A bully crew and a captain true,
[ʌ ˈbʊlɪ kɹu ænd ʌ ˈkæptæ(ɪ)n tɹu]
to carry me o'er the seas.
[tu ˈkæʁɪ mi ɔːʌ ðʌ siz]
To carry me o'er the seas, my boys,
[tu ˈkæʁɪ mi ɔːʌ ðʌ siz mɑːɪ bɔːɪz]
to my true love so gay,
[tu mɑːɪ tɹu lʌv soːʊ ɡɛːɪ]
Who went on a trip on a Government ship
[hu wɛnt ɑn ʌ tɹɪp ɑn ʌ ˈɡʌvʌnmɛnt ʃɪp]
ten thousand miles away!
[tɛn ˈθɑːʊzæ(ʌ)nd mɑːɪlz ʌˈwɛːɪ]
Oh, blow, ye winds, hi oh! A roaming I will go.
[oːʊ bloːʊ ji wɪndz hɑːɪ oːʊ ʌ ˈɹoːʊmɪŋ ɑːɪ wɪl ɡoːʊ]
I'll stay no more on England's shore
[ɑːɪl stɛːɪ noːʊ mɔːʌʁ ɑn ˈɪŋɡlæ(ʌ)ndz ʃɔːʌ]
so let the music play.
[soːʊ lɛt ðʌ ˈmjuzɪk plɛːɪ]
I'll start by the morning train
[ɑːɪl stat bɑːɪ ðʌ ˈmɔnɪŋ tɹɛːɪn]

to cross the raging main,
[tu kɹɑs ðʌ ˈɹɛːɪdʒɪŋ meːɪn]
For I'm on the road to my own true love,
[fɔʁ⁽ʳ⁾ ɑːɪm ɑn ðʌ ɹoːʊd tʊ mɑːɪ oːʊn tɹu lʌv]
ten thousand miles away.
[tɛn ˈθɑːʊzæ(ʌ)nd mɑːɪlz ʌˈwɛːɪ]
My true love she was handsome,
[mɑːɪ tɹu lʌv ʃi waz ˈhænsʌm]
My true love she was young.
[mɑːɪ tɹu lʌv ʃi waz jʌŋ]
Her eyes were blue as the violet's hue,
[hɜ ɑːɪz wɜ blu æz ðʌ ˈvɑːɪo(ʌ)lɛ(ɪ)ts hju]
and silv'ry was the sound of her tongue.
[ænd ˈsɪlvɹɪ waz ðʌ sɑːʊnd ʌv hɜ tʌŋ]
And silv'ry was the sound of her tongue,
[ænd ˈsɪlvɹɪ waz ðʌ sɑːʊnd ʌv hɜ tʌŋ]
my boys, and while I sing this lay,
[mɑːɪ bɔːɪz ænd ʌɑːɪl ɑːɪ sɪŋ ðɪs lɛːɪ]
She's a doing of the grand in a far off land,
[ʃiz ʌ ˈduɪŋ ʌv ðʌ ɡɹænd ɪn ʌ fɑʁ af lænd]
ten thousand miles away.
[tɛn ˈθɑːʊzæ(ʌ)nd mɑːɪlz ʌˈwɛːɪ]
Oh, blow, ye winds, hi oh! A roaming I will go.
[oːʊ bloːʊ ji wɪndz hɑːɪ oːʊ ʌ ˈɹoːʊmɪŋ ɑːɪ wɪl ɡoːʊ]
I'll stay no more on England's shore,
[ɑːɪl stɛːɪ noːʊ mɔːʁ ɑn ˈɪŋglæ(ʌ)ndz ʃɔːʌ]
so let the music play.
[soːʊ lɛt ðʌ ˈmjuzɪk plɛːɪ]
I'll start by the morning train
[ɑːɪl stɑt bɑːɪ ðʌ ˈmɔnɪŋ tɹɛːɪn]
to cross the raging main!
[tu kɹɑs ðʌ ˈɹɛːɪdʒɪŋ meːɪn]
For I'm on the road to my own true love,
[fɔʁ⁽ʳ⁾ ɑːɪm ɑn ðʌ ɹoːʊd tʊ mɑːɪ oːʊn tɹu lʌv]
ten thousand miles away.
[tɛn ˈθɑːʊzæ(ʌ)nd mɑːɪlz ʌˈwɛːɪ]

2. On the Other Shore
[ɑn ði ˈʌðʁ ʃɔːʁ]

I have a mother gone to glory,
[ɑːɪ hæv ʌ ˈmʌðʌ ɡɑn tʊ ˈglɔʁɪ]
On the other shore.
[ɑn ði ˈʌðʌ ʃɔːʌ]
By and by I'll go to meet her,
[bɑːɪ ænd bɑːɪ ɑːɪl ɡoːʊ tʊ mit hɜ]
On the other shore.
[ɑn ði ˈʌðʌ ʃɔːʌ]
Won't that be a happy meetin'?
[woːʊnt ðæt bi ʌ ˈhæpɪ ˈmitɪn]
On the other shore.
[ɑn ði ˈʌðʌ ʃɔːʌ]
There we'll see our good old neighbors,
[ðɛːʌ wil si ɑːʊʌ ɡʊd oːʊld ˈnɛːɪbɔ(ʌ)z]
On the other shore.
[ɑn ði ˈʌðʌ ʃɔːʌ]

There we'll see our blessed Savior
[ðɛːʌ wil si ɑːʊʌ ˈblɛsɛ(ɪ)d ˈsɛːɪvjɔ(ʌ)]
On the other shore.
[ɑn ði ˈʌðʌ ʃɔːʌ]

3. The Farmer's Curst Wife
[ðʌ ˈfɑʁmʁz kɜst wɑːɪf]

There was an old man at the foot of the hill.
[ðɛːʌ waz æn oːʊld mæn æt ðʌ fʊt ʌv ðʌ hɪl]
If he ain't moved away, he's a' livin' there still.
[ɪf hi ɛːɪnt muvd ʌˈwɛːɪ hiz ʌ ˈlɪvɪn ðɛːʌ stɪl]
Sing hi diddle i diddle i fi,
[sɪŋ hɑːɪ ˈdɪdʊl ɑːɪ ˈdɪdʊl ɑːɪ fɑːɪ]
diddle i diddle i day.
[ˈdɪdʊl ɑːɪ ˈdɪdʊl ɑːɪ dɛːɪ]
The devil he come to his house one day,
[ðʌ ˈdɛvɪ(ʊ)l hi kʌm tu hɪz hɑːʊs wʌn dɛːɪ]
says "one of your fam'ly I'm gonna take away."
[sɛz wʌn ʌv jɔːʌ ˈfæmɪlɪ ɑːɪm ˈɡʌnʌ tɛːɪk ʌˈwɛːɪ]
Sing hi diddle i diddle i fi
[sɪŋ hɑːɪ ˈdɪdʊl ɑːɪ ˈdɪdʊl ɑːɪ fɑːɪ]
diddle i diddle i day.
[ˈdɪdʊl ɑːɪ ˈdɪdʊl ɑːɪ dɛːɪ]
"Take her, my wife, with all a' my heart,
[tɛːɪk hɜ mɑːɪ wɑːɪf wɪð ɔl ʌ mɑːɪ hɑt]
and I hope, by golly, you never part."
[ænd ɑːɪ hoːʊp bɑːɪ ˈɡɑlɪ ju ˈnɛvʌ pɑt]
Sing hi diddle i diddle i fi
[sɪŋ hɑːɪ ˈdɪdʊl ɑːɪ ˈdɪdʊl ɑːɪ fɑːɪ]
diddle i diddle i day.
[ˈdɪdʊl ɑːɪ ˈdɪdʊl ɑːɪ dɛːɪ]
The devil he put her up on his back,
[ðʌ ˈdɛvɪ(ʊ)l hi pʊt hɜ ʌp ɑn hɪz bæk]
and off to Hell he went, clickity clack.
[ænd af tʊ hɛl hi wɛnt ˈklɪkɪtɪ klæk]
Sing hi diddle i diddle i fi
[sɪŋ hɑːɪ ˈdɪdʊl ɑːɪ ˈdɪdʊl ɑːɪ fɑːɪ]
diddle i diddle i day.
[ˈdɪdʊl ɑːɪ ˈdɪdʊl ɑːɪ dɛːɪ]
When he got her down to the gates of Hell,
[ʌɛn hi gat hɜ dɑːʊn tu ðʌ gɛːɪts ʌv hɛl]
he says "punch up the fire, we'll scorch her well."
[hi sɛz pʌntʃ ʌp ðʌ fɑːɪʌ wil skɔtʃ hɜ wɛl]
Sing hi diddle i diddle i fi,
[sɪŋ hɑːɪ ˈdɪdʊl ɑːɪ ˈdɪdʊl ɑːɪ fɑːɪ]
diddle i diddle i day.
[ˈdɪdʊl ɑːɪ ˈdɪdʊl ɑːɪ dɛːɪ]
In come a little devil draggin' a chain,
[ɪn kʌm ʌ ˈlɪtʊl ˈdɛvɪ(ʊ)l ˈdɹægɪn ʌ tʃɛːɪn]
She upped with a hatchet and split his brain!
[ʃi ʌpt wɪð ʌ ˈhætʃɛ(ɪ)t ænd splɪt hɪz bɹɛːɪn]
Sing hi diddle i diddle i fi,
[sɪŋ hɑːɪ ˈdɪdʊl ɑːɪ ˈdɪdʊl ɑːɪ fɑːɪ]
diddle i diddle i day.
[ˈdɪdʊl ɑːɪ ˈdɪdʊl ɑːɪ dɛːɪ]

Now nine little devils went a climbin' the wall
[nɑːʊ naːɪn ˈlɪtʊl ˈdɛvɪ(ʊ)lz wɛnt ʌ ˈklɑːɪmɪn ðʌ wɔl]
sayin' "take her back, daddy!
[ˈsɛːɪɪn tɛːɪk hɜ bæk ˈdædɪ]
She'll a' murder us all!"
[ʃɪl ʌ ˈmɜdʌʁ ʌs ɔl]
Sing hi diddle i diddle i fi
[sɪŋ hɑːɪ ˈdɪdʊl ɑːɪ ˈdɪdʊl ɑːɪ fɑːɪ]
diddle i diddle i day!
[ˈdɪdʊl ɑːɪ ˈdɪdʊl ɑːɪ dɛːɪ]
The old man was a' peepin' out of a crack,
[ði oːʊld mæn wɑz ʌ ˈpipɪn ɑːʊt ʌv ʌ kɹæk]
And he saw the old Devil come draggin' her back.
[ænd hi sɔ ði oːʊld ˈdɛvɪ(ʊ)l kʌm ˈdɹægɪn hɜ bæk]
Sing hi diddle i diddle i fi
[sɪŋ hɑːɪ ˈdɪdʊl ɑːɪ ˈdɪdʊl ɑːɪ fɑːɪ]
diddle i diddle i day.
[ˈdɪdʊl ɑːɪ ˈdɪdʊl ɑːɪ dɛːɪ]
Now, there's one advantage
[nɑːʊ ðɛːʌz wʌn ædˈvæntæ(ɪ)dʒ]
women have over men.
[ˈwɪmɛ(ɪ)n hæv ˈoːʊvʌ mɛn]
They can all go to Hell!
[ðɛːɪ kæn ɔl goːʊ tʊ hɛl]
and come back, again.
[ænd kʌm bæk ʌˈgɛn]
Sing hi diddle i diddle i fi
[sɪŋ hɑːɪ ˈdɪdʊl ɑːɪ ˈdɪdʊl ɑːɪ fɑːɪ]
diddle i diddle i day!
[ˈdɪdʊl ɑːɪ ˈdɪdʊl ɑːɪ dɛːɪ]

4. Wanderin'
[ˈwandʌʁɪn]

I been a wanderin' early,
[ɑ bɪn ʌ ˈwandɹɪn ˈɜlɪ]
I been a wanderin' late,
[ɑ bɪn ʌ ˈwandɹɪn lɛːɪt]
From New York City
[fɹʌm nju jɔk ˈsɪdɪ]
To the Golden Gate.
[tʊ ðʌ ˈgoːʊldɛ(ɪ)n gɛːɪt]
And it looks like
[ænd ɪt lʊks lɑːɪk]
I'm never gonna cease
[ɑm ˈnɛvʌ ˈgʌnʌ sis]
My wanderin'.
[mɑ ˈwandʌʁɪn]
Been a' workin' in the army,
[bɪn ʌ ˈwɜkɪn ɪn ði ˈɑmɪ]
An' workin' on a farm,
[æn ˈwɜkɪn an ʌ fam]
All I got to show for it
[ɔl ɑ gat tʊ ʃoːʊ fʌʁ ɪt]
Is the muscle in my arm.
[ɪz ðʌ ˈmʌsʊl ɪn mɑ am]

An' it looks like
[æn ɪt lʊks lɑːɪk]
I'm never gonna cease
[am ˈnɛvʌ ˈgʌnʌ sis]
My wanderin'.
[mɑ ˈwandʌʁɪn]
There's snakes upon the mountain,
[ðɛːʌz snɛːɪks ʌˈpan ðʌ ˈmaːʊntæ(ɪ)n]
And eels in the sea.
[ænd ilz ɪn ðʌ si]
'Twas a red headed woman
[twaz ʌ ɹɛd ˈhɛdɛ(ɪ)d ˈwʊmæ(ʌ)n]
Made a wreck of me.
[mɛːɪd ʌ ɹɛk ʌv mi]
An' it looks like
[æn ɪt lʊks lɑːɪk]
I'm never gonna cease
[am ˈnɛvʌ ˈgʌnʌ sis]
My wanderin'.
[mɑ ˈwandʌʁɪn]
Ashes to ashes
[ˈæʃɛ(ɪ)z tu ˈæʃɛ(ɪ)z]
And dust to dust.
[ænd dʌst tʊ dʌst]
If whiskey don't get you,
[ɪf ˈʍɪskɪ doːʊnt gɛt jʊ]
Then the woman must.
[ðɛn ðʌ ˈwʊmæ(ʌ)n mʌst]
An' it looks like
[æn ɪt lʊks lɑːɪk]
I'm never gonna cease
[am ˈnɛvʌ ˈgʌnʌ sis]
My wanderin'.
[mɑ ˈwandʌʁɪn]

5. Red Iron Ore
[ɹɛd ɑːɪʁn ɔːʁ]

Come all ye bold sailors that follow the Lakes,
[kʌm ɔl ji boːʊld ˈsɛːɪlɔ(ʌ)z ðæt ˈfaloːʊ ðʌ lɛːɪks]
on an iron ore vessel your living to make.
[an æn ˈɑːɪʌn ɔːʌ ˈvɛsʊl jɔːʌ ˈlɪvɪŋ tʊ mɛːɪk]
I shipped in Chicago, bid adieu to the shore,
[ɑːɪ ʃɪpt ɪn ʃɪˈkagoːʊ bɪd aˈdjø tʊ ðʌ ʃɔːʌ]
Bound away to Escanaba for red iron ore,
[bɑːʊnd ʌˈwɛːɪ tu ɛskʌˈnabʌ fɔ ɹɛd ˈɑːɪʌn ɔːʌ]
Derry down, down, down, derry down.
[ˈdɛʁɪ dɑːʊn dɑːʊn dɑːʊn ˈdɛʁɪ dɑːʊn]
In the month of September, the seventeenth day,
[ɪn ðʌ mʌnθ ʌv sɛpˈtɛmbʌ ðʌ ˈsɛvɛ(ɪ)nˈtinθ dɛːɪ]
two dollars and a quarter was all they would pay,
[tu ˈdalʌz ænd ʌ ˈkwɔtʌ waz ɔl ðɛːɪ wʊd pɛːɪ]
And on Monday morning the Bridgeport did take
[ænd an ˈmʌndɛːɪ ˈmɔnɪŋ ðʌ ˈbɹɪdʒpɔt dɪd tɛːɪk]
the E. C. Roberts out into the lake.
[ði i si ˈɹabʌts ɑːʊt ˈɪntʊ ðʌ lɛːɪk]

Derry down, down, down, derry down.

[ˈdɛʁɪ daːʊn daːʊn daːʊn ˈdɛʁɪ daːʊn]

This packet she howled 'cross the mouth of Green Bay,

[ðɪs ˈpækɛ(ɪ)t ʃi haːʊld kʁas ðʌ maːʊθ ʌv gʁin bɛːɪ]

and before her cut water she dashed the white spray.

[ænd bɪˈfɔːʌ hɜ kʌt ˈwɔtʌ ʃi dæʃt ðʌ ʍaːɪt spʁɛːɪ]

We rounded the sand point,

[wi ˈʁaːʊndɛ(ɪ)d ðʌ sænd pɔːɪnt]

our anchor let go,

[aːʊʌʁ ˈæŋkɔ(ʌ) lɛt goːʊ]

We furled in our canvas and the watch went below.

[wi fɜld ɪn aːʊʌ ˈkænvʌs ænd ðʌ watʃ wɛnt bɪˈloːʊ]

Derry down, down, down, derry down.

[ˈdɛʁɪ daːʊn daːʊn daːʊn ˈdɛʁɪ daːʊn]

Next morning we hove in along the Exile,

[nɛkst ˈmɔnɪŋ wi hoːʊv ɪn ʌˈlaŋ ði ˈɛgzaːɪl]

and soon was made fast to an iron ore pile.

[ænd sun waz mɛːɪd fæst tu æn ˈaːɪʌn ɔːʌ paːɪl]

They lowered their chutes and like thunder did roar.

[ðɛːɪ ˈloːʊʌd ðɛːʌ ʃuts ænd laːɪk ˈθʌndʌ dɪd ʁɔːʌ]

They spouted into us that red iron ore.

[ðɛːɪ spaːʊtɛ(ɪ)d ˈɪntu ʌs ðæt ʁed ˈaːɪʌn ɔːʌ]

Derry down, down, down, derry down.

[ˈdɛʁɪ daːʊn daːʊn daːʊn ˈdɛʁɪ daːʊn]

Some sailors took shovels while others got spades,

[sʌm ˈsɛːɪlɔ(ʌ)z tʊk ˈʃʌvʊlz ʍaːɪl ˈʌðʌz gat spɛːɪdz]

and some took wheelbarrows, each man to his trade.

[ænd sʌm tʊk ˈʍilbæʁoːʊz itʃ mæn tʊ hɪz tʁɛːɪd]

We looked like red devils, our fingers got sore,

[wi lʊkt laːɪk ʁed ˈdɛvɪ(ʊ)lz aːʊʌ ˈfɪŋgʌz gat sɔːʌ]

We cursed Escanaba an' that damned iron ore.

[wi kɜst ɛskʌˈnabʌ æn ðæt dæmd ˈaːɪʌn ɔːʌ]

Derry down, down, down, derry down.

[ˈdɛʁɪ daːʊn daːʊn daːʊn ˈdɛʁɪ daːʊn]

The tug Escanaba she towed out the Minch.

[ðʌ tʌg ɛskʌˈnabʌ ʃi toːʊd aːʊt ðʌ mɪntʃ]

The Roberts she thought she had left in a pinch,

[ðʌ ˈʁabʌts ʃi θɔt ʃi hæd lɛft ɪn ʌ pɪntʃ]

And as she passed by us she bid us goodbye,

[ænd æz ʃi pæst baːɪ ʌs ʃi bɪd ʌs gʊdˈbaːɪ]

Saying "We'll meet in Cleveland next fourth of July."

[ˈsɛːɪɪŋ wil mit ɪn ˈklivlæ(ʌ)nd nɛkst fɔθ ʌv dʒuˈlaːɪ]

Derry down, down, down, derry down.

[ˈdɛʁɪ daːʊn daːʊn daːʊn ˈdɛʁɪ daːʊn]

'Cross Saginaw Bay the Roberts did ride with dark

[kʁas ˈsægɪnɔ bɛːɪ ðʌ ˈʁabʌts dɪd ʁaːɪd wɪð dak]

and deep water rolling over her side.

[ænd dip ˈwɔtʌ ˈʁoːʊlɪŋ ˈoːʊvʌ hɜ saːɪd]

And now for Port Huron the Roberts must go

[ænd naːʊ fɔ pɔt ˈhjʊʁan ðʌ ˈʁabʌts mʌst goːʊ]

where the tug Katey Williams will take us in tow.

[ʍɛːʌ ðʌ tʌg ˈkɛːɪti ˈwɪljæ(ɪ)mz wɪl tɛːɪk ʌs ɪn toːʊ]

Derry down, down, down, derry down.

[ˈdɛʁɪ daːʊn daːʊn daːʊn ˈdɛʁɪ daːʊn]

We went through North Passage, O Lord, how it blew!

[wi wɛnt θʁu nɔθ ˈpæsæ(ɪ)dʒ oːʊ lɔd haːʊ ɪt blu]

And all 'round the Dummy a fleet there came too.

[ænd ɔl ʁaːʊnd ðʌ ˈdʌmɪ ʌ flit ðɛːʌ kɛːɪm tu]

The night being dark, Old Nick it would scare.

[ðʌ naːɪt ˈbiɪŋ dak oːʊld nɪk ɪt wʊd skɛːʌ]

We hove up next morn and for Cleveland did steer.

[wi hoːʊv ʌp nɛkst mɔn ænd fɔ ˈklivlæ(ʌ)nd dɪd stɪːʌ]

Derry down, down, down, derry down.

[ˈdɛʁɪ daːʊn daːʊn daːʊn ˈdɛʁɪ daːʊn]

Now the Roberts in Cleveland made fast stem

[naːʊ ðʌ ˈʁabʌts ɪn ˈklivlæ(ʌ)nd mɛːɪd fæst stɛm]

and stern, and over the bottle we'll spin a big yarn.

[ænd stɜn ænd ˈoːʊvʌ ðʌ ˈbatʊl wil spɪn ʌ bɪg jan]

But Cap Harvey Shannon had ought to stand treat,

[bʌt kæp ˈhavɪ ˈʃænʌn hæd ɔt tʊ stænd tʁit]

for getting to Cleveland ahead of the fleet.

[fɔ ˈgɛtɪŋ tʊ ˈklivlæ(ʌ)nd ʌ ˈhɛd ʌv ðʌ flit]

Derry down, down, down, derry down.

[ˈdɛʁɪ daːʊn daːʊn daːʊn ˈdɛʁɪ daːʊn]

Now my song is ended. I hope you won't laugh.

[naːʊ maːɪ saŋ ɪz ˈɛndɛ(ɪ)d aːɪ hoːʊp ju woːʊnt læf]

Our dunnage is packed and all hands are paid off.

[aːʊʌ ˈdʌnæ(ɪ)dʒ ɪz pækt ænd ɔl hændz a pɛːɪd af]

Here's health to the Roberts,

[hɪːʌz hɛlθ tʊ ðʌ ˈʁabʌts]

she's staunch, strong and true;

[ʃiz stɔntʃ stʁaŋ ænd tʁu]

Not forgotten, the bold boys that make up her crew.

[nat fɔˈgatɛ(ɪ)n ðʌ boːʊld bɔːɪz ðæt mɛːɪk ʌp hɜ kʁu]

Derry down, down, down, derry down!

[ˈdɛʁɪ daːʊn daːʊn daːʊn ˈdɛʁɪ daːʊn]

American Folk Set, Book 2 (Song Cycle)

[ʌˈmɛʁɪkɪn foːʊk sɛt bʊk tu]

Folksongs

1. The Bachelor's Lay

[ðʌ ˈbætʃʊlʁz lɛːɪ]

As I was a trav'ling one morning in May,

[æz aːɪ waz ʌ ˈtʁævlɪŋ wʌn ˈmɔnɪŋ ɪn mɛːɪ]

I heard an old bachelor beginning a lay:

[aːɪ hɜd æn oːʊld ˈbætʃʊlʌ(ʌ) bɪˈgɪnɪŋ ʌ lɛːɪ]

"Oh, I can't tell why the reason may be

[oːʊ aːɪ kænt tɛl ʍaːɪ ðʌ ˈʁizʌn mɛːɪ bi]

that none of those girls will marry me.

[ðæt nʌn ʌv ðoːʊz gɜlz wɪl ˈmæʁɪ mi]

I've courted the rich and I've courted the poor,

[aːɪv ˈkɔtɛ(ɪ)d ðʌ ʁɪtʃ ænd aːɪv ˈkɔtɛ(ɪ)d ðʌ pɔːʌ]

I've often been snubbed at the meeting house door,

[aːɪv ˈafɛ(ɪ)n bɪn snʌbd æt ðʌ ˈmitɪŋ haːʊs dɔːʌ]

And I can't tell why the reason may be

[ænd aːɪ kænt tɛl ʍaːɪ ðʌ ˈʁizʌn mɛːɪ bi]

that none of those girls will marry me.

[ðæt nʌn ʌv ðoːʊz gɜlz wɪl ˈmæʁɪ mi]

I've offered them silver, I've offered them gold,

[aːɪv ˈafʌd ðɛm ˈsɪlvʌ aːɪv ˈafʌd ðɛm goːʊld]

and many fine stories to them I have told,
[ænd 'mɛnɪ faːɪn 'stɔʁɪz tu ðɛm aːɪ hæv toːʊld]
But gold and silver won't do, I can see.
[bʌt goːʊld ænd 'sɪlvʌ woːʊnt du aːɪ kæn si]
For none of those girls have married me.
[fɔ nʌn ʌv ðoːʊz gɜlz hæv 'mæʁɪd mi]
I've been through the mountains,
[aːɪv bɪn θru ðʌ 'maːʊntæ(ɪ)nz]
I've traveled the plains.
[aːɪv 'tɹævʊld ðʌ pleːɪnz]
I courted the missus, I've courted the dames.
[aːɪ 'kɔtɛ(ɪ)d ðʌ 'mɪsʌz aːɪv 'kɔtɛ(ɪ)d ðʌ dɛːɪmz]
And I can't tell why the reason may be
[ænd aːɪ kænt tɛl ʍaːɪ ðʌ 'ɹizan mɛːɪ bi]
that none of those girls will marry me.
[ðæt nʌn ʌv ðoːʊz gɜlz wɪl 'mæʁɪ mi]
I've sailed on the main and I've followed the coast.
[aːɪv sɛːɪld an ðʌ mɛːɪn ænd aːɪv 'faloːʊd ðʌ koːʊst]
No conquest of love can I honestly boast.
[noːʊ 'kaŋkwɛst ʌv lʌv kæn aːɪ 'ane(ɪ)stlɪ boːʊst]
And I can't tell what the reason may be
[ænd aːɪ kænt tɛl ʍat ðʌ 'ɹizʌn mɛːɪ bi]
that none of those girls will marry me.
[ðæt nʌn ʌv ðoːʊz gɜlz wɪl 'mæʁɪ mi]
I've asked them to tell me what stood in their way.
[aːɪv æskt ðɛm tʊ tɛl mi ʍat stʊd ɪn ðɛːʌ wɛːɪ]
And all of them answered 'I'd rather not say.'
[ænd ɔl ʌv ðɛm 'ænsʌd aːɪd 'ɹæðʌ nat sɛːɪ]
So I can't tell why the reason may be
[soːʊ aːɪ kænt tɛl ʍaːɪ ðʌ 'ɹizʌn mɛːɪ bi]
that none of those girls will marry me.
[ðæt nʌn ʌv ðoːʊz gɜlz wɪl 'mæʁɪ mi]
Go shave off your whiskers and powder your hair!
[goːʊ ʃɛːɪv af jɔːʌ 'ʍɪskʌz ænd 'paːʊdʌ jɔːʌ hɛːʌ]
Go dress yourself up with the greatest of care.
[goːʊ dɹɛs jɔːʌ'sɛlf ʌp wɪð ðʌ 'gɹɛːɪtɛ(ɪ)st ʌv kɛːʌ]
Put on your broad sword and bright buckles too
[pʊt an jɔːʌ bɹɔd sɔd ænd bɹaːɪt 'bʌkʊlz tu]
if you want a young lady to marry you."
[ɪf ju want ʌ jʌŋ 'lɛːɪdɪ tu 'mæʁɪ ju]

2. Down, Down, Down
[daːʊn daːʊn daːʊn]

With your kind attention a song I will trill
[wɪð jɔːʌ kaːɪnd ʌ'tɛnʃʌn ʌ saŋ aːɪ wɪl tɹɪl]
for ye who must toil with the pick and the drill.
[fɔ jiː hu mʌst tɔːɪl wɪð ðʌ pɪk ænd ðʌ dɹɪl]
And sweat for your bread in that hole at Oak Hill
[ænd swɛt fɔ jɔːʌ bɹɛd ɪn ðæt hoːʊl æt oːʊk hɪl]
that goes down, down, down.
[ðæt goːʊz daːʊn daːʊn daːʊn]
When I was a boy, said my daddy to me,
[ʍɛn aːɪ waz ʌ bɔːɪ sɛd maːɪ 'dædɪ tʊ mi]
"Stay out of Oak Hill, take my warnin'," said he,
[stɛːɪ aːʊt ʌv oːʊk hɪl tɛːɪk maːɪ 'wanɪn sɛd hi]

"Or with dust you'll be choked and a pauper you'll be,
[ɔ wɪð dʌst jul bi ʧoːʊkt ænd ʌ 'pɔpʌ jul bi]
broken down, down, down."
['bɹoːʊkɛ(ɪ)n daːʊn daːʊn daːʊn]
But I went to Oak Hill and I asked for a job,
[bʌt aːɪ wɛnt tu oːʊk hɪl ænd aːɪ æskt fɔʁ ʌ dʒab]
a mule for to drive or a gangway to rob.
[ʌ mjul fɔ tʊ dɹaːɪv ɔʁ ʌ 'gæŋwɛːɪ tʊ ɹab]
So the boss said "Come out, Bill and follow the mob
[soːʊ ðʌ bas sɛd kʌm aːʊt bɪl ænd 'faloːʊ ðʌ mab]
that goes down, down, down."
[ðæt goːʊz daːʊn daːʊn daːʊn]
"All aboard for the bottom" the topman did yell.
[ɔl ʌ'bɔd fɔ ðʌ 'batʌm ðʌ 'tapmæn dɪd jɛl]
We stepped on the cage and he gave her the bell.
[wi stɛpt an ðʌ kɛːɪdʒ ænd hi gɛːɪv hɜ ðʌ bɛl]
Then from under our feet like a bat out of... well,
[ðɛn fɹʌm 'ʌndʌʁ aːʊʌ fit laːɪk ʌ bæt aːʊt ʌv wɛl]
We went down, down, down.
[wi wɛnt daːʊn daːʊn daːʊn]
You could look at the rib, or the face or the top,
[ju kʊd lʊk æt ðʌ ɹɪb ɔ ðʌ fɛːɪs ɔ ðʌ tap]
Ne'er a sign of a laggin' or slab or of prop.
[nɛːʁ ʌ saːɪn ʌv ʌ 'lægɪn ɔ slæb ɔʁ ʌv pɹap]
Some day I expect this old mountain to drop,
[sʌm dɛːɪ aːɪ ɪk'spɛkt ðɪs oːʊld 'maːʊntæ(ɪ)n tu dɹap]
and come down, down, down.
[ænd kʌm daːʊn daːʊn daːʊn]

3. The Old Woman's Courtship
[ði oːʊld 'wʊmʌnz 'kɔʁtʃɪp]

Old woman, old woman,
[oːʊld 'wʊmæ(ʌ)n oːʊld 'wʊmæ(ʌ)n]
will you go a shearing?
[wɪl ju goːʊ ʌ 'ʃiːʌʁ(ʳ)ɪŋ]
"Speak a little louder, sir,
[spik ʌ 'lɪtʊl 'laːʊdʌ sɜ]
I'm rather hard of hearing."
[aːɪm 'ɹæðʌ had ʌv 'hiːʌʁ(ʳ)ɪŋ]
Old woman, old woman,
[oːʊld 'wʊmæ(ʌ)n oːʊld 'wʊmæ(ʌ)n]
are you good at weaving?
[a ju gʊd æt 'wivɪŋ]
"Pray speak a little louder sir,
[pɹɛːɪ spik ʌ 'lɪtʊl 'laːʊdʌ sɜ]
my hearing is deceiving."
[maːɪ 'hiːʌʁ(ʳ)ɪŋ ɪz dɪ'sivɪŋ]
Old woman, old woman,
[oːʊld 'wʊmæ(ʌ)n oːʊld 'wʊmæ(ʌ)n]
will you go a' walking?
[wɪl ju goːʊ ʌ 'wɔkɪŋ]
"Speak a little louder sir,
[spik ʌ 'lɪtʊl 'laːʊdʌ sɜ]
or what's the use of talking?"
[ɔ ʍats ðʌ jus ʌv 'tɔkɪŋ]

Old woman, old woman,
[oːʊld ˈwʊmæ(ʌ)n oːʊld ˈwʊmæ(ʌ)n]
are you fond of spinning?
[ɑ ju fɑnd ʌv ˈspɪnɪŋ]
"Pray speak a little louder sir,
[pɹɛːɪ spik ʌ ˈlɪtʊl ˈlaːʊdʌ sɜ]
I only see you grinning."
[ɑːɪ ˈoːʊnlɪ si ju ˈɡɹɪnɪŋ]
Old woman! Old woman!
[oːʊld ˈwʊmæ(ʌ)n oːʊld ˈwʊmæ(ʌ)n]
Will you do my knitting?
[wɪl ju du maːɪ ˈnɪtɪŋ]
"My hearing's getting better now.
[maːɪ ˈhɪːʌʁ⁽ʳ⁾ɪŋz ˈɡɛtɪŋ ˈbɛtʌ naːʊ]
Come near to where I'm sitting."
[kʌm nɪːʌ tu ʍɛːʌʁ⁽ʳ⁾ aːɪm ˈsɪtɪŋ]
Old woman! Old woman!
[oːʊld ˈwʊmæ(ʌ)n oːʊld ˈwʊmæ(ʌ)n]
Shall I kiss you dearly?
[ʃæl aːɪ kɪs ju ˈdɪːʌlɪ]
"Oh, Lord have mercy on my soul, sir.
[oːʊ lɔd hæv ˈmɜsɪ ɑn maːɪ soːʊl sɜ]
Now I hear you clearly."
[naːʊ aːɪ hɪːʌ ju ˈklɪːʌlɪ]

4. The Ocean Burial
[ði ˈoːʊʃɪn ˈbɛʁɪʊl]

"Oh, bury me not in the deep, deep sea."
[oːʊ ˈbɛʁ⁽ʳ⁾ɪ mi nɑt ɪn ðʌ dip dip si]
These words came low and mournfully
[ðiz wɜdz kɛːɪm loːʊ ænd ˈmɔnfʊlɪ]
from the pallid lips of a youth who lay
[fɹʌm ðʌ ˈpælɪd lɪps ʌv ʌ juθ hu lɛːɪ]
in his small cabin bed at the close of day.
[ɪn hɪz smɔl ˈkæbɪn bɛd æt ðʌ kloːʊz ʌv dɛːɪ]
"Oh bury me not in the deep, deep sea,
[oːʊ ˈbɛʁ⁽ʳ⁾ɪ mi nɑt ɪn ðʌ dip dip si]
where the billowy shroud will roll over me,
[ʍɛːʌ ðʌ ˈbɪloːʊɪ ʃɹaːʊd wɪl ɹoːʊl ˈoːʊvʌ mi]
where no light will break through the cold dark wave,
[ʍɛːʌ noːʊ laːɪt wɪl bɹɛːɪk θɾu ðʌ koːʊld dɑk wɛːɪv]
and no sunbeam rest upon my grave.
[ænd noːʊ ˈsʌnbim ɹɛst ʌˈpɑn maːɪ ɡɹ⁽ʳ⁾ɛːɪv]
Oh it matters not, I have oft been told,
[oːʊ ɪt ˈmætʌz nɑt aːɪ hæv ɑft bɪn toːʊld]
where the body may lie
[ʍɛːʌ ðʌ ˈbɑdɪ mɛːɪ laːɪ]
when the heart grows cold.
[ʍɛn ðʌ hɑt ɡɹoːʊz koːʊld]
But grant, oh grant me this one final plea,
[bʌt ɡɹænt oːʊ ɡɹænt mi ðɪs wʌn ˈfaːɪnʊl pli]
to bury me not in the deep, deep sea.
[tu ˈbɛʁ⁽ʳ⁾ɪ mi nɑt ɪn ðʌ dip dip si]
I have always hoped to be laid when I died,
[aːɪ hæv ˈɔlwɛːɪz hoːʊpt tu bi lɛːɪd ʍɛn aːɪ daːɪd]

in the old church yard, on the green hillside.
[ɪn ði oːʊld ˈʧɜʧ jɑd ɑn ðʌ ɡɹin ˈhɪlsaːɪd]
By the bones of my father, oh, there let me be.
[baːɪ ðʌ boːʊnz ʌv maːɪ ˈfɑðʌ oːʊ ðɛːʌ lɛt mi bi]
Oh, bury me not in the deep, deep sea.
[oːʊ ˈbɛʁ⁽ʳ⁾ɪ mi nɑt ɪn ðʌ dip dip si]
Oh bury me not!" And his voice failed there.
[oːʊ ˈbɛʁ⁽ʳ⁾ɪ mi nɑt ænd hɪz vɔːɪs fɛːɪld ðɛːʌ]
But they gave no heed to his dying prayer.
[bʌt ðɛːɪ ɡɛːɪv noːʊ hid tu hɪz ˈdaːɪɪŋ pɹɛːʌ]
They have lowered him over the vessel's side,
[ðɛːɪ hæv ˈloːʊʌd hɪm ˈoːʊvʌ ðʌ ˈvɛsʊlz saːɪd]
and above him has closed the cold dark tide.
[ænd ʌˈbʌv hɪm hæz kloːʊzd ðʌ koːʊld dɑk taːɪd]

5. California
[kælɪˈfɔʁnjʌ]

When formed our band, we are all well manned
[ʍɛn fɔmd aːʊʌ bænd wi ɑʁ ɔl wɛl mænd]
To journey far to the promised land.
[tu ˈʤɜnɪ fɑ tʊ ðʌ ˈpɹɑmɪst lænd]
The golden ore is rich in store
[ðʌ ˈɡoːʊldɛ(ɪ)n ɔːʁ ɪz ɹɪʧ ɪn stɔːʌ]
On the banks of the Sacramento shore.
[ɑn ðʌ bæŋks ʌv ðʌ sækɹʌˈmɛntoːʊ ʃɔːʌ]
Then ho, boys, ho! To California go!
[ðɛn hoːʊ bɔːɪz hoːʊ tʊ kælɪˈfɔnjʌ ɡoːʊ]
There's plenty of gold, or so I'm told,
[ðɛːʌz ˈplɛntɪ ʌv ɡoːʊld ɔ soːʊ aːɪm toːʊld]
On the banks of the Sacramento!
[ɑn ðʌ bæŋks ʌv ðʌ sækɹʌˈmɛntoːʊ]
We all expect the coarsest fare,
[wi ɔl ɪkˈspɛkt ðʌ ˈkoːsɛ(ɪ)st fɛːʌ]
Sleeping out in the open air.
[ˈslipɪŋ aːʊt ɪn ði ˈoːʊpɛ(ɪ)n ɛːʌ]
On the ground we'll all sleep sound
[ɑn ðʌ ɡɹaːʊnd wɪl ɔl slip saːʊnd]
'cept when the wolves go howling round!
[sɛpt ʍɛn ðʌ wʊlvz ɡoːʊ ˈhaːʊlɪŋ ɹaːʊnd]
Then ho, boys, ho! To California go!
[ðɛn hoːʊ bɔːɪz hoːʊ tʊ kælɪˈfɔnjʌ ɡoːʊ]
There's plenty of gold, or so I'm told,
[ðɛːʌz ˈplɛntɪ ʌv ɡoːʊld ɔ soːʊ aːɪm toːʊld]
On the banks of the Sacramento!
[ɑn ðʌ bæŋks ʌv ðʌ sækɹʌˈmɛntoːʊ]
As we explore the distant shore,
[æz wi ɪkˈsplɔːʌ ðʌ ˈdɪstæ(ɪ)nt ʃɔːʌ]
Filling our pockets up with ore.
[ˈfɪlɪŋ aːʊʌ ˈpɑkɛ(ɪ)ts ʌp wɪð ɔːʌ]
Hear the sound, the shout goes 'round,
[hɪːʌ ðʌ saːʊnd ðʌ ʃaːʊt ɡoːʊz ɹaːʊnd]
Filling our pockets with a dozen pounds!
[ˈfɪlɪŋ aːʊʌ ˈpɑkɛ(ɪ)ts wɪð ʌ ˈdʌzɛ(ɪ)n paːʊndz]
Then ho, boys, ho! To California go!
[ðɛn hoːʊ bɔːɪz hoːʊ tʊ kælɪˈfɔnjʌ ɡoːʊ]

There's plenty of gold, or so I'm told,
[ðɛːʌz 'plɛntɪ ʌv goːʊld ɔ soːʊ aːɪm toːʊld]
On the banks of the Sacramento!
[ɑn ðʌ bæŋks ʌv ðʌ sækɪʌ'mɛntoːʊ]
The gold is almost ev'rywhere,
[ðʌ goːʊld ɪz 'ɔlmoːʊst 'ɛvɪʌʍɛːʌ]
We dig it out with an iron bar!
[wi dɪɢ ɪt aːʊt wɪð æn 'aːɪʌn bɑ]
But where it's thick, with spade or pick,
[bʌt ʍɛːʌʀ ɪts θɪk wɪð spɛːɪd ɔ pɪk]
We take out chunks as big as a brick!
[wi tɛːɪk aːʊt tʃʌŋks æz bɪg æz ʌ bɪɪk]
Then ho, boys, ho! To California go!
[ðɛn hoːʊ bɔːɪz hoːʊ tʊ kælɪ'fɔnjʌ goːʊ]
As oft we roam the dark sea foam,
[æz ɑft wi ɪoːʊm ðʌ dak si foːʊm]
We'll not forget our friends at home.
[wil nat fɔ'gɛt aːʊʌ fɪɛndz æt hoːʊm]
For memory kind will bring to mind
[fɔ 'mɛmɔʀɪ kaːɪnd wɪl bɪɪŋ tʊ maːɪnd]
The love of those we left behind.
[ðʌ lʌv ʌv ðoːʊz wi lɛft bɪ'haːɪnd]
Then ho, boys, ho. To California go.
[ðɛn hoːʊ bɔːɪz hoːʊ tʊ kælɪ'fɔnjʌ goːʊ]
There's plenty of gold, or so I'm told,
[ðɛːʌz 'plɛntɪ ʌv goːʊld ɔ soːʊ aːɪm toːʊld]
On the banks of the Sacramento!
[ɑn ðʌ bæŋks ʌv ðʌ sækɪʌ'mɛntoːʊ]

American Folk Set, Book 3 (Song Cycle)
[ʌ'mɛʀɪkɪn foːʊk sɛt bʊk θri]
Folksongs

1. The Gallows Tree
[ðʌ 'gæloːʊz tɹi]

Slack your rope, hangs a man!
[slæk jɔːʌ ɹoːʊp hæŋz ʌ mæn]
Slack it for a while.
[slæk ɪt fɔʀ⁽ʳ⁾ ʌ ʍaːɪl]
I think I see my mother comin',
[a θɪŋk a si ma 'mʌðʌ 'kʌmɪn]
ridin' many a mile.
['ɹaːɪdɪn 'mɛnɪ ʌ maːɪl]
Oh mother have you brought me gold,
[oːʊ 'mʌðʌ hæv jʊ bɹɔt mi goːʊld]
or have you paid my fee?
[ɔ hæv jʊ pɛːɪd ma fi]
Or have you come to see me hangin'
[ɔ hæv jʊ kʌm tʊ si mi 'hæŋɪn]
on the gallows tree?
[ɑn ðʌ 'gæloːʊz tɹi]
"I have not brought you gold.
[aːɪ hæv nat bɹɔt ju goːʊld]
I have not paid your fee.
[aːɪ hæv nat pɛːɪd jɔːʌ fi]

But I have come to see you hanging
[bʌt aːɪ hæv kʌm tʊ si ju 'hæŋɪn]
on the gallows tree."
[ɑn ðʌ 'gæloːʊz tɹi]
Slack your rope, hangs a man!
[slæk jɔːʌ ɹoːʊp hæŋz ʌ mæn]
Slack it for a while.
[slæk ɪt fɔʀ⁽ʳ⁾ ʌ ʍaːɪl]
I think I see my father comin',
[a θɪŋk a si ma 'faðʌ 'kʌmɪn]
ridin' many a mile.
['ɹaːɪdɪn 'mɛnɪ ʌ maːɪl]
Oh father have you brought me gold
[oːʊ 'faðʌ hæv jʊ bɹɔt mi goːʊld]
or have you paid my fee?
[ɔ hæv jʊ pɛːɪd ma fi]
Or have you come to see me hangin'
[ɔ hæv jʊ kʌm tʊ si mi 'hæŋɪn]
on the gallows tree?
[ɑn ðʌ 'gæloːʊz tɹi]
"I have not brought you gold.
[a hæv nat bɹɔt jʊ goːʊld]
I have not paid your fee.
[a hæv nat pɛːɪd jɔːʌ fi]
But I have come to see you hanging
[bʌt a hæv kʌm tʊ si jʊ 'hæŋɪn]
on the gallows tree."
[ɑn ðʌ 'gæloːʊz tɹi]
Slack your rope, hangs a man!
[slæk jɔːʌ ɹoːʊp hæŋz ʌ mæn]
Slack it for a while.
[slæk ɪt fɔʀ⁽ʳ⁾ ʌ ʍaːɪl]
I think I see my true love comin',
[a θɪŋk a si ma tɹu lʌv 'kʌmɪn]
ridin' many a mile.
['ɹaːɪdɪn 'mɛnɪ ʌ maːɪl]
Oh, darlin' have you brought me gold,
[oːʊ 'dalɪn hæv jʊ bɹɔt mi goːʊld]
or have you paid my fee?
[ɔ hæv jʊ pɛːɪd ma fi]
Or have you come to see me hangin'
[ɔ hæv jʊ kʌm tʊ si mi 'hæŋɪn]
on the gallows tree?
[ɑn ðʌ 'gæloːʊz tɹi]
"Yes, I have brought you gold.
[jɛs aːɪ hæv bɹɔt ju goːʊld]
Yes, I have paid your fee.
[jɛs aːɪ hæv pɛːɪd jɔːʌ fi]
I have not come to see you hanging
[aːɪ hæv nat kʌm tʊ si ju 'hæŋɪn]
on the gallows tree."
[ɑn ðʌ 'gæloːʊz tɹi]

2. I'm a Stranger Here
[aːɪm ʌ ˈstɹɛːɪndʒʁ hɪːʁ]

Hitch up my buggy, saddle up my old black mare.
[hɪtʃ ʌp ma ˈbʌgɪ ˈsædʊl ʌp ma oːʊld blæk mɛːʌ]
Goin' to find me an angel
[ˈgoːʊm tʊ faːɪnd mi æn ˈɛːɪndʒɛ(ʊ)l]
in this world somewhere.
[ɪn ðɪs wɜld ˈsʌmmɛːʌ]
I'm a stranger here. I'm a stranger ev'rywhere.
[am ʌ ˈstɹɛːɪndʒʌ hɪːʌ am ʌ ˈstɹɛːɪndʒʌ ˈɛvɹɪmɛːʌ]
I would go home but honey, I'm a stranger there.
[a wʊd goːʊ hoːʊm bʌt ˈhʌnɪ am ʌ ˈstɹɛːɪndʒʌ ðɛːʌ]
I'm worried now, but I won't be worried long.
[am ˈwʊʁɪd naːʊ bʌt a woːʊnt bi ˈwʊʁɪd lan]
It takes a worried man to sing a worried song.
[ɪt teːɪks ʌ ˈwʊʁɪd mæn tʊ sɪŋ ʌ ˈwʊʁɪd san]
I'm a stranger here, I'm a stranger everywhere.
[am ʌ ˈstɹɛːɪndʒʌ hɪːʌ am ʌ ˈstɹɛːɪndʒʌ ˈɛvɹɪmɛːʌ]
I would go home, but honey, I'm a stranger there.
[a wʊd goːʊ hoːʊm bʌt ˈhʌnɪ am ʌ ˈstɹɛːɪndʒʌ ðɛːʌ]
Looked down that road far as I could see.
[lʊkt daːʊn ðæt ɹoːʊd faʁ⁽ⁱ⁾ æz a kʊd si]
And a little bitty hand kept wavin' back at me.
[ænd ʌ ˈlɪdʊl ˈbɪdɪ hænd kɛpt ˈwɛːɪvɪn bæk æt mi]
I'm a stranger here,
[am ʌ ˈstɹɛːɪndʒʌ hɪːʌ]
I'm a stranger everywhere.
[am ʌ ˈstɹɛːɪndʒʌʁ ˈɛvɹɪmɛːʌ]
I would go home, but honey, I'm a stranger there.
[a wʊd goːʊ hoːʊm bʌt ˈhʌnɪ am ʌ ˈstɹɛːɪndʒʌ ðɛːʌ]

3. The Drunken Old Fool
[ðʌ ˈdɹʌŋkɪn oːʊld ful]

Note: the silent "r" may be pronounced

Oh, the old man he came home
[oːʊ ði oːʊld mæn hi kɛːɪm hoːʊm]
one night as drunk as he could be.
[wʌn naːɪt æz dɹʌŋk æz hi kʊd bi]
He saw a coat upon the rack
[hi sɔ ʌ koːʊt ʌˈpan ðʌ ɹæk]
where his coat ought to be.
[ʍɛːʌ hɪz koːʊt ɔt tʊ bi]
"My good wife, my dear wife,
[maːɪ gʊd waːɪf maːɪ dɪːʁ waːɪf]
my darlin' wife" said he,
[maːɪ ˈdaɹlɪn waːɪf sɛd hi]
"whose coat is that upon the rack
[huz koːʊt ɪz ðæt ʌˈpan ðʌ ɹæk]
where my coat ought to be?"
[ʍɛːʁ maːɪ koːʊt ɔt tʊ bi]
"Oh, you old fool, you blind fool,
[oːʊ ju oːʊld ful ju blaːɪnd ful]
you doddering fool" says she.
[ju ˈdadʌʁɪŋ ful sɛz ʃi]

"It's nothing but a bed quilt
[ɪts ˈnʌθɪŋ bʌt ʌ bɛd kwɪlt]
me uncle sent to me."
[mi ˈʌŋkʊl sɛnt tu mi]
"I've traveled the whole world over
[aːɪv ˈtɹævʊld ðʌ hoːʊl wɜld ˈoːʊvʁ]
ten thousand times or more
[tɛn ˈθaːʊzæ(ʌ)nd taːɪmz ɜ mɔːʁ]
but buttons on a bed quilt
[bʌt ˈbʌtʌnz an ʌ bɛd kwɪlt]
I've never seen before!"
[aːɪv ˈnɛvʁ sin bɪˈfɔːʁ]
Oh, the old man, he came home again
[oːʊ ði oːʊld mæn hi kɛːɪm hoːʊm ʌˈgɛn]
as drunk as he could be.
[æz dɹʌŋk æz hi kʊd bi]
He saw some boots beneath the bed
[hi sɔ sʌm buts bɪˈniθ ðʌ bɛd]
where his boots ought to be.
[ʍɛːʌ hɪz buts ɔt tu bi]
"My good wife, my dear wife,
[maːɪ gʊd waːɪf maːɪ dɪːʁ waːɪf]
my darlin' wife" said he,
[maːɪ ˈdaɹlɪn waːɪf sɛd hi]
"whose boots are these beneath the bed
[huz buts a ðiz bɪˈniθ ðʌ bɛd]
where my boots ought to be?"
[ʍɛːʁ maːɪ buts ɔt tu bi]
"Oh, you old fool, you blind fool,
[oːʊ ju oːʊld ful ju blaːɪnd ful]
you doddering fool" says she.
[ju ˈdadʌʁɪŋ ful sɛz ʃi]
"It's nothing but some milk jugs
[ɪts ˈnʌθɪŋ bʌt sʌm mɪlk dʒʌgz]
me uncle sent to me."
[mi ˈʌŋkʊl sɛnt tu mi]
"I've traveled the whole world over
[aːɪv ˈtɹævʊld ðʌ hoːʊl wɜld ˈoːʊvʁ]
ten thousand times or more,
[tɛn ˈθaːʊzæ(ʌ)nd taːɪmz ɜ mɔːʁ]
but spurs upon a milk jug
[bʌt spɜz ʌˈpan ʌ mɪlk dʒʌg]
I've never seen before!"
[aːɪv ˈnɛvʁ sin bɪˈfɔːʁ]
He stumbled home the next night,
[hi ˈstʌmbʊld hoːʊm ðʌ nɛkst naːɪt]
as drunk as he could be.
[æz dɹʌŋk æz hi kʊd bi]
He saw a face between the sheets
[hi sɔ ʌ fɛːɪs bɪˈtwin ðʌ ʃits]
where no face ought to be.
[ʍɛːʌ noːʊ fɛːɪs ɔt tu bi]
"My good wife, my dear wife,
[maːɪ gʊd waːɪf maːɪ dɪːʁ waːɪf]
my darlin' wife" said he,
[maːɪ ˈdaɹlɪn waːɪf sɛd hi]

"whose face is that between the sheets
[huz fɛːɪs ɪz ðæt bɪˈtwin ðʌ ʃits]
where my face ought to be?"
[ʍɛːʁ maːɪ fɛːɪs ɔt tʊ bi]
"Oh, you old fool, you blind fool,
[oːʊ ju oːʊld ful ju blaːɪnd ful]
you doddering fool" says she.
[ju ˈdadʌʁɪŋ ful sɛz ʃi]
"It's nothing but a cabbage head
[ɪts ˈnʌθɪŋ bʌt ʌ ˈkæbæ(ɪ)ʤ hɛd]
me uncle sent to me."
[mi ˈʌŋkʊl sɛnt tu mi]
"I've traveled the whole world over
[aːɪv ˈtʁævʊld ðʌ hoːʊl wɜld ˈoːʊvʁ]
ten thousand times or more…
[tɛn ˈθaːʊzæ(ʌ)nd taːɪmz ɜ moːʁ]
but a mustache on a cabbage head?
[bʌt ʌ mʌˈstæʃ an ʌ ˈkæbæ(ɪ)ʤ hɛd]
I've never seen before!"
[aːɪv ˈnɛvʁ sin bɪˈfɔːʁ]

4. Poor Wayfaring Stranger (see "Wayfaring Stranger" by Niles)

5. Hell in Texas
[hɛl ɪn ˈtɛksʌs]

Oh, the Devil in hell they say he was chained.
[oːʊ ðʌ ˈdɛvɪ(ʊ)l ɪn hɛl ðɛːɪ sɛːɪ hi waz ʧɛːɪnd]
And there for a thousand years he remained.
[ænd ðɛːʌ fɔʁ ʌ ˈθaːʊzæ(ʌ)nd jɪːʌz hi ʁɪˈmɛːɪnd]
He never complained, no, nor did he groan,
[hi ˈnɛvʌ kʌmˈplɛːɪnd noːʊ nɔ dɪd hi gʁoːʊn]
But decided he'd start up a hell of his own,
[bʌt dɪˈsaːɪdɛ(ɪ)d hid stat ʌp ʌ hɛl ʌv hɪz oːʊn]
He'd start up a hell of his own!
[hid stat ʌp ʌ hɛl ʌv hɪz oːʊn]
Where he could torment the souls of men
[ʍɛːʌ hi kʊd tɔˈment ðʌ soːʊlz ʌv mɛn]
Free from the walls of his prison pen.
[fʁi fʁʌm ðʌ wɔlz ʌv hɪz ˈpʁɪzʌn pɛn]
So he asked the Lord if he had any sand
[soːʊ hi æskt ðʌ lɔd ɪf hi hæd ˈɛnɪ sænd]
Left over from making this great land,
[lɛft ˈoːʊvʌ fʁʌm ˈmɛːɪkɪŋ ðɪs gʁɛːɪt lænd]
Left over from making this land!
[lɛft ˈoːʊvʌ fʁʌm ˈmɛːɪkɪŋ ðɪs lænd]
The Lord said, "why, yes! I have plenty on hand.
[ðʌ lɔd sɛd ʍaːɪ jɛs aːɪ hæv ˈplɛntɪ an hænd]
It's way down south on the Rio Grande,
[ɪts wɛːɪ daːʊn saːʊθ an ðʌ ˈʁioːʊ gʁænd]
But I got to be honest, the stuff is so poor
[bʌt aːɪ gat tu bi ˈanɛ(ɪ)st ðʌ stʌf ɪz soːʊ pʊːʌ]
That I wouldn't use it for hell anymore.
[ðæt aːɪ ˈwʊdɛ(ɪ)nt juz ɪt fɔ hɛl ˌɛnɪˈmɔːʌ]

It won't do for hell anymore!"
[ɪt woːʊnt du fɔ hɛl ˌɛnɪˈmɔːʌ]
So the Devil went down to look over his truck.
[soːʊ ðʌ ˈdɛvɪ(ʊ)l wɛnt daːʊn tu lʊk ˈoːʊvʌ hɪz tʁʌk]
It came as a gift, so he figured he's stuck.
[ɪt kɛːɪm æz ʌ gɪft soːʊ hi ˈfɪgjʒd hɪz stʌk]
And when he examined it careful and well,
[ænd ʍɛn hi ɪgˈzæmɪnd ɪt ˈkɛːʌfʊl ænd wɛl]
He decided the place was too dry for hell.
[hi dɪˈsaːɪdɛ(ɪ)d ðʌ plɛːɪs waz tu dʁaːɪ fɔ hɛl]
The place was too dry for his hell!
[ðʌ plɛːɪs waz tu dʁaːɪ fɔ hɪz hɛl]
Well, the Lord, he just wanted the stuff off his hands,
[wɛl ðʌ lɔd hi ʤʌst ˈwantɛ(ɪ)d ðʌ stʌf af hɪz hændz]
So he promised the Devil he'd water the land.
[soːʊ hi ˈpʁamɪst ðʌ ˈdɛvɪ(ʊ)l hid ˈwɔtʌ ðʌ lænd]
He had some old water that wasn't no use,
[hi hæd sʌm oːʊld ˈwɔtʌ ðæt ˈwazɛ(ɪ)nt noːʊ jus]
A rancid old puddle that stunk like the deuce,
[ʌ ˈʁænsɪd oːʊld ˈpʌdʊl ðæt stʌŋk laːɪk ðʌ dus]
I tell you it stunk like the deuce!
[aːɪ tɛl ju ɪt stʌŋk laːɪk ðʌ dus]
The Lord, he was crafty, the deal was arranged.
[ðʌ lɔd hi waz ˈkʁæftɪ ðʌ dil waz ʌˈʁɛːɪnʤd]
He laughed to himself as the deed was exchanged.
[hi læft tu hɪmˈsɛlf æz ðʌ did waz ɪksˈʧɛːɪnʤd]
But the Devil was ready to go with his plan
[bʌt ðʌ ˈdɛvɪ(ʊ)l waz ˈʁɛdi tu goːʊ wɪð hɪz plæn]
To make up a hell and so he began!
[tu mɛːɪk ʌp ʌ hɛl ænd soːʊ hi bɪˈgæn]
He scattered tarantulas over the roads,
[hi ˈskætʌd tʌˈʁænʧʊlʌz ˈoːʊvʌ ðʌ ʁoːʊdz]
Put thorns on the cactus and horns on the toads,
[pʊt θɔnz an ðʌ ˈkæktʌs ænd hɔnz an ðʌ toːʊdz]
He sprinkled the sand with millions of ants,
[hi ˈspʁɪŋkʊld ðʌ sænd wɪð ˈmɪljʌnz ʌv ænts]
So if you sit down, you need soles on your pants!
[soːʊ ɪf ju sɪt daːʊn ju nid soːʊlz an jɔːʌ pænts]
He put water puppies in all of the lakes,
[hi pʊt ˈwɔtʌ ˈpʌpɪz ɪn ɔl ʌv ðʌ lɛːɪks]
And under the rocks he put poisonous snakes.
[ænd ˈʌndʌ ðʌ ʁaks hi pʊt ˈpɔːɪzʌnʌs snɛːɪks]
He mixed all the dust up with jiggers and fleas,
[hi mɪkst ɔl ðʌ dʌst ʌp wɪð ˈʤɪgʌz ænd fliz]
Hung thorns and brambles all over the trees,
[hʌŋ θɔnz ænd ˈbʁæmbʊlz ɔl ˈoːʊvʌ ðʌ tʁiz]
The heat in the summer's a-hundred and ten,
[ðʌ hit ɪn ðʌ ˈsʌmʌz ʌ ˈhʌndʁɛ(ɪ)d ænd tɛn]
Not bad for the Devil but way too hot for men!!
[nat bæd fɔ ðʌ ˈdɛvɪ(ʊ)l bʌt wɛːɪ tu hat fɔ mɛn]
And after he'd fixed things so thorny and well
[ænd ˈæftʌ hid fɪkst θɪŋz soːʊ ˈθɔnɪ ænd wɛl]
He said "I'll be damned if this don't beat hell!"
[hi sɛd aːɪl bi dæmd ɪf ðɪs doːʊnt bit hɛl]
Then he flapped up his wings and away he flew
[ðɛn hi flæpt ʌp hɪz wɪŋz ænd ʌˈwɛːɪ hi flu]

And vanished from earth in a blaze of blue!
[ænd ˈvænɪʃt fɹʌm ɜθ ɪn ʌ bleːɪz ʌv blu]
So, if you ever end up in Texas
[soːʊ ɪf ju ˈɛvʌʀ ɛnd ʌp ɪn ˈtɛksʌs]
Let me know if it's true!!
[lɛt mi noːʊ ɪf ɪts tɹu]

L

 Laitman, Lori (Am. b. 1955)

Mystery (Song Cycle)
[ˈmɪstʌʀi]
Teasdale, Sara (Am. 1884-1933)

1. Nightfall
[ˈnɑːɪtfɔl]

We will never walk again
[wi wɪl ˈnɛvʌ wɔk ʌˈgɛn]
As we used to walk at night,
[æz wi just tu wɔk æt nɑːɪt]
Watching our shadows lengthen
[ˈwɑtʃɪŋ ɑːʊʌ ˈʃædoːʊz ˈlɛŋθɛ(ɪ)n]
Under the gold street-light
[ˈʌndʌ ðʌ goːʊld stɹit lɑːɪt]
When the snow was new and white
[ʌɛn ðʌ snoːʊ wɑz nju ænd ʌɑːɪt]
We will never walk again, Slowly, we two,
[wi wɪl ˈnɛvʌ wɔk ʌˈgɛn ˈsloːʊli wi tu]
In spring when the park is sweet
[ɪn spɹɪŋ ʌɛn ðʌ pɑk ɪz swit]
With midnight, and with dew,
[wɪð ˈmɪdnɑːɪt ænd wɪð dju]
And the passers-by are few.
[ænd ðʌ ˈpæsʌz bɑːɪ ɑ fju]
I sit and think of it all,
[ɑːɪ sɪt ænd θɪŋk ʌv ɪt ɔl]
And the blue June twilight dies,
[ænd ðʌ blu dʒun ˈtwɑːɪlɑːɪt dɑːɪz]
Down in the clanging square
[dɑːʊn ɪn ðʌ ˈklæŋɪŋ skwɛːʌ]
A street piano cries
[ʌ stɹit ˈpjænoːʊ kɹɑːɪz]
And stars come out in the skies.
[ænd stɑz kʌm ɑːʊt ɪn ðʌ skɑːɪz]

2. Spray
[spɹɛːɪ]

I knew you thought of me all night,
[ɑːɪ nju ju θɔt ʌv mi ɔl nɑːɪt]

I knew, though you were far away;
[ɑːɪ nju ðoːʊ ju wɜ fɑʀ⁽ʳ⁾ ʌˈwɛːɪ]
I felt your love blow over me
[ɑːɪ fɛlt jɔːʌ lʌv bloːʊ ˈoːʊvʌ mi]
As if a dark wind-riven sea
[æz ɪf ʌ dɑk wɪnd ˈɹɪvɛ(ɪ)n si]
Drenched me with quivering spray.
[dɹɛntʃt mi wɪð ˈkwɪvʌʀ⁽ʳ⁾ɪŋ spɹɛːɪ]
There are so many ways to love
[ðɛːʌʀ⁽ʳ⁾ ɑ soːʊ ˈmɛnɪ wɛːɪz tu lʌv]
And each way has its own delight–
[ænd ɪtʃ wɛːɪ hæz ɪts oːʊn dɪˈlɑːɪt]
Then be content to come to me
[ðɛn bi kʌnˈtɛnt tu kʌm tu mi]
Only as spray the beating sea
[ˈoːʊnlɪ æz spɹɛːɪ ðʌ ˈbitɪŋ si]
Drives inland through the night.
[dɹɑːɪvz ˈɪnlæ(ʌ)nd θɹu ðʌ nɑːɪt]

3. The Kiss
[ðʌ kɪs]

I hoped that she would love me,
[ɑːɪ hoːʊpt ðæt ʃi wʊd lʌv mi]
And she has kissed my mouth,
[ænd ʃi hæz kɪst mɑːɪ mɑːʊθ]
But I am like a stricken bird
[bʌt ɑːɪ æm lɑːɪk ʌ ˈstɹɪkɛ(ɪ)n bɜd]
That cannot reach the south.
[ðæt kæˈnɑt ɹitʃ ðʌ sɑːʊθ]
For though I know she loves me,
[fɔ ðoːʊ ɑːɪ noːʊ ʃi lʌvz mi]
To-night my heart is sad;
[tu nɑːɪt mɑːɪ hɑt ɪz sæd]
Her kiss was not so wonderful
[hɜ kɪs wɑz nɑt soːʊ ˈwʌndʌfʊl]
As all the dreams I had.
[æz ɔl ðʌ dɹimz ɑːɪ hæd]

4. The Mystery
[ðʌ ˈmɪstʌʀi]

Your eyes drink of me,
[jɔːʌʀ⁽ʳ⁾ ɑːɪz dɹɪŋk ʌv mi]
Love makes them shine,
[lʌv mɛːɪks ðɛm ʃɑːɪn]
Your eyes that lean
[jɔːʌʀ⁽ʳ⁾ ɑːɪz ðæt lin]
So close to mine.
[soːʊ kloːʊs tu mɑːɪn]
We have long been lovers,
[wi hæv lɑŋ bɪn ˈlʌvʌz]
We know the range
[wi noːʊ ðʌ ɹɛːɪndʒ]
Of each other's moods
[ʌv ɪtʃ ˈʌðʌz mudz]

And how they change;
[ænd haːʊ ðɛːɪ ʧɛːɪndʒ]
But when we look
[bʌt ʍɛn wi lʊk]
At each other so
[æt iʧ ˈʌðʌ soːʊ]
Then we feel
[ðɛn wi fil]
How little we know;
[haːʊ ˈlɪtʊl wi noːʊ]
The spirit eludes us,
[ðʌ ˈspɪʀ⁽ʳ⁾ɪt ɪˈljudz ʌs]
Timid and free
[ˈtɪmɪd ænd fʀi]
Can I ever know you
[kæn aːɪ ˈɛvʌ noːʊ ju]
Or you know me?
[ɔ ju noːʊ mi]

5. The Rose
[ðʌ ʀoːʊz]

Beneath my chamber window
[bɪˈniθ maːɪ ˈʧɛːɪmbʌ ˈwɪndoːʊ]
Pierrot was singing, singing, La la...
[pjɛˈʀo waz ˈsɪŋɪŋ ˈsɪŋɪŋ la la]
I heard his lute the whole night thru
[aːɪ hɜd hɪz ljut ðʌ hoːʊl naːɪt θru]
Until the east was red.
[ʌnˈtɪl ði ist waz ʀɛd]
Alas, alas, Pierrot,
[ʌˈlæs ʌˈlæs pjɛˈʀo]
I have no rose for flinging, Ah...
[aːɪ hæv noːʊ ʀoːʊz fʌ ˈflɪŋɪŋ a]
Save one that drank my tears for dew
[sɛːɪv wʌn ðæt dʀæŋk maːɪ tɪːʌz fʌ dju]
Before its leaves were dead.
[bɪˈfɔːʌʀ⁽ʳ⁾ ɪts livz wɜ dɛd]
I found it in the darkness
[aːɪ faːʊnd ɪt ɪn ðʌ ˈdaknɛ⁽ɪ⁾s]
I kissed it once and threw it, Ta ta...
[aːɪ kɪst ɪt wʌns ænd θʀu ɪt ta ta]
The petals scattered over him,
[ðʌ ˈpɛtʊlz ˈskætʌd ˈoːʊvʌ hɪm]
His song was turned to joy;
[hɪz saŋ waz tɜnd tu dʒɔːɪ]
And he will never know—
[ænd hi wɪl ˈnɛvʌ noːʊ]
Alas, the one who knew it!
[ʌˈlæs ðʌ wʌn hu nju ɪt]
The rose was plucked when dusk was dim
[ðʌ ʀoːʊz waz plʌkt ʍɛn dʌsk waz dɪm]
Beside a laughing boy. Ha ha...
[bɪˈsaːɪd ʌ ˈlæfɪŋ bɔːɪ ha ha]

The Metropolitan Tower and Other Songs
[ðʌ mɛtʀʌˈpalɪtɪn taːʊʀ ænd ˈʌðʀ saŋz]
(Song Cycle)
Teasdale, Sara (Am. 1884-1933)

1. The Metropolitan Tower
[ðʌ mɛtʀʌˈpalɪtɪn taːʊʀ]

We walked together in the dusk
[wi wɔkt tuˈgɛðʌʀ⁽ʳ⁾ ɪn ðʌ dʌsk]
To watch the tower grow dimly white,
[tu waʧ ðʌ taːʊʌ gʀoːʊ ˈdɪmlɪ ʍaːɪt]
And saw it lift against the sky
[ænd sɔ ɪt lɪft ʌˈgɛnst ðʌ skaːɪ]
Its flower of amber light.
[ɪts flaːʊʌʀ⁽ʳ⁾ ʌv ˈæmbʌ laːɪt]
You talked of half a hundred things,
[ju tɔkt ʌv hæf ʌ ˈhʌndʀɛ⁽ɪ⁾d θɪŋz]
I kept each hurried word you said:
[aːɪ kɛpt iʧ ˈhʊʀ⁽ʳ⁾ɪd wɜd ju sɛd]
And when at last the hour was full,
[ænd ʍɛn æt læst ði aːʊʌ waz fʊl]
I saw the light turn red.
[aːɪ sɔ ðʌ laːɪt tɜn ʀɛd]
You did not know the time had come.
[ju dɪd nat noːʊ ðʌ taːɪm hæd kʌm]
You did not see the sudden flower,
[ju dɪd nat si ðʌ ˈsʌdɛ⁽ɪ⁾n flaːʊʌ]
Nor know that in my heart Love's birth
[nɔ noːʊ ðæt ɪn maːɪ hat lʌvz bɜθ]
Was reckoned from that hour.
[waz ˈʀɛkʌnd fʀʌm ðæt aːʊʌ]

2. A Winter Night
[ʌ ˈwɪntʀ naːɪt]

My window-pane is starred with frost,
[maːɪ ˈwɪndoːʊ pɛːɪn ɪz stad wɪð fʀast]
The world is bitter cold to-night,
[ðʌ wɜld ɪz ˈbɪtʌ koːʊld tu naːɪt]
The moon is cruel, and the wind
[ðʌ mun ɪz ˈkʀ⁽ʳ⁾uːɛ⁽ʊ⁾l ænd ðʌ wɪnd]
Is like a two-edged sword to smite.
[ɪz laːɪk ʌ tu ɛdʒd sɔd tu smaːɪt]
God pity all the homeless ones,
[gad ˈpɪtɪ ɔl ðʌ ˈhoːʊmlɛ⁽ɪ⁾s wʌnz]
The beggars pacing to and fro.
[ðʌ ˈbɛgʌz ˈpɛːɪsɪŋ tu ænd fʀoːʊ]
God pity all the poor to-night
[gad ˈpɪtɪ ɔl ðʌ puːʌ tu naːɪt]
Who walk the lamp-lit streets of snow.
[hu wɔk ðʌ læmp lɪt stʀits ʌv snoːʊ]
My room is like a bit of June,
[maːɪ ʀ⁽ʳ⁾um ɪz laːɪk ʌ bɪt ʌv dʒun]
Warm and close-curtained fold on fold,
[wɔm ænd kloːʊz ˈkɜtæ⁽ɪ⁾nd foːʊld an foːʊld]

But somewhere, like a homeless child,
[bʌt 'sʌmʍɛːʌ laːɪk ʌ 'hoːʊmlɛ(ɪ)s ʧaːɪld]
My heart is crying in the cold.
[maːɪ hat ɪz 'kɪ⁽ʳ⁾aːɪɪŋ ɪn ðʌ koːʊld]

3. Old Tunes
[oːʊld tjunz]

As the waves of perfume, heliotrope, rose,
[æz ðʌ wɛːɪvz ʌv pɜ'fjum 'hilɪo͵tɪoːʊp ɹoːʊz]
Float in the garden when no wind blows,
[floːʊt ɪn ðʌ 'gadɛ(ɪ)n ʍɛn noːʊ wɪnd bloːʊz]
Come to us, go from us, whence no one knows;
[kʌm tu ʌs goːʊ fɪʌm ʌs ʍɛns noːʊ wʌn noːʊz]
So the old tunes float in my mind,
[soːʊ ði oːʊld tjunz floːʊt ɪn maːɪ maːɪnd]
And go from me leaving no trace behind,
[ænd goːʊ fɪʌm mi 'livɪŋ noːʊ tɪɛːɪs bɪ'haːɪnd]
Like fragrance borne on the hush of the wind.
[laːɪk 'fɪɛːɪgɪæ(ɪ)ns bon an ðʌ hʌʃ ʌv ðʌ wɪnd]
But in the instant the airs remain,
[bʌt ɪn ði 'ɪnstæ(ɪ)nt ði ɛːʌz ɹɪ'mɛːɪn]
I know the laughter and the pain
[aːɪ noːʊ ðʌ 'læftʌʁ⁽ʳ⁾ ænd ðʌ pɛːɪn]
Of times that will not come again.
[ʌv taːɪmz ðæt wɪl nat kʌm ʌ'gɛn]
I try to catch at many a tune
[aːɪ tɪaːɪ tu kæʧ æt 'mɛnɪ ʌ tjun]
Like petals of light fallen from the moon,
[laːɪk 'pɛtʊlz ʌv laːɪt 'fɔlɛ(ɪ)n fɪʌm ðʌ mun]
Broken and bright on a dark lagoon.
['bɪoːʊkɛ(ɪ)n ænd bɪaːɪt an ʌ dak lʌ'gun]
But they float away for who can hold
[bʌt ðɛːɪ floːʊt ʌ'wɛːɪ fɔ hu kæn hoːʊld]
Youth, or perfume or the moon's gold?
[juθ ɔ pɜ'fjum ɔ ðʌ munz goːʊld]

4. The Strong House
[ðʌ stɪaŋ haːʊs]

Our love is like a strong house
[aːʊʌ lʌv ɪz laːɪk ʌ stɪaŋ haːʊs]
Well roofed against the wind and rain
[wɛl ɹ⁽ʳʳ⁾uft ʌ'gɛnst ðʌ wɪnd ænd ɹɛːɪn]
Who passes darkly in the sun again and again?
[hu 'pæsɛ(ɪ)z 'daklɪ ɪn ðʌ sʌn ʌ'gɛn ænd ʌ'gɛn]
The doors are fast, the lamps are lit,
[ðʌ dɔːʌz a fæst ðʌ læmps a lɪt]
We sit together talking low
[wi sɪt tu'gɛðʌ 'tɔkɪŋ loːʊ]
Who is it in the ghostly dusk goes to and fro?
[hu ɪz ɪt ɪn ðʌ 'goːʊstlɪ dʌsk goːʊz tu ænd fɪoːʊ]
Surely ours is a strong house,
['ʃʊːʌlɪ aːʊʌz ɪz ʌ stɪaŋ haːʊs]
I will not trouble any more
[aːɪ wɪl nat 'tɪʌbʊl 'ɛnɪ mɔːʌ]

But who comes stealing at midnight
[bʌt hu kʌmz 'stilɪŋ æt 'mɪdnaːɪt]
To try the locked door?
[tu tɪaːɪ ðʌ lakt dɔːʌ]

5. The Hour
[ði aːʊʁ]

Was it foreknown, was it foredoomed
[waz ɪt fɔ'noːʊn waz ɪt fɔ'dumd]
Before I drew my first small breath?
[bɪ'fɔːʌʁ⁽ʳ⁾ aːɪ dɪ⁽ʳ⁾u maːɪ fɜst smɔl bɪɛːθ]
Will it be with me to the end,
[wɪl ɪt bi wɪð mi tu ði ɛnd]
Will it go down with me to death?
[wɪl ɪt goːʊ daːʊn wɪð mi tu dɛθ]
Or was it chance, would it have been
[ɔ waz ɪt ʧæns wʊd ɪt hæv bɪn]
Another if it was not you?
[ʌ'nʌðʌʁ⁽ʳ⁾ ɪf ɪt waz nat ju]
Could any other voice or hands
[kʊd 'ɛnɪ 'ʌðʌ vɔːɪs ɔ hændz]
Have done for me what yours can do?
[hæv dʌn fɔ mi ʍat jɔːʌz kæn du]
Now without sorrow and without elation
[naːʊ wɪð'aːʊt 'saʁ⁽ʳ⁾oːʊ ænd wɪð'aːʊt ɪ'lɛːɪʃʌn]
I say the day I found you was foreknown,
[aːɪ sɛːɪ ðʌ dɛːɪ aːɪ faːʊnd ju waz fɔ'noːʊn]
Let the years blow like sand around that hour,
[lɛt ðʌ jɪːʌz bloːʊ laːɪk sænd ʌ'ʁ⁽ʳ⁾aːʊnd ðæt aːʊʌ]
Changeless and fixed as Memnon carved in stone.
['ʧɛːɪnʤlɛ(ɪ)s ænd fɪkst æz 'mɛmnan kavd ɪn stoːʊn]

6. To a Loose Woman
[tu ʌ lus 'wʊmʌn]

My dear, your face is lovely,
[maːɪ dɪːʌ jɔːʌ fɛːɪs ɪz 'lʌvlɪ]
And you have lovely eyes,
[ænd ju hæv 'lʌvlɪ aːɪz]
I do not cavil at your life,
[aːɪ du nat 'kævɪ(ʊ)l æt jɔːʌ laːɪf]
But only at your lies.
[bʌt 'oːʊnlɪ æt jɔːʌ laːɪz]
You are not brave,
[ju a nat bɪɛːɪv]
You are not wild,
[ju a nat waːɪld]
You merely ride the crest of fashion;
[ju 'mɪːʌlɪ ɹaːɪd ðʌ kɪɛst ʌv 'fæʃʌn]
Ambition is your special ware
[æm'bɪʃʌn ɪz jɔːʌ 'spɛʃʊl wɛːʌ]
And you have dared to call it passion.
[ænd ju hæv dɛːʌd tu kɔl ɪt 'pæʃʌn]

Song Selections

"I'm Nobody" (see Gordon)

"If I Can Stop One Heart from Breaking" (see Hall)

"Over the Fence" (Days and Nights)
[ˈoːʊvʁ ðʌ fɛns]
Dickinson, Emily (Am. 1830-1886)

Over the fence–
[ˈoːʊvʌ ðʌ fɛns]
Strawberries– grow–
[ˈstɹɔbɛʁ⁽ʳ⁾ɪz ɡɹoːʊ]
Over the fence–
[ˈoːʊvʌ ðʌ fɛns]
I could climb– if I tried, I know–
[aːɪ kʊd klaːɪm ɪf aːɪ tɹaːɪd aːɪ noːʊ]
Berries are nice!
[ˈbɛʁ⁽ʳ⁾ɪz a naːɪs]
But– if I stained my Apron–
[bʌt ɪf aːɪ stɛːɪnd maːɪ ˈɛːɪpɹʌn]
God would certainly scold!
[ɡad wʊd ˈsɜtæ⁽ɪ⁾nlɪ skoːʊld]
Oh, dear,– I guess if He were a Boy–
[oːʊ dɪːʌ aːɪ ɡɛs ɪf hi wɜ⁽ʳ⁾ ʌ bɔːɪ]
He'd– climb– if He could!
[hid klaːɪm ɪf hi kʊd]

"She Died" (Four Dickinson Songs)
[ʃi daːɪd]
Dickinson, Emily (Am. 1830-1886)

She died – this is the way she died;
[ʃi daːɪd ðɪs ɪz ðʌ wɛːɪ ʃi daːɪd]
And when her breath was done,
[ænd ʍɛn hɜ bɹɛθ waz dʌn]
Took up her simple wardrobe
[tʊk ʌp hɜ ˈsɪmpʊl ˈwɔdɹoːʊb]
And started for the sun. She died.
[ænd ˈstatɛ⁽ɪ⁾d fɔ ðʌ sʌn ʃi daːɪd]
Her little figure at the gate
[hɜ ˈlɪtʊl ˈfɪɡjʊ(ʌ)ʁ⁽ʳ⁾ æt ðʌ ɡɛːɪt]
The angels must have spied,
[ði ˈɛːɪndʒɛ(ʊ)lz mʌst hæv spaːɪd]
Since I could never find her
[sɪns aːɪ kʊd ˈnɛvʌ faːɪnd hɜ]
Upon the mortal side.
[ʌˈpan ðʌ ˈmɔtʊl saːɪd]

"Song" (Days and Nights)
[saŋ]
Rossetti, Christina Georgina (Eng. 1830-1894)

When I am dead, my dearest,
[ʍɛn aːɪ æm dɛd maːɪ ˈdɪːʁ⁽ʳ⁾ɛ⁽ɪ⁾st]

Sing no sad songs for me;
[sɪŋ noːʊ sæd saŋz fɔ mi]
Plant no roses at my head,
[plænt noːʊ ˈɹoːʊzɛ⁽ɪ⁾z æt maːɪ hɛd]
Nor shady cypress tree:
[nɔ ˈʃɛːɪdɪ ˈsaːɪpɹɛ⁽ɪ⁾s tɹi]
Be the green grass above me
[bi ðʌ ɡɹin ɡɹæs ʌˈbʌv mi]
With showers and dewdrops wet;
[wɪð ʃaːʊʌz ænd ˈdjudɹaps wɛt]
And if thou wilt, remember,
[ænd ɪf ðaːʊ wɪlt ɹɪˈmɛmbʌ]
And if thou wilt, forget.
[ænd ɪf ðaːʊ wɪlt fɔˈɡɛt]
I shall not see the shadows,
[aːɪ ʃæl nat si ðʌ ˈʃædoːʊz]
I shall not feel the rain;
[aːɪ ʃæl nat fil ðʌ ɹɛːɪn]
I shall not hear the nightingale
[aːɪ ʃæl nat hɪːʌ ðʌ ˈnaːɪtɪŋɡɛːɪl]
Sing on, as if in pain:
[sɪŋ an æz ɪf ɪn pɛːɪn]
And dreaming through the twilight
[ænd ˈdɹimɪŋ θɹu ðʌ ˈtwaːɪlaːɪt]
That doth not rise nor set,
[ðæt dʌθ nat ɹaːɪz nɔ sɛt]
Haply I may remember,
[ˈhæplɪ aːɪ mɛːɪ ɹɪˈmɛmbʌ]
And haply may forget.
[ænd ˈhæplɪ mɛːɪ fɔˈɡɛt]

"The Ballad Singer"
[ðʌ ˈbælɪd ˈsɪŋʁ]
Hardy, Thomas (Eng. 1840-1928)

Sing, Ballad-singer, raise a hearty tune;
[sɪŋ ˈbælæ⁽ɪ⁾d ˈsɪŋʌ ɹɛːɪz ʌ ˈhatɪ tjun]
Make me forget there was ever a one
[mɛːɪk mi fɔˈɡɛt ðɛːʌ waz ˈɛvʌʁ⁽ʳ⁾ ʌ wʌn]
I walked with in the meek light of the moon
[aːɪ wɔkt wɪð ɪn ðʌ mik laːɪt ʌv ðʌ mun]
When the day's work was done.
[ʍɛn ðʌ dɛːɪz wɜk waz dʌn]
Rhyme, Ballad-rhymer, start a country song;
[ɹaːɪm ˈbælæ⁽ɪ⁾d ˈɹaːɪmʌ stat ʌ ˈkʌntɹɪ saŋ]
Make me forget that she whom I loved well
[mɛːɪk mi fɔˈɡɛt ðæt ʃi hum aːɪ lʌvd wɛl]
Swore she would love me dearly, love me long,
[swɔːʌ ʃi wʊd lʌv mi ˈdɪːʌlɪ lʌv mi laŋ]
Then– what I cannot tell!
[ðɛn ʍat aːɪ kæˈnat tɛl]
Sing, Ballad-singer, from your little book;
[sɪŋ ˈbælæ⁽ɪ⁾d ˈsɪŋʌ fɹʌm jɔːʌ ˈlɪtʊl bʊk]
Make me forget those heart-breaks, achings, fears;
[mɛːɪk mi fɔˈɡɛt ðoːʊz hat bɹɛːɪks ˈɛːɪkɪŋz fɪːʌz]

Make me forget her name, her sweet sweet look–
[mɛːɪk mi fɔˈgɛt hɜ nɛːɪm hɜ swit swit lʊk]
Make me forget her tears.
[mɛːɪk mi fɔˈgɛt hɜ tɪːʌz]

"The Night Has a Thousand Eyes" (Days and Nights)
[ðʌ naːɪt hæz ʌ ˈθaːʊzʌnd aːɪz]
Bourdillon, Francis William (Eng. 1852-1921)

The night has a thousand eyes,
[ðʌ naːɪt hæz ʌ ˈθaːʊzæ(ʌ)nd aːɪz]
 And the day but one;
[ænd ðʌ dɛːɪ bʌt wʌn]
Yet the light of the bright world dies
[jɛt ðʌ laːɪt ʌv ðʌ bɹaːɪt wɜld daːɪz]
With the dying sun.
[wɪð ðʌ ˈdaːɪɪŋ sʌn]
The mind has a thousand eyes,
[ðʌ maːɪnd hæz ʌ ˈθaːʊzæ(ʌ)nd aːɪz]
And the heart but one;
[ænd ðʌ hat bʌt wʌn]
Yet the light of a whole life dies
[jɛt ðʌ laːɪt ʌv ʌ hoːʊl laːɪf daːɪz]
When its love is done.
[ʍɛn ɪts lʌv ɪz dʌn]

"They Might Not Need Me" (Days and Nights)
[ðɛːɪ maːɪt nat nid mi]
Dickinson, Emily (Am. 1830-1886)

They might not need me; yet they might–
[ðɛːɪ maːɪt nat nid mi jɛt ðɛːɪ maːɪt]
I'll let my heart just be in sight–
[aːɪl lɛt maːɪ hat dʒʌst bi ɪn saːɪt]
A smile as small as mine might be
[ʌ smaːɪl æz smɔl æz maːɪn maːɪt bi]
Precisely their necessity–
[pɹɪˈsaːɪslɪ ðɛːʌ nɪˈsɛsɪtɪ]

"Will There Really Be a Morning" (see Gordon)

Larsen, Libby (Am. b. 1950)

Songs from Letters (Song Cycle)
[saŋz fɪʌm ˈlɛtʁz]
Cannary, Martha Jane (Am. 1856-1903)

1. So like Your Father's (1880)
[soːʊ laːɪk jɔːʁ ˈfaðʁz ˈɛːɪtin ˈɛːɪdi]

Janey, a letter came today
[ˈdʒɛːɪnɪ ʌ ˈlɛtʌ kɛːɪm tuˈdɛːɪ]
and a picture of you.
[ænd ʌ ˈpɪktʃʊ(ʌ)ʁ(r) ʌv ju]

Your expression so like your father's,
[jɔːʌʁ(r) ɪkˈspɹɛʃʌn soːʊ laːɪk jɔːʌ ˈfaðʌz]
brought back all the years.
[bɹɔt bæk ɔl ðʌ jɪːʌz]

2. He Never Misses (1880)
[hi ˈnɛvʁ ˈmɪsɪz ˈɛːɪtin ˈɛːɪdi]

I met your father "Wild Bill Hickok" near Abilene.
[aːɪ mɛt jɔːʌ ˈfaðʌ waːɪld bɪl ˈhɪkak nɪːʌ ˈæbɪˌlin]
A bunch of outlaws were trying to kill him,
[ʌ bʌntʃ ʌv ˈaːʊtˌlɔz wɜ ˈtɹaːɪɪŋ tu kɪl hɪm]
I crawled through the brush to warn him,
[aːɪ kɹɔld θɹu ðʌ bɹʌʃ tu wɔn hɪm]
Bill killed them all.
[bɪl kɪld ðɛm ɔl]
I'll never forget
[aːɪl ˈnɛvʌ fɔˈgɛt]
Blood running down his face
[blʌd ˈɹʌnɪŋ daːʊn hɪz fɛːɪs]
while he used two guns.
[ʍaːɪl hi juzd tu gʌnz]
He never aimed and he was never known to miss.
[hi ˈnɛvʌʁ(r) ɛːɪmd ænd hi waz ˈnɛvʌ noːʊn tu mɪs]

3. A Man Can Love Two Women (1880)
[ʌ mæn kæn lʌv tu ˈwɪmɪn ˈɛːɪtin ˈɛːɪdi]

Don't let jealousy get you, Janey.
[doːʊnt lɛt ˈdʒɛlʌsɪ gɛt ju ˈdʒɛːɪnɪ]
It kills love and all nice things.
[ɪt kɪlz lʌv ænd ɔl naːɪs θɪŋz]
It drove your father from me.
[ɪt dɹoːʊv jɔːʌ ˈfaðʌ fɹʌm mi]
I lost everything I loved except for you.
[aːɪ last ˈɛvɹɪθɪŋ aːɪ lʌvd ɪkˈsɛpt fɔ ju]
A man can love two women at a time.
[ʌ mæn kæn lʌv tu ˈwɪmɛ(ɪ)n æt ʌ taːɪm]
He loved her and he still loved me
[hi lʌvd hɜ ænd hi stɪl lʌvd mi]
Because of you, Janey.
[bɪˈkɔz ʌv ju ˈdʒɛːɪnɪ]

4. A Working Woman
[ʌ ˈwɜkɪŋ ˈwʊmʌn]

Your mother works for a living.
[jɔːʌ ˈmʌðʌ wɜks fɔʁ(r) ʌ ˈlɪvɪŋ]
One day I have chickens, and the next day feathers.
[wʌn dɛːɪ aːɪ hæv ˈtʃɪkɛ(ɪ)nz ænd ðʌ nɛkst dɛːɪ ˈfɛðʌz]
These days I'm driving a stagecoach.
[ðiz dɛːɪz aːɪm ˈdɹaːɪvɪŋ ʌ ˈstɛːɪdʒˌkoːʊtʃ]
For a while I worked in Russell's saloon.
[fɔʁ(r) ʌ ʍaːɪl aːɪ wɜkt ɪn ˈɹʌsʊlz sʌˈlun]
But when I worked there all the virtuous women
[bʌt ʍɛn aːɪ wɜkt ðɛːʌ ɔl ðʌ ˈvɜtʃuʌs ˈwɪmɛ(ɪ)n]

planned to run me out of town,
[plænd tu ɹʌn mi ɑːʊt ʌv taːʊn]
so these days I'm driving a stagecoach.
[soːʊ ðiz deːɪz ɑːɪm ˈdɪɑːɪvɪŋ ʌ ˈsteːɪdʒˌkoːʊtʃ]
Your mother works for a living.
[jɔːʌ ˈmʌðʌ wɜks fɔʁ⁽ʳ⁾ ʌ ˈlɪvɪŋ]
I'll be leaving soon to join Bill Cody's Wild West Show.
[ɑːɪl bi ˈlivɪŋ sun tu dʒɔːɪn bɪl ˈkoːʊdɪz wɑːɪld wɛst ʃoːʊ]
I'll ride a horse bare-back, standing up,
[ɑːɪl ɹɑːɪd ʌ hɔs beːʌ bæk ˈstændɪŋ ʌp]
shooting my Stetson hat twice,
[ˈʃutɪŋ mɑːɪ ˈstɛtsʌn hæt twɑːɪs]
throwing it into the air–
[ˈθɹoːʊɪŋ ɪt ˈɪntu ði ɛːʌ]
and landing on my head.
[ænd ˈlændɪŋ ɑn mɑːɪ hɛd]
These are hectic days, like hell let out for noon.
[ðiz ɑ ˈhɛktɪk deːɪz lɑːɪk hɛl lɛt ɑːʊt fɔ nun]
I mind my own business, but remember
[ɑːɪ mɑːɪnd mɑːɪ oːʊn ˈbɪznɛ⁽ɪ⁾s bʌt ɹɪˈmɛmbʌ]
the one thing the world hates is a woman
[ðʌ wʌn θɪŋ ðʌ wɜld heːɪts ɪz ʌ ˈwʊmæ⁽ʌ⁾n]
who minds her own business.
[hu mɑːɪndz hɜ oːʊn ˈbɪznɛ⁽ɪ⁾s]
All the virtuous women
[ɔl ðʌ ˈvɜtʃuʌs ˈwɪmɛ⁽ɪ⁾n]
have bastards and shot-gun weddings.
[hæv ˈbæstʌdz ænd ʃat gʌn ˈwɛdɪŋz]
I have nursed them through childbirth and
[ɑːɪ hæv nɜst ðɛm θɹu ˈtʃɑːɪldˌbɜθ ænd]
my only pay is a kick in the pants
[mɑːɪ ˈoːʊnlɪ peːɪ ɪz ʌ kɪk ɪn ðʌ pænts]
when my back is turned.
[ʍɛn mɑːɪ bæk ɪz tɜnd]
These other women are pot bellied, hairy legged
[ðiz ˈʌðʌ ˈwɪmɛ⁽ɪ⁾n ɑ pat ˈbɛlɪd ˈheːʌʁ⁽ʳ⁾ɪ lɛgd]
and look like something the cat dragged in.
[ænd lʊk lɑːɪk ˈsʌmθɪŋ ðʌ kæt dɹægd ɪn]
I wish I had the power to damn their souls to hell!
[ɑːɪ wɪʃ ɑːɪ hæd ðʌ pɑːʊʌ tu dæm ðeːʌ soːʊlz tu hɛl]
Your mother works for a living.
[jɔːʌ ˈmʌðʌ wɜks fɔʁ⁽ʳ⁾ ʌ ˈlɪvɪŋ]

5. All I Have
[ɔl ɑːɪ hæv]

I am going blind.
[ɑːɪ æm ˈgoːʊɪŋ blɑːɪnd]
All hope of seeing you again is dead, Janey.
[ɔl hoːʊp ʌv ˈsiɪŋ ju ʌˈgɛn ɪz dɛd ˈdʒeːɪnɪ]
What have I ever done
[ʍat hæv ɑːɪ ˈɛvʌ dʌn]
except one blunder after another?
[ɪkˈsɛpt wʌn ˈblʌndʌʁ⁽ʳ⁾ ˈæftʌʁ⁽ʳ⁾ ʌˈnʌðʌ]
All I have left are these pictures of you,
[ɔl ɑːɪ hæv lɛft ɑ ðiz ˈpɪktʃʊ⁽ʌ⁾z ʌv ju]

You and your father.
[ju ænd jɔːʌ ˈfɑðʌ]
I am going blind.
[ɑːɪ æm ˈgoːʊɪŋ blɑːɪnd]
Don't pity me, Janey,
[doːʊnt ˈpɪtɪ mi ˈdʒeːɪnɪ]
forgive my faults and all the wrong I did you.
[fɔˈgɪv mɑːɪ fɔlts ænd ɔl ðʌ ɹaŋ ɑːɪ dɪd ju]
Good night, little girl, little girl,
[gʊd nɑːɪt ˈlɪtʊl gɜl ˈlɪtʊl gɜl]
And may God keep you from harm.
[ænd meːɪ gad kip ju fɹʌm hɑm]

Sonnets from the Portuguese (Song Cycle)
[ˈsanɪts fɹʌm ðʌ ˈpɔʁtʃʌˌgiz]
Browning, Elizabeth Barrett (Eng. 1806-1861)

1. I Thought Once How Theocritus Had Sung
[ɑːɪ θɔt wʌns hɑːʊ θiˈakɹɪtʊs hæd sʌŋ]

I thought once how Theocritus had sung
[ɑːɪ θɔt wʌns hɑːʊ θiˈakɹɪtʊs hæd sʌŋ]
Of the sweet years, the dear and wished-for years,
[ʌv ðʌ swit jɪːʌz ðʌ dɪːʌʁ⁽ʳ⁾ ænd wɪʃt fɔ jɪːʌz]
Who each one in a gracious hand appears
[hu itʃ wʌn ɪn ʌ ˈgɹeːɪʃʌs hænd ʌˈpɪːʌz]
To bear a gift for mortals, old or young:
[tu beːʌʁ⁽ʳ⁾ ʌ gɪft fɔ ˈmɔtʊlz oːʊld ɔ jʌŋ]
And, as I mused it in his antique tongue,
[ænd æz ɑːɪ mjuzd ɪt ɪn hɪz ænˈtik tʌŋ]
I saw, in gradual vision through my tears,
[ɑːɪ sɔ ɪn ˈgɹædʒuʊl ˈvɪʒʌn θɹu mɑːɪ tɪːʌz]
The sweet, sad years, the melancholy years,
[ðʌ swit sæd jɪːʌz ðʌ ˈmɛlæ⁽ɪ⁾nˌkalɪ jɪːʌz]
Those of my own life, who by turns had flung
[ðoːʊz ʌv mɑːɪ oːʊn lɑːɪf hu bɑːɪ tɜnz hæd flʌŋ]
A shadow across me. Straightway I was 'ware,
[ʌ ˈʃædoːʊ ʌˈkɹas mi ˈstɹeːɪtweːɪ ɑːɪ waz weːʌ]
So weeping, how a mystic Shape did move
[soːʊ ˈwipɪŋ hɑːʊ ʌ ˈmɪstɪk ʃeːɪp dɪd muv]
Behind me and drew me backward by the hair:
[bɪˈhɑːɪnd mi ænd dɹɪ⁽ʳ⁾u mi ˈbækwʊd bɑːɪ ðʌ heːʌ]
And a voice said in mast'ry, while I strove,–
[ænd ʌ vɔːɪs sɛd ɪn ˈmæstɹɪ ʍɑːɪl ɑːɪ stɹoːʊv]
"Guess now who holds thee?"
[gɛs nɑːʊ hu hoːʊldz ði]
"Death," I said. But, there,
[dɛθ ɑːɪ sɛd bʌt ðeːʌ]
The silver answer rang, "Not Death, but Love."
[ðʌ ˈsɪlvʌ ˈænsʌ ɹæŋ nat dɛθ bʌt lʌv]

2. My Letters!
[mɑːɪ ˈlɛtʁz]

My letters! all dead paper, mute and white!
[mɑːɪ ˈlɛtʌz ɔl dɛd ˈpeːɪpʌ mjut ænd ʍɑːɪt]

And yet they seem alive and quiv'ring
[ænd jɛt ðɛːɪ sim ʌˈlaːɪv ænd ˈkwɪvɹɪŋ]
Against my trem'lous hands which loose the string
[ʌˈgɛnst maːɪ ˈtɹɛmlʌs hændz ʍɪtʃ lus ðʌ stɹɪŋ]
And let them drop down on my knee to-night.
[ænd lɛt ðɛm dɹap daːʊn an maːɪ ni tu naːɪt]
This said, he wished to have me in his sight
[ðɪs sɛd hi wɪʃt tu hæv mi ɪn hɪz saːɪt]
Once, as a friend: this fixed a day in spring
[wʌns æz ʌ fɹɛnd ðɪs fɪkst ʌ dɛːɪ ɪn spɹɪŋ]
To come and touch my hand, a simple thing,
[tu kʌm ænd tʌtʃ maːɪ hænd ʌ ˈsɪmpʊl θɪŋ]
Yet I wept for it! This, the paper's light
[jɛt aːɪ wɛpt fɔʁ⁽ʳ⁾ ɪt ðɪs ðʌ ˈpɛːɪpʌz laːɪt]
Said, Dear, I love thee; and I sank and quailed
[sɛd dɪːʌʁ⁽ʳ⁾ aːɪ lʌv ði ænd aːɪ sæŋk ænd kwɛːɪld]
As if God's future thundered on my past.
[æz ɪf gadz ˈfjutʃʊ(ʌ) ˈθʌndʌd an maːɪ pæst]
This said, I am thine, and so its ink has paled
[ðɪs sɛd aːɪ æm ðaːɪn ænd soːʊ ɪts ɪŋk hæz pɛːɪld]
With lying at my heart that beat too fast.
[wɪð ˈlaːɪɪŋ æt maːɪ hat ðæt bit tu fæst]
And this, O Love, thy words have ill availed
[ænd ðɪs oːʊ lʌv ðaːɪ wɜdz hæv ɪl ʌˈvɛːɪld]
If, what this said, I dared repeat at last!
[ɪf ʍat ðɪs sɛd aːɪ dɛːʌd ɹɪˈpit æt læst]

3. With the Same Heart, I Said, I'll Answer Thee
[wɪθ ðʌ sɛːɪm haʁt aːɪ sɛd aːɪl ˈænsʁ ði]

With the same heart, I said, I'll answer thee,
[wɪð ðʌ sɛːɪm hat aːɪ sɛd aːɪl ˈænsʌ ði]
As those, when thou shalt call me by my name,
[æz ðoːʊz ʍɛn ðaːʊ ʃælt kɔl mi baːɪ maːɪ nɛːɪm]
Lo, the vain promise! is the same,
[loːʊ ðʌ vɛːɪn ˈpɹamɪs ɪz ðʌ sɛːɪm]
Perplexed and ruffled by life's strategy?
[pɜˈplɛkst ænd ˈɹʌfʊld baːɪ laːɪfs ˈstɹætɛ(ɪ)dʒɪ]
When called before, I told how hast'ly
[ʍɛn kɔld bɪˈfɔːʌ aːɪ toːʊld haːʊ ˈhɛːɪstlɪ]
I dropped my flowers or brake off from a game,
[aːɪ dɹapt maːɪ flaːʊʌz ɔ bɹɛːɪk af fɹʌm ʌ gɛːɪm]
To run and answer the smile that came
[tu ɹʌn ænd ˈænsʌ ðʌ smaːɪl ðæt kɛːɪm]
At play last moment, and went on with me
[æt plɛːɪ læst ˈmoːʊmɛnt ænd wɛnt an wɪð mi]
Through my obedience. When I answer now,
[θɹu maːɪ oˈbidɪɛ(ɪ)ns ʍɛn aːɪ ˈænsʌ naːʊ]
I drop a grave thought, break from solitude:
[aːɪ dɹap ʌ gɹɛːɪv θɔt bɹɛːɪk fɹʌm ˈsaːɪtjud]
Yet still my heart goes out to thee– ponder how–
[jɛt stɪl maːɪ hat goːʊz aːʊt tu ði ˈpandʌ haːʊ]
Not as to a single good, but all my good!
[nat æz tu ʌ ˈsɪŋgʊl gʊd bʌt ɔl maːɪ gʊd]
Lay thy hand on it, best one, and allow
[lɛːɪ ðaːɪ hænd an ɪt bɛst wʌn ænd ʌˈlaːʊ]

That no child's foot could run fast as this blood.
[ðæt noːʊ tʃaːɪldz fʊt kʊd ɹʌn fæst æz ðɪs blʌd]

4. If I Leave All for Thee
[ɪf aːɪ liv ɔl fɔʁ ði]

If I leave all for thee, wilt thou exchange
[ɪf aːɪ liv ɔl fɔ ði wɪlt ðaːʊ ɪksˈtʃɛːɪndʒ]
And be all to me? Shall I never miss
[ænd bi ɔl tu mi ʃæl aːɪ ˈnɛvʌ mɪs]
Home-talk and blessing and the common kiss
[hoːʊm tɔk ænd ˈblɛsɪŋ ænd ðʌ ˈkamʌn kɪs]
That comes to each in turn, nor count it strange,
[ðæt kʌmz tu itʃ ɪn tɜn nɔ kaːʊnt ɪt stɹɛːɪndʒ]
When I look up, to drop on a new range
[ʍɛn aːɪ lʊk ʌp tu dɹap an ʌ nju ɹɛːɪndʒ]
Of walls and floors, another home than this?
[ʌv wɔlz ænd flɔːʌz ʌˈnʌðʌ hoːʊm ðæn ðɪs]
Nay, wilt thou fill that place by me which is
[nɛːɪ wɪlt ðaːʊ fɪl ðæt plɛːɪs baːɪ mi ʍɪtʃ ɪz]
Filled by dead eyes too tender to know change
[fɪld baːɪ dɛd aːɪz tu ˈtɛndʌ tu noːʊ tʃɛːɪndʒ]
That's hardest. If to conquer love, has tried,
[ðæts ˈhadɛ(ɪ)st ɪf tu ˈkaŋkʌ lʌv hæz tɹaːɪd]
To conquer grief, tries more, as all things prove;
[tu ˈkaŋkʌ gɹɪ⁽ʳ⁾ɪf tɹaːɪz mɔːʌ æz ɔl θɪŋz pɹ⁽ʳ⁾uv]
For grief indeed is love and grief beside.
[fɔ gɹɪ⁽ʳ⁾ɪf ɪnˈdid ɪz lʌv ænd gɹɪ⁽ʳ⁾ɪf bɪˈsaːɪd]
Alas, I have grieved so I am hard to love.
[ʌˈlæs aːɪ hæv gɹɪ⁽ʳ⁾ivd soːʊ aːɪ æm had tu lʌv]
Yet love me, wilt thou? Op'n thine heart wide,
[jɛt lʌv mi wɪlt ðaːʊ oːʊpn ðaːɪn hat waːɪd]
And fold within the wet wings of thy dove.
[ænd foːʊld wɪðˈɪn ðʌ wɛt wɪŋz ʌv ðaːɪ dʌv]

5. Oh, Yes!
[oːʊ jɛs]

Oh, Yes! they love through all this world of ours!
[oːʊ jɛs ðɛːɪ lʌv θɹu ɔl ðɪs wɜld ʌv aːʊʌz]
I will not gainsay love, called love forsooth.
[aːɪ wɪl nat ˈgɛːɪnˌsɛːɪ lʌv kɔld lʌv fɔˈsuθ]
I have heard love talked in my early youth
[aːɪ hæv hɜd lʌv tɔkt ɪn maːɪ ˈɜlɪ juθ]
And since, not so long back but that the flowers
[ænd sɪns nat soːʊ laŋ bæk bʌt ðæt ðʌ flaːʊʌz]
Then gathered, smell still. Mussulmans and Giaours
[ðɛn ˈgæðʌd smɛl stɪl ˈmʌsʊlmæ(ʌ)nz ænd ˈgaːɪʌz]
Throw kerchiefs at a smile, and have no ruth
[θɹoːʊ ˈkɜtʃɪfs æt ʌ smaːɪl ænd hæv noːʊ ɹ⁽ʳʳ⁾uθ]
For any weeping. Polypheme's white tooth
[fɔʁ⁽ʳ⁾ ˈɛnɪ ˈwipɪŋ ˈpalɪˌfimz ʍaːɪt tuθ]
Slips on the nut, if after frequent showers,
[slɪps an ðʌ nʌt ɪf ˈæftʌ ˈfɹikwɛnt ʃaːʊʌz]
The shell is over smooth; and not so much
[ðʌ ʃɛl ɪz ˈoːʊvʌ smuð ænd nat soːʊ mʌtʃ]

Will turn the thing called love to hate
[wɪl tɜn ðʌ θɪŋ kɔld lʌv tu heːɪt]
Or else to oblivion. But thou art not such
[ɔʁ⁽ʳ⁾ ɛls tu oˈblɪvɪʌn bʌt ðɑːʊ at nat sʌʧ]
A lover, my Beloved! thou canst wait
[ʌ ˈlʌvʌ maːɪ bɪˈlʌvɛ(ɪ)d ðɑːʊ kænst weːɪt]
Through sorrow and sickness, to bring souls to touch
[θru ˈsaʁ⁽ʳ⁾oːʊ ænd ˈsɪknɛ(ɪ)s tu bɹɪŋ soːʊlz tu tʌʧ]
And think it soon when others cry "Too late!"
[ænd θɪŋk ɪt sun ʍɛn ˈʌðʌz kɹ⁽ʳ⁾aːɪ tu leːɪt]

6. How Do I Love Thee?
[haːʊ du aːɪ lʌv ði]

How do I love thee? Let me count the ways.
[haːʊ du aːɪ lʌv ði lɛt mi kaːʊnt ðʌ weːɪz]
I love thee from the depth and breadth and height
[aːɪ lʌv ði fɹʌm ðʌ dɛpθ ænd bɹedθ ænd haːɪt]
My soul can reach, when feeling out of sight
[maːɪ soːʊl kæn ɹiʧ ʍɛn ˈfilɪŋ aːʊt ʌv saːɪt]
For the ends of Being and ideal Grace.
[fɔ ði ɛndz ʌv ˈbiɪŋ ænd aːɪˈdiʌl gɹeːɪs]̚
I love thee to the level of every day's
[aːɪ lʌv ði tu ðʌ ˈlɛvʊl ʌv ˈɛvɹɪ deːɪz]
Most quiet need, by sun and candlelight.
[moːʊst ˈkwaːɪɛ(ɪ)t nid baːɪ sʌn ænd ˈkændʊlaːɪt]
I love thee freely, as men strive for Right;
[aːɪ lʌv ði ˈfɹili æz mɛn stɹaːɪv fɔ ɹaːɪt]
I love thee purely, as they turn from Praise.
[aːɪ lʌv ði ˈpjʊːʌlɪ æz ðeːɪ tɜn fɹʌm pɹeːɪz]
I love thee with the passion put to use
[aːɪ lʌv ði wɪð ðʌ ˈpæʃʌn pʊt tu jus]
In my old griefs, and with my childhood's faith.
[ɪn maːɪ oːʊld gɹ⁽ʳ⁾ifs ænd wɪð maːɪ ˈʧaːɪldhʊdz feːɪθ]
I love thee with a love I seemed to lose
[aːɪ lʌv ði wɪð ʌ lʌv aːɪ simd tu luz]
With my lost saints, I love thee with the breath,
[wɪð maːɪ last seːɪnts aːɪ lʌv ði wɪð ðʌ bɹeθ]
Smiles, tears, of all my life! and, if God choose,
[smaːɪlz tɪːʌz ʌv ɔl maːɪ laːɪf ænd ɪf gad ʧuz]
I shall but love thee better after death.
[aːɪ ʃæl bʌt lʌv ði ˈbɛtʌ ˈæftʌ dɛθ]

Three Cowboy Songs (Song Cycle)
[θɹi ˈkaːʊˌbɔːɪ saŋz]

1. Bucking Bronco
[ˈbʌkɪŋ ˈbɹaŋkoːʊ]
Starr, Belle (Am. 1848-1889)

My love is a rider, my love is a rider,
[maːɪ lʌv ɪz ʌ ˈɹaːɪdʌ maːɪ lʌv ɪz ʌ ˈɹaːɪdʌ]
My true love is a rider, wild broncos he breaks,
[maːɪ tɹ⁽ʳ⁾u lʌv ɪz ʌ ˈɹaːɪdʌ waːɪld ˈbɹaŋkoːʊz hi bɹeːɪks]
though he promised to quit for my sake.
[ðoːʊ hi ˈpɹamɪst tu kwɪt fɔ maːɪ seːɪk]

It's one foot in the stirrup and the saddle put on
[ɪts wʌn fʊt ɪn ðʌ ˈstɜʌp ænd ðʌ ˈsædʊl pʊt an]
with a swing and a jump he is mounted and gone.
[wɪð ʌ swɪŋ ænd ʌ dʒʌmp hi ɪz ˈmaːʊntɛ(ɪ)d ænd gan]
The first time I met him it was early one spring
[ðʌ fɜst taːɪm aːɪ met hɪm ɪt waz ˈɜlɪ wʌn spɹɪŋ]
a riding a bronco a high headed thing.
[ʌ ˈɹaːɪdɪŋ ʌ ˈbɹaŋkoːʊ ʌ haːɪ ˈhedɛ(ɪ)d θɪŋ]
The next time I saw him, it was late in the fall
[ðʌ nɛkst taːɪm aːɪ sɔ hɪm ɪt waz leːɪt ɪn ðʌ fɔl]
a swinging the girls at Tomlinson's ball.
[ʌ ˈswɪŋɪŋ ðʌ gɜlz æt ˈtamlɪnsʌnz bɔl]
He gave me some presents among them a ring
[hi geːɪv mi sʌm ˈpɹezents ʌˈmʌŋ ðɛm ʌ ɹɪŋ]
the return that I gave him was a far better thing;
[ðʌ ɹɪˈtɜn ðæt aːɪ geːɪv hɪm waz ʌ fa ˈbɛtʌ θɪŋ]
A young maiden's heart, I'd have you all know,
[ʌ jʌŋ ˈmeːɪdɛ(ɪ)nz hat aːɪd hæv ju ɔl noːʊ]
that he won it by riding his bucking bronco.
[ðæt hi wʌn ɪt baːɪ ˈɹaːɪdɪŋ hɪz ˈbʌkɪŋ ˈbɹaŋkoːʊ]
Now all young maidens, where're you reside,
[naːʊ ɔl jʌŋ ˈmeːɪdɛ(ɪ)nz ʍɛːʌˈɛːʌ ju ɹɪˈzaːɪd]
beware of the cowboy who swings rawhide,
[bɪˈweːʌʁ⁽ʳ⁾ ʌv ðʌ ˈkaːʊˌbɔːɪ hu swɪŋz ɹɔˈhaːɪd]
He'll court you and pet you and leave you to go
[hɛl kɔt ju ænd pet ju ænd liv ju tu goːʊ]
in the spring up the trail on his bucking bronco.
[ɪn ðʌ spɹɪŋ ʌp ðʌ tɹeːɪl an hɪz ˈbʌkɪŋ ˈbɹaŋkoːʊ]

2. Lift Me into Heaven Slowly
[lɪft mi ˈɪntu ˈhɛvɪn ˈsloːʊli]
Creeley, Robert (Am. 1926-2005)

Lift me into heaven slowly,
[lɪft mi ˈɪntu ˈhɛvɛ(ɪ)n ˈsloːʊli]
cause my back's sore
[kɔz maːɪ bæks sɔːʌ]
and my mind's thoughtful
[ænd maːɪ maːɪndz ˈθɔtfʊl]
and I'm not even sure
[ænd aːɪm nat ˈivɛ(ɪ)n ʃʊːʌ]
I want to go.
[aːɪ want tu goːʊ]

3. Billy the Kid
[ˈbɪli ðʌ kɪd]
Anonymous

Billy was a bad man
[ˈbɪli waz ʌ bæd mæn]
Carried a big gun,
[ˈkæʁ⁽ʳ⁾ɪd ʌ bɪg gʌn]
He was always after good folks
[hi waz ˈɔlweːɪz ˈæftʌ gʊd foːʊks]
And he kept them on the run.
[ænd hi kɛpt ðɛm an ðʌ ɹʌn]

He shot one every morning
[hi ʃɑt wʌn ˈɛvɹɪ ˈmɔnɪŋ]
To make his morning meal.
[tu meːɪk hɪz ˈmɔnɪŋ mil]
Let a man sass him,
[lɛt ʌ mæn sæs hɪm]
He was sure to feel his steel.
[hi wɑz ʃʊːʌ tu fil hɪz stil]
He kept folks in hot water,
[hi kɛpt foːʊks ɪn hɑt ˈwɔtʌ]
Stole from ev'ry stage,
[stoːʊl fɹʌm ˈɛvɹɪ steːɪdʒ]
When he was full of liquor
[ʍɛn hi wɑz fʊl ʌv ˈlɪkɔ(ʌ)]
He was always in a rage.
[hi wɑz ˈɔlweːɪz ɪn ʌ ɹeːɪdʒ]
He kept things boilin' over,
[hi kɛpt θɪŋz ˈbɔːɪlɪŋ ˈoːʊvʌ]
he stayed out in the brush,
[hi steːɪd ɑːʊt ɪn ðʌ bɹʌʃ]
when he was full of dead eye,
[ʍɛn hi wɑz fʊl ʌv dɛd ɑːɪ]
other folks I'd better hush.
[ˈʌðʌ foːʊks ɑːɪd ˈbɛtʌ hʌʃ]
Billy was a bad man, but one day
[ˈbɪlɪ wɑz ʌ bæd mæn bʌt wʌn deːɪ]
He met a man a whole lot badder
[hi mɛt ʌ mæn ʌ hoːʊl lʊt ˈbædʌʁ]
and now he's dead
[ænd nɑːʊ hiz dɛd]
and we ain't none the sadder.
[ænd wi ɛːɪnt nʌn ðʌ ˈsædʌʁ]

Lawes, William (Eng. 1602-1645)

Song Selections

"Beauty and Love"
[ˈbjuti ænd lʌv]
Lawes, Henry (Eng. 1595-1662)

1. Beauty and love once fell at odds,
[ˈbjuti ænd lʌv wʌns fɛl æt ɑdz]
And thus revil'd each other:
[ænd ðʌs ɹɪˈvaːɪld itʃ ˈʌðʌ]
Quoth love, "I am one of the gods,
[kwoːʊθ lʌv ɑːɪ æm wʌn ʌv ðʊ gɑdz]
And you wait on my mother;
[ænd ju weːɪt ɑn mɑːɪ ˈmʌðʌ]
Thou hast no pow'r o'er man at all
[ðɑːʊ hæst noːʊ pɑːʊɑɾ ɔːʌ mæn æt ɔl]
But what I gave to thee;
[bʌt ʍɑt ɑːɪ geːɪv tu ði]
Nor art thou longer fair or sweet,
[nɔʁ(ʳ) ɑt ðɑːʊ ˈlɑŋgʌ feːʌɾ ɔ swit]

Than men acknowledge me."
[ðɛn mɛn ækˈnɑlɛ(ɪ)dʒ mi]
2. "Away fond boy," then Beauty said,
[ʌˈweːɪ fɑnd bɔːɪ ðɛn ˈbjuti sɛd]
"We see that thou art blind:
[wi si ðæt ðɑːʊ ɑt blɑːɪnd]
But men have knowing eyes, and can
[bʌt mɛn hæv ˈnoːʊɪŋ ɑːɪz ænd kæn]
My graces better find:
[mɑːɪ ˈgɹɛːɪsɛ(ɪ)z ˈbɛtʌ fɑːɪnd]
'Twas I begot thee, mortals know,
[twɑz ɑːɪ bɪˈgɑt ði ˈmɔtʊlz noːʊ]
And call'd thee blind desire;
[ænd kɔld ði blɑːɪnd dɪˈzɑːɪʌ]
I made thy arrows and thy bow,
[ɑːɪ meːɪd ðɑːɪ ˈæɾoːʊz ænd ðɑːɪ boːʊ]
And wings to kindle fire."
[ænd wɪŋz tu ˈkɪndʊl fɑːɪʌ]
3. Love here in anger flew away
[lʌv hiːʌɾ ɪn ˈæŋgʌ flu ʌˈweːɪ]
And straight to Vulcan pray'd
[ænd stɹeːɪt tu ˈvʌlkæ(ɪ)n pɹeːɪd]
That he would tip his shafts with scorn
[ðæt hi wʊd tɪp hɪz ʃɑfts wɪð skɔn]
To punish this proud maid.
[tu ˈpʌnɪʃ ðɪs pɹɑːʊd meːɪd]
So Beauty ever since hath been
[soːʊ ˈbjuti ˈɛvʌ sɪns hæθ bin]
But courted for an hour;
[bʌt ˈkɔtɛ(ɪ)d fɔʁ(ʳ) æn ɑːʊʌ]
To love a day is now a sin
[tu lʌv ʌ deːɪ ɪz nɑːʊ ʌ sɪn]
'Gainst Cupid and his pow'r.
[gɛnst ˈkjupɪd ænd hɪz pɑːʊʌ]

"Gather Your Rosebuds While You May"
[ˈgæðʌ jɔːʌ ˈɹoːʊzbʌdz ʍɑːɪl ju meːɪ]
Herrick, Robert (Eng. 1591-1674)

Gather your Rosebuds while you may,
[ˈgæðʌ jɔːʌ ˈɾoːʊzbʌdz ʍɑːɪl ju meːɪ]
Old Time is still a flying;
[oːʊld tɑːɪm ɪz stɪl ʌ ˈflɑːɪŋ]
And that same Flow'r that smiles today,
[ænd ðæt seːɪm flɑːʊʌ ðæt smɑːɪlz tuˈdɛːɪ]
tomorrow will be dying.
[tuˈmɑɾoːʊ wɪl bi ˈdɑːɪŋ]
The glorious Lamp of Heav'n the Sun,
[ðʊ ˈglɔɾɪʌs læmp ʌv ˈhɛvɪn ðʊ sʌn]
the higher he is a getting;
[ðʊ ˈhɑːɪʌ hi ɪz ʌ ˈgɛtɪŋ]
The sooner must his race be run,
[ðʊ ˈsunʌ mʌst hɪz ɹeːɪs bi ɾʌn]
And nearer he's to setting.
[ænd ˈnɪːʌɾʌ hiz tu ˈsɛtɪŋ]

That age is best that is the first,
[ðæt ɛːɪʤ ɪz bɛst ðæt ɪz ðʊ fɜst]
while youth and blood are warmer,
[ʍaːɪl juθ ænd blʌd ɑ 'wɔmʌ]
Expect not the last and worst,
[ɪk'spɛkt nat ðʊ last ænd wɜst]
Time still succeeds the former.
[taːɪm stɪl sʌk'sidz ðʊ 'fɔmʌ]
Then be not coy, but use your time,
[ðɛn bi nat kɔːɪ bʌt juz jɔːʌ taːɪm]
While ye may go marry,
[ʍaːɪl ji mɛːɪ goːʊ 'mæɪɪ]
For having once but lost your prime,
[fɔ 'hævɪŋ wʌns bʌt last jɔːʌ pɪaːɪm]
you may forever tarry.
[ju mɛːɪ fɔʁ⁽ʳ⁾'ɛvʌ 'tæɪɪ]

Lehmann, Liza (Eng. 1862-1918)

Bird Songs (Song Cycle)
[bɜd sɑŋz]
Anonymous

1. The Woodpigeon
[ðʊ 'wʊdpɪʤʌn]

When the harvest all was gathered
[ʍɛn ðʊ 'havɛ(ɪ)st ɔl waz 'gæðʌd]
In the sunny Autumn weather,
[ɪn ðʊ 'sʌnɪ 'ɔtʌm 'wɛðʌ]
To the greenwood, blithe and merry,
[tu ðʊ 'gɪinwʊd blaːɪð ænd 'mɛɪɪ]
We went nutting all together;
[wi wɛnt 'nʌtɪŋ ɔl tu'gɛðʌ]
And as the woods we wander'd,
[ænd æz ðʊ wʊdz wi 'wandʌd]
So dim and dark and green,
[soːʊ dɪm ænd dak ænd gɪin]
We heard a sweet voice calling
[wi hɜd ʌ swit vɔːɪs 'kɔlɪŋ]
Though no one could be seen:
[ðoːʊ noːʊ wʌn kʊd bi sin]
"Two sticks across,
[tu stɪks ʌ'kɪas]
And a little bit of moss;
[ænd ʌ 'lɪtʊl bɪt ʌv mɔs]
It'll do, it'll do it'll do, Coo, coo, coo."
['ɪtʌl du 'ɪtʌl du 'ɪtʌl du ku ku ku]
The wild things of the woodlands
[ðʊ waːɪld θɪŋz ʌv ðʊ 'wʊdlæ(ʌ)ndz]
Scarce seemed of us afraid;
[skɛːʌs simd ʌv ʌs ʌ'fɪɛːɪd]
The blue jay flash'd before us,
[ðʊ blu ʤɛːɪ flæʃt bɪ'fɔːʌʌ ʌs]

And the Squirrel near us played.
[ænd ðʊ 'skwʊɪʊl niːʌʌ ʌs plɛːɪd]
We ate our nuts and rested
[wi ɛːɪt aːʊʌ nʌts ænd 'ɪɛstɛ(ɪ)d]
On a fallen tree, moss-grown,
[an ʌ 'fɔlɛ(ɪ)n tɪi mɔs gɪoːʊn]
And still a voice kept calling
[ænd stɪl ʌ vɔːɪs kɛpt 'kɔlɪŋ]
In softest, tend'rest tone:
[ɪn 'saftɛ(ɪ)st 'tɛndʌɪɛ(ɪ)st toːʊn]
"Two sticks across,
[tu stɪks ʌ'kɪas]
And a little bit of moss;
[ænd ʌ 'lɪtʊl bɪt ʌv mɔs]
It'll do, it'll do it'll do, Coo, coo, coo."
['ɪtʌl du 'ɪtʌl du 'ɪtʌl du ku ku ku]

2. The Starling
[ðʊ 'stalɪŋ]

On her nest, with her young,
[an hɜ nɛst wɪð hɜ jʌŋ]
Sat the Starling in the steeple,
[sæt ðʊ 'stalɪŋ ɪn ðʊ 'stipʊl]
While below the great bell swung
[ʍaːɪl bɪ'loːʊ ðʊ gɪɛːɪt bɛl swʌŋ]
To the church to call the people.
[tu ðʊ ʧɜʧ tu kɔl ðʊ 'pipʊl]
"Mother, mother," cried the starlings,
['mʌðʌ 'mʌðʌ kɪaːɪd ðʊ 'stalɪŋz]
"What is that? Oh mother, tell!"
[ʍat ɪz ðæt oːʊ 'mʌðʌ tɛl]
"Don't be frightened, little darlings,
[doːʊnt bi 'fɪaːɪtɛ(ɪ)nd 'lɪtʊl 'dalɪŋz]
'Tis the great church bell,
[tɪz ðʊ gɪɛːɪt ʧɜʧ bɛl]
Ringing out its solemn warning,
['ɪɪŋɪŋ aːʊt ɪts 'salʌm 'wɔnɪŋ]
That the people far and near
[ðæt ðʊ 'pipʊl far ænd niːʌ]
All may know 'tis Sunday morning,
[ɔl mɛːɪ noːʊ tɪz 'sʌndɛːɪ 'mɔnɪŋ]
And make haste to gather here.
[ænd mɛːɪk hɛːɪst tu 'gæðʌ hiːʌ]
While the organ's sweetly playing
[ʍaːɪl ði 'ɔgæ(ɪ)nz 'switlɪ 'plɛːɪɪŋ]
Little birds need have no fear!
['lɪtʊl bɜdz nid hæv noːʊ fiːʌ]
While below the folk are praying,
[ʍaːɪl bɪ'loːʊ ðʊ foːʊk ɑ 'pɪɛːɪɪŋ]
You can sing your hymns up here!"
[ju kæn sɪŋ jɔːʌ hɪmz ʌp hiːʌ]

3. The Yellowhammer
[ðʊ ˈjɛloːʊhæmʌ]

On a sultry Summer morning
[ɑn ʌ ˈsʌltɪɪ ˈsʌmʌ ˈmɔnɪŋ]
Down the dusty road we stray'd,
[daːʊn ðʊ ˈdʌstɪ roːʊd wi stɪɛːɪd]
And plucked the wayside flowers,
[ænd plʌkt ðʊ ˈwɛːɪsaːɪd flaːʊʌz]
And ran and laughed and played!
[ænd ɹæn ænd lɑft ænd plɛːɪd]
There was not the slightest breeze,
[ðɛːʌ wɑz nɑt ðʊ ˈslaːɪtɛ(ɪ)st bɹiz]
And we wearied of our play,
[ænd wi ˈwɪːʌɪd ʌv aːʊʌ plɛːɪ]
And then we heard the yellowhammer say:
[ænd ðɛn wi hɜd ðʊ ˈjɛloːʊhæmʌz sɛːɪ]
"A little bit of bread and no cheese!"
[ʌ ˈlɪtʊl bɪt ʌv bɹɛd ænd noːʊ ʧiz]
Once again we roamed the woodland,
[wʌns ʌˈgɛn wi roːʊmd ðʊ ˈwʊdlæ(ʌ)nd]
When the years had fleeted by,
[ʍɛn ðʊ jɪːʌz hæd ˈflitɛ(ɪ)d baːɪ]
And, poor as mice, we pledged Our vows,
[ænd pʊːʌɾ æz maːɪs wi plɛʤd aːʊʌ vaːʊz]
My love and I.
[maːɪ lʌv ænd aːɪ]
We had kiss'd beneath the tress,
[wi hæd kɪst bɪˈniθ ðʊ tɹɛs]
And then we heard again
[ænd ðɛn wi hɜd ʌˈgɛn]
The yellowhammer say, quite plain:
[ðʊ ˈjɛloːʊhæmʌ sɛːɪ kwaːɪt plɛːɪn]
"A little bit of bread and no cheese!"
[ʌ ˈlɪtʊl bɪt ʌv bɹɛd ænd noːʊ ʧiz]

4. The Wren
[ðʊ ɹɛn]

A wren just under my window
[ʌ ɾɛn ʤʌst ˈʌndʌ maːɪ ˈwɪndoːʊ]
Has suddenly, sweetly sung;
[hæz ˈsʌdɛ(ɪ)nlɪ ˈswitlɪ sʌŋ]
He woke me from my slumbers
[hi woːʊk mi fɹʌm maːɪ ˈslʌmbʌz]
With his sweet shrill tongue.
[wɪð hɪz swit ʃɹɪl tʌŋ]
It was so very early,
[ɪt wɑz soːʊ ˈvɛɾɪ ˈɜlɪ]
The dew-drops were not dry,
[ðʊ dju dɹɑps wɜ nɑt dɹaːɪ]
And pearly cloudlets floated
[ænd ˈpɜlɪ ˈklaːʊdlɛ(ɪ)ts ˈfloːʊtɛ(ɪ)d]
Across the rosy sky. Ah
[ʌˈkɹɑs ðʊ ˈroːʊzɪ skaːɪ ɑ]

His nest is in the ivy
[hɪz nɛst ɪz ɪn ði ˈaːɪvi]
Where his little wife sits all day,
[ʍɛːʌ hɪz ˈlɪtʊl waːɪf sɪts ɔl dɛːɪ]
And by her side he sings to her,
[ænd baːɪ hɜ saːɪd hi sɪŋz tu hɜ]
And never flies far away.
[ænd ˈnɛvʌ flaːɪz faɾ ʌˈwɛːɪ]

5. The Owl
[ði aːʊl]

Three little owlets
[θɾi ˈlɪtʊl ˈaːʊlɛ(ɪ)ts]
In a hollow tree,
[ɪn ʌ ˈhaloːʊ tɹi]
Cuddled up together
[ˈkʌdʊld ʌp tuˈgɛðʌ]
Close as could be.
[kloːʊs æz kʊd bi]
When the moon shone out
[ʍɛn ðʊ mun ʃoːʊn aːʊt]
And the dew lay wet,
[ænd ðʊ dju lɛːɪ wɛt]
Mother flew about
[ˈmʌðʌ flu ʌˈbaːʊt]
To see what she could get.
[tu si ʍat ʃi kʊd gɛt]
She caught a little mouse
[ʃi kɔt ʌ ˈlɪtʊl maːʊs]
So velvety and soft,
[soːʊ ˈvɛlvɛ(ɪ)tɪ ænd saft]
She caught some little sparrows,
[ʃi kɔt sʌm ˈlɪtʊl ˈspæɾoːʊz]
And then she flew aloft
[ænd ðɛn ʃi flu ʌˈlaft]
To the three little owlets
[tu ðʊ θɾi ˈlɪtʊl ˈaːʊlɛ(ɪ)ts]
In a hollow tree,
[ɪn ʌ ˈhaloːʊ tɹi]
Cuddled up together
[ˈkʌdʊld ʌp tuˈgɛðʌ]
Close as could be.
[kloːʊs æz kʊd bi]
"Tu-whoo," said the old owl,
[tu ʍu sɛd ði oːʊld aːʊl]
"Isn't this good cheer?"
[ˈɪzɛ(ɪ)nt ðɪs gʊd ʧiːʌ]
"Tu-whit," said the owlets,
[tu ʍɪt sɛd ði ˈaːʊlɛ(ɪ)ts]
"Thank you, mother dear,
[θæŋk ju ˈmʌðʌ dɪːʌ]
Tu-whit, tu-whit, tu-whit, tu-whit, Tu-whoo!"
[tu ʍɪt tu ʍɪt tu ʍɪt tu ʍɪt tu ʍu]

Liddle, Samuel (Eng. 1867-1951)

Song Selection

"How Lovely Are Thy Dwellings"
[hɑːʊ ˈlʌvli ɑ ðɑːɪ ˈdwɛlɪŋz]
Psalm 84:1, 2, 4

How lovely are Thy dwellings, O Lord of Hosts!
[hɑːʊ ˈlʌvlɪ ɑ ðɑːɪ ˈdwɛlɪŋz oːʊ lɔd ʌv hoːʊsts]
My soul longeth, yea, fainteth,
[mɑːɪ soːʊl ˈlɑŋɛ(ɪ)θ jɛːɪ ˈfɛːɪntɛ(ɪ)θ]
For the courts of the Lord:
[fɔ ðʊ kɔts ʌv ðʊ lɔd]
My heart and my flesh cry out for the living God.
[mɑːɪ hɑt ænd mɑːɪ flɛʃ kɹ⁽ʳ⁾ɑːɪ ɑːʊt fɔ ðʊ ˈlɪvɪŋ gɑd]
Yea, the sparrow hath found her a house,
[jɛːɪ ðʊ ˈspæroːʊ hæθ fɑːʊnd hɜ⁽ʳ⁾ ʌ hɑːʊs]
And the swallow a nest,
[ænd ðʊ ˈswɑloːʊ ʌ nɛst]
Where she may lay her young,
[ʍɛːʌ ʃi mɛːɪ lɛːɪ hɜ jʌŋ]
Even Thine altars, O Lord of Hosts,
[ˈivɛ(ɪ)n ðɑːɪn ˈɔltʌz oːʊ lɔd ʌv hoːʊsts]
my King and my God.
[mɑːɪ kɪŋ ænd mɑːɪ gɑd]
O Lord God of Hosts, hear my prayer.
[oːʊ lɔd gɑd ʌv hoːʊsts hiːʌ mɑːɪ pɹɛːʌ]
I would rather be a doorkeeper
[ɑːɪ wʊd ˈɹɑðʌ bi ʌ ˈdɔːʌˌkipʌɾ]
in the house of my God,
[ɪn ðʊ hɑːʊs ʌv mɑːɪ gɑd]
Than to dwell in the tents of wickedness
[ðæn tu dwɛl ɪn ðʊ tɛnts ʌv ˈwɪkɛ(ɪ)dnɛ(ɪ)s]
For a day in Thy courts is better than a thousand.
[fɔʁ⁽ʳ⁾ ʌ dɛːɪ ɪn ðɑːɪ kɔts ɪz ˈbɛtʌ ðæn ʌ ˈθɑːʊzæ(ʌ)nd]
How lovely are thy dwellings, O Lord of Hosts!
[hɑːʊ ˈlʌvlɪ ɑ ðɑːɪ ˈdwɛlɪŋz oːʊ lɔd ʌv hoːʊsts]
My soul longeth, yea fainteth,
[mɑːɪ soːʊl ˈlɑŋɛ(ɪ)θ jɛːɪ ˈfɛːɪntɛ(ɪ)θ]
For the courts of the Lord:
[fɔ ðʊ kɔts ʌv ðʊ lɔd]
My heart and my flesh cry out for the living God.
[mɑːɪ hɑt ænd mɑːɪ flɛʃ kɹɑːɪ ɑːʊt fɔ ðʊ ˈlɪvɪŋ gɑd]
Yea, the sparrow hath found her a house,
[jɛːɪ ðʊ ˈspæroːʊ hæθ fɑːʊnd hɜ⁽ʳ⁾ ʌ hɑːʊs]
And the swallow a nest,
[ænd ðʊ ˈswɑloːʊ ʌ nɛst]
Where she may lay her young,
[ʍɛːʌ ʃi mɛːɪ lɛːɪ hɜ jʌŋ]
Even Thine altars, O Lord of Hosts,
[ˈivɛ(ɪ)n ðɑːɪn ˈɔltʌz oːʊ lɔd ʌv hoːʊsts]
my King and my God.
[mɑːɪ kɪŋ ænd mɑːɪ gɑd]

M

MacDowell, Edward (Am. 1860-1908)

Song Selections

"The Sea" (Eight Love Songs)
[ðʌ si]
Howells, William Dean (Am. 1837-1920)

One sails away to sea, to sea,
[wʌn sɛːɪlz ʌˈwɛːɪ tu si tu si]
One stands on the shore and cries;
[wʌn stændz ɑn ðʌ ʃɔːʌʁ⁽ʳ⁾ ænd kɹɑːɪz]
The ship goes down the world, and the light
[ðʌ ʃɪp goːʊz dɑːʊn ðʌ wɜld ænd ðʌ lɑːɪt]
On the sullen water dies.
[ɑn ðʌ ˈsʌlɛ(ɪ)n ˈwɔtʌ dɑːɪz]
The whispering shell is mute,
[ðʌ ˈʍɪspʌʁ⁽ʳ⁾ɪŋ ʃɛl ɪz mjut]
And after is evil cheer;
[ænd ˈæftʌʁ⁽ʳ⁾ ɪz ˈivɪ(ʊ)l ʧɪːʌ]
She shall stand on the shore and cry in vain,
[ʃi ʃæl stænd ɑn ðʌ ʃɔːʌʁ⁽ʳ⁾ ænd kɹɑːɪ ɪn vɛːɪn]
Many and many a year.
[ˈmɛni ænd ˈmɛni ʌ jɪːʌ]
But the stately wide-winged ship lies wrecked,
[bʌt ðʌ ˈstɛːɪtlɪ wɑːɪd wɪŋgd ʃɪp lɑːɪz ɹɛkt]
Lies wrecked on the unknown deep;
[lɑːɪz ɹɛkt ɑn ði ʌnˈnoːʊn dip]
Far under, dead in his coral bed,
[fɑʁ⁽ʳ⁾ ˈʌndʌ dɛd ɪn hɪz ˈkɔʁ⁽ʳ⁾ʊl bɛd]
The lover lies asleep.
[ðʌ ˈlʌvʌ lɑːɪz ʌˈslip]

"To a Wild Rose"
[tu ʌ wɑːɪld ɹoːʊz]
Hagedorn, Herman (Am. 1882-1964)

Come, oh, songs! Come, oh, dreams!
[kʌm oːʊ sɑŋz kʌm oːʊ dɹimz]
Soft the gates of day close,
[sɑft ðʌ gɛːɪts ʌv dɛːɪ kloːʊz]
Sleep, my birds! Sleep, streams!
[slip mɑːɪ bɜdz slip stɹimz]
Sleep, my wild rose!
[slip mɑːɪ wɑːɪld ɹoːʊz]
Pool and bud, hill and deep,
[pul ænd bʌd hɪl ænd dip]
You who wore my robes, sleep!
[ju hu wɔːʌ mɑːɪ ɹoːʊbz slip]

Droop, east! Die, west!
[dɹ⁽ʳ⁾up ist dɑːɪ wɛst]
Let my land rest.
[lɛt mɑːɪ lænd ɹɛst]
Woods, I woke your boughs,
[wʊdz ɑːɪ woːʊk jɔːʌ bɑːʊz]
Hills, I woke your elf-throngs!
[hɪlz ɑːɪ woːʊk jɔːʌʁ⁽ʳ⁾ ɛlf θɹɔŋz]
Land, all thy hopes and woes
[lænd ɔl ðɑːɪ hoːʊps ænd woːʊz]
Rang from me in songs!
[ɹæŋ fɹʌm mi ɪn sɑŋz]
Come, oh, songs! Come, oh, dreams!
[kʌm oːʊ sɑŋz kʌm oːʊ dɹimz]
In our house is deep rest,
[ɪn ɑːʊʌ hɑːʊs ɪz dip ɹɛst]
Through the pines, gleams, gleams,
[θɹu ðʌ pɑːɪnz glimz glimz]
Bright the gold west,
[bɹɑːɪt ðʌ goːʊld wɛst]
There the flutes shall cry,
[ðɛːʌ ðʌ fluts ʃæl kɹɑːɪ]
There the viols weep,
[ðɛːʌ ðʌ ˈvɑːɪʊlz wip]
Laugh, my dreams and sigh!
[læf mɑːɪ dɹimz ænd sɑːɪ]
Sing, and vigil keep,
[sɪŋ ænd ˈvɪdʒɪ⁽ʊ⁾l kip]
"Awake, wild rose!"
[ʌˈwɛːɪk wɑːɪld ɹoːʊz]

Malotte, Albert Hay (Am. 1895-1964)

Song Selections

"The Lord's Prayer"
[ðʌ lɔʁdz pɹɛːʁ]
Matthew 6:9-13 KJV

Our Father, which art in heaven,
[ɑːʊʌ ˈfɑðʌ ʍɪtʃ at ɪn ˈhɛvɛ⁽ɪ⁾n]
Hallowed be thy Name.
[ˈhæloɛ⁽ɪ⁾d bi ðɑːɪ nɛːɪm]
Thy kingdom come. Thy will be done in earth,
[ðɑːɪ ˈkɪŋdʌm kʌm ðɑːɪ wɪl bi dʌn ɪn ɜθ]
As it is in heaven.
[æz ɪt ɪz ɪn ˈhɛvɛ⁽ɪ⁾n]
Give us this day our daily bread.
[gɪv ʌs ðɪs dɛːɪ ɑːʊʌ ˈdɛːɪli bɹɛd]
And forgive us our debts,
[ænd fɔˈgɪv ʌs ɑːʊʌ dɛts]
As we forgive our debtors.
[æz wi fɔˈgɪv ɑːʊʌ ˈdɛtɔ⁽ʌ⁾z]
And lead us not into temptation;
[ænd lid ʌs nat ˈɪntu tɛmˈtɛːɪʃʌn]

But deliver us from evil:
[bʌt dɪˈlɪvʌʁ⁽ʳ⁾ ʌs fɹʌm ˈivɪ⁽ʊ⁾l]
For thine is the kingdom, and the power,
[fɔ ðɑːɪn ɪz ðʌ ˈkɪŋdʌm ænd ðʌ pɑːʊʌ]
and the glory, for ever. Amen.
[ænd ðʌ ˈglɔʁ⁽ʳ⁾ɪ fɔʁ⁽ʳ⁾ ˈɛvʌ ɑˈmɛn]

"The Twenty-Third Psalm"
[ðʌ ˈtwɛnti θɜd sam]
Psalm 23:1-6 KJV

The Lord is my shepherd; I shall not want.
[ðʌ lɔd ɪz mɑːɪ ˈʃɛpʌd ɑːɪ ʃæl nat want]
He maketh me to lie down in green pastures:
[hi ˈmɛːɪkɛ⁽ɪ⁾θ mi tu lɑːɪ dɑːʊn ɪn gɹin ˈpæstʃʊ⁽ʌ⁾z]
He leadeth me beside the still waters.
[hi ˈlidɛ⁽ɪ⁾θ mi bɪˈsɑːɪd ðʌ stɪl ˈwɔtʌz]
He restoreth my soul:
[hi ɹɪˈstɔːʁ⁽ʳ⁾ɛ⁽ɪ⁾θ mɑːɪ soːʊl]
He leadeth me in the paths of righteousness
[hi ˈlidɛ⁽ɪ⁾θ mi ɪn ðʌ pæðz ʌv ˈɹɑːɪtʃʌsnɛ⁽ɪ⁾s]
for His name's sake.
[fɔ hɪz nɛːɪmz sɛːɪk]
Yea, though I walk through the valley
[jɛːɪ ðoːʊ ɑːɪ wɔk θɹu ðʌ ˈvælɪ]
of the shadow of death,
[ʌv ðʌ ˈʃædoːʊ ʌv dɛθ]
I will fear no evil: for Thou art with me;
[ɑːɪ wɪl fɪːʌ noːʊ ˈivɪ⁽ʊ⁾l fɔ ðɑːʊ at wɪð mi]
thy rod and thy staff they comfort me.
[ðɑːɪ ɹad ænd ðɑːɪ stæf ðɛːɪ ˈkʌmfɔt mi]
Thou preparest a table before me
[ðɑːʊ pɹɪˈpɛːʁ⁽ʳ⁾ɛ⁽ɪ⁾st ʌ ˈtɛːɪbʊl bɪˈfɔːʌ mi]
in the presence of mine enemies:
[ɪn ðʌ ˈpɹɛzɛ⁽ɪ⁾ns ʌv mɑːɪn ˈɛnɪ⁽ʌ⁾mɪz]
thou anointest my head with oil;
[ðɑːʊ ʌˈnɔːɪntɛ⁽ɪ⁾st mɑːɪ hɛd wɪð ɔːɪl]
my cup runneth over.
[mɑːɪ kʌp ˈɹʌnɛ⁽ɪ⁾θ ˈoːʊvʌ]
Surely goodness and mercy shall follow me
[ˈʃʊːʌlɪ ˈgʊdnɛ⁽ɪ⁾s ænd ˈmɜsi ʃæl ˈfaloːʊ mi]
all the days of my life:
[ɔl ðʌ dɛːɪz ʌv mɑːɪ lɑːɪf]
and I will dwell in the house of the Lord for ever.
[ænd ɑːɪ wɪl dwɛl ɪn ðʌ hɑːʊs ʌv ðʌ lɔd fɔʁ⁽ʳ⁾ ˈɛvʌ]
And evermore.
[ænd ˈɛvʌ mɔːʌ]

Moeran, Ernest John
(Eng. 1894-1950)

Song Selections

"A Cottager" (Six Poems by Seumas O'Sullivan)
[ʌ ˈkatɪdʒʌ]
O'Sullivan, Seumas (Ir. 1879-1958)

The rafters blacken year by year,
[ðʊ ˈraftʌz ˈblækɛ(ɪ)n jɪːʌ baːɪ jɪːʌ]
And the roof beams under that once were green.
[ænd ðʊ rruf bimz ˈʌndʌ ðæt wʌns wɜ gɹin]
'Twas himself that cut them and brought them here,
[twɑz hɪmˈsɛlf ðæt kʌt ðɛm ænd bɹɔt ðɛm hɪːʌ]
But who has count of the years between?
[bʌt hu hæz kɑːʊnt ʌv ðʊ jɪːʌz bɪˈtwin]
And Autumn comes, and its withering,
[ænd ˈɔtʌm kʌmz ænd ɪts ˈwɪðʌrɪŋ]
And Spring again and the fields are green.
[ænd spɹɪŋ ʌˈgɛn ænd ðʊ fildz a gɹin]
Winter and Summer and Autumn and Spring,
[ˈwɪntʌr ænd ˈsʌmʌr ænd ˈɔtʌm ænd spɹɪŋ]
Yet who has count of the years between?
[jɛt hu hæz kɑːʊnt ʌv ðʊ jɪːʌz bɪˈtwin]
The big old clock by the window screen
[ðʊ bɪg oːʊld klak baːɪ ðʊ ˈwɪndoːʊ skɹin]
Keeps count of the hours both day and night.
[kips kɑːʊnt ʌv ði aːʊʌz boːʊθ deːɪ ænd naːɪt]
I mind the time when its face was white,
[aːɪ maːɪnd ðʊ taːɪm ʍɛn ɪts feːɪs wɑz ʍaːɪt]
But who has count of the years between?
[bʌt hu hæz kɑːʊnt ʌv ðʊ jɪːʌz bɪˈtwin]

"Impromptu in March"
[ɪmˈpɹamptju ɪn matʃ]
Wallace, Doreen A. E. (Eng. 1897-1989)

I will cut you wands of willow,
[aːɪ wɪl kʌt ju wandz ʌv ˈwɪloːʊ]
I will fetch you catkins yellow
[aːɪ wɪl fetʃ ju ˈkætkɪnz ˈjɛloːʊ]
For a sign of March.
[fɔʁ(r) ʌ saːɪn ʌv matʃ]
I've a snowy silken pillow
[aːɪv ʌ ˈsnoːʊɪ ˈsɪlkɛ(ɪ)n ˈpɪloːʊ]
For my head, you foolish fellow–
[fɔ maːɪ hɛd ju ˈfulɪʃ ˈfeloːʊ]
I've no love for March!
[aːɪv noːʊ lʌv fɔ matʃ]
Get me buckles, bring me laces,
[gɛt mi ˈbʌkʊlz bɹɪŋ mi ˈlɛːɪsɛ(ɪ)z]
Amber beads and chrysoprases,
[ˈæmbʌ bidz ænd ˈkɹɪso(ʌ)ˌpɹɛːɪzɛ(ɪ)z]

Fans and castanets.
[fænz ænd ˈkæstʌnɛts]
Lady, in the sunny places
[ˈlɛːɪdɪ ɪn ðʊ ˈsʌnɪ ˈplɛːɪsɛ(ɪ)z]
I can find you early daisies
[aːɪ kæn faːɪnd ju ˈɜlɪ ˈdɛːɪzɪz]
And sweet violets.
[ænd swit ˈvaːɪo(ʌ)lɛ(ɪ)ts]

"In Youth Is Pleasure"
[ɪn juθ ɪz ˈplɛʒʌ]
Wever, Richard (Eng. 1505-1560)

In an arbour green, asleep whereas I lay,
[ɪn æn ˈabʊ(ʌ) gɹin ʌˈslip ʍɛːʌrˈæz aːɪ lɛːɪ]
The birds sang sweet in the middle of the day;
[ðʊ bɜdz sæŋ swit ɪn ðʊ ˈmɪdʊl ʌv ðʊ dɛːɪ]
I dreamed fast of mirth and play:
[aːɪ ˈdɹimɛ(ɪ)d fast ʌv mɜθ ænd plɛːɪ]
In youth is pleasure, in youth is pleasure.
[ɪn juθ ɪz ˈplɛʒʊ(ʌ) ɪn juθ ɪz ˈplɛʒʊ(ʌ)]
Methought I walked still to and fro,
[ˌmiˈθɔt aːɪ wɔkt stɪl tu ænd fɹoːʊ]
And from her company I could not go;
[ænd fɹʌm hɜ ˈkʌmpæ(ɪ)nɪ aːɪ kʊd nat goːʊ]
But when I waked it was not so:
[bʌt ʍɛn aːɪ wɛːɪkt ɪt wɑz nat soːʊ]
In youth is pleasure, in youth is pleasure.
[ɪn juθ ɪz ˈplɛʒʊ(ʌ) ɪn juθ ɪz ˈplɛʒʊ(ʌ)]
Therefore my heart is surely pight
[ˈðɛːʌfɔːʌ maːɪ hat ɪz ˈʃʊːʌlɪ paːɪt]
Of her alone to have a sight,
[ʌv hɜ(r) ʌˈloːʊn tu hæv ʌ saːɪt]
Which is my joy and heart's delight:
[ʍɪtʃ ɪz maːɪ dʒɔːɪ ænd hats dɪˈlaːɪt]
In youth is pleasure, in youth is pleasure.
[ɪn juθ ɪz ˈplɛʒʊ(ʌ) ɪn juθ ɪz ˈplɛʒʊ(ʌ)]

"Oh Fair Enough Are Sky and Plain"
[oːʊ fɛːʁ ɪˈnʌf a skaːɪ ænd plɛːɪn]
Housman, Alfred Edward (Eng. 1859-1936)

Oh fair enough are sky and plain,
[oːʊ fɛːʌr ɪˈnʌf a skaːɪ ænd plɛːɪn]
But I know fairer far:
[bʌt aːɪ noːʊ ˈfɛːʌrʌ fa]
Those are as beautiful again
[ðoːʊz ar æz ˈbjutɪfʊl ʌˈgɛːɪn]
That in the water are;
[ðæt ɪn ðʊ ˈwɔtʌr a]
The pools and rivers wash so clean
[ðʊ pulz ænd ˈɹɪvʌz waʃ soːʊ klin]
The trees and clouds and air,
[ðʊ tɹiz ænd klaːʊdz ænd ɛːʌ]
The like on earth was never seen,
[ðʊ laːɪk an ɜθ wɑz ˈnɛvʌ sin]

And oh that I were there.
[ænd oːʊ ðæt aːɪ wɜ ðɛːʌ]
These are the thoughts I often think
[ðiz a ðʊ θɔts aːɪ ˈafɛ(ɪ)n θɪŋk]
As I stand gazing down
[æz aːɪ stænd ˈgɛːɪzɪŋ daːʊn]
In act upon the cressy brink
[ɪn ækt ʌˈpan ðʊ ˈkɹɛsɪ bɹɪŋk]
To strip and dive and drown;
[tu stɹɪp ænd daːɪv ænd dɹaːʊn]
But in the golden sanded brooks
[bʌt ɪn ðʊ ˈgoːʊldɛ(ɪ)n ˈsændɛ(ɪ)d bɹʊks]
And azure meres I spy
[ænd ˈæʒʊ(ʌ) mɪːʌz aːɪ spaːɪ]
A silly lad that longs and looks
[ʌ ˈsɪlɪ læd ðæt laŋz ænd lʊks]
And wishes he were I.
[ænd ˈwɪʃɛ(ɪ)z hi wɜ aːɪ]

"Rain Has Fallen All the Day"

[ɹɛːɪn hæz ˈfɔlɪn ɔl ðʊ dɛːɪ]
Joyce, James (Ir. 1882-1941)

Rain has fallen all the day.
[ɹɛːɪn hæz ˈfɔlɛ(ɪ)n ɔl ðʊ dɛːɪ]
O come among the laden trees:
[oːʊ kʌm ʌˈmʌŋ ðʊ ˈlɛːɪdɛ(ɪ)n tɹiz]
The leaves lie thick upon the way
[ðʊ livz laːɪ θɪk ʌˈpan ðʊ wɛːɪ]
Of memories.
[ʌv ˈmɛmɔɹɪz]
Staying a little by the way
[ˈstɛːɪɪŋ ʌ ˈlɪtʊl baːɪ ðʊ wɛːɪ]
Of memories shall we depart.
[ʌv ˈmɛmɔɹɪz ʃæl wi dɪˈpat]
Come, my beloved, where I may
[kʌm maːɪ bɪˈlʌvɛ(ɪ)d ʍɛːʌɾ aːɪ mɛːɪ]
Speak to your heart.
[spik tu jɔːʌ hat]

"Rosefrail"

[ˈɹoːʊzfɹɛːɪl]
Joyce, James (Ir. 1882-1941)

Frail the white rose and frail are
[fɹɛːɪl ðʊ ʍaːɪt ɹoːʊz ænd fɹɛːɪl a]
Her hands that gave
[hɜ hændz ðæt gɛːɪv]
Whose soul is sere and paler
[huz soːʊl ɪz sɪːʌɾ ænd ˈpɛːɪlʌ]
Than time's wan wave.
[ðæn taːɪmz wan wɛːɪv]
Rosefrail and fair– yet frailest
[ˈɹoːʊzfɹɛːɪl ænd fɛːʌ jɛt ˈfɹɛːɪlɛ(ɪ)st]
A wonder wild
[ʌ ˈwʌndʌ waːɪld]

In gentle eyes thou veilest,
[ɪn ˈdʒɛntʊl aːɪz ðaːʊ ˈvɛːɪlɛ(ɪ)st]
My blueveined child.
[maːɪ ˈbluvɛːɪnd tʃaːɪld]

"The Dustman" (Six Poems by Seumas O'Sullivan)

[ðʊ ˈdʌstmʌn]
O'Sullivan, Seumas (Ir. 1879-1958)

At night when everyone's asleep
[æt naːɪt ʍɛn ˈɛvɹɪwʌnz ʌˈslip]
It must be very late! I creep
[ɪt mʌst bi ˈvɛɾɪ lɛːɪt aːɪ krip]
Softly down the darkened stairs
[ˈsaftlɪ daːʊn ðʊ ˈdakɛ(ɪ)nd stɛːʌz]
To the big room where we have prayers,
[tu ðʊ bɪg ɹum ʍɛːʌ wi hæv pɹɛːʌz]
And, standing at the window,
[ænd ˈstændɪŋ æt ðʊ ˈwɪndoːʊ]
I watch the Dustman going by.
[aːɪ watʃ ðʊ ˈdʌstmæ(ʌ)n ˈgoːʊɪŋ baːɪ]
Perched up on his high seat he looks
[pɜːʃt ʌp an hɪz haːɪ sit hi lʊks]
Like charioteers in those old books,
[laːɪk tʃæɹɪʌˈtɪːʌz ɪn ðoːʊz oːʊld bʊks]
And his long coat, when the lights are dim,
[ænd hɪz laŋ koːʊt ʍɛn ðʊ laːɪts a dɪm]
Makes funny shadows all over him.
[mɛːɪks ˈfʌnɪ ˈʃædoːʊz ɔl ˈoːʊvʌ hɪm]

"The Merry Green Wood" (7 Poems by James Joyce)

[ðʊ ˈmɛʁi gɹin wʊd]
Joyce, James (Ir. 1882-1941)

Who goes amid the green wood
[hu goːʊz ʌˈmɪd ðʊ gɹin wʊd]
With springtide all adorning her?
[wɪð spɹɪŋtaːɪd ɔl ʌˈdɔnɪŋ hɜ]
Who goes amid the merry green wood
[hu goːʊz ʌˈmɪd ðʊ ˈmɛɾɪ gɹin wʊd]
To make it merrier?
[tu mɛːɪk ɪt ˈmɛɾɪʌ]
Who passes in the sunlight
[hu ˈpasɛ(ɪ)z ɪn ðʊ ˈsʌnlaːɪt]
By ways that know the light footfall?
[baːɪ wɛːɪz ðæt noːʊ ðʊ laːɪt ˈfʊtfɔl]
Who passes in the sweet sunlight
[hu ˈpasɛ(ɪ)z ɪn ðʊ swit ˈsʌnlaːɪt]
With mien so virginal?
[wɪð min soːʊ ˈvɜdʒɪnʊl]
The ways of all the woodland
[ðʊ wɛːɪz ʌv ɔl ðʊ ˈwʊdlæ(ʌ)nd]
Gleam with a soft and golden fire,
[glim wɪð ʌ saft ænd ˈgoːʊldɛ(ɪ)n faːɪʌ]
For whom does all the sunny woodland
[fɔ hum dʌz ɔl ðʊ ˈsʌnɪ ˈwʊdlæ(ʌ)nd]

Carry so brave attire?
['kærɪ soːʊ bɹɛːɪv ʌ'taːɪʌ]
O, it is for my true love
[oːʊ ɪt ɪz fɔ maːɪ tru lʌv]
The woods their rich apparel wear
[ðʊ wʊdz ðɛːʌ rɪʧ ʌ'pærʊl weːʌ]
O, it is for my own true love,
[oːʊ ɪt ɪz fɔ maːɪ oːʊn tru lʌv]
That is so young and fair.
[ðæt ɪz soːʊ jʌŋ ænd fɛːʌ]

"When June Is Come"
[ʍɛn ʤun ɪz kʌm]
Bridges, Robert Seymour (Eng. 1844-1930)

When June is come, then all the day
[ʍɛn ʤun ɪz kʌm ðɛn ɔl ðʊ deːɪ]
I'll sit with my love in the scented hay:
[aːɪl sɪt wɪð maːɪ lʌv ɪn ðʊ 'sɛntɛ(ɪ)d heːɪ]
And watch the sun shot palaces high,
[ænd waʧ ðʊ sʌn ʃat 'pælæ(ʌ)sɛ(ɪ)z haːɪ]
That the white clouds build in the breezy sky.
[ðæt ðʊ ʍaːɪt klaːʊdz bɪld ɪn ðʊ 'bɹizɪ skaːɪ]
She singeth, and I do make her a song,
[ʃi 'sɪŋɛ(ɪ)θ ænd aːɪ du meːɪk hɜ(r) ʌ saŋ]
And read sweet poems the whole day long:
[ænd ɹid swit 'poːʊɛ(ɪ)mz ðʊ hoːʊl deːɪ laŋ]
Unseen as we lie in our haybuilt home,
[ʌn'sin æz wi laːɪ ɪn aːʊʌ 'heːɪbɪlt hoːʊm]
O, life is delight when June is come.
[oːʊ laːɪf ɪz dɪ'laːɪt ʍɛn ʤun ɪz kʌm]

Monro, George (Eng. 1680-1731)

Song Selection

"My Lovely Celia"
[maːɪ 'lʌvli 'silja]
Munro, George (Eng. 1825-1896)

My lovely Celia, heav'nly fair,
[maːɪ 'lʌvlɪ 'silja 'hɛvɛ(ɪ)nlɪ fɛːʌ]
As lilies sweet, as soft as air;
[æz 'lɪlɪz swit æz saft æz ɛːʌ]
No more then torment me, but be kind,
[noːʊ mɔːʌ ðɛn tɔ'mɛnt mi bʌt bi kaːɪnd]
And with thy love ease my troubled mind.
[ænd wɪð ðaːɪ lʌv iz maːɪ 'tɹʌbʊld maːɪnd]
O, let me gaze on your bright eyes,
[oːʊ lɛt mi ɡeːɪz an jɔːʌ bɹaːɪt aːɪz]
Where melting beams so oft arise;
[ʍɛːʌ 'mɛltɪŋ bimz soːʊ aft ʌ'raːɪz]
My heart's enchanted with thy charms,
[maːɪ hats ɪn'ʧantɛ(ɪ)d wɪð ðaːɪ ʧamz]

O, take me, dying, to your arms.
[oːʊ teːɪk mi 'daːɪɪŋ tu jɔːʌr amz]

 # Moore, Ben (Am. b. 1960)

Song Selections

"Ah, Happy, Happy Boughs!"
[a 'hæpi 'hæpi baːʊz]
Keats, John (Eng. 1795-1821)

Ah, happy, happy boughs! that cannot shed
[a 'hæpɪ 'hæpi baːʊz ðæt kæ'nat ʃɛd]
Your leaves nor ever bid the spring adieu;
[jɔːʌ livz nɔʁ(r) 'ɛvʌ bɪd ðʌ spɹɪŋ a'djø]
And happy melodist unwearied
[ænd 'hæpɪ 'mɛlodɪst ʌn'wɪːʌʁ(r)ɪd]
For ever piping songs forever new;
[fɔʁ(r) 'ɛvʌ 'paːɪpɪŋ saŋz fɔʁ(r) 'ɛvʌ nju]
More happy love! more happy, happy love!
[mɔːʌ 'hæpɪ lʌv mɔːʌ 'hæpɪ 'hæpi lʌv]
Forever warm and still to be enjoyed,
[fɔʁ(r) 'ɛvʌ wɔm ænd stɪl tu bi ɪn'ʤɔːɪd]
Forever panting, and forever young;
[fɔʁ(r) 'ɛvʌ 'pæntɪŋ ænd fɔʁ(r) 'ɛvʌ jʌŋ]
All breathing human passion far above,
[ɔl 'bɹiðɪŋ 'hjumæ(ʌ)n 'pæʃʌn faʁ(r) ʌ'bʌv]
That leaves the heart high sorrowful and cloy'd,
[ðæt livz ðʌ hat haːɪ 'saʁ(r)oːʊfʊl ænd klɔːɪd]
A burning forehead and a parching tongue.
[ʌ 'bɜnɪŋ 'fɔhɛd ænd ʌ 'paʧɪŋ tʌŋ]

"Hope Is the Thing with Feathers"
[hoːʊp ɪz ðʌ θɪŋ wɪθ 'fɛðʁz]
Dickinson, Emily (Am. 1830-1886)

Hope is the thing with feathers
[hoːʊp ɪz ðʌ θɪŋ wɪð 'fɛðʌz]
That perches in the soul,
[ðæt 'pɜʧɛ(ɪ)z ɪn ðʌ soːʊl]
And sings the tune without the words,
[ænd sɪŋz ðʌ tjun wɪð'aːʊt ðʌ wɜdz]
And never stops at all,
[ænd 'nɛvʌ staps æt ɔl]
And sweetest in the gale is heard;
[ænd 'switɛ(ɪ)st ɪn ðʌ geːɪl ɪz hɜd]
And sore must be the storm
[ænd sɔːʌ mʌst bi ðʌ stɔm]
That could abash the little bird
[ðæt kʊd ʌ'bæʃ ðʌ 'lɪtʊl bɜd]
That kept so many warm.
[ðæt kɛpt soːʊ 'mɛnɪ wɔm]
I've heard it in the chillest land,
[aːɪv hɜd ɪt ɪn ðʌ 'ʧɪlɛ(ɪ)st lænd]

And on the strangest sea;
[ænd ɑn ðʌ ˈstɹɛːɪndʒɛ(ɪ)st si]
Yet never in extremity,
[jɛt ˈnɛvʌʁ⁽ʳ⁾ ɪn ɪkˈstɹɛmɪtɪ]
It asked a crumb of me.
[ɪt æskt ʌ kɹʌm ʌv mi]

"In the Dark Pine-Wood"
[ɪn ðʌ daʁk pɑːɪn wʊd]
Joyce, James (Ir. 1882-1941)

In the dark pine-wood
[ɪn ðʌ dɑk pɑːɪn wʊd]
I would we lay,
[ɑːɪ wʊd wi lɛːɪ]
In deep cool shadow
[ɪn dip kul ˈʃædoːʊ]
At noon of day.
[æt nun ʌv dɛːɪ]
How sweet to lie there,
[hɑːʊ swit tu lɑːɪ ðɛːʌ]
Sweet to kiss,
[swit tu kɪs]
Where the great pine-forest
[ʍɛːʌ ðʌ ɡɹɛːɪt pɑːɪn ˈfɔʁ⁽ʳ⁾ɛ(ɪ)st]
Enaisled is!
[ɪnˈɑːɪlɛ(ɪ)d ɪz]
Thy kiss descending
[ðɑːɪ kɪs dɪˈsɛndɪŋ]
Sweeter were
[ˈswitʌ wɜ]
With a soft tumult
[wɪð ʌ saft ˈtjumʊlt]
Of thy hair.
[ʌv ðɑːɪ hɛːʌ]
O unto the pine-wood
[oːʊ ˈʌntu ðʌ pɑːɪn wʊd]
At noon of day
[æt nun ʌv dɛːɪ]
Come with me now,
[kʌm wɪð mi nɑːʊ]
Sweet love, away.
[swit lʌv ʌˈwɛːɪ]

"Lullaby"
[ˈlʌlʌbɑːɪ]
Rossetti, Christina Georgina (Eng. 1830-1894)

Lullaby, oh, lullaby!
[ˈlʌlʌbɑːɪ oːʊ ˈlʌlʌbɑːɪ]
The flowers are closed,
[ðʌ flɑːʊʌz a kloːʊzd]
The lambs are sleeping;
[ðʌ læmz a ˈslipɪŋ]
Nothing will wake the frogs by the lake,
[ˈnʌθɪŋ wɪl wɛːɪk ðʌ fɹɑgz bɑːɪ ðʌ lɛːɪk]

Stars are up, and the moon is peeping;
[stɑz ɑʁ⁽ʳ⁾ ʌp ænd ðʌ mun ɪz ˈpipɪŋ]
Nothing will stir the toads and spiders
[ˈnʌθɪŋ wɪl stɜ ðʌ toːʊdz ænd ˈspɑːɪdʌz]
All are silence keeping.
[ɔl a ˈsɑːɪlɛ(ɪ)ns ˈkipɪŋ]
Oh, lullaby, oh, lullaby!
[oːʊ ˈlʌlʌbɑːɪ oːʊ ˈlʌlʌbɑːɪ]
Sleep, my baby, fall a-sleeping,
[slip mɑːɪ ˈbɛːɪbɪ fɔl ʌ ˈslipɪŋ]
Oh, lullaby, lullaby!
[oːʊ ˈlʌlʌbɑːɪ ˈlʌlʌbɑːɪ]
The flowers are closed,
[ðʌ flɑːʊʌz a kloːʊzd]
The lambs are sleeping;
[ðʌ læmz a ˈslipɪŋ]
Sleep my baby, sleep.
[slip mɑːɪ ˈbɛːɪbɪ slip]

"Requiem"
[ˈɹɛkwiɛm]
Stevenson, Robert Louis (Sc. 1850-1894)

Under the wide and starry sky
[ˈʌndʌ ðʌ wɑːɪd ænd ˈstɑʁ⁽ʳ⁾ɪ skɑːɪ]
Dig the grave and let me lie;
[dɪg ðʌ gɹ⁽ʳ⁾ɛːɪv ænd lɛt mi lɑːɪ]
Glad did I live and gladly die,
[glæd dɪd ɑːɪ lɪv ænd ˈglædlɪ dɑːɪ]
And I laid me down with a will.
[ænd ɑːɪ lɛːɪd mi dɑːʊn wɪð ʌ wɪl]
This be the verse you grave for me:
[ðɪs bi ðʌ vɜs ju gɹ⁽ʳ⁾ɛːɪv fɔ mi]
"Here he lies where he longed to be;
[hɪːʌ hi lɑːɪz ʍɛːʌ hi laŋd tu bi]
Home is the sailor, home from sea,
[hoːʊm ɪz ðʌ ˈsɛːɪlɔ(ʌ) hoːʊm fɹʌm si]
And the hunter home from the hill."
[ænd ðʌ ˈhʌntʌ hoːʊm fɹʌm ðʌ hɪl]

"When You Are Old"
[ʍɛn ju ɑʁ oːʊld]
Yeats, William Butler (Ir. 1865-1939)

When you are old and gray and full of sleep,
[ʍɛn ju ɑʁ⁽ʳ⁾ oːʊld ænd gɹɛːɪ ænd fʊl ʌv slip]
And nodding by the fire, take down this book,
[ænd ˈnadɪŋ bɑːɪ ðʌ fɑːɪʌ tɛːɪk dɑːʊn ðɪs bʊk]
And slowly read, and dream of the soft look
[ænd ˈsloːʊlɪ ɹid ænd dɹim ʌv ðʌ saft lʊk]
Your eyes had once, and of their shadows deep;
[jɔːʌʁ⁽ʳ⁾ ɑːɪz hæd wʌns ænd ʌv ðɛːʌ ˈʃædoːʊz dip]
How many loved your moments of glad grace,
[hɑːʊ ˈmɛnɪ lʌvd jɔːʌ ˈmoːʊmɛnts ʌv glæd gɹɛːɪs]
And loved your beauty with love false or true,
[ænd lʌvd jɔːʌ ˈbjutɪ wɪð lʌv fɔls ɔ tɹ⁽ʳ⁾u]

But one man loved the pilgrim soul in you,
[bʌt wʌn mæn lʌvd ðʌ ˈpɪlgɹɪm soːʊl ɪn ju]
And loved the sorrows of your changing face;
[ænd lʌvd ðʌ ˈsaʁ⁽ʳ⁾oːʊz ʌv jɔːʌ ˈʧɛːɪndʒɪŋ fɛːɪs]
And bending down beside the glowing bars,
[ænd ˈbɛndɪŋ daːʊn bɪˈsaːɪd ðʌ ˈgloːʊɪŋ baz]
Murmur, a little sadly, how love fled
[ˈmɜmʊ(ʌ) ʌ ˈlɪtʊl ˈsædlɪ haːʊ lʌv flɛd]
And paced upon the mountains overhead
[ænd pɛːɪst ʌˈpan ðʌ ˈmaːʊntæ(ɪ)nz ˈoːʊvʌhɛd]
And hid his face amid a crowd of stars.
[ænd hɪd hɪz fɛːɪs ʌˈmɪd ʌ kɹaːʊd ʌv staz]

Moore, Dorothy Rudd (Am. b. 1940)

Song Selection

"For a Poet" (From the Dark Tower)
[tu ʌ ˈpoːʊɪt]
Cullen, Countee (Am. 1903-1946)

I have wrapped my dreams in a silken cloth,
[aːɪ hæv ɹæpt maːɪ dɹimz ɪn ʌ ˈsɪlkɛ(ɪ)n klaθ]
And laid them away in a box of gold;
[ænd lɛːɪd ðɛm ʌˈwɛːɪ ɪn ʌ baks ʌv goːʊld]
Where long will cling the lips of the moth,
[ʍɛːʌ laŋ wɪl klɪŋ ðʌ lɪps ʌv ðʌ maθ]
I have wrapped my dreams in a silken cloth;
[aːɪ hæv ɹæpt maːɪ dɹimz ɪn ʌ ˈsɪlkɛ(ɪ)n klaθ]
I hide no hate; I am not even wroth
[aːɪ haːɪd noːʊ hɛːɪt aːɪ æm nat ˈiːvɛ(ɪ)n ɹoθ]
Who found earth's breath so keen and cold;
[hu faːʊnd ɜθs bɹɛθ soːʊ kin ænd koːʊld]
I have wrapped my dreams in a silken cloth,
[aːɪ hæv ɹæpt maːɪ dɹimz ɪn ʌ ˈsɪlkɛ(ɪ)n klaθ]
And laid them away in a box of gold.
[ænd lɛːɪd ðɛm ʌˈwɛːɪ ɪn ʌ baks ʌv goːʊld]

Moore, Undine Smith (Am. 1905-1989)

Song Selection

"Love Let the Wind Cry"
[lʌv lɛt ðʌ wɪnd kɹaːɪ]
Carman, Bliss (Ca. 1861-1929)

Love, let the wind cry
[lʌv lɛt ðʌ wɪnd kɹaːɪ]
On the dark mountain,
[an ðʌ dak ˈmaːʊntæ(ɪ)n]
Bending the ash trees
[ˈbɛndɪŋ ði æʃ tɹiz]

And the tall hemlocks
[ænd ðʌ tɔl ˈhɛmlaks]
With the great voice of
[wɪð ðʌ gɹeːɪt vɔːɪs ʌv]
Thunderous legions.
[ˈθʌndʌʁ⁽ʳ⁾ʌs ˈlidʒʌnz]
How I adore thee.
[haːʊ aːɪ ʌˈdɔːʌ ði]
Let the hoarse torrent
[lɛt ðʌ hɔs ˈtɔʁ⁽ʳ⁾ɛnt]
In the blue canyon,
[ɪn ðʌ blu ˈkænjʌn]
Murmuring mightily
[ˈmɜmʊʁ⁽ʳ⁾ɪŋ ˈmaːɪtɪlɪ]
Out of the gray mist
[aːʊt ʌv ðʌ gɹeːɪ mɪst]
Of primal chaos
[ʌv ˈpɹɑːɪmʊl ˈkeas]
Cease not proclaiming
[sɪs nat pɹoˈklɛːɪmɪŋ]
How I adore thee.
[haːʊ aːɪ ʌˈdɔːʌ ði]
Let the long rhythm
[lɛt ðʌ laŋ ˈɹɪðmʌn]
Of crunching rollers,
[ʌv ˈkɹʌnʧɪŋ ˈɹoːʊlʌz]
Breaking and bursting
[ˈbɹɛːɪkɪŋ ænd ˈbɜstɪŋ]
On the white seaboard
[an ðʌ ʍaːɪt ˈsibɔd]
Titan and tireless,
[ˈtaːɪtæ(ɪ)n ænd ˈtaːɪʌlɛ(ɪ)s]
Tell, while the world stands,
[tɛl ʍaːɪl ðʌ wɜld stændz]
How I adore thee.
[haːʊ aːɪ ʌˈdɔːʌ ði]
Love, let the clear call
[lʌv lɛt ðʌ klɪːʌ kɔl]
Of the tree cricket,
[ʌv ðʌ tɹi ˈkɹɪkɛ(ɪ)t]
Frailest of creatures,
[ˈfɹɛːɪlɛ(ɪ)st ʌv ˈkɹiʧʊ(ʌ)z]
Green as the young grass,
[gɹin æz ðʌ jʌŋ gɹæs]
Mark with his trilling
[mak wɪð hɪz ˈtɹɪlɪŋ]
Resonant bell-note,
[ˈɹɛzonæ(ɪ)nt bɛl noːʊt]
How I adore thee.
[haːʊ aːɪ ʌˈdɔːʌ ði]
But, more than all sounds,
[bʌt mɔːʌ ðæn ɔl saːʊndz]
Surer, serener,
[ˈʃʊːʌʁ⁽ʳ⁾ʌ sɪˈʁ⁽ʳ⁾inʌ]
Fuller of passion
[ˈfʊlʌʁ⁽ʳ⁾ ʌv ˈpæʃʌn]

And exultation,
[ænd ɛgzu(ʊ)lˈtɛːɪʃʌn]
Let the hushed whisper
[lɛt ðʌ hʌʃt ˈʍɪspʌ]
In thine own heart say,
[ɪn ðaːɪn oːʊn hɑt sɛːɪ]
How I adore thee.
[haːʊ ɑːɪ ʌˈdɔːʌ ði]

Morley, Thomas (Eng. 1557-1603)

Song Selection

"It Was a Lover and His Lass"
[ɪt wɑz ʌ ˈlʌvʁ ænd hɪz læs]
Shakespeare, William (Eng. 1564-1616)

1. It was a lover and his lass,
[ɪt wɑz ʌ ˈlʌvʌɾ ænd hɪz læs]
With a hey, and a ho, and a hey nonny no,
[wɪð ʌ hɛːɪ ænd ʌ hoːʊ ænd ʌ hɛːɪ ˈnoːʊnɪˌnoːʊ]
That o'er the green cornfields did pass.
[ðæt ɔːʌ ðʊ gɹin ˈkɔnfildz dɪd pas]
CHORUS:
In spring time, the only pretty ring time,
[ɪn spɹɪŋ taːɪm ðɪ ˈoːʊnlɪ ˈpɹɪtɪ ɹɪŋ taːɪm]
When birds do sing, hey ding a ding a ding,
[ʍɛn bɜdz du sɪŋ hɛːɪ dɪŋ ʌ dɪŋ ʌ dɪŋ]
Sweet lovers love the spring.
[swit ˈlʌvʌz lʌv ðʊ spɹɪŋ]
2. Between the acres of the rye,
[bɪˈtwin ðɪ ˈɛːɪkʌz ʌv ðʊ ɾaːɪ]
With a hey, and a ho, and a hey nonny no,
[wɪð ʌ hɛːɪ ænd ʌ hoːʊ ænd ʌ hɛːɪ ˈnoːʊnɪˌnoːʊ]
These pretty country fools would lie,
[ðiz ˈpɹɪtɪ ˈkʌntɹɪ fulz wʊd laːɪ]
CHORUS
3. This carol they began that hour,
[ðɪs ˈkæɾʊl ðɛːɪ bɪˈgæn ðæt aːʊʌ]
With a hey, and a ho, and a hey nonny no,
[wɪð ʌ hɛːɪ ænd ʌ hoːʊ ænd ʌ hɛːɪ ˈnoːʊnɪˌnoːʊ]
How that a life was but a flower,
[haːʊ ðæt ʌ laːɪf wɑz bʌt ʌ flaːʊʌ]
CHORUS
4. Then, pretty lovers take the time,
[ðɛn ˈpɹɪtɪ ˈlʌvʌz tɛːɪk ðʊ taːɪm]
With a hey, and a ho, and a hey nonny no,
[wɪð ʌ hɛːɪ ænd ʌ hoːʊ ænd ʌ hɛːɪ ˈnoːʊnɪˌnoːʊ]
For love is crowned with the prime,
[fɔ lʌv ɪz ˈkɹɑːʊnɛ(ɪ)d wɪð ðʊ pɹaːɪm]
CHORUS

Müller, Wenzel (Aut. 1767-1817)

Song Selection

"Create In Me A Clean Heart"
[kɹɪˈɛːɪt ɪn mi ʌ klin hɑt]
Psalm 51:10-19 KJV

Create in me a clean heart, O God;
[kɹɪˈɛːɪt ɪn mi ʌ klin hɑt oːʊ gɑd]
and renew a right spirit within me.
[ænd ɹɪˈnju ʌ ɾaːɪt ˈspɪɾɪt wɪðˈɪn mi]
Cast me not away from Thy presence;
[kɑst mi nɑt ʌˈwɛːɪ fɹʌm ðaːɪ ˈpɹɛzɛ(ɪ)ns]
and take not Thy holy spirit from me.
[ænd tɛːɪk nɑt ðaːɪ ˈhoːʊlɪ ˈspɪɾɪt fɹʌm mi]
Restore unto me the joy of Thy salvation;
[ɹɪˈstɔːʌɾ ˈʌntu mi ðʊ dʒɔːɪ ʌv ðaːɪ sælˈvɛːɪʃʌn]
and uphold me with Thy free spirit.
[ænd ʌpˈhoːʊld mi wɪð ðaːɪ fɹi ˈspɪɾɪt]
Then will I teach transgressors Thy ways;
[ðɛn wɪl ɑːɪ tiʃ tɹænzˈgɹɛsɔ(ʌ)z ðaːɪ wɛːɪz]
and sinners shall be converted unto Thee.
[ænd ˈsɪnʌz ʃæl bi kʌnˈvɜtɛ(ɪ)d ˈʌntu ði]

 # Musto, John (Am. b. 1954)

Song Selection

"Recuerdo" (Recuerdo)
[reˈkwɛɾðo]
Millay, Edna St. Vincent (Am. 1892-1950)

We were very tired, we were very merry –
[wi wɜ ˈvɛʁɪ taːɪʌd wi wɜ ˈvɛʁɪ ˈmɛʁɪ]
We had gone back and forth all night on the ferry.
[wi hæd gɑn bæk ænd fɔθ ɔl naːɪt ɑn ðʌ ˈfɛʁɪ]
It was bare and bright, and smelled like a stable –
[ɪt wɑz bɛːʌʁ ænd bɹaːɪt ænd smɛld laːɪk ʌ ˈstɛːɪbʊl]
But we looked into a fire, we leaned across a table,
[bʌt wi lʊkt ˈɪntu ʌ faːɪʌ wi lind ʌˈkɹɑs ʌ ˈtɛːɪbʊl]
We lay on a hill-top underneath the moon;
[wi lɛːɪ ɑn ʌ hɪl tɑp ʌndʌˈniθ ðʌ mun]
And the whistles kept blowing,
[ænd ðʌ ˈʍɪsʊlz kɛpt ˈbloːʊɪŋ]
and the dawn came soon.
[ænd ðʌ dɔn kɛːɪm sun]
We were very tired, We were very merry –
[wi wɜ ˈvɛʁɪ taːɪʌd wi wɜ ˈvɛʁɪ ˈmɛʁɪ]
We had gone back and forth all night on the ferry.
[wi hæd gɑn bæk ænd fɔθ ɔl naːɪt ɑn ðʌ ˈfɛʁɪ]
You ate an apple, and I ate a pear,
[ju ɛːɪt æn ˈæpʊl ænd ɑːɪ ɛːɪt ʌ pɛːʌ]

From a dozen of each we had bought somewhere;
[fɹʌm ʌ 'dʌzɛ(ɪ)n ʌv ɪʧ wi hæd bɒt 'sʌmmɛːʌ]
And the sky went wan, and the wind came cold,
[ænd ðʌ skɑːɪ wɛnt wɑn ænd ðʌ wɪnd kɛːɪm koːʊld]
And the sun rose dripping, a bucketful of gold.
[ænd ðʌ sʌn ɹoːʊz 'dɹɪpɪŋ ʌ 'bʌkɛ(ɪ)tfʊl ʌv goːʊld]
We were very tired, we were very merry,
[wi wɜ 'vɛʁɪ tɑːɪʌd wi wɜ 'vɛʁɪ 'mɛʁɪ]
We had gone back and forth all night on the ferry.
[wi hæd gɑn bæk ænd fɔθ ɔl nɑːɪt ɑn ðʌ 'fɛʁɪ]
We hailed, "Good morrow, mother!"
[wi hɛːɪld gʊd 'maʁoːʊ 'mʌðʌ]
to a shawl-covered head,
[tu ʌ ʃɔl 'kʌvʌd hɛd]
And bought a morning paper, which neither of us read;
[ænd bɒt ʌ 'mɔnɪŋ 'pɛːɪpʌ ʍɪʧ 'nɑːɪðʌʁ ʌv ʌs ɹɛd]
And she wept, "God bless you!"
[ænd ʃi wɛpt gɑd blɛs ju]
for the apples and pears,
[fɔ ði 'æpʊlz ænd pɛːʌz]
And we gave her all our money but our subway fares.
[ænd wi gɛːɪv hɜ ɔl ɑːʊʌ 'mʌnɪ bʌt ɑːʊʌ 'sʌbwɛːɪ fɛːʌz]

Myers, Gordon, arr. (Am. 1919-2006)

Song Selection

"Jesus Walked This Lonesome Valley"
['ʤizʌs wɔkt ðɪs 'loːʊnsʌm 'væli]
Traditional Hymn

1. Jesus walked this lonesome valley,
['ʤizʌs wɔkt ðɪs 'loːʊnsʌm 'væli]
He had to walk it by Himself.
[hi hæd tu wɔk ɪt bɑːɪ hɪm'sɛlf]
Oh, nobody else could walk it for Him,
[oːʊ 'noːʊbɑdɪ ɛls kʊd wɔk ɪt fɔ hɪm]
He had to walk it by Himself.
[hi hæd tu wɔk ɪt bɑːɪ hɪm'sɛlf]
2. We must walk this lonesome valley,
[wi mʌst wɔk ðɪs 'loːʊnsʌm 'væli]
We have to walk it by ourselves.
[wi hæv tu wɔk ɪt bɑːɪ ɑːʊʌ'sɛlvz]
Oh, nobody else can walk it for us,
[oːʊ 'noːʊbɑdɪ ɛls kæn wɔk ɪt fɔʁ(ʳ) ʌs]
We have to walk it by ourselves.
[wi hæv tu wɔk ɪt bɑːɪ ɑːʊʌ'sɛlvz]
3. We must clasp our hands together,
[wi mʌst klæsp ɑːʊʌ hændz tu'gɛðʌ]
We have to clasp them in the air.
[wi hæv tu klæsp ðɛm ɪn ði ɛːʌ]
Oh, nobody else can clasp them for us,
[oːʊ 'noːʊbɑdɪ ɛls kæn klæsp ðɛm fɔʁ(ʳ) ʌs]
We have to clasp them by ourselves.
[wi hæv tu klæsp ðɛm bɑːɪ ɑːʊʌ'sɛlvz]

4. We must lift our hearts to heaven
[wi mʌst lɪft ɑːʊʌ hɑts tu 'hɛvɛ(ɪ)n]
We have to lift them up ourselves
[wi hæv tu lɪft ðɛm ʌp ɑːʊʌ'sɛlvz]
Oh, nobody else can lift them for us,
[oːʊ 'noːʊbɑdɪ ɛls kæn lɪft ðɛm fɔʁ(ʳ) ʌs]
The prayer of brotherhood is there.
[ðʌ pɹɛːʌʁ(ʳ) ʌv 'bɹʌðʌˌhʊd ɪz ðɛːʌ]
5. Jesus walked this lonesome valley,
['ʤizʌs wɔkt ðɪs 'loːʊnsʌm 'væli]
He had to walk it by Himself.
[hi hæd tu wɔk ɪt bɑːɪ hɪm'sɛlf]
Oh, nobody else could walk it for Him,
[oːʊ 'noːʊbɑdɪ ɛls kʊd wɔk ɪt fɔ hɪm]
He had to walk it by Himself.
[hi hæd tu wɔk ɪt bɑːɪ hɪm'sɛlf]

N

Neidlinger, William (Am. 1863-1924)

Song Selection

"The Birthday of a King"
[ðʌ 'bɜθdɛːɪ ʌv ʌ kɪŋ]
Neidlinger, William Harold (Am. 1863-1924)

1. In the little village of Bethlehem,
[ɪn ðʌ 'lɪtʊl 'vɪlæ(ɪ)ʤ ʌv 'bɛθlɪhɛm]
There lay a Child one day,
[ðɛːʌ lɛːɪ ʌ ʧɑːɪld wʌn dɛːɪ]
And the sky was bright with a holy light,
[ænd ðʌ skɑːɪ wɑz bɹɑːɪt wɪð ʌ 'hoːʊli lɑːɪt]
O'er the place where Jesus lay:
[ɔːʌ ðʌ plɛːɪs ʍɛːʌ 'ʤizʌs lɛːɪ]
REFRAIN:
Alleluia! O how the angels sang,
[alɛ'luja oːʊ hɑːʊ ði 'ɛːɪnʤɛ(ʊ)lz sæŋ]
Alleluia! How it rang;
[alɛ'luja hɑːʊ ɪt ɹæŋ]
And the sky was bright with a holy light,
[ænd ðʌ skɑːɪ wɑz bɹɑːɪt wɪð ʌ 'hoːʊli lɑːɪt]
'Twas the birthday of a King.
[twɑz ðʌ 'bɜθdɛːɪ ʌv ʌ kɪŋ]
2. 'Twas a humble birth-place, but oh! how much
[twɑz ʌ 'hʌmbʊl bɜθ plɛːɪs bʌt oːʊ hɑːʊ mʌʧ]
God gave to us that day,
[gɑd gɛːɪv tu ʌs ðæt dɛːɪ]
From the manger bed, what a path has led,
[fɹʌm ðʌ 'mɛːɪnʤʌ bɛd ʍɑt ʌ pæθ hæz lɛd]
What a perfect, holy way:
[ʍɑt ʌ 'pɜfɛ(ɪ)kt 'hoːʊli wɛːɪ]
REFRAIN

Niles, John Jacob (Am. 1892-1980)

Song Selections

"Black Is the Color of My True Love's Hair"
[blæk ɪz ðʌ ˈkʌlʁ ʌv maːɪ tɹu lʌvz hɛːʁ]
Folksong

Black, black, black is the color
[blæk blæk blæk ɪz ðʌ ˈkʌlɔ(ʌ)ʁ⁽ʳ⁾]
of my true love's hair,
[ʌv maːɪ tɹ⁽ʳ⁾u lʌvz hɛːʌ]
Her lips are something rosy fair,
[hɜ lɪps ɑ ˈsʌmθɪŋ ˈɹoːʊzɪ fɛːʌ]
The pertest face and the daintiest hands
[ðʌ ˈpɜtɛ(ɪ)st fɛːɪs ænd ðʌ ˈdeːɪntɪɛ(ɪ)st hændz]
I love the grass whereon she stands.
[aːɪ lʌv ðʌ ɡɹæs ʍɛːʌʁ⁽ʳ⁾ɑn ʃi stændz]
I love my love and well she knows,
[aːɪ lʌv maːɪ lʌv ænd wɛl ʃi noːʊz]
I love the grass whereon she goes;
[aːɪ lʌv ðʌ ɡɹæs ʍɛːʌʁ⁽ʳ⁾ɑn ʃi goːʊz]
If she on earth no more I see,
[ɪf ʃi ɑn ɜθ noːʊ mɔːʌʁ⁽ʳ⁾ aːɪ si]
My life will quickly leave me.
[maːɪ laːɪf wɪl ˈkwɪklɪ liv mi]
I go to Troublesome to mourne, to weep,
[aːɪ goːʊ tu ˈtɹʌbʊlsʌm tu mɔn tu wip]
But satisfied I ne'er can sleep;
[bʌt ˈsætɪsfaːɪd aːɪ nɛːʌ kæn slip]
I'll write her a note in a few little lines,
[aːɪl ɹaːɪt hɜ⁽ʳ⁾ ʌ noːʊt ɪn ʌ fju ˈlɪtʊl laːɪnz]
I'll suffer death ten thousand times.
[aːɪl ˈsʌfʌ dɛθ tɛn ˈθaːʊzæ(ʌ)nd taːɪmz]

"Go 'Way from My Window"
[goːʊ wɛːɪ fɹʌm maːɪ ˈwɪndoːʊ]
Niles, John Jacob (Am. 1892-1980)

Go 'way from my window,
[goːʊ wɛːɪ fɹʌm maːɪ ˈwɪndoːʊ]
Go 'way from my door,
[goːʊ wɛːɪ fɹʌm maːɪ dɔːʌ]
Go 'way, 'way, 'way from my bedside
[goːʊ wɛːɪ wɛːɪ wɛːɪ fɹʌm maːɪ ˈbɛdsaːɪd]
and bother me no more.
[ænd ˈbɑðʌ mi noːʊ mɔːʌ]
I'll give you back your letters,
[aːɪl ɡɪv ju bæk jɔːʌ ˈlɛtʌz]
I'll give you back your ring,
[aːɪl ɡɪv ju bæk jɔːʌ ɹɪŋ]
But I'll ne'er forget my own true love
[bʌt aːɪl nɛːʌ fɔˈɡɛt maːɪ oːʊn tɹ⁽ʳ⁾u lʌv]
As long as songbirds sing.
[æz lɑŋ æz ˈsɑŋbɜdz sɪŋ]

I'll go tell all my brothers,
[aːɪl goːʊ tɛl ɔl maːɪ ˈbɹʌðʌz]
Tell all my sisters, too,
[tɛl ɔl maːɪ ˈsɪstʌz tu]
That the reason why my heart is broke
[ðæt ðʌ ˈɹizʌn ʍaːɪ maːɪ hɑt ɪz bɹoːʊk]
Is on account of you.
[ɪz ɑn ʌˈkaːʊnt ʌv ju]
Go on your way, be happy,
[goːʊ ɑn jɔːʌ wɛːɪ bi ˈhæpɪ]
Go on your way and rest,
[goːʊ ɑn jɔːʌ wɛːɪ ænd ɹɛst]
Remember, dear, that you're the one
[ɹɪˈmɛmbʌ dɪːʌ ðæt jɔːʌ ðʌ wʌn]
I really did love best.
[aːɪ ˈɹɪlɪ dɪd lʌv bɛst]

"I Wonder as I Wander"
[aːɪ ˈwʌndʁ æz aːɪ ˈwandʁ]
Niles, John Jacob (Am. 1892-1980)

I wonder as I wander, out under the sky,
[aːɪ ˈwʌndʌʁ⁽ʳ⁾ æz aːɪ ˈwandʌʁ⁽ʳ⁾ aːʊt ˈʌndʌ ðʌ skaːɪ]
How Jesus the Saviour did come for to die
[haːʊ ˈdʒizʌs ðʌ ˈsɛːɪvjɔ(ʌ) dɪd kʌm fɔ tu daːɪ]
For poor ordn'ry people like you and like I...
[fɔ pʊːʌʁ⁽ʳ⁾ ˈɔdɪnɹɪ ˈpipʊl laːɪk ju ænd laːɪk aːɪ]
I wonder as I wander, out under the sky.
[aːɪ ˈwʌndʌʁ⁽ʳ⁾ æz aːɪ ˈwandʌ aːʊt ˈʌndʌ ðʌ skaːɪ]
When Mary birthed Jesus, 'twas in a cow stall,
[ʍɛn ˈmæʁ⁽ʳ⁾ɪ bɜθt ˈdʒizʌs twaz ɪn ʌ kaːʊ stɔl]
With wise men and farmers and shepherds and all.
[wɪð waːɪz mɛn ænd ˈfɑmʌz ænd ˈʃɛpʌdz ænd ɔl]
But high from God's Heavens a star's light did fall,
[bʌt haːɪ fɹʌm ɡɑdz ˈhɛvɛ(ɪ)nz ʌ staz laːɪt dɪd fɔl]
And the promise of ages it then did recall.
[ænd ðʌ ˈpɹɑmɪs ʌv ˈɛːɪdʒɛ(ɪ)z ɪt ðɛn dɪd ɹɪˈkɔl]
If Jesus had wanted for any wee thing,
[ɪf ˈdʒizʌs hæd ˈwantɛ(ɪ)d fɔʁ⁽ʳ⁾ ˈɛnɪ wi θɪŋ]
A star in the sky, or a bird on the wing,
[ʌ staʁ⁽ʳ⁾ ɪn ðʌ skaːɪ ɔʁ⁽ʳ⁾ ʌ bɜd ɑn ðʌ wɪŋ]
Or all of God's angels in Heav'n to sing,
[ɔʁ⁽ʳ⁾ ɔl ʌv ɡɑdz ˈɛːɪdʒɛ(ʊ)lz ɪn ˈhɛvɪn tu sɪŋ]
He surely could have it, 'cause he was the King.
[hi ˈʃʊːʌlɪ kʊd hæv ɪt kɔz hi waz ðʌ kɪŋ]

"Jesus, Jesus Rest Your Head"
[ˈdʒizʌs ˈdʒizʌs ɹɛst jɔːʁ hɛd]
Southern Appalachian Folksong

REFRAIN:
Jesus, Jesus, rest your head,
[ˈdʒizʌs ˈdʒizʌs ɹɛst jɔːʌ hɛd]
You has got a manger bed.
[ju hæz ɡat ʌ ˈmɛːɪndʒʌ bɛd]

All the evil folk on earth
[ɔl ði ˈivɪ(ʊ)l foːʊk ɑn ɜθ]
Sleep in feathers at their birth.
[slip ɪn ˈfɛðʌz æt ðeːʌ bɜθ]
Jesus, Jesus, rest your head,
[ˈdʒizʌs ˈdʒizʌs ɹɛst jɔːʌ hɛd]
You has got a manger bed.
[ju hæz gɑt ʌ ˈmeːɪndʒʌ bɛd]
1. Have you heard about our Jesus?
[hæv ju hɜd ʌˈbɑːʊt ɑːʊʌ ˈdʒizʌs]
Have you heard about his fate?
[hæv ju hɜd ʌˈbɑːʊt hɪz feːɪt]
How his mammy went to that stable
[hɑːʊ hɪz ˈmæmɪ wɛnt tu ðæt ˈsteːɪbʊl]
On that Christmas Eve so late?
[ɑn ðæt ˈkɹɪsmʌs iv soːʊ lɛːɪt]
Winds were blowing, cows were lowing,
[wɪndz wɜ ˈbloːʊɪŋ kɑːʊz wɜ ˈloːʊɪŋ]
Stars were glowing, glowing, glowing.
[stɑz wɜ ˈgloːʊɪŋ ˈgloːʊɪŋ ˈgloːʊɪŋ]
REFRAIN
2. To that manger came then wise men,
[tu ðæt ˈmeːɪndʒʌ keːɪm ðen wɑːɪz mɛn]
Bringing things from hin and yon.
[ˈbɹɪŋɪŋ θɪŋz fɹʌm hɪn ænd jɑn]
For the mother and the father
[fɔ ðʌ ˈmʌðʌʁ⁽ʳ⁾ ænd ðʌ ˈfɑðʌ]
And the blessed little Son.
[ænd ðʌ ˈblɛsɛ(ɪ)d ˈlɪtʊl sʌn]
Milkmaids left their fields and flocks
[ˈmɪlkmeːɪdz lɛft ðeːʌ fildz ænd flɑks]
And sat beside the ass and ox.
[ænd sæt bɪˈsɑːɪd ði æs ænd ɑks]
REFRAIN

"My Lover Is a Farmer Lad"
[mɑːɪ ˈlʌvʁ ɪz ʌ ˈfɑmʁ læd]
Niles, John Jacob (Am. 1892-1980)

My lover is a farmer lad
[mɑːɪ ˈlʌvʌʁ⁽ʳ⁾ ɪz ʌ ˈfɑmʌ læd]
who comes to me at twilight.
[hu kʌmz tu mi æt ˈtwɑːɪlɑːɪt]
Meanwhile my other suitors woo me
[ˈminʍɑːɪl mɑːɪ ˈʌðʌ ˈsjutɔ(ʌ)z wu mi]
while it is yet daylight.
[ʍɑːɪl ɪt ɪz jɛt ˈdeːɪlɑːɪt]
A butcher's boy, a cavalier,
[ʌ ˈbʊtʃʌz bɔːɪ ʌ ˌkævʌˈliːʌ]
and one of his Majesty's
[ænd wʌn ʌv hɪz ˈmædʒɛ(ɪ)stɪz]
most magnificent dragoons.
[moːʊst mægˈnɪfɪˌsɛnt dɹʌˈgunz]
But my lover is a farmer lad
[bʌt mɑːɪ ˈlʌvʌʁ⁽ʳ⁾ ɪz ʌ ˈfɑmʌ læd]

who comes to me at twilight.
[hu kʌmz tu mi æt ˈtwɑːɪlɑːɪt]
Meanwhile my other suitors woo me
[ˈminʍɑːɪl mɑːɪ ˈʌðʌ ˈsjutɔ(ʌ)z wu mi]
while it is yet daylight.
[ʍɑːɪl ɪt ɪz jɛt ˈdeːɪlɑːɪt]
The keeper of a public house, a commissionaire
[ðʌ ˈkipʌʁ⁽ʳ⁾ ʌv ʌ ˈpʌblɪk hɑːʊs ʌ kʌmɪʃʌnˈɛːʌ]
and one of his Majesty's
[ænd wʌn ʌv hɪz ˈmædʒɛ(ɪ)stɪz]
most magnificent dragoons.
[moːʊst mægˈnɪfɪˌsɛnt dɹʌˈgunz]
My farmer lad loves his farming
[mɑːɪ ˈfɑmʌ læd lʌvz hɪz ˈfɑmɪŋ]
and he loves the rising moon,
[ænd hi lʌvz ðʌ ˈɹɑːɪzɪŋ mun]
And he cunningly watches my garden gate
[ænd hi ˈkʌnɪŋlɪ ˈwɑtʃɛ(ɪ)z mɑːɪ ˈgɑdɛ(ɪ)n geːɪt]
for that pompous, proud dragoon.
[fɔ ðæt ˈpɑmpʌs pɹɑːʊd dɹʌˈgun]
Oh, my lover has neither city clothes,
[oːʊ mɑːɪ ˈlʌvʌ hæz ˈnɑːɪðʌ ˈsɪtɪ kloːʊðz]
nor a comb for his tousled hair,
[nɔʁ⁽ʳ⁾ ʌ koːʊm fɔ hɪz ˈtɑːʊzʊld hɛːʌ]
But his handsome hands are strong and brown,
[bʌt hɪz ˈhænsʌm hændz ɑ stɹɑŋ ænd bɹɑːʊn]
and his manner is debonaire.
[ænd hɪz ˈmænʌʁ⁽ʳ⁾ ɪz dɛboˈnɛːʌ]
My lover is a farmer lad
[mɑːɪ ˈlʌvʌʁ⁽ʳ⁾ ɪz ʌ ˈfɑmʌ læd]
who comes to me at twilight.
[hu kʌmz tu mi æt ˈtwɑːɪlɑːɪt]
Meanwhile my other suitors woo me
[ˈminʍɑːɪl mɑːɪ ˈʌðʌ ˈsjutɔ(ʌ)z wu mi]
while it is yet daylight.
[ʍɑːɪl ɪt ɪz jɛt ˈdeːɪlɑːɪt]
A butcher's boy, a cavalier,
[ʌ ˈbʊtʃʌz bɔːɪ ʌ ˌkævʌˈliːʌ]
and one of his Majesty's
[ænd wʌn ʌv hɪz ˈmædʒɛ(ɪ)stɪz]
most magnificent dragoons.
[moːʊst mægˈnɪfɪˌsɛnt dɹʌˈgunz]
But my lover is a farmer lad
[bʌt mɑːɪ ˈlʌvʌʁ⁽ʳ⁾ ɪz ʌ ˈfɑmʌ læd]
who comes to me at twilight.
[hu kʌmz tu mi æt ˈtwɑːɪlɑːɪt]

"The Black Dress"
[ðʌ blæk dɹɛs]
Folksong

Oh she'll take off the black dress
[oːʊ ʃil teːɪk ɑf ðʌ blæk dɹɛs]
And put on the green,
[ænd pʊt ɑn ðʌ gɹin]

For she is forsaken and only nineteen.
[fɔ ʃi ɪz fɔˈsɛːɪkɛ(ɪ)n ænd ˈoːʊnlɪ naːɪnˈtin]
Fa la la...
[fɑ lɑ lɑ]
Oh he courted her and he kissed her
[oːʊ hi ˈkɔtɛ(ɪ)d hɜ ænd hi kɪst hɜ]
And he made her heart warm.
[ænd hi mɛːɪd hɜ hɑt wɔm]
And then when he left her
[ænd ðɛn ʍɛn hi lɛft hɜ]
He laughed her to scorn.
[hi læft hɜ tu skɔn]
Fa la la...
[fɑ lɑ lɑ]
Forsaken, forsaken her heart is forlorn,
[fɔˈsɛːɪkɛ(ɪ)n fɔˈsɛːɪkɛ(ɪ)n hɜ hɑt ɪz fɔˈlɔn]
But he is mistaken if he thinks she will mourn.
[bʌt hi ɪz mɪˈstɛːɪkɛ(ɪ)n ɪf hi θɪŋks ʃi wɪl mɔn]
Fa la la...
[fɑ lɑ lɑ]
For we'll build her a cabin
[fɔ wil bɪld hɜ ʌ ˈkæbɪn]
On yon mountain high
[ɑn jɑn ˈmaːʊntæ(ɪ)n haːɪ]
Where the wild birds can't find her
[ʍɛːʌ ðʌ waːɪld bɜdz kænt faːɪnd hɜ]
Nor hear her heart cry
[nɔ hiːʌ hɜ hɑt kɾaːɪ]
Fa la la...
[fɑ lɑ lɑ]
Take warning, take warning, young ladies pray do,
[tɛːɪk ˈwɔnɪŋ tɛːɪk ˈwɔnɪŋ jʌŋ ˈlɛːɪdɪz pɹɛːɪ du]
For you are quite lucky that this is not you. Fa la la...
[fɔ ju ɑ kwaːɪt ˈlʌkɪ ðæt ðɪs ɪz nɑt ju fɑ lɑ lɑ]

"The Lass from the Low Countree"
[ðʌ læs fɪʌm ðʌ loːʊ ˈkʌntɹi]
Niles, John Jacob (Am. 1892-1980)

Oh, he was a lord of high degree
[oːʊ hi waz ʌ lɔd ʌv haːɪ dɪˈgɹi]
And she was a lass from the low countree
[ænd ʃi waz ʌ læs fɪʌm ðʌ loːʊ ˈkʌntɹi]
But she loved his lordship so tenderly.
[bʌt ʃi lʌvd hɪz ˈlɔdʃɪp soːʊ ˈtendʌlɪ]
Oh sorrow, sing sorrow
[oːʊ ˈsaʁ⁽ʳ⁾oːʊ sɪŋ ˈsaʁ⁽ʳ⁾oːʊ]
Now she sleeps in the valley
[naːʊ ʃi slips ɪn ðʌ ˈvælɪ]
where the wild flowers nod
[ʍɛːʌ ðʌ waːɪld flaːʊʌz nɑd]
And no one knows she loved him but herself and God
[ænd noːʊ wʌn noːʊz ʃi lʌvd hɪm bʌt hɜˈsɛlf ænd gɑd]
One morn when the sun was on the mead
[wʌn mɔn ʍɛn ðʌ sʌn waz ɑn ðʌ mid]

He passed by her door on a milk white steed
[hi pæst baːɪ hɜ dɔːʌʁ⁽ʳ⁾ ɑn ʌ mɪlk ʍaːɪt stid]
She smiled and she spoke, but he paid no heed
[ʃi smaːɪld ænd ʃi spoːʊk bʌt hi pɛːɪd noːʊ hid]
Oh sorrow, sing sorrow
[oːʊ ˈsaʁ⁽ʳ⁾oːʊ sɪŋ ˈsaʁ⁽ʳ⁾oːʊ]
Now she sleeps in the valley where the wild flowers nod
[naːʊ ʃi slips ɪn ðʌ ˈvælɪ ʍɛːʌ ðʌ waːɪld flaːʊʌz nɑd]
And no one knows she loved him but herself and God
[ænd noːʊ wʌn noːʊz ʃi lʌvd hɪm bʌt hɜˈsɛlf ænd gɑd]
If you be a lass from the low countree
[ɪf ju bi ʌ læs fɪʌm ðʌ loːʊ ˈkʌntɹi]
Don't love of no lord of high degree
[doːʊnt lʌv ʌv noːʊ lɔd ʌv haːɪ dɪˈgɹi]
They ain't got a heart for sympathy
[ðɛːɪ ɛːɪnt gɑt ʌ hɑt fɔ ˈsɪmpæ(ʌ)θɪ]
Oh sorrow, sing sorrow
[oːʊ ˈsaʁ⁽ʳ⁾oːʊ sɪŋ ˈsaʁ⁽ʳ⁾oːʊ]
Now she sleeps in the valley where the wild flowers nod
[naːʊ ʃi slips ɪn ðʌ ˈvælɪ ʍɛːʌ ðʌ waːɪld flaːʊʌz nɑd]
And no one knows she loved him but herself and God.
[ænd noːʊ wʌn noːʊz ʃi lʌvd hɪm bʌt hɜˈsɛlf ænd gɑd]

"The Rovin' Gambler"
[ðʌ ˈɹoːʊvɪŋ ˈgæmblʁ]
Folksong

I am a rovin' gambler,
[aːɪ æm ʌ ˈɹoːʊvɪn ˈgæmblʌ]
I've been in many a town.
[aːɪv bɪn ɪn ˈmɛnɪ ʌ taːʊn]
Where-e'er I see a pack of cards
[ʍɛːʌʁ⁽ʳ⁾ ɛːʌʁ⁽ʳ⁾ aːɪ si ʌ pæk ʌv kɑdz]
I lay my money down.
[aːɪ lɛːɪ maːɪ ˈmʌnɪ daːʊn]
With a click clack oh and a high johnny ho,
[wɪð ʌ klɪk klæk oːʊ ænd ʌ haːɪ ˈdʒɑnɪ hoːʊ]
I lay my money down.
[aːɪ lɛːɪ maːɪ ˈmʌnɪ daːʊn]
I hadn't been a packet man
[aːɪ ˈhædɛ(ɪ)nt bɪn ʌ ˈpækɛ(ɪ)t mæn]
Many more weeks than three,
[ˈmɛnɪ mɔːʌ wiks ðæn θri]
When I fell in love with a St. Louis girl
[ʍɛn aːɪ fɛl ɪn lʌv wɪð ʌ sɛːɪnt ˈlui gɜl]
And she in love with me.
[ænd ʃi ɪn lʌv wɪð mi]
With a click clack oh and a high johnny ho,
[wɪð ʌ klɪk klæk oːʊ ænd ʌ haːɪ ˈdʒɑnɪ hoːʊ]
And she in love with me.
[ænd ʃi ɪn lʌv wɪð mi]
We went in the back parlor,
[wi wɛnt ɪn ðʌ bæk ˈpalɔ(ʌ)]
She cooled me with her fan,
[ʃi kuld mi wɪð hɜ fæn]

And she whispered soft in her mother's ear,
[ænd ʃi ˈʍɪspʌd saft ɪn hɜ ˈmʌðʌz iːʌ]
"I love my gamblin' man,
[ɑːɪ lʌv mɑːɪ ˈgæmblɪn mæn]
With a click clack oh and a high johnny ho,
[wɪð ʌ klɪk klæk oːʊ ænd ʌ hɑːɪ ˈdʒɑnɪ hoːʊ]
I love my gamblin' man."
[ɑːɪ lʌv mɑːɪ ˈgæmblɪn mæn]
"Oh daughter dear, dear daughter,
[oːʊ ˈdɔtʌ diːʌ diːʌ ˈdɔtʌ]
How could you do me so,
[hɑːʊ kʊd ju du mi soːʊ]
To leave your dear old mother-er,
[tu liv jɔːʌ diːʌʁ⁽ʳ⁾ oːʊld ˈmʌðʌ ɜ]
And with this gambler go?
[ænd wɪð ðɪs ˈgæmblʌ goːʊ]
With a click clack oh and a high johnny ho,
[wɪð ʌ klɪk klæk oːʊ ænd ʌ hɑːɪ ˈdʒɑnɪ hoːʊ]
And with the gambler go?"
[ænd wɪð ðʌ ˈgæmblʌ goːʊ]
"'Tis true I love you dearly,
[tɪz tɪ⁽ʳ⁾u ɑːɪ lʌv ju ˈdiːʌlɪ]
'Tis true I love you well,
[tɪz tɪ⁽ʳ⁾u ɑːɪ lʌv ju wɛl]
But the love I have for the gamblin' man
[bʌt ðʌ lʌv ɑːɪ hæv fɔ ðʌ ˈgæmblɪn mæn]
No human tongue can tell.
[noːʊ ˈhjumæ(ʌ)n tʌŋ kæn tɛl]
With a click clack oh and a high johnny ho,
[wɪð ʌ klɪk klæk oːʊ ænd ʌ hɑːɪ ˈdʒɑnɪ hoːʊ]
No human tongue can tell."
[noːʊ ˈhjumæ(ʌ)n tʌŋ kæn tɛl]
She picked up her satchel
[ʃi pɪkt ʌp hɜ ˈsætʃʊl]
And she did leave her home,
[ænd ʃi dɪd liv hɜ hoːʊm]
And on the steamer "Morning Star"
[ænd ɑn ðʌ ˈstimʌ ˈmɔnɪŋ stɑ]
The two of them did roam,
[ðʌ tu ʌv ðɛm dɪd ɹoːʊm]
With a click clack oh and a high johnny ho,
[wɪð ʌ klɪk klæk oːʊ ænd ʌ hɑːɪ ˈdʒɑnɪ hoːʊ]
The two of them did roam.
[ðʌ tu ʌv ðɛm dɪd ɹoːʊm]
With a click clack oh and a high johnny ho...

"Wayfaring Stranger"
[ˈwɛːɪˌfɛʁɪŋ ˈstɹɛːɪndʒʁ]
Traditional

I am a poor wayfaring stranger,
[ɑːɪ æm ʌ pʊːʌ ˈwɛːɪ fɛːʌʁ⁽ʳ⁾ɪŋ ˈstɹɛːɪndʒʌ]
While traveling (journ'ying) through this world of woe,
[ʍɑːɪl ˈtɹævʊlɪŋ (ˈdʒɜnɪɪŋ) θru ðɪs wɜd ʌv woːʊ]
And (Yet) there's no sickness, toil, nor danger
[ænd (jɛt) ðɛːʌz noːʊ ˈsɪknɛ(ɪ)s tɔːɪl nɔ ˈdɛːɪndʒʌ]

In that fair land to which I go.
[ɪn ðæt fɛːʌ lænd tu ʍɪtʃ ɑːɪ goːʊ]
I'm going there to see my Mother,
[ɑːɪm ˈgoːʊɪŋ ðɛːʌ tu si mɑːɪ ˈmʌðʌ]
I'm going there, no more to roam;
[ɑːɪm ˈgoːʊɪŋ ðɛːʌ noːʊ mɔːʌ tu ɹoːʊm]
I am only going over Jordan,
[ɑːɪ æm ˈoːʊnlɪ ˈgoːʊɪŋ ˈoːʊvʌ ˈdʒɔdʌ(ɪ)n]
I am only going over home.
[ɑːɪ æm ˈoːʊnlɪ ˈgoːʊɪŋ ˈoːʊvʌ hoːʊm]
I know dark clouds will gather o'er me,
[ɑːɪ noːʊ dɑk klɑːʊdz wɪl ˈgæðʌʁ⁽ʳ⁾ ɔːʌ mi]
I know my way is rough and steep;
[ɑːɪ noːʊ mɑːɪ wɛːɪ ɪz ɹʌf ænd stip]
Yet beauteous fields lie just before me,
[jɛt ˈbjutɪʌs fildz lɑːɪ dʒʌst bɪˈfɔːʌ mi]
Where God's redeemed their vigils keep.
[ʍɛːʌ gɑdz ɹɪˈdimd ðɛːʌ ˈvɪdʒɪ(ʊ)lz kip]
I'm going there to see my Father,
[ɑːɪm ˈgoːʊɪŋ ðɛːʌ tu si mɑːɪ ˈfɑðʌ]
He said He'd meet me when I come.
[hi sɛd hid mit mi ʍɛn ɑːɪ kʌm]
I'm only going over Jordan,
[ɑːɪm ˈoːʊnlɪ ˈgoːʊɪŋ ˈoːʊvʌ ˈdʒɔdʌ(ɪ)n]
I'm only going over home.
[ɑːɪm ˈoːʊnlɪ ˈgoːʊɪŋ ˈoːʊvʌ hoːʊm]
I want to wear a crown of glory
[ɑːɪ wɑnt tu wɛːʌʁ⁽ʳ⁾ ʌ kɹɑːʊn ʌv ˈglɔʁ⁽ʳ⁾ɪ]
When I get home to that good land,
[ʍɛn ɑːɪ gɛt hoːʊm tu ðæt gʊd lænd]
I want to shout Salvation's story
[ɑːɪ wɑnt tu ʃɑːʊt sælˈvɛːɪʃʌnz ˈstɔʁ⁽ʳ⁾ɪ]
In concert with the blood-washed Band.
[ɪn ˈkɑnˌsɜt wɪð ðʌ blʌd wɑʃt bænd]
I'm going there to meet my Saviour,
[ɑːɪm ˈgoːʊɪŋ ðɛːʌ tu mit mɑːɪ ˈsɛːɪvjʊ(ʌ)]
To sing His praise forevermore,
[tu sɪŋ hɪz pɹɛːɪz fɔʁ⁽ʳ⁾ˈɛvʌmɔːʌ]
I'm only going over Jordan,
[ɑːɪm ˈoːʊnlɪ ˈgoːʊɪŋ ˈoːʊvʌ ˈdʒɔdʌ(ɪ)n]
I'm only going over home.
[ɑːɪm ˈoːʊnlɪ ˈgoːʊɪŋ ˈoːʊvʌ hoːʊm]

 # Nombeko, Nailah (Am. b. 1976)

Four Songs to Poems by William Blake (Song Cycle)
[fɔːʁ sɑŋz tu ˈpoːʊɪmz bɑːɪ ˈwɪljɪm blɛːɪk]
Blake, William (Eng. 1757-1827)

1. The Lily
[ðʌ ˈlɪli]

The modest Rose puts forth a thorn,
[ðʌ ˈmɑdɛ(ɪ)st ɹoːʊz pʊts fɔθ ʌ θɔn]

The humble sheep a threat'ning horn:
[ðʌ ˈhʌmbʊl ʃip ʌ ˈθrɛtnɪŋ hɔn]
While the Lily white shall in love delight,
[ʍaːɪl ðʌ ˈlɪlɪ ʍaːɪt ʃæl ɪn lʌv dɪˈlaːɪt]
Nor a thorn nor a threat stain her beauty bright.
[nɔʁ⁽ʳ⁾ ʌ θɔn nɔʁ⁽ʳ⁾ ʌ θrɛt stɛːɪn hɜ ˈbjutɪ bɹaːɪt]

2. The Garden of Love
[ðʌ ˈgaʁdɪn ʌv lʌv]

I went to the Garden of Love,
[aːɪ wɛnt tu ðʌ ˈgadɛ(ɪ)n ʌv lʌv]
And saw what I never had seen;
[ænd sɔ ʍat aːɪ ˈnɛvʌ hæd sin]
A Chapel was built in the midst,
[ʌ ˈtʃæpʊl waz bɪlt ɪn ðʌ mɪdst]
Where I used to play on the green.
[ʍɛːʌʁ⁽ʳ⁾ aːɪ just tu plɛːɪ an ðʌ gɹin]
And the gates of this Chapel were shut,
[ænd ðʌ gɛːɪts ʌv ðɪs ˈtʃæpʊl wɜ ʃʌt]
And 'Thou shalt not' writ over the door;
[ænd ðaːʊ ʃælt nat ɹɪt ˈoːʊvʌ ðʌ dɔːʌ]
So I turned to the Garden of Love
[soːʊ aːɪ tɜnd tu ðʌ ˈgadɛ(ɪ)n ʌv lʌv]
That so many sweet flowers bore.
[ðæt soːʊ ˈmɛnɪ swit flaːʊʌz bɔːʌ]
And I saw it was filled with graves,
[ænd aːɪ sɔ ɪt waz fɪld wɪð gɹɛːɪvz]
And tombstones where flowers should be;
[ænd ˈtumstoːʊnz ʍɛːʌ flaːʊʌz ʃʊd bi]
And priests in black gowns were walking their rounds,
[ænd pɹists ɪn blæk gaːʊnz wɜ ˈwɔkɪŋ ðɛːʌ ɹaːʊndz]
And binding with briars my joys and desires.
[ænd ˈbaːɪndɪŋ wɪð ˈbɹaːɪʌz maːɪ dʒɔːɪz ænd dɪˈzaːɪʌz]

3. The Divine Image (see Thomson)

4. My Pretty Rose Tree
[maːɪ ˈpɹɪtɪ ɹoːʊz tɹi]

A flower was offered to me,
[ʌ flaːʊʌ waz ˈafʌd tu mi]
Such a flower as May never bore;
[sʌtʃ ʌ flaːʊʌʁ⁽ʳ⁾ æz mɛːɪ ˈnɛvʌ bɔːʌ]
But I said, 'I've a pretty rose tree,'
[bʌt aːɪ sɛd aːɪv ʌ ˈpɹɪtɪ ɹoːʊz tɹi]
And I passed the sweet flower o'er.
[ænd aːɪ pæst ðʌ swit flaːʊʌʁ⁽ʳ⁾ ɔːʌ]
Then I went to my pretty rose tree,
[ðɛn aːɪ wɛnt tu maːɪ ˈpɹɪtɪ ɹoːʊz tɹi]
To tend her by day and by night;
[tu tɛnd hɜ baːɪ dɛːɪ ænd baːɪ naːɪt]
But my rose turned away with jealousy,
[bʌt maːɪ ɹoːʊz tɜnd ʌˈwɛːɪ wɪð ˈdʒɛlʌsɪ]
And her thorns were my only delight.
[ænd hɜ θɔnz wɜ maːɪ ˈoːʊnlɪ dɪˈlaːɪt]

O

Orr, Charles Wilfred
(Eng. 1893-1976)

Song Selection

"'Tis Time, I Think, by Wenlock Town"
[tɪz taːɪm aːɪ θɪŋk baːɪ ˈwɛnlak taːʊn]
(Two Songs from "A Shropshire Lad")
Housman, Alfred Edward (Eng. 1859-1936)

'Tis time, I think, by Wenlock town
[tɪz taːɪm aːɪ θɪŋk baːɪ ˈwɛnlak taːʊn]
The golden broom should blow;
[ðʊ ˈgoːʊldɛ(ɪ)n brum ʃʊd bloːʊ]
The hawthorn sprinkled up and down
[ðʊ ˈhɔθɔn ˈspɹɪŋkʊld ʌp ænd daːʊn]
Should charge the land with snow.
[ʃʊd tʃadʒ ðʊ lænd wɪð snoːʊ]
Spring will not wait the loiterer's time
[spɹɪŋ wɪl nat wɛːɪt ðʊ ˈlɔːɪtʌɾʌz taːɪm]
Who keeps so long away;
[hu kips soːʊ laŋ ʌˈwɛːɪ]
So others wear the broom and climb
[soːʊ ˈʌðʌz wɛːʌ ðʊ brum ænd klaːɪm]
The hedgerows heaped with may.
[ðʊ ˈhɛdʒɹoːʊz hipt wɪð mɛːɪ]
Oh tarnish late on Wenlock Edge,
[oːʊ ˈtanɪʃ lɛːɪt an ˈwɛnlak ɛdʒ]
Gold that I never see;
[goːʊld ðæt aːɪ ˈnɛvʌ si]
Lie long, high snowdrifts in the hedge
[laːɪ laŋ haːɪ ˈsnoːʊdɹɪfts ɪn ðʊ hɛdʒ]
That will not shower on me.
[ðæt wɪl nat ʃaːʊʌɾ an mi]

Owens, Robert (Am. 1925-2017)

Song Selections

"For a Poet" (see Moore, Dorothy)

"If We Must Die" (3 Songs for Baritone and Piano)
[ɪf wi mʌst daːɪ]
Mckay, Claude (Jam. 1890-1948)

If we must die– let it not be like hogs
[ɪf wi mʌst daːɪ lɛt ɪt nat bi laːɪk hagz]
Hunted and penned in an inglorious spot,
[ˈhʌntɛ(ɪ)d ænd pɛnd ɪn æn ɪnˈglɔʁ⁽ʳ⁾ɪʌs spat]

While round us bark the mad and hungry dogs,
[ʍaːɪl ɹaːʊnd ʌs bak ðʌ mæd ænd ˈhʌŋɡɹɪ dɑgz]
Making their mock at our accursed lot.
[ˈmeːɪkɪŋ ðɛːʌ mak æt ɑːʊʌʁ⁽ʳ⁾ ʌˈkɜːsɛ⁽ɪ⁾d lat]
If we must die– oh, let us nobly die,
[ɪf wi mʌst daːɪ oːʊ lɛt ʌs ˈnoːʊblɪ daːɪ]
So that our precious blood may not be shed
[soːʊ ðæt ɑːʊʌ ˈpɹɛʃʌs blʌd meːɪ nat bi ʃɛd]
In vain; then even the monsters we defy
[ɪn vɛːɪn ðɛn ˈivɛ⁽ɪ⁾n ðʌ ˈmanstʌz wi dɪˈfaːɪ]
Shall be constrained to honor us though dead!
[ʃæl bi kʌnˈstɹɛːɪnd tu ˈanʌʁ⁽ʳ⁾ ʌs ðoːʊ dɛd]
Oh, Kinsmen! We must meet the common foe;
[oːʊ ˈkɪnzmɛ⁽ɪ⁾n wi mʌst mit ðʌ ˈkamʌn foːʊ]
Though far outnumbered, let us still be brave,
[ðoːʊ faʁ⁽ʳ⁾ ɑːʊtˈnʌmbʌd lɛt ʌs stɪl bi bɹɛːɪv]
And for their thousand blows deal one death-blow!
[ænd fɔ ðɛːʌ ˈθaːʊzæ⁽ʌ⁾nd bloːʊz dil wʌn dɛθ bloːʊ]
What though before us lies the open grave?
[ʍat ðoːʊ bɪˈfɔːʁ⁽ʳ⁾ ʌs laːɪz ði ˈoːʊpɛ⁽ɪ⁾n ɡɹɛɪv]
Like men we'll face the murderous, cowardly pack,
[laːɪk mɛn wil fɛːɪs ðʌ ˈmɜdʌʁ⁽ʳ⁾ʌs ˈkaːʊʌdlɪ pæk]
Pressed to the wall, dying, but– fighting back!
[pɹɛst tu ðʌ wɔl ˈdaːɪŋ bʌt ˈfaːɪtɪŋ bæk]

"No Images"
[noːʊ ˈɪmɪdʒɪz]
Cuney, Waring (Am. 1906-1976)

She does not know her beauty,
[ʃi dʌz nat noːʊ hɜ ˈbjutɪ]
she thinks her brown body has no glory.
[ʃi θɪŋks hɜ bɹaːʊn ˈbadɪ hæz noːʊ ˈɡlɒʁ⁽ʳ⁾ɪ]
If she could dance naked under palm trees
[ɪf ʃi kʊd dæns ˈnɛːɪkɛ⁽ɪ⁾d ˈʌndʌ pam tɹiz]
and see her image in the river, she would know.
[ænd si hɜ ˈɪmæ⁽ɪ⁾dʒ ɪn ðʌ ˈɹɪvʌ ʃi wʊd noːʊ]
But there are no palm trees on the street,
[bʌt ðɛːʌʁ⁽ʳ⁾ a noːʊ pam tɹiz an ðʌ stɹit]
and dish water gives back no images.
[ænd dɪʃ ˈwɔtʌ ɡɪvz bæk noːʊ ˈɪmæ⁽ɪ⁾dʒɛ⁽ɪ⁾z]

"When We Two Parted"
[ʍɛn wi tu ˈpaʁtɪd]
Gordon, Lord Byron (Eng. 1788-1824)

When we two parted, In silence and tears,
[ʍɛn wi tu ˈpatɛ⁽ɪ⁾d ɪn ˈsaːɪlɛ⁽ɪ⁾ns ænd tɪːʌz]
Half broken-hearted, To sever for years,
[hæf ˈbɹoːʊkɛ⁽ɪ⁾n ˈhatɛ⁽ɪ⁾d tu ˈsɛvʌ fɔ jɪːʌz]
Pale grew thy cheek and cold, Colder thy kiss;
[pɛːɪl ɡɹ⁽ʳ⁾u ðaːɪ tʃik ænd koːʊld ˈkoːʊldʌ ðaːɪ kɪs]
Truly that hour foretold, Sorrow to this.
[ˈtɹ⁽ʳ⁾ulɪ ðæt aːʊʌ fɔˈtoːʊld ˈsaʁ⁽ʳ⁾oːʊ tu ðɪs]
The dew of the morning, Sunk chill on my brow –
[ðʌ dju ʌv ðʌ ˈmɔnɪŋ sʌŋk tʃɪl an maːɪ bɹaːʊ]

It felt like the warning, I feel now.
[ɪt fɛlt laːɪk ðʌ ˈwɔnɪŋ aːɪ fil naːʊ]
Thy vows all broken, And light is thy fame;
[ðaːɪ vaːʊz ɔl ˈbɹoːʊkɛ⁽ɪ⁾n ænd laːɪt ɪz ðaːɪ fɛːɪm]
I hear thy name spoken, And share in its shame.
[aːɪ hiːʌ ðaːɪ nɛːɪm ˈspoːʊkɛ⁽ɪ⁾n ænd ʃɛːʁ⁽ʳ⁾ ɪn ɪts ʃɛːɪm]
They name thee before me, A knell to mine ear;
[ðɛːɪ nɛːɪm ði bɪˈfɔːʌ mi ʌ nɛl tu maːɪn iːʌ]
A shudder comes o'er me – Why wert thou so dear?
[ʌ ˈʃʌdʌ kʌmz ɔːʌ mi ʍaːɪ wɜt ðaːʊ soːʊ dɪːʌ]
They know not I knew thee, Who knew thee too well:–
[ðɛːɪ noːʊ nat aːɪ nju ði hu nju ði tu wɛl]
Long, long shall I rue thee, Too deeply to tell.
[laŋ laŋ ʃæl aːɪ ɹ⁽ʳ⁾u ði tu ˈdiplɪ tu tɛl]
In secret we met – In silence I grieve
[ɪn ˈsikɹɛ⁽ɪ⁾t wi mɛt ɪn ˈsaːɪlɛ⁽ɪ⁾ns aːɪ ɡɹ⁽ʳ⁾iv]
That thy heart could forget, Thy spirit deceive.
[ðæt ðaːɪ hat kʊd fɔˈgɛt ðaːɪ ˈspɪʁ⁽ʳ⁾ɪt dɪˈsiv]
If I should meet thee, After long years,
[ɪf aːɪ ʃʊd mit ði ˈæftʌ laŋ jɪːʌz]
How shall I greet thee? – With silence and tears.
[haːʊ ʃæl aːɪ ɡɹit ði wɪð ˈsaːɪlɛ⁽ɪ⁾ns ænd tɪːʌz]

"Yet Do I Marvel"
[jɛt du aːɪ ˈmaʁvʊl]
Cullen, Countee (Am. 1903-1946)

I doubt not God is good, well-meaning, kind
[aːɪ daːʊt nat gad ɪz gʊd wɛl ˈminɪŋ kaːɪnd]
And did He stoop to quibble could tell why
[ænd dɪd hi stup tu ˈkwɪbʊl kʊd tɛl ʍaːɪ]
The little buried mole continues blind,
[ðʌ ˈlɪtʊl ˈbɛʁ⁽ʳ⁾ɪd moːʊl kʌnˈtɪnjuz blaːɪnd]
Why flesh that mirrors Him must some day die,
[ʍaːɪ flɛʃ ðæt ˈmɪʁ⁽ʳ⁾ɔ⁽ʌ⁾z hɪm mʌst sʌm dɛːɪ daːɪ]
Make plain the reason tortured Tantalus
[mɛːɪk plɛːɪn ðʌ ˈɹizʌn ˈtɔtʃʊ⁽ʌ⁾d ˈtæntʊlʊs]
Is baited by the fickle fruit, declare
[ɪz ˈbɛːɪtɛ⁽ɪ⁾d baːɪ ðʌ ˈfɪkʊl fɹ⁽ʳ⁾ut dɪˈklɛːʁ⁽ʳ⁾]
If merely brute caprice dooms Sisyphus
[ɪf ˈmiːʌlɪ bɹ⁽ʳ⁾ut kʌˈpɹis dumz ˈsɪsɪfʊs]
To struggle up a never-ending stair.
[tu ˈstɹʌgʊl ʌp ʌ ˈnɛvʌ ˈɛndɪŋ stɛːʌ]
Inscrutable His ways are, and immune
[ɪnˈskɹ⁽ʳ⁾utʌbʊl hɪz wɛːɪz a ænd ɪˈmjun]
To catechism by a mind too strewn
[tu ˈkætɪkɪzʌm baːɪ ʌ maːɪnd tu stɹ⁽ʳ⁾un]
With petty cares to slightly understand
[wɪð ˈpɛtɪ kɛːʌz tu ˈslaːɪtlɪ ʌndʌˈstænd]
What awful brain compels His awful hand.
[ʍat ˈɔfʊl bɹɛːɪn kʌmˈpɛlz hɪz ˈɔfʊl hænd]
Yet do I marvel at this curious thing:
[jɛt du aːɪ ˈmavʊl æt ðɪs ˈkjuːʁ⁽ʳ⁾ɪʌs θɪŋ]
To make a poet black, and bid him sing!
[tu mɛːɪk ʌ ˈpoːʊɛ⁽ɪ⁾t blæk ænd bɪd hɪm sɪŋ]

P

Parry, Charles Hubert
(Eng. 1848-1918)

"Crabbed Age and Youth" (see Dring)

"Willow" (see "The Willow Song" Coleridge-Taylor)

Pasatieri, Thomas (Am. b. 1945)

Three Poems of Oscar Wilde (Song Cycle)
[θɾi 'poːʊɪmz ʌv 'askʁ waːɪld]
Wilde, Oscar (Ir. 1854-1900)

1. Helas
[e'las]

To drift with every passion till my soul
[tu dɹɪft wɪð 'ɛvɹɪ 'pæʃʌn tɪl maːɪ soːʊl]
Is a stringed lute on which all winds can play.
[ɪz ʌ 'stɹɪŋɛ(ɪ)d ljut ɑn ʍɪʧ ɔl wɪndz kæn pleːɪ]
Is it for this that I have given away
[ɪz ɪt fɔ ðɪs ðæt aːɪ hæv 'gɪvɛ(ɪ)n ʌ'wɛːɪ]
Mine ancient wisdom and austere control?
[maːɪn 'ɛːɪnʧɛnt 'wɪzdʌm ænd ɔ'stiːʌ kʌn'tɹoːʊl]
Methinks my life is a twice-written scroll,
[ˌmi'θɪŋks maːɪ laːɪf ɪz ʌ twaːɪs 'ɹɪtɛ(ɪ)n skɹoːʊl]
Scrawled over on some boyish holiday
[skɹɔld 'oːʊvʌʁ(ᶠ) ɑn sʌm 'bɔːɪʃ 'halɪdeːɪ]
With idle songs for pipe and virelay,
[wɪð 'aːɪdʊl sɑŋz fɔ paːɪp ænd 'vɪːʌʁ(ᶠ)ʌleːɪ]
Which do but mar the secret of the whole.
[ʍɪʧ du bʌt ma ðʌ 'sikɹɛ(ɪ)t ʌv ðʌ hoːʊl]
Surely there was a time I might have trod
['ʃʊːʌlɪ ðɛːʌ waz ʌ taːɪm aːɪ maːɪt hæv tɹad]
The sunlit heights, and from life's dissonance
[ðʌ 'sʌnlɪt haːɪts ænd fɹʌm laːɪfs 'dɪsɔnæ(ɪ)ns]
Struck one clear chord to reach the ears of God.
[stɹʌk wʌn kliːʌ kɔd tu ɹiːʧ ði iːʌz ʌv gad]
Is that time dead? Lo, with a little rod
[ɪz ðæt taːɪm dɛd loːʊ wɪð ʌ 'lɪtʊl ɹad]
I did but touch the honey of romance.
[aːɪ dɪd bʌt tʌʧ ðʌ 'hʌnɪ ʌv ɹo'mæns]
And must I lose a soul's inheritance?
[ænd mʌst aːɪ luz ʌ soːʊlz ɪn'hɛʁ(ᶠ)ɪtæ(ɪ)ns]

2. The Harlot's House
[ðʌ 'haʁlʌts haːʊs]

We caught the tread of dancing feet,
[wi kɔt ðʌ tɹɛd ʌv 'dænsɪŋ fit]

We loitered down the moonlit street
[wi 'lɔːɪtʌd daːʊn ðʌ 'munlɪt stɹit]
And stopped beneath the Harlot's house.
[ænd stɑpt bɪ'niθ ðʌ 'halʌts haːʊs]
Inside, above the din and fray,
['ɪnsaːɪd ʌ'bʌv ðʌ dɪn ænd fɹɛːɪ]
We heard the loud musicians play
[wi hɜd ðʌ laːʊd mju'zɪʃæ(ɪ)nz pleːɪ]
The "Treues Liebes Herz" of Strauss.
[ðʌ 'trɔːøəs 'liːbəs hɛrts ʌv ʃtɹaːoss]
Like strange mechanical grotesques
[laːɪk stɹɛːɪndʒ mɪ'kænɪkʊl gɹ(ᶠ)o'tɛsks]
Making fantastic arabesques,
['meːɪkɪŋ fæn'tæstɪk æɹʌ'bɛsks]
The shadows raced across the blind.
[ðʌ 'ʃædoːʊz ɹɛːɪst ʌ'kɹas ðʌ blaːɪnd]
We watched the ghostly dancers spin
[wi wɑʧt ðʌ 'goːʊstlɪ 'dænsʌz spɪn]
To sound of horn and violin,
[tu saːʊnd ʌv hɔn ænd vaːɪo'lɪn]
Like black leaves wheeling in the wind.
[laːɪk blæk livz 'ʍilɪŋ ɪn ðʌ wɪnd]
Like wire-pulled automatons,
[laːɪk waːɪʌ pʊld ɔ'tamʌtanz]
Slim silhouetted skeletons
[slɪm ˌsɪlu'wɛtɛ(ɪ)d 'skelɛ(ɪ)tʌnz]
Went sliding through the slow quadrille.
[wɛnt 'slaːɪdɪŋ θɾu ðʌ sloːʊ kwa'dɹɪl]
They took each other by the hand,
[ðɛːɪ tʊk iʧ 'ʌðʌ baːɪ ðʌ hænd]
And danced a stately saraband.
[ænd dænst ʌ 'stɛːɪtlɪ 'sæɾʌbænd]
Their laughter echoed thin and shrill.
[ðɛːʌ 'læftʌʁ(ᶠ) 'ɛkoːʊd θɪn ænd ʃɹɪl]
Sometimes a clockwork puppet pressed
['sʌmtaːɪmz ʌ 'klɑkwɜk 'pʌpɛ(ɪ)t pɹɛst]
A phantom lover to her breast,
[ʌ 'fæntʌm 'lʌvʌ tu hɜ bɹɛst]
Sometimes they seemed to try and sing.
['sʌmtaːɪmz ðɛːɪ simd tu tɹaːɪ ænd sɪŋ]
Sometimes a horrible marionette
['sʌmtaːɪmz ʌ 'hɔʁ(ᶠ)ɪbʊl mæɾɪo(ʌ)'nɛt]
Came out and smoked its cigarette
[kɛːɪm aːʊt ænd smoːʊkt ɪts sɪgaˈʁ(ᶠ)ɛt]
Upon the steps like a live thing.
[ʌ'pɑn ðʌ stɛps laːɪk ʌ laːɪv θɪŋ]
Then turning to my love, I said,
[ðɛn 'tɜnɪŋ tu maːɪ lʌv aːɪ sɛd]
"The dead are dancing with the dead.
[ðʌ dɛd a 'dænsɪŋ wɪð ðʌ dɛd]
The dust is whirling with the dust."
[ðʌ dʌst ɪz 'ʍɜlɪŋ wɪð ðʌ dʌst]
But she, she heard the violin
[bʌt ʃi ʃi hɜd ðʌ vaːɪo'lɪn]
And left my side and entered in.
[ænd lɛft maːɪ saːɪd ænd 'ɛntʌd ɪn]

Love passed into the House of Lust.
[lʌv pæst ˈɪntu ðʌ hɑːʊs ʌv lʌst]
Then suddenly the tune went false,
[ðɛn ˈsʌdɛ(ɪ)nlɪ ðʌ tjun wɛnt fɔls]
The dancers wearied of the waltz.
[ðʌ ˈdænsʌz ˈwɪːʌʁ⁽ʳ⁾ɪd ʌv ðʌ wɔlts]
The shadows ceased to wheel and whirl.
[ðʌ ˈʃædoːʊz sist tu ʍil ænd ʍɜl]
And down the long and silent street,
[ænd dɑːʊn ðʌ lɑŋ ænd ˈsɑːɪlɛnt stɹit]
The dawn with silver-sandalled feet,
[ðʌ dɔn wɪð ˈsɪlvʌ ˈsændʊld fit]
Crept like a frightened girl.
[kɹɛpt lɑːɪk ʌ ˈfɹɑːɪtɛ(ɪ)nd ɡɜl]

3. Requiescat
[ɹɛkwiˈɛskɑt]

Tread lightly, she is here, under the snow.
[tɹɛd ˈlɑːɪtlɪ ʃi ɪz nɪːʌ ˈʌndʌ ðʌ snoːʊ]
Speak gently;
[spik ˈdʒɛntlɪ]
She can hear the daisies grow.
[ʃi kæn hɪːʌ ðʌ ˈdɛːɪzɪz ɡɹoːʊ]
All her bright golden hair, Tarnished with rust.
[ɔl hɜ bɹɑːɪt ˈɡoːʊldɛ(ɪ)n hɛːʌ ˈtɑnɪʃt wɪð ɹʌst]
She that was young and fair, fallen to dust.
[ʃi ðæt waz jʌŋ ænd fɛːʌ ˈfɔlɛ(ɪ)n tu dʌst]
Lily-like, white as snow,
[ˈlɪlɪ lɑːɪk ʍɑːɪt æz snoːʊ]
She hardly knew she was a woman,
[ʃi ˈhɑdlɪ nju ʃi waz ʌ ˈwʊmæ(ʌ)n]
So sweetly she grew.
[soːʊ ˈswitlɪ ʃi ɡɹ⁽ʳ⁾u]
Coffin-board, heavy stone, lie on her breast.
[ˈkɑfɪn bɔd ˈhɛvɪ stoːʊn lɑːɪ an hɜ bɹɛst]
I vex my heart alone.
[ɑːɪ vɛks mɑːɪ hat ʌˈloːʊn]
She is at rest.
[ʃi ɪz æt ɹɛst]
Peace, Peace, she cannot hear lyre or sonnet,
[pis pis ʃi kæˈnat hɪːʌ ˈlɑːɪʌʁ⁽ʳ⁾ ɔ ˈsanɛ(ɪ)t]
All my life's buried here. Heap earth upon it.
[ɔl mɑːɪ lɑːɪfs ˈbɛʁ⁽ʳ⁾ɪd hɪːʌ hip ɜθ ʌˈpan ɪt]

Song Selections

"Beneath the Cypress Shade" (A Rustling of Angels)
[bɪˈniθ ðʌ ˈsɑːɪpɹɪs ʃɛːɪd]
Peacock, Thomas Love (Eng. 1785-1866)

I dug, beneath the cypress shade,
[ɑːɪ dʌg bɪˈniθ ðʌ ˈsɑːɪpɹɛ(ɪ)s ʃɛːɪd]
What well might seem an elfin's grave;
[ʍat wɛl mɑːɪt sim æn ˈɛlfɪnz ɡɹ⁽ʳ⁾ɛːɪv]

And every pledge in earth I laid,
[ænd ˈɛvɹɪ plɛdʒ ɪn ɜθ ɑːɪ lɛːɪd]
That erst thy false affection gave.
[ðæt ɜst ðɑːɪ fɔls ʌˈfɛkʃʌn ɡɛːɪv]
I pressed them down the sod beneath;
[ɑːɪ pɹɛst ðɛm dɑːʊn ðʌ sad bɪˈniθ]
I placed one mossy stone above;
[ɑːɪ plɛːɪst wʌn ˈmɔsɪ stoːʊn ʌˈbʌv]
And twined the roses' fading wreath
[ænd twɑːɪnd ðʌ ˈɹoːʊzɛ(ɪ)z ˈfɛːɪdɪŋ ɹiθ]
Around the sepulchre of love.
[ʌˈʁ⁽ʳ⁾ɑːʊnd ðʌ ˈsɛpʊlkʌʁ⁽ʳ⁾ ʌv lʌv]
Frail as thy love, the flowers were dead,
[fɹɛːɪl æz ðɑːɪ lʌv ðʌ flɑːʊʌz wɜ dɛd]
Ere yet the evening sun was set:
[ɛːʌ jɛt ði ˈivnɪŋ sʌn waz sɛt]
But years shall see the cypress spread,
[bʌt jɪːʌz ʃæl si ðʌ ˈsɑːɪpɹɛ(ɪ)s spɹɛd]
Immutable as my regret.
[ɪˈmjutʌbʊl æz mɑːɪ ɹɪˈɡɹɛt]

"How Sweet the Answer" (A Rustling of Angels)
[hɑːʊ swit ði ˈænsʁ]
Moore, Thomas (Ir. 1779-1852)

How sweet the answer Echo makes
[hɑːʊ swit ði ˈænsʌ ˈɛkoːʊ mɛːɪks]
To Music at night,
[tu ˈmjuzɪk æt nɑːɪt]
When, roused by lute or horn, she wakes,
[ʍɛn ɹɑːʊzd bɑːɪ ljut ɔ hɔn ʃi wɛːɪks]
And far away o'er lawns and lakes
[ænd fɑʁ⁽ʳ⁾ ʌˈwɛːɪ ɔːʌ lɔnz ænd lɛːɪks]
Goes answering light!
[ɡoːʊz ˈænsʌʁ⁽ʳ⁾ɪŋ lɑːɪt]
Yet Love hath echoes truer far,
[jɛt lʌv hæθ ˈɛkoːʊz ˈtɹ⁽ʳ⁾uʌ fa]
And far more sweet,
[ænd fɑ mɔːʌ swit]
Than e'er beneath the moonlight's star,
[ðæn ɛːʌ bɪˈniθ ðʌ ˈmunlɑːɪts sta]
Of horn, or lute, or soft guitar,
[ʌv hɔn ɔ ljut ɔ saft ɡɪˈta]
The songs repeat.
[ðʌ sɑŋz ɹɪˈpit]
'Tis when the sigh, in youth sincere,
[tɪz ʍɛn ðʌ sɑːɪ ɪn juθ sɪnˈsɪːʌ]
And only then,–
[ænd ˈoːʊnlɪ ðɛn]
The sigh that's breathed for one to hear,
[ðʌ sɑːɪ ðæts bɹiðd fɔ wʌn tu hɪːʌ]
Is by that one, that only dear,
[ɪz bɑːɪ ðæt wʌn ðæt ˈoːʊnlɪ dɪːʌ]
Breathed back again.
[bɹiðd bæk ʌˈɡɛn]

"What Would I Give" (A Rustling of Angels)
[ʍat wʊd ɑːɪ gɪv]
Rossetti, Christina Georgina (Eng. 1830-1894)

What would I give for a heart of flesh
[ʍat wʊd ɑːɪ gɪv fɔʁ⁽ʳ⁾ ʌ hɑt ʌv flɛʃ]
to warm me through,
[tu wɔm mi θɾu]
Instead of this heart of stone ice-cold
[ɪnˈstɛd ʌv ðɪs hɑt ʌv stoːʊn ɑːɪs koːʊld]
whatever I do;
[ʍatˈɛvʌʁ⁽ʳ⁾ ɑːɪ du]
Hard and cold and small,
[hɑd ænd koːʊld ænd smɔl]
of all hearts the worst of all.
[ʌv ɔl hɑts ðʌ wɜst ʌv ɔl]
What would I give for words,
[ʍat wʊd ɑːɪ gɪv fɔ wɜdz]
if only words would come;
[ɪf ˈoːʊnlɪ wɜdz wʊd kʌm]
But now in its misery
[bʌt nɑːʊ ɪn ɪts ˈmɪzʌʁ⁽ʳ⁾ɪ]
my spirit has fallen dumb:
[mɑːɪ ˈspɪʁ⁽ʳ⁾ɪt hæz ˈfɔlɛ(ɪ)n dʌm]
O merry friends, go your way,
[oːʊ ˈmɛʁ⁽ʳ⁾ɪ fɹɛndz goːʊ jɔːʌ wɛːɪ]
I have never a word to say.
[ɑːɪ hæv ˈnɛvʌʁ⁽ʳ⁾ ʌ wɜd tu sɛːɪ]
What would I give for tears,
[ʍat wʊd ɑːɪ gɪv fɔ tɪːʌz]
Not smiles but scalding tears,
[nat smɑːɪlz bʌt ˈskɔldɪŋ tɪːʌz]
To wash the black mark clean,
[tu waʃ ðʌ blæk mak klin]
and to thaw the frost of years,
[ænd tu θɔ ðʌ fɹɑst ʌv jɪːʌz]
To wash the stain ingrain,
[tu waʃ ðʌ stɛːɪn ɪnˈgɹɛːɪn]
and to make me clean again.
[ænd tu mɛːɪk mi klin ʌˈgɛn (ʌˈgɛːɪn)]

Price, Florence (Am. 1887-1953)

Song Selections

"An April Day"
[æn ˈɛːɪpɹʊl dɛːɪ]
Cotter Jr., Joseph Seamon (Am. 1895-1919)

On such a day as this I think,
[an sʌʧ ʌ dɛːɪ æz ðɪs ɑːɪ θɪŋk]
On such a day as this,
[an sʌʧ ʌ dɛːɪ æz ðɪs]
When earth and sky and nature's world
[ʍɛn ɜθ ænd skɑːɪ ænd ˈnɛːɪʧʊ(ʌ)z wɜld]

Are clad in April's bliss;
[ɑ klæd ɪn ˈɛːɪpɹɪ(ʊ)lz blɪs]
And balmy zephyrs gently waft
[ænd ˈbɑmɪ ˈzɛfʌz ˈʤɛntlɪ wæft]
Upon your cheek a kiss,
[ʌˈpɑn jɔːʌ ʧik ʌ kɪs]
Sufficient is it just to live,
[sʌˈfɪʃɛnt ɪz ɪt ʤʌst tu lɪv]
On such a day as this.
[an sʌʧ ʌ dɛːɪ æz ðɪs]

"Because"
[bɪˈkɔz]
Dunbar, Paul Laurence (Am. 1872-1906)

Because I had loved so deeply,
[bɪˈkɔz ɑːɪ hæd lʌvd soːʊ ˈdiplɪ]
Because I had loved so long,
[bɪˈkɔz ɑːɪ hæd lʌvd soːʊ laŋ]
God in His great compassion
[gad ɪn hɪz gɹɛːɪt kʌmˈpæʃʌn]
Gave me the gift of song.
[gɛːɪv mi ðʌ gɪft ʌv saŋ]
Because I have loved so vainly,
[bɪˈkɔz ɑːɪ hæv lʌvd soːʊ ˈvɛːɪnlɪ]
And sung with such faltering breath,
[ænd sʌŋ wɪð sʌʧ ˈfɔltʌʁ⁽ʳ⁾ɪŋ bɹɛθ]
The Master in infinite mercy
[ðʌ ˈmæstʌʁ⁽ʳ⁾ ɪn ˈɪnfɪnɪt ˈmɜsɪ]
Offers the boon of Death.
[ˈafʌz ðʌ bun ʌv dɛθ]

"My Soul's Been Anchored in the Lord"
[mɑːɪ soːʊlz bɪn ˈæŋkʁd ɪn ðʌ lɔʁd]
Spiritual

In de Lord, in de Lord,
[ɪn dʌ lɔd ɪn dʌ lɔd]
My soul's been anchored in de Lord.
[ma soːʊlz bɪn ˈæŋkɔ(ʌ)d ɪn dʌ lɔd]
Befo' I'd stay in hell one day,
[bɪˈfɔ ɑːɪd stɛːɪ ɪn hɛl wʌn dɛːɪ]
My soul's been anchored in de Lord;
[ma soːʊlz bɪn ˈæŋkɔ(ʌ)d ɪn dʌ lɔd]
I'd sing an' pray myself away,
[ɑːɪd sɪŋ æn pɹɛːɪ maˈsɛlf ʌˈwɛːɪ]
My soul's been anchored in de Lord.
[ma soːʊlz bɪn ˈæŋkɔ(ʌ)d ɪn dʌ lɔd]
I'm goin' to pray an' never stop,
[ɑːɪm ˈgoːʊɪn tu pɹɛːɪ æn ˈnɛvʌ stap]
My soul's been anchored in de Lord;
[ma soːʊlz bɪn ˈæŋkɔ(ʌ)d ɪn dʌ lɔd]
Until I've reached the mountain top,
[ʌnˈtɪl ɑːɪv ɹiʧt ðʌ ˈmaːʊntæ(ɪ)n tap]
My soul's been anchored in de Lord.
[ma soːʊlz bɪn ˈæŋkɔ(ʌ)d ɪn dʌ lɔd]

"Sympathy"
[ˈsɪmpʌθi]
Dunbar, Paul Laurence (Am. 1872-1906)

I know what the caged bird feels, alas!
[ɑːɪ noːʊ ʍɑt ðʌ kɛːɪʤd bɜd filz ʌˈlæs]
When the sun is bright on the upland slopes;
[ʍɛn ðʌ sʌn ɪz bɹɑːɪt ɑn ði ˈʌplæ(ʌ)nd sloːʊps]
When the wind stirs soft through the springing grass,
[ʍɛn ðʌ wɪnd stɜz sɑft θɾu ðʌ ˈspɹɪŋɪŋ ɡɹæs]
And the river flows like a stream of glass;
[ænd ðʌ ˈɹɪvʌ floːʊz lɑːɪk ʌ stɹim ʌv ɡlæs]
When the first bird sings and the first bud opes,
[ʍɛn ðʌ fɜst bɜd sɪŋz ænd ðʌ fɜst bʌd oːʊps]
And the faint perfume from its chalice steals–
[ænd ðʌ fɛːɪnt pɜˈfjum fɹʌm ɪts ˈtʃælɪs stilz]
I know what the caged bird feels.
[ɑːɪ noːʊ ʍɑt ðʌ kɛːɪʤd bɜd filz]
I know why the caged bird beats his wing
[ɑːɪ noːʊ ʍɑːɪ ðʌ kɛːɪʤd bɜd bits hɪz wɪŋ]
Till the blood is red on the cruel bars;
[tɪl ðʌ blʌd ɪz ɹed ɑn ðʌ ˈkɹ(ʳ)uːɛ(ʊ)l bɑz]
For he must fly back to his perch and cling
[fɔ hi mʌst flɑːɪ bæk tu hɪz pɜtʃ ænd klɪŋ]
When he fain would be on the bough a-swing;
[ʍɛn hi fɛːɪn wʊd bi ɑn ðʌ bɑːʊ ʌ swɪŋ]
And the pain still throbs in the old, old scars
[ænd ðʌ pɛːɪn stɪl θɾɑbz ɪn ði oːʊld oːʊld skɑz]
And they pulse again with a keener sting.
[ænd ðɛːɪ pʌls ʌˈɡen wɪð ʌ ˈkinʌ stɪŋ]
I know why he beats his wing,
[ɑːɪ noːʊ ʍɑːɪ hi bits hɪz wɪŋ]
I know why the caged bird sings, ah me,
[ɑːɪ noːʊ ʍɑːɪ ðʌ kɛːɪʤd bɜd sɪŋz ɑ mi]
When his wing is bruised and his bosom sore,
[ʍɛn hɪz wɪŋ ɪz bɹ(ʳ)ʊzd ænd hɪz ˈbʊzʌm sɔːʌ]
When he beats his bars and he would be free.
[ʍɛn hi bits hɪz bɑz ænd hi wʊd bi fɹi]
It is not a carol of joy or glee,
[ɪt ɪz nɑt ʌ ˈkæɾ(ʳ)ʊl ʌv ʤɔːɪ ɔ gli]
But a prayer that he sends from his heart's deep core,
[bʌt ʌ pɹɛːʌ ðæt hi sɛndz fɹʌm hɪz hɑts dip kɔːʌ]
But a plea that upward to Heaven he flings.
[bʌt ʌ pli ðæt ˈʌpwʊd tu ˈhɛvɛ(ɪ)n hi flɪŋz]
I know why the caged bird sings!
[ɑːɪ noːʊ ʍɑːɪ ðʌ kɛːɪʤd bɜd sɪŋz]

"The Glory of the Day Was in Her Face"
[ðʌ ˈɡlɔɾi ʌv ðʌ dɛːɪ wɑz ɪn hɜ fɛːɪs]
Johnson, James Weldon (Am. 1871-1938)

The glory of the day was in her face.
[ðʌ ˈɡlɔɾ(ʳ)i ʌv ðʌ dɛːɪ wɑz ɪn hɜ fɛːɪs]
The beauty of the night was in her eyes
[ðʌ ˈbjuti ʌv ðʌ nɑːɪt wɑz ɪn hɜ ɑːɪz]

And over all her loveliness the grace
[ænd ˈoːʊvʌɾ(ʳ) ɔl hɜ ˈlʌvlɪnɛ(ɪ)s ðʌ ɡɹɛːɪs]
Of morning blushing in the early skies.
[ʌv ˈmɔnɪŋ ˈblʌʃɪŋ ɪn ði ˈɜlɪ skɑːɪz]
And in her voice the calling of the dove
[ænd ɪn hɜ vɔːɪs ðʌ ˈkɔlɪŋ ʌv ðʌ dʌv]
Like music of a sweet, melodious part.
[lɑːɪk ˈmjuzɪk ʌv ʌ swit mɛˈloːʊdjʌs pɑt]
And in her smile the breaking light of love;
[ænd ɪn hɜ smɑːɪl ðʌ ˈbɹɛːɪkɪŋ lɑːɪt ʌv lʌv]
And all the gentle virtues in her heart.
[ænd ɔl ðʌ ˈʤɛntʊl ˈvɜtʃuz ɪn hɜ hɑt]
And now the glorious day, the beauteous night,
[ænd nɑːʊ ðʌ ˈɡlɔɾ(ʳ)ɪʌs dɛːɪ ðʌ ˈbjutɪʌs nɑːɪt]
The birds that signal to their mates at dawn,
[ðʌ bɜdz ðæt ˈsɪɡnʊl tu ðɛːʌ mɛːɪts æt dɑn]
To my dull ears, to my tear-blinded sight
[tu mɑːɪ dʌl ɪːʌz tu mɑːɪ tɪːʌ ˈblɑːɪndɛ(ɪ)d sɑːɪt]
Are one with all the dead since she is gone.
[ɑ wʌn wɪð ɔl ðʌ dɛd sɪns ʃi ɪz ɡɑn]

"The Poet and His Song"
[ðʌ ˈpoːʊɪt ænd hɪz sɑŋ]
Dunbar, Paul Laurence (Am. 1872-1906)

A song is just a little thing,
[ʌ sɑŋ ɪz ʤʌst ʌ ˈlɪtʊl θɪŋ]
And yet what joy it is to sing!
[ænd jɛt ʍɑt ʤɔːɪ ɪt ɪz tu sɪŋ]
In hours of toil it gives me zest,
[ɪn ɑːʊʌz ʌv tɔːɪl ɪt ɡɪvz mi zɛst]
And when at last I long for rest;
[ænd ʍɛn æt læst ɑːɪ lɑŋ fɔ ɹɛst]
When cows come home along the bars,
[ʍɛn kɑːʊz kʌm hoːʊm ʌˈlɑŋ ðʌ bɑz]
And in the fold I hear the bell!
[ænd ɪn ðʌ foːʊld ɑːɪ hɪːʌ ðʌ bɛl]
At Night, the shepherd herds his stars,
[æt nɑːɪt ðʌ ˈʃɛpʌd hɜdz hɪz stɑz]
I sing my song and all is well.
[ɑːɪ sɪŋ mɑːɪ sɑŋ ænd ɔl ɪz wɛl]
My days are never filled with ease.
[mɑːɪ dɛːɪz ɑ ˈnɛvʌ fɪld wɪð iz]
I till my ground and prune my trees.
[ɑːɪ tɪl mɑːɪ ɡɹɑːʊnd ænd pɹ(ʳ)un mɑːɪ tɹiz]
When ripened gold is all the grain,
[ʍɛn ˈɹɑːɪpɛ(ɪ)nd ɡoːʊld ɪz ɔl ðʌ ɡɹɛːɪn]
I labor hard and toil and sweat,
[ɑːɪ ˈlɛːɪbɔ(ʌ) hɑd ænd tɔːɪl ænd swɛt]
While others dream within the dell;
[ʍɑːɪl ˈʌðʌz dɹim wɪðˈɪn ðʌ dɛl]
But even while my brow is wet,
[bʌt ˈivɛ(ɪ)n ʍɑːɪl mɑːɪ bɹɑːʊ ɪz wɛt]
I sing my song, and all is well.
[ɑːɪ sɪŋ mɑːɪ sɑŋ ænd ɔl ɪz wɛl]

Sometimes the sun, unkindly hot,
[ˈsʌmtɑːɪmz ðʌ sʌn ʌnˈkɑːɪndlɪ hɑt]
My garden makes a desert spot;
[mɑːɪ ˈɡɑdɛ(ɪ)n meːɪks ʌ ˈdɛzʌt spɑt]
Sometimes a blight upon the tree
[ˈsʌmtɑːɪmz ʌ blɑːɪt ʌˈpɑn ðʌ tɹɪ]
Takes all my fruit away from me;
[teːɪks ɔl mɑːɪ fɹ⁽ʳ⁾ut ʌˈweːɪ fɹʌm mi]
And then with throes of bitter pain
[ænd ðɛn wɪð θroːʊz ʌv ˈbɪtʌ peːɪn]
Rebellious passions rise and swell;
[ɹɪˈbɛljʌs ˈpæʃʌnz ɹɑːɪz ænd swɛl]
But—life is more than fruit or grain,
[bʌt lɑːɪf ɪz mɔːʌ ðæn fɹ⁽ʳ⁾ut ɔ ɡɹeːɪn]
And so I sing and all is well.
[ænd soːʊ ɑːɪ sɪŋ ænd ɔl ɪz wɛl]

Purcell, Henry (Eng. 1658-1695)

Song Selections

"Dido's Lament" (Dido and Aeneas)
[ˈdɑːɪdoːʊz lʌˈmɛnt]
Tate, Nahum (Eng. 1652-1715)

Thy hand, Belinda; darkness shades me,
[ðɑːɪ hænd bɪˈlɪndʌ ˈdɑknɛ(ɪ)s ʃɛːɪdz mi]
On thy bosom let me rest;
[ɑn ðɑːɪ ˈbʊzʌm lɛt mi ɹɛst]
More I would, but Death invades me;
[mɔːʌɾ ɑːɪ wʊd bʌt dɛθ ɪnˈveːɪdz mi]
Death is now a welcome guest.
[dɛθ ɪz nɑːʊ ʌ ˈwɛlkʌm ɡɛst]
When I am laid in earth,
[ʍɛn ɑːɪ æm lɛːɪd ɪn 3θ]
may my wrongs create
[meːɪ mɑːɪ ɾɑŋz kɹɪˈɛːɪt]
No trouble in thy breast.
[noːʊ ˈtɹʌbʊl ɪn ðɑːɪ bɹɛst]
Remember me! But ah! forget my fate.
[ɹɪˈmɛmbʌ mi bʌt ɑ fʌˈɡɛt mɑːɪ fɛːɪt]

"Fairest Isle"
[ˈfɛːɹɪst ɑːɪl]
Dryden, John (Eng. 1631-1700)

Fairest Isle, all isles excelling,
[ˈfɛːʌɾɛ(ɪ)st ɑːɪl ɔl ɑːɪlz ɪkˈsɛlɪŋ]
Seat of pleasures and of loves
[sit ʌv ˈplɛʒʊ(ʌ)z ænd ʌv lʌvz]
Venus here will choose her dwelling,
[ˈvinʊs hɪːʌ wɪl tʃuz hɜ ˈdwɛlɪŋ]
And forsake her Cyprian groves.
[ænd fʌˈseːɪk hɜ ˈsɪpɹɪæ(ɪ)n ɡɹoːʊvz]

Cupid, from his fav'rite nation,
[ˈkjupɪd fɹʌm hɪz ˈfɛːɪvɹɪt ˈneːɪʃʌn]
Care and envy will remove;
[kɛːʌɾ ænd ˈɛnvɪ wɪl ɹɪˈmuv]
Jealousy, that poisons passion,
[ˈdʒɛlʌsɪ ðæt ˈpɔːɪzʌnz ˈpæʃʌn]
And despair that dies for love.
[ænd dɪˈspeːʌ ðæt dɑːɪz fɔ lʌv]
Gentle murmurs, sweet complaining,
[ˈdʒɛntʊl ˈmɜmʊ(ʌ)z swit kʌmˈpleːɪnɪŋ]
Sighs that blow the fire of love,
[sɑːɪz ðæt bloːʊ ðʊ fɑːɪʌɾ ʌv lʌv]
Soft repulses, kind disdaining,
[sɑft ɹɪˈpʌlsɛ(ɪ)z kɑːɪnd dɪsˈdeːɪnɪŋ]
Shall be all the pains you prove.
[ʃæl bi ɔl ðʊ peːɪnz ju pɹuv]
Ev'ry swain shall pay his duty,
[ˈɛvɹɪ sweːɪn ʃæl peːɪ hɪz ˈdjutɪ]
Grateful ev'ry nymph shall prove;
[ˈɡɹeːɪtfʊl ˈɛvɹɪ nɪmf ʃæl pɹuv]
And as these excel in beauty,
[ænd æz ðiz ɪkˈsɛl ɪn ˈbjutɪ]
Those shall be renown'd for love.
[ðoːʊz ʃæl bi ɹɪˈnɑːʊnd fɔ lʌv]

"Hark! The Echoing Air" (The Fairy Queen)
[hɑk ði ˈɛkoːʊɪŋ ɛːʌ]
Anonymous adaptation of "A Midsummer Night's Dream" by William Shakespeare

Hark! hark! the echoing air a triumph sings.
[hɑk hɑk ði ˈɛkoːʊɪŋ ɛːʌɾ ʌ ˈtɹɑːɪʌmf sɪŋz]
And all around, pleas'd Cupids clap their wings.
[ænd ɔl ʌˈɾɑːʊnd plizd ˈkjupɪdz klæp ðɛːʌ wɪŋz]

"I Attempt from Love's Sickness"
[ɑːɪ ʌˈtɛmpt fɹʌm lʌvz ˈsɪknɪs]
(The Indian Queen)
Dryden, John (Eng. 1631-1700)

I attempt from love's sickness to fly in vain,
[ɑːɪ ʌˈtɛmpt fɹʌm lʌvz ˈsɪknɛ(ɪ)s tu flɑːɪ ɪn veːɪn]
Since I am, myself, my own fever and pain.
[sɪns ɑːɪ æm mɑːɪˈsɛlf mɑːɪ oːʊn ˈfivʌ⁽ʳ⁾ ænd peːɪn]
No more now, fond heart, with pride no more swell,
[noːʊ mɔːʌ nɑːʊ fɑnd hɑt wɪð pɹɑːɪd noːʊ mɔːʌ swɛl]
Thou canst not raise forces enough to rebel.
[ðɑːʊ kænst nɑt ɹɛːɪz ˈfɔsɛ(ɪ)z ɪˈnʌf tu ɹɪˈbɛl]
I attempt from love's sickness...
[ɑːɪ ʌˈtɛmpt fɹʌm lʌvz ˈsɪknɛ(ɪ)s]
For love has more pow'r and less mercy than fate,
[fɔ lʌv hæz mɔːʌ pɑːʊʌɾ ænd lɛs ˈmɜsɪ ðæn fɛːɪt]
To make us seek ruin, and love those that hate.
[tu meːɪk ʌs sik ˈɾɾuin ænd lʌv ðoːʊz ðæt hɛːɪt]
I attempt from love's sickness...
[ɑːɪ ʌˈtɛmpt fɹʌm lʌvz ˈsɪknɛ(ɪ)s]

"I Love and I Must"
[ɑːɪ lʌv ænd ɑːɪ mʌst]
Anonymous

I love and I must, and yet I would fain
[ɑːɪ lʌv ænd ɑːɪ mʌst ænd jɛt ɑːɪ wʊd fɛːɪn]
With a large dose of reason cure my pain.
[wɪð ʌ lɑdʒ doːʊs ʌv ˈɹizʌn kjʊːʌ mɑːɪ pɛːɪn]
But I am past hope, and yet it seems strange
[bʌt ɑːɪ æm past hoːʊp ænd jɛt ɪt simz stɹɛːɪndʒ]
A thing that's call'd Man not subject to change.
[ʌ θɪŋ ðæts kɔld mæn nɑt ˈsʌbdʒɛkt tu ʧɛːɪndʒ]
Had I power to scorn, as she to despise,
[hæd ɑːɪ pɑːʊʌ tu skɔn æz ʃi tu dɪˈspɑːɪz]
I might at once be inconstant and wise.
[ɑːɪ mɑːɪt æt wʌns bi ɪnˈkɑnstæ(ɪ)nt ænd wɑːɪz]
Then tell me, oh tell me, how it should be
[ðɛn tɛl mi oːʊ tɛl mi hɑːʊ ɪt ʃʊd bi]
So easy to men, yet so hard to me.
[soːʊ ˈizɪ tu mɛn jɛt soːʊ had tu mi]

"I'll Sail upon the Dog Star"
[ɑːɪl sɛːɪl ʌˈpɑn ðʊ dag sta]
D'Urfey, Thomas (Eng. 1653-1723)

I'll sail upon the Dog Star,
[ɑːɪl sɛːɪl ʌˈpɑn ðʊ dag sta]
And then pursue the morning,
[ænd ðɛn pɜˈsju ðʊ ˈmɔnɪŋ]
I'll chase the moon 'till it be noon,
[ɑːɪl ʧɛːɪs ðʊ mun tɪl ɪt bi nun]
But I'll make her leave her horning.
[bʌt ɑːɪl mɛːɪk hɜ liv hɜ ˈhɔnɪŋ]
I'll climb the frosty mountain,
[ɑːɪl klɑːɪm ðʊ ˈfɹɑstɪ ˈmɑːʊntæ(ɪ)n]
And there I'll coin the weather;
[ænd ðɛːʌr ɑːɪl kɔːɪn ðʊ ˈwɛðʌ]
I'll tear the rainbow from the sky,
[ɑːɪl tɛːʌ ðʊ ˈɹɛːɪnboːʊ fɹʌm ðʊ skɑːɪ]
And tie both ends together.
[ænd tɑːɪ boːʊθ ɛndz tuˈgɛðʌ]
The stars pluck from their orbs, too,
[ðʊ staz plʌk fɹʌm ðɛːʌ⁽ʳ⁾ ɔbz tu]
And crowd them in my budget!
[ænd kɹɑːʊd ðɛm ɪn mɑːɪ ˈbʌdʒɛ(ɪ)t]
And whether I'm a roaring boy,
[ænd ˈʍɛðʌ⁽ʳ⁾ ɑːɪm ʌ ˈɹɔːʌɹɪŋ bɔːɪ]
Let all the nations judge it.
[lɛt ɔl ðʊ ˈnɛːɪʃʌnz dʒʌdʒ ɪt]

"If Music Be the Food of Love"
[ɪf ˈmjuzɪk bi ðʊ fud ʌv lʌv]
Heveningham, Colonel Henry (Eng. 1651-1700)

If music be the food of love,
[ɪf ˈmjuzɪk bi ðʊ fud ʌv lʌv]

Sing on till I am fill'd with joy;
[sɪŋ ɑn tɪl ɑːɪ æm fɪld wɪð dʒɔːɪ]
For then my list'ning soul you move
[fɔ ðɛn mɑːɪ ˈlɪsnɪŋ soːʊl ju muv]
To pleasures that can never cloy.
[tu ˈplɛʒʊ(ʌ)z ðæt kæn ˈnɛvʌ klɔːɪ]
Your eyes, your mien, your tongue declare
[jɔːʌ ɑːɪz jɔːʌ min jɔːʌ tʌŋ dɪˈklɛːʌ]
That you are music ev'rywhere.
[ðæt ju ʌ ˈmjuzɪk ˈɛvɹɪmɛːʌ]
Pleasures invade both eye and ear,
[ˈplɛʒʊ(ʌ)z ɪnˈvɛːɪd boːʊθ ɑːɪ ænd ɪːʌ]
So fierce the transports are, they wound,
[soːʊ fɪːʌs ðʊ ˈtɹænspɔts ɑ ðɛːɪ wund]
And all my senses feasted are,
[ænd ɔl mɑːɪ ˈsɛnsɛ(ɪ)z ˈfistɛ(ɪ)d ɑ]
Tho' yet the treat is only sound,
[ðoːʊ jɛt ðʊ tɹit ɪz ˈoːʊnlɪ sɑːʊnd]
Sure I must perish by your charms,
[ʃʊːʌ ɑːɪ mʌst ˈpɛɹɪʃ bɑːɪ jɔːʌ ʧamz]
Unless you save me in your arms.
[ʌnˈlɛs ju sɛːɪv mi ɪn jɔːʌ amz]

"Music for a While"
[ˈmjuzɪk fɔʁ ʌ ʍɑːɪl]
Dryden, John (Eng. 1631-1700)

Music for a while
[ˈmjuzɪk fɔʁ⁽ʳ⁾ ʌ ʍɑːɪl]
Shall all your cares beguile:
[ʃæl ɔl jɔːʌ kɛːʌz bɪˈgɑːɪl]
Wond'ring how your pains were eas'd
[ˈwʌndɹɪŋ hɑːʊ jɔːʌ pɛːɪnz wɜ izd]
And disdaining to be pleas'd
[ænd dɪsˈdɛːɪnɪŋ tu bi plizd]
Till Alecto free the dead
[tɪl ʌˈlɛktoːʊ fɹi ðʊ dɛd]
From their eternal bands,
[fɹʌm ðɛːʌr ɪˈtɜnʊl bændz]
Till the snakes drop from her head,
[tɪl ðʊ snɛːɪks dɹɑp fɹʌm hɜ hɛd]
And the whip from out her hands.
[ænd ðʊ ʍɪp fɹʌm ɑːʊt hɜ hændz]

"Next, Winter Comes Slowly" (The Fairy Queen)
[nɛkst ˈwɪntʌ kʌmz ˈsloːʊli]
Anonymous

Next, Winter comes slowly,
[nɛkst ˈwɪntʌ kʌmz ˈsloːʊli]
Pale, meagre and old,
[pɛːɪl ˈmigʌr ænd oːʊld]
First trembling with age
[fɜst ˈtɹɛmblɪŋ wɪð ɛːɪdʒ]
and then quiv'ring with cold,
[ænd ðɛn ˈkwɪvɹɪŋ wɪð koːʊld]

Benumb'd with hard frosts
[bɪˈnʌmd wɪð had fɹɑsts]
and with snow cover'd o'er,
[ænd wɪð snoːʊ ˈkʌvʌd ɔːʌ]
Prays the sun to restore him,
[pɹɛːɪz ðʊ sʌn tu ɹɪˈstɔːʌ hɪm]
and sings as before.
[ænd sɪŋz æz bɪˈfɔːʌ]

"Nymphs and Shepherds"
[nɪmfs ænd ˈʃɛpʌdz]
Shadwell, Thomas (Eng. 1642?-1692)

Nymphs and shepherds, come away!
[nɪmfs ænd ˈʃɛpʌdz kʌm ʌˈwɛːɪ]
In ye grove let's sport and play,
[ɪn ji ɡɹoːʊv lɛts spɔt ænd plɛːɪ]
For this is Flora's holiday,
[fɔ ðɪs ɪz ˈflɔɾʌz ˈhalɪdɛːɪ]
Sacred to ease and happy love,
[ˈsɛːɪkɹɛ(ɪ)d tu iz ænd ˈhæpɪ lʌv]
To dancing, to music and to poetry;
[tu ˈdansɪŋ tu ˈmjuzɪk ænd tu ˈpoːʊɛ(ɪ)tɹɪ]
Your flocks may now securely rove;
[jɔːʌ flaks mɛːɪ naːʊ sɪˈkjʊːʌlɪ roːʊv]
Whilst you express your jollity!
[ʍaːɪlst ju ɪkˈspɹɛs jɔːʌ ˈdʒalɪtɪ]
Nymphs and shepherds, come away!
[nɪmfs ænd ˈʃɛpʌdz kʌm ʌˈwɛːɪ]

"Sound the Trumpet"
[saːʊnd ðʊ ˈtɹʌmpɪt]
Tate, Nahum (Eng. 1652-1715)

Sound the Trumpet and beat the warlike Drum;
[saːʊnd ðʊ ˈtɹʌmpɛ(ɪ)t ænd bit ðʊ ˈwɔlaːɪk dɹʌm]
The Prince will be with laurels crown'd
[ðʊ pɹɪns wɪl bi wɪð ˈlɔɾʊlz kɹaːʊnd]
Before his manhood comes.
[bɪˈfɔːʌ hɪz ˈmænhʊd kʌmz]
Ah! how pleas'd he is and gay,
[ɑ haːʊ plizd hi ɪz ænd ɡɛːɪ]
When the Trumpet strikes his ear.
[ʍɛn ðʊ ˈtɹʌmpɛ(ɪ)t stɹaːɪks hɪz ɪːʌ]
His hands like shaking lilies play
[hɪz hændz laːɪk ˈʃɛːɪkɪŋ ˈlɪlɪz plɛːɪ]
And catch at ev'ry spear.
[ænd kæʧ æt ˈɛvɹɪ spɪːʌ]

"Strike the Viol"
[stɹɑːɪk ðʊ ˈvaːɪʊl]
Tate, Nahum (Eng. 1652-1715)

Strike the Viol, touch the Lute;
[stɹɑːɪk ðʊ ˈvaːɪʊl tʌʧ ðʊ ljut]

Wake the Harp, inspire the Flute,
[wɛːɪk ðʊ hap ɪnˈspaːɪʌ ðʊ flut]
Sing your Patronesse's Praise,
[sɪŋ jɔːʌ ˈpɛːɪtɹʌnɛ(ɪ)sɛ(ɪ)z pɹɛːɪz]
Sing, in cheerful and harmonious Lays.
[sɪŋ ɪn ˈʧiːʌfʊl ænd haˈmoːʊnɪʌs lɛːɪz]

"Sweeter than Roses" (The Indian Queen)
[ˈswitʌ ðæn ˈɹoːʊzɪz]
Anonymous

Sweeter than roses, or cool evening breeze,
[ˈswitʌ ðæn ˈɹoːʊzɛ(ɪ)z ɔ kul ˈivnɪŋ bɹiz]
On a warm flowery shore, was the dear kiss,
[an ʌ wɔm ˈflaːʊʌɾɪ ʃɔːʌ waz ðʊ diːʌ kɪs]
First trembling made me freeze,
[fɜst ˈtɹɛmblɪŋ mɛːɪd mi fɹiz]
Then shot like fire all o'er.
[ðɛn ʃat laːɪk faːɪʌɾ ɔl ɔːʌ]
What magic has victorious love!
[ʍat ˈmædʒɪk hæz vɪkˈtɔɾɪʌs lʌv]
For all I touch or see, Since that dear kiss,
[fɔʁ(ⁱ) ɔl aːɪ tʌʧ ɔ si sɪns ðæt diːʌ kɪs]
I hourly prove, All is love to me.
[aːɪ ˈaːʊʌlɪ pɹuv ɔl ɪz lʌv tu mi]

"Turn Then Thine Eyes" (The Fairy Queen)
[tɜn ðɛn ðaːɪn aːɪz]
Anonymous adaptation of "A Midsummer Night's
Dream" by William Shakespeare

Turn, turn, then thine eyes upon those glories there,
[tɜn tɜn ðɛn ðaːɪn aːɪz ʌˈpan ðoːʊz ˈɡlɔɾɪz ðɛːʌ]
And catching, catching flames will on thy torch appear.
[ænd ˈkæʧɪŋ ˈkæʧɪŋ flɛːɪmz wɪl an ðaːɪ tɔʧ ʌˈpɪːʌ]

"What Can We Poor Females Do?"
[ʍat kæn wi pʊːʌ ˈfimɛːɪlz du]
Anonymous

What can we poor females do,
[ʍat kæn wi pʊːʌ ˈfimɛːɪlz du]
When pressing, teasing lovers sue?
[ʍɛn ˈpɹɛsɪŋ ˈtizɪŋ ˈlʌvʌz sju]
What can we poor females do?
[ʍat kæn wi pʊːʌ ˈfimɛːɪlz du]
Fate affords no other way,
[fɛːɪt ʌˈfɔdz noːʊ ˈʌðʌ wɛːɪ]
But denying or complying,
[bʌt dɪˈnaːɪɪŋ ɔ kʌmˈplaːɪɪŋ]
And resenting, or consenting,
[ænd ɹɪˈzɛntɪŋ ɔ kʌnˈsɛntɪŋ]
Does alike our hopes betray.
[dʌz ʌˈlaːɪk aːʊʌ hoːʊps bɪˈtɹɛːɪ]

Q

Quilter, Roger (Eng. 1877-1953)

To Julia (Song Cycle)
[tu ˈdʒuliʌ]
Herrick, Robert (Eng. 1591-1674)

1. The Bracelet
[ðʊ ˈbɹɛːɪslɪt]

Why I tie about thy wrist,
[ʍaːɪ aːɪ taːɪ ʌˈbaːʊt ðaːɪ ɹɪst]
Julia, this my silken twist;
[ˈdʒuliʌ ðɪs maːɪ ˈsɪlkɛ(ɪ)n twɪst]
For what other reason is't,
[fɔ ʍat ˈʌðʌ ˈɹizʌn ɪzt]
But to show thee how in part
[bʌt tu ʃoːʊ ði haːʊ ɪn pat]
Thou my pretty captive art?
[ðaːʊ maːɪ ˈpɹɪtɪ ˈkæptɪv at]
But thy bondslave is my heart.
[bʌt ðaːɪ ˈbandslɛːɪv ɪz maːɪ hat]
'Tis but silk that bindeth thee,
[tɪz bʌt sɪlk ðæt ˈbaːɪndɛ(ɪ)θ ði]
Knap the thread and thou art free
[næp ðʊ θɹɛd ænd ðaːʊ at fɹi]
But 'tis otherwise with me:
[bʌt tɪz ˈʌðʌwaːɪz wɪð mi]
I am bound, and fast bound so
[aːɪ æm baːʊnd ænd fast baːʊnd soːʊ]
That from thee I cannot go;
[ðæt fɹʌm ði aːɪ kæˈnat goːʊ]
If I could I would not so.
[ɪf aːɪ kʊd aːɪ wʊd nat soːʊ]

2. The Maiden Blush
[ðʊ ˈmɛːɪdɪn blʌʃ]

So look the mornings when the sun
[soːʊ lʊk ðʊ ˈmɔnɪŋz ʍɛn ðʊ sʌn]
Paints them with fresh vermilion:
[pɛːɪnts ðɛm wɪð fɹɛʃ vɜˈmɪljʌn]
So cherries blush, and Kathern pears,
[soːʊ ˈtʃɛɹɪz blʌʃ ænd ˈkæθʌn pɛːʌz]
And apricocks in youthful years;
[ænd ˈɛːɪpɹɪkaks ɪn ˈjuθfʊl jɪːʌz]
So corals look more lovely red,
[soːʊ ˈkɔɹʊlz lʊk mɔːʌ ˈlʌvlɪ ɹɛd]
And rubies lately polished:
[ænd ˈɹɹubɪz ˈlɛːɪtlɪ ˈpalɪʃɛ(ɪ)d]
So purest diaper doth shine,
[soːʊ ˈpjʊːʌɹɛ(ɪ)st ˈdaːɪʌpʌ dʌθ ʃaːɪn]

Stain'd by the beams of claret wine:
[stɛːɪnd baːɪ ðʊ bimz ʌv ˈklæɹɛ(ɪ)t waːɪn]
As Julia looks when she doth dress
[æz ˈdʒuliʌ lʊks ʍɛn ʃi dʌθ dɹɛs]
Her either cheek with bashfulness.
[hɜ ˈaːɪðʌ tʃik wɪð ˈbæʃfʊlnɛ(ɪ)s]

3. To Daisies
[tu ˈdɛːɪziz]

Shut not so soon, the dull-eyed night
[ʃʌt nat soːʊ sun ðʊ dʌl aːɪd naːɪt]
Has not as yet begun
[hæz nat æz jɛt bɪˈgʌn]
To make a seizure on the light,
[tu mɛːɪk ʌ ˈsiʒʊ(ʌ)ɹ an ðʊ laːɪt]
Or to seal up the sun.
[ɔ tu sil ʌp ðʊ sʌn]
No marigolds yet closed are,
[noːʊ ˈmæɹɪgoːʊldz jɛt ˈkloːʊzɛ(ɪ)d a]
No shadows great appear,
[noːʊ ˈʃædoːʊz gɹɛːɪt ʌˈpɪːʌ]
Nor doth the early shepherd's star
[nɔ dʌθ ði ˈɜlɪ ˈʃɛpʌdz sta]
Shine like a spangle here.
[ʃaːɪn laːɪk ʌ ˈspæŋgʊl hɪːʌ]
Stay but till my Julia close
[stɛːɪ bʌt tɪl maːɪ ˈdʒuliʌ kloːʊz]
Her life begetting eye;
[hɜ laːɪf bɪˈgɛtɪŋ aːɪ]
And let the whole world then dispose
[ænd lɛt ðʊ hoːʊl wɜld ðɛn dɪˈspoːʊz]
Itself to live or die.
[ɪtˈsɛlf tu lɪv ɔ daːɪ]

4. The Night Piece
[ðʊ naːɪt pis]

Her eyes the glow-worm lend thee,
[hɜ aːɪz ðʊ gloːʊ wɜm lɛnd ði]
The shooting stars attend thee;
[ðʊ ˈʃutɪŋ staz ʌˈtɛnd ði]
And the elves also,
[ænd ði ɛlvz ˈɔlsoːʊ]
Whose little eyes glow
[huz ˈlɪtʊl aːɪz gloːʊ]
Like the sparks of fire, befriend thee.
[laːɪk ðʊ spaks ʌv faːɪʌ bɪˈfɹɛnd ði]
No Will-o'-th'-Wisp mislight thee,
[noːʊ wɪl oːʊ ð wɪsp mɪsˈlaːɪt ði]
Nor snake, or slow-worm bite thee;
[nɔ snɛːɪk ɔ sloːʊ wɜm baːɪt ði]
But on, on thy way
[bʌt an an ðaːɪ wɛːɪ]
Not making a stay,
[nat ˈmɛːɪkɪŋ ʌ stɛːɪ]

Since ghost there's none to affright thee.
[sɪns ɡoːʊst ðɛːʌz nʌn tu ʌˈfɹɑːɪt ði]
Let not the dark thee cumber:
[lɛt nat ðʊ dak ði ˈkʌmbʌ]
What though the moon does slumber?
[ʍat ðoːʊ ðʊ mun dʌz ˈslʌmbʌ]
The stars of the night
[ðʊ staz ʌv ðʊ nɑːɪt]
Will lend thee their light,
[wɪl lɛnd ði ðɛːʌ lɑːɪt]
Like tapers clear without number.
[lɑːɪk ˈtɛːɪpʌz klɪːʌ wɪðˈɑːʊt ˈnʌmbʌ]
Then, Julia, let me woo thee,
[ðɛn ˈdʒulɪʌ lɛt mi wu ði]
Thus, thus to come unto me;
[ðʌs ðʌs tu kʌm ˈʌntu mi]
And when I shall meet
[ænd ʍɛn ɑːɪ ʃæl mit]
Thy silvery feet,
[ðɑːɪ ˈsɪlvʌɾɪ fit]
My soul I'll pour into thee.
[mɑːɪ soːʊl ɑːɪl pɔːʌɾ ˈɪntu ði]

5. Julia's Hair
[ˈdʒulɪʌz hɛːʌ]

Dew sat on Julia's hair,
[dju sæt an ˈdʒulɪʌz hɛːʌ]
And spangled too,
[ænd ˈspæŋɡʊld tu]
Like leaves that laden are
[lɑːɪk livz ðæt ˈlɛːɪdɛ(ɪ)n a]
With trembling dew;
[wɪð ˈtɹɛmblɪŋ dju]
Or glittered to my sight,
[ɔ ˈɡlɪtʌd tu mɑːɪ sɑːɪt]
As when the beams
[æz ʍɛn ðʊ bimz]
Have their reflected light
[hæv ðɛːʌ ɾɪˈflɛktɛ(ɪ)d lɑːɪt]
Danced by the streams.
[danst bɑːɪ ðʊ stɹimz]

6. Cherry Ripe
[ˈtʃɛʁi ɹɑːɪp]

"Cherry-ripe, ripe, ripe," I cry,
[ˈtʃɛɾɪ ɾɑːɪp ɹɑːɪp ɹɑːɪp ɑːɪ kɹɑːɪ]
"Full and fair ones, come and buy."
[fʊl ænd fɛːʌ wʌnz kʌm ænd bɑːɪ]
If so be you ask me where
[ɪf soːʊ bi ju ask mi ʍɛːʌ]
They do grow, I answer: "There,
[ðɛːɪ du ɡɹoːʊ ɑːɪ ˈansʌ ðɛːʌ]
Where my Julia's lips do smile;
[ʍɛːʌ mɑːɪ ˈdʒulɪʌz lɪps du smɑːɪl]

There's the land, or cherry-isle,
[ðɛːʌz ðʊ lænd ɔ ˈtʃɛɾɪ ɑːɪl]
Whose plantations fully show
[huz plænˈtɛːɪʃʌnz ˈfʊlɪ ʃoːʊ]
All the year where cherries grow."
[ɔl ðʊ jɪːʌ ʍɛːʌ ˈtʃɛɾɪz ɡɹoːʊ]

Five Shakespeare Songs (Song Cycle)
[fɑːɪv ˈʃɛːɪkspɪːʌ sɑŋz]
Shakespeare, William (Eng. 1564-1616)

1. Fear No More the Heat O' the Sun
[fɪːʌ noːʊ mɔːʌ ðʊ hit ʌ ðʊ sʌn]

Fear no more the heat o' the sun,
[fɪːʌ noːʊ mɔːʌ ðʊ hit ʌ ðʊ sʌn]
Nor the furious winter's rages;
[nɔ ðʊ ˈfjʊːʌɾɪʌs ˈwɪntʌz ˈɹɛːɪdʒɛ(ɪ)z]
Thou thy worldly task hast done,
[ðɑːʊ ðɑːɪ ˈwɜldlɪ task hæst dʌn]
Home art gone, and ta'en thy wages:
[hoːʊm at ɡan ænd ˈtɛːɪn ðɑːɪ ˈwɛːɪdʒɛ(ɪ)z]
Golden lads and girls all must,
[ˈɡoːʊldɛ(ɪ)n lædz ænd ɡɜlz ɔl mʌst]
As chimney sweepers, come to dust.
[æz ˈtʃɪmnɪ ˈswipʌz kʌm tu dʌst]
Fear no more the frown o' the great;
[fɪːʌ noːʊ mɔːʌ ðʊ fɹɑːʊn ʌ ðʊ ɡɹɛːɪt]
Thou art past the tyrant's stroke;
[ðɑːʊ at past ðʊ ˈtɑːɪɾæ(ɪ)nts stɹoːʊk]
Care no more to clothe and eat;
[kɛːʌ noːʊ mɔːʌ tu kloːʊð ænd it]
To thee the reed is as the oak:
[tu ði ðʊ ɹid ɪz æz ði oːʊk]
The sceptre, learning, physic, must
[ðʊ ˈsɛptʌ ˈlɜnɪŋ ˈfɪzɪk mʌst]
All follow this, and come to dust.
[ɔl ˈfaloːʊ ðɪs ænd kʌm tu dʌst]
Fear no more the light'ning flash,
[fɪːʌ noːʊ mɔːʌ ðʊ ˈlɑːɪtnɪŋ flæʃ]
Nor the all-dreaded thunder-stone;
[nɔ ði ɔl ˈdɹɛdɛ(ɪ)d ˈθʌndʌ stoːʊn]
Fear not slander, censure rash;
[fɪːʌ nat ˈslændʌ ˈsɛnʃʊ(ʌ) ræʃ]
Thou hast finish'd joy and moan:
[ðɑːʊ hæst ˈfɪnɪʃt dʒɔːɪ ænd moːʊn]
All lovers young, all lovers must
[ɔl ˈlʌvʌz jʌŋ ɔl ˈlʌvʌz mʌst]
Consign to thee, and come to dust.
[kʌnˈsɑːɪn tu ði ænd kʌm tu dʌst]
No exorciser harm thee!
[noːʊ ˈɛksɔsɑːɪzʌ ham ði]
Nor no witchcraft charm thee!
[nɔ noːʊ ˈwɪtʃkɹaft tʃam ði]
Ghost unlaid forbear thee!
[ɡoːʊst ʌnˈlɛːɪd fɔˈbɛːʌ ði]

Nothing ill come near thee!
[ˈnʌθɪŋ ɪl kʌm niːʌ ði]
Quiet consummation have;
[ˈkwaːɪɛ(ɪ)t kɑnsʌˈmeːɪʃʌn hæv]
And renowned be thy grave!
[ænd ɹɪˈnaːʊnɛ(ɪ)d bi ðaːɪ gɹɛːɪv]

2. Under the Greenwood Tree
[ˈʌndʌ ðʊ ˈgɹinwʊd tɹi]

Under the greenwood tree
[ˈʌndʌ ðʊ ˈgɹinwʊd tɹi]
Who loves to lie with me,
[hu lʌvz tu laːɪ wɪð mi]
And turn his merry note
[ænd tɜn hɪz ˈmɛɹɪ noːʊt]
Unto the sweet bird's throat,
[ˈʌntu ðʊ swit bɜdz θroːʊt]
Come hither, come hither, come hither:
[kʌm ˈhɪðʌ kʌm ˈhɪðʌ kʌm ˈhɪðʌ]
Here shall he see
[hɪːʌ ʃæl hi si]
No enemy
[noːʊ ˈɛnɪ(ʌ)mɪ]
But winter and rough weather.
[bʌt ˈwɪntʌr ænd ɹʌf ˈwɛðʌ]
Who doth ambition shun,
[hu dʌθ æmˈbɪʃʌn ʃʌn]
And loves to live i' the sun,
[ænd lʌvz tu lɪv ɪ ðʊ sʌn]
Seeking the food he eats,
[ˈsikɪŋ ðʊ fud hi its]
And pleased with what he gets,
[ænd plizd wɪð ʍat hi gɛts]
Come hither, come hither, come hither:
[kʌm ˈhɪðʌ kʌm ˈhɪðʌ kʌm ˈhɪðʌ]
Here shall he see
[hɪːʌ ʃæl hi si]
No enemy
[noːʊ ˈɛnɪ(ʌ)mɪ]
But winter and rough weather.
[bʌt ˈwɪntʌ(ʳ) ænd ɹʌf ˈwɛðʌ]

3. It Was a Lover and His Lass (see Morley)

4. Take, O Take Those Lips Away (see Beach)

5. Hey, Ho, the Wind and the Rain
[hɛːɪ hoːʊ ðʊ wɪnd ænd ðʊ ɹɛːɪn]
Shakespeare, William (Eng. 1564-1616)

When that I was and a little tiny boy,
[ʍɛn ðæt aːɪ waz ænd ʌ ˈlɪtol ˈtaːɪnɪ bɔːɪ]
With hey, ho, the wind and the rain;
[wɪð hɛːɪ hoːʊ ðʊ wɪnd ænd ðʊ ɹɛːɪn]

A foolish thing was but a toy,
[ʌ ˈfuliʃ θɪŋ waz bʌt ʌ tɔːɪ]
For the rain it raineth every day.
[fɔ ðʊ ɹɛːɪn ɪt ˈɹɛːɪnɛ(ɪ)θ ˈɛvɹɪ dɛːɪ]
But when I came to man's estate,
[bʌt ʍɛn aːɪ kɛːɪm tu mænz ɪˈstɛːɪt]
With hey, ho, the wind and the rain;
[wɪð hɛːɪ hoːʊ ðʊ wɪnd ænd ðʊ ɹɛːɪn]
'Gainst knaves and thieves men shut their gate,
[gɛnst nɛːɪvz ænd θivz mɛn ʃʌt ðɛːʌ gɛːɪt]
For the rain it raineth every day,
[fɔ ðʊ ɹɛːɪn ɪt ˈɹɛːɪnɛ(ɪ)θ ˈɛvɹɪ dɛːɪ]
But when I came, alas! to wive,
[bʌt ʍɛn aːɪ kɛːɪm ʌˈlæs tu waːɪv]
With hey, ho, the wind and the rain;
[wɪð hɛːɪ hoːʊ ðʊ wɪnd ænd ðʊ ɹɛːɪn]
By swaggering could I never thrive,
[baːɪ ˈswægʌrɪŋ kʊd aːɪ ˈnɛvʌ θraːɪv]
For the rain it raineth every day.
[fɔ ðʊ ɹɛːɪn ɪt ˈɹɛːɪnɛ(ɪ)θ ˈɛvɹɪ dɛːɪ]
A great while ago the world begun,
[ʌ gɹɛːɪt ʍaːɪl ʌˈgoːʊ ðʊ wɜld bɪˈgʌn]
With hey, ho, the wind and the rain;
[wɪð hɛːɪ hoːʊ ðʊ wɪnd ænd ðʊ ɹɛːɪn]
But that's all one, our play is done,
[bʌt ðæts ɔl wʌn aːʊʌ plɛːɪ ɪz dʌn]
And we'll strive to please you every day.
[ænd wil stɹaːɪv tu pliz ju ˈɛvɹɪ dɛːɪ]

Seven Elizabethan Lyrics (Song Cycle)
[ˈsɛvɪn ˌɛlɪzʌˈbiθɪn ˈlɪɹɪks]

1. Weep You No More
[wip ju noːʊ mɔːʌ]
Anonymous

Weep you no more, sad fountains;
[wip ju noːʊ mɔːʌ sæd ˈfaːʊntæ(ɪ)nz]
What need you flow so fast?
[ʍat nid ju floːʊ soːʊ fast]
Look how the snowy mountains
[lʊk haːʊ ðʊ ˈsnoːʊɪ ˈmaːʊntæ(ɪ)nz]
Heav'n's sun doth gently waste!
[ˈhɛvɪnz sʌn dʌθ ˈdʒɛntlɪ wɛːɪst]
But my sun's heav'nly eyes
[bʌt maːɪ sʌnz ˈhɛvɪnlɪ aːɪz]
View not your weeping,
[vju nat jɔːʌ ˈwipɪŋ]
That now lies sleeping,
[ðæt naːʊ laːɪz ˈslipɪŋ]
Softly now softly lies
[ˈsaftlɪ naːʊ ˈsaftlɪ laːɪz]
Sleeping.
[ˈslipɪŋ]
Sleep is a reconciling,
[slip ɪz ʌ ɹɛkʌnˈsaːɪlɪŋ]

A rest that peace begets;
[ʌ ɹɛst ðæt pis bɪˈgɛts]
Doth not the sun rise smiling
[dʌθ nat ðʊ sʌn ɹɑːɪz ˈsmɑːɪlɪŋ]
When fair at even he sets?
[ʍɛn fɛːɹ æt ˈivɛ(ɪ)n hi sɛts]
Rest you, then, rest, sad eyes!
[ɹɛst ju ðɛn ɹɛst sæd ɑːɪz]
Melt not in weeping,
[mɛlt nat ɪn ˈwipɪŋ]
While she lies sleeping,
[ʍɑːɪl ʃi lɑːɪz ˈslipɪŋ]
Softly now softly lies
[ˈsaftlɪ nɑːʊ ˈsaftlɪ lɑːɪz]
Sleeping.
[ˈslipɪŋ]

2. My Life's Delight
[mɑːɪ lɑːɪfs dɪˈlɑːɪt]
Campion, Thomas (Eng. 1567-1620)

Come, O come, my life's delight!
[kʌm oːʊ kʌm mɑːɪ lɑːɪfs dɪˈlɑːɪt]
Let me not in languor pine:
[lɛt mi nat ɪn ˈlæŋgɔ(ʌ) pɑːɪn]
Love loves no delay; thy sight
[lʌv lʌvz noːʊ dɪˈlɛːɪ ðɑːɪ sɑːɪt]
The more enjoyed, the more divine.
[ðʊ mɔːɹ ɪnˈdʒɔːɪd ðʊ mɔːʌ dɪˈvɑːɪn]
O come, and take from me
[oːʊ kʌm ænd tɛːɪk fɹʌm mi]
The pain of being depriv'd of thee.
[ðʊ pɛːɪn ʌv ˈbiɪŋ dɪˈpɹɑːɪvd ʌv ði]
Thou all sweetness dost enclose,
[ðɑːʊ ɔl ˈswitnɛ(ɪ)s dʌst ɪnˈkloːʊz]
Like a little world of bliss:
[lɑːɪk ʌ ˈlɪtʊl wɜld ʌv blɪs]
Beauty guards thy looks: the rose
[ˈbjuti gɑdz ðɑːɪ lʊks ðʊ ɹoːʊz]
In them pure and eternal is.
[ɪn ðɛm pjʊːʌɹ ænd ɪˈtɜnʊl ɪz]
Come then! O come, and make thy flight
[kʌm ðɛn oːʊ kʌm ænd mɛːɪk ðɑːɪ flɑːɪt]
As swift to me as heav'nly light!
[æz swɪft tu mi æz ˈhɛvnlɪ lɑːɪt]

3. Damask Roses
[ˈdæmɪsk ˈɹoːʊzɪz]
Anonymous

Lady, when I behold the roses sprouting,
[ˈlɛːɪdɪ ʍɛn ɑːɪ bɪˈhoːʊld ðʊ ˈɹoːʊzɛ(ɪ)z ˈspɹɑːʊtɪŋ]
Which, clad in damask mantles, deck the arbours,
[ʍɪtʃ klæd ɪn ˈdæmæ(ɪ)sk ˈmæntʊlz dɛk ði ˈɑbʊ(ʌ)z]
And then behold your lips, where sweet love harbours,
[ænd ðɛn bɪˈhoːʊld jɔːʌ lɪps ʍɛːʌ swit lʌv ˈhɑbʊ(ʌ)z]

My eyes present me with a double doubting:
[mɑːɪ ɑːɪz pɹɪˈzɛnt mi wɪð ʌ ˈdʌbʊl ˈdɑːʊtɪŋ]
For viewing both alike,
[fɔ ˈvjuɪŋ boːʊθ ʌˈlɑːɪk]
hardly my mind supposes
[ˈhadlɪ mɑːɪ mɑːɪnd sʌˈpoːʊzɛ(ɪ)z]
Whether the roses be your lips,
[ˈʍɛðʌ ðʊ ˈɹoːʊzɛ(ɪ)z bi jɔːʌ lɪps]
or your lips the roses.
[ɔ jɔːʌ lɪps ðʊ ˈɹoːʊzɛ(ɪ)z]

4. The Faithless Shepherdess
[ðʊ ˈfɛːɪθlɪs ˈʃɛpʌdɪs]
Anonymous

While that the sun with his beams hot
[ʍɑːɪl ðæt ðʊ sʌn wɪð hɪz bimz hat]
Scorched the fruits in vale and mountain,
[ˈskɔtʃɛ(ɪ)d ðʊ fruts ɪn vɛːɪl ænd ˈmɑːʊntæ(ɪ)n]
Philon, the shepherd, late forgot,
[ˈfɑːɪlan ðʊ ˈʃɛpʌd lɛːɪt fɔˈgat]
Sitting beside a crystal fountain,
[ˈsɪtɪŋ bɪˈsɑːɪd ʌ ˈkɹɪstʊl ˈfɑːʊntæ(ɪ)n]
In shadow of a green oak tree,
[ɪn ˈʃædoːʊ ʌv ʌ gɹin oːʊk tɹi]
Upon his pipe this song play'd he:
[ʌˈpan hɪz pɑːɪp ðɪs saŋ plɛːɪd hi]
Adieu, Love, adieu, Love, untrue Love,
[aˈdjø lʌv aˈdjø lʌv ʌnˈtru lʌv]
Untrue Love, untrue Love, adieu, Love!
[ʌnˈtru lʌv ʌnˈtru lʌv aˈdjø lʌv]
Your mind is light, soon lost for new love.
[jɔːʌ mɑːɪnd ɪz lɑːɪt sun last fɔ nju lʌv]
So long as I was in your sight
[soːʊ laŋ æz ɑːɪ waz ɪn jɔːʌ sɑːɪt]
I was your heart, your soul, your treasure;
[ɑːɪ waz jɔːʌ hat jɔːʌ soːʊl jɔːʌ ˈtɹɛʒʊ(ʌ)]
And evermore you sobb'd and sigh'd
[ænd ɛvʌˈmɔːʌ ju sabd ænd sɑːɪd]
Burning in flames beyond all measure:
[ˈbɜnɪŋ ɪn flɛːɪmz bɪˈjand ɔl ˈmɛʒʊ(ʌ)]
Three days endured your love to me,
[θɹi dɛːɪz ɪnˈdjʊːʌd jɔːʌ lʌv tu mi]
And it was lost in other three!
[ænd ɪt waz last ɪn ˈʌðʌ θɹi]
Adieu, Love, adieu, Love, untrue Love,
[aˈdjø lʌv aˈdjø lʌv ʌnˈtru lʌv]
Untrue Love, untrue Love, adieu, Love!
[ʌnˈtru lʌv ʌnˈtru lʌv aˈdjø lʌv]
Your mind is light, soon lost for new love.
[jɔːʌ mɑːɪnd ɪz lɑːɪt sun last fɔ nju lʌv]

5. Brown Is My Love
[bɹɑːon ɪz maːɪ lʌv]
Anonymous

Brown is my Love, but graceful,
[bɹɑːon ɪz maːɪ lʌv bʌt ˈɡɹɛːɪsfʊl]
And each renowned whiteness,
[ænd iʧ ɹɪˈnɑːʊnɛ(ɪ)d ˈʍɑːɪtnɛ(ɪ)s]
Match'd with her lovely brown, loseth its brightness.
[mæʧt wɪð hɜ ˈlʌvlɪ bɹɑːon ˈluzɛ(ɪ)θ ɪts ˈbɹɑːɪtnɛ(ɪ)s]
Fair is my Love, but scornful,
[fɛːʌɾ ɪz maːɪ lʌv bʌt ˈskɔnfʊl]
Yet have I seen despised
[jɛt hæv aːɪ sin dɪˈspɑːɪzɛ(ɪ)d]
Dainty white lilies, and sad flow'rs well prized.
[ˈdɛːɪntɪ ʍɑːɪt ˈlɪlɪz ænd sæd flɑːʊɑz wɛl ˈpɹɑːɪzɛ(ɪ)d]

6. By a Fountainside
[baːɪ ʌ ˈfɑːʊntɪnsɑːɪd]
Jonson, Ben (Eng. 1572-1637)

Slow, slow, fresh fount, keep time with my salt tears;
[sloːʊ sloːʊ fɹɛʃ fɑːʊnt kip taːɪm wɪð maːɪ sɔlt tɪːʌz]
Yet slower, yet: O faintly, gentle springs:
[jɛt ˈsloːʊʌ jɛt oːʊ ˈfɛːɪntlɪ ˈʤɛntʊl spɹɪŋz]
List to the heavy part the music bears,
[lɪst tu ðʊ ˈhɛvɪ pɑt ðʊ ˈmjuzɪk bɛːʌz]
Woe weeps out her division when she sings.
[woːʊ wips aːʊt hɜ dɪˈvɪʒʌn ʍɛn ʃi sɪŋz]
Droop herbs and flow'rs,
[dɹup ɜbz ænd flɑːʊʌz]
Fall grief in show'rs,
[fɔl ɡɹif ɪn ʃɑːʊʌz]
Our beauties are not ours;
[ɑːʊʌ ˈbjutɪz ɑ nɑt ɑːʊʌz]
Or I could still,
[ɔʁ⁽ʳ⁾ aːɪ kʊd stɪl]
Like melting snow upon some craggy hill,
[lɑːɪk ˈmɛltɪŋ snoːʊ ʌˈpɑn sʌm ˈkɹægɪ hɪl]
Drop, drop, drop, drop,
[dɹɑp dɹɑp dɹɑp dɹɑp]
Since nature's pride is now a wither'd daffodil.
[sɪns ˈnɛːɪʧʊ(ʌ)z pɹɑːɪd ɪz nɑːʊ ʌ ˈwɪðʌd ˈdæfo(ʌ)dɪl]

7. Fair House of Joy
[fɛːʌ hɑːʊs ʌv ʤɔːɪ]
Anonymous

Fain would I change that note
[fɛːɪn wʊd aːɪ ʧɛːɪnʤ ðæt noːʊt]
To which fond Love hath charm'd me
[tu ʍɪʧ fɑnd lʌv hæθ ʧɑmd mi]
Long, long to sing by rote,
[lɑŋ lɑŋ tu sɪŋ bɑːɪ ɹoːʊt]
Fancying that that harm'd me:
[ˈfænsɪɪŋ ðæt ðæt hɑmd mi]

Yet when this thought doth come
[jɛt ʍɛn ðɪs θɔt dʌθ kʌm]
"Love is the perfect sum
[lʌv ɪz ðʊ ˈpɜfɛ(ɪ)kt sʌm]
Of all delight!"
[ʌv ɔl dɪˈlɑːɪt]
I have no other choice
[aːɪ hæv noːʊ ˈʌðʌ ʧɔːɪs]
Either for pen or voice
[ˈɑːɪðʌ fɔ pɛn ɔ vɔːɪs]
To sing or write.
[tu sɪŋ ɔ ɹɑːɪt]
O Love! they wrong thee much
[oːʊ lʌv ðɛːɪ ɹɑŋ ði mʌʧ]
That say thy sweet is bitter,
[ðæt sɛːɪ ðɑːɪ swit ɪz ˈbɪtʌ]
When thy rich fruit is such
[ʍɛn ðɑːɪ ɹɪʧ frut ɪz sʌʧ]
As nothing can be sweeter.
[æz ˈnʌθɪŋ kæn bi ˈswitʌ]
Fair house of joy and bliss,
[fɛːʌ hɑːʊs ʌv ʤɔːɪ ænd blɪs]
Where truest pleasure is,
[ʍɛːʌ ˈtruɛ(ɪ)st ˈplɛʒʊ(ʌ)ɾ ɪz]
I do adore thee:
[aːɪ du ʌˈdɔːʌ ði]
I know thee what thou art,
[aːɪ noːʊ ði ʍat ðɑːʊ at]
I serve thee with my heart,
[aːɪ sɜv ði wɪð maːɪ hat]
And fall before thee.
[ænd fɔl bɪˈfɔːʌ ði]

Three Shakespeare Songs (Song Cycle)
[θɹi ˈʃɛːɪkspɪːʌ sɑŋz]
Shakespeare, William (Eng. 1564-1616)

1. Come Away, Death (see "Dirge" by Argento)

2. O Mistress Mine
[oːʊ ˈmɪstɹɪs maːɪn]

O mistress mine, where are you roaming?
[oːʊ ˈmɪstɹɛ(ɪ)s maːɪn ʍɛːʌɾ ɑ ju ˈɹoːʊmɪŋ]
O stay and hear, your true love's coming,
[oːʊ stɛːɪ ænd hɪːʌ jɔːʌ tru lʌvz ˈkʌmɪŋ]
That can sing both high and low;
[ðæt kæn sɪŋ boːʊθ hɑːɪ ænd loːʊ]
Trip no further, pretty sweeting;
[tɹɪp noːʊ ˈfɜðʌ ˈpɹɪtɪ ˈswitɪŋ]
Journeys end in lovers' meeting,
[ˈʤɜnɪz ɛnd ɪn ˈlʌvʌz ˈmitɪŋ]
Ev'ry wise man's son doth know.
[ˈɛvɪ waːɪz mænz sʌn dʌθ noːʊ]
What is love? 'Tis not hereafter;
[ʍat ɪz lʌv tɪz nat hɪːʌɾˈaftʌ]

Present mirth hath present laughter;
['pɹɛzɛnt mɜθ hæθ 'pɹɛzɛnt 'laftʌ]
What's to come is still unsure:
[ʍats tu kʌm ɪz stɪl ʌn'ʃʊːʌ]
In delay there lies no plenty;
[ɪn dɪ'lɛːɪ ðɛːʌ laːɪz noːʊ 'plɛntɪ]
Then come kiss me, Sweet and twenty,
[ðɛn kʌm kɪs mi swit ænd 'twɛntɪ]
Youth's a stuff will not endure.
[juθs ʌ stʌf wɪl nat ɪn'djʊːʌ]

3. Blow, Blow Thou Winter Wind
[bloːʊ bloːʊ ðaːʊ 'wɪntʌ wɪnd]

Blow, blow, thou winter wind,
[bloːʊ bloːʊ ðaːʊ 'wɪntʌ wɪnd]
Thou art not so unkind
[ðaːʊ at nat soːʊ ʌn'kaːɪnd]
As man's ingratitude;
[æz mænz ɪn'gɹætɪtjud]
Thy tooth is not so keen,
[ðaːɪ tuθ ɪz nat soːʊ kin]
Because thou art not seen,
[bɪ'kɔz ðaːʊ at nat sin]
Although thy breath be rude.
[ɔl'ðoːʊ ðaːɪ bɹɛθ bi ɹrud]
Heigh ho! sing heigh ho! unto the green holly;
[hɛːɪ hoːʊ sɪŋ hɛːɪ hoːʊ 'ʌntu ðʊ gɹin 'halɪ]
Most friendship is feigning, most loving mere folly:
[moːʊst 'fɹɛndʃɪp ɪz 'fɛːɪnɪŋ moːʊst 'lʌvɪŋ mɪːʌ 'falɪ]
Then heigh ho! the holly!
[ðɛn hɛːɪ hoːʊ ðʊ 'halɪ]
This life is most jolly.
[ðɪs laːɪf ɪz moːʊst 'dʒalɪ]
Freeze, freeze, thou bitter sky,
[fɹiz fɹiz ðaːʊ 'bɪtʌ skaːɪ]
That dost not bite so nigh
[ðæt dʌst nat baːɪt soːʊ naːɪ]
As benefits forgot:
[æz 'bɛnɪfɪts fɔ'gat]
Though thou the waters warp,
[ðoːʊ ðaːʊ ðʊ 'wɔtʌz wɔp]
Thy sting is not so sharp
[ðaːɪ stɪŋ ɪz nat soːʊ ʃap]
As friend remembered not.
[æz fɹɛnd ɹɪ'mɛmbʌd nat]
Heigh ho! sing heigh ho! unto the green holly:
[hɛːɪ hoːʊ sɪŋ hɛːɪ hoːʊ 'ʌntu ðʊ gɹin 'halɪ]
Most friendship is feigning, most loving mere folly:
[moːʊst 'fɹɛndʃɪp ɪz 'fɛːɪnɪŋ moːʊst 'lʌvɪŋ mɪːʌ 'falɪ]
Then heigh ho! the holly!
[ðɛn hɛːɪ hoːʊ ðʊ 'halɪ]
This life is most jolly.
[ðɪs laːɪf ɪz moːʊst 'dʒalɪ]

Three Songs from Old English Popular Songs
[θɹi saŋz fɹʌm oːʊld 'ɪŋglɪʃ 'papjulʌ saŋz]
(Song Cycle)

1. Drink to Me Only with Thine Eyes
[dɹɪŋk tu mi 'oːʊnli wɪθ ðaːɪn aːɪz]
Jonson, Ben (Eng. 1572-1637)

Drink to me only with thine eyes,
[dɹɪŋk tu mi 'oːʊnli wɪð ðaːɪn aːɪz]
And I will pledge with mine;
[ænd aːɪ wɪl plɛdʒ wɪð maːɪn]
Or leave a kiss within the cup
[ɔ liv ʌ kɪs wɪð'ɪn ðʊ kʌp]
And I'll not ask for wine.
[ænd aːɪl nat ask fɔ waːɪn]
The thirst that from the soul doth rise
[ðʊ θɜst ðæt fɹʌm ðʊ soːʊl dʌθ ɹaːɪz]
Doth ask a drink divine;
[dʌθ ask ʌ dɹɪŋk dɪ'vaːɪn]
But might I of Jove's nectar sup,
[bʌt maːɪt aːɪ ʌv dʒoːʊvz 'nɛktʌ sʌp]
I would not change for thine.
[aːɪ wʊd nat tʃɛːɪndʒ fɔ ðaːɪn]
I sent thee late a rosy wreath,
[aːɪ sɛnt ði lɛːɪt ʌ 'ɹoːʊzɪ ɹiθ]
not so much honouring thee,
[nat soːʊ mʌtʃ 'anʊɹɪŋ ði]
As giving it a hope that there
[æz 'gɪvɪŋ ɪt ʌ hoːʊp ðæt ðɛːʌ]
It could not withered be.
[ɪt kʊd nat 'wɪðʌd bi]
But thou thereon didst only breathe
[bʌt ðaːʊ ðɛːʌɹ'an dɪdst 'oːʊnlɪ bɹɪð]
And send'st it back to me:
[ænd sɛndst ɪt bæk tu mi]
Since when it grows, and smells, I swear,
[sɪns ʍɛn ɪt gɹoːʊz ænd smɛlz aːɪ swɛːʌ]
not of itself, but thee.
[nat ʌv ɪt'sɛlf bʌt ði]

2. Barbara Allen
['babɹʌ 'ælɪn]
Folksong

In Scarlet Town, where I was born,
[ɪn 'skalɛ(ɪ)t taːʊn ʍɛːʌɹ aːɪ waz bɔn]
There was a fair maid dwellin',
[ðɛːʌ waz ʌ fɛːʌ mɛːɪd 'dwɛlɪn]
Made ev'ry youth cry "Well-a-day!"
[mɛːɪd 'ɛvɹɪ juθ kɹaːɪ wɛl ʌ dɛːɪ]
Her name was Barb'ra Allen.
[hɜ nɛːɪm waz 'babɹʌ 'ælɛ(ɪ)n]
All in the merry month of May
[ɔl ɪn ðʊ 'mɛɹɪ mʌnθ ʌv mɛːɪ]

When green buds they were swellin',
[ʍɛn gɹin bʌdz ðeːɪ wɜ ˈswɛlɪn]
Young Jemmy Grove on his death-bed lay
[jʌŋ ˈdʒɛmɪ gɹoːʊv ɑn hɪz dɛθ bɛd leːɪ]
For love of Barb'ra Allen.
[fɔ lʌv ʌv ˈbɑbɹʌ ˈælɛ(ɪ)n]
Then slowly, slowly she came up,
[ðɛn ˈsloːʊlɪ ˈsloːʊlɪ ʃi keːɪm ʌp]
And slowly she came nigh him,
[ænd ˈsloːʊlɪ ʃi keːɪm naːɪ hɪm]
And all she said when there she came
[ænd ɔl ʃi sɛd ʍɛn ðeːʌ ʃi keːɪm]
"Young man, I think you're dying."
[jʌŋ mæn aːɪ θɪŋk jɔːʌ ˈdaːɪɪŋ]
As she was walking o'er the fields
[æz ʃi wɑz ˈwɔkɪŋ ɔːʌ ðʊ fildz]
She heard the dead-bell knellin',
[ʃi hɜd ðʊ dɛd bɛl ˈnɛlɪn]
And ev'ry stroke the dead-bell gave
[ænd ˈɛvɹɪ stɹoːʊk ðʊ dɛd bɛl geːɪv]
Cried "Woe to Barb'ra Allen!"
[kɹaːɪd woːʊ tu ˈbɑbɹʌ ˈælɛ(ɪ)n]
When he was dead and laid in grave
[ʍɛn hi wɑz dɛd ænd leːɪd ɪn gɹeːɪv]
Her heart was struck with sorrow,
[hɜ hɑt wɑz stɹʌk wɪð ˈsaɹoːʊ]
"O mother, mother, make my bed,
[oːʊ ˈmʌðʌ ˈmʌðʌ meːɪk maːɪ bɛd]
For I shall die tomorrow."
[fɔʁ⁽ʳ⁾ aːɪ ʃæl daːɪ tuˈmaɹoːʊ]
"Farewell," she said, "ye virgins all,
[fɛːʌˈwɛl ʃi sɛd ji ˈvɜdʒɪnz ɔl]
And shun the fault I fell in;
[ænd ʃʌn ðʊ fɔlt aːɪ fɛl ɪn]
Henceforth take warning by the fall
[ˈhɛnsfɔθ teːɪk ˈwɔnɪŋ baːɪ ðʊ fɔl]
Of cruel Barb'ra Allen."
[ʌv ˈkɹuːɛ(ʊ)l ˈbɑbɹʌ ˈælɛ(ɪ)n]

3. Over the Mountains
[ˈoːʊvʌ ðʊ ˈmaːʊntɪnz]
Folksong

Over the mountains
[ˈoːʊvʌ ðʊ ˈmaːʊntæ(ɪ)nz]
And over the waves,
[ænd ˈoːʊvʌ ðʊ weːɪvz]
Under the fountains
[ˈʌndʌ ðʊ ˈfaːʊntæ(ɪ)nz]
And under the graves,
[ænd ˈʌndʌ ðʊ gɹ⁽ʳ⁾eːɪvz]
Under floods that are deepest
[ˈʌndʌ flʌdz ðæt ɑ ˈdipɛ(ɪ)st]
Which Neptune obey,
[ʍɪtʃ ˈnɛptjun oˈbeːɪ]

Over rocks that are steepest,
[ˈoːʊvʌ ɹɑks ðæt ɑ ˈstipɛ(ɪ)st]
Love will find out the way.
[lʌv wɪl faːɪnd aːʊt ðʊ weːɪ]
Where there is no place
[ʍɛːʌ ðɛːʌɹ ɪz noːʊ pleːɪs]
For the glow-worm to lie,
[fɔ ðʊ gloːʊ wɜm tu laːɪ]
Where there is no space
[ʍɛːʌ ðɛːʌɹ ɪz noːʊ speːɪs]
For receipt of a fly:
[fɔ ɹɪˈsit ʌv ʌ flaːɪ]
Where the midge dare not venture
[ʍɛːʌ ðʊ mɪdʒ dɛːʌ nɑt ˈvɛntʃʊ(ʌ)]
Lest herself fast she lay,
[lɛst hɜˈsɛlf fɑst ʃi leːɪ]
If love come he will enter
[ɪf lʌv kʌm hi wɪl ˈɛntʌ]
And will find out the way.
[ænd wɪl faːɪnd aːʊt ðʊ weːɪ]
Some think to loose him
[sʌm θɪŋk tu lus hɪm]
Or have him confined.
[ɔ hæv hɪm kʌnˈfaːɪnd]
Some do suppose him,
[sʌm du sʌˈpoːʊz hɪm]
Poor thing, to be blind;
[pʊːʌ θɪŋ tu bi blaːɪnd]
But if ne'er so close ye wall him,
[bʌt ɪf nɛːʌ soːʊ kloːʊs ji wɔl hɪm]
Do the best that ye may,
[du ðʊ bɛst ðæt ji meːɪ]
Blind Love, if so ye call him,
[blaːɪnd lʌv ɪf soːʊ ji kɔl hɪm]
Soon will find out his way.
[sun wɪl faːɪnd aːʊt hɪz weːɪ]
You may train the eagle
[ju meːɪ tɹeːɪn ði ˈigʊl]
To stoop to your fist
[tu stup tu jɔːʌ fist]
Or you may inveigle
[ɔ ju meːɪ ɪnˈveːɪgʊl]
The phoenix of the East.
[ðʊ ˈfinɪks ʌv ði ist]
The lioness you may move her
[ðʊ ˈlaːɪʌnɛ(ɪ)s ju meːɪ muv hɜ]
To get o'er her prey,
[tu gɛt ɔːʌ hɜ pɹɛːɪ]
But you'll ne'er stop a lover,
[bʌt jul nɛːʌ stɑp ʌ ˈlʌvʌ]
Love shall find out the way.
[lʌv ʃæl faːɪnd aːʊt ðʊ weːɪ]

Song Selections

"By the Sea" (Four Songs of the Sea)
[baːɪ ðʊ si]
Quilter, Roger (Eng. 1877-1953)

I stood today by the shimmering sea;
[aːɪ stʊd tuˈdeːɪ baːɪ ðʊ ˈʃɪmʌɾɪŋ si]
Never was wind so mild and free;
[ˈnɛvʌ waz wɪnd soːʊ maːɪld ænd fɹi]
The light and the loveliness dazzled me.
[ðʊ laːɪt ænd ðʊ ˈlʌvlɪnɛ(ɪ)s ˈdæzʊld mi]
The waves did frolic and curve and roll;
[ðʊ weːɪvz dɪd ˈfɹalɪk ænd kɜv ænd ɹoːʊl]
They sigh'd and sang to my list'ning soul,
[ðɛːɪ saːɪd ænd sæŋ tu maːɪ ˈlɪsnɪŋ soːʊl]
And the might of their mystery made me whole.
[ænd ðʊ maːɪt ʌv ðɛːʌ ˈmɪstʌɾɪ meːɪd mi hoːʊl]
I stood today by the shimmering sea.
[aːɪ stʊd tuˈdeːɪ baːɪ ðʊ ˈʃɪmʌɾɪŋ si]
Never was wind so mild and free;
[ˈnɛvʌ waz wɪnd soːʊ maːɪld ænd fɹi]
The light and the loveliness dazzled me, dazzled me.
[ðʊ laːɪt ænd ðʊ ˈlʌvlɪnɛ(ɪ)s ˈdæzʊld mi ˈdæzʊld mi]

"Come Back!"
[kʌm bæk]
Quilter, Roger (Eng. 1877-1953)

I dream'd I heard your voice in the night,
[aːɪ dɹimd aːɪ hɜd jɔːʌ vɔːɪs ɪn ðʊ naːɪt]
Deep and tender with loving words.
[dip ænd ˈtɛndʌ wɪð ˈlʌvɪŋ wɜdz]
I dream'd I saw your wondrous eyes
[aːɪ dɹimd aːɪ sɔ jɔːʌ ˈwʌndɹʌs aːɪz]
Aglow with love and light divine:
[ʌˈgloːʊ wɪð lʌv ænd laːɪt dɪˈvaːɪn]
"Come back! come back! my love," I cried.
[kʌm bæk kʌm bæk maːɪ lʌv aːɪ kɾaːɪd]
"Come back, come back, my love, my life!"
[kʌm bæk kʌm bæk maːɪ lʌv maːɪ laːɪf]

"Go, Lovely Rose" (see "Song" by Rorem)

"June"
[dʒun]
Hopper, Nora (Eng. 1871-1906)

Dark red roses in a honeyed wind swinging,
[dak ɹed ˈɹoːʊzɛ(ɪ)z ɪn ʌ ˈhʌnɪd wɪnd ˈswɪŋɪŋ]
Silk-soft hollyhock, coloured like the moon;
[sɪlk saft ˈhalɪhak ˈkʌlʊ(ʌ)d laːɪk ðʊ mun]
Larks high overhead lost in light, and singing;
[laks haːɪ ˈoːʊvʌhɛd last ɪn laːɪt ænd ˈsɪŋɪŋ]
That's the way of June.
[ðæts ðʊ weːɪ ʌv dʒun]

Dark red roses in the warm wind falling,
[dak ɹed ˈɹoːʊzɛ(ɪ)z ɪn ðʊ wɔm wɪnd ˈfɔlɪŋ]
Velvet leaf by velvet leaf, all the breathless noon;
[ˈvɛlvɛ(ɪ)t lif baːɪ ˈvɛlvɛ(ɪ)t lif ɔl ðʊ ˈbɹɛθlɛ(ɪ)s nun]
Far off sea waves calling, calling, calling;
[far af si weːɪvz ˈkɔlɪŋ ˈkɔlɪŋ ˈkɔlɪŋ]
That's the way of June.
[ðæts ðʊ weːɪ ʌv dʒun]
Sweet as scarlet strawberry under wet leaves hidden,
[swit æz ˈskalɛ(ɪ)t ˈstɹɔbɛɾɪ ʌndʌ wɛt livz ˈhɪdɛ(ɪ)n]
Honey'd as the damask rose, lavish as the moon,
[ˈhʌnɪd æz ðʊ ˈdæmæ(ɪ)sk ɹoːʊz ˈlævɪʃ æz ðʊ mun]
Shedding lovely light on things forgotten,
[ˈʃɛdɪŋ ˈlʌvlɪ laːɪt an θɪŋz fɔˈgatɛ(ɪ)n]
hope forbidden,
[hoːʊp fɔˈbɪdɛ(ɪ)n]
That's the way of June.
[ðæts ðʊ weːɪ ʌv dʒun]

"Love's Philosophy"
[lʌvz fɪˈlasʌfi]
Shelley, Percy Bysshe (Eng. 1792-1822)

The fountains mingle with the river
[ðʊ ˈfaːʊntæ(ɪ)nz ˈmɪŋgʊl wɪð ðʊ ˈɾɪvʌ]
And the rivers with the ocean;
[ænd ðʊ ˈɾɪvʌz wɪð ði ˈoːʊʃæ(ɪ)n]
The winds of Heav'n mix for ever
[ðʊ wɪndz ʌv ˈhɛvɪn mɪks fɔʁ⁽ʳ⁾ ˈɛvʌ]
With a sweet emotion.
[wɪð ʌ swit ɪˈmoːʊʃʌn]
Nothing in the world is single;
[ˈnʌθɪŋ ɪn ðʊ wɜld ɪz ˈsɪŋgʊl]
All things, by a law divine,
[ɔl θɪŋz baːɪ ʌ lɔ dɪˈvaːɪn]
In one another's being mingle,
[ɪn wʌn ʌˈnʌðʌz ˈbiɪŋ ˈmɪŋgʊl]
Why not I with thine?
[ʍaːɪ nat aːɪ wɪð ðaːɪn]
See, the mountains kiss high Heav'n
[si ðʊ ˈmaːʊntæ(ɪ)nz kɪs haːɪ ˈhɛvɪn]
And the waves clasp one another;
[ænd ðʊ weːɪvz klasp wʌn ʌˈnʌðʌ]
No sister flower would be forgiv'n
[noːʊ ˈsɪstʌ flaːʊʌ wʊd bi fɔˈgɪvɪn]
If it disdained its brother.
[ɪf ɪt dɪsˈdeːɪnd ɪts ˈbɹʌðʌ]
And the sunlight clasps the earth,
[ænd ðʊ ˈsʌnlaːɪt klasps ði ɜθ]
And the moonbeams kiss the sea,
[ænd ðʊ ˈmunbimz kɪs ðʊ si]
What are all these kissings worth,
[ʍat aɾ ɔl ðiz ˈkɪsɪŋz wɜθ]
If thou kiss not me?
[ɪf ðaːʊ kɪs nat mi]

"Moonlight"
[ˈmunlɑːɪt]
Quilter, Roger (Eng. 1877-1953)

Under the silver moonlight,
[ˈʌndʌ ðʊ ˈsɪlvʌ ˈmunlɑːɪt]
flutter the great white wings,
[ˈflʌtʌ ðʊ ɡɹɛːɪt ʍɑːɪt wɪŋz]
Woo'd by the soft night breezes
[wud bɑːɪ ðʊ saft nɑːɪt ˈbɹizɛ(ɪ)z]
tender with whispered things.
[ˈtɛndʌ wɪð ˈʍɪspʌd θɪŋz]
Silently onward gliding into the silent night,
[ˈsɑːɪlɛntlɪ ˈɑnwʊd ˈɡlɑːɪdɪŋ ˈɪntu ðʊ ˈsɑːɪlɛnt nɑːɪt]
Like to a fairy vessel crowned with a fairy light.
[lɑːɪk tu ʌ ˈfɛːʌɾɪ ˈvɛsʊl kɹɑːʊnd wɪð ʌ ˈfɛːʌɾɪ lɑːɪt]
Whisper O soft night breezes,
[ˈʍɪspʌɾ oːʊ saft nɑːɪt ˈbɹizɛ(ɪ)z]
murmur your tender tune,
[ˈmɜmʊ(ʌ) jɔːʌ ˈtɛndʌ tjun]
Carry the white wings onward, under the silver moon.
[ˈkæɾɪ ðʊ ʍɑːɪt wɪŋz ˈɑnwʊd ˈʌndʌ ðʊ ˈsɪlvʌ mun]

"Now Sleeps the Crimson Petal"
[nɑːʊ slips ðʊ ˈkɹɪmzʌn ˈpɛtʊl]
Tennyson, Lord Alfred (Eng. 1809-1892)

Now sleeps the crimson petal, now the white;
[nɑːʊ slips ðʊ ˈkɹɪmzʌn ˈpɛtʊl nɑːʊ ðʊ ʍɑːɪt]
Nor waves the cypress in the palace walk;
[nɔ wɛːɪvz ðʊ ˈsɑːɪpɹɛ(ɪ)s ɪn ðʊ ˈpælæ(ʌ)s wɔk]
Nor winks the gold fin in the porph'ry font:
[nɔ wɪŋks ðʊ ɡoːʊld fɪn ɪn ðʊ ˈpɔfɹɪ fant]
The fire-fly wakens: waken thou with me.
[ðʊ fɑːɪʌ flɑːɪ ˈwɛːɪkɛ(ɪ)nz ˈwɛːɪkɛ(ɪ)n ðɑːʊ wɪð mi]
Now folds the lily all her sweetness up,
[nɑːʊ foːʊldz ðʊ ˈlɪlɪ ɔl hɜ ˈswitnɛ(ɪ)s ʌp]
And slips into the bosom of the lake;
[ænd slɪps ˈɪntu ðʊ ˈbʊzʌm ʌv ðʊ lɛːɪk]
So fold thyself, my dearest, thou, and slip,
[soːʊ foːʊld ðɑːɪˈsɛlf mɑːɪ ˈdɪːʌɾɛ(ɪ)st ðɑːʊ ænd slɪp]
Into my bosom and be lost in me.
[ˈɪntu mɑːɪ ˈbʊzʌm ænd bi last ɪn mi]

"Over the Land Is April"
[ˈoːʊvʌ ðʊ lænd ɪz ˈɛːɪpɹʊl]
Stevenson, Robert Louis (Sc. 1850-1894)

Over the land is April,
[ˈoːʊvʌ ðʊ lænd ɪz ˈɛːɪpɹɪ(ʊ)l]
Over my heart a rose;
[ˈoːʊvʌ mɑːɪ hat ʌ ɾoːʊz]
Over the high, brown mountain
[ˈoːʊvʌ ðʊ hɑːɪ bɹɑːʊn ˈmɑːʊntæ(ɪ)n]
The sound of singing goes.
[ðʊ sɑːʊnd ʌv ˈsɪŋɪŋ ɡoːʊz]

Say, love, do you hear me,
[sɛːɪ lʌv du ju hɪːʌ mi]
Hear my sonnets ring?
[hɪːʌ mɑːɪ ˈsanɛ(ɪ)ts ɹɪŋ]
Over the high, brown mountain,
[ˈoːʊvʌ ðʊ hɑːɪ bɹɑːʊn ˈmɑːʊntæ(ɪ)n]
Love, do you hear me sing?
[lʌv du ju hɪːʌ mi sɪŋ]
By highway, love, and byway
[bɑːɪ ˈhɑːɪwɛːɪ lʌv ænd ˈbɑːɪwɛːɪ]
The snows succeed the rose.
[ðʊ snoːʊz sʌkˈsid ðʊ ɾoːʊz]
Over the high, brown mountain
[ˈoːʊvʌ ðʊ hɑːɪ bɹɑːʊn ˈmɑːʊntæ(ɪ)n]
The wind of winter blows.
[ðʊ wɪnd ʌv ˈwɪntʌ bloːʊz]
Say, love, do you hear me,
[sɛːɪ lʌv du ju hɪːʌ mi]
Hear my sonnets ring?
[hɪːʌ mɑːɪ ˈsanɛ(ɪ)ts ɹɪŋ]
Over the high, brown mountain,
[ˈoːʊvʌ ðʊ hɑːɪ bɹɑːʊn ˈmɑːʊntæ(ɪ)n]
I sound the song of spring
[ɑːɪ sɑːʊnd ðʊ saŋ ʌv spɹɪŋ]
Over the land is April,
[ˈoːʊvʌ ðʊ lænd ɪz ˈɛːɪpɹɪ(ʊ)l]
Over my heart a rose;
[ˈoːʊvʌ mɑːɪ hat ʌ ɾoːʊz]
Over the high, brown mountain
[ˈoːʊvʌ ðʊ hɑːɪ bɹɑːʊn ˈmɑːʊntæ(ɪ)n]
The sound of singing goes.
[ðʊ sɑːʊnd ʌv ˈsɪŋɪŋ ɡoːʊz]
Say, love, do you hear me,
[sɛːɪ lʌv du ju hɪːʌ mi]
Hear my sonnets ring?
[hɪːʌ mɑːɪ ˈsanɛ(ɪ)ts ɹɪŋ]
Over the high, brown mountain,
[ˈoːʊvʌ ðʊ hɑːɪ bɹɑːʊn ˈmɑːʊntæ(ɪ)n]
Love, do you hear me, do you hear,
[lʌv du ju hɪːʌ mi du ju hɪːʌ]
Do you hear the song of spring?
[du ju hɪːʌ ðʊ saŋ ʌv spɹɪŋ]

"Song of the Blackbird" (see "The Blackbird"
by Faith)

"Where Go the Boats" (Four Child Songs)
[ʍɛːʌ ɡoːʊ ðʊ boːʊts]
Stevenson, Robert Louis (Sc. 1850-1894)

Dark brown is the river,
[dak bɹɑːʊn ɪz ðʊ ˈɾɪvʌ]
Golden is the sand.
[ˈɡoːʊldɛ(ɪ)n ɪz ðʊ sænd]
It flows along for ever,
[ɪt floːʊz ʌˈlaŋ fɔʁ⁽ⁱ⁾ ˈɛvʌ]

With trees on either hand.
[wɪð tɹiz an ˈɑːɪðʌ hænd]
Green leaves a-floating,
[gɹin livz ʌ ˈfloːʊtɪŋ]
Castles of the foam,
[ˈkasʊlz ʌv ðʊ foːʊm]
Boats of mine a-boating–
[boːʊts ʌv maːɪn ʌ ˈboːʊtɪŋ]
Where will all come home?
[ʍɛːʌ wɪl ɔl kʌm hoːʊm]
On goes the river
[an goːʊz ðʊ ˈɹɪvʌ]
And out past the mill,
[ænd ɑːʊt past ðʊ mɪl]
Away down the valley,
[ʌˈwɛːɪ daːʊn ðʊ ˈvælɪ]
Away down the hill.
[ʌˈwɛːɪ daːʊn ðʊ hɪl]
Away down the river,
[ʌˈwɛːɪ daːʊn ðʊ ˈɹɪvʌ]
A hundred miles or more,
[ʌ ˈhʌndɹɛ(ɪ)d maːɪlz ɔ moːʌ]
Other little children
[ˈʌðʌ ˈlɪtʊl ˈʧɪldɹɛ(ɪ)n]
Shall bring my boats ashore.
[ʃæl bɹɪŋ maːɪ boːʊts ʌˈʃɔːʌ]

"Why So Pale and Wan"
[ʍaːɪ soːʊ pɛːɪl ænd wan]
Suckling, Sir John (Eng. 1609-1642)

Why so pale and wan, fond lover?
[ʍaːɪ soːʊ pɛːɪl ænd wan fand ˈlʌvʌ]
Prithee, why so pale?
[ˈpɹɪðɪ ʍaːɪ soːʊ pɛːɪl]
Will if looking well can't move her,
[wɪl ɪf ˈlʊkɪŋ wɛl kant muv hɜ]
Will thy looking ill prevail?
[wɪl ðaːɪ ˈlʊkɪŋ ɪl pɹɪˈvɛːɪl]
Prithee, why so pale?
[ˈpɹɪðɪ ʍaːɪ soːʊ pɛːɪl]
Why so dull and mute, young sinner?
[ʍaːɪ soːʊ dʌl ænd mjut jʌŋ ˈsɪnʌ]
Prithee, why so mute?
[ˈpɹɪðɪ ʍaːɪ soːʊ mjut]
Will, when speaking well can't win her,
[wɪl ʍɛn ˈspikɪŋ wɛl kant wɪn hɜ]
Will thy saying nothing do't?
[wɪl ðaːɪ ˈsɛːɪɪŋ ˈnʌθɪŋ dut]
Prithee, why so mute?
[ˈpɹɪðɪ ʍaːɪ soːʊ mjut]
Quit, for shame, this will not gain her,
[kwɪt fɔ ʃɛːɪm ðɪs wɪl nat gɛːɪn hɜ]
This will never, never do.
[ðɪs wɪl ˈnɛvʌ ˈnɛvʌ du]

If thy wooing can't attain her,
[ɪf ðaːɪ ˈwuɪŋ kant ʌˈtɛːɪn hɜ]
Then no more, no more, pursue,
[ðɛn noːʊ mɔːʌ noːʊ mɔːʌ pɜˈsju]
Then no more, no more, pursue.
[ðɛn noːʊ mɔːʌ noːʊ mɔːʌ pɜˈsju]

R

 Ragland, Dave (Am. b. 19??)

Song Selections (please visit website - many selections are not included here due to copyright restrictions)

"Balm in Gilead" (see Burleigh)

"I Believe"
[aːɪ bɪˈliv]
Anonymous

I believe in the sun,
[aːɪ bɪˈliv ɪn ðʌ sʌn]
Even when it is not shining,
[ˈivɛ(ɪ)n ʍɛn ɪt ɪz nat ˈʃaːɪnɪŋ]
I believe in love,
[aːɪ bɪˈliv ɪn lʌv]
Even when I feel it not.
[ˈivɛ(ɪ)n ʍɛn aːɪ fil ɪt nat]
I believe in God,
[aːɪ bɪˈliv ɪn gad]
Even when He is silent,
[ˈivɛ(ɪ)n ʍɛn hi ɪz ˈsaːɪlɛnt]
I believe in the sun, in love, in God.
[aːɪ bɪˈliv ɪn ðʌ sʌn ɪn lʌv ɪn gad]

"Steal Away" (see Burleigh)

Rainier, Priaulx (S. Af. 1903-1986)

Cycle for Declamation (Song Cycle)
[ˈsaːɪkʊl fɔ ˌdɛklʌˈmɛːɪʃʌn]
Donne, John (Eng. 1572-1631)

1. Wee Cannot Bid the Fruits
[wi kæˈnat bɪd ðʊ fɹuts]

We cannot bid the fruits come in May,
[wi kæˈnat bɪd ðʊ fɹuts kʌm ɪn mɛːɪ]
nor the leaves to sticke on in December.
[nɔ ðʊ livz tu stɪk an ɪn dɪˈsɛmbʌ]

There are of them that will give,
[ðɛːʌr ɑr ʌv ðem ðæt wɪl gɪv]
that will do justice, that will pardon,
[ðæt wɪl du ˈdʒʌstɪs ðæt wɪl ˈpɑdʌn]
but they have their owne seasons for all these,
[bʌt ðeːɪ hæv ðɛːʌr oːʊn ˈsizʌnz fɔʁ⁽ʳ⁾ ɔl ðiz]
and he that knowes not them,
[ænd hi ðæt noːʊz nɑt ðem]
shall starve before that gift come.
[ʃæl stɑv bɪˈfɔːʌ ðæt gɪft kʌm]
Reward is the season of one man,
[ɹɪˈwɔd ɪz ðʊ ˈsizʌn ʌv wʌn mæn]
and importunitie of another;
[ænd ˌɪmpɔˈtjunɪti ʌv ʌˈnʌðʌ]
feare is the season of one man,
[fiːʌr ɪz ðʊ ˈsizʌn ʌv wʌn mæn]
and favour of another;
[ænd ˈfɛːɪvɔ(ʌ)r ʌv ʌˈnʌðʌ]
friendship the season of one man,
[ˈfɹɛndʃɪp ðʊ ˈsizʌn ʌv wʌn mæn]
and naturall affection of another;
[ænd ˈnætʃʊɾʊl ʌˈfekʃʌn ʌv ʌˈnʌðʌ]
and hee that knowes not their seasons,
[ænd hi ðæt noːʊz nɑt ðɛːʌ ˈsizʌnz]
nor cannot stay them, must lose the fruits.
[nɔ kæˈnɑt stɛːɪ ðem mʌst luz ðʊ fɹuts]

2. In the Wombe of the Earth
[ɪn ðʊ wum ʌv ði ɜθ]

In the wombe of the earth, wee diminish,
[ɪn ðʊ wum ʌv ði ɜθ wi dɪˈmɪnɪʃ]
and when shee is delivered of us,
[ænd ʍɛn ʃi ɪz dɪˈlɪvʌd ʌv ʌs]
our grave opened for another,
[ɑːʊʌ gɹɛːɪv ˈoːʊpɛ(ɪ)nd fɔʁ⁽ʳ⁾ ʌˈnʌðʌ]
wee are not transplanted, but transported, our
[wi ɑ nɑt tɹænˈsplantɛ(ɪ)d bʌt tɹænˈspɔtɛ(ɪ)d ɑːʊʌ]
dust blowne away with prophane dust, with every wind.
[dʌst bloːʊn ʌˈwɛːɪ wɪð pɹoˈfɛːɪn dʌst wɪð ˈɛvɹɪ wɪnd]

3. Nunc, lento, sonitu dicunt, morieris
[nuŋk ˈlɛntɔ sɔˈnitu ˈdikunt mɔriˈɛris]

Nunc, lento, sonitu dicunt, morieris.
[nuŋk ˈlɛntɔ sɔˈnitu ˈdikunt mɔriˈɛris]
The bell doth toll for him that thinks it doth.
[ðʊ bɛl dʌθ toːʊl fɔ hɪm ðæt θɪŋks ɪt dʌθ]
Morieris.
[mɔriˈɛris]
Who casts not up his eye to the sun when it rises?
[hu kɑsts nɑt ʌp hɪz ɑːɪ tu ðʊ sʌn ʍɛn ɪt ˈɹɑːɪzɛ(ɪ)z]
but who takes off his eye from a comet
[bʌt hu tɛːɪks ɑf hɪz ɑːɪ fɹʌm ʌ ˈkɑmɛ(ɪ)t]
when that breaks out?
[ʍɛn ðæt bɹɛːɪks ɑːʊt]

Who bends not his ear to any bell,
[hu bɛndz nɑt hɪz iːʌ tu ˈɛni bɛl]
which upon any occasion rings?
[ʍɪtʃ ʌˈpɑn ˈɛni oˈkɛːɪʒʌn ɹɪŋz]
Morieris.
[mɔriˈɛris]
But who can remove it from that bell which is passing
[bʌt hu kæn ɹɪˈmuv ɪt fɹʌm ðæt bɛl ʍɪtʃ ɪz ˈpɑsɪŋ]
a piece of himself out of this world?
[ʌ pis ʌv hɪmˈsɛlf ɑːʊt ʌv ðɪs wɜld]
Nunc, lento, sonitu dicunt, morieris.
[nuŋk ˈlɛntɔ sɔˈnitu ˈdikunt mɔriˈɛris]
No man is an island, entire of itself;
[noːʊ mæn ɪz æn ˈɑːɪlæ(ʌ)nd ɪnˈtɑːɪʌr ʌv ɪtˈsɛlf]
every man is a piece of the continent,
[ˈɛvɹɪ mæn ɪz ʌ pis ʌv ðʊ ˈkɑntɪnɛnt]
a part of the main.
[ʌ pat ʌv ðʊ mɛːɪn]
If a clod bè washed away by the sea, Europe is the less,
[ɪf ʌ klɑd bi wɑʃt ʌˈwɛːɪ bɑːɪ ðʊ si ˈjʊːʌɾʌp ɪz ðʊ lɛs]
as well as if a promontory were,
[æz wɛl æz ɪf ʌ ˈpɹɑmʌntɹɪ wɜ]
as well as if a manor
[æz wɛl æz ɪf ʌ ˈmænɔ(ʌ)r]
of thy friends or of thine own were.
[ʌv ðɑːɪ fɹɛndz ɔʁ⁽ʳ⁾ ʌv ðɑːɪn oːʊn wɜ]
Morieris.
[mɔriˈɛris]
Any man's death diminishes me,
[ˈɛni mænz dɛθ dɪˈmɪnɪʃɛ(ɪ)z mi]
because I am involved in mankind.
[bɪˈkɔz ɑːɪ æm ɪnˈvɔlvd ɪn mænˈkɑːɪnd]
Morieris.
[mɔriˈɛris]
And therefore never send to know
[ænd ˈðɛːʌfɔːʌ ˈnɛvʌ sɛnd tu noːʊ]
for whom the bell tolls;
[fɔ hum ðʊ bɛl toːʊlz]
it tolls for thee.
[ɪt toːʊlz fɔ ði]
Nunc, lento, sonitu dicunt, morieris.
[nuŋk ˈlɛntɔ sɔˈnitu ˈdikunt mɔriˈɛris]

 # Rhodenizer, Donna (Ca. b. 1961)

Song Selections for Youth

Texts reprinted by permission of Red Castle Publishing
© Donna Rhodenizer. Web: www.donnarhodenizer.com

"Computer Cat"
[kʌmˈpjutʁ kæt]

I was using my computer the other day.
[ɑːɪ wɑz ˈjuzɪŋ mɑːɪ kʌmˈpjutʌ ði ˈʌðʌ dɛːɪ]

I was using my computer in the usual way,
[ɑːɪ waz ˈjuzɪŋ maːɪ kʌmˈpjutʌʁ⁽ʳ⁾ ɪn ðʌ ˈjuʒʊʊl weːɪ]
With my hand on the mouse and the mouse on the pad;
[wɪð maːɪ hænd an ðʌ maːʊs ænd ðʌ maːʊs an ðʌ pæd]
Then something happened,
[ðɛn ˈsʌmθɪŋ ˈhæpɛ⁽ɪ⁾nd]
something that was really bad.
[ˈsʌmθɪŋ ðæt waz ˈɹɪlɪ bæd]
My cat ate the mouse,
[maːɪ kæt ɛːɪt ðʌ maːʊs]
but it's more complicated than that.
[bʌt ɪts mɔːʌ ˈkʌmplɪ ˌkɛːɪtɛ⁽ɪ⁾d ðæn ðæt]
Now I can't use my mouse,
[naːʊ ɑːɪ kænt juz maːɪ maːʊs]
unless I also use my cat.
[ʌnˈlɛs ɑːɪ ˈɔlsoːʊ juz maːɪ kæt]
Now when we want to play computer games
[naːʊ wɛn wi want tu pleːɪ kʌmˈpjutʌ geːɪmz]
it's diff'rent at our house.
[ɪts ˈdɪfɹɛnt æt ɑːʊʌ haːʊs]
We all use a cat, where ordinary people use a mouse.
[wi ɔl juz ʌ kæt weːʌ ˈɔdɪnɛʁ⁽ʳ⁾ɪ ˈpipʊl juz ʌ maːʊs]
I must call, "Kitty, Kitty," and hope she will come,
[ɑːɪ mʌst kɔl ˈkɪtɪ ˈkɪtɪ ænd hoːʊp ʃi wɪl kʌm]
And using my computer is no longer fun.
[ænd ˈjuzɪŋ maːɪ kʌmˈpjutʌʁ⁽ʳ⁾ ɪz noːʊ ˈlaŋgʌ fʌn]
It is hard to get Kitty to lie down and rest
[ɪt ɪz had tu gɛt ˈkɪtɪ tu laːɪ daːʊn ænd ɹɛst]
And it is harder still to push
[ænd ɪt ɪz ˈhadʌ stɪl tu pʊʃ]
that cat around on the desk!
[ðæt kæt ʌˈʁ⁽ʳ⁾aːʊnd an ðʌ dɛsk]
It is highly inconvenient for us and for her,
[ɪt ɪz ˈhaːɪlɪ ɪnkʌnˈvinjɛnt fɔʁ⁽ʳ⁾ ʌs ænd fɔ hɜ]
And it's difficult to point and click
[ænd ɪts ˈdɪfɪkʊlt tu pɔːɪnt ænd klɪk]
through all of that fur.
[θɹu ɔl ʌv ðæt fɜ]
All the same I must say how thankful I am
[ɔl ðʌ sɛːɪm ɑːɪ mʌst sɛːɪ haːʊ ˈθæŋkfʊl ɑːɪ æm]
That she didn't try for bigger prey
[ðæt ʃi ˈdɪdɛ⁽ɪ⁾nt tɹaːɪ fɔ ˈbɪgʌ pɹɛːɪ]
and swallow the 'RAM'!
[ænd ˈswaloːʊ ðʌ ɹæm]

"Ed the Invisible Dragon"
[ɛd ði ɪnˈvɪzɪbʊl ˈdɹægʌn]

I have a dragon and his name is Ed.
[ɑːɪ hæv ʌ ˈdɹægʌn ænd hɪz nɛːɪm ɪz ɛd]
He sleeps in the space at the foot of my bed.
[hi slips ɪn ðʌ spɛːɪs æt ðʌ fʊt ʌv maːɪ bɛd]
He follows along wherever I go,
[hi ˈfaloːʊz ʌˈlaŋ weːʌʁ⁽ʳ⁾ˈɛvʌʁ⁽ʳ⁾ ɑːɪ goːʊ]
But he keeps himself invisible so no one will know.
[bʌt hi kips hɪmˈsɛlf ɪnˈvɪzɪbʊl soːʊ noːʊ wʌn wɪl noːʊ]

He's Ed the invisible dragon,
[hiz ɛd ði ɪnˈvɪzɪbʊl ˈdɹægʌn]
oh where did that dragon go?
[oːʊ weːʌ dɪd ðæt ˈdɹægʌn goːʊ]
When I'm home after school
[wɛn ɑːɪm hoːʊm ˈæftʌ skul]
and I'm looking for a snack,
[ænd ɑːɪm ˈlʊkɪŋ fɔʁ⁽ʳ⁾ ʌ snæk]
It's all I can do to hold Ed back,
[ɪts ɔl ɑːɪ kæn du tu hoːʊld ɛd bæk]
And when the kitchen's in a mess and Mom has a fit,
[ænd wɛn ðʌ ˈkɪtʃɛ⁽ɪ⁾nz ɪn ʌ mɛs ænd mam hæz ʌ fɪt]
I look at Ed and shrug and say, "I didn't do it!"
[ɑːɪ lʊk æt ɛd ænd ʃɹʌg ænd sɛːɪ ɑːɪ ˈdɪdɛ⁽ɪ⁾nt du ɪt]
It was Ed the invisible dragon,
[ɪt waz ɛd ði ɪnˈvɪzɪbʊl ˈdɹægʌn]
It was Ed the invisible dragon,
[ɪt waz ɛd ði ɪnˈvɪzɪbʊl ˈdɹægʌn]
oh where did that dragon go?
[oːʊ weːʌ dɪd ðæt ˈdɹægʌn goːʊ]
Playing in the rec-room with a bat and a ball
[ˈpleːɪɪŋ ɪn ðʌ ɹɛk ɹum wɪð ʌ bæt ænd ʌ bɔl]
A lamp gets smashed but it's not my fault at all
[ʌ læmp gɛts smæʃt bʌt ɪts nat maːɪ fɔlt æt ɔl]
It was Ed who knocked it down
[ɪt waz ɛd hu nakt ɪt daːʊn]
with his pointy, pointy tail,
[wɪð hɪz ˈpɔːɪntɪ ˈpɔːɪntɪ tɛːɪl]
But no one seems to listen
[bʌt noːʊ wʌn simz tu ˈlɪsɛ⁽ɪ⁾n]
when I begin to wail:
[wɛn ɑːɪ bɪˈgɪn tu weːɪl]
It was Ed the invisible dragon,
[ɪt waz ɛd ði ɪnˈvɪzɪbʊl ˈdɹægʌn]
oh where did that dragon go?
[oːʊ weːʌ dɪd ðæt ˈdɹægʌn goːʊ]
So if you notice in your house
[soːʊ ɪf ju ˈnoːʊtɪs ɪn jɔːʌ haːʊs]
that things begin to break
[ðæt θɪŋz bɪˈgɪn tu bɹɛːɪk]
And you've taken all the blame that you can take,
[ænd juv ˈtɛːɪkɛ⁽ɪ⁾n ɔl ðʌ blɛːɪm ðæt ju kæn tɛːɪk]
You might try looking at the foot of your bed
[ju maːɪt tɹaːɪ ˈlʊkɪŋ æt ðʌ fʊt ʌv jɔːʌ bɛd]
Don't be surprised if there you see invisible Ed!
[doːʊnt bi sɜˈpɹaːɪzd ɪf ðɛːʌ ju si ɪnˈvɪzɪbʊl ɛd]
He's Ed the invisible dragon,
[hiz ɛd ði ɪnˈvɪzɪbʊl ˈdɹægʌn]
oh where did that dragon go?
[oːʊ weːʌ dɪd ðæt ˈdɹægʌn goːʊ]

"Forty Little Birdies"
[ˈfɔʁti ˈlɪtʊl ˈbɜdiz]

Forty little birdies sittin' on the wire.
[ˈfɔti ˈlɪtʊl ˈbɜdɪz ˈsɪtɪn an ðʌ waːɪʌ]

Forty little birdies a-practicing for choir.
[ˈfɔtɪ ˈlɪtʊl ˈbɜdɪz ʌ ˈpɹæktɪsɪŋ fɔ ˈkwɑːɪʌ]
Some sing low. Tweet, tweet, tweet.
[sʌm sɪŋ loːʊ twit twit twit]
Some sing higher. Tweet en deet en dee deet.
[sʌm sɪŋ ˈhɑːɪʌ twit ɛn dit ɛn di dit]
All of them together sounding mighty pretty,
[ɔl ʌv ðɛm tuˈgɛðʌ ˈsɑːʊndɪŋ ˈmɑːɪtɪ ˈpɹɪtɪ]
Singin' in the choir on the telephone wire.
[ˈsɪŋɪn ɪn ðʌ ˈkwɑːɪʌʁ⁽ʳ⁾ an ðʌ ˈtɛli(ʌ)foːʊn wɑːɪʌ]
Forty little birdies sittin' on the wire.
[ˈfɔtɪ ˈlɪtʊl ˈbɜdɪz ˈsɪtɪn an ðʌ wɑːɪʌ]
Forty little birdies, all of them retired.
[ˈfɔtɪ ˈlɪtʊl ˈbɜdɪz ɔl ʌv ðɛm ɹɪˈtɑːɪʌd]
They don't work. Tweet, tweet, tweet.
[ðɛːɪ doːʊnt wɜk twit twit twit]
They cannot be fired. Tweet en deet en dee deet.
[ðɛːɪ kæˈnat bi fɑːɪʌd twit ɛn dit ɛn di dit]
If work is for the birds, oh, what an occupation;
[ɪf wɜk ɪz fɔ ðʌ bɜdz oːʊ wat æn akjuˈpɛːɪʃʌn]
Restin' and retirin' on the telephone wire.
[ˈɹɛstɪn ænd ɹɪˈtɑːɪʌʁ⁽ʳ⁾ɪn an ðʌ ˈtɛli(ʌ)foːʊn wɑːɪʌ]
Forty little birdies sittin' on the wire.
[ˈfɔtɪ ˈlɪtʊl ˈbɜdɪz ˈsɪtɪn an ðʌ wɑːɪʌ]
Doin' just whatever their little hearts desire.
[ˈduɪn dʒʌst watˈɛvʌ ðɛːʌ ˈlɪtʊl hats dɪˈzɑːɪʌ]
Chat all day. Tweet, tweet, tweet.
[tʃæt ɔl dɛːɪ twit twit twit]
Read circulars and flyers. Tweet en deet en dee deet.
[ɹid ˈsɜkju(ʌ)lʌz ænd ˈflɑːɪʌz twit ɛn dit ɛn di dit]
Doin' mainly nothin' 'cause nothin' is required;
[ˈduɪn ˈmɛːɪnlɪ ˈnʌθɪn kɔz ˈnʌθɪn ɪz ɹɪˈkwɑːɪʌd]
Visitin' with neighbours on the telephone wire.
[ˈvɪzɪtɪn wɪð ˈnɛːɪbʊ(ʌ)z an ðʌ ˈtɛli(ʌ)foːʊn wɑːɪʌ]

"I Need a Home for My Dinosaur"
[ɑːɪ nid ʌ hoːʊm fɔʁ mɑːɪ ˈdɑːɪnʌsɔːʁ]

I need a home for my dinosaur
[ɑːɪ nid ʌ hoːʊm fɔ mɑːɪ ˈdɑːɪnʌsɔːʌ]
I need it right away.
[ɑːɪ nid ɪt ɹɑːɪt ʌˈwɛːɪ]
I need a home for my dinosaur
[ɑːɪ nid ʌ hoːʊm fɔ mɑːɪ ˈdɑːɪnʌsɔːʌ]
My mom wants to give him away.
[mɑːɪ mam wants tu gɪv hɪm ʌˈwɛːɪ]
I gave him some corn flakes for breakfast
[ɑːɪ gɛːɪv hɪm sʌm kɔn flɛːɪks fɔ ˈbɹɛkfæ(ɪ)st]
In a china bowl with a spoon
[ɪn ʌ ˈtʃɑːɪnʌ boːʊl wɪð ʌ spun]
He sure did love those corn flakes
[hi ʃʊːʌ dɪd lʌv ðoːʊz kɔn flɛːɪks]
But he also ate the spoon.
[bʌt hi ˈɔlsoːʊ ɛːɪt ðʌ spun]
He saw my dad's new slippers
[hi sɔ mɑːɪ dædz nju ˈslɪpʌz]

In his favourite shade of blue
[ɪn hɪz ˈfɛːɪvɔʁ⁽ʳ⁾ɪt ʃɛːɪd ʌv blu]
He ate my dad's new slippers
[hi ɛːɪt mɑːɪ dædz nju ˈslɪpʌz]
Now what am I gonna do?
[nɑːʊ wat æm ɑːɪ ˈgʌnʌ du]
I'd like to let my sister
[ɑːɪd lɑːɪk tu lɛt mɑːɪ ˈsɪstʌ]
Go play in the dinosaur pen
[goːʊ plɛːɪ ɪn ðʌ ˈdɑːɪnʌsɔːʌ pɛn]
Except he'd probably eat her
[ɪkˈsɛpt hid ˈpɹabʌblɪ it hɜ]
And I'd be in trouble again.
[ænd ɑːɪd bi ɪn ˈtɹʌbʊl ʌˈgɛn]
My mom wants to give him away.
[mɑːɪ mam wants tu gɪv hɪm ʌˈwɛːɪ]
My mom wants to give him away.
[mɑːɪ mam wants tu gɪv hɪm ʌˈwɛːɪ]
Anybody want a dinosaur? CHEAP!
[ˈɛnɪbadɪ want ʌ ˈdɑːɪnʌsɔːʌ tʃip]

"I Wonder"
[ɑːɪ ˈwʌndʁ]

I wonder if a penguin has closets
[ɑːɪ ˈwʌndʌʁ⁽ʳ⁾ ɪf ʌ ˈpɛŋgwɪn hæz ˈklazɛ(ɪ)ts]
full of clothes,
[fʊl ʌv kloːʊðz]
To be dressed up so finely
[tu bi dɹɛst ʌp soːʊ ˈfɑːɪnlɪ]
wherever he may go.
[wɛːʌʁ⁽ʳ⁾ˈɛvʌ hi mɛːɪ goːʊ]
You never see him sloppy,
[ju ˈnɛvʌ si hɪm ˈslapɪ]
in sweatshirts or blue jeans.
[ɪn ˈswɛtʃɜts ɔ blu dʒinz]
He's always in a suit coat,
[hiz ˈɔlwɛːɪz ɪn ʌ sjut koːʊt]
all pressed and washed and clean.
[ɔl pɹɛst ænd waʃt ænd klin]
A very tidy eater our penguin friend must be,
[ʌ ˈvɛʁ⁽ʳ⁾ɪ ˈtɑːɪdɪ ˈitʌʁ⁽ʳ⁾ ɑːʊʌ ˈpɛŋgwɪn fɹɛnd mʌst bi]
For spots upon his shirt-front
[fɔ spats ʌˈpan hɪz ʃɜt fɹʌnt]
is something you won't see.
[ɪz ˈsʌmθɪŋ ju woːʊnt si]
Perhaps he wears an apron or a bib upon his chest.
[pɜˈhæps hi wɛːʌz æn ˈɛːɪpɹʌn ɔʁ⁽ʳ⁾ ʌ bɪb ʌˈpan hɪz tʃɛst]
Immaculate perfection, he always looks his best.
[ɪˈmækjulæt pɜˈfɛkʃʌn hi ˈɔlwɛːɪz lʊks hɪz bɛst]
I wonder if a penguin
[ɑːɪ ˈwʌndʌʁ⁽ʳ⁾ ɪf ʌ ˈpɛŋgwɪn]
gets tired of black and white.
[gɛts tɑːɪʌd ʌv blæk ænd wɑːɪt]
I wonder if he ever says,
[ɑːɪ ˈwʌndʌʁ⁽ʳ⁾ ɪf hi ˈɛvʌ sɛz]

"I'm wearing red tonight!"
[ɑːɪm ˈwεːʌʁ⁽ʳ⁾ɪŋ ɹεd tuˈnaːɪt]
But when he checks his closet
[bʌt wεn hi tʃεks hɪz ˈklɑzε⁽ɪ⁾t]
the choice is very plain.
[ðʌ tʃɔːɪs ɪz ˈvεʁ⁽ʳ⁾ɪ plεːɪn]
His options are: wear white and black,
[hɪz ˈɑpʃʌnz ɑ wεːʌ waːɪt ænd blæk]
or black and white again.
[ɔ blæk ænd waːɪt ʌˈgεn]

"I'm Wishing"
[ɑːɪm ˈwɪʃɪŋ]

I'm wishin', oh, I'm wishin',
[ɑːɪm ˈwɪʃɪn oːʊ ɑːɪm ˈwɪʃɪn]
I am wishing very hard.
[ɑːɪ æm ˈwɪʃɪŋ ˈvεʁ⁽ʳ⁾ɪ hɑd]
I'm wishin', oh, I'm wishin'
[ɑːɪm ˈwɪʃɪn oːʊ ɑːɪm ˈwɪʃɪn]
On that distant star.
[ɑn ðæt ˈdɪstæ⁽ɪ⁾nt stɑ]
Know what I would wish for, if you're listening?
[noːʊ wɑt ɑːɪ wʊd wɪʃ fɔ ɪf jɔːʌ ˈlɪsε⁽ɪ⁾nɪŋ]
Know what I would wish for if I could?
[noːʊ wɑt ɑːɪ wʊd wɪʃ fɔʁ⁽ʳ⁾ ɪf ɑːɪ kʊd]
I'd just wish a few, perhaps just one or two,
[ɑːɪd dʒʌst wɪʃ ʌ fju pɜˈhæps dʒʌst wʌn ɔ tu]
I wouldn't waste your time, I'd make them good.
[ɑːɪ ˈwʊdε⁽ɪ⁾nt wεːɪst jɔːʌ taːɪm ɑːɪd mεːɪk ðεm gʊd]
Don't you think we ought to have more laughter?
[doːʊnt ju θɪŋk wi ɔt tu hæv mɔːʌ ˈlæftʌ]
Children playing safely everywhere.
[ˈtʃɪldɹε⁽ɪ⁾n ˈplεːɪŋ ˈsεːɪflɪ ˈεvɹɪwεːʌ]
Peace instead of war, love each other more,
[pis ɪnˈstεd ʌv wɔ lʌv ɪtʃ ˈʌðʌ mɔːʌ]
And then we'd have the world I'm wishing for.
[ænd ðεn wɪd hæv ðʌ wɜld ɑːɪm ˈwɪʃɪŋ fɔ]
I know I am not a famous person;
[ɑːɪ noːʊ ɑːɪ æm nɑt ʌ ˈfεːɪmʌs ˈpɜsʌn]
But still, I am someone who can dream
[bʌt stɪl ɑːɪ æm ˈsʌmwʌn hu kæn dɹim]
That wishes might come true,
[ðæt ˈwɪʃε⁽ɪ⁾z maːɪt kʌm tɹ⁽ʳ⁾u]
and so I'm asking you,
[ænd soːʊ ɑːɪm ˈæskɪŋ ju]
Please won't you try to see what you can do?
[pliz woːʊnt ju tɹɑːɪ tu si wɑt ju kæn du]
I know I have used up all my wishes,
[ɑːɪ noːʊ ɑːɪ hæv juzd ʌp ɔl maːɪ ˈwɪʃε⁽ɪ⁾z]
But I do have one last small request.
[bʌt ɑːɪ du hæv wʌn læst smɔl ɹɪˈkwεst]
Let me do my part, and promise, cross my heart,
[lεt mi du maːɪ pɑt ænd ˈpɹɑmɪs kɹɑs maːɪ hɑt]
To make my world a place worth wishing for.
[tu mεːɪk maːɪ wɜld ʌ plεːɪs wɜθ ˈwɪʃɪŋ fɔ]

"Jolly Sailors"
[ˈdʒɑlɪ ˈsεːɪlʌz]

I am a jolly, jolly soul
[ɑːɪ æm ʌ ˈdʒɑlɪ ˈdʒɑlɪ soːʊl]
and I sail the ocean blue.
[ænd ɑːɪ sεːɪl ði ˈoːʊʃæ⁽ɪ⁾n blu]
I have me a bonny, bonny boat
[ɑːɪ hæv mi ʌ ˈbɑnɪ ˈbɑnɪ boːʊt]
and the very finest crew.
[ænd ðʌ ˈvεʁ⁽ʳ⁾ɪ ˈfɑːɪnε⁽ɪ⁾st kɹ⁽ʳ⁾u]
We sail and sail around the world,
[wi sεːɪl ænd sεːɪl ʌˈʁ⁽ʳ⁾aːʊnd ðʌ wɜld]
adventure is our job;
[ædˈvεntʃʊ⁽ʌ⁾ʁ⁽ʳ⁾ ɪz ɑːʊʌ dʒɑb]
And if any sailor dares complain,
[ænd ɪf ˈεnɪ ˈsεːɪlɔ⁽ʌ⁾ dεːʌz kʌmˈplεːɪn]
the deck, I make them swab.
[ðʌ dεk ɑːɪ mεːɪk ðεm swɑb]
We eat a yummy, runny stew
[wi it ʌ ˈjʌmɪ ˈɹʌnɪ stju]
that the cook prepares each day.
[ðæt ðʌ kʊk pɹɪˈpεːʌz ɪtʃ dεːɪ]
There's all sorts of funny, bumpy lumps,
[ðεːʌz ɔl sɔts ʌv ˈfʌnɪ ˈbʌmpɪ lʌmps]
but we eat it anyway.
[bʌt wi it ɪt ˈεnɪwεːɪ]
We eat and sail around the world
[wi it ænd sεːɪl ʌˈʁ⁽ʳ⁾aːʊnd ðʌ wɜld]
and see what we can see;
[ænd si wɑt wi kæn si]
And there is no better life, we know,
[ænd ðεːʌʁ⁽ʳ⁾ ɪz noːʊ ˈbεtʌ laːɪf wi noːʊ]
than sailing on the sea!
[ðæn ˈsεːɪlɪŋ ɑn ðʌ si]
We sleep in comfy, cozy bunks
[wi slip ɪn ˈkʌmfɪ ˈkoːʊzɪ bʌnks]
when our time on deck is through.
[wεn ɑːʊʌ taːɪm ɑn dεk ɪz θɹu]
We hear lots of loud and snorty snores,
[wi hɪːʌ lɑts ʌv laːʊd ænd ˈsnɔtɪ snɔːʌz]
but there's nothing we can do.
[bʌt ðεːʌz ˈnʌθɪŋ wi kæn du]
We wake up with the rising sun, as happy as can be;
[wi wεːɪk ʌp wɪð ðʌ ˈɹaːɪzɪŋ sʌn æz ˈhæpɪ æz kæn bi]
To be sailing on the open sea, a jolly bunch are we!
[tu bi ˈsεːɪlɪŋ ɑn ði ˈoːʊpε⁽ɪ⁾n si ʌ ˈdʒɑlɪ bʌntʃ ɑ wi]

"Singin' the Blues"
[ˈsɪŋɪn ðʌ bluz]

Please take my bicycle,
[pliz tεːɪk maːɪ ˈbɑːɪsɪkʊl]
my shiny red bicycle.
[maːɪ ˈʃaːɪnɪ ɹεd ˈbɑːɪsɪkʊl]

It's let me down for the very last time.
[ɪts lɛt mi daːʊn fɔ ðʌ 'vɛʁ⁽ʳ⁾ɪ læst taːɪm]
I have skinned both my knees,
[aːɪ hæv skɪnd boːʊθ maːɪ niz]
I'm hurtin', so baby, please,
[aːɪm 'hɜtɪn soːʊ 'beːɪbɪ pliz]
please take my bicycle,
[pliz teːɪk maːɪ 'baːɪsɪkʊl]
I'm singing the blues.
[aːɪm 'sɪŋɪŋ ðʌ bluz]
Please take my chewing gum,
[pliz teːɪk maːɪ 'ʧuɪŋ gʌm]
my very best bubble gum.
[maːɪ 'vɛʁ⁽ʳ⁾ɪ bɛst 'bʌbʊl gʌm]
It's let me down for the very last time.
[ɪts lɛt mi daːʊn fɔ ðʌ 'vɛʁ⁽ʳ⁾ɪ læst taːɪm]
Bubbles have busted,
['bʌbʊlz hæv 'bʌstɛ(ɪ)d]
they cannot be trusted.
[ðeːɪ kæ'nat bi 'tɪʌstɛ(ɪ)d]
Please take my chewing gum,
[pliz teːɪk maːɪ 'ʧuɪŋ gʌm]
I'm singing the blues.
[aːɪm 'sɪŋɪŋ ðʌ bluz]
Bicycles and chewing gum,
['baːɪsɪkʊlz ænd 'ʧuɪŋ gʌm]
busted bubble dreams.
['bʌstɛ(ɪ)d 'bʌbʊl dɪimz]
Age, it makes no matter when
[ɛːɪʤ ɪt meːɪks noːʊ 'mætʌ wɛn]
blue is how everything seems.
[blu ɪz haːʊ 'ɛvɹɪθɪŋ simz]
You see I'm not old enough
[ju si aːɪm nat oːʊld ɪ'nʌf]
To own my own pickup truck
[tu oːʊn maːɪ oːʊn 'pɪk ʌp tɪʌk]
Too young to date and my Momma's not in jail.
[tu jʌŋ tu deːɪt ænd maːɪ 'mamʌz nat ɪn ʤeːɪl]
I don't mind rainy days,
[aːɪ doːʊnt maːɪnd 'ɹeːɪnɪ deːɪz]
my dog has not run away,
[maːɪ dag hæz nat ɹʌn ʌ'weːɪ]
but all the same I am singing the blues.
[bʌt ɔl ðʌ seːɪm aːɪ æm 'sɪŋɪŋ ðʌ bluz]
Oh yeah.
[oːʊ jæʌ]

"Star Above"
[staʁ ʌ'bʌv]

Star above, shine down your light on me.
[staʁ⁽ʳ⁾ ʌ'bʌv ʃaːɪn daːʊn jɔːʌ laːɪt an mi]
Star of love, you speak to all who see.
[staʁ⁽ʳ⁾ ʌv lʌv ju spik tu ɔl hu si]
Come, share with me the light,
[kʌm ʃɛːʌ wɪð mi ðʌ laːɪt]

feel the hope in this dark night.
[fil ðʌ hoːʊp ɪn ðɪs dak naːɪt]
Star above, shine down your light on me.
[staʁ⁽ʳ⁾ ʌ'bʌv ʃaːɪn daːʊn jɔːʌ laːɪt an mi]
Christmas star way up yonder,
['kɪɪsmʌs sta weːɪ ʌp 'jandʌ]
All around the world gonna shine, shine.
[ɔl ʌ'ʁ⁽ʳ⁾aːʊnd ðʌ wɜld 'gʌnʌ ʃaːɪn ʃaːɪn]
Star above, like you I want to be,
[staʁ⁽ʳ⁾ ʌ'bʌv laːɪk ju aːɪ want tu bi]
shining bright for all the world to see.
['ʃaːɪnɪŋ bɪaːɪt fɔʁ⁽ʳ⁾ ɔl ðʌ wɜld tu si]
Sharing with all my might,
['ʃɛːʌʁ⁽ʳ⁾ɪŋ wɪð ɔl maːɪ maːɪt]
hope and love will be my light.
[hoːʊp ænd lʌv wɪl bi maːɪ laːɪt]
Star above, like you, I want to be.
[staʁ⁽ʳ⁾ ʌ'bʌv laːɪk ju aːɪ want tu bi]
Star above, shine down your light on me.
[staʁ⁽ʳ⁾ ʌ'bʌv ʃaːɪn daːʊn jɔːʌ laːɪt an mi]
Star of love, you speak to all who see.
[staʁ⁽ʳ⁾ ʌv lʌv ju spik tu ɔl hu si]
Come, share with me the light,
[kʌm ʃɛːʌ wɪð mi ðʌ laːɪt]
feel the hope in this dark night.
[fil ðʌ hoːʊp ɪn ðɪs dak naːɪt]
Star above, shine down your light on me.
[staʁ⁽ʳ⁾ ʌ'bʌv ʃaːɪn daːʊn jɔːʌ laːɪt an mi]

Rorem, Ned (Am. 1923-2022)

War Scenes (Song Cycle)
[wɔʁ sinz]
Whitman, Walt (Am. 1819-1892)

1. A Night Battle
[ʌ naːɪt 'bætʊl]

What scene is this? –is this indeed humanity –
[ʌat sin ɪz ðɪs ɪz ðɪs ɪn'did hju'mænɪtɪ]
these butchers' shambles?
[ðiz 'bʊʧʌz 'ʃæmbʊlz]
There they lie, in an open space in the woods,
[ðɛːʌ ðeːɪ laːɪ ɪn æn 'oːʊpɛ(ɪ)n speːɪs ɪn ðʌ wʊdz]
Three hundred poor fellows, The groans and screams
[θri 'hʌndɪɛ(ɪ)d pʊːʌ 'fɛloːʊz ðʌ gɪ⁽ʳ⁾oːʊnz ænd skɪimz]
mixed with the fresh scent of the night,
[mɪkst wɪð ðʌ fɪɛʃ sɛnt ʌv ðʌ naːɪt]
that slaughter-house! O well it is
[ðæt 'slɔtʌ haːʊs oːʊ wɛl ɪt ɪz]
their mothers cannot see them.
[ðɛːʌ 'mʌðʌz kæ'nat si ðɛm]
Some have their legs blown off,
[sʌm hæv ðɛːʌ lɛgz bloːʊn af]

some bullets through the breast,
[sʌm ˈbʊlɛ(ɪ)ts θru ðʌ bɹɛst]
some indescribably horrid wounds –
[sʌm ɪndɪsˈkɹɑːɪbʌblɪ ˈhɔʁ⁽ʳ⁾ɪd wundz]
in the face or head, all mutilated,
[ɪn ðʌ fɛːɪs ɔ hɛd ɔl ˈmjutɪlɛːɪtɛ(ɪ)d]
sickening, torn, gouged out, some mere boys, –
[ˈsɪkɛ(ɪ)nɪŋ tɔn gɑːʊdʒd ɑːʊt sʌm mɪːʌ bɔːɪz]
they take their turns with the rest.
[ðɛːɪ tɛːɪk ðɛːʌ tɜnz wɪð ðʌ ɹɛst]
Such is the camp of the wounded,
[sʌtʃ ɪz ðʌ kæmp ʌv ðʌ ˈwundɛ(ɪ)d]
while over all the clear,
[ʍɑːɪl ˈoːʊvʌʁ⁽ʳ⁾ ɔl ðʌ klɪːʌ]
large moon comes out at times softly,
[lɑdʒ mun kʌmz ɑːʊt æt tɑːɪmz ˈsaftlɪ]
amid the crack and crash – and yelling sounds. –
[ʌˈmɪd ðʌ kɹ⁽ʳ⁾æk ænd kɹ⁽ʳ⁾æʃ ænd ˈjɛlɪŋ sɑːʊndz]
the clear obscure up there,
[ðʌ klɪːʌʁ⁽ʳ⁾ ʌbˈskjʊːʁ⁽ʳ⁾ ʌp ðɛːʌ]
those buoyant upper oceans,
[ðoːʊz ˈbɔːɪæ(ɪ)nt ˈʌpʌʁ⁽ʳ⁾ ˈoːʊʃæ(ɪ)nz]
a few large placid stars beyond,
[ʌ fju lɑdʒ ˈplæsɪd staz bɪˈjand]
coming languidly out, then disappearing,
[ˈkʌmɪŋ ˈlæŋgwɪdlɪ ɑːʊt ðɛn ˌdɪsʌˈpɪːʌʁ⁽ʳ⁾ɪŋ]
the melancholy, draperied night around.
[ðʌ ˈmɛlæ(ɪ)n ˌkalɪ ˈdɹɛːɪpʌʁ⁽ʳ⁾ɪd nɑːɪt ʌˈʁ⁽ʳ⁾ɑːʊnd]
And there, upon the roads and in those woods,
[ænd ðɛːʌʁ⁽ʳ⁾ ʌˈpɑn ðʌ ɹoːʊdz ænd ɪn ðoːʊz wʊdz]
that contest, never one more desperate
[ðæt ˈkɑntɛst ˈnɛvʌ wʌn mɔːʌ ˈdɛspʌʁ⁽ʳ⁾æ(ɪ)t]
in any age or land.
[ɪn ˈɛnɪ ɛːɪdʒ ɔ lænd]
What history can ever give
[ʍat ˈhɪstɔʁ⁽ʳ⁾ɪ kæn ˈɛvʌ gɪv]
(for who can know) the mad,
[fɔ hu kæn noːʊ ðʌ mæd]
determin'd tussle of the armies?
[dɪˈtɜmɪnd ˈtʌsʊl ʌv ði ˈɑmɪz]
Who knows the many conflicts in
[hu noːʊz ðʌ ˈmɛnɪ ˈkanflɪkts ɪn]
flashing moonbeam'd woods, the
[ˈflæʃɪŋ ˈmunbimd wʊdz ðʌ]
writhing squads, the cries, the din,
[ˈɹɑːɪðɪŋ skwadz ðʌ kɹ⁽ʳ⁾ɑːɪz ðʌ dɪn]
the distant cannon, the –
[ðʌ ˈdɪstæ(ɪ)nt ˈkænʌn ðʌ]
cheers and calls and threats
[tʃɪːʌz ænd kɔlz ænd θɹɛts]
and awful music of the oaths,
[ænd ˈɔfʊl ˈmjuzɪk ʌv ði oːʊðz]
the indescribable mix,– the officers' orders,
[ði ɪndɪsˈkɹɑːɪbʌbʊl mɪks ði ˈafɪsʌz ˈɔdʌz]
the devils fully rous'd in human hearts,–
[ðʌ ˈdɛvɪ(ʊ)lz ˈfʊlɪ ɹɑːʊzd ɪn ˈhjumæ(ʌ)n hats]

the strong shout, Charge, men, charge.
[ðʌ stɹaŋ ʃɑːʊt tʃɑdʒ mɛn tʃɑdʒ]
And still again the moonlight pouring
[ænd stɪl ʌˈgɛn ðʌ ˈmunlɑːɪt ˈpɔːʌʁ⁽ʳ⁾ɪŋ]
silvery soft its radiant patches over all.
[ˈsɪlvʌʁ⁽ʳ⁾ɪ saft ɪts ˈɹɛːɪdɪæ(ɪ)nt ˈpætʃɛ(ɪ)z ˈoːʊvʌʁ⁽ʳ⁾ ɔl]
Who paint the scene,
[hu pɛːɪnt ðʌ sin]
the sudden partial panic of the afternoons, at dusk?
[ðʌ ˈsʌdɛ(ɪ)n ˈpaʃʊl ˈpænɪk ʌv ði æftʌˈnunz æt dʌsk]

2. A Specimen Case
[ʌ ˈspɛsɪmɪn kɛːɪs]

Poor youth, so handsome, athletic,
[pʊːʌ juθ soːʊ ˈhænsʌm æθˈlɛtɪk]
with profuse shining hair.
[wɪð pɹoˈfjus ˈʃɑːɪnɪŋ hɛːʌ]
One time as I sat looking at him
[wʌn tɑːɪm æz ɑːɪ sæt ˈlʊkɪŋ æt hɪm]
while he lay asleep, he suddenly,
[ʍɑːɪl hi lɛːɪ ʌˈslip hi ˈsʌdɛ(ɪ)nlɪ]
without the least start, awaken'd,
[wɪðˈɑːʊt ðʌ list stat ʌˈwɛːɪkɛ(ɪ)nd]
open'd his eyes, gave me a long steady look,
[ˈoːʊpɛ(ɪ)nd hɪz ɑːɪz gɛːɪv mi ʌ laŋ ˈstɛdɪ lʊk]
turning his face very slightly to gaze easier,
[ˈtɜnɪŋ hɪz fɛːɪs ˈvɛʁ⁽ʳ⁾ɪ ˈslɑːɪtlɪ tu gɛːɪz ˈizɪʌ]
one long, clear, silent look, a slight sigh,
[wʌn laŋ klɪːʌ ˈsɑːɪlɛnt lʊk ʌ slɑːɪt sɑːɪ]
then turn'd back and went into his doze – again.
[ðɛn tɜnd bæk ænd wɛnt ˈɪntu hɪz doːʊz ʌˈgɛn]
Little he knew, poor death-stricken boy,
[ˈlɪtʊl hi nju pʊːʌ dɛθ ˈstɹɪkɛ(ɪ)n bɔːɪ]
the heart of the stranger that hover'd near.
[ðʌ hat ʌv ðʌ ˈstɹɛːɪndʒʌ ðæt ˈhʌvʌd nɪːʌ]

3. An Incident
[æn ˈɪnsɪdɛnt]

In one of the fights before Atlanta,
[ɪn wʌn ʌv ðʌ fɑːɪts bɪˈfɔːʁ⁽ʳ⁾ ætˈlæntʌ]
a rebel soldier, of large size,
[ʌ ˈɹɛbʊl ˈsoːʊldʒʌʁ⁽ʳ⁾ ʌv lɑdʒ sɑːɪz]
evidently a young man,
[ɛvɪˈdɛntlɪ ʌ jʌŋ mæn]
was mortally wounded top of head,
[waz ˈmɔtʊlɪ ˈwundɛ(ɪ)d tap ʌv hɛd]
so that the brains partially exuded.
[soːʊ ðæt ðʌ bɹɛːɪnz ˈpaʃʊlɪ ɪgˈzjudɛ(ɪ)d]
He lived three days,
[hi lɪvd θri dɛːɪz]
lying on his back – on the spot where – he first – dropt.
[ˈlɑːɪɪŋ an hɪz bæk an ðʌ spat ʍɛːʌ hi fɜst dɹapt]
He dug with his heel – in the ground – during that time
[hi dʌg wɪð hɪz hil ɪn ðʌ gɹɑːʊnd ˈdjʊːʁ⁽ʳ⁾ɪŋ ðæt tɑːɪm]

a hole – big enough to put in
[ʌ hoːʊl bɪg ɪˈnʌf tu pʊt ɪn]
a couple of ordinary knapsacks.
[ʌ ˈkʌpʊl ʌv ˈɔdɪnɛʁ⁽ʳ⁾ɪ næpsæks]
He just lay there in the open air,
[hi dʒʌst lɛːɪ ðɛːʌʁ⁽ʳ⁾ ɪn ði ˈoːʊpɛ⁽ɪ⁾n ɛːʌʁ⁽ʳ⁾]
and with little intermission kept his heel going
[ænd wɪð ˈlɪtʊl ˌɪntʌˈmɪʃʌn kɛpt hɪz hil ˈgoːʊɪŋ]
night and day.
[naːɪt ænd dɛːɪ]
Some of our soldiers then moved him to a house,
[sʌm ʌv ɑːʊʌ ˈsoːʊldʒʌz ðɛn muvd hɪm tu ʌ haːʊs]
but he died – in a few minutes.
[bʌt hi daːɪd ɪn ʌ fju ˈmɪnɪ⁽ʌ⁾ts]

4. Inauguration Ball
[ɪnˈɔgjʊʁɛːɪʃʌn bɔl]

At the dance and supper room –
[æt ðʌ dæns ænd ˈsʌpʌ ʁ⁽ʳʳ⁾um]
I could not help thinking,
[ɑːɪ kʊd nat hɛlp ˈθɪŋkɪŋ]
what a different scene they presented –
[ʍat ʌ ˈdɪfʌʁ⁽ʳ⁾ent sin ðɛːɪ pʌɪˈzɛntɛ⁽ɪ⁾d]
to my view a while since.
[tu maːɪ vju ʌ ʍaːɪl sɪns]
Filled with a crowded mass of the worst wounded
[fɪld wɪð ʌ ˈkʌɑːʊdɛ⁽ɪ⁾d mæs ʌv ðʌ wɜst ˈwundɛ⁽ɪ⁾d]
of the war.
[ʌv ðʌ wɔ]
Tonight, beautiful women, perfumes,
[tuˈnaːɪt ˈbjutɪfʊl ˈwɪmɛ⁽ɪ⁾n pɜˈfjumz]
the violins' sweetness, the polka and the waltz;
[ðʌ vɑːɪoˈlɪnz ˈswitnɛ⁽ɪ⁾s ðʌ ˈpoːʊlka ænd ðʌ wɔlts]
Then the amputation, the blue face, the groan,
[ðɛn ði æmpjuˈtɛːɪʃʌn ðʌ blu fɛːɪs ðʌ gʌɪ⁽ʳ⁾oːʊn]
the glassy eye of the dying, the clotted rag,
[ðʌ ˈglæsɪ ɑːɪ ʌv ðʌ ˈdaːɪɪŋ ðʌ ˈklatɛ⁽ɪ⁾d ʌæg]
the odor of blood,
[ði ˈoːʊdɔ⁽ʌ⁾ʁ⁽ʳ⁾ ʌv blʌd]
And many a mother's son amid strangers,
[ænd ˈmɛnɪ ʌ ˈmʌðʌz sʌn ʌˈmɪd ˈstʌɛːɪndʒʌz]
passing away untended there.
[ˈpæsɪŋ ʌˈwɛːɪ ʌnˈtɛndɛ⁽ɪ⁾d ðɛːʌ]

5. The Real War Will Never Get in the Books
[ðʌ ʌɪːʌl wɔʁ wɪl ˈnɛvʁ gɛt ɪn ðʌ bʊks]

And so good-bye to the war.
[ænd soːʊ gʊd baːɪ tu ðʌ wɔ]
I know not how it may have been to others.
[ɑːɪ noːʊ nat haːʊ ɪt mɛːɪ hæv bɪn tu ˈʌðʌz]
To me the main interest
[tu mi ðʌ mɛːɪn ˈɪntʌʁ⁽ʳ⁾ɛ⁽ɪ⁾st]
was in the rank and file of the armies,
[waz ɪn ðʌ ʌæŋk ænd faːɪl ʌv ði ˈɑmɪz]

both sides, and even the dead on the field.
[boːʊθ saːɪdz ænd ˈivɛ⁽ɪ⁾n ðʌ dɛd an ðʌ fild]
The points illustrating the latent character
[ðʌ pɔːɪnts ˈɪlʌstʌɛːɪtɪŋ ðʌ ˈlɛːɪtɛnt ˈkæʁ⁽ʳ⁾æ⁽ɪ⁾ktʌ]
of the American young
[ʌv ði ʌˈmɛʁ⁽ʳ⁾ɪkʌn jʌŋ]
were of more significance
[wɜ⁽ʳ⁾ ʌv mɔː sɪgˈnɪfɪkæ⁽ɪ⁾ns]
than the political interests involved.
[ðæn ðʌ poˈlɪtɪkʊl ˈɪntʌɛ⁽ɪ⁾sts ɪnˈvɔlvd]
Future years will never know the seething hell
[ˈfjuʧʊ⁽ʌ⁾ jɪːʌz wɪl ˈnɛvʌ noːʊ ðʌ ˈsiðɪŋ hɛl]
of countless minor scenes.
[ʌv ˈkaːʊntlɛ⁽ɪ⁾s ˈmaːɪnɔ⁽ʌ⁾ sinz]
The real war will never get in the books,
[ðʌ ʌɪːʌl wɔ wɪl ˈnɛvʌ gɛt ɪn ðʌ bʊks]
perhaps must not and should not be.
[pɜˈhæps mʌst nat ænd ʃʊd nat bi]
The whole land, North and South,
[ðʌ hoːʊl lænd nɔθ ænd saːʊθ]
was one vast hospital, greater (like life's)
[waz wʌn væst ˈhaspɪtʊl ˈgʌɛːɪtʌ laːɪk laːɪfs]
than the few distortions ever told.
[ðæn ðʌ fju dɪˈstɔʃʌnz ˈɛvʌ toːʊld]
Think how much, and of importance,
[θɪŋk haːʊ mʌʧ ænd ʌv ɪmˈpɔtæ⁽ɪ⁾ns]
will be, – has already been– buried in the grave.
[wɪl bi hæz ɔlˈʌɛdɪ bɪn ˈbɛʁ⁽ʳ⁾ɪd ɪn ðʌ gʌɪ⁽ʳ⁾ɛːɪv]

Song Selections

"Ferry Me Across the Water" (Nantucket Songs)
[ˈfɛʁɪ mi ʌˈkʌɑs ðʌ ˈwɔtʁ]
Rossetti, Christina Georgina (Eng. 1830-1894)

"Ferry me across the water, Do, boatman, do."
[ˈfɛʁ⁽ʳ⁾ɪ mi ʌˈkʌɑs ðʌ ˈwɔtʌ du ˈboːʊtmæ⁽ʌ⁾n du]
"If you've a penny in your purse, I'll ferry you."
[ɪf juv ʌ ˈpɛnɪ ɪn jɔːʌ pɜs ɑːɪl ˈfɛʁ⁽ʳ⁾ɪ ju]
"I have a penny in my purse, And my eyes are blue;
[ɑːɪ hæv ʌ ˈpɛnɪ ɪn maːɪ pɜs ænd maːɪ ɑːɪz a blu]
So ferry me across the water, Do, boatman, do!"
[soːʊ ˈfɛʁ⁽ʳ⁾ɪ mi ʌˈkʌɑs ðʌ ˈwɔtʌ du ˈboːʊtmæ⁽ʌ⁾n du]
"Step into my ferry-boat, Be they black or blue,
[stɛp ˈɪntu maːɪ ˈfɛʁ⁽ʳ⁾ɪ boːʊt bi ðɛːɪ blæk ɔ blu]
And for the penny in your purse I'll ferry you."
[ænd fɔ ðʌ ˈpɛnɪ ɪn jɔːʌ pɜs ɑːɪl ˈfɛʁ⁽ʳ⁾ɪ ju]

"Gliding O'er All"
[ˈglaːɪdɪŋ ɔːʁ ɔl]
Whitman, Walt (Am. 1819-1892)

Gliding o'er all, through all,
[ˈglaːɪdɪŋ ɔːʌʁ⁽ʳ⁾ ɔl θʌu ɔl]
Through Nature, Time, and Space,
[θʌu ˈnɛːɪʧʊ⁽ʌ⁾ taːɪm ænd spɛːɪs]

As a ship on waters advancing,
[æz ʌ ʃɪp ɑn ˈwɔtʌz æd ˈvænsɪŋ]
The voyage of the soul–not Life alone,
[ðʌ ˈvɔːɪæ(ɪ)ʤ ʌv ðʌ soːʊl nɑt lɑːɪf ʌˈloːʊn]
Death, many deaths I'll sing.
[dɛθ ˈmɛnɪ dɛθs ɑːɪl sɪŋ]

"Go, Lovely Rose" (Nantucket Songs)
[goːʊ ˈlʌvli ɹoːʊz]
Waller, Edmund (Eng. 1608-1687)
and Henry Kirke White (1785-1806)

Go, lovely Rose
[goːʊ ˈlʌvlɪ ɹoːʊz]
Tell her, that wastes her time and me,
[tɛl hɜ ðæt weːɪsts hɜ tɑːɪm ænd mi]
That now she knows,
[ðæt nɑːʊ ʃi noːʊz]
When I resemble her to thee,
[ʍɛn ɑːɪ ɹɪˈzɛmbʊl hɜ tu ði]
How sweet and fair she seems to be.
[hɑːʊ swit ænd feːʌ ʃi simz tu bi]
Tell her that's young,
[tɛl hɜ ðæts jʌŋ]
And shuns to have her graces spied,
[ænd ʃʌnz tu hæv hɜ ˈɡɹeːɪsɛ(ɪ)z spɑːɪd]
That hadst thou sprung
[ðæt hædst ðɑːʊ spɹʌŋ]
In deserts where no men abide,
[ɪn ˈdɛzʌts ʍeːʌ noːʊ mɛn ʌˈbɑːɪd]
Thou must have uncommended died.
[ðɑːʊ mʌst hæv ʌnkʌˈmɛndɛ(ɪ)d dɑːɪd]
Small is the worth
[smɔl ɪz ðʌ wɜθ]
Of beauty from the light retired:
[ʌv ˈbjutɪ fɹʌm ðʌ lɑːɪt ɹɪˈtɑːɪd]
Bid her come forth,
[bɪd hɜ kʌm fɔθ]
Suffer herself to be desired,
[ˈsʌfʌ hɜˈsɛlf tu bi dɪˈzaːɪɹd]
And not blush so to be admired.
[ænd nɑt blʌʃ soːʊ tu bi ædˈmɑːɪɹd]
Then die that she
[ðɛn dɑːɪ ðæt ʃi]
The common fate of all things rare
[ðʌ ˈkɑmʌn feːɪt ʌv ɔl θɪŋz ɹeːʌ]
May read in thee:
[meːɪ ɹid ɪn ði]
How small a part of time they share
[hɑːʊ smɔl ʌ pɑt ʌv tɑːɪm ðeːɪ ʃeːʌ]
That are so wondrous sweet and fair!
[ðæt ɑ soːʊ ˈwʌndɹʌs swit ænd feːʌ]

"I Am Rose"
[ɑːɪ æm ɹoːʊz]
Stein, Gertrude (Am. 1874-1946)

I am Rose my eyes are blue
[ɑːɪ æm ɹoːʊz mɑːɪ ɑːɪz a blu]
I am Rose and who are you?
[ɑːɪ æm ɹoːʊz ænd hu a ju]
I am Rose and when I sing
[ɑːɪ æm ɹoːʊz ænd ʍɛn ɑːɪ sɪŋ]
I am Rose like anything.
[ɑːɪ æm ɹoːʊz lɑːɪk ˈɛnɪθɪŋ]

"In a Gondola"
[ɪn ʌ ˈɡɑndʌlʌ]
Browning, Robert (Eng. 1812-1889)

The moth's kiss, first!
[ðʌ mɑðz kɪs fɜst]
Kiss me as if you made me believe
[kɪs mi æz ɪf ju meːɪd mi bɪˈliv]
You were not sure, this eve,
[ju wɜ nɑt ʃʊːʌ ðɪs iv]
How my face, your flower, had pursed
[hɑːʊ mɑːɪ feːɪs jɔːʌ flɑːʊʌ hæd pɜst]
Its petals up; so, here and there
[ɪts ˈpɛtʊlz ʌp soːʊ hɪːʌɾ ænd ðeːʌ]
You brush it, till I grow aware
[ju bɹʌʃ ɪt tɪl ɑːɪ ɡɹoːʊ ʌˈweːʌ]
Who wants me, and wide ope I burst.
[hu wɑnts mi ænd waːɪd oːʊp ɑːɪ bɜst]
The bee's kiss, now!
[ðʌ biz kɪs nɑːʊ]
Kiss me as if you enter'd gay
[kɪs mi æz ɪf ju ˈɛntʌd ɡeːɪ]
My heart at some noonday,
[mɑːɪ hɑt æt sʌm ˈnundeːɪ]
A bud that dares not disallow
[ʌ bʌd ðæt deːʌz nɑt dɪsʌˈlɑːʊ]
The claim, so all is render'd up,
[ðʌ kleːɪm soːʊ ɔl ɪz ˈɹɛndʌd ʌp]
And passively its shatter'd cup
[ænd ˈpæsɪvlɪ ɪts ˈʃætʌd kʌp]
Over your head to sleep I bow.
[ˈoːʊvʌ jɔːʌ hɛd tu slip ɑːɪ bɑːʊ]

"Little Elegy" (Six Songs)
[ˈlɪtʊl ˈɛlɪʤi]
Wylie, Elinor (Am. 1885-1928)

Without you, No rose can grow:
[wɪðˈaːʊt ju noːʊ ɹoːʊz kæn ɡɹoːʊ]
No leaf be green, If never seen
[noːʊ lif bi ɡɹin ɪf ˈnɛvʌ sin]
Your sweetest face; No bird have grace
[jɔːʌ ˈswitɛ(ɪ)st feːɪs noːʊ bɜd hæv ɡɹeːɪs]

Or power to sing; Or anything
[ɔ pɑːʊʌ tu sɪŋ ɔʁ⁽ʳ⁾ ˈɛnɪθɪŋ]
Be kind, or fair, And you nowhere.
[bi kɑːɪnd ɔ fɛːʌ ænd ju ˈnoːʊʍɛːʌ]

"Look Down, Fair Moon"
[lʊk dɑːʊn fɛːʁ mun]
Whitman, Walt (Am. 1819-1892)

Look down, fair moon, and bathe this scene,
[lʊk dɑːʊn fɛːʌ mun ænd bɛːɪð ðɪs sin]
Pour softly down night's nimbus floods
[pɔːʌ ˈsɑftlɪ dɑːʊn nɑːɪts ˈnɪmbʌs flʌdz]
on faces ghastly, swollen, purple,
[ɑn ˈfɛːɪsɛ⁽ɪ⁾z ˈgæstlɪ ˈswoːʊlɛ⁽ɪ⁾n ˈpɜpʊl]
On the dead on their backs with arms toss'd wide,
[ɑn ðʌ dɛd ɑn ðɛːʌ bæks wɪð ɑmz tɑst wɑːɪd]
Pour down your unstinted nimbus,
[pɔːʌ dɑːʊn jɔːʌʁ⁽ʳ⁾ ʌnˈstɪntɛ⁽ɪ⁾d ˈnɪmbʌs]
sacred moon.
[ˈsɛːɪkɹɛ⁽ɪ⁾d mun]

"Love"
[lʌv]
Lodge, Thomas (Eng. 1558-1625)

Turn I my looks unto the skies,
[tɜn ɑːɪ mɑːɪ lʊks ˈʌntu ðʌ skɑːɪz]
Love with his arrows wounds my eyes;
[lʌv wɪð hɪz ˈæʁ⁽ʳ⁾oːʊz wundz mɑːɪ ɑːɪz]
If so I gaze upon the ground,
[ɪf soːʊ ɑːɪ gɛːɪz ʌˈpɑn ðʌ gɹɑːʊnd]
Love then in every flower is found;
[lʌv ðɛn ɪn ˈɛvɹɪ flɑːʊʁ⁽ʳ⁾ ɪz fɑːʊnd]
Search I the shade to fly my pain,
[sɜʧ ɑːɪ ðʌ ʃɛːɪd tu flɑːɪ mɑːɪ pɛːɪn]
Love meets me in the shade again;
[lʌv mits mi ɪn ðʌ ʃɛːɪd ʌˈgɛn]
Want I to walk in secret grove,
[wɑnt ɑːɪ tu wɔk ɪn ˈsikɹɛ⁽ɪ⁾t gɹoːʊv]
E'en there I meet with sacred love;
[ˈiːn ðɛːʌʁ⁽ʳ⁾ ɑːɪ mit wɪð ˈsɛːɪkɹɛ⁽ɪ⁾d lʌv]
If so I bathe me in the spring,
[ɪf soːʊ ɑːɪ bɛːɪð mi ɪn ðʌ spɹɪŋ]
E'en on the brink I hear him sing;
[ˈiːn ɑn ðʌ bɹɪŋk ɑːɪ hɪːʌ hɪm sɪŋ]
If so I meditate alone,
[ɪf soːʊ ɑːɪ ˈmɛdɪtɛːɪt ʌˈloːʊn]
He will be partner to my moan;
[hi wɪl bi ˈpɑtnʌ tu mɑːɪ moːʊn]
If so I mourn, he weeps with me,
[ɪf soːʊ ɑːɪ mɔn hi wips wɪð mi]
And where I am there will he be.
[ænd ʍɛːʌʁ⁽ʳ⁾ ɑːɪ æm ðɛːʌ wɪl hi bi]

"Mother, I Cannot Mind My Wheel" (see Barber)

"O Do Not Love Too Long"
[oːʊ du nɑt lʌv tu lɑŋ]
Yeats, William Butler (Ir. 1865-1939)

Sweetheart, do not love too long:
[ˈswithɑt du nɑt lʌv tu lɑŋ]
I loved long and long,
[ɑːɪ lʌvd lɑŋ ænd lɑŋ]
And grew to be out of fashion
[ænd gɹ⁽ʳ⁾u tu bi ɑːʊt ʌv ˈfæʃʌn]
Like an old song.
[lɑːɪk æn oːʊld sɑŋ]
All through the years of our youth
[ɔl θru ðʌ jɪːʌz ʌv ɑːʊʌ juθ]
Neither could have known
[ˈnɑːɪðʌ kʊd hæv noːʊn]
Their own thought from the other's,
[ðɛːʌʁ⁽ʳ⁾ oːʊn θɔt fɹʌm ði ˈʌðʌz]
We were so much at one.
[wi wɜ soːʊ mʌʧ æt wʌn]
But O, in a minute she changed–
[bʌt oːʊ ɪn ʌ ˈmɪnʌt ʃi ʧɛːɪndʒd]
O do not love too long,
[oːʊ du nɑt lʌv tu lɑŋ]
Or you will grow out of fashion
[ɔ ju wɪl gɹoːʊ ɑːʊt ʌv ˈfæʃʌn]
Like an old song.
[lɑːɪk æn oːʊld sɑŋ]

"Reconciliation" [ˌɹɛkʌnsɪliˈɛːɪʃʌn]
Whitman, Walt (Am. 1819-1892)

Word over all, beautiful as the sky!
[wɜd ˈoːʊvʌʁ⁽ʳ⁾ ɔl ˈbjutɪfʊl æz ðʌ skɑːɪ]
Beautiful that war, and all its deeds of carnage,
[ˈbjutɪfʊl ðæt wɔʁ⁽ʳ⁾ ænd ɔl ɪts didz ʌv ˈkɑnæ⁽ɪ⁾dʒ]
must in time be utterly lost;
[mʌst ɪn tɑːɪm bi ˈʌtʌlɪ lɑst]
That the hands of the sisters Death and Night,
[ðæt ðʌ hændz ʌv ðʌ ˈsɪstʌz dɛθ ænd nɑːɪt]
incessantly softly wash again,
[ɪnˈsɛsæ⁽ɪ⁾ntlɪ ˈsɑftlɪ wɑʃ ʌˈgɛn]
and ever again, this soiled world:
[ænd ˈɛvʌʁ⁽ʳ⁾ ʌˈgɛn ðɪs sɔːɪld wɜld]
For my enemy is dead–
[fɔ mɑːɪ ˈɛnɪ(ʌ)mɪ ɪz dɛd]
a man divine as myself is dead;
[ʌ mæn dɪˈvɑːɪn æz mɑːɪˈsɛlf ɪz dɛd]
I look where he lies, white-faced and still,
[ɑːɪ lʊk ʍɛːʌ hi lɑːɪz ʍɑːɪt fɛːɪst ænd stɪl]
in the coffin– I draw near;
[ɪn ðʌ ˈkɑfɪn ɑːɪ dɹɔ nɪːʌ]
Bend down, and touch lightly
[bɛnd dɑːʊn ænd tʌʧ ˈlɑːɪtlɪ]
with my lips the white face in the coffin.
[wɪð mɑːɪ lɪps ðʌ ʍɑːɪt fɛːɪs ɪn ðʌ ˈkɑfɪn]

"Rondelay"
[ˈɹɑːʊndɪlɛːɪ]
Dryden, John (Eng. 1631-1700)

Chloe found Amyntas lying,
[ˈkloːʊɪ fɑːʊnd əˈmɪntəs ˈlɑːɪŋ]
All in tears, upon the plain,
[ɔl ɪn tɪːʌz ʌˈpɑn ðʌ pleːɪn]
Sighing to himself, and crying,
[ˈsɑːɪŋ tu hɪmˈsɛlf ænd ˈkɹ⁽ʳ⁾ɑːɪŋ]
Wretched I, to love in vain!
[ˈɹɛtʃɛ⁽ɪ⁾d ɑːɪ tu lʌv ɪn veːɪn]
Kiss me, Dear, before my dying;
[kɪs mi dɪːʌ bɪˈfɔːʌ mɑːɪ ˈdɑːɪŋ]
Kiss me once, and ease my pain.
[kɪs mi wʌns ænd iz mɑːɪ peːɪn]
Sighing to himself and crying,
[ˈsɑːɪŋ tu hɪmˈsɛlf ænd ˈkɹ⁽ʳ⁾ɑːɪŋ]
Wretched I, to love in vain!
[ˈɹɛtʃɛ⁽ɪ⁾d ɑːɪ tu lʌv ɪn veːɪn]
Ever scorning, and denying
[ˈɛvʌ ˈskɔnɪŋ ænd dɪˈnɑːɪŋ]
To reward your faithful Swain:
[tu ɹɪˈwɔd jɔːʌ ˈfeːɪθfʊl sweːɪn]
Kiss me, Dear, before my dying;
[kɪs mi dɪːʌ bɪˈfɔːʌ mɑːɪ ˈdɑːɪŋ]
Kiss me once, and ease my pain!
[kɪs mi wʌns ænd iz mɑːɪ peːɪn]
Ever scorning and denying
[ˈɛvʌ ˈskɔnɪŋ ænd dɪˈnɑːɪŋ]
To reward your faithful Swain.
[tu ɹɪˈwɔd jɔːʌ ˈfeːɪθfʊl sweːɪn]
Chloe laughing at his crying,
[ˈkloːʊɪ ˈlæfɪŋ æt hɪz ˈkɹ⁽ʳ⁾ɑːɪŋ]
Told him that he lov'd in vain:
[toːʊld hɪm ðæt hi lʌvd ɪn veːɪn]
Kiss me once, before my dying:
[kɪs mi wʌns bɪˈfɔːʌ mɑːɪ ˈdɑːɪŋ]
Kiss me once, and ease my pain!
[kɪs mi wʌns ænd iz mɑːɪ peːɪn]
Chloe laughing at his crying,
[ˈkloːʊɪ ˈlæfɪŋ æt hɪz ˈkɹ⁽ʳ⁾ɑːɪŋ]
Told him that he loved in vain;
[toːʊld hɪm ðæt hi lʌvd ɪn veːɪn]
But repenting, and complying,
[bʌt ɹɪˈpɛntɪŋ ænd kʌmˈplɑːɪŋ]
When he kiss'd, she kiss'd again:
[ʍɛn hi kɪst ʃi kɪst ʌˈgɛn]
Kiss'd him up, before his dying;
[kɪst hɪm ʌp bɪˈfɔːʌ hɪz ˈdɑːɪŋ]
Kiss'd him up, and eas'd his pain.
[kɪst hɪm ʌp ænd izd hɪz peːɪn]

"Sometimes with One I Love"
[ˈsʌmtɑːɪmz wɪθ wʌn ɑːɪ lʌv]
Whitman, Walt (Am. 1819-1892)

Sometimes with one I love,
[ˈsʌmtɑːɪmz wɪð wʌn ɑːɪ lʌv]
I fill myself with rage,
[ɑːɪ fɪl mɑːɪˈsɛlf wɪð ɹɛːɪdʒ]
for fear I effuse unreturn'd love;
[fɔ fɪːʁ⁽ʳ⁾ ɑːɪ ɪ ˈfjuz ʌnɹɪˈtɜnd lʌv]
But now I think there is no unreturn'd love
[bʌt nɑːʊ ɑːɪ θɪŋk ðɛːʁ⁽ʳ⁾ ɪz noːʊ ʌnɹɪˈtɜnd lʌv]
-the pay is certain, one way or another;
[ðʌ pɛːɪ ɪz ˈsɜtæ⁽ɪ⁾n wʌn wɛːɪ ɔʁ⁽ʳ⁾ ʌˈnʌðʌ]
I loved a certain person ardently,
[ɑːɪ lʌvd ʌ ˈsɜtæ⁽ɪ⁾n ˈpɜsʌn ˈɑdɛntlɪ]
my love was not return'd;
[mɑːɪ lʌv wɑz nɑt ɹɪˈtɜnd]
Yet out of that I have written these songs.
[jɛt ɑːʊt ʌv ðæt ɑːɪ hæv ˈɹɪtɛ⁽ɪ⁾n ðiz sɑŋz]

"Song for a Girl" [sɑŋ fɔʁ ʌ gɜl]
Dryden, John (Eng. 1631-1700)

Young I am, and yet unskilled
[jʌŋ ɑːɪ æm ænd jɛt ʌnˈskɪld]
How to make a lover yield,
[hɑːʊ tu mɛːɪk ʌ ˈlʌvʌ jild]
How to keep, or how to gain,
[hɑːʊ tu kip ɔ hɑːʊ tu gɛːɪn]
When to love, and when to feign.
[ʍɛn tu lʌv ænd ʍɛn tu fɛːɪn]
Take me, take me, some of you,
[tɛːɪk mi tɛːɪk mi sʌm ʌv ju]
While I yet am young and true;
[ʍɑːɪl ɑːɪ jɛt æm jʌŋ ænd tɹ⁽ʳ⁾u]
E're I can my soul disguise,
[ɛːʁ⁽ʳ⁾ ɑːɪ kæn mɑːɪ soːʊl dɪsˈgɑːɪz]
Heave my breasts, and roll my eyes.
[hiv mɑːɪ bɹɛsts ænd ɹoːʊl mɑːɪ ɑːɪz]
Stay not till I learn the way,
[stɛːɪ nɑt tɪl ɑːɪ lɜn ðʌ wɛːɪ]
How to lie, and to betray:
[hɑːʊ tu lɑːɪ ænd tu bɪˈtɹɛːɪ]
He that has me first, is blest,
[hi ðæt hæz mi fɜst ɪz blɛst]
For I may deceive the rest.
[fɔʁ⁽ʳ⁾ ɑːɪ mɛːɪ dɪˈsiv ðʌ ɹɛst]
Could I find a blooming youth,
[kʊd ɑːɪ fɑːɪnd ʌ ˈblumɪŋ juθ]
Full of love and full of truth,
[fʊl ʌv lʌv ænd fʊl ʌv tɹ⁽ʳ⁾uθ]
Brisk and of a jaunty mien,
[bɹɪsk ænd ʌv ʌ ˈdʒɔntɪ min]
I should long to be fifteen.
[ɑːɪ ʃʊd lɑŋ tu bi fɪfˈtin]

"The Dancer" (Nantucket Songs)
[ðʌ ˈdænsʁ]
Waller, Edmund (Eng. 1608-1687)

Behold the brand of beauty tossed!
[bɪˈhoːʊld ðʌ bɹænd ʌv ˈbjutɪ tast]
See how the motion does dilate the flame!
[si haːʊ ðʌ ˈmoːʊʃʌn dʌz ˈdaːɪlɛːɪt ðʌ flɛːɪm]
Delighted love his spoils does boast,
[dɪˈlaːɪtɛ(ɪ)d lʌv hɪz spoːɪlz dʌz boːʊst]
And triumph in this game.
[ænd ˈtɹɑːɪʌmf ɪn ðɪs gɛːɪm]
Fire, to no place confined,
[faːɪʌ tu noːʊ plɛːɪs kʌnˈfaːɪnd]
Is both our wonder and our fear;
[ɪz boːʊθ aːʊʌ ˈwʌndʌʁ(ʳ) ænd aːʊʌ fiːʌ]
Moving the mind,
[ˈmuvɪŋ ðʌ maːɪnd]
As lightning hurled through the air.
[æz ˈlaːɪtnɪŋ hɜld θɹu ði ɛːʌ]
High heaven the glory does increase
[haːɪ ˈhɛvɛ(ɪ)n ðʌ ˈgloʁ(ʳ)ɪ dʌz ɪnˈkɹis]
Of all her shining lamps, this artful way;
[ʌv ɔl hɜ ˈʃaːɪnɪŋ læmps ðɪs ˈatfʊl wɛːɪ]
The sun, in figures such as these,
[ðʌ sʌn ɪn ˈfɪgjʊ(ʌ)z sʌtʃ æz ðiz]
Joys with the moon to play;
[dʒɔːɪz wɪð ðʌ mun tu plɛːɪ]
To the sweet strains they advance,
[tu ðʌ swit stɹɛːɪnz ðɛːɪ ædˈvæns]
Which do result from their own spheres,
[ʍɪtʃ du ɹɪˈzʌlt fɹʌm ðɛːʌʁ(ʳ) oːʊn sfiːʌz]
As this nymph's dance
[æz ðɪs nɪmfs dæns]
Moves with the numbers which she hears.
[muvz wɪð ðʌ ˈnʌmbʌz ʍɪtʃ ʃi hiːʌz]

"The Nightingale"
[ðʌ ˈnaːɪtɪŋgɛːɪl]
Anonymous (about AD 1500)

The little pretty nightingale
[ðʌ ˈlɪtʊl ˈpɹɪtɪ ˈnaːɪtɪŋgɛːɪl]
Among the leaves so green
[ʌˈmʌŋ ðʌ livz soːʊ gɹin]
Would I were with her all the night!
[wʊd aːɪ wɜ wɪð hɜ ɔl ðʌ naːɪt]
But ye know not whom I mean,
[bʌt ji noːʊ nat hum aːɪ min]
But ye know not whom I mean!
[bʌt ji noːʊ nat hum aːɪ min]
The nightingale sat on a briar
[ðʌ ˈnaːɪtɪŋgɛːɪl sæt an ʌ ˈbɹaːɪʌʁ(ʳ)]
Among the thorns so keen
[ʌˈmʌŋ ðʌ θɔnz soːʊ kin]

And comforted my heart's desire
[ænd ˈkʌmfɔtɛ(ɪ)d maːɪ hats dɪˈzaːɪʌ]
But ye know not whom I mean,
[bʌt ji noːʊ nat hum aːɪ min]
Ye know not whom I mean.
[ji noːʊ nat hum aːɪ min]
It did me good on her to look;
[ɪt dɪd mi gʊd an hɜ tu lʊk]
She was all clothed in green.
[ʃi waz ɔl kloːʊðd ɪn gɹin]
Away from me her heart she took
[ʌˈwɛːɪ fɹʌm mi hɜ hat ʃi tʊk]
But ye know not whom I mean.
[bʌt ji noːʊ nat hum aːɪ min]
"Lady," I cried with rueful moan,
[ˈlɛːɪdɪ aːɪ kɹ(ʳ)aːɪd wɪð ˈɹ(ʳʳ)ufʊl moːʊn]
Mind ye how true I have been.
[maːɪnd ji haːʊ tɹ(ʳ)u aːɪ hæv bɪn (bin)]
For I loved but you alone–
[fɔʁ(ʳ) aːɪ lʌvd bʌt ju ʌˈloːʊn]
Yet ye know whom I mean.
[jɛt ji noːʊ hum aːɪ min]

"The Serpent" (see Hoiby)

"To the Willow-Tree" (Flight for Heaven)
[tu ðʌ ˈwɪloːʊ tɹi]
Herrick, Robert (Eng. 1591-1674)

Thou art to all lost love the best,
[ðaːʊ at tu ɔl last lʌv ðʌ bɛst]
The only true plant found,
[ði ˈoːʊnlɪ tɹ(ʳ)u plænt faːʊnd]
Wherewith young men and maids distress'd,
[ʍɛːʌˈwɪð jʌŋ mɛn ænd mɛːɪdz dɪˈstɹɛst]
And left of love, are crown'd.
[ænd lɛft ʌv lʌv a kɹaːʊnd]
When once the lover's rose is dead,
[ʍɛn wʌns ðʌ ˈlʌvʌz ɹoːʊz ɪz dɛd]
Or laid aside forlorn:
[ɔ lɛːɪd ʌˈsaːɪd fɔˈlɔn]
Then willow-garlands 'bout the head
[ðɛn ˈwɪloːʊ ˈgalæ(ʌ)ndz baːʊt ðʌ hɛd]
Bedew'd with tears are worn.
[bɪˈdjud wɪð tiːʌz a wɔn]
When with neglect, the lover's bane,
[ʍɛn wɪð nɪˈglɛkt ðʌ ˈlʌvʌz bɛːɪn]
Poor maids rewarded be,
[pʊːʌ mɛːɪdz ɹɪˈwɔdɛ(ɪ)d bi]
For their love lost, their only gain
[fɔ ðɛːʌ lʌv last ðɛːʌʁ(ʳ) ˈoːʊnlɪ gɛːɪn]
Is but a wreath from thee.
[ɪz bʌt ʌ ɹiθ fɹʌm ði]
And underneath thy cooling shade,
[ænd ʌndʌˈniθ ðaːɪ ˈkulɪŋ ʃɛːɪd]

When weary of the light,
[ʍɛn ˈwɪːʀ⁽ʳ⁾ɪ ʌv ðʌ lɑːɪt]
The love-spent youth and love-sick maid
[ðʌ lʌv spɛnt juθ ænd lʌv sɪk mɛːɪd]
Come to weep out the night.
[kʌm tu wip ɑːʊt ðʌ nɑːɪt]

"To You"
[tu ju]
Whitman, Walt (Am. 1819-1892)

Stranger, if you passing, meet me,
[ˈstɹɛːɪndʒʌ ɪf ju ˈpæsɪŋ mit mi]
And desire to speak to me,
[ænd dɪˈzɑːɪʌ tu spik tu mi]
Why should you not speak to me?
[ʍɑːɪ ʃʊd ju nɑt spik tu mi]
And why should I not speak to you?
[ænd ʍɑːɪ ʃʊd ɑːɪ nɑt spik tu ju]

"Up-Hill" (The Nantucket Songs)
[ʌp hɪl]
Rossetti, Christina Georgina (Eng. 1830-1894)

Does the road wind up-hill all the way?
[dʌz ðʌ ɹoːʊd wɑːɪnd ʌp hɪl ɔl ðʌ wɛːɪ]
Yes, to the very end.
[jɛs tu ðʌ ˈvɛʀ⁽ʳ⁾ɪ ɛnd]
Will the day's journey take the whole long day?
[wɪl ðʌ dɛːɪz ˈdʒɜnɪ tɛːɪk ðʌ hoːʊl lɑŋ dɛːɪ]
From morn to night my friend.
[fɹʌm mɔn tu nɑːɪt mɑːɪ fɹɛnd]
But is there for the night a resting place?
[bʌt ɪz ðɛːʌ fɔ ðʌ nɑːɪt ʌ ˈɹɛstɪŋ plɛːɪs]
A roof for when the slow dark hours begin.
[ʌ ɹ⁽ʳʳ⁾uf fɔ ʍɛn ðʌ sloːʊ dak ɑːʊʌz bɪˈɡɪn]
May not the darkness hide it from my face?
[mɛːɪ nɑt ðʌ ˈdaknɛ(ɪ)s hɑːɪd ɪt fɹʌm mɑːɪ fɛːɪs]
You cannot miss that inn.
[ju kæˈnɑt mɪs ðæt ɪn]
Shall I meet other wayfarers at night?
[ʃæl ɑːɪ mit ˈʌðʌ ˈwɛːɪ fɛːʀ⁽ʳ⁾ʌz æt nɑːɪt]
Those who have gone before.
[ðoːʊz hu hæv ɡan bɪˈfɔːʌ]
Then must I knock, or call when just in sight?
[ðɛn mʌst ɑːɪ nak ɔ kɔl ʍɛn dʒʌst ɪn sɑːɪt]
They will not keep you standing at that door.
[ðɛːɪ wɪl nɑt kip ju ˈstændɪŋ æt ðæt dɔːʌ]
Shall I find comfort, travel-sore and weak?
[ʃæl ɑːɪ fɑːɪnd ˈkʌmfɔt ˈtɹævʊl sɔːʌʀ⁽ʳ⁾ ænd wik]
Of labour you shall find the sum.
[ʌv ˈlɛːɪbʊ(ʌ) ju ʃæl fɑːɪnd ðʌ sʌm]
Will there be beds for me and all who seek?
[wɪl ðɛːʌ bi bɛdz fɔ mi ænd ɔl hu sik]
Yes, beds for all who come.
[jɛs bɛdz fɔʀ⁽ʳ⁾ ɔl hu kʌm]

"Upon Julia's Clothes" (Flight for Heaven)
[ʌˈpɑn ˈdʒuliʌz kloːʊðz]
Herrick, Robert (Eng. 1591-1674)

Whenas in silks my Julia goes,
[ʍɛnˈæz ɪn sɪlks mɑːɪ ˈdʒuliʌ ɡoːʊz]
Then, then, methinks, how sweetly flows
[ðɛn ðɛn ˌmiˈθɪŋks hɑːʊ ˈswitlɪ floːʊz]
That liquefaction of her clothes.
[ðæt lɪkwɪˈfækʃʌn ʌv hɜ kloːʊðz]
Next, when I cast mine eyes, and see
[nɛkst ʍɛn ɑːɪ kæst mɑːɪn ɑːɪz ænd si]
That brave vibration each way free,
[ðæt bɹɛːɪv vɑːɪˈbɹɛːɪʃʌn itʃ wɛːɪ fɹi]
O how that glittering taketh me!
[oːʊ hɑːʊ ðæt ˈɡlɪtʌʀ⁽ʳ⁾ɪŋ ˈtɛːɪkɛ(ɪ)θ mi]

Rosseter, Philip (Eng. 1568-1623)

Song Selection

"What Then Is Love but Mourning?"
[ʍat ðɛn ɪz lʌv bʌt ˈmɔnɪŋ]
Campion, Thomas (Eng. 1567-1620)

What then is love but mourning?
[ʍat ðɛn ɪz lʌv bʌt ˈmɔnɪŋ]
What desire but a self burning?
[ʍat dɪˈzɑːɪʌ bʌt ʌ self ˈbɜnɪŋ]
Till she that hates doth love return,
[tɪl ʃi ðæt hɛːɪts dʌθ lʌv ɹɪˈtɜn]
Thus will I mourn, thus will I sing,
[ðʌs wɪl ɑːɪ mɔn ðʌs wɪl ɑːɪ sɪŋ]
Come away, come away, my darling.
[kʌm ʌˈwɛːɪ kʌm ʌˈwɛːɪ mɑːɪ ˈdalɪŋ]
Beauty is but a blooming,
[ˈbjutɪ ɪz bʌt ʌ ˈblumɪŋ]
Youth in his glory entombing;
[juθ ɪn hɪz ˈɡlɔɪ ɪnˈtumɪŋ]
Time hath a while, which none can stay,
[tɑːɪm hæθ ʌ ʍɑːɪl ʍɪtʃ nʌn kæn stɛːɪ]
Then come away while thus I sing,
[ðɛn kʌm ʌˈwɛːɪ mɑːɪl ðʌs ɑːɪ sɪŋ]
Come away, come away my darling.
[kʌm ʌˈwɛːɪ kʌm ʌˈwɛːɪ mɑːɪ ˈdalɪŋ]
Summer in winter fadeth,
[ˈsʌmʌ ɪn ˈwɪntʌ ˈfɛːɪdɛ(ɪ)θ]
Gloomy night heavn'ly light shadeth,
[ˈɡlumɪ nɑːɪt ˈhɛvnlɪ lɑːɪt ˈʃɛːɪdɛ(ɪ)θ]
Like to the morn are Venus' flowers,
[lɑːɪk tu ðʊ mɔn ʌ ˈvinʊs flɑːʊʌz]
Such are her hours: then will I sing,
[sʌtʃ ɑ hɜ ɑːʊʌz ðɛn wɪl ɑːɪ sɪŋ]
Come away, come away my darling.
[kʌm ʌˈwɛːɪ kʌm ʌˈwɛːɪ mɑːɪ ˈdalɪŋ]

Roy, William (Am. 1928-2003)

Song Selection

"This Little Rose" (See "Nobody Knows" by Duke)

S

Sacco, John (Am. 1905-1987)

Song Selection

"Brother Will, Brother John"
[ˈbɹʌðʁ wɪl ˈbɹʌðʁ dʒan]
Welborn, Elizabeth Charles (Eng. 1828-1896)

You can't take it with you, Brother Will, Brother John,
[ju kænt tɛːɪk ɪt wɪð ju ˈbɹʌðʌ wɪl ˈbɹʌðʌ dʒan]
It ain't no use, Mister, after you're gone,
[ɪt ɛːɪnt noːʊ jus ˈmɪstʌ ˈæftʌ jɔːʌ gan]
You can't take it with you, Brother Will, Brother John.
[ju kænt tɛːɪk ɪt wɪð ju ˈbɹʌðʌ wɪl ˈbɹʌðʌ dʒan]
You needn't squeeze your coin tight in your hand,
[ju ˈnidɛ(ɪ)nt skwiz jɔːʌ kɔːɪn taːɪt ɪn jɔːʌ hænd]
No place for small change in the Promised Land.
[noːʊ plɛːɪs fɔ smɔl tʃɛːɪndʒ ɪn ðʌ ˈpɹamɪst lænd]
It ain't no use, Mister, after you're gone,
[ɪt ɛːɪnt noːʊ jus ˈmɪstʌ ˈæftʌ jɔːʌ gan]
You can't take it with you, Brother Will, Brother John.
[ju kænt tɛːɪk ɪt wɪð ju ˈbɹʌðʌ wɪl ˈbɹʌðʌ dʒan]
Shake a leg here, shake a leg there,
[ʃɛːɪk ʌ lɛg hiːʌ ʃɛːɪk ʌ lɛg ðɛːʌ]
laugh a little, smile a little, spread a little cheer,
[læf ʌ ˈlɪtʊl smaːɪl ʌ ˈlɪtʊl spɹɛd ʌ ˈlɪtʊl tʃiːʌ]
Brother Will, Brother John...
[ˈbɹʌðʌ wɪl ˈbɹʌðʌ dʒan]
Why mope around with funereal faces,
[ʍaːɪ moːʊp ʌˈʁ(ɾ)aːʊnd wɪð fju ˈniːʌʁ(ɾ)ɪʊl ˈfɛːɪsɛ(ɪ)z]
Whip up your nag and loosen the traces.
[ʍɪp ʌp jɔːʌ næg ænd ˈlusɛ(ɪ)n ðʌ ˈtɹɛːɪsɛ(ɪ)z]
Take a little joy, take a little pleasure,
[tɛːɪk ʌ ˈlɪtʊl dʒɔːɪ tɛːɪk ʌ ˈlɪtʊl ˈplɛʒʊ(ʌ)]
Bow to the ladies, dance a measure,
[baːʊ tu ðʌ ˈlɛːɪdɪz dæns ʌ ˈmɛʒʊ(ʌ)]
Brother Will, Brother John...
[ˈbɹʌðʌ wɪl ˈbɹʌðʌ dʒan]
You'll have to leave it when the coffin lid's on,
[jul hæv tu liv ɪt ʍɛn ðʌ ˈkafɪn lɪdz an]
You can't take it with you, Brother Will, Brother John!
[ju kænt tɛːɪk ɪt wɪð ju ˈbɹʌðʌ wɪl ˈbɹʌðʌ dʒan]

Schuman, William (Am. 1910-1992)

Song Selections

"Holiday Song"
[ˈhalɪdɛːɪ saŋ]
Taggard, Genevieve (Am. 1894-1948)

When was it ever a waste of time to climb hills?
[ʍɛn waz ɪt ˈɛvʌʁ(ɾ) ʌ wɛːɪst ʌv taːɪm tu klaːɪm hɪlz]
When was it ever a useless thing to sing the song
[ʍɛn waz ɪt ˈɛvʌʁ(ɾ) ʌ ˈjuslɛ(ɪ)s θɪŋ tu sɪŋ ðʌ saŋ]
of a long jolly day in the sun? Mm Lo!
[ʌv ʌ laŋ ˈdʒalɪ dɛːɪ ɪn ðʌ sʌn m loːʊ]
Deedelee dee, deedelee dee, Lo!
[ˈdidɪli di ˈdidɪli di loːʊ]
When was it ever a waste of time to climb hills
[ʍɛn waz ɪt ˈɛvʌʁ(ɾ) ʌ wɛːɪst ʌv taːɪm tu klaːɪm hɪlz]
or to sing on our hills the song
[ɔ tu sɪŋ an aːʊʌ hɪlz ðʌ saŋ]
of a long jolly day in the sun?
[ʌv ʌ laŋ ˈdʒalɪ dɛːɪ ɪn ðʌ sʌn]
All of us, ev'ryone, ev'ryone, all of us, all of us,
[ɔl ʌv ʌs ˈɛvɹɪwʌn ˈɛvɹɪwʌn ɔl ʌv ʌs ɔl ʌv ʌs]
Everyone of us,
[ˈɛvɹɪwʌn ʌv ʌs]
Has something to sing about,
[hæz ˈsʌmθɪŋ tu sɪŋ ʌˈbaːʊt]
to sing and shout, shout! Lo!
[tu sɪŋ ænd ʃaːʊt ʃaːʊt loːʊ]

"Orpheus with His Lute" (see Hundley)

Somervell, Arthur (Eng. 1863-1937)

A Shropshire Lad (Song Cycle)
[ʌ ˈʃɹapʃaːɪʌ læd]
Housman, Alfred Edward (Eng. 1859-1936)

1. Loveliest of Trees the Cherry Now
(see Butterworth)

2. When I Was One-and-Twenty (see Butterworth)

3. There Pass the Careless People
[ðɛːʌ pas ðʊ ˈkɛːʌlɪs ˈpipʊl]

There pass the careless people
[ðɛːʌ pas ðʊ ˈkɛːʌlɛ(ɪ)s ˈpipʊl]
That call their souls their own:
[ðæt kɔl ðɛːʌ soːʊlz ðɛːʌr oːʊn]
Here by the road I loiter,
[hiːʌ baːɪ ðʊ roːʊd aːɪ ˈlɔːɪtʌ]

How idle and alone.
[haːʊ ˈaːɪdʊl ænd ʌˈloːʊn]
His folly has not fellow
[hɪz ˈfalɪ hæz nat ˈfɛloːʊ]
Beneath the blue of day,
[bɪˈniθ ðʊ blu ʌv deːɪ]
That gives to man or woman
[ðæt gɪvz tu mæn ɔ ˈwʊmæ(ʌ)n]
His heart and soul away.
[hɪz hat ænd soːʊl ʌˈweːɪ]

4. In Summer-Time on Bredon
[ɪn ˈsʌmʌtaːɪm an ˈbɹɪdʌn]

In summertime on Bredon
[ɪn ˈsʌmʌtaːɪm an ˈbɹɪdʌn]
The bells they sound so clear;
[ðʊ bɛlz ðɛːɪ saːʊnd soːʊ klɪːʌ]
Round both the shires they ring them,
[ɹaːʊnd boːʊθ ðʊ ˈʃaːɪʌz ðɛːɪ rɪŋ ðɛm]
In steeples far and near,
[ɪn ˈstipʊlz far ænd nɪːʌ]
A happy noise to hear.
[ʌ ˈhæpɪ nɔːɪz tu hɪːʌ]
Here of a Sunday morning
[hɪːʌɾ ʌv ʌ ˈsʌndɛːɪ ˈmɔnɪŋ]
My love and I would lie,
[maːɪ lʌv ænd aːɪ wʊd laːɪ]
And see the coloured counties,
[ænd si ðʊ ˈkʌlʊ(ʌ)d ˈkaːʊntɪz]
And hear the larks so high
[ænd hɪːʌ ðʊ laks soːʊ haːɪ]
About us in the sky.
[ʌˈbaːʊt ʌs ɪn ðʊ skaːɪ]
The bells would ring to call her
[ðʊ bɛlz wʊd rɪŋ tu kɔl hɜ]
In valleys miles away
[ɪn ˈvælɪz maːɪlz ʌˈweːɪ]
"Come all to church, good people;
[kʌm ɔl tu ʧɜʧ gʊd ˈpipʊl]
Good people, come and pray"
[gʊd ˈpipʊl kʌm ænd pɹɛːɪ]
But here my love would stay.
[bʌt hɪːʌ maːɪ lʌv wʊd stɛːɪ]
And I would turn and answer
[ænd aːɪ wʊd tɜn ænd ˈansʌɾ]
Among the springing thyme,
[ʌˈmʌŋ ðʊ ˈspɹɪŋɪŋ taːɪm]
'O peal upon our wedding,
[oːʊ pil ʌˈpan aːʊʌ ˈwɛdɪŋ]
And we will hear the chime,
[ænd wi wɪl hɪːʌ ðʊ ʧaːɪm]
And come to church in time.'
[ænd kʌm tu ʧɜʧ ɪn taːɪm]
But when the snows at Christmas
[bʌt ʍɛn ðʊ snoːʊz æt ˈkɹɪsmʌs]

On Bredon top were strown,
[an ˈbɹɪdʌn tap wɜ stɹoːʊn]
My love rose up so early
[maːɪ lʌv ɹoːʊz ʌp soːʊ ˈɜlɪ]
And stole out unbeknown,
[ænd stoːʊl aːʊt ˌʌnbɪˈnoːʊn]
And went to church alone.
[ænd wɛnt tu ʧɜʧ ʌˈloːʊn]
They toll'd the one bell only,
[ðɛːɪ toːʊld ðʊ wʌn bɛl ˈoːʊnlɪ]
Groom there was none to see,
[gɹum ðɛːʌ waz nʌn tu si]
The mourners follow'd after,
[ðʊ ˈmɔnʌz ˈfaloːʊd ˈaftʌ]
And so to church went she,
[ænd soːʊ tu ʧɜʧ wɛnt ʃi]
And would not wait for me.
[ænd wʊd nat wɛːɪt fɔ mi]
The bells they sound on Bredon,
[ðʊ bɛlz ðɛːɪ saːʊnd an ˈbɹɪdʌn]
And still the steeples hum.
[ænd stɪl ðʊ ˈstipʊlz hʌm]
"Come all to church, good people,"–
[kʌm ɔl tu ʧɜʧ gʊd ˈpipʊl]
Oh, noisy bells, be dumb;
[oːʊ ˈnɔːɪzɪ bɛlz bi dʌm]
I hear you, I will come.
[aːɪ hɪːʌ ju aːɪ wɪl kʌm]

5. The Street Sounds to the Soldiers' Tread
[ðʊ stɹit saːʊndz tu ðʊ ˈsoːʊldjʌz tɹɛd]

The street sounds to the soldiers' tread,
[ðʊ stɹit saːʊndz tu ðʊ ˈsoːʊldjʌz tɹɛd]
And out we come to see:
[ænd aːʊt wi kʌm tu si]
A single redcoat turns his head,
[ʌ ˈsɪŋgʊl ˈɹɛdˌkoːʊt tɜnz hɪz hɛd]
He turns and looks at me.
[hi tɜnz ænd lʊks æt mi]
My man, from sky to sky's so far,
[maːɪ mæn fɹʌm skaːɪ tu skaːɪz soːʊ fa]
We never cross'd before;
[wi ˈnɛvʌ kɹʌst bɪˈfɔːʌ]
Such leagues apart the world's ends are
[sʌʧ ligz ʌˈpat ðʊ wɜldz ɛndz a]
We're like to meet no more.
[wɪːʌ laːɪk tu mit noːʊ mɔːʌ]
What thoughts at heart have you and I,
[ʍat θɔts æt hat hæv ju ænd aːɪ]
We cannot stop to tell,
[wi kæˈnat stap tu tɛl]
But, dead or living, drunk or dry,
[bʌt dɛd ɔ ˈlɪvɪŋ dɹʌŋk ɔ dɹaːɪ]
Soldier, I wish you well.
[ˈsoːʊldjʌ aːɪ wɪʃ ju wɛl]

6. On the Idle Hill of Summer
[ɑn ði ˈɑːɪdʊl hɪl ʌv ˈsʌmʌ]

On the idle hill of summer,
[ɑn ði ˈɑːɪdʊl hɪl ʌv ˈsʌmʌ]
Sleepy with the flow of streams,
[ˈslipɪ wɪð ðʊ floːʊ ʌv stɹimz]
Far I hear the steady drummer,
[fɑɹ ɑːɪ hɪːʌ ðʊ ˈstɛdɪ ˈdɹʌmʌ]
Drumming like a noise in dreams.
[ˈdɹʌmɪŋ lɑːɪk ʌ nɔːɪz ɪn dɹimz]
Far and near and low and louder
[fɑɹ ænd nɪːʌɾ ænd loːʊ ænd ˈlaːʊdʌ]
On the roads of earth go by,
[ɑn ðʊ roːʊdz ʌv ɜθ goːʊ bɑːɪ]
Dear to friends and food for powder,
[dɪːʌ tu fɹɛndz ænd fud fɔ ˈpaːʊdʌ]
Soldiers marching, all to die.
[ˈsoːʊldjʌz ˈmɑʧɪŋ ɔl tu dɑːɪ]
East and west, on fields forgotten,
[ist ænd wɛst ɑn fildz fɔˈgɑtɛ(ɪ)n]
Bleach the bones of comrades slain,
[bliʧ ðʊ boːʊnz ʌv ˈkʌmɹædz slɛːɪn]
Lovely lads and dead and rotten;
[ˈlʌvlɪ lædz ænd dɛd ænd ˈɹɑtɛ(ɪ)n]
None that go return again.
[nʌn ðæt goːʊ ɹɪˈtɜn ʌˈgɛːɪn]
Far the calling bugles hollo,
[fɑ ðʊ ˈkɔlɪŋ ˈbjugʊlz ˈhaloːʊ]
High the screaming fife replies,
[hɑːɪ ðʊ ˈskɹimɪŋ fɑːɪf ɹɪˈplɑːɪz]
Gay the files of scarlet follow:
[gɛːɪ ðʊ fɑːɪlz ʌv ˈskɑlɛ(ɪ)t ˈfaloːʊ]
Woman bore me, I will rise.
[ˈwʊmæ(ʌ)n bɔːʌ mi ɑːɪ wɪl ɹɑːɪz]

7. White in the Moon the Long Road Lies
[ʍɑːɪt ɪn ðʊ mun ðʊ lɑŋ ɹoːʊd lɑːɪz]

White in the moon the long road lies,
[ʍɑːɪt ɪn ðʊ mun ðʊ lɑŋ ɹoːʊd lɑːɪz]
The moon stands blank above;
[ðʊ mun stændz blæŋk ʌˈbʌv]
White in the moon the long road lies
[ʍɑːɪt ɪn ðʊ mun ðʊ lɑŋ ɹoːʊd lɑːɪz]
That leads me from my love.
[ðæt lidz mi fɹʌm mɑːɪ lʌv]
Still hangs the hedge without a gust,
[stɪl hæŋz ðʊ hɛʤ wɪðˈaːʊt ʌ gʌst]
Still, still the shadows stay:
[stɪl stɪl ðʊ ˈʃædoːʊz stɛːɪ]
My feet upon the moonlit dust
[mɑːɪ fit ʌˈpɑn ðʊ ˈmunlɪt dʌst]
Pursue the ceaseless way.
[pɜˈsju ðʊ ˈsislɛ(ɪ)s wɛːɪ]

The world is round, so trav'llers tell,
[ðʊ wɜld ɪz ɹɑːʊnd soːʊ ˈtɹævlʌz tɛl]
And straight thou' reach the track,
[ænd stɹɛːɪt ðoːʊ ɹiʧ ðʊ tɹæk]
Trudge on, trudge on, 'twill all be well,
[tɹʌʤ ɑn tɹʌʤ ɑn twɪl ɔl bi wɛl]
The way will guide one back.
[ðʊ wɛːɪ wɪl gɑːɪd wʌn bæk]
But ere the circle homeward hies,
[bʌt ɛːʌ ðʊ ˈsɜkʊl ˈhoːʊmwʊd hɑːɪz]
Far, far must it remove:
[fɑ fɑ mʌst ɪt ɹɪˈmuv]
White in the moon the long road lies
[ʍɑːɪt ɪn ðʊ mun ðʊ lɑŋ ɹoːʊd lɑːɪz]
That leads me from my love.
[ðæt lidz mi fɹʌm mɑːɪ lʌv]

8. Think No More, Lad (see Butterworth)

9. Into My Heart an Air That Kills
[ˈɪntu mɑːɪ hɑt æn ɛːʌ ðæt kɪlz]

Into my heart an air that kills
[ˈɪntu mɑːɪ hɑt æn ɛːʌ ðæt kɪlz]
From yon far country blows:
[fɹʌm jɑn fɑ ˈkʌntɹɪ bloːʊz]
What are those blue remember'd hills,
[ʍɑt ɑ ðoːʊz blu ɹɪˈmɛmbʌd hɪlz]
What spires, what farms are those?
[ʍɑt spɑːɪʌz ʍɑt fɑmz ɑ ðoːʊz]
That is the land of lost content,
[ðæt ɪz ðʊ lænd ʌv lɑst kʌnˈtɛnt]
I see it shining plain,
[ɑːɪ si ɪt ˈʃɑːɪnɪŋ plɛːɪn]
The happy highways where I went
[ðʊ ˈhæpɪ ˈhɑːɪwɛːɪz ʍɛːʌɾ ɑːɪ wɛnt]
And cannot come again.
[ænd kæˈnɑt kʌm ʌˈgɛːɪn]

10. The Lads in Their Hundreds (see Butterworth)

Speaks, Oley (Am. 1874-1948)

Song Selections

"On the Road to Mandalay"
[ɑn ðʌ ɹoːʊd tu ˈmændʌ leːɪ]
Kipling, Rudyard (Eng. 1865-1936)

1. By the old Moulmein Pagoda,
[bɑːɪ ði oːʊld ˈmʊlmɛːɪn pʌˈgoːʊdʌ]
lookin' eastward to the sea,
[ˈlʊkɪn ˈistwʊd tu ðʌ si]
There's a Burma girl a-settin',
[ðɛːʌz ʌ ˈbɜmʌ gɜl ʌ ˈsɛtɪn]

an' I know she thinks o' me;
[æn ɑːɪ noːʊ ʃi θɪŋks ʌ mi]
For the wind is in the palm-trees,
[fɔ ðʌ wɪnd ɪz ɪn ðʌ pɑm tɹiz]
An' the temple bells they say:
[æn ðʌ 'tɛmpʊl bɛlz ðɛːɪ sɛːɪ]
"Come you back, you British soldier;
[kʌm ju bæk ju 'bɹɪtɪʃ 'soːʊldʒʌ]
Come you back to Mandalay!"
[kʌm ju bæk tu 'mændʌˌlɛːɪ]
REFRAIN:
Come you back to Mandalay,
[kʌm ju bæk tu 'mændʌˌlɛːɪ]
Where the old Flotilla lay:
[ʍɛːʌ ði oːʊld floˈtɪlʌ lɛːɪ]
Can't you 'ear their paddles chunkin'
[kænt ju ɪːʌ ðɛːʌ 'pædʊlz 'tʃʌŋkɪn]
from Rangoon to Mandalay?
[fɹʌm ɹæŋˈgun tu 'mændʌˌlɛːɪ]
On the road to Mandalay,
[ɑn ðʌ ɹoːʊd tu 'mændʌˌlɛːɪ]
Where the flyin' fishes play,
[ʍɛːʌ ðʌ 'flɑːɪɪn 'fɪʃɛ(ɪ)z plɛːɪ]
An' the dawn comes up like thunder
[æn ðʌ dɔn kʌmz ʌp lɑːɪk 'θʌndʌ]
out of China 'crost the bay.
[ɑːʊt ʌv 'tʃɑːɪnʌ kɹɑst ðʌ bɛːɪ]
2. 'Er petticoat was yaller,
[ɜ 'pɛtɪkoːʊt wɑz 'jælɜ]
an' 'er little cap was green,
[æn ɜ 'lɪ(t)ʊl kæp wɑz gɹin]
An' 'er name was Supiyawlat
[æn ɜ nɛːɪm wɑz supɪ'jɔlæt]
Jes' the same as Thebaw's Queen,
[dʒɛs ðʌ sɛːɪm æz 'θibɔz kwin]
An' I seed her first a smokin'
[æn ɑːɪ sid hɜ fɜst ʌ 'smoːʊkɪn]
Of a whackin' white cheroot,
[ʌv ʌ 'ʍækɪn ʍɑːɪt ʃɛˈʁ⁽ʳ⁾ut]
An' a-wastin' Christian kisses
[æn ʌ 'wɛːɪstɪn 'kɹɪstʃæ(ɪ)n 'kɪsɛ(ɪ)z]
On an 'eathen idol's foot:
[ɑn æn 'iðɛ(ɪ)n 'ɑːɪdʊlz fʊt]
Bloomin' idol made o' mud–
['blumɪn 'ɑːɪdʊl mɛːɪd ʌ mʌd]
What they called the great Gawd Budd–
[ʍɑt ðɛːɪ kɔld ðʌ gɹɛːɪt gɔd bʌd]
Plucky lot she cared for idols
['plʌkɪ lɑt ʃi kɛːʌd fɔʁ⁽ʳ⁾ 'ɑːɪdʊlz]
When I kissed her where she stood!
[ʍɛn ɑːɪ kɪst hɜ ʍɛːʌ ʃi stʊd]
REFRAIN
3. Ship me somewheres east of Suez
[ʃɪp mi 'sʌmʍɛːʌz ist ʌv 'suˈɛz]
where the best is like the worst,
[ʍɛːʌ ðʌ bɛst ɪz lɑːɪk ðʌ wɜst]

Where there ain't no Ten Commandments,
[ʍɛːʌ ðɛːʌʁ⁽ʳ⁾ ɛːɪnt noːʊ tɛn kʌˈmændmɛnts]
an' a man can raise a thirst;
[æn ʌ mæn kæn ɹɛːɪz ʌ θɜst]
For the temple bells are callin',
[fɔ ðʌ 'tɛmpʊl bɛlz ɑ 'kɔlɪn]
an' it's there that I would be–
[æn ɪts ðɛːʌ ðæt ɑːɪ wʊd bi]
By the old Moulmein Pagoda,
[bɑːɪ ði oːʊld 'mʊlmɛːɪn pʌˈgoːʊdʌ]
lookin' lazy at the sea.
['lʊkɪn 'lɛːɪzɪ æt ðʌ si]
REFRAIN

"Sylvia"
['sɪlvɪa]
Scollard, Clinton (Am. 1860-1932)

Sylvia's hair is like the night,
['sɪlvɪaz hɛːʌʁ⁽ʳ⁾ ɪz lɑːɪk ðʌ nɑːɪt]
Touched with glancing starry beams;
[tʌtʃt wɪð 'glænsɪŋ 'stɑʁ⁽ʳ⁾ɪ bimz]
Such a face as drifts thro' dreams,
[sʌtʃ ʌ fɛːɪs æz dɹɪfts θru dɹimz]
This is Sylvia to the sight.
[ðɪs ɪz 'sɪlvɪa tu ðʌ sɑːɪt]
And the touch of Sylvia's hand
[ænd ðʌ tʌtʃ ʌv 'sɪlvɪaz hænd]
Is as light as milkweed down,
[ɪz æz lɑːɪt æz 'mɪlkwid dɑːʊn]
When the meads are golden brown,
[ʍɛn ðʌ midz ɑ 'goːʊldɛ(ɪ)n bɹɑːʊn]
And the autumn fills the land.
[ænd ði 'ɔtʌm fɪlz ðʌ lænd]
Sylvia:- just the echoing
['sɪlvɪa dʒʌst ði 'ɛkoːʊɪŋ]
Of her voice brings back to me,
[ʌv hɜ vɔːɪs bɹɪŋz bæk tu mi]
From the depths of memory,
[fɹʌm ðʌ dɛpθs ʌv 'mɛmʌʁ⁽ʳ⁾ɪ]
All the loveliness of spring:
[ɔl ðʌ 'lʌvlɪnɛ(ɪ)s ʌv spɹɪŋ]
Sylvia! Such a face as drifts thro' dreams,
['sɪlvɪa sʌtʃ ʌ fɛːɪs æz dɹɪfts θru dɹimz]
This is Sylvia to the sight.
[ðɪs ɪz 'sɪlvɪa tu ðʌ sɑːɪt]

Sullivan, Arthur (Eng. 1842-1900)

Song Selections

"Arabian Love Song"
[ʌˈʁɛːɪbin lʌv saŋ]
Shelley, Percy Bysshe (Eng. 1792-1822)

My faint spirit was sitting in the light
[maːɪ fɛːɪnt ˈspɪrɪt waz ˈsɪtɪŋ ɪn ðʊ laːɪt]
Of thy looks, my love;
[ʌv ðaːɪ lʊks maːɪ lʌv]
It panted for thee like the hind at noon
[ɪt ˈpæntɛ(ɪ)d fɔ ði laːɪk ðʊ haːɪnd æt nun]
For the brooks, my love.
[fɔ ðʊ bɹʊks maːɪ lʌv]
Thy barb, whose hoofs outspeed the tempest's flight,
[ðaːɪ bab huz huvz aːʊtˈspid ðʊ ˈtɛmpɛ(ɪ)sts flaːɪt]
Bore thee far from me;
[bɔːʌ ði fa fɹʌm mi]
My heart, for my weak feet were weary soon,
[maːɪ hat fɔ maːɪ wik fit wɜ ˈwiːʌrɪ sun]
Did companion thee.
[dɪd kʌmˈpænjʌn ði]
Ah! fleeter far than fleetest storm or steed,
[a ˈflitʌ fa ðæn ˈflitɛ(ɪ)st stɔm ɔ stid]
Or the death they bear,
[ɔ ðʊ dɛθ ðɛːɪ bɛːʌ]
The heart which tender thought clothes like a dove
[ðʊ hat ʍɪʧ ˈtɛndʌ θɔt kloːʊðz laːɪk ʌ dʌv]
With the wings of care;
[wɪð ðʊ wɪŋz ʌv kɛːʌ]
In the battle, in the darkness, in the need,
[ɪn ðʊ ˈbætʊl ɪn ðʊ ˈdaknɛ(ɪ)s ɪn ðʊ nid]
Shall mine cling to thee,
[ʃæl maːɪn klɪŋ tu ði]
Nor claim one smile for all the comfort, love,
[nɔ klɛːɪm wʌn smaːɪl fɔʁ(ʳ) ɔl ðʊ ˈkʌmfɔ(ʌ)t lʌv]
It may bring to thee.
[ɪt mɛːɪ bɹɪŋ tu ði]

"Crabbed Age and Youth" (see Dring)

"On the Hill"
[an ðʊ hɪl]
(The Window, or The Songs of the Wrens)
Tennyson, Lord Alfred (Eng. 1809-1892)

The lights and shadows fly.
[ðʊ laːɪts ænd ˈʃædoːʊz flaːɪ]
Yonder it brightens and darkens
[ˈjandʌr ɪt ˈbɹaːɪtɛ(ɪ)nz ænd ˈdakɛ(ɪ)nz]
down on the plain
[daːʊn an ðʊ plɛːɪn]
A jewel, a jewel dear to a lover's eye.
[ʌ ˈʤuːɛ(ʊ)l ʌ ˈʤuːɛ(ʊ)l diːʌ tu ʌ ˈlʌvʌz aːɪ]

Oh is it the brook, or a pool,
[oːʊ ɪz ɪt ðʊ bɹʊk ɔʁ(ʳ) ʌ pul]
or her window pane,
[ɔ hɜ ˈwɪndoːʊ pɛːɪn]
When the winds are up in the morning?
[ʍɛn ðʊ wɪndz ar ʌp ɪn ðʊ ˈmɔnɪŋ]
Clouds that are rising above,
[klaːʊdz ðæt a ˈraːɪzɪŋ ʌˈbʌv]
O winds and lights and shadows
[oːʊ wɪndz ænd laːɪts ænd ˈʃædoːʊz]
that cannot be still,
[ðæt kæˈnat bi stɪl]
All running on one way to
[ɔl ˈɹʌnɪŋ an wʌn wɛːɪ tu]
the home of my love, All running on,
[ðʊ hoːʊm ʌv maːɪ lʌv ɔl ˈɹʌnɪŋ an]
And I stand on the slope of the hill
[ænd aːɪ stænd an ðʊ sloːʊp ʌv ðʊ hɪl]
And the winds are up in the morning!
[ænd ðʊ wɪndz ar ʌp ɪn ðʊ ˈmɔnɪŋ]
Follow, I follow the chase.
[ˈfaloːʊ aːɪ ˈfaloːʊ ðʊ ʧɛːɪs]
And my thoughts are as quick,
[ænd maːɪ θɔts ar æz kwɪk]
are as quick running on, running on.
[ar æz kwɪk ˈɹʌnɪŋ an ˈɹʌnɪŋ an]
O Lights, are you flying over her sweet little face?
[oːʊ laːɪts a ju ˈflaːɪŋ ˈoːʊvʌ hɜ swit ˈlɪtʊl fɛːɪs]
And my heart is there before you are come and gone,
[ænd maːɪ hat ɪz ðɛːʌ bɪˈfɔːʌ ju a kʌm ænd gan]
When the winds are up in the morning.
[ʍɛn ðʊ wɪndz ar ʌp ɪn ðʊ ˈmɔnɪŋ]
Follow them down the slope,
[ˈfaloːʊ ðɛm daːʊn ðʊ sloːʊp]
And I follow them down to the window pane
[ænd aːɪ ˈfaloːʊ ðɛm daːʊn tu ðʊ ˈwɪndoːʊ pɛːɪn]
of my dear.
[ʌv maːɪ diːʌ]
Oh it brightens and darkens and brightens
[oːʊ ɪt ˈbɹaːɪtɛ(ɪ)nz ænd ˈdakɛ(ɪ)nz ænd ˈbɹaːɪtɛ(ɪ)nz]
like my hope, It darkens and brightens
[laːɪk maːɪ hoːʊp ɪt ˈdakɛ(ɪ)nz ænd ˈbɹaːɪtɛ(ɪ)nz]
and darkens like my fear,
[ænd ˈdakɛ(ɪ)nz laːɪk maːɪ fiːʌ]
When the winds are up in the morning!
[ʍɛn ðʊ wɪndz ar ʌp ɪn ðʊ ˈmɔnɪŋ]

"Sigh No More, Ladies" (see Dowland)

"The Lost Chord"
[ðʊ last kɔd]
Procter, Adelaide Anne (Eng. 1825-1864)

Seated one day at the organ,
[ˈsitɛ(ɪ)d wʌn dɛːɪ æt ði ˈɔgæ(ɪ)n]

I was weary and ill at ease,
[ɑːɪ waz ˈwiːʌɾɪ ænd ɪl æt iz]
And my fingers wandered idly
[ænd mɑːɪ ˈfɪŋgʌz ˈwandʌd ˈɑːɪdlɪ]
Over the noisy keys;
[ˈoːʊvʌ ðʊ ˈnɔːɪzɪ kiz]
I know not what I was playing,
[ɑːɪ noːʊ nat ʌat ɑːɪ waz ˈplɛːɪɪŋ]
Or what I was dreaming then,
[ɔ ʌat ɑːɪ waz ˈdɹimɪŋ ðɛn]
But I struck one chord of music,
[bʌt ɑːɪ stɹʌk wʌn kɔd ʌv ˈmjuzɪk]
Like the sound of a great Amen.
[lɑːɪk ðʊ saːʊnd ʌv ʌ gɹɛːɪt ɑˈmɛn]
It flooded the crimson twilight,
[ɪt ˈflʌdɛ(ɪ)d ðʊ ˈkɹɪmzʌn ˈtwaːɪlɑːɪt]
Like the close of an Angel's Psalm,
[lɑːɪk ðʊ kloːʊz ʌv æn ˈɛːɪndʒɛ(ʊ)lz sɑm]
And it lay on my fevered spirit,
[ænd ɪt lɛːɪ an mɑːɪ ˈfivʌd ˈspɪɾɪt]
With a touch of infinite calm,
[wɪð ʌ tʌtʃ ʌv ˈɪnfɪnɪt kɑm]
It quieted pain and sorrow,
[ɪt ˈkwaːɪɛ(ɪ)tɛ(ɪ)d pɛːɪn ænd ˈsaɾoːʊ]
Like love overcoming strife,
[lɑːɪk lʌv ˈoːʊvʌˌkʌmɪŋ stɹaːɪf]
It seemed the harmonious echo,
[ɪt simd ðʊ haˈmoːʊnɪʌs ˈɛkoːʊ]
From our discordant life.
[fɹʌm aːʊʌ dɪsˈkɔdæ(ɪ)nt lɑːɪf]
It linked all perplexed meanings,
[ɪt lɪŋkt ɔl pɜˈplɛksɛ(ɪ)d ˈminɪŋz]
Into one perfect peace,
[ˈɪntu wʌn ˈpɜfɛ(ɪ)kt pis]
And trembled away into silence,
[ænd ˈtɹɛmbʊld ʌˈwɛːɪ ˈɪntu ˈsaːɪlɛ(ɪ)ns]
As if it were loth to cease;
[æz ɪf ɪt wɜ loːʊð tu sis]
I have sought, but I seek it vainly,
[ɑːɪ hæv sɔt bʌt ɑːɪ sik ɪt ˈvɛːɪnlɪ]
That one lost chord divine,
[ðæt wʌn last kɔd dɪˈvaːɪn]
Which came from the soul of the organ,
[ʌɪtʃ kɛːɪm fɹʌm ðʊ soːʊl ʌv ði ˈɔgæ(ɪ)n]
And entered into mine.
[ænd ˈɛntʌd ˈɪntu maːɪn]
It may be that Death's bright Angel,
[ɪt mɛːɪ bi ðæt dɛθs bɹaːɪt ˈɛːɪndʒɛl]
Will speak in that chord again;
[wɪl spik ɪn ðæt kɔd ʌˈgɛːɪn (ʌˈgɛn)]
It may be that only in heav'n,
[ɪt mɛːɪ bi ðæt ˈoːʊnlɪ ɪn hɛvn]
I shall hear that grand Amen.
[ɑːɪ ʃæl hiːʌ ðæt gɹænd ʌˈmɛn]

"The Willow Song" (see Coleridge-Taylor)

"Winter" (The Window, or The Songs of the Wrens)
[ˈwɪntʌ]
Tennyson, Lord Alfred (Eng. 1809-1892)

The frost is here,
[ðʊ fɹast ɪz hiːʌ]
And fuel is dear,
[ænd ˈfjuːʊl ɪz diːʌ]
And woods are sear,
[ænd wʊdz a siːʌ]
And fires burn clear,
[ænd faːɪʌz bɜn klɪːʌ]
And frost is here,
[ænd fɹast ɪz hiːʌ]
And has bitten the heel of the going year.
[ænd hæz ˈbɪtɛ(ɪ)n ðʊ hil ʌv ðʊ ˈgoːʊɪŋ jiːʌ]
Bite, frost, bite!
[baːɪt fɹast baːɪt]
You roll up away from the light.
[ju roːʊl ʌp ʌˈwɛːɪ fɹʌm ðʊ laːɪt]
The blue wood louse,
[ðʊ blu wʊd laːʊs]
And the plump dormouse,
[ænd ðʊ plʌmp ˈdɔmaːʊs]
And the bees are still'd,
[ænd ðʊ biz a stɪld]
And the flies are kill'd,
[ænd ðʊ flaːɪz a kɪld]
And you bite far far into the heart of the house,
[ænd ju baːɪt fa far ˈɪntu ðʊ hat ʌv ðʊ haːʊs]
But not into mine,
[bʌt nat ˈɪntu maːɪn]
And you bite far far into the heart of the house,
[ænd ju baːɪt fa far ˈɪntu ðʊ hat ʌv ðʊ haːʊs]
But not into mine.
[bʌt nat ˈɪntu maːɪn]
Bite, frost, bite!
[baːɪt fɹast baːɪt]
The woods are all the searer,
[ðʊ wʊdz ar ɔl ðʊ ˈsiːʌɾʌ]
The fuel is all the dearer,
[ðʊ ˈfjuːʊl ɪz ɔl ðʊ ˈdiːʌɾʌ]
The fires are all the clearer,
[ðʊ faːɪʌz ar ɔl ðʊ ˈklɪːʌɾʌ]
My spring is all the nearer,
[maːɪ spɹɪŋ ɪz ɔl ðʊ ˈniːʌɾʌ]
You have bitten into the heart of the earth,
[ju hæv ˈbɪtɛ(ɪ)n ˈɪntu ðʊ hat ʌv ði ɜθ]
But not into mine,
[bʌt nat ˈɪntu maːɪn]
You have bitten into the heart of the earth,
[ju hæv ˈbɪtɛ(ɪ)n ˈɪntu ðʊ hat ʌv ði ɜθ]
But not, not into mine.
[bʌt nat nat ˈɪntu maːɪn]

Sutherland, Margaret
(Aus. 1897-1984)

Four Blake Songs (Song Cycle)
[fɔːʌ blɛːɪk sɑŋz]
Blake, William (Eng. 1757-1827)

1. Memory, Hither Come
[ˈmɛmɔʁi ˈhɪðʌ kʌm]

Memory, hither come,
[ˈmɛmɔɹi ˈhɪðʌ kʌm]
And tune your merry notes;
[ænd tjun jɔːʌ ˈmɛɹi noːʊts]
And, while upon the wind
[ænd ʍɑːɪl ʌˈpan ðʊ wɪnd]
Your music floats,
[jɔːʌ ˈmjuzɪk floːʊts]
I'll pore upon the stream
[ɑːɪl pɔːʌɾ ʌˈpan ðʊ stɹim]
Where sighing lovers dream,
[ʍɛːʌ ˈsɑːɪɪŋ ˈlʌvʌz dɹim]
And fish for fancies as they pass
[ænd fɪʃ fɔ ˈfænsɪz æz ðɛːɪ pas]
Within the watery glass.
[wɪðˈɪn ðʊ ˈwɔtʌɾi glas]
I'll drink of the clear stream,
[ɑːɪl dɹɪŋk ʌv ðʊ klɪːʌ stɹim]
And hear the linnet's song;
[ænd hɪːʌ ðʊ ˈlɪnɛ(ɪ)ts saŋ]
And there I'll lie and dream
[ænd ðɛːʌɾ ɑːɪl lɑːɪ ænd dɹim]
The day along:
[ðʊ dɛːɪ ʌˈlaŋ]
And, when night comes, I'll go
[ænd ʍɛn nɑːɪt kʌmz ɑːɪl goːʊ]
To places fit for woe,
[tu ˈplɛːɪsɛ(ɪ)z fɪt fɔ woːʊ]
Walking along the darkened valley
[ˈwɔkɪŋ ʌˈlaŋ ðʊ ˈdakɛ(ɪ)nd ˈvæli]
With silent Melancholy.
[wɪð ˈsɑːɪlɛnt ˈmɛlæ(ɪ)n̩ˌkali]

2. Piping Down the Valleys Wild
[ˈpɑːɪpɪŋ dɑːʊn ðʊ ˈvæliz wɑːɪld]

Piping down the valleys wild,
[ˈpɑːɪpɪŋ dɑːʊn ðʊ ˈvæliz wɑːɪld]
Piping songs of pleasant glee,
[ˈpɑːɪpɪŋ saŋz ʌv ˈplɛzæ(ɪ)nt gli]
On a cloud I saw a child,
[an ʌ klɑːʊd ɑːɪ sɔ ʌ tʃɑːɪld]
And he laughing said to me:
[ænd hi ˈlafɪŋ sɛd tu mi]

"Pipe a song about a lamb!"
[pɑːɪp ʌ saŋ ʌˈbaːʊt ʌ læm]
So I piped with merry cheer.
[soːʊ ɑːɪ pɑːɪpt wɪð ˈmɛɹɪ tʃiːʌ]
"Piper, pipe that song again;"
[ˈpɑːɪpʌ pɑːɪp ðæt saŋ ʌˈgɛːɪn]
So I piped: he wept to hear.
[soːʊ ɑːɪ pɑːɪpt hi wɛpt tu hɪːʌ]
"Drop thy pipe, thy happy pipe;
[dɹap ðɑːɪ pɑːɪp ðɑːɪ ˈhæpɪ pɑːɪp]
Sing thy songs of happy cheer!"
[sɪŋ ðɑːɪ saŋz ʌv ˈhæpɪ tʃiːʌ]
So I sang the same again,
[soːʊ ɑːɪ sæŋ ðʊ sɛːɪm ʌˈgɛːɪn]
While he wept with joy to hear.
[ʍɑːɪl hi wɛpt wɪð dʒɔːɪ tu hɪːʌ]
"Piper, sit thee down and write
[ˈpɑːɪpʌ sɪt ði dɑːʊn ænd ɹɑːɪt]
In a book, that all may read."
[ɪn ʌ bʊk ðæt ɔl mɛːɪ ɹid]
So he vanished from my sight;
[soːʊ hi ˈvænɪʃt fɹʌm mɑːɪ sɑːɪt]
And I pluck'd a hollow reed,
[ænd ɑːɪ plʌkt ʌ ˈhaloːʊ ɹid]
And I made a rural pen,
[ænd ɑːɪ mɛːɪd ʌ ˈɾʊːʌɾʊl pɛn]
And I stain'd the water clear,
[ænd ɑːɪ stɛːɪnd ðʊ ˈwɔtʌ klɪːʌ]
And I wrote my happy songs
[ænd ɑːɪ ɾoːʊt mɑːɪ ˈhæpɪ saŋz]
Every child may joy to hear.
[ˈɛvɹɪ tʃɑːɪld mɛːɪ dʒɔːɪ tu hɪːʌ]

3. How Sweet I Roam'd
[hɑːʊ swit ɑːɪ ɹoːʊmd]

How sweet I roam'd from field to field,
[hɑːʊ swit ɑːɪ ɾoːʊmd fɹʌm fild tu fild]
And tasted all the summer's pride
[ænd ˈtɛːɪstɛ(ɪ)d ɔl ðʊ ˈsʌmʌz pɹɑːɪd]
'Till I the prince of love beheld
[tɪl ɑːɪ ðʊ pɹɪns ʌv lʌv bɪˈhɛld]
Who in the sunny beams did glide!
[hu ɪn ðʊ ˈsʌnɪ bimz dɪd glɑːɪd]
He shew'd me lilies for my hair
[hi ʃoːʊd mi ˈlɪlɪz fɔ mɑːɪ hɛːʌ]
And blushing roses for my brow;
[ænd ˈblʌʃɪŋ ˈɹoːʊzɛ(ɪ)z fɔ mɑːɪ bɹɑːʊ]
He led me through the gardens fair,
[hi lɛd mi θɾu ðʊ ˈgadɛ(ɪ)nz fɛːʌ]
Where all his golden pleasures grow.
[ʍɛːʌɾ ɔl hɪz ˈgoːʊldɛ(ɪ)n ˈplɛʒʊ(ʌ)z gɹoːʊ]
With sweet May dews my wings were wet,
[wɪð swit mɛːɪ djuz mɑːɪ wɪŋz wɜ wɛt]
And Phoebus fir'd my vocal rage
[ænd ˈfibʊs fɑːɪʌd mɑːɪ ˈvoːʊkʊl ɹɛːɪdʒ]

He caught me in his silken net,
[hi kɔt mi ɪn hɪz 'sɪlkɛ(ɪ)n nɛt]
And shut me in his golden cage.
[ænd ʃʌt mi ɪn hɪz 'go:ʊldɛ(ɪ)n kɛ:ɪʤ]
He loves to sit and hear me sing,
[hi lʌvz tu sɪt ænd hɪ:ʌ mi sɪŋ]
Then, laughing, sports and plays with me;
[ðɛn 'lafɪŋ spɔts ænd plɛ:ɪz wɪð mi]
He stretches out my golden wing,
[hi 'stɹɛtʃɛ(ɪ)z a:ʊt ma:ɪ 'go:ʊldɛ(ɪ)n wɪŋ]
And mocks my loss of liberty.
[ænd maks ma:ɪ las ʌv 'lɪbʌtɪ]

4. I Love the Jocund Dance

[a:ɪ lʌv ðʊ 'ʤakʌnd dans]

I love the jocund dance,
[a:ɪ lʌv ðʊ 'ʤakʌnd dans]
The softly breathing song,
[ðʊ 'saftlɪ 'bɹiðɪŋ saŋ]
Where innocent eyes do glance
[ʍɛ:ʌʁ(ʳ) 'ɪno(ʌ)sɛnt a:ɪz du glans]
And where lisps the maiden's tongue.
[ænd ʍɛ:ʌ lɪsps ðʊ 'mɛ:ɪdɛ(ɪ)nz tʌŋ]
I love the laughing vale,
[a:ɪ lʌv ðʊ 'lafɪŋ vɛ:ɪl]
I love the echoing hill,
[a:ɪ lʌv ði 'ɛko:ʊɪŋ hɪl]
Where mirth does never fail,
[ʍɛ:ʌ mɜθ dʌz 'nɛvʌ fɛ:ɪl]
And the jolly swain laughs his fill.
[ænd ðʊ 'ʤalɪ swɛ:ɪn lafs hɪz fil]
I love the pleasant cot,
[a:ɪ lʌv ðʊ 'plɛzæ(ɪ)nt kat]
I love the innocent bower,
[a:ɪ lʌv ði 'ɪno(ʌ)sɛnt 'ba:ʊʌ]
Where white and brown is our lot
[ʍɛ:ʌ ʍa:ɪt ænd bɹa:ʊn ɪz a:ʊʌ lat]
Or fruit in the midday hour.
[ɔ frut ɪn ðʊ 'mɪdɛ:ʌ a:ʊʌ]
I love the oaken seat,
[a:ɪ lʌv ði 'o:ʊkɛ(ɪ)n sit]
Beneath the oaken tree,
[bɪ'niθ ði 'o:ʊkɛ(ɪ)n tɹi]
Where all the old villagers meet,
[ʍɛ:ʌʁ ɔl ði o:ʊld 'vɪlæ(ɪ)ʤʌz mit]
And laugh our sports to see.
[ænd laf a:ʊʌ spɔts tu si]
I love our neighbors all,
[a:ɪ lʌv a:ʊʌ 'nɛ:ɪbɔ(ʌ)z ɔl]
But, Kitty, I better love thee
[bʌt 'kɪtɪ a:ɪ 'bɛtʌ lʌv ði]
And love them I ever shall,
[ænd lʌv ðɛm a:ɪ 'ɛvʌ ʃæl]
But thou art all to me.
[bʌt ða:ʊ at ɔl tu mi]

Song Selection

"The Orange Tree"
[ði 'ɔʁɪnʤ tɹi]
Neilson, John Shaw (Au. 1872-1942)

The young girl stood beside me.
[ðʊ jʌŋ gɜl stʊd bɪ'sa:ɪd mi]
I saw not what her young eyes could see:
[a:ɪ sɔ nat ʍat hɜ jʌŋ a:ɪz kʊd si]
- A light, she said, not of the sky
[ʌ la:ɪt ʃi sɛd nat ʌv ðʊ ska:ɪ]
Lives somewhere in the orange tree.
[lɪvz 'sʌmʍɛ:ʌɾ ɪn ði 'ɔræ(ɪ)nʤ tɹi]
- is it, I said, of east or west?
[ɪz ɪt a:ɪ sɛd ʌv ist ɔ wɛst]
The heart beat of a luminous boy
[ðʊ hat bit ʌv ʌ 'ljumɪnʌs bɔ:ɪ]
Who with his faltering flute confessed
[hu wɪð hɪz 'fɔltʌɾɪŋ flut kʌn'fɛst]
Only the edges of his joy?
['o:ʊnlɪ ði 'ɛdʒɛ(ɪ)z ʌv hɪz ʤɔ:ɪ]
- Was he, I said, home to the blue
[waz hi a:ɪ sɛd ho:ʊm tu ðʊ blu]
In a mad escapade of Spring
[ɪn ʌ mæd 'ɛskʌ'pɛ:ɪd ʌv spɹɪŋ]
Ere he could make a fond adieu
[ɛ:ʌ hi kʊd mɛ:ɪk ʌ fand a'djø]
To his love in the blossoming?
[tu hɪz lʌv ɪn ðʊ 'blasʌmɪŋ]
- Listen! The young girl said. There calls
['lɪsɛ(ɪ)n ðʊ jʌŋ gɜl sɛd ðɛ:ʌ kɔlz]
No voice, no music beats on me;
[no:ʊ vɔ:ɪs no:ʊ 'mjuzɪk bits an mi]
But it is almost sound: it falls
[bʌt ɪt ɪz 'ɔlmo:ʊst sa:ʊnd ɪt fɔlz]
This evening on the orange tree.
[ðɪs 'ivnɪŋ an ði 'ɔræ(ɪ)nʤ tɹi]
- Does he, I said, so fear the Spring
[dʌz hi a:ɪ sɛd so:ʊ fɪ:ʌ ðʊ spɹɪŋ]
Ere the white sap too far can climb?
[ɛ:ʌ ðʊ ʍa:ɪt sæp tu fa kæn kla:ɪm]
See in the full gold evening
[si ɪn ðʊ fʊl go:ʊld 'ivnɪŋ]
All happenings of the olden time?
[ɔl 'hæpɪnɪŋz ʌv ði 'o:ʊldɛ(ɪ)n ta:ɪm]
Is he so goaded by the green?
[ɪz hi so:ʊ 'go:ʊdɛ(ɪ)d ba:ɪ ðʊ gɹin]
Does the compulsion of the dew
[dʌz ðʊ kʌm'pʌlʃʌn ʌv ðʊ dju]
Make him unknowable but keen
[mɛ:ɪk hɪm ʌn'no:ʊʌbʊl bʌt kin]
Asking with beauty of the blue?
['askɪŋ wɪð 'bjutɪ ʌv ðʊ blu]
- Listen! The young girl said. For all
['lɪsɛ(ɪ)n ðʊ jʌŋ gɜl sɛd fɔʁ(ʳ) ɔl]

Your hapless talk you fail to see
[jɔːʌ 'hæplɛ(ɪ)s tɔk ju fɛːɪl tu si]
There is a light, a step, a call,
[ðɛːʌɾ ɪz ʌ laːɪt ʌ stɛp ʌ kɔl]
This evening on the orange tree.
[ðɪs 'ivnɪŋ ɑn ði 'ɔɾæ(ɪ)ndʒ tɹi]
- is it, I said, a waste of love
[ɪz ɪt aːɪ sɛd ʌ wɛːɪst ʌv lʌv]
Imperishably old in pain,
[ɪm'pɛɾɪʃʌblɪ oːʊld ɪn pɛːɪn]
Moving as an affrighted dove
['muvɪŋ æz æn ʌ'fɹaːɪtɛ(ɪ)d dʌv]
Under the sunlight or the rain?
['ʌndʌ ðʊ 'sʌnlaːɪt ɔ ðʊ ɾɛːɪn]
Is it a fluttering heart that gave
[ɪz ɪt ʌ 'flʌtʌɾɪŋ hat ðæt gɛːɪv]
Too willingly and was reviled?
[tu 'wɪlɪŋlɪ ænd wɑz ɹɪ'vaːɪld]
Is it the stammering at a grave,
[ɪz ɪt ðʊ 'stæmʌɾɪŋ æt ʌ gɹɛːɪv]
The last word of a little child?
[ðʊ last wɜd ʌv ʌ 'lɪtʊl ʧaːɪld]
- Silence! The young girl said. Oh why,
['saːɪlɛ(ɪ)ns ðʊ jʌŋ gɜl sɛd oːʊ ʍaːɪ]
Why will you talk to weary me?
[ʍaːɪ wɪl ju tɔk tu 'wɪːʌɾɪ mi]
Plague me no longer now, for I
[plɛːɪg mi noːʊ 'laŋgʌ naːʊ fɔʁ⁽ʳ⁾ aːɪ]
Am listening like the orange tree.
[æm 'lɪsɛ(ɪ)nɪŋ laːɪk ði 'ɔɾæ(ɪ)ndʒ tɹi]

T

Thiman, Eric (Eng. 1900-1975)

Song Selection

"Jesus, the Very Thought of Thee"
['dʒizʌs ðʊ 'vɛʁi θɔt ʌv ði]
Bernard of Clairvaux (tr. by Edward Caswall)

Jesus, the very thought of Thee
['dʒizʌs ðʊ 'vɛɾi θɔt ʌv ði]
With sweetness fills my breast,
[wɪð 'switnɛ(ɪ)s fɪlz maːɪ bɹɛst]
But sweeter far Thy face to see,
[bʌt 'switʌ fa ðaːɪ fɛːɪs tu si]
And in Thy presence rest.
[ænd ɪn ðaːɪ 'pɹɛzɛ(ɪ)ns ɹɛst]
Nor voice can sing, nor heart can frame,
[nɔ vɔːɪs kæn sɪŋ nɔ hat kæn fɹɛːɪm]
Nor can the mem'ry find
[nɔ kæn ðʊ 'mɛmɹɪ faːɪnd]

A sweeter sound than Thy blest name,
[ʌ 'switʌ saːʊnd ðæn ðaːɪ blɛst nɛːɪm]
O Saviour of mankind.
[oːʊ 'sɛːɪvjɔ(ʌ)ɾ ʌv mæn'kaːɪnd]
O Hope of every contrite heart,
[oːʊ hoːʊp ʌv 'ɛvɹɪ 'kantɹaːɪt hat]
O Joy of all the meek,
[oːʊ dʒɔːɪ ʌv ɔl ðʊ mik]
To those who fall, how kind Thou art,
[tu ðoːʊz hu fɔl haːʊ kaːɪnd ðaːʊ at]
How good to those who seek!
[haːʊ gʊd tu ðoːʊz hu sik]
But what to those who find? ah, this
[bʌt ʍat tu ðoːʊz hu faːɪnd a ðɪs]
Nor tongue nor pen can show;
[nɔ tʌŋ nɔ pɛn kæn ʃoːʊ]
The love of Jesus, what it is
[ðʊ lʌv ʌv 'dʒizʌs ʍat ɪt ɪz]
None but His loved ones know.
[nʌn bʌt hɪz lʌvd wʌnz noːʊ]
Jesus, our only joy be Thou,
['dʒizʌs aːʊʌɾ 'oːʊnlɪ dʒɔːɪ bi ðaːʊ]
As Thou our prize will be;
[æz ðaːʊ aːʊʌ pɹaːɪz wɪl bi]
Jesus, be Thou our glory now,
['dʒizʌs bi ðaːʊ aːʊʌ 'glɔɾɪ naːʊ]
And through eternity.
[ænd θɹu ɪ'tɜnɪtɪ]

Thomson, Virgil (Am. 1896-1989)

Five Songs from William Blake (Song Cycle)
[faːɪv saŋz fɹʌm 'wɪljɪm blɛːɪk]
Blake, William (Eng. 1757-1827)

1. The Divine Image
[ðʌ dɪ'vaːɪn 'ɪmɪdʒ]

To Mercy, Pity, Peace and Love
[tu 'mɜsɪ 'pɪtɪ pis ænd lʌv]
All pray in their distress;
[ɔl pɹɛːɪ ɪn ðɛːʌ dɪ'stɹɛs]
And to these virtues of delight
[ænd tu ðiz 'vɜʧuz ʌv dɪ'laːɪt]
Return their thankfulness.
[ɹɪ'tɜn ðɛːʌ 'θæŋkfʊlnɛ(ɪ)s]
For Mercy, Pity, Peace, and Love
[fɔ 'mɜsɪ 'pɪtɪ pis ænd lʌv]
Is God, our Father dear;
[ɪz gad aːʊʌ 'faðʌ dɪːʌ]
And Mercy, Pity, Peace, and Love
[ænd 'mɜsɪ 'pɪtɪ pis ænd lʌv]
Is man, His child and care.
[ɪz mæn hɪz ʧaːɪld ænd kɛːʌ]

For Mercy has a human heart,
[fɔ ˈmɜsɪ hæz ʌ ˈhjumæ(ʌ)n hɑt]
Pity a human face,
[ˈpɪtɪ ʌ ˈhjumæ(ʌ)n fɛːɪs]
And Love, the human form divine,
[ænd lʌv ðʌ ˈhjumæ(ʌ)n fɔm dɪˈvɑːɪn]
And Peace, the human dress.
[ænd pis ðʌ ˈhjumæ(ʌ)n dɹɛs]
Then every man, of every clime,
[ðɛn ˈɛvɹɪ mæn ʌv ˈɛvɹɪ klɑːɪm]
That prays in his distress,
[ðæt pɹɛːɪz ɪn hɪz dɪˈstɹɛs]
Prays to the human form divine,
[pɹɛːɪz tu ðʌ ˈhjumæ(ʌ)n fɔm dɪˈvɑːɪn]
Love, Mercy, Pity, Peace.
[lʌv ˈmɜsɪ ˈpɪtɪ pis]
And all must love the human form,
[ænd ɔl mʌst lʌv ðʌ ˈhjumæ(ʌ)n fɔm]
In heathen, Turk, or Jew;
[ɪn ˈhiðɛ(ɪ)n tɜk ɔ dʒu]
Where Mercy, Love, and Pity dwell
[ʍɛːʌ ˈmɜsɪ lʌv ænd ˈpɪtɪ dwɛl]
There God is dwelling too.
[ðɛːʌ ɡɑd ɪz ˈdwɛlɪŋ tu]

2. Tiger! Tiger!
[ˈtɑːɪɡʁ ˈtɑːɪɡʁ]

Tiger! Tiger! burning bright,
[ˈtɑːɪɡʌ ˈtɑːɪɡʌ ˈbɜnɪŋ bɹɑːɪt]
In the forests of the night;
[ɪn ðʌ ˈfɔʁ⁽ʳ⁾ɛ(ɪ)sts ʌv ðʌ nɑːɪt]
What immortal hand or eye,
[ʍɑt ɪˈmɔtʊl hænd ɔʁ⁽ʳ⁾ ɑːɪ]
Could frame thy fearful symmetry?
[kʊd fɹɛːɪm ðɑːɪ ˈfɪːʌfʊl ˈsɪmɛ(ɪ)tɹɪ]
In what distant deeps or skies
[ɪn ʍɑt ˈdɪstæ(ɪ)nt dips ɔ skɑːɪz]
Burnt the fire of thine eyes?
[bɜnt ðʌ fɑːɪʌʁ⁽ʳ⁾ ʌv ðɑːɪn ɑːɪz]
On what wings dare he aspire?
[ɑn ʍɑt wɪŋz dɛːʌ hi ʌˈspɑːɪʌ]
What the hand dare seize the fire?
[ʍɑt ðʌ hænd dɛːʌ siz ðʌ fɑːɪʌ]
And what shoulder, and what art,
[ænd ʍɑt ˈʃoːʊldʌʁ⁽ʳ⁾ ænd ʍɑt ɑt]
Could twist the sinews of thy heart?
[kʊd twɪst ðʌ ˈsɪnjuz ʌv ðɑːɪ hɑt]
And when the heart began to beat,
[ænd ʍɛn ðʌ hɑt bɪˈɡæn tu bit]
What dread hand? and what dread feet?
[ʍɑt dɹɛd hænd ænd ʍɑt dɹɛd fit]
What the hammer? what the chain?
[ʍɑt ðʌ ˈhæmʌ ʍɑt ðʌ ʧɛːɪn]
In what furnace was thy brain?
[ɪn ʍɑt ˈfɜnæ(ɪ)s wɑz ðɑːɪ bɹɛːɪn]

What the anvil? what dread grasp,
[ʍɑt ði ˈænvɪ(ʊ)l ʍɑt dɹɛd ɡɹæsp]
Dare its deadly terrors clasp?
[dɛːʌ ɪts ˈdɛdlɪ ˈtɛʁ⁽ʳ⁾ɔ(ʌ)z klæsp]
When the stars threw down their spears
[ʍɛn ðʌ stɑz θɹu dɑːʊn ðɛːʌ spɪːʌz]
And water'd heaven with their tears:
[ænd ˈwɔtʌd ˈhɛvɪn wɪð ðɛːʌ tɪːʌz]
Did he smile his work to see?
[dɪd hi smɑːɪl hɪz wɜk tu si]
Did he who made the Lamb make thee?
[dɪd hi hu mɛːɪd ðʌ læm mɛːɪk ði]
Tiger! Tiger! Burning bright,
[ˈtɑːɪɡʌ ˈtɑːɪɡʌ ˈbɜnɪŋ bɹɑːɪt]
In the forests of the night,
[ɪn ðʌ ˈfɔʁ⁽ʳ⁾ɛ(ɪ)sts ʌv ðʌ nɑːɪt]
What immortal hand or eye,
[ʍɑt ɪˈmɔtʊl hænd ɔʁ⁽ʳ⁾ ɑːɪ]
Dare frame thy fearful symmetry?
[dɛːʌ fɹɛːɪm ðɑːɪ ˈfɪːʌfʊl ˈsɪmɛ(ɪ)tɹɪ]

3. The Land of Dreams
[ðʌ lænd ʌv dɹimz]

Awake, awake, my little boy!
[ʌˈwɛːɪk ʌˈwɛːɪk mɑːɪ ˈlɪtʊl bɔːɪ]
Thou wast thy mother's only joy.
[ðɑːʊ wɑst ðɑːɪ ˈmʌðʌz ˈoːʊnlɪ dʒɔːɪ]
Why dost thou weep in thy gentle sleep?
[ʍɑːɪ dʌst ðɑːʊ wip ɪn ðɑːɪ ˈdʒɛntʊl slip]
Awake! thy father does thee keep.
[ʌˈwɛːɪk ðɑːɪ ˈfɑðʌ dʌz ði kip]
O, what land is the land of dreams?
[oːʊ ʍɑt lænd ɪz ðʌ lænd ʌv dɹimz]
What are its mountains, and what are its streams?
[ʍɑt ɑʁ⁽ʳ⁾ ɪts ˈmɑːʊntæ(ɪ)nz ænd ʍɑt ɑʁ⁽ʳ⁾ ɪts stɹimz]
O, father! I saw my mother there,
[oːʊ ˈfɑðʌ ɑːɪ sɔ mɑːɪ ˈmʌðʌ ðɛːʌ]
Among the lilies by waters fair.
[ʌˈmʌŋ ðʌ ˈlɪlɪz bɑːɪ ˈwɔtʌz fɛːʌ]
Among the lambs, clothed in white,
[ʌˈmʌŋ ðʌ læmz ˈkloːʊðɛ(ɪ)d ɪn ʍɑːɪt]
She walked with her Thomas in sweet delight.
[ʃi wɔkt wɪð hɜ ˈtɑmʌs ɪn swit dɪˈlɑːɪt]
I wept for joy, like a dove I mourn.
[ɑːɪ wɛpt fɔ dʒɔːɪ lɑːɪk ʌ dʌv ɑːɪ mɔn]
O! when shall I again return?
[oːʊ ʍɛn ʃæl ɑːɪ ʌˈɡɛn ɹɪˈtɜn]
Dear child, I also by pleasant streams
[dɪːʌ ʧɑːɪld ɑːɪ ˈɔlsoːʊ bɑːɪ ˈplɛzæ(ɪ)nt stɹimz]
Have wandered all night in the land of dreams;
[hæv ˈwɑndʌd ɔl nɑːɪt ɪn ðʌ lænd ʌv dɹimz]
But though calm and warm the waters wide,
[bʌt ðoːʊ kɑm ænd wɔm ðʌ ˈwɔtʌz wɑːɪd]
I could not get to the other side.
[ɑːɪ kʊd nɑt ɡɛt tu ði ˈʌðʌ sɑːɪd]

Father, O father! what do we here,
[ˈfaðʌʁ⁽ʳ⁾ oːʊ ˈfaðʌ ʍat du wi hɪːʌ]
In this land of unbelief and fear?
[ɪn ðɪs lænd ʌv ʌnbɪˈlif ænd fɪːʌ]
The land of dreams is better far–
[ðʌ lænd ʌv dɹimz ɪz ˈbɛtʌ fa]
Above the light of the morning star.
[ʌˈbʌv ðʌ laːɪt ʌv ðʌ ˈmɔnɪŋ sta]

4. The Little Black Boy
[ðʌ ˈlɪtʊl blæk bɔːɪ]

My mother bore me in the southern wild,
[maːɪ ˈmʌðʌ bɔːʌ mi ɪn ðʌ ˈsʌðʌn waːɪld]
And I am black, but O! my soul is white;
[ænd aːɪ æm blæk bʌt oːʊ maːɪ soːʊl ɪz ʍaːɪt]
White as an angel is the English child,
[ʍaːɪt æz æn ˈɛːɪndʒɛ⁽ʊ⁾l ɪz ði ˈɪŋglɪʃ ʧaːɪld]
But I am black, as if bereaved of light.
[bʌt aːɪ æm blæk æz ɪf bɪˈʁ⁽ʳ⁾ivd ʌv laːɪt]
My mother taught me underneath a tree,
[maːɪ ˈmʌðʌ tɔt mi ʌndʌˈniθ ʌ tɹi]
And, sitting down before the heat of day,
[ænd ˈsɪtɪŋ daːʊn bɪˈfɔːʌ ðʌ hit ʌv dɛːɪ]
She took me on her lap and kissed me,
[ʃi tʊk mi ɑn hɜ læp ænd ˈkɪsɛ⁽ɪ⁾d mi]
And, pointing to the east, began to say:
[ænd ˈpɔːɪntɪŋ tu ði ist bɪˈgæn tu sɛːɪ]
"Look at the rising sun, there God does live,
[lʊk æt ðʌ ˈɹaːɪzɪŋ sʌn ðɛːʌ gad dʌz lɪv]
And gives His light, and gives His heat away;
[ænd gɪvz hɪz laːɪt ænd gɪvz hɪz hit ʌˈwɛːɪ]
And flowers and trees and beasts and men receive
[ænd flaːʊʌz ænd tɹiz ænd bists ænd mɛn ɹɪˈsiv]
Comfort in morning, joy in the noonday.
[ˈkʌmfɔt ɪn ˈmɔnɪŋ dʒɔːɪ ɪn ðʌ ˈnundɛːɪ]
And we are put on earth a little space,
[ænd wi ɑ pʊt ɑn ɜθ ʌ ˈlɪtʊl spɛːɪs]
That we may learn to bear the beams of love;
[ðæt wi mɛːɪ lɜn tu bɛːʌ ðʌ bimz ʌv lʌv]
And these black bodies and this sunburnt face
[ænd ðiz blæk ˈbadɪz ænd ðɪs ˈsʌnbɜnt fɛːɪs]
Is but a cloud, and like a shady grove.
[ɪz bʌt ʌ klaːʊd ænd laːɪk ʌ ˈʃɛːɪdɪ gɹoːʊv]
For when our souls have learn'd the heat to bear,
[fɔ ʍɛn aːʊʌ soːʊlz hæv lɜnd ðʌ hit tu bɛːʌ]
The cloud will vanish; we shall hear His voice,
[ðʌ klaːʊd wɪl ˈvænɪʃ wi ʃæl hɪːʌ hɪz vɔːɪs]
Saying: "Come out from the grove, my love and care,
[ˈsɛːɪɪŋ kʌm aːʊt fɹʌm ðʌ gɹoːʊv maːɪ lʌv ænd kɛːʌ]
And round my golden tent like lambs rejoice."
[ænd ɹaːʊnd maːɪ ˈgoːʊldɛ⁽ɪ⁾n tɛnt laːɪk læmz ɹɪˈdʒɔːɪs]
Thus did my mother say, and kissed me;
[ðʌs dɪd maːɪ ˈmʌðʌ sɛːɪ ænd ˈkɪsɛ⁽ɪ⁾d mi]
And thus I say to little English boy:
[ænd ðʌs aːɪ sɛːɪ tu ˈlɪtʊl ˈɪŋglɪʃ bɔːɪ]

When I from black and he from white cloud free,
[ʍɛn aːɪ fɹʌm blæk ænd hi fɹʌm ʍaːɪt klaːʊd fɹi]
And round the tent of God like lambs we joy,
[ænd ɹaːʊnd ðʌ tɛnt ʌv gad laːɪk læmz wi dʒɔːɪ]
I'll shade him from the heat till he can bear,
[aːɪl ʃɛːɪd hɪm fɹʌm ðʌ hit tɪl hi kæn bɛːʌ]
To lean in joy upon our Father's knee;
[tu lin ɪn dʒɔːɪ ʌˈpan aːʊʌ ˈfaðʌz ni]
And then I'll stand and stroke his silver hair,
[ænd ðɛn aːɪl stænd ænd stɹoːʊk hɪz ˈsɪlvʌ hɛːʌ]
And be like him, and he will then love me.
[ænd bi laːɪk hɪm ænd hi wɪl ðɛn lʌv mi]

5. And Did Those Feet
[ænd dɪd ðoːʊz fit]

And did those feet in ancient times
[ænd dɪd ðoːʊz fit ɪn ˈɛːɪntʃɛnt taːɪmz]
Walk upon England's mountains green?
[wɔk ʌˈpan ˈɪŋglæ⁽ʌ⁾ndz ˈmaːʊntɛ⁽ɪ⁾nz gɹin]
And was the holy Lamb of God
[ænd waz ðʌ ˈhoːʊlɪ læm ʌv gad]
On England's pleasant pastures seen?
[an ˈɪŋglæ⁽ʌ⁾ndz ˈplɛzæ⁽ɪ⁾nt ˈpasʧʊ⁽ʌ⁾z sin]
And did the Countenance Divine
[ænd dɪd ðʌ ˈkaːʊntɛ⁽ɪ⁾næ⁽ɪ⁾ns dɪˈvaːɪn]
Shine forth upon our clouded hills?
[ʃaːɪn fɔθ ʌˈpan aːʊʌ ˈklaːʊdɛ⁽ɪ⁾d hɪlz]
And was Jerusalem builded here
[ænd waz dʒɛˈʁ⁽ʳ⁾usʌlɛm ˈbɪldɛ⁽ɪ⁾d hɪːʌ]
Among these dark Satanic Mills?
[ʌˈmʌŋ ðiz dak sɛːɪˈtænɪk mɪlz]
Bring me my bow of burning gold!
[bɹɪŋ mi maːɪ boːʊ ʌv ˈbɜnɪŋ goːʊld]
Bring me my arrows of desire!
[bɹɪŋ mi maːɪ ˈæʁ⁽ʳ⁾oːʊz ʌv dɪˈzaːɪʌ]
Bring me my spear! O clouds, unfold!
[bɹɪŋ mi maːɪ spɪːʌ oːʊ klaːʊdz ʌnˈfoːʊld]
Bring me my chariot of fire!
[bɹɪŋ mi maːɪ ˈʧæʁ⁽ʳ⁾ɪʌt ʌv faːɪʌ]
I will not cease from mental fight,
[aːɪ wɪl nat sis fɹʌm ˈmɛntʊl faːɪt]
Nor shall my sword sleep in my hand,
[nɔ ʃæl maːɪ sɔd slip ɪn maːɪ hænd]
Till we have built Jerusalem
[tɪl wi hæv bɪlt dʒɛˈʁ⁽ʳ⁾usʌlɛm]
In England's green and pleasant land.
[ɪn ˈɪŋglæ⁽ʌ⁾ndz gɹin ænd ˈplɛzæ⁽ɪ⁾nt lænd]

Song Selections

"If Thou a Reason Dost Desire to Know"
[ɪf ðɑːʊ ʌ ˈɹizʌn dʌst dɪˈzɑːɪʁ tu noːʊ]
Kynaston, Sir Francis (Eng. 1587-1642)

If thou a reason dost desire to know,
[ɪf ðɑːʊ ʌ ˈɹizʌn dʌst dɪˈzɑːɪʌ tu noːʊ]
My dearest Cynthia, why I love thee so,
[mɑːɪ ˈdɪːʌʁ⁽ʳ⁾ɛ⁽ɪ⁾st ˈsɪnθɪʌ ʍɑːɪ ɑːɪ lʌv ði soːʊ]
As when I do enjoy all thy love's store,
[æz ʍɛn ɑːɪ du ɪnˈʤɔːɪ ɔl ðɑːɪ lʌvz stɔːʌ]
I am not yet content, but seek for more;
[ɑːɪ æm nɑt jɛt kʌnˈtɛnt bʌt sik fɔ mɔːʌ]
When we do kiss so often as the tale
[ʍɛn wi du kɪs soːʊ ˈɑfɛ⁽ɪ⁾n æz ðʌ tɛːɪl]
Of kisses doth out vie the winter's hail:
[ʌv ˈkɪsɛ⁽ɪ⁾z dʌθ ɑːʊt vɑːɪ ðʌ ˈwɪntʌz hɛːɪl]
When I do print them on more close and sweet
[ʍɛn ɑːɪ du pɹɪnt ðɛm ɑn mɔːʌ kloːʊs ænd swit]
Than shells of scallops, cockles when they meet,
[ðæn ʃɛlz ʌv ˈskælʌps ˈkɑkʊlz ʍɛn ðɛːɪ mit]
Yet am not satisfied: when I do close
[jɛt æm nɑt ˈsætɪsfɑːɪd ʍɛn ɑːɪ du kloːʊz]
Thee nearer to me than the ivy grows
[ði ˈnɪːʌʁ⁽ʳ⁾ʌ tu mi ðæn ði ˈɑːɪvi ɡɹoːʊz]
unto the oak: when those white arms of thine
[ˈʌntu ði oːʊk ʍɛn ðoːʊz ʍɑːɪt ɑmz ʌv ðɑːɪn]
Clip me more close than doth the elm the vine:
[klɪp mi mɔːʌ kloːʊs ðæn dʌθ ði ɛlm ðʌ vɑːɪn]
When naked both, thou seemest not to be
[ʍɛn ˈnɛːɪkɛ⁽ɪ⁾d boːʊθ ðɑːʊ ˈsimɛ⁽ɪ⁾st nɑt tu bi]
Contiguous, but continuous parts of me:
[kʌnˈtɪɡjuʌs bʌt kʌnˈtɪnjuʌs pɑts ʌv mi]
And we in bodies are together brought
[ænd wi ɪn ˈbɑdɪz ɑ tuˈɡɛðʌ bɹɔt]
So near, so near, our souls may know each
[soːʊ nɪːʌ soːʊ nɪːʌ ɑːʊʌ soːʊlz mɛːɪ noːʊ itʃ]
other's thought without a whisper: yet I do aspire
[ˈʌðʌz θɔt wɪðˈɑːʊt ʌ ˈʍɪspʌ jɛt ɑːɪ du ʌˈspɑːɪʌ]
To come more close to thee, and to be nigher,
[tu kʌm mɔːʌ kloːʊs tu ði ænd tu bi ˈnɑːɪʌ]
Know, 'twas well said, that spirits are too high
[noːʊ twaz wɛl sɛd ðæt ˈspɪʁ⁽ʳ⁾ɪts ɑ tu hɑːɪ]
For bodies, when they meet, to satisfy.
[fɔ ˈbɑdɪz ʍɛn ðɛːɪ mit tu ˈsætɪsfɑːɪ]

"Sigh No More, Ladies" (See Dowland)

"Take, O Take Those Lips Away" (See Beach)

"Tell Me Where Is Fancy Bred"
[tɛl mi ʍɛːʁ ɪz ˈfænsi bɹɛd]
Shakespeare, William (Eng. 1564-1616)

Tell me where is Fancy bred,
[tɛl mi ʍɛːʌʁ ɪz ˈfænsɪ bɹɛd]
Or in the heart, or in the head,
[ɔʁ⁽ʳ⁾ ɪn ðʌ hat ɔʁ⁽ʳ⁾ ɪn ðʌ hɛd]
How begot, how nourished?
[hɑːʊ bɪˈɡat hɑːʊ ˈnʊɾɪʃɛ⁽ɪ⁾d]
Reply, reply!
[ɹɪˈplɑːɪ ɹɪˈplɑːɪ]
It is engender'd in the eyes,
[ɪt ɪz ɪnˈʤɛndʌd ɪn ði ɑːɪz]
With gazing fed; and Fancy dies–
[wɪð ˈɡɛːɪzɪŋ fɛd ænd ˈfænsɪ dɑːɪz]
In the cradle where it lies.–
[ɪn ðʌ ˈkɹɛːɪdʊl ʍɛːʌʁ ɪt lɑːɪz]
Let us all ring– Fancy's knell.
[lɛt ʌs ɔl ɹɪŋ ˈfænsɪz nɛl]
Ding, dong, ding, dong, bell.
[dɪŋ daŋ dɪŋ daŋ bɛl]

Tosti, Paolo (It. 1846-1916)

Song Selections

"Goodbye"
[ɡʊdˈbɑːɪ]
Whyte-Melville, George John (Sc. 1821-1878)

Falling leaf and fading tree,
[ˈfɔlɪŋ lif ænd ˈfɛːɪdɪŋ tɹi]
Lines of white in a sullen sea,
[lɑːɪnz ʌv ʍɑːɪt ɪn ʌ ˈsʌlɛ⁽ɪ⁾n si]
Shadows rising on you and me;
[ˈʃædoːʊz ˈɹɑːɪzɪŋ an ju ænd mi]
The swallows are making them ready to fly,
[ðʊ ˈswaloːʊz ɑ ˈmɛːɪkɪŋ ðɛm ˈɹɛdɪ tu flɑːɪ]
Wheeling out on a windy sky.
[ˈʍilɪŋ ɑːʊt an ʌ ˈwɪndɪ skɑːɪ]
Goodbye, Summer! Goodbye, Goodbye!
[ɡʊdˈbɑːɪ ˈsʌmʌ ɡʊdˈbɑːɪ ɡʊdˈbɑːɪ]
Hush! A voice from the far away!
[hʌʃ ʌ vɔːɪs fɹʌm ðʊ far ʌˈwɛːɪ]
"Listen and learn," it seems to say,
[ˈlɪsɛ⁽ɪ⁾n ænd lɜn ɪt simz tu sɛːɪ]
"All the tomorrows shall be as today."
[ɔl ðʊ tuˈmaɾoːʊz ʃæl bi æz tuˈdɛːɪ]
"All the tomorrows shall be as today."
[ɔl ðʊ tuˈmaɾoːʊz ʃæl bi æz tuˈdɛːɪ]
The cord is frayed, the cruse is dry,
[ðʊ kɔd ɪz fɹɛːɪd ðʊ kruz ɪz dɹɑːɪ]
The link must break, and the lamp must die.
[ðʊ lɪŋk mʌst bɹɛːɪk ænd ðʊ læmp mʌst dɑːɪ]

Goodbye, to Hope! Goodbye, Goodbye!
[gʊdˈbaːɪ tu hoːʊp gʊdˈbaːɪ gʊdˈbaːɪ]
What are we waiting for? Oh! my heart!
[ʍat a wi ˈwɛːɪtɪŋ fɔ oːʊ maːɪ hat]
Kiss me straight on the brows! And part! Again!
[kɪs mi stɹɛːɪt an ðʊ bɹaːʊz ænd pat ʌˈgɛːɪn]
Again! my heart! my heart!
[ʌˈgɛːɪn maːɪ hat maːɪ hat]
What are we waiting for, you and I?
[ʍat a wi ˈwɛːɪtɪŋ fɔ ju ænd aːɪ]
A pleading look, a stifled cry.
[ʌ ˈplidɪŋ lʊk ʌ ˈstaːɪfʊld kɹ⁽ʳ⁾aːɪ]
Goodbye, for ever! Goodbye, for ever!
[gʊdˈbaːɪ fɔʁ⁽ʳ⁾ ˈɛvʌ gʊdˈbaːɪ fɔʁ⁽ʳ⁾ ˈɛvʌ]
Goodbye, Goodbye, Goodbye!
[gʊdˈbaːɪ gʊdˈbaːɪ gʊdˈbaːɪ]

"I Dare to Love Thee"
[aːɪ dɛːʌ tu lʌv ði]
Mackay, Mary (Eng. 1855-1924)

As the billow flings shells on the shore,
[æz ðʊ ˈbɪloːʊ flɪŋz ʃɛlz an ðʊ ʃɔːʌ]
As the sun poureth light on the sea
[æz ðʊ sʌn ˈpɔːʌɹɛ⁽ɪ⁾θ laːɪt an ðʊ si]
As a lark on the wing scatters song to the spring,
[æz ʌ lak an ðʊ wɪŋ ˈskætʌz saŋ tu ðʊ spɹɪŋ]
So rushes my love to thee.
[soːʊ ˈɹʌʃɛ⁽ɪ⁾z maːɪ lʌv tu ði]
As the ivy clings close to the tower,
[æz ði ˈaːɪvɪ klɪŋz kloːʊs tu ðʊ taːʊʌ]
As the dew lieth deep in a flower,
[æz ðʊ dju ˈlaːɪɛ⁽ɪ⁾θ dip ɪn ʌ flaːʊʌ]
As the shadow to light, as the day unto night,
[æz ðʊ ˈʃædoːʊ tu laːɪt æz ðʊ dɛːɪ ˈʌntu naːɪt]
So clings my wild soul to thee!
[soːʊ klɪŋz maːɪ waːɪld soːʊl tu ði]
As the moon glitters coldly alone,
[æz ðʊ mun ˈglɪtʌz ˈkoːʊldlɪ ʌˈloːʊn]
Above earth on her cloud-woven throne
[ʌˈbʌv ɜθ an hɜ klaːʊd ˈwoːʊvɛ⁽ɪ⁾n θroːʊn]
As the rocky-bound cave repulses a wave,
[æz ðʊ ˈɹaki baːʊnd kɛːɪv ɹɪˈpʌlsɛ⁽ɪ⁾z ʌ wɛːɪv]
So thy anger repulseth me.
[soːʊ ðaːɪ ˈæŋgʌ ɹɪˈpʌlsɛ⁽ɪ⁾θ mi]
As the bitter black frost of a night
[æz ðʊ ˈbɪtʌ blæk fɹast ʌv ʌ naːɪt]
Slays the roses with pitiless might,
[slɛːɪz ðʊ ˈɹoːʊzɛ⁽ɪ⁾z wɪð ˈpɪtɪlɛ⁽ɪ⁾s maːɪt]
As a sharp dagger-thrust hurls a king to the dust,
[æz ʌ ʃap ˈdægʌ θɹʌst hɜlz ʌ kɪŋ tu ðʊ dʌst]
So thy cruelty murdereth me.
[soːʊ ðaːɪ ˈkruːɛ⁽ʊ⁾ltɪ ˈmɜdʌɹɛ⁽ɪ⁾θ mi]
Yet in spite of thy queenly disdain,
[jɛt ɪn spaːɪt ʌv ðaːɪ ˈkwinlɪ dɪsˈdɛːɪn]

Thou art seared by my passion and pain;
[ðaːʊ at sɪːʌd baːɪ maːɪ ˈpæʃʌn ænd pɛːɪn]
Thou shalt hear me repeat,
[ðaːʊ ʃælt hɪːʌ mi ɹɪˈpit]
Till I die for it sweet!
[tɪl aːɪ daːɪ fɔʁ⁽ʳ⁾ ɪt swit]
I love thee! I love thee! I love thee!
[aːɪ lʌv ði aːɪ lʌv ði aːɪ lʌv ði]
I dare to love thee, To love...
[aːɪ dɛːʌ tu lʌv ði tu lʌv]

"In the Hush of the Night"
[ɪn ðʊ hʌʃ ʌv ðʊ naːɪt]
Weatherly, Frederick E. (Eng. 1848-1929)

In the hush of the night, by the waves of the sea,
[ɪn ðʊ hʌʃ ʌv ðʊ naːɪt baːɪ ðʊ wɛːɪvz ʌv ðʊ si]
I am looking and waiting and longing for thee;
[aːɪ æm ˈlʊkɪŋ ænd ˈwɛːɪtɪŋ ænd ˈlaŋɪŋ fɔ ði]
And I stretch out my arms to the night, to the star,
[ænd aːɪ stɹɛtʃ aːʊt maːɪ amz tu ðʊ naːɪt tu ðʊ sta]
But a gulf is between us, the light is so far!
[bʌt ʌ gʌlf ɪz bɪˈtwin ʌs ðʊ laːɪt ɪz soːʊ fa]
O love of my life, in what land may'st thou be?
[oːʊ lʌv ʌv maːɪ laːɪf ɪn ʍat lænd ˈmɛːɪɛ⁽ɪ⁾st ðaːʊ bi]
I am looking and waiting and longing for thee!
[aːɪ æm ˈlʊkɪŋ ænd ˈwɛːɪtɪŋ ænd ˈlaŋɪŋ fɔ ði]
In the hush of the night, by the foam of the sea,
[ɪn ðʊ hʌʃ ʌv ðʊ naːɪt baːɪ ðʊ foːʊm ʌv ðʊ si]
I hear thee, I see thee, thou comest to me,
[aːɪ hɪːʌ ði aːɪ si ði ðaːʊ ˈkʌmɛ⁽ɪ⁾st tu mi]
With thine eyes shining through me,
[wɪð ðaːɪn aːɪz ˈʃaːɪnɪŋ θru mi]
like stars in the night,
[laːɪk staz ɪn ðʊ naːɪt]
And I lie on thy breast in a storm of delight.
[ænd aːɪ laːɪ an ðaːɪ bɹɛst ɪn ʌ stɔm ʌv dɪˈlaːɪt]
O God! 'tis a dream! 'tis a wraith from the sea!
[oːʊ gad tɪz ʌ dɹim tɪz ʌ ɹɛːɪθ fɹʌm ðʊ si]
Thou art gone! thou art dead! thou art parted from me!
[ðaːʊ at gan ðaːʊ at dɛd ðaːʊ at ˈpatɛ⁽ɪ⁾d fɹʌm mi]
In the hush of the night, by the desolate sea,
[ɪn ðʊ hʌʃ ʌv ðʊ naːɪt baːɪ ðʊ ˈdɛso⁽ʌ⁾lætɛ⁽ɪ⁾t si]
I am weeping and kneeling and praying for thee,
[aːɪ æm ˈwipɪŋ ænd ˈnilɪŋ ænd ˈpɹɛːɪɪŋ fɔ ði]
And thy spirit comes back with the passion of yore,
[ænd ðaːɪ ˈspɪɹɪt kʌmz bæk wɪð ðʊ ˈpæʃʌn ʌv jɔːʌ]
And the gulf shall divide us, my darling, no more!
[ænd ðʊ gʌlf ʃæl dɪˈvaːɪd ʌs maːɪ ˈdalɪŋ noːʊ mɔːʌ]
O love of the past! O love yet to be!
[oːʊ lʌv ʌv ðʊ past oːʊ lʌv jɛt tu bi]
I have found thee at last! I am coming to thee!
[aːɪ hæv faːʊnd ði æt last aːɪ æm ˈkʌmɪŋ tu ði]

V

Vaughan Williams, Ralph
(Eng. 1872-1958)

Five Mystical Songs (Song Cycle)
[fɑːɪv 'mɪstɪkʊl sɑŋz]
Herbert, George (Wel. 1593-1633)

1. Easter ['istʌ]

Rise heart; thy Lord is risen. Sing his praise
[ɹɑːɪz hat ðaːɪ lɔd ɪz 'ɹɪzɛ(ɪ)n sɪŋ hɪz pɹɛːɪz]
Without delays,
[wɪðˈɑːʊt dɪˈlɛːɪz]
Who takes thee by the hand, that thou likewise
[hu tɛːɪks ði baːɪ ðʊ hænd ðæt ðaːʊ 'laːɪkwaːɪz]
With him may'st rise;
[wɪð hɪm 'mɛːɪɛ(ɪ)st ɹɑːɪz]
That, as his death calcined thee to dust,
[ðæt æz hɪz dɛθ kælˈsaːɪnɛ(ɪ)d ði tu dʌst]
His life may make thee gold, and much more, Just.
[hɪz laːɪf mɛːɪ mɛːɪk ði goːʊld ænd mʌʧ mɔːʌ ʤʌst]
Awake, my lute, and struggle for thy part
[ʌˈwɛːɪk maːɪ ljut ænd 'stɹʌgʊl fɔ ðaːɪ pat]
With all thy art.
[wɪð ɔl ðaːɪ at]
The cross taught all wood to resound his name
[ðʊ kɹas tɔt ɔl wʊd tu ɹɪ'zaːʊnd hɪz nɛːɪm]
Who bore the same.
[hu bɔːʌ ðʊ sɛːɪm]
His stretched sinews taught all strings, what key
[hɪz 'stɹɛʧɛ(ɪ)d 'sɪnjuz tɔt ɔl stɹɪŋz ʍat ki]
Is best to celebrate this most high day.
[ɪz bɛst tu 'sɛlɪbɹɛːɪt ðɪs moːʊst haːɪ dɛːɪ]
Consort both heart and lute, and twist a song
[kʌnˈsɔt boːʊθ hat ænd ljut ænd twɪst ʌ sɑŋ]
Pleasant and long:
['plɛzæ(ɪ)nt ænd lɑŋ]
Or since all music is but three parts vied,
[ɔ sɪns ɔl 'mjuzɪk ɪz bʌt θri pats vaːɪd]
And multiplied;
[ænd 'mʌltɪplaːɪd]
O let thy blessed Spirit bear a part,
[oːʊ lɛt ðaːɪ 'blɛsɛ(ɪ)d 'spɪɹɪt bɛːʌɾ ʌ pat]
And make up our defects with his sweet art.
[ænd mɛːɪk ʌp aːʊʌ 'difɛkts wɪð hɪz swit at]

2. I Got Me Flowers
[aːɪ gat mi flaːʊʌz]

I got me flowers to strew thy way;
[aːɪ gat mi flaːʊʌz tu stɹu ðaːɪ wɛːɪ]

I got me boughs off many a tree:
[aːɪ gat mi baːʊz af 'mɛnɪ ʌ tɹi]
But thou wast up by break of day,
[bʌt ðaːʊ wast ʌp baːɪ bɹɛːɪk ʌv dɛːɪ]
And brought'st thy sweets along with thee.
[ænd bɹɔtst ðaːɪ swits ʌ'lɑŋ wɪð ði]
The Sun arising in the East,
[ðʊ sʌn ʌ'ɹaːɪzɪŋ ɪn ði ist]
Though he give light, and the East perfume;
[ðoːʊ hi gɪv laːɪt ænd ði ist pɜ'fjum]
If they should offer to contest
[ɪf ðɛːɪ ʃʊd 'afʌ tu kʌn'tɛst]
With thy arising, they presume.
[wɪð ðaːɪ ʌ'ɹaːɪzɪŋ ðɛːɪ pɹɪ'zjum]
Can there be any day but this,
[kæn ðɛːʌ bi 'ɛnɪ dɛːɪ bʌt ðɪs]
Though many suns to shine endeavour?
[ðoːʊ 'mɛnɪ sʌnz tu ʃaːɪn ɪn'dɛvʊ(ʌ)]
We count three hundred, but we miss:
[wi kaːʊnt θri 'hʌndɹɛ(ɪ)d bʌt wi mɪs]
There is but one, and that one ever.
[ðɛːʌɾ ɪz bʌt wʌn ænd ðæt wʌn 'ɛvʌ]

3. Love Bade Me Welcome
[lʌv bæd mi 'wɛlkʌm]

Love bade me welcome: yet my soul drew back,
[lʌv bæd mi 'wɛlkʌm jɛt maːɪ soːʊl dɹu bæk]
Guilty of dust and sin.
['gɪltɪ ʌv dʌst ænd sɪn]
But quick-ey'd Love, observing me grow slack
[bʌt kwɪk aːɪd lʌv ʌb'zɜvɪŋ mi gɹoːʊ slæk]
From my first entrance in,
[fɹʌm maːɪ fɜst 'ɛntɹæ(ɪ)ns ɪn]
Drew nearer to me, sweetly questioning,
[dɹu 'nɪːʌɾʌ tu mi 'switlɪ 'kwɛsʧʌnɪŋ]
If I lack'd anything.
[ɪf aːɪ lækt 'ɛnɪθɪŋ]
"A guest," I answer'd, "worthy to be here:"
[ʌ gɛst aːɪ 'ansʌd 'wɜðɪ tu bi hɪːʌ]
Love said, "You shall be he."
[lʌv sɛd ju ʃæl bi hi]
"I the unkind, ungrateful? Ah, my dear,
[aːɪ ði ʌn'kaːɪnd ʌn'gɹɛːɪtfʊl a maːɪ dɪːʌ]
I cannot look on thee."
[aːɪ kæ'nat lʊk an ði]
Love took my hand, and smiling did reply,
[lʌv tʊk maːɪ hænd ænd 'smaːɪlɪŋ dɪd ɹɪ'plaːɪ]
"Who made the eyes but I?"
[hu mɛːɪd ði aːɪz bʌt aːɪ]
Truth, Lord, but I have marr'd them: let my shame
[tɹuθ lɔd bʌt aːɪ hæv mad ðɛm lɛt maːɪ ʃɛːɪm]
Go where it doth deserve.
[goːʊ ʍɛːʌɾ ɪt dʌθ dɪ'zɜv]
"And know you not," says Love,
[ænd noːʊ ju nat sɛz lʌv]

"who bore the blame?"
[hu bɔːʌ ðʊ blɛːɪm]
"My dear, then I will serve."
[maːɪ dɪːʌ ðɛn aːɪ wɪl sɜv]
"You must sit down," says Love, "and taste my meat:"
[ju mʌst sɪt daːʊn sɛz lʌv ænd tɛːɪst maːɪ mit]
So I did sit and eat.
[soːʊ aːɪ dɪd sɪt ænd it]

4. The Call
[ðʊ kɔl]

Come, my Way, my Truth, my Life:
[kʌm maːɪ wɛːɪ maːɪ truθ maːɪ laːɪf]
Such a Way, as gives us breath:
[sʌtʃ ʌ wɛːɪ æz ɡɪvz ʌs bɹɛθ]
Such a Truth, as ends all strife:
[sʌtʃ ʌ truθ æz ɛndz ɔl stɹaːɪf]
Such a Life, as killeth death.
[sʌtʃ ʌ laːɪf æz ˈkɪlɛ(ɪ)θ dɛθ]
Come, My Light, my Feast, my Strength:
[kʌm maːɪ laːɪt maːɪ fist maːɪ stɹɛŋθ]
Such a Light, as shows a feast:
[sʌtʃ ʌ laːɪt æz ʃoːʊz ʌ fist]
Such a Feast, as mends in length:
[sʌtʃ ʌ fist æz mɛndz ɪn lɛŋθ]
Such a Strength, as makes his guest.
[sʌtʃ ʌ stɹɛŋθ æz mɛːɪks hɪz ɡɛst]
Come, my Joy, my Love, my Heart:
[kʌm maːɪ dʒɔːɪ maːɪ lʌv maːɪ hat]
Such a Joy, as none can move:
[sʌtʃ ʌ dʒɔːɪ æz nʌn kæn muv]
Such a Love, as none can part:
[sʌtʃ ʌ lʌv æz nʌn kæn pat]
Such a Heart, as joys in love.
[sʌtʃ ʌ hat æz dʒɔːɪz ɪn lʌv]

5. Antiphon
[ˈæntɪfʌn]

Let all the world in every corner sing,
[lɛt ɔl ðʊ wɜld ɪn ˈɛvɹɪ ˈkɔnʌ sɪŋ]
My God and King!
[maːɪ ɡad ænd kɪŋ]
The heavens are not too high,
[ðʊ ˈhɛvɛ(ɪ)nz a nat tu haːɪ]
His praise may thither fly:
[hɪz pɹɛːɪz mɛːɪ ˈθɪðʌ flaːɪ]
The earth is not too low,
[ði ɜθ ɪz nat tu loːʊ]
His praises there may grow.
[hɪz ˈpɹɛːɪzɛ(ɪ)z ðɛːʌ mɛːɪ ɡɹoːʊ]
Let all the world in every corner sing,
[lɛt ɔl ðʊ wɜld ɪn ˈɛvɹɪ ˈkɔnʌ sɪŋ]
My God and King!
[maːɪ ɡad ænd kɪŋ]

The church with Psalms must shout.
[ðʊ tʃɜtʃ wɪð samz mʌst ʃaːʊt]
No door can keep them out:
[noːʊ dɔːʌ kæn kip ðɛm aːʊt]
But above all, the heart
[bʌt ʌˈbʌv ɔl ðʊ hat]
Must bear the longest part.
[mʌst bɛːʌ ðʊ ˈlaŋɡɛ(ɪ)st pat]
Let all the world in every corner sing,
[lɛt ɔl ðʊ wɜld ɪn ˈɛvɹɪ ˈkɔnʌ sɪŋ]
My God and King!
[maːɪ ɡad ænd kɪŋ]

On Wenlock Edge (Song Cycle)
[an ˈwɛnlak ɛdʒ]
Housman, Alfred Edward (Eng. 1859-1936)

1. On Wenlock Edge
[an ˈwɛnlak ɛdʒ]

On Wenlock Edge the wood's in trouble;
[an ˈwɛnlak ɛdʒ ðʊ wʊdz ɪn ˈtɹʌbʊl]
His forest fleece the Wrekin heaves;
[hɪz ˈfɔɹɛ(ɪ)st flis ðʊ ˈrikɪn hivz]
The gale, it plies the saplings double,
[ðʊ ɡɛːɪl ɪt plaːɪz ðʊ ˈsæplɪŋz ˈdʌbʊl]
And thick on Severn snow the leaves.
[ænd θɪk an ˈsɛvʌn snoːʊ ðʊ livz]
'Twould blow like this through holt and hanger
[twʊd bloːʊ laːɪk ðɪs θru hoːʊlt ænd ˈhæŋʌ]
When Uricon the city stood:
[ʍɛn ˈjuɹɪkan ðʊ ˈsɪtɪ stʊd]
'Tis the old wind in the old anger,
[tɪz ði oːʊld wɪnd ɪn ði oːʊld ˈæŋɡʌ]
But then it threshed another wood.
[bʌt ðɛn ɪt θɹɛʃt ʌˈnʌðʌ wʊd]
Then, 'twas before my time, the Roman
[ðɛn twaz bɪˈfɔːʌ maːɪ taːɪm ðʊ ˈroːʊmæ(ʌ)n]
At yonder heaving hill would stare:
[æt ˈjandʌ ˈhivɪŋ hɪl wʊd stɛːʌ]
The blood that warms an English yeoman,
[ðʊ blʌd ðæt wamz æn ˈɪŋɡlɪʃ ˈjoːʊmæ(ʌ)n]
The thoughts that hurt him, they were there.
[ðʊ θɔts ðæt hɜt hɪm ðɛːɪ wɜ ðɛːʌ]
There, like the wind through woods in riot,
[ðɛːʌ laːɪk ðʊ wɪnd θru wʊdz ɪn ˈɹaːɪʌt]
Through him the gale of life blew high;
[θru hɪm ðʊ ɡɛːɪl ʌv laːɪf blu haːɪ]
The tree of man was never quiet:
[ðʊ tɹi ʌv mæn waz ˈnɛvʌ ˈkwaːɪɛ(ɪ)t]
Then 'twas the Roman, now 'tis I.
[ðɛn twaz ðʊ ˈroːʊmæ(ʌ)n naːʊ tɪz aːɪ]
The gale, it plies the saplings double,
[ðʊ ɡɛːɪl ɪt plaːɪz ðʊ ˈsæplɪŋz ˈdʌbʊl]
It blows so hard, 'twill soon be gone:
[ɪt bloːʊz soːʊ had twɪl sun bi ɡan]

Today the Roman and his trouble
[tuˈdɛːɪ ðʊ ˈroːʊmæ(ʌ)n ænd hɪz ˈtɹʌbʊl]
Are ashes under Uricon.
[ɑ ˈæʃɛ(ɪ)z ˈʌndʌ ˈjuɹɪkan]

2. From Far, from Eve and Morning
[fɪʌm fɑ fɪʌm iv ænd ˈmɔnɪŋ]

From far, from eve and morning
[fɪʌm fɑ fɪʌm iv ænd ˈmɔnɪŋ]
And yon twelve-winded sky,
[ænd jan twelv ˈwɪndɛ(ɪ)d skɑːɪ]
The stuff of life to knit me
[ðʊ stʌf ʌv lɑːɪf tu nɪt mi]
Blew hither: here am I.
[blu ˈhɪðʌ hɪːʌɾ æm ɑːɪ]
Now– for a breath I tarry
[nɑːʊ fɔʁ⁽ʳ⁾ ʌ bɹɛθ ɑːɪ ˈtæɹɪ]
Nor yet disperse apart–
[nɔ jɛt dɪˈspɜs ʌˈpɑt]
Take my hand quick and tell me,
[tɛːɪk mɑːɪ hænd kwɪk ænd tɛl mi]
What have you in your heart.
[ʌ̃at hæv ju ɪn jɔːʌ hat]
Speak now, and I will answer;
[spik nɑːʊ ænd ɑːɪ wɪl ˈansʌ]
How shall I help you, say;
[hɑːʊ ʃæl ɑːɪ help ju sɛːɪ]
Ere to the wind's twelve quarters
[ɛːʌ tu ðʊ wɪndz twelv ˈkwɔtʌz]
I take my endless way.
[ɑːɪ tɛːɪk mɑːɪ ˈɛndlɛ(ɪ)s wɛːɪ]

3. Is My Team Ploughing (see Butterworth)

4. Oh, When I Was in Love with You
[oːʊ ʌ̃ɛn ɑːɪ waz ɪn lʌv wɪθ ju]

Oh, when I was in love with you,
[oːʊ ʌ̃ɛn ɑːɪ waz ɪn lʌv wɪð ju]
Then I was clean and brave,
[ðɛn ɑːɪ waz klin ænd bɹɛːɪv]
And miles around the wonder grew
[ænd mɑːɪlz ʌˈɹɑːʊnd ðʊ ˈwʌndʌ gɹu]
How well did I behave.
[hɑːʊ wɛl dɪd ɑːɪ bɪˈhɛːɪv]
And now the fancy passes by,
[ænd nɑːʊ ðʊ ˈfænsɪ ˈpasɛ(ɪ)z bɑːɪ]
And nothing will remain,
[ænd ˈnʌθɪŋ wɪl ɹɪˈmɛːɪn]
And miles around they'll say that I
[ænd mɑːɪlz ʌˈɹɑːʊnd ðɛːɪl sɛːɪ ðæt ɑːɪ]
Am quite myself again.
[æm kwɑːɪt mɑːɪˈsɛlf ʌˈgɛːɪn]

5. Bredon Hill (see "In Summer-Time on Bredon" by Somervell)

6. Clun
[klʌn]

In valleys of springs of rivers,
[ɪn ˈvælɪz ʌv spɹɪŋz ʌv ˈɹɪvʌz]
By Ony and Teme and Clun,
[bɑːɪ ˈanɪ ænd tim ænd klʌn]
The country for easy livers,
[ðʊ ˈkʌntɹɪ fɔʁ⁽ʳ⁾ ˈizɪ ˈlɪvʌz]
The quietest under the sun,
[ðʊ ˈkwɑːɪɛ(ɪ)tɛ(ɪ)st ˈʌndʌ ðʊ sʌn]
We still had sorrows to lighten,
[wi stɪl hæd ˈsaɹoːʊz tu ˈlɑːɪtɛ(ɪ)n]
One could not be always glad,
[wʌn kʊd nat bi ˈɔlwɛːɪz glæd]
And lads knew trouble at Knighton,
[ænd lædz nju ˈtɹʌbʊl æt ˈnɑːɪtʌn]
When I was a Knighton lad.
[ʌ̃ɛn ɑːɪ waz ʌ ˈnɑːɪtʌn læd]
By bridges that Thames runs under,
[bɑːɪ ˈbɹɪdʒɛ(ɪ)z ðæt tɛmz ɹʌnz ˈʌndʌ]
In London, the town built ill,
[ɪn ˈlʌndʌn ðʊ tɑːʊn bɪlt ɪl]
'Tis sure small matter for wonder
[tɪz ʃʊːʌ smɔl ˈmætʌ fɔ ˈwʌndʌ]
If sorrow is with one still.
[ɪf ˈsaɹoːʊ ɪz wɪð wʌn stɪl]
And if as a lad grows older
[ænd ɪf æz ʌ læd gɹoːʊz ˈoːʊldʌ]
The troubles he bears are more,
[ðʊ ˈtɹʌbʊlz hi bɛːʌz ɑ mɔːʌ]
He carries his griefs on a shoulder
[hi ˈkæɹɪz hɪz grifs an ʌ ˈʃoːʊldʌ]
That handselled them long before.
[ðæt ˈhændsɛld ðɛm laŋ bɪˈfɔːʌ]
Where shall one halt to deliver
[ʌ̃ɛːʌ ʃæl wʌn hɔlt tu dɪˈlɪvʌ]
This luggage I'd lief set down?
[ðɪs ˈlʌgæ(ɪ)dʒ ɑːɪd lif sɛt dɑːʊn]
Not Thames, not Teme is the river,
[nat tɛmz nat tim ɪz ðʊ ˈɹɪvʌ]
Nor London nor Knighton the town:
[nɔ ˈlʌndʌn nɔ ˈnɑːɪtʌn ðʊ tɑːʊn]
'Tis a long way further than Knighton,
[tɪz ʌ laŋ wɛːɪ ˈfɜðʌ ðæn ˈnɑːɪtʌn]
A quieter place than Clun,
[ʌ ˈkwɑːɪɛ(ɪ)tʌ plɛːɪs ðæn klʌn]
Where doomsday may thunder and lighten
[ʌ̃ɛːʌ ˈdumzˌdɛːɪ mɛːɪ ˈθʌndʌɾ ænd ˈlɑːɪtɛ(ɪ)n]
And little 'twill matter to one.
[ænd ˈlɪtʊl twɪl ˈmætʌ tu wʌn]

Songs of Travel (Song Cycle)
[sɑŋz ʌv ˈtɹævʊl]
Stevenson, Robert Louis (Sc. 1850-1894)

1. The Vagabond
[ðʊ ˈvægʌband]

Give to me the life I love,
[gɪv tu mi ðʊ lɑːɪf ɑːɪ lʌv]
Let the lave go by me,
[lɛt ðʊ lɛːɪv goːʊ bɑːɪ mi]
Give the jolly heaven above,
[gɪv ðʊ ˈdʒɑlɪ ˈhɛvɪn ʌˈbʌv]
And the byway nigh me.
[ænd ðʊ ˈbɑːɪwɛːɪ nɑːɪ mi]
Bed in the bush with stars to see,
[bɛd ɪn ðʊ bʊʃ wɪð stɑz tu si]
Bread I dip in the river–
[bɹɛd ɑːɪ dɪp ɪn ðʊ ˈɹɪvʌ]
There's the life for a man like me,
[ðɛːʌz ðʊ lɑːɪf fɔʁ⁽ʳ⁾ ʌ mæn lɑːɪk mi]
There's the life for ever.
[ðɛːʌz ðʊ lɑːɪf fɔʁ⁽ʳ⁾ ˈɛvʌ]
Let the blow fall soon or late,
[lɛt ðʊ bloːʊ fɔl sun ɔ lɛːɪt]
Let what will be o'er me;
[lɛt ʍat wɪl bi ɔːʌ mi]
Give the face of earth around,
[gɪv ðʊ fɛːɪs ʌv ɜθ ʌˈɹɑːʊnd]
And the road before me.
[ænd ðʊ roːʊd bɪˈfɔːʌ mi]
Wealth I seek not, hope nor love,
[wɛlθ ɑːɪ sik nat hoːʊp nɔ lʌv]
Nor a friend to know me;
[nɔʁ⁽ʳ⁾ ʌ fɹɛnd tu noːʊ mi]
All I seek, the heaven above
[ɔl ɑːɪ sik ðʊ ˈhɛvɪn ʌˈbʌv]
And the road below me.
[ænd ðʊ roːʊd bɪˈloːʊ mi]
Or let autumn fall on me
[ɔ lɛt ˈɔtʌm fɔl an mi]
Where afield I linger,
[ʍɛːʌʁ ʌˈfild ɑːɪ ˈlɪŋgʌ]
Silencing the bird on tree,
[ˈsɑːɪlɛ⁽ɪ⁾nsɪŋ ðʊ bɜd an tɹi]
Biting the blue finger.
[ˈbɑːɪtɪŋ ðʊ blu ˈfɪŋgʌ]
White as meal the frosty field–
[ʍɑːɪt æz mil ðʊ ˈfɹɑstɪ fild]
Warm the fireside haven–
[wɔm ðʊ ˈfɑːɪʌsɑːɪd ˈhɛːɪvɛ⁽ɪ⁾n]
Not to autumn will I yield,
[nat tu ˈɔtʌm wɪl ɑːɪ jild]
Not to winter even!
[nat tu ˈwɪntʌ ˈivɛ⁽ɪ⁾n]

Let the blow fall soon or late,
[lɛt ðʊ bloːʊ fɔl sun ɔ lɛːɪt]
Let what will be o'er me;
[lɛt ʍat wɪl bi ɔːʌ mi]
Give the face of earth around,
[gɪv ðʊ fɛːɪs ʌv ɜθ ʌˈɹɑːʊnd]
And the road before me.
[ænd ðʊ roːʊd bɪˈfɔːʌ mi]
Wealth I ask not, hope nor love,
[wɛlθ ɑːɪ ask nat hoːʊp nɔ lʌv]
Nor a friend to know me;
[nɔʁ⁽ʳ⁾ ʌ fɹɛnd tu noːʊ mi]
All I ask, the heaven above
[ɔl ɑːɪ ask ðʊ ˈhɛvɪn ʌˈbʌv]
And the road below me.
[ænd ðʊ roːʊd bɪˈloːʊ mi]

2. Let Beauty Awake
[lɛt ˈbjuti ʌˈwɛːɪk]

Let Beauty awake in the morn from beautiful dreams,
[lɛt ˈbjuti ʌˈwɛːɪk ɪn ðʊ mɔn fɹʌm ˈbjutɪfʊl dɹimz]
Beauty awake from rest!
[ˈbjuti ʌˈwɛːɪk fɹʌm ɹɛst]
Let Beauty awake
[lɛt ˈbjuti ʌˈwɛːɪk]
For Beauty's sake
[fɔ ˈbjutɪz sɛːɪk]
In the hour when the birds awake in the brake
[ɪn ði ɑːʊʌ ʍɛn ðʊ bɜdz ʌˈwɛːɪk ɪn ðʊ bɹɛːɪk]
And the stars are bright in the west!
[ænd ðʊ stɑz ɑ bɹɑːɪt ɪn ðʊ wɛst]
Let Beauty awake in the eve from the slumber of day,
[lɛt ˈbjuti ʌˈwɛːɪk ɪn ði iv fɹʌm ðʊ ˈslʌmbʌʁ ʌv dɛːɪ]
Awake in the crimson eve!
[ʌˈwɛːɪk ɪn ðʊ ˈkɹɪmzʌn iv]
In the day's dusk end
[ɪn ðʊ dɛːɪz dʌsk ɛnd]
When the shades ascend,
[ʍɛn ðʊ ʃɛːɪdz ʌˈsɛnd]
Let her wake to the kiss of a tender friend,
[lɛt hɜ wɛːɪk tu ðʊ kɪs ʌv ʌ ˈtɛndʌ fɹɛnd]
To render again and receive!
[tu ˈɹɛndʌʁ ʌˈgɛːɪn ænd ɹɪˈsiv]

3. The Roadside Fire
[ðʊ ˈɹoːʊdsɑːɪd fɑːɪʌ]

I will make you brooches and toys for your delight
[ɑːɪ wɪl mɛːɪk ju ˈbɹoːʊʃɛ⁽ɪ⁾z ænd tɔːɪz fɔ jɔːʌ dɪˈlɑːɪt]
Of bird-song at morning and star-shine at night,
[ʌv bɜd saŋ æt ˈmɔnɪŋ ænd stɑ ʃɑːɪn æt nɑːɪt]
I will make a palace fit for you and me,
[ɑːɪ wɪl mɛːɪk ʌ ˈpælæ⁽ʌ⁾s fɪt fɔ ju ænd mi]
Of green days in forests and blue days at sea.
[ʌv gɹin dɛːɪz ɪn ˈfɔɹɛ⁽ɪ⁾sts ænd blu dɛːɪz æt si]

I will make my kitchen, and you shall keep your room,
[ɑːɪ wɪl meːɪk mɑːɪ ˈkɪʧɛ(ɪ)n ænd ju ʃæl kip jɔːʌ ɾɾum]
Where white flows the river
[ʌɛːʌ ʌɑːɪt floːʊz ðʊ ˈɾɪvʌ]
and bright blows the broom;
[ænd bɹɑːɪt bloːʊz ðʊ bɾum]
And you shall wash your linen
[ænd ju ʃæl waʃ jɔːʌ ˈlɪnɛ(ɪ)n]
and keep your body white
[ænd kip jɔːʌ ˈbadɪ ʌɑːɪt]
In rainfall at morning and dewfall at night.
[ɪn ˈɹɛːɪnfɔl æt ˈmɔnɪŋ ænd ˈdjufɔl æt nɑːɪt]
And this shall be for music when no one else is near,
[ænd ðɪs ʃæl bi fɔ ˈmjuzɪk ʌɛn noːʊ wʌn ɛls ɪz nɪːʌ]
The fine song for singing, the rare song to hear!
[ðʊ fɑːɪn saŋ fɔ ˈsɪŋɪŋ ðʊ ɾɛːʌ saŋ tu hɪːʌ]
That only I remember, that only you admire,
[ðæt ˈoːʊnlɪ ɑːɪ ɾɪ ˈmɛmbʌ ðæt ˈoːʊnlɪ ju æd ˈmɑːɪʌ]
Of the broad road that stretches
[ʌv ðʊ bɹɔd ɹoːʊd ðæt ˈstɹɛʧɛ(ɪ)z]
and the roadside fire.
[ænd ðʊ ˈɾoːʊdsɑːɪd fɑːɪʌ]

4. Youth and Love
[juθ ænd lʌv]

To the heart of youth the world is a highway side.
[tu ðʊ hat ʌv juθ ðʊ wɜld ɪz ʌ ˈhɑːɪwɛːɪ sɑːɪd]
Passing for ever, he fares; and on either hand,
[ˈpɑsɪŋ fɔʁ(ⁱ) ˈɛvʌ hi fɛːʌz ænd an ˈɑːɪðʌ hænd]
Deep in the gardens golden pavilions hide,
[dip ɪn ðʊ ˈgadɛ(ɪ)nz ˈgoːʊldɛ(ɪ)n pʌˈvɪljʌnz hɑːɪd]
Nestle in orchard bloom, and far on the level land
[ˈnɛsʊl ɪn ˈɔʧʌd blum ænd far an ðʊ ˈlɛvʊl lænd]
Call him with lighted lamp in the eventide.
[kɔl hɪm wɪð ˈlɑːɪtɛ(ɪ)d læmp ɪn ði ˈivɛ(ɪ)ntɑːɪd]
Thick as stars at night when the moon is down,
[θɪk æz staz æt nɑːɪt ʌɛn ðʊ mun ɪz dɑːʊn]
Pleasures assail him. He to his nobler fate
[ˈplɛʒʊ(ʌ)z ʌˈsɛːɪl hɪm hi tu hɪz ˈnoːʊblʌ fɛːɪt]
Fares; and but waves a hand as he passes on,
[fɛːʌz ænd bʌt wɛːɪvz ʌ hænd æz hi ˈpasɛ(ɪ)z an]
Cries but a wayside word to her at the garden gate,
[kɾɑːɪz bʌt ʌ ˈwɛːɪsɑːɪd wɜd tu hɜ æt ðʊ ˈgadɛ(ɪ)n gɛːɪt]
Sings but a boyish stave and his face is gone.
[sɪŋz bʌt ʌ ˈbɔːɪʃ stɛːɪv ænd hɪz fɛːɪs ɪz gan]

5. In Dreams
[ɪn dɹimz]

In dreams unhappy, I behold you stand
[ɪn dɹimz ʌnˈhæpɪ ɑːɪ bɪˈhoːʊld ju stænd]
As heretofore:
[æz ˈhɪːʌtuˈfɔːʌ]
The unremembered tokens in your hand
[ði ˌʌnɹɪˈmɛmbʌd ˈtoːʊkɛ(ɪ)nz ɪn jɔːʌ hænd]

Avail no more.
[ʌˈvɛːɪl noːʊ mɔːʌ]
No more the morning glow, no more the grace,
[noːʊ mɔːʌ ðʊ ˈmɔnɪŋ gloːʊ noːʊ mɔːʌ ðʊ gɹɛːɪs]
Enshrines, endears.
[ɪnˈʃɹɑːɪnz ɪnˈdɪːʌz]
Cold beats the light of time upon your face
[koːʊld bits ðʊ lɑːɪt ʌv tɑːɪm ʌˈpan jɔːʌ fɛːɪs]
And shows your tears.
[ænd ʃoːʊz jɔːʌ tɪːʌz]
He came and went. Perchance you wept awhile
[hi kɛːɪm ænd wɛnt pɜˈʧans ju wɛpt ʌˈʌɑːɪl]
And then forgot.
[ænd ðɛn fɔˈgat]
Ah me! but he that left you with a smile
[ɑ mi bʌt hi ðæt lɛft ju wɪð ʌ smɑːɪl]
Forgets you not.
[fɔˈgɛts ju nat]

6. The Infinite Shining Heavens
[ði ˈɪnfɪnɪt ˈʃɑːɪnɪŋ ˈhɛvɪnz]

The infinite shining heavens
[ði ˈɪnfɪnɪt ˈʃɑːɪnɪŋ ˈhɛvɛ(ɪ)nz]
Rose, and I saw in the night
[ɹoːʊz ænd ɑːɪ sɔ ɪn ðʊ nɑːɪt]
Uncountable angel stars
[ʌnˈkɑːʊntʌbʊl ˈɛːɪndʒɛ(ʊ)l staz]
Showering sorrow and light.
[ˈʃɑːʊɾɪŋ ˈsaɾoːʊ ænd lɑːɪt]
I saw them distant as heaven,
[ɑːɪ sɔ ðɛm ˈdɪstæ(ɪ)nt æz ˈhɛvɛ(ɪ)n]
Dumb and shining and dead,
[dʌm ænd ˈʃɑːɪnɪŋ ænd dɛd]
And the idle stars of the night
[ænd ði ˈɑːɪdʊl staz ʌv ðʊ nɑːɪt]
Were dearer to me than bread.
[wɜ ˈdɪːʌɾʌ tu mi ðæn bɹɛd]
Night after night in my sorrow
[nɑːɪt ˈaftʌ nɑːɪt ɪn mɑːɪ ˈsaɾoːʊ]
The stars looked over the sea,
[ðʊ staz lʊkt ˈoːʊvʌ ðʊ si]
Till lo! I looked in the dusk
[tɪl loːʊ ɑːɪ lʊkt ɪn ðʊ dʌsk]
And a star had come down to me.
[ænd ʌ sta hæd kʌm dɑːʊn tu mi]

7. Whither Must I Wander?
[ˈʌɪðʌ mʌst ɑːɪ ˈwandʌ]

Home no more home to me,
[hoːʊm noːʊ mɔːʌ hoːʊm tu mi]
whither must I wander?
[ˈʌɪðʌ mʌst ɑːɪ ˈwandʌ]
Hunger my driver, I go where I must.
[ˈhʌŋgʌ mɑːɪ ˈdɹɑːɪvʌ ɑːɪ goːʊ ʌɛːʌɾ ɑːɪ mʌst]

Cold blows the winter wind over hill and heather;
[koːʊld bloːʊz ðʊ ˈwɪntʌ wɪnd ˈoːʊvʌ hɪl ænd ˈhɛðʌ]
Thick drives the rain, and my roof is in the dust.
[θɪk dɹaːɪvz ðʊ ɾɛːɪn ænd maːɪ rruf ɪz ɪn ðʊ dʌst]
Loved of wise men was the shade of my roof-tree.
[lʌvd ʌv waːɪz mɛn waz ðʊ ʃɛːɪd ʌv maːɪ rruf tɹi]
The true word of welcome was spoken in the door:
[ðʊ tru wɜd ʌv ˈwɛlkʌm waz ˈspoːʊkɛ(ɪ)n ɪn ðʊ dɔːʌ]
Dear days of old, with the faces in the firelight;
[dɪːʌ dɛːɪz ʌv oːʊld wɪð ðʊ ˈfɛːɪsɛ(ɪ)z ɪn ðʊ ˈfaːɪʌlaːɪt]
Kind folks of old, you come again no more.
[kaːɪnd foːʊks ʌv oːʊld ju kʌm ʌˈgɛːɪn noːʊ mɔːʌ]
Home was home then, my dear,
[hoːʊm waz hoːʊm ðɛn maːɪ dɪːʌ]
full of kindly faces,
[fʊl ʌv ˈkaːɪndlɪ ˈfɛːɪsɛ(ɪ)z]
Home was home then, my dear, happy for the child.
[hoːʊm waz hoːʊm ðɛn maːɪ dɪːʌ ˈhæpɪ fɔ ðʊ ʧaːɪld]
Fire and the windows bright glittered
[faːɪʌɾ ænd ðʊ ˈwɪndoːʊz bɹaːɪt ˈglɪtʌd]
on the moorland:
[ɑn ðʊ ˈmʊːʌlæ(ʌ)nd]
Song, tuneful song, built a palace in the wild.
[sɑŋ ˈtjunfʊl sɑŋ bɪlt ʌ ˈpælæ(ʌ)s ɪn ðʊ waːɪld]
Now when day dawns on the brow of the moorland,
[naːʊ ʍɛn dɛːɪ dɔnz ɑn ðʊ bɹaːʊ ʌv ðʊ ˈmʊːʌlæ(ʌ)nd]
Lone stands the house,
[loːʊn stændz ðʊ haːʊs]
and the chimney-stone is cold.
[ænd ðʊ ˈʧɪmnɪ stoːʊn ɪz koːʊld]
Lone let it stand, now the friends are all departed,
[loːʊn lɛt ɪt stænd naːʊ ðʊ fɹɛndz ɑɾ ɔl dɪˈpatɛ(ɪ)d]
The kind hearts, the true hearts,
[ðʊ kaːɪnd hats ðʊ tru hats]
that loved the place of old.
[ðæt lʌvd ðʊ plɛːɪs ʌv oːʊld]
Spring shall come, come again,
[spɹɪŋ ʃæl kʌm kʌm ʌˈgɛːɪn]
calling up the moorfowl,
[ˈkɔlɪŋ ʌp ðʊ ˈmʊːʌfaːʊl]
Spring shall bring the sun and rain,
[spɹɪŋ ʃæl bɹɪŋ ðʊ sʌn ænd ɹɛːɪn]
bring the bees and flowers;
[bɹɪŋ ðʊ biz ænd flaːʊʌz]
Red shall the heather bloom over hill and valley,
[ɹɛd ʃæl ðʊ ˈhɛðʌ blum ˈoːʊvʌ hɪl ænd ˈvælɪ]
Soft flow the stream through the even-flowing hours.
[saft floːʊ ðʊ stɹim θɾu ði ˈivɛ(ɪ)n ˈfloːʊɪŋ aːʊʌz]
Fair the day shine as it shone on my childhood;
[fɛːʌ ðʊ dɛːɪ ʃaːɪn æz ɪt ʃoːʊn ɑn maːɪ ˈʧaːɪldhʊd]
Fair shine the day on the house with open door.
[fɛːʌ ʃaːɪn ðʊ dɛːɪ ɑn ðʊ haːʊs wɪð ˈoːʊpɛ(ɪ)n dɔːʌ]
Birds come and cry there and twitter in the chimney—
[bɜdz kʌm ænd kɹaːɪ ðɛːʌɾ ænd ˈtwɪtʌɾ ɪn ðʊ ˈʧɪmnɪ]
But I go for ever and come again no more.
[bʌt aːɪ goːʊ fɔʁ⁽ʳ⁾ ˈɛvʌ ænd kʌm ʌˈgɛːɪn noːʊ mɔːʌ]

8. Bright Is the Ring of Words
[bɹaːɪt ɪz ðʊ ɹɪŋ ʌv wɜdz]

Bright is the ring of words
[bɹaːɪt ɪz ðʊ ɾɪŋ ʌv wɜdz]
When the right man rings them,
[ʍɛn ðʊ ɾaːɪt mæn ɹɪŋz ðɛm]
Fair the fall of songs
[fɛːʌ ðʊ fɔl ʌv sɑŋz]
When the singer sings them.
[ʍɛn ðʊ ˈsɪŋʌ sɪŋz ðɛm]
Still they are carolled and said—
[stɪl ðɛːɪ ɑ ˈkærʊld ænd sɛd]
On wings they are carried—
[ɑn wɪŋz ðɛːɪ ɑ ˈkærɪd]
After the singer is dead
[ˈaftʌ ðʊ ˈsɪŋʌɾ ɪz dɛd]
And the maker buried.
[ænd ðʊ ˈmɛːɪkʌ ˈbɛɾɪd]
Low as the singer lies
[loːʊ æz ðʊ ˈsɪŋʌ laːɪz]
In the field of heather,
[ɪn ðʊ fild ʌv ˈhɛðʌ]
Songs of his fashion bring
[sɑŋz ʌv hɪz ˈfæʃʌn bɹɪŋ]
The swains together.
[ðʊ swɛːɪnz tuˈgɛðʌ]
And when the west is red
[ænd ʍɛn ðʊ wɛst ɪz ɹɛd]
With the sunset embers,
[wɪð ðʊ ˈsʌnsɛt ˈɛmbʌz]
The lover lingers and sings
[ðʊ ˈlʌvʌ ˈlɪŋgʌz ænd sɪŋz]
And the maid remembers.
[ænd ðʊ mɛːɪd ɹɪˈmɛmbʌz]

9. I Have Trod the Upward
[aːɪ hæv tɹad ði ˈʌpwʊd]
and the Downward Slope
[ænd ðʊ ˈdaːʊnwʊd sloːʊp]

I have trod the upward and the downward slope;
[aːɪ hæv tɹad ði ˈʌpwʊd ænd ðʊ ˈdaːʊnwʊd sloːʊp]
I have endured and done in days before;
[aːɪ hæv ɪnˈdjʊːʌd ænd dʌn ɪn dɛːɪz bɪˈfɔːʌ]
I have longed for all, and bid farewell to hope;
[aːɪ hæv lɑŋd fɔʁ⁽ʳ⁾ ɔl ænd bɪd fɛːʌˈwɛl tu hoːʊp]
And I have lived and loved, and closed the door.
[ænd aːɪ hæv lɪvd ænd lʌvd ænd kloːʊzd ðʊ dɔːʌ]

Song Selections

"Linden Lea"
[ˈlɪndɪn li]
Barnes, William (Eng. 1801-1886)

Within the woodlands, flow'ry gladed,
[wɪð ˈɪn ðʊ ˈwʊdlæ(ʌ)ndz ˈflaˈʊʌɾi ˈglɛːɪdɛ(ɪ)d]
By the oak trees' mossy moot,
[baːɪ ði oːʊk tɹiz ˈmɔsɪ mut]
The shining grass blades, timber-shaded,
[ðʊ ˈʃaːɪnɪŋ gɹas blɛːɪdz ˈtɪmbʌ ˈʃɛːɪdɛ(ɪ)d]
Now do quiver underfoot;
[naːʊ du ˈkwɪvʌɾ ʌndʌˈfʊt]
And birds do whistle overhead,
[ænd bɜdz du ˈʍɪsʊl ˈoːʊvʌhɛd]
And water's bubbling in its bed;
[ænd ˈwɔtʌz ˈbʌblɪŋ ɪn ɪts bɛd]
And there for me, the apple tree
[ænd ðɛːʌ fɔ mi ði ˈæpʊl tɹi]
Do lean down low in Linden Lea.
[du lin daːʊn loːʊ ɪn ˈlɪndɛ(ɪ)n li]
When leaves, that lately were a-springing,
[ʍɛn livz ðæt ˈlɛːɪtlɪ wɜ(ʳ) ʌ ˈspɹɪŋɪŋ]
Now do fade within the copse,
[naːʊ du fɛːɪd wɪðˈɪn ðʊ kɔps]
And painted birds do hush their singing,
[ænd ˈpɛːɪntɛ(ɪ)d bɜdz du hʌʃ ðɛːʌ ˈsɪŋɪŋ]
Up upon the timber tops;
[ʌp ʌˈpɔn ðʊ ˈtɪmbʌ tɔps]
And brown-leaved fruits a-turning red,
[ænd bɹaːʊn livd fruts ʌ ˈtɜnɪŋ ɹɛd]
In cloudless sunshine overhead,
[ɪn ˈklaːʊdlɛ(ɪ)s ˈsʌnʃaːɪn ˈoːʊvʌhɛd]
With fruit for me, the apple tree
[wɪð frut fɔ mi ði ˈæpʊl tɹi]
Do lean down low in Linden Lea.
[du lin daːʊn loːʊ ɪn ˈlɪndɛ(ɪ)n li]
Let other folk make money faster;
[lɛt ˈʌðʌ foːʊk mɛːɪk ˈmʌnɪ ˈfastʌ]
In the air of dark-roomed towns;
[ɪn ði ɛːʌɾ ʌv dak ɹɾumd taːʊnz]
I don't dread a peevish master,
[aːɪ doːʊnt dɹɛd ʌ ˈpivɪʃ ˈmastʌ]
Though no man may heed my frowns.
[ðoːʊ noːʊ mæn mɛːɪ hid maːɪ fɹaːʊnz]
I be free to go abroad,
[aːɪ bi fɹi tu goːʊ ʌˈbɹɔd]
Or take again my homeward road
[ɔ tɛːɪk ʌˈgɛːɪn maːɪ ˈhoːʊmwʊd ɹoːʊd]
To where, for me, the apple tree
[tu ʍɛːʌ fɔ mi ði ˈæpʊl tɹi]
Do lean down low in Linden Lea.
[du lin daːʊn loːʊ ɪn ˈlɪndɛ(ɪ)n li]

"Orpheus with His Lute" (see Hundley)

"Silent Noon"
[ˈsaːɪlɛnt nun]
Rossetti, Dante Gabriel (Eng. 1828-1882)

Your hands lie open in the long fresh grass,
[jɔːʌ hændz laːɪ ˈoːʊpɛ(ɪ)n ɪn ðʊ laŋ fɹɛʃ gɹas]
The finger-points look through like rosy blooms:
[ðʊ ˈfɪŋgʌ pɔːɪnts lʊk θru laːɪk ˈɹoːʊzɪ blumz]
Your eyes smile peace. The pasture gleams and glooms
[jɔːʌ aːɪz smaːɪl pis ðʊ ˈpastʃʊ(ʌ) glimz ænd glumz]
'Neath billowing skies that scatter and amass.
[niθ ˈbɪloːʊɪŋ skaːɪz ðæt ˈskætʌɾ ænd ʌˈmæs]
All round our nest, far as the eye can pass,
[ɔl ɹaːʊnd aːʊʌ nɛst far æz ði aːɪ kæn pas]
Are golden kingcup fields with silver edge,
[ɑ ˈgoːʊldɛ(ɪ)n ˈkɪŋkʌp fildz wɪð ˈsɪlvʌɾ ɛdʒ]
Where the cow parsley skirts the hawthorn hedge.
[ʍɛːʌ ðʊ kaːʊ ˈpaslɪ skɜts ðʊ ˈhɔθɔn hɛdʒ]
'Tis visible silence, still as the hour glass.
[tɪz ˈvɪzɪbʊl ˈsaːɪlɛ(ɪ)ns stɪl æz ði aːʊʌ glas]
Deep in the sunsearched growths the dragonfly
[dip ɪn ðʊ ˈsʌnsɜtʃt gɹoːʊθs ðʊ ˈdɹægʌnflaːɪ]
Hangs like a blue thread loosened from the sky:
[hæŋz laːɪk ʌ blu θɹɛd ˈlusɛ(ɪ)nd fɹʌm ðʊ skaːɪ]
So this winged hour is dropt to us from above.
[soːʊ ðɪs wɪŋgd aːʊʌɾ ɪz dɹɑpt tu ʌs fɹʌm ʌˈbʌv]
Oh, clasp we to our hearts, for deathless dower,
[oːʊ klasp wi tu aːʊʌ hats fɔ ˈdɛθlɛ(ɪ)s daːʊʌ]
This close-companioned inarticulate hour,
[ðɪs kloːʊs kʌmˈpænjʌnd ɪnaˈtɪkju(ʊ)læ(ɪ)t aːʊʌ]
When twofold silence was the song of love.
[ʍɛn ˈtuˈfoːʊld ˈsaːɪlɛ(ɪ)ns wɑz ðʊ saŋ ʌv lʌv]

"The Sky above the Roof"
[ðʊ skaːɪ ʌˈbʌv ðʊ ɹuf]
Dearmer, Mabel (Eng. 1872-1915)

The sky above the roof
[ðʊ skaːɪ ʌˈbʌv ðʊ ɹɾuf]
Is calm and sweet:
[ɪz kɑm ænd swit]
A tree above the roof
[ʌ tɹi ʌˈbʌv ðʊ ɹɾuf]
Bends in the heat.
[bɛndz ɪn ðʊ hit]
A bell from out the blue
[ʌ bɛl fɹʌm aːʊt ðʊ blu]
Drowsily rings:
[ˈdɹaːʊzɪlɪ ɹɪŋz]
A bird from out the blue
[ʌ bɜd fɹʌm aːʊt ðʊ blu]
Plaintively sings.
[ˈplɛːɪntɪvlɪ sɪŋz]
Ah God! A life is here,
[ɑ gɑd ʌ laːɪf ɪz hɪːʌ]

Simple and fair,
[ˈsɪmpʊl ænd fɛːʌ]
Murmurs of strife are here
[ˈmɜːmʊ(ʌ)z ʌv stɹɑːɪf a hiːʌ]
Lost in the air.
[lɑst ɪn ði ɛːʌ]
Why dost thou weep, O heart,
[ʍaːɪ dʌst ðaːʊ wip oːʊ hɑt]
Poured out in tears?
[pɔːʌd aːʊt ɪn tɪːʌz]
What hast thou done, O heart,
[ʍat hæst ðaːʊ dʌn oːʊ hɑt]
With thy spent years?
[wɪð ðaːɪ spɛnt jɪːʌz]

W

Walker, Gwyneth (Am. b. 1947)

Song Selection

"thy fingers make early flowers"
[ðaːɪ ˈfɪŋgʁz meːɪk ˈɜːli ˈflaːʊʁz]
(though love be a day)
Cummings, E. E. (Am. 1894-1962)

thy fingers make early flowers
[ðaːɪ ˈfɪŋgʌz meːɪk ˈɜːli flaːʊʌz]
of all things.
[ʌv ɔl θɪŋz]
thy hair mostly the hours love:
[ðaːɪ hɛːʌ ˈmoːʊstli ði aːʊʌz lʌv]
a smoothness which
[ʌ ˈsmuðnɛ(ɪ)s ʍɪʧ]
sings, saying
[sɪŋz ˈsɛːɪɪŋ]
do not fear, though love be a day,
[du nat fiːʌ ðoːʊ lʌv bi ʌ dɛːɪ]
we will go a-maying.
[wi wɪl goːʊ ʌˈmeːɪɪŋ]
thy whitest feet crisply are straying.
[ðaːɪ ˈʍaːɪtɛ(ɪ)st fit ˈkɹɪspli a ˈstɹɛːɪɪŋ]
always
[ˈɔlwɛːɪz]
thy moist eyes are at kisses playing,
[ðaːɪ mɔːɪst aːɪz aʁ(ʳ) æt ˈkɪsɛ(ɪ)z ˈplɛːɪɪŋ]
whose strangeness much says;
[huz ˈstɹɛːɪndʒnɛ(ɪ)s mʌʧ sɛz]
singing
[ˈsɪŋɪŋ]
for which girl art thou flowers bringing?
[fɔ ʍɪʧ gɜl at ðaːʊ flaːʊʌz ˈbɹɪŋɪŋ]

though love be a day, flowers bringing
[ðoːʊ lʌv bi ʌ dɛːɪ flaːʊʌz ˈbɹɪŋɪŋ]
to be thy lips is a sweet thing
[tu bi ðaːɪ lɪps ɪz ʌ swit θɪŋ]
and small.
[ænd smɔl]
Death, thee i call rich beyond wishing
[dɛθ ði aːɪ kɔl ɹɪʧ bɪˈjand ˈwɪʃɪŋ]
if this thou catch,
[ɪf ðɪs ðaːʊ kæʧ]
else missing.
[ɛls ˈmɪsɪŋ]
and life be nothing, though love be a day
[ænd laːɪf bi ˈnʌθɪŋ ðoːʊ lʌv bi ʌ dɛːɪ]
it shall not stop kissing.
[ɪt ʃæl nat stap ˈkɪsɪŋ]

Walton, William (Eng. 1902-1983)

A Song for the Lord Mayor's Table (Song Cycle)
[ʌ saŋ fɔ ðʊ lɔd ˈmeːɪʌz ˈteːɪbʊl]

1. The Lord Mayor's Table
[ðʊ lɔd ˈmeːɪʌz ˈteːɪbʊl]
Jordan, Thomas (Eng. 1612-1685)

Let all the Nine Muses lay by their abuses,
[lɛt ɔl ðʊ naːɪn ˈmjuzɛ(ɪ)z leːɪ baːɪ ðɛːʌr ʌˈbjuzɛ(ɪ)z]
Their railing and drolling on tricks of the Strand,
[ðɛːʌ ˈrɛːɪlɪŋ ænd ˈdɹoːʊlɪŋ an tɹɪks ʌv ðʊ stɹænd]
To pen us a ditty in praise of the City,
[tu pɛn ʌs ʌ ˈdɪti ɪn pɹɛːɪz ʌv ðʊ ˈsɪti]
Their treasure, and pleasure,
[ðɛːʌ ˈtɹɛʒʊ(ʌ)r ænd ˈplɛʒʊ(ʌ)]
their pow'r and command.
[ðɛːʌ paːʊʌr ænd kʌˈmand]
Their feast, and guest, so temptingly drest,
[ðɛːʌ fist ænd gɛst soːʊ ˈtɛmptɪŋli dɹɛst]
Their kitchens all kingdoms replenish;
[ðɛːʌ ˈkɪʧɛ(ɪ)nz ɔl ˈkɪŋdʌmz ɹɪˈplɛnɪʃ]
In bountiful bowls they do succour their souls,
[ɪn ˈbaːʊntɪfʊl boːʊlz ðɛːɪ du ˈsʌkʊ(ʌ) ðɛːʌ soːʊlz]
With claret, Canary, and Rhenish:
[wɪð ˈklærɛ(ɪ)t kʌˈnærɪ ænd ˈɹɛnɪʃ]
Their lives and wives in plenitude thrives,
[ðɛːʌ laːɪvz ænd waːɪvz ɪn ˈplɛnɪtjud θɹaːɪvz]
They want not for meat nor money;
[ðɛːɪ want nat fɔ mit nɔ ˈmʌnɪ]
The Promised Land's in a Londoner's hand,
[ðʊ ˈpɹamɪst lændz ɪn ʌ ˈlʌndʌnʌz hænd]
They wallow in milk and honey.
[ðɛːɪ ˈwaloːʊ ɪn mɪlk ænd ˈhʌnɪ]
Let all the Nine Muses lay by their abuses,
[lɛt ɔl ðʊ naːɪn ˈmjuzɛ(ɪ)z leːɪ baːɪ ðɛːʌr ʌˈbjuzɛ(ɪ)z]

Their railing and drolling on tricks of the Strand
[ðɛːʌ ˈɾɛːɪlɪŋ ænd ˈdɹoːʊlɪŋ an tɹɪks ʌv ðʊ stɹænd]
To pen us a ditty in praise of the City,
[tu pɛn ʌs ʌ ˈdɪtɪ ɪn pɹɛːɪz ʌv ðʊ ˈsɪtɪ]
Their treasure, and pleasure,
[ðɛːʌ ˈtɹɛʒʊ(ʌ)r ænd ˈplɛʒʊ(ʌ)]
their pow'r and command.
[ðɛːʌ paːʊʌr ænd kʌˈmand]

2. Glide Gently
[glaːɪd ˈdʒɛntli]
Wordsworth, William (Eng. 1770-1850)

Glide gently, thus for ever, ever glide,
[glaːɪd ˈdʒɛntlɪ ðʌs fʊ(ɾ) ˈɛvʌ ˈɛvʌ glaːɪd]
O Thames! that other bards may see
[oːʊ tɛmz ðæt ˈʌðʌ badz mɛːɪ si]
As lovely visions by thy side
[æz ˈlʌvlɪ ˈvɪʒʌnz baːɪ ðaːɪ saːɪd]
As now, fair river! come to me.
[æz naːʊ fɛːʌ ˈɾɪvʌ kʌm tu mi]
O glide, fair stream, for ever so,
[oːʊ glaːɪd fɛːʌ stɹim fʊ(ɾ) ˈɛvʌ soːʊ]
Thy quiet soul on all bestowing,
[ðaːɪ ˈkwaːɪɛ(ɪ)t soːʊl an ɔl bɪˈstoːʊɪŋ]
Till all our minds for ever flow
[tɪl ɔl aːʊʌ maːɪndz fʊ(ɾ) ˈɛvʌ floːʊ]
As thy deep waters now are flowing.
[æz ðaːɪ dip ˈwɔtʌz naːʊ a ˈfloːʊɪŋ]

3. Wapping Old Stairs
[ˈwapɪŋ oːʊld stɛːʌz]
Anonymous

Your Molly has never been false, she declares,
[jɔːʌ ˈmalɪ hæz ˈnɛvʌ bin fɔls ʃi dɪˈklɛːʌz]
Since last time we parted at Wapping Old Stairs,
[sɪns last taːɪm wi ˈpatɛ(ɪ)d æt ˈwapɪŋ oːʊld stɛːʌz]
When I swore that I still would continue the same,
[ʍɛn aːɪ swɔːʌ ðæt aːɪ stɪl wʊd kʌnˈtɪnju ðʊ sɛːɪm]
And gave you the 'bacco box, marked with your name.
[ænd gɛːɪv ju ðʊ ˈbækoːʊ baks makt wɪð jɔːʌ nɛːɪm]
When I pass'd a whole fortnight
[ʍɛn aːɪ past ʌ hoːʊl ˈfɔtnaːɪt]
between decks with you,
[bɪˈtwin dɛks wɪð ju]
Did I e'er give a kiss, Tom, to one of the crew?
[dɪd aːɪ ɛːʌ gɪv ʌ kɪs tam tu wʌn ʌv ðʊ kɹu]
To be useful and kind, with my Thomas I stay'd,
[tu bi ˈjusfʊl ænd kaːɪnd wɪð maːɪ ˈtamʌs aːɪ stɛːɪd]
For his trousers I wash'd, and his grog, too, I made.
[fɔ hɪz ˈtɹaːʊzʌz aːɪ waʃt ænd hɪz gɹag tu aːɪ mɛːɪd]
Though you threaten'd, last Sunday, to walk in the Mall
[ðoːʊ ju ˈθɾɛtɛ(ɪ)nd last ˈsʌndɛːɪ tu wɔk ɪn ðʊ mɔl]
With Susan from Deptford, and likewise with Sal,
[wɪð ˈsuzæ(ʌ)n fɹʌm ˈdɛptfɔt ænd ˈlaːɪkwaːɪz wɪð sæl]

In silence I stood your unkindness to hear,
[ɪn ˈsaːɪlɛ(ɪ)ns aːɪ stʊd jɔːʌr ʌnˈkaːɪndnɛ(ɪ)s tu hiːʌ]
And only upbraided my Tom, with a tear.
[ænd ˈoːʊnlɪ ʌpˈbɹɛːɪdɛ(ɪ)d maːɪ tam wɪð ʌ tiːʌ]
Why should Sal, or should Susan,
[ʍaːɪ ʃʊd sæl ɔ ʃʊd ˈsuzæ(ʌ)n]
than me be more priz'd?
[ðæn mi bi mɔːʌ pɹaːɪzd]
For the heart that is true, Tom,
[fɔ ðʊ hat ðæt ɪz tɾu tam]
should ne'er be despis'd;
[ʃʊd nɛːʌ bi dɪˈspaːɪzd]
Then be constant and kind, nor your Molly forsake,
[ðɛn bi ˈkanstæ(ɪ)nt ænd kaːɪnd nɔ jɔːʌ ˈmalɪ fɔˈsɛːɪk]
Still your trousers I'll wash,
[stɪl jɔːʌ ˈtɹaːʊzʌz aːɪl waʃ]
and your grog, (too) I'll make.
[ænd jɔːʌ gɹag tu aːɪl mɛːɪk]

4. Holy Thursday
[ˈhoːʊli ˈθɜzdɛːɪ]
Blake, William (Eng. 1757-1827)

'Twas on a holy Thursday,
[twaz an ʌ ˈhoːʊli ˈθɜzdɛːɪ]
their innocent faces clean,
[ðɛːʌr ˈɪno(ʌ)sɛnt ˈfɛːɪsɛ(ɪ)z klin]
The children walking two and two,
[ðʊ ˈtʃɪldɹɛ(ɪ)n ˈwɔkɪŋ tu ænd tu]
in red, and blue, and green:
[ɪn ɹɛd ænd blu ænd gɹin]
Gray-headed beadles walked before,
[gɹɛːɪ ˈhɛdɛ(ɪ)d ˈbidʊlz wɔkt bɪˈfɔːʌ]
with wands as white as snow,
[wɪð wandz æz ʍaːɪt æz snoːʊ]
Till into the high dome of St Paul's
[tɪl ˈɪntu ðʊ haːɪ doːʊm ʌv sɛːɪnt pɔlz]
they like Thames waters flow.
[ðɛːɪ laːɪk tɛmz ˈwɔtʌz floːʊ]
O what a multitude they seemed,
[oːʊ ʍat ʌ ˈmʌltɪtjud ðɛːɪ simd]
these flowers of London town!
[ðiz flaːʊʌz ʌv ˈlʌndʌn taːʊn]
Seated in companies they sit,
[ˈsitɛ(ɪ)d ɪn ˈkʌmpæ(ɪ)nɪz ðɛːɪ sɪt]
with radiance all their own.
[wɪð ˈɹɛːɪdɪæ(ɪ)ns ɔl ðɛːʌr oːʊn]
The hum of multitudes was there,
[ðʊ hʌm ʌv ˈmʌltɪtjudz waz ðɛːʌ]
but multitudes of lambs,
[bʌt ˈmʌltɪtjudz ʌv læmz]
Thousands of little boys and girls
[ˈθaːʊzæ(ʌ)ndz ʌv ˈlɪtʊl bɔːɪz ænd gɜlz]
raising their innocent hands.
[ˈɹɛːɪzɪŋ ðɛːʌ ˈɪno(ʌ)sɛnt hændz]

Now like a mighty wind
[naːʊ laːɪk ʌ ˈmaːɪtɪ wɪnd]
they raise to heaven the voice of song,
[ðεːɪ rεːɪz tu ˈhεvε(ɪ)n ðʊ vɔːɪs ʌv saŋ]
Or like harmonious thunderings
[ɔ laːɪk haˈmoːʊnɪʌs ˈθʌndʌrɪŋz]
the seats of heaven among;
[ðʊ sits ʌv ˈhεvε(ɪ)n ʌ ˈmʌŋ]
Beneath them sit the aged men,
[bɪˈniθ ðεm sɪt ði ˈεːɪdʒε(ɪ)d mεn]
wise guardians of the poor.
[waːɪz ˈgadɪæ(ɪ)nz ʌv ðʊ pʊːʌ]
Then cherish pity,
[ðεn ˈtʃεɪʃ ˈpɪtɪ]
lest you drive an angel from your door.
[lεst ju dɪaːɪv æn ˈεːɪndʒε(ʊ)l fɪʌm jɔːʌ dɔːʌ]

5. The Contrast
[ðʊ ˈkantɪast]
Morris, Charles (Eng. 1745-1838)

In London I never know what I'd be at,
[ɪn ˈlʌndʌn aːɪ ˈnεvʌ noːʊ ʍat aːɪd bi æt]
Enraptured with this, and enchanted by that;
[ɪnˈɪæptʃʊ(ʌ)d wɪð ðɪs ænd ɪnˈtʃantε(ɪ)d baːɪ ðæt]
I'm wild with the sweets of variety's plan,
[aːɪm waːɪld wɪð ðʊ swits ʌv vʌˈɪaːɪɪtɪz plæn]
And life seems a blessing too happy for man.
[ænd laːɪf simz ʌ ˈblεsɪŋ tu ˈhæpɪ fɔ mæn]
But the country, Lord help me!, sets all matters right,
[bʌt ðʊ ˈkʌntɪɪ lɔd hεlp mi sεts ɔl ˈmætʌz ɪaːɪt]
So calm and composing from morning to night;
[soːʊ kam ænd kʌmˈpoːʊzɪŋ fɪʌm ˈmɔnɪŋ tu naːɪt]
Oh! it settles the spirit when nothing is seen
[oːʊ ɪt ˈsεtʊlz ðʊ ˈspɪrɪt ʍεn ˈnʌθɪŋ ɪz sin]
But an ass on a common, a goose on a green.
[bʌt æn æs an ʌ ˈkamʌn ʌ gus an ʌ gɪin]
Your magpies and stockdoves may flirt among trees,
[jɔːʌ ˈmæg͵paːɪz ænd ˈstakdʌvz mεːɪ flɜt ʌˈmʌŋ tɪiz]
And chatter their transports in groves, if they please:
[ænd ˈtʃætʌ ðεːʌ ˈtɪænspɔts ɪn gɪoːʊvz ɪf ðεːɪ pliz]
But a house is much more to my taste than a tree,
[bʌt ʌ haːʊs ɪz mʌtʃ mɔːʌ tu maːɪ tεːɪst ðæn ʌ tɪi]
And for groves, O! a good grove of chimneys for me.
[ænd fɔ gɪoːʊvz oːʊ ʌ gʊd gɪoːʊv ʌv ˈtʃɪmnɪz fɔ mi]
In the country, if Cupid should find a man out,
[ɪn ðʊ ˈkʌntɪɪ ɪf ˈkjupɪd ʃʊd faːɪnd ʌ mæn aːʊt]
The poor tortured victim mopes hopeless about;
[ðʊ pʊːʌ ˈtɔtʃʊ(ʌ)d ˈvɪktɪm moːʊps ˈhoːʊplε(ɪ)s ʌ ˈbaːʊt]
But in London, thank Heaven! Our peace is secure,
[bʌt ɪn ˈlʌndʌn θæŋk ˈhεvε(ɪ)n aːʊʌ pis ɪz sɪˈkjʊːʌ]
Where for one eye to kill, there's a thousand to cure.
[ʍεːʌ fɔ wʌn aːɪ tu kɪl ðεːʌz ʌ ˈθaːʊzæ(ʌ)nd tu kjʊːʌ]
I know love's a devil, too subtle to spy,
[aːɪ noːʊ lʌvz ʌ ˈdεvɪ(ʊ)l tu ˈsʌtʊl tu spaːɪ]

That shoots through the soul, from the beam of an eye;
[ðæt ʃuts θɾu ðʊ soːʊl fɪʌm ðʊ bim ʌv æn aːɪ]
But in London these devils so quick fly about,
[bʌt ɪn ˈlʌndʌn ðiz ˈdεvɪ(ʊ)lz soːʊ kwɪk flaːɪ ʌˈbaːʊt]
That a new devil still drives an old devil out.
[ðæt ʌ nju ˈdεvɪ(ʊ)l stɪl dɪaːɪvz æn oːʊld ˈdεvɪ(ʊ)l aːʊt]

6. Rhyme [ɪaːɪm]
Anonymous

Gay go up and gay go down,
[gεːɪ goːʊ ʌp ænd gεːɪ goːʊ daːʊn]
To ring the bells of London Town.
[tu rɪŋ ðʊ bεlz ʌv ˈlʌndʌn taːʊn]
Oranges and lemons
[ˈɔɾæ(ɪ)ndʒε(ɪ)z ænd ˈlεmʌnz]
Say the bells of St. Clement's.
[sεːɪ ðʊ bεlz ʌv sεːɪnt ˈklεmεnts]
Bull's eyes and targets,
[bʊlz aːɪz ænd ˈtagε(ɪ)ts]
Say the bells of St. Margaret's.
[sεːɪ ðʊ bεlz ʌv sεːɪnt ˈmagɪε(ɪ)ts]
Brickbats and tiles,
[ˈbɪɪkbæts ænd taːɪlz]
Say the bells of St. Giles'.
[sεːɪ ðʊ bεlz ʌv sεːɪnt dʒaːɪlz]
Half-pence and farthings,
[haf pεns ænd ˈfaðɪŋz]
Say the bells of St. Martin's.
[sεːɪ ðʊ bεlz ʌv sεːɪnt ˈmatɪnz]
Pancakes and fritter's,
[ˈpænkεːɪks ænd ˈfɪɪtʌz]
Say the bells of St. Peter's.
[sεːɪ ðʊ bεlz ʌv sεːɪnt ˈpitʌz]
Two sticks and an apple,
[tu stɪks ænd æn ˈæpʊl]
Say the bells of Whitechapel.
[sεːɪ ðʊ bεlz ʌv ˈʍaːɪtˈtʃæpʊl]
Pokers and tongs,
[ˈpoːʊkʌz ænd taŋz]
Say the bells of St. John's.
[sεːɪ ðʊ bεlz ʌv sεːɪnt dʒanz]
Kettles and pans,
[ˈkεtʊlz ænd pænz]
Say the bells of St. Anne's.
[sεːɪ ðʊ bεlz ʌv sεːɪnt ænz]
Old father baldpate,
[oːʊld ˈfaðʌ ˈbɔldpεːɪt]
Say the slow bells of Aldgate.
[sεːɪ ðʊ sloːʊ bεlz ʌv ˈɔldgεːɪt]
You owe me ten shillings,
[ju oːʊ mi tεn ˈʃɪlɪŋz]
Say the bells of St. Helen's.
[sεːɪ ðʊ bεlz ʌv sεːɪnt ˈhεlε(ɪ)nz]
When will you pay me?
[ʍεn wɪl ju pεːɪ mi]

Say the bells of Old Bailey.
[sɛːɪ ðʊ bɛlz ʌv ɔːʊld ˈbɛːɪlɪ]
When I grow rich,
[ʍɛn aːɪ ɡɹoːʊ ɹɪtʃ]
Say the bells of Shoreditch.
[sɛːɪ ðʊ bɛlz ʌv ˈʃɔːʌdɪtʃ]
Pray when will that be?
[pɹɛːɪ ʍɛn wɪl ðæt bi]
Say the bells of Stepney.
[sɛːɪ ðʊ bɛlz ʌv ˈstɛpnɪ]
I do not know,
[aːɪ du nat noːʊ]
Says the great bell of Bow.
[sɛz ðʊ ɡɹɛːɪt bɛl ʌv boːʊ]
Gay go up and gay go down,
[ɡɛːɪ ɡoːʊ ʌp ænd ɡɛːɪ ɡoːʊ daːʊn]
To ring the bells of London Town.
[tu ɹɪŋ ðʊ bɛlz ʌv ˈlʌndʌn taːʊn]

 # Warlock, Peter (Eng. 1894-1930)

Lillygay (Song Cycle)
[ˈlɪliɡɛːɪ]
Anonymous

1. The Distracted Maid
[ðʊ dɪˈstɹæktɪd mɛːɪd]

One morning very early, one morning in the spring,
[wʌn ˈmɔnɪŋ ˈvɛɹɪ ˈɜlɪ wʌn ˈmɔnɪŋ ɪn ðʊ spɹɪŋ]
I heard a maid in Bedlam who mournfully did sing.
[aːɪ hɜd ʌ mɛːɪd ɪn ˈbɛdlæ(ʌ)m hu ˈmɔnfʊlɪ dɪd sɪŋ]
Her chains she rattled on her hands
[hɜ tʃɛːɪnz ʃi ˈɹætʊld an hɜ hændz]
while sweetly thus sang she,
[ʍaːɪl ˈswitlɪ ðʌs sæŋ ʃi]
I love my love because I know my love loves me.
[aːɪ lʌv maːɪ lʌv bɪˈkɔz aːɪ noːʊ maːɪ lʌv lʌvz mi]
Oh cruel were his parents who sent my love to sea,
[ɔːʊ ˈkɹuːɛ(ʊ)l wɜ hɪz ˈpæɹɛnts hu sɛnt maːɪ lʌv tu si]
And cruel, cruel was the ship
[ænd ˈkɹuːɛ(ʊ)l ˈkɹuːɛ(ʊ)l waz ðʊ ʃɪp]
that bore my love from me.
[ðæt bɔːʌ maːɪ lʌv fɹʌm mi]
Yet I love his parents since they're his,
[jɛt aːɪ lʌv hɪz ˈpæɹɛnts sɪns ðɛːʌ hɪz]
although they've ruined me,
[ɔlˈðoːʊ ðɛːɪv ˈɹɹuɪnd mi]
And I love my love because I know my love loves me.
[ænd aːɪ lʌv maːɪ lʌv bɪˈkɔz aːɪ noːʊ maːɪ lʌv lʌvz mi]
Oh should it please the pitying powers
[ɔːʊ ʃʊd ɪt pliz ðʊ ˈpɪtɪŋ paːʊʌz]
to call me to the sky,
[tu kɔl mi tu ðʊ skaːɪ]

I'll claim a guardian angel's charge
[aːɪl klɛːɪm ʌ ˈɡadɪæ(ɪ)n ˈɛːɪndʒɛ(ʊ)lz tʃadʒ]
around my love to fly.
[ʌˈɹaːʊnd maːɪ lʌv tu flaːɪ]
To guard him from all dangers how happy I should be,
[tu ɡad hɪm fɹʌm ɔl ˈdɛːɪndʒʌz haːʊ ˈhæpɪ aːɪ ʃʊd bi]
For I love my love because I know my love loves me.
[fɔʁ⁽ʳ⁾ aːɪ lʌv maːɪ lʌv bɪˈkɔz aːɪ noːʊ maːɪ lʌv lʌvz mi]
I'll make a strawy garland,
[aːɪl mɛːɪk ʌ ˈstɹɔɪ ˈɡalæ(ʌ)nd]
I'll make it wondrous fine,
[aːɪl mɛːɪk ɪt ˈwʌndɹʌs faːɪn]
With roses, lilies, daisies, I'll mix the eglantine,
[wɪð ˈɹoːʊzɛ(ɪ)z ˈlɪlɪz ˈdɛːɪzɪz aːɪl mɪks ði ɛɡlænˈtaːɪn]
And I'll present it to my love when he returns from sea,
[ænd aːɪl pɹɪˈzɛnt ɪt tu maːɪ lʌv ʍɛn hi ɹɪˈtɜnz fɹʌm si]
For I love my love because I know my love loves me.
[fɔʁ⁽ʳ⁾ aːɪ lʌv maːɪ lʌv bɪˈkɔz aːɪ noːʊ maːɪ lʌv lʌvz mi]
Oh if I were a little bird to build upon his breast,
[ɔːʊ ɪf aːɪ wɜ⁽ʳ⁾ ʌ ˈlɪtʊl bɜd tu bɪld ʌˈpan hɪz bɹɛst]
Or if I were a nightingale to sing my love to rest,
[ɔʁ⁽ʳ⁾ ɪf aːɪ wɜ⁽ʳ⁾ ʌ ˈnaːɪtɪŋɡɛːɪl tu sɪŋ maːɪ lʌv tu rɛst]
To gaze upon his lovely eyes all my reward should be,
[tu ɡɛːɪz ʌˈpan hɪz ˈlʌvlɪ aːɪz ɔl maːɪ ɹɪˈwɔd ʃʊd bi]
For I love my love because I know my love loves me.
[fɔʁ⁽ʳ⁾ aːɪ lʌv maːɪ lʌv bɪˈkɔz aːɪ noːʊ maːɪ lʌv lʌvz mi]
Oh if I were an eagle to soar in to the sky,
[ɔːʊ ɪf aːɪ wɜ⁽ʳ⁾ æn ˈiɡʊl tu sɔːʌr ɪn tu ðʊ skaːɪ]
I'd gaze around with piercing eyes
[aːɪd ɡɛːɪz ʌˈɹaːʊnd wɪð ˈpɪʌsɪŋ aːɪz]
where I my love might spy.
[ʍɛːʌr aːɪ maːɪ lʌv maːɪt spaːɪ]
But ah, unhappy maiden, that love you ne'er shall see,
[bʌt a ʌnˈhæpɪ ˈmɛːɪdɛ(ɪ)n ðæt lʌv ju nɛːʌ ʃæl si]
Yet I love my love because I know my love loves me.
[jɛt aːɪ lʌv maːɪ lʌv bɪˈkɔz aːɪ noːʊ maːɪ lʌv lʌvz mi]

2. Johnnie wi'the Tye
[ˈdʒani wɪ ðʊ taːɪ]

Johnnie cam' to our toun,
[ˈdʒanɪ kɛːɪm tu aːʊʌ taːʊn]
To our toun, to our toun,
[tu aːʊʌ taːʊn tu aːʊʌ taːʊn]
Johnnie cam' to our toun,
[ˈdʒanɪ kɛːɪm tu aːʊʌ taːʊn]
the body wi'the tye;
[ðʊ ˈbadɪ wɪ ðʊ taːɪ]
And o as he kittl'd me,
[ænd oːʊ æz hi ˈkɪtʊld mi]
Kittl'd me, kittl'd me!
[ˈkɪtʊld mi ˈkɪtʊld mi]
O, as he kittl'd me!
[oːʊ æz hi ˈkɪtʊld mi]
But I forgot to cry.
[bʌt aːɪ fɔˈɡat tu kɹaːɪ]

He gaed thro' the fields wi' me,
[hi gɛːɪd θɾu ðʊ fildz wɪ mi]
The fields wi' me, the fields wi' me,
[ðʊ fildz wɪ mi ðʊ fildz wɪ mi]
He gaed thro' the fields with me
[hi gɛːɪd θɾu ðʊ fildz wɪð mi]
And down among the rye.
[ænd daːʊn ʌˈmʌŋ ðʊ ɾaːɪ]
Then o, as he kittl'd me,
[ðɛn oːʊ æz hi ˈkɪtʊld mi]
Kittl'd me, kittl'd me!
[ˈkɪtʊld mi ˈkɪtʊld mi]
O, as he kittl'd me!
[oːʊ æz hi ˈkɪtʊld mi]
But I forgot to cry.
[bʌt aːɪ fɔˈgat tu kɪaːɪ]

3. The Shoemaker
[ðʊ ˈʃuˌmɛːɪkʌ]

Shoemaker, shoemaker, are ye within?
[ˈʃuˌmɛːɪkʌ ˈʃuˌmɛːɪkʌ ɑ ji wɪðˈɪn]
A fal a fall addie fallee!
[ʌ fal ʌ fal ɑˈdi ˈfali]
Hae ye got shoes to fit me so trim
[ha ji gat ʃuz tu fɪt mi soːʊ tɪɪm]
For a kiss in the morning early?
[fɔʁ(ɾ) ʌ kɪs ɪn ðʊ ˈmɔnɪŋ ˈɜlɪ]
O fair may, come in and see,
[oːʊ fɛːʌ mɛːɪ kʌm ɪn ænd si]
A fal a fall addie fallee!
[ʌ fal ʌ fal ɑˈdi ˈfali]
I've got but ae pair and I'll gie them to thee
[aːɪv gat bʌt ʌ pɛːʌɾ ænd aːɪl gi ðɛm tu ði]
For a kiss in the morning early.
[fɔʁ(ɾ) ʌ kɪs ɪn ðʊ ˈmɔnɪŋ ˈɜlɪ]
He's ta'en her in behind the bench,
[hiz tɛːɪn hɜ(ɾ) ɪn bɪˈhaːɪnd ðʊ bɛntʃ]
A fal a fall addie fallee!
[ʌ fal ʌ fal ɑˈdi ˈfali]
And there he has fitted his own pretty wench.
[ænd ðɛːʌ hi hæz ˈfɪtɛ(ɪ)d hɪz oːʊn ˈpɪɪtɪ wɛntʃ]
With a kiss in the morning early.
[wɪð ʌ kɪs ɪn ðʊ ˈmɔnɪŋ ˈɜlɪ]

4. Burd Ellen and Young Tamlane
[bɜd ˈɛlɪn ænd jʌŋ ˈtæmlɛːɪn]

Burd Ellen sits in her bower windowe,
[bɜd ˈɛlɪn sɪts ɪn hɜ ˈbaːʊʌ ˈwɪndoːʊ]
With a double laddy double, and for the double dow,
[wɪð ʌ ˈdʌbʊl ˈlædɪ ˈdʌbʊl ænd fɔ ðʊ ˈdʌbʊl daːʊ]
Twisting the red silk and the blue,
[ˈtwɪstɪŋ ðʊ ɾed sɪlk ænd ðʊ blu]
With the double rose and the May hay.
[wɪð ðʊ ˈdʌbʊl ɾoːʊz ænd ðʊ mɛːɪ hɛːɪ]

And whiles she twisted and whiles she twan,
[ænd ʍaːɪlz ʃi ˈtwɪstɛ(ɪ)d ænd ʍaːɪlz ʃi twɑn]
With a double laddy double and for the double dow,
[wɪð ʌ ˈdʌbʊl ˈlædɪ ˈdʌbʊl ænd fɔ ðʊ ˈdʌbʊl daːʊ]
And whiles the tears fell down amang,
[ænd ʍaːɪlz ðʊ tɪːʌz fɛl daːʊn ʌˈmʌŋ]
With the double rose and the May hay.
[wɪð ðʊ ˈdʌbʊl ɾoːʊz ænd ðʊ mɛːɪ hɛːɪ]
Till once there cam' by young Tamlane,
[tɪl wʌns ðɛːʌ kʌm baːɪ jʌŋ ˈtæmlɛːɪn]
With a double laddy double and for the double dow,
[wɪð ʌ ˈdʌbʊl ˈlædɪ ˈdʌbʊl ænd fɔ ðʊ ˈdʌbʊl daːʊ]
"Come light, oh light and rock your young son!"
[kʌm laːɪt oːʊ laːɪt ænd ɾak jɔːʌ jʌŋ sʌn]
With the double rose and the May hay.
[wɪð ðʊ ˈdʌbʊl ɾoːʊz ænd ðʊ mɛːɪ hɛːɪ]
"If ye winna rock him, ye may let him rair,
[ɪf ji ˈwɪnʌ ɾak hɪm ji mɛːɪ lɛt hɪm ɾɛːʌ]
With a double laddy double and for the double dow,
[wɪð ʌ ˈdʌbʊl ˈlædɪ ˈdʌbʊl ænd fɔ ðʊ ˈdʌbʊl daːʊ]
For I ha'e rockit my share and mair!"
[fɔʁ(ɾ) aːɪ hæ ˈɾakɪt maːɪ ʃɛːʌɾ ænd mɛːʌ]
With the double rose and the May hay.
[wɪð ðʊ ˈdʌbʊl ɾoːʊz ænd ðʊ mɛːɪ hɛːɪ]
Young Tamlane to the seas he's gone,
[jʌŋ ˈtæmlɛːɪn tu ðʊ siz hiz gɑn]
With a double laddy double and for the double dow,
[wɪð ʌ ˈdʌbʊl ˈlædɪ ˈdʌbʊl ænd fɔ ðʊ ˈdʌbʊl daːʊ]
And a' woman's curse in his company's gane!
[ænd ʌ ˈwʊmæ(ʌ)nz kɜs ɪn hɪz ˈkʌmpæ(ɪ)nɪz gɑn]
With the double rose and the May hay.
[wɪð ðʊ ˈdʌbʊl ɾoːʊz ænd ðʊ mɛːɪ hɛːɪ]

5. Rantum Tantum
[ˈɾæntʌm ˈtæntʌm]

Who'll play at Rantum Tantum
[hul plɛːɪ æt ˈɾæntʌm ˈtæntʌm]
Over the fields in May?
[ˈoːʊvʌ ðʊ fildz ɪn mɛːɪ]
Oh, maidens fair, 'od grant 'em
[oːʊ ˈmɛːɪdɛ(ɪ)nz fɛːʌ ɔd gɹant ɛm]
Rantum Tantum play!
[ˈɾæntʌm ˈtæntʌm plɛːɪ]
The dawning fields are rimy,
[ðʊ ˈdɔnɪŋ fildz ɑ ˈɾaːɪmɪ]
White in the sunrise way,
[ʍaːɪt ɪn ðʊ ˈsʌnɾaːɪz wɛːɪ]
But oh! the fields smell thymy
[bʌt oːʊ ðʊ fildz smel ˈtaːɪmɪ]
Later in the day.
[ˈlɛːɪtʌɾ ɪn ðʊ dɛːɪ]
And oh! may the fields be pearly
[ænd oːʊ mɛːɪ ðʊ fildz bi ˈpɜlɪ]
With dawn and virgin dew,
[wɪð dɔn ænd ˈvɜdʒɪn dju]

And may my love come early
[ænd mɛːɪ maːɪ lʌv kʌm ˈɜlɪ]
And may my love be true...
[ænd mɛːɪ maːɪ lʌv bi tɾu]
Oh, the fields are green in daytime
[oːʊ ðʊ fildz ɑ gɹin ɪn ˈdɛːɪtɑːɪm]
And the trees are white in May,
[ænd ðʊ tɾiz ɑ ʍɑːɪt ɪn mɛːɪ]
And Rantum Tantum
[ænd ˈɹæntʌm ˈtæntʌm]
Maytime's the time for lovers' play.
[ˈmɛːɪtɑːɪmz ðʊ tɑːɪm fɔ ˈlʌvʌz plɛːɪ]

Three Belloc Songs (Song Cycle)
[θɾi ˈbɛlɔk sɑŋz]
Belloc, Joseph Hilaire (Eng. 1870-1953)

1. Ha'nacker Mill
[ˈhænʌkʌ mɪl]

Sally is gone that was so kindly
[ˈsælɪ ɪz gɑn ðæt wɑz soːʊ ˈkɑːɪndlɪ]
Sally is gone from Ha'nacker Hill.
[ˈsælɪ ɪz gɑn fɹʌm ˈhænʌkʌ hɪl]
And the Briar grows ever since then so blindly
[ænd ðʊ ˈbɹɑːɪʌ gɹoːʊz ˈɛvʌ sɪns ðɛn soːʊ ˈblɑːɪndlɪ]
And ever since then the clapper is still,
[ænd ˈɛvʌ sɪns ðɛn ðʊ ˈklæpʌɾ ɪz stɪl]
And the sweeps have fallen from Ha'nacker Mill.
[ænd ðʊ swips hæv ˈfɔlɛ(ɪ)n fɹʌm ˈhænʌkʌ mɪl]
Ha'nacker Hill is in Desolation:
[ˈhænʌkʌ hɪl ɪz ɪn ˌdɛso(ʌ)ˈlɛːɪʃʌn]
Ruin a-top and a field unploughed.
[ˈrɾuɪn ʌ tɑp ænd ʌ fild ʌnˈplɑːʊd]
And Spirits that call on a fallen nation,
[ænd ˈspɪɾɪts ðæt kɔl ɑn ʌ ˈfɔlɛ(ɪ)n ˈnɛːɪʃʌn]
Spirits that loved her calling aloud:
[ˈspɪɾɪts ðæt lʌvd hɜ ˈkɔlɪŋ ʌˈlɑːʊd]
Spirits abroad in a windy cloud.
[ˈspɪɾɪts ʌˈbɹɔd ɪn ʌ ˈwɪndɪ klɑːʊd]
Spirits that call and no one answers;
[ˈspɪɾɪts ðæt kɔl ænd noːʊ wʌn ˈɑnsʌz]
Ha'nacker's down and England's done.
[ˈhænʌkʌz dɑːʊn ænd ˈɪŋglæ(ʌ)ndz dʌn]
Wind and thistle for pipe and dancers
[wɪnd ænd ˈθɪsʊl fɔ pɑːɪp ænd ˈdansʌz]
And never a ploughman under the Sun.
[ænd ˈnɛvʌɾ ʌ ˈplɑːʊmæ(ʌ)n ˈʌndʌ ðʊ sʌn]
Never a ploughman. Never a one.
[ˈnɛvʌɾ ʌ ˈplɑːʊmæ(ʌ)n ˈnɛvʌɾ ʌ wʌn]

2. The Night
[ðʊ nɑːɪt]

Most Holy Night, that still dost keep
[moːʊst ˈhoːʊlɪ nɑːɪt ðæt stɪl dʌst kip]

The keys of all the doors of sleep,
[ðʊ kiz ʌv ɔl ðʊ dɔːʌz ʌv slip]
To me when my tired eyelids close
[tu mi ʍɛn mɑːɪ tɑːɪʌd ˈɑːɪlɪdz kloːʊz]
Give thou repose.
[gɪv ðɑːʊ ɾɪˈpoːʊz]
And let the far lament of them
[ænd lɛt ðʊ fɑ lʌˈmɛnt ʌv ðɛm]
That chaunt the dead day's requiem
[ðæt ʧɔnt ðʊ dɛd dɛːɪz ˈɹɛkwɪɛm]
Make in my ears, who wakeful lie,
[mɛːɪk ɪn mɑːɪ ɪːʌz hu ˈwɛːɪkfʊl lɑːɪ]
Soft lullaby.
[sɑft ˈlʌlʌbɑːɪ]
Let them that guard the horned moon
[lɛt ðɛm ðæt gɑd ðʊ ˈhɔnɛ(ɪ)d mun]
By my bedside their memories croon.
[bɑːɪ mɑːɪ ˈbɛdsɑːɪd ðɛːʌ ˈmɛmɹɪz kɾun]
So shall I have new dreams and blest
[soːʊ ʃæl ɑːɪ hæv nju dɹimz ænd blɛst]
In my brief rest.
[ɪn mɑːɪ bɹif ɹɛst]
Fold your great wings about my face,
[foːʊld jɔːʌ gɹɛːɪt wɪŋz ʌˈbɑːʊt mɑːɪ fɛːɪs]
Hide dawning from my resting-place,
[hɑːɪd ˈdɔnɪŋ fɹʌm mɑːɪ ˈɹɛstɪŋ plɛːɪs]
And cheat me with your false delight,
[ænd ʧit mi wɪð jɔːʌ fɔls dɪˈlɑːɪt]
Most Holy Night.
[moːʊst ˈhoːʊlɪ nɑːɪt]

3. My Own Country
[mɑːɪ oːʊn ˈkʌntɹɪ]

I shall go without companions,
[ɑːɪ ʃæl goːʊ wɪðˈɑːʊt kʌmˈpænjʌnz]
And with nothing in my hand;
[ænd wɪð ˈnʌθɪŋ ɪn mɑːɪ hænd]
I shall pass through many places
[ɑːɪ ʃæl pɑs θɾu ˈmɛnɪ ˈplɛːɪsɛ(ɪ)z]
That I cannot understand–
[ðæt ɑːɪ kæˈnɑt ʌndʌˈstænd]
Until I come to my own country,
[ʌnˈtɪl ɑːɪ kʌm tu mɑːɪ oːʊn ˈkʌntɹɪ]
Which is a pleasant land!
[ʍɪʧ ɪz ʌ ˈplɛzæ(ɪ)nt lænd]
The trees that grow in my own country
[ðʊ tɾiz ðæt gɹoːʊ ɪn mɑːɪ oːʊn ˈkʌntɹɪ]
Are the beech tree and the yew;
[ɑ ðʊ biʧ tɾi ænd ðʊ ju]
Many stand together, And some stand few.
[ˈmɛnɪ stænd tuˈgɛðʌ ænd sʌm stænd fju]
In the month of May in my own country
[ɪn ðʊ mʌnθ ʌv mɛːɪ ɪn mɑːɪ oːʊn ˈkʌntɹɪ]
All the woods are new.
[ɔl ðʊ wʊdz ɑ nju]

When I get to my own country
[ʍɛn ɑːɪ gɛt tu mɑːɪ oːʊn ˈkʌntɹɪ]
I shall lie down and sleep;
[ɑːɪ ʃæl lɑːɪ dɑːʊn ænd slip]
I shall watch in the valleys
[ɑːɪ ʃæl wɑʧ ɪn ðʊ ˈvælɪz]
The long flocks of sheep.
[ðʊ lɑŋ flɑks ʌv ʃip]
And then I shall dream, for ever and all,
[ænd ðɛn ɑːɪ ʃæl dɹim foʁ⁽ʳ⁾ ˈɛvʌr ænd ɔl]
A good dream and deep.
[ʌ gʊd dɹim ænd dip]

Song Selections

"Autumn Twilight"
[ˈɔtʌm ˈtwaːɪlɑːɪt]
Symons, Arthur (Eng. 1865-1945)

The long September evening dies
[ðʊ lɑŋ sɛpˈtɛmbʌr ˈivnɪŋ dɑːɪz]
In mist along the fields and lanes.
[ɪn mɪst ʌˈlɑŋ ðʊ fildz ænd lɛːɪnz]
Only a few faint stars surprise
[ˈoːʊnlɪ ʌ fju fɛːɪnt stɑz sɜˈpɹɑːɪz]
The lingering twilight as it wanes.
[ðʊ ˈlɪŋgʌrɪŋ ˈtwaːɪlɑːɪt æz ɪt wɛːɪnz]
Night creeps across the darkening vale;
[nɑːɪt krips ʌˈkɹɑs ðʊ ˈdɑkɛ(ɪ)nɪŋ vɛːɪl]
On the horizon tree by tree
[ɑn ðʊ hɔˈrɑːɪzʌn tɹi bɑːɪ tɹi]
Fades into shadowy skies as pale
[fɛːɪdz ˈɪntu ˈʃædoːʊɪ skɑːɪz æz pɛːɪl]
As moonlight on a shadowy sea.
[æz ˈmunlɑːɪt ɑn ʌ ˈʃædoːʊɪ si]
And down the mist-enfolded lanes,
[ænd dɑːʊn ðʊ mɪst ɪnˈfoːʊldɛ(ɪ)d lɛːɪnz]
Grown pensive now with evening,
[gɹoːʊn ˈpɛnsɪv nɑːʊ wɪð ˈivnɪŋ]
See, lingering as the twilight wanes,
[si ˈlɪŋgʌrɪŋ æz ðʊ ˈtwaːɪlɑːɪt wɛːɪnz]
Lover with lover wandering.
[ˈlʌvʌ wɪð ˈlʌvʌ ˈwandʌrɪŋ]

"I Have a Garden"
[ɑːɪ hæv ʌ ˈgɑdɪn]
Moore, Thomas (Eng. (1779-1852)

I have a garden of my own
[ɑːɪ hæv ʌ ˈgɑdɛ(ɪ)n ʌv mɑːɪ oːʊn]
Shining with flow'rs of ev'ry hue;
[ˈʃaːɪnɪŋ wɪð flɑːʊʌz ʌv ˈɛvɹɪ hju]
I lov'd it dearly while alone,
[ɑːɪ lʌvd ɪt ˈdɪːʌlɪ ʍɑːɪl ʌˈloːʊn]
But I shall love it more with you:
[bʌt ɑːɪ ʃæl lʌv ɪt mɔːʌ wɪð ju]

And there the golden bees shall come
[ænd ðɛːʌ ðʊ ˈgoːʊldɛ(ɪ)n biz ʃæl kʌm]
In summer time at break of morn,
[ɪn ˈsʌmʌ tɑːɪm æt bɹɛːɪk ʌv mɔn]
And wake us with their busy hum
[ænd wɛːɪk ʌs wɪð ðɛːʌ ˈbɪzɪ hʌm]
Around the Siha's fragrant thorn.
[ʌˈrɑːʊnd ðʊ ˈsɪtɑz ˈfɹɛːɪgɹæ(ɪ)nt θɔn]
I have a fawn from Aden's land,
[ɑːɪ hæv ʌ fɔn fɹʌm ˈɛːɪdɪnz lænd]
On leafy buds and berries nurst;
[ɑn ˈlifɪ bʌdz ænd ˈbɛrɪz nɜst]
And you shall feed him from your hand,
[ænd ju ʃæl fid hɪm fɹʌm jɔːʌ hænd]
Though he may start with fear at first.
[ðoːʊ hi mɛːɪ stɑt wɪð fɪːʌr æt fɜst]
And I will lead you where he lies
[ænd ɑːɪ wɪl lid ju ʍɛːʌ hi lɑːɪz]
For shelter in the noontide heat,
[fɔ ˈʃɛltʌr ɪn ðʊ ˈnuntɑːɪd hit]
And you may touch his sleeping eyes,
[ænd ju mɛːɪ tʌʧ hɪz ˈslipɪŋ ɑːɪz]
And feel his little silv'ry feet.
[ænd fil hɪz ˈlɪtʊl ˈsɪlvɹɪ fit]

"Jillian of Berry"
[ˈdʒɪliɪn ʌv ˈbɛʁɪ]
Anonymous

For Jillian of Berry she dwells on a hill,
[fɔ ˈdʒɪlɪæ(ɪ)n ʌv ˈbɛrɪ ʃi dwɛlz ɑn ʌ hɪl]
And she hath good beer and ale to sell,
[ænd ʃi hæθ gʊd bɪːʌr ænd ɛːɪl tu sɛl]
And of good fellows she thinks no ill,
[ænd ʌv gʊd ˈfɛloːʊz ʃi θɪŋks noːʊ ɪl]
And thither will we go now, now, now.
[ænd ˈθɪðʌ wɪl wi goːʊ nɑːʊ nɑːʊ nɑːʊ]
And thither will we go now.
[ænd ˈθɪðʌ wɪl wi goːʊ nɑːʊ]
And when you have made a little stay,
[ænd ʍɛn ju hæv mɛːɪd ʌ ˈlɪtʊl stɛːɪ]
You need not ask what is to pay,
[ju nid nɑt ask ʍɑt ɪz tu pɛːɪ]
But kiss your hostess and go your way,
[bʌt kɪs jɔːʌ ˈhoːʊstɛ(ɪ)s ænd goːʊ jɔːʌ wɛːɪ]
And thither will we go now, now, now,
[ænd ˈθɪðʌ wɪl wi goːʊ nɑːʊ nɑːʊ nɑːʊ]
And thither will we go now.
[ænd ˈθɪðʌ wɪl wi goːʊ nɑːʊ]

"Mourn No Moe"
[mɔn noːʊ mɔːʌ]
Fletcher, John (Eng. 1579-1625)

Weep no more, nor sigh, nor groan,
[wip noːʊ mɔːʌ nɔ sɑːɪ nɔ gɹoːʊn]

Sorrow calls no time that's gone:
[ˈsɑɾoːʊ kɔlz noːʊ tɑːɪm ðæts gɑn]
Violets plucked the sweetest rain
[ˈvɑːɪo(ʌ)lɛ(ɪ)ts plʌkt ðʊ ˈswitɛ(ɪ)st ɹɛːɪn]
Makes not fresh nor grow again;
[mɛːɪks nɑt fɹɛʃ nɔ gɹoːʊ ʌˈgɛːɪn]
Trim thy locks, look cheerfully;
[tɹɪm ðɑːɪ lɑks lʊk ˈtʃɪːʌfʊlɪ]
Fate's hid ends eye can not see;
[fɛːɪts hɪd ɛndz ɑːɪ kæn nɑt si]
Joys as winged dreams fly fast,
[dʒɔːɪz æz ˈwɪŋɛ(ɪ)d dɹimz flɑːɪ fast]
Why should sadness longer last?
[ʍɑːɪ ʃʊd ˈsædnɛ(ɪ)s ˈlɑŋgʌ last]
Grief is but a wound to woe;
[gɹif ɪz bʌt ʌ wund tu woːʊ]
Gentlest fair! Mourn, mourn no moe.
[ˈdʒɛntlɛ(ɪ)st fɛːʌ mɔn mɔn noːʊ mɔːʌ]

"Passing By" (see "There Is a Lady Sweet and Kind"
by Dello Joio)

"Rest Sweet Nymphs"
[ɹɛst swit nɪmfs]
Anonymous

Rest, sweet nymphs, let golden sleep
[ɹɛst swit nɪmfs lɛt ˈgoːʊldɛ(ɪ)n slip]
Charm your star-brighter eyes,
[tʃɑm jɔːʌ stɑ ˈbɹɑːɪtʌ⁽ʳ⁾ ɑːɪz]
While my lute her watch doth keep
[ʍɑːɪl mɑːɪ ljut hɜ watʃ dʌθ kip]
With pleasing sympathies.
[wɪð ˈplizɪŋ ˈsɪmpæ(ʌ)θɪz]
Lullaby, lullaby,
[ˈlʌlʌbɑːɪ ˈlʌlʌbɑːɪ]
Sleep sweetly, sleep sweetly,
[slip ˈswitlɪ slip ˈswitlɪ]
Let nothing affright ye,
[lɛt ˈnʌθɪŋ ʌˈfɹɑːɪt ji]
In calm contentments lie.
[ɪn kɑm kʌnˈtɛntmɛnts lɑːɪ]
Thus, dear damsels, I do give
[ðʌs dɪːʌ ˈdæmzʊlz ɑːɪ du gɪv]
Good night, and so am gone;
[gʊd nɑːɪt ænd soːʊ æm gɑn]
With your hearts' desires long live,
[wɪð jɔːʌ hats dɪˈzɑːɪʌz lɑŋ lɪv]
Still joy and never mourn.
[stɪl dʒɔːɪ ænd ˈnɛvʌ mɔn]
Lullaby, lullaby,
[ˈlʌlʌbɑːɪ ˈlʌlʌbɑːɪ]
Hath eas'd you and pleas'd you,
[hæθ izd ju ænd plizd ju]
And sweet slumber seized you,
[ænd swit ˈslʌmbʌ sizd ju]

And now to bed I hie.
[ænd nɑːʊ tu bɛd ɑːɪ hɑːɪ]

"Take, O Take Those Lips Away" (see Beach)

"The Bachelor"
[ðʊ ˈbætʃʊlʌ]
Anonymous

In all this warld nis a meriar life
[ɪn ɔl ðɪs wɜld nɪz ʌ ˈmɛɹɪʌ lɑːɪf]
Than is a yong man withouten a wife;
[ðæn ɪz ʌ jʌŋ mæn wɪðˈɑːʊtɛ(ɪ)n ʌ wɑːɪf]
For he may liven withouten strife,
[fɔ hi mɛːɪ ˈlɪvɛ(ɪ)n wɪðˈɑːʊtɛ(ɪ)n stɹɑːɪf]
In every place where so he go.
[ɪn ˈɛvʌɹɪ plɛːɪs ʍɛːʌ soːʊ hi goːʊ]
In every place he is loved over all,
[ɪn ˈɛvʌɹɪ plɛːɪs hi ɪz lʌvd ˈoːʊvʌɹ ɔl]
Among the maidens grete and small,
[ʌˈmʌŋ ðʊ ˈmɛːɪdɛ(ɪ)nz gɹɛːɪt ænd smɔl]
In dauncing, in piping, and renning at the ball,
[ɪn ˈdansɪŋ ɪn ˈpɑːɪpɪŋ ænd ˈɹʌnɪŋ æt ðʊ bɔl]
In every place where so he go.
[ɪn ˈɛvʌɹɪ plɛːɪs ʍɛːʌ soːʊ hi goːʊ]
Then sey maidens, "Farewell, Jacke!
[ðɛn sɛːɪ ˈmɛːɪdɛ(ɪ)nz fɛːʌˈwɛl dʒæk]
Thy love is pressed all in thy pake;
[ðɑːɪ lʌv ɪz pɹɛst ɔl ɪn ðɑːɪ pæk]
Thou berest thy love behind thy back,"
[ðɑːʊ ˈbɛːʌɹɛ(ɪ)st ðɑːɪ lʌv bɪˈhɑːɪnd ðɑːɪ bæk]
In every place where so he go.
[ɪn ˈɛvʌɹɪ plɛːɪs ʍɛːʌ soːʊ hi goːʊ]

"The Bayly Berith the Bell Away"
[ðʊ ˈbɛːɪli ˈbɛʁɪθ ðʊ bɛl ʌˈwɛːɪ]
Anonymous

The maidens came
[ðʊ ˈmɛːɪdɛ(ɪ)nz kɛːɪm]
when I was in my mother's bow'r.
[ʍɛn ɑːɪ waz ɪn mɑːɪ ˈmʌðʌz ˈbɑːʊʌ]
I had all that I would.
[ɑːɪ hæd ɔl ðæt ɑːɪ wʊd]
The bailey beareth the bell away,
[ðʊ ˈbɛːɪli ˈbɛːʌɾɛ(ɪ)θ ðʊ bɛl ʌˈwɛːɪ]
The lily, the rose, the rose I lay.
[ðʊ ˈlɪlɪ ðʊ ɾoːʊz ðʊ ɾoːʊz ɑːɪ lɛːɪ]
The silver is white, Red is the gold
[ðʊ ˈsɪlvʌɾ ɪz ʍɑːɪt ɹɛd ɪz ðʊ goːʊld]
The robes they lay in fold.
[ðʊ ɾoːʊbz ðɛːɪ lɛːɪ ɪn foːʊld]
The bailey beareth the bell away,
[ðʊ ˈbɛːɪli ˈbɛːʌɾɛ(ɪ)θ ðʊ bɛl ʌˈwɛːɪ]
The lily, the rose, the rose I lay.
[ðʊ ˈlɪlɪ ðʊ ɾoːʊz ðʊ ɾoːʊz ɑːɪ lɛːɪ]

And through the glass window shines the sun.
[ænd θɾu ðʊ glas ˈwɪndoːʊ ʃaːɪnz ðʊ sʌn]
How should I love, and I so young?
[haːʊ ʃʊd aːɪ lʌv ænd aːɪ soːʊ jʌŋ]
The bailey beareth the bell away;
[ðʊ ˈbɛːɪlɪ ˈbɛːʌɾɛ(ɪ)θ ðʊ bɛl ʌˈwɛːɪ]
The lily, the lily, the rose I lay.
[ðʊ ˈlɪlɪ ðʊ ˈlɪlɪ ðʊ ɾoːʊz aːɪ lɛːɪ]

"The Everlasting Voices"
[ði ɛvʌˈlastɪŋ ˈvɔːɪsɪz]
Yeats, William Butler (Ir. 1865-1939)

O sweet everlasting Voices, be still;
[oːʊ swit ɛvʌˈlastɪŋ ˈvɔːɪsɛ(ɪ)z bi stɪl]
Go to the guards of the heavenly fold
[goːʊ tu ðʊ gadz ʌv ðʊ ˈhɛvɛ(ɪ)nlɪ foːʊld]
And bid them wander obeying your will,
[ænd bɪd ðɛm ˈwandʌɾ oˈbɛːɪɪŋ jɔːʌ wɪl]
Flame under flame, till Time be no more;
[flɛːɪm ˈʌndʌ flɛːɪm tɪl taːɪm bi noːʊ mɔːʌ]
Have you not heard that our hearts are old,
[hæv ju nat hɜd ðæt aːʊʌ hats ɑɾ oːʊld]
That you call in birds, in wind on the hill,
[ðæt ju kɔl ɪn bɜdz ɪn wɪnd an ðʊ hɪl]
In shaken boughs, in tide on the shore?
[ɪn ˈʃɛːɪkɛ(ɪ)n baːʊz ɪn taːɪd an ðʊ ʃɔːʌ]
O sweet everlasting Voices, be still.
[oːʊ swit ɛvʌˈlastɪŋ ˈvɔːɪsɛ(ɪ)z bi stɪl]

"The Lover's Maze"
[ðʊ ˈlʌvʌz mɛːɪz]
Campion, Thomas (Eng. 1567-1620)

O be still, be still, unquiet thoughts,
[oːʊ bi stɪl bi stɪl ʌnˈkwaːɪɛ(ɪ)t θɔts]
and rest on love's adventer.
[ænd ɾɛst an lʌvz ædˈvɛntʌ]
Go no more astray, my wanton eyes,
[goːʊ noːʊ mɔːʌ ʌˈstɾɛːɪ maːɪ ˈwantʌn aːɪz]
but keep within your centre.
[bʌt kip wɪðˈɪn jɔːʌ ˈsɛntʌ]
Delight not yourselves for to stand and gaze
[dɪˈlaːɪt nat jɔːʌˈsɛlvz fɔ tu stænd ænd gɛːɪz]
On the alluring looks of a beautyous face,
[an ði ʌˈljuːʌɾɪŋ lʊks ʌv ʌ ˈbjutɪʌs fɛːɪs]
For love is like to an endless maze,
[fɔ lʌv ɪz laːɪk tu æn ˈɛndlɛ(ɪ)s mɛːɪz]
More hard to get out than to enter.
[mɔːʌ had tu gɛt aːʊt ðæn tu ˈɛntʌ]
O but why should I complain of love,
[oːʊ bʌt ʌaːɪ ʃʊd aːɪ kʌmˈplɛːɪn ʌv lʌv]
since once I have affected?
[sɪns wʌns aːɪ hæv ʌˈfɛktɛ(ɪ)d]
My hopes are not yet quite so dead
[maːɪ hoːʊps ɑ nat jɛt kwaːɪt soːʊ dɛd]

but that I might be respected.
[bʌt ðæt aːɪ maːɪt bi ɾɪˈspɛktɛ(ɪ)d]
Yet her often replies say no, no, no,
[jɛt hɜ ˈafɛ(ɪ)n ɹɪˈplaːɪz sɛːɪ noːʊ noːʊ noːʊ]
It is danger to say so, so, so,
[ɪt ɪz ˈdɛːɪndʒʌ tu sɛːɪ soːʊ soːʊ soːʊ]
Which makes my heart very woe, woe, woe,
[ʌɪtʃ mɛːɪks maːɪ hat ˈvɛɾɪ woːʊ woːʊ woːʊ]
For fear I should be rejected.
[fɔ fiːʌɾ aːɪ ʃʊd bi ɾɪˈdʒɛktɛ(ɪ)d]
O but wherefore should so fair a face
[oːʊ bʌt ʌɛːʌˈfɔːʌ ʃʊd soːʊ fɛːʌɾ ʌ fɛːɪs]
retain a heart so cruel?
[ɹɪˈtɛːɪn ʌ hat soːʊ ˈkruːɛ(ʊ)l]
Then despair, despair, aspiring thoughts,
[ðɛn dɪˈspɛːʌ dɪˈspɛːʌɾ ʌˈspaːɪʌɾɪŋ θɔts]
to gain so rare a jewel.
[tu gɛːɪn soːʊ ɾɛːʌɾ ʌ ˈdʒuːɛ(ʊ)l]
O but when I cull and clip and kiss,
[oːʊ bʌt ʌɛn aːɪ kʌl ænd klɪp ænd kɪs]
Methinks there hidden treasure is,
[ˌmiˈθɪŋks ðɛːʌ ˈhɪdɛ(ɪ)n ˈtɾɛʒʊ(ʌ)ɾ ɪz]
Which whispers in mine ears all this:
[ʌɪtʃ ˈʌɪspʌz ɪn maːɪn ɪːʌz ɔl ðɪs]
Love's flames require more fuel.
[lʌvz flɛːɪmz ɹɪˈkwaːɪʌ mɔːʌ ˈfjuːʊl]

"The Magpie"
[ðʊ ˈmægˌpaːɪ]
Hunter, Harry

I lingered near a cottage door,
[aːɪ ˈlɪŋgʌd niːʌɾ ʌ ˈkatæ(ɪ)dʒ dɔːʌɾ]
And the magpie said "Come in! come in!"
[ænd ðʊ ˈmægˌpaːɪ sɛd kʌm ɪn kʌm ɪn]
And the magpie said "Come in!"
[ænd ðʊ ˈmægˌpaːɪ sɛd kʌm ɪn]
The door was open, I went in
[ðʊ dɔːʌ waz ˈoːʊpɛ(ɪ)n aːɪ wɛnt ɪn]
And I saw standing there
[ænd aːɪ sɔ ˈstændɪŋ ðɛːʌ]
A maiden with a dimpled chin
[ʌ ˈmɛːɪdɛ(ɪ)n wɪð ʌ ˈdɪmpʊld tʃɪn]
A-combing her back hair, back hair,
[ʌ ˈkoːʊmɪŋ hɜ bæk hɛːʌ bæk hɛːʌ]
A-combing her back hair.
[ʌ ˈkoːʊmɪŋ hɜ bæk hɛːʌ]
A sweet surprise was in her eyes,
[ʌ swit sɜˈpɹaːɪz waz ɪn hɜ aːɪz]
But still she did not frown,
[bʌt stɪl ʃi dɪd nat fɹaːʊn]
But even smiled, the pretty child,
[bʌt ˈivɛ(ɪ)n smaːɪld ðʊ ˈpɹɪtɪ tʃaːɪld]
And the magpie said "Sit down! Sit down!"
[ænd ðʊ ˈmægˌpaːɪ sɛd sɪt daːʊn sɪt daːʊn]

And the magpie said "Sit down!"
[ænd ðʊ 'mæg͵paːɪ sɛd sɪt daːʊn]
I sat down in her father's chair
[aːɪ sæt daːʊn ɪn hɜ 'faðʌz ʧɛːʌ]
And the magpie said "Kiss her! Kiss her!"
[ænd ðʊ 'mæg͵paːɪ sɛd kɪs hɜ kɪs hɜ]
And the magpie said "Kiss her!"
[ænd ðʊ 'mæg͵paːɪ sɛd kɪs hɜ]
And yet the maiden didn't speak
[ænd jɛt ðʊ 'mɛːɪdɛ(ɪ)n 'dɪdɛ(ɪ)nt spik]
Which made me think "I will!"
[ʌɪʧ mɛːɪd mi θɪŋk aːɪ wɪl]
For as the red rushed to her cheek
[fɔʁ⁽ʳ⁾ æz ðʊ ɾɛd ɾʌʃt tu hɜ ʧik]
She looked more lovely still, still, still,
[ʃi lʊkt mɔːʌ 'lʌvlɪ stɪl stɪl stɪl]
She looked more lovely still.
[ʃi lʊkt mɔːʌ 'lʌvlɪ stɪl]
But when in haste I clasped her waist
[bʌt ʌɛn ɪn hɛːɪst aːɪ klaspt hɜ wɛːɪst]
She screamed out "No! No! No!"
[ʃi skɾimd aːʊt noːʊ noːʊ noːʊ]
But 'twas so nice I kissed her twice
[bʌt twaz soːʊ naːɪs aːɪ kɪst hɜ twaːɪs]
And the magpie said "Bravo! Bravo!"
[ænd ðʊ 'mæg͵paːɪ sɛd 'bravo 'bravo]
And the magpie said "Bravo!"
[ænd ðʊ 'mæg͵paːɪ sɛd 'bravo]
Her father then came rushing in,
[hɜ 'faðʌ ðɛn kɛːɪm 'ɾʌʃɪŋ ɪn]
And the magpie said "Get out! Get out!"
[ænd ðʊ 'mæg͵paːɪ sɛd gɛt aːʊt gɛt aːʊt]
And the magpie said "Get out!"
[ænd ðʊ 'mæg͵paːɪ sɛd gɛt aːʊt]
Her father's voice was like a rasp
[hɜ 'faðʌz vɔːɪs waz laːɪk ʌ ɾasp]
And swearing he began–
[ænd 'swɛːʌɾɪŋ hi bɪ'gæn]
And I experienced the grasp,
[ænd aːɪ ɪk'spɪːʌɾɪ͵ɛ(ɪ)nst ðʊ gɾasp]
The grasp of an honest man, man, man,
[ðʊ gɾasp ʌv æn 'anɛ(ɪ)st mæn mæn mæn]
The grasp of an honest man.
[ðʊ gɾasp ʌv æn 'anɛ(ɪ)st mæn]
He rained such blows upon my clothes
[hi ɾɛːɪnd sʌʧ bloːʊz ʌ'pan maːɪ kloːʊðz]
I feel them to this day;
[aːɪ fil ðɛm tu ðɪs dɛːɪ]
He kicked me too as out I flew,
[hi kɪkt mi tu æz aːʊt aːɪ flu]
And the magpie said "Hooray! Hooray!"
[ænd ðʊ 'mæg͵paːɪ sɛd hʊ'ɾɛːɪ hʊ'ɾɛːɪ]
And the magpie said "Hooray!"
[ænd ðʊ 'mæg͵paːɪ sɛd hʊ'ɾɛːɪ]

Watts, Wintter (Am. 1884-1962)

Vignettes Overseas (Song Cycle)
[vɪ'njɛts ͵oːʊvʁ'siz]
Teasdale, Sara (Am. 1884-1933)

1. Addio
[ad'diːo]

Oh give me neither love nor tears,
[oːʊ gɪv mi 'naːɪðʌ lʌv nɔ tɪːʌz]
Nor dreams that sear the night with fire.
[nɔ dɾimz ðæt sɪːʌ ðʌ naːɪt wɪð faːɪʌ]
Go lightly on your pilgrimage
[goːʊ 'laːɪtlɪ an jɔːʌ 'pɪlgɾɪmæ(ɪ)ʤ]
Unburdened by desire.
[ʌn'bɜdɛ(ɪ)nd baːɪ dɪ'zaːɪʌ]
Forget me for a month, a year,
[fɔ'gɛt mi fɔʁ⁽ʳ⁾ ʌ mʌnθ ʌ jɪːʌ]
But oh, beloved, think of me
[bʌt oːʊ bɪ'lʌvɛ(ɪ)d θɪŋk ʌv mi]
When unexpected beauty burns
[ʌɛn ʌnɪks'pɛktɛ(ɪ)d 'bjutɪ bɜnz]
Like sudden sunlight on the sea.
[laːɪk 'sʌdɛ(ɪ)n 'sʌnlaːɪt an ðʌ si]

2. Naples
['nɛːɪpʊlz]

Nisida and Prosida are laughing in the light,
['nizida ænd 'pɾozida ɑ 'læfɪŋ ɪn ðʌ laːɪt]
Capri is a dewy flower lifting into sight.
['kapri ɪz ʌ 'djuɪ flaːʊʌ 'lɪftɪŋ 'ɪntu saːɪt]
Posilipo kneels and looks in the burnished sea,
[po'zilipo nilz ænd lʊks ɪn ðʌ 'bɜnɪʃt si]
Naples crowds her million roofs
['nɛːɪpʊlz kɾaːʊdz hɜ 'mɪljʌn ɾ⁽ʳʳ⁾ufs]
close as close can be;
[kloːʊs æz kloːʊs kæn bi]
Round about the mountain crest
[ɾaːʊnd ʌ'baːʊt ðʌ 'maːʊntæ(ɪ)n kɾɛst]
a flag of smoke is hung,–
[ʌ flæg ʌv smoːʊk ɪz hʌŋ]
Oh, when God made Italy He was gay and young!
[oːʊ ʌɛn gad mɛːɪd 'ɪtʌlɪ hi waz gɛːɪ ænd jʌŋ]

3. Capri ['kapri]

When beauty grows too great to bear
[ʌɛn 'bjutɪ gɾoːʊz tu gɾɛːɪt tu bɛːʌ]
How can I ease me of its ache,
[haːʊ kæn aːɪ iz mi ʌv ɪts ɛːɪk]
For beauty more than bitterness
[fɔ 'bjutɪ mɔːʌ ðæn 'bɪtʌnɛ(ɪ)s]
Makes the heart break.
[mɛːɪks ðʌ hɑt bɾɛːɪk]

Now while I watch the dreaming sea
[nɑːʊ ʍaːɪl aːɪ watʃ ðʌ ˈdɹimɪŋ si]
With isles like flowers against her breast,
[wɪð aːɪlz laːɪk flaːʊʌz ʌˈgɛnst hɜ bɹɛst]
Only one voice in all the world
[ˈoːʊnlɪ wʌn vɔːɪs ɪn ɔl ðʌ wɜld]
Could give me rest.
[kʊd gɪv mi ɹɛst]

4. Night Song at Amalfi
[naːɪt saŋ æt aˈmalfi]

I asked the heav'n of stars
[aːɪ æskt ðʌ hɛvn ʌv staz]
What I should give my love,
[ʍat aːɪ ʃʊd gɪv maːɪ lʌv]
It answered me with silence,
[ɪt ˈænsʌd mi wɪð ˈsaːɪlɛ(ɪ)ns]
Silence above.
[ˈsaːɪlɛ(ɪ)ns ʌˈbʌv]
I asked the darkened sea,
[aːɪ æskt ðʌ ˈdakɛ(ɪ)nd si]
Down where the fishers go,
[daːʊn ʍɛːʌ ðʌ ˈfɪʃʌz goːʊ]
It answered me with silence,
[ɪt ˈænsʌd mi wɪð ˈsaːɪlɛ(ɪ)ns]
Silence below.
[ˈsaːɪlɛ(ɪ)ns bɪˈloːʊ]
Oh, I could give him weeping,
[oːʊ aːɪ kʊd gɪv hɪm ˈwipɪŋ]
Or I could give him song,
[ɔʁ⁽ʳ⁾ aːɪ kʊd gɪv hɪm saŋ]
But how can I give silence
[bʌt haːʊ kæn aːɪ gɪv ˈsaːɪlɛ(ɪ)ns]
My whole life long?
[maːɪ hoːʊl laːɪf laŋ]

5. Ruins of Paestum
[ˈɹuɪnz ʌv ˈpɛstum]

On lowlands where the temples lie
[an ˈloːʊlæ(ʌ)ndz ʍɛːʌ ðʌ ˈtɛmpʊlz laːɪ]
The marsh-grass mingles with the flowers,
[ðʌ maʃ gɹæs ˈmɪŋgʊlz wɪð ðʌ flaːʊʌz]
Only the little songs of birds
[ˈoːʊnlɪ ðʌ ˈlɪtʊl saŋz ʌv bɜdz]
Link the unbroken hours.
[lɪŋk ði ʌnˈbɹoːʊkɛ(ɪ)n aːʊʌz]
So in the end, above my heart
[soːʊ ɪn ði ɛnd ʌˈbʌv maːɪ hat]
Once like a city, wild and gay,
[wʌns laːɪk ʌ ˈsɪtɪ waːɪld ænd gɛːɪ]
The slow white stars will pass by night,
[ðʌ sloːʊ ʍaːɪt staz wɪl pæs baːɪ naːɪt]
The swift brown birds by day.
[ðʌ swɪft bɹaːʊn bɜdz baːɪ dɛːɪ]

6. From a Roman Hill
[fɹʌm ʌ ˈɹoːʊman hɪl]

Oh for the rising moon
[oːʊ fɔ ðʌ ˈɹaːɪzɪŋ mun]
Over the roofs of Rome,
[ˈoːʊvʌ ðʌ ɹ⁽ʳ⁾ufs ʌv ɹoːʊm]
And swallows in the dusk
[ænd ˈswaloːʊz ɪn ðʌ dʌsk]
Circling a darkened dome!
[ˈsɜkʊlɪŋ ʌ ˈdakɛ(ɪ)nd doːʊm]
O for the measured dawns
[oːʊ fɔ ðʌ ˈmɛʒʊ(ʌ)d dɔnz]
That pass with folded wings!
[ðæt pæs wɪð ˈfoːʊldɛ(ɪ)d wɪŋz]
How can I let them go
[haːʊ kæn aːɪ lɛt ðɛm goːʊ]
With unremembered things?
[wɪð ˌʌnɹɪˈmɛmbʌd θɪŋz]

7. Ponte Vecchio, Florence
[ˈponte ˈvekkjo ˈflɔɹɛns]

The bells ring over the Arno,
[ðʌ bɛlz ɹɪŋ ˈoːʊvʌ ði ˈarno]
Midnight, the long, long chime;
[ˈmɪdnaːɪt ðʌ laŋ laŋ tʃaːɪm]
Here in the quiv'ring darkness
[hiːʌʁ⁽ʳ⁾ ɪn ðʌ ˈkwɪvɹɪŋ ˈdaknɛ(ɪ)s]
I am afraid of time.
[aːɪ æm ʌˈfɹɛːɪd ʌv taːɪm]
O gray bells, cease your tolling,
[oːʊ gɹɛːɪ bɛlz sis jɔːʌ ˈtoːʊlɪŋ]
Time takes too much from me,
[taːɪm tɛːɪks tu mʌtʃ fɹʌm mi]
And yet to rock and river
[ænd jɛt tu ɹak ænd ˈɹɪvʌ]
He gives eternity.
[hi gɪvz ɪˈtɜnɪtɪ]

8. Villa Serbelloni, Bellaggio
[ˈvilla serbelˈloni belˈladdʒo]

The fountain shivers lightly in the rain,
[ðʌ ˈfaːʊntæ(ɪ)n ˈʃɪvʌz ˈlaːɪtlɪ ɪn ðʌ ɹɛːɪn]
The laurels drip, the fading roses fall.
[ðʌ ˈlɔʁ⁽ʳ⁾ʊlz dɹɪp ðʌ ˈfɛːɪdɪŋ ˈɹoːʊzɛ(ɪ)z fɔl]
The marble satyr plays a mournful strain
[ðʌ ˈmabʊl ˈsɛːɪtʌ plɛːɪz ʌ ˈmɔnfʊl stɹɛːɪn]
That leaves the rainy fragrance musical.
[ðæt livz ðʌ ˈɹɛːɪnɪ ˈfɹɛːɪgɹæ(ɪ)ns ˈmjuzɪkʊl]
O dripping laurel, Phoebus' sacred tree,
[oːʊ ˈdɹɪpɪŋ ˈlɔʁ⁽ʳ⁾ʊl ˈfibʊs ˈsɛːɪkɹɛ(ɪ)d tɹi]
Would that swift Daphne's lot might come to me,
[wʊd ðæt swɪft ˈdæfnɪz lat maːɪt kʌm tu mi]

Then would I still my soul and for an hour
[ðɛn wʊd ɑːɪ stɪl maːɪ soːʊl ænd fɔʁ⁽ʳ⁾ æn ɑːʊʌ]
Change to a laurel in the glancing shower.
[ʧɛːɪndʒ tu ʌ ˈlɔʁ⁽ʳ⁾ʊl ɪn ðʌ ˈglænsɪŋ ʃaːʊʌ]

9. Stresa [ˈstreza]

The moon grows out of the hills
[ðʌ mun gɹoːʊz ɑːʊt ʌv ðʌ hɪlz]
A yellow flower.
[ʌ ˈjɛloːʊ flaːʊʌ]
The lake is a dreamy bride
[ðʌ lɛːɪk ɪz ʌ ˈdɹɪmɪ bɹaːɪd]
Who waits her hour.
[hu wɛːɪts hɜ ɑːʊʌ]
Beauty has filled my heart,
[ˈbjutɪ hæz fild maːɪ hat]
It can hold no more,
[ɪt kæn hoːʊld noːʊ mɔːʌ]
It is full as the lake is full,
[ɪt ɪz fʊl æz ðʌ lɛːɪk ɪz fʊl]
From shore to shore.
[fɹʌm ʃɔːʌ tu ʃɔːʌ]
Oh, beloved, think of me,
[oːʊ bɪˈlʌvɛ⁽ɪ⁾d θɪŋk ʌv mi]
When unexpected beauty burns
[ʍɛn ʌnɪksˈpɛktɛ⁽ɪ⁾d ˈbjutɪ bɜnz]
Like sunlight on the sea.
[laːɪk ˈsʌnlaːɪt an ðʌ si]
Beloved, think of me!
[bɪˈlʌvɛ⁽ɪ⁾d θɪŋk ʌv mi]

Song Selections

"Hushing Song"
[ˈhʌʃɪŋ saŋ]
Sharp, William (Sc. 1855-1905)

Eilidh, Eilidh,
[ˈɛːɪlɪ ˈɛːɪlɪ]
My bonny wee lass:
[maːɪ ˈbanɪ wi læs]
The winds blow,
[ðʌ wɪndz bloːʊ]
And the hours pass.
[ænd ði aːʊʌz pæs]
But never a wind
[bʌt ˈnɛvʌʁ⁽ʳ⁾ ʌ wɪnd]
Can do thee wrong,
[kæn du ði ɹaŋ]
Brown Birdeen, singing
[bɹaːʊn ˈbɜˈdin ˈsɪŋɪŋ]
Thy bird-heart song.
[ðaːɪ bɜd hat saŋ]
And never an hour
[ænd ˈnɛvʌʁ⁽ʳ⁾ æn ɑːʊʌ]

But has for thee
[bʌt hæz fɔ ði]
Blue of the heaven
[blu ʌv ðʌ ˈhɛvɛ⁽ɪ⁾n]
And green of the sea:
[ænd gɹin ʌv ðʌ si]
Blue for the hope of thee,
[blu fɔ ðʌ hoːʊp ʌv ði]
Eilidh, Green for the joy of thee,
[ˈɛːɪlɪ gɹin fɔ ðʌ dʒɔːɪ ʌv ði]
Eilidh, Sing in thy nest, then,
[ˈɛːɪlɪ sɪŋ ɪn ðaːɪ nɛst ðɛn]
Here on my heart,
[hɪːʌʁ⁽ʳ⁾ an maːɪ hat]
Birdeen, Birdeen, Here on my heart.
[ˈbɜˈdin ˈbɜˈdin hɪːʌʁ⁽ʳ⁾ an maːɪ hat]

"Like Music on the Waters"
[laːɪk ˈmjuzɪk an ðʌ ˈwɔtʁz]
Byron, George Gordon Noel (Eng. 1788-1824)

There be none of Beauty's daughters
[ðɛːʌ bi nʌn ʌv ˈbjutɪz ˈdɔtʌz]
With a magic like thee,
[wɪð ʌ ˈmædʒɪk laːɪk ði]
And like music on the waters
[ænd laːɪk ˈmjuzɪk an ðʌ ˈwɔtʌz]
Is thy sweet voice to me:
[ɪz ðaːɪ swit vɔːɪs tu mi]
When as if its sound were causing
[ʍɛn æz ɪf ɪts saːʊnd wɜ ˈkɔzɪŋ]
The charmed ocean's pausing,
[ðʌ ˈʧamɛ⁽ɪ⁾d ˈoːʊʃæ⁽ɪ⁾nz ˈpɔzɪŋ]
The waves lie still and gleaming
[ðʌ wɛːɪvz laːɪ stɪl ænd ˈglimɪŋ]
And the lull'd winds seem dreaming;
[ænd ðʌ lʌld wɪndz sim ˈdɹimɪŋ]
And the midnight moon is weaving
[ænd ðʌ ˈmɪdnaːɪt mun ɪz ˈwivɪŋ]
Its bright chain o'er the deep,
[ɪts bɹaːɪt ʧɛːɪn ɔːʌ ðʌ dip]
Whose breast is gently heaving–
[huz bɹɛst ɪz ˈdʒɛntlɪ ˈhivɪŋ]
As an infant's asleep:
[æz æn ˈɪnfæ⁽ɪ⁾nts ʌˈslip]
So the spirit bows before thee,
[soːʊ ðʌ ˈspɪʁ⁽ʳ⁾ɪt baːʊz bɪˈfɔːʌ ði]
To listen and adore thee;
[tu ˈlɪsɛ⁽ɪ⁾n ænd ʌˈdɔːʌ ði]
With a full but soft emotion,
[wɪð ʌ fʊl bʌt saft ɪˈmoːʊʃʌn]
Like the swell of Summer's ocean.
[laːɪk ðʌ swɛl ʌv ˈsʌmʌz ˈoːʊʃæ⁽ɪ⁾n]
There be none of Beauty's daughters
[ðɛːʌ bi nʌn ʌv ˈbjutɪz ˈdɔtʌz]

With a magic like thee,
[wɪð ʌ ˈmædʒɪk laːɪk ði]
And like music on the waters
[ænd laːɪk ˈmjuzɪk ɑn ðʌ ˈwɔtʌz]
Is thy sweet voice to me.
[ɪz ðaːɪ swit vɔːɪs tu mi]

"The Poet Sings"
[ðʌ ˈpoːʊɪt sɪŋz]
Gallienne, Richard Le (Eng. 1866-1947)

She's somewhere in the sunlight strong,
[ʃiz ˈsʌmʍɛːʌʁ(ʳ) ɪn ðʌ ˈsʌnlaːɪt stɹɑŋ]
Her tears are in the falling rain,
[hɜ tiːʌz ɑʁ(ʳ) ɪn ðʌ ˈfɔlɪŋ ɹɛːɪn]
She calls me in the wind's soft song,
[ʃi kɔlz mi ɪn ðʌ wɪndz saft sɑŋ]
And with the flowers she comes again.
[ænd wɪð ðʌ flaːʊʌz ʃi kʌmz ʌˈɡɛn]
Yon bird is but her messenger,
[jɑn bɜd ɪz bʌt hɜ ˈmɛsɛ(ɪ)ndʒʌ]
The moon is but her silver car,
[ðʌ mun ɪz bʌt hɜ ˈsɪlvʌ kɑ]
Yea! sun and moon are sent by her,
[jɛːɪ sʌn ænd mun ɑ sɛnt baːɪ hɜ]
And every wistful, waiting star.
[ænd ˈɛvɹɪ ˈwɪstfʊl ˈwɛːɪtɪŋ stɑ]

"Wings of Night"
[wɪŋz ʌv naːɪt]
Teasdale, Sara (Am. 1884-1933)

Dreamily over the roofs
[ˈdɹimɪlɪ ˈoːʊvʌ ðʌ ɹ(ʳʳ)ufs]
The cold spring rain is falling;
[ðʌ koːʊld spɹɪŋ ɹɛːɪn ɪz ˈfɔlɪŋ]
Out in a lonely tree
[aːʊt ɪn ʌ ˈloːʊnlɪ tɹi]
A bird is calling, calling.
[ʌ bɜd ɪz ˈkɔlɪŋ ˈkɔlɪŋ]
Softly over the earth
[ˈsaftlɪ ˈoːʊvʌ ðɪ ɜθ]
The wings of night are falling;
[ðʌ wɪŋz ʌv naːɪt ɑ ˈfɔlɪŋ]
My heart, like the bird in the tree,
[maːɪ hɑt laːɪk ðʌ bɜd ɪn ðʌ tɹi]
Is calling, calling, calling.
[ɪz ˈkɔlɪŋ ˈkɔlɪŋ ˈkɔlɪŋ]

"Wood-Song"
[wʊd sɑŋ]
Lee-Hamilton, Eugene (Eng. 1845-1907)

When we are gone, love,
[ʍɛn wi ɑ ɡɑn lʌv]

Gone as the breeze,
[ɡɑn æz ðʌ bɹiz]
Woods will be sweet, love,
[wʊdz wɪl bi swit lʌv]
Even as these.
[ˈivɛ(ɪ)n æz ðiz]
Sunflecks will dance, love,
[ˈsʌnflɛks wɪl dæns lʌv]
Even as now,
[ˈivɛ(ɪ)n æz naːʊ]
Here on the moss, love,
[hiːʌʁ(ʳ) ɑn ðʌ mɔs lʌv]
Under the bough.
[ˈʌndʌ ðʌ baːʊ]
Others unborn, love,
[ˈʌðʌz ʌnˈbɔn lʌv]
Maybe will sit
[ˈmɛːɪbi wɪl sɪt]
Here in the woods, love,
[hiːʌʁ(ʳ) ɪn ðʌ wʊdz lʌv]
Leafily lit;
[ˈlifɪlɪ lɪt]
Harking as now, love,
[ˈhɑkɪŋ æz naːʊ lʌv]
Treble of birds;
[ˈtɹɛbʊl ʌv bɜdz]
Breathing as we, love,
[ˈbɹiðɪŋ æz wi lʌv]
Wondering words.
[ˈwʌndʌʁ(ʳ)ɪŋ wɜdz]

 # Weill, Kurt (Am. 1900-1950)

Three Walt Whitman Songs (Song Cycle)
[θri wɔlt ˈʍɪtmɪn sɑŋz]
Whitman, Walt (Am. 1819-1892)

1. O Captain! My Captain! (see Hoiby)

2. Beat! Beat! Drums!
[bit bit dɹʌmz]

Beat! beat! drums!– blow! bugles! blow!
[bit bit dɹʌmz bloːʊ ˈbjuɡʊlz bloːʊ]
Through the windows– through doors–
[θru ðʌ ˈwɪndoːʊz θru dɔːʌz]
burst like a ruthless force,
[bɜst laːɪk ʌ ˈɹ(ʳʳ)uθlɛ(ɪ)s fɔs]
Into the solemn church, and scatter the congregation,
[ˈɪntu ðʌ ˈsalʌm tʃɜtʃ ænd ˈskætʌ ðʌ kɑŋɡɹɪˈɡɛːɪʃʌn]
Into the school where the scholar is studying;
[ˈɪntu ðʌ skul ʍɛːʌ ðʌ ˈskɑlʌʁ(ʳ) ɪz ˈstʌdɪɪŋ]
Leave not the bridegroom quiet–
[liv nɑt ðʌ ˈbɹaːɪdɡɹ(ʳ)um ˈkwaːɪɛ(ɪ)t]

no happiness must he have now with his bride,
[noːʊ ˈhæpɪnɛ(ɪ)s mʌst hi hæv naːʊ wɪð hɪz bɹaːɪd]
Nor the peaceful farmer any peace,
[nɔ ðʌ ˈpisfʊl ˈfamʌ ˈɛnɪ pis]
ploughing his field or gathering his grain,
[ˈplaːʊɪŋ hɪz fild ɔ ˈgæðʌʁ(ʳ)ɪŋ hɪz gɹeːɪn]
So fierce you whirr and pound, your drums–
[soːʊ fiːʌs ju ʍɜ(ʳ) ænd paːʊnd jɔːʌ dɹʌmz]
so shrill your bugles blow.
[soːʊ ʃɹɪl jɔːʌ ˈbjugʊlz bloːʊ]
Beat! beat! drums!– blow! bugles! blow!
[bit bit dɹʌmz bloːʊ ˈbjugʊlz bloːʊ]
Over the traffic of cities–
[ˈoːʊvʌ ðʌ ˈtɹæfik ʌv ˈsɪtɪz]
over the rumble of wheels in the streets;
[ˈoːʊvʌ ðʌ ˈɹʌmbʊl ʌv ʍilz ɪn ðʌ stɹits]
Are beds prepared for sleepers at night in the houses?
[a bɛdz pɹɪˈpɛːʌd fɔ ˈslipʌz æt naːɪt ɪn ðʌ ˈhaːʊzɛ(ɪ)z]
No sleepers must sleep in those beds–
[noːʊ ˈslipʌz mʌst slip ɪn ðoːʊz bɛdz]
No bargainers bargains by day–
[noːʊ ˈbagæ(ɪ)nʌz ˈbagæ(ɪ)nz baːɪ deːɪ]
no brokers or speculators– would they continue?
[noːʊ ˈbɹoːʊkʌz ɔ ˈspɛkju ˌleːɪlɔ(ʌ)z wʊd ðeːɪ kʌnˈtɪnju]
Would the talkers be talking?
[wʊd ðʌ ˈtɔkʌz bi ˈtɔkɪŋ]
Would the singer attempt to sing?
[wʊd ðʌ ˈsɪŋʌʁ(ʳ) ʌˈtɛmpt tu sɪŋ]
Would the lawyer rise in the court
[wʊd ðʌ ˈlɔjʌ ɹaːɪz ɪn ðʌ kɔt]
to state his case before the judge?
[tu steːɪt hɪz kɛːɪs bɪˈfɔːʌ ðʌ dʒʌdʒ]
Then rattle quicker, heavier drums–
[ðɛn ˈɹætʊl ˈkwɪkʌ ˈhɛvɪʌ dɹʌmz]
your bugles wilder blow.
[jɔːʌ ˈbjugʊlz ˈwaːɪldʌ bloːʊ]
Beat! beat! drums!– blow! bugles! blow!
[bit bit dɹʌmz bloːʊ ˈbjugʊlz bloːʊ]
Make no parley– stop for no expostulation,
[meːɪk noːʊ ˈpalɪ stap fɔ noːʊ ɛkspastjuˈleːɪʃʌn]
Mind not the timid– mind not the weeper or prayer,
[maːɪnd nat ðʌ ˈtɪmɪd maːɪnd nat ðʌ ˈwipʌʁ(ʳ) ɔ pɹeːʌ]
Mind not the old man beseeching the young man,
[maːɪnd nat ði oːʊld mæn bɪˈsitʃɪŋ ðʌ jʌŋ mæn]
Let not the child's voice be heard,
[lɛt nat ðʌ tʃaːɪldz vɔːɪs bi hɜd]
nor the mother's entreaties,
[nɔ ðʌ ˈmʌðʌz ɪnˈtɹitɪz]
Make even the trestles to shake the dead
[meːɪk ˈivɛ(ɪ)n ðʌ ˈtɹɛsʊlz tu ʃeːɪk ðʌ dɛd]
where they lie awaiting the hearses,
[ʍɛːʌ ðeːɪ laːɪ ʌˈweːɪtɪŋ ðʌ ˈhɜsɛ(ɪ)z]
So strong you thump O terrible drums–
[soːʊ stɹaŋ ju θʌmp oːʊ ˈtɛʁ(ʳ)ɪbʊl dɹʌmz]
so loud you bugles blow.
[soːʊ laːʊd ju ˈbjugʊlz bloːʊ]

Beat! beat! drums!– blow! bugles! blow!
[bit bit dɹʌmz bloːʊ ˈbjugʊlz bloːʊ]

3. Dirge for Two Veterans
[dɜdʒ fɔʁ tu ˈvɛtɹɪnz]

The last sunbeam
[ðʌ læst ˈsʌnbim]
Lightly falls from the finish'd Sabbath,
[laːɪtlɪ fɔlz fɹʌm ðʌ ˈfɪnɪʃt ˈsæbæ(ʌ)θ]
On the pavement here, and there beyond it is looking,
[an ðʌ ˈpeːɪvmɛnt hiːʌ ænd ðɛːʌ bɪˈjand ɪt ɪz ˈlʊkɪŋ]
Down a new-made double grave.
[daːʊn ʌ nju meːɪd ˈdʌbʊl gɹ(ʳ)eːɪv]
Lo, the moon ascending,
[loːʊ ðʌ mun ʌˈsɛndɪŋ]
Up from the east the silvery round moon,
[ʌp fɹʌm ði ist ðʌ ˈsɪlvʌʁ(ʳ)ɪ ɹaːʊnd mun]
Beautiful over the house-tops, ghastly, phantom moon,
[ˈbjutɪfʊl ˈoːʊvʌ ðʌ haːʊs taps ˈgæstlɪ ˈfæntʌm mun]
Immense and silent moon.
[ɪˈmɛns ænd ˈsaːɪlɛnt mun]
I see a sad procession,
[aːɪ si ʌ sæd pɹoˈsɛʃʌn]
And I hear the sound of coming full-key'd bugles,
[ænd aːɪ hiːʌ ðʌ saːʊnd ʌv ˈkʌmɪŋ fʊl kid ˈbjugʊlz]
All the channels of the city streets they're flooding,
[ɔl ðʌ ˈtʃænʊlz ʌv ðʌ ˈsɪtɪ stɹits ðɛːʌ ˈflʌdɪŋ]
As with voices and with tears.
[æz wɪð ˈvɔːɪsɛ(ɪ)z ænd wɪð tɪːʌz]
I hear the great drums pounding,
[aːɪ hiːʌ ðʌ gɹeːɪt dɹʌmz ˈpaːʊndɪŋ]
And the small drums steady whirring
[ænd ðʌ smɔl dɹʌmz ˈstɛdɪ ˈʍʌʁ(ʳ)ɪŋ]
And every blow of the great convulsive drums,
[ænd ˈɛvɹɪ bloːʊ ʌv ðʌ gɹeːɪt kʌnˈvʌlsɪv dɹʌmz]
Strikes me through and through.
[stɹaːɪks mi θɹu ænd θɹu]
For the son is brought with the father,
[fɔ ðʌ sʌn ɪz bɹɔt wɪð ðʌ ˈfaðʌ]
(In the foremost ranks of the fierce assault they fell,
[ɪn ðʌ ˈfɔmoːʊst ɹæŋks ʌv ðʌ fiːʌs ʌˈsɔlt ðɛːɪ fɛl]
Two veterans son and father dropt together,
[tu ˈvɛtɹæ(ɪ)nz sʌn ænd ˈfaðʌ dɹapt tuˈgɛðʌ]
And the double grave awaits them.)
[ænd ðʌ ˈdʌbʊl gɹ(ʳ)eːɪv ʌˈweːɪts ðɛm]
Now nearer blow the bugles,
[naːʊ ˈnɪːʌʁ(ʳ)ʌ bloːʊ ðʌ ˈbjugʊlz]
And the drums strike more convulsive,
[ænd ðʌ dɹʌmz stɹaːɪk mɔːʌ kʌnˈvʌlsɪv]
And the daylight o'er the pavement
[ænd ðʌ ˈdeːɪlaːɪt ɔːʌ ðʌ ˈpeːɪvmɛnt]
quite has faded,
[kwaːɪt hæz ˈfeːɪdɛ(ɪ)d]
And the strong dead-march enwraps me.
[ænd ðʌ stɹaŋ dɛd maːtʃ ɪnˈɹæps mi]

O strong dead-march you please me!
[oːʊ stɹɑŋ dɛd matʃ ju pliz mi]
O moon immense with your silvery face you soothe me!
[oːʊ mun ɪˈmɛns wɪð jɔːʌ ˈsɪlvʌʁ⁽ʳ⁾ɪ fɛːɪs ju suð mi]
O my soldiers twain!
[oːʊ maːɪ ˈsoːʊldʒʌz twɛːɪn]
O my veterans passing to burial!
[oːʊ maːɪ ˈvɛtɹæ⁽ɪ⁾nz ˈpæsɪŋ tu ˈbɛʁ⁽ʳ⁾ɪʊl]
What I have I also give you.
[ʍat aːɪ hæv aːɪ ˈɔlsoːʊ gɪv ju]
The moon gives you light,
[ðʌ mun gɪvz ju laːɪt]
And the bugles and the drums give you music,
[ænd ðʌ ˈbjugʊlz ænd ðʌ dɹʌmz gɪv ju ˈmjuzɪk]
And my heart, O my soldiers, my veterans,
[ænd maːɪ hat oːʊ maːɪ ˈsoːʊldʒʌz maːɪ ˈvɛtɹæ⁽ɪ⁾nz]
My heart gives you love.
[maːɪ hat gɪvz ju lʌv]

Weir, Judith (Eng. b. 1954)

Scotch Minstrelsy (Song Cycle)
[skatʃ ˈmɪnstɹʊlsi]
Folksongs

1. Bessie Bell and Mary Gray
[ˈbɛsi bɛl ænd ˈmæʁi gɹɛːɪ]

Bessie Bell and Mary Gray,
[ˈbɛsɪ bɛl ænd ˈmæɹɪ grɛːɪ]
They were two bonnie lasses.
[ðɛːɪ wɜ tu ˈbanɪ ˈlæsɛ⁽ɪ⁾z]
They biggit a bow'r on the banks of the river,
[ðɛːɪ ˈbɪgɪt ʌ ˈbaːʊʌɾ an ðʊ bæŋks ʌv ðʊ ˈɹɪvʌ]
And theekit it over with rashes O!
[ænd ˈθikɪt ɪt ˈoːʊvʌ wɪð ˈɹæʃɛ⁽ɪ⁾z oːʊ]
They theekit it over with rashes green,
[ðɛːɪ ˈθikɪt ɪt ˈoːʊvʌ wɪð ˈɹæʃɛ⁽ɪ⁾z grin]
They theekit it over with heather;
[ðɛːɪ ˈθikɪt ɪt ˈoːʊvʌ wɪð ˈhɛðʌ]
The plague came into the river bank,
[ðʊ plɛːɪg kɛːɪm ˈɪntu ðʊ ˈɹɪvʌ bæŋk]
And slew them both together.
[ænd slu ðɛm boːʊθ tuˈgɛðʌ]

2. Bonnie James Campbell
[ˈbani dʒɛːɪmz ˈkæmbʊl]

It's up in the highlands, along the sweet Tay,
[ɪts ʌp ɪn ðʊ ˈhilæ⁽ʌ⁾ndz ʌ ˈlɛːɪŋ ðʊ swit tɛːɪ]
Bonnie James Campbell rode many a day.
[ˈbani dʒɛːɪmz ˈkæmbʊl roːʊd ˈmʌnɪ ʌ dɛːɪ]
He saddled, he bridled and gallant rode he,
[hi ˈsædʊld hi ˈbraːɪdʊld ænd ˈgælæ⁽ɪ⁾nt roːʊd hi]

And home came his good horse but never came he.
[ænd hɛːɪm kɛːɪm hɪz gɛːɪd hɔs bʌt ˈnɛvʌ kɛːɪm hi]
Out came his old mother a-crying full sair,
[aːʊt kɛːɪm hɪz oːʊld ˈmʌðʌɾ ʌ ˈkɹaːɪɪŋ fʊl sɛːʌ]
Out came his bonny bride tearing her hair.
[aːʊt kɛːɪm hɪz ˈbanɪ braːɪd ˈtɛːʌɾɪŋ hɜ hɛːʌ]
'My meadow lies green and my corn is unshorn,
[ma ˈmɛdoːʊ laːɪz grin ænd ma kɔn ɪz ʌnˈʃɔn]
But bonny James Campbell will never return'.
[bʌt ˈbanɪ dʒɛːɪmz ˈkæmbʊl wɪl ˈnɛvʌ ɹɪˈtɜn]
Saddled and bridled and booted rode he,
[ˈsædʊld ænd ˈbraːɪdʊld ænd ˈbutɛ⁽ɪ⁾d roːʊd hi]
A plume in his helmet, a sword at his knee.
[ʌ plum ɪn hɪz ˈhɛlmɛ⁽ɪ⁾t ʌ sɔd æt hɪz ni]
Empty his saddle all bloody to see;
[ˈɛmptɪ hɪz ˈsædʊl ɔl ˈblʌdɪ tʊ si]
Oh home came his good horse, but never came he.
[oːʊ hɛːɪm kɛːɪm hɪz gɛːɪd hɔs bʌt ˈnɛvʌ kɛːɪm hi]

3. Lady Isobel and the Elf-Knight
[ˈlɛːɪdi ˈɪzʌˌbɛl ænd ði ɛlf naːɪt]

Fair Lady Isobel sits in her bower sewing:
[fɛːʌ ˈlɛːɪdi ˈɪzo⁽ʌ⁾ˌbɛl sits ɪn hɜ ˈbaːʊʌ ˈsoːʊɪŋ]
There she heard the Elf-Knight blowing his horn.
[ðɛːʌ ʃi hɜd ði ɛlf naːɪt ˈbloːʊɪŋ hɪz hɔn]
'If I had yon horn that I hear blowing,
[ɪf aːɪ hæd jan hɔn ðæt a hiːʌ ˈbloːʊɪŋ]
And yon Elf-Knight to sleep in my bosom.'
[ænd jan ɛlf naːɪt tu slip ɪn maːɪ ˈbʊzʌm]
The maiden had scarcely these words spoken;
[ðʊ ˈmɛːɪdɛ⁽ɪ⁾n hæd ˈskɛːʌslɪ ðiz wɜdz ˈspoːʊkɛ⁽ɪ⁾n]
When in at her window the Elf-Knight has luppen.
[ʍɛn ɪn æt hɜ ˈwɪndoːʊ ði ɛlf naːɪt hæz ˈloːʊpɛ⁽ɪ⁾n]
'It's a very strange matter, fair maiden' said he,
[ɪts ʌ ˈvɛɾi strɛːɪndʒ ˈmætʌ fɛːʌ ˈmɛːɪdɛ⁽ɪ⁾n sɛd hi]
'I canna blow my horn but ye call on me.
[aːɪ ˈkænʌ bloːʊ ma hɔn bʌt ji kɔl an mi]
But will ye go to yon Greenwood side?
[bʌt wɪl ji goːʊ tu jan ˈgrinwʊd saːɪd]
If ye canna gang, I will cause you to ride.'
[ɪf ji ˈkænʌ gæŋ a wɪl kɔz ju tu ɾaːɪd]
He leapt on a horse and she on another,
[hi lɛpt an ʌ hɔs ænd ʃi an ʌˈnʌðʌ]
And they rode on to the Greenwood together.
[ænd ðɛːɪ roːʊd an tu ðʊ ˈgrinwʊd tuˈgɛðʌ]
'Light down, light down, Lady Isobel' said he,
[laːɪt daːʊn laːɪt daːʊn ˈlɛːɪdi ˈɪzo⁽ʌ⁾ˌbɛl sɛd hi]
'We are come to the place where you are to die'.
[wi a kʌm tʊ ðʊ plɛːɪs ʍɛːʌ ji a tʊ di]
'Have mercy, have mercy, kind sir, on me,
[hæv ˈmɜsi hæv ˈmɜsi kaːɪnd sɜ an mi]
Till once my dear father and mother I see.'
[tɪl ʍʌns maːɪ dɪːʌ ˈfaðʌ ænd ˈmʌðʌ aːɪ si]
'Sev'n king's daughters here have I slain,
[ˈsɛvɪn kɪŋz ˈdɔtʌz hiːʌ hæv aːɪ slɛːɪn]

And you shall be the eighth of them.'
[ænd ju ʃæl bi ði ɛːɪtθ ʌv ðɛm]
'O sit down a while, rest your head upon my knee,
[oːʊ sɪt daːʊn ʌ ʍaːɪl rɛst jɔːʌ hɛd ʌˈpɑn maːɪ ni]
That we may have some rest before I die.'
[ðæt wi mɛːɪ hæv sʌm rɛst bɪˈfɔːʌr a di]
She stroked him so softly the nearer he did creep;
[ʃi stroːʊkt hɪm soːʊ ˈsaftlɪ ðʊ ˈnɪːʌɾʌ hi dɪd krip]
With a small, secret charm she lulled him fast asleep.
[wɪð ʌ smɔl ˈsikrɛ(ɪ)t tʃam ʃi lʌld hɪm fast ʌˈslip]
With his own sword belt so softly she bound him;
[wɪð hɪz oːʊn sɔd bɛlt soːʊ ˈsaftlɪ ʃi baːʊnd hɪm]
With his own dagger so softly she killed him.
[wɪð hɪz oːʊn ˈdægʌ soːʊ ˈsaftlɪ ʃi kɪld hɪm]

4. The Gypsy Laddie
[ðʊ ˈdʒɪpsi ˈlædi]

The gypsies came to our good lord's castle gates,
[ðʊ ˈdʒɪpsiz kɛːɪm tʊ aːʊʌ gʊd lɔdz ˈkasʊl gɛːɪts]
And O! but they sang sweetly, O!
[ænd oːʊ bʌt ðɛːɪ sæŋ ˈswitlɪ oːʊ]
They sang so sweet, and so complete,
[ðɛːɪ sæŋ soːʊ swit ænd soːʊ kʌmˈplit]
That down came our fair lady, O!
[ðæt daːʊn kɛːɪm aːʊʌ fɛːʌ ˈlɛːɪdɪ oːʊ]
They gave to her the nutmeg brown;
[ðɛːɪ gɛːɪv tʊ hɜ ðʊ ˈnʌtˌmɛg braːʊn]
They gave the finest ginger.
[ðɛːɪ gɛːɪv ðʊ ˈfaːɪnɛ(ɪ)st ˈdʒɪndʒʌ]
The gypsies saw her well-fared face,
[ðʊ ˈdʒɪpsiz sɔ hɜ wɛl fɛːʌd fɛːɪs]
And cast their glamour over her:
[ænd kast ðɛːʌ ˈglæmʊ(ʌ)r ˈoːʊvʌ hɜ]
'Go, take from me this silver cloak
[goːʊ tɛːɪk frʌm mi ðɪs ˈsɪlvʌ kloːʊk]
And bring to me a plaidie.
[ænd brɪŋ tʊ mi ʌ ˈplɛːɪdɪ]
I will forget my kith and kin,
[aːɪ wɪl fɔˈgɛt maːɪ kɪθ ænd kɪn]
And follow the gypsy laddie.
[ænd ˈfaloːʊ ðʊ ˈdʒɪpsi ˈlædɪ]
Last night I lay on a feather bed,
[last naːɪt aːɪ lɛːɪ an ʌ ˈfɛðʌ bɛd]
My wedded lord beside me;
[maːɪ ˈwɛdɛ(ɪ)d lɔd bɪˈsaːɪd mi]
Tonight I lie with stars and moon and sky,
[tuˈnaːɪt aːɪ laːɪ wɪð staz ænd mun ænd skaːɪ]
Ah! Whatever shall betide me!'
[ɑ ʍatˈɛvʌ ʃæl bɪˈtaːɪd mi]
'Go, saddle to me the black' he said,
[goːʊ ˈsædʊl tʊ mi ðʊ blæk hi sɛd]
'The brown rides never so speedy:
[ðʊ braːʊn raːɪdz ˈnɛvʌ soːʊ ˈspidɪ]
And I will neither eat nor drink nor sleep,
[ænd aːɪ wɪl ˈnaːɪðʌr it nɔ drɪŋk nɔ slip]

Till I avenge my lady.'
[tɪl aːɪ ʌˈvɛndʒ maːɪ ˈlɛːɪdɪ]
There were fifteen valiant gypsies;
[ðɛːʌ wɜ ˈfɪftin ˈvæljæ(ɪ)nt ˈdʒɪpsiz]
They were black, O! but they were bonny;
[ðɛːɪ wɜ blæk oːʊ bʌt ðɛːɪ wɜ ˈbanɪ]
They are all to be hanged on a tree,
[ðɛːɪ aɾ ɔl tu bi hæŋd an ʌ tri]
For stealing our good lord's lady.
[fɔ ˈstilɪŋ aːʊʌ gʊd lɔdz ˈlɛːɪdɪ]

5. The Braes of Yarrow
[ðʊ bɹɛːɪz ʌv ˈjæʁoːʊ]

I dreamed a dreary dream last night,
[aːɪ drimd ʌ ˈdɾɪːʌɾɪ drim last naːɪt]
That filled my heart with sorrow:
[ðæt fɪld maːɪ hat wɪð ˈsaɾoːʊ]
I dreamt I pulled the heather green,
[aːɪ drɛmt aːɪ pʊld ðʊ ˈhɛðʌ grin]
Upon the braes of Yarrow.
[ʌˈpan ðʊ brɛːɪz ʌv ˈjæɾoːʊ]
I dreamed a dreary dream last night,
[aːɪ drimd ʌ ˈdɾɪːʌɾɪ drim last naːɪt]
That filled my heart with sorrow;
[ðæt fɪld maːɪ hat wɪð ˈsaɾoːʊ]
I dreamt my love came headless home,
[aːɪ drɛmt maːɪ lʌv kɛːɪm ˈhɛdlɛ(ɪ)s hoːʊm]
Upon the braes of Yarrow.
[ʌˈpan ðʊ brɛːɪz ʌv ˈjæɾoːʊ]
O gentle wind that bloweth south,
[oːʊ ˈdʒɛntʊl wɪnd ðæt ˈbloːʊɛ(ɪ)θ saːʊθ]
to where my love repaireth;
[tu ʍɛːʌ maːɪ lʌv ɾɪˈpɛːʌɾɛ(ɪ)θ]
Convey a kiss from her dear mouth,
[kʌnˈvɛːɪ ʌ kɪs frʌm hɜ dɪːʌ maːʊθ]
And tell me how she fareth!
[ænd tɛl mi haːʊ ʃi ˈfɛːʌɾɛ(ɪ)θ]

Songs from the Exotic (Song Cycle)
[saŋz fɾʌm ði ɪgˈzatɪk]
Folksongs

1. A Serbian Folk-Song
[ʌ ˈsɜbiɪn foːʊk saŋ]

Sevdalino, my little one,
[sɛvdaˈlino maːɪ ˈlɪtʊl wʌn]
are you still at home, my sweetheart?
[a ju stɪl æt hoːʊm maːɪ ˈswithat]
You took all my money away:
[ju tʊk ɔl maːɪ ˈmʌni ʌˈwɛːɪ]
five thousand piastres!
[faːɪv ˈθaːʊzæ(ʌ)nd piˈastrɛs]
Give me back a little money my sweetheart,
[gɪv mi bæk ʌ ˈlɪtʊl ˈmʌni maːɪ ˈswithat]

Give me back a little money
[gɪv mi bæk ʌ ˈlɪtʊl ˈmʌnɪ]
that I might buy a pair of trousers.
[ðæt ɑːɪ mɑːɪt bɑːɪ ʌ pɛːʌɾ ʌv ˈtɹɑːʊzʌz]
Sevdalino, my little one...
[sɛvdaˈlino mɑːɪ ˈlɪtʊl wʌn]

2. From a Serbian Epic
[fɹʌm ʌ ˈsɜbiɪn ˈɛpɪk]

In the lovely village of Nevesinje,
[ɪn ðʊ ˈlʌvlɪ ˈvɪlæ(ɪ)dʒ ʌv njɛvɛˈsinjɛ]
Bey Lujibovic writes a letter
[bɛːi ljuˈjibavɪʧ ɹɑːɪts ʌ ˈlɛtʌ]
and sends it to the Rocky Piva,
[ænd sɛndz ɪt tu ðʊ ˈɾɑkɪ ˈpiva]
into the hands of Bey Pivlyanahin:
[ˈɪntu ðʊ hændz ʌv bɛːi pɪvˈljanɑhɪn]
"Listen you, Bey Pivlyanahin,
[ˈlɪsɛ(ɪ)n ju bɛːi pɪvˈljanɑhɪn]
You bit right into my heart,
[ju bɪt ɹɑːɪt ˈɪntu mɑːɪ hɑt]
for you killed my brother. Ahi! Ahi!
[fɔ ju kɪld mɑːɪ ˈbɹʌðʌ ɑːi ɑːi]
Come out you, I dare you to fight!
[kʌm ɑːʊt ju ɑːɪ dɛːʌ ju tu fɑːɪt]
I give you three choices:
[ɑːɪ gɪv ju θɾi ˈʧɔːɪsɛ(ɪ)z]
First at the rocky Korita,
[fɜst æt ðʊ ˈɾɑkɪ koˈɾita]
second on Trusina Hill,
[ˈsɛkʌnd an ˈtrusina hɪl]
the third, where ever we should meet by chance:
[ðʊ θɜd ʍɛːʌɾ ˈɛvʌ wi ʃʊd mit bɑːɪ ʧans]
If you lack the courage to fight,
[ɪf ju læk ðʊ ˈkʊɾæ(ɪ)dʒ tu fɑːɪt]
I will send you an embroidering frame and a distaff,
[ɑːɪ wɪl sɛnd ju æn ɪmˈbɹɔːɪdʌɾɪŋ fɹæːɪm ænd ʌ ˈdɪstaf]
and moreover an Egyptian cotton reel
[ænd mɔːʌɾˈɔːʊvʌɾ æn ɪˈdʒɪpʃæ(ɪ)n ˈkatʌn ɹil]
with a boxwood spindle;
[wɪð ʌ ˈbaksˌwʊd ˈspɪndʊl]
you may weave for me a shirt
[ju mɛːɪ wiv fɔ mi ʌ ʃɜt]
and a lacy apron."
[ænd ʌ ˈlɛːɪsɪ ˈɛːɪpɹʌn]
When the letter reached Baya,
[ʍɛn ðʊ ˈlɛtʌ ɹiʧt ˈbaja]
he understood the contents:
[hi ʌndʌˈstʊd ðʊ ˈkantɛnts]
he reached for his inkwell,
[hi ɹiʧt fɔ hɪz ˈɪŋkwɛl]
and wrote the Bey an answer.
[ænd ɹɔːʊt ðʊ bɛːi æn ˈansʌ]

3. The Romance of Count Arnaldos
[ðʊ ɹoˈmæns ʌv kaˈʊnt arˈnaldos]

¡Quien hubiese tal ventura sobre las aguas del mar,
[kjɛn uˈβjese tal βɛnˈtura ˈsoβre las ˈaɣwas ðɛl mar]
como hubo el conde Arnaldos
[ˈkomo ˈuβo ɛl ˈkonde arˈnaldos]
la mañana de San Juan!
[la maˈɲana ðe san xwan]
Con un falcón en la mano, la caza iba a cazar
[kon um falˈkon ɛn la ˈmano la ˈkaθa ˈiβa a kaˈθar]
vió venir una galera que a tierra quiere llegar.
[biˈo βeˈnir ˈuna ɣaˈlera ke a ˈtjera ˈkjere ʎeˈɣar]
Las velas traía de seda, la ejarcia de un cendal,
[las ˈβelas traˈia ðe ˈseða la eˈxarθia ðe un θɛnˈdal]
marinero que la manda diciendo viene un cantar
[mariˈnero ke la ˈmanda ðiˈθjɛndo ˈβjɛne un kanˈtar]
que la mar facía en calma los vientos hace amainar,
[ke la mar faˈθia ɛn ˈkalma los ˈβjɛntos ˈaθe amajˈnar]
las peces que andan n'el hondo arriba los haces andar
[las ˈpeθes ke ˈandan nɛl ˈondo aˈriβa los ˈaθes anˈdar]
las aves que andan volando
[las ˈaβes ke ˈandam boˈlando]
n'el mastel las faz' posar
[nɛl masˈtɛl las faθ poˈsar]
allí fabló el conde Arnaldos bien oréis lo que dirá:
[aˈʎi faβˈlo ɛl ˈkonde arˈnaldos βjɛn oˈreis lo ke ðiˈra]
"Por Dios te ruego
[por ˈdios te ˈrweɣo]
marinero dígasme ora ese cantar."
[mariˈnero ˈðiɣasme ˈora ˈese kanˈtar]
Respondióle el marinero tal respuesta le fué a dar:
[respondiˈole ɛl mariˈnero tal resˈpwesta le fue a ðar]
"Yo no digo esta cancion sino a quien comigo va:"
[jo no ˈðiɣo ˈesta kanθiˈon ˈsino a kjɛn koˈmiɣo βa]

4. The Song of a Girl Ravished Away
[ðʊ saŋ ʌv ʌ gɜl ˈɹævɪʃt ʌˈwɛːɪ]
by the Fairies in South Uist
[bɑːɪ ðʊ ˈfɛɾiz ɪn sɑːʊθ ˈjuɪst]

My love, my love, let me home to my mother;
[mɑːɪ lʌv mɑːɪ lʌv lɛt mi hoːʊm tu mɑːɪ ˈmʌðʌ]
my love, my love, let me home, let me home;
[mɑːɪ lʌv mɑːɪ lʌv lɛt mi hoːʊm lɛt mi hoːʊm]
my love, my love, let me home as you found me;
[mɑːɪ lʌv mɑːɪ lʌv lɛt mi hoːʊm æz ju fɑːʊnd mi]
I came to call the cattle home.
[ɑːɪ kɛːɪm tu kɔl ðʊ ˈkætʊl hoːʊm]
I heard last night that my love was surrounded;
[ɑːɪ hɜd last nɑːɪt ðæt mɑːɪ lʌv waz sɜˈɾɑːʊndɛ(ɪ)d]
I climbed the hill by the light of the moon;
[ɑːɪ klɑːɪmd ðʊ hɪl bɑːɪ ðʊ lɑːɪt ʌv ðʊ mun]
my love, my love, let me home as you found me:
[mɑːɪ lʌv mɑːɪ lʌv lɛt mi hoːʊm æz ju fɑːʊnd mi]

I came to call the cattle home.
[ɑːɪ kɛːɪm tu kɔl ðʊ ˈkætʊl hoːʊm]
Though you gave me horses on halters,
[ðoːʊ ju gɛːɪv mi ˈhɔsɛ(ɪ)z an ˈhɔltʌz]
though you gave me cattle and sheep,
[ðoːʊ ju gɛːɪv mi ˈkætʊl ænd ʃip]
though you gave me servants and footmen,
[ðoːʊ ju gɛːɪv mi ˈsɜvæ(ɪ)nts ænd ˈfʊtmɛ(ɪ)n]
I came to call the cattle home.
[ɑːɪ kɛːɪm tu kɔl ðʊ ˈkætʊl hoːʊm]
My love, my love, let me home to my mother;
[mɑːɪ lʌv mɑːɪ lʌv lɛt mi hoːʊm tu mɑːɪ ˈmʌðʌ]
my love, my love, let me home, let me home;
[mɑːɪ lʌv mɑːɪ lʌv lɛt mi hoːʊm lɛt mi hoːʊm]
My love, my love, let me home as you found me;
[mɑːɪ lʌv mɑːɪ lʌv lɛt mi hoːʊm æz ju fɑːʊnd mi]
I came to call the cattle home.
[ɑːɪ kɛːɪm tu kɔl ðʊ ˈkætʊl hoːʊm]

The Voice of Desire (Song Cycle)
[ðʊ vɔːɪs ʌv dɪˈzɑːɪʌ]

1. The Voice of Desire
[ðʊ vɔːɪs ʌv dɪˈzɑːɪʌ]
Bridges, Robert Seymour (Eng. 1844-1930)

Beautiful must be the mountains whence ye come,
[ˈbjutɪfʊl mʌst bi ðʊ ˈmɑːʊntæ(ɪ)nz ʍɛns ji kʌm]
And bright in the fruitful valleys the streams,
[ænd bɹɑːɪt ɪn ðʊ ˈfrutfʊl ˈvælɪz ðʊ stɹimz]
Wherefrom ye learn your song:
[ʍɛːʌˈfɹʌm ji lɜn jɔːʌ sɑŋ]
Where are those starry woods? O might I wander there,
[ʍɛːʌr a ðoːʊz ˈstaɹɪ wʊdz oːʊ mɑːɪt ɑːɪ ˈwandʌ ðɛːʌ]
Among the flowers, which in that heavenly air
[ʌˈmʌŋ ðʊ flɑːʊʌz ʍɪtʃ ɪn ðæt ˈhɛvɛ(ɪ)nlɪ ɛːʌ]
Bloom the year long!
[blum ðʊ jɪːʌ lɑŋ]
Barren are those mountains and spent the streams:
[ˈbæɹɛ(ɪ)n a ðoːʊz ˈmɑːʊntæ(ɪ)nz ænd spɛnt ðʊ stɹimz]
Our song is the voice of desire, that haunts our dreams,
[ɑːʊʌ sɑŋ ɪz ðʊ vɔːɪs ʌv dɪˈzɑːɪʌ ðæt hɔnts ɑːʊʌ dɹimz]
A throe of the heart,
[ʌ θroːʊ ʌv ðʊ hat]
Whose pining visions dim,
[huz ˈpɑːɪnɪŋ ˈvɪʒʌnz dɪm]
forbidden hopes profound,
[fɔˈbɪdɛ(ɪ)n hoːʊps pɹoːˈfɑːʊnd]
No dying cadence nor long sigh can sound,
[noːʊ ˈdɑːɪɪŋ ˈkɛːɪdɛ(ɪ)ns nɔ lɑŋ sɑːɪ kæn sɑːʊnd]
For all our art.
[fɔʁ(ɪ) ɔl ɑːʊʌ at]
Alone, aloud in the raptured ear of men
[ʌˈloːʊn ʌˈlɑːʊd ɪn ðʊ ˈræptʃʊ(ʌ)d iːʌr ʌv mɛn]
We pour our dark nocturnal secret; and then,
[wi pɔːʌr ɑːʊʌ dak nakˈtɜnʊl ˈsikɹɛ(ɪ)t ænd ðɛn]

As night is withdrawn
[æz nɑːɪt ɪz wɪðˈdɹɔn]
Dream, while the innumerable choir of day
[dɹim ʍɑːɪl ði ɪnˈnumʌɹʌbʊl ˈkwɑːɪʌɾ ʌv dɛːɪ]
Welcome the dawn.
[ˈwɛlkʌm ðʊ dɔn]

2. White Eggs in the Bush (copyright)

3. Written on Terrestrial Things
[ˈɹɪtɪn an tʊ ˌʁɛstɹiʊl θɪŋz]
Hardy, Thomas (Eng. 1840-1928)

I leant upon a coppice gate
[ɑːɪ lint ʌˈpan ʌ ˈkapɪs gɛːɪt]
When frost was specter-gray,
[ʍɛn fɹast waz ˈspɛktʌ gɹɛːɪ]
And Winter's dregs made desolate
[ænd ˈwɪntʌz dɹɛgz mɛːɪd ˈdɛsolæ(ɪ)t]
The weakening eye of day.
[ðʊ ˈwiknɪŋ ɑːɪ ʌv dɛːɪ]
The tangled bine-stems scored the sky
[ðʊ ˈtæŋgʊld bɑːɪn stɛmz skɔːʌd ðʊ skɑːɪ]
Like strings of broken lyres,
[lɑːɪk stɹɪŋz ʌv ˈbɹoːʊkɛ(ɪ)n ˈlɑːɪʌz]
And all mankind that haunted nigh
[ænd ɔl mænˈkɑːɪnd ðæt ˈhɔntɛ(ɪ)d nɑːɪ]
Had sought their household fires.
[hæd sɔt ðɛːʌ ˈhɑːʊshoːʊld fɑːɪʌz]
The land's sharp features seemed to be
[ðʊ lændz ʃap ˈfitʃʊ(ʌ)z simd tu bi]
The Century's corpse outleant,
[ðʊ ˈsɛntʃʊɹɪz kɔps ɑːʊtˈlɛnt]
His crypt the cloudy canopy,
[hɪz kɹɪpt ðʊ ˈklɑːʊdɪ ˈkæno(ʌ)pɪ]
The wind his death-lament.
[ðʊ wɪnd hɪz dɛθ lʌˈmɛnt]
The ancient pulse of germ and birth
[ði ˈɛːɪntʃɛnt pʌls ʌv dʒɜm ænd bɜθ]
Was shrunken hard and dry,
[waz ˈʃɹʌŋkɛ(ɪ)n had ænd dɹɑːɪ]
And every spirit upon earth
[ænd ˈɛvɹɪ ˈspɪrɪt ʌˈpan ɜθ]
Seemed fervourless as I.
[simd ˈfɜvʊ(ʌ)lɛ(ɪ)s æz ɑːɪ]
At once a voice arose among
[æt wʌns ʌ vɔːɪs ʌˈroːʊz ʌˈmʌŋ]
The bleak twigs overhead
[ðʊ blik twɪgz ˈoːʊvʌhɛd]
In a full-hearted evensong
[ɪn ʌ fʊl ˈhatɛ(ɪ)d ˈivɛ(ɪ)nsɑŋ]
Of joy illimited;
[ʌv dʒɔːɪ ɪˈlɪmɪtɛ(ɪ)d]
An aged thrush, frail, gaunt and small,
[æn ˈɛːɪdʒɛ(ɪ)d θɹʌʃ fɹɛːɪl gɔnt ænd smɔl]

In blast-beruffled plume,
[ɪn blɑst bɪˈɾʌfʊld plum]
Had chosen thus to fling his soul
[hæd ˈʧoːʊzɛ(ɪ)n ðʌs tu flɪŋ hɪz soːʊl]
Upon the growing gloom.
[ʌˈpɑn ðʊ ˈɡɹoːʊɪŋ glum]
So little cause for carolings
[soːʊ ˈlɪtʊl kɔz fɔ ˈkærʊlɪŋz]
Of such ecstatic sound
[ʌv sʌʧ ɪkˈstætɪk sɑːʊnd]
Was written on terrestrial things
[wɑz ˈɹɪtɛ(ɪ)n ɑn tʊˈɾɛstɹɪʊl θɪŋz]
Afar or nigh around,
[ʌˈfɑɾ ɔ naːɪ ʌˈɾɑːʊnd]
That I could think there trembled through
[ðæt ɑːɪ kʊd θɪŋk ðɛːʌ ˈtɹɛmbʊld θru]
His happy goodnight air
[hɪz ˈhæpɪ ˌɡʊdˈnɑːɪt ɛːʌ]
Some blessed Hope, whereof I knew
[sʌm ˈblɛsɛ(ɪ)d hoːʊp ʍɛːʌˈɾʌv ɑːɪ nju]
And I was unaware.
[ænd ɑːɪ wɑz ʌnʌˈwɛːʌ]

4. Sweet Little Red Feet
[swit ˈlɪtʊl ɹɛd fit]
Keats, John (Eng. 1795-1821)

I had a dove and the sweet dove died;
[ɑːɪ hæd ʌ dʌv ænd ðʊ swit dʌv dɑːɪd]
And I have thought it died of grieving:
[ænd ɑːɪ hæv θɔt ɪt dɑːɪd ʌv ˈɡɹɪ(ʲ)ivɪŋ]
Oh, what could it grieve for? Its feet were tied,
[oːʊ ʍɑt kʊd ɪt ɡɹɪ(ʲ)iv fɔʁ(ʲ) ɪts fit wɝ tɑːɪd]
With a silken thread of my own hand's weaving;
[wɪð ʌ ˈsɪlkɛ(ɪ)n θɹɛd ʌv mɑːɪ oːʊn hændz ˈwivɪŋ]
Sweet little red feet! why should you die–
[swit ˈlɪtʊl ɹɛd fit ʍɑːɪ ʃʊd ju dɑːɪ]
Why should you leave me, sweet dove! why?
[ʍɑːɪ ʃʊd ju liv mi swit dʌv ʍɑːɪ]
You lived alone on the forest tree,
[ju lɪvd ʌˈloːʊn ɑn ðʊ ˈfɔɾɛ(ɪ)st tɹi]
Why, pretty thing! could you not live with me?
[ʍɑːɪ ˈpɹɪtɪ θɪŋ kʊd ju nɑt lɪv wɪð mi]
I kissed you oft and gave you white peas:
[ɑːɪ kɪst ju ɑft ænd ɡɛːɪv ju ʍɑːɪt piz]
Why not live sweetly, as in the green trees?
[ʍɑːɪ nɑt lɪv ˈswitlɪ æz ɪn ðʊ ɡɹin tɹiz]

Whitacre, Eric (Am. b. 1970)

Song Selection

"Goodnight Moon"
[ˌɡʊdˈnɑːɪt mun]
Brown, Margaret Wise (Am. 1910-1952)

In the great green room
[ɪn ðʌ ɡɹɛːɪt ɡɹin ɹum]
There was a telephone
[ðɛːʌ wɑz ʌ ˈtɛlɪ(ʌ)foːʊn]
And a red balloon
[ænd ʌ ɹɛd bʌˈlun]
And a picture of
[ænd ʌ ˈpɪkʧʊ(ʌ)ʁ ʌv]
The cow jumping over the moon
[ðʌ kɑːʊ ˈʤʌmpɪŋ ˈoːʊvʌ ðʌ mun]
And there were three little bears sitting on chairs
[ænd ðɛːʌ wɝ θri ˈlɪtʊl bɛːʌz ˈsɪtɪŋ ɑn ʧɛːʌz]
And two little kittens
[ænd tu ˈlɪtʊl ˈkɪtɛ(ɪ)nz]
And a pair of mittens
[ænd ʌ pɛːʌʁ ʌv ˈmɪtɛ(ɪ)nz]
And a little toy house
[ænd ʌ ˈlɪtʊl tɔːɪ hɑːʊs]
And a young mouse
[ænd ʌ jʌŋ mɑːʊs]
And a comb and a brush and a bowl full of mush
[ænd ʌ koːʊm ænd ʌ bɹʌʃ ænd ʌ boːʊl fʊl ʌv mʌʃ]
And a quiet old lady who was whispering "hush"
[ænd ʌ ˈkwɑːɪɛ(ɪ)t oːʊld ˈlɛːɪdɪ hu wɑz ˈʍɪspʌʁɪŋ hʌʃ]
Goodnight room
[ˌɡʊdˈnɑːɪt ɹum]
Goodnight moon
[ˌɡʊdˈnɑːɪt mun]
Goodnight cow jumping over the moon
[ˌɡʊdˈnɑːɪt kɑːʊ ˈʤʌmpɪŋ ˈoːʊvʌ ðʌ mun]
Goodnight light
[ˌɡʊdˈnɑːɪt lɑːɪt]
And the red balloon
[ænd ðʌ ɹɛd bʌˈlun]
Goodnight bears
[ˌɡʊdˈnɑːɪt bɛːʌz]
Goodnight chairs
[ˌɡʊdˈnɑːɪt ʧɛːʌz]
Goodnight kittens
[ˌɡʊdˈnɑːɪt ˈkɪtɛ(ɪ)nz]
Goodnight mittens
[ˌɡʊdˈnɑːɪt ˈmɪtɛ(ɪ)nz]
Goodnight clocks
[ˌɡʊdˈnɑːɪt klɑks]
And goodnight socks
[ænd ˌɡʊdˈnɑːɪt sɑks]
Goodnight little house
[ˌɡʊdˈnɑːɪt ˈlɪtʊl hɑːʊs]

And goodnight mouse
[ænd ˌɡʊdˈnɑːɪt mɑːʊs]
Goodnight comb
[ˌɡʊdˈnɑːɪt koːʊm]
And goodnight brush
[ænd ˌɡʊdˈnɑːɪt bɹʌʃ]
Goodnight nobody
[ˌɡʊdˈnɑːɪt ˈnoːʊbɑdɪ]
Goodnight mush
[ˌɡʊdˈnɑːɪt mʌʃ]
And goodnight to the old lady whispering "hush"
[ænd ˌɡʊdˈnɑːɪt tu ði oːʊld ˈleːɪdɪ ˈʍɪspʌʁɪŋ hʌʃ]
Goodnight stars
[ˌɡʊdˈnɑːɪt stɑz]
Goodnight air
[ˌɡʊdˈnɑːɪt ɛːʌ]
Good night noises everywhere
[ɡʊd nɑːɪt ˈnɔːɪzɛ(ɪ)z ˈɛvɹɪʍɛːʌ]

Y

Yon, Pietro A. (It. 1886-1943)

Song Selection

"Gesù, Bambino"
[dʒeˈzu bamˈbino]
Martens, Frederick H. (Am. 1874-1932)

1. When blossoms flowered
[ʍɛn ˈblasʌmz flɑːʊʌd]
'mid the snows Upon a winter night
[mɪd ðʌ snoːʊz ʌˈpan ʌ ˈwɪntʌ nɑːɪt]
Was born the Child, the Christmas Rose,
[wɑz bɔn ðʌ ʧɑːɪld ðʌ ˈkɹɪsmʌs ɹoːʊz]
The King of Love and Light.
[ðʌ kɪŋ ʌv lʌv ænd lɑːɪt]
The angels sang, the shepherds sang,
[ði ˈɛːɪndʒɛ(ʊ)lz sæŋ ðʌ ˈʃɛpʌdz sæŋ]
The grateful earth rejoiced,
[ðʌ ˈɡɹɛːɪtfʊl ɜθ ɹɪˈdʒɔːɪst]
And at His blessed birth the stars
[ænd æt hɪz ˈblɛsɛ(ɪ)d bɜθ ðʌ stɑz]
Their exultation voiced.
[ðɛːʌʁ(ʳ) ɛgzu(ʊ)lˈtɛːɪʃʌn vɔːɪst]
CHORUS
O come let us adore Him,
[oːʊ kʌm lɛt ʌs ʌˈdɔːʌ hɪm]
Christ the Lord.
[kɹɑːɪst ðʌ lɔd]

2. Again the heart with rapture glows
[ʌˈɡɛn ðʌ hɑt wɪð ˈɹæpʧʊ(ʌ) gloːʊz tu]
To greet the holy night
[ɡɹit ðʌ ˈhoːʊlɪ nɑːɪt]
That gave the world its Christmas Rose,
[ðæt ɡɛːɪv ðʌ wɜld ɪts ˈkɹɪsmʌs ɹoːʊz]
Its king of Love and Light.
[ɪts kɪŋ ʌv lʌv ænd lɑːɪt]
Let ev'ry voice acclaim His name,
[lɛt ˈɛvɹɪ vɔːɪs ʌˈkleːɪm hɪz neːɪm]
The grateful chorus swell,
[ðʌ ˈɡɹɛːɪtfʊl ˈkɔʁ(ʳ)ʌs swɛl]
From paradise to earth He came
[fɹʌm ˈpæʁ(ʳ)ʌdɑːɪs tu ɜθ hi kɛːɪm]
That we with Him might dwell.
[ðæt wi wɪð hɪm mɑːɪt dwɛl]
CHORUS
O come let us adore Him,
[oːʊ kʌm lɛt ʌs ʌˈdɔːʌ hɪm]
Christ the Lord.
[kɹɑːɪst ðʌ lɔd]

Index of Composers

Index of Songs

Bibliography

Adams, Leslie, D., Margaret Bonds Baker, et al. *An Anthology of African and African Diaspora Songs* / Louise Toppin, Editor; Scott Piper, Associate Editor. Ann Arbor, MI: Videmus, 2021.

Adams, Leslie, and Edna St. Vincent Millay. *Five Millay Songs: for Voice and Piano*. New York: American Composers Alliance, 2019.

Adderley, Cedric, Lettie Beckon Alston, Shelton Becton, Valerie Capers, Roland M. Carter, Roy Cotton, and Adolphus C. Hailstork. *Art Songs and Spirituals by Contemporary African American Composers* / Edited by Kathy W. Bullock and Donna M. Cox. Xenia, OH: PBM Press, 2012.

Adler, Samuel. *Four Poems of James Stephens*. New York: Oxford University Press, 1963.

Anon. *Contemporary Art Songs: 28 Songs by American and British Composers*. New York: G. Schirmer, 1970.

Argento, Dominick. *Collected Song Cycles* / Dominick Argento. London: Boosey & Hawkes, 2006.

Arne, Thomas, Michael Pilkington, and T. A. Arne. *Twelve Songs: Thomas Arne* / Edited by Michael Pilkington. London: Stainer & Bell, 1979.

Barber, Samuel, and Matthew Arnold. *Dover Beach for Medium Voice and String Quartet*. New York: G. Schirmer, 1936.

Bax, Arnold. *Five Irish Songs* / by Arnold Bax. New York: Chappell & Co., 1943.

Bennett, Richard, J. Clare, A. T. Tennyson, P. B. Shelley, and S. Coleridge-Taylor. *The Aviary: Five Songs for Unison Voices and Piano* / Richard Rodney Bennett. New York: Universal Edition, 2017.

Bernstein Leonard, R. Walters, and L. Bernstein. *Art Songs and Arias: 33 Selections* / Leonard Bernstein; Edited by Richard Walters. New York: Bernstein Music Publishing: Boosey & Hawkes; Milwaukee, WI: 2007.

Bolcom, William. *Concert Songs. Volume 1 (1975–2000): 35 Songs for High Voice and Piano*. New York: Edward B. Marks Music, 2014.

Boytim, J. Frey, Arthur Goodhart, R. C. Clarke, et al. *The First Book of Baritone/Bass Solos* / Compiled by Joan Frey Boytim. New York: G. Schirmer, 1991.

Boytim, J. Frey, G. Rich, C. Chaminade, et al. *The First Book of Mezzo-Soprano/Alto Solos* / Compiled by Joan Frey Boytim. New York: G. Schirmer, 1991.

Boytim, J. Frey, A. H. Malotte, G. F. Handel, et al. *The First Book of Soprano Solos* / Compiled by Joan Frey Boytim. New York: G. Schirmer, 1991.

Boytim, J. Frey, D. W. Guion, W. David, P. I. Tchaikovsky, et al. *The First Book of Tenor Solos* / Compiled by Joan Frey Boytim. New York: G. Schirmer, 1991.

Bridge, Frank. *Ten Songs for Voice and Piano* / Frank Bridge. Boca Raton, FL: Masters Music Publications, 1992.

Britten, Benjamin. *A Charm of Lullabies: Op. 41: for Mezzo-Soprano and Piano* / Benjamin Britten. London, NY: Boosey & Hawkes, 1949.

Britten, Benjamin, R. Walters, C. Matthews, and B. Britten. *Complete Folksong Arrangements: 61 Songs* / Benjamin Britten; Edited by Richard Walters. London: Boosey & Hawkes, 2006.

Britten, Benjamin, and John Donne. *The Holy Sonnets of John Donne: Op. 35: High Voice and Piano* / Benjamin Britten. London: Boosey & Hawkes, 1946.

Britten, Benjamin, J. Weldon, and H. Purcell. *The Purcell Collection: 50 Songs: Realizations by Benjamin Britten* / Music by Henry Purcell; the figured basses realized by Benjamin Britten; the vocal parts edited by Peter Pears; Edited by Richard Walters. New York: Boosey & Hawkes, 2008.

Britten, Benjamin, and Thomas Hardy. *Winter Words, Op. 52, Lyrics and Ballads of Thomas Hardy for High Voice and Piano*. London: Boosey & Hawkes, 1954.

Burleigh, H. (Harry T.). *The Spirituals of Harry T. Burleigh*. Melville, NY: Belwin-Mills, 1984.

Campbell, Ross (Compiler), Robert Forbes (Compiler), and Lilija Zobens (Compiler). *The ABRSM Songbook*. London: ABRSM, 2008.

Campion, T., and P. Rosseter. *Songs from Rosseter's Book of Airs, 1601*. London: Stainer & Bell, Ltd., 1922–1924.

Chanler, Theodore, and Paul Sperry. *The Collected Songs of Theodore Chanler: Medium/High Voice and Piano*. New York: G. Schirmer, 1994.

Chanler, Theodore, and Walter De La Mare. *Eight Epitaphs for Voice and Piano*. New York: Boosey & Hawkes, 1939.

Charles, Ernest. *And So, Goodbye. Song for Voice and Piano.* New Yrok: G. Schirmer, 1938.

Charles, Ernest. *Songs of Ernest Charles, Low Voice and Piano.* New York: G. Schirmer, 1990.

Cipullo, Tom, Emily Dickinson, and Thomas Wentworth Higgginson. *A Visit with Emily: Songs for Soprano, Two Baritones, and Piano.* New York: Oxford University Press, 2003.

Clarke, Rebecca, and W. B. Yeats. *The Cloths of Heaven.* London, Boston: W. Rogers; Boston Music Co., 1920.

Clarke, Rebecca. *Songs with Violin.* New York: Oxford University Press, 2001.

Clarke, Rebecca. *Three Irish Country Songs.* London: Oxford University Press, 1928.

Cloud, Judith. *Five Edgar Allan Poe Songs.* CloudWalk Press, 2013.

Cloud, Judith, and e. e. cummings. *I Spill My Soul.* CloudWalk Press, 2009.

Conte, David. *American Death Ballads: for High Voice and Piano.* St. Louis, MO: E.C. Schirmer Music Company, 2006.

Conte, David. *Sexton Songs, for Soprano and Piano or Optional Chamber Ensemble.* St. Louis, MO: E.C. Schirmer Music Company, Inc., 2012.

Copland, Aaron. *Art Songs and Arias* / Aaron Copland. Boosey & Hawkes, 2007.

Copland, Aaron. *Old American Songs: Complete.* New York: Boosey & Hawkes Voice, 2009.

Delius, Frederick, P. Pears, and Robert Threlfall. *Nineteen Songs* / Frederick Delius; English words Edited by Peter Pears. New York: Oxford University Press, 1969.

Dougherty, Celius. *Love in The Dictionary: For Voice and Piano.* New York: G. Schirmer, 1949.

Duke, John, and Emily Dickinson. *Six Poems by Emily Dickinson.* New York: Southern Music Publishing Co. 1978.

Faith, Richard. *The Songs of Richard Faith: for Voice and Piano.* Geneseo, NY: Leyerle Publications, 1993.

Fine, Irving. *Childhood Fables for Grownups* / Verses by Gertrude Norman; Music by Irving Fine. New York: G. Schirmer, 1984.

Finzi, Gerald, and Thomas Hardy. *I Said to Love: Six Songs for Low Voice and Piano* / Words by Thomas Hardy. London: Boosey & Hawkes, 1958.

Gordon, Ricky Ian, and Emily Dickinson. *Too Few the Mornings Be: Eleven Songs for Soprano and Piano* / Music by Ricky Ian Gordon; Words by Emily Dickinson. New York: Carl Fischer, 2009.

Griffes, Charles Tomlinson, and Fiona Macleod. *Three Poems by Fiona MacLeod: for Voice and Piano, Op. 11.* Boca Raton, Fla.: Masters Music, 1994.

Hall, Juliana, and E. Dickinson E. St. V. Millay, E. Brontë, and E. Bishop. *Night Dances: 6 Songs for Soprano and Piano* / Juliana Hall; Boston, MA: E.C. Schirmer Music Company, 2017.

Hall, Juliana. *Setting Sail, Songs for Soprano, Mezzo-Soprano, or Tenor and Piano.* St. Louis, MO: E.C. Schirmer Music Company, 2006.

Hall, Juliana, Amy Lowell, Edna St. Vincent Millay, and Carl Sandburg. *Theme in Yellow: Six Songs for Mezzo-Soprano and Piano on Poems by Amy Lowell, Edna St. Vincent Millay, and Carl Sandburg.* St. Louis, MO: E. C. Schirmer Music Company, 2017.

Hall, Juliana, and Emily Dickinson. *Syllables of Velvet, Sentences of Plush: Seven Songs for Soprano and Piano on Letters of Emily Dickinson.* New York: Boosey & Hawkes, 1995.

Hall, Juliana, Walter De la Mare, Henry Wadsworth Longfellow, Edna St. Vincent Millay, and Percy Bysshe Shelley. *Winter Windows: 7 Songs for Baritone and Piano.* St. Louis, MO: E. C. Schirmer Music Company, 2017.

Head, Michael. *Michael Head Song Album.* New York: Boosey & Hawkes, 1985.

Head, Michael, and F. Ledwidge. *Over the Rim of the Moon: Song Cycle for High Voice and Piano* / Michael Head; Words by Francis Ledwidge. Boosey & Hawkes; Distributed by Hal Leonard Corp., London, New York, 1930.

Head, Michael. *Songs of Romance and Delight* / Michael Head. New York: Boosey & Hawkes, 1985.

Heggie, Jake. *Before the Storm, Four Songs for Mezzo-Soprano, Cello, and Piano.* San Francisco, CA: Bent Pen Music, 1998.

Heggie Jake. *The Faces of Love: The Songs of Jake Heggie: Complete, Books 1–3.* New York: Associated Music Publishers, 2015.

Heggie, Jake, and V. Lindsay. *The Moon Is a Mirror (2001): Five Songs for Baritone and Piano* / Music by Jake Heggie; Poetry by Vachel Lindsay. San Francisco, CA: Bent Pen Music, 2002.

Heggie, Jake, E. Dickinson, K. Te Kanawa, and W. Kauffman. *Newer Every Day: For Soprano and Piano* / Music by Jake Heggie; Poetry by Emily Dickinson. San Francisco, CA: Bent Pen Music, 2014.

Heggie, Jake. *On the Road to Christmas: For Mezzo-Soprano and String.* San Francisco, CA: Bent Pen Music, 2015.

Heggie, Jake. *Passing By: For Voice and Piano* / Songs by Jake Heggie. San Francisco, CA: Bent Pen Music, 2010.

Heggie, Jake, and E. Dickinson. *How Well I Knew the Light: Two Songs for Soprano and Piano* / Music by Jake Heggie; Poetry by Emily Dickinson. San Francisco, CA: Bent Pen Music, 2000.

Higdon, Jennifer, and Amy Lowell. *Love Sweet.* Philadelphia, PA: Lawdon Press, 2013.

Hoiby, Lee. *Eleven Songs: For Middle Voice and Piano* / Lee Hoiby. New York: G. Schirmer, 1995.

Hoiby, Lee, and Walt Whitman. *I Was There: Five Poems of Walt Whitman: Baritone and Piano* / Lee Hoiby. New York: G. Schirmer, 1993.

Hoiby, Lee, and Emily Dickinson. *The Shining Place: Five Poems of Emily Dickinson: For High Voice and Piano* / Lee Hoiby. New York: Peermusic Classical, 2002.

Hundley, Richard, J. Behr, A. Moffo, T. Stratas, et al. *Eight Early Songs* / Richard Hundley; [foreword by] Paul Sperry. New York: Boosey & Hawkes, 2016.

Hundley, Richard. *Eight Songs: Voice and Piano* / Richard Hundley. New York: Boosey & Hawkes, 1989.

Hundley, Richard. *Four Songs, Voice and Piano* / Richard Hundley. New York: Boosey & Hawkes, 1989.

Hundley, Richard. *Octaves and Sweet Sounds: For Voice and Piano* / Richard Hundley. New York: Boosey & Hawkes, 1993.

Hundley, Richard, E. Dickinson, J. Fletcher, R. L. Stevenson, et al. *Ten Songs for High Voice and Piano* / Richard Hundley. New York: Boosey & Hawkes, 2005.

Ives, Charles, and H. W. (Hugh W.) Hitchcock. *129 Songs* / Charles Ives. New York: Charles Ives Society, 1998.

Johnson, Hall. *The Green Pastures Spirituals*. New York: Carl Fischer, 1930.

Johnson, Hall. *Thirty Spirituals: for High Voice and Piano* / [arranged by] Hall Johnson. New York: G. Schirmer, Inc., 2020.

Kimball, Carol, Dominick Argento, J. Beeson, et al. *Art Song in English: 50 Songs by 21 American and British Composers* / Edited by Carol Kimball. New York: Boosey & Hawkes, 2006.

Kimball, Carol. *Song: A Guide to Art Song Style and Literature*, Revised Edition. New York: Hal Leonard Corporation, 2006.

Kohn, Steven Mark. *American Folk Set Arranged by Steven Mark Kohn*. New York: E.C. Schirmer Publishing, 2000.

Laitman, Lori, and E. Dickinson. *Four Dickinson Songs: Soprano Voice, Piano Accompaniment* / Lori Laitman; [poems by] Emily Dickinson. Enchanted Knickers Music, [United States], 1996.

Laitman, Lori, and S. Teasdale. *The Metropolitan Tower and Other Songs: For Soprano and Piano* / Lori Laitman; Poems by Sara Teasdale. Enchanted Knickers Music; Selling agent, Classical Vocal Reprints, [United States], Riverdale, NY, 1991.

Laitman, Lori, and S. Teasdale. *Mystery: For Mezzo-soprano and Piano* / Music by Lori Laitman; Poems by Sara Teasdale. Enchanted Knickers Music, BMI; Selling agent, Classical Vocal Reprints, Fayetteville, AR, [2009?].

Larsen, Libby, and Jane Calamity. *Songs from Letters: Calamity Jane to Her Daughter Janey, 1880–1902* / Libby Larsen. New York: Oxford University Press , 1994.

Larsen, Libby, and Elizabeth Barrett Browning. *Sonnets from the Portuguese: For Soprano Solo and Piano* / Libby Larsen. New York: Oxford University Press, 1998.

Liebergen, P. M., and Thomas Goeman. *Favorite Christmas Classics for Solo Singers* / Compiled and Edited by Patrick M. Liebergen. Los Angeles, CA: Alfred, 1998.

Marshall, Madeleine. *The Singer's Manual of English Diction*. New York: G. Schirmer, 1953.

Moeran, E. J., and J. Talbot, ed. *Collected Solo Songs* / E. J. Moeran; Edited by John Talbot. London: Thames Pub., 1998.

Moeran, E. J. *Two Songs: The Bean Flower; Impromptu in March* / E. J. Moeran. London: Chester Music, 1924.

Montgomery, Cheri. *A Picture Workbook of English Spellings and Phonetics*. Nashville, TN: S.T.M. Publishers, 2023.

Montgomery, Cheri. *Singer's Diction*. Nashville, TN: S.T.M. Publishers, 2019.

Moore, Ben, C. G. Rossetti, R. L. Stevenson, E. Dickinson, W. B. (William B.) Yeats, and J. Joyce. *Keats Eight Songs: On Poems by Various Poets: Christina Rossetti* [and others]*: Voice and Piano* / Ben Moore. New York: Benjamin C. Moore Publishing, 2009.

Moore, Dorothy, J. W. Johnson, A. Bontemps, H. C. Johnson, et al. *From the Dark Tower: For Voice, Cello, and Piano: 1972* / Dorothy Rudd Moore. New York: American Composers Alliance Inc., 2020.

Musto, John. *Selected Songs: For High Voice and Piano* / John Musto. Macomb, IL: Western Illinois University, 2009.

Niles, John Jacob. *The Songs of John Jacob Niles*. New York: G. Schirmer, 1990.

Northcote, S. *Bass Songs, Compiled, Edited, and Arranged by Sydney Northcote*. London: Boosey & Hawkes, 1950.

Orr, C.W., and A. E. (Alfred Edward) Housman. *Two Songs from a Shropshire Lad: For Voice and Piano* / by C. W. Orr; [poems by] A. E. Housman. London: Chester Music, 2011.

Pasatieri, Thomas. *A Rustling of Angels: 12 Songs for Voice and Piano* / Thomas Pasatieri. King of Prussia, PA: Theodore Presser Co., 2003.

Patterson, W. C., L. Adams, D. Baker, et al. *Anthology of Art Songs by Black American Composers* / Compiled by Willis C. Patterson; Preface by George Shirley; Introduction by Wendell P. Whalum. New York: E. B. Marks Music Corp., 1977.

Price, Florence, and R. E. Heard, ed. *44 Art Songs and Spirituals* / by Florence B. Price; Edited by Richard Heard. Fayetteville, AR: ClarNan Editions, a division of Classical Vocal Reprints, 2015.

Purcell, Henry, and J. Edmunds. *Henry Purcell Songs* / with Realizations of the Figured Bass by John Edmunds. New York: R. D. Row Music Co.; Carl Fischer Inc., sole selling agents, [Boston], 1960.

Quilter, Roger, and Richard Walters, ed. *55 Songs of Roger Quilter*. Milwaukee, WI: H. Leonard, 2003.

Ragland, Dave, G. Brooks, and Dave Ragland. *Spirituals and Art Songs. Volume 1* / by Dave Ragland. Nashville, TN: Dave Ragland, 2017.

Rich, Adrienne, William Blake, Dorothy Aldis, Henri-Léandre Rittener, A. E. (Alfred Edward) Housman, Klaus George Roy, Starling A. Cumberworth, John David White, Frederick. Koch, Susan Krausz, and Raymond Wilding-White. *Contemporary Art Song Album: For High Voice*. NY, London: Galaxy Music Corporation; Galliard Limited, 1969.

Rhodenizer, Donna, and Andy Duinker. *Blue Skies and Pirates Song Collection* (E-book ed.). New Minas, NS: Red Castle Publishing, 2008.

Rhodenizer, Donna. *Computer Cat Song Collection* (E-book Ed.). New Minas, NS: Red Castle Publishing, 1998.

Rhodenizer, Donna. *Dinosaurs, Dragons and Me Song Collection* (E-book ed.). New Minas, NS: Red Castle Publishing, 2005.

Rhodenizer, Donna. *It's Christmas Time Song Collection* (E-book ed.). New Minas, NS: Red Castle Publishing, 2005.

Rhodenizer, Donna, and Andy Duinker. *Jolly Sailors* (single-song digital download). New Minas, NS: Red Castle Publishing, 2023.

Rorem, Ned, and W. Whitman. *Five Poems of Walt Whitman: For Voice and Piano* / Ned Rorem. NY: Boosey & Hawkes, 1970.

Rorem, Ned, and Robert Herrick. *Flight for Heaven: A Cycle of Robert Herrick Songs*, for Bass Voice and Piano / Ned Rorem. New York: Mercury Music Corp, 1952.

Rorem, Ned. *The Nantucket Songs: Ten Songs for Voice and Piano* / Ned Rorem. New York: Boosey & Hawkes, 1981.

Rorem, Ned. *I Am Rose* / Ned Rorem; [text by] Gertrude Stein. New York: Henmar Press; Sole selling agents, C. F. Peters, 1963.

Rorem, Ned, Robert Browning, and John Dryden. *Six Songs for High Voice: Voice and Piano* / Ned Rorem. New York: Henmar Press; Sole selling agents, C. F. Peters, 1963.

Rorem, Ned. *Song Album, (Voice and Piano)* / Ned Rorem. New York: Boosey & Hawkes, 1980.

Rorem, Ned, and Whitman W. *War Scenes for Medium-Low Voice and Piano*. New York: Boosey & Hawkes, 1969.

Royal Conservatory of Music. *Voice*. Repertoire Series. RCM Publishing: Frederick Harris Music, Toronto, ON, 2019.

Sullivan, Anthony. *Irish Traditional Music: Session Tunes: A Selection of Popular Tunes for All Instruments* / by Anthony Sullivan. Macclesfield, England: Halshaw Music, [197–?].

Taylor, Bernard, David Diamond, John Duke, Vincent Persichetti, Hugo Weisgall, Ernst Bacon, George Rochberg, Charles Ives, Wintter Watts, Ned Rorem, Mary Howe, Louis Calabro, and Sergius Kagen. *Contemporary American Art Songs* / Compiled and Edited by Bernard Taylor. O. Ditson Co., Bryn Mawr, Pennsylvania, 1977.

Taylor, Bernard. *Songs by 22 Americans: A Collection of Songs by Outstanding American Composers* / Compiled by Bernard Taylor. New York: G. Schirmer, 1960.

Tear, Robert. *Sing Solo Tenor* / Edited by Robert Tear. Oxford [Oxfordshire]: Oxford University Press, 1985.

Thomson, Virgil, and William Shakespeare. *Shakespeare Songs for Voice and Piano*. New York: Southern Music Publishing Co. Inc., 1961.

Vaughan Williams, Ralph, and George Herbert. *Five Mystical Songs* / Words by George Herbert; Set to Music for Baritone Solo, Chorus (Ad. Lib.) and Orchestra by R. Vaughan Williams. Miami, FL: Kalmus, 1987.

Vaughan Williams, Ralph, and John W. Stout. *Linden Lea / Vaughan Williams*; Arr. John W. Stout. London: Boosey and Hawkes, 1939.

Vaughan Williams, Ralph, and A. E. (Alfred Edward) Housman. *On Wenlock Edge: A Cycle of Six Songs: For Tenor Voice, with Accompaniment of Pianoforte and String Quartet (Ad Lib)* / The Words by A. E. Housman, from A. Shropshire Lad; Music by R. Vaughan Williams. London: Boosey & Co., 1911.

Vaughan Williams, Ralph, Roy Douglas, and Robert Louis Stevenson. *Songs of Travel: For Voice and Orchestra* / R. Vaughan Williams; Orchestrated by the Composer and by Roy Douglas; Poems by Robert Louis Stevenson. London: Boosey & Hawkes, 2018.

Walker, Gwyneth, and E. E. (Edward Estlin) Cummings. *Though Love Be a Day: Five Songs for High Voice and Piano on Poems by E. E. Cummings and Gwyneth Walker* / [music by] Gwyneth Walker. Boston, MA: E. C. Schirmer Music Company, 1993.

Walters, Richard, Kurt Ollmann, P. Goodman, et al. *50 Collected Songs of Ned Rorem*. New York: Boosey & Hawkes, 2008.

Walters, Richard, E. Bacon, A. Beach, et al. *Romantic American Art Songs: 50 Songs by 14 Composers*. [compiled by Richard Walters]. New York: G. Schirmer, 1990.

Walton, William, William Blake, William Drummond, Thomas Jordan, Louis MacNeice, Charles Morris, William Shakespeare, Edith Sitwell, Algernon Charles Swinburne, William Wordsworth, and William Walton. *Vocal Music* / William Walton; Edited by Steuart Bedford. Oxford: Oxford University Press Music Department, 2011.

Warlock, Peter. *Collected Songs, for Voice and Piano* / Peter Warlock. Miami Lakes, FL: Masters Music Pub., 1989.

Warlock, Peter, Philip Wilson, Thomas Campion, Thomas Greaves, William Corkine, John Dowland, John Danyel, Philip Rosseter, Michael Cavendish, and Robert Jones. *English Ayres, Elizabethan and Jacobean. Volume 1* / Transcribed and Edited from the Original Editions by Peter Warlock and Philip Wilson. London: Oxford University Press, 1927.

Weir, Judith, and Anon. *Scotch Minstrelsy: For Tenor (or Soprano) and Piano* / Judith Weir. London: Novello, 1986.

Weir, Judith, and Anon. *Songs from the Exotic: for Medium Voice and Piano* / Judith Weir. Chester Music; Exclusive distributor, Music Sales, London, Bury St. Edmonds, Suffolk, 1991.

Weir, Judith, Bridges, Robert, Ulli Beier, Thomas Hardy, and John Keats. 2005. *The Voice of Desire: Song Cycle for Mezzo-Soprano and Piano (2003)* / Judith Weir. Chester Music; Exclusive distributor, Music Sales Ltd., London, Bury St Edmonds, Suffolk, 2007.

About the Authors

Versatile artist, teacher, arts administrator, and baritone **Allen Henderson** is executive director of the National Association of Teachers of Singing (NATS), the world's largest professional association of voice teachers, supervising a talented staff in promoting continuing education for voice teachers; publishing a recognized scholarly journal, *Journal of Singing*; and promoting voice education among a wide array of constituencies, from recreational singers to voice educators and medical doctors. In this position, he serves as administrator for the International Congress of Voice Teachers held every four years at locations around the world. He is also professor of music at Georgia Southern University where he teaches voice and for many years taught foreign language diction.

As baritone soloist, Henderson has appeared in concert, opera, and oratorio with opera companies and symphonies around the United States. A district winner and regional finalist in the Metropolitan Opera auditions, Henderson was a winner of the National Federation of Music Clubs Artist Awards. He can be heard on Aeolian Records release titled *Dimensions* and on his world-premier recording with guitarist Stanley Yates titled *Shadows* featuring works by John Rutter, Michael Fink, and Castelnuovo-Tedesco.

Henderson's students have graced the stages of venues around the world. They have been associated with leading young artist programs and have been winners of numerous NATS and other national and regional competitions. His students also are gracing the stages of cruise ships, teaching in public schools, colleges, and universities, and even working for TESLA.

In demand as a clinician internationally, Henderson has had multiple residencies teaching in Singapore at the Yong Siew Toh Conservatory of Music and in China. He has served on the faculty of SongFest(2015), Savannah Voice and Choral Institute, and is cofounder of the NATS Science Informed Voice Pedagogy Institute. In 2018 he was inducted into membership in the American Academy of Teachers of Singing.

Henderson helped conceive of and launch two major national level voice competitions, the National Musical Theatre Competition and National Student Auditions sponsored by NATS. He also served as president of the American Traditions Vocal Competition, a unique vocal competition celebrating the diversity of American vocal music.

As an author and creator, Henderson conceived of and is executive editor of the So You Want to Sing series published by Rowman & Littlefield. Twenty volumes have been published in the critically successful series. Additionally, he has published articles in *Choral Journal*, *Journal of Singing*, and *Creator Magazine*, and has a regular column in *Inter Nos*.

As a church musician, Henderson has served churches in Tennessee, Ohio, Oklahoma, and Georgia and recently retired as director of music at First Presbyterian Church, Statesboro, Georgia.

Cheri Montgomery is a member of the voice faculty at the Blair School of Music at Vanderbilt University and an author and lecturer on the topics of voice and diction. Her published texts include: the Lyric Diction Workbook Series (for English, Italian, Latin, German, French, Spanish, and Russian lyric diction courses); the *IPA Handbook for Singers*, *Phonetic Readings for Lyric Diction*, and *Phonetic Transcription for Lyric Diction* (for the abbreviated lyric diction course); and *A Sketchbook Atlas of the Vocal Tract* and *The Singer's Daily Practice Journal*, volumes 1, 2, 3 (for private and class voice). Book reviews are available at www.stmpublishers.com.

She is coauthor of *Exploring Art Song Lyrics* published by Oxford University Press. In her work with Oxford, she provided pronunciation and phonetic symbols for more than 750 Italian, German, and French art songs. Her method of transcription and choice of phonetic symbols are published in the appendix.

Her articles published in the National Association of Teachers of Singing, *Journal of Singing,* include: "Defining the Schwa for English, German, French, and Russian Lyric Diction"; "IPA Braille for Lyric Diction"; "Diction (Still) Belongs in the Music Department"; "The Voice and Diction Connection: A Diction Instructor's Approach to Voice Pedagogy"; and "The Dynamic Diction Classroom."

The National Association of Teachers of Singing, the National Opera Association, and the Nashville Opera's HBCU Fellowship Program have invited her to present on various topics related to voice and diction.

Performance credits include the operatic roles of Gilda (Rigoletto) and the Shepherd Boy (Tosca) with the Nashville Opera. Oratorio engagements include appearances with the Knoxville and Nashville Symphonies as soprano soloist for the *Messiah*.